MAGAZINE OF THE NORTH AMERICAN A.L.F. SUPPORTER S GROUP

UNDERGROUND

THE A.L.F. IN THE 1990S

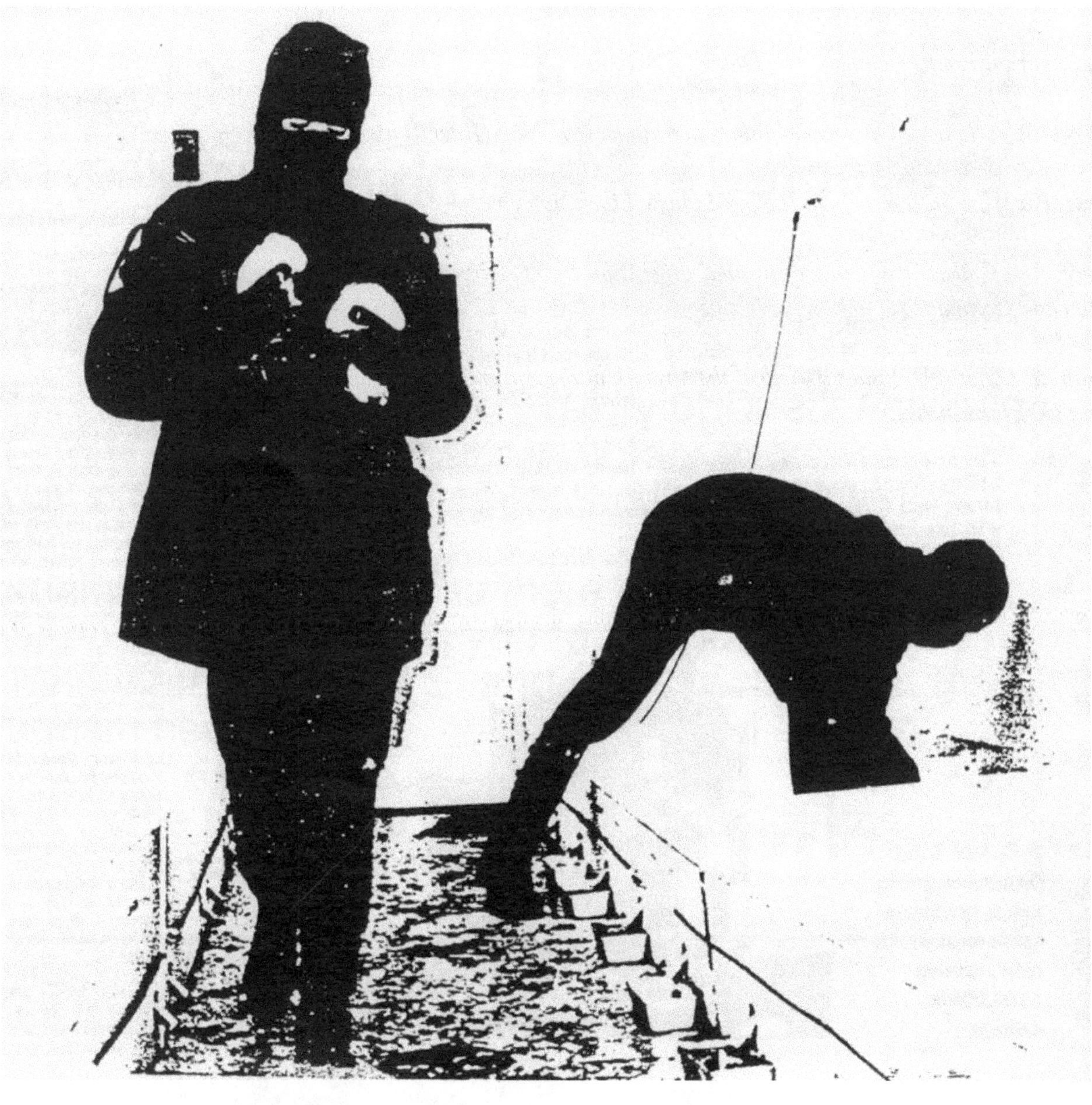

Underground: The Animal Liberation Front in the 1990's, Collected Issues of the A.L.F. Supporters Group Magazine

This compilation first published in the United States in 2011 by Warcry.

ISBN 978-0984284443

For information, submission guidelines, bulk requests, or general inquiries, please contact:

peter@peteryoung.me

Also published by Warcry:

The A.L.F. Strikes Again: Collected Writings Of The Animal Liberation Front In North America (Animal Liberation Front)

Animal Liberation Front: Complete US Diary Of Actions

Liberate: Stories & Lessons On Animal Liberation Above The Law (Peter Young)

Last Words, For War: Statements Of The Symbionese Liberation Army

Flaming Arrows: Collected Writings of Animal Liberation Front Activist Rod Coronado (Rod Coronado)

From Dusk 'til Dawn: An Insider's View of the Growth of the Animal Liberation Movement (Keith Mann)

INTRODUCTION

In 1996, I bought a copy of *Underground #3* at my first animal right group meeting. I was 18, and learning about the A.L.F. before I had attended my first protest. Perhaps sensing my interest in the publication, which I carried with me at all times and read zealously, one of the group's founders took me aside later that month and asked my feelings about direct action. He said he had an action planned, and needed help.

Having received no further details, I met up with him at 10pm at his house in Seattle. He handed me a pair of gloves, and took me into the bathroom. We spent the next two hours filling light bulbs with red paint. As per his instructions, I had brought a backpack with disposable, dark clothing. As we filled paint bombs, he went over the plan: Walk the three miles to a large taxidermy warehouse in Seattle's industrial neighborhood (we had no cars, and taking the bus, he explained, would present the risk of a bus driver remembering us, and giving our description to police). I would unleash a half-dozen paint bombs on the building's front, while he spray painted animal liberation messages before we disappeared into the night.

It was my first illegal action for animals. Although we did not claim it as an A.L.F. action (or report it to *Underground*), we followed the model first been introduced to me by that copy of *Underground #3*.

For over a year we continued these small-scale attacks around Seattle. Although most went unreported, they eventually grew too numerous to ignore, and the media began taking notice. And so did the police, who began staking out my friend's homes. Soon we were finding ourselves pulled at 2am over near past A.L.F. targets under "suspicious circumstances," and the media was reporting my home as a "suspected A.L.F. safe house."

With the stakes raised and an arrest appearing imminent, I began to question the efficacy of small-scale A.L.F. "smash attacks" — the type which filled the pages of *Underground*. Anything action aiming for less than maximum impact was to fail the animals. With greater victories in mind, soon I would be pulling back shed doors to enter chicken farms, and rolling under photoelectric beams to access local mink prisons. As I strove for more effective tiers of A.L.F. activity, *Underground* was both instructional and catalytic.

This book compiles the first 15 issues of *Underground: The Official Newsletter of the North American Animal Liberation Front Supporter's Group*. (The magazine continued until issue 17, but the last two issues slipped in quality, and have not been included).

Underground came early in a chain of U.S. A.L.F.-focused publications that continue to this day. In the 1980's, a smattering of small, limited-circulation publications made appearances, including *The Liberator*. The first (to my knowledge) sustained U.S. direct action animal liberation publication came in the form of *The Militant Vegan*, which published 8 issues in the early to mid-1990s. *Underground* debuted in 1994, followed soon after by *No Compromise. Bite Back* published its first issue in 2002, and at the time of this writing has published its 16th issue covering A.L.F. actions worldwide.

This project had one goal: offer the most comprehensive look at North American A.L.F. activity in the 90s available. Much of the history documented here has never been covered anywhere but the pages of *Underground*, and would be lost forever were these issues not rescued from obscurity.

Notable articles from *Underground* include "Raiding Arizona" — the story of the A.L.F.'s largest U.S. lab raid to date, the extensive debate over Rod Coronado, history of the splinter-group Justice Department, and a first-hand account of a raid on the University of Alberta. With an explicit willingness to publish anonymous articles (and offering guidelines for making forensic-free submissions), *Underground* gave the A.L.F. a voice.

Reading these magazines for the first time in over a decade reminds me of the power of print. How the first issue of *Underground* I read fueled my fight more than anything I've read on the internet. There is an organic energy to printed matter somehow absent from a website or PDF. While no one has isolated what is lost when information is digested from a digital medium, I know that one piece of printed matter has greater impact that a thousand "website hits." The internet strips a work of an analog electricity vital to any book. When I want someone to merely know *of* something, I give them a website. When I want them to feel and act on it, I give them a book.

Top among the complications in editing this project was how to include everything while keeping the size (and price) manageable. It was tempting to keep the book restrained to a "reasonable" page number, yet I couldn't allow this book to see print without going making the collection (nearly) complete — and very big. Keeping with this, the only cuts from the originals were redundant prisoner listings, ads, and intro pages; a section on constructing incendiary devices; and articles on political prisoners from outside the animal liberation movement. In the end, I cut as little as I could in keeping with the book's mission: To provide the best document to date of the Animal Liberation Front in the 1990s.

With *Underground* inextricably tied into my personal history, editing was an emotional journey. Through the process, I confronted how many of my life's experiences could be traced to the early issues of *Underground*. Had I chosen more conservative periodicals, I may never have been chased through woods by farmers, pulled friends form vats of chicken blood inside slaughterhouses, dropped through unhinged skylights, or gone to prison.

While legislative "victories" mandating extra cage space in puppy mills gains national media coverage, this history of those who strike blows to animal abusers under darkness goes largely unrecorded and uncelebrated, but for small publications like *Underground*.

Read this history of those who fight for animals under the radar, and above the law.

And then, make your own.

Peter Young, editor

CONTENTS

UNDERGROUND

"Drill through the roof, break through a wall, cut through the window.... The best way in is never the front door."

Animal rights activists suspected in firebombing

By Susan Feyder
Staff Writer

Five trucks belonging to a Minneapolis meat wholesaler were firebombed Sunday after being spray-painted with slogans including "Meat is murder" and the initials of an animal rights group.

The five trucks were destroyed, said LeRoy Mann, owner of Swanson Meats Inc., 2700 26th Av. S. Mann, who has operated the business for 12 years, estimated the damage at about $100,000, and said insurance will cover some of that.

The firebombing appears to be the worst local case of vandalism related to protests against the meat industry.

Mann said this is the second time in recent weeks his business has been targeted by vandals who left messages behind claiming they support animal rights. Four weeks ago, the windshields of all his delivery trucks

Vandals continued on page 4A

► **On Nov. 8, ALF firebombed trucks owned by a Minneapolis meat wholesaler, causing $100,000 in damage.**

A note on this collection: Compiling this material required drawing from some very old sources. A certain level of quality loss is inevitable when reprinting a 15+ year-old publications. This material was taken from the highest quality sources available.

UNDERGROUND

#1
Aug 94

The magazine of the North American Animal Liberation Front Supporters Group

$ 2

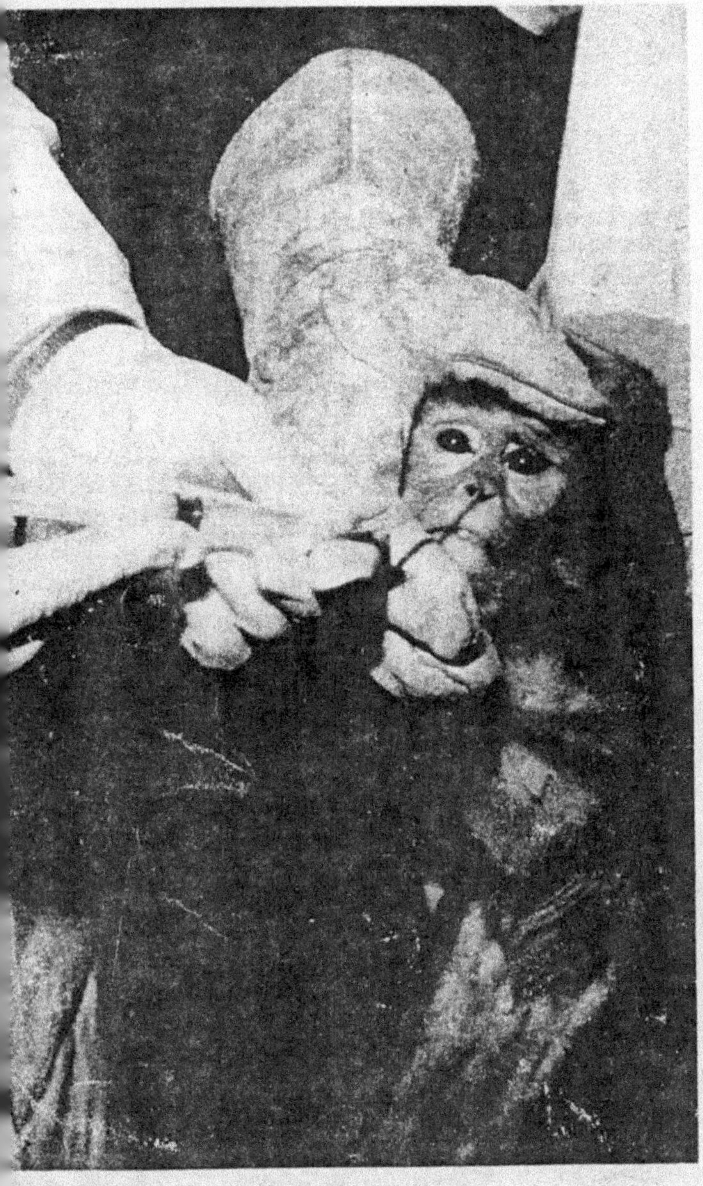

WHICH SIDE ARE YOU ON?

NORTH AMERICAN A.L.F.S.G. NEWS

WELCOME to the first edition of the North American Animal Liberation Front Supporters Group (N.A.-A.L.F.S.G.). newsletter, *Underground*!

DISCLAIMER: The information in *Underground* is not intended to encourage or discourage anyone to do anything illegal; it is for entertainment only. Material within *Underground* is not necessarily that of the A.L.F. or the North American A.L.F.S.G.

We have received several letters recently asking what has happened to the A.L.F.S.G.-Canada publication, *Combat*, which last came out in 1992. And also several letters saying "you never responded to my last letter".

The last two years have been very difficult. Since June 1992, our good friend and comrade Darren Thurston has been fighting a terrible legal battle, mostly from behind bars, for charges stemming from A.L.F. actions in Edmonton, the home of the old A.L.F.S.G.

In addition, state harassment of the animal rights movement in the USA has increased dramatically. Several people have been imprisoned for refusing to testify before Grand Juries, and we have watched our brother Rod Coronado ruthlessly hunted by the F.B.I. It is a testimony to Rod's courage that he remains outside the grasp of the police.

It is sometimes hard to remember, when watching your friends go through hell, what this movement is about: liberation.

Given the obvious need for an active A.L.F.S.G. that could support animal liberation prisoners in Canada <u>and</u> the USA, the old A.L.F.S.G.-Canada ended and the North American A.L.F.S.G. was born.

Of course we are not here only to support our human friends who are caged, but to do what we can to assist the Animal Liberation Front in freeing our animal friends from the cages of the animal abuse industries.

We have recently completed the process of moving from Edmonton to Victoria, B.C. and have almost finished sifting through the huge stack of mail. So please be patient with us for a short while longer. We are making efforts to ensure that your letters are answered quickly.

What we need now, more than your patience, is your generosity. We are, at present, unable to mail to the S.G.'s full membership and cover the costs of jail support. This puts us in the frustrating position of having to choose whether to limit our work to provide an educational/ communication forum for the A.L.F. and its supporters, or to limit our assistance to animal rights prisoners.

We are dealing with the lack of funds by limiting our mailouts. The N.A.-A.L.F.S.G. has a huge mailing list, and to mail every update or newsletter to our 1000+ supporters is, at this point, impossible.

Because the A.L.F. is a movement that must survive underground, communication between active cells, and between activists and supporters, is almost impossible. It is easy for people who are taking direct action on behalf of the animals to feel as if they are the only ones. Supporters of the A.L.F. sometimes feel that the Front has withered away because they do not hear of any actions.

In the face of the state's attempt to destroy the animal liberation movement, it is crucial, now more than ever, to communicate with each other and support each other. Running the N.A.-A.L.F.S.G. is hard work but it is worth it every time we get a report of animals freed or economic damage done to animal abusers. We all need to know that there are people out there who are translating their caring for animals into successful actions, that as individuals we can make a difference.

We have been touched by the generosity of you, the A.L.F. supporters, in recent months. We ask once again that you continue to give what you can, so that we can do our job more fully.

For the animals,

NORTH AMERICAN ANIMAL LIBERATION FRONT SUPPORTERS GROUP

NOTE: We welcome letters, articles, artwork, action reports, poetry, or anything else for publication in *Underground*. Please be sure to write "FOR PUBLICATION" on anything you send us for the newsletter, so that we know what should and should not be publicized. Also please make it clear whether or not you will accept editing of your contribution.

NORTH AMERICAN
ANIMAL LIBERATION FRONT
SUPPORTERS GROUP
(N.A.-A.L.F.S.G.)
P.O. BOX 8673
VICTORIA, BC
CANADA V8W 3S2
e-mail: un028@freenet.victoria.bc.ca

MAIL SECURITY

If you are a member of an active cell, send any clippings, or your own report, with date, time, place, and a few details about the action. Send your reports on plain paper, using block capital letters, or a public typewriter that many people have access to. Wear gloves at all times so your fingerprints are not on the paper, envelope, or stamp. Do not give your address, and don't lick the stamp or envelope -- wet it with a sponge. Remember you should expect that all of our mail and any other support groups' mail is opened and read by the authorities. Do not tell us about upcoming actions.

ANIMAL LIBERATION FRONT (A.L.F.) GUIDE-LINES:

The Animal Liberation Front carries out direct action against animal abuse in the form of rescuing animals and causing financial loss to animal exploiters, usually through the damage and destruction of property.

The A.L.F.'s short term aim is to save as many animals as possible and directly disrupt the practice of animal abuse. Their long term aim is to end all animal suffering by forcing animal abuse companies out of business.

It is a nonviolent campaign, activists taking all precautions not to harm any animal (human or otherwise).

Because A.L.F. actions are against the law, activists work anonymously, either in small groups or individually, and do not have any centralized organization or coordination.

Any group of people who are vegetarians or vegans and who carry out actions according to A.L.F. guidelines have the right to regard themselves as part of the A.L.F.

ANIMAL LIBERATION FRONT SUPPORTERS GROUP GUIDELINES:

The purpose of the Supporters Group is to support the work of the Animal Liberation Front by ALL LAWFUL MEANS POSSIBLE. This includes:

* support of imprisoned activists
* support and defense of the A.L.F.
* educating the public as to the need and rationale of direct action
* providing a communication forum through the Supporters Group newsletter
* raising funds for all the above activities

The Supporters Group is for those who wish to support the A.L.F. without breaking the law. We encourage the participation of all activists -- including those who are unable to, or who do not wish to, take part in direct action.

The Animal Liberation Front consists of small autonomous groups of people all over the world who carry out direct action according to the A.L.F. guidelines. You cannot become a member of the A.L.F. -- or an A.L.F. activist -- through the North American A.L.F. Supporters Group, which is a completely separate organization.

LITERATURE DISTRIBUTION

NOTE: All of the following prices include postage costs for North American orders. Overseas orders please add 25% postage charge. *Make cheques or money orders out to "A.L.F.S.G." and send to :* ***A.L.F.S.G., P.O. Box 8763, Victoria, BC, V8W 3S2, Canada***

For comparison shoppers: prices listed for some of these items are way cheaper if ordered through Vegan Action, P.O. Box 4353, Berkeley, CA 94704, USA. We have no idea how they can afford doing it so cheaply, but would encourage you to look into their catalogue.

BOOKLETS

A Declaration of War: Killing People To Save Animals and The Environment. Written by Screaming Wolf. 64 pp; cerlox binding. $8.

A very controversial contribution to the debate about violence as an acceptable tactic for animal liberation.

An Animal Liberation Primer, 2nd ed. Compiled and edited by @nu. 32 1/2size pp. $2.50.

A DIY booklet of direct action tactics: how to stake out an action site, tips for breaking into buildings, how to react to police interrogation, etc.

as long as there are slaughterhouses....then there shall be battlefields--into the nineties. 30 pp. $5.

"a historical look at the actions against animal abuse, from 1991 onwards and a critique of the branch upon which we're sitting". An invaluable look at the A.L.F. in Britain, and some interesting analyses of the A.L.F. [One of these is reprinted in this issue of *Underground.*]

Grand Jury Comix: A Guide to Federal Grand Juries. 1978. 13 8x14 pp. $3.

Although put out almost 20 years ago, this booklet provides useful information on Grand Juries for our movement today--and is a great tool for public education.

Huddersfield: 4; The State: 0--a storybook tale of a trial. 36 1/2size pp. $3.

The story of a 1992 trial of four people accused of being A.L.F. activists in England. The trial "*did not* produce sensationalised lies in the papers, *did not* make threatening examples of the defendants and *did not* produce harsh prison sentences..."

Interviews with Animal Liberation Front Activists. 52 pp. $6.50.

Compiled in England with interviews with many different A.L.F. cells. Covers most aspects of the A.L.F.

Into the 1990's With the A.L.F. 18 pp. $3.

A how-to book from England, on A.L.F. tactics.

The Power is Ours: A Manual on Saving the Earth and the Animals. 15 pp. $2.50.

A reprint of *Into the 1990's* with slightly different layout and a few last minute additions.

MAGAZINES

Combat. Published by the ALFSG-Canada.

#1, 1990: 16 pp. $2.50 #2, 1992: 8 pp. $1.

Front Line News. Published by the ALFSG-Canada.

#3, 1986: 12 11x17pp; newsprint (some pictures will not reproduce well). $4.
#4, Spring 1988: 32 11x17pp; newsprint (some pictures will not reproduce well). $8.

HOWL: Magazine of the Hunt Saboteurs Association. #46, Spring 1991. 24 pp. $4.

Liberator: News of Animal Liberation Direct Actions in the U.S. 1988 edition. 16 11x17pp; newsprint (some pictures will not reproduce well). $5.

Out of the Cages! #9. Published by People for Animal Liberation. 24 pp. $4.

South East Liberator! #2, Autumn 1992. 14 pp. $2.50.

The Militant Vegan

#1, 1993: 20 pp. $3.50. #2-5: 12 pp. $2.

LEAFLETS/BROADSHEETS

$0.50 each

- *Direct Action for Animal Rights: A Member of the Animal Liberation Front tells why she broke the law for animals.*
- *Information about Djurens Hamnars / Diary of Animal Avengers Actions.*
- *Natives and the Fur Industry: Native / Animal Brotherhood.*

PRISONER NEWS

NORTH AMERICAN PRISONERS

Kim Trimiew, Spokane County Jail, 1100 West Mallon, Spokane, WA 99260 USA
Kim has been in prison since February for refusing to testify before a Grand Jury in Washington. Previous prisoners hav spent 158 and 159 days for refusing to testify; Kim reached day 153 as of July 19. For news on Deb Stout, who was also ir the Spokey Pokey, see p. 9.

David Barbarash, Edmonton Remand Centre, 9660 - 104 Ave, Edmonton, AB, T5H 4B5, Canada
David is awaiting trial on charges related to a 1992 A.L.F. raid on the University of Alberta which resulted in the liberatio of 29 cats and significant damage to the laboratories. David was arrested in California in May and deported at the beginnin of June. He has been refused bail several times and will most likely be held in the ERC until his trial. His preliminary hearin is scheduled for August 31.

Darren Thurston, Fort Saskatchewan Correctional Facility, Bag 10, 7802-101 st, Fort. Sask., AB, T8L 2P3, Canada
Darren is serving a two year sentence for charges relating to a 1992 raid on the University of Alberta (29 cats were liberate and the lab trashed) and the burning and spraypainting of lobster trucks in 1991. Darren was arrested in 1992 and serve 14 1/2 months while awaiting trial. Darren was tried in 1993 and received time served and an order to pay $75,000 i restitution. In March 1994 the Crown appealed the sentence and asked for three more years; in May the Alberta Court o Appeal sentenced Darren to two more years less a day.

[NOTE: Darren has applied to be transferred to Fort Saskatchewan and is expecting to move there some time in August. His mail will be forwarded there. Also, please do NOT put any stickers on his letters or envelopes.]

U.K. PRISONERS

New Prisoner:

Gurjeet Aujla, HMP Birmingham, Winston Green Road, Birmingham, B18 4AS, England; 011-44-021-554-3838
On Friday June 3, Gurjett Aujla was arrested at his home. He was questioned over the weekend and was then formally charged with "Conspiracy to cause explosions" on June 6. He was remanded for a week to HMP Birmingham and according to the UK-ALFSG "it is expected that he will remain there for some time".

The following three prisoners were convicted early in 1994 for causing tens of thousands of dollars damage to butchers' shops and a zoo:
Terry Helsby EF0761, HMP Risley, Warrington Road, Risley, Warrington, Cheshire, WA3 6BP, England
Allison McKeon RE2370, HMP Askham Grange, Askham, Richard, York, Y02 3PT, England
Max Watson BJ2477, HMP Haverigg, Haverigg Camp, Millom, Cumbria, LA18 4NA, England

Annette is serving 4 years for conspiracy to commit arson against animal abusers.
Annette Tibbles TT2215, HMP Holloway, Parkhurst Road, Holloway, London, N7 0NU, England

Angie and Keith were arrested in the spring of 1994 at an animal sanctuary. Keith, after being arrested for numerous arson attacks on the meat trade in England in 1991, escaped from police custody in Liverpool on June 23, 1993.
Angie Hamp TW1687, HMP Holloway, Parkhurst Road, Holloway, London, N7 0NU, England
Keith Mann, HMP Manchester, 1 Southall Street, Manchester, M60 9AH, England

MARK DAVIS #23106-008, Federal Prison Camp, PO Box 1000, Boron, CA 93596 USA

Legal Defense Fund, HC 29, Box 424, Prescott, AZ 86301 USA

Mark Davis is one of the "Arizona 5" arrested in an F.B.I. sting of Earth First! in 1989. He is currently serving the third year of a six year sentence, after repeatedly being denied parole. Although Mark is not an animal rights prisoner per se, his actions to prevent wilderness destruction (and wildlife habitat) deserve support and we would encourage people to consider Mark as part of our extended movement.

LETTER FROM DAVID BARBARASH, JAILED ANIMAL RIGHTS PRISONER

Greetings! 7-10-94

Once again I'm facing charges related to Animal Liberation Front activities. The first time was in Toronto back in the late 80's when I was convicted of several offences along with four friends, in connection with attacks on animal abuse businesss. This time, the charges - Break and Enter/Theft Over $1000 and Mischief - are in connection with the ALF action of June 1/92 when 29 cats were liberated from the University of Alberta's Bio Animal Kennels. The cats, facing broken spines for spinal cord research, have never been recaptured and remain free. Currently, Darren Thurston is serving a 2 year sentence for this & other actions.

photo sent to the NA-ALFSG: one of the 29 cats freed by the A.L.F.'s June 29/92 raid of the University of Alberta , well-loved in its new home.

Although I had a Canada-wide warrant for my arrest for two years, I was never served it by the RCMP. My capture in California on May 9th was a result of FBI and local police surveillance on several homes, and was carried out with a show of extreme force. I am thought to be such a dangerous person that every one of the two dozen or so cops they apparently needed at the roadblock had their guns out and pointed at myself and a friend. I don't know if it's all the years of media desensitization, but I wasn't really scared; instead, I thought I was in some sort of surreal movie.

At any rate, now, months later, I sit here in the Edmonton Remand Centre having been denied bail. The Crown Attorney fears I would disappear into the "animal rights underground", and the judge has called the "zealousness" of my beliefs "frightening", and believes I pose a "danger to the public". Whatever. Let them play their little power games. They have my physical body for this relatively short period of time. They will never have my spirit, or my mind, or my will. And that's where the real power lies. It doesn't matter whether I'm innocent or guilty; I'm happy the cats are free to live out their lives in peace.

Recently I read a report in a "Security" magazine which states that the ALF are reported to be active now in 45 countries! Actions continue in spite of police crackdowns everywhere, including the insidious Grand Juries in the U.S. (which have jailed numerous people for simply exercising their right to remain silent). The authorities and power mongers are getting desperate as the world moves toward a more enlightened consciousness. It is only a matter of time.

Future generations will look back on these times of animal abuse with disgust and amazement. For now, I sit in my cell and wait for the wheels of "justice" to roll over me, but they won't crush me. The struggle cannot be stopped either, simply by jailing a few people here and there. I send all my love and prayers to all of you courageous warriors on the front lines. Be safe!

Love and Liberation,

David Barbarash
9660-104 Ave.
Edmonton, Alberta
T5H 4B5 Canada

P.S. My Preliminary Hearing is set for Aug. 31. I would love to hear from any who care to write; letters are my sustenance in this pit.

GRAND JURIES AND THE

By Crescenzo Vellucci, National Activist Network

(Author's note: This is an update of a story written in 1991 after federal grand juries in northern California cripple progressive activist groups in that area. That article cautioned that activists were not taking the grand jury threat seriously and because of that, the government's use of grand juries would expand, further disrupting the animal liberation cause. Th prophecy has come true. Today, there are six sitting grand juries.)

Some activists may not want to hear this, but it is folly to believe otherwise: the repressive and illegal use, under the direction of the U.S. Justice Department, of federal grand juries against animal liberation and environmental activists has severely disrupted these social justice movements since 1990.

It serves no useful purpose--in fact it hurts the cause--to ignore the threat, or the reality. But, to face it is to be able to deal with it in a rational, and political sense. To understand the threat, and power, of grand juries is to empower yourself.

And, if you can become empowered, you will not feel fear. And, without fear, the state, and the abusive grand jury system, cannot do anything to you.

The good news is that once we face this fact, and become more familiar with the grand jury and its abuses, we can resist the unconstitutional use of these undemocratic tribunals. We can even turn the power of the government back against itself. The "Lexington Six", an anti-war group jailed for non-collaboration with a grand jury decades ago, said it best:

> "*People must* <u>*mobilize around these issues*</u>*. To do this, people must first become familiar with the grand jury and its abuses,* <u>*publicizing the facts and educating others as to their rights*</u>*. Secondly it is important to engender in others a commitment to the resistance of these abuses including, but not limited to one's refusal to testify before the grand jury. Thirdly, it is necessary to keep in mind that while court battles can be fought and sometimes won, these abuses of the law are not abnormalities in a basically good system--they rather illustrate the true intentions of a* <u>*BAD*</u> *system more openly and graphically than other more insidious practices (and)* <u>*this should dominate our thinking as we organize*</u>."

We are now experiencing the most intensive use of the illegal authority of grand juries since the repression against the peace and civil rights movements of the 1960s and 70s. Not that it helps an awful lot, but we are in good company. And the state would not employ such draconian methods if the movements hadn't achieved something for the animals and the earth.

As of this date (July, 1994), there are, from the best information we have, <u>at least six current federal grand juries</u>. There has been a total, <u>to the best of our knowledge</u>, of at least eight different federal grand juries since 1990.

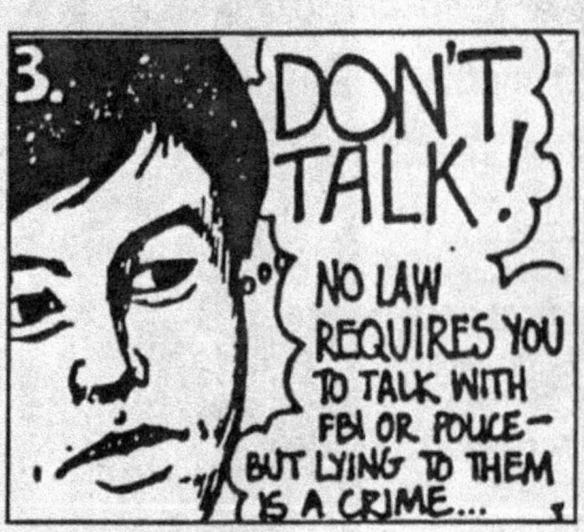

The current federal grand juries include those in Portland, Oregon; Spokane, Washington; Grand Rapids, Michigan; Albuquerque, New Mexico; New Orleans, Louisiana; Salt Lake City, Utah. A Eugene, Oregon U.S. panel, begun in 1991, reportedly ended last year and a series of three grand juries in Sacramento, California, ended in 1991 after nearly four years of intimidation and abuse.

We caution that because of the ultra-secret nature of federal grand juries there could be <u>more grand juries at work</u>.

At least four good activists have been jailed for up to 159 days by the newest of these grand juries, and the government continues to gather information, intimidate activists, their families, support networks and others associated with the liberation of animals and the planet.

The federal grand jury in Spokane has incarcerated activists Jonathan Paul (158 days) and Rik Scarce (159 days). Kim Trimiew has been jailed since Feb. 18, 1994; Deb Stout, who was jailed on Feb. 18 as well, was released only days ago, on July 19 . Henry Hutto was the first activist to successfully resist the grand jury when he spent 45 days in jail in Sacramento in 1990.

Equally disturbing is that the government, and the powerful corporate entities it represents, is, unfortunately, obtaining what it really wanted all along--**<u>INFORMATION ABOUT THE STRUCTURE AND WORK-</u>**

ANIMAL RIGHTS MOVEMENT

Special to the North American A.L.F.S.G.

INGS OF THE GRASSROOTS MOVEMENT.

There is some recent good news. The Portland grand jury hs yet to hear (to our knowledge) any testimony (since January). Its most recent attempt to harass activist Beth Fries (June 28) failed when a motion to quash was filed by her attorney. And, because of the motion, two other potential witnesses (parents of an activist) were able to avoid grand jury testimony.

And, in Albuquerque, where there is a new grand jury, only one of three activists actually went into the grand jury room. The two others, after motions were filed to quash their subpoenas, were excused, and must be re-subpoenaed.

However, too many activists have collaborated with the state, and too many activists have become informants, some unwittingly and others knowingly, to "save" themselves. But, if activists know their rights, they can protect them--and those of others.

There is no doubt the FBI, ATF and Justice Department have abused the legal system, and under the guise of attacking "terrorism," have become the real terrorists by harassing people because of their

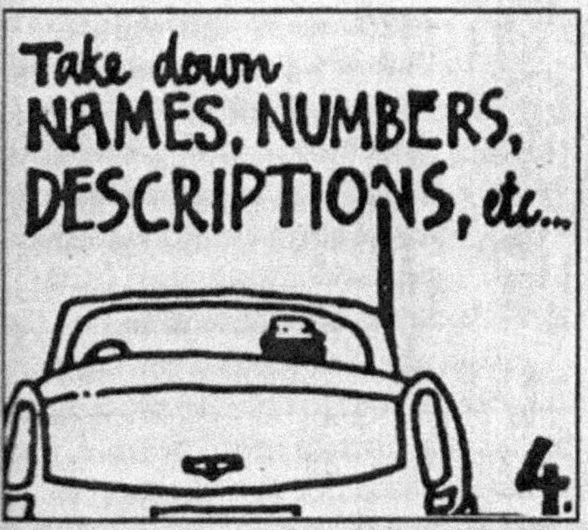
Take down
NAMES, NUMBERS,
DESCRIPTIONS, etc...
4.

political views and beliefs.

The grand jury is being used by the government as an instrument of political repression because it does, in fact, frighten many activists, forcing them out of a political movement and causes others to inform on their former friends and activists out of fear.

In California, where the first federal grand juries were held in the late 1980s and early 1990s, activists--turned informants--attempted to justify turning over activists' names, addresses and phone numbers--in addition to possibly incriminating information.

To make matters worse, other activists, instead of acknowledging the ethical wrongs of the informants, embraced them, inviting them back into the movement. This is how things can go wrong, very wrong, if we are not prepared to resist.

If any of this sounds familiar, it is because the tactic of "isolating hardcore activists (read committed)" from the rest of the movement is EXACTLY what was proposed in the American Medical Association's "battle plan" against the animal rights movement in 1989. Interestingly enough, the AMA also called for Justice Dept. intervention, which is what has happened.

RELATIVES & BOSS

LET YOU KNOW IF THEY'VE

As the National Lawyer Guild's primer on grand juries says, "For many political activsts, the historic and principled way to avoid these dilemmas (informing, perjury) has been the invocation of **<u>absolute noncollaboration with grand jury investigations of political movements</u>**. While this has resulted in many instances with the witness' incarceration for contempt, it has also **<u>discouraged the subpoenaing of further witnesses</u>**, and on some occasions, the **<u>withdrawal of all subpoenas."</u>**

Remember that <u>you have no right to remain silent in a grand jury room.</u> That is why you need assistance <u>before your appearance</u>. Following are some other thoughts, and examples, to ponder:

1. **<u>The goal of grand juries is to terrorize, not investigate crimes. Period.</u>** When you hear, from agents, lawyers, or other activists, that a grand jury has been empaneled to "investigate" this crime or another, DO NOT BELIEVE IT. The goal of the government, as has been documented in dozens of grand juries from movements past, is to intimidate, disrupt and, if they can, destroy movements. This is the truth and this is what you should tell the media and others who ask. It is the government's claim they are investigating a crime--that is their excuse for trampling our rights. DO NOT BUY

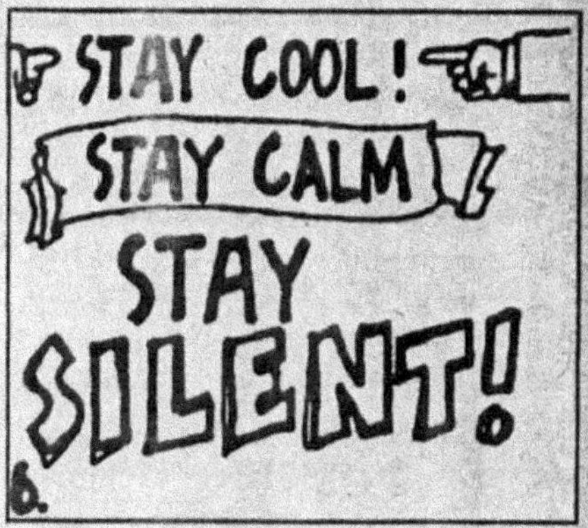
STAY COOL!
STAY CALM
STAY
SILENT!
6.

INTO THE STATE'S RATIONALE. We know their true intent--to harass activists, and gain information about individuals and political organizations. That, by the way, is illegal and unconstitutional. By the way, it is dangerous to talk freely about why you think, or someone else thinks, a grand jury has been started. <u>EXAMPLE:</u> In California, activists and the media were told the grand jury was investigating a research lab fire. In truth, the questions asked were about groups and activists in general, even those in other states. Also, in Albuquerque, everyone "heard" the state was investigating power line disruptions. However, the questions dealt with activists' political association, not alleged crimes.

2. <u>**You do not have to talk to the FBI or other agents.**</u> However, it is a crime to lie to them. The best response is no response. Contact a lawyer and your defense team (see below). <u>EXAMPLE:</u> Recently, some activists were located, and served subpoenas and now face jail time, because grassroots groups

and individuals willingly, and without subpoena, gave the FBI the activists' new address. Remember, you don't have to answer your door, and law enforcement cannot enter unless they have a warrant. Just keep the door closed until you know who's on the other side.

3. <u>**Do not believe ANYTHING the government says**</u>. A typical FBI/ATF comment goes something like, "We already know everything, we just want you to confirm it." Gee, if they already knew everything (whatever that might be), why do they need it confirmed? In fact, they DO NOT have anything; that's why they've come to see you. And, they're acting on illegally obtained information (wiretap or rumor/innuendo from another activist) that is not admissible in court. Act accordingly. And, if they say you are, or are not, a target, don't believe them! Their job is to lie, and to say whatever they think will scare you into cooperating. Again, act accordingly.

4. <u>**There is no such thing as a "innocent" question.**</u> <u>EXAMPLE</u>: The Leslie Bacon Case. The National Lawyers Guild, which has produced a wealth of information about grand juries, cites the Leslie Bacon case. Leslie was an antiwar activist who agreed to appear before a grand jury that was allegedly investigating a bombing in the U.S. capitol. Since she knew nothing about it, Leslie decided to go to the grand jury room alone. As it turned out, the government was really interested in other individuals and other activities, not at all connected to any bombing. By answering one question, Leslie was had. She, and others, later were indicted anyway. The lessons learned include (a) the government was much more intersted in pumping Leslie for information about friends than the so-called bombing plot; (b) her case shows how easy it is to waive what rights you may have by <u>answering a single question;</u> (c) Leslie learned that testifying doesn't mean you'll save your own skin; and (d) this is the most important: as a result of her testimony, new grand juries were begun in three other cities, and many other people were harassed.

5. <u>**Form a defense committee.**</u> If you are subpoenaed, or think you will be, form a defense committee with friends, witnesses, legal workers. As activists, we determine the correct strategy for the liberationist cause, not lawyers, who we hire to defend our righ The committee will discuss issues li how to coordinate media, demonst tions, what legal strategies to take a what legal motions to file. <u>EXAMPL</u> In several cases, good activists, aft hiring lawyers, shunned help from oth activists and legal workers, and i stead followed the guidance of th lawyers, which has not been in the be interest of the cause. This results ir lack of coordinated strategy to end gra juries, and the threat to political fre dom. It may help save the individu activist, but even that is d batable (see Leslie Bac Case). It also isolates acti ists, when we should be pu ing closer together.

6. <u>**Share informatio community unity.**</u> The go ernment's goal is to obta information. So should ou The more information v have as a movement abo the actions of a grand ju the better prepared we are resist abusive actions. All l gal motions, among other i formation, should be shar between movement lawye and defense committees. To do so faci tates trust during a difficult time, ar also makes it easier for one legal tea to pick up on a good legal strategy use by another legal team. <u>EXAMPLE</u>: I practice, there has been little shari of information between lawyers in o movements (and then only whe pressed by the activist clients). In th California cases, the grand jury ha been going on for months, but activis who had been subpoenaed did not i form other activists. If there had bee more advance warning, maybe no or would have been jailed, and maybe th current grand jury onslaught could hav been avoided.

7. <u>**Resist attempts to intimidat you.**</u> Make the government do its jo Use every <u>legal</u> means to resist th illegal and abusive actions of a feder grand jury. <u>EXAMPLE</u>: As opposed t the Albuquerque case where activis filed motions to quash, and were r

CONTINUED

eased from having to appear, a Califor-
nia organization recently made the mistake of turning over records about certain individuals to the government rather than fight a subpoena. The group could have delayed, and possibly even had the subpoena quashed (withdrawn) if they had taken some basic steps to protect their rights, and everyone else's. Of course, don't break the law by obstructing a grand jury, or avoiding a subpoena. There are legal ways to fight these terrorist-like attempts to repress our rights.

8. <u>Avoid the temptation to "just get it over with."</u> The Lawyers Guild rightly suggests that activists, and lawyers, should avoid the temptation to "just get it over with," by either testifying, or even going to jail, without first exhausting legal and constitutional remedies. <u>EXAMPLE</u>: While it is honorable to go to jail rather than cooperate, it can still have a negative impact because the government (in the Spokane grand juries) uses the jailing of activists as an example to others to "cooperate." It is important to resist as long as possible. To do so uses up the government resources so that they have less time to harass other activists.

9. <u>What happens if you testify?</u> First of all, you have made real what they were only guessing, you have increased your chances of being subpoenaed again and you may be responsible for someone, perhaps even yourself, for going to prison, maybe for something they didn't do. Because, in a grand jury proceeding, people can be indicted on hearsay (rumours) and innuendo.

10. <u>Do not be afraid.</u> Easy to say, but it is also practical. <u>EXAMPLE</u>: An activist subpoened in California in 1990 showed no fear, and even refused to show up at the grand jury, opting instead to read a statement defying the grand jury. She was <u>never bothered again</u>. Likewise, activists in California who cooperated were harassed repeatedly. Remember: the state feeds on fear. Do not show fear, and you'll starve the monster.

11. <u>If you go in alone: The Jonathan Paul Case.</u> In the case of Jonathan Paul, an activist who eventually spent 158 days behind bars for not cooperating with the Spokane Grand Jury, you can see why <u>no one should go to a grand jury alone.</u> He decided, because like Leslie Bacon he had "nothing to hide," to go into the grand jury room by himself. The result was hours of prosecutorial harassment, questions about everything from his family to his girlfriends, and then his jailing (all in the same day!) when he refused to answer questions about other activists and his political activities. He wasn't even allowed a postponement to obtain an attorney. The lesson learned is that although you have few rights in the grand jury room, a good activist lawyer and a faithful support team can make it easier for you.

[Jonathan Paul, Henry Hutto and Crescenzo Vellucci, all jailed as a result of grand jury harassment, helped form the National Activist Network's Grand Jury Project. It provides free information (gleaned from several years of research about grand juries and other movements), legal assistance and lawyer referrals to all grassroots activists threatened by grand juries, and associated government harassment. All calls are confidential. Call (916) 452-7179 for more information, or write: PO Box 19515, Sacramento, CA 95819]

DEB STOUT IS OUT!

Deb Stout was released from Spokane County Jail on July 18, after spending 151 days behind bars for refusing to testify before a grand jury. While this is somewhat bittersweet, as Kim Trimiew (who was imprisoned with Deb on Feb 18) is still being held, we are ecstatic that Deb is finally out and hope that she has a good time celebrating! Thank you to everyone who supported Deb. Please do not forget that Kim is still in need of help. Contact the Activist Support Group, P.O. Box 9286, Missoula, MT, 59807 USA.

A recent article in the magazine *New Scientist* suggests new legislation for Britain:
"...medical researchers have been responsible for major advances that benefit us all. Something beyond normal criminal law is required to cope with the pattern of growing violence against them. The first step is to look carefully at some of the legislation introduced in the US to tackle the problem of animal-rights extremism."
YIKES! What's next? Grand Juries in the UK?

Direct Action for

CANADA

DEC 14/93: Whitehorse, Yukon -- Department of Renewable Resources (DRR): 54 tires slashed, locks of 17 trucks glued, barbed wire of security fence cut. The DDR is carrying out a wolf kill program.
-- A.L.F.

CROATIA

no date specified: location not specified -- Meat, leather shops: locks glued; the A.L.F. is also involved in opposing the war.
-- A.L.F.

ENGLAND

In England, actions happen every day, and it is impossible to report them all. Here are some recent highlights.

Jan/94: Hampshire -- 17 animal abusers windows smashed in the Portsmouth/Fareham area.
--A.L.F.

Jan/94 : Kent -- Horse rescued in the Swale area. The "owners" of the horse had been taken to court, by the RSPCA, for animal cruelty.
--A.L.F.

Jan/94: London -- The Home Secretary recieves about 100 letters from vivisectors frightened of Justice Department letterbombs.

Jan/94: Sussex, Steyning --Shamrock workers car trashed.
--A.L.F.

Jan/94: Sussex, Eastbourne -- Shamrock vets car trashed.
--A.L.F.

Jan/94: Sussex,Brighton -- Shamrock Farm Minibus trashed.
--A.L.F.

Jan/94: Yorkshire -- Barnsley, two badgers rescued from baiters. A polecat was re-homed at the same time.

Feb/94: Cambridgeshire -- Dr. Pamela Mullins, vet for Huntingdon Research Centre, recieves mouse trap primed with razor blades and coated in dead HIV infected blood.
--JUSTICE DEPARTMENT

Feb/94: Cambridgeshire -- Dr. Harley Farmer, vet for Ichor Ltd, receives mouse trap primed with razor blades and coated in dead HIV infected blood.
--JUSTICE DEPARTMENT

Feb/94: Hampshire -- Wickham Laboratories visited. Three cars outside the lab had etching fluid sprayed over their windowscreens.
-- A.L.F.

Feb/94: Hampshire,Wickham -- The notorious Garetmar Ken nels. A speedboat outside the cottage is given a new coat of blac paint.
--A.L.F.

Feb/94: Hampshire -- First ever Women Only mass sab take place.

Feb/94: Hertfordshire -- Hoax parcel bomb to Hertfordshir South Beagle Hunt supporter.
--JUSTICE DEPARTMENT

Feb/94:Humberside -- Hoax parcel bombs sent to Chiddingfold Leconfield and Cowdray hunt supporters.
--JUSTICE DEPARTMENT

Feb/94: Lancashire -- Three stolen land mines claim to be plante at the Waterloo Cup.
--HUNT RETRIBUTION SQUAD

Feb/94: London -- Hoax parcel bomb sent to Enfield Chas supporter.
--JUSTICE DEPARTMENT

Feb/94: Merseyside,Altcar --Waterloo Cup stopped by a combina tion of Sabs and weather.

Feb/94: Nottinghamshire -- Gordon Houston, Managing Directo of Boots the Chemist, recieves mouse trap primed with razo blades and coated in dead HIV infected blood.
--JUSTICE DEPARTMENT

Feb/94: Nottinghamshire -- Terry Richardson, Managing Direc tor of Boots Pharmaceuticals recieves mouse trap primed wit razor blades and coated in dead HIV infected blood.
--JUSTICE DEPARTMENT

Feb/94: Nottinghamshire -- Tony Rollings, Director of Biotech recieves mouse trap primed with razor blades and coated in dea HIV infected blood.
--JUSTICE DEPARTMENT

Feb/94: Sussex -- Shamrock workers, driving home, have bricks thrown through their vehicle windows.

Feb/94: Sussex, Hastings -- Incendiary device dropped through Boots letter box.
-- A.L.F.

Feb/94: Sussex, Bexhill-on-Sea -- Incendiary device dropped through Boots letter box.
-- A.L.F.

Animal Liberation

Feb/94: Sussex, St Leonards-on-Sea --Incendiary device dropped through Boots letter box.
-- A.L.F.

Feb/94: Sussex, Brighton -- A.L.F. raid Standean Farm to visit the notorious gamekeeper Nigel Javis. Javis traps wild birds, keeps them in a cage and then uses them as lures for other birds. A.L.F. free the birds and trash every vehicle in sight. Warning given of future actions.
--A.L.F.

Feb/94: Sussex, Eastbourne -- Shamrock worker, Paul West, discovers his car vandalized.
--A.L.F.

Feb/94: Sussex, Crowborough -- Home of badger baiter Michael Head visited. His vehicles were trashed.
--A.L.F.

Feb/94: Sussex -- David Cooper, Director of Shamrock Farm recieves mouse trap primed with razor blades and coated in dead HIV infected blood.
--JUSTICE DEPARTMENT

Feb/94: Warwickshire -- Michael Keighly, Birmingham University vivisector, recieves mouse trap primed with razor blades and coated in dead HIV infected blood.
--JUSTICE DEPARTMENT

Feb/94: West Midlands -- Nicholas Green, Birmingham university vivisector, recieves mouse trap primed with razor blades and coated in dead HIV infected blood.
--JUSTICE DEPARTMENT

Feb/94: Yorkshire -- Georgina Watson, Leeds university vivisector, recieves mouse trap primed with razor blades and coated in dead HIV infected blood.
--JUSTICE DEPARTMENT

Feb/94: Yorkshire -- Brian Cass, Director of Hazleton Contract Testing Services, recieves mouse trap primed with razor blades and coated in dead HIV infected blood.
--JUSTICE DEPARTMENT

March/94: Cornwall -- Hunt supporters are attacked. 4 scum injured. One is beaten unconcious.
--Hunt Retribution Squad

March/94: Cornwall -- Concrete block thrown through hunt supporters window.
-- Hunt Retribution Squad

March/94: Hampshire, Wickam -- Garetmar Kennels visited. Animals liberated include: 5 month old labrador, a four month old labrador, a 6 month old Golden retriever, two 4 four month old Old English sheepdogs, an 8 week old dalmation, two 6 week old Shetland sheepdogs, an 8 week old collie cross and a 2 year old chihuahua. All 10 dogs were in poor condition.
-- A.L.F.

March/94: London -- Leyden Street slaughterhouse visited. 58 hens rescued.
-- A.L.F.

March/94: Sussex -- Kingswood Eggs farm raided. 100 hens rescued. 3 lorries were also damaged by the activists etching the window screens, putting sugar and water/whitespirit in petrol tank and a nice A.L.F. logo replaced the boring Kingswood logo.
-- A.L.F.

March/94: Sussex, Gatwick -- Incendiary device discovered. Device thought to be planted by animal liberation activists.

March/94: West Midlands -- 5 demonstrators try to break into Crufts arena. One demonstrator was assaulted and kidnapped by security guards, who drove him to junction 4 of the M6 before dumping him.

March/94: Yorkshire, Leeds -- 3 sheep rescued from University factory farming research lab. Lab equipment also smashed in action.
-- A.L.F.

March/94: location not specified -- Claims that battery eggs from Stonegate Farm have been contaminated and placed in shops and supermarkets.
-- POULTRY LIBERATION ORGANIZATION (PLO)

APR/94: Cambridgeshire, Cambridge -- Incendiary discovered inside Boots. Device "made safe".
--JUSTICE DEPARTMENT

APR/94: Cheshire -- Activists cause damage to Aintree (the Grand National) race course. Sadly, three people are remanded.

APR/94: Hampshire -- The night before the Grand National, locks of 20 Southhampton bookies are glued
--A.L.F.

APR/94: Cheshire -- 800 police and security, including armed police on roof, used for security operation at 1994 Grand National. Helicopters and 1 million pound chain link fence also available for use.

APR/94: Cheshire -- Mass protests outside the Grand National. Many people are arrested outside race course including a man carrying darts and a hammer.

APR/94: Gloucestershire, Winchombe -- Incendiary device sent to W. Gilder whose family is involved with farming, haulage, buchery and live exports.
--JUSTICE DEPARTMENT

APR/94: Lancashire, Garstang -- Castle Foods meat factory attacked. Slogans painted on the door and 3 vans have their windows smashed and tires slashed. Estimated damage is $20,000.
-- A.L.F.

APR/94: London -- Letter bomb recieved at BNP headquarters. Administration Officer, Alfred Waite injured.
-- JUSTICE DEPARTMENT

APR/94: Northamptonshire, Coventry -- Justice Department device accidently activates inside mail sorting office.

APR/94: Oxford -- Activists occupy MuckDonalds for half an hour and distribute the original "What's wrong with McDonalds" leaflet. Eventually police were called and the activists evicted.

APR/94: Surrey -- More than 200 laboratory animals are rescued from North East Surrey College. These included 15 rabbits, 52 guinea pigs, 58 hamsters and 90+ rats. After rescuing the animals the cages were smashed and rooms flooded.
-- A.L.F.

APR/94: Sussex, Crowborough -- Letter bomb sent to badger baiter Michael Head.
-- JUSTICE DEPARTMENT

APR 30/94: Plymouth — Boots (target of National Day of Action and repeated actions, for their support of vivisection): Part of Plymouth City Centre was closed off as it was feared a Justice Department device that could have resulted in an explosion was inside Boots. This turned out to be a hoax.
-- JUSTICE DEPARTMENT

APR/94: Unspecified location -- 100 guinea pigs rescued as response to arrest of Angie and Keith.
--A.L.F.

MAY/94: Cornwall -- The home of Geoffery and Tracy Broster is threatened with a firebomb attack after the scum starved a dog to death.

MAY/94: Hampshire -- Mouse traps, primed with razor blades, sent to Days of Torbay Farm (breeders who supply Wickham Research Labs. David Walker, owner of Animal Pharmaceutical and Toxicology and former vet at Wickham Research Labs. Froxfield Farms, suppliers of animals to vivisection labs. William Cartmell, owner of Wickham Research Labs. Paddy Edwards, manager of Wickham Research Labs. Nicola Scarr, 50% owner of Garetmar Kennels. David Witcher, worker at Garetmar and live-in lover of Nicola Scarr. Nick Fawcett of Chiddingfold, Leconfield and Cowdray hunt. Also, P. Humphrey of Webb's Poultry and known Hunt supporter.
-- JUSTICE DEPARTMENT

MAY 11/94: Plymouth — Boots: Incendiary discovered inside.
-- A.L.F.

MAY 14/94: Plymouth — Boots: Windows smashed, locks glued; $12,000 of damage done.
-- A.L.F.

MAY/94: Nothants, Moulton -- Video type bomb left on t doorstep of Genus, the artificial insemination company. R bomb disposal unit called in.
-- JUSTICE DEPARTMENT

MAY/94: Sussex, Eastbourne -- 7 carloads of activists visit t home of Paul West, the Shamrock vet, on his birthday. A dem held. Chants include "Shamrock Farm, Burn it down!"

MAY/94: Sussex -- Activists visit the home of David Cooper, senior technician at Shamrock Farm. One person arrested b not charged.

MAY/94: Sussex -- Activists chan and padlock the gates Shamrock Farm. One activists was handcuffed to the ou perimiter fence.

MAY/94: Sussex, Brighton -- Activists hold mass demo outsi the home of John Worrow, the Shamrock driver who colle primates from the airport.

MAY/94: Sussex -- Mouse trap primed with razor blades sent Paul West, Vet at Shamrock Farm; Andy Bradwell, Manager Shamrock Farm; S. Grinyer, Shamrock employee; J. Worro Shamrock employee; and Michael Head, the badger baiter.
-- JUSTICE DEPARTMENT

JUN/94: Devon, Tavistock -- Boots windows smashed, sloga sprayed on walls.
-- A.L.F.

JUN/94: Devon, Ilfracombe -- $14,000 fishing boat destroyed fire.

JUN/94: Devon, Torquay -- 4 butchers shops and 3 Boots sto are spraypainted. Some windows smashed.
-- A.L.F.

JUN/94: Gloucestershire, Elstone Hardwick -- The Gilder fam recieve their second letter bomb. This time it goes to Graha Gilder.
-- JUSTICE DEPARTMENT

JUN/94: Gloucestershire, Bourton-on-the-Water -- The Gild family recieves its third letter bomb. Device sent to Gild Haulage company.
-- JUSTICE DEPARTMENT

JUN/94: Kent, Ashford -- Letter bomb explodes at Sena Sealin A secretary recieves minor cuts and burns.
-- JUSTICE DEPARTMENT

JUN/94: Lincoln, Rothwell -- Letter bomb sent to Cherry Valk Farm is made safe.
-- JUSTICE DEPARTMENT

JUN/94: London -- Incendiary device found inside Boots.
-- A.L.F.

JUN/94: Northants -- 82 hens leave poultry breeder for new li
--A.L.F.

JUN 3/94:
Oxfordshire -- Pig company: Cardboard tube that arrived in t post exploded. One man was injured.
Gloucester -- Meat company: Bomb exploded. Damages not spe

fied.

JUN 20/94: Newton Abbott -- Boots: Several hours after the grand opening of a new $8,000,000 store, it was temporarily closed after someone phoned a local newspaper and said a bomb was inside the store. No bomb was found.

JUN/94: Warwickshire, Exhall -- a man is arrested and later charged with sending out a number of Justice Department letter bombs.

JUN/94: The Animal Liberation Front celebrates its "Coming of Age" 18th birthday.

JULY/94: Cambridgeshire, Cambridge -- Two incendiaries ignite inside Boots and Edinburgh Woolen Mill stores. Damage was severe and 15 fire crews were called to tackle the blazes. Two more devices found inside Marr's Leather and Eaden Lilley.
-- ANIMAL LIBERATION MILITIA

FINLAND

OCT-DEC/93: location not specified -- Fur stores: locks glued, windows smashed; part of Operation Bite Back.
-- A.L.F.

GERMANY

DEC 25/93: Marburg -- University: 173 animals liberated from lab: 148 hamsters, 86 rabbits.
-- AUTONOME TIERSCHUTZERLNNEN

JAN/94: Bingen -- 5 hunting platforms destroyed.
AUTONOMEN TRIERSCHUTZES

JAN/94: Kirweiler -- 6 hunting platforms destroyed
-- AUTONOME TIERSCHUTZERLNNEN

JAN/94: Hamburg -- 9 fur shops attacked with stinkbombs.
-- TIERMORDMAFIA

MARCH/94: Hunting platforms destroyed. 4 in Vinnum/Coesfeld, 4 in Sachsenwald, 3 in Bad Harzburg and 2 in Heinischer Bruch. Damage over 200,000 DM
-- AUTONOMEN TIERSCHUTZERIN

MARCH/94: Location unspecified. Angling Sabs managed to liberate 2500 worms and maggots.

APR 30, MAY 1/94: Frankfurt -- McDonald's, Burger King, Wienerwald: Toilets blocked; 10,000 DM damage.

HOLLAND

NOV/93: location not specified -- Hunting platforms destroyed.
-- A.L.F.

NOV/93: Amsterdam -- Scientific Council: Locks glued and slogans painted on the walls.
-- AMNESTY FOR ANIMALS

NORTHERN IRELAND

DEC 4/93: location not specified -- McDonald's: windows smashed.
-- A.L.F.

Feb/94: Animal Liberation Activists in Northern Ireland mail timed incendiaries to various blood-junkies in Britain and Ireland. Targets include Irish Coursing Club HQ, Horse and Hound and Countryman's Weekly. Warnings given of further actions.

MAY/94: Belfast -- Activists destroy a research lab by fire.

NORWAY

date not specified: Hamar -- Fur stores and the building almost all furs there go through: sabotage.
-- A.L.F.

JAN 24/93: Slevik-kilen -- *Senet*, a Norwegian-registered outlaw whaler: Ship scuttled; engine room flooded. This is the second Norwegian whaler the Sea Shepherds have sunk. On June 3 Sea Shepherd Captain Paul Watson and Lisa DiStefano were convicted in absentia for their part in this action.
-- SEA SHEPHERD CONSERVATION SOCIETY

SCOTLAND

JUN 3/94: Edinburgh -- Chicken breeding company: Letter bomb exploded. One man injured.
--JUSTICE DEPARTMENT

SWEDEN

SUMMER/93: Stockholm -- Fur stores, butchers, vivisectors: Paint bombs, locks glued.
-- DJURENS HAMNARS/ANIMAL AVENGERS

OCT 16/93: South Sweden -- McDonald's: Anti-McDonald's posters superglued to windows.
-- DJURENS HAMNARS/ANIMAL AVENGERS

NOV 8/93: Stockholm -- Animal breeder: Nine guinea pigs and two rabbits liberated. These animals were being bred for vivisection.
-- DJURENS HAMNARS/ANIMAL AVENGERS

DEC 18/93: Stockholm -- Slaughterhouse district: One meat truck painted and gravel put into petrol tank; many walls to meat factories painted.
-- DJURENS HAMNARS/ANIMAL AVENGERS

DEC 21/93: location not specified -- Angling shop: repainted, locks glued; Meat shop -- repainted; small amount of damage done by arson.
-- DJURENS HAMNARS/ANIMAL AVENGERS

DEC 27/93: Stockholm -- Animal breeder: 7 guinea pigs liberated. This is the same animal breeder that was hit on Nov. 8.
-- DJURENS HAMNARS/ANIMAL AVENGERS

JAN 22/94: Stockholm -- Södersjukhuset (a hospital): Thirty-two lab animals liberated from vivisection lab. The 18 guinea pigs, 9 hamsters, and 5 rabbits were put in safe homes after receiving veterinary treatment. This was Action No. 44 of the Swedish A.L.F.
-- DJURENS BEFRIELSE FRONT (D.B.F.)/A.L.F.

FEB 18/94: Stockholm -- Slaughterhouse district: 3 meat trucks painted with slogans, sugar put in gas tanks, one window smashed, and a small amount of damage by fire.
-- DJURENS HAMNARS/ANIMAL AVENGERS

FEB 26/94: Stockholm -- Slaughterhouse district: walls to factories painted with slogans such as "Meat is Murder", "Death", "Animals have rights", etc.
-- DJURENS HAMNARS/ANIMAL AVENGERS

MAR 3/94: Stockholm -- Two fur stores: "repainted", anti-fur sticker stuck onto window, locks glued.

-- DJURENS HAMNARS/ANIMAL AVENGERS

APR/94: Stockholm -- Djurens Hamnare announce change in policy. Group no longer opposes violence and says it will use violence against animal abusers.

APR 5/94: Stockholm -- Twelve fur stores: spraypainted, locks glued.
-- DJURENS HAMNARS/ANIMAL AVENGERS

MAY 7, 19/94: Stockholm -- Scan (Sweden's biggest meat company): One meat truck burned; other trucks damaged. Slogans such as "murder" and "death" spraypainted in red on every truck. Estimated $180,000 damage.
-- DJURENS AKTIONS GRUPP/ANIMAL ACTION GROUP

U.S.A.

for reports on actions in California, see the next page.

DEC 26/93: Brookfield, Wisconsin -- Chudiks' West Inc (fur store): At least $125,000 damage caused by arson and spraypainting "ALF" and "We skin you alive". Prior to this action the store and the owner's van have been attacked repeatedly with acid, painted slogans, and glued locks.
-- A.L.F.

JAN/94: Ohio -- Unspecified action against animal abusers.

JAN 8/94: Seattle, Washington --
Eddie Bauer: $5,000 worth of merchandise slashed, including down-filled parkas and leather chairs; the store manager reported to police that Eddie Bauer had received several letters telling it to stop selling items made from animal material.
On the street: A woman wearing a parka with a fake fur collar had red paint squirted on the back of her coat. She remembers seeing two men walking past her carrying a sign reading "Fur is dead".

JAN 13/94: Tillamook County, Oregon -- Clearcut site: survey stakes pulled to sabotage those who destroy wildlife habitat.
-- A.L.F.

FEB/94: Detroit area, Michigan: Fur stores: Locks glued, week after week.

FEB/94: Philadelphia area, Pennsylvania -- Ham Sweet Ham: Paint-filled ornaments thrown; lock glued.
Other animal abusers have also been attacked.

FEB 8/94: Pittsburg, Pennsylvania -- Abraville Furriers: Paint bombed.
-- PAINT PANTHERS

FEB 9/94: Columbus, Ohio; Cincinatti, Ohio -- At least two fur stores: Paint bombed.
-- PAINT PANTHERS

FEB 10/94: Chicago, Illinois -- American Fur Mart, Chicago Fur Outlet: Paint bombed.
-- PAINT PANTHERS

FEB 11/94: Omaha, Nebraska -- Julia Talent Fur Store: Paint bombed.
-- PAINT PANTHERS

FEB 14/94:
Denver, Colorado -- Koslough Furs: Paint bombed.
Colorado Springs, Colorado -- Lay Limited Furs: Paint bombed.
-- PAINT PANTHERS
FEB 15/94: Kansas City, Missouri -- Fenhardt Furs, Sident Furs: Paint bombed.
-- PAINT PANTHERS

FEB 16/94: St. Louis, Missouri -- St. Louis Fur and Leather Gallery: Paint bombed.
-- PAINT PANTHERS

FEB 21/94: New York City, New York -- Elizabeth Arden Furs, Fendi Furs: Paint bombed.
-- PAINT PANTHERS

LATE FEB/94: Louisville, Kentucky -- Bowhunting trade show: Elaborate fake bomb left that contained a note saying a real bomb was hidden in the building; 5000 convention-goers evacuated for hours.

MAR 7/94: Atlanta, Georgia -- Capitol City Carriage Co: Five horse-drawn carriages torched. According to a news report, the fire put the company out of business.

APR 4/94: Parma, Ohio -- State Meats, Geiler Meats, another unidentified butcher shop: Doors smashed, locks glued, windows broken, "Meat is Murder" and "A-L-F-" spraypainted. Geiler Meats has been hit three times in the past three years.
-- A.L.F.

APR 25/94: Tempe, Arizona -- Arizona State University: Doors of psychology building padlocked; front gate of Animal Care Program glued; "Stop animal research" and other slogans spraypainted in both locations. According to the chair of the psych department, experiments on rats and pigeons are being done at the psych building.

JUL 10/94: Memphis, Tennessee -- "Especially Leather" Furniture Shop, Southern Meat Market: Locks glued.

JUL/94: Miami,Florida -- 33 Primates liberated from an animal lab supplier. Minor damage. No responsibility claimed.

IF NOT YOU, WHO?
IF NOT NOW, WHEN?

REPORT FROM THE A.L.F. U.S. CONGRESSIONAL CELL

MAY 1994 -- A fur store in Washington, DC had a ball bearing shot through their display window.

MAY 1994 -- A Gillette billboard in Silver Spring, MD was spraypainted with "GILLETTE KILLS ANIMALS" for their continued use of animals in product testing.

JUNE 1994 -- A Roy Rogers/Hardees fast-food restaurant in Kensington, MD had "MEAT IS MURDER" painted on their wall and a brick delivered through their window!

...MORE TO COME
- the U.S. Congressional Cell

HEADACHES FOR ANIMAL EXPLOITERS IN CALIFORNIA, USA, COURTESY OF THE A.L.F.

SEP 15: Alameda County -- Butcher shop, meat jobber: Several windows broken, slogans sprayed.

SEP 20: Alameda County -- Butcher shop, poultry shop: Locks glued, slogans etched on the windows with acid.

OCT 17: Walnut Creek -- Fur store: Spraypainted with slogans, locks glued.

OCT 31: Alameda County --
Butcher shop: locks glued, windows etched with acid, slogans painted on the walls.
Ham retailer: locks glued, windows etched with acid, large front window smashed.
McDonald's: window broken.
Fur store: locks glued, slogans painted on walls, windows etched with acid.

NOV: Los Angeles -- 2 cars belonging to fur store owners: Windows broken.

NOV 22: location not specified --
Van of a veal distributor: windshield etched with acid, tires slashed.
Ham retailer: windows broken, slogans painted, locks glued.
Two butcher shops: locks glued, slogans painted on walls, windows etched.

NOV 26: Oakland, San Francisco, Walnut Creek --
Furman Fur Service (private home): paint bombed.
Bernard's Fine Furs (private home): front windows smashed, paint bombs thrown.
Saga Fur and Leather: paint bombed, locks glued, most windows etched.
Herbert's Furs: locks glued.
Michelle's Furs: locks to building glued.
Sheepskin store: paint bombed.
Kane's Furs: locks glued, slogans painted, front windows broken.
J.E. Harl Furs: locks glued, windows etched, slogans painted, expensive light fixture destroyed.
Middent's Furs: locks glued, windows etched, slogans sprayed.
California Fur Industry skyscraper: locks glued, windows etched.

DEC 23: San Francisco -- Superglue, razor blades, and scissors were used to damage 25-30 fur garments in stores and on the streets.

AN 5: San Jose -- Tarlow's Furs: Several windows smeared with tching fluid.

AN 7: Stockton -- Mansoor Furs, Chuck E. Cheese restaurant: locks glued, slogans spraypainted. Mansoor Furs is the only furrier in Stockton.

AN 15: Beverly Hills -- American Express: Display window smashed to protest promotion of fur.

AN 16: San Francisco -- Robert's Furs: Paint-bombed with red paint.
[Non A.L.F. action]

JAN 17: Oakland -- Middent's Furs: Windows etched, locks glued, slogans painted, canvas awning shredded.

JAN 22: San Francisco -- Kane's Furs: Lock glued, slogans painted on walls, windows broken.

JAN 27: Beverly Hills, Santa Monica:
Somper Furs: Display window smashed.
Adrienne Furs: Display window smashed.
"An escalation in actions is planned for the succeeding months."
-- A.L.F., NOV. 26 CELL

JAN 27: San Francisco -- Nagano Furs: Windows etched.

JAN 29: San Francisco -- Kane's Furs: Holes put through windows.

JAN - FEB: San Diego -- Meat companies: Several companies hit; at least one arson attack in which a refrigerated meat truck was burned and the building was spraypainted with "Meat is Murder".
[-- Farm Animal Revenge Militia]

FEB: Oakland -- At least 2 Hormel meat chili billboards: Spraypainted with slogans like "Go Vegan".

FEB 5: San Francisco --
Kane's Furs: locks glued, slogans painted, neon sign smashed.
Herbert's Furs: door etched, lock glued.
Veal restaurant: windows etched.

FEB 19: Pleasant Hill -- Diablo Valley College: Six rabbits liberated. After students informed the A.L.F. of a professor who killed a rabbit by snapping its neck and then bragged about it, the A.L.F. took the rabbits from the Horticulture garden and placed the rabbits in a permanent home.

FEB 20: Oakland, Walnut Creek --
Middent's Furs: locks glued, windows smashed, paint bombs thrown inside.
J.E. Harl Furs: locks glued, exterior painted.

MARCH: San Francisco / Bay Area --
Hanes Furs: Locks glued, sign partially smashed, slogans painted in front of the store.
Honey Baked Hams: front door lock glued, windows etched, slogans painted on store front.
Butcher shop: windows etched, slogans spraypainted.
Milk ad on street: smashed.
McDonald's: windows smashed.
Sheepskin store: two windows broken.
Robert's Furs: lock glued, slogans painted.
Harris Steak House: locks glued, slogans painted, window etched.
Robert's Corned Beef: two trucks -- slashed tires, painted slogans, etched or broken windows; one had its locks glued.

APRIL, EARTH DAY: San Jose, San Francisco -- "Durham's

Meat in San Jose and Columbus Sausage and Meat in San Francisco were hit by the A.L.F. in an effort to radicalize Earth Day. The attack was an attempt to radicalize Earth Day actions, opposing the usual 'green' corporate bullshit that the general public is being duped into believing will make a difference." (From report of the action in *Out of the Cages.*)

APR 28: San Francisco -- Restaurant serving live lobster: Windows etched, locks glued.
[-- Crustacean Liberation Front]

MAY 1: Hollywood -- Contemporary Hides of West Hollywood: Display window smashed.
-- A.L.F., NOVEMBER 26 CELL
"Increased police patrols and surveillance have limited our number of actions" - communique
The following list of actions is printed as received.

The following is an Action Report listing the activities of the Animal Liberation Front, Southland Unit, which operates in Southern California. The ensuing actions occurred in the period from 1993-1994.

SOMPER'S FURS in Beverly Hills: slogans were spray-painted in back of the store saying, "FUR IS DEAD; and "FUR IS MURDER" as well as "WEAR YOUR OWN SKIN." Front and back locks were glued. The ALF left its calling card. They were targeted twice.

THE RED LOBSTER in Studio City had slogans spray-painted on its walls, and had its locks glued. They were hit twice. The action was tagged "ALF."

WOODLAND HILLS FURRIERS and FASHION FURS in Woodland Hills were spray-painted with slogans "FUR IS DEAD," "FUR IS MURDER," and "FUR BLEEDS." Their locks were glued. The latest action was tagged "PAINT PANTHERS" and pressed-released, appearing on Channel 5 News at 10:00 P.M. and 1:00 A.M. These two stores have been hit about nine times all told. The previous eight actions were tagged "ALF."

HONEYBAKED HAMS in Calabasas had its front windows blown out with explosives as well as its locks glued. The action was tagged "ALF."

THE LEATHER FACTORY in Van Nuys was spray-painted with the slogan 'WEAR YOUR OWN SKIN" and had its locks glued. The action was signed, "ALF." They were targeted twice.

WINNICKS FURS in SHERMAN OAKS was spray-painted with a variety of slogans pertaining to the subject, and had its locks glued. After three hits, they changed their product line to women's clothing. It has recently come to the attention of the ALF that they are once again selling furs. "ALF" was credited.

BURGER KING in Reseda had slogans painted saying "MEAT STINKS" and MEAT IS MURDER," as well as a message regarding their policy of clearcutting rainforest acreage. Their locks were glued. Courtesy of ALF.

ANGELO'S ITALIAN RESTAURANT in Chatsworth had 'VEAL IS CHILD ABUSE" and "VEAL IS MURDER" spray-painted on its walls, and its locks glued. They were targeted twice. ALF.

VITELLO'S ITALIAN RESTAURANT in Encino had "NO VEAL THIS MEAL" spray-painted on its walls and its locks glued. ALF.

TANDY LEATHER in Reseda had appropriate slogans spray-painted on its walls and windows, and had its locks glued. The ALF took credit.

MR. KOSHER MEATS in Sherman Oaks had "MEAT STINKS" and "MEAT IS MURDER" spray-painted on its walls and had its locks glued. They were hit three times. The action was tagged "ALF."

TACO BELL in Tarzana was spray-painted "MEAT STINKS" and "MEAT IS MURDER" and had its locks glued. The ALF took credit.

A veal restaurant had its front window smashed. We cannot supply the name and location of this action for security reasons.

CAFE RENI's in Santa Monica, which serves veal, had "VEAL IS CHILD ABUSE" spray-painted all over its walls, and had its locks glued. The action was tagged "ALF." They were hit twice.

A building owned by Procter & Gamble was spray-painted with slogans saying "ANIMAL ASSASSINS" and "ANIMAL TORTURERS" and had its locks glued. The city cannot be mentioned for security reasons. ALF.

BURGER KING had its walls spray-painted with the slogans "RAINFOREST RAZERS" and "BOVINE BUTCHERS" and had its locks glued. The ALF took credit.

A "B" dealer had his walls, gates, and driveway spray-painted; the ALF took credit. The city cannot be stated for security reasons.

A store selling hunting equipment in Reseda had its walls spray-painted "ANIMAL ASSASSINS" and had its locks glued. They were hit twice. The ALF took credit.

A sheepskin store in Woodland Hills had its locks glued twice. No painting or tagging was done, as the business is located on a main boulevard.

A McDonald's billboard in Santa Cruz was altered to read, "Over One Billion Slaughtered" and tagged "ALF."

A fur store in the New York garment district had its front windows smashed with the aid of a projectile brick. Under the circumstances, the activist thought it prudent to exit the premises immediately, and no painting or tagging was done.

A vivisector in the Playa Del Rey area had animal rights bumper stickers placed on his car. Not a particularly severe action, but one that hopefully embarrassed him, as he would have had to drive to "work" with A.R. messages visible to his psychotic colleagues. No official credit was taken as such.

We hope the above will serve to let you know that the ALF is active in Southern California. We extend our greetings and gratitude to all activists fighting for the rights of animals. In a world where those in power will literally do anything for a buck, torturing and murdering animals, destroying the planet, and thereby harming humans as well, we do what little we can to make their demonic agendas more difficult to execute.

WHY DIRECT ACTION?

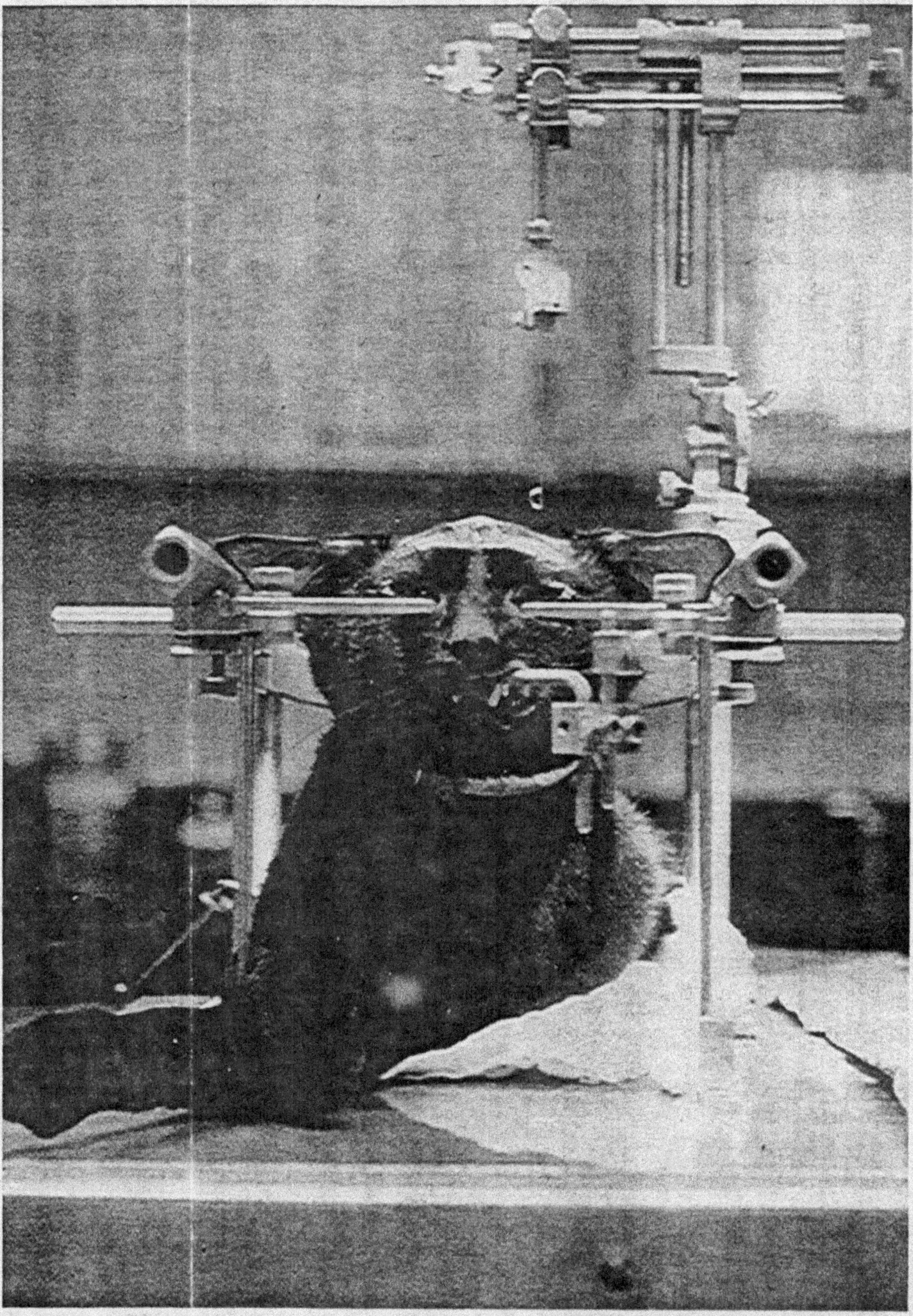

WHY ASK WHY?

THE MANY FACES OF

UNIVERSITY RESEARCH

The fur industry relies on research done in labs to increase their profits through further genetic manipulation of furbearers.

FUR FARM FEED SUPPLIERS

The unnatural state of the pelts of murdered fur farm prisoners is partly due to the types of special feeds developed by feed suppliers.

FUR PROCESSORS

These are the people who clean up the pelts for their future use as vanity items.

FUR AUCTION HOUSES

This is where trappers and fur farmers sell the skins to retailers. This is a particularly weak point in the industry, as only a few auction houses remain open.

FUR FARM ORGANIZATIONS

These are small groups of fur farmers who meet to produce propaganda, lobby state legislators, and manage sales of skins. Only a few are listed in this article.

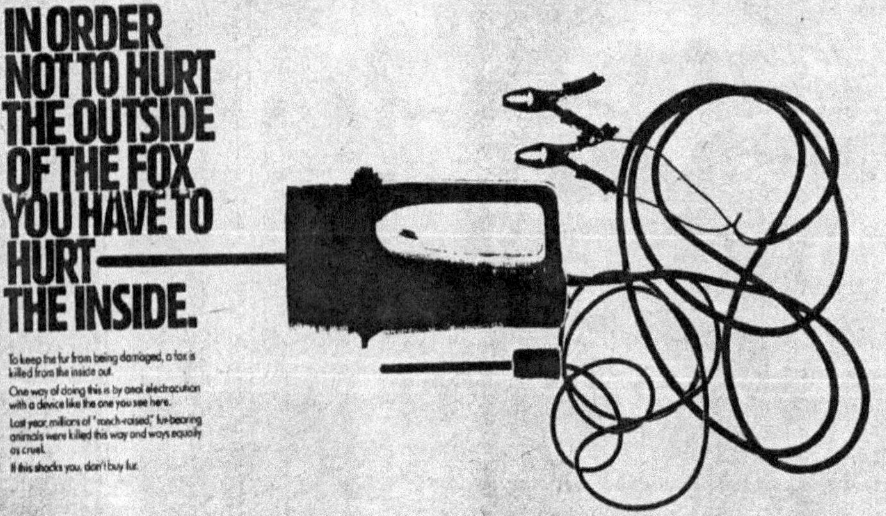
IN ORDER NOT TO HURT THE OUTSIDE OF THE FOX YOU HAVE TO HURT THE INSIDE.
To keep the fur from being damaged, a fox is killed from the inside out.
One way of doing this is by anal electrocution with a device like the one you see here.
Last year, millions of "ranch-raised," fur-bearing animals were killed this way and ways equally as cruel.
If this shocks you, don't buy fur.

FUR FARM EQUIPMENT SUPPLIERS

TRAPPING SUPPLIERS

FUR FARMS

CHINCHILLA -- There are 6 or 7 farms left which imprison over 1000 animals, and a few smaller ones. There are only four buyers for chinchilla pelts in North America.

MINK -- As of 1993, there were 571 mink farms left in the USA, down from 2,000 a few years ago. 57 of these farms also imprison fox. Wisconsin "produces" the most mink pelts but Utah has the most mink farms.

Numbers of mink farms in the USA:

Utah: 150	Wisconsin: 114	Minnesota: 72
Oregon: 29	Washington: 28	Idaho: 27
Iowa: 25	Pennsylvania: 21	Illinois: 15
New York: 12	Ohio: 11	South Dakota: 7

[Other states: 45]

UR - University Research

FFES - Fur Farm Equipment Supplier

CANADA

FAH - North American Fur Auctions: 65 Skyway, Rexdale, ONT, M9W 6C7

FFO - Canada Mink Breeders Association: 65 Skyway Ave, Suite B, Rexdale, ONT, M9W 6C7

USA

COLORADO

FFES - Wildlife Pharmaceuticals: 1401 Duff Drive, Suite 600, Fort Collins, CO 80524; call them at 1-800-222-WILD. This company is the only US company that makes melatonin implants, which are used to speed the process of fur-bearing animals producing a prime coat (which saves fur farms money on food and labor).

GEORGIA

FF - Crider Furs, Inc: Route 2, Box 150, Nicholls, GA 31554; the largest fur farm in the USA, with 82,000 mink imprisoned there (most mink farms are much smaller).

IDAHO

TS - Rocky Mountain Fur Co: 1507 Willis Rd, Caldwell, ID 83605

FF/M - Jeffrey Hobbs, Body T. Hobbs, Larry D. Kingsford (3 separate mink farms): Franklin, ID

ILLINOIS

FP - National Superior: 4447 West Cortland St, Chicago, IL 60634

FFES - Valentine Equipment Co: 4259 S. Western Blvd, Chicago, IL 60609; Call them at 1-800-GET-STUF.

FP - Platinum Co-op Processing: 113 Whiteside, Columbia, IL 62236

FFES - Illinois Mink Wire Co: 38614 North Fairfield Rd, Lake Villa, IL 60046

FF/M - Gengel Mink Farm: 38614 North Fairfield Road, Lake Villa, IL

INDIANA

FF - Hoosier Hills Fur Farm: RFD 1, Lawrenceburg, IN 47025

THE FUR INDUSTRY

CODING FOR THE ADDRESS LIST BELOW

FF - Fur Farm

FF/M - Mink Fur Farm

FP - Fur Processor

FAH - Fur Auction House

FFFS - Fur Farm Feed Supplier

TS - Trapping Supplier

FFO - Fur Farm Organiation

IOWA

FF/M - Twilight Mink Farm: RR 2, Box 119, Webster City, Iowa 50595

FF/M - Hillpipre Mink Farm: 136 Parkview Dr, Webster City, Iowa 50595

MASSACHUSETTS

FF/M - Carmel's Mink Ranch: Route 143, Hinsdale, MA 01235

FFES - Riverdale Mills: 130 Riverdale St, Northbridge, MA 01534; sells cage wire.

MICHIGAN

FF/M - Robert Roell: Star Route, Box 92, Channing, MI 49815

FF/M - Jim & Vince Roell: Box 88, Channing, MI 49815

UR - Michigan State University: East Lansing, MI; still hurting badly from an A.L.F. raid.

MINNESOTA

FFES - Friesens Inc: Box 889, Detroit Lakes, MN 56502

FFES - Mills Fur Farm Supply: Box 348, Eden Valley, MN 55329

FFES - Crown of Minnesota: 1200 Central Ave. NE, Minneapolis, MN 55413

FFFS - Heger Co: 545 Hardman Ave, South St. Paul, MN

FFO - Fur Farm "Animal Welfare" Coalition: 225 E. 6th St. #230, St. Paul, MN 55101; described in *The Militant Vegan* as "the biggest and most evil".

MISSISSIPPI

TS - Duke Traps: West Point, Mississippi

MISSOURI

FF/M - Cary Mink Farm: Route 1, Box 98-A, California, Missouri 65018

MONTANA

FF/M - Crowell Mink Farm: 1109 Church Ave, Bozeman, MT 59715

UR - Rocky Mountain Laboratories: Hamilton, MT

NEBRASKA

FF - Kirkpatrick Fur Farm: 2304 South Memorial Park Road, Grand Island, NE 68803

FFFS - Heartand Blends: Route 1, Scribner, NE 68057

NEW JERSEY

FAH - North American Fur Auctions: 1275 Valley Brook, Lyndhurst, NJ

FP - Tubari Ltd: 3 Rosol Lane, Saddle Brook, NJ 07662

COURTESY OF COALITION AGAINST FUR FARMS

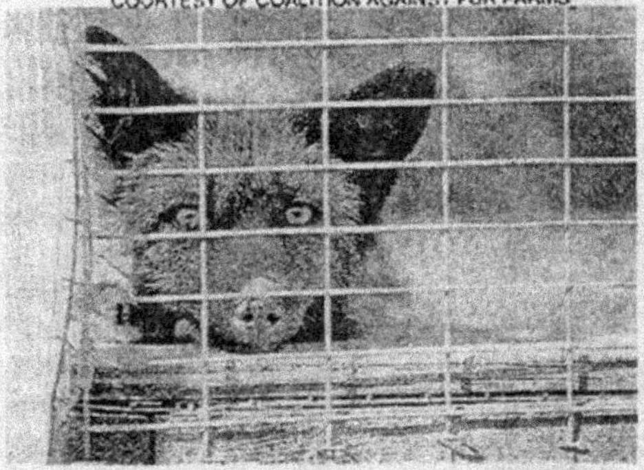

A fox, prior to its release into the wild by animal liberators

NEW YORK

FF/M - Merle Main Mink Ranch: Route 60, Gerry, NY 14740

NORTH DAKOTA

FFO - American Fox Association: Max, ND

OHIO

TS - Northern Fur and Sport: 9191 Leavitt Rd, Elyria, OH 44035; the largest trapping supplier.

FF/M - Mohoric Mink Ranch: 7035 Chatham Rd, Medina, OH 44256

TS - Verleeng Trappers: Smithville, OH

OREGON

FF/M - Trails End Fur Farm: Route 3, Box 546, Astoria, OR 97103

FF/M - Bill & Nancy Tynkila, Ray & Verna Tynkila (2 separate mink farms): Route 6, Box 118, Astoria, OR 97103

PENNSYLVANIA

TS - Krufick Outdoor Supplies: 30 Lightcap Rd, Latrobe, PA 15650

TS - Woodstream Traps: Lititz, PA

TS - Russ Carmen: New Milford, PA; described in *The Militant Vegan* as "a real scumbag".

FF/M - Burns Mink Ranch: Box 377, RD3 Bend Rd, New Wilmington, PA 16142

UTAH

UR - Utah State University: Logan, UT

TS - Montgomery Fur Co: Ogden, UT

FFES - Utah Fur Breeds Agricultural Co-op: 8700 South 700 W, Sandy, UT 84070

FFO - Fur Breeders Agricultural Cooperative: 8700 South 700 W, Sandy, UT 84070

WASHINGTON

FFFS - Northwest Fur Feeds Cooperative: Edmonds, WA

FAH - Seattle Fur Exchange: 240 Andover Park West, Seattle, WA

UR - Washington State University: Spokane, WA

WISCONSIN

FFFS - Wisco Fur Foods: Box 10, Abbotsford, WI 54405

FFES - Continental Fur Farm Supplies: Box C, Delavan, WI 53115

UR - University of Wisconsin: Madison and Milwaukee, WI

FFFS - National Fur Foods: Box 220, New Holstein, WI 53061; crucial feed supplier for the industry; runs an experimental mink ranch in Oshkosh, near New Holstein. Call them at 1-800-558-5803.

FP - B&W Pelt Processing: Route 2, Oranton, WI 54436

Information from "The Militant Vegan" #4, Jan 1994. The North American A.L.F.S.G. takes no responsibility for any of these listings being incorrect or out of date.

WHEN STAR TREK ISN'T ON:

For all you Pacific Northwesties, an anonymous note sent to the North American ALFSG reads:

"Dr. Max Cynader, who blinds kittens at Vancouver General Hospital (been doing blinding in various places for years) may live at 3595 S.W. Marine Drive, West Vancouver". West Vancouver is in southwest BC, Canada.

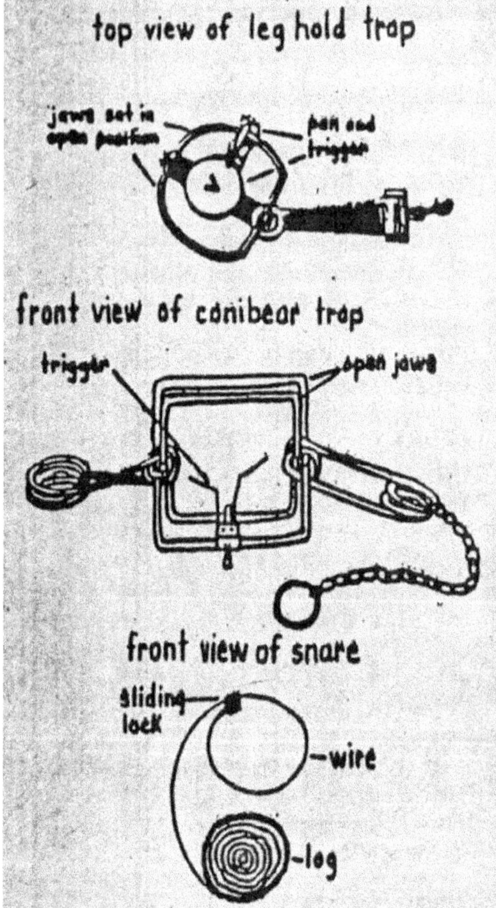

FOR PHONE FUN, CALL 1-800

Linda Lundtrom: 1-800-66LINDA
Canadian outdoor clothing designer who recently began promoting the use of fur as an ecologically sound product.

United Vaccines: 1-800-283-6465
Fur farm supplier.

Central Ohio Chinchilla Supply: 1-800-742-6024

Valley Industries: 1-800-722-6455
Fur farm equipment supplier.

Shady Brook Farms/Turkey Processing: 1-900-297-4077

Trapper and Predator Caller (magazine): 1-800-258-0929

ADVANCED

In response to the reader who was unable to locate traplines based on advice in "Ecodefense" (ed. note: see box on bottom corner of next page), it is possible that there were simply no traps in their area at the time they searched. The key to finding traps is to understand how the trapper operates, to "think" like a trapper. Equally critical is a knowledge of the area you are working. You must know the busy roads, the back roads, the snowmobile trails, and how they are used by locals in the trapping season. Know where the target species travel by looking for their tracks in loose dirt, streamside mud or fresh snow.

Trappers are usually highly mobile and will trap an area for a week or two before moving on to another location. Their goal is to "trap out" the available animals and then find a new source of blood money. If the number of catches drops off, or fails to materialize at all, the traps are pulled out and moved elsewhere.

A good time to start trap hunting is in the early weeks of the trapping season (see your state regulations) when trappers are competing with one another for the easy pickings. Another surge in trapping often occurs in late winter/early spring when the mating urge increases travel among target species, especially solitaries like cats, making them vulnerable to trapping even in areas that were trapped out earlier in the season.

As mentioned in *Ecodefense* most trappers are part-timers, working their trapping in around their other obligations (like a job or school.) This means that they are most likely to be traveling their trapline early or late in the day. Others are only seasonally employed and trapping is their winter "job." Mornings are favored by some to reduce the chance of losing an overnight catch to a "trap thief," who is usually another trapper. Checking back roads, jeep trails, and other likely access routes after an overnight snow may reveal a trapper's tire tracks left in the early hours. Still others may work their trapline after getting off work later in the day.

You can monitor a number of back roads by carefully brushing out a narrow strip of old tire tracks and waiting for fresh tracks to appear on top of the smoothed soil or snow, indicating recent use. To do this, pick a spot near where the road leaves a major traveled route--aided, if necessary, by a landmark alongside the road that you can remember, such as a rock, bush or tree. Adjacent to this, brush smooth a narrow (3-6 inch) strip across either the left or right hand set of tire tracks. Don't brush a wide swath or brush out tracks all the way across the road as this is both unnecssary and much too noticeable. Don't leave obvious scrape marks to reveal what you've done. A daily check, such as a drive-by, will reveal fresh tracks at a glance that may lead you to a trapline. By erasing the fresh tracks you find, you can determine the approximate frequency with which the back road is used. Because trapping regulations usually specify a frequency for trapline checks by the trapper (often 24 or 48 hours--check your copy of the regs), daily or every-other-day use may reveal a trapper at work.

ALWAYS have a rehearsed cover story for being in the area, along with the necessary props. A rifle and small game license can make an acceptable "instant redneck." If you encounter a person or a parked motor vehicle, DON'T STOP. Memorize the location with the aid of a landmark and keep on going. A friendly wave may be appropriate.

Trappers' vehicles are subject to the abuse of back road driving, and are often older, dirty rattletraps. Pickups are popular because smelly items like rotting bait, odorous lures and animal carcasses can be carried in back along with traps, a shovel, a hammer for driving tap stakes, and assorted

HOW TO LEGALLY

At all costs, hunters want to avoid the following:
1. Noise
2. Scents & odors (gun smoke, human smell, etc.)
3. Visibility

Bogus hunters can supply the above three deterrents to successful hunting. First of all, the anti-hunter must look like a hunter, act like a hunter, and talk like a hunter. To make it absolutely legal, it is necessary to secure a hunting license. Then, engage in the following tactics:
1. Have some common type of flagrant, bright colored piece of clothing (hat, vest, etc.)
2. Plot your area of coverage and travel in pairs (cover as much of a hunting area as possible).
3. Get a safe shooting shotgun & use high power shells -- they make more noise.
4. Alternately and periodically shoot into a dead stump or dirt bank (Also, talk & chatter

small accessories. Because most trappers work locally, you should know the license plate letters that are typical in the area you're working so as to keep from being distracted by a visitor who's out from the city.

Finding the actual trap set requires practice and a trapper's knowledge of animal movements. Traplines are set along natural wildlife travel routes. Traps set for coyote and fox favor roads, trails, canyon bottoms, streambeds, and saddles in ridges. Bobcats are usually taken on canyon ledges or rocky ridges. Target species mark their territories with scent posts that favor prominent visual features in the landscape, like solitary trees, isolated stumps and rocks, old bones and dried carcasses, and are similarly favored by trappers. I've found traps beside large rocks overlooking a canyon bottom (for bobcat), underneath a tree that stood out slightly from the edge of a clearing, alongside a tree stump in a meadow, and in the middle of narrow paths paralleling streambeds. Experienced trappers like to set traps under evergreens so that eagles don't spot the trapped animal and "steal" it.

Once the trapper locates a probable area for a trap set, he has to think about getting the animal to place its foot on a small spot of ground where the trap is buried. Some will shoot an animal (sometimes illegal if it's a "game" animal) or place a chunk of an animal carcass in a prominent spot to lure animals to the area. If you see ravens, crows, eagles or hawks circling an area, or taking off on your approach, they may be feeding on such a bait. The trapper Claude Dallas, who murdered two Idaho game wardens, was notorious for killing raptors in traps set alongside this type of bait (and it's usually legal!) Most trappers will make their trap sets nearby, on trails, beneath nearby trees, or near potential scent posts, to catch animals traveling to and from the bait.

Along animal travel routes, the trapper will look for something to attract a predator. First he'll look at what is naturally there. I've found several traps set at the mouths of small animal burrows. Others were buried in spots where a trail crossed through a narrow passage between shrubs or rocks. An additional attraction may be necessary. An animal bone, even a single vertebra, may draw a hungry and curious animal to the trap. Always popular is a dead animal, like a rabbit or skunk, wired to a low tree limb with one or more traps set immediately below it. A small bundle of feathers hung from a tree and flapping in the breeze is visually attractive, especially for cats.

Often these obvious visual and odor lures are backed up by one or more "blind sets," traps without any attractant nearby, usually set on a trail leading to or from a baited trap set. A smooth spot in the dirt, often with rocks or tree branches set on either side to direct the animal's foot directly onto the trap, are all that reveals these sets.

After finding a likely trapping area, post a lookout or keep an ear cocked for approaching vehicles while trap hunting. It is easy at ths point to develop "tunnel vision" and overlook warning sounds and sights.

Before you try to locate the trap, it is important to study the appearance of the spot carefully. It is essential that you restore the area to its original appearance before you leave so that the trapper will not suspect trouble and simply replace the missing trap. To locate the actual trap you can probe the ground with a stout stick, or with your booted foot. The trap will be secured, by chain or wire, to either a stake or a "drag" like a large tree limb designed to hang up in the brush when a trapped animal tries to flee. The drag must be left exactly as you found it. Stakes can usually be pulled up and disposed of along with the trap. If you can't pull up the stake or cut the trap loose (the multi-purpose Leatherman-type tool is handy!) try bending as many parts of the trap as you can by smashing it with a rock. Then, re-bury it and restore the spot to its original appearance.

Throw all traps and stakes Away where they will be hard to find. NEVER carry anything incriminating out with you. Erase your own tracks as you leave. In snow, I carry a cheap pair of insulated "moon boots" so that only these tracks are left at the scene, and they can be discarded with little loss. An important note about winter tracks: unless you can wipe the tracks away, avoid stepping in mud as these tracks can harden like concrete and last weeks or months. Stepping in snow is usually preferred since melting can distort or destroy them. The local game warden may investigate trap sabotage, and these people are usually reasonably competent trackers. From the standpoint of evidence, good forensic photographing or impressioning of footprints in snow is difficult and the necessary skills are not usually available in rural areas for low priority crimes. Don't be intimidated if law enforcement tells you they found "your" footprints. The evidence may simply be of a similar sole that is of common manufacture (you are, of course, intelligent enough to only buy common discount house brands a size or two different from your normal shoe size!)

Finally, don't trust your memory. Study all the available trapping manuals and trap sabotage material again before you go trap hunting, and NEVER forget your security precautions.

reprinted from *Earth First! Journal*, Litha 1994

[ed. note: *Ecodefense: A Field Guide to Monkeywrenching*, 3rd edition, which is mentioned a couple times in the above article, is available from the EF! Journal, PO Box 1415, Eugene, OR 97440 USA. This is an invaluable resource and action manual. Highly recommended. 350 pages; $US 18.

Also available from these folks is *If An Agent Knocks*, a pamphlet to help you deal with visits from F.B.I. agents or other federal investigators. The legal specs apply to the USA only but there are some good general tips.]

SAB A HUNT

as you hike through the woods).

5. Smoke cigars & cigarettes (don't burn down the forest). Use other odors, e.g. gun oil, ammonia, stink bombs, citronella oil, camphor, etc.
6. Get some of those military training whistles for dogs -- above the frequency of human hearing. If a dog can hear those high cycles so can all other wild game animals.
7. Watch for the sitters, i.e. hunters who wait for the drivers to push game toward them.

The above will alert the game and make them very wary. It will also cause them to hole up and scatter to safer areas. Oh, I know! It spooks them, but would you rather be spooked a bit or dead? It will work and it is all legal. No warden or law enforcement officer can do a thing about it.

- Yuka N. Shutem II

reprinted from "Out of the Cages" #9

PICKING OUR TARGETS: THINKING ABOUT RACISM, CLASSISM AND THE ANIMAL LIBERATION FRONT

As a Jew, everything I do, including work I have done as an A.L.F. activist, I do as a Jew. As a Jewish animal liberation activist, it turns my stomach to hear of A.L.F. actions against kosher butchers.

I am not saying that Jewish people should be "allowed" to profit from the animal abuse industry. But I would encourage other A.L.F. activists to think very carefully about who to target in their actions.

In "animal rightism and the ideology of the single issue" (ed. note: see next page), the author writes, "...the struggle to relieve animals from cruel exploitation is very political. Each particular aspect (i.e. who owns the land on which hunts devastate the wildlife, who dictates psychological control experiments...who profits from the vast food industries...etc) is intimately linked to our own lives and the problems we face."

There are many potential targets for direct action against animal abuse. I would suggest that it is in the best interests of the animals for A.L.F. activists to choose targets wisely, with attention to maximum impact on the animal abuse industry and some thought to the political ramifications of our actions.

For example, it is relatively easy to glue locks of a small kosher butcher shop. What are the effects of this kind of action, in terms of stopping animal abuse? Well, if you do it enough times you may put the shop out of business. Big deal. Small shops are tiny cogs in the animal abuse industry. We can pick off hundreds of these shops and the industry itself will keep on ticking. What we must strive to do, in my opinion, is strike closer to the heart of the animal abuse industry. In terms of the meat branch of the exploitation industry, let's do our research and find out who are the main suppliers of the animals. Let's work harder on large actions: repeatedly hitting the big players in the industry, instead of carrying out many small actions.

We can see how class can be used by the profiteers as a weapon against change, and how racism and classism intersect, by looking at how the earth-destroyers have manipulated environmental struggles into a "jobs vs the earth" corner. One example of this is in local struggles against industrial forestry, where loggers and "environmentalists" (mostly white and middle/upper-class) have been pitted against each other, while the shareholders and the industry thugs sit comfortably in their plush chairs. Meanwhile, the local indigenous people are tokenized, ignored, or bought off by the environmentalists, government, and/or industry--all with the agenda of minimizing native liberation struggles.

The same perils hold true for the animal liberation movement if we continue to blur the distinctions between those who make a huge proft from animal abuse and those who work in the industry and make enough money to get by.

There are other ramifications of A.L.F. actions in terms of the impact on the diversity of our movement. I am not crying diversity for any "politically correct" reasons, but because I firmly believe that unless we are a diverse movement, with the variety of skills and experience that diversity brings, we will fail.

When we choose targets such as kosher butchers, we are targeting people who are very used to having to fight desperately in order to survive. Jewish people are some of the most tenacious, skilled fighters and I would seriously think about the ramifications of making Jewish communities into our enemies rather than potential allies.

Non-Jewish people must understand that Jewish food laws have been an important part of Jewish culture, and Jewish resistance to assimilation and genocide, for thousands of years. The Jewish community is NEVER going to accept the demands of non-Jewish animal rights activists. It is up to people <u>within</u> these communities to bring about change.

The willingness of some animal rights activists to ally with the neo-Nazis (ed. note: see article on next page) shows ho prevalent racism still is in our movement. I have seen many othe examples of racism in general and anti-Jewish racism in particula within our movement. This serves to alienate Jewish animal right activists.

I would suggest that any animal liberation activists who ar serious about making alliances with Jewish people, without sellin out the animals, should think about how to assist Jewish anima liberation activists in taking on the task of changing our communi ties' abuse of animals. By targeting kosher butchers, you make tha change more difficult for us.

I do not mean to belittle the work of other A.L.F. activists who have risked their freedom to try to make a difference for th animals. But if we are going to successfully end animal exploita tion, I believe we must move beyond focussing on our short-tern aims of ending the suffering of individual animals and look at long term strategy, which includes examinations of how racism an classism affect our ability to put the animal abuse industry out o business.

- article and recipe by devora

FOOD FOR US: VEGAN TREATS

This recipe is for my great-grandma, who at 92 still scares the pant off anyone who tries to help in her kitchen. See Bobo, I <u>can</u> be vegetarian and still eat Jewish!

VEGAN KNISHES

from *New Farm Vegetarian Cookbook*

Dough:	Filling:
1 cup cooked potatoes, peeled & mashed	1 1/2 cups mashed potatoes
1/4 cup oil	1/4 tsp. pepper
1 tsp. salt	1/2 tsp. salt
3 cups flour	1/2 cup onions, sauteed in 1/4 cup margarine
1 tsp. baking powder	
1/2 cup cold water	

Dough: Mix potatoes, oil, and salt. In a separate bowl, mix the flour and baking powder and add to the potato mix. Mix together thoroughly. Make a well in the center and add the water. Knead into smooth dough; place on a lightly floured board and cover with a bowl or cloth and let it rest for 1/2 hour.

Filling: Combine all ingredients and mix well.

To make the knishes: Cut dough into 4 sections. Roll each section out as thin as possible. Cut into 4" x 6" rectangles for nice big knishes, smaller for appetizers. Place some filling in the center of each rectangle and fold the two shorter ends toward the centre, then fold the longer ends over to make a double-folded dumpling. Bake on a well-oiled baking sheet, fold side down, at 350 F for about 1/2 hour (until golden).

Serve with tofu sour cream.

• •

"Food for Thought" will be a regular feature of "Underground". This is a space for discussion <u>with the intention of furthering the work the of the A.L.F.</u> Articles that merely bash or trash will not be printed here; articles that attempt to contribute to analysis and strategy will. In order to balance a free discussion of ideas with the limitations of the "Underground" editor's patience, reasons will be given any time an article is not printed in this space and the editor will make some attempt to discuss the editorial concerns with the author of the article.

animal rightism and the ideology of the single issue

reprinted from "as long as there are slaughterhouses...then there shall be battlefields.", 1991.

What single issue politics does is attend to 'symptoms' but not tack the disease itself. It presents such issues as if they are errations or faults in the system. In reality such problems are the evitable consequence of a social order based on exploitation and erarchical power.

The animal rights movement has unfortunately become a single sue. Rather than extend its disgust with the way non-human ecies are treated in this society to a criticism of this society itself, e movement tends to disappear up its own arse and wallows in its vn cliquey issues. Rarely do the 'voices' of the animal rights ovement speak about anything other than animal rights, almost if nothing else existed...but it does.

"there is an undercurrent of misanthropy in the movement; the ea that all people are evil and if only they could be done away with some way everything would be alright" - P. Gravett, Arkangel #5.

The fact is that the animal liberation movement is made up of ıman beings and we can't get away from that. Issues relating to JR lives are important to us, as individuals, yet somehow the ovement presents the image that the only true struggle is that for imal rights. Somewhere down the line the animal rights movement has lost its critical tongue, it has ceased to analyse society. ıy critical look at society would show that all of the issues are ıked together, that the thread of exploitation spins a web in which are all trapped.

Just like our lives, the struggle to relieve animals from cruel ploitation is very political. Each particular aspect (i.e. who owns e land on which hunts devastate the wildlife, who dictates ychological control experiments (tested on animals before being plied to humans), who profits from the vast food industries, who cides to mount the huge surveilance operations etc, etc) is timately linked to our own lives and the problems we face. There a huge political system out there, which perpetuates the abuse of imals, the wholescale destruction of the environment and our n enslavement into lives dulled by work and alienation, because do so is profitable for a small class of people.

However, some people have forgotten this:

"What reason for living do ordinary, unenlightened people have, agging out their tiny meaningless lives, changing nothing, achiev- g nothing, merely taking up space in an already grossly over- owded world? As I look out of the window of a train, gazing down a town or a city, and see all the rows and rows of houses stretching to the distance my mind recoils in horror with the thought, "How n they stand to live?", "How can there be enough within their lives make it worth the effort." - Ronnie Lee, Arkangel #5

The notion of a passive and guilty public - of public opinion as it were something real and concrete is becoming worryingly evalent. Individuals struggling for a better world often become ter and cynical, suggesting that "ordinary people" really do lieve everything that is said to them by the media - as if they don't ink or talk about it. Often individuals involved in the animal eration movement talk about the public as if it were an abstract ing not a vast collection of individuals, each capable of thought d subjective opinion.

Because the public is *seen* or *perceived* to be not listening or anging, a contemptuous attitude emerges in which ordinary ople are condemned as being non-thinkers, passive or ignorant. rdinary" people even become the enemy to some people.

This is undoubtably one of the main reasons why working clas ple are so under represented, and why the animal rights move- nt hasn't developed even the vaguest hint of class analysis.

The fact that the media tends to be the key information source society, that it is perpetuating the status quo (and that most finitely includes animal abuse), and that it is but one of a whole host of factors playing upon every individual cannot be just conveniently ignored.

Society makes life a bit easier if individuals appear to be inconsiderate, passive or naive. Most people have little control over events in their lives and all around images and information is displayed re-enforcing this notion.

Single issue campaigns fragment the struggle for a sane, free world by containing each problem within its own isolated campaign. Dedication to the campaign is what is required. To concentrate energy - which might otherwise be expended in activities which would really change society - into campaigns for specific issues. Once confronted with concrete, moderate and "realistic" demands, the state can grant them, partially grant them or stall them indefinately. (The long awaited ban on hunting with hounds being a clear example)

It's unfortunate that even the most ardent and sussed activsts can become sucked into the all pervasive single issue ideology of it all; even to such an extent that people who should know better, accept the idea of petitions to the government or the European parliament or consumer boycotts. Animal rights campaigners excuse such things by saying that they attract people to stalls etc. - maybe so, but in doing so it is just re-inforcing the notion that we have no control - we sign away our control to THEM with petitions. "Someone will sort it out, legislate about it." Really? When?

Even more repulsive is the inclusion of articles by blatantly fascist people in Arkangel (an animal rights magazine) under the pathetic excuse that it has a policy of non-censorship. Fascists are the ultimate censors - you cannot allow freedom of speech to those whose ideology promotes the restriction of freedom of speech. Such scum have latched onto every issue out to try and bolster some support for their archaic cause. Those in the animal rights movement who want unity with fascists and still describe abbattoirs and laboratories as Belsens or Auschwitzes are not only incredulously hypocritical but also dangerous. Some of us won't accept fascists on our streets never mind being allowed a voice in our publications. Fascism is based on hierarchical power and the notion of superiority, in exactly the same way animal abuse is. There can be no unity with authoritarians and as ever the song remains the same "the only good fascist is a dead one". Some of us are not afraid to include the police in this equation.

those who's revolution only goes half way dig their own graves

The legislation cited as victories by animal rights magazines etc. are no more than token gestures and a whole lot less than half measures. All too often the adaptive flexibility of the economic market and its protecting ideologies in parliament and the media are totally ignored. Since animal abuse is, in the end, about making money supported by the idea that animals are ours to do with as we please - by ignoring and avoiding criticising the market we are going nowhere.

Capitalism is the totalitarianism of economics over life. All life becomes a commodity in this society. That's what animals have been reduced to, that is what the majority of people in the world have become. How long are we going to waste all our compassionate anger quibbling about the small details? For animals and ourselves liberation must be total or it will be nothing.

One of the ways the actions going under the name of the a.l.f. are so crucial is that **they demonstrate by example that we need not be passive, that we need not have our struggles fought by representatives and that there are ways in which everyone can, quite easily, act against the enemies *and* cause them considerable damage.**

BEWARE

Armed bands are roaming the highways and marching through your neighborhood. They may even try to enter your home! Watch for these gang identifiers:

Vehicles: Sports cars, four-door sedans, and vans, often painted black and white or blue and white, with sirens and flashing red and blue lights.

Clothing: Well kempt dress uniforms, usually blue or black (gang colors), and adorned with patches and badges. Head-wear varies. Other accessories include gun belts, handcuffs, hand-held radios, and large flashlights.

Armaments: Handguns, shotguns, assault rifles, tear-gas rifles, billy clubs, shields, bullet-proof armor, helmets and face-shields.

Demeanor: Surly and hostile or aggressively friendly

These gangs are highly organized, well armed, and potentially violent. Warn your friends and neighbors

Do Not Provoke Them!

Do Not Let Them Corner You!

Protect Yourself

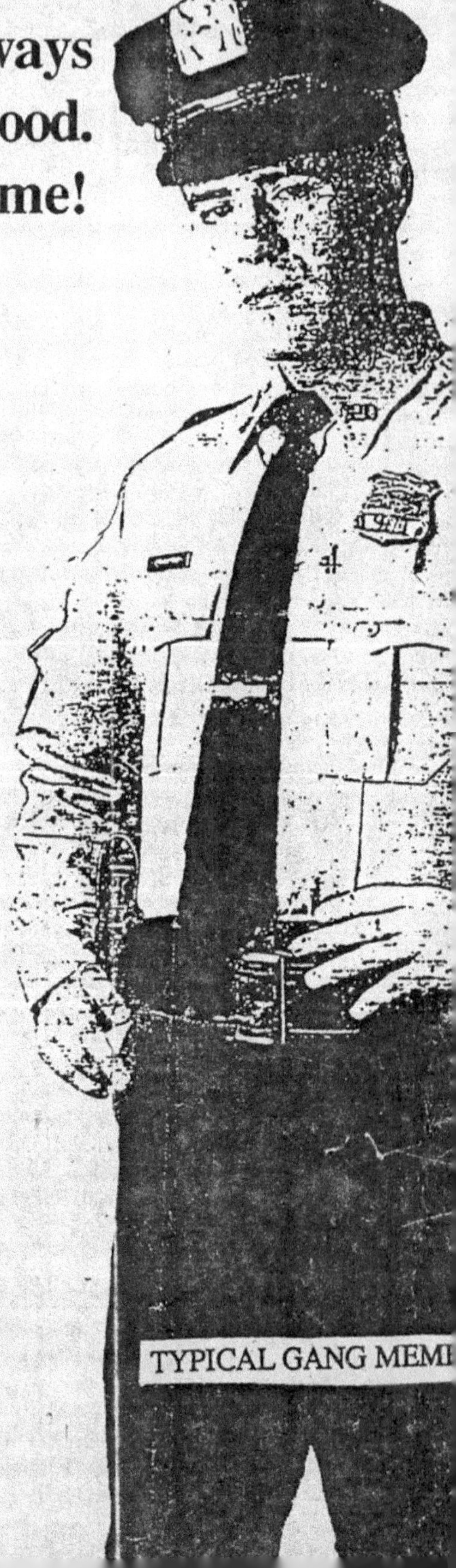

UNDERGROUND

#2
Nov 94

THE MAGAZINE OF THE NORTH AMERICAN ANIMAL LIBERATION FRONT SUPPORTERS GROUP

$ 4

cording to a
ɔort by the U.S.
partments of
stice and
riculture,
tween 1977 - June
93, in the US alone
ere were:

313 documented actions involving property damage or personal injury against medical researchers, furriers, and meat producers

this includes 21 arsons, 14 fire bombings, 186 other acts of property damage, 28 bomb threats/ hoaxes/attempts, and 77 thefts

43% of these actions targeted bio-medical research facilities, mostly at universities and National Institutes of Health

- estimated monetary value was $137 million dollars in damage
- years of research has also been destroyed: one attack alone (at Michigan State University) cost 32 years of research on minks
- nearly 60% of these actions were claimed by the A.L.F.
- 43 of the incidents involved threats or injury to individuals or damage to their homes

from article by Robert Cassidy, Editor-In-Chief of "R&D Magazine", as printed in "The People's Agenda" October 1994 (Putting People First's newsletter)

16 YEARS OF DIRECT ACTION FOR ANIMAL LIBERATION

$137 MILLION DAMAGE

O B L I G A T O R Y   S T U F F

DEDICATION ~ LINDA COTNAM
Sept 27 1959 - Nov 5 1994
This issue is dedicated to Linda, who was a tireless activist in so many movements, including women's, queer, and animal liberation. Linda was arrested in 1987 with four other activists for A.L.F. actions in the Toronto area. For the last 4 years of her life Linda worked at a women's shelter helping women who were living on the street.
Her favorite sound was the sound of breaking glass.

THANKS to all those who helped us put out this issue of *Underground*, particularly: Annette Tibbles, Darren Thurston, David Barbarash, devorah, John Perotti, Rod Coronado, and all other contributors; R@bbix, Vegan Resistance, the UK ALFSG, and all the groups that gave us the o.k. to reprint information from their newsletters; *Prison News Service* and the Prison Activist Resource Centre for their immense contributions; *Schism*'s Neat-Gizmos-&-All-Round-Swell-Guy-Editor and everyone else who put so many hours into production; all folks taking direct action for earth/animal/human liberation; friends and comrades who helped support us after the burglary; and last but definitely not least our financial angels, anonymous and otherwise. A special thank you to Corndog for organizing so many benefits in such a short period of time!

LOUD HOWLS to all political prisoners, especially: Darren Thurston, John Perotti and the Lucasville brothers, Lise Olsen, Little Rock Reed, Mark Davis, Milton Born With A Tooth, Rod Coronado, W.C. Lassell, Allison McKeon, Angie Hamp, Annette Tibbles, Colin Chatfield, Dave Callender, Greg Avery, Gurjeet Aujla, Keith Mann, Max Watson, Terry Helsby, Paul S, and others who are raging against the machine. And no, it is not true that Darren is going to show off his new jail-acquired muscles in an ALFSG calendar—that is a vicious rumor.

NO THANKS to the fuckers who robbed our home/office; whoever led to Rod's arrest; Jessica Sandham and all other snitches; Putting People First/Kathleen Marquardt and their ilk; groups that insist on promoting unnecessary conflict and divisive infighting; and of course CSIS/NSIS/FBI/BATF/other federal agencies.

HOW TO GET INCLUDED IN THE THANKS SECTION: Give us presents. Right now we are really in desperate need of equipment (or money for equipment), to replace what was stolen. We are also looking for donations of additional equipment, so we can stop spending so much money on printing/photocopying/faxing and put the money to better uses. On our wish list, from most urgent to least urgent: fax machine, laser printer, photocopier, graphics scanner, 9400/higher modem, or other Mac-compatible gadgets or computers. We can also use donations of unused Canadian stamps or international postal orders. All gifts, large and small, are sincerely appreciated.

~~SUBMISSIONS~~ ASSERTIONS TO *UNDERGROUND*

We welcome letters, articles, artwork, action reports, or anything else for publication in *Underground*. Please be sure to write "FOR PUBLICATION" on anything you send us for the newsletter, so that we know what should and should not be published. Also please make it clear whether or not you will accept editing of your contribution.

We do not believe in censorship. If we have serious concerns about printing something that is sent to us, we will make every effort to discuss our concerns with the author. As part of taking responsibility for *Underground*, we will let readers know if we have a serious problem with something we end up printing. Keep in mind that this is a magazine by and for people who support the A.L.F. and please strive to keep your letters / articles respectful.

On Friday, October 22, between 8 and 9:30 pm, the ALFSG coordinators' home, which doubles as the SG office, was broken into. Items stolen include the SG computer, modems, telephone, almost all our work on this issue of *Underground*, the SG petty cash, materials from the SG files, and a few personal items of no commercial value—an address book, date book, socks (!), and diary. Although some of our non-ALFSG housemate's valuables were taken, the thieves left other items of hers that would have been of high resale value. The house next door was burgled that same night as well. Not much was taken; again, valuables were left. Of all the rooms in each house, only one room was thoroughly ransacked—the magazine editor's bedroom/office. It seems clear that this was, at least in part, an attack on the ALFSG.

NORTH AMERICAN ALFSG NEWS --

On behalf of the NA-ALFSG, I am pleased to say that all was not lost. We are confident that the thieves will not be able to decode the information stored on our computer. Most of our data was backed up on disks that were not stolen. However, we <u>have</u> lost some data. So if you do not receive merchandise you ordered or an answer to your letter, or if you receive a letter saying "your subscription has expired" even though you just sent us a cheque, please write us again. We apologize for any delays or confusion this may cause.

THOUGHTS ON THE BURGLARY

I cannot say I was surprised at being targeted in this way. At some point, those of us who are committed to seeing radical changes in the way society is structured are going to have to accept that radical change is going to really piss some people off. But do we really accept what that means? Or do we cling to the privileged and illusory notion that we can effect change without threatening the security of the current order? George Jackson, a black liberationist and revolutionary who was imprisoned and then assassinated in the 1970s, said, "If we accept revolution, we must accept all that it implies: repression, counter-terrorism, days filled with work, nervous strain, prison, funerals." If we are to stand behind our commitments, we must come to grips with the reality of what being part of a liberation movement means, let go of our illusions of living in a benevolent society, and do what we can to prepare ourselves for intensified levels of repression that will

---

The purpose of the North American Animal Liberation Front Supporters Group (NA-ALFSG) is to support the work of the Animal Liberation Front (A.L.F.) by ALL LAWFUL MEANS POSSIBLE. This includes:

* support of imprisoned A.L.F. activists
* support and defense of the A.L.F.
* educating the public as to the need and rationale of direct action
* providing a communication forum through the Supporters Group newsletter
* raising funds for all the above activities

The Supporters Group is for those who wish to support the A.L.F. without breaking the law. We encourage the participation of all activists — including those who are unable to, or who do not wish to, take part in direct action.

Any individual or group of people who are vegetarians or vegans and who carry out actions according to A.L.F. guidelines have the right to regard themselves as part of the A.L.F.

The Animal Liberation Front consists of small autonomous groups of people all over the world who carry out direct action according to the A.L.F. guidelines. You cannot become a member of — or an A.L.F. activist — by joining or writing to the North American ALFSG, which is a completely separate organization.

ANIMAL LIBERATION FRONT (A.L.F.) GUIDELINES:

The Animal Liberation Front carries out direct action against animal abuse in the form of rescuing animals and causing financial loss to animal exploiters, usually through the damage and destruction of property.

The A.L.F.'s short term aim is to save as many animals as possible and directly disrupt the practice of animal abuse. Their long term aim is to end all animal suffering by forcing animal abuse companies out of business. It is a nonviolent campaign, activists taking all precautions not to harm any animal (human or otherwise).

Because A.L.F. actions are against the law activists work anonymously, either in small groups or individually, and do not have any centralized organization or coordination.

happen as we become more effective.

On October 2, 1994, an explosive device was placed on or underneath the car of a well-known hunt saboteur in England. The device exploded at 9 am, in a crowded area. This was, as far as we know, the first time that a timed device has been used against a member of the animal liberation movement—but you can bet it won't be the last. At a recent conference a friend informed me that Judi Bari, a well known American environmental/trade union/feminist activist, is receiving death threats again, four years after surviving a bomb attack that left her permanently wounded.

The nature of this kind of harassment is that those around us will get dragged in. The parents of an activist who has been the target of grand jury investigations were subpoenaed to the grand jury investigating an ALF raid at the University of Washington. It is enraging that innocents such as her parents, or my housemate & neighbours, were affected simply because of their neighbours'/friends'/child's perceived political activities. It is true indeed, as the author of "What's It Gonna Take?" writes, that anyone can be a target—whether they are activists or not.

We have GOT to wake up and stop denying/romanticizing what is happening. This wave of repression is not from a Hollywood movie, it is our movement's reality. We are not the first. This has happened to other movements. How many of us, though, have educated ourselves about police tactics used against the Black Panthers and other black liberationists, the American Indian Movement and other indigenous sovereigntists, the Puerto Rican independentistas, the Sanctuary movement, unionists, etc? We'd better open

What was helpful: people letting me talk as much as I needed to; people thinking about practical details such as whether or not I was eating and sleeping; people offering to help recoup the work that was lost; and, very importantly, people offering to help with money. An extraordinary activist, who doesn't know me that well and is not at all rich, offered 100% financial (and other) assistance to get me to a conference where I would get tons of support, even at the expense of his own participation in the conference—this kind of unconditional, selfless support REALLY made a difference. Which is not to say the emotional support people offered was not as helpful as the money; all of us can support each other in different ways, no matter what our resources are.

I was shocked by is how few people asked me what I needed, assuming instead that they knew what would be the best way to give support. Other attempts that were NOT helpful (no matter how well-intentioned): people who spent my long distance phone time and money discussing various conspiracy theories; clichéd rhetoric such as "keep up the fight, sister", "we're all targets", etc. (even if it's true, it's not the first thing I wanted to hear given that I was the one who had my home trashed); people who tried to "distract me"; and people who did not take the burglary seriously (yes I know it could have been worse—I've had nightmares about how much worse it could have been).

4) DEAL WITH PARANOIA. There is a difference between paranoia and security. Paranoia causes us to be fearful and/or apathetic, wastes our time & energy on pointless speculation and sloppy judgements, and leads us to being isolated from each other. When something happens that you think was directed at you for political reasons, stop, breathe, and GET HELP. This stuff is simply too

GETTING ROBBED, GETTING PARANOID, AND GETTING THE MAGAZINE OUT

our circles wider than a narrowly defined animal liberation community, or we will not know how to prepare for survival.

On the topic of education—as with every situation, we can learn from the recent break-in at the NA-ALFSG office. Some of our precautions in anticipation of this type of harassment worked; others didn't. Lessons for the future. The following are a few of my still-scrambled thoughts on how to prepare for & deal with incidents such as this, on a political and personal level:

1) PROTECT YOUR WORK. The thieves have failed to seriously set the SG back. Part of this was good planning on our part; part of it was luck. This burglary is a potent reminder of the need to take the time to safeguard the work we do. ALWAYS make back-ups of computer information or hard copies; store these somewhere other than your house. On this same theme, one person should NEVER have all the information—because if that person is seriously harmed or killed (or imprisoned and kept incommunicado), all the work will be lost. DO NOT KEEP POTENTIALLY DANGEROUS PAPERS IN YOUR HOME. Before the police arrived I spent some time ignoring 911's warnings to "not touch anything" and cleaned up some papers, booklets, literature, etc. that I did not think the police would take kindly to. These papers should not have been in my house in the first place. ENCODE ALL COMPUTER WORK. Make sure that your hard drive, disks, and backup disks are also encoded/encrypted and that you store the decoding program on disks kept elsewhere (it won't do you much good to encode anything if you can't decode it, or if the thieves can easily access your decoding program). PGP is an excellent encoder (available for IBM-compatibles from Hidden Agenda, PO Box 1TA, Newcastle Upon Tyne, NE99 1TA, England; we are still trying to determine whether or not it is legal to distribute PGP as shareware for Macintoshes)—other algorithmic encoding programs are also useful. Do NOT rely on password-protect programs in software such as Excel, Word, etc. -- they are exceedingly easy to break.

2) STRENGTHEN THE PLACES YOU ARE WEAK. Assessing your weaknesses may be difficult on your own; ask trusted comrades to assist you. Where could your work be disrupted? Where is your security poor? Where could you be broken? Where do your ways of relating to comrades/friends/family leave you vulnerable to agitators and infiltrators? Where are tensions that can be exploited by provocateurs? Under what circumstances do you lose clearheaded thinking? Devise plans to work on these areas. Have no illusions: dealing with your weaknesses is extraordinarily difficult, and ongoing, work.

3) SUPPORT YOUR COMRADES WHO HAVE BEEN HARASSED. Different people will need different kinds of support; the following are not any concrete rules, but observations of my own reactions to the support offered by friends, family, and other activists.

overwhelming when we are isolated and alone.

Dealing with paranoia means educating yourself on the history of repression of political movements, becoming acquainted with police/state repression tactics and techniques, and trying to realistically assess what is currently happening in your locale in terms of government, corporate, or private surveillance/harassment. Avoid the temptation to make every little thing a big political deal. Compare different tactics: frame-ups, surveillance, incitement, provocation, infiltration, etc. Do not let your ego get grandiose (this is not as easy as it sounds!) and do not be afraid of showing weakness by asking for help.

OTHER NA-ALFSG NEWS

On the "when it rains, it pours" theme: our local Internet/e-mail system crashed in early October. For several weeks, all e-mail was returned to the sender. Our modems are being replaced by mid-November, so we should be back on line soon, assuming that the Freenet is back on-line by the time we return from our visit with an imprisoned activist. We will have a backlog of hundreds of postings to go through so please be patient, and if you got a posting bounced, please re-send it or send it via regular mail.

The main challenge for us now is to intensively fundraise. The huge influx of imprisoned activists and the costs of their support work, in addition to the recent burglary, have forced us to borrow almost $2000. This money must be paid back **by December 31**—above and beyond the costs of our day to day work. We need your ideas for fundraising and we need you to continue your personal financial support of our work. As A.L.F. prisoner Darren Thurston writes, your financial assistance is necessary to "help the SG support those of us inside." We cannot do it alone.

I should say that it has not all been grim lately. Direct action for animal liberation continues, with some important victories. Two prisoners were recently released. The support we have received from other activists has been immensely helpful. And we have received other assistance—a surprise visit by a huge buck and roe, who suddenly appeared in the middle of the city. The deer stopped & stared directly at the SG coordinators, then took off down the road. Incidents such as this give us renewed commitment and courage.

Despite the setbacks, this issue of the magazine WAS published (and almost on time, too!!). Even though all our work on this issue was stolen one week before it was due to be sent to the printers, we were able, through fiercely hard work, to put it together a second time. We hope you enjoy the second issue of *Underground* and welcome your deas for the third issue (due out in Feb/95). In the meantime stay safe and stay active!

NORTH AMERICAN ANIMAL LIBERATION FRONT SUPPORTERS GROUP

UK A.L.F. PRESS OFFICE REPORT

- by Robin Webb
special to the North American ALFSG

RIDING SHOTGUN FOR THE MOVEMENT?

During August the press office was raided by the police on two occasions; this seems to be a change of tactics from the period of relative calm that had existed in recent months.

The first raid was on Friday 5th August, a few days after the latest battery egg contamination hoax by the Poultry Liberation Organisation which claimed to have placed eggs in Tesco stores throughout the South. It also happened to be the day before NAHC's anti-bloodsport march and rally in London.

Two detectives arrived on my doorstep unannounced during the afternoon to be met with my standard reply along the lines of "No, I won't answer your questions; please contact my solicitor. His name and telephone number is...Thank you." As usual, they left. Later that evening they returned with some Cambridgeshire police and a newly-sworn-out warrant to search for correspondence. Hell hath no fury like a police officer scorned! Clearly, the search was only carried out through vindictiveness. Even the answering and fax machines were taken; they also want to question me and have said they will arrest me to do so if I don't agree voluntarily. Whichever way it goes I still have the right to silence, no thanks to Michael Howard.

Two weeks later, on 19th August, I was in Hove on the South coast to visit a few people in the area. As I went to leave my first visit my car was stopped in TV-drama style by the Special Operations Unit (SOU) from new Scotland Yard who I guess were on a day trip to the seaside. Almost immediately from around the corner came several Sussex police patrol cars appeared from around the corner where it is suggested they had been having a cup of tea.

I can't go into details at this time except to say that David Hammond, who I had just left, and myself have both been charged with offenses relating to a sawn-off double-barrelled shotgun and 22 rounds of ammunition. I have been further charged with possessing ammunition of a different type. Needless to say, both Dave and I are strenuously denying the charges.

We were both held incommunicado until our respective houses were "made secure" (i.e. police arrived to search them). At my little terraced cottage in the sleepy village I call home no less than one unmarked SOU car, 4 patrol cars and 2 police personnel carriers turned up! Turning the house over until midnight on that Fateful Friday they stationed a WPC overnight and came back in force at 9.00 am on Saturday to continue the search. I just hope the Hampshire police haven't got anything they want or it could make things difficult.

In the meantime, Dave and I are out on bail, our current conditions being no communication whatsoever with each other, to reside at our home addresses and to report every day at our respective police stations every day. My additional restriction is that I must not travel further than 20 miles from the centre of Cambridge.

May I take this opportunity to thank the High Court in London for relaxing my bail condition on appeal. I am now allowed to travel more than 20 miles if it is to attend court or to visit my solicitor in London by prior written appointment. On those days I don't have to report to the police station! As you can imagine, that has made life easier to bear!

A BLATANT APPEAL FOR MONEY - 1

This case is likely to last some time, with the trial not taking place until sometime next year. Our next court appearance is scheduled for 14th November at Brighton and Hove Magistrates Court.

A defense fund has been set up to which donations are invited. **Please make cheques/postal orders payable to "Hove Two Defense Fund" and send them c/o BM4400, London, WC1N 3XX, England.** For those with an interest in things nautical I apologize for the unintentional pun in the defense fund title.

"And I say we go outside and we *play with this ball!*"

A BLATANT APPEAL FOR MONEY - 2

The first time we had to report back to court in answer to bail a number of requests were made by the defense, one of which was to relax or remove my travel restrictions. This was opposed by the prosecution on the grounds that I travel up and down the country appearing on television and speaking at meetings and rallies which could be inciting. As I have never been charged with incitement and appearing on TV seems to have nothing to do with the charges against me I can only assume that this is a thinly-disguised attempt to close down the press office. However, I can happily deal with the radio, magazines and newspapers by telephone. As for TV, I can travel into Cambridge and link up with any BBC studio in the country from the satellite television studio at BBC Radio Cambridgeshire; for ITV companies throughout the UK the same can be achieved from Anglia TV's Cambridge studios. So, all is not lost.

The real problem comes from not being able to attend meetings, demos, etc. where most of the fund-raising takes place through donations and sale of merchandise. I feel sure that this is another reason for the travel restrictions which have been imposed on me and that the establishment know that their swingeing and unjust actions will financially impede the work of the press office.

So, please don't let them get away with it! I can continue the work of the ALF Press Office but only if the money is there to pay the bills. If you want to see it continue then any fundraising you can do or donations you can offer would be greatly appreciated. Maybe your local group has a bit of spare cash and would like to help...don't forget that the press office is a lawful undertaking and I am a member of the NUJ [National Union of Journalists-ed.] running it as almost any other news agency would be run. Thanks to those who have already begun to rally round by doing anything from car boot sales to coffee mornings.

from UK Press Office report for "Underground"; for Press Office news on actions in Britain, see "Diary of Actions" on the next page.

Report from R@T, a great British anarchist bi-monthly broadsheet with a strong focus on animal/earth liberation and prisoner support:

"Swedish customs/police have confiscated a Blackwiddow [slingshot—ed.] that was being sent to Djurens Hamnare. It is alleged that R@T sent the slingshot. One Swedish person was threatened with prosecution over the incident. But there was no real case against them."
For more info, or to subscribe to *R@T*'s editor's new bi-monthly, *Eco-Veg@n* (R@T is now defunct), write to:
BM HEAL, London WC1N 3XX, England

Direct Action FOR ANIMAL LIBERATION

(This list includes time-periods that were covered in the last issue, where actions not included in the last issue have since been reported.)

BELGIUM

MAR/94: Near Lommel — Thirty-eight dogs that were facing death in dog fights were liberated.

CANADA

(more actions, from Dec 94 - Jul 94, covered in last issue)

FEB 18/94: Victoria, British Columbia - McDonald's: Destroyed by arson; took 6 months to rebuild. This same branch had their windows smashed and walls painted with slogans by the A.L.F. in December 1992.

AUG 8/94: Vancouver, British Columbia - Western Freezer Meats: Locks glued, Van windows smashed, tires slashed. *A.L.F.*

AUG 9/94: Vancouver, British Columbia — Capilano Furs: Tires slashed, paint-bombed. Speiser Furs: Locks glued, all windows etched. *A.L.F.*

AUG 10/94: Vancouver, British Columbia — Western Freezer Meats: Locks glued, windows etched, truck tires slashed and windows etched, paint-bombed. *A.L.F.*

AUG 18/94: North Vancouver, British Columbia — Home-operated fur business: Paint-bombed with red paint, resulting in "extensive cleaning work".

ENGLAND

In England, according to police estimates, an average of five A.L.F. actions happen every day (or night). That does not include the work of the Justice Department, Animal Rights Militia, Hunt Retribution Squad, Poultry Liberation Organization, etc. According to a British newspaper, "Animal rights campaigners have been more active in the past 12 months than any other time in their 18-year history. And none more so than the Animal Liberation Front, which caused £15 million [approx. $30 million-ed.] worth of damage last year." ('Daily Express', Aug 25/94) Here are some recent highlights of actions in England. (more actions, from Jan 94- Jul 94, covered in last issue)

JAN 1/94: Heytsbury — Wiltshire & Infantry Beagles: Sabbed--no kills! *Bristol, Bath, & Pewsey Vale Hunt Saboteurs*

FEB/94: location unspecified — Badger baiter: Attacked by members of the public after appearing on BBC TV.

FEB/94: Southwest — Shoots near Lackham Agricultural College: Pheasant shoot, Duck shoot, and rough shoots successfully sabbed. Lackham runs a game management course. *Bath and Bristol Hunt Saboteurs*

MAR/94: Cheshire — Hylyne Rabbits: Car torched. *A.L.F.*

MAR/94: Hampshire — Southampton Medical School: 2 rats liberated. *A.L.F.*

DEVON WEEK, MAR/94: Devon — South West hunts: Hunt sabs successfully sabbed for one week. One sabber was handcuffed to a tree by hunt supporters.

MAR 4/94: Northampton — Bridge Home Farm: 82 hens liberated. *Poultry Liberation Organization (P.L.O.)*

MAR 4/94: Southampton — Southampton University: Two white rats were rescued in the confusion after fire alarms were set off inside the university during a demonstration/banner hanging by the Students Campaign for Animal Rights.

MAR 5/94: Prees, Shropshire — Thames Valley Eggs: incendiary "planned"; the action had to be aborted at the last minute. *Poultry Liberation Organization (P.L.O.)*

MAR 14/94: Edgware — Price's Butchers, Hussein's Halal Meat: Front windows smashed; the $2000+ windows of the Halal shop had only just been replaced from a similar attack 3 weeks previously. *A.L.F.*

MAR 17/94: Bexhill-on -Sea, Sussex — The Egg Store: Small explosive devices placed inside fuel tanks of 4 trucks and outside 2 wooden buildings. *Poultry Liberation Organization (P.L.O.)*

MAR 24/94: Mobberley, Cheshire — Sovereign Stud Farm: 11 Persian cats in awful condition, some heavily pregnant, liberated. This rescue represented the entire breeding colony of the farm's owner. *A.L.F.*

APR/94: Essex — A. Tuck and Sons (lab animal breeders): 100 guinea pigs rescued, unit "redecorated" and flooded. Action dedicated to Angie Hamp and Keith Mann. *A.L.F.* (This action was partially reported in the last *Underground*; since then we have learned more details of the action.)

APR/94: Fareham, Hampshire — Tom Parker Dairies: large vat of milk contaminated with creosote; 50 milk floats have tires slashed, windscreens smashed, wipers pulled off, bodywork paint stripped, and slogans painted. *A.L.F.*

APR 1/94: Hampshire — At least seventeen animal abuse shops: Sprayed with creosote. *A.L.F.*

APR 2/94: Charing — Ashford Valley Hunt Secretary: Hoax bomb device left near the Secretary's tent. The biscuit tin had all the elements of a bomb but did not contain explosive; it was removed by Richard Pemble, the hunt joint master, and later detonated by the police, who chastised Pemble for taking the risk of removing the device.

APR 15/94: Garstang, Preston — Barry Crowe Cooked Meats: Every window smashed on one building; 3 vans had tires slashed, body work paint stripped and spraypainted, windows smashed, internal fittings trashed, engines damaged. Over $20,000 damage. Action dedicated to Keith Mann and Angie Hamp. *A.L.F.*

Direct Action FOR ANIMAL LIBERATION

MAY/94: Cheshire — Hylyne Rabbits: 30 rabbits liberated. One week later, incendiaries destroy empty sheds. *A.L.F.*

MAY 1/94: Northwest England — Six cats sentenced to death in their "owner"'s will liberated. Strangely enough, the sole beneficiaries of the will were five animal welfare charities. *A.L.F.*

JUN/94: Reading, Berkshire — Meat firm: Device mailed.

JUL/94: Bedfordshire — Two hundred pheasants liberated from pens. *A.L.F.*

JUL/94: Birmingham — Butcher shops: Windows smashed. *A.L.F.*

JUL/94: Bucks — Penn Pharmaceuticals (contracts testing to Wickham Research Labs): Mouse traps primed with razor blades sent. *Justice Department*

JUL/94: Truro, Cornwall — MAFF Wildlife Unit (responsible for trapping and killing badgers): Activists wielding clubs intimidate MAFF staff; slogans painted over front doors of MAFF workers' homes; MAFF workers intimidated in street. "Badgers Not Guilty" painted on A30 flyover.

JUL/94: Twyford, Hampshire — Stonegate Farm: 8 vehicles had locks glued, tires slashed, windowscreens smashed, and paint ruined. *A.L.F.*

JUL/94: Hampshire — Tour de France route (British section): Incendiaries placed under police bollards. Action to highlight the live exports between France and Britain.

JUL/94: Oxfordshire — Vivisectors' conference, Exeter College: 20 activists wearing combat gear and masks entered conference, smashed dining room and shouted slogans. All 5 activists who were arrested were sentenced to community service hours.

JUL/94: Lancashire — Cooper Lancaster Brewers (company dealing with liquidation of Hylyne Rabbits): Letter sent that threatens direct action against all animal abusers' property. *A.L.F.*

JUL 15/94: Hampshire — Mouse traps primed with razor blades sent to: David Walker, owner of Animal Pharmaceutical & Toxicology and former vet at Wickham Research Labs; James Phillips of Froxfield Farms, supplier of animals to vivisection labs; Deborah Dowsett, 50% owner of Garetmar Kennels; Nicola Scarr, 50% owner of Garetmar Kennels; Simon Day of Torbay Farm, breeders for Wickham Research Labs; P. Humphrey of Webb's Poultry and a known hunter; and last but not least William Cartmell, owner of Wickham Research Labs, who "got a little bit extra". *Justice Department*

above: two of the 11 Persian cats rescued by the A.L.F. March 24/94

JUL 15/94: Herts — Roche Products (contracts testing to Wickham Research Labs): Mouse traps primed with razor blades sent. *Justice Department*

JUL 15/94: London — Pitman Moore Ltd (contracts testing to Wickham Research Labs): Mouse trap primed with razor blades sent. *Justice Department*

JUL 15/94: Sussex — Nicholas Fawcett (Chiddingfold, Leconfield & Cowdray hunt): Mouse trap primed with razor blades sent. *Justice Department*

JUL 15/94: Tayside — HMC (Manufacturing chemists that contract testing to Wickham Research Labs): Mouse trap primed with razor blades sent. *Justice Department*

JUL 24/94: North Harrow — Microbiological Lab (56 Northumberland Rd.): Locks glued, windows smashed, paint daubed on walls, 2 vehicles trashed. Homes of two of the lab's employees: Covered in red paint, cars smashed. This is the third attack on this lab in recent months. "The A.L.F. will close this lab and end the suffering of the animals here once and for all...The A.L.F. will close this lab down by any means necessary." (note sent to press) *A.L.F.*

JUL 28/94: Hampshire — Garetmar Kennels: Two speedboats firebombed. *Justice Department*

JUL 28/94: various locations — Hoax letter bombs sent to: Horsley Hunt Kennels (in Droxfield); Chiddingfold, Leconfield & Cowdray Hunt Kennels (in Petworth); David Walker, owner of Animal Pharmaceutical & Toxicology (breeds dogs for vivisection) and former vet at Wickham Research Labs; and Nicholas Fawcett, of the Chiddingfold, Leconfield & Cowdray hunt. *Justice Department*

AUG/94: Channel Island — Jersey Zoo: Shop destroyed by fire.

AUG/94: Plymouth, Devon — Boots the Chemist (supports animal testing): Suspect package found. Controlled explosion of package revealed the package contained soft toys.

AUG 4/94: Hampshire — Tesco's: Urgent checks on all eggs in stores across the south of England ordered after claims that battery eggs had been injected with poison. No tampered eggs were found. *Poultry Liberation Organization (P.L.O.)*

AUG 6/94: Great Billing, Northamptonshire — Padbury's livestock haulage company: Twelve powerful firebombs planted. Two truck tractor units, three trailers, two rigid vehicles severely damaged; one of the $60,000 vehicles completely burnt out. *Justice Department*

AUG 10/94: Oxford — C.H. Brown's saddlery & leather shop, Edinburgh Woolen Mill: Incendiaries caused tens of thousands of dollars damage done to saddlery; minor damage to wool shop. Three other firebombs hidden in two leather shops (Madison's and Westworld) and a fur store (Nurse's) were found and defused after the first firebomb ignited and police ordered other local businesses to allow police to search their premises. According to the UK A.L.F. Press Office, "No reports of anything at Boots but this may have been a deliberate piece of censorship as they have been featured in all of the other attacks." *Animal Rights Militia (A.R.M.)*

AUG 15/94: Torquay, Devon — Co-Op Dairy: Nine trucks covered in paint stripper, tires slashed, painted with slogans, refrigeration units turned off. Four milk floats severely damaged. *A.L.F.*

AUG 22/94: Winsford, Cheshire — Manufacturer of animal traps: Letter bomb sent. The target is also a member of the British Field Sports Society. No official claim; assumed to be the work of the Justice Department. According to the UK A.L.F. Press Officer, "Although JD devices have usually been sent out in waves it is just possible that it is an isolated individual attack. More likely, the 'powers that be' have censored news of the other devices that may have been sent at the same time. The shroud of secrecy on this one incident was so great that even the local media couldn't find out the victims name at the time!"

AUG 22/94: Avon — Myrtle Farm: 50 hens liberated. *A.L.F.*

Direct Action FOR ANIMAL LIBERATION

AUG 24/94: Newport & Ryde, Isle of Wight — In Newport—Boots the Chemist (supports animal testing); in Ryde—Sports and Model Shop (selling leather goods), Suede and Leather Shop, Cancer Research Fund shop: Four incendiaries; over $4,000,000 damage. Incendiaries at Scotties fishing tackle shop, Halfords motorcycle shop (owned by Boots) were discovered and made safe. *Animal Rights Militia (A.R.M.)*

SEP 11/94: Battlesbridge, Essex — A. Tuck & Sons (breed animals for vivisection): Entire stock of unit, 470 guinea pigs, liberated despite on-site security patrols. Tuck's was raided in April as well. The activists say they "will be back — again and again — until Tuck's closes down."

SEP 16/94: York & Harrogate, Yorkshire — In Harrogate—Boots the Chemist (supports animal testing), Fads DIY store (subsidiary of Boots), Linsley Brother bloodsports shop, Imperial Cancer Research Foundation shop; in York—Boots the Chemist (newly refurbished branch!), Fads DIY store (subsidiary of Boots): Incendiaries ignite. Over $4,000,000 damages for the fires in both towns. *Animal Rights Militia (A.R.M.)*

SEP 25/94: Huntingdon — Boots the Chemist (supports animal testing), butchers shop: Windows etched.

SEP 25/94: location unspecified — Interfauna animal breeders: Van damaged.

OCT 5 & 6/94: High Wycombe, York, Plymouth, Ronford — Boots the Chemist (supports animal testing): Boots' own-brand formula toothpaste (Freshmint and Original) contaminated with mercury. Samples of contaminated toothpaste with stenciled statements claiming the action were sent to Boots and the media. Certain media outlets received the toothpaste and statements that the police had confiscated all the toothpaste, and "requesting" no coverage by the media. *Animal Rights Militia (A.R.M.)*

According to a UK A.L.F. Press Office mole, Boots are losing no less than $4,000,000 each week through animal liberation activities.

OCT 7/94: Treburley, near Launceston (West Country) — One of the largest family owned slaughterhouses in the West Country: Completely gutted by fire; five refrigerated trucks destroyed. Incendiaries placed in three other transporters and a tractor failed to activate. *A.L.F.*

FINLAND

(more actions, from Oct/93 - Dec/93, covered in last issue)

AUG-SEP/94: at least 59 reported A.L.F. actions, including the following:

AUG 19/94: Helsinki — Ten fur stores: Locks glued. *A.L.F.*

AUG 20/94: Mikkeli — Fur store, Shell gas station, Coca-Cola billboard: vandalized with paint. A man was arrested at the scene and was soon released. He now awaits trial.

AUG 23/94: Helsinki — Eight fur stores: Locks glued. *A.L.F.*

AUG 26/94: Helsinki — Six fur stores: Locks glued. Fur store: Locks glued, window smashed, walls spraypainted, advertisement sign torn down from wall. Fur store: 10 windows smashed; according to the report, "A month has passed and the broken windows are still there. This place is going down!" *A.L.F.*

SEP 3/94: Mikkeli — Two fur stores: Locks glued, walls spraypainted. *A.L.F.*

SEP 11/94: Tampere — Three fur stores: Locks glued. Fur store: Locks glued, walls and windows spraypainted. Fur store: Locks glued, walls and windows spraypainted, window smashed. *A.L.F.*

SEP 12/94: Lahti — Two fur stores: Locks glued. Wholesale fur store: 4 locks glued, 5 windows smashed, walls spraypainted with "boycott fur", "fur is murder", and "A.L.F.". Meat factory: Locks of 3 doors glued shut, walls spraypainted. Eight meat trucks: locks glued, 6 trucks spraypainted. *A.L.F.*

FRANCE

MAY/94: Pyrenees — Demonstration against tunnel-building plan that will destroy the last French bear population turned into direct action as 5000 demonstrators clashed with riot police; activists tore down sheds & fences and threw rocks at the cops as police used tear gas and batons.

GERMANY

(more actions, from Dec/93 - May/94, covered in last issue)

MAR/94: Dortmund — Twelve hunting platforms: Destroyed.

APR/94: Near Hanau — Animal abuser: 24 beagles, 18 rabbits liberated. *Autonome Befrieungsfront*

MAY 9/94: Mecklenburg-Vorpommern — Three hunting platforms: Destroyed.

JUN 15/94: Landkreis Harburg — Three large hunting platforms: Destroyed. Near Weiterstadt — Six hunting platforms: Destroyed.

JUN 21/94: Woods near Bad Soden — Hunting platforms: Every single one destroyed. Each one was worth 4,500 DM. A 5,000 DM reward has been offered for the capture of the activists responsible. *Autonome TierrechtlerInnen*

JUL/94: location unspecified — Braunschweig Zoo: Cash desk destroyed. *Autonome TierschutzerInnen*

NETHERLANDS

(more actions, from Nov/93 - Dec/93, covered in last issue)

AUG/94: Tsjechian (spelling unclear) — McDonald's: Attacked four times in one week. Activists tried to demolish the branches; according to a McDonald's spokesperson, "just minor damage" was caused. *Animal S.O.S.*

AUG/94: Amsterdam — Frank Govers Shop: Windows smashed for ninth time. According to the report, "the most famous Dutch pro-fur campaigner, 'haute-couture' designer Frank Govers had to take extra security-measures and rollershutters for his shop in the centre of Amsterdam, because his insurance-company threatened not to compensate damage anymore".

NORTHERN IRELAND

(more actions, from Dec/93 - May/94, covered in last issue)

JUL/94: location unspecified — Family home of Ian Buchanan (joint master of County Down Staghounds): Slogans painted, car covered in paint stripper. *A.L.F.*

JUL/94: location unspecified — Burger King, Leather Centre: Windows smashed. *A.L.F.*

JUL/94: location unspecified — Various hunters and pro-hunting groups, including the organizers of the Game Fair (major Irish blood-sports event organized by BFSS & BASC): Postal devices sent.

SPAIN

date and location unspecified — Bullfighter and his chief: Warned to get out of bull fighting or face a possible car bomb attack. *Tierschutzfront*

SWEDEN

(more actions, from Summer/93 - May/94, covered in last issue)

APR 17/94: location unspecified — Restaurant with aquarium in shop window: Spray-painted with slogan "CAPTIVITY KILL". According to the report, it was a "very little aquarium with very big fishes".

MAY 12/94: Gothenburg — Butcher shop: Walls, windows painted. *Djurens Hamnare/Animal Avengers*

MAY 14/94: Gothenburg — Fur shop: Spraypainted, windows smashed. Same butcher shop as May 12: Re-spraypainted, windows smashed. *Djurens Hamnare/Animal Avengers*

MAY 19/94: Stockholm — Slaughterhouse district: Two trucks totally destroyed by arson; large fence destroyed to gain access to the trucks. *Djurens Aktions Grupp/Animal Action Group*

MAY 30/94: South Sweden — Fur farm: 100 minks liberated.

JUN 27/94: Stockholm — Butcher shop: Slogans painted, locks glued; this is the 5th time this butcher has been hit. Fur shop: locks glued. *Djurens Hamnare/Animal Avengers*

JUN 30/94 Stockholm — Södersjukhuset (South Hospital): Forty slogans painted. Södersjukhuset D.B.F. hit #3. *Djurens Befrielse Front (D.B.F.)/A.L.F.*

JUN 30/94: Stockholm — Skansen Zoo: Daubed with slogans such as "ANIMAL PRISON".

JUL/94: Stockholm — Fur shop: Slogans painted. *Djurens Hamnare/Animal Avengers*

JUL 5/94: Outside Stockholm — SBL (primate research lab): Two expensive computer/electronic locks destroyed. *Djurens Hamnare/Animal Avengers*

JUL 14/94: Stockholm — Meat shop: Locks glued. *Djurens Hamnare/Animal Avengers*

JUL 24/94: Stockholm — Södersjukhuset (South Hospital): Anti-vivisection slogans painted. This is the 4th time this hospital has been hit by the D.B.F./A.L.F. *Djurens Befrielse Front (D.B.F.)/A.L.F.*

JUL 24/94: Stockholm — Fish store: Painted with slogans.

JUL 25/94: location unspecified — Fur shop: Locks glued. *Djurens Hamnare/Animal Avengers*

JUL 30/94: Stockholm — Fur shop: Syrup poured over furs. *Djurens Hamnare/Animal Avengers*

END OF JUL/94: Stockholm — Slaughterhouse district: Anti-meat slogans spraypainted on truck. *Djurens Hamnare/Animal Avengers*

AUG/94: Stockholm — Slaughterhouse district: Factories spraypainted, locks glued. Fur shop: spraypainted, locks glued. *Djurens Hamnare/Animal Avengers*

SEP/94: location unspecified — Hunting leader: Fell from a hunting platform when the sabotaged floor collapsed. He survived the fall.

SEP 16/94: Stockholm — SCAN (Sweden's biggest meat company): Offices spraypainted. Slaughterhouse district: Locks glued. Meat shop: Spraypainted, locks glued. *Djurens Hamnare/Animal Avengers*

SEP 24/94: Stockholm — Fur shop, two butcher shops: Locks glued, slogans spraypainted. According to the report, there was "again no name, but this sounds as if it might be Djurens Hamnare."

SEP 24/94: Stockholm — Södersjukhuset (South Hospital): Slogans painted. This is the 5th time this hospital has been hit; although the D.B.F. did not claim this action, the tactics and target are identical to previous D.B.F. actions.

Direct Action FOR ANIMAL LIBERATION

NORTHERN SWEDEN ACTION REPORT

SPRING/94: Umeå, northern Sweden — SCAN (Sweden's biggest meat company): Slogans painted.

MAY 14/94: Umeå, northern Sweden — Meat company: Locks glued.

JUL 21/94: Northern Sweden — Leather shop: Slogans "Wear your own skin", "ALF", "The war has begun" written on shop window.

JUL 23/94: Umeå, northern Sweden — Charko (subsidiary of SCAN, Sweden's biggest meat company): Slogans painted, windows smashed.

AUG 13/14: Umeå, northern Sweden — SCAN (Sweden's biggest meat company): Slogans spraypainted.

SEP/94: Northern Sweden — Hot dog bar: Burned down; "Animal Rights" painted.

SEP 24/94: Umeå, northern Sweden — Three meat trucks: Totally destroyed by arson; "ALF" and "THE WAR HAS BEGUN" written in English.

Neither Djurens Hamnare or the D.B.F. (A.L.F.) have claimed responsibility for any of these actions; according to the Djurens Hamnare Press Officer, "it seems as it is a new group...Now there is direct action groups in 3 places in Sweden". After a bomb exploded at Umeå University (possibly the work of animal liberation activists), the D.B.F. began receiving intense media attention, including an interview with "Expressen", Sweden's biggest newspaper.

D.B.F./A.L.F. PRESS OFFICER REPORT

According to Swedish media an unknown group (not connected to the Swedish A.L.F. - Djurens Befrielse Front) has destroyed three slaughter vehicles by fire.

This happened outside a slaughter house in Umeå (a town in the northern Sweden) in the early morning on Saturday September 24th. Shortly after 2 o'clock in the morning an explosion was heard and three very expensive vehicles was ruined. The damaged was estimated to around 3 million Swedish krona.

During summer other slaughter vehicles at a slaughter house near Skellefteå got their dashboards destroyed.

Also during summer two hot-dog-stand was put to fire in Umeå.

On Sep 29th a short note arrived by mail to Djurens Befrielse Front's press officer, postmarked Umeå but without any name/address, confirming the raid at the slaughterhouse. The note also suggests that this raid was not the last one.

In Sweden around 67 million animals are murdered in slaughter houses each year (cows, sheep, pigs and horses).

After this raid the media went crazy and most of them putting the blame on Djurens Befrielse Front and D.B.F.'s press officer is now waiting for the police and interrogation.

Emilie E:son
DJURENS BEFRIELSE FRONT, BOX 2051, S-265 02 ÅSTORP, SWEDEN.

SWITZERLAND

AUG/94: locations unspecified — Cows and calves liberated. *Tierbefreiungsfront (T.B.F.)*

AUG/94: Stink bombs set off in animal abuse establishments. *Tierbefreiungsfront (T.B.F.)*

AUG 8/94: location unspecified — Rabbit farm: "a lot of rabbits" liberated. *Tierbefreiungsfront (T.B.F.)*

USA

(more actions, from Dec/93 - Jul/94, covered in last issue)

JAN 28/94: San Diego, California — San Diego Meat Company: Two refrigerator trucks, used for delivering meat to restaurants, destroyed by fire. *Farm Animal Revenge Militia (F.A.R.M.)*

JAN 30/94: San Diego, California — San Diego Meat Company: Boarded-over window broken into, building set on fire (flammable liquid splashed around, fire started in two rooms). "FARM", "Meat is Murder" painted at scene. Estimated damages: $75,000. *Farm Animal Revenge Militia (F.A.R.M.)*

FEB 12/94: Syracuse, New York — Fur store: Bucket of paint thrown on front of shop.

FEB 12/94: Memphis, Tennessee — Hataway Taxidermy: Truck engine damaged. *A.L.F.*

MAR/94: New Jersey — Unspecified actions against animal abusers.

MAR/94: Woodbridge, New Jersey — Fur billboard: Splattered with red paint three times.

MAR 5/94: Memphis, Tennessee — Jack Lewis Furs: Paint-bombed, locks glued. *A.L.F.*

MAR 30/94: Memphis, Tennessee — Jack Lewis Furs: Locks glued. *A.L.F.*

LATE MAR/94: Cleveland, Ohio — Meat packing plant: Broken into, serious damage caused to equipment and supplies. Security cameras filmed the masked activists and

footage was shown on local TV stations; police have questioned local animal rights supporters but have made no arrests. *A.L.F.*

APR/94: Pueblo, California — Animal abuse billboards: Spraypainted.

APR 5/94: San Francisco, California — McDonald's: Slogans spraypainted on walls and smeared on windows with etching cream. *A.L.F.*

MAY/94: Oakland, California — Butchers, fish shops: Attacked. *A.L.F.*

MAY/94: Newtown, Pennsylvania — Ham Sweet Ham: Windows shot out. *A.L.F.*

MAY/94: Southampton, Pennsylvania — Fur store: Windows shot out. *A.L.F.*

MAY 25/94: Santa Cruz, California — University of California Campus: Slogans (including "A.L.F.") spraypainted on building where vivisection takes place. *A.L.F.*

MAY 31/94: Fond Du Lac, Wisconsin — McDonald's (699 S. Military Rd): "Meat is Murder" spraypainted on wall, seven windows shattered by ball-bearings fired from slingshot. A local paper reported a $700 reward offered by the local police and McDonald's for info on the attackers. *A.L.F.*

JUN/94: Oakland, California — Butcher shop: "A.L.F." etched on windows in very large letters. The shop, located in a crowded shopping district, has visible damage from previous attacks. *A.L.F.*

JUL/94: Olney, Maryland — Boston Chicken: "Meat is Murder" spraypainted on wall, brick thrown through window. *U.S. Congressional Cell, A.L.F.*

JUL/94: Olney, Maryland — KFC: Rock thrown through window. *U.S. Congressional Cell, A.L.F.*

JUL/94: Washington, DC — Jennifer Leather (1-800-JENNIFER): Ad displayed in the metro subway station destroyed. *U.S. Congressional Cell, A.L.F.*

JUL 10/94: Little Rock, Arkansas — Honeybaked Ham: window shot out with ball bearing. *A.L.F.*

JUL 11/94: Little Rock, Arkansas — Spector Furs: Paint-bombed, locks glued. *A.L.F.*

JUL 21/94: San Francisco, California — Pacific Cafe: Windows etched, including with slogan "Lobster Liberation". According to Ross Warren, owner of the restaurant, approximately four months ago his windows were etched (no slogans or legible words), and a month later a man called asking if the restaurant sold live lobsters; when Warren replied "no" the man said killing lobsters was cruel and hung up. Warren also told the newspaper that the morning after the cafe was hit, a man called and said "We hit your place last night. We are the Crustacean Liberation Front. We're protesting your sale of live lobsters. Stop serving live lobsters." According to Warren, The Pacific Cafe sold live lobsters for three weeks in March but stopped because customers were not buying. *Crustacean Liberation Front (C.L.F.)*

JUL 29/94: Madison, Wisconsin — Two pro-animal exploitation billboards: Cut down and spraypainted. According to one news report, one adult and 2 minors were arrested for one of the billboards; we are still tryingto get details.

AUG/94: Washington, DC — Jennifer Leather (1-800-JENNIFER): Ad displayed in the metro subway station destroyed. *A.L.F., U.S. Congressional Cell*

AUG/94: Washington, DC — DC-101 Annual Championship Barbecue: Ad "with two happy dancing pigs" (from A.L.F. communiqué) in the metro subway station destroyed. *A.L.F., U.S. Congressional Cell*

AUG/94: location unspecified — County fair: Starving, emaciated goat liberated and "is now happily and healthily living on a spacious farm". (from F.A.R.M. communiqué) *Farm Animal Revenge Militia (F.A.R.M.)*

AUG/94: Oshkosh, Wisconsin — Pet store: Persian cat liberated. Three teenagers were arrested several days later. One of the arrestees told police "he took the cat because he is an animal rights activist and didn't want the cat caged against its will". The cat was turned over to the Humane Society pending notification of the "owner".

AUG/94: Memphis, Tennessee — Goldsmiths department store (sells fur): Windows smashed 4 times. *A.L.F.*
AUG 6/94: Memphis, Tennessee — Jack Lewis Furs: Paint-bombed, locks glued. *A.L.F.*

AUG 25/94: Memphis, Tennessee — Jack Lewis Furs: Paint-bombed. *A.L.F.*

AUG 31/94: Memphis, Tennessee — Factory farm: Pigs liberated. *A.L.F.*

SEP 4/94: Memphis, Tennessee — McDonald's, KFC: Windows smashed. Fur Fashions of Memphis: Locks glued. Goldsmith's department store (sells furs): spraypainted, windows smashed, truck tires slashed, truck windshield broken, locks glued. *A.L.F.*

SEP 17/94: New York City, New York — Billy Martin Leather: Paper clips and glue in 2 locks. Ballys: Paper clip and glue in one lock. Limited: Paper clip and glue in main lock. Elizabeth Arden: Paper clip and glue in main lock. Rubin Furs: Display window defaced with glass cutter. *A.L.F.*

SEP 18/94: Beverly Hills, California — Beverly Hills Fur Company: Display windows smashed. "Every fur store in the area has now had some action performed against them. More to come." (from A.L.F. communiqué) *A.L.F., November 26 Cell*

OCT 18/94: Sebastopol, California — Jose LaCalle (chinchilla rancher facing charges of killig chinchillas with genital electrocution; forensic pyschologist; co-owner of Bella Chinchilla International in Freestone, CA): Office spraypainted with anti-fur slogans.

WALES

SUMMER/94: location unspecified — Mink hunters: Regularly sabbed.

4-Hers get animal-rights brochures

GILROY, Calif. (AP) — Young 4-H Club members who raise livestock say they're used to animal-rights protests at county fairs. But they're shaken by anonymous mailings of anti-meat brochures sent to their homes.

"I feel kind of violated. ... It isn't right for them to have my address," said club member Melanie Coffman, 16.

Nearly 100 children in southern Santa Clara County involved in 4-H farm programs received the pamphlets this week. The mailings, sent from San Jose with no return address, were addressed to the young club members and contained brochures with pictures of farm animals and text condemning the use of animals for food.

The pamphlet asks, "Would you kill your buddy?"

Aug 12/94

Direct Action FOR ANIMAL LIBERATION

WAS IT DIRECT ACTION FOR ANIMAL LIBERATION?

MAY 10/94: Burlington, Vermont, USA — Carolina Biological Supply Company: A fire in a chemical storage building at the company's Burlington campus forced the evacuation of 1000 workers and residents for fear of toxic chemicals being released. Carolina Biological is one of the USA's largest suppliers of animals for dissection in school and research labs, and animal rights groups have actively campaigned against the company. According to the newspaper report, fire investigators are certain the fire was deliberately started, but "there has been no indication that animal rights people have been involved in it."
- info from "Alamance Bureau", July 28/94

MID JUL/94: Miami, Florida, USA — Thirty-three baby cynomolgous (aka Asian crab-eating) monkeys, due to be sold for animal research when they reached the age of two, were stolen from Matthew Block, primate dealer and animal lab supplier. We erroneously reported in the last issue that this was an animal liberation; it is actually not clear whether this was an animal liberation or a theft for profit. Block says he does not believe the theft was the work of animal liberation activists because the action has not been claimed. Block is one of the USA's largest primate dealers and one of the few abusers ever sentenced for his actions. In 1993 he was sentenced to 13 months for international orangutan smuggling; he originally plead guilty but then withdrew his plea, and is now free pending his appeal.
- information from "Miami Herald", July 11/94

JUL 19 or 20/94: Mohawk Nation, North America — Vandals cut a 10-foot hole in netting and allowed about 8000 trout fingerlings to swim away into the St. Lawrence River, ruining a fish farming program at the St. Regis (in what is known as northern New York, near Canadian border) Mohawk Nation, according to a Mohawk official. Estimated damage and loss of fish was $10,000.
- info from "New York Times", July 31/94

EARLY SEP/94: Umeå, Northern Sweden — Three people were injured when a bomb exploded in the Chemistry Department at Umeå University. Mice are used at the university and Umeå has been the site of many animal liberation actions in the last six months. According to the press officer for Djurens Hamnare/Animal Avengers, "I do not think it was AR-people because it was in the chemistry department. The police up there in Umeå say they have asked 10 people about this action, but it is a lie!"

SEP 6/94: Abbotsford, British Columbia, Canada — Arson destroyed the McClary family's rear stock-yard barn. The hundreds of animals that would normally be kept in the barn for grading and auction were not in the barn, as the long weekend resulted in a postponement of the auction. The four horses and two cows that were in the barn were freed before the fire consumed the building. This arson is one of a recent string of arsons in the Abbotsford-Matsqui area; none of the other fires were animal-related.
- "Vancouver Sun"

OCT 31/94: Duncan, British Columbia, Canada — A pipe bomb exploded at the Running With Eggs poultry farm (1700 Herd Rd). Glass was smashed but there were no injuries. Approximately $300 damage was caused.
- "Times-Colonist", November 1/94

EARTH/ANIMAL LIBERATION DIRECT ACTION

NO DATES SPECIFIED: Holland, various locations — Amsterdam Airport: fire started as protest of expansion of the airport. Hundreds of cars trashed (229 destroyed in a single action). Hunting platforms destroyed. Oil exploration equipment wrecked. According to the Dutch government, all these recent actions have happened because of British eco-terrorists who have crossed the North Sea. *Earth Liberation Front*

NO DATES SPECIFIED: Russia, around Kaliningrad — Seven bulldozers: Trashed. *Radical Brigades for Ecological Defence*

LATE AUG/94: USA, near Santa Fe, New Mexico — Albuquerque Asphalt paving operations on the Las Campanas subdivision: Shut down for 3-4 days when heavy-equipment machines worth $500,000 - $700,000 was damaged. Two front-end loaders were used simultaneously to cause the following damage: $250,000-$500,000 16-ton paving machine rolled on its back and destroyed; $80,000 - $100,000 steel-wheel roller machine flipped over on its side and destroyed; $25,000 water truck destroyed by the cab being smashed in; pneumatic rubber machine damaged but possibly salvageable.

EARTH WEEK, APR 1-7/94: Germany

Bremen — Meat company: Vehicles burned; 250,000 DM damage. *Okoguerilla Norddeutschland*

Frankfurt — McDonald's: Toilets blocked. *Autonome KamperferInnen*

Leer/Ostfriesland — CDU-Zentrale: Windows smashed, powerful stinkbomb thrown in. *an Autonome Gruppe*

Muenster — Hunting platforms: Wrecked. Butcher shops: Windows smashed. Thousands of DM damage.

EARTH NIGHT, JUN 21/94: Germany, near Frankfurt — Dredgers: Destroyed. According to a letter sent to a German animal liberation group, the dredgers were destroying a wood that was in the way of urban expansion, thereby destroying animals, plants and a whole ecological system. The destruction of the dredgers was a "show of resistance...More is to be expected." *Autonome Befrieungsfront*

IT'S NEVER TOO LATE — MAKE EVERY WEEK EARTH WEEK

The Earth Liberation Front, Germany, has declared Oct. 31 through Nov. 6, 1994, an International Action Week. We want to stop the development that leads to nothing. We don't think that the ruling class will give up their role or their way of destruction. We don't believe that the industry will search for or find an antidote for a single one of its poisons. Disrespectful behavior and exploitation of the environment—mainly by the imperialist industrial nations—is responsible for the imminent breakdown of all cycles of life. The consequences would be without example in the history of planet earth. But even today humanity suffers punishment for its attempts to control nature, in the form of deteriorating quality of life, famines, innumerable illnesses, etc. Unfortunately innocent animals and humans who are not to blame become the first victims of the senseless destruction. This makes it even more important to act now. All over the world people are just beginning to search for appropriate answers. Targets of sabotage have stretched right across the spectrum. Last November and April, earth-trashing projects, companies and organizations were hit, even those which force us into material dependence on their money. This system tells us to take responsibility, when in fact we're facing an inheritance of ravages and poisons. That's why we will liberate ourselves and the earth from it. Any action should not endanger life, only property. Please document your actions. Send details to either:

The Verge, Postbox 92066, 1090 AB Amsterdam, Netherlands

E.B.O., c/o Kopierladen M99, Nanteuffelstr. 96, 10997 Berlin, Germany

info from "Earth First! Journal", Mabon 1994, & R@bbix

even though we know that unless all forms of oppression are destroyed, animal liberation cannot be a reality
even though we know small victories are not enough
no victory for animal liberation is too small to mention

ONE STEP CLOSER TO

ARGENTINA: AIRLINES REFUSE TO TRANSPORT MONKEYS
Argentinian airlines is refusing to transport monkeys for experimentation. - *"Arkangel" #12, Tierbefreiung Aktuell June 94*

CANADA: ELEPHANT PROMO AT SKI RESORT NOT REPEATED
In the winter of 1993, ARK II activists crashed a publicity stunt at Dagmar Ski Resort in Ashburn, Ontario. Angus, an African elephant, was being pulled backwards by approximately 100 people on a snow slope. Just as his "opponents" began pulling Angus backwards, an amplified voice was heard saying "wild animals belong in the wild". Thanks to the resulting chaos, the advertising stunt was cut short. A letter writing campaign ensued. This year, Dagmar did not repeat the elephant tug-of-war advertising gimmick. - *ARK II's newsletter "The Activist", Summer 94*

CANADA: AIR CANADA PULLS PATÉ
After learning how foie gras producers force-feed ducks and geese, Air Canada announced it will no longer serve the pâté on any of its flights. Virgin Atlantic Airlines (a British company) and Swiss Air made similar announcements. - *"Arkangel" #12, "Animal Times" June/July 94*

ENGLAND: MEAT AND LIVESTOCK TRADES GOES DOWN
The Meat and Livestock Commission closed the Taunton and Bury St. Edmunds regional offices, the abattoir design services, and meat industry management services. Wadebridge Quality Meats, a North Cornwall abattoir with a throughput of 100 bullocks, 400 pigs, and 400 sheep per week, has closed. - *"Arkangel" #12, "Meat Trades Journal" Jan 27/94*

ENGLAND: FERRIES DISCONTINUE LIVESTOCK TRANSPORT
Brittany Ferries, P&O, and Stena Sealink have announced that they would stop carrying live animals for slaughter in Europe, "because of fears over the suffering caused." (not to mention being repeatedly targeted by animal liberation activists) According to P&O, unless there is an imminent prospect of improved European Union standards they will stop carrying live animals as of October. Brittany ceased carrying livestock on August 22. Stena was expected to announce an immediate ban on carrying live animals for fattening or slaughter, going one step further than P&O or Brittany. - *"Arkangel" #12*

ENGLAND: BRITAIN'S LARGEST HUNTING FESTIVAL CANCELLED
The 1994 Northumberland Beagling Festival, after being targeted for 7 years by hunt sabbers, announced its cancellation. According to Stephen Loveridge, spokesperson for the British Field Sports Society (BFSS), "The main reason it was cancelled is because over the last few years saboteurs have targeted it considerably." - *"HOWL" #55*

ISRAEL: FUR STORE CLOSES
After pickets and leafletting by a new animal rights organization, "Anonymous", Tel Aviv's Chinchilla Furs closed. The fur trade in Israel consists of 13 remaining shops, supported almost completely by the tourist trade. For more information, contact: Anonymous, PO Box 6315, Tel Aviv, 61062, Israel. - *"UK ALFSG Newsletter"*

SWEDEN: DJURENS AKTIONS GRUPP SETS BACK MEAT TRADE
As reported in the last issue, in May, Djurens Aktions Grupp (Animal Action Group) set fire to a number of meat trucks owned by Scan, Sweden's largest meat company. Damage was estimated at $180,000. Since then the Swedish meat traders have claimed, in their own publication, that it will take six months to build the replacement trucks, resulting in a "break" in the production and selling of meat. - *R@bbix, Djurens Hamnare*

UGANDA: BABY CHIMPS RESCUED FROM CIRCUS
Following an inspection four baby chimpanzees were confiscated from the Akef Egyptian Circus. The chimps will either go to a new 100 acre chimpanzee sanctuary in Kenya or be integrated into a family group in an established sanctuary near Lake Victoria.

USA: GREAT AMERICAN MEATOUT CAMPAIGN SHOWS SUCCESS
From its inception in 1985, the Great American Meatout has grown rapidly to become one of the nations' largest grass-roots public interest campaigns. Over 30 million Americans have now explored a meatless diet. National beef and veal consumption have dropped by 30 and 70 % respectively. - *"Arkangel" #12, Great American Meatout 94*

Dwayne paused. As usual, the forest was full of happy little animals -- but this time something seemed awry.
Larson

USA: MINK RANCH CLOSES
McArthur Mink Ranch in Wisconsin has gone out of business. - *"Arkangel" #12, "Militant Vegan" Jan 94*

USA: LOBSTER RELEASED
Concerned citizens in Sacramento, California persuaded a restaurant owner to part with a 126-year old lobster so it could be released back into the sea. - *"Arkangel" #12, "Ceefax" Mar 21/94*

USA: NUMBER OF SCHOOLS REQUIRING MED STUDENTS TO VIVISECT DROPS
The University of Nevada-Reno no longer insists that medical students carry out animal

experiments as part of their training, meaning there are now only 2 US medical schools that require animal experimentation. - *"Arkangel" #12*

USA: UC'S "SURPLUS" BEAGLES REHOMED, NOT KILLED
After a campaign by animal protection organizations, the University of California at Davis allowed 177 "surplus" lab beagles to be rehomed instead of killing them for use in dissection. - *"Arkangel" #12, "Civil Abolitionist" Spring 94*

USA: WHALE IMPORT PREVENTED
The Animal and Environmental Defense Association and Earth Island Institute successfully prevented the import (into the U.S.) of four false killer whales (smaller than orcas) from Japan to Indianapolis Zoo, after the zoo was unable to prove the whales were not imported through the Japanese drive fisheries method. - *"Arkangel" #12*

USA: CIRCUS DROPS ELEPHANT ACTS
Circus Vargas has redesigned its show to feature people instead of animal acts after the Elephant Alliance produced video evidence of the elephant abuse taking place there. - *"Arkangel" #12*

USA: BOURGIE DESIGNERS STOP USING FUR
America's most popular woman designer, Donna Karan, joined Calvin Klein and Anne Klein in dropping the use of fur in designs. - *"Arkangel" #12*

USA: THE FUR INDUSTRY IS DYING
"From Alaska to Maine the numbers of those trapping, fur hunting and buying fur has plummeted to the lowest level yet recorded." - *"The Trapper" Feb/94, as in "Dressed in Black" #1*

USA: PLASTICS INDUSTRY STARTS SWITCH FROM TALLOW TO VEGGIE OILS
Most plastic food packaging includes ingredients called release agents, which come from tallow (animal fat). Rabbi Jonah Gewirtz has been leading a campaign to get the animal fat out of the packaging on the grounds that the tallow leaches into food, contravening dietary codes of some Jewish, Islamic, Seventh-day Adventist, and vegetarian groups. In response to the campaign, in June 1994 Solvay Polymers (Deer Park, Texas) began the switch to an animal-free plastics-making process that uses palm and cottonseed oils. Solvay has promised to make the new process available to the entire plastics industry. This is Gewirtz's second victory: three years ago he successfully led the campaign that persuaded every North American steel company to discontinue using animal-based ingredients. - *"Vegetarian Times" Nov/94*

WALES: OSTRICH FARM STOPPED
The campaign (organized by South Wales animal rights group FAUNA) to stop an ostrich farm from being set up at Penmark in the Vale of Glamorgan persuaded local Councillors to vote against planning permission for the farm. Council had previously given the go ahead to ostrich farm planner Frank Lister, but after receiving detailed letters from FAUNA and a leaflet demo at the meeting at which the decision was due to be ratified, various councillors spoke out against the proposal. - *"Turning Point" #31*

NOW THAT'S WHAT I CALL JUSTICE...
Texas Judge Michael Peters ordered that a man convicted of cruelly starving a dog be fed only bread and water during his prison sentence, "so he'll know in some small measure what his dog went through". - "Arkangel" #12

That's nice, dear. And what does your 'Animal Liberation Club' do?

ENGLAND: HYLYNE RABBITS CLOSES

On June 27, 1994 Hylyne Rabbits Ltd. and Coney Europa Ltd both went into voluntary liquidation. Edwin Sutton, Hylyne Director (phone 011-44-925-756737), said "You can't keep looking for bombs under cars". Hylyne has been repeatedly targeted by the A.L.F. and other animal liberation groups. In 1993, Hylyne received a Justice Department letter bomb, and in May 1993, an inflatable boat was used to rescue 80 rabbits, including nursing mothers with their young. In May 1994 ALF liberated 30 Hylyne rabbits, and a week later incendiaries were placed in all sheds. At the time of their closure Hylyne had 600 remaining rabbits. The RSPCA distributed 60 rabbits to animal homes (claiming 60 rabbits was "all they could manage"); the rest went to labs and other breeders. The A.L.F. sent a warning about what these other animal abusers could expect. On July 22 the Animal Liberation Investigative Unit (A.L.I.U.) visited Hylyne. There were no rabbits, but many documents that contained "lots of juicy stuff". All the documents were photocopied and returned.- *R@bbix, A.L.I.U., A.L.F., "UK ALFSG Newsletter", "Merseyside Daily Post" June 29/94*

Hylyne's Press Release

Due to recent severe fire bomb and parcel bomb attacks on Hylyne Rabbit Farm at Lymm, Cheshire the company has been forced to cease trading and go into liquidation. The company has no desire to subject its staff and families to further fear of harm and harassment.

Several recent attacks have destroyed staff vehicles, burnt down rabbit breeding and nursery units and in the most recent incident caused severe problems with new born baby rabbits and lactating females. Many rabbits have been stolen.

Hylyne Rabbits Ltd. have become known world wide for the development of modern rabbit farming technology improvements in housing standards, animal health and environmental enrichment. Visitors from all over the World have visited the modern rabbit maternity facility at Lymm and attending training courses held at the farm.

The business was founded in 1955 with a capital of 30p [sic] has traded world wide more than once being considered for export achievement awards.

...Coney Europa Ltd the associated rabbit marketing company has also been placed in liquidation as their housing has also been burnt down only months after complete refurbishment.

Ends.
27 June 1994
Further information from Edwin Sutton 0925 756737

SEA SHEPHERDS LEGAL UPDATE

On March 24/94, Captain Paul Watson was tried on six counts of the Canada Shipping Act. he was fined $5,000 and his former ship the "Cleveland Amory" was fined $30,000 in connection with a high seas incident with a Cuban-registered factory trawler on the Grand Banks of Newfoundland. In anticipation of the ruling against the "Cleveland Amory", Watson sold the ship in September 1993; he cannot be legally held responsible for fines against a ship he no longer owns.

Captain Paul also faces a judge & jury trial for three counts of Mischief stemming for the same incident. A trial date has not yet been set. If found guilty, he could be sentenced to life in prison on two counts and ten years on the third count.

Paul Watson Legal Defence Fund
c/o Sea Shepherds
PO Box 48466 Vancouver, BC,
V7X 1A2 Canada 604-688-SEAL
info from *Ark II Activist*, Summer '94

GRAND JURY UPDATES

At this time, there are at least three active grand juries (in Washington, Oregon, and Michigan) allegedly investigating A.L.F.'s 1991-1992 "Operation Bite Back" actions the fur industry. So far, at least eight grand juries have questioned approximately 60 people about these actions. Four people were jailed for over 5 months for refusing to testify before the grand jury In Spokane, WA. Although Rod Coronado was supposedly the target of these grand juries, Rod's arrest and subsequent incarceration has not put an end to the harassment of activists by grand juries in the USA.

According to Beth Fries' attorney Larry Weiss, federal authorities plan to serve Fries with a new subpoena to appear before the grand jury in Portland, Oregon. According to Weiss, the assistant US Attorney in Portland has said that Beth Fries is neither a target nor a suspect of the grand jury investigations. Beth was once a staff member at the Sea Shepherd Conservation Society, where Rod worked. She was originally supposed to appear before the Portland grand jury in June 1994, but the subpoena was delayed and then dropped after Weiss petitioned the government for information as to whether Beth was subjected to wiretap surveillance. Marsh later ordered federal law enforcement to prove whether it tapped any telephone lines Beth regularly used. If the government had produced evidence showing it had illegally tapped phone lines, then no new subpoena would have been issued.

The Portland Grand Jury's subpoena of PeTA (People for the Ethical Treatment of Animals)'s financial records was dropped after a request for wiretap information similar to Beth Fries' request. The grand jury was allegedly looking for payments from PeTA to Rod Coronado. Kym Boyman, a former assistant to PeTA Chair Ingrid Newkirk, was subpoenaed and appeared before the federal Grand Jury in Michigan in late October.

information from "Coronado arrest doesn't stop grand juries' investigations", in 'Moscow-Pullman Daily News', Nov 8/94

---

statement and poem from "South Africa—A Different Kind of War", ed. Julie Frederikse

FORMER SECURITY DETAINEE WHO REFUSED TO SERVE AS A STATE WITNESS

Unless you've thrashed through this issue before you get detained, there's no way you can work it out for yourself inside. There's the problem that once your interrogators tell you they want you as a state witness, there is a sort of feeling of relief: 'Whew! I'm not going to be in the accused box." Whereas before, you were the detainee, and they're hammering you, now you've actually got a bit of leverage behind you because they need you as a state witness.

Fortunately, I had dealt with the issue before, and I had told people outside before I'd been picked up, that if I was ever called to be a witness I wouldn't do it. So in a sense it was off my chest, knowing that the people outside, whom I couldn't communicate with, at least knew that was the position I was going to take. But then you have to start gearing yourself for a prison sentence. Because you know then that it won't be just a few weeks till you're out, but it'll be a few years—that's the kind of sentence you get these days for refusing to testify, and it will probably get worse and worse.

Not that I didn't go through doubts. It seemed that they had found so much on the accused, in terms of evidence, that I really didn't see that they needed me as a witness. So that led me to thinking, well, they've actually got it in for me and they want to intimidate me at this point. And then, of course—I'm sure everybody thinks it—I'd think, one person is going to jail anyway, so why should two go? I'd think, maybe I would be more effective outside; if I'm stuck in jail, I can't make any contribution at all—so that's another reason to cave in and testify. But I'd keep coming back to the principal of the thing. It would be such a betrayal of whoever you worked with. I mean, you have to be able to assume that people are going to refuse to give evidence when you do political work with somebody, because that's the basic minimum of trust that you have to develop. And then there's also the fact that to be a state witness you're giving evidence for a state that we actually regard as being illegitimate anyway, because it doesn't represent the people. So to be a state witness would be to just totally sell out your principles and those of the people you worked with.

But maybe the most important to me is the personal aspect. I knew that I was in a far more advantageous position to serve a prison sentence than a lot of other people who would also choose to refuse. I had no dependents, I was young, I was healthy, I had a whole life ahead of me, and a four or five year prison sentence was not going to kill me. I mean, if I wasn't prepared to make a small sacrifice, who would be? And, of course, my personal relationship with the accused was a big factor. I can't imagine how he feels about the people who did give evidence against him, because of the betrayed trust. I mean, for one of your friends to stand up in court and contribute to your prison sentence! You just don't do that to people who are involved in the same struggle as you, the same cause, who are your friends.

INFORMER

by Nhlanhla Paul Maake

happy birthday
star of the auction
black
born in the ghetto
bred in the brick
and mortar pillars

who can forget
your ubiquitous
ear
that can hear
whispers in a
tremor

none
so dull as
to miss your forked
eyes
that cut through the dark
to look at things
they cannot
see

perverted seller
of human
souls
diseased with deceit

feet
nimble with tales
and mouth talented
in lies

in darkness
your shadow
becomes blacker than
blackness
while your purchased soul
remains pale

suggested reading:

Agents of Repression: FBI Attacks on the Black Panthers and the American Indian Movement, Ward Churchill and Jim Vander Wall. Boston: South End Press, 1988.

COINTELPRO Papers, Ward Churchill and Jim Vander Wall. Boston: South End Press, 1989.

Break-ins, Death Threats and the FBI: The Covert War Against the Central America Movement, Ross Gelspan. Boston: South End Press, 1991.

War at Home: Covert Action Against U.S. Activists and What We Can Do About It, Brian Glick. Boston: South End Press, 1989.

back issues of the *Earth First! Journal,* 1989-1994: information on the Arizona 5 (particularly issues between 1989-1991), Grand Juries (particularly 1992-1994), and the bombing of Judi Bari/Darryl Cherney (1990 onward).

DEALING WITH POSSIBLE INFORMANTS / INFILTRATORS

Dear readers,

Recently, we received a letter which caused much discussion, and after a lot of thought we decided the best way to handle it (since it was not marked for publication) would be to publish a summary of the letter in order to give some context to our response. So here goes: The letter named a specific person who was reportedly asking too many questions. The writer asked us to stop sending any information or publications to this person. This is our response:

Dear ALFSG supporter,

Your letter troubled us deeply and we felt it was important enough to publish and respond to. I offered to do it, as I have had several years experience dealing with issues around infiltration/frame-ups through my work in different groups that have come under police scrutiny.

Firstly, we believe that security and safety of A.L.F. activists must be our #1 priority and we would hope that we never do anything to jeopardize that security. If you are as concerned about your safety as you express in your letter, then we must take it seriously. However, your request poses several problems for us. Unmasking infiltrators is a very treacherous process and must be done very carefully.

We have discussed at length the ramifications of denying people subscriptions to *Underground* or membership to the NA-ALFSG, and the greater issues of security and infiltration. At this point, we do not see how sending any of the information the NA-ALFSG distributes, including this magazine, is a threat to anyone's security. This magazine, like all other literature we distribute, is completely public; it is sold in bookstores. Similarly, we do not see how responding to a letter could in any way jeopardize anyone's security. We never reveal any personal information about any of the NA-ALFSG members in letters to other members, and we do not reveal any personal information about ourselves in response to inquiries about the NA-ALFSG.

As I mentioned at the beginning of this letter, I have had some experience dealing with infiltrators (known and suspected), police informants, and the like. I have also been accused of being an infilitrator due to people's suspicion of my eagerness to become involved in different groups. Through these experiences I have developed a system that I use to deal with the very real threat of police infiltration. Hopefully these ideas will help you develop a system for yourself that you feel comfortable with.

1) *Keep a careful log of your interactions with the person you are suspicious of.* Write down as many details as possible, as close to the exact wording as possible. Focus on questions that s/he asked or other aspects of her/his behaviour that disturb you.

2) *Challenge behaviour that disturbs you rather than challenging the motives behind the behaviour.* Use the log you have kept to bring up specific examples rather than broad generalizations—saying "I was uncomfortable when you said ____ the other day" lets the person know that you are paying attention, whereas broad generalizations are easily shrugged off as paranoia. For example, in your case, tell this woman that you are not comfortable with her asking you about your friends and their addresses when you hardly know her.

She may indeed be an infiltrator; or she may just be doing something inappropriate with totally benevolent motives. You will probably never know. It is the behaviour that threatens your security, not her motives behind it.

3) *Do not reveal any personal or political information that you feel could be used against you or others.* Some of us are more public about or lives than other, more private folks. You are never under any obligation to provide information about yourself or others, and this can be avoided in a respectful, low-key way simply by saying "I'd rather not discuss that right now". If you are a serious target of the police, your phone will be tapped and there may be surveillance devices in your home/car/personal belongings. However, most of us are NOT under this intense a level of scrutiny and it is not practical to be 100% secret about your life. Consider what could reasonably be used against you (personally and politically) and develop clear boundaries around who you share that information with. Remember that infiltrators can only use what they are given. We can squash their efforts by not giving them what they want. Do not be naive about this, though—read about Mike Fain and the Arizona 5 (old issues of the *Earth First! Journal* are excellent) for an example of how special agents are trained to use people's soft spots to build trust and distract from inconsistencies or questionable behaviour.

4) *If the person persists with the behaviour that you are uncomfortable with, let the person know you do not want to have contact with them in the future.* Again, be as specific and low-key as possible. There's no need to give the person any reason to suspect that you are freaked out about the possibility of them being an informer—it is counterproductive to make them think you have something to hide. Remember that you are never under ANY obligation to work or associate with people who make you uncomfortable, for personal or political reasons—this can be done in a respectful way that does not breed rumour and dissension.

5) *Avoid calling anyone an infiltrator, police informant, etc. unless you are absolutely sure that is their motive, based on hard evidence beyond your own suspicions.* Accusations of this nature can totally destroy a movement as mistrust and division causes internal conflict and splits. Share information with other activists in terms of what *specific* behaviour disturbed you. Trained infiltrators are experts at using suspicion and fear to destroy movements.

6) *Trust your instincts and pay attention.* Peg Millett, in a recent speaking engagement, said these are two of the most important things to do, and that she knew that there was something wrong with Mike Fain but did not trust her instincts and stopped paying attention to inconsistencies in his behaviour.

7) If someone confesses to being an informant or infiltrator, try to get as much information about them as quickly as possible. Photos are extremely useful. Send this information to the NA-ALFSG., the *Earth First! Journal*, or anyone else who could publicize it within the movement. ONLY DO THIS IF YOU ARE 100% SURE THAT THE PERSON IS AN INFILTRATOR.Back up your info on the person with detailed proof of your claim that s/he is an informant.

From what we know about how the police work in terms of repression against animal liberation activists in North America, the police have not, at this point, attempted to frame anyone. They have used snitches to gather information used to prosecute activists (e.g. Jessica Sandham against Darren Thurston), used infiltrators to entrap activists (e.g. Mary Lou Sapone against Fran Trutt), used Grand Juries to obtain testimony from other activists and breed suspicion and division (eg. activists assisting Grand Juries in Washington, Oregon, New Mexico, Michigan) and used infiltrators to spread misinformation (e.g. Barry Klaussen against Pacific Northwest Earth First! groups). This is not to say that frame-ups are not possible, but I think part of dealing with the threat of infiltration is to try to be as well-educated as possible and try to keep analysis grounded rather than sinking into our own quagmire of paranoia.

A classic counter-activist tactic is to use paranoia and fear to split groups apart. In the past, COINTELPRO very successfully used this tactic against the Black Panther, American Indian Movement (AIM), and others by forging letters in activists' names, writing "anonymous" letters accusing activists of being infiltrators, etc. When a letter comes to us accusing someone of being an informant, we take it seriously, but in the context of knowing that letters like this have actually been manufactured by counter-activist agencies in the past.

Attached is a list of suggested readings for more information. I hope this letter has been helpful.

In struggle towards animal liberation and freedom for all political prisoners,

Zabaglione / for the NA-ALFSG

the enemies within

THE END OF THE INNOCENCE:

In 1988, the "Fran Trutt" case—where a government/industry infiltrator set up an animal activist—should have signalled to activists that the movement was about to be hit hard by infiltrators, informers and government agents. Instead, the movement, for the most part, has refused to see that Trutt was the victim of a bigger hidden agenda, a covert war against the movement.

The government's covert attack has reached a level of intensity reminiscent of the 1980s when the Central American Sanctuary Movement was heavily infiltrated by the government and activists were harassed. The tactic of creating a climate of fear and mistrust which undermines the efforts of animal activists has been used over and over against other social justice causes, including the civil rights, anti-war and feminist movements.

According to attorney Brian Glick, who authored "War at Home—Covert Action Against U.S. Activists", attacks on progressive movements

are part of a "vast government program to neutralize domestic political opposition." The government, he adds, carries out political repression secretly or under the "guise" of law enforcement necessary to stop "terrorists". Virtually every scenario outlined by Glick—and others who have documented government harassment of political groups—has been used against activists in California [and elsewhere-ed.], including burglaries of activists' homes, disinformation campaigns against key activists and infiltration by informers.

As in past movements, informers not only spy on political activists, but are used to discredit and disrupt. As Glick notes, "The FBI and police exploit (fear) to smear genuine activists as agents," which is exactly what happened [in 1990] in Sacramento when activists attempted to expose known agents and informants.

A disinformation campaign has spread rumors to inflame disagreements among activists. Campaigns have been sabotaged... Informants have provoked jealousy and embarrassed progressive groups. Dedicated activists have even been accused of being government agents, a common play to undermine the activists' effectiveness and focus attention away from the actual informer.

Activists, generally, do not yet realize what has happened. In fact, most still do not understand that they have been "set-up" as Glick states, and instead honestly believe the disruptions involving different factions are caused by "personality" conflicts.

They are unaware that the FBI routinely produces phony phone calls, letters and leaflets to discredit groups and turn them against one another. In the 1960s, covert operations fueled antagonism between factions in the anti-war movement when one activist received a threatening phone call allegedly made by another activist. It was more than 20 years later before it was learned the real activist never made the call.

In Sacramento, something very close to that took place [in the early 1990s] when fabricated evidence was planted in an attempt to implicate key activists. Bogus threatening letters were sent to several activists, and implicated the other activists who were scheduled to reveal the existence of a government informer at an upcoming meeting. It became clear that agents must be involved, because the letters were mailed in envelopes from an office no longer frequented by the key activists, but where police believed their office was located.

Glick says that the FBI and police have abused the legal system—under the guise of attacking "terrorism"—by harassing activists with grand jury subpoenas. The use of subpoenas has intimidated activists in past social justice movements—and the same has occurred [throughout the U.S.], where dozens of subpoenas since 1987 have been distributed by the FBI, who used the occasion of presenting the subpoenas to harass, frighten and intimidate activists at home and at work.

Some activists—now turned informants—have rationalized their cooperation, or collaboration. They have attempted to justify turning over activists' names, addresses, and phone numbers—in addition to possibly incriminating information—to the government.

A group of Sacramento activists—including several who may have...informed on other activists—even embraced a confessed informant. Although the informant admitted in a public meeting she would "inform again" if asked by the government, and the activists were warned such a person could jeopardize the campaigns in the area, they invited her back.

The government's war is working. In part, it is effective because the animal rights movement is so young and naive. But it is successful also because many in it refuse to see the political realities, and decide to traffic in lies and innuendo that fuel differences and invite splits, rather than work for true animal liberation.

Glick says in his book that the strategy of the government in dealing with political groups has been consistent for years—isolate the most militant and radical groups for direct attack and promise others that "things would be much easier" for them if they disassociated from such "violent disruptive elements".

If any of this sounds familiar, it is because the tactic is the same one espoused by the American Medical Association (AMA) in its "battle plan" against the animal rights movement. In the plan, it is suggested that those opposed to animal rights work with government agencies to "isolate" hardcore activists from the rest of the movement, which the AMA plan described as "weak".

Glick, and others who have observed government repression firsthand since the 1960s, believe covert action—despite being undemocratic and terrorist in nature—will probably not end in the near future in this country. But, they suggest that movements should fight back, and put the police, political informants and operatives on the defense by publicizing attacks on genuine activists and exposing those who inform to the rest of the movement.

The animal rights movement can minimize the effectiveness of covert agents and informants by refusing to spread lies and rumors about dedicated activists—who are the subject of the government campaign—and tracing those rumors back to their source, where government informants can usually be found. Activists can wholeheartedly support other activists, especially those who are the targets of break-ins, grand jury harassment and defendants in political trials.

THE INFILTRATION — INFORMANTS AND COLLABORATORS

Although the federal government and state agencies have been tight-lipped about exactly who their informants are, or how deep they have infiltrated the animal rights movement, the [1990] grand jury investigation in Sacramento, CA and arrest of several key activists stemming out of the probe have provided some valuable facts.

Apparently, at least four key informants [were] working for the government on the West Coast, and, several animal activists have decided to collaborate freely, and also act as informants. Until the federal grand jury records are unsealed, it may be impossible to know how many activists have informed on their fellow activists. Those activists apparently have given up names, numbers, and other information to the FBI and other repressive police groups in return for being "left alone".

The really frightening specter is that those people—who have informed on other activists—are still active in the movement, free to gather still more information to pass on to government, and industry, grand inquisitors.

And, the very real truth of the matter is that when you hold a picket sign at a protest, or talk to another activist on the phone, you don't know who is listening—and who is going to talk about it to a government bent on taking away your freedom so that you cannot fight for the freedom of billions of animals.

As in past social justice movements, informants or government agents serve a multipurpose role. They pass on information to the government, allowing it to arrest and otherwise

A.L.F.S.G.

THE LEGAL FILES

THE HIDDEN GOVERNMENT WAR ON ANIMAL ACTIVISTS

from article by Cresc Velluci (with permission)

harass key activists. Or, they can disrupt, confuse, and misdirect other activists. Informants also frighten off good activists by their very, or suspected, presence.

It doesn't do any good to ignore the threat, or the reality. But, to face it is be able to deal with it in rational, and political sense. To understand the threat is to empower yourself, and the movement.

If activists know their rights, they can protect them—and those of others. Basically, an activist—or any other U.S. citizen—does not have to talk to the police, FBI or a grand jury without having a lawyer. Any small bit of "innocent' information helps oppressors, if not to convict someone then to lead them to another activist to harass.

Activists have often been asked only to "confirm" information. If they collaborated, they were told by the government, they would save themselves. But, to cooperate in any sense with government repression has to be likened to collaborating with the enemy in a time of war—and surely if we, as activists, are not at war, then the animals are (at war).

And, to collaborate with the government will only insure that the killing—by the billions—of animals will continue for an even longer time than it should.

To thwart government repression will take courage and ethical behavior. But, that is exactly and simply what is needed to not only stop repression of us, but the oppression of all animals on this planet.

THE PLAYERS

In 1992 & 1993 *Jessica Michelle Charlotte Sandham* (birthdate Dec '73) made a 4-1/2 hour videotaped statement to police and testified against Darren Thurston at his preliminary hearing on charges related to A.L.F. actions in Edmonton, Alberta (Canada). Her testimony has cost Darren 21 months and counting. Unfortunately we do not have a photo of Jessica available. She is approx. 5'9", sandy brown hair that was shoulder length as of 1993, heavy set, no glasses, caucasian. She is, as far as we know, currently living in Edmonton and is not presently active in animal rights/animal lib work.

Mark Mead and *Mary Lou Sapone* (below) were, and are possibly still, two agents employed by Perceptions International, a security company contracted by US Surgical (USS), a vivisection corporation. The two agents set up Fran Trutt, an animal rights activist, by supplying her with the money, transportation, and encouragement to plant a bomb outside USS. Mead even rehearsed the arrest scenario with police before driving Trutt to the site. Sapone has attempted to infiltrate numerous animal rights and environmental groups.

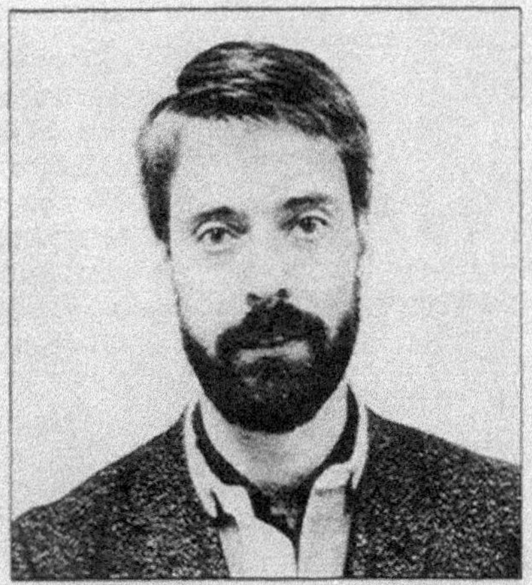

Martin Lane Gorda
Gorda has informed on, and fabricated evidence about, at least 15 different animal activists on the West Coast, according to documents filed by the FBI and Lane County District Attorney's Office in Oregon. His unsworn testimony has yet to be tested at trial, but his claims could result in the imprisonment of activists for up to 20 years. Gorda has posed as a sincere animal rights activist, and environmentalist, in the Sacramento/Davis area since at least 1983. He participated in demonstrations, and even was arrested. However, he was a loner who even his closet activist "friends" could not get close to. His income was also a mystery, and he would disappear for weeks—even missing court dates—without explanation. It is not clear if he has been a government agent from the beginning, or an activist who has decided to collaborate with government repressors. He has received immunity from prosecution in return for turning in activists. He now lives in Mt. View, CA, south of San Francisco.

Lynne Ann Trulio
Like Gorda, Trulio has provided dozens of pages of unseen testimony to the FBI and Oregon authorities, according to government agencies involved. She also has bought immunity from prosecution if she informs on activists. Trulio, who lived with Gorda, also was active in the animal rights movement in the Sacramento/Davis area. She was a graduate student at UC Davis for at least six years, and worked as a staff biologist for the Mountain Lion Coalition in the late 1980s. She also is believed to be living in Mt. View, CA, and may be attempting to infiltrate environmental organizations there.

Gayle Smart
She admitted to a roomful of activists in late February 1991 that she had informed on other activists for nearly three hours last year before a U.S. Grand Jury. She received limited immunity for helping to harass other activists. Smart became active in the Sacramento area in 1985, and about one year later, she dropped out. However, since she was asked to inform on others, she became active again, and attempted to disrupt meetings being held by activists threatened by government harassment. She has said she would "inform again" if pressured by the government. Some Sacramento activists—who may not know better—have refused to bar her from important meetings where she could glean information that would be valuable to the government.

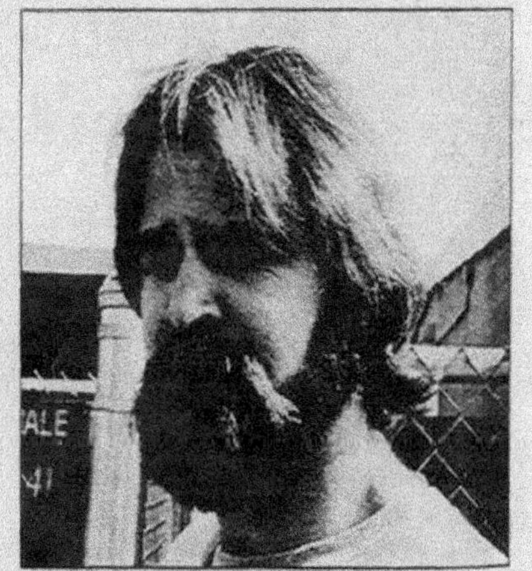

William Ferguson
One of the key informants in the current intimidation campaign against the animal rights movement is William (aka Bill) Ferguson, who was involved in Los Angeles-area animal rights since the mid-1980s. Prone to using violence to settle disputes—he shot Chris DeRose, founder and president of Last Chance for Animals, in the back, nearly killing him—Ferguson has also sent numerous threatening letters to animal activists. DeRose says that while he agrees that the movement is "young and naive," he believes that because "we are in the embryo stages of development that we must weed out infiltrators, and informants. We are in the middle of a revolution, said DeRose. "And we should not be afraid of words like 'revolution.' I feel strongly about this. To revolt in the face of oppression, government control and atrocities, is what this great nation was built on. We will prevail." ■

THE MCLIBEL TRIAL CONTINUES

Information from the McLibel Support Campaign, c/o London Greenpeace, 5 Caledonian Road, London N1 9DX, England
Tel/fax +44-171-713 1269

October 3, 1994

After several years of pre-trial hearings, the McDonald's libel case against two unwaged campaigners - who were allegedly involved in distribution in 1989/1990 of the London Greenpeace leaflet "What's Wrong With McDonald's" - finally began at the end of June.

REMINDER OF THE BACKGROUND

A total of approximately 170 UK and international witnesses will give evidence in court about the effects of the company's advertising and the impact of its operating practices and food products on the environment, on millions of farmed animals, on human health, on the Third World, and on McDonald's own staff. They will include environmental and nutritional experts, trade unionists, McDonald's employees, customers and top executives.

McDonald's have claimed that wide-ranging criticisms of their operations, in a leaflet produced by London Greenpeace, have defamed them, so they have launched this libel action against two people (Dave Morris & Helen Steel) involved with the group.

Prior to the start of the case, McDonald's issued leaflets nationwide calling their critics liars. So Helen and Dave themselves took out a counterclaim for libel against McDonald's which will run concurrently with McDonald's libel action.

Helen and Dave were denied their right to a jury trial, at McDonald's request. And, with no right to Legal Aid in libel cases, they are forced to conduct their own defence against the McDonald's team of top libel lawyers.

The trial is open to members of the press and public (Court 35, Royal Courts of Justice, Strand, London WC2 - nearest Underground Temple or Holborn) and is set to run until March 1995.

THE SIXTH AND SEVENTH WEEKS OF THE TRIAL

(weeks beginning 12 and 19 Sept) were taken up with McDonald's witnesses on DIET & CANCER, ADDITIVES, DIET & DIABETES, and MARKETING; and with a Defence witness on ADVERTISING and NUTRITION.

DR SIDNEY ARNOTT: On 12 & 13th September, Dr Arnott (McDonald's expert on cancer) returned to be cross-examined by the Defendants. He argued that although there had been a great deal of research into cancer the exact causes were not proven. He was not convinced by the evidence linking a high fat/low fibre diet to cancers of the breast and bowel, although he accepted that a high fat diet was linked to heart disease, diabetes and also obesity (which he agreed might increase the risks of some forms of cancer).

MODERN DIET LINKED TO CHRONIC DISEASES - The Defendants referred him to the conclusions and recommendations of a wide range of authoritative medical, scientific, advisory and governmental bodies including the major 1990 World Health Organisation (WHO) Report which stated "dietary factors are now known to influence the development of ... heart disease, various cancers, hypertension ... and diabetes. These conditions are the commonest cause of premature death in developed countries. ...The 'affluent' type of diet that often accompanies economic development is energy dense. People consuming these diets characteristically have a high intake of fat (especially saturated fat) and free sugars and a relatively low intake of complex carbohydrates (from starchy, fibre-containing foods). Such diets are well established in developed countries, and are now becoming more common in most developing countries. ...This change in diet can now be linked to the increasing incidence of chronic diseases and of premature death. Evidence suggests that many of these premature deaths should be preventable by changes in diet and in other aspects of lifestyle. ...Their prevention or reduction is both a social responsibility and an economic necessity." Dr Arnott reluctantly admitted that the World Health Organisation was "probably" the most influential health organisation in the world.

The Defendants quoted similar views linking diet with cancer from one of McDonald's own booklets from 1985 (not displayed in their stores), which Dr Arnott said was "reasonable" and "sensible" advice.

"KISS OF DEATH" - In addition, the Defendants asked Dr Arnott's opinion of the following statement: "A diet high in fat, sugar, animal products and salt, and low in fibre, vitamins and minerals, is linked with cancer of the breast and bowel and heart disease." He replied: "If it is being directed to the public then I would say it is a very reasonable thing to say." The court was then informed that the statement was an extract from the London Greenpeace Factsheet. This section had been characterised at pre-trial hearings as the central and most "defamatory" allegation, which if proven would be the "kiss of death"(*) for a fast-food company like McDonald's. On the strength of the supposed scientific complexities surrounding this issue the Defendants had been denied their right to a jury.

(* — Richard Rampton QC for McDonald's, Court of Appeal, 16th March 1994.)

STEVEN GARDNER: On 15th & 16th September Stephen Gardner, former Assistant Attorney General of Texas, gave evidence for the Defence. Mr Gardner told how, in April 1986, a number of States including Texas held meetings with the major fast-food companies in order to force them to comply with food labelling regulations. They were told to provide ingredient and nutritional information to customers about each product sold. He said that McDonald's had been the most "recalcitrant" and "had to be dragged kicking and screaming into the fold". Eventually general agreement was reached and it was planned to make announcements to the press that the information was available from all the major chains. McDonald's told the Attorneys General that they needed more time before they were ready. However, the company then issued a unilateral press release claiming they were voluntarily pioneering a unique project to provide this information. The huge public row which followed led to extensive press coverage attacking McDonald's deception. An internal company memo sent out at that time was read to the court which revealed that McDonald's had produced ingredient brochures "to help blunt the growing interest of state and federal lawmakers for ingredient labelling legislation".

ADVERTISING DECEIT - The former Assistant Attorney General continued by explaining how, in the following year, McDonald's began a major, but deceptive, advertising campaign. The company claimed it was an "informational" campaign about the content of their food. However, the company's own internal magazine stated that the aim was "a long term commitment beginning with a year-long advertising schedule" ... "to neutralise the junk food misconceptions about McDonald's good food." The buzz words in almost all the ads were "nutrition", "balance" and "McDonald's good food". After the series of ads hit the news-stands, the Attorney General of Texas, in conjunction with the two other major states, wrote a letter to McDonald's on 24th April 1987 stating:

> "The Attorneys General of Texas, California and New York have concluded our joint review of McDonald's recent advertising campaign which claims that McDonald's food is nutritious. Our mutual conclusion is that this advertising campaign is deceptive. We therefore request that McDonald's immediately cease and desist further use of this advertising campaign. The reason for this is simple: McDonald's food is, as a whole, not nutritious. The intent and result of the current campaign is to deceive customers into believing the opposite. Fast food customers often choose to go to McDonald's because it is inexpensive and convenient. They should not be fooled into eating there because you have told them it is also nutritious. ...The new campaign appears intended to pull the wool over the public's eyes."

Mr Gardener also referred the court to some of the specific examples of inaccuracies and distortions in the 16 individual advertisements. He related how, after the three States had threatened legal action if the ads were repeated, McDonald's promised to stop the ads.

At the current trial McDonald's claim that the ads were not dropped and were later printed again. However, of the four ads they said had been run after the threats, three were not the specific ads referred to in the complaints, one was not from the original series of ads at all, and none mentioned "nutrition", "balance" or "McDonald's good food".

PROFESSOR RONALD WALKER - ADDITIVES: McDonald's called Professor Walker, their expert on additives and toxicology. The company uses dozens of additives in its food. The Defendants have cited nine of these (E110/Sunset Yellow, E124/Amaranth, E250/Sodium Nitrite, E252/Potassium Nitrate, E320/BHA, E321/BHT, E407/Carrageenan, 621/Monosodium Glutamate, 924/Potassium Bromate) as potentially detrimental to health; most of them are banned in one or more countries.

Professor Walker explained that the main basis for permitting additives as "safe" was that they had been tested on animals. (He said tests on humans were unethical.) He admitted that animals had a different metabolism to humans, that the small number of animals used in each experiment would not reflect the vast diversity of human situations, and that the results were not always consistent. However, as a result of these tests an "Acceptable Daily Intake" for humans is usually set.

ALLERGIES - The animal tests, Professor Walker admitted, failed to predict allergies and some other "intolerances", and he went on to accept that many people (about "one in a thousand") were allergic to the colouring additives E110 & E124. He stated there was also "anecdotal" evidence that four of the additives provoked hyperactivity in kids. His opinion was that food should be properly labelled so that people could avoid the additives.

Professor Walker agreed that one of the nine additives, Potassium Bromate, was known to be carcinogenic. It had been used in the manufacture of all McDonald's bread buns until 1990 when it was banned.

Walker also acknowledged that the basis for permitting the use of additives varied from country to country, taking into consideration "the balance of safety and need" (i.e. the food industry's modern processing needs).

STYRENE MIGRATION INTO FOOD - Finally, Professor Walker agreed that styrene can migrate from polystyrene packaging into food (especially fatty foods). He said that the International Agency for the Research on Cancer had classified styrene as possibly carcinogenic to humans. Also styrene can be transformed in the body into styrene oxide, which he said appeared to be much more hazardous to human health. He said that more styrene from "the polluted urban atmosphere" also gets into the body. He referred to a survey which claimed that "100% of subjects studied in the USA had detectable levels of styrene in their body fat".

ALISTAIR FAIRGRIEVE - MARKETING: Alistair Fairgrieve, McDonald's UK Marketing Services Manager, outlined some of the research undertaken by the company to discover what customers were thinking and the effects of advertising, with the aim of increasing the number of customers visiting McDonald's and the frequency of visits. They are part of a fast food "syndicate" which does an annual phone survey of eating habits of 60,000 people. They also do their own "customer profile" questionnaires etc.

Mr Fairgrieve explained that questions were asked about seventeen "functional" and "emotional" attributes which were "ranked in terms of importance" to McDonald's. "At the top there are the ones by which we stand or fall." At the bottom were four categories: "Food is Filling", "Good Value For Money", "Use Top Quality Ingredients", and finally "Nutritious Food".

Some interesting conclusions were reported for 1994: 91% agreed that McDonald's was a "place kids enjoy", whereas only 47% a "place adults enjoy" (up from 31% in 1992). Only 34% agreed it "offers low price" and only 30% felt that it sold "nutritious food" (up from 19% in 1992).

ADVERTISING AND EMOTIONAL PULL - Fairgrieve explained how the company boosted some of the lower percentages by building people's "trust" and their "emotional pull" to the company - this was achieved by "a repositioning of McDonald's as a brand in late 1992 and the launch of a new advertising theme". He later stated "it is our objective to dominate the communications area ... because we are competing for a share of the customer's mind". Further interpretation of various survey results was hampered by a lack of background information and statistics; Mr Fairgrieve was told to return at a later date with such details.

PROFESSOR HARRY KEEN - DIET & DIABETES: On the links between diet and diabetes, McDonald's called Professor Harry Keen, former chair of the World Health Organisation's (WHO) Expert Committee on Diabetes. He stated that diabetes and its complications are estimated to affect about 5% of "western" populations. There were two main types of diabetes. The more common type, non-insulin-dependent diabetes mellitus, was usually diagnosed after middle life. He said that obesity was shown to be clearly linked with increased risk of this type of diabetes. He said that "the link between obesity and diabetes development is universally accepted". In general the whole UK population was becoming more obese, and as physical activity falls (with use of cars etc) people need to cut back even more on energy intake (fat is the most concentrated form of energy in the diet).

The Defendants referred Professor Keen to sections of the 1990 WHO Report on Diet, Nutrition and the Prevention of Chronic Diseases. One extract suggested that the optimal percentage of food energy obtained from dietary fat should be 15-20%. (UK governmental recommendations are 30% - these were set as an "achievable" target given the average current levels of fat intake which are much higher. McDonald's have admitted that most of their main meals are above even that figure.) Professor Keen said that "dietary factors are now known to be associated with the development of a wide range of chronic diseases", including heart disease, hypertension, cancer and diabetes. His view of WHO reports was that they "represent state of the art and the state of the scientific opinion so they are regarded with considerable respect".

++ *The case continues.* +++

CAMPAIGN STATEMENT

The McLibel Support Campaign was set up to generate solidarity and financial backing for the McLibel Defendants, who are not themselves responsible for Campaign publicity. The Campaign is also supportive of, but independent from, general, worldwide, grassroots anti-McDonalds activities and protests.

The trial is open to members of the press and public, starting at 10.30am daily: Court 35, Royal Courts of Justice, Strand, London WC2.

Previous updates are available on the World Wide Web on Chris Harrison's page at http://www.cs.ucl.ac.uk/~harrison/Environment/Environment.html or via Nick Fiddes pages at http://anthfirst.san.ed.ac.uk/

Please distribute the update far and wide.
cheers, Richard

ed. note: we printed the McLibel update in entirety, even though it is a non-North American case, because SLAPPs (Strategic Lawsuits Against Public Participation) are happening with increased frequency against environmental activists in both Canada and the USA, and we felt the McLibel case was a good example of how SLAPPs work. We will keep you updated as the North American SLAPPs progress.

WHAT 'S IT GONNA TAKE?

reprinted, with author's permission, from *Live Wild Or Die! #4*

the first in a series of articles, by various authors, dealing with life underground.

Hey! You out there! Are you awake? Have you really taken a good look around lately? Have you noticed what's going on? We have less forests now. We have more roads and concrete. We have less species of animals and plants now. We have more polluted air, water, and food. Life dying all around us while corporate fucks and the brainless masses concern themselves with money and things. Have you noticed? If you get your news primarily from the corporations through tv and newspaper, you probably haven't noticed. The struggle for liberation and freedom for all species and the Earth continues. It's time to notice. It's time to help the struggle. It's time to get involved, because there just isn't much time left. If you're interested, read on. If not, go back to watching America's Most Wanted. You never know, you might just see your friends there. Then will you care?

The April 94 issue of Militant Vegan reports that there have be "more than 20 acts of sabotage and liberation in just the first 2 months" of 1994 in North America. By including vandalism and other minor attacks, the list grows to over 40. That's not counting what we'll never hear about. These figures mean that some kind of action happens almost every day.

This year we've taken some blows as well. In Edmonton, the prosecutor of an A.L.F. activist appealed the sentence handed down to Darren Thurston and put him in a cell for 6 1/2 months so far (of a 2 year sentence) on top of the 14 1/2 months he already spent inside. In Spokane, Kim Trimiew and Deb Stout were imprisoned for months for refusing to talk to the grand jury about the A.L.F.; this was Kim's second time beind bars for refusing to testify. David Barbarash served 4 months after being picked up at gunpoint by the FBI/BATF. The latest news is that Rod Coronado has been arrested after 2 years of freedom from the feds—now they want to keep him in jail until he is 99 years old. Arizona has become the most recent state to create laws specifically to criminalize animal liberation activists. There are already federal laws in place. Grand juries are continuing until at least mid-1995 in five states (OR, WA, MI, UT, LA). Direct FBI harassment of activists continues in at least 3 states so far this year.

Does this sound pretty bad to you? We need to remember that what this all really means, what it reflects, is the growth of our movement. There are now more brave sister and brother warriors forming cells and tribes and taking action. What it also means is that we have to be much more careful and smart in our daily activities. The "political climate" is not what it was ten or even five years ago. Now, in the mid-nineties, mistakes will be hard and costly. Follow the basic rules: don't use phones for anything, use only safe addresses for mail, shut your mouth — do not say anything to anyone, etc., etc. You know it all, right? Well, I hope so.

"Again? Why is it that the revolution always gets this far and then everyone just chickens out?"

As the evolution of the struggle continues in this way and the attempts to squash it increase, we will see more of our brothers and sisters either in jail or on the run. We need to accept this as a reality because people do fuck up, and sometimes the feds do get lucky. We need to prepare ourselves for the increased repression. The first steps to take are to thoroughly clean your home, to get new i.d., and to start stashes of needed things such as money, food, gear, etc.

It doesn't matter whether you are active or not. If you have any friends or connections at all to active resistance fighters, then you may find yourself in need of i.d. at some point. Making your home safe means having all personal letters, diaries, photos, papers and magazines advocating illegal activities, and any related items such as that timing device you have been working on for months, it means having all this stuff out of your home and into a safe place. It may seem a bit inconvenient and perhaps unnecessary, but I tell ya, 5-10 years in a cell will be a lot more inconvenient. Also remember that someone else's actions in your city or neighborhood could precipitate a raid on your home even if you had nothing to do with it.

If you are an active warrior, you should consider ending your public life and begin your private one. There are a few activists who are living this way now, and so far none have been caught [since this was written, two underground North American activists have been captured by the feds.-ed]. One thing to consider is that all the people the feds are physically harassing right now, and all the activists who are or have gone to jail, have all been public people with all connections leading to their homes, jobs, friends, etc. An activist is much more secure and safe away from prying eyes, if s/he is a private person. A private life as an activist means not going to any public political rallies and demos, meetings or similar events. It means dropping out of a public existence as much as possible.

In this private life many new issues will come up that are sometimes not so easily dealt with. This includes loneliness and isolation, especially if you make a complete break from traditional friends and family. This is why the idea of a tribe is so important. We need each other for our psychic and emotional well-being, to enable us to cope and survive. This break from those friends and family does become necessary when you realize that those who lead public lives often do not fully understand your security needs. Many mistakes will happen such as mentioning your name over the phone or in the presence of others who will repeat the information to someone else. Your friends will do this, no matter how many times you've tried to explain the situation to them. Until your friends and relatives really and truly understand the level of security you need, it is wisest to have as little contact as possible with them. For those who do begin to understand, encourage them to get a safe address, and if you have one yourself (which you should) you can now safely communicate with each other through the mail.

Other issues that will come up tend to revolve around home and money. About the former, it is best not to live with people who can testify as to whether you were home on a certain day, or what firearms you have, or where you might have travelled. Will your housemates be brave enough and have the integrity to refuse to answer questions to an agent or a grand jury? Will they too choose jail over talking? Do you really know their breaking point? Think about it. Perhaps your current home situation needs to be changed. Living on your own or with your comrades is the best. Living on the road is also an alternative. Whatever you decide to do, do it safely. No phones, no mail, do not arouse the suspicions of your neighbours. We are now in the era of safe actions and safe living.

LIFE UNDERGROUND

The central issue that will keep coming up is the one of money. If you've been thinking ahead and have been part of the slave force, maybe you've put away a few thousand. Or maybe you've got some left over from grandma's inheritance. Eventually though, your personal supply will run out. A job is out of the question when you're leading a private activist life. Besides, there's so much real work to be done. So how will you survive? Surviving costs money ,whether it's for food (you will need to cut down on shoplifting as it poses a huge risk to your survival) or for research work or for those tools, or for gas or for the occasional car rental or motel room. It all adds up.

Unfortunately, money is the one thing I haven't completely figured out yet. You can try your folks or your working friends to donate to your needs, or maybe you or they know of richer sympathetic folks. For those of you reading this who have been approached for money, or know of activists who need it, put your thinking caps on to figure this one out. The reality is, without the cash flow, ain't nothing much gonna happen.

This may sound so dire and depressing and especially difficult. This road is certainly not for everyone. Careful consideration must be given to this decision. Hard questions must be asked of yourself: Do I really think that letter writing, petitioning, marching, shouting, civil disobedience, and banner hanging will really change anything before it's too late? Is it almost too late already? Is there something more than needs to be done? Am I one of those people who needs to be doing that "something more"? There's nothing more this planet needs right now than committed Earth warriors. Think about it.

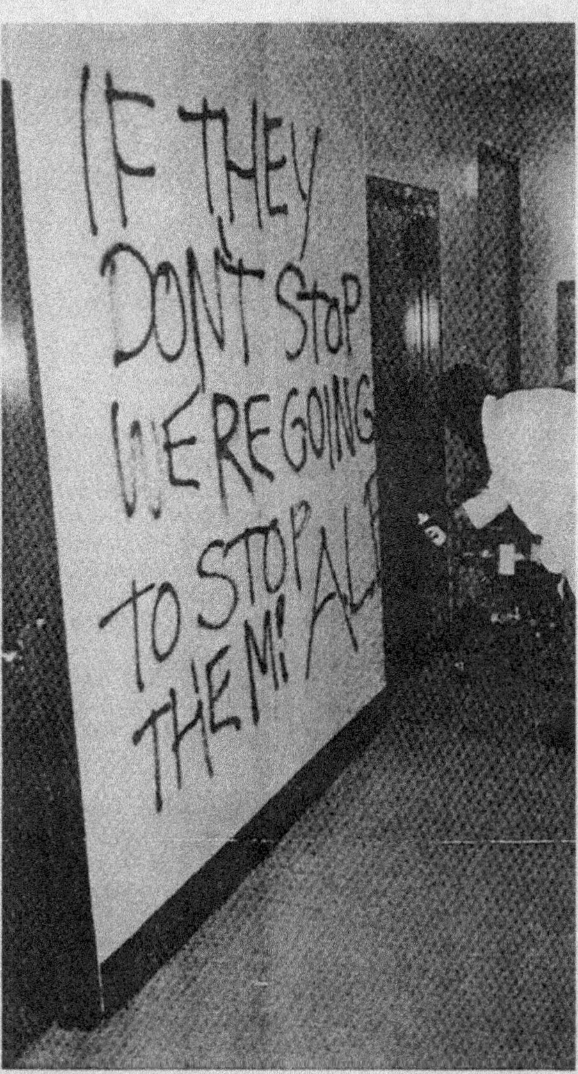

One thing I would like to touch on briefly is one not many people give much thought or credit to. That thing is magic, specifically, magical protection. Amid your scoffing and teasing I can happily say that there is magical energy to tap into. Most of my protection, outside of all the practical precautions I take, comes from my faith in the magical realm. This is not to say I've ignored my own advice or acted callously, but much of my safety and security is greatly enhanced by my knowledge and understanding and "tuning in" to the magic around me. I look at it as a kind of chaos of energy which engulfs and connects every being and place. Once you learn to see signs of the energy, and begin to connect with the chaos around you, you can tap into the protective energies. There is no rule of how to do this; everybody must find their own way which suits their particular way of relating. A lot of it has to do with faith and a lot has to do with your connection to other like-minded souls and well as the natural world. Anyway, I'm not writing to convert you non-believers. All I'm saying is just open yourself up to the potentials and the possibilities. What have you got to lose?

We have an incredibly enormous task on our hands, which is to help bring the madness to an end. The planet and all creatures on it have suffered long enough at the hands of humans. As conscious people we have the responsibility to stop the destruction, and to do that we must stop the humans and their criminal corporate enterprises. Earth warriors need help from you as soon as possible, and we need as many new dedicated souls as possible to join in the struggle. And, we need all the help magic can provide for us as well.

I want to talk a bit more about the support role. Fact is, most of you reading this, no matter how much you agree with the idea of resistance and direct action, will not participate in it or be prepared to involve yourselves in full-scale resistance. That's unfortunate, but not a complete waste. Truth is, in order for any level of direct action campaigns to continue and flourish, we need people who are not directly involved to offer much needed support. Here are some ideas, some of which have already been mentioned but they can be stressed over and over again.

You likely know someone who is involved in illegal actions. Help to maintain their security. How? By not asking them questions such as "Where are you going?" or "Where have you been?" By not talking about these people to your friends or strangers, casually, over the phone, or otherwise. By refusing to answer questions about them posed to you by anyone, either a close friend or the fbi. By opening your door to them when they need a place to crash, no questions asked. By offering them money when they come through town, because they need it, and their sources are few and far between. Like I said before, money is the main issue as far as support for an underground life and for continued actions. If you've got a job, consider putting away a set amount each month to support the underground. You may not know anyone now who is in need but in all probability you will sometime in the future. Hit up your wealthy friends and relatives, and they don't need to know what it's for.

There are other things to start acquiring and stashing. Non-perishable food such as grains and canned goods will always be useful. Know anyone who works in a health food store or even a safeway? With the approach of world disorder, you yourself might just benefit from a well thought out survival plan. Aside from stashing food and money, you might also want to consider acquiring a gun and lots of ammo. Personally, I have no use for such things in 1994, but who's to say what might happen in 5-10 years. Every year it's getting harder to get a weapon for personal defense, so the smart thing to do would be to get that stuff now while you still can and simply stash it in one of those army ammo boxes buried in a spot in a national forest or somewhere. I would suggest either a 9mm or 38 with as much ammo as you can afford. If you never need it, great! But if you do need to defend yourself in the future, you will be prepared.

The important thing to remember here is that there are people now, our friends, our brothers and sisters, who are, in 1994, on the run, avoiding police detection, trying to continue this struggle which we all believe in, carrying out actions for the Earth and the animals, and who are barely surviving and only just surviving due to the support, minimal though it is, and good will of some people and friends like you. Ideally, in my fantasy world, every one of you would immediately quit your jobs and your public lives and start your private underground life of activism and resistance. I know that won't happen, so the next best thing is for ya'll to start putting into place measures to support our comrades. Remember, we're out here on the front lines, and we need you! Let's support our troops!

NEW PRISONER

Rodney Adam Coronado F4445
Newaygo County Jail, PO Box 845, White Cloud, MI, 49349 USA

On Wednesday, September 27, Rod Coronado was arrested by officials of the FBI, BATF, and BIA at the Pascua Yaqui Reservation for allegedly participating in the Feb 28,1992 arson at Michigan State University in East Lansing. The fire destroyed a mink research facility and the work of researchers Richard Aulerich (who fed dioxins and other toxins to minks) and Karen Chou.

In July 1993 a federal grand jury in Michigan indicted Rod of five charges: arson, extortion, possession of stolen property, using fire to commit extortion, and interstate travel to commit arson. Rod is also "considered a suspect" in the 1991 raid on Washington State University. Grand juries have been investigating 1991-2 fires and burglaries at 4 universities, a defunct mink farm, and a mink food plant. These actions, claimed by the A.L.F. as part of "Operation Bite Back", caused over $1.5 million damage.

Numerous bail applications were unsuccessful. On October 27, despite pleas from Rod's community to return him to the Pascua Yaqui reservation, Rod was extradited to Michigan. His trial is expected to begin in early 1995.

ROD CORONADO SUPPORT COMMITTEE
PO Box 1891, Tucson, AZ 85702
Phone: 602-322-9819 Fax: 602-795-2527
e-mail: <seac-sw@seac.com>

General donations for Rod's support work should go to the Rodney Coronado Support Committee in Tucson.

The Activist Support Group in Missoula is fundraising to pay for Pasqua Yaqui children and elders to visit Rod in Michigan; send donations for this project to the Activist Support Group, Box 9286, Missoula, MT, 59807 USA, marked "Rod".

Yaqui cross with circle of all life extending from it. Within this circle are all the earth's creatures. The stars in the cross are those that represent the heavens above.

Further information on Rod's case can be obtained from the Rodney Coronado Support Committee (RCSC): PO Box 1891, Tucson, AZ, 85702 USA

Also see "A Letter to my Friends" in the Samhain '94 *Earth First Journal.*

My name is Rodney Adam Coronado. I'm 28 years old and a mixed-blood Yaqui. Before my arrest, I lived on our small reservation Pascua Yaqui Pueblo south of Tucson, Arizona with our tribe's Traditional Elder and Spiritual Leader, Anselmo Valencia. This is a short history of my life.

Our tribe's homeland is in present day Sonora, Mexico but my grandparents parents fled the region when Yaquis were being murdered wholesale. After a time in Tucson, they followed farmwork to the Central Valley of California where my parents met and were married. They were both active in the United Farm Workers movement, and my father was a Brown Beret. When my mother was pregnant with me, she attended a demonstration against

ROD CORONADO

the then racist governor of California.

I grew up mostly in San Jose, California and got used to the name-calling by white kids, "Beaner", "Spic", and worse. In the 3rd grade I remember having my mouth taped because the teacher said I talked too much, then she summoned my 2nd grade teacher Mr. Hill who was native american also to come look. I'll never forget that.

All my life I was drawn to nature and animals and would be the first to intercede when someone was being cruel. I always remember my mom telling me I was Yaqui, and should be proud. When I was 12 I saw a PBS documentary on the Canadian harp seal hunt and after crying through the whole thing, refused to turn it off. I swore that night that I would devote my life to ending such disrespect and cruelty. When I was 14 my mother gave me Dee Brown's *Bury My Heart at Wonded Knee* and I struggled through it convincing myself that I must never be ashamed to be an indigenous person. I saved my lawn-cutting money, and work wages and sent them to various animal-welfare groups. I also wrote many letters of protest.

When I graduated from high school I immediately left home to work full-time as a volunteer for the Sea Shepherd Society and their Captain Paul Watson, the same man I saw on PBS defending the harp seals. In 1979 when I had heard of his ramming and later sinking of the pirate whaling ship "Sierra" I told myself, "These are the people I will work with". From 1984 to 1987 I helped the Sea Shepherds. Sailing on their ship the Sea Shepherd to the North Atlantic and Pacific to interfere with the illegal killing of ocean wildlife. In the Faroe Islands in 1986 I was arrested and beaten and held for 5 days until Amnesty International helped secure my release. In Iceland in 1986 a comrade and I disabled the country's illegal whaling station, and later that evening sank two of the country's four whaling ships. In all these actions I always accepted full responsibility.

In Britain in 1986 & 1987 I also participated with the Hunt Saboteurs, a legitimate anti-hunting group, in disrupting fox hunts non-violently. Through 1987-1989 I again sailed with the Sea Shepherd, was a Director for a short time, and also participated with various animal rights groups in staging anti-vivisection rallies and demonstrations. I also participated with various Earth First! groups in protesting trophy hunts for protected Mtn. Lions, and wilderness destruction. In 1987 I helped found the Hunt Saboteurs of America to interfere with the trophy hunt of protected Bighorn Sheep in California's Mojave Desert.

Through all these activities I adhered to non-violence and never hurt anyone. I also was one of the few non-white people in the struggles and felt my participation was based on the beliefs as a Yaqui that all creations were deserving of respect and reverence.

In 1987-1990 I worked for People for the Ethical Treatement of Animals as a researcher and investigator and in 1990 a friend and I founded our own investigation agency called "Global Investigations". In Spring 1990 we were hired by "Friends of Animals" to investigate and document allegations of abuse on fur farms in America. For the next eleven months we worked undercover and infiltrated the industry as prospective fur ranchers and were witness to horrible conditions on mink, fox, bobcat, lynx, and chinchilla farms throughout the United States.

ANIMAL LIBERATION PRISONER SUPPORT

North America

In December of 1990 we purchased Campbell's Fur Farm in Montana where we had witnessed the worst abuse and immediately transferred the 66 mink, bobcats and lynx to a rehabilitation site in Washington State. At this same time, friends and I formed the "Coalition Against Fur Farms" to disseminate the information and evidence gathered in our eleven month investigation some of which was aired on the news program "60 Minutes" in 1991. The sixty-six animals in our care were nursed back to health, rehabilitated and released back into their native habitat. We then issued a press release accepting responsibility and invited authorities to press charges if we had broken any law. There were never any charges filed.

When the Animal Liberation Front began a direct action campaign against the fur industry, various media representatives asked CAFF for information about the fur farm industry. I obliged, did numerous interviews and was quickly identified by the FBI and fur farmers as Jim Perez, the fur farmer from Oregon. I began to recieve death threats in the fall of 1991 and so decided to do some backpacking before winter set in. When the threats continued, and were acknowledged by the FBI I decided to lie low with other indians on various reservations across the country.

During this time I became involved with native issues to protect the land, and helped identify the religious as well as ecological benefits of native lands restoration. In 1993 I moved to Tucson, Arizona to be near my Yaqui culture and people and became involved with the traditional religious ceremonies of our people. On Christmas Eve 1993 I became a member of the Wikoi Yau üra, or Bow Leaders, the traditional Yaqui warrior society. As a member it is our responsibility to protect the culture, people and lands of our tribe.

In 1994 I began volunteering my services to the Yoemem Tekia Foundation who are entrusted by the tribe to preserve the cultrue. I immediately became aware to the threat posed to our culture and youth by drugs, alcohol and gang activity, so with the approval of various traditional elders began a weekly youth retreat to expose Yaqui kids to our still living culture and heritage. The Yoeme Nation Youth Junta taught desert survival skills, demonstrated traditional dance, showed educational videos on indigenous issues, provided a free healthy meal, elders told stories of our ancestors struggles to retain cultural identity, made traditional arts and crafts, and most importantly stressed the importance of maintaining a pure life free from the poisons of drugs, alcohol, or violence.

This work was the pinnacle of my career as an advocate for peace and justice. I had returned home to my people. My elders and other traditionals welcomed me into their lives and gave me back my family. All my lessons learned, and friends made in other movements were welcome and people began to have hope. My elder Anselmo Valencia welcomed me as he would his own son, and taught me lessons of respect, love and understanding that only an elder can. In ceremonies we danced to our fallen warriors of the past, and to our animal relations whom are our sisters and brothers. We began to build bridges with non-native environmentalists and joined them in their resistance to the desecration of sacred places on our earth mother.

The Federal gov't. call me a threat to the community. They want to jail me for 56 years though I've never hurt anyone or caused loss of life. I am innocent of the charges laid against me. I have lived my life as my elders taught me. I have practiced my traditional religion. It is against my ethics as a human being to stand witness to atrocites against life without speaking out. I only want to live with my people and help fight the skyrocketing levels of domestic violence, alcoholism, drug abuse, suicide, and gang violence. I want to pursue a life of peace where the hand of friendship is extended to all, even my captors and persecutors.

If the above mentioned facts can be seen as a crime, then I would rather spend the rest of my life in jail than retract a single contribution I've made. I have an obligation as a Bow Leader of the Yaqui Nation. I made a pledge to give my life to the people, and to the creations we live with. I must remember the sacrifices made by my ancestors of not long ago. The raped women, the babies whose heads were smashed against tree trunks, the men hung with barbed wire, the women and children who in 1910 by the hundreds plunged off of cliffs rather than be taken prisoner at a place called Masacoba.

It is year 502 of the Invader and still he cannot live in peace with the children of earth. We want friendship not anger, love not hate, respect not desecration. Please join me. Stand together as sisters and brothers, do not forget the lessons of our grandmothers. Let us live in harmony. Enough blood has been spilled, too many loved ones sacrificed. Remember that we are all related, all children of the same earth mother. I love you all, and will die if necessary so that others may live. With prayers for the Rebirth.

In Her Service,
Rod Coronado
Wikoi Yau üra
Pascua Yaqui Tribe

LISE OLSEN B48426
PO Box 5001, Dwight, IL, 60420 USA

In November 1992, Chicago activist Lise Olsen was arrested at her home. Earlier that year, on the US "Independence Day", Lise had hung 21 home-made lanterns fueled with a very small amount of gasoline near a railroad trestle to illuminate a 30-foot red, white and blue "Freedom" banner suspended over a pro-fur billboard painted on the metal siding of a railway overpass. Lise had designed these lanterns to burn like small torches, for about five minutes, and then go out.

In her latest letter to the ALFSG, Lise writes, "It seems important to mention...that I did a July 4 Independence Day Action. I guess most people know that means lots of fireworks, that was my idea to make a "Spirit of 1776" connection with the lanterns. Like an old-timey, authentic look."

Only one of the lanterns actually lit; it burned for five minutes with a very small flame. Because most of the lanterns had failed to light, Lise decided it was useless to take pictures for the media, and removed her banner. Lise has an immune deficiency called Chronic Fatigue Syndrome and felt physically unable to remove the 21 lanterns, so she left them there. Four months later, she was arrested for attempted arson, and released on a $20,000 bond.

NEW PRISONER

According to Lise, "although I denied it categorically, the detective who arrested me, Robert Schatzel, told the media and the Grand Jury that I had confessed to it. The terrible media I received convicted me before my trial. When the detective was challenged by my attorney at my trial to produce the supposed signed confession, of course he couldn't. he just said he had made an 'error' about it."

Lise describes her July 1994 trial as a "farce" and lists countless procedural "irregularities", including manipulation of evidence, use of past records and fingerprints that were ordered expunged when charges against Lise were dropped (from an attempted animal liberation years ago), and obvious judicial bias. The prosecution's manipulation of the evidence included placing the lanterns in plastic bags labelled "BOMB" in large red letters. Despite a military explosives consultant's testimony that the lanterns were candles, not incendiaries, Lise was convicted of possession of incendiary devices, manufacture of incendiary devices, and unlawful use of a weapon, i.e. possession of more than 3 teaspoonfuls of gasoline.

After her conviction Lise spent over a month in appalling conditions at the Cook County Jail, awaiting sentencing. During this time she undertook a hunger strike in protest of her incarceration as a political prisoner. On August 31, Lise was sentenced to four years imprisonment and ordered to pay a $1000 fine.

In Lise's words, "My case rests on the fact that I manufactured illuminating devices which were distorted by the prosecution to be called incendiary devices, simply in order to convict me and make an <u>example of me as an animal rights activist</u>, although they <u>did not burn anything</u>." (underlining as in original letter).

Since Lise's conviction, she has had to spend massive energy and time fighting further attempts to harass her from behind bars.

"I...have serious security problems. Although I live on a minimum security unit, my official status is still 'pending'. As long as this continues, the necessary paperwork even to get on the work release waiting list (5 mo. long at this prison, much shorter at other Illinois prisons) cannot be submitted. Howard Peters [Director of Illinois Corrections-ed.] has already received appeal letters in response to the appeal I sent out. In an answer to one of them, it was stated that I had been charges with 'Possession of Explosives'! I almost fainted with shock. My trial attorney, Barry Gross, had told me there was nothing more they could do to hurt me now that they had sentenced me to prison—at least it was over. Surprise! My sole charge now consolidated at my sentencing, is 'Possession of Incendiary Devices'. And a match, gas oven, lantern, etc, can all potentially be these. But explosives?! That is <u>NOT</u> on my mittimus (court papers)..."

"The prosecutor (State's attorney) submitted an 'Official Statement of Facts' to the Records Office here. All this on Oct. 12. In it he stated my action as 'July 4', never mentioning the year, as it if had happened this year and of course OMITTING the bit about free on bond for 2 years. Then he said the banner had never been recovered—and it was submitted into evidence at my trial! He specifically stated I had 'endangered the lives of children' and held up traffic (the latter was laboriously ad nauseam belabored at my trial—as if that was the <u>real</u> charge against me). The 'endangering children' bit can have terribly serious consequences. People who have done violent crimes (ie murder, reckless homicide, heinous battery, child pornography) are not eligible for a 2nd '3 months good time' off their sentences. One such charge is 'endangering the life or health of a child.' By putting this in, he is attempting to not let me be awarded this good time. He also recommended I not get early release."

One of the prisoncrats, Sgt. Kinkaid, is doing what he can do make Lise's time more difficult. When Lise's boyfriend visited Lise, they embraced—as within prison guidelines—and the staff promptly terminated the visit and ordered Lise's boyfriend to leave. Kinkaid then ordered Lise be charged with "sexual misconduct" and receive a 7-day cell lock as a punishment—the sexual misconduct charge was later dropped, but the punishment remains on Lise's record. This could mean a higher security classification or problems for Lise when she applies for work release.

To make matters worse, despite a second visit with her boyfriend with no problems, on Oct 12 the warden issued a memo that her boyfriend could not visit her for three months.

LISE OLSEN

Lise's boyfriend was never notified of this and arrived the following week with a box of Lise's clothes. The usual procedure is to put a box of clothes in the prisoner's personal property, unopened, to be opened in the prisoner's presence—Sgt. Kinkaid decided to deviate from the regular procedure and ordered Lise's box of clothes opened; he then denied them because of a questionable custom-painted towel design. (?!)

As of Oct 24, Lise was told she could no longer walk outside because her minimum security classification was still "pending". No recognition was given to the fact that she had been walking outside for 33 days, without problems, while living on the minimum security unit.

Despite two court orders for a vegetarian diet, Lise is not getting a proper diet.

HOW YOU CAN HELP LISE

In addition to the usual prisoner support (writing to the prisoner, fundraising, sending reading materials, etc) Lise has asked that people help by:

1) Circulating petitions that read "We, the undersigned, support clemency in the form of release to work release and/or reduction of sentence for Lise Olsen, a non-violent activist who is no threat to the community, does an unusual amount of community volunteer work, and who has proved her commitment to a legal, constructive lifestyle during the two years she was free on bond prior to incarceration. We believe in her good character and honorable intentions." Send filled petitions to the North American ALFSG—we will pass them on to Lise, the Warden, the head of Illinois Corrections, other government officials, etc.

2) Writing to the Warden and to the Director of Illinois Department of Corrections, requesting that Lise be assigned to work release and listed for electronic detention immediately. State that Lise is non-violent, etc. as in the petition wording above. Also mention that Lise is imprisoned for an action that never caused any property damage or harm to any life and never seriously posed a threat in either of these regards; also that Lise suffers from Chronic Fatigue Syndrome and her health will continue to deteriorate the longer she is incarcerated. Send copies of these letters to Lise and to the North American ALFSG—please do NOT send your only copy directly to the jail, we need to make sure Lise actually <u>gets</u> the letters for her appeals.

LISE'S ADDRESSES

Warden Gwen Thornton: PO Box 5001, Dwight, IL, 60420 USA

Howard Peters III, Director, Illinois Dept of Corrections: 1301 Concordia Court, PO Box 19277, Springfield, IL, 62794-9277 USA

DAVID BARBARASH & KIM TRIMIEW RELEASED!

On August 29, Kim Trimiew was finally released after spending more than 6 months in the Spokane County Jail for refusing to testify before a Spokane Grand Jury. Kim's 193 days in jail marked a significant increase in length of incarceration for refusing to testify before a Grand Jury: of the five people (three of them in Spokane) other than Kim who have been jailed since 1989 for not talking to Grand Juries about the A.L.F, none have served over 5 months. This was Kim's second time around; in October she was jailed for 2 weeks for refusing to testify before a different grand jury. Deborah Stout, who also refused to testify and was sent to jail at the same time as Kim, was released in July. Both Kim and Deb were released on the grounds that the incarceration was obviously not going to persuade them to talk to the Grand Jury and was, instead, being used to punish them for crimes they had never been charged with.

On September 8, David Barbarash pled guilty to a lesser charge of "accessory after the fact" and was sentenced to 200 community service hours and a suspended sentence of 18 months probation. He was released later that day. David, a Canadian activist, was arrested in the USA in May after successfully avoiding Canadian police for almost 2 years. He originally faced three charges stemming from a 1992 A.L.F. raid on the University of Alberta, where 29 cats were freed an estimated $22,000 damage caused to the lab. David was held without bail for a month in various American jails, then deported to Canada and held for another 3 months. This was David's second A.L.F.-related conviction.

Oct. 19 FULL MOON O

Since the last full moon I have again had tears of anger and sorrow. Rod was arrested on September 28 in Arizona. Once again they've locked up another warrior. The wheels of the 'Just-Us' system try to trample another one.

In just so coincidental timing Security here has told me they're holding back magazines, newsletters and newsclippings sent to me!? Taking away one of the biggest things keeping me happy. I've been on the dreaded telephone (they haven't taken that away, yet). Keeping up to date and more often than not keeping others up to date.

I've seen egos and attitudes come out of the woodwork in the last three weeks. It's made me quite angry, sad and frustrated that some people can't work together even when someone needs them most. All too many people and groups (big and small) seem to need to control as much as they can. If you can't for just this one time do as Rod has asked, "...put petty differences aside, time to hold each others hands TOGETHER" then stand back, shut-up and let others do what needs to be done. Rod's trial will be next year some time and I expect a fair amount of people will be subpoenaed. How many of you will refuse to testify for the so called just-us system? It's time to start gathering your strength and support soon, you may need it.

Most of you know the FBI's "Cointelpro" tactics of the past. Beware they still go on, probably more than ever. You can be sure they're just loving it as some of us argue, fight and spread rumors. Beware of what you hear and be even more careful of what you say.

I've been trying to keep as busy as possible both physically and mentally. The time has been going by fairly quickly which I'm thankful for. When times are tough I've always told myself 'it could be worse'. I'm surviving and look forward to the day when I can once again be with the mountains and trees.

Darren Thurston

One last word regarding the North American A.L.F. Supporters Group. At the moment but one person does 80%+ of the day to day work. That person is unpaid and yet regularly puts in 8-12 hour days doing support work. Their office has been broken into and computer equipment and files stolen and they're still doing more work than ever. With so many people imprisoned this year in North America the SG has been forced to borrow approx. $2000 to cover costs of support work. Any help in raising money in your area or personal donations will help the SG support those of us inside.

Darren Thurston
FSCC, Bag 10-7802 101 St., Fort Saskatchewan, AB, T8L 2P3 Canada

Darren is approx. 6 1/2 months into the 2-year sentence he received from the Alberta Court of Appeal in May 94, after the Crown Prosecutor successfully appealed Darren's original sentence and release from jail last year. In September 1993, after serving 14 1/2 months pre-trial time in the Edmonton Remand Hellhole, Darren was convicted of charges relating to two A.L.F. actions in Edmonton that caused over $70,000 in damages: an arson at Billingsgate Fish Company and the liberation of 29 cats from the University of Alberta/severe damage to the lab. He was originally sentenced to time served and ordered to pay almost $75,000 in restitution. He is still having some trouble receiving certain mail items but as of late October some magazines and newsletters were getting through.

Sept. 5 New Moon

...early one morning I lie very still, I'm under a pine tree my whole body pressed into the earth. I'd been there for six hours already, watching the Ellerslie Research Station, a University of Alberta animal laboratory. When all of a sudden a field mouse ran over my hand and stopped to stare at me, this strange one lying under a tree with binoculars and a radio to his ear. It talked but a short moment and went back on it's way, needless to say I didn't understand what it said but it moved me. It made me think again of my commitment to the earth and just why I'd been lying under a pine tree eight hours a night for seven days straight. Later that week I helped liberate 29 cats and damage equipment in that laboratory.

Unfortunately not all stories end up happy, nineteen days later I was arrested by the RCMP. Fortunately 29 cats are still out there, living their lives in loving and caring homes. I spent 15 months locked up awaiting trial and finally in September '93 I was given a suspended sentence, two years probation and ordered to pay $73,725 restitution. The state was not impressed, they wanted blood oops I mean three more years prison time and immediately appealed the judge's sentence. On May 12 '94 after a very short eight months of freedom the Alberta Court of Appeals issued a written decision sentencing me to an additional two years less a day. On friday the 13th after saying many tearful goodbyes, I took the long walk and turned myself in.

I'm well into my government vacation now and I've just recently been transferred to "the fort" which is definitely nicer than the last two government resorts. Not to say it's all been fun, I'm not too happy to be back inside after only eight months out, but I've gotten used to my temporary home. I think of it as a strengthening process, one where we can harden ourselves in our struggle. For the battle has begun and it is not going to be easy. More people will go underground. And more people will go to prison, in England activists are serving four, six, ten year sentences. Yet actions there continue unabated. Sisters and Brothers (mothers, fathers, uncles, aunts, and even second removed cousins), earth and animal warriors we must join hands with others fighting for their own liberation. You must realize that we all have tremendous power, it takes but one person to cost them millions. When you see the pictures of a masked liberator, stop asking who's behind the mask and look in the mirror!

Many thanks to all those that have written me during my time inside, it sure helps me survive. And to the few people that have travelled thousands of miles and put hundreds of hours into my support, a huge thank you. To those on the front lines, stay strong, stay free, and keep fighting the good fight.

Clenched Fist Salutations,
Darren Thurston

DARREN THURSTON

KEITH MANN EE3588
HMP Wandsworth, PO Box 757, 23 Heathfield Rd, Wandsworth, London SW18 3HS England

In June 1992, Keith Mann and Vivien Smith pled guilty to attempted arson at Madstone Crown Court. Because he was also facing charges in the Manchester conspiracy case (with Allison McKeon, Max Watson, and Terry Helsby), his sentence was deferred until the Manchester case was concluded. When Keith found himself unattended in an unlocked police van last year, he decided to take a vacation from being interviewed by the police and took off. In the early morning of April 8, police officers raided the Celia Hammond Animal Trust Sanctuary in East Sussex, and arrested Angie Hamp (another activist on the lam) and Keith Mann.

After being remanded to HMP Holloway, Keith was classified as an "A" category prisoner and as such faces extremely strict regulations (see sidebar). He also has had to deal with all the idiotic rules applying to all prisoners who attempt or succeed in escaping from custody. Several months after his incarceration, Keith's "high escape risk" status was dropped so he no longer has to put lovely yellow-striped clothes outside his cell at night.

On June 10, Keith was "properly" convicted of the 1992 arson charges and received even more rules and regs, this time for convicted prisoners—which means visits must be accompanied by Visiting Orders (V.O.), with one V.O. issued per week. As of November, Keith was still having severe problems getting visits. Most visitors have been denied, apparently for no reason other than to harass Keith.

In early November he was moved from Manchester to London pending a court appearance.

GURJEET AUJLA HV2047
HMP Birmingham, Winson Green Road, Birmingham, B18 4AS

On June 3, Gurj was arrested at his home. He was questioned over the weekend and was then formally charged with "Conspiracy to cause explosions" on June 6. He has been classified as an "A" category prisoner, like Keith Mann, and as such faces extremely strict regulations (see sidebar). Only family have been allowed to see Gurj, in closed visits. Despite this, Gurj says "apart from hassle over visits...it's not a problem, I've got a single cell and I'm in good spirits."

NEW PRISONERS

DAVE CALLENDER HV3314
GREG AVERY HV3313
HMP Birmingham, Winson Green Road, Birmingham, B18 4AS, England

(Write to each separately; do NOT address envelope to both)

On October 21 Dave and Greg were remanded to HMP Birmingham after being charged with "conspiracy to cause criminal damage". They had both been arrested a few days earlier near Cambridge, on bicycles & wearing backpacks. Nothing which could be called "illegal" was found on them but they were arrested and taken to Cambridge Police Station. Later that day they were released on police bail only to be re-arrested immediately by the West Midlands police, who took them both to Birmingham. They have been arrested in connection with a raid on a house which neither of them live at, where items which could be used to make incendiaries have been found—and were accused of a "bomb-making factory"! No actual incendiaries were located and no other persons have been arrested. Both have been remanded for a week and will appear in court again on October 28. The day after being put in remand, they were put into "A" category status (see sidebar), like Gurjeet Aujla and Keith Mann; they have since been lowered to a less restrictive security status. This is Dave Callender's second time in jail (first time—1985).

COLIN CHATFIELD CB2966
HMP Acklington, Acklington, Morpeth, Northumberland, NE65 9XF, England

In early October Colin was sentenced to 121 days (approx. 4 months) in prison by Barrow-in-Furness magistrates court, for sending a hoax bomb call to a branch of Boots the Chemist (vivisectors). If all goes well he will be released on November 25. This is the third time Colin has been imprisoned for animal liberation actions and he has vowed to continue upon his release.

"A" STATUS—STATUS QUO FOR NEW ANIMAL LIBERATION PRISONERS?

Four animal liberation prisoners, Gurjeet Aujla, Keith Mann, Dave Callender, and Greg Avery, were classified as "A" category prisoners after their arrest. In a letter in the *UK ALFSG Newsletter*, Keith writes, "Exactly why I've been Cat 'A'd hasn't been officially explained (more secrets) but I was told it's because I've been accused of causing explosions; not charged, just accused and bailed..."

All four of these animal lib prisoners who were put in "A" category are in remand, i.e. have not been convicted/sentenced. According to the UK ALFSG, "It seems clear that it is being used to victimize animal liberation prisoners and to make their time in prison that more unpleasant."

Dave and Greg were recently given a lower security category.

Keith's description of "A" status is: he is escorted every time he leaves his cell; all his movements around the prison are written down; all visitors must be checked out by the police and issued passes (most of Keith's visitors have been refused); all phone calls are taped and filed, and, along with all letters, passed on to the feds; and he is not allowed to go to the gym or to education. We can only assume that Gurj is under similar restrictions.

"A" category is supposedly for prisoners who are violent and/or likely to break out of prison using extreme force, with or without outside help. It is usually reserved for IRA prisoners, armed robbers, and other members of organized crime. These four are the first animal liberation prisoners to be given "A" status since Ronnie Lee; will category "A" be the status quo for animal lib prisoners from here on in?

ANGIE HAMP TW1687
HMP Holloway, Parkhurst Road, Holloway, London, N7 0NU, England

About 2 1/2 years ago, Angie decided against appearing in court for animal liberation charges and went on the run. In the early morning of April 8, police officers raided the Celia Hammond Animal Trust Sanctuary in East Sussex, and arrested Angie Hamp and Keith Mann (another activist on the lam).

Angie faced many charges. Her first, the Swalesmoor fur farm investigation, ended favorably when she was found not guilty. Her co-defendants fared similarly, either acquittals or extremely light sentences—no jail terms.

Pleas on other charges were arranged prior to sentencing. Angie pleaded not guilty to violent disorder but guilty to affray (for an incident concerning a huntsman), and not guilty to conspiracy to commit criminal damage but guilty to conspiracy to cause arson.

On September 30 Angie went to court for sentencing. According to another animal lib prisoner, "if she gets 4 years she will be quite happy but that's hoping they run the sentences for different charges together rather than one after the other." Angie did indeed get 4 years: 3 years for conspiracy to commit arson (for which Annette Tibbles is serving four years), 6 months for affray, and 6 months for breach of bail on three counts (i.e. failing to appear in court). All in all this is lighter than expected!

She is still facing the police's threat of charges for a raid on London Hospital. She was originally arrested for actions in Hastings (against Boots, some trucks, and for items sent through the mail) but apparently Keith Mann will be the only one charged for these

• •

ALLISON MCKEON RE2370
HMP Askham Grange, Askham Richard, York, Y02 3PT, England

MAX WATSON BJ2477
HMP Haverigg, Haverigg Camp, Millom, Cumbria, LA18 4NA, England

TERRY HELSBY EF0761
HMP Risley, Warrington Road, Risley, Warrington, WA3 6BP, England

These three prisoners were jailed in October 1993 following a lengthy and very expensive conspiracy trial in Manchester. The charges related to alleged damage (tens of thousands of dollars) against a zoo and various butchers' shops. Co-defendant Keith Mann was able to escape from police before the trial got under way but was captured earlier this year (see Keith update above). Terry Helsby was sentenced to 3 1/2 years, Max Watson received 3 years, and Allison was given a 2 year sentence. In December 1993 the remaining defendant, a woman who had been sentenced to two years in prison, was released by the Court of Appeal. Shortly after sentencing, one of the prisoners commented, "Our case was quite exceptional, so we had been dealt with particularly severely. The judge had to compensate for the millions of pounds spent on investigation and legal procedures."

On April 29, the High Court announced that all the appeals had been rejected by the first Judge at leave to appeal. Max Watson writes, in a letter to the UK ALFSG, "He said that: The Judge was entitled to impose a deterrent sentence of 3 years imprisonment for this planned and vicious conspiracy. What exactly he means by vicious I'm not exactly sure, except to say that through the eyes of a bigoted fuck-head anything goes when talking down to us criminals." (from *UK ALFSG Newsletter* Summer 94)

The charges against Allison from the Swalesmoor fur farm investigation ended favorably when she was found not guilty. All other defendants were either found not guilty or received extremely light sentences (no jail terms).

ANNETTE TIBBLES TT2215
HMP Holloway, Parkhurst Road, Holloway, London N7 0NU, England

Annette is serving a 4 year sentence for conspiracy to commit arson against animal abusers.

Dear Friends,

Things here are pretty good. P & O ferries have finally decided that they won't transport animals to Europe for slaughter and they handle 60% of the trade, so the other companies are making noises like they will be following. Its been a long campaign, but at least we have won. Kind of a strange victory though — even though the 100's of thousands of animals wont suffer long journeys & slaughter with barbaric methods outlawed here — they will still die at the end of the day. Most of the transport lorry firms are the ones regularly attacked by ALF—have to move on to other things haha. So maybe we will be seeing more varied targets soon.

Thanks for your newsletter—very professional looking and a good read. Nice to know that you are so busy over there too. I'll keep sending you cuttings as things happen.

love & liberation

Annette

Hello to my friends in America. Just wanted to let you know that we prisoners are doing OK and say thanks for your letters and news. Personally, I am doing really well. Now that Angie is with me and quite happy about getting 4 years (as opposed to 6 or more) I have started to clear my head and get some work done. With only 6 months to parole I have been allowed out 5 days a week to attend college and am studying media. It's all practical stuff that I can put to use in the future — editing video, Black & white photography, computerised magazine layout etc. Only a couple of months ago I even went on a course and learned rock climbing/abseiling/canoeing. They don't seem to have considered that rock climbing may be useful for my future lawbreaking ha ha!

There has been some wonderful support from around the world too, and I am beginning to feel just how big our movement is. I am first with all the gossip about actions and victories and do my best to pass it all on to others. There are a few things I have to tell you about, like the ban the ferry companies have put on carrying live animals to slaughter in Europe. It's been a long hard campaign but we have won massive public support and a response from the companies. Now all we have to do is get the population to go veggie and stop the murder for good. You gotta aim high! There has also been some aiming high on the High Streets—in the last 3 months Oxford, Isle of Wight, and York have all lost £2 million in fire damage at animal abuse shops. There have also been two major riots in central London at protests at a new law—The Criminal Justice Bill. The bill will affect all forms of protest and most 'alternative' lifestyles (ie squatters, travellers - new age and gypsies, rave parties and gatherings) plus it takes away the right to silence when questioned by the police and makes people trespassers potentially everywhere. People are at last waking up to what the State is planning and there is a lot of dissent around.

Sometimes I really miss being out there and joining in! Ah well, we'll be back. All the prisoners over here are in good spirits and no-one is in the least bit changed by the experience of prison—except a little bit wiser of course. Talk about a university of crime! Anyone want to know how to hot wire a car........

NEW PRISONERS

PHIL DESOUZA EJ3496

House Block 2, HMP Elmley, Church Road, Eastchurch, Shearness, Kent, ME12 4D2 England

Phil Desouza, an animal rights activist and well-known hunt saboteur, was imprisoned after pleading guilty to charges relating to anti-fascist activities and events surrounding the demonstration against the new Criminal Justice Bill in Hyde Park in early November. He is currently awaiting sentencing.

PAUL S. c/o EYFA

P.O. Box 92066, 1090 AB, Amsterdam, Netherlands

In early 1994, Paul S., a Dutch activist, was convicted of 18 counts of criminal damage relating to environmental actions. He was originally sentenced to 5 years imprisonment, but the state then turned around and tried to have Paul classified as "insane", which could have meant a life sentence. We are still trying to confirm the latest details but as far as we know Paul was classed as "partially insane" and placed in a mental hospital. Paul desperately needs international support. We are pleased to announce that in response to Paul's incarceration, the Earth Liberation Front in Holland has stepped up their activities (see diary of actions).

MILTON BORN WITH A TOOTH

In September 1994, Lonefighter Society leader Milton Born With A Tooth was sentenced to 16 months in jail for firing two shots into the air during the Sept 1990 Alberta Govt/RCMP invasion of the Peigan Nation.

Milton Born With A Tooth and the Lonefighter Society of the Peigan Nation have been vigorously resisting the construction of a dam on the Oldman River, in Peigan territory, for over four years. The development of the Oldman River Dam has been marked not only by usurpation of Peigan sovereignty and jurisdiction, but also by extreme examples of federal and provincial government corruption and a refusal to even follow their own environmental regulations. In March 1994 the Alberta Environment Ministry was found by the courts to have made fraudulent misrepresentations in the construction of the Paddle River dam in central Alberta during the early 1980s'—the same government staff responsible for this dam are responsible for the Oldman River Dam.

In the summer of 1990 the Lonefighter Society began digging channels to return the Oldman River back into its original bed by diverting it around a canal constructed by the Lethbridge Northern Irrigation District. On September 6 1990, provincial officials and 50-80 fully armed and camouflaged RCMP "tactical squad" officers invaded Peigan land and surrounded the Lonefighter Society camp. Two shots were fired into the air to warn the RCMP that they were trespassing. On September 12, Milton Born With A Tooth was arrested and jailed for over three months before obtaining bail.

In March 1991, Milton Born With A Tooth was convicted on 7 fire-arm charges stemming from the two shots being fired into the air and was sentenced to serve 18 months. An appeal of the decision was immediately launched. In September 1992, the Alberta Court of Appeal granted Milton Born With A Tooth a new trial. Alberta's chief justice instructed that 50% of the panel from which the jury be selected be Native people. In May 1993, Justice Willis O'Leary refused to allow the selection of a jury from a panel of 25 Native and non-Native people selected by the sheriff's office.

In March 1994, a 12-member jury found Milton Born With A Tooth guilty after an unusual handling of a "hung jury" verdict. After four days of deliberating, one juror refused to agree. After the verdict was read, the judge immediately returned the jury to its deliberations and after another 90 minutes the guilty verdict was returned.

In November 1994, Milton Born With A Tooth announced he will appeal the trial and sentence to the Alberta Court of Appeal. **$13,000 must be raised** to pay for court transcripts. Over $8000 has already been raised. Cheques are payable to the Mother Earth Defense Fund.

Lorraine Sinclair, of the Mother Earth Defense Fund, writes, "Milton should not be in jail—the politicians who made the decisions to construct the Oldman dam without an environmental assessment, sent in armed police officers to trespass on Peigan territory and who continue to violate FEARO (Federal Environmental Assessment Review Office) Panel recommendations are the ones who should be prosecuted. As an indigenous person, Milton had every right to protect and defend his territory."

Milton Born With A Tooth has asked Lorraine Sinclair of the Mother Earth Healing Society to coordinate a campaign and defense fund on his behalf. The Mother Earth Defense Fund is "being set up to support indigenous people who protect and defend Mother Earth in conflict with the Canadian legal system." - Lorraine Sinclair

MOTHER EARTH DEFENSE FUND
Box 53, 10024-82 Ave, Edmonton, AB, Canada T6E 1Z3
Phone: 403-461-9532 / Fax: 403-450-2665

info used, with permission, from "Mother Earth Defense Fund Bulletin", Fall 1994

MARK DAVIS #23106-008

FPC, P.O. Box 1000, Boron, CA, 93596 USA

Mark Davis is the only remaining defendant in the Arizona Five case who is still in prison. The Arizona Five (Mark, Peg Millett, Marc Baker, Ilse Asplund, and Dave Foreman) went on trial in June 1991 for allegedly participating in "ecoterrorist" conspiracies to cut down a power line providing power to a nuclear power plant. The Five were set up by FBI Special Agent Mike Fain and other FBI agents. Mark's release date (no parole) is June 1995, four years after being imprisoned in 1991. His co-defendant Peg Millett spent the last several months of her 2-year jail time in a halfway house; Mark similarly expected to get his last 4-6 months in a transitional work-furlough type program, as is standard for nonviolent inmates with a record of good behavior. Mark recently learned that he will only be granted 2 months in a halfway house, which means he faces another 7 months in prison. This is a great disappointment. Please let Mark know he is not forgotten and offer encouragement.

WAYNE CODY LASSELL D71733

Box 7500 B3 Cell 214, Pelican Bay State Prison, Crescent City, CA, 95531-7500 USA

Cody is incarcerated in Pelican Bay, one of the most horrific maximum security jails in the USA. He is kept in a 7' x 10' cell for 22 1/2 hours a day, and the entire prison is under intense security regulations. Cody writes "I'm not surprised you've heard of the conditions here at Pelican Bay. Just last wed. another prisoner was shot and killed for fighting with another prisoner. We have been on full scale lockdown since the incident, but this means little more than we are locked in our cells 24 hours a day, rather than 22 hours a day. the rate of violence here is unbelievable. It's nearly an everyday occurrence. So perhaps you appreciate the discomfort it is for a non-meat eating, non-violent person such as ourselves (the few that are among the 4000 men here)."

Cody describes himself as "a long time animal rights activist and a die hard supporter of all earth first causes...My love is with all of you that dedicate yourselves to the movement. He has been arrested at various civil disobedience actions.

Cody has not asked for any money; as he says, "my first and most important need/desire is to be remembered and cared about. In my situation, this means letters. Someone who thinks they have little to share, would be so desired and such a joy to someone who spends 22+ hours every day of his life in the confines of a small cell." He has also asked for postcards and photographs of wildlife to put up in his cell. He can receive 5 postcards or 12 photographs at a time, sent in a manila envelope. He can also use writing tablets, envelopes, American stamps, and magazine subscriptions (which must be sent directly from the publishers or bookstores).

Let Cody know that he is remembered by kindred spirits. He has never made any pretensions to be incarcerated for animal liberation charges (unlike Anthony Miller, for example) and we are certain from our correspondence that he is not looking to milk the movement (unlike Anthony Miller).

"It's important to me to lastly express my love, pride, and appreciation to one and all who dedicate their time in efforts to help those unable to help themselves." - Cody *prison struggles in north america*

JUSTICE DENIED

From this issue onward, *Underground* will include an expanded "prisoner support" section, to look at not only how we can help people imprisoned for animal liberation action, but also at what is going on in prisons in North American today and inform ourselves about how we can assist with prisoner struggles for justice, freedom, and dignity. Initial issues will cover struggles within specific prisons that are among the worst of the worst in North America.

editorial

BEHIND BARS: ANTI-PRISON WORK AS PART OF ANIMAL LIBERATION

This issue features articles about Lucasville; the struggle against control units will be featured in the next issue, including information about Pelican Bay.

I am anticipating receiving letters saying "stick to animal issues" so I wanted to head some of these letters off at the pass and, at the same time, explain a little about the direction the North American ALFSG is heading in right now.

What does the slogan "animal liberation=human liberation" really mean? Most animal liberation activists I have talked with see it as a reminder that humans cannot be free until animals are free. I tend to see it from another angle—that a commitment to animal liberation reminds us that all animals must be freed from their cages.

This sentiment is echoed by John Winter in the summer issue of the UK ALFSG newsletter: "How can we in the Animal Rights movement even hope for society to accept that other species have rights, when due to negative influences, a significant number of people have trouble in even accepting that groups within their own species have rights? Those involved in direct action should consider widening their scope of targets ... an 'Animal Liberation Front' should aim to liberate ALL animals." A short time later the Justice Department delivered an incendiary device to the headquarters of the fascistic British National Party (an openly racist, neo-nazi political party in England).

REMEMBER!
We're still here
support class struggle
& anarchist prisoners

There are some specific distinctions between (non-human) animal liberation struggles and human liberation struggles. That said, there are some obvious similarities between the work to free animals and the work to free prisoners. Prisoners are "dehumanized" -- treated like animals -- imprisoned in cages and subject to brutality, slavery for the corporate captors' profit, and, in some cases, experimentation, torture, and murder. Keep in mind that this is not Guatemala, China, or any other country we hear about so much about for human rights violations -- it is happening here, in North America, where prisons provide incredible profits for powerful industries.

It is not a question of taking pity on prisoners. We on the outside can learn a lot from people who are incarcerated. Many prison activists put their freedom and their lives on the line every day in their struggles for dignity and justice. A.L.F. and other animal liberation activists put their freedom, and in some cases their lives, on the line in the struggle for justice for animals. We can learn from prisoners about how to resist in the most brutal and hopeless of conditions.

I hope that people within the animal liberation movement are open to discussion and analysis about human liberation movements that are connected with (non-human) animal liberation. If you want to see *Underground* cover why vivisection, the meat industry, etc. are bad then you are probably reading the wrong magazine. We are assuming that anyone who picks up this magazine has a basic level of awareness and support for animal liberation. What we are trying to do with *Underground* is use it as a communication tool, to cover some new ground with the intention of contributing to the constant process of broadening and refining our analysis so that we become more effective activists.

Working on analysis does not mean sitting on our asses and intellectualizing so we do not have to take action (oh no, it's the Animal Deliberation Front!). It means looking at our mistakes, our successes, and the work of other liberation movements and determining what we should change about the work we do so that we avoid the pitfalls set for us by our own egos and the state, corporations, and those who would otherwise like to see us become a fragmented, ineffective clique.

I do not want to defend my personal politics, since I think the time could be better spent in other ways. But I do want to make it clear that I, and other people working on the NA-ALFSG, have a particular orientation that does determine the direction of the SG and the direction of this magazine. We come to the SG from a context of working in a range of social justice and environmental (and of course animal) liberation struggles. All of us see connections between these different "issues".

I know that some of you will disagree with the expansion of animal liberation to include so-called "human-centred" liberation. I would hope that this movement is big enough to include diversity and different kinds of analysis and commitment. The goals of animal liberation are too urgent and serious to waste time and energy arguing with each other about what "true" animal liberation is, or what a "true" activist is.

That said, if you disagree with the direction *Underground* or the ALFSG is heading in, then write and let us know. Without your feedback it is difficult to know whether or not we are doing a good job. Please remember that it is difficult to have any kind of dialogue with people who are making accusations based on judgments about ideological purity (we would hope this is obvious, but judging by some of the letters we get, apparently not).

Animal liberation activists who include humans in their definition of animal liberation and animal liberationists who prefer to focus on non-human animals need not be enemies. We do not need to slag each other off and boast about who is more committed or righteous or more purely allied with the animals. To do so accomplishes not much more than diverting energy away from the enormous tasks at hand: to work our asses off towards the goal of animal liberation, and assist each other in freeing animals from their cages.

Eddie Tor

YOUR FUR COAT IS ALMOST DEAD.

Every year in the United States, 20 million furbearing animals are brutally killed in steel-jawed leghold traps—devices which imprison a wild animal by one or two legs until they die, either by starvation, exposur to weather, thirst, or they are killed by the trapper, usually by being beaten or stompe to death (so as to not damage their fur).

It takes up to 60 mink to make one coat, 25 foxes to make another, 40 raccoons, 35 coyotes, and 180 rabbits. In this photo, a trapper is suffocating a coyote to death by standing on its throat; the coyote has been caught by the legs in two traps.

FOR THE SAKE OF VANITY, INNOCENT ANIMALS ARE BRUTALLY KILLED

Another four million mink and foxes are raised on "fur farms"—inside tiny cages where these wild animals are driven insane by their confinement. Killing methods vary: animals are either asphyixiated, bludgeoned to death, have their necks primitively broken or they are anally electrocuted—as is this fox in the photo at the right.

DON'T BUY FUR.

BEHIND *FOOD FOR THOUGHT*: DEEPENING OUR ANALYSIS TO BECOME MORE EFFECTIVE; TREATING EACH OTHER WITH RESPECT

"We need to go beyond human needs and desires and begin to look at the animal and environmental crises from an eco-centric viewpoint. We need to ask ourselves not, what is good for the humans and their communities? But instead, what is good for the Earth and her critters?...The questions now are: Are we ready to ally ourselves with the animal nations? Are we ready to ally ourselves with the earth?"

- David Barbarash, from Picking Our Targets: Thinking About Animals and the Earth

Food for Thought came about because I (the editor) came to believe, from my observations over the last couple years as an animal/earth activist, that there is a general lack of strategic analysis within the animal liberation movement (with some exceptions). From my involvement in other social justice movements over the last 10 years I have seen how constant struggle to refine and broaden analysis is necessary to keep from stagnating and becoming increasingly less effective.

I had hoped that readers would view this section of the magazine as a place to examine more deeply issues that affect our effectiveness, so that, as David says, we can ally ourselves with animals and the earth. These are difficult questions, ones that require us to continually examine where we have gone wrong and where we have had successes, and ones that challenge us to change our own behaviour that contributes to animal/earth exploitation or hinder the struggle for animal/earth liberation.

In my experience, conflicts between humans (on an individual and group level) have a huge impact on our effectiveness as activists. This includes conflicts based on the complexities of issues of oppression.

As I said in the last issue of *Underground*, "This is a space for discussion with the intention of furthering the work of the A.L.F. Articles that merely bash or trash will not be printed here; articles that attempt to contribute to analysis and strategy will." (underlining from original)

Some of us in the SG agreed with the analysis in devorah's article in *Underground* #1; others did not. Nevertheless, we printed the article because we felt it would be stimulating and thought-provoking, and was a good first step in looking at one way that issues of human-centred oppression affect our efforts towards animal/earth liberation. *Food for Thought*, like the rest of the magazine, is intended to be in the interests of supporting the work of the A.L.F., and animal/earth liberation in general. We felt devorah's article was in this spirit.

I have been appalled at some of the letters that have come to *Underground* in response to devorah's article in the last issue. Because none of the writers indicated they wanted their letters published, all I can say is that the sentiments in some of the letters ranged from "how could you print her article, she can obviously not be trusted" to "she is a Jew, not an animal liberation activist" and other openly anti-Semitic comments.

I had hoped that a fundamental part of this section of the magazine would be that all contributors would work towards treating each other with respect, so that we may work together instead of falling prey to divisive in-fighting. I believe that even when we disagree strongly with each other, and even when there is intense emotion behind the disagreement, we can express that disagreement in a respectful way.

I believe very strongly that criticism and self-criticism, when it is done in a thoughtful way conducive to assisting in change, is an important part of becoming a more effective activist. I do NOT believe that telling other contributors that they are "stupid", "narrow-minded", etc. is productive. I do not want us all to become nicey-nice people, nor do I want to stifle creativity and diversity of expression—we can still have vigor and spice, and vehemently disagree with each other, without telling people they are fucked and worthless.

It became clear after reading a number of the responses to devorah's article that our interpretation of the article was quite different than most of the interpretations from the people who wrote in response. In discussing this with devorah we all came to the conclusion that she had not communicated clearly enough what she was trying to say (since so many people misunderstood it) and offered her space to try to clarify her points, in the form of a response to the only person who made it clear he wanted his article published.

We welcome responses to articles. Promoting discussion is what *Food for Thought* is all about. I would request, though, that if you write a letter or article, you think carefully about what you are trying to say and whether or not it will be conducive to a discussion that will further the work of the A.L.F. — and this includes furthering the understanding of each other. Do not forget that the A.L.F. is not just "out there", it is also readers and contributors to the magazine. It is important that we strive towards being responsible activists in every sense of the word, and that means not doing the work of the FBI, CSIS, Putting People First, and others who would happily see us disintegrate from snipy in-fighting.

(Also, please CLEARLY indicate whether your responses are intended for publication, i.e. write "for publication" or "not for publication" at the beginning or end of the article.)

In struggle towards liberation,
Eddie Tor

PICKING OUR TARGETS:

by David Barbarash

Devorah's article "Picking Our Targets..." in the premiere issue of *Underground* begs for a response. In it I find accusations of racism and anti-semitism against the ALF, and veiled threats of repercussions from the "Jewish communities" should the ALF continue to attack kosher butchers. I believe the whole premise of the article is a false one, and it distorts the real goals and motivations of the animal liberation movement.

Before I go on, I want to identify myself as a long time animal liberation and environmental activist. I was born and raised Jewish, but I have rejected that religion for an eco-centric, Earth-based philosophy and belief system known as Paganism.

From my experience, activists do not go out seeking specifically Jewish-owned butchers (at least, not here in N. America), and the accusation is an outrageous distortion of reality. If and when kosher butchers are attacked, I do not believe, and have seen no evidence to support Devorah's claim, that these actions were carried out with racist motivations.

Does one now need to verify that a business is owned by a white male before taking action against it? Many butchers and furriers are owned by those of east european descent. Are they off limits? What about McDonald's, Burger King, and other fast food places? They are predominantly the workplaces and eating places of african americans, as well as the economically disadvantaged. Is it now racist and classist to attack african americans or asian animal abusers? Hell, let's not stop with race and class; all women animal abusers are off limits too, right? Where does this end?

Aside from the racial issue, devorah brings up the tactical point that a hit on a supplier is a much better use of time and resources, and does much more to end animal abuse. I agree that this may be true, but I do not agree that these are reasons to not hit the storefront butcher and furrier.

Those small businesspeople who only "make enough money to get by" are not exempt from being responsible for their lives, filled as they are with animal deaths. Further, just because a community is "very used to having to fight desperately in order to survive", or that they may be "some of the most

Dear *Underground*,

David Barbarash wrote a response to my article for publication in *Underground*, and in discussing his response we realized that he had misunderstood several of the points I was trying to make. In discussions with others who disagreed with the original article, it became clear that they had also misunderstood what I was trying to say. Obviously I didn't say it clearly enough! I apologize and thank you for the chance to clarify. I suspect many of the people who wrote to *Underground* in disagreement with my first article will still disagreethis time round, but I want to make sure that they are clear on what they are disagreeing with. Thanks to David for contributing to the discussion.

Towards animal liberation,

devorah

Whew! I have received a lot of flack for the article I wrote in *Underground* #1. The premise of my original article was that it is important that we look at how our choices of targets for direct action determine our effectiveness towards animal liberation. I referred specifically to what I perceive as racism and classism clouding our analysis in terms of picking the targets that will have the most impact towards animal liberation.

One of the criticisms of my article was that I tried to include too much in a short article, and that in doing so I did not adequately examine issues of either racism or classism. Given that most of the feedback disagreeing with my article was in reference to my points on racism, this time I'll stick to looking at how racism (in this instance, anti-Jewish racism) limits our effectiveness as animal liberation activists.

THINKING ABOUT ANIMALS AND THE EARTH

tenacious, skilled fighters", does not mean that we should back off. Perhaps instead, we should be prepared to fight even harder for animal lives.

Just because a culture/people have been persecuted for centuries, does that mean we must give them the okay to take part in the atrocities committed against the animal nations? For how many centuries have animals been persecuted? I would say for many more than Judaism has existed.

There are other, more practical reasons why I think that abandoning attacks on small businesses is a major mistake. First, there is the community aspect. Part of taking more control over our lives means having more say about what takes place in our communities and neighbourhoods. You are more likely to find a butcher or furrier on your street rather than a major supplier or slaughterhouse. It's our responsibility to keep our streets clean of these scum, especially if they are just doors away from your home, regardless of what god they pray to. Secondly, what better way for the novice activist to begin to take personal responsibility in his or her own life? It makes more sense to begin small at the storefront level, then with larger operations.

I do not believe that attacking small businesses does little to end animal abuse. Experience has shown us that a business repeatedly hit will, eventually, pack it in. Over time we can eliminate all butchers or all furriers from a geographical area such as a community or neighbourhood.

I believe that devorah's whole premise is wrong. The main problem is that she is approaching the animal liberation movement from a human-centred point-of-view. We need to go beyond human needs and desires and begin to look at the animal and environmental crises from an eco-centric viewpoint. We need to ask ourselves not, what is good for the humans and their communities? But instead, what is good for the Earth and her critters?

In this world of extreme Earth and animal exploitation, it is no longer important or relevant what traditions and practices a particular culture adheres to. No religious community that engages in animal death as a part of its culture will ever "accept the demands" of animal activists. The question is not whether we want to "make alliances with Jewish people" or any other religious sect. The questions now are: Are we ready to ally ourselves with the animal nations? Are we ready to ally ourselves with the earth?

PICKING OUR TARGETS: THINKING ABOUT THE IMPACT RACISM HAS ON OUR EFFECTIVENESS AS ANIMAL LIBERATIONISTS

a response to the responses

In my first article, I used kosher butchers as an example of a poor choice of targets. The A.L.F. Southland Unit, operating in California, hit "Mr. Kosher Meats" in Sherman Oaks in 1993-1994 (reported in *Underground* #1). In the UK, kosher butchers, halal butchers, and other butchers that cater to specific ethnic/religious communities targeted by racism have also been hit.

I am not saying that the motivations behind these attacks was racist, necessarily; I assume that the activists who did these actions sincerely believed that they were working for animal liberation. But I do believe that part of racism is ignorance about how different cultures operate, on many levels, including a political level; I think that the A.L.F. activists who carried out these actions were ignorant about how the Jewish community would react to the action and the ramifications for the animals. My intention is to educate other activists about my experiences within the Jewish community, so that they can make act from a more fully informed analysis, and not let ignorance lead the A.L.F. to making mistakes that hamper animal liberation.

From my experience working with the local Jewish community, I have observed that when the Jewish community perceives itself as being attacked, people within the community become very defensive and pull together to fight the attacker(s). Rightly or wrongly, this is the way the community operates. It must be seen in the context of Jewish people being attacked for thousands of years—we are sensitive to what seems to be attempts to force our culture and traditions to change. Remember that in the past these pushes to change have been accompanied by wide-scale murder, torture, and other state repression.

I agree that the Jewish community needs to change, and stop the exploitation of animals. I believe, as a Jew and as an animal/earth liberation activist, that kosher dietary laws are outmoded and inhumane, much as I disagree with other aspects of Jewish tradition that are sexist, homo and lesbophobic, ethnocentric, etc. But from what I have seen, the best way to get the Jewish community to change is NOT to attack it directly, but to work within the community and build trust, so that people within the community understand that in seeking change we are not seeking to destroy the Jewish people.

In his response, David says "...just because a community is 'very used to having to fight desperately in order to survive,' or that they may be 'some of the most tenacious, skilled fighters,' does not mean that we should back off. Perhaps instead, we should be prepared to fight even harder for animal lives."

I believe this approach is counter-productive when dealing with the Jewish community, or any other ethnic community that has been persistently historically targeted. Push them hard, and they will push even harder. I have seen that when the Jewish community perceives itself as being attacked, it becomes even more reactionary and resistant to change. What a waste of effort on the part of animal liberationists, given that there are so many other places to put our energy!

In his article David says, "Does one now need to verify that a business is owned by a white male before taking action against it? Many butchers and furriers are owned by those of eastern european descent Are they off limits? What about McDonalds, Burger King, and other fast food places? They are predominantly the workplaces and eating places of african americans, as well as the economically disadvantaged. Is it now racist and classist to attack these businesses? What about Jewish vivisectors, or african american or asian animal abusers? Hell, let's not stop with race and class; all women animal abusers are off limits too, right? Where does this end?"

It is disappointing to me that attempts to include looking at how racism and classism affect our effectivness as part of a greater analysis of our effectiveness are subverted into accusations of "political correctness". I am not saying that Jewish animal exploiters should be "off limits" because they are Jewish, I am saying that when the Jewish community perceives itself as being attacked, it becomes more resistant to change.

If we are not looking at the effects of our actions, then in my opinion we cannot seriously assess our effectiveness. Taking the examples that David uses (which I would question—what is the basis of his claim that fast food places are predominantly the workplaces and eating places of African-Americans?), we can look at the response when a local McDonald's was burned to the ground 6 months ago. There was no outcry from any ethnic community or the "economically disadvantaged", as David puts it. This attack on McDonald's was not perceived as an attack on poor people or ethnic groups. Similarly, I have never heard grumblings within the Jewish community about actions that target individual Jewish furriers, vivisectors, or other animal exploiters. However, attacks on kosher butchers, or any other Jewish-owned business that caters specifically to Jewish traditions, ARE perceived as attacks on the Jewish people.

I am not saying this perception is justified, although I certainly understand where it comes from. I would hope, though, that animal liberationists strive to be aware of the impact that such actions have. Even a gesture of including the statement that "we are not striving to attack the Jewish community" in a press release, or some other indication that activists are at least aware of issues of racism and other "isms", would have been helpful. In order to prevent a backlash, it is important to let the Jewish community know that animal liberationists have no desire to destroy Jewish culture or the Jewish people.

David writes, "No religious community that engages in animal death as a part of its culture will ever 'accept the demands' of animal activists". I disagree. There are numerous Jewish vegetarian groups that are working hard to educate Jewish communities and change Jewish traditions, from the inside. There are Jewish animal liberation activists, including myself, who are working hard to pressure our local Jewish groups to not serve meat at community functions (incidentally, my local rabbi is vegetarian and prohibits the serving of meat at synagogue). In showing Jewish people we can still "cook Jewish" in vegan ways, we are showing Jewish people the alternatives to animal abuse, but we are doing so from being active and involved in our Jewish communities, not as outsiders. This makes it easier for Jewish people to hear us. Yes, these are miniscule victories, but they are victories nonetheless, and I believe that every victory for animal liberation is worth examining.

I had an interesting discussion yesterday with a white, middle-class male who is also an earth liberation activist. He expressed an increasing amount of rage towards white, middle-class Canadians who do nothing other than pick up a beer and watch TV. I have felt the same frustrations at times working within the Jewish community, when people are so reluctant to take responsibility to change their own behaviour and change the oppressive societal structures that are based on exploitation of animals, the earth, and humans.

David says that he thinks my major error is coming at this from a human-centred perspective instead of an an animal/eco-centred perspective. Perhaps this is a worthwhile challenge for some of us animal liberation activists, to take full responsibilities for working persistently and committedly for animal liberation within our communities (whether they be defined around ethnicity, sexual orientation, gender, class, etc) and not just say "fuck you all". If we are to do this, though, it will not be practical to approach everyone who contributes to animal exploitation as "scum", no matter how much we feel that way at times. It is easy in some ways to work for earth/animal liberation because those we are working for cannot tell us they don't like what we are doing, want us to work differently, etc. But I believe it is dangerous to ignore the human element of animal liberation, for it is humans who are doing the exploiting. And not all of us are equally involved in the profits of the exploitation, either...let's not fall into generalized misanthropy that obscures the classism/racism/sexism that is inherent in the structures of capitalism & the exploitation of animals for profit.

David's analysis of targeting small businesses as an aspect of responsibility for our neighbourhoods/communities is an interesting one. I agree, although I do not necessarily agree with his statement that "it's our responsibility to keep our streets clean of these scum, especially if they are just doors away from your home". This resonates too closely for me with the violent racism, homo and lesbophobia, etc. so often spouted by the right-wing. I prefer to use different language and a different analysis; I think this type of rhetoric obscures the structures that support (and to some extent rely on) animal exploitation.

We must not forget that animal exploitation is not just a matter of individual, personal lifestyle choice, it is also built into North American society's capitalist structure. In my opinion, we must look at how we can effect change both on an individual and a societal level.

An A.L.F. campaign such as "Operation Bite Back", when combined with the work of the Coalition Against Fur Farming (and other such groups) that do educational work about fur from a radical perspective, is one example of how direct action and radical education are both parts of the animal liberation struggle. Yes, individuals must be held accountable. Owners of kosher butcher shops must be held accountable. But in what way?

I believe that it is a mistake to leave "mainstream" tactics such as education and community outreach to mainstream groups; a radical perspective is needed in these areas as well. In terms of changing the exploitative practices of ethnic communities, I believe that these mainstream tactics, when done consistently and persistently, from a radical perspective, combined with careful and well-thought direct action that will not be perceived as a direct attack, are more effective when it comes to bringing about change within groups that have been historically targeted by racism.

In the last issue of *Underground* there was a cartoon called "Cows Bash Back", about some cows who decide to blow up a leather bar. I loved this cartoon, as a queer, partly because it was reprinted from a queer magazine and I knew that it was queers pointing out what's fucked within our community, not homo/lesbophobes trying to say "queers are disgusting and their exploitation of animals proves it". Queers targeting queer leather bars/leather shops makes much more of an impact, I believe, than hets targeting these businesses.

I must stress that I am not saying that any ethnic/religious group, or any other oppressed group, has the "right" to abuse animals. I am saying that we must not only act, but also THINK about how our actions affect our efforts to bring about maximum change. We cannot ignore how racism and other "isms" shape our strategies; to do so is, I believe, to ensure that the animal exploitation industries are allowed to continue.

(P.S. It is interesting to note, too, that Kathleen Marquardt (head of Putting People First), in her horrendous book *Animal Scam*, devotes a full 8 pages (almost an entire chapter) on pointing out examples of extreme anti-Semitism by so-called animal liberationists to support her theory that animal liberation will lead to a Nazi regime(!). If the head of Putting People First is so interested in promoting division between Jewish people and animal liberationists, and can so easily find examples that will achieve this, shouldn't we be concerned? By the way, her examples of anti-Semitism are all footnoted and have appeared in Jewish magazines at some time—I am sad to say I think they may be real incidents, easily used as propaganda against animal liberation but not fiction designed by these people.)

FOOD FOR US: VEGAN DEATH-BY-CHOCOLATE aka Wacky Cake

This is one of those great totally indestructible, foolproof recipes that you can't go wrong with. Excellent to use on your friends/relatives who are squeamish about vegan food. Make sure that your sugar is vegan or use another type of sweetener. I have to say, though, I've tried this recipe with carob, rice syrup, brown flour, etc. and it just isn't the same. This cake may be indestructible, but it's simply not a cake that wants to be in the health food racks! So enjoy the disgustingness of it.

1 1/2 cups flour
1 cup sugar
1 tsp. @ baking powder, baking soda, salt
5 tbsp. cocoa
1 tsp vanilla
5 tbsp. oil
1 tbsp. vinegar
1 cup warm water

Mix the dry ingredients (flour, sugar, baking powder, soda, salt, and cocoa). If your cocoa is really lumpy then try to squish the lumps into smaller lumps. Using your fingers to do this allows you to pop the lumps and squirt cocoa powder at your friends. Don't worry about squishing all the lumps, as they will be OK in the end.

Add the vanilla, oil, and vinegar and mix in. Again, don't worry about thoroughly mixing. Finally add the warm water and now mix vigorously. Pour the whole slew into a greased 9-inch pan and bake at 350 F for 30-45 minutes.

This cake is really rich and yummy on its own and doesn't need icing.

GIVE THE DOG A BONE

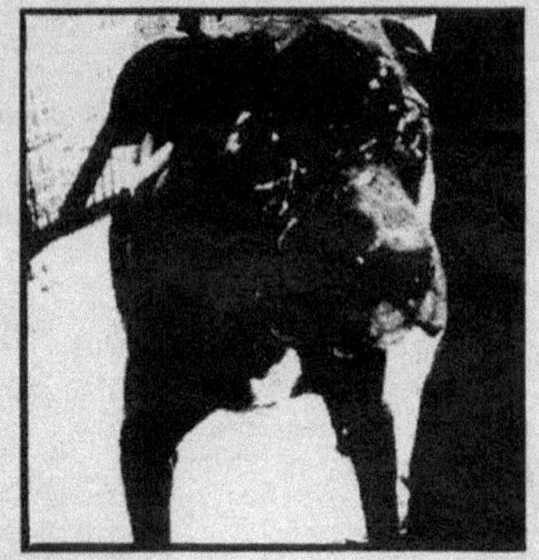

PART ONE: If you've ever wondered about that 'special relationship' between police dogs and their handlers, then this exclusive little snippet is for you...

An inside source has given us the dirt on how the police manage to train their animals to perform their scabby tasks. And we mean *dirt*. In order to get their dogs to sniff out drugs, cops will slowly wank them off and then slip a lump of hash (or whatever) under the dog's nose right at the crucial moment. The theory is that the next time the dogs sniff out a bit of blow (blow?!), they'll associate the smell with orgasm and go sex-crazy.

Now I know why those sick bastards are called dog handlers...

...BUT THEY DO PROVIDE US WITH SOME AMUSEMENT

NO-BRAIN COPS IN THE UK

On Nov 22/93, 13 anti-bloodsport activists raided the British Field Sports Society (BFSS)'s offices in London. While one group of activists barricaded themselves in the first-floor suite, another group (including one dressed as a fox) entertained reporters outside. Eventually the police arrived, and that's when the fun really started.

No-brain police incident #1: Police bashed their way into the occupied suite with a sledgehammer, damaging a BFSS photocopier and filing cabinets in the process.

No-brain police incident #2: After sledgehammering their way into the suite, "two officers leapt into the room, knocking their third colleague over and causing him to cut off the top of one of his fingers."

All charges against the activists were dismissed. Civil action against the Metropolitan police is pending.

- from "HOWL" #54, "Arkangel" #12

NO-BRAIN COPS IN CANADA

In September, several Earth First! activists were arrested during a demonstration. As they were piled into a paddy wagon, one of the activists managed to conceal a cellular phone. While the paddy wagon proceeded to the police station, the giggling EF!ers dialed the police station and said "We've been kidnapped by two men, they threw us into their van, we're heading north!". A cop car was dispatched to try to track the "kidnappers". When everyone finally arrived at the police station, both sets of cops were more than slightly red-faced.

- from conversation with a merry prankster

MORE NO-BRAIN COPS IN THE UK

Acting on a tip that an ARM meeting would be held in Yorkshire, cops busted up the meeting half-way through...only to discover that instead of the Animal Rights Militia, it was a meeting of the Association of Radical Midwives. The local paper's headline the next day was "The wrong ARM of the law".

- info from "UK ALFSG Newsletter" Autumn 1994

SOME WORDS SPEAK AS LOUDLY AS ACTIONS

reprinted from "HOWL" #54; originally in "Talking Blues"

"I had a dream about all of us, about the section, going round in a car. We were in plain clothes and we were indiscriminately murdering everybody in the daytime that was causing the troubles in the night time. I've never enjoyed a dream so much in my life..."

"You have to make the first move, use your vehicles, drive the Land Rovers straight at the bastards. Then they scatter. You deal with the rest with your sticks. No problem. I don't give a fuck about the kids who got hurt."

quotes from two police officers, each with over ten years' service, referring to their experiences during the Toxteth riots, in which a disabled man was knocked over and killed by a police Land Rover.

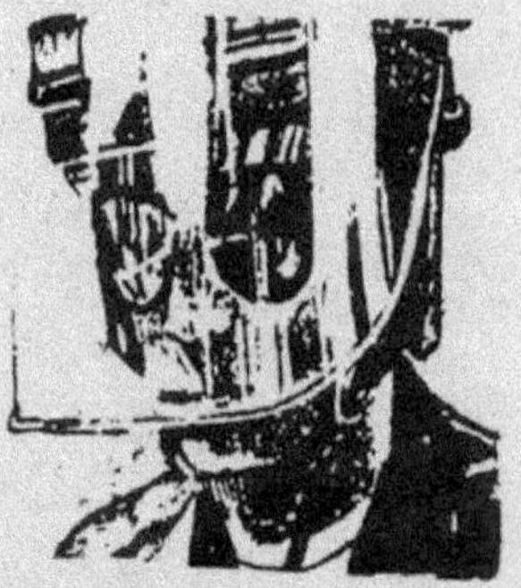

Pigs are our friends	Cops are not
Pigs mind their own business	Cops do not
Pigs have curly tails	Cops have guns
Pigs excrete un-self-consciously	Cops are anal
Pigs are highly intelligent creatures	Cops are known to possess a certain small cunning but are not generally characterized as intelligent
Pigs grunt with joy	Cops grunt with aggression
Pigs are oppressed	Cops oppress
Pigs are maligned by those in power	Cops are glorified by those in power

SO who are we really insulting?

Fascist pig, Imperialist pig, Capitalist pig, Male Chauvinist Pig... We label pigs with the most unappealing characteristics that human culture has ever produced, but WE put the pigs in those conditions in the first place. Pigs are consistently abused, tortured, raped, confined, and slaughtered because of the very structures they are so often identified with. They are victims, not aggressors. The last thing they need is to be associated with the police state. In a society founded on the oppression of all who do not possess heterosexuality, all who do not possess whiteness and maleness and wealth, how can we fail to recognize the oppression of those who simply lack humanness?

by P. bean

UNDERGROUND #3

The Official Newsletter of the North American A.L.F. Supporters Group

DEC.'94 TO NOV.'95 - ONE YEAR OF DIRECT ACTION FOR ANIMALS -$3-

THIS ISSUE IS DEDICATED TO THE MEMORY OF BRITISH ACTIVIST JILL PHIPPS
MURDERED BY ANIMAL ABUSERS while fighting to save animals lives.

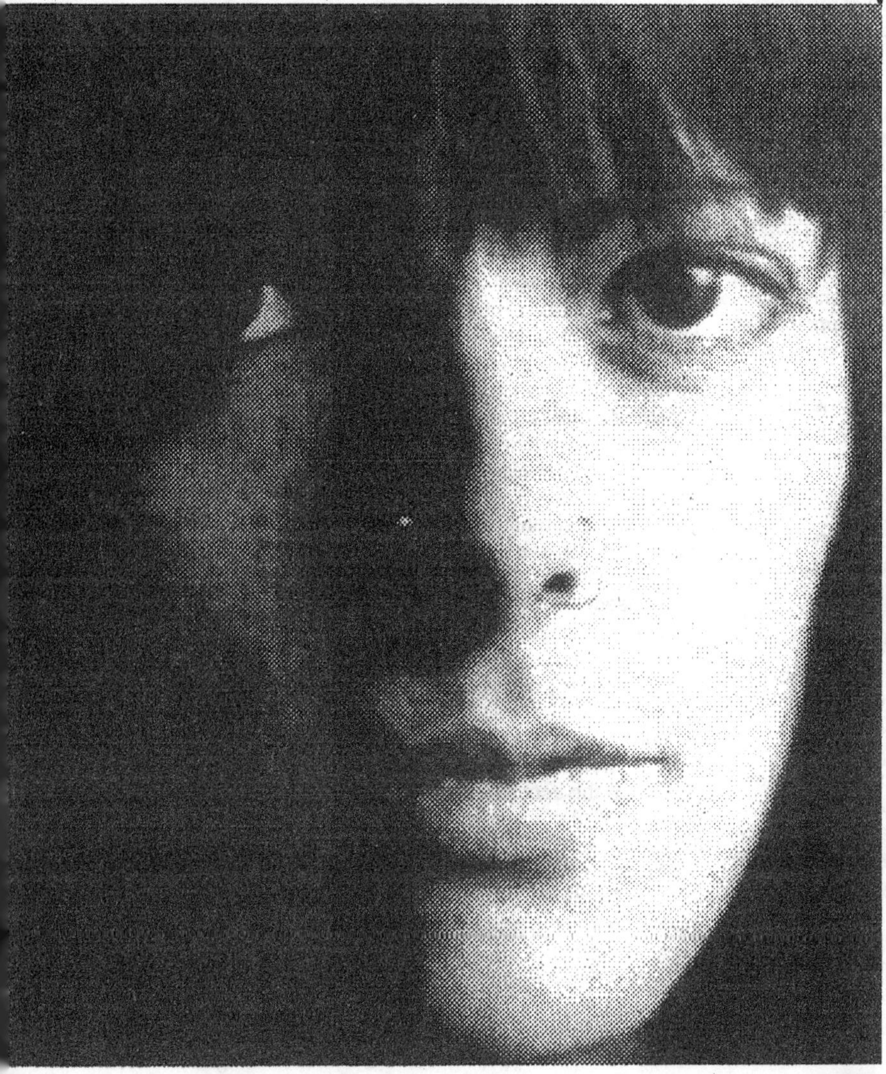

IN THIS ISSUE:

NA-ALFSG Coordinator Change Over

Helpful Hints on Keeping Your Privacy

"The First Ten Years" - The Story of the Swedish A.L.F.

Prisoner News, Updates, and Addresses

...AND LOTS MORE GREAT ANIMAL LIB ACTIONS, UPDATES AND INFO!

A.L.F. STRIKE! -

16 pages of ALF actions!

A.L.F. HAVE A BONFIRE AT HOFMANN'S SAUSAGE FACTORY →

NA-ALFSG NEWS, PART 1: CHANGES IN THE SG

A Word from the Former SG Coordinator

It's been a real time of upheaval for the SG over the last couple months. Three people who were helping with the SG have moved on to other political projects. I had originally agreed to coordinate the SG until January 1995, but with the other people gone I felt I should stick with it for the time being.

It became fairly obvious fairly quickly that I didn't have the time, energy, or commitment to stick it thru as coordinator past January. *Underground #3*'s deadline passed, letters to be answered piled up ... it was clear that a new SG crew was needed. Unfortuantely, there was no new crew waiting to take on the SG. So from January to June, the SG was in limbo. Part of the problem was the debt accumulated from 1994, and the unfinished business left by the departure of the other SGers. I had my hands full with trying to complete projects and take care of the debt.

In looking for a new crew to take over the SG, there were some good discussions with activists in the USA, Canada, and the UK. What became clear was the need for a fully-functioning, stable SG in North America. Many people expressed hope that this time round the SG would be here to stay, not just here for a couple years as in the past.

Right now there is a slow but steady revitalization of direct action for animal liberation within North America. As an aboveground, legal organization, there's a lot a Supporters Group can do to support those who are either on the front lines or in jail as a result of their actions for liberation movements. With the demise of *Out of the Cages,* and *Militant Vegan, Underground*(or some similar mag) seems needed right now. In addition, we Canadians have the capacity to legally publish information on methods of illegal direct action, unlike our compadres at the SG in England.

In June, discussions began with a group of activists in Ontario who were interested in taking on the SG. In August and September, these arrangements were finalized.

The transition has gone amazingly smoothly, but please bear with the new crew as they become familiar with all the SG baggage! the new crew has a lot of work ahead of them, and I have every confidence that they will be able to do an excellent job with the SG.

Whatever happens in the future, our past and present members and other generous souls who have helped keep the SG financially afloat deserve a tremendous thank you. There is no way we could have done what we have without your monetary and political support. Certain prisoners have also invested a great deal of energy in making the SG work, particularly in making Underground happen and in kicking the butts of the people running the SG when we got tired and whiny. We hope that none of you feel your efforts were wasted, and we will continue to do what we can to further the work of the A.L.F. and bring about freedom for all political prisoners.

Towards liberation,

Z.

NORTH AMERICAN A.L.F. SUPPORTERS GROUP

NA-ALFSG NOTES, PART 2

As many of you may already be aware, there have been some serious internal changes taking place within the SG. Throughout the month of August and into September steps were taken in which the SG changed hands, moving the coordination of the SG from Victoria, B.C. across the country to Toronto, Ont. Now, perhaps more than ever, as the animal liberation movement increases the pressure on animal ab/users on all fronts, there exists the need for a North American A.L.F. Supporters Group, providing updates and hard-to get information, and supporting animal liberation, direct action and political prisoners. Following discussions with activists across North America and the UK, a number of activists in different groups began discussing spreading the SG work out amongst (known & trusted) activists in different cities -- people who were to make long-term commitments to the SG, and people from different areas of expertise/interest. Well, the process is now complete and the NA- ALFSG is ready to take up where it left off.

A.L.F. actions have continued unabated, during the SG change-over, and within days of our taking over the SG's e-mail address in late August, we were receiving word of an ALF action in which 500 pigeons were freed near Hegins, Pennsylvania (see pg 30 for details). At the same time, other ALF action reports have been pouring in from around the world. For those of you who have written the SG, don't worry - you've not been forgotten. Right now it feels like the Toronto SG office is living out of boxes, but as we unload and file away all the updates, letters, correspondences and information forwarded from B.C., we are taking the time to answer each letter needing a reply.

Apologies to those of you who have been anxiously wondering what happened to *Underground #3*. Yes, it has been one year since issue #2. There are many reasons why we were unable to go to print before now, as Zab metioned above. An important reason was the $2000 debt accumulated as a result of the sharp increase in prison support work needed in 1994. It has taken a lot of work, and there is still $300 owing, but thanks to very generous donations from supporters we have been able to come into this new SG with far less worry than the old crew.

Financial woes aside, the 12 months since *Underground #2* have been...interesting. Lots of UK news, but we'll leave it to the UK SG and A.L.F. Press Officer to fill everyone in (see pages 10 to 17). On a more local note, there were some important victories for our imprisoned comrades. Darren Thurston was released in January 1995, and has now served all his time. Lise Olson has also been freed, having served her time. New prisoners include Rod Coronado, who was sentenced to 4 yrs for A.L.F. related activities (pg 56 for his address).

Our insurance company has informed us they will not replace the equipment that was stolen in the October burglary of the former SG office. Donations of IBM computer equipment and a photocopier are sorely needed right now, for any of you who feel like being particularly generous.

Speaking of insurance companies and burglaries, just as we were beginning to relax after the relative post-burglary calm, our e-mail account, <un028@freenet.victoria.bc.ca>, was shut down. The panicked service providers (Victoria Freenet) informed us that they had "disabled" the account after seeing a TV news story about "illegal documents" (i.e. the article on how to build incendiaries that appeared in Underground #2) being distributed on the World Wide Web (WWW) AR Frontline Information Service pages, at http://envirolink.org/adn/alf.html. Our Freenet address appeared on TV as part of the broadcast (and of course the predictable interviews with the police about the terroristic nature of the SG, ha ha). So now the situation with that account is that e-mail is possibly still being received, but we cannot access the account. The only people who can access the account are the Victoria Freenet maintainers. Freenet maintains that they are not reading our mail or passing it on the police. Yeah right. We'll leave you folks to decide where our mail is now going...

But as always there are ways around these things, and so we are back on-line without too much fuss. Our new address is <an246614@anon.penet.fi>.

We have been getting quite a bit of mail lately. Many of you have asked either (1) how to donate money from outside Canada, or (2) why it takes us so long to get merchandise orders out. Here's the scoop on both questions, for all of you who have been wondering.

1) We accept cheques or money orders in either US or Canadian dollars. Any other currency must be exchanged, and we lose almost half of the money in exchange fees, so we ask overseas supporters to send

money orders in US or Canadian currency ONLY. All cheques and money orders should be made out to: NA-ALFSG. Please do NOT send cheques if you are outside the USA or Canada; our bank only accepts cheques from Canadian and US banks. The same principles apply for those of you wanting to donate to the UK ALFSG. According to the UK-ALFSG, "Due to high exchange rates we cannot accept cheques or notes in Canadian or USA dollars as we lose so much in the transaction. A bank will organize a cheque in pounds sterling which is the best solution."

2) We have had a lot of problems with distribution. Basically, the person handling distribution was unable to do the job properly. Distribution is now being run by SG activists in Memphis, and we are hoping the problems will be taken care of. The new NA-ALFSG Distro address is as follows:

NA-ALFSG Distro
Box 241532
Memphis, TN
38124 USA

In general, it can take a while for merchandise orders to be processed and sent because we are so short-staffed. We are trying to improve the system so that orders are filled more quickly. Please be patient with us. Also -- if you have not received your merchandise within 6 weeks of ordering it, please send us a note. We do make mistakes, and sometimes orders are not processed properly.

So why all this blather about us, with no news on how animals are faring? Well, because, as always, our critter friends are being mutilated, tortured, murdered, and otherwise generally exploited. Not much new about that. It's sad but true that although we can report some setbacks for the animal abuse industries, overall not much has changed in the last ten months. But then this isn't a battle that will be won by short-term victories. Do not be discouraged by what may appear to be slow progress. Like any liberation movement, we have a great deal of work ahead of us, and we must see the process of animal liberation in the context of the long, hard fight it will surely be.

Underground #3 is chock full of updates, actions and articles from the last 12 or so months, from Nov 94 to Nov 95. Inside you'll find information about animal liberation activities, some you may already know about, and many that you probably don't. Obviously, this is a fairly large issue, however, once we start producing Underground on a (hopefully) quarterly basis our printing and mailing costs will go down in accordance to the size and bulk of the magazine. Unfortunately, after having published *Underground #3,* we're pretty much broke! Much of our costs will be recouped through the sale of *Underground* and S.G. merchandise (hint hint!), but right now we have other financial obligations (prisoner support, etc.) that just can't be put on hold. As always, any donations, no matter how small are greatly appreciated, and will be put to good use.

One thing that is striking about some of the information listed in this issue of *Underground* is the level of intimidation and physical violence currently being directed at animal activists. While government and industry continue to scream themselves hoarse about "terrorism" and "animal fanatics" who will "stop at nothing," the body count only climbs on one side, as animal lib activists are murdered by those directly involved in animal exploitation. The Animal Liberation Front's campaign of economic sabotage through the damage and destruction of property actively seeks to aviod the harming of any animal (human or otherwise). Those bent on destroying the animal liberation movement are not so careful with their actions. In their world, life is cheap (human and otherwise), and murder is justified in the name of profit. As you know, *Underground #3* is dedicated to one such person killed while trying to protect animals. Jill Phipps had the life crushed out of her under the wheels of a cattle truck as it drove through a crowd of protesters campaigning against the export of veal calves. Jill's death is a terrible loss for everyone. She was a tireless campaigner for a number of social justice causes, and she will be sorely missed by everyone, including the animals she has helped during her lifetime. One thing has become clear: her death has strengthened this movement, bringing together people from all walks of life, increasing our determination to bring an end to animal expoitation on all levels. With love, courage and anger, we continue where Jill left off.

Ok then, kick up your heels, stay active, and stay safe. We hope you find this issue of *Underground* enjoyable and useful.

Towards animal liberation and freedom for all political prisoners,
NORTH AMERICAN A.L.F. SUPPORTERS GROUP

ANIMAL LIBERATION FRONT (A.L.F.) GUIDELINES:

The Animal Liberation Front carries out direct action against animal abuse in the form of rescuing animals and causing financial loss to animal exploiters, usually through the damage and distruction of property.

The A.L.F.'s short term aim is to save as many animals as possible and direcitly disrupt the practice of animal abuse. their long term aim is to end all animal suffering by forcing animal abuse companies out of business. It is a nonviolent campaign, activists taking all precautions not to harm any animal (human or otherwise).

Because A.L.F. actions are against the law, activists work anonymously, either in small groups or individually, and do not have any centralized organization or coordination.

The purpose of the North American Animal Liberation Front Supporters Group (NA-ALFSG) is to support the work of the Animal Liberation Front (A.L.F.) by ALL LAWFUL MEANS POSSIBLE. This includes:

*** support of imprisoned A.L.F. activists**
*** support and defence of the A.L.F.**
*** educating the public as to the need and rationale of direct action**
*** providing a communication forum through the Supporters Group newsletter**
*** raising funds for all the above activities**

The Supporters Group is for those who wish to support the A.L.f. without breaking the law. We encourage the participation of all activists - including those who are unable to, or who do not wish to, take part in direct action.

Any individual or group of people who are vegetarians or vegans and who carry out actions according to A.L.F. guidelines have the right to regard themselves as part of the A.L.F.

The Animal Liberation Front consists of small atonomous groups of people all over the world who carry out direct action according to the A.L.F. guidelines. You cannot become a member of - or an A.L.F. activist - by joining or writing to the North American ALFSG, which is a completely separeate organization.

Got Somethin' To Say? Give Us A Shout!

We welcome letters, articles, artwork, action reports, or anything else for publication in Underground. Please be sure to write "FOR PUBLICATION" on anything you send us for the newsletter, so that we know what should and should not be published. Also please make it clear whether or not you will accept editing of your contribution.

We do not believe in censorship. If we have serious concerns about printing something that is sent to us, we will make every effort to discuss our concerns with the author. As part of taking responsibility for Underground, we will let readers know if we have a serious problem with something we end up printing. Keep in mind that this is a magazine by and for people who support the A.L.F. and please strive to keep your letters/articles respectful.

North American ALFSG Membership

Suggested costs for a membership to the NA-ALFSG, including a year's subscription to Undrground are on a $20-$30 sliding scale. Canadian and US checks or money orders only (overseas subscribers please pay in US currency). Prisoner subscriptions are free. Make cheques payable to: NA-ALFSG..

Send all corispondances and money orders to:

NA-ALFSG
Po Box 96597
5845 Younge St.

HOW TO REGAIN YOR PRIVACY

Troubled by phone tapping?
Someone interfering with your post?
BIG BROTHER IS WATCHING YOU!

In this the age of national computer databases, video surveillance cameras, DNA finger-printing, eroding civil rights and ever increasing police powers, the privacy of the individual is seriously at risk. However, some of the very technology that helps to deprive us of privacy may now help us to regain it.

When a citizens' movement questions authority or challenges the status quo, there is a possibility that the interests threatened will attempt to monitor their actions. This may be done in order to ascertain the danger posed, identify the individuals involved, discover ways to reduce the effectiveness of the movement or, if possible, destroy it. It is the communications between the members of the movement that are perhaps the most useful to the opposition and it should come as no surprise that phone tapping and intercepting mail are amongst the methods commonly used against citizens' movements.

Thankfully, there are methods that can be used to help minimize the problem, but most traditional methods are far from foolproof and are hardly convenient. Traditional methods are, in fact, so inconvenient that it is doubtful that they are used by many to any great degree.

When making phone calls, some form of code could be implemented, substituting incriminating words with "innocent" ones and also disguising sensitive information like times, dates and places. Producing an effective and flexible code is very difficult, rather like trying to invent a new language. All the people you wish to understand the code must have been taught how to use it, and the information about the workings of the code must be passed in private and must not be allowed to fall into the wrong hands at any time since all messages (past, present, and future) would then be compromised. Most codes are also cumbersome in use, restrictive, and easy to crack unless the code is changed frequently.

Slightly harder to crack and less restrictive would be the use of written messages that have been manually encrypted and then sent through the post. A safe method of passing the key is still necessary, and manual encryption can be very cumbersome to use.

The drawbacks may make these encryption methods impractical to use routinely, and so when you do use them, the encoded message itself would appear highly suspicious. Even if the opposition could not immediately understand the message, they might have their interest raised sufficiently to step-up surveillance, while putting resources into cracking the code.

So what's left? With a computer you can use military standard encryption algorithms that are virtually impossible to crack. You get flexibility, ease, and speed of use. And since it is so easy to use, you can use it all the time, so the importance of a very sensitive message is not revealed.

While encryption offers a solution to the problems of phone tapping or mail interception, conventional methods have their own problems. To de-cipher a message requires the recipient to have the same key as that used by the sender to encrypt it. If the sender and recipient get the opportunity to meet face to face then the key can be exchanged, but there are situations when no safe channel is available.

MAIL SECURITY

If you are a member of an active A.L.F. Cell, send us any clippings, or your own report, with date, time, place and details of the action. Wear gloves at all times to aviod leaving fingerprints on the paper, envelope or stamp. Do not give your address, and don't lick the stamp or envelope (use a wet sponge). REMEMBER you should expect that all of our mail is opened and read by the authorities.

DO NOT inform us of upcoming actions BEFORE they happen.

Public key cryptology provides the solution. Each person using the system has two related keys; one secret, one public. The public key can be distributed freely; it doesn't matter if it falls into the hands of the opposition. Possessing the public key does not enable anyone to deduce the corresponding secret key. Ideally, the secret key must be kept secure; however the best laid plans to go astray, so in order to add further protection, the best systems require a "pass-phrase", known only by the owner, whenever the key is used.

Before sending a message, the sender encrypts the message using the public key belonging to the intended recipient. The resulting encrypted file can then be sent by electronic mail (or by disk in the standard post). The encrypted message can not be read by anyone (even with the public key), only by the person with the matching secret key and its "pass-phrase".

The system also provides message authentication. The sender's own secret key can be used to encrypt a message, thereby "signing" it. This creates a digital signature of a message, which anyone can check by using the sender's public key to decrypt it. This proves that the sender was the true originator of the message, and that the message has not been subsequently altered by anyone else. Forgery is not feasible, and the sender cannot later disown his/her signature. Both privacy and authentication can be provided by first signing a message with your own secret key, then encrypting it with the recipient's public key. The recipient reverses these steps by first decrypting the message with their own secret key, then checking the enclosed signature with your public key.

The advanced algorithms used by Public Key Cryptology and conventional single-key cryptology may be practically uncrackable, and potentially helpful in solving the problems of phone tapping and mail interception. However, no system can free us from the threat of infiltration or stupidity! The person you send the encrypted messages to may be the only person who can read them, but if that person is careless or, not as trustworthy as you thought, all your efforts will have been wasted. Beware! - be careful, be free and be useful.

Anon.
For privacy, freedom and the animals.

PRETTY GOOD PRIVACY

Pretty Good Privacy (PGP) is a high security cryptographic software application based on "public key" cryptography (described above). PGP allows people to exchange files or messages with privacy, authentication, and convenience.

The original versions of PGP were written by Philip Zimmerman. If the US government has its way, he will spend a long time in prison since he is being prosecuted by US Customs for exporting encryption technology without a licence. This apparently is covered by the same laws as the export of arms, explosives, ammunition or military technology, so he could be spending a very long time behind bars. However, he has achieved what he set out to achieve -- he has provided a public key cryptology system for the masses. PGP is available for most major computers and operating systems including IBM PC, Apple, Amiga, Atari and UNIX systems. It's "free-ware", which means it costs nothing and is easy to obtain from any decent shareware library, computer bulletin board or anonymous FTP site. With a computer and this software, we can gain back some of the privacy that modern technology has allowed others to take away from us.

-ben

So You Want To Send Us A Letter - by @nu

It has been brought to our attention that not only has mail addressed to the old North American A.L.F. Supporters Group address (P.O. Box 8673, Victoria) been very blatantly opened but that a fair amount of mail is never making it to us. Obviously ending up in someone else's hands (hummm RCMP...CSIS?) See page 4 for mail security tips, but here's some good advice: go to a college/school photo-copy shop and type a press release on a computer (do not save to computer or disk) and print. At a public photocopier, find some scrap paper and place one piece on the tray where copies come out. Make your copies but do NOT touch them Place the second scrap paper on top of the finished copies and keep your original separate (to burn later). Buy some pre-packed stamps and wrapped envelopes. At a clean work area (beware of DNA traces!) using gloves, remove the scraps of paper, load evelopes and seal with a sponge. Beware of traces of hair, fibers, etc!! Address with a common bic pen and place in a larger envelope to carry and tip contents into a distant mail box. Be sure to destroy the stamps, envelopes, large envelope, etc. This may seem extreme, but if saves you from prison, its worth it!

SOME BASIC TIPS ON GENERAL SECURITY

As animal liberation activists, we must expect that at some point we will be victims of surveillance, disruption and attacks (legal and illegal) instigated by the state and/or political opponents. Just look what happened to the NA-ALFSG in B.C. last year *[Underground #2 for details]* if you're not sure what we mean. Just remember, you are not helpless. There are some basic ways to deal with the problem of surveillance, generally the rules apply everywhere. *(info taken from REALITY NOW #38)*

Telephones

The general rule: act as if the phone you are using is tapped.
Why the rule? Because:
!. If you are known to police as an activist or someone who you openly associate with is a known activist you are a candidate for a phone tap.
2. You cannot assume that your meek and mild friend, who's phone you are using does not have an open association with someone who is "heavy."
3. Pay phones are also tapped. Perhaps the payphone you're using is also the one "Teddy the Torch" uses, and he's not as cautious as you. The police solve many crimes by "accident" when they stumble across evidence while investigating something completely different.
Only a fool or a hermit assumes her or his phone is not tapped.

Tracing Calls

Yes they can do it without legal restrictions.
-long distance phone bills are checked to see who you've called and how often, etc.
-equipment is attached which can identify the numbers being called and the time.

Your House and Other Places
Surreptitous Entries

Purpose of Entries: i) to look around: at documents, files, letters, address books, weapons etc. ii) to plant bugs or remove them later. iii) to steal or destroy documents or to torch the place. iv) to plant documents or prohibited items. Cars are also easily broken into. Don't assume that conversation in a car is safe.

Your Garbage

Yes, they look through you garbage too. Try burning the papers you don't want read. You can take your garbage elsewhere too.

Combatting the Problem

* Consider the advantages of living with others. It makes it hard for them to predict when the house will be empty, if you have enough people. But don't count on this.
* Keep sensitive material in locked containers. At least you know that its been tampered with or taken.
* Keep really sensitive materials in "safe houses."
* Duplicate hard to replace documents and store the copies in safe places.

Weigh the relative importance of writing down every history making decision you make against the importance of not providing the police with the evidence they need for the conspiracy trial.

BE CAREFUL. GOOD LUCK.

*The person who wrote this is aware of the possible legal ramifications of the article being printed. We encourage all activists to think **VERY CAREFULLY** before writing anything that links specific people to specific actions.*

THE FIRST TEN YEARS

The story about the Swedish A.L.F., Djurens Befrielse Front

After being interested in animal welfare almost all of my life, being a member in ordinary animal welfare associations, the turning point came in the autumn 1984. Swedish TV broadcast a film about all the horrible and cruel things done to animals. Things that I already knew of and a lot of things I didn't. While watching Victor Schonfelt's film, hatred began to grow inside me. The film showed things worse than slavery, worse than the extermination camps in Nazi-Germany. I had always avoided watching such terrible pictures, but this time I forced myself to see every single film frame.

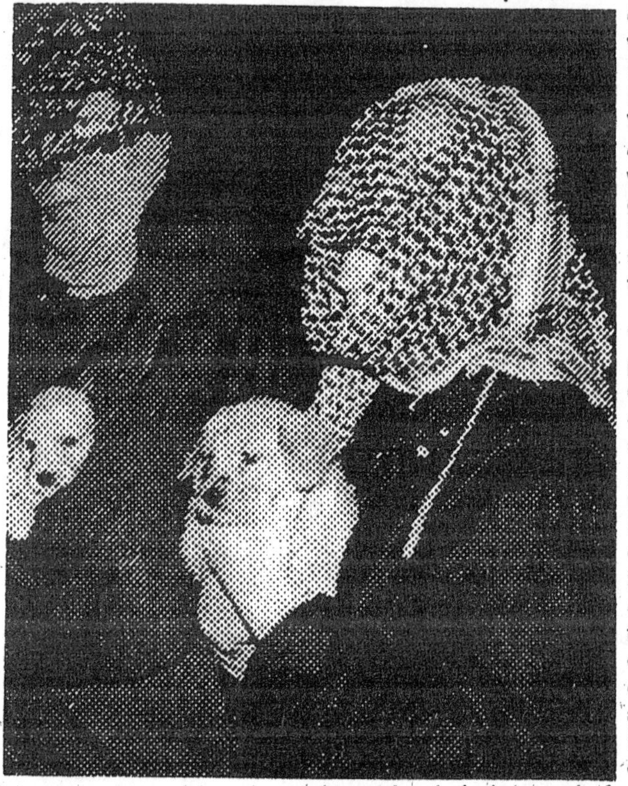

That night I felt sick with anger and guilt, sick with myself who had let this happen, sick with humans doing this to animals. When the dawn had set in I understood I had to do something -- really do something, to take action. But how? I had never felt so lonely as I did that night, as if I was the only human being in the whole universe.

Of course I had heard of the Animal Liberation Front and always had felt sympathetic to their work. Could I do that? Not me, a middle class, divorced, then 35 year old woman. After spending days thinking about this, the answer came up. The only way to get the abused animals saved was to just go in and bring them out. But that's a crime. So what? The bigger crime is to expose animals to abuse.

As I couldn't do anything on my own I had to find other people to work with me, I couldn't put out an advertisement, could I? Well I did, under the personals in the newspaper, seeking people interested in animal welfare work the English way. Then I spent a couple of nervous days waiting and then answers came dropping in. Thirteen answers. After two meetings talking After two meetings talking around things, saying what I wanted without actually saying anything, a small group of four was left after the rest found it too radical. There were "Asa", "Kevin", "Eric" and me. Discussions took place about how to do it and most of all where. We didn't know that much about vivisection and how to break in. How to use a crowbar? What name should we use?

Well that question was easy of course we should take on the name Animal Liberation Front which is Djurens Befrielse Front in Swedish. Some months of investigation took place and also some field trips. We had heard rumors that the University of Lund's, Dept. of Dentistry, was experimenting on animals. We went to the large building where the school is located in the center of Malmo. We could hear the dogs bark on the top floor.

On June 16th 1985 three of us went to our first night shift. One crowbar and a couple of screwdrivers was all we brought. It was late at night and very quiet and we walked around the huge building in order to find the perfect place to break in. We found it, a small, rather old door in the basement. Being the first time for us, we really got a good grip on the crowbar; after a short while the door just flew open with a terrible noise. in we went. We ran up and down various stairways but we couldn't get to the top floor. Back down to the basement again and we found an elevator. With pounding heart and a sweat-production that was unbelievable we stepped in, pushed the button marked top floor. What would be waiting there? After what seemed like many hours, the elevator stopped. We now were in a narrow hallway looking at a steel door and some ordinary simple doors. On the other side of the steel door we could hear the dogs bark.

A steel door with a complicated lock. No idea. We tried the ordinary doors, no luck and the crowbar was no good on the door. But what about the door frame? Now the crowbar was working. We came into a small office and on the desk was some sort of pot with keys in it. Back to the steel door. The first, second, and third keys didn't fit. Lucky for us the steel door had no alarm. Finally the fourth key fit.

Three very tired and scared people set foot in the vivisection department. The first time any outsiders ever set foot in a vivisection lab in Sweden. At this point we didn't care, didn't understand we were actually writing history. We just wanted to get the dogs we had been working so hard for. We noticed rats in several rooms and finally we came to the dog room. Could it be dangerous -- big angry dogs? Slowly we opened the door into a dark room and the barking became louder. By the sound of the barking it didn't seem dangerous. The light went on and we looked at a pack of Beagles.

So many and we could only take two. We spent a little time with the dogs. They were all so beautiful but a bit scared. We looked around in the dog room. There were open pens so at least the dogs could be together but there were no bedding, no toys for them. But how to choose which ones to bring? This dilemma worked out by itself. The two dogs that were most interested in us and had the guts to sniff at our hands told us they were the ones. We ran out, into the elevator and down and out into the night air. We couldn't believe what we had done now when reality set in. We were happy but still unhappy for the dogs we had to leave behind.

We took them to a safe house and gave them water and a big soft blanket. We could see that one of the female dogs had a metal thing in her mouth instead of teeth. The other one had teeth but her gums were swollen and had a strange color. Slowly we began to understand what the experiment was all about. Periodontoclasia. The dogs had been given soft food, and of course had no bedding and toys, in order to make them lose their teeth. The metal thing in the dog's mouth was screwed in her jaw-bone. This required a vet to remove.

Four days later when the dogs were well taken care of and moved a long way from Malmo, we wrote a press release explaining what and why we had done this. Of course the newspapers had written about this, without knowing anything. They actually speculated the British A.L.F. had come over. We had painted the letters D B F together with "animal abuser" on the walls outside the dog room. People in various animal well fare organizations condemned the action saying we had acted as kidnappers and they felt sorry for the dogs and believed the dogs had a better life at the lab.

Well we were in business and during the rest of 1985 another three rescue actions took place. All together 47 dogs were rescued from animal abusers and also a raid at a mink farm took place. The media went nuts due to all this drama.

1986 started good. Fifteen beagles were rescued in a day light raid at Sweden's largest dog breeder for vivisection, then owned by Mary and Rolf Andersson at Vastrarps farm near Orkelljunga. Later on this place was bought by ASTRA and Kabi Pharmacia. Boy are we glad that people have their lunch break at noon. Thanks to their hunger, 15 dogs didn't have to end their lives in a lab.

Two more actions were taken care of that year. Guineapigs and more dogs. We were beginning to get rather good at this and the second action that year was a real cheeky one. We knew that a vivisection breeder outside Malmo transported guineapigs by train from Malmo to Stockholm in the evening. We walked into the crowded train station in plain clothes looking very normal. The station had police and security guards. We ran fast towards the trains goods wagon, which was unlocked, after we had place a couple of look-outs. We found the guineapigs easily and took the cardboard boxes in our arms walking away. When we were close to the entrance door a pair of policeman walked by us. They seemed to find everything normal.

Away we went with 39 white lovely guineapigs. Our rescue wasn't noticed until the next morning in Stockholm, when the lab went crazy. No guineapigs to torture. Now we were really in the mood. We had for some time had our eyes on the University of Lund where almost every department has vivisection labs. We went on a field trip to the department of Pharmacology. It looked as if it was possible to carry out action #10 there. On Sept. 27th 1987 we went in at midnight. While the look-outs were on a roof the troops went in. The look-outs spotted a security guard walking towards the door we had just broken into. We got the signal for danger. Inside the rabbit room none of the activists breathed for a long while. Security guards aren't the brightest people, this one just closed the door and that was that. The eight rabbits were carefully put into special bags and were brought out.

Several rescues at the University took place and also some sheep and private owned dogs were rescued from their abusers together with a few raids at mink farms.

In 1987 a terrible thing happened. Someone (and I know who) told the police about me. Up to now the police didn't have a clue where I was or who I was. Early one morning a police car came up to the house where I lived. I knew at once what was happening and I felt as if I could die knowing someone has told the police. It was terrible that someone once involved could do this. I was almost in shock and was not prepared to face the police, and also the house was full of evidence, no rescued animals, but working tools, names, address and so on.

The police went away and I'm sure they thought "we'll get her next time". OK the next time I was prepared, invited the police in and I was charming and absolutely lovely. I was brought to a police station in the next town, had to wait in the arrest area but not in a cell, but a police women kept her eye on me. I still didn't know exactly why I was there. I was told to wait for the police from Lund. After a couple of hours they came and interrogated me for a few hours. After that I was prosecuted for theft of a monkey from a lab. Since the prosecutor didn't have any evidence and the person who had told on me couldn't face me on trial, the case was thrown out by the judge. Lucky me.

Action #22 took place on Nov. 22 1988, when 25 chinchillas were rescued from a fur farm. That same night seven hens were rescued from an egg factory. 1989 started good too. On March 4th, fourteen cats were rescued from a lab-breeder in Halmstead. One cat was pregnant and later gave birth to two kittens. After another three rescue actions, we carried out our first sabotage raid. Eight hunting platforms (a sort of tower where deer and elk are shot from). In the newspapers hunters said that if and when they got a hold of me they would beat me up. Violent people those hunters.

For some time now we had both a phone number and a post office box and money started to come in and letters, letters and more letters, journalists, TV and radio. The whole thing was like a mad house. By now we also had established contact with colleagues in the UK.

Action #34 on April 21st 1990 was an unusual one. We had gathered a lot of unconnected people for a demo outside the place in Orkelljunga that we had rescued dogs from. The owners knew we were coming and had prepared themselves with thugs who more or less beat us up while the place was crowded with police who looked the other way. We weren't really badly hurt but I'll never forget the disgusting feeling when vivisection-defenders/animal-abusers touched me with their violent hands. When I came home that same day I sat down and has a good long cry. But there wasn't time for feeling sorry for oneself.

A few days later some more hunting platforms became history and four dogs were rescued from a notorious dog breeder. On May 14th 1991 we visited four fur shops in Helsingborg with red paint, glue and so on. This, our action #39, was in honor of the young hunt sab Mike Hill who was killed in the UK by hunters. It was a sad time knowing that a young wonderful person who did right, who did good, had to end in such a terrible way.

For some time now we had talked about having me go to London, and in April 1992 it was time. I went on an air plane for the first and last time in my life. Rescuing animals at night - piece of cake, but traveling by air, no thanks, not again. In London, I met activists who I had been in touch with while they were in prison. My dear sweet friends took care of me as if I was a queen.

I would have liked to meet Ronnie Lee but he was still in prison. But I did meet with the ALF Press Officer, a wonderful warm and caring man who gave me an ALF SG hat which I wear on special occasions. We had a long nice talk and I felt as if he was, and still is, my brother. Later on I got a chance to say Hi to his wonderful supportive partner.

I also had a chance to take part in a demo outside Boots arranged by London Boots Action Group. I also was introduced to a man who had a real impact on my life. This intense little guy spoke in soft 'musical' English how he had to give up football. Stupid me asked why. He explained about the football and shoes were made of leather. Thanks B for making me aware of the fact that it's not enough to be vegetarian. Vegan is the thing. Vegan power can make us move mountains.

The last day of my visit was the big march against vivisection arranged by the NAVS. I was amazed how big the march was, all those people in the same place for one reason only. I met a priest who, after I told him who I was, gave me his blessing. Even if I'm an atheist and 50% Buddhist it felt good. Of course I met with even more colleagues. I would had wished the march could end up outside a vivisection lab and I felt it was sad to see how many people had brought dogs. Leave the animals home where they are safe.

After a week I was back home safe (no the plane didn't crash!), full of energy, feeling good.

At home we had problems. Hardly any activists left, no homes for rescued animals, no money and not even a car. I had to move from my old home to a new little town. People knew who I was and I was attacked with spit and stones, and finally my car burned. The new place was quiet, still is. The police come and want to know a lot of stupid things which I, of course, don't answer.

Only one action took place in 1992 and the next year none. But 1994 started well. Action #44 took place on Jan. 22nd. 18 guineapigs, 9 hamsters and 5 rabbits were rescued from a hospital vivisection lab in the capital of Sweden.

In May something interesting occurred and for once it was not us. Some slaughter vehicles were burned outside a slaughterhouse in Stockholm. The damage was valued at a couple of million (Swedish krona). I felt great that others had finally started to do something. In September it happened again, this time in northern Sweden. In Umea three slaughter vehicles were burned out: three million kronas damage. Unfortunately the group who did this had painted our name on a car outside the place.

Again the media went nuts and phoned me over and over again. All I could say was "No we didn't do it, I don't know who did it, yes I agree with their action because 67 million animals are killed in slaughterhouses in Sweden each year." TV phoned, interviews were made, radio and so on. A lot of hard work but I say thanks for all the free PR we got.

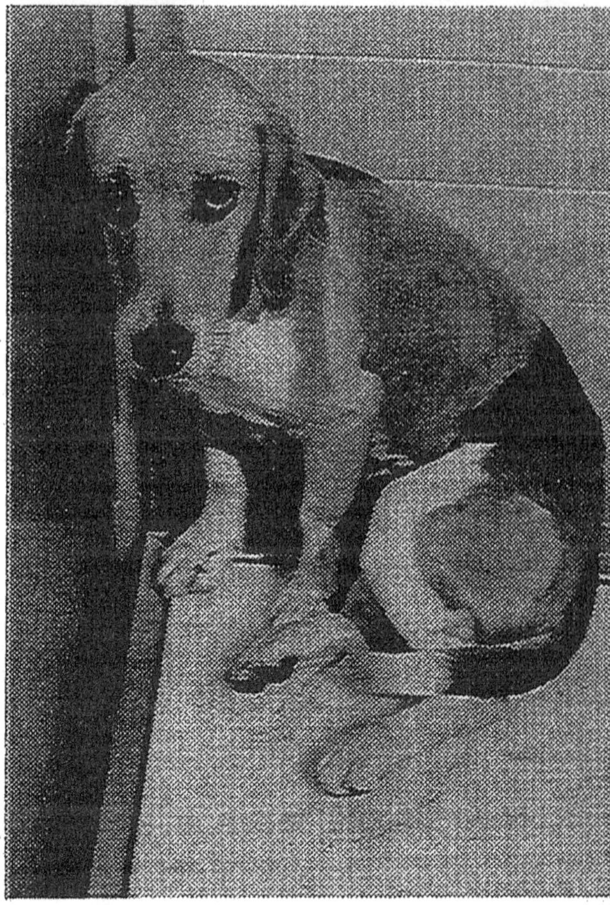

Death threats and such are almost an everyday thing for me but after the slaughterhouse vehicle raids something else has occurred. People, not reporters or police, have been asking questions in the neighborhood about me. Even the post office has gotten these questions. This might mean trouble. But I have taken steps to protect myself. A police man gave me some ideas on how to protect myself. I will not let anyone scare me into closing down an organization that is almost 10 years old. No way, threats or no threats. Yes I'm a bit afraid, but there is a saying that gives me strength: "When the going gets tough, the tough get going".

Still I consider myself lucky, no prison (yet) and I have been treated rather well by the police. It's not at all as activists are treated in the UK, USA and Canada. And it has been ten great years, weird but great even though I'm now 20 years older instead of ten! I have no regrets, well maybe one. Why didn't I start the DBF sooner. Reporters keep asking me if I'm going to slow down now at my age (a few more years and I'm turning 50). To that there is only one answer "You ain't seen nothing yet".

1994 ended rather well, on Dec. 22nd we visited three meatshops and one fur shop in Stockholm (smashed window, red paint and glue).

Four days later I became a grandmother to baby Luke.

I wish all activists, and especially those in prison, a happy, safe and successful 1995.

Astorp, Sweden
January 2 1995
Emilie E:son - DBF (the Swedish ALF)

DJURENS BEFRIELSE FRONT
BOX 179
S - 265 22 ÅSTORP, SWEDEN
Tel: +46 42 576 93

THOSE FOLK SAY THE STRANGEST THINGS...

"It Takes A Virile Man To Make A Chicken Pregnant."
- Perdue chicken ad, as seen mistranslated abroad (original caption: "It Takes A Tough Man To Make A Tender Chicken")

"Wish--To end all the killing in the world."
"Hobbies--Hunting and fishing."
- from personal statistics of California Angel Bryan Harvey, flashed on the scoreboard at Anaheim Stadium

On the Little-known Importance of Poultry Inspectors:
"The crime bill passed by the Senate would reinstate the Federal death penalty for certain violent crimes: assassinating the President; hijacking an airliner; and murdering a government poultry inspector."
- Knight Ridder News Service dispatch

On Pesticides:
"Sure, it's going to kill a lot of people, but they may be dying of something else anyway."
- Othal Brand, member of a Texas pesticide review board, on chlordane.

- from post to AR-Talk, Mar 4/95

From the Daily Telegraph (Mon. 6,March 1995, p1) UK

Terror Police Target Animal Extremists

By Neil Darbyshire, Crime Correspondent

ANIMAL RIGHTS extremists, whose increasingly violent campaigns have alarmed chief constables, are to be targeted for the first time by a national police unit to be set up under the direction of Scotland Yard's anti-terrorist branch. Cdr David Tucker, head of the branch, is expected to be named as national co-ordinator and the unit sited at his existing London offices.

The decision is a measure of chief constables' fears that violence in support of animal causes is becoming more widespread and better organised.

They are also concerned that such violent protest or quasi-terrorist activity often occurs without warning in remote parts of the country, where the local police may not be fully equipped to cope.

The move is likely to provoke fears within some non-violent animal groups that part of the intention may be to stifle legitimate protest.

Draft terms of reference are still being studied by the Association of Chief Police Officers, but the main task of the anti-terrorist detectives would be to bring to animal extremist cases their investigative skills, gathered over more than 20 years of tackling IRA and international terrorism.

They would help county forces in the recovery of forensic and scientific material from the scenes of explosive or arson attacks and, where necessary, visit forces to give technical advice. Local forces would remain in control of individual inquiries on their territory.

Scotland Yard already houses the animal rights national index, a computer that collates intelligence on animal rights extremists. It contains the names and details of between two and three thousand people who have committed or are suspected of having committed criminal offences.

The computer will remain under the authority of the Special Branch. But Cdr Tucker and his officers would work closely with their Special Branch colleagues, as they already do in many other security policing matters.

Deputy assistant commissioner John Howley, overall head of both the Special Branch and the anti-terrorist branch, told The Daily Telegraph that neither the Special Branch nor the new unit would be interested in the many people who simply turn up to vent their feelings during animal rights protests.

"The people we are interested in are extremists who are prepared to use criminal tactics or commit public order offences to achieve their ends in pursuit of animal rights," he said.

"I want to emphasise that animal rights extremist activity is not terrorism. There is a definition of terrorism contained in the Prevention of Terrorism Act and it is basically the advancement ofpolitical objectives by means of violence with a view to over throwing the government.

'What these sorts of people are indulging in while it is akin to what we would call terrorism or political violence, is not quite on the same level yet. But it could be and requires very similar methods of investigation."

Mr Howley said it would be a mistake to see Cdr Tucker's new role as an extension of his counter terrorism function, despite some similariies in approach.

Special Branch figures show that there were about 800 reported animal extemist offences in England and Wales last year, including the placing or sending of 50 explosive, mostly incendiary, devices.

Apart from 1991, when groups such as the Animal Rights Militia and the Justice Department were at their most active before a number of key arrests, that was the highest total of devices in a single year since reliable recording began in 1986. While no one has yet been killed in an animal related attack, there have been two attemped murders.

There are believed to be fewer than 100 violent activists, many of them more interested in anarchist causes than animals.

"They have latched on to animal rights because there is a lot of public support for it at the moment," Mr Howley said.

"If there was a tremendous national protest about closing post offices, they would probably leap on that bandwagon as well."

Many have been associated with protests over new road developments and the recent Criminal Justice Act demonstrations. They tend to gain their explosives expertise from underground publications such as the Anarchist Cook Book.

Mr Howley said the computer index did not exist to log the details of people simply because they had turned up at a hunt sabotage or anti-veal protest. But some such events were monitored for evidence of serious criminal activity.

"Almost all the people who are in prison now for animal rights extremist activities have come up through that system. You can see their progress over the years and the extremist groups do most of their recruiting from among the people who turn out for these mass protests."

Mr Howley added: "The risk is that you could have Northamptonshire police investigating a store burnt down in their force area, Wiltshire looking at damage to three butchers' shops and sussex investigating some damage to docks without realising that the people who were pulling the strings were the same in each case."

This article has been bought to you by the Daily Telegraph, Scotland Yard, ARNI and the letters A L and F.

THE JUSTICE DEPARTMENT: THE STORY... SO FAR!

On Wednesday 6th October 1993 a package exploded in the sorting office at Watford, Hertfordshire. The police claimed that it was addressed to a person involved in bloodsports and that other devices had been intercepted.

At the time it was thought that it may be the Animal Rights Militia, an attempt at 'dirty tricks' against the animal liberation movement or just a coincidence. Much later the Justice Department claimed that these had been the first wave of their devices and proved the authenticity by listing all the targets; information that the police had never revealed.

Just three weeks and a day later, Thursday 28th October 1993, two animal abusers were injured when parcel bombs detonated at their homes. This was clearly the work of an animal liberation group but, again, no claim of responsibility was made at the time.

Tuesday 23rd November saw everything becoming clearer when the ALF(UK) Press Office received a statement from a new group calling itself the Justice Department. Claiming that it had sent the devices that had caused such a stir on 28th October the statement was accompanied by a video film showing the internal components and construction of a device and its subsequent detonation. No further proof was needed that this new group's claims were both genuine and serious. The statement read:-

THE JUSTICE DEPARTMENT.

On the 28th October two animal abusers were injured and given the shock of their pathetic lives when they opened parcel-bombs sent by us. We don't need to explain why these two - Colin French, farm animal abuser, and Christopher Brown, laboratory cat supplier - were targeted, suffice it to say they cause animals to suffer great cruelty, and they deserve it.

In spite of their relatively minor injuries they will now be very much aware we mean business and, were they not our 'guinea pigs' for the testing of our experimental devices, would have been more permanently physically injured. This will be the case next time.

We've sat back for years and watched the AR activists ask nicely for all the abuse to stop - the more daring risk their lives and liberty but still the unacceptable number of tortured animals keeps rising.

The torturers become more extreme; they attack and kill their non-violent opponents to. All this without fear of retribution from the authorities and at worst damaged property c/o the ALF, which we wholeheartedly encourage.

On November 15th two much more powerful devices were despatched in search of Arlin Rickard, BFSS p.r.o., and George Murray, Cheshire Beagles hunt master and 'Alan Summersgill benefit fund organiser. In light of the recent parcel bombs sent by the HRS to bloodsport fanatics most are aware of the threat and may well call the police upon receipt of parcels!! Paranoia sets in! The lack of media hysteria suggests we didn't get through but we will. We only have to get lucky once.........

We won't be asking anyone to stop messing with animals and will make no excuses for our violent intervention - they've had it too good for too long. NO MORE TORTURE NO MORE LIES.......

ENDS

The ALF Press Office gave the story, in the first instance, to the Daily Telegraph as the newspaper most likely to go into the homes of animal abusers and most likely to report the facts accurately. The report appeared in the first edition next day and was dropped from all subsequent print runs.
Meanwhile, the statement and video film had been taken into the Cambridge studios of BBC-tv News, again as an exclusive. They made a copy of the video and carried out a lengthy interview with Robin Webb, ALF Press Officer. The news item appeared as the primary story but in the Eastern region only with the video film not being shown at all "on policy grounds" and none of the interview being screened. The copy tape was given to the police that same evening by BBC- tv.

The following months saw the video-cassette devices joined by poster-tube designs and powerful timed incendiaries, most of which received ever-increasing publicity. However, on Wednesday 16th February 1994 the first wave of metal mouse traps primed and fitted with razor blades were sent out. With pieces of razor blade super-glued to the snap bar of the trap it was then primed (set), wrapped in paper and packed in a small Jiffy bag.

This saw the beginning of a real media blackout, possibly because the authorities recognised the first devices as too complicated for many people, while the new mouse-trap devices were within the capability of anyone who could use a catapult or glue a lock.

At about this time the Hight Court announced its decision to overturn the ban introduced by Somerset County Council against the Quantock Staghounds using local authority land. Received by the ALF Press Office on 19th february a communication from the Justice Department made its reaction clear:

JUSTICE DEPARTMENT STATEMENT

If our arguments weren't believable before the latest example of political corruption perhaps now there are a few more converts.

80% of the population are opposed to bloodsports; clearly the majority of local councils - which have banned hunting - did so because the majority voted for that, now we're told it's not proper to go with a democratic decision. So be it.

We never had faith in the political system so used direct action to fight the many obscenities inflicted on the animal kingdom, and proved its worth.

Now we hope and anticipate more will join the war being fought by so many good people outside the hopelessness of asking people with nasty habits nicely to stop destroying animals' lives. They insult humanity so deserve to be insulted and humiliated.

They deserve more we think, soon they'll get it. JD and Company.

ENDS

As the JD's campaign continued and increased so solid victories were at last achieved......

Hyline Rabbits in Cheshire had long been fighting a rearguard action against the Animal Liberation Front with rabbits of all ages being regularly rescued and property being damaged and destroyed. With the device sent to Hyline's owner, Edwin Sutton, during December 1993 and the increased intensity of the ALF's actions both Hyline Rabbits and its sister company Coney Europa announced on Monday 27th June 1994 that they were going into voluntary liquidation.

The 'live exports' trade has seen active campaigning for about forty years during which things have just got worse. The first device from the Justice Department against the trade was despatched on 18th April 1994 with six more following on 3rd June. For the first time in all those years major ferry companies announced that they would no longer be carrying live animals for slaughter.

With such a sudden and unexpected withdrawal of facilities the exporters began frantically trying to find alternative routes through smaller ports and smaller companies. Up and down the country animal rights groups have joined forces with local people who are now outraged enough to take part in campaigns to prevent the trade continuing.

The Justice Department is also continuing the pressure with a device being sent to the manager of Shoreham Port Authority as recently as 20th October. Through the JD there finally seems real hope that this trade will be ended with the help of firm and spirited local and national campaigning.

Following is the complete listing of Justice Department actions to date. They would want everyone to remember what they said at the time of the December 1993 poster-tube devices.....
...It hasn't even started yet. Now is the time to give them everything you've got....

JUSTICE DEPARTMENT: 1

6th October 1993. The first devices sent by the Justice Department were housed in VHS-size video cassette boxes. One device detonated and six others were intercepted and "made safe' at the sorting office in Watford, Hertfordshire. The targets were:

Frank Evans (Gtr Man) - Matador
G. Jones (S Yorks) - Fell & Moorland Working Terrier Club rep.
J.J Kirkpatrick (Dorset) - Assoc. of Masters of Harriers & Beagles.
P.J Caddy (Cumbria) - Central Committee of Fell Packs.
W.A. Mackenzie (Suffolk) - Coursing Supporters Club.
P. Wild (Berkshire) - Masters of Minkhounds Assoc.
T.I. Whitley (Devon) - Master & Huntsman North Dartmoor Beagles.

28th October 1993. Similar devices were delivered. Both detonated when opened. The targets were:-
Colin French (Bucks) - Farmer.
Christopher Brown (Oxon) - Breeder of cats for laboratories.

17th November 1993. Another video delivered to :-
George Murray (Cheshire) Master of Cheshire Beagles.

18th November 1993. Again, a video device delivered to: -
Arlin Rickard (Cornwall) West country PRO for the BFSS.

24th November 1993. Video-type device delivered to: -
Leo Sawrij (W Yorks) Swalesmoor Mink Farm.

30th November 1993. Video devices, the first one of which detonated, delivered to: -
Haydon Noble (London) - Noble Furs.
Rosalie Noble (London) - Noble Furs.

21st and 22nd December 1993. The first wave of poster-tube devices, each with six hypodermic needles packed in with the explosive materials. A claim was made that, as AIDS had apparently been created in a laboratory, some HIV-infected blood had been stolen and may be used in the future to return the virus to the vivisection community responsible for its creation. The targets were:-

Mark Matfield (London) - Research Defence Society.
Edwin Sutton (Cheshire) - Hylyne Rabbits.
W.H. Mellor (Gtr Man) - H.G. Rabbitry, Oldham.
Harlan Porcellus (E Sussex) - Guinea pig breeders, Cross-in-Hand.
E.D.S. (Surrey) - Publish a directory of animal suppliers.
Peter Savage (W Sussex) - Shamrock Farms/Vet Diagnostics.
Chas Gentry (Her & Worc) - Consort of Ross-on-Wye, beagle breeders.
Terry Hornett (Herts) - Glaxo breeding unit & FIAT Council.
Phil Ruddock (Surrey) - Editor of IAT Bulletin/Lillico feed sup.
Louise Philips (Hants) - Selborne Biological Services.
D. Hall (Staffs) - Guinea pig breeders, Burton-upon-Trent.
Colin Blakemore (Oxon) - Well-known blinder of kittens.
FELASA (London) - Federation of European Laboratory Animal Science Association.

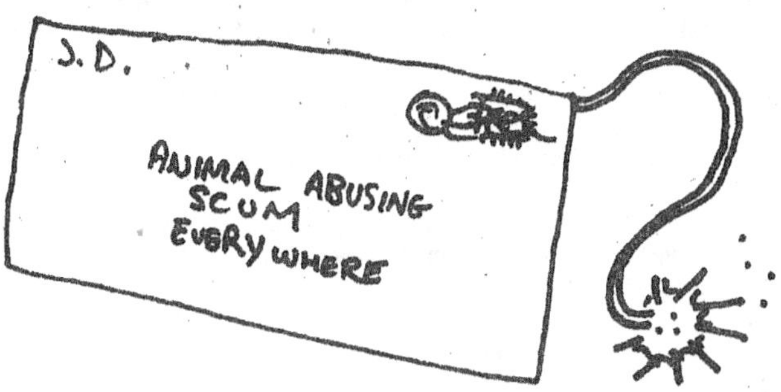

24th December 1993. The third type of device, a powerful timed incendiary, was placed in thee Boots store, Northampton:
Boots (Northants) - Boots the Chemist, Nothants.

28th December 1933. Two more timed incendiaries:-
Boots (Cornwall) - Boots the Chemist, Bodmin.
Boots (Cornwall) - Boots the Chemist, Liskeard.

29th December 1993. Another powerful timed incendiary:-
Boots (Corwall) - Boots the Chemist, Helston.

2nd February 1994. The first elaborate hoax devices sent by the Justice Department. Based on the video cassette design. Reason given for using hoax packages was "Operative devices won't get through to even the dumbest just now". The targets were:

Terry Bambridge (Herts) - Enfield Chace hunt.
Lt Cdr D.C. Douglas (W Sussex) - Point to Point Sec: Chiddingfold, Deconfield and Cowdray hunt.
Mrs S.J. Ashby (Beds) - Jt Master: Herts South Beagles.

16th February 1994. Powerful metal mousetraps primed and fitted with razor blades on the snap bar, allegedly contaminated with the stolen HIV-infected blood (see 21st and 22nd December 1993). Sent to:

Dr Palmela Mullins (Cambs) - Huntingdon Research Centre vet.
Dr Harley Farmer (Cambs) - Ichor Ltd vet.
Georgina Watson (N Yorks) - Leeds University.
Brian Cass (N Yorks) - Director, Hazelton contract Testing Services.
Tony Rollings (Northants) - Director, Biotech.
Gordon Houston (Notts) - Managing Director, Boots the Chemist.
Terry Richardson (Notts) - Managing Director, Boots Pharmaceutical.
Nicholas Green (W Midlands) Vivisectionist at Birmingham University.
Michael Keighley (Warks) - Vivisectionist at Birmingham University.
David Cooper (E Sussex) - Director, Shamrock Farm.

7th April 1984. Two video-type devices delivered, the second to show that the chant "Human freedom, animal rights: one struggle, one fight" isn't just empty rhetoric:

Boots (Cambs) - Boots the Chemist, Cambridge.
BNP headquarters (Gtr London) - British National Party HQ.

18th April 1994. Two more video-type devices were sent. The second, which detonated in Coventry sorting office, was claimed as "the first wave of a new campaign against live exports":

Michael head (E Sussex) - Badger baiter featured on Channel 4 TV.
W. Gilder (Glos) - Member of prominent "live exports" family, this one lives at Winchombe.

30th April 1994. A Justice Department hoax call cleared Boots huge store in Plymouth together with neighbouring businesses including McDonald's. City centre closed off for several hours. McDonald's didn't reopen until 4.00pm. This was a busy Saturday on May Bank Holiday weekend. No device was actually placed:

Boots (Devon) - Boots the Chemist, Plymouth.

12th May 1994 Fifteen mousetrap devices fitted with razor blades were despatched to various targets; 10 vivisection, 2 puppy breeders, 2 bloodsports, 1 slaughterhouse:

Days of Torbay farms (Hants) - Breeds for Wickham Research Laboratories.
David Walker (Hants) - Owner of Animal Pharmaceutical & toxicology, formerly vet at Wickham.
SBS (Hants) Selborne Biological Services, breeds large animals for use in serum production.
Froxfield Farms (Hants) - Breeds rabbits, ferrets, rats mice etc.
Paul West (E Sussex) - Vet at Shamrock Farm.
Andy Bradwell (W Sussex) - Manager, Shamrock Farm.
S Grinyer (W Sussex) - Shamrock Farm employee.
William Cartmell (Hants) - Owner of Wickham Research Laboratories.
J Worrow (E Sussex) - Shamrock Farm employee.
Paddy Edwards (Hants) - Manager, Wickham Research Laboratories.
Deborah Dowset (Hants) - Owns 50% of Garetmar Kennels, formerly the notorious Cottagepatch.
N Scarr/D Witcher (Hants) - Nicola Scarr owns the other 50% of Garetmar. David Witcher works at Garetmar and is Scarr's live-in boyfriend.
Nick fawcett (W Sussex) - Chiddingfold, Leconfield and Cowdray hunt.
Michael Head (E Sussex) - Badger baiter, see 18th April.
P Humphrey (Hants) - Webb's Poultry, also hunting.

27th May 1994. What is believed to have been a video-type device of slightly different construction to those previously used was left on a doorstep. Subsequently the RAF bomb disposal unit detonated it by "controlled explosion":- Genus (Northants) - Artificial insemination company, Moulton.

3rd June 1994. Six poster-tube devices delivered to targets involved in the 'live export trade'. These devices lacked the hypodermic needles used in the earlier tubes but had a greater explosive capability.
Stena Sealink (Kent) - Head office of ferry company.
Ross Breeeders (Lothian) -Poultry breeder HQ near Edinburgh.
Pig Improvement Co (Oxon) - Fyfield Wick, near Oxford.
Cherry Valley Farm (Lincs) - Breeds much for export, near Rothwell.
Graham Gilder (Glos) - The infamous family, see 7th April. This one is at Elmstone Hardwicke.
Gilder Haulage (Glos) - The same family. This time based at Bourton-on-the-Water.

15th July 1994. The third wave of mousetrap devices fitted with razor blades are mailed out; 9 vivisection, 3 hunt, 2 puppy breeders, 1 slaughterhouse:-
Porton Products (Wilts) - Contracts testing to Wickham Research Labs.
HMC (MFg Chemist) (Tayside) - Contracts testing to Wicham Research Labs.
Roche Products (Herts) - Contracts testing to Wickham Research Labs.
Pitman Moore Ltd (Grt London) - Contracts testing to Wickham Research Labs.
Penn Pharmaceutical (Bucks) - Contracts testing to Wickham Research labs.
*Deborah Dowsett (Hants) - Owns 50% of Garetmar Kennels.
*Nicola Walker (Hants) - Owns 50% of Garetmar Kennels.
*David Walker (Hants) - Owner of APT, formerly vet at Wickham.
*Simon Day (Hants) - Torbay Farm, breeds for Wickham.
*Nicholas Fawcett (W Sussex) - Chiddingfold, Leconfield and Cowdray hunt.
D Hunt (Hants) - Hursley Hambledon hunt.
*P Humphreys (Hants) - Webb's Poultry/Hursley Hambledon hunt.
*James Philips (Hants) - Froxfield Farm; breeds for vivisection.
Webb's Country Foods (Hants) - Chicken slaughterhouse.
*William Cartmell (Hants) - Owner of Wickham Research Laboratories claimed that Cartmell "also got a little bit extra".
* See also target for 12th May 1994; these appear to have been repeats.

28th July 1994. Powerful incendiaries destroy speedboat kept on a trailer which had been subjected to regular damage attacks by the ALF. Four hoax devices were also sent out at the same time. The speedboat was destroyed at:-
*Garetmar Kennels (Hants) - Formerly Cottagepatch.

Hoax devices sent to: -
*Nicholas Fawcett (W Sussex) - Chiddingfold, Leconfield and Cowdray Hunt.
*David Walker (Hants) - Owner of Animal Pharmaceutical Toxicology, formerly vet at Wickham.
*D Hunt (Hants) - Hursley Hambledon Hunt Kennels.
Hunt kennels (W Sussex) - Chiddingfold, Leconfield and Cowdray Hunt kennels at Petworth.
* See also 12th May 1994 and 15th July 1994.

6th August 1994. Twelve powerful incendiaries planted at a livestock haulage company. It had been intended to damage buildings as well but more vehicles and two rigid lorries were severely damaged. One £30,000 vehicle completely burnt out:-
J T Padbury (Northants) - Livestock haulage company.

22nd August 1994. Letter bomb delivered to a manufacturer of animal traps. Police refused to give the name of the target to local media but it appeared eventually in the Sunday Times. No claim was received and it is not known whether any other devices were despatched at the same time to other targets. It is fairly certain that this was a JD action:-
William Stedman (Cheshire) - Manufactures animal traps, BFSS member.

9th September 1994. Hoax devices placed at a hunt kennels and at a public house used by the hunt. These may have been placed the previous day:-
*Hunt kennels (Hants) - Hursley Hambledon Hunt Kennels.
Bucks Head (Hants) - Public house in Meonstoke.
* See also 12th May, 15th July and 28th July 1994.

12th September 1994. New group announced as an offshoot of the Justice Department; AC/DC (Anti-Carmell & Dowsett Campaign) formed to commemorate the 10th Anniversary of the SEALL's "Wickham 19". Powerful incendiary devices were placed under two cars. The one placed under Walker's vehicle is known to have detonated, destroying the target vehicle:-
*David Walker (Hants) - Owner of Animal Pharmaceutical & Toxicology.
*Paddy Edwards (Hants) - Manager, Wickham Research Laboratories.
* See also 12th May, 15th July and 28th July 1994.

20th October 1994. Mousetraps feature again as 13 are delivered, primed and fitted with razor blades. A further 19 letters are booby-trapped with razor blades. The mousetrap devices were sent to: -
*Bucks Head, Meonstoke (Hants) - Public House used by Hursley Hambledon Hunt.

*P Humphreys (Hants) - Webb's Poultry/Hursley Hambledon Hunt.
*D Hunt (Hants) - Hursley Hambledon Hunt.
J Beechinoor (W Sussex) - Shamrock Farm.
V Villiers (W Sussex) - Chidingfold, Leconfield & Cowdray Hunt.
C Bishop (Hants) - Wickham Research Laboratories.
*Days of Torbay Farm (Hants) - Breeds for Wickham Research Laboratories.
P Lacey (W Sussex) - Shorham Port Authority Manager, subject of 'Live Exports Campaign.
L Ford (E Sussex) - Shamrock Farm.
*P Philips (Hants) - Froxfield Farm; breeds for vivisection.
*N Fawcett (W Sussex) - Chiddingfold, Leconfield and Cowdray Hunt.
T Welburn (E Sussex) - Shamrock Farm.
K Coker (Hants) - Hursley Hambledon Hunt.

The razor blade letters were sent to: -
*Shamrock Farm (W Sussex) - The infamous primate supply establishment.
V Hall (W Sussex) - Shamrock Farm.
*William Cartmell (Hants) - Owner of Wickham Research Laboratories.
*Paddy Edwards (Hants) - Manager, Wickham Research Laboratories.
*David Walker (Hants) - Owner of APT, formerly vet at Wickham.
*Nicola Scarr (Hants) - Owns 50% of Garetmar Kennels.
*Deborah Dowsett (Hants) - Owns 50% of Garetmar Kennels.
*Hunt Kennels (Hants) - Hursley Hambledon Hunt Kennels.
Claredon Estate (Wilts) - Used by Hursley Hambledon Hunt.
The Shoe, Exton (Hants) - Public House used by Hursley Hambledon Hunt.
Mr Rousell (Hants) - New Farm, Exton; supports Hursley Hambledon Hunt.
Mr Wallace(Hants) - Hursley Hambledon Hunt.
Mr Bingham (Hants) - Hursley Hambledon Hunt.
D Grey (Hants) - Webb's Poultry.
K Webb (Hants) - Webb's Poultry.
Spread Eagle, Midhurst (W Sussex) - Public House used by Chiddingfold, Leconfield and Cowdray Hunt.
J Stoner (W Sussex) - Shamrock Farm.
*Paul West (E Sussex) - Vet for Shamrock Farm.
T Richards (Hants) - Hursley Hambledon Hunt.
* See also 12th May, 15th July, 28th July, 9th September and 12th September 1994. In addition to those marked * see also 21st/22nd December 1993 and 16th February 1994.

14th November 1994 An escalation as rat-traps primed and fitted with razor blades are sent to two prominent targets in a display of the anger felt at the continuation of hunting and the introduction of the Criminal Justice Act to curtail lawful protest. The devices were despatched to:

Michael Howard (Grt London) - The Home Secretary, Westminster.
Prince Charles (Norfolk) - The Royal Estate, Sandringham.

22nd November 1994. The Justice Department decide to set up in the Irish Republic. Hearing that Captain Mark Philips was visiting that country to hunt and bearing in mind claims that "there is no opposition to hunting there" they sought to prove otherwise. Devices of an unidentified type were sent to the hunts which were to play host. Later comments from on of the hunts to sabs at a later date indicate that something certainly got through. The JD also "advised Captain Mark Philip to go home ASAP". Devices were sent to:
North Galway Hunt - (Co Galway) - Hunt in the Republic of Ireland.
Galway Blazers (Co Galway) - Hunt in the Republic of Ireland.

NEWS FROM FINLAND

Some very daring animal liberation actions have taken place in Finland this year, including the liberation of over 600 foxes from various fur farms throughout the west of the country by three 19 year old women. The following letter was sent to Underground by one of the activists, Mia Salli, who was arrested along with two others by Finnish police for the actions:

Hello!
I want to tell you animal liberation greetings from Finland! As you know, Finland is the biggest fur breeder of foxes. Just now it's bigger news here than ever before. I'm one of three 19 year old girls who liberated about 600 foxes from fur farms at the end of May this year. We visited for fox farms in Western Finland. We just opened the doors of cages. We were very quiet, we didn't frighten, harass or touch any fox. They made their own decision about coming out and being free.

We are long time animal rights activists. For example, I've been already for years a kind of coordinator in different groups active against animal abuse. I've arranged events, demonstrations, support concerts and so on. Work for animal rights has always been the most important part of my life. I've been vegetarian since I was 7 years old and now I'm vegan. I've always been interested in fighting against other problems also - for human rights, original citizens, individual freedom, environmental things. I believe that these problems are parts of bigger totalities. Animal liberation and human rights aren't opposites. They are all the same fight.

We thought it was really time now to get fox farming under discussion and in the news in Finland. There is now a new animal protection law being prepared in Finnish national Parliament. Proposition of new law isn't almost at all better than old law about fur farming. We want that fur farming of foxes will be refused. And of course our main motivation of liberations was to give possibilities to live free for foxes as individuals who lived in terrible conditions.

We didn't do any vandalism. Ok, we sprayed some slogans to farming buildings which are just old boards but that's all. However, we couldn't believe the reaction of the media. It was absolutely terrible. There were fur farmers interviewed everywhere. They could say whatever they wanted without any criticisms from the media. It was the main news on TV news programs for two days, on the radio, in every newspaper, in every magazine... They called us terrorists, murderers, vandals, torturers of animals and so on. They claimed that we'd bothered foxes, made noises so much that foxdams were killing their cubs in very great numbers and that some dams had miscarriages. They also exaggerated numbers of liberated foxes. For example, one of them said that we had opened 350 cages, when it was really we only opened 70 on his farm. They also claimed acts of vandalism that we didn't do.

We knew fur farming in Finland is the kind of livelihood which receives lots of support money from the state and good media (because advertising of furs is big income to newspapers) and is almost the main source of livelihood in some pats of Western Finland. E.g. a little town called Uusikaarlepyy (there we liberated foxes from two farms) has got most of the fur farms in all of Finland. There is 7000 inhabitants and 400 fur farms in town. So we knew to expect negative reactions about the liberations - but not ever so negative. Also Finland's biggest animal protection group, Animalia, has judged the liberations, calling them "dastardly" in the news.

LIBERATION NEWS FROM FINLAND

That was the situation after our liberations in June. Then it all happened. Early one morning at the start of July, seven policemen came to my house while I was taking a shower. They started a house-search which took many hours in my little one room flat. They took me with them - to police- examination as they said. Then I was in the main criminal station, where they put me under arrest. I didn't tell anything in examinations and that's why after my legal arresting time (3 days in Finland) they wanted to get me as an "examination-prisoner." I had a so-called lawsuit about it in Western Finland, and they decided to put me in for one week more at the police prison as an isolation prisoner. I was in a little cell in total isolation - it was a very hard time.

Just before a second lawsuit about my being held in prison, my friend Minna Salonen was arrested and later put in prison also. I soon found out that the third girl of us who lives in Western Finland (we two are from the capital) told the whole story to the police and was then not arrested or anything. In addition, she told lots of lies about us and the liberations. She tried to clear herself of the actions to avoid sentencing herself. She tells incredible lies like she has been just the driver and that I was a kind of leader in the liberations.

After a difficult lawsuit to get free, Minna and I started very actively to take the truth to the media. We arranged a press conference where we told facts about farming foxes in Finland and what we really did in the farms. Believe me, it's very hard to get out only a little positive reaction in the media about our actions, but the press conference was a success. After that there was news in every newspaper, TV and radio program - and it was incredible - the news was absolutely different. We weren't terrorists anymore. News was great. Well, of course already the next day the same media claimed that because our press conference was so well organized there must be some other people or even groups behind us telling us what to do and say.

So, that's the situation now. The truth is -and almost sad- there is not any group behind us. We have to do almost all the work alone. Of course there are some other animal rights activists who try to help, but only a few. Now we have plans to create a support group ourselves and to tour the largest Finnish towns in August to tell about conditions in fur farms and what we did.

It seems that lawsuits about the liberations will begin at the earliest at the end of September or October. It will be a hard lawsuit because this is a so-called precedent in Finnish law. The lawsuit will be in a little town in Western Finland where fur farming is the main source of livelihood. All the people there, including the judge and lay members of the court, have something to do with the fur trade. They want hard sentences for us. there are predictions even about quite long absolute prison sentences.

However, we are hopeful because now there are more discussions in the media about animal rights than ever before. Maybe we will even have an effect on the new animal protection law. We have discussed it with some political people.

Our ability to work for all of this will be better if we could get all the support possible. We need everything: economic support, materials (investigations, magazines, leaflets and particularly photos and posters about the fur farming of foxes) and letters/calls etc to the Finnish media from abroad. We need groups, associations and individuals abroad who can speak out against Finnish fur farming.

We also need vets, biologist and leaders of large associations which work against fur farming as witnesses in our lawsuit to tell the facts about fur farming. I hope you can help us in some way - everything is really needed. And please, tell this story to other people ... We can win, but we need your support to do it! Animal rights fighting has to continue here in Finland! Thanks in advance for everything. I'd like hear from you all soon.

FOR ANIMAL LIBERATION
Mia Salli

As the situation currently stands, the police are watching Mia's post, so she is unable to recieve any letters or support money directly. Until we receive word from Mia of an address that can be made public for supporters, we ask that you specifically earmark all letters and donations destined for the Finnish activists, and send them directly to the NA-ALFSG. We will gladly pass them on.

S A L F G
TORONTO

Diary of Actions

Please Note: The Diary of Actions is intended to report the news of direct action to save animals, not to encourage crime. All reports come from other publications, the internet, or communiques sent to animal rights groups.

As we reported in the last issue, it seems that the Animal Liberation Front, which made headlines in the 1980's with scores of lab break-ins in California and the east coast, has changed tactics and spread to many other areas of the U.S.

Since around the middle of 1993, a flood of small actions concentrated against the meat and fur trades have taken place at the rate of 8-15 a month. A state/province breakdown for 1994 alone from reported actions is as follows:

Arizona: At least 1 action. Unclaimed.
Arkansas: 2+ Animal Liberation Front active.
British Columbia: 6+. ALF, Animal Rights Militia active.
California: 77+. ALF, ALF Stockton Unit, ALF Golden Gate Unit, ALF Southland Unit, ALF November 26 Cell, Crustacean Liberation Front, Farm Animal Revenge Militia active.
Colorado: 3+. Paint Panthers active.
District of Columbia: 5+. ALF active.
Georgia: 1+. Unclaimed.
Indiana: 3+. ALF active.
Illinois: 1+. Paint Panthers active.
Kentucky 1+. Unclaimed.
Maryland: 9+. ALF active.
Michigan: 1+. Unclaimed.
Minnesota: 7+. ALF active.
Missouri: 2+. Paint Panthers active.
Nebraska: 1+. Paint Panthers active.
New Jersey: 2+. Unclaimed.
New York: 10+ ALF, Paint Panthers active.
Ohio: 6+. ALF, Paint Panthers active.
Oregon: 1+. ALF active.
Pennsylvania: 6+. ALF active.
South Dakota: 2+. Unclaimed.
Tennessee: 11+ ALF active.
Utah: 3+. Vegan Revolution active.
Washington: 3+. Paint Panthers active.
Wisconsin: 5+. ALF active.
location unspecified: 2.

Totals: At least 171 actions in 23 states, D.C., and 1 province.

This increase in actions since mid 1993 corresponds to anincrease in actions across Europe, which has seen numerous arsons, break ins, and smaller attacks across the continent, and in England, where the already high level of actions increased with tens of millions of pounds of damages and scores of bombings and arson attacks in 1994.

New York A.L.F. turn up the heat

NOTE: THE FOLLOWING LIST INCLUDES ACTIONS THAT TOOK PLACE IN TIME PERIODS COVERED IN _UNDERGROUND_ #1 AND #2, BUT WERE NOT REPORTED UNTIL RECENTLY. SOME ACTIONS ARE NOT LISTED BEYOND MAY '95, EVEN THOUGH MORE ACTIONS HAVE TAKEN PLACE SINCE MAY. WE DO NOT HAVE A COMPLETE LIST OF ALL ACTIONS TO OCTOBER '95 AS OF YET. ALL COMMUNIQUES WERE SENT ANONYMOUSLY TO THE SG.

AUSTRALIA

SEP 7/94: Victoria - Happy Hens Egg World: 12 sick hens rescued, 9 dead hens removed and delivered to Minister for Agriculture. Animal Liberation Investigation Unit (A.L.I.U.)

CANADA

1993: Guelph, Ontario - Red Lobster: Windows smashed; "Killing the oceans to feed your greed", "Meat is murder", "Red Lobster - Rapists of the sea" painted on building.

● ●

COMMUNIQUE

On May 11/94 ALF firebombed boat at home of guide outfitter BOB WELSH in port alberni
ALF HATES THIS SCUM
timer delay used then kaboom
HA HA BOB ALF BURNED YOUR TOY
scared bob? who next?

sorry for delay SG

ALF PLAYS SAFE
Truck taged (alf)
truck burned too?
alf not sure

● ●

SEP/94: Vancouver, British Columbia - Vancouver Aquarium billboard: "Free the whales" spraypainted. A.L.F.

THANKSGIVING/94: West Vancouver, British Columbia - Saskatchewan Pavilion Restaurant (serves turkey dinners): Painted with slogans, including "Happy Thanksgiving, butchers!", "Bloodfeast", "Turkey Liberation", and "ALF". Paint remains six months later. A.L.F.

OCT/94: Vancouver, British Columbia - Eaton's department store: Several fur coats slashed. A.L.F.

NOV/94: Vancouver, British Columbia - Pappas Furs: Building spraypainted. A.L.F.

NOV/94: Vancouver, British Columbia - Several pet stores: Spraypainted with slogans, including "Free the animals", "Stop the pet slave trade", "Killers!" A.L.F.

NOV/94: Burnaby, British Columbia - Kensington Meats: Picture windows smashed, fluorescent signs smashed, storefront spraypainted. A.L.F.

NOV/94: Vancouver, British Columbia - Several KFC outlets: Spraypainted; locks glued. A.L.F.

DEC/94: Vancouver, British Columbia - Community hall hosting hunting party: Spraypainted, stinkbombed. A.L.F.

DEC 23/94: Lower Mainland, British Columbia - Safeway, Save-On-Foods: Frozen turkey bodies reportedly injected with rat poison; no evidence of actual poisoning. Over $1 million of turkeys pulled off shelves. Animal Rights Militia

● ●

Communiqué:

ATTENTION MEAT-EATING SCUM

The holidays have finally arrived--and so has the Animal Rights Militia. We are here to avenge the mass murder of millions of "Christmas turkeys". Numerous turkey bodies have been injected with rat poison in the past week. The poisonings have been random and widely-dispersed throughout the Lower Mainland at various Safeway and Save-On-Foods locations, with Lucerne and Butterball being the main targets. Various police departments, grocery stores, and media outlets have been notified and sample chickens have been given to the media.

THIS IS NO PRANK Ignore this warning and you will be accountable. Nobody eats the turkeys, nobody gets hurt.

Animal Rights Militia
ARM

JAN/95: Vancouver, British Columbia - Vancouver Aquarium billboard: Hacked down with saw. The billboard had just been replaced after being spraypainted by the A.L.F. in September. A.L.F.

JAN/95: Burnaby, British Columbia - Kensington Meats: Windows smashed. Hit #2. According to the communique, "WE'LL BE BACK!!!!!!!!!!!". A.L.F.

● ● ● ● ● ● ● ● ● ● ● ● ● ● ● ● ● ● ● ●

JAN/95: Vancouver, British Columbia - Friendly Meats: Rocks thrown through front window. A.L.F.

MAR/95: Vancouver, British Columbia - Fish market, Meat market: Windows shattered. A.L.F.

APR 13/95: Guelph, Ontario - Guelph Fashion Furs: "Fur is Dead" painted on main windows. In the past this shop has had windows smashed; twice the two-story side wall was covered in red paint splashes, requiring extensive re-painting.

● ●

COMMUNIQUE

The Justice Department Arrives in Canada

April 24, 1995.....In commemoration of World Day for Laboratory Animals, we sent a razor blade mouse trap device to the workplaçe of scumbag, Dick Johl, the director of Simon Fraser University's Animal Torture Facility. We let him know that as soon as he loses his fingers, the sooner the animals will stop suffering.

● ●

COMMUNIQUE

June 19, 1995

GUIDE OUTFITTER FIREBOMBED

In the early morning hours of June 19, several commandos of the Earth Liberation Army attacked the main camp of BC Guide Outfitter Volker Scherm
(604-837-3538). The camp, situated on the west shore of Lake Revelstoke, consisted of two cabins for Scherm's outfitting operation Monashee Outfitting. Both cabins were firebombed.

Trophy hunting is one of the most despicable practices carried out by the human species, and the Earth Liberation Army intends to do their utmost to put an end to it. Guide outfitters are nothing more than hired assassins, pimps of the hunting world. Volker Scherm charges $8.030.00 for the death of a Grizzly Bear; $6,820.00 for the death of a Black Bear, $5,445.00 for the deaths of a Mountain Goat, Moose and Deer, $4,620.00 for the deaths of a Cougar and Deer. His clients are mostly from Germany, Sweden, and the U.S.

We ask you... Which is more valuable to this planet Earth... the lives of beautiful animals or the property of those who kill them?
We decided to attack Volker Scherm and Monashee Outfitting partly because of his use of dogs for hunting Black Bear and Cougar; dogs which he glorifies in breeding and pimping to other hunters, and which he
takes particular delight in using to chase and terrorize these wild animals.

The Earth Liberation Army issues this warning: Anyone doing business in the massacre of wild animals, as well as those in related industries, are "fair game". We will not rest until the war against Earth ceases. End trophy
hunting now!
E.L.A.

AUG/95:Vancouver/Victoria: Windows smashed at 6 Starbucks Coffee shops in Vancouver and 1 in Victoria. "Stop supporting the death of animals or it will get worse!" -A.L.F.

AUG/95: Burlington, Ontario: REPORT - When numerous complaints from neighbours failed to get action against a family of animal abusers, two or more unknown animal liberation activists took matters into their own hands, showing the Humane Society how it's done. Ontario laws essentually ties the hands of Humane Societies and animal welfare groups, who are unable to prosecute animal abusers unless they are caught red-handed by H.S. Officers. At worse, convicted abusers are told they can't have animals for one year (no list of convicted abusers exists to prevent them from buying/stealing animals again to abuse). Well, frustrated neighbours were sick and tire of seeing and hearing an entire family torture and abuse a young kitten and a Yorkshire terrier cross (including beatings with brooms, an unbrella and torture with plastic bags being tied around the animal's heads), and word went out asking for help. On Sunday, August 6, at aprox 1pm in the afternoon, 2 activists knocked on the door. Having observed the family and investigating their background, the two female activists gained the wife's confidence as they spoke through the door, stating they had a message to pass on from an old friend. When the door opened, the two women burst in, dressed in very offical uniform-like clothing. The reportedly stated "We are confiscating your animals. Call the police if you want, we'd be more than happy to talk to them about how you've tortured these animals." The two liberationists took the animals and walked out in broad daylight. When the husband later returned, the police were called in to investigate. Out of an entire apartment building of hundreds of residents, nobody would talk to the police, except to express their happiness at what had happened!
Both animals are now in happy, loving homes. The dog, Paddington, has been neutered, but is unfortunately not well, having suffered medical complications due to the abuse. A.L.F. (?)

● ●

SEPT 15/95: Sutton, Ontario - A conference hosted by furriers hoping to form a new Canadian furriers federation was targetted at the Sutton Arena. Trappers arrived to the words "NO FUR" and an entire bucket load of blood-red paint splashed on the side of the arena. The public was invited to attend the conference on Saturday, and it is unlikely the furrier scum had time clean it all up before people arrived. A.L.F.

CZECH REPUBLIC

1995: Brno - Vivisection laboratory: Window smashed. A.L.F.

1995: Brno - Fur stores: Splashed with red paint; locks glued. A.L.F.

1995: Vyskov, near Brno - Circus vans: Tires slashed; one van turned on its side. A.L.F.

1995: Vyskov, near Brno - One hunting platform: Destroyed. A.L.F.

ENGLAND

date not specified: Petworth - Chiddingfold, Leconfield and Cowdray Hunt: Tires slashed on 15 hunt vehicles; video recorder broken.

date not specified: Petworth - Chiddingfold, Leconfield and Cowdray Hunt: Three hunt vehicles trashed.

date not specified: location not specified - Sally Baker, Chiddingfold hunt supporter: Wheel nuts removed from horse trailer. The wheel fell off but there were no injuries.

date not specified: Hants - Philip Lacey, Shoreham Port Manager: Received over 150 unsolicited goods and services; recipient of two hoax bombs.

date not specified: near Launceston - H. R. Jasper's abbatoir: Destroyed by fire. Thousands of pounds of damage.

JUL/94: Lower Upham - Torbay Farm: Incendiary device left. A.L.F.

JUL/94: Droxford - Kings Head, hunt supporters' pub: Incendiary device left. A.L.F.

AUG 17/94: Jersey - Zoo visitors' centre: roof covered in gasoline, set alight; approx. $650,000 damage (a briefer version of this was reported in *Underground #2).*

AUG 22/94: Howard Davis Farm artificial insemination centre: $12,000 damage caused by smoke bomb.

AUG 23/94: Lewes - Fur, Feathers 'n Fins (pet store selling exotic animals): Kitten liberated and rehomed.

SEP/94: Hants - Hursley & Hambledon Hunt Kennels: Two small barns set on fire. A.L.F.

SEP/94: location not specified - Hursley & Hambledon Hunt cheese and wine event: Hoax bomb call prompted evacuation of building. A.L.F.

SEP 9/94: Hants - Hursley and Hambledon Hunt Kennels, public house used by the hunt: Hoax devices left. Justice Department

SEP 12/94: Hants - David Walker, Owner of APT/former partner, Wickham Labs; Paddy Edwards, Manager of Wickham of labs: Powerful incendaries totally destroyed their cars outside their homes. Justice Department: Anti-Cartmell/Dowsett* Campaign (AC/DC)

*: NOTES ON AC/DC: William Cartmell is the owner of Wickham labs; Deborah Dowsett owns 50% of Garetmar Kennels. AC/DC was apparently formed to mark the 10th anniversary of the arrest of 19 activists during a raid at Wickham Animal Research Laboratories (the SEALL 19).

SEP 24/94: Whitechurch Farm, Stoneaton - Tom Osborne, Mendip Farmers Hunt Club: Hit with a spiked club, acid squirted in his face. Taken to hospital, no serious injury.

SEP 24/94: location not specified - The 8th Earl of Yarborough: Attacked en route to a hunt meet. Nine activists smashed his Mercedes' windows and dented the car. Hunt Retribution Squad

OCT/94: location not specified: William Cartmell, owner of Wickham Labs: Driveway covered in animal shit. A.L.F.

OCT 20/94: Various locations - Justice Department 13 mousetraps primed with razor blades (see report on Justice Department for details)

NOV/94: Small Dole, near Henfield - Shamrock Farm (holding centre for animals used for vivisection): Hoax bomb left on a road leading to the farm. A.L.F.

NOV/94: Hampshire - Car of William Cartmell, owner of Wickham Labs: Paintstripped; tires slashed; windows etched.

NOV/94: Shoreham, Sussex - Texaco Oil Refinery at Shoreham port: Incendiary left as "a warning to show what could happen if live exports are not banned". A.L.F.

NOV/94: Southwick, Sussex - Lacy & Middlemiss Ltd, agents that arrange Shoreham shipping schedules: Claim that incendiary has been planted. A.L.F.

NOV/94: Small Dole, Sussex - Shamrock Farm: Incendiary device ignited. A.L.F.

NOV/94: Coventry, West Midlands - Christopher Barret-Jolley, managing director of Phoenix Aviation (transports live animals): Recipient of death threats, nuisance phone calls, death threats against family, threats to damage Phoenix planes; house daubed in slogans.

NOV 14/94: Greater London - Michael Howard, Home Secretary; Norfolk - Prince Charles: Rat traps primed with razor blades sent to both targets "in display of the anger felt at the continuation of hunting and the introduction of the Criminal Justice Bill". Justice Department

NOV 19/94: Good Easter, near Chelmsford - Essex Hunt: One policeman kicked unconscious; one policeman's arm broken during clashes between hunt sabbers and police. One sabber was taken to hospital with head injuries.

DEC/94: location not specified - Upham Village Hall: The night before the hall was to host a Hursley & Hambledon Hunt social event, the building was spraypainted with anti-hunt slogans; windows etched; locks glued; hoax bomb left. A.L.F.

DEC/94: Chiddingfold, Hampshire - Chiddingfold Fox Hunt Kennels; Chiddingfold Fox Hunt security manager's home: Sophisticated incendiaries discovered in both locations.

DEC/94: Southern England - Boots: Shoplifted items donated to animal protection charity shops.

DEC/94: Coventry, West Midlands - Christopher Barret-Jolley, managing director of Phoenix Aviation (transports live animals): Recipient of further phone calls, death threats.

DEC/94: Coventry, West Midlands - Truck that transported live animals: All ten tires slashed. A.L.F.

DEC/94: Fernhurst, Sussex - Meat truck: Coated in brake fluid. A.L.F.

JUST BEFORE CHRISTMAS/94: Shoreham, West Sussex - Shoreham Harbour (site of live exports): Hoax bomb left on a ferry. A.L.F.

DEC 28/94: location not specified: David Boulter, South Dorset Fox Hunt kennel-huntsman - "Attacked someone's fist with his nose whilst out hunting."

JAN/95: Shoreham, West Sussex - Trucks carrying cows and calves: Windscreens smashed; lights smashed; lines cut; rocks and other objects thrown through windows during protest against live exports. At least one $250,000 truck completely destroyed.

JAN/95: Exeter, Devon - Roadsigns leading to and from A30 (road leading to Plymouth docks, site of live exports): Painted with anti-live export slogans.

JAN/95: Chewton Mendip, Somerset - William Waldegrave, Agriculture Minister: Recipient of letter containing a razor blade. Second razor blade letter sent to Waldergrave via Westminster.

JAN/95: Lancing, Sussex - Four butchers: Windows etched. A.L.F.

MID-JAN/95: Plymouth, Devon - Richard Otely (farmer who organizes live exports from Plymouth docks): Incendiary left on doorstep; house covered in paint.

From AR-News, Jan 26: "The latest Weekly Telegraph from the UK has two items of interest. One concerns Auberon Waugh, the offensive columnist who is apparently in favour of cruelty to animals and who writes that Americans stink and are infested with diseases. He has had his house burgled; jewellery and other effects to the value of 25,000 pounds were stolen. One can but hope the burglar was some smelly diseased American animal rights terrorist."

COMMUNIQUE

JAN 21/95: Essex - Police left standing as saboteurs stop bloodsports across Essex. Hunt Saboteurs today effectively imposed a blanket ban on bloodsports in Essex. In a well-coordinated and sophisticated operation, nearly 100 saboteurs reduced three foxhunts and a pheasant shoot in locations across the county to a shambles, forcing all of them to pack up early in disarray.

Saboteurs hit the Essex Farmers' & Union Foxhunt meet at the Fox and Hounds, Tillingham; the Essex & Suffolk Foxhunt meet at Tendring Lodge; the Essex Foxhunt meet at Hatfield Broadoak; and a pheasant shoot at Bradwell. Saboteurs took effective action to ensure that no animals were killed at any of the locations and by 2 p.m. all the hunts and the shoot had given up: Essex was a bloodsports-free zone and saboteurs claimed victory.

Meanwhile, Essex police were caught entirely off-guard and were forced into a humiliating climbdown from their previous hardline policy against anti-hunt protesters as their command system more or less collapsed. Previous anti-hunt protests in Essex have been dealt with by the same hardline tactics that have caused such outrage in Brightlingsea this week, with mass arrests and saboteurs being beaten by police. On this day, however, Essex police seemed bewildered by the tactic of hitting all across the county and struggled to cope as reports came in from all across the county. Police coverage of the hunts was, to say the least, patchy and appallingly coordinated: while the Essex Farmers' and Union Hunt initially got only a couple of traffic patrol cars, police numbers at the hunt eventually climbed to some 60 officers and the force helicopter; meanwhile the Essex Hunt received only four officers and the Essex and Suffolk only about eight. The shoot had to make do with "spares" from the Essex Farmers' and Union Hunt. The police made no arrests at any of the four locations in what must be considered a serious reversal for Geoffrey Markham's hardline policy of attempting to crush saboteurs at any opportunity.

• •

FEB/95: Rugby, Warwickshire - Head Office of Phoenix Aviation, veal calf exporters: Fake bomb sent.

FEB/95: Lancing, Sussex - Boots (vivisectors): Bomb hoax #1.

FEB/95: Lancing, Sussex - Boots (vivisectors): Bomb hoax #2.

FEB/95: Brighton, Sussex - 6 butcher shops: Jars filled with paint/ creosote thrown at windows.

FEB/95: Sussex - Paddy Edwards, manager of Wickham Labs: Car blown up, for the second time.

FEB/95: Coventry, West Midlands - Home of Christopher Barret-Jolley, head of Phoenix Aviation (transports live animals): Ground-floor windows
smashed by group of masked activists after death of Jill Phipps.

FEB 3/95: Shoreham, West Sussex - Shoreham Harbor: Two trucks damaged during live export protest; according to the Daily Mail, "500 militants" set up roadblocks, threw "missiles", and dropped tacks onto roads.

FEB 4/95: Northamptonshire - Hunt supporters: Recipients of letter bombs.

FEB 4/95: North Yorkshire - Farm involved in livestock exports: Recipient of letter bomb.

FEB 5/95: Billing, near Northamptonshire - Haulage company specialising in transport of livestock: Four incendiary devices left on trucks. The devices were discovered before igniting and dismantled by an army bomb-disposal unit.

FEB 17/95: London - Department of Transport central London offices: One hundred computers vandalized; hard disks (computers' databank) stolen. Believed to be the work of anti-road activists.

MAR/95: Chadshunt, Warwickshire - Car driven by hunt supporter: Attacked by 20 activists; mirrors and headlights smashed. Two arrests.

MAR/95: Rugby, Warwickshire - Bridge: Anti-fur slogan painted.

MAR/95: Sussex - Wickham Labs, Hurley & Hambledon hunt kennels: Recipients of hoax bombs
MAR/95: Brighton, Sussex - Booth Museum: Incendiary device discovered. Action against live exports. A.L.F.

MAR/95: Rugby, Warwickshire - Phoenix Aviation headquarters: Recipients of hoax bomb.

MAR/95: Coventry - Airport: Fire started by arsonists. Action against live exports.

MAR/95: Coventry - Airport: Fencing pulled down. Action against live exports.

MAR/95: location not specified - Sun Valley Poultry: Claim of contamination with cold medicine. Chickens Incorporated Against Wicked Farms (CIWF)

MAR 25/95: Enfield, North London - Boots: Incendiary discovered. A.L.F.

MAR 25/95: Southend, Essex - Boots: Incendiary discovered. A.L.F.

APR/95: Hampshire - Peter Barfoot, Joint Master of New Forest buckhounds: Discovered incendiary device planted under his car.

APR/95: Sussex - Wickham Labs employee's car: Paint stripped.

APR/95: Lancing, Sussex - Bomb hoaxed.

APR/95: Sussex - Paul Dowsett, Garetmar Kennels: Car destroyed by fire.

APR/95: Sussex - Hursley & Hambledon Hunt Kennels: Empty bungalow destroyed by fire.

APR/95: Rugby, Warwickshire - Bridge: Anti-fur slogan painted.

APR/95: Coventry, West Midlands - Road signs: Anti-live export slogans painted.

APR 25/95: various locations - letter bombs sent to William Waldegrave, MAFF Minister and farmer who exports veal calves; and Tom King, a MP who supports hunting. Justice Department

MAY/95: Paddlington, Cheshire - Milk Marque: 12 milk tankers burned. Wardall, near Crewe: 26 more milk tankers burned. Estimated damage: $4,000,000. A.L.F.

(Here's a news report on the incident):

Milk Tankers Destroyed in UK Attack:
Police in England were investigating an incendiary device attack which wrecked 38 milk tankers and other vehicles at two depots in the county of Cheshire,UK.

The attack has all the hallmarks of a coordinated ALF action although no claims had been made to the press at present. This is no great surprise as the the ALF Press Officer is currently awaiting trial. This means that activists have to contact the press direct, which they have proved to be reluctant to do in the past. The company attacked, Milk Marque, has asked for security to be stepped up at 55 depots across the county and has warned other companies.

The raids, which caused an estimated L2 million worth of damage, happened in the early hours of the morning. Twelve vehicles were attacked at the Aldington depot and 26 at the Wardle depot. All lorries were contracted out to the company by other firms. Most were small tankers but a few were bigger vehicles, capable of carrying up to 2300 litres of milk. At Wardle, vehicles were parked close together in rows. The cabs had been reduced to steel shells and the police have stated that many incendiaries had been used. Some that failed to go off have been taken away for forensic tests.

Peter Stevenson of Compassion in World Farming (CIWF) said "This kind of thing is wrong in principle."

Although there has been no formal claim, this action has all signs of being an ALF attack, and a highly successful one by an organized team.

Source: The Guardian, May 30, 1995, page 5 story by David Ward.

MAY/95: Coventry, West Midlands - Road signs: Anti-live export slogans painted again. A.L.F.

FINLAND

OCT 7-8/94: Kuopio - University of Kuopio vivisection lab: Spraypainted.

DEC/94: Turku - Turkey farm: Contamination hoax.

DEC 31/94: Helsinki - Three fur stores: Locks glued.

JAN 1/95: Helsinki - Fur store: Two large windows smashed.

JAN 4/95: Turku - Fur store: Locks glued shut.

JAN 12/95: Lahti - Two fur stores: Locks glued; according to the report, "someone visited the 3rd one before us!"

JAN 19/95: Helsinki - Meat factory: Slogans spraypainted. Butcher shop: Locks glued. Dresmaker's shop (handles fur): Locks glued, window spraypainted. Eläinten Vapautus Rintama (E.V.R.) / A.L.F.

JAN 19/95: Helsinki - Fur store: Locks glued. Fur store: Window spraypainted. Fur store: Lock glued, window smashed. Fur store: Locks glued, walls and windows spraypainted, 5 large windows smashed. Eläinten Vapautus Rintama (E.V.R.) / A.L.F.

JAN 22/95: Helsinki - Fur store: Four windows damaged, "Death-store of Valtonen the Sadist" (Valtonen is the name of the store's owner) spraypainted on wall. Butcher store: Locks glued. Eläinten Vapautus Rintama (E.V.R.) / A.L.F.

JAN 24/95: Helsinki - Fur store: Slogans spraypainted, window smashed. Eläinten Vapautus Rintama (E.V.R.) / A.L.F.

JAN 28/95: Kuopio - Fur store: Locks glued, walls spraypainted, windows smashed. Eläinten Vapautus Rintama (E.V.R.) / A.L.F.

JAN 28/95: Hämeenlinna - Dairy: building spraypainted; 10 trailers spraypainted; 3 refrigeration units unplugged. Fur store: Locks glued. Eläinten Vapautus Rintama (E.V.R.) / A.L.F.

JAN 28/95: Tampere - Two fur stores, two leather stores, Dolphin aquarium: Slogans painted. Eläinten Vapautus Rintama (E.V.R.) / A.L.F.

JAN 30/95: Helsinki - Fur store: Slogans spraypainted. Eläinten Vapautus Rintama (E.V.R.) / A.L.F.

FEB/95: Helsinki - Fur store: Windows smashed. Eläinten Vapautus Rintama (E.V.R.) / A.L.F.

FEB/95: Helsinki - Two fur stores: Locks glued, window smashed. Eläinten Vapautus Rintama (E.V.R.) / A.L.F.

EARLY FEB/95: Tuusula - Fur wholesale trader: Slogans like "sadist" spraypainted on owner's building; "fur is murder" spraypainted on sign.

FEB 2/95: Helsinki - Fur store: Two windows smashed. Eläinten Vapautus Rintama (E.V.R.) / A.L.F.

FEB 4/95: Loviisa - Fur advertisement sign: Spraypainted.

FEB 4/95: Kuopio - Fur store: "Fur is dead", "Murder" spraypainted. Meat company's office: "Murderers" spraypainted. Eläinten Vapautus Rintama (E.V.R.) / A.L.F.

FEB 5/95: Lahti - Fur wholesale trader: Slogans spraypainted, 5 windows smashed. Eläinten Vapautus Rintama (E.V.R.) / A.L.F.

FEB 11/95: Helsinki - Fur store: Lock glued, 6 windows smashed. Fur store: "Murder" spraypainted on door, locks glued, window smashed. Eläinten Vapautus Rintama (E.V.R.) / A.L.F.

FEB 14/95: Helsinki - Fur store: Four slogans spraypainted. Leather store: Two slogans spraypainted. Eläinten Vapautus Rintama (E.V.R.) / A.L.F.

FEB 18/95: Helsinki - Fur store: Seventeen slogans spraypainted. Eläinten Vapautus Rintama (E.V.R.) / A.L.F.

FEB 20/95: Helsinki - Fur store: Locks glued, "EVR" spraypainted. Eläinten Vapautus Rintama (E.V.R.) / A.L.F.

FEB 25/95: Lahti - Meat factory: Locks glued, "EVR" spraypainted on door; 6 meat trucks had windscreens destroyed, 12 tires slashed, slogans (including "EVR", "Stop the Slaughter, or else...", "For the animals and the environment, EVR!") spraypainted. Eläinten Vapautus Rintama (E.V.R.) / A.L.F.

FEB 27/95: Helsinki - Fur store: Six windows smashed. Eläinten Vapautus Rintama (E.V.R.) / A.L.F.

MAR 2/95: Vaasa - Meat truck: Spraypainted. Eläinten Vapautus Rintama (E.V.R.) / A.L.F.

MAR 4/95: Kuopio - Slaughterhouse: "Murder" spraypainted. Eläinten Vapautus Rintama (E.V.R.) / A.L.F.

MAR 5/95: Vaasa - Meat factory: Slogans spraypainted.

MAR 7/95: Kuopio - Two fur stores: Windows smashed, locks glued, slogans spraypainted. Eläinten Vapautus Rintama (E.V.R.) / A.L.F.

MAR 8/95: Helsinki - Meat factory: Approx 30 slogans spraypainted. Eläinten Vapautus Rintama (E.V.R.) / A.L.F.

MAR 10/95: Helsinki - Fur store: Two windows smashed. Eläinten Vapautus Rintama (E.V.R.) / A.L.F.

MAR 10-11/95: Helsinki - Large fur store: Spraypainted.

MAR 20/95: Helsinki - Fur factory: Advertisement spraypainted. Fur store: Two windows smashed. L'Oreal shop: Window smashed. Eläinten Vapautus Rintama (E.V.R.) / A.L.F.

MAR 25/95: Vaasa - Meat truck: Spraypainted, locks glued.

Report from new Finland ALFSG: *"The Finnish version of ALF is Eläinten Vapautus Rintama (EVR). EVR has been busy, really busy. According to action reports and rumors there seems to be (this is just a guess) active cells in Kuopio, Turku, Tampere, Lahti, and 2 in*

Helsinki! Some cells are more and some less active, but anyway....So far the actions have been vandalizing etc. Nevertheless, we see huge potentiality here as far as direct action goes."

GERMANY

SEP 25-26/94: Köppen - Six hunting platforms: Destroyed. Autonomous Animal Protectors

SEP 25-26/94: Bad Soden - Hunting stand: A stand that was under repair after June 21 (Earth Liberation Night) destruction of hunting platforms was knocked over.

SEP 27-28/94: Offenbach - Several fur and butcher shops: Windows damaged by acid; locks glued. "With this action we want to show that behind the shiny
glass facades are the corpses of animals." The group promised more actions, until "every business that does business with animal corpses is forced to close". Autonome Befreiungsgruppe / Autonomous Liberation
Front

OCT/94: Hamburg - Hunting organization office: Sour butter stinkbomb sprayed in entranceway. Hunter's vehicle: sour butter stinkbomb sprayed in ventilation system; 3 tires slashed. Autonomous Animal Protectors

NOV 5/94 (International Night for Earth Liberation): Taunus - 8 hunting platforms: Destroyed. "With this and future actions we want to expose the killing of animals as the bloody hobby which it is....we will not give peace until the animals in the forest can again live peacefully and no hunting platforms ruin the forests and meadows." Smart Fox Hunting Platform Group

CHRISTMAS TIME/94: Hamburg - 20 carp liberated.

CHRISTMAS TIME/94: Stuttgart - 58 rabbits liberated.

CHRISTMAS TIME/94: Oldenburg - 43 geese liberated.

CHRISTMAS TIME/94: location not specified - A fourth animal rescue. No other details at this time.

DEC 31/94: Hamburg - Hunting organization office: Arson attack. 100,000 DM
damage. Hit #2. Hunters have claimed that "Animal Rights Action" is responsible.

DEC 31/94: Bayern - 15 hunting platforms: Destroyed.

DEC 31/94: Karlsruhe - 12 hunting platforms: Destroyed.

DEC 31/94: all over Germany - Butchers' furriers' shops: Windows smashed to celebrate New Year's Eve.

JAN/95: near Erfstadt/Köttingen - Four hunting platforms: Smashed.

FEB/95: near Wuppertal - Six hunting platforms: Destroyed.

IRELAND

NOV/94: Galway - Captain Mark Phillips, Queen's husband and notorious hunt supporter: Recipient of warning to "go home ASAP". North Galway and
Galway Blazers hunts: Recipients of letter bombs. Justice Department

ISRAEL

NOV/94: Tel Aviv - Fur shops: Windows etched/smashed; locks glued. A.L.F.

DEC/94: Tel Aviv - 5 fur shops: Windows smashed. A.L.F.

FEB/95: Hoolon - Three meat vans: Destroyed. A.L.F.

FEB/95: Hoolon - Six butcher shops: Destroyed. A.L.F.

MAR/95: Tel Aviv - Fur shop: Vandalized. A.L.F.

NEW ZEALAND / AOTEAROA

FEB/94: Christchurch - Meat truck: Trashed. A.L.F.

JUNE-JULY/94: Christchurch - Stanmore Butchery: Locks glued twice; slogans painted 3 times. Owner's car: tires slashed; "Meat is Murder" painted. A.L.F.

AUG/94: Christchurch - Cancer Society Headquarters: Spraypainted twice within a two week period. A.L.F.

AUG/94: Christchurch - National Bank (major sponsor of Cancer Society Daffodil Day): 5 branches spraypainted; locks of 3 branches glued; billboards painted with anti-vivisection messages. A.L.F.

NOV/94: Christchurch - Tegal Chicken truck parked by roadside: Vandalized. A.L.F.

NOV/94: Christchurch - Two butchers: Paintbombed. A.L.F.

WORLD VEGAN DAY, NOV/94: Christchurch - Canterbury Frozen Meat: Company office sloganised, splattered in paint, locks glued; frozen chicken van redecorated, tires slashed. A.L.F.

DEC - JAN/95: Christchurch - Several butchers: Paintbombed; windows smashed at one location. A.L.F.

DEC - JAN/95: Christchurch - Ratcliffe Circus: Unspecified action. A.L.F.

JAN/95: Wellington - Hataiai Butchers: Locks glued. A.L.F.

FEB/95: Wellington - Cuba St. butchers: Locks glued. A.L.F.

FEB/95: Auckland - Butcher shop: Trash can thrown through window.

MAR/95: Wellington - New World Supermarket: Hoax advertising of supermarket free battery-farmed eggs for every shopper.

APR 24/95: Wellington - Lever-Rexona, subsidiary of Unilever (vivisectors): Activists announced they had tampered with AIM brand toothpaste tubes, in recognition of World Day for Lab Animals. Several AIM toothpaste tubes filled with ketchup were found by supermarket staff. According to a press statement, "the tomato sauce symbolised the blood of many animals in vivisection labs run by Unilever and other companies". According to a newspaper report, police "visited the homes of known activists" and viewed supermarket videotapes in an attempt to identify the activists who pulled off the action. Lever-Rexona is now looking at introducing tamper-proof containers; National Manager Murray Papps encouraged anyone with concerns about the tampering to phone Lever's customer advisory centre at 0800-108-806 (conveniently toll-free!).

LATE APR/95: Auckland - A week before duck shooting season was scheduled to begin, a fake bomb was discovered in a post office and was blown up by a bomb sqaud. A message on the package said "stop killing our ducks".

APRIL/95: Christchurch - Animal Liberation Front paints anti meat slogans on two butcher shops in Colombo St and redecorates Sydenham KFC with red painted messages.

MAY/95: Christchurch - Animal Liberation Front activists return to a Colombo St butcher and Sydenham KFC with more paint! "Smash Factory Farming" painted.

MAY/95: Christchurch - A week later more ALF activists put superglue into locks at (you guessed it) Sydenham KFC and paint slogans all over it, the same night a meat wholesaler in Sydenham gets glue in the locks and grafitti all over it, including "MEAT IS MURDER" in six foot letters along one wall. This was not cleaned off for several days. A Colombo St butcher gets repainted with slogans again.

MAY/95: Christchurch - Activists remove the Ratcliffe Circus banner from outside a performance site in Belfast.

MAY/95: Christchurch - A week later, Ratcliffes circus was in Bromley Park, Christchurch when somebody painted the words "LET ME OUT" on the Elephants trailer! Eyewitnesses report that the grafitti wasn't noticed by circus staff until the next afternoon when, as the show was about to begin, and several families were gathered around the elephant trailer, the owner came running out screaming "I'll fucking kill the bastards".

MAY/95: Christchurch - (same night as "let me out" above) A.L.F. activists painted slogans on Riccarton McDonald's and destroyed two large advertising banners outside the McMurder branch.

MAY/95: Wellington - Two trucks belonging to a fish company covered in slogans and a lobster exporting business next door sprayed with "let lobsters live" and other slogans A.L.F.

JUNE/95: Levin - KFC covered in spraypainted slogans like "KENTUCKY FRIED CORPSE", "SMASH FACTORY FARMING" etc and rocks through the front window. (ALF)

JUNE/95: Palmerston North - Three McDonalds advertising signs had "McSHIT" written all over them.

JUNE/95: Dunedin - Front window of McDonald's smashed causing $1300 damage. Unfortunately one person arrested.

JULY/95: Auckland - Several butcher and fish shops in Ponsonby Rd get their locks superglued. (ALF)

JULY/95: Wellington - KFC in Cambridge Terrace gets superglued and splattered in red paint. (ALF)

JULY/95: Wellington - Front window smashed at "Charcoal Chicken" in Cuba St.(ALF)

JULY/95: Wellington - Town Hall locks glued and slogan painted on door on eve of a vivisectors conference there. (ALF)

JULY/95: Wellington - Vivisectors conference dinner at Skyline restaurant disrupted by fifteen masked activists who banged on doors and windows, shouted, and threw stuff.

JULY/95: Christchurch - Animal libbers make hoax bomb threats to two National Banks in Colombo St on Daffodil Day, closing both branches for several hours. National Bank is the major sponsor of Daffodil Day, a cancer research (vivisection) fundraising event. They raise money by selling sausages outside bank branches.

AUGUST/95: Auckland - Medical school at Auckland university covered in multi coloured anti vivisection slogans including "viviSICKtion" and "ALF". (ALF)

POLAND

DEC/94: Bialystock - Fur shops: Locks glued. A.L.F.

DEC/94: Bialystock - Hospital lab: Guinea pigs, rats liberated. A.L.F.

DEC/94: Bialystock - Various locations: Anti-hunt graffiti. A.L.F.

JAN/95: Bialystock - Hunt shop, butcher's store: Spraypainted; A.L.F. posters stuck on windows. A.L.F.

FEB/95: Bialystock - Butchers' shops: Locks glued. A.L.F.

FEB/95: Zielona Goar - Furriers' stores: Windows smashed, slogans demo.

SCOTLAND

APR 24/95: Glasgow - Alaska Fur Company, Glasgow branch: Recipient of letter bomb. Justice Department

EARLY 1995: Edinburgh - Ethicon (vivisectors): Recipient of letter bomb. Justice Department

SWEDEN

SEP 24/94: Umea - Three meat trucks burnt out. Millions of dollars worth of damage.

NOV 12/94: Stockholm - Arla's Dairy: Seven milk trucks burnt out. Militant Vegans

END OF 94: Jonkoping - Meat shops: Slogans painted; locks glued; windows smashed.

JAN/95: Jonkoping - Fur shop: Burned to the ground.

EARLY JAN/95: Gothenburg - Meat and fish vehicles: Attempted arson; minor damage. Militant Vegans

JAN 19/95: Östersund - Slaughterhouse: Containers with acetylene gas opened, no damage. Frösö Zoo: 10 foxes, 2 wolves, 13 lynx and a few owls set free.

FEB 10/95: Stockholm - 3 fur shops, 2 meat shops, 1 hot dog bar: Red slogans painted; windows scratched; advertising banners destroyed. Actions dedicated to Jill Phipps. One of the butchers targeted in this attack has been hit 15 times; damage from the D.B.F. (A.L.F.)'s last hit in December was still showing at the time of this hit. Djurens Hämnare / Animal Avengers

FEB 22/95: Stockholm - Burger King: Painted with red anti-meat slogans. Djurens Hämnare / Animal Avengers

MAR 10/95: Stockholm - Skansen Zoo: Spraypainted with red anti-zoo slogans, windows scratched. Djurens Hämnare / Animal Avengers

APR/95: Stockholm - Solna Korv meat truck: Destroyed by fire. Djurens Hämnare / Animal Avengers

APR 4/95: Gothenburg - Hot dog bar: Totally destroyed by explosion caused by either arson or a bomb. No group has claimed responsibility, but according to the Djurens Hämnare press officer, "I think it is animal liberationists involved".

APR 10/95: Stockholm - Meat shop: Spraypainted. Djurens Befrielse Front (D.B.F.) / A.L.F.

USA

no date: Red paint sprayed on thousands of dollars of fur coats while they were being worn by "their cruel and ignorant 'owners'". A.L.F.

FEB/94: Madison, Wisconsin - Herschlender's Furs "Fur Her"

billboard: Paintbombed; local papers reported $11,000 damage (!); the sign was permanently removed. Savidusky's Furs: Windows smashed. A.L.F.

APR/94: Madison, Wisconsin - Taxidermist: Windows smashed on three occasions. A.L.F.

JUN/94: San Francisco, California - Several businesses which sell live lobster: Attacked. Crustacean Liberation Front (C.L.F.)

SUMMER/94: Minneapolis, Minnesota - KFC: Walls spraypainted with "ALF", "Meat is Murder", other slogans; locks glued. Fish restaurant: Spraypainted
with "stop raping the oceans"; locks glued; screen door ripped off.

Butcher shop: Locks glued; "veal is child abuse" and "Meat is Murder" spraypainted. A.L.F.

SUMMER/94: Fond du Lac, Wisconsin - Many downtown restaurants: Spraypainted with vegan slogans. A.L.F.

MID-OCT/94: Pleasant View, Tennessee - McEllis fur farm: Cages holding 20-25 foxes opened so the animals could escape. A.L.F.

OCT 17/94: Salt Lake County, Utah - Honey Baked Hams: Three windows worth $500 smashed. Vegan Revolution

OCT 18/95: Sebastopol, CA - Work place of Jose LaCalle, chinchilla rancher and forensic psychologist currently facing charges of killing chinchillas with genital electrocution spraybombed with anti-fur slogans.

OCT 26/94: Salt Lake County, Utah -- Honey Baked Hams: Hit again. Meier's Meat Market: Windows smashed; note left said "Murderers. Next time it
won't be windows...." Vegan Revolution

OCT 31/94: Dover, New Jersey - Farm Fresh Meats: delivery trucks damaged. A.L.F.

OCT-NOV 94: West Valley City, Utah - Jordan Meat Company: Pipe bomb thrown through window. Approximately $1,500 damages. Vegan Revolution

NOV/94: Olney, Maryland - Kentucky Fried Chicken: Spraypainted; windows smashed out. A.L.F.

NOV/94: New York City, New York - Fur salon: Large steel garbage can tossed through front picture window. A.L.F.

NOV/94: Spokane, Washington - Exclusifurs: Painted. Paint Panthers

NOV/94: Seattle, Washington - Kentucky Fried Chicken: Trashed. A.L.F.

NOV/94: Washington, DC - Fur store: Window shot out. A.L.F.

NOV/94: Maryland - Best Kept Secrets: Fake blood sprayed on thousands of dollars worth of fur coats. A.L.F.

NOV 7/95: Memphis, Tennessee - New location of Jean Benham Furs: Firebombed before it opened. The BATF investigated, questioning nearby shop owners and trying to question at least one local activist, who refused to speak to them. It appears that the investigation has gone nowhere, but the fur store is now open for business. A.L.F.

NOV 17/94: San Francisco, California - Robert's Furs: Hit; other unspecified actions. Berkeley's Milk Board: Paint bombed. A.L.F.

NOV 29/94: Dayton, Ohio - Lazurus Department store: Delivery truck spraypainted with anti-fur slogans. A.L.F.

LATE NOV/94: Mankato, Minnesota - Fur store: "Fur is Dead" spraypainted. A.L.F.

NOV-DEC/94: location not specified - Local grocery store: Rodent glue traps, UPC re-order tags for the traps damaged and thrown in in-store garbage cans. Result: store no longer sells devices. A.L.F.

EARLY DEC/94: Portland, Oregon - Numerous fast food restaurants: Vandalized, spraypainted with animal lib slogans.

DEC/94: Maryland - Used clothing store: Fur coats spraypainted. A.L.F.

DEC/94: Maryland - Best Kept Secrets: Hundreds dollars of furs splattered with fake blood. Hit #2. A.L.F.

DEC/94: Berkeley, CA - Clothing store: Gum in fur trims; fur hats torn. A.L.F. Golden Gate Unit

DEC/94: location unspecified - "Giant" grocery chain: Large number of trucks with meat advertisements spray painted with "Meat is Murder", "Meat Kills,", other anti-meat slogans. A.L.F.

DEC/94: location unspecified - Large fur store: Bomb threat.

DEC/94: Colorado - Egg farm: One hen liberated from abandoned wing of farm, and subsequently rehomed. Publicly done action, resulting in a trespassing charge.

DEC 2/94: Bloomington, Indiana - Lazurus department store delivery truck: Anti-fur slogans painted; windows smashed. A.L.F.

DEC 2/94: Indianapolis, Indiana - Lazurus department store: Slogans painted, windows broken. A.L.F.

DEC 16/94: Berkeley, California - Northwest Animal Research Facility: Hit with six large paint bombs. A.L.F.

DEC 23/94: San Francisco, California - Roberts Furs: Locks glued. A.L.F. Stockton Unit

DEC 23/94: San Francisco, California - Home Fine Sausage: Locks glued; paint bombed. A.L.F. Stockton Unit

DEC 24/94: Memphis, Tennessee - Tandy Leather: Windows smashed. A.L.F.

DEC 25/94: Oakland, California - Barney's Gourmet Hamburgers: Front lock glued. A.L.F. Golden Gate Unit

DEC/94 - JAN/95: outside Philadelphia, Pennsylvania - Numerous meat industry ads: Paint enamel used to paint anti-meat/ environmental slogans.

DEC/94 - JAN/95: outside Philadelphia, Pennsylvania - Eight billboards: Altered.

LATE 1994 OR EARLY 1995: San Francisco, California - Herbert's Furs: "Fur Scum" burnt into glass front door with acid, during their going out of business sale. A.L.F.

EARLY 1995: Salt Lake City, UT - Burger King, KFC, Leather Factory, Main Street Poultry, H and D Food Services, Consolidated Field Sports Taxidermy: Ball bearings shot through windows. A.L.F.

JAN 15/95: San Francisco, California - Herberts Furs: Locks glued, "FUR SCUM": etched on glass door. A.L.F. Stockton Unit
JAN 15/95: San Francisco, California - Home Fine Sausage: Locks glued. A.L.F. Stockton Unit

JAN 21/95: Virginia Beach, Virginia - Lowenthal Furs: Slogans painted. A.L.F.

JAN 28/95: Virginia Beach, Virginia - Central Meats and Packing: Unspecified damage. A.L.F.

JAN 30/95: Virginia Beach, Virginia - Central Meats and Packing: Vehicle windows smashed; slogans painted on vehicles and main building; central cooling system destroyed; truck tires slashed. Estimated $4000 damage. "We won't stop until the senseless slaughtering of animals is stopped." A.L.F.

FEB 1/95: Dover, New Jersey - Farm Fresh Meats: 10 tires on delivery trucks slashed, slogans painted on trucks and trailer; compressor damaged Total of $2100 damage. Hit #2. A.L.F.

FEB 13/95: Minneapolis, Minnesota - Ribnick Furs: Every first-floor window smashed. Ambassador Sausage: Every sign spraypainted; locks glued. A.L.F.

FEB 16/95: San Francisco, California - Robert's Furs: Paint bombed. Hit #2. A.L.F. Stockton Unit

FEB 27/95: San Francisco, California - Robert's Furs: Door etched. Hit #3. A.L.F. Stockton Unit

MAR/95: Eden Prairie, Minneapolis - Communications Marketing (publisher of Fur Rancher): Locks glued. A.L.F.

MAR/95: Indianapolis, Indiana - Kinkaid's Meat Market: Windows broken, locks glued, slogans painted. A.L.F.

MAR/95: Winnebago County Courthouse, Illinois - Richard Ramos: Chased out of courthouse by several AR activists. In November 1994, Ramos and two other men were arrested in Rockton, Illinois for killing and then decapitating a poodle for "entertainment". According to one animal rights activist, Ramos' court appearance was "one of those scenes you might remember for the rest of your life. Richard Ramos, big, bad poodle slayer, being chased out of the Winnebago County Courthouse by several female members of the Chicago Animal Rights Coalition (CHARC). 'Coward, you coward' the women yelled, as Ramos and his attorney fled for parts unknown. Both print and television media recorded the event. We can only hope the killer wasn't too badly scared."

MAR 8/95: Salt Lake City, Utah - Egg Products: Trucks painted with slogans. A.L.F.

MAR 13/95: Minneapolis, Minnesota - Crown of MN, Inc (fur ranch supplier): "Fur Trade, Death Trade" spraypainted; locks glued. Ambassador Sausage: Rock thrown through glass front door; hit #2. A.L.F.

MAR 13/95: St. Paul, Minnesota - MidAmerica Seafood: Windows etched, locks glued. A.L.F.

APR/95: Washington, DC - Miller's Furs: Paint bombed. A.L.F.

APR 2/95: Indianapolis, Indiana - Kinkaid's Meat Market: Windows smashed, locks glued, slogans painted. Hit #2. A.L.F.

APR 5/95: Washington, DC - Capitol Building: A dozen costumed animal liberation activists dressed as elephants, mice, and zebras ran past a phalanx of policemen guarding a circus performance organized by congressional Republicans. Half the activists leaped a police barricade, heading for the trailer holding "King Tusk" and other circus elephants. All were wrestled to the ground and carried away handcuffed. U.S. Capitol police said 18 were arrested, charged with unlawful entry and obstructing passage on Capitol grounds.

APR 11/95: Virginia Beach, Virginia - Lowenthals Furs: Windows smashed. Central Meats and Packing: Windows smashed, slogans painted. A.L.F.

APR 27/95: Virginia Beach, Virginia - Lowenthal's Furs: Windows smashed. Hit #2. A.L.F.

APR 28/95: Minneapolis, Minnesota - George Garden International Circus/Minneapolis Shrine Circus: Two semi-trailer trucks paint-bombed, front windows smashed. Crown of MN, Inc. (fur ranch supplier): paint-bombed; hit #2. Simek's Meat: Billboard paint-bombed. A.L.F.

MAY 1/95: Minneapolis, Minnesota - Brotherson's Meats: Locks glued; "death" spraypainted on front and back of building. Johnson Meat Company: Locks glued; "murder" spraypainted on front window Finer Meat Company: Locks glued; "ALF", "death" spraypainted on front window. Ribnick Furs: Locks glued; "scum", "murder", "ALF" spraypainted on front windows; hit #2. A.L.F.

MAY 21/95: Syracuse, New York - Liehs & Steigerwald Meats: Windows shot out; A.L.F. slogans painted. Honeybaked Hams: Windows shot out: A.L.F. slogans painted all over store; paint splattered on windows.
Eastern Milk Producers: A.L.F. slogans painted, front door windows shot out, air conditioning system sabotaged. A.L.F.

JUN 1/95: Syracuse, New York - Sugar Mountain Leather: Front window shot out; locks glued; A.L.F./Vegans Against Animal Abuse slogans painted. Dairy Queen: A.L.F./V3A slogans painted on all sides of building; several windows etched; several windows shot out. "The liberation crusade has begun in Syracuse. More to come..." (from communique) A.L.F. V3A (Vegans Against Animal Abuse) Cell.

"To Inflict Economic Damage on Those Who Profit From the Suffering and Exploitation of Animals -
Don't Wait to Act"
- from Minneapolis A.L.F. communique

BUSY IN NEW YORK

(more 1994 actions listed in Underground #1 and #2)

MAR/94: Rochester, New York -- Rodeo: Truck windows smashed; trucks painted. A.L.F.

MAY 1/94: Rochester, New York -- Hunting Store: Windows smashed.
A.L.F.

MAY 1/94: Rochester, New York -- Lipsitz Furs: Windows smashed. A.L.F.

MAY 2/94: Rochester, New York -- Federal Meats: Locks glued; windows smashed; slogans painted. A.L.F.

MAY 4/94: Rochester, New York -- Federal Meats: Paint damage. Hit #2. A.L.F.

NOV/94: Henrietta, New York -- Conti Packing Company (meat packing plant): Windows smashed; buildings and vehicles graffitied. A.L.F., Rochester cell

NOV 30/94: Brighton, New York -- Berman's Fur Fashion: "Fur is Dead" and "Stop or be Stopped" written in black paint on building walls; streaks of red paint poured along ground; window smashed with a brick; "A.L.F." etched into windows. A.L.F., Rochester cell

DEC 2/94: Henrietta, New York -- Conti Packing Company (meat packing plant): Windows of seven trucks and three trailers smashed; $5,000+ damage. "Meat is murder", "Veggie power", "Stop or Be Stopped", "This is Just a Warning" painted in green on trucks Firebombed; slogans painted. A.L.F.

DEC 22/94: Mendon, New York -- Hillcrest Turkey Products: Windshields of two trucks smashed; sugar poured into both gasoline tanks; "Meat is murder", "We're going to come back to get you and your turkeys" painted on trucks and sides of building. $35,000 damage. A.L.F., Rochester cell

DEC 22/94: Brighton, New York -- Berman's Fur Fashion: Brick thrown through window. Fur coat inside damaged by glass from smashed window. $1000 damage. Hit #2. A.L.F., Rochester cell

JAN 12/95: Syracuse, New York -- NY Eastern Milk Producers: Slogans painted. A.L.F.

JAN 16/95: Syracuse, New York -- Georgios Furs: Paint bombed. A.L.F.

JAN 16/95: Syracuse, New York -- Mazzye's Meats: Windows smashed.
A.L.F.

mid-Jan/95: Henrietta, New York -- Conti Packing Company (meat packing plant): Two Mack trucks used to deliver meat set on fire; interior of truck cabs heavily damaged. "We're just getting warmed up" spraypainted on trailer. Hit #2. A.L.F., Rochester cell

FEB 23/95: Syracuse, New York -- Georgio's Furs: Paint bombed, slogans painted. A.L.F.

APR 14/95: Syracuse, New York -- Oneanta Beef Company: Incendiary devices ignited. $6000 damage. A.L.F.

APR 27/95: Rochester, New York -- TD Cohn Meat Packing Plant: The FBI is currently investigating the actions near Rochester and Syracuse, and have threatened at least one activist with a subpoena. At this point we do not know if a grand jury has been convened. Stay tuned for more details.

ANIMAL LIBERATION FRONT RELEASES 500 PIGEONS DESTINED FOR HEGINS PIGEON SHOOT

(From a Fund For Animals press release) On the morning of Monday, August 28, The Fund for Animals received an anonymous telephone call from someone claiming to be a member of the Animal Liberation Front. The caller indicated that, late last night, ALF activists liberated 500 pigeons from Mike's Feed Barn, on Middle Road, in Weishample, Pennsylvania (in Schuylkill County, only a few miles from Hegins).

The caller said that these 500 birds were destined for the Hegins pigeon shoot on Labor Day. The caller described ALF activists cutting the locks on the barn, stealing six crates from the property, working late into the night to place the birds into crates one by one, and spray painting "ALF" on the barn. The activists reportedly released the birds in a park where hunting is not allowed.

According to the anonymous caller, "We have been waiting all year for someone to stop the shoot, but these 500 birds had no more time to wait."

Says Heidi Prescott, National Director of The Fund for Animals, "We, too, have been waiting all year for someone to stop the insidious Hegins pigeon shoot. The State Legislature, the State Police, Governor Ridge, and the Courts have all failed to end this cruelty. It is nice to see that someone in Pennsylvania has some guts."

Adds Cleveland Amory, President of The Fund and best-selling author, "The Fund for Animals does not encourage anyone to break the law. But when I think of 500 birds flying free, instead of being stuffed in tiny boxes and tortured for fun, it puts a big smile on my face."

The Hegins pigeon shoot is the world's largest and most gruesome live bird shooting contest. Of the 5,000 birds shot each year, investigators from The Fund have documented that approximately 70 percent of the birds are not killed immediately, but wounded. Young children collect crippled birds, ripping off their heads, stomping on them, or throwing them into barrels to suffocate.

On Labor Day at the Hegins pigeon shoot, The Fund for Animals will organize a massive bird rescue effort with veterinarians, wildlife rehabilitators, and a mobile MASH unit on hand to treat wounded birds. Last year, Fund volunteers rescued over 300 birds from the pigeon shoot, treated them with medical care, and transported them to various rehabilitation facilities.

TAKING DIRECT ACTION AGAINST McDONALD'S

BELGIUM

NOV 9/94: Gent - Building site of new McDonald_s branch: Smashed up. Property of the contracting firm building the new branch was also destroyed. Commando No Pain for Gain

CANADA

APR 22/95: Guelph, Ontario - McDonald's: Hundreds of "grease" stickers glued on drive-thru and main building; posters glued on building. Posters read "Happy Birthday McDonald's?"; golden arch with "McCancer"; "40 years of environmental damage, human rights abuses, rainforest destruction and cruelty to animals. Chew on that with your next big mac"; "McDonald's: You deserve a BRICK today".

CZECH REPUBLIC

MAY 1/95: Prague - 200 people turned out for an anti-McDonald's demo; over $15,000 of damage was caused in battles with the police when bricks and paint were thrown. Two McDonald's windows were smashed.

DENMARK

JAN 1/95: Copenhagen - McDonald's branch: Broken into and smashed up by hundreds of "left wing anarchists" because it "symbolises capitalism and money". Furniture was ripped out and burnt on a bonfire.

FINLAND

JAN 28/95: Tampere - McDonald's branch: Slogans painted, sign smashed. Eläinten Vapautus Rintama (E.V.R.) / A.L.F.

JAN 30/95: Vantaa - McDonald's branch: At least 20 slogans spraypainted, 5 windows smashed. Eläinten Vapautus Rintama (E.V.R.) / A.L.F.

EARLY FEB/95: Kerava - McDonald's branch: Slogans spraypainted.

FEB 14/95: Helsinki - McDonald's branch: Slogans spraypainted. Eläinten Vapautus Rintama (E.V.R.) / A.L.F.

FEB 18/95: Vantaa - McDonald's branch: "Meat is murder", "A.L.F." spraypainted on windows; 4 large windows smashed.

FEB 25/95: Helsinki - McDonald's branch: Smashed window reported.

MAR 30/95: Vantaa - McDonald's branch: Walls spraypainted, 17 windows smashed. Another McDonald's branch: Walls, garbage cans spraypainted; 9 windows smashed. Eläinten Vapautus Rintama (E.V.R.) / A.L.F.

FRANCE

JUL 9/94: North Paris - Branch in Massy: 67 workers pulled a surprise strike, closing the store down during its busiest period. They were demanding "respect of their rights to engage in union activity, paid vacations, the right to choose their own delegates and recognition of their personal needs." Less than 24 hours after the strike an agreement was signed between management and the General Confederation of Workers (CGT) union representing the workers. A few days later McDonald's workers in the town of Ulis walked out. In Nantes, west France, McDonald's workers prepared a week of action with CGT trade unionists.

GERMANY

SEP 19/94: New Ulm - Not-yet-opened McDrive at McDonald's branch: 24 window panes damaged with acid shortly before the opening; "Revenge for every murdered animal", "McMurder" written on walls. Estimated 30,000 DM damages. The Organization of Animal Liberators acted as press officers for the activists responsible. In the press statement points were made about the connections of animal oppression, environmental destruction and use of animal feed out of the "Third World". Autonomous Animal Protectors

MEXICO

NOV 9/94: Mexico City - McDonald's branch: 40 masked activists caused considerable damage. The action took place during a protest against a ballot that would cut social benefits for immigrants in California, as activists saw McDonald's as "a symbol of US mperialism".

NEW ZEALAND

AUG/94: Christchurch - McDonald's branch: Paintbombed. A.L.F.

SWEDEN

APR 15/95: all over Sweden - Various McDonald's branches: Toilets blocked, slogans painted, arsons, non-specified minor damage. Actions done to mark McDonald's 50th birthday.

SWITZERLAND

JAN 21/95: Zürich - Several McDonald's branches: Toilets blocked with cement.

THE NETHERLANDS

Oct 15/94: Groningen - McDonald's branch: Windows smashed, slogans painted as an act of solidarity with the McLibel Two in England. Commando Helen Steel

USA

SUMMER/94: Minneapolis, Minnesota - McDonald's branch: Spraypainted with "McDeath", other slogans; locks glued. A.L.F.

DEC/94: Gaithersburg, Maryland - McDonald's branch: Extensively spray-painted; windows smashed out. A.L.F.

Police and anti-McDonald's activists battle in Prague

DEC 6/94: Madison, Wisconsin - McDonald's branch: Paintbombed. A.L.F.

DEC/94 - JAN/95: outside Philadelphia, Pennsylvania - McDonald's branch: "Meat is Murder" painted on two separate occasions.

MAR/95: Minneapolis, Minnesota - McDonald's branch: Locks glued. A.L.F.

APR 13/95: Syracuse, New York - McDonald's billboard: Slogans painted. A.L.F.

MAY 1/95: Minneapolis, Minnesota - McDonald's drive-through: Menu spraypainted with "death". A.L.F.

Other actions against McDonald's and in solidarity of Helen Steel and David Morris (the McLibel Two) have been reported in Aotearoa (New Zealand), Australia, Belgium, Canada, Croatia, the Czech Republic, Denmark, France, Germany, Hong Kong, Hungary,

FINISHING OFF THE FUR INDUSTRY

Let me begin by listing the fur store closings we know of for the end of 1994.

Thomas McElroy 3 stores in Chicago, IL
Himmel Furs in Chicago, IL
Salvator Trippy Furs in Seattle, WA
Jack Lewis Furs in Memphis, TN
Fur Fashions of Memphis in Memphis, TN
Weinsteins Fur Faire in Long Island, NY
Yorkman Furs in Minneapolis, MN
unnamed location in Reno, NV
unnamed location in Boston, MA

Seems great doesn't it? Well, here's a list of stores that opened this Winter or will open soon.

Olympus Furs in Indianapolis, IN
Maxmillian Furs at Bloomingdales in Miami, FL
Saks 6 new salons, bringing them up to 38 salons
Henig Furs about 6 new stores, bringing them up to 12 or 13locations
Fur Vault 1 new store, bringing them up to 5 stores
Burlington Coat Factories 8 new operations, meaning fur will be in 88 of their 256 locations
Modas Longoria 3 new locations, in Julian Reed stores across Texas

The Fur Information Council of America (FICA) reports sales increases in the last 2 years. While their figures are debatable, it is not debatable that more animals died at the hands of the fur trade in 1994 than in years previous. Furriers killed 22 million minks in 1993 and 28 million in 1994. They killed 2.5 million foxes in 1993 and 3.1 million in 1994 (90% of all fox fur is going to fur trimmed coats). Fur farmers are making money again as pelts from all commonly ranch raised species are now bringing in enough cashto cover costs and then some. Why is this happening? Probably because too many groups have become complacent, thinking that we have won this battle. It's time for an all out campaign against the fur trade with tons of action on all fronts.

This is an industry that can be beat. A victory would means millions and millions of lives saved, tons of momentum and energy for the animal liberation movement, increased credibility in the public's eye, and a smaller base of opposition as an industry which has fought us harder than any other would have been eliminated.

The A.L.F. can defeat the fur industry. Remember all of the lab raids and animal liberations that took place in the eighties? Imagine if the same amount of energy and enthusiasm was put into attacking fur farms in the nineties. I think that the fur industrywould be crushed. All fur animal species, except chinchilla, can bereleased into the wild and survive. They disperse quickly andtravel many miles in a single day so there is no need to fear a huge ecological imbalance as a result of a massive mink liberation.

Malecky Mink Ranch was torched in Dec. 1992. The fur farm industry tried to decline that this was an A.L.F. action for quite some time. Eventually they could no longer hide from the truth as pieces of an incendiary device were found. Presumably they wanted to covethis up so that other mink ranchers wouldn't be scared out of the business. If scores of fur farms were raided then the industry would be devastated and many would stop raising fur animals for fear of losing their entire investment. Remember, most fur farmers do this part time and are not solely dependent on mink and fox to make a living. Therefore they are much easier to push out of business as opposed to a chicken farmer, etc.

If A.L.F. cells were to raid fur farms, one thing should beremembered. The animals aren't old enough to release until after May. Also, they must be liberated before late October because otherwise Winter will have set in and they won't have time to learn how to efficiently hunt for food as most prey species will now be more difficult to catch.

National Fur Foods in New Holstein, WI is doing major research to make fur farming more profitable. The same is true for Wildlife Pharmaceutical in Fort Collins, CO. I'm surprised that these twocompanies haven't been targeted yet. The A.L.F. completely shut down the mink research center at Oregon State University and crippled several other fur animal research centers. National FurFoods could be the strongest remaining.

On the retail level, I think all activist groups should really hammer the department stores that still sell fur. I would bet that they sell as much, if not more fur, than regular retail furriers. This is because they have more walk-in traffic, a better advertising budget, and their own charge accounts. Also, they can be forced to get rid of fur because they aren't solely dependent on the sale of such items. The thing to remember is that one or twospaced out actions aren't enough. Persistence is the key!

The Coalition to Abolish the Fur Trade, PO Box 40641, Memphis, TN 38174, has a list of fur farms which they sent out to anyone. For yours and their protection, claim you need it for research andnvestigations. Then, pass the lists around to everyone. Let's not let them hide these hellholes anymore! I really believe that the A.L.F. can finish the furriers off. The body count is rising in the fur concentration camps. Are we going to lose ground and then the whole battle, or are w going to fight harder than ever and liberate every last animal?

TOTAL LIBERATION
anonymous

USING DIRECT ACTION EFFECTIVELY AGAINST THE FUR TRADE

I would like to discuss ways in which DA (direct action) can be effectively used against the fur trade. I will discuss live animal liberations first. Basically, there are three ranch-raised fuanimals: mink, fox, and chinchilla. Mink and fox are genetically wild and will survive when released into the woods. Minks cantravel five miles a day while fox can travel twelve. They disperse quickly so there should be no worry that a habitat will be wrecked by a massive release of fur farm animals.

Mink and fox do bite so heavy gloves are a necessity. They can be grabbed and dropped on the other side of the fence. Don't ever put them into bags together as many A.L.F. cells do when dealing with other animals. These particular species are very likely to start fighting when piled on top of each other. One idea is to cut holes in the fence around the compound and then open all the cages so that the animals can find their own way out. Plenty of escaperoutes should be provided. None should lead the animals towards a busy road. Also, release type actions should take place between late May and late October. If before then, the animals will be too young and if after this period, there may not be enough food available.

The chinchilla is a small herbivore that is native to the Andes mountains in South America. They can't be released into the wild and if liberated, should be given good homes. There are several things that should be taken into consideration concerning post-raidchinchilla care. An important one is that they have a hard time tolerating extremes above 80 degrees F. If you should liberate chinchillas, please make sure that the person providing their newhome has been educated about their special needs. Chinchilla rare. Boks are available at the book store and library.

Fur farms can still be hit even if a live liberation is not possible at that time. In October through December, the pelting stock (those about to be killed) will be the same size as the breeding stock (those kept to produce more animals). If all of the animals are released into the compound then the fur farmer won't know which are the breeders and which are the pelters. He will have to pelt them all out and spend thousands of dollars on new breeding stock. This is so annoying that sometimes they just give up for good. If anyone uses this tactic, they should make sure every animal cage is opened as it is hard for us to know which shed contains breeders and which doesn't. If a couple sheds are left untouched, then you might miss the breeding stock completely and the purpose of the hit will not have been achieved.

Non-toxic dyes can be sprayed on the animals' backs to ruin the economic value of their pelt. This is better than nothing, but as with the last described tactic, the animals will still be killed. The processing room and the feed storage barns can be hit as well. Malecky Mink Ranch in Yamhill, OR was put out of business when theA.L.F. burned down their processing barn. Arson should only be usedwhen it can be guaranteed that the fire will not spread to thesheds the animals are in.

Fur farmers have specialized tractors that dispense feed on top of the cages. These vehicles can be trashed in a number of ways. One easy one is to buy a bottle of muriatic acid at the hardware store. This costs about three dollars for one or two gallons. Simply pour it all over the engine and leave.

Your state department of agriculture may have a list of fur farms in your state. You can call and ask and if they ask questions sayyou're a potential fur farmer looking for breeding stock. It may be wiser to contact the Coalition to Abolish the Fur Trade. They have a small fur farm list, and while their list may not be complete, at least they won't tell who ordered the lists from them. For security purposes, claim you need the list for research and investigations. Their address is: PO Box 40641, Memphis, TN, 38174, USA. Try and send $1 to cover postage and printing.

Economic sabotage can also be employed. This simply involves smashing fur shops' windows, squirting super glue into the locks, spray painting, filling bell peppers or Christmas ornaments with paint and "paint bombing" the building, etc. To be effective, a place should be hit repeatedly. Every hit causes security to increase so go for maximum destruction.

Send press releases about fur hits to the Coalition to Abolish the Fur Trade [and the NA-ALFSG, of course!-ed].

It's past time to end the fur trade for good. Let's take to thestreets and stop the killing. Action speaks louder than words.

NEW HUNT SAB POSSIBILITY?

Russ Mason, Dale Nolte, and Gisela Epple of the Denver Wildlife Research Center's Monell Field Station have been studying theeffects of coyote urine. Mountain beavers, deer, and other mammalian herbivores are bothered by certain fractions within the urine. Recent experiments have shown that when roots are immersed, plants will translocate aversive substances. Analytical chemistry is being utilized to uncover the identity of thetranslocated fractions. If the fractions can be identified, it may be possible to develop an effective, biologically-based, systemic repellent for mammalian herbivores.

- posted to ar-news Jan 23/95; coyote urine info originally from "The Probe", Dec/92, Issue 128

The poster wrote, *"Now I don't know how or where they get the coyote pee, BUT this sounds like it has some potential. If we can follow this development, we may be able to sabotage hunts, without even being there-hence avoiding that new damned 'Hunter Harrassment' law."*

COMBINING TACTICS TO STOP THE VIVISECTORS: A REPORT OF SORTS FROM ENGLAND

Just writing to inform you about a protest I heard about in England. Apparently there was a vivisection conference that wasgoing to go on, but the animal rights groups found out about it as well as the A.L.F.

Before the conference happened the hotel was notified of whatvivisectors are and what evil things they do by concerned peoplewho phoned them up. These people also demanded that the hotel stop letting such nazis hold conferences there beginning now or they would boycott their hotels nation-wide. This gave the hotel ample time to pull out, but they continued to rationalize their involvement in the conference.

Activists then called and made many bogus reservations at the hotel to try and cause the hotel economic hardship or at least frustrate them in trying to determine between the real reservations and the fake ones.

A few days before the conference began, the A.L.F. spraypainted "go home vivisectors" and similar slogans on all major roadways heading toward the hotel, especially the one from the airport as most of them flew in. Posters were also hung all over the city regarding vivisection and the evil conference that was to come.

The day the vivisectors arrived, they were greeted by a loud bunch of protesters who had numerous banners telling the vivisectors how evil they are and that they should feel free to leave at once. One protester with a megaphone quite vehemently attacked all the vivisectors as they tried to enter the building by telling them exactly what she thought of them. Almost 100 of the vivisectors, witnessing the many sights, took the activists up on their offers and, at great cost, whent home. A great victory.

The activists continued to be loud once the convention had started by banging on drums and chanting. They especially rose their voices loudly when the police asked them to quiet down asthe vivisectors could not hear the people giving the speeches.

The A.L.F. was also busy. They had dumped lots of red food coloring and laundry liquid in the hotel's fountains, sprayed slogans on the side of the hotel, and dumped motor oil in their pool. All of this was to put economic pressure on the hotel to not hold such murderous conventions now or ever again as well asput the vivisectors on edge. It worked tremendously well. Now the hotel was claiming that they had thought the conference was on animal welfare, and that they were ashamed that they had ever let them hold a vivisection conference there.

At lunch, some vivisectors wanted to leave the hotel to grab a bite to eat. Protestors followed them around and leafletted everyone around them and told them what the vivisectors did. If the vivisector went into a store, some would leaflet outside the store while others would go inside and tell everyone who that peson was and what they did. Pretty soon, no more of the vivisectors left the hotel.

Some activists managed to get inside the convention and cause problems. Once when the vivisectors were sitting down to eat, an activist who had been waiting their table threw the food, told them what she thought of vivisectors in general, and then what she thought of them in particular and stormed out of the place At another conference, well dressed activists who had been hiding out in bathrooms stormed into the dining hall, overturned tables and exited before anyone else could catch them. Other activistsreserved one room so they could have access inside of the hotel for further disruptions.

Activists willing to get arrested would enter the conference rooms, and disrupt the speeches by starting arguments about animal rights. After three or four of these, the vivisectors' nerves were shot and morale amongst them was low.

These actions have had far reaching effects on vivisection conferences in England. Many of them have been cancelled when thevivisectors have found out that animal rights activists wereaware of when and where they are going to take place. Likewise, numerous hotels and even cities refuse to let the conference take place in their borders as activists send them news cuttings of what happened at this past conference and they quickly pull out.It cost the city almost 100 pounds (approx. $200-ed) to police the week long conference, and the hotel suffered financially as well. Hopefully vivisectors soon will no longer be able to meetand communicate better ways to exploit animals and to fight those of us who stand up for animals.

Ann Nonamous
originally printed in "Dressed in Black" #3

"Well! No wonder! ... Look who's been loose the whole evening!"

The following is a review of attacks against animal activists over the last year.

CZECH REPUBLIC

DEC 7/94: Moravian city of Brno: a McDonald's asssistant manager sprayed tear gas in a photographer's face during a protest at the opening of the county's seventh McDonald's. After initially denying that the offender was a McDonald's employee, the company issued a formal apology to the Czech Press Agency photographer. The incident occurred when about 30 people, mainly from the environmental group Duha were pushed and carried out of a
McDonald's restaurant where they had been eating vegetables in a peaceful protest. "Just taking up the space is a form of violence" said McDonald's public relations manager Drahomira Jirakova. The McDonald's employee was asked to pay a small fine but is still working at McDonald's.
For more information, contact: Hnuti Duha Brno, Jakuska nam 7, 602 00 Brno, Czech Republic and Hnuti Duha Plzen, Skolni 309, 330 08 Zruc, Czech Republic.

DEC 17/94: Kingston McDonald's: demonstrators were threatened with having their legs broken by a McDonald's manager - protests continue.

PORTUGAL

Protesters were beaten up and arrested by police after a demonstration outside a Lisbon McDonald's where 80 demonstrators voiced their opposition to the BigMac. Leafletting continues across the country.

USA

During the Mink Producers Convention, an animal liberation activist's wrist was broken when police tried to remove her from handcuffs that she had used to lock herself to a conference area.
- from "U animal-rights group targets hunters", Minnesota Daily, Jan 20 1995

NEW ZEALAND

Date: Tue, 07 Feb 95
Subject: New Zealand protesters board Whaling Ship

On Tuesday Feb 7 in a protest organised by Greenpeace, several people tryed to board a Japanese whaling ship as it made an emergency stop at Wellington Harbour.
The Toshi Maru 18 is one of four catcher ships that kill whales for a factory ship in the Southern whale sanctuary. The reason they can do this is cos they are 'research' whalers . . .

The ship was forced to visit Wellington after one of the crew chopped his finger off. As the ship approached the harbour entrance, the harbour pilot boat sped out to meet it followed by a police boat, and two greenpeace inflatables, and a greenpeace boat carrying a video crew.

The pilot boat met the whaler, transferred the injured 'scientist' and NZ police on board loaded fresh supplies for the whaler. As soon as the pilot boat was clear, the whaler turned and headed out to sea with greenpeace chasing it. As protesters tryed to get onto the ship NZ police stepped on their hands, kicked and hit protesers and threw several overboard. At this stage the whaler was about 20 miles from land and going about 15 knots.

One person was dragged onto the ship, handcuffed and then beaten by a cop. another person suffered a dislocated shoulder as she was pushed off the ship. Eventually the ship was too far from land and Greenpeace turned back. As they returned to shore some dolphins appeared and escorted them back.

The police have denied assaulting anyone although pictures of a cop kicking a person overboard are on the front pages of all the papers here and a TV news helicopter filmed cops dragging a handcuffed man across the deck and throwing people into the sea.

The government is demanding an explanation from the Japanese embassy as the ship was granted permission to transfer the injured sailor to land but not to resupply. The police have also been criticised for helping load the supplies.

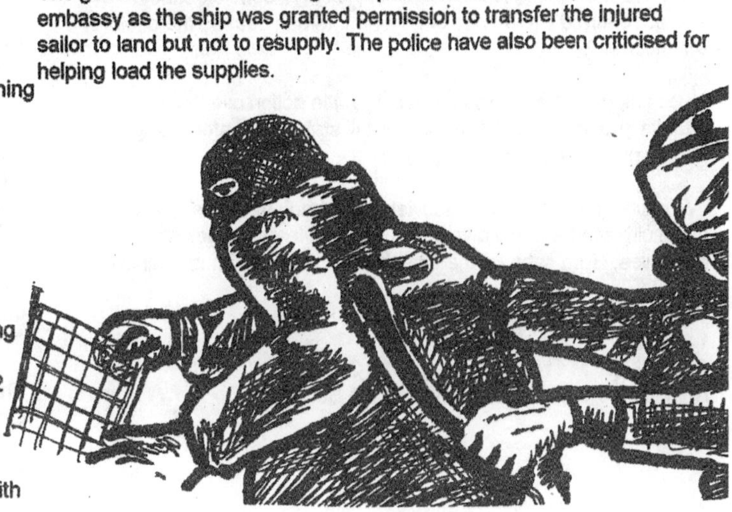

HUNTS: FIND THEM.. SAB THEM!!

Attack on activists house

18th February 95

Late yesterday (18-02-95), just before midnight, the home of John Curtins house was attacked by a group of masked men, armed with sticks and bricks. They smashed all the windows of the house and attempted to break down the door while screaming threats at John who was inside the house with his partner and a number of rescued dogs. failing to gain entry, or to do any harm to John, his partner or the animals they fled before help arrived.

John is a well known ALF activist of many years, having been sent to prison twice, the last time for liberating 89 beagles from a company called Interfauna which breeds for vivisection. He took over as spokesperson for the ALF when Robin Webb the then Press Officer was remanded to prison, and over the past weeks has appeared on TV and been quoted in many papers concerning the Live exports campaign and the ALF in general.

Although unhurt in this attack John fears mostly for the safety of the animals under his protection and arrangements are being made to move him to a safe location, he is to continue as spokesperson for the ALF.

Since the attack on John Curtins home in Liverpool there have been two more 'incidents'.

On the same night as the attack already reported 4 men armed and masked as in the other attack, broke down the 4 doors to get to the flat in Manchester, lived in by Dave Blenkinsop, who is a Hunt saboteur and ex-prisoner. Dave went to prison following the 'riot' which occurred outside the home of Huntsman Ian Summersgill who run over and killed saboteur Mike Hill a few years ago. Although entry to the flat was successful Dave was out and the men left.

Two day later at the home of a number of animal rights activists in Manchester, two men broke into the home and badly beat a number of dogs and a 19 year old female activists who was there alone at the time (other members of the household were at a demo). She was beaten with staves and knuckle dusters and was left concussed and with two fractured ribs and bruising to her face. She was told by the two men that they would kill her if she attended another hunt.

All attackers in the three incidents had Liverpool accents and it is widely believed that they are members of supporters of the Cheshire hunt which is known for its violent attacks on saboteurs and as reported above, one of its ex-huntsman caused the death of a saboteur.

Needless to say the police are making little action over the attacks and have failed to return for full statements after being initially contacted.

We expect no less, animal activists have been treated as second class citizens for many a year and we have learnt to look after ourselves. Hunt sabs on the Cheshire hunt will continue unabated.

The struggle continues.

ALF SG, BCM 1160, London WC1N 3XX
Animal Liberation Frontline Information Service

HUNT THUGS CONVICTED: SABOTEURS CALL FOR CRACKDOWN ON HUNT VIOLENCE

news release 3rd March 1995

Hunt saboteurs in the Northwest applauded the conviction today of two thugs from the Cheshire Foxhunt on charges of violent disorder. The two men, Geoffrey Park, 30, of The Elms, Tushingham, Whitchurch, Shropshire and Anthony Ronald Kirkham, 50, of Ridley Farm, Ridley, Cheshire had been charged after a vicious gang attack on saboteurs on Saturday 11th December 1993 in which their vehicle was wrecked and a woman was savagely beaten up. Both men have a track record of violence against protesters and Kirkham is said to have served prison sentences for grievous bodily harm and attempted murder. They are to be sentenced for this latest attack next Friday.

On the day in question, Cheshire Police had arrested all the occupants of the van, about a dozen saboteurs, "to prevent a breach of the peace", a common tactic in Cheshire when anti-hunt protesters have committed no offence but the police want to "intern" them for the duration of the hunt. It is, of course, completely illegal, but such niceties have never bothered Cheshire Police when it comes to dealing with hunt saboteurs. Astonishingly the police refused to move the saboteurs' vehicle but instead left it parked in the middle of very hostile hunt supporters at Faddiley, near Nantwich, saying they would ensure it was safe. All those arrested were released without charge at the end of the hunting day and returned to the van about 6.15 p.m. to find it had been so badly vandalised it eventually had to be written off, the windscreen had been put through, extensive damage was caused to the side panels and doors, and several tyres were slashed, over =A31,000 worth of damage in total.

Saboteurs rang the AA, but while they were waiting for a truck to come out, the hunt thugs, armed with pickaxe handles and coshes, returned to finished the job. This time the ten-strong gang were able to attack not just the van but also its occupants. A 24-year old woman attempted to run for help but was cornered by the gang, punched to the ground by Kirkham, and then kicked and beaten about the head and body as she lay on the floor helpless. She sustained two black eyes, damaged kidneys, and extensive cuts and bruising to her head and body in the vicious attack. The gang then dragged her back to the van and resumed their attack on the van, jumping on the roof and causing further damage to the exterior. While his friends were occupied in trashing the vehicle, Park climbed inside the van and beat up several of the occupants with a cosh.

Kirkham had already shown his propensity for brutal violence against saboteurs, in particular on Boxing Day 1992, when the Cheshire Beagles met at The Poacher in Bickerton near Kirkham's farm. He beat a woman unconscious with a piece of wood and left her lying unconscious in a stream, where she had to be rescued by her fellow saboteurs, who called an ambulance. Her injuries were so severe she had to be airlifted to hospital by a helicopter yet police refused to arrest Kirkham. When her fellow sabs went to Nantwich police station to make statements identifying Kirkham as the culprit they were themselves arrested. Conveniently, all charges were dropped before the case reached court and no-one was ever prosecuted.

These attacks fit into a disturbing pattern of hunt supporters in Cheshire using extreme violence against protesters, seemingly with impunity, while the police seem interested only in arresting saboteurs on the pretext of minor offences, usually fictitious. The police in Cheshire must now begin a major crackdown on the hunt company called Interfauna which breeds for vivisection. He took over as spokesperson for the ALF when Robin Webb the then Press Officer was remanded to prison, and over the past weeks has appeared on TV and been quoted in many papers concerning the Live exports campaign and the ALF in general.

Although unhurt in this attack John fears mostly for the safety of the animals under his protection and arrangements are being made to move him to a safe location, he is to continue as spokesperson fór the ALF.

Since the attack on John Curtins home in Liverpool there have been two more 'incidents'.

On the same night as the attack already reported 4 men armed and masked as in the other attack, broke down the 4 doors to get to the flat in Manchester, lived in by Dave Blenkinsop, who is a Hunt saboteur and ex-prisoner. Dave went to prison following the 'riot' which occurred outside the home of Huntsman Ian Summersgill who run over and killed saboteur Mike Hill a few years ago. Although entry to the flat was successful Dave was out and the men left.

Two day later at the home of a number of animal rights activists in Manchester, two men broke into the home and badly beat a number of dogs and a 19 year old female activists who was there alone at the time (other members of the household were at a demo). She was beaten with staves and knuckle dusters and was left concussed and with two fractured ribs and bruising to her face. She was told by the two men that they would kill her if she attended another hunt.

All attackers in the three incidents had Liverpool accents and it is widely believed that they are members of supporters of the Cheshire hunt which is known for its violent attacks on saboteurs and as reported above, one of its ex-huntsman caused the death of a saboteur.

Needless to say the police are making little action over the attacks and have failed to return for full statements after being initially contacted.

We expect no less, animal activists have been treated as second class citizens for many a year and we have learnt to look after ourselves. Hunt sabs on the Cheshire hunt will continue unabated.

Animal Liberation Frontline Information Service

From: hsa@gn.apc.org (Hunt Saboteurs Association)

Subject: Hunt Thugs Convicted of Attacks on Sabs

HUNT THUGS CONVICTED: SABOTEURS CALL FOR CRACKDOWN ON HUNT VIOLENCE
news release 3rd March 1995

Hunt saboteurs in the Northwest applauded the conviction today of two thugs from the Cheshire Foxhunt on charges of violent disorder. The two men, Geoffrey Park, 30, of The Elms, Tushingham, Whitchurch, Shropshire and Anthony Ronald Kirkham, 50, of Ridley Farm , Ridley, Cheshire had been charged after a vicious gang attack on saboteurs on Saturday 11th December 1993 in which their vehicle was wrecked and a woman was savagely beaten up. Both men have a track record of violence against protesters and Kirkham is said to have served prison sentences for grievous bodily harm and attempted murder.They are to be sentenced for this latest attack next Friday.

On the day in question, Cheshire Police had arrested all the occupants of the van, about a dozen saboteurs, "to prevent a breach of the peace", a common tactic in Cheshire when anti-hunt protesters have committed no offence but the police want to "intern" them for the duration of the hunt. It is, of course, completely illegal, but such niceties have never bothered Cheshire Police when it comes to dealing with hunt saboteurs. Astonishingly the police refused to move the saboteurs' vehicle but instead left it parked in the middle of very hostile hunt supporters at Faddiley, near Nantwich, saying they would ensure it was safe. All those arrested were released without charge at the end of thehunting day and returned to the van about 6.15 p.m. to find it had been so badly vandalised it eventually had to be written off, the windscreen had been put through, extensive damage was caused to the side panels and doors, and several tyres were slashed, over =A31,000 worth of damage in total.

Saboteurs rang the AA, but while they were waiting for a truck to come out, the hunt thugs, armed with pickaxe handles and coshes, returned to finished the job. This time the ten-strong gang wereable to attack not just the van but also its occupants. A 24-year old woman attempted to run for help but was cornered by the gang, punched to the ground by Kirkham, and then kicked and beaten about the head and body as she lay on the floor helpless. She sustained two black eyes, damaged kidneys, and extensive cuts and bruising to her head and body in the vicious attack. The gang then dragged her back to the van and resumed their attack on the van, jumping on the roof and causing further damage to the exterior. While his friendswere occupied in trashing the vehicle, Park climbed inside the vanand beat up several of the occupants with a cosh.

Kirkham had already shown his propensity for brutal violence against saboteurs, in particular on Boxing Day 1992, when the Cheshire Beagles met at The Poacher in Bickerton near Kirkham's farm. He beat a woman unconscious with a piece of wood and left her lying unconscious in a stream, where she had to be rescued by her fellow saboteurs, who called an ambulance. Her injuries were so severe she had to be airlifted to hospital by a helicopter yet police refused to arrest Kirkham. When her fellow sabs went to Nantwich police station to make statements identifying Kirkham as the culprit they were themselves arrested. Conveniently, all charges were dropped before the case reached court and no-one was ever prosecuted.

These attacks fit into a disturbing pattern of hunt supporters in Cheshire using extreme violence against protesters, seemingly with impunity, while the police seem interested only in arresting saboteurs on the pretext of minor offences, usually fictitious. The police in Cheshire must now begin a major crackdown on the hunt thugs who think they can have a free hand in attacking protesters.

CHESHIRE HUNTS: A CULTURE OF VIOLENCE

The attack on the 12th December was by no means an isolated incident. Other similar attacks around that time include:

January 30th 1993 Cheshire Foxhounds: an ITV camera crew filmed Park and Kirkham punching a sab to the ground and beating him up. The police took no action over the attack.

In the first six weeks of the cubbing season of 1993, at least one sab was taken to hospital by ambulance every week as a result of being beaten up by hunt thugs.

October 23rd 1993 Cheshire Foxhounds: a sab required six stitches to a head wound after being beaten around the head by a hunt rider with the bone handle of his riding whip.

October 30th 1993 North Staffs Foxhounds: Park and Kirkham turned up at the hunt meet at Knighton near Worre, Staffs, and beat up aman who required seven stitches to a head wound after a ferocious beating with baseball bats.

November 2nd 1993 Cheshire Foxhounds: a sab required 8 stitches to a head wound after being attacked by fifteen men with baseball bats.

Thurs March (22) 95
ALF SG (UK) Raided

According to SG (UK) co-ordinators, "Three coppers turned up while I was at University, dragged my partner out of work and searched our house. the warrant was for 'inciting materials and items which could be used to make incendiaries or explosives'.

They left after three and half hours with a pile of letters, newsletters, press cuttings and the computer! We were not the only ones to be done. They raided three addresses the day before looking for the editor of Green Anarchist magazine (which is very pro-ALF and advertises 'Into the 90's and 'interviews'). They found him on the third attempt took a pile of stuff and arrested and charged him with inciting others to cause damage by fire. He's out on policebail so it can't be that serious."

Green Anarchist Magazine Raided by Police

Date: Thu, 11 May 1995

In an act of repression worthy of East Germany, police believed to be from Hampshire Special Branch raided the Inner Bookshop in Magalene Road, Oxford, *GA*'s mail box location.

Shortly after this on 14th March 1995, Special Branch raided theeditor of *GA* and the printer. Many of the magazine records were taken, together with copy for next issue, cheque books, computerdiscs and a computer.

Back ground

Founded in 1984, *Green Anarchist* is a militant technology and callsfor sustainable self-sufficient villages.

GA deals with travellers, sqatters, animal rights, environmental issues, anti-motorway protests, anti-fascism, sexual liberation and counter culture. We reject non-violence [typist notes in my opinion this is not true they do report support non-violent direct action but also support violent resistance and revolution] and reportactions carried out by ALF and ELF. (Earth Liberation Front.)

In 1991, Frontline Books Manchester was raided after police took exception to *GA* issue 27. Frontline subsequently doubled their order.

In 1993, *Green Anarchist* helped to expose Searchlight as a destabilising influence on the left and an arm of the state in the booklets 'A Lie too Far' (ALTF) and 'At War with The Truth'(AWWTT).

GA was linked with campaign to stop the Grand National in an article by Chester Stern, Mail on Sunday 6th Feb 1994

These police raids follow on from the July Sunday Times John Harlow 'Summer of Hate' smear campaign against radical greens and arepetition of the unsubstantiated Harlow smears on TV and other places, especially the false and slanderous description of *Green Anarchist* as a terrorist organisation by Jason Bennetto in the Independent, 28th December 1994.

New contact address
Green Anarchist
BM 1715, London WC1N 3XX

*THIS JUST IN * THIS JUST IN * THIS JUST IN*
HAMPSHIRE CID TARGET GREEN ANARCHIST MAGAZINE

GREEN ANARCHIST is an international militant eco magazine, published in Britain. In recent months sections of the British media have described GA as Britain's "most radical underground newspaper on the animal and roads protests fringe" (Observer 9.7.95) and Britain's "most notorious and seditious radical newspaper (Student Outlook - Summer 1995).

In Mid March 1995, members of Hampshire CID raided three addresses in Oxford. The outcome of these raids was the confiscation of much property and the arrest of one man who the British police claim is the General Editor of *Green Anarchist* magazine.

A couple of weeks later Hampshire CID raided another two addresses, on in the North West of England and the other in the South East of England. The outcome was two more arrests and more confiscation of property.

A couple of days after that, Hampshire CID raided two houses in the South West of England searching for a fourth person. Having failed to locate the person at the two addresses in Devon (but having sadly confiscated much property from one of the addresses), Hampshire CID then went on a 150-200 mile drive and located their target in the English Midlands. Again this person was arrested and more of their property was confiscated.

After their arrest, each person was taken to an appropriate local police station and questioned. When it became clear to the police that none of the people they had arrested intended to give them any information, each one was released on Police Bail (on condition they all appeared at a cop shop in Hampshire on the 7th of June or face fines/imprisonment for failing to surrender to police custody).

In Mid May, each of the four received a letter from Hampshire CID telling them the did not need to turn up to the Hampshire cop shop as the police were continuing with their enquiries. These "continuing enquiries" have taken the form of a number of radical bookstores that sell *GA* being raided.

Now despite the raids/arrests, at the end of June *GA* managed to produce another issue of their magazine. This seemed to anger Hampshire CID who had obviously hoped they had decommissioned *GA* magazine. The response of the police was to launch three more raids against suspected Green Anarchists. Two of these raids were in England and the third was in Scotland. One of the raids proved unsuccessful for Hampshire CID and they failed to locate the person they wanted. However, the other two raids did result in two more arrests.

Since then Hampshire CID have just been plain barmy! Hampshire CID appear to be going through all and any letters they managed to seize during the raids and paying anyone who has written to the alleged *Green Anarchists* a visit. On the 2nd of August, at 7:10am, two Hampshire CID officers raided the home of a *GA* reader who just happened to of written to *GA* back in November 1994! The search warrant the police showed the *GA* reader entitled Hampshire CID to search for "any article/record connected with *Green Anarchist* magazine, together with any article/record related to similar publications/ advertisements, and any other material inciting acts of arson/criminal damage." The *GA* reader is not a known arsonist or into anything like that.

If anyone has contacted *Green Anarchist* magazine there is a chance you might also be raided by Hampshire CID, who seem to be going to ever more desperate measures to try and set up those who they have arrested. If anyone does receive a visit by Hampshire CID, as a result of their reading/communicating with *Green Anarchist* magazine (or similar publications) then please let *Green Anarchist* magazine have the details. And if anyone reading this does not already subscribe to GA, then as a mark of solidarity with those arrested you might like to consider taking out a subscription to *GA*.
-anon.

SEAL WARS BACK ON

Date: Thu, 16 Mar 1995

Martin Sheen, Captain Paul Watson and Sea Shepherd Crew violently attacked by angry sealing mob on the Canadian Magdalen Islands. The seal wars are back on. Angered by Paul Watson's conservationist actions in the early 1980s which ultimately led to the reversal of the "Seal Protection Act" and ended the commercial seal hunt, Canadian sealers were out to "settle a score." Captain Watson, Sea Shepherd, and Martin Sheen were in the Magdalen Islands to try to promote their project to create a cruelty-freen non-lethal alternative to sealing, by collecting hair fibers by brushing harp seal pups as they molt. The fibers could be used for fill inquilts, down jackets, and other products needing insulation. Infact, a large German company was already offering to purchase all the molted hair that could be harvested. "I believe we have found a way to provide full employment for traditional sealers without having to kill a single seal," said Martin Sheen.

"Seals are meant to be clubbed, not coddled," said one representative of the Sealing Association. "Who does Watson think he is? Does he think we will exchange the club for a hairbrush? We are men, sealing men. We are not women."

The sealers attacked Watson in his hotel room, during which Watson received a number of cuts from flying glass, but had recieved serious injuries. Photojournalist Marc Gaede indicated the Germans were beaten, according to Carla Robinson at the Sea Shepherd Conservation Society headquarters in Santa Monica, California.

A German television crew were told by police that their safety could not be guaranteed unless the videos were turned over to the sealers. They gave them five cassettes to appease them. Their main story had been successfully hidden in a snow bank.

Satisfied that there was no documentation, the Quebec police told the outside world that nothing had happened. Oh, they said, "There was a peaceful demonstration, but no violence and Paul Watson voluntarily left the Magdalens when politely requested to do so by the sealers."

According to Watson, "All of us who were involved were astounded at the blatant lies from the police. We were even more astounded when much of the Canadian media echoed the lies and refused to run comments by journalists who had witnessed the incident.

The next day when I called to request that charges be laid, the Quebec police spokesperson told me, 'you were lucky to get off the island alive so don't push it.'"

Excerpts from Lies, Damn Lies and Green Wellies

Hunt Saboteurs Association <hsa@gn.apc.org>
WWW site at : http://envirolink.org/arrs/HSA/hsa.html

In the past three years, the hunting community has realised it has a serious image problem and has put substantial effort and millions of pounds into trying to make themselves more acceptable. Much of this effort has consisted of a smear campaign coordinated by the British Field Sports Society (BFSS) to cover up the brutality and violence of hunt supporters by "exposing" saboteurs as class war militants bent on violence and destruction. There is precious little evidence to support this theory, but the hardy folk of the hunting community will not let such trivia deter them and simply make up their "proof". We regard the issue of class as entirely irrelevant to the central moral issue of cruelty. Saboteurs come from all backgrounds, age groups, professions and political points of view. On the other side of the coin, the worst perpetrators of cruelty and violence at hunts are terriermen who are solidly working class. So-called class struggle is deliberately used to cloud the issue and provide a handy diversion for hunters unable to defend themselves on mora l grounds to spread alarm about "sinister political extremists". Perhaps they mean people like the now-famous "Granny Group" of saboteurs in Surrey? Every one of this brave group of senior citizens is over 60 and there's not a punk rocker among them. Unfortunately this does not seem to exempt them from violent attacks by hunt thugs. Or perhaps the hunt lobby mean such notorious class warriors as Rev. Bert Jones, a 65-year old church minister, who has been a hunt saboteur for three years.

Similarly, the word terrorist is frequently flung about in an attempt to smear genuine animal lovers, often coupled with lurid tales of bomb attacks. In June 1990, hunt supporter John Newberry-Street gained much valuable anti-saboteur publicity when a nail-bomb was found under his Land Rover. Further investigation revealed that he had planted the bomb himself and he later told police "I did it to discredit the animal rights saboteurs". He was jailed for nine months for his bomb hoax and asked for several other similar offences to be taken into a ccount.

A Catologue of Violence

There is a very real problem of violence at hunts . It overwhelmingly consists of assaults by hunt thugs against saboteurs. In the first 3 months of 1993 alone, some 75 saboteurs were victims of violent attacks by hunts, 13 of them requiring hospital attention as a result. In recent years saboteurs have been kicked, whipped, beaten with staves, spades and other weapons, ridden down by horses and vehicles, throttled, threatened with knives and shotguns, knocked unconscious and sexually assaulted in a range of attacks all across the country. There has also been an alarming rise in the use of vehicles as weapons despite the deaths of two saboteurs in recent years under the wheels of hunt vehicles.

Beaten With a Hammer

January 1994 Old Surrey & Burstow Hunt. Three saboteurs driving home after the hunt spotted a hunt official thrashing his horse to get it in a horsebox. They stopped to take photographs and the huntsman attacked them with a hammer, terrifying his horse which was only prevented from bolting when the female saboteur held and calmed the petrified animal. Her compassion was rewarded when the huntsman turned on her too, inflicting similar serious head wounds to those of her friends.

Scythe Attack

January 1993 Bramham Moor Foxhunt supporter Raymond Walker attacked saboteurs with a scythe, leaving two with head wounds and smashing van windows. In February 1994, he was convicted of a fray and causing criminal damage along with two other hunt supporters, Mr & Mrs Winstanley, who pleaded guilty to affray for their part in the psychotic attack. All walked free from court with community service orders.

Five Days in Hospital

March 1994 Four Burrow Foxhunt. A mass attack on saboteurs started with the hunt whipper-in riding his horse several times over saboteur John Prescott, causing him massive internal injuries including 3 fractured ribs and serious internal bleeding. Saboteurs defended themselves and injuries were sustained on both sides. Only saboteurs were arrested even though many of them were injured in the unprovoked attack, including Mr Prescott who spent several hours in police cells vomiting blood before being allowed to go to hospital. He remained in hospital for five days, much of that time on a drip feed.

"From now on, we're going to start hunting the saboteurs..."

This is BFSS spokesman Nick Herbert's chilling announcement of the introduction of "stewards" " to deal with" saboteurs. The full sinister potential of his words was soon realised, as all over the country violent attacks on saboteurs reached epidemic proportions. It quickly became apparent that stewards, ostensibly introduced to tackle trespass, were actually being used as a quasi-legal cover for a new wave of violence designed to create unprecedented levels of tension at hunts. As violent attacks on saboteurs reached the point that at least one saboteur was being taken to hospital by ambulance every week, hunters launched renewed calls for legislation against peaceful protesters, citing their own violence in support.

Targeting Women

Many stewards have directed their attacks against female saboteurs, either simply beating them up or using the threat of sexual attacks.

* February 1994 At the Hursley Hambledon Foxhunt, a woman was trapped and held down; her breasts were molested and she was threatened with having a lighted cigarette stubbed out in her face.

* August 1992 Four stewards at a grouse shoot in Yorkshire surrounded a woman and subjected her to a lengthy sexual assault. Under the pretext of searching her, they pinned her to the ground and groped her body, thrusting their hands inside her clothing. The main instigator of this attack was subsequently employed by several other hunts where he continued to single out female saboteurs for sexual attacks.

* January 1993 At the Garth & South Berks Foxhunt, a woman was beaten unconscious and left lying in a pool of blood by a Reading bouncer drafted in to intimidate saboteurs. She was the most seriously injured of the 20 saboteurs attacked by stewards during the day.

Rotten to the Core

The hunting community often tries to dismiss violence against saboteurs as isolated incidents resulting from provocation and in fact the BFSS has published confidential guidelines urging hunt masters to adopt just such a defence if questioned by the media. The HSA has long felt that many hunts have allowed a culture of violence to develop in which engineering confrontational situations, intimidation and outright violence, both threatened and actual, are acceptable approaches to dealing with saboteurs. The deployment of stewards, in particular, has been a cynical step that has provided useful cover for such activity. It cannot be mere coincidence that since the introduction of stewarding, under the guiding hand of the BFSS, more saboteurs have been hospitalised and more hunt supporters jailed than at any time in the HSA's 32-year history.

Now, one brave woman, a former hunt supporter of many years standing, has decided to stand up and speak out against this culture of violence. Her name is Lynn Sawyer and she was at one time as committed to hunting as she is now repelled by it. She acted as a mole for the BFSS and found that saboteurs were not violent extremists motivated by class hatred, a tale she and every other hunt supporter had been force-fed for years. Instead, she found that saboteurs were on the whole deeply committed, sincere individuals who acted out of great and genuine concern for animals and that her own side were deliberately distorting the truth and provoking violence simply to suit their long-term political aims. Ironically, it was only the depth of her involvement in hunting that allowed her access to the inner echelons denied to most hunt supporters, where she encountered the brutality behind the respectable facade which was to make her question her support for bloodsports and ultimately turn her back on that world for ever.

The rest of this section is in Lynn's own words. We have left her tale as she wrote it as well as her open letter to the hunting world. Both pieces speak eloquently of the determination of the hunting hierarchy to continue on the path of violence and confrontation and the inability of the bloodsports community to set its own house in order.

Lynn's Story

My hunting career began with the Essex Foxhounds in 1982 when I was fourteen. By 1990, I had hunted with many different packs, including the East Essex, Essex Farmers' & Union, Puckeridge & Thurlow, Cottesmore, and West Kent Foxhounds; the Eastern Counties, Northamptonshire and Kent & Sussex Minkhounds; the Epping Coursing Club; and many West Country foxhound and staghound packs. Those eight years were spent running, or occasionally riding, to hounds; wielding a spade at digouts; helping out with hound exercise and doing odd jobs around hunt kennels; stewarding at point-to-points, collecting signatures on pro-hunt petitions and donations for the BFSS; and working on BFSS stalls and persuading the public at shows and by writing to the press.

From 1984-90, much of my time was spent gathering information for the field sports fraternity on anti-hunting activity. This meant doing anything to gather information including taking vehicle registrations (over 130 on file by 1990!), photographing sabs, delving through animal rights literature and music bought in specialist shops, attending animal rights meetings and gigs, chatting to the police and generally finding out what I could (none of which I am proud of now).

For several reasons in 1990, I could no longer continue these activities and I then spent four years trying to ascertain what exactly my feelings were. I spent time with the Shire hunts (the Quorn, Cottesmore, and Belvoir Foxhounds) and revisited the Essex before deciding earlier this year that it was time to speak out in the hope of stemming the tide of grossly exaggerated anti-sab propaganda and the violence it has brought to the field.

I went to great lengths to discuss the issue of hunt violence with the BFSS and other pro-hunting people [including John Hopkinson, Stephen Loveridge, Peter Smith and Nick Herbert of the BFSS and John Swift, director of the British Association for Shooting and Conservation (BASC)] before, and indeed for some time after, it became clear that I could not permeate their rather narrow-minded way of thinking or change or influence any of them without being patronised or being singled out as a trouble-maker.

An Open Letter to the Hunting World

This is an open letter to those who I feel have a right to be informed of my recent decision to abandon my position of neutrality on the hunting issue in favour of the animal rights movement. For those who are not already aware, I ceased to be a hunt supporter four years ago because I was very uncomfortable with the way in which I was expected to behave in that role and due to the reaction I received from some pro-hunt leaders when I disagreed with their tactics. Four years of sitting on the fence has given me time to reflect upon my past as a hunt follower, a BFSS voluntary worker, a farm worker, a meat-eater, etc. Endless hours have been spent studying animal rights literature, keeping up to date via the sporting press, attending hunt meets and listening whilst in the field to the views of a wide spectrum of people from both sides. This decision is probably the most difficult that I have ever had to make, it has not been taken lightly and I am simply being honest with the readers of this letter and with myself. My reasons are as follows:

1. Whilst maintaining my deep respect for the sanctity of human life and dignity, I have extended my concern to ALL sentient beings. I now believe that it is abhorrent to kill, unless in exceptional cases such as euthanasia, or to cause suffering to any living creature for our own benefit. This means that I am now a dietary vegan and I will be boycotting leather, silk, wool, etc. in the future. I can no longer ignore my remorse at the large amount of suffering that I have caused, nor can I ignore what is happening in the abattoirs, in the laboratories, in the oceans, down on the farm and out in the field.

2. Whilst I will admit that saboteurs are not all paragons of virtue, I can testify that during twelve years of observing sabs active in the field, including six years of information gathering for the BFSS, I was treated with courtesy on most occasions, witnessed others being treated in a similar fashion and non-violent, effective tactics. I am fully satisfied that most sabs are altruists and that there is more than adequate legislation to deal with anyone, from either side, who threatens or uses violence.

3. British history is full of cases when people have had no option but to use non-violent direct action unless they wanted their grievances to be totally ignored by a self-serving establishment. The suffragettes were not deterred by prison and their modern counterparts, the sabs, the road protesters, CND, or any other group or individual who refuse to be patronised by the state are not going to abandon deeply held beliefs when they face the same historical fate. The Criminal Justice and Public Order Bill seeks to criminalise all those seen by the government as weak enough, unconventional enough or easy enough to brand as a threat to society to use as scapegoats for their incompetence. This endangers the civil liberties of EVERYONE and it obliterates the right to protest effectively, the right of freedom of movement, the right of freedom of association and the right to live in a way that differs from what the government thinks is normal. I suggest that people read this draconian piece of literature and consider its implications very carefully. I cannot maintain a position of neutrality in the face of such a vicious attack on civil liberties.

4. The instigators of the use of stewards in the field could not have possibly thought up a more effective way of raising the levels of violence to unprecedented levels. It seems rather too convenient that when sabs used the inevitable, time honoured mass hit tactic when faced with large, less than diplomatic hordes of "the lads", who dragged them off public rights of way under the aegis of the BFSS, that Mr Howard then launched his attack on the less powerful, less influential group involved in the resulting battles. I hope that I am wrong in assuming that this was the desired outcome of those who put the lives of hunting folk, stewards, sabs and police officers at considerable risk by their confrontational tactics, because if I am right then the ramifications of this bill are even more sinister. Once again I cannot turn a blind eye to this sort of manipulation and bullying.

I apologise to those who will feel betrayed by this change of heart, especially those who have had the decency and integrity to listen. I will never support the use of violence against people and I guarantee that past confidences will remain confidential.

Hunt Master Hospitalises Saboteur

Kettering Hunt Saboteurs news release 11th February 1995
A hunt saboteur was taken to hospital in an ambulance Saturday, February 11, after being ridden down by a Master of Foxhounds at a joint meet of the Fitzwilliam Hunt and the Woodland Pytchley Hunt at Chapel End, Great Gidding, Northants.

While walking along a public footpath near Little Gidding and causing no disruption to the hunt, a saboteur was confronted by DAVID REYNOLDS, Master of the Woodland Pytchley Hunt who rode his horse over him, causing serious internal injureis. The attack took place in full view of the police, who called an ambulance and the Tactical Support Group (TSG) to the scene. Some indication of police priorities can be seen from the fact that the TSG arrived some 20 minutes before the ambulance. Some hunt saboteurs were arrested when the TSG arrived, unlike Mr Reynolds who was allowed to calmly ride away from the scene.

A spokesman for Cambridgeshire Police later claimed that 10-15 arrests had been made. In fact there were four arrests, of whom 3 were saboteurs and one a hunt steward. Saboteurs pronounced the day a victory as they had ensured that the two hunts between them killed no animals that day.

The injured saboteur has since been released from hospital following treatment but the incident has highlighted the brutality of those who get their kicks from blood.

This is the second violent attack in as many weeks involving the Woodland Pytchley Hunt which numbers Richard Otley (sheep exporter) among its riders. Other supporters of this hunt have been arrested for public order and assault offences and specific saboteurs have been targetted with threats of death and violence and have also suffered damage to vehicles.

Northamptonshire Police have admitted that they no longer have the resources to deal with this kind of problem. We hope that the Wild Mammals (Protection) Bill, which gets its second reading in the Commons on March 3rd will see an end to this barbaric excuse for a sport and none too soon.

HUNT THUGS GIVEN 12-MONTH PRISON SENTENCES

news release 10th March 1995
Two thugs from the Cheshire Foxhunt, a favourite hunt of Prince Charles, were given twelve month prison sentences at Chester Crown Court today after being found guilty last week of violent disorder. The two men, Geoffrey Park, 30, of The Elms, Tushingham, Whitchurch, Shropshire and Anthony Ronald Kirkham, 50, of Ridley Farm, Ridley, Cheshire had been charged after a vicious gang attack on saboteurs on Saturday 11th December 1993 in which their vehicle was wrecked and a woman was savagely beaten up. Both men have a track record of violence against protesters and Kirkham is said to have served prison sentences for grievous bodily harm and attempted murder.

Park and Kirkham were part of a ten-strong gang of hunt thugs, armed with pickaxe handles and coshes, who smashed up a saboteurs' van and beat up the occupants. A 24-year old woman who attempted to run for help during the attack was cornered by the gang, punched to the ground by Kirkham, and then kicked and beaten about the head and body as she lay on the floor helpless. She sustained two black eyes, damaged kidneys, and extensive cuts and bruising to her head and body in the vicious attack. The gang then dragged her back to the van and resumed their attack on the van, jumping on the roof and causing further damage to the exterior. While his friends were occupied in trashing the vehicle, Park climbed inside the van and beat up several of the occupants with a cosh.

Kirkham had already shown his propensity for brutal violence against saboteurs, in particular on Boxing Day 1992, when the

Cheshire Beagles met at The Poacher in Bickerton near Kirkham's farm. He beat a woman unconscious with a piece of wood and left her lying unconscious in a stream, where she had to be rescued by her fellow saboteurs, who called an ambulance. Her injuries were so severe she had to be airlifted to hospital by a helicopter yet police refused to arrest Kirkham. When her fellow sabs went to Nantwich police station to make statements identifying Kirkham as the culprit they were themselves arrested. Conveniently, all charges were dropped before the case reached court and no-one was ever prosecuted.

Despite these sentences, it is doubtful whether hunt thugs in Cheshire will be deterred from violent attacks on saboteurs: Kirkham certainly has not learnt any sort of lesson from his conviction. He was arrested at the Cheshire Hunt only yesterday after he rammed two saboteurs' vehicles and then rammed a car belonging to a passer-by who was not connected with the hunt or protesters. And this the day before he was to appear in court to be sentenced for one of his many other violent attacks on saboteurs! In another of several violent attacks on saboteurs at the Cheshire Hunt yesterday, a hunt supporter was arrested for threatening a saboteur with an axe.

It seems that thugs in Cheshire think they can have a free hand in attacking anyone who objects to hunting: the police must take firm action to crack down on these hooligans before someone else is killed in Cheshire.

Saboteurs are also calling on Prince Charles, who was hunting with the Cheshire as recently as last week, to stop endorsing this extremely violent hunt by refusing to ride with them until they cease attacking anyone who disagrees with them and expel the violent lunatics within their ranks such as Kirkham and Park.

Police turn blind eye as minkhunt yobs ambush saboteurs: 10 in hospital

news release May 29th 1995

Ten saboteurs received hospital treatment in Dorset today after a terrifying ambush by hunt heavies at the Ytene Minkhunt. Twenty-three saboteurs had attended the hunt meet on the River Stour in Marnhull, near Shaftesbury, Dorset: only four escaped injury. One woman who was present said "It was like something out of a film ... it was just a bloodbath."

At about 1 p.m., saboteurs in the field spotted known thugs from the New Forest Foxhunt hiding in bushes. The 15 heavies, armed with sticks, cudgels, and a slingshot, immediately launched a sustained attack on the protesters. The attack started with a barrage of rocks the size of housebricks and the thugs then moved in to attack individuals. While some were beaten with cudgels, others were punched to the ground and kicked and stamped on. The thugs had been brought in specially for the day in what appears to be a carefully planned attack, resulting in serious injuries to several sabs. Ten of the injured were taken to Shaftesbury Casualty Department for treatment to a host of injuries:

* a Bristol woman treated for a broken wrist after she was stamped on as she lay on the ground
* a North Dorset woman treated for a weal on her left shoulder after being beaten with a heavy stick while another woman from the area suffered a dislocated finger
* a Cambridge woman had her camera smashed and was kicked and punched
* two men from Cambridge were treated for leg wounds after being hit by a 2-inch piece of lead shot fired from a slingshot
* a man from Bath had his camera and glasses smashed and sustained severe head injuries from being kicked and punched in a sustained assault so vicious he was left with a boot mark on his head
* a Peterborough man suffered a broken finger and heavy bruising to his back after he was repeatedly kicked and punched as he lay on the floor
* a man from Ross-on-Wye received two stitches in a vicious cut above his eye
* a woman from Bath had to be rushed to Yeovil hospital by ambulance after she suffered a severe asthma attack induced by the trauma of the attack. Two thugs stamped on her back as she lay helpless on the ground.
* a video camera and a van window were smashed.

Amazingly, it appears that the local police knew in advance that an ambush had been planned and took no steps to prevent it. There was just one officer present at the hunt, a PC Cotton from Blandford, who hinted to protesters that they should not go near the hunt as "there's more of them than you ... and they're twice the size". He then went on to say that "if anything happened ... I'm not going to be here to pick up the pieces." Just quarter of an hour later the thugs launched their attack and PC Cotton was conveniently nowhere to be seen. The Ytene Minkhunt have an appalling track record for violence of the worst order and while the police turn a blind eye to these sort of mob attacks there is little to deter them from the sort of hooliganism that would bring shame on any football club.

Top English Huntsman arrested for assault

HSA news release Oct 7th 1995

Alistair Jackson, the southeast region press spokesman of the British Field Sports Society (BFSS), the pro-bloodsports lobby group has been arrested for assault after punching a saboteur to the ground at a cubhunting meet of the Cattistock Foxhunt. In a morning of violence, balaclava-clad thugs at the Crawley and Horsham Foxhunt in Sussex also smashed a saboteur van's windscreen.

Jackson spends most of his time when he's not killing foxcubs for fun loudly slandering saboteurs as violent thugs. Who are the thugs now then, Alistair?

The activist: Jill Phipps with son Luke

JILL PHIPPS died the way she had always lived, as a fanatical animal rights protester.

Unlike many drawn into the campaign against live animal exports, she had been a hardcore activist for years.

It was a cause for which she had nearly gone to jail and which brought her death, crushed under the wheels of a lorry carrying veal calves into Bagington Airport, Coventry, on Wednesday.

By TONY HALPIN

She, her mother Nancy, and sister Lesley, were once branded 'enemies of society' by a judge for their part in a raid on Unilever, in which equipment worth £14,000 was smashed.

Jill received a two-year suspended prison sentence at Leicester Crown Court in 1986.

Dramatic

Her mother was jailed for six months and Lesley received six months' youth custody. All three were convicted of conspiring to burgle.

Jill first took part in a demonstration when she was 11, joining her mother in a protest outside a fur farm.

A bright girl who excelled at English and Art at Lyng Hall School, Coventry, she turned her back on the chance of A-levels and a possible university career to leave school at 16.

Headmistress Jane McGinn recalled: 'She wanted to do something dramatic with her life.

'Jill was never going to end up doing something ordinary. She wanted to change the world.'

Jill, who was 31 when she died, left school in 1980 and took a job at the Post Office. She became involved with the Coventry Animal Alliance, a group of activists led by her mother.

Fellow activist Rob White, 22, recalled how she would travel around the country in a clapped-out van with a group of hunt saboteurs to protest against bloodsports.

'She was a real radical prepared to do anything for her cause,' he said.

In 1984, Jill married Alan Cockrill and she later gave birth to her son Luke, now nine.

The marriage broke up when Luke was a few months old and she drifted for a time, living in squats before being given a flat in a council block in rundown Hillfields, Coventry.

Five years ago she met Australian Justin Timson, who became her boyfriend.

Angered

Yesterday Mr Timson, a 26-year-old self-employed craftsman making didgeridoos, was heartbroken.

He and Jill travelled all over the country to animal rights protests.

'We were with a small group that waxed and waned in size,' he said. 'Lately the apathy of people really angered her.'

Now Mr Timson intends to look after Luke.

Woman is killed in veal lorry protest

By Michael Hornsby

A YOUNG mother protesting against the export of veal calves died under the wheels of a delivery lorry at Coventry airport yesterday, prompting the company involved to cancel livestock flights.

Jill Phipps, 31, who had a nine-year-old son, Luke, was crushed to death by the slow-moving lorry after she and three other protesters leapt at the cab. Her mother and sister, Lesley, who were among 40 people trying to obstruct the vehicle, saw the accident.

Police freed Ms Phipps, of Coronation Road, Coventry, and she was taken to Warwick Hospital but was dead on arrival. The three other people who tried to climb on the cab were unhurt.

Police said the demonstrators had ignored repeated requests to clear the road. The calves were to have been exported to Amsterdam.

Last night Phoenix Aviation, the air freight company operating veal flights out of Coventry Airport, announced it was cancelling all flights until further notice. John Bradshaw said: "We are all so shocked and upset at what has happened."

Gill Gates, a friend of Ms Phipps and a fellow protester, fought back tears as she described the incident. "Jill was just behind me. I turned around for a second and she was on the ground. I don't know if she slipped, fell or was knocked over by the truck. Police yelled for the truck to stop and it did but with the wheels on her body."

Ms Phipps's Australian husband, Justin, was told of her death as he prepared to stage an Anti-Nazi League concert in a local pub. Her sister was treated for shock.

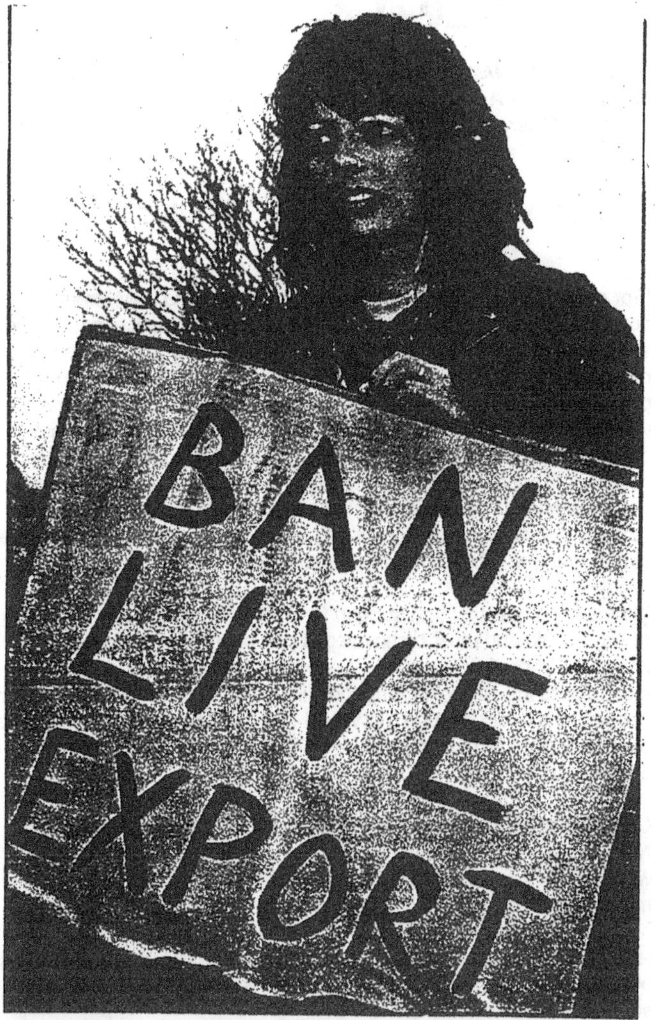

Animal lover . . Dreadlocked Jill was committed to ending veal trade

By ANDREW PARKER

A WOMAN animal rights protester died last night after being run over by a lorry carrying live calves for export.

Jill Phipps — mother of a seven-year-old boy — was crushed by the wheels of the huge artic as activists tried to stop it reaching an airport.

Jill's mum Nancy and sister Lesley, 26, watched in horror as the lorry rolled over her after she tried to climb on to the cab. Police said Jill, 31, was in a group that dodged their cordon outside Coventry airport.

Two months ago she condemned five people who died when a cargo plane — leased by Coventry-based Phoenix Aviation to transport calves — crashed near the city. She said: "I don't feel sorry for the dead people. They are just as guilty as Phoenix's owner Christopher Barrett-Jolly.

"If he was not trying to get rich quick this would not have happened. This is all down to greed."

'A headstrong girl deeply committed to animal rights'

Last night Phoenix announced that all its livestock flights would be cancelled "for the foreseeable future."

Warwickshire Acting Chief Constable Chris Fox said there were about 40 protesters being marshalled by 70 police.

He said: "As the lorry approached, protesters moved towards it, despite repeated requests to keep back.

Awful

"The lorry slowed down and a woman tried to grab hold of the front of the cab. She appeared to slip and fell under the front wheels."

The dead woman's shocked pal Gill Gates said: "It was awful.

"Police yelled for the lorry driver to stop and it did, but the wheels were right over her."

Jill's uncle James Phipps said: "It is horrifying to think Nancy watched her daughter die."

But he said Jill had laid down her life for a cause she passionately believed in.

"She was a headstrong girl deeply committed to animal rights."

Jill lived with her Australian husband Justin and son Luke in Hillfields, Coventry.

Phoenix had flown out 500 calves a day to Holland and France until the air crash.

The Civil Aviation Authority halted the flights amid residents' protests that they were unsafe.

Flights resumed this week after Phoenix carried out a "proving" flight

Phoenix spokesman John Bradshaw said last night: "We are deeply shocked and upset.

"We did not hire the lorry — we are just a link in the chain.

"In the past people have thrown themselves under the vehicles, but until now there have been no injuries.

"This is the sort of thing that one has always feared in the darker recesses of one's mind."

THE SUN, Thursday, February 2, 1995

FOOD FOR THOUGHT

a space for discussion and analysis with the intention of furthering the work of the A.L.F. This issue: the role of prison justice work in the animal liberation movement

WHERE WE ARE AT IN TERMS OF PRISON JUSTICE

[For new readers: In September 1994, we decided to start expanding our prisoner support work to include general prison justice issues and supporting political prisoners who were incarcerated for actions not related to the A.L.F. In the last issue of Underground, in addition to publishing information about 12 prisoners incarcerated for alleged involvement in animal liberation activities, we also published information on: 2 prisoners incarcerated for alleged involvement in earth lliberation activities, 2 prisoners incarcerated as a result of their work for indigenous liberation, 2 prisoners who are animal rights activists but are incarcerated on other charges, and several prison activists incarcerated in the Southern Ohio Correctional Facility in Lucasville, OH.

"There is no question that support for political prisoners and prisoners of war should and must be an integral part of any movement for liberation. There is no question, that is, for people who have dedicated their lives to the struggle for freedom in this country and realize that it is not possible to talk about a movement for liberation if you fail to liberate people who are incarcerated as a result of that struggle for liberation." - Safiya Bukhari *

Our explanation for our desire to include prison justice as a part of the NA-ALFSG's work can be found in the last issue of Underground; we won't repeat it here. The articles by Little Rock Reed and "a field marshall" in this issue of Underground do much to expand on why we are taking that position. The following is our attempt to respond to the letters we have received since Underground #2 was published and to let our members know where we are at in terms of developing prisoner support guidelines.

In regards to the queries of why we are covering prison justice struggles and not other human liberation struggles, there are many reasons why we are making prison justice a priority.

Prison justice activist John Perotti comments, "the editorial by Eddie T [in Underground #2] was on time. It's not just the A.L.F. who needs to start focusing on their 'human' prisoners. With the spiralling growth of the prison industry and public attitude what it is, they're slowly imprisoning the majority of us, with no actions geared toward liberation." The increase in incarceration is so extreme that by the middle of the 21st century, if incarceration rates continue as they have been, then 1/2 of the US will be jail and the other 1/2 will be guarding those in jail. We avoid dealing with this issue at our own peril.

As people who support illegal direct action in a wide variety of movements, we find ourselves having first-hand experience of the need for prison justice. Members of our movements are in jail; more will end up in jail as time passes. This means that we must consider how to deal with jail, as a movement. If our movement is to be successful, we must rely on each other to do what needs to be done for the animals; can we rely on each other to do what needs to be done when we are kept in cages? If not, who can we rely on?

Personally, I would prefer to face imprisonment with some knowledge of how the prison system works, and how to fight it, than to face imprisonment in ignorance. People who are on the front lines of fighting the prison system (i.e. prison activists) are the people with the most to teach about prisons, in my opinion. So it is natural for us to connect with these people and work with them, and in doing so to become part of that struggle. And of course the issues are not unconnected; prison justice involves ending racism, homophobia, sexism, classism, and other forms of oppression.

The bottom line is that we know some animal liberation activists will NOT feel the need to work on prison justice struggles. We can't possibly dictate how the movement proceeds (nor would we want to!), but we can give our thoughts on where we feel it is productive to put our energies.

Having said that, determining guidelines around prison justice work as part of the NA-ALFSG's responsibilities is a very important issue, one that we have been struggling with. At this time we are still attempting to lay down clear guidelines on who will we support, and what support we can offer. The following may give you some idea of where we are at in the discussion.

What appears to be developing is a group that will work on general prison abolition/prison justice issues in cooperation with, but independently of, the NA-ALFSG. We have been reluctant to form another group, given that we don't want to split our energies too far between different groups. As time has gone on, though, we have come to believe that it would be easier and more efficient to have two separate groups, rather than try to radically change the NA-ALFSG's mandate. We recognize that the NA-ALFSG may not be the best vehicle for doing prison justice work.

This does not mean that the NA-ALFSG will stop supporting political prisoners. At this point, what we are looking at in terms of a draft NA-ALFSG prison support policy is:

- we will provide financial support, to the best of our abilities, to people incarcerated for actions that fall under A.L.F. guidelines
- providing publicity and letter-writing appeals for political prisoners who ask for our assistance, and working on clear guidelines for who we will assist in this way (i.e. what do we mean by "political prisoner"?)
- continuing prison justice education work in Underground so that people within the animal liberation movement are more aware of what is happening in North American prisons.

There are still a lot of questions about what Underground will cover--where to focus our energies. Some basic limits are clear. We don't have the resources to provide information on every political prisoner/prisoner of war within North America. We don't want to cover ground that is being covered by specific defense committees for certain prisoners (eg. the Leonard Peltier Defense Committee).

Underground may be the area where the NA-ALFSG and the emerging prison justice group can operate cooperatively but independently of each other. We are still discussing the idea of keeping a certain number of pages in Underground for prison justice issues--to be designed by the new prison justice group, in collaboration with the prisoners they work with. We want Underground to continue covering some of the specific issues North American prisoners and their allies are working on, from a prison abolitionist perspective.

At this time we are unable to provide full financial assistance to A.L.F. prisoners, and this must be the NA-ALFSG's priority over the needs of non-A.L.F. prisoners. At the same time, several of us within the NA-ALFSG see an urgent need for fundraising for non-A.L.F. prisoners. We will continue our fundraising efforts for these prisoners outside the NA-ALFSG.

As always, it is up to our members to decide to what extent they want to be involved in prisoner support, whether it be A.L.F. prisoners or other prisoners. Some of our members donate money to specific prisoners, some write letters regularly, and some do not become involved in that aspect of supporting the A.L.F.

As we said, the NA-ALFSG position on where to draw the line in terms of prisoner support is not yet wholly clear. Still, we hope this provides you with a better picture of where the NA-ALFSG is at in terms of answering the question of which prisoners we do and don't support.

Z. - Prison Justice Coordinator for the NA-ALFSG

After having read P.'s comments on the AR-bombings in Britain and his suspicion that there might be a state controlled dirty-tricks campaign under way, I feel compelled to support this view.

I joined the AR movement in Britain 6 years ago and what I initially felt was paranoia on beha lf of some people overestimating their importance, I fully see now as being justified: the feeling of constantly being scrutinized, taped, surveilled and assest by state security. In those 6 years I experienced on many occasions to what length the state is prepared to go to deter AR activism even on the most minor levels. I witnessed a number of raids on activists homes (5 this year alone in Cambridge), we had at least two confirmed police infiltrators in our AR groups in Cambridge, we had mysterious break-ins in houses and cars, where diaries and similar things were removed, and parts of taped telephone calls were played to people during interviews. I personally was also surveilled for 4 months and my employer was shown results of this surveillance and talked to on two occasions. In addition, totally peaceful and non-violent, sophisticatedly planned actions to blokade Brightlingsea docks, for example, were busted by police, which proved that they must have been bugging a certain house, which was actually not connected to animal rights (in that the inhabitants were not AR activists but sympathizers). Two weeks later exactly that house was raided by police.

People were brutally manhandled and scared by police for no obvious reasons. I, for example, was put in a prison cell and questioned for 2 days allegedly because of a fire-bombing that happened hundreds of miles away and there was no apparent reason why Ishould have been involved, etc. In short, the police is very veryinterested in our activities, even in the most harmless ones andthey try their best to scare and bully people in passivity. You can be sure that this list, as many other AR lists, will be monitoredby police as well (incidentally that makes any honest discussionover the ethics of (fire-)bombings and the like impossible, at least if you are an activist who might face conspiracy charges at some stage in your life - and if you don't fully and whole-heartedly condemn any illegal acts).

Looking on historical developments in the late 60ties in Germany, for example, it is definitely a policy of state security to try to radicalize a movement in order to be able to justify (to the public as well as to the politicians who spend the money) draconian measures against the movement. For such means it has been an approved tactic to supply people with weapons and to start out with the initial attacks. Considering that so many of those Justice Department bombs were intercepted and no-one was ever seriously injured, I would not be surprised if they were police initiated. I also received a magazine (as did many other groups), which was sent anonymous and tried to incite its readers not to waste their time with animal liberation (including literally liberating animals in ALF raids), but to attack the animal abusers. Any other action would be a waste of time and resources. Many people felt, as I did, that this writing was not from within the movement, not the least because of its writing style, the little compassion even for animals it expressed, and the fact that about half the volume wasused to smear other groups and individuals. Interestingly, all this bombing and radicalizing on the AR front coincides also with the Criminal Justice Act and other measures to curb peaceful protest. Again, I would be surprised if that was not a concerted effort on the side of the state to push the AR movement from a mass movement to a terrorist activity shunned by the public. I suggest we don't debate the ethics of bombings or any illegalityfor that matter, at all, since the consequence might be that someone, feeling strongly about it all, feels inclined to say something s/he might regret on a later date in the court room. Indeed, it might be wise to treat someone, who insists in discussing this topic, with care.
M.

YEAH, IT USED TO BE WORLD ANIMAL LIBERATION WEEK... NOW IT'S "EARTH DAY" WEEK
... WHEN YOU'RE HOT, YOU'RE HOT - AND WHEN YOU'RE NOT, YOU'RE... DEAD...
EZ, ONE STINKIN' EEK OUTTA THE AR... IS THAT O MUCH TO ASK?
I GUESS WE DIDN'T DO TOO WELL IN THE RATINGS...

N.A.-A.L.F.S.G. *LEGAL FILES*

It is impossible for us to keep track of all animal liberation-related arrests for civil disobedience or other forms of protest. Groups such as PeTA or the Network (see activist directory) may be helpful in this regard. The following is a partial list of arrests and convictions for actions that fall under A.L.F. guidelines.

SWEDEN

NOV 16/94: location unspecified --Two female activists, aged 17 and 18, were arrested for allegedly throwing a rock through a fur and leather shop window.

DEC 15/94: 17 year old female activist found guilty of damaging a fur shop window. She was given approx. $300 in a fine and ordered to pay the furrier approx. $350 to replace the damaged window.

JAN 19/95: 25-year old man arrested after letting animals out of zoo.

D.B.F. PRESS RELEASE:

According to Swedish TV news on Jan 19th, a 25-year old man had opened containers with acetylene gas outside a slaughterhouse in Östersund (town in the middle/centre of Sweden. No damage was made!

After that he went on to Fröső Zoo (on an island outside Östersund) and had opened cages with owls, foxes, wolves and lynx. He had tried to open the cages with tigers and lions, but failed. 10 foxes, 2 wolfs and around 13 lynx and a few owls were out. Some animals were later caught and some were shot dead by the zoo personel and police. At least 6 lynx and 1 or 2 wolves were killed.

The man was later caught by the police and arrested. The police says the man was confused and has psychological problems. At the arrest the man said he felt sorry for the imprisoned animals. The police don't think he's connected to any A/R group.

On Jan 20th Swedish newspaper report on that case, saying the man was mentally ill (schizophrenia) and had been let out from the mental hospital a couple days earlier. The night before he had ran naked around town in the cold winter night.

The 25-year old has now been transferred to the hospital.

REPORT FROM MICHIGAN: ACTIVISTS THREATENED FOR WEARING MASKS IN PUBLIC

After an anti-fur demonstration in Birmingham, MI on December 26, 1994, three activists received summons in the mail for wearing masks in public. The masks were "death" masks -- hoods with skulls painted on them.

The three activists were arraigned and pled not guilty to the charges. They will be asking for a jury trial when the date is set for their case to be heard. The Michigan American Civil LibertiesUnion (ACLU) has accepted the case and will challenge the constitutionality of MI's state law prohiting the wearing of masks in public.

Michigan state law on masks, dating back to the 1950s, reads:

Chapter LVII. Masks and Disguises
750.396 Wearing masks or face coverings in public

Sec. 396. "Wearing masks or face coverings in public--Any person who shall assemble, march or parade on any street, highway or public place in this state while wearing a mask or covering which conceals in whole or part, the face of the wearer, shall be guilty of a misdemeanor: Provided, This chapter shall not apply to the pranks of children on Hallowe'en, to those going to and from masquarade parties, to those participating in any public parade of an educational, religious or historical character and to those participating in the parades of minstrel troupes, circuses or other amusement or dramatic shows."

It's ironic that this law protects minstrel troupes...generallydefined here as "a troupe of comedians, usually white men made upas Negroes (in 'blackface') ..."[!]. It's also interesting that recently the KKK had a rally in Lansing (MI's capitol) wearingtheir hoods. All the police did about it was to approach them and tell them they were breaking the law, and asked them to removetheir hoods or they would be given citations. The KKK members thenremoved their hoods. The KKK apparently talked to the ACLU about this incident but the ACLU was not interested in promoting the KKK's case.

In a somewhat ludicrous postscript to the Dec. 26 demo, Michael Ceresnie, of Ceresnie & Offen Furs, presented a petition signed by more than 20 other merchants and managers in the business district to the Birmingham City Commission. They want "something done" about the animal rights protesters marching in front of Ceresnie's store. Ceresnie & Offen Furs was plastered with anti-fur stickers andposters on December 26. Commissioner Rex Martin, who is sympathetic to Ceresnie, said, "When the radical fringe groups come out, we need to know where we stand." Ceresnie stated: I'd like the cityto put some restrictions on these protests so normal business can be conducted. People were unable to walk in and out of our store." Poor baby...
information provided by a Michigan animal liberation activist

Omnibus Counterterrorism Bill
S. 390 and H.R. 896

New FBI Charter to Investigate Political Groups

February 10, 1995 the Omnibus Counterterrorism Bill was introduced as S. 390 into the Senate and as H.R. 896 in the House. It was initiated by the FBI, and passed on by the Justice Department and the White House. Senators Biden (D-DE) and Specter (R- PA) initiated it in the Senate, Rep. Schumer (D-NY) and Dicks (D-WA) inthe House. It has bipartisan support and could get expedited action.

SUMMARY

THIS IS A GENERAL CHARTER FOR THE FBI AND OTHER AGENCIES, INCLUDING THE MILITARY, TO INVESTIGATE POLITICAL GROUPS AND CAUSESAT WILL. The bill is a wide-ranging federalization of different kinds of actions applying to both citizens and non-citizens. The range includes acts of violence (attempts, threats and conspiracies) as well as giving funds for humanitarian, legal activity.

* It would allow up to 10 year sentences for citizens and deportation for permanent resident non-citizens for the "crime" of supporting the lawful activities of an organization the President declares to be "terrorist", as the African National Congress, FMLN in El Salvador, IRA in Northern Ireland, and PLO have beenlabelled. It broadens the definition of terrorism. The President's determination of who is a terrorist is unappealable, and specifically can include groups regardless of any legitimate activity they might pursue.

* It authorizes secret trials for immigrants who are not charged with a crime but rather who are accused of supporting lawful activity by organizations which have also been accused of committing illegal acts. Immigrants could be deported: 1) using evidence they or their lawyers would never see, 2) in secret proceedings 3) with one sided appeals 4) using illegally obtained evidence.

* It suspends posse comitatus - allowing the use of the military to aid the police regardless of other laws.

* It reverses the presumption of innocence - the accused ispresumed ineligible for bail and can be detained until trial.

* It loosens the rules for wiretaps. It would prohibit probation as a punishment under the act - even for minor nonviolent offenses.

IMPLICATIONS

* Those who remember the McCarran Walter Act will recognize this m bill, only in some ways this is broader and potentially more dangerous.

* This bill is highly political: the President can determine who is a terrorist and change his/her mind at will and even for economic reasons. The breadth of its coverage would make it impossible for the government to prosecute all assistance to groups around the world that have made or threatened to commit violent acts of any sort. Necessarily its choices would be targeted at organizations the government found currently offensive. People to be deported would be chosen specifically because of their political associations and beliefs.

* The new federal crime: international terrorism doesn't cover anything that is not already a crime. As the Center for National Security Studies notes: "Since the new offense does not cover anything that is not already a crime, the main purpose of theproposal seems

to be to avoid certain constitutional and statutory protections that would otherwise apply."

* While many provisions of this bill could well be found unconstitutional after years of litigation, in the mean time the damage could be enormous to the First Amendment and other constitutional rights including presumption of innocence and right to bail.

FOR MORE INFORMATION:

Kit Gage
Washington Liaison, National Lawyers Guild
3321-12th St NE, Washington, DC 20017, USA
Phone: 202-529-4225 / Fax: 202-526-4611
e-mail: kgage@igc.apc.org

ATTACKS AND INTIMIDATION: GRAND JURIES AS A TOOL OF REPRESSION

by Eli Rosenblatt, Prison Activist Resource Center

Reading Crescenzo Vellucci's excellent article on grand juries and the animal rights movement (see Underground #1), I was inspired to look more deeply into the way that grand juries have historically been used against our movements as a powerful weapon to repress activism and dissent. What I found, of course,is that someone needs to write a book on the subject. What I offer here,instead, is a slice of some of the more significant modern cases and pointers as to where to learn more. Apparently, the US government has used grand juries since its inception. In the late 1700s and in the 1800s, the targets included confederates, colonial dissidents, and activists in the labor, communist, anti-slavery and feminist movements. Much more has been written about the modern history of grand juries, especially as they have been used against militants in the various anti-imperialist and national liberation movements.

The Movimiento de Liberacion Nacional (MLN) produced an essay in the early 1980s on "Collaboration and Non-collaboration" in which they detailed the repression against Puerto Ricans:

"In 1975, following the emergence of the FALN (Fuerzas Armadas de Liberacion Nacional) in the United States, several members of the Puerto Rican Socialist Party were threatened with subpoenaes, and one-Lureida Torres-was actually imprisoned for six months. In 1977-78, eleven persons-some associated with the National Commission on Hispanic Affairs of the Episcopal Church-were subpoenaed in New York and Chicago, and nine were imprisoned for periods ranging from three months to eleven months, for refusing to collaborate."

With the grand jury, the state built into its laws a mechanism to cover up its true motivations of quashing dissent and threats to oppressive institutions. By claiming some great threat to "public safety" or "national security" from "terrorist" activity, the state can imprison anyone who refuses to talk, anyone who won't provide information to the government about themselves or others. The Justice Department and intelligence agencies have thus targeted, disrupted, and caged numerous people in recent decades, simply for their opposition to US government policies.

The MLN goes on in its essay to detail the political basis for the repression brought down on the Puerto Rican independence movement. They describe how the US attorneys had an explicit rationale that "lengthy imprisonment of open, legal organizations and members which seek to mobilize public opinion in support of [independence]... is both a legal and valid way of pursuing the campaign against the independence movement."

In the summer 1984 issue of Breakthrough, Prairie Fire Organizing Committee (PFOC) put together a brief chronology of recent political internment. Outlined in this piece were the cases of Puerto Rican, Mexican, New Afrikan, and North American anti-imperialists who refused to collaborate with grand jury investigations, and who were arrested and convicted of criminal contempt. In all, dozens of activists were jailed from several months to many years for not answering the questions of the grand juries. PFOC explained how these grand juries were (and are) a violation of basic civil and political rights:

"Many people think of the grand jury as an impartial body that reviews evidence to determine if criminal indictments should be issued. But the political grand jury is nothing less than an interrogation center without the bright light. You cannot have a lawyer present. The government is not required to inform you of the nature of the investigation, or whether you yourself are under investigation. There are no limits to the scope of their questions, which you are required to answer under threat of contempt. ...By standing behind those who refuse to collaborate, by refusing to cooperate in any government investigation, we begin to build an awareness of the State and its repressive goals."

In 1984, a grand jury was convened in New York which targeted the those in support of the Puerto Rican independence movement. One Euro-american woman who was subpoenaed and who did not collaborate, wrote a lengthy statement to the Grand Jury in which she explained her support for liberation movements everywhere. As was the case for many activists of the era, her opposition grew out of the movement against the US war in Vietnam, and in fighting fopeace and justice at home. Far from being alone, she was part of a much larger movement:

"Like any other person, I have no desire to go to jail. I might be much more fearful to take this step if I were alone, though I would still refuse to talk. But I know that I do not stand alone. That while I take this position of non-collaboration as an individual, I am part of a much larger struggle-a struggle for a humane and just society for all of our children. And if my taking this stand can enable even one other person to have the strength and conviction to say 'No, I won't collaborate' then I am happy to make this contribution."

In the January/February 1984 Guild Notes, Michael Deutsch and Dennis Cunningham wrote a piece entitled "Developments in the Judicial Art of Repression," in which they outlined not only the recent use of grand juries, but several other of the "panoply of highly repressive legal devices which involve further radical perversions of fundamental constitutional rights." They highlight the resubpoenaing of a number of activists who had already resisted grand juries, and done jail time:

"...and public statements have made it absolutely clear that they would never testify=8A [T]he government has no expectation of gathering evidence. Their intention is nothing more or less than the incarceration of political and community activists without any charge of criminal wrongdoing: this is political internment, American style."

The political targets of grand juries have, of course, not been limited to activists. One of the more famous recent cases of grand jury repression involved a New York/Philadelphia attorney who did about six months at the Bucks County Correctional Facility for refusing to testify against a client who was accused of being involved with a "revolutionary group that was storing a cache of arms and explosives=8A [to be used on] the United States Congress." That's how the New York Times put it on 15 February 1991, in their article on Linda Backiel titled, "Defense Lawyer is Jailed Over Client Confidentiality" Clearly, however, Linda's case was about more than simply attorney-client privilege. It was also about the government trying to break the will of a committed advocate for justice. In Linda's statement, she told the court, "*I became a lawyer because I believe in justice. To each and every one of my clients I say: 'you must trust me with the truth; I will defend you with all my wit and skill and integrity. I am your advocate. I will never betray you.*"

The government did not happen upon Linda's case and decide to pick on her, out of the blue. Linda was subpoenaed to a Grand Jury by a prosecutor who wanted to use her testimony against a client. The government had long known of Linda's opposition to US government policies, and to the use of grand juries in particular. She testified against grand jury abuses in Congress and hadwritten briefs about the illegality of efforts to force lawyers to testify against clients. She had also appealed to the international human rightscommunity to recognize the human rights violations committed by the USespecially those committed against Puerto Rico and against political prisoners. Linda was targeted, as so many are, because of her effectiveness. She was (and likely is!) seen as a threat. Just our kind of lawyer, I'd say.

After acknowledging the inhumanity of jails and stating that she did not want to go to jail, Linda concluded her statement by affirming, *"...my dignity, and my commitment to my clients, which is my commitment to justice, are not intimidated by the threat of jail. Nor will a few months or even years in jail force me to exchange my ideals for a walk in the sun. Without dignity there can be no justice."*

So whether the target is community activists, folks doing direct action, or radical/progressive attorneys, the goal is the same. The government wants information. More than that, though, they want to scare us and all our friends, family, and neighbors into not carrying forward whatever urgent work it is we are doing that pisses off the powers that be. The numerous examples of people who've said NO to the government's scare tactics are so inspiring. We need to hear more stories of grand jury resistance. In my view, knowing the names and stories in the her/history of resistance to legal repression will help strengthen our movements so that we can't be bought or broken. Because we know that power and capital won't stop when this or that particular legal maneuvering ceases working. It may sound obvious, but I believe it deserves being said here: Defending our ideals, and indeed our communities will be as much about solidarity, and a keen awareness of those who came before us as it will be about knowing how to do a press release, trip a lock, or make a bomb.

HUNTER HARASSMENT" LAWS USED TO HARASS ACTIVISTS IN MINNESOTA...

Minnesota adopted a "hunters' rights" law in 1989. The law prohibits pickets or any other kind of anti-hunting demonstration, including singing, on public lands.

On November 12, 1994, over a dozen members of the Student Organization for Animal Rights (SOAR) entered the Murphey-Hanrahan Regional Park in Scott County to protest the killing of wildlife by speaking directly to the bow-hunters. Ten activists then received mailed citations for four misdemeanor charges: "Hunter Harassment", "Disturbing Wildlife", "Trespass Harassment", and "Trespass in a closed park". The first three charges stem from the "hunters' rights" law.

This is the first time that the "hunters' rights" law has been used in Minnesota, and SOAR hopes it will be the last. The "SOAR 10" are using the citations to legally challenge the "hunters' rights" law in the grounds that it is discriminatory and unconstitutional, and that hunters should not have the right to close a public park. The "SOAR 10" face up to 360 days in jail and a $2800 fine if convicted.

information from SOAR pamphlet
Student Organization for Animal Rights (SOAR)
235 CMU, 300 Washington Ave SE, Minneapolis, MN 55455, USA
SOAR hotline: 612-624-0422

...IN MONTANA...

On the week of April 17, Court TV aired the "hunter harassment" trial of Montana activist John Lilburn. Lilburn was charged with Montana's "hunter harassment" law a few years ago when he spoke out against the sport killing of bison. A Montana court declared the law unconstitutional, but a higher court overturned that decision. At the time of press we had no news on the verdict.

from Internet posting by Fund for Animals
<fund4animals@igc.apc.org>

...AND IN MICHIGAN

"Michigan is a VERY pro-hunting state with many hunter-harassment laws to protect the 5% that hunt here." - a Michigan animal liberation activist.

A Michigan couple was arrested under Michigan's "Hunter Harassment" law after approaching a hunter who was on a neighbor's property. The couple intended to speak to the man about his hunting activities on the property. Department of Natural Resources (DNR)staff then "jumped out of the bushes", after waiting for over two hours for the activists to come out and say something to the hunter. Obviously a sting arranged between the hunter and the DNR, to entrap this couple.

In the end, the activists had the last laugh. The charges against them were dropped because, as it turns out, this hunter was hunting illegally--he was too close to an occupied building.
information from a Michigan animal liberation activist

AND FINALLY, SOME GOOD NEWS

Ohio and Connecticut repealed their "hunters' rights" laws after challenges from animal liberation activists.

TED NUGENT SHELLS OUT BIG BUCKS AFTER DEFAMING ANTI-HUNTER!

DETROIT - Rock star and hunting advocate Ted Nugent has settled a defamation lawsuit stemming from a WRIF radio interview, agreeing to pay $75,000 to the plaintiff Heidi Prescott, National Director of The Fund for Animals.

On the November 19, 1992 morning talk show, only weeks after a Michigan anti-hunting protest organized by Ms. Prescott and The Fund for Animals, Mr. Nugent made several false statements aboutMs. Prescott.

"Ted Nugent is one hunter who shot himself in the foot," says Patricia Stamler, Southfield, Michigan-based attorney for Ms. Prescott. "We feel that our client's reputation, which was deeply tarnished by Mr. Nugent's patently false comments to the public, is on its way to restoration."

WRIF, a Detroit radio station which was also a defendant in the suit, settled out of court last year for a sizable sum, but Nugent settled just three days before the case was scheduled to go to trial.

"The Nuge is accustomed to attacking defenseless animals who do not have a fair chance to fight back," declares Ms. Prescott. "This time he took aim at the wrong target."

Ms. Prescott vows, "Ted's money will go far to fight hunting and to protect animals."
from Fund for Animals press release, April 4/95
For more information, contact Heidi Prescott at 301-585-2591

Nugent on guard

Rocker Ted Nugent says he has been the subject of death threats from animal rights activists over his avid promotion of animal hunting, which the singer claims keeps the balance of nature and land. He says he has been stalked in several cities by activists and has beefed up security on his latest tour.

WHAT YOU CAN DO TO SUPPORT PRISONERS

* Prisoners REALLY appreciate mail. It is often the only link they have to the outside world.

* Prisoners also appreciate money. Some prisoners can receive money sent directly to the jail; others cannot. Your best bet is to send money to one of the SGs, *clearly* marked "for (name of prisoner)". The SG can then pass it on to the prisoner in whatever form is necessary.

* Some prisoners can get other items sent to them in jail, eg. postcards, stamps, letter paper, envelopes, photos, books, clothing. Write the prisoner and ask what they can be mailed. Regulations vary from jail to jail.

* Buy magazine subscriptions so prisoners have reading material. In most cases, the magazine will get through if it is sent directly from the publisher.

* At certain times, in certain cases, letter-writing appeals may be requested. Often prisoners ask that letters be written to newspapers, state officials, or prison officials, to protest treatment of the prisoner or to protest a sentence. Again, the SGs are the best way to find out what letter-writing campaigns are currently happening.

This is only a general list. Individual prisoners may have needs above and beyond the points listed here. Your best bet is to write the prisoners themselves and ask what you can do for them.

Prisoners are frequently moved, occasionally released, and there are often people going in and out of jail on short sentences. It is best to contact the prisoner support groups that exist for up-to-date information.

The UK A.L.F. Supporters Group and the North American A.L.F. Supporters Group can provide you with updated info on each animal liberation prisoner.

UK-ALFSG: BCM 1160, London, WC1N 3XX, England
NA-ALFSG: PO Box 69597, 5845 Yonge St. Willowdale, Ont. Canada, M2M 4K3

PRISON AS INDUSTRY

by Lise Olsen, recently released animal rights activist

Prison. We tend to think of it, if we think of it at all, as a remote place in which dangerous violent persons who threaten our safety and way of life are contained. It is a place totally beyond the pale, out of the public eye. We are shocked when we read about the abuse of innocent people imprisoned in "foreign countries". The very foreignness of those distant countries is what enables us to be so righteously shocked. I was the same. I wrote many many letters on the behalf of prisoners of conscience persecuted in countries not my own. I was aware, as were most educated persons I knew, that human rights violations were going on, justified as punishment by "criminal-justice systems", in the former Soviet Union, Peoples Republic of China, Burma. I knew that the general population in Nazi Germany had said they "didn't know"; I also knew how self-righteous Americans (U.S.) could be in criticizing them for that "excuse". But I was totally unaware of the law-and-order-out-of-control, the imprisonment binge on the rampage in my own country, until I, a political prisoner, fell into the grip of the monster, the American penal system, myself.

The state in which I am incarcerated is Illinois. A state in which imprisoning non-violent people, charging taxpayers for their incarceration and attempting to thwart any efforts at rehabilitation is a multi-million dollar industry. The aims of this arrest-conviction-incarceration are two-fold: imprisonment and recidivism. I have now been in prison 6 1/2 months, and in this time I have interviewed hundreds of fellow-prisoners. The average middle-class taxpayer would be amazed to know what petty "offenses" or violations of the law eat up his tax dollars in order to pay the $25,000 per annum per prisoner that the Illinois Department of Corrections [IDOC-ed.] receives. Driving on a revoked license, one year in prison. This works out to six months in prison and six on parole. With the two 3-month periods of "good time" legislated by the state awarded to the prisoner, in actual fact there is no time to be served. Inasmuch as the IDOC cannot receive the actual payment until the prisoner has been incarcerated sixty days, therefore the inmate will be kept in prison sixty days so that the money can be collected. During that time the person cannot take care of her rent, loses her job and cannot pay her bills. Not one bit of "rehabilitation" is offered the prisoner. The objective is to exhaust her bank account, leave her jobless, disoriented and emotionally distraught and (hopefully) to get her to take to a life of crime, prostitution, retail theft and drug addiction. Having shattered a responsible lifestyle, the objective of recidivism becomes much more likely, along with the tempting prospect of another $25,000 when the "offender" is incarcerated the next time round.

Would you like to be imprisoned for the theft of three watermelons and a gallon of milk? Impossible, you say. Not in the United States, the land of the free, not in Illinois, the land of Lincoln. Yet my roommate in Dwight Penitentiary was serving a one-year sentence for exactly that. Her problem, kleptomania caused by a loveless, arranged marriage, was being treated by psychiatric counseling. Having once been arrested for stealing a carton of cigarettes while in a fugue state (she didn't even smoke), she was given probation. She never missed a probation date, yet stole again, again in a fugue state, and was arrested a second time for the watermelons-and-milk. Next followed a two-year period on bond in which therapy continued, no court dates were missed and no violations occurred. Despite selling her home to pay a $35,000 legal fee, her sentence was a year in prison. Her psychiatrist's testimony that the psychological trigger to the retail thefts was resolved as well as the proof of her own behavior for two years on bond made no difference. How could it in a court where the conviction rate is 99%?

A 99% conviction statistic already tells us that something is dreadfully wrong somewhere. True, media and our own eyes show us every day that our society is violent, drug-ridden and dangerous. Yet even given the fact that violence, generalized, gang-related and domestic is on the upswing, 99% conviction is too high, too unbalanced. Even in childbirth there is a 50-50 chance of male or female babies. So how do so many convictions occur? And why, if they are occurring, does violent crime in our country never seem to be reduced? Are the means meeting the ends, or are the wrong people going to prison?

As in any dictatorship, conviction is a virtually foregone conclusion when a person is arrested. This is a fact so abhorrent to the American public that they are in complete denial about it. The media promotes the conspiracy by providing the current diet of tabloid journalism. Gone, seemingly forever, are the days of fair, investigative reporting. "The strength of the vampire lies in the fact that no-one will believe in him," it states in Bram Stoker's Dracula. Who would believe that our "democratic" government is the author of a conspiracy to set people up for lives of ignorance, poverty and petty crime, to paint them as dangerous criminals in the media and then to imprison them as a subterranean slave-class for which it is paid so-much-per-head by the middle class, who is kept in the dark about the reality of the situation and who wants to be kept in the dark about it, in order to maintain their illusion of safety and normalcy in their own everyday lives?

My own case provides a typical example of how the destruction of a life can be accomplished in order to assure incarceration and collection of the annual fee. The one difference between myself (thus far) and those who have no savings, education or financial backup is that I do have resources and a profession with which to reclaim my life after prison, difficult as that will be to do. Even if my profession is taken from me, as is certainly the State Attorney's desire and design, I should still be able to re-enter the work force in some other sphere, thus thwarting the recidivist-goal. The vast majority of prisoners can not.

How did I get from being a "respectable" member of society, a registered nurse and nurse-practitioner, to being fuel for the prison industry mill? By challenging the system of money which is the lord of the United States society. As an animal rights activist, the only one imprisoned in the United States, I challenged the vested interests of the fur industry. Although this article is not really about me per se, my case serves to illustrate the operation, built on a network of deceptive practices, of the prison industry conspiracy.

Deceptive practice #1 requires an arrest. As Americans, we are adverse to admitting that any person not actually fleeing from police can be arrested without a warrant. Yet it happened to me. Not only was I not fleeing anywhere, I was in my bed at home. Deceptive practice #2 requires a confession. The antidote to this practice is refusing to talk to the police under any circumstances until your attorney arrives. The difficulty here is that many people may not have a criminal attorney to call upon. Or they may be so innocent of any wrong-doing, as I was, that they openly and earnestly speak to the police in order to explain the reality of the situation. In my case, I explained how four months earlier I had attempted, on the U.S. Independence Day, to illuminate a large "Freedom" banner (red-white-blue) hung over a steel railway overpass viaduct on which pro-fur advertising was painted. This banner was to be illuminated with 21 home-made gas lanterns affixed in metal holders, the idea being to make a 1776-style display that could last for five minutes, long enough to take a photo for the media. Only one lit, though, burned with a small flame as designed, and went out on its own, candle-style, when the fuel was consumed. The festive display did not work and I, discouraged, had collected my banner and gone home, leaving the lanterns along with all the spent rockets and firecrackers lying about everywhere. The detective listened sympathetically; however, even he was telling me that he now understood that this was just a fourth of July anti-fur protest and he wasn't "going to make a big deal out of it", he was writing down that the lanterns were "Molotov cocktails designed to blow up the whole bridge" and that I (Lise Olsen) had "signed a confession to arson". This lying statement, common to most arrests, is witnessed by nobody; in my case, the detective also told the media and the Grand Jury the same pack of lies. Not until my trial almost two years later, when confronted by my attorney to produce his "signed confession", did he admit that he had "made an error" about it.

Armed now with an arrest and a "confession", and with the States' Attorney and trial judge on his side, as well as the Director of the Department of Corrections, it is easy to move on to the next deceptive practice, which ensures conviction. This process is two-fold and requires manipulation of evidence and discreditation of the defendant's character. Both are easy to accomplish and are set up, at some point during the multiple continuances that make salaries for detectives, court clerks, bailiffs, sheriffs and judges each time one occurs (taxpayers paying all the while, of course, as well as the defendant, exhausting more of her savings with every appearance, missing more time from work and generally setting the stage for the depletion of resources that is the basis of the desired end-goal, recidivism), in a conference called the "402". It is at this point in the proceedings, which can be over a year after the arrest yet is always prior to the trial, that plea-bargains occur. One must remember that many defendants, unable to pay astronomical bonds, are in jail all this time, under conditions of dire privation. So plea-bargaining is a great temptation. The positive side of the plea-bargain, in theory, is that the sentence will be lighter in return for a guilty plea. I, however, was not offered a plea-bargain: I was asked to plead guilty to the same contrived felony counts I had already been charged with (possession, manufacture and transportation of incendiary devices, attempted arson plus unlawful use of a weapon, in my case meaning possession of more than three tablespoons of gasoline). In the "402 conference" a little stage play is enacted between judge and States' Attorney -- depending on the level of collusion, they can dupe even an experienced criminal attorney completely. This is because promises are made in this conference (defendant is not permitted to participate, of course), that are never put in writing. The entire process is based upon honesty and trust.

In my 402 conference the States' Attorney maintained that I should be given a prison sentence; he was "morally outraged" by my protest action which caused no injury nor property damage. So the judge pointed out that this "offense" was probationable and that he could hardly imprison a person who had caused no harm. The States' Attorney then begged for 6 months in Cook County Jail: the judge again pointed out that such a sentence was disproportionate to any damage or injury done. This act led my attorney to believe that we had a realistic chance of justice at my trial, which we then decided to go for. Unfortunately my attorney failed to see beyond the act.

This leads to the point of manipulation of evidence. Again, my trial serves as a good example, worthy of the former Soviet Union. Yet thousands of trials contain these same elements. Paid informers can provide "eye-witness" testimony, for example. Introduction of testimony from a previous offense in which the defendant was acquitted can be allowed. Because the judge is in a position of complete omnipotent power, nothing can be done to acquit an innocent person if he assumes, or in a sense becomes, the States' Attorney. It is comparable to the situation when the government turns military artillery against the people. When tanks enter the streets, the populace doesn't stand a chance.

In my trial, manipulation of evidence (over my attorney's objections) included: admission of testimony by a security policeman against me for a rescue attempt of two cats from the research lab at the hospital where I was employed, although the attempt had failed and the charge against me had been dismissed. Not only dismissed, even legally expunged. Surprise, though, the expungement order had never been carried out and fingerprints on the lanterns, an action done not-secretly but in full view of all fourth of July holiday-makers around and noticed, presumably by any and all policemen driving by to and from the police station one block from the railway overpass, were matched with the "expunged" record. That is what led to my arrest four months later, without a warrant. Now, at my trial, the security policeman was asked to testify against me in a case that was legally expunged (equal to never having existed) when he had never done that even in the first case. Another manipulation of evidence included bringing my lanterns from the police warehouse in plastic bags, each labelled BOMB in big red letters, and placing them in a ring around the courtroom for the jury to see. It was also permissible for the jury to see large color photos of the lanterns removed from their original dangling positions (over the billboard) and lined up along train tracks with a train coming towards them. It was also acceptable to deny an actual video made by my expert witness, a renowned explosives consultant for the military, of a replica lantern alight. Needless to say, when the arresting detective was forced to admit that he had made an "error" in his Grand Jury statement about a signed confession, the judge never charged him with perjury. The fact that I was arrested without a warrant on an expunged record were also totally acceptable. Testimony against me from the previously dismissed "cat" action was sanctioned as showing "intent of previous Crimes" (note plural).

This leads to the important point of character defamation, a tremendously effective deceptive practice vital to obtaining convictions and imprisonments. Popular thinking is that only poor blacks suffer from this, yet is a vital element in the conviction and imprisonment of everybody. it was held against me, in particular, for example, that I am a registered nurse. The most outrageous thing about my Independence Day protest seemed to be, in the eyes of the judge-and-States' Attorney, that I, Lise Olsen, had betrayed my race, my class and my education by challenging a monied industry, one similar to the industry in which they are involved. What the fur-bearing animals are to the fur industry, defendants are to the prison industry: fodder. It was clear that my education was totally held against me, as evidenced by the judge's statement when a motion to dismiss was filed on the basis that I had never been given the Miranda warnings (whatever you say to the police can and will be used against

you -- what this actually means is, don't open your mouth at all, because if you speak at all, totally different things will be written down and used against you in court). The judge ruled that it was just the detective's word against mine, but even if I had not been read my rights, it didn't matter because I had a high level of education and should have known them anyway. This kind of discrimination against me, as an educated person, or "intellectual" as it is known in other countries, colored my trial, sentencing and conviction. The court-and-prison system are designed to prevent the defendant from ever speaking in his/her defense. This aids the defamation of character deceptive practice tremendously. A typical example of this occurred at my sentencing: having been offered probation by the trial judge at the 402 conference I openly and honestly filled out the probation forms done with me by a probation officer. This included revealing the name of the last place I had worked, a clinic in which six employees were fired when a patient treated us to an after-work champagne toast on New Year's Eve after the patient care was concluded. Almost all employees appealed this summary mass firing at Unemployment Compensation. At my own hearing, the company's witness against me said nothing worse about me than that I had "tasted one sip of champagne". This was distorted by the States' Attorney at my sentencing into my being fired "for being drunk on the job". The States' Attorney is under no accountability whatsoever to say anything truthful or accurate about the defendant -- and yet the defendant is totally not permitted by the structure of the court system to defend herself; she cannot speak in order to refute such slanders. Thus conviction is assured.

Having explored the legally-sanctioned deceptive practice of warrant-less arrest, introduction of material from expunged/dismissed cases, fabrication of evidence and character-assassination, it is time to address the ultimate goal of the industry conspiracy, recidivism. Having assured conviction and the longest possible prison sentence, justified in my case by making an "example" of me since one could hardly claim damage or injury done, and any potential for same was totally refuted by the testimony of the expert witness, the government is assured of a healthy income from the taxpayers for the inmate for several years. based on any claims of endangerment that the States' Attorney feels inclined to write in his Official Statement of Facts (a document required by law, allegedly to furnish the Department of Corrections with the "facts and circumstances of the offense" which in actual fact contains personal opinions, animus and lies), a prisoner's actual time in prison can be extended enormously by denial of work release, electronic detention or meritorious good time. But eventually the prisoner will have to be released. Now it becomes imperative for the perpetuation of the prison industry for new charges or cases to be brought against the prisoner, whether on parole or before. One can do this by waiting to serve any outstanding warrants until she is coming right out of the prison door, giving her no chance to go to court and solve things while already in prison. Fabricating reasons for indictment at FBI Grand Juries is another good way. And there are other ways too, all of which can commence while a first sentence is being served, in preparation for having a second one.

The first way is to set up a prisoner while she is still in prison to insure that she will be totally uneducated and unprepared to support herself in society in a meaningful way when she gets out of prison. Contrary to popular belief, educational opportunities are minimal in prison. That some exist is because it is necessary to maintain the popular myth in the public eye that prisons are "rehabilitative" in nature. Government, however, is working hard to make sure that rehabilitation does not occur, and this can be accomplished in several ways. One is by vetoing money to fund education, the grant called the Pell Grant in the United States. This cancellation of federal money for prison education has already been accomplished in the U.S. under the new Crime Bill. Sentences will be longer too -- 85% of time now requires to be served rather than 50%. Prisoners can wait 4-8 months just to get into a GED (high school substitute) program, meanwhile wasting vast amounts of time assigned as janitors, playing cards and watching endless amounts of television. Giving prisoners free cheap cigarettes or arrival (even those who are fighting to be assigned to non-smoking cells) and stocking the commissary with every sort of junk food while making constructive items like sewing kits, manila envelopes and school folders rare contributes to the goal-less lifestyle. Certain prisoners are eligible to receive time off their sentences for going to school, but it is easy to make sure that the person won't complete her contract (certain amount of time required to be in school in order to accrue these "good days") by transferring the prisoner to another prison before her contract is completed. Another effective method is to accuse the prisoner or almost anything (sticking out her tongue playfully in a joke can be called "sexual misconduct", tossing a half-pint of milk in play "assault"), write a "disciplinary ticket" on her (guilt of whatever the "charge" is is decided prior to the mock "hearing" that follows the ticket) which will lead to her being locked up in "segregation" (solitary confinement 23 hours a day, unfortunately with another prisoner, overcrowding being what it is). If a prisoner is attacked by another, both go to "seg". After four classes are missed (easy to arrange since people are always being sent to "seg" for weeks), the prisoner is expelled from class and all "good time" is lost.

Needless to say, the token "state pay" that each prisoner is given in order to buy necessary personal items from the commissary is lowest for students -- a miserable $10 per month. Therefore, for those unfortunate enough to be entirely dependent upon state pay, going to school is not a high priority compared to competing for a non-student assignment that could pay as high as a whopping $30/month.

It is also important to make it difficult and arduous for prisoners to get to the library or to typewriters or to xerox copiers. The original typing of this article is a marvelous testimonial to that. So if a prisoner achieves any education while in prison, it is due to her own intiative and determination in spite of the obstructiveness of the system, not because of all the opportunities offered to her.

So uneducated she came, uneducated she returns. Being just where she was when arrested originally, uneducated, without savings (any she had went to attornies' fees and court costs, plus paying life expenses for her children while imprisoned), she is much more likely to return to her former ways of making money and former associations than if she was not actually prepared to assume a role in the mainstream work force. Of course, the court records may be viewed by anyone wishing to hire her, alongside with the slanderous Official Statement of Fact. Who would want to hire anyone deliberately depicted by the States' Attorney as being the most horrible criminal on earth?

The Official Statement of Facts has been a major weapon both in terms of ensuring that prison sentences are as long as possible (if it serves as a tool for preventing people from going to work release, then it maintains them in the meaningless limbo existence of the prison and keeps them from working gainfully and/or going to school in the outside world, where they would be able to complete their classes without the constant threat of being transferred to another prison or going to "seg" over their heads), and keeping people from getting productive jobs once out. Because it is so biased and harmful to building a meaningful life and future, it has been challenged legally several times. Despite claims by prisoner-plaintiffs that the States' Attorney has no accountability to anyone in terms of what he writes (true), the court ruled in 1946 and again in 1973 that the official statement of facts of an individual's case imposes no limitations on the States' Attorney, that although it is is mandated by law that the "statement be transmitted to the institution to which the defendant is committed to furnish it with the facts and circumstances of the offense...which may aid the department during its custody of such a person" that it is also allowable for the statement to contain opinions and recommendations as well. Since these are of course going to be very negative, the "facts" will only serve to condemn. Furthermore, the Act which describes the content of the Official Statement (Illinois Revised Statute 1971, ch. 108, par. 203) was revised in 1973 (West's Illinois Court Decisions, 194, 628 N.E. 2d 370, page 873), thusly: "The legislature removed the trial judge from the process...and placed in his stead the defense counsel, thus giving the State and the defendant the opportunity to submit statements to Illinois Department of Corrections in an attempt to achieve some objective balance between the statements offered by the real parties in interest." However, the Department of Corrections does not even include the defense counsel's statement in the prisoner's file -- it is discarded once submitted, thus rendering it valueless when making any decisions about the prisoner's life that would require an "objective balance". Nor is it included in the court record that future employers may examine when they decide whether to hire an ex-convict or not. The Official Statement is also used as a perpetual justification in denying extra good time (different from school "good days") for which some prisoners are eligible. Even the lowest class of felony can be denied this good time based upon any allegation of endangerment the States' Attorney feels motivated to include, while Class X offenders convicted of "violent crimes" can receive it if the States' Attorney has no personal agenda to pursue against an individual prisoner via his "Official Statement".

Because of the political agenda against me in making an"example" of me as an animal rights activist, I, a Class 2"offense" called "Possession of Incendiary Devices" was denied the extra good time I was eligible for, when Class X offenders who had actually done bodily harm or property damage received it. Moreover, the Department of Corrections insisted upon entering the charge against me in their computer as "Possession of Explosives" because that happened to be in the same statute although I had not been charged or convicted of that. In spite of an Appellate Court order to remove the prejudicial "Possession of Explosives" from their computer, which had justified denying me a transfer to a minimum-security prison where one could visit with relatives in a relaxed way and go to the library as in the normal world, IDOC defied the court order and let the frightening and volatile word "explosives" remain.

In some instances, due to a prisoner's determination to help herself in spite of the agendas the system has against her, she acquires a marketable skill while in prison and later succeeds in getting a job. How to assure recidivism now? By placing so many obstacles in her path as she attempts to rebuild her life that she will get caught in some sort of wrong-doing and thereby be sent to prison again. This is quite simple to accomplish. Take, for example, the case of a single divorced mother who was renting part of a house for herself and her two children. They had lived there a year, the children were in school and the mother's beautician license bore the address, naturally, where they were residing. The owner of the house who rented out the flat was engaged at the time she and her children moved in. But during the course of the year, his engagement was broken off. One night he appeared in the woman's room and said she would have to sleep with him in order to go on living there. The next day she took her children and herself to her ex-husband's apartment to stay temporarily, then returned a few days later to move their belongings. Two months later she was arrested for residential burglary. The man from whom she had rented had charged her with stealing his computer discs. Although she did not possess a computer, she was arrested. And she convicted herself, just as I did, through her naivete in speaking to the police without an attorney present. Remember Deceptive Practice #1? I told I had made lanterns to light up a banner. She admitted she had moved her belongings from her own address. Was her name on the lease? No. She remained in the county jail 1 1/2 months, unable to post bond, observing how many continuances everyone went out on, to court, and how interminable the proceedings were before one was able to get to trial. Unable to be away from her children, she plea-bargained with a guilty plea -- and got 2 1/2 years in prison. This adds up to 9 months of actual time, but at least she was able to make arrangements for their care before going away. However, she ended up with a felony conviction for moving her own belongings from her own address. Another $25,000 of the taxpayer's money into the pocket of the State. Mission accomplished!

Another simple technique to send innocent people back to prison is by planting drugs on them. One woman I met in Cook County Jail had been to prison "four times, unfortunately", as she stated ruefully. Her problem, a heroin addiction of many years, had finally been conquered over by participation in a drug rehabilitation program. At last she had her own apartment and a job in a restaurant, and was on the verge of bringing her children to live with her, after relying for many years on help from her own mother. Because of her history, the neighborhood police recognized her easily. One day, riding home on her bicycle from visiting a person to whom she had lent money and to whom she had gone to get it back, the police "pulled her over". Why? Because the person whom she had visited sold drugs. She told me that everyone in her neighborhood was in some way involved with drugs; just because she visited someone did not implicate her though. The police searched her beside her bicycle, in full daylight -- nothing. Suddenly the police picked up a "rock" of cocaine from the grass, saying it was hers. Although she was a heroin addict and did not use cocaine, this "evidence" was enough. Busted. Loss of job. Loss of apartment. Loss of children. Prison.

Probably the most useful tool of the police in the recidivism crusade is a person's "history". No matter how exaggerated or fabricated this history is, even if it involves a dismissed case legally expunged, as mine did, one is automatically guilty of anything and everything the police wish to charge one with based upon any previous arrest. It is best if new cases can be fabricated even before one finishes the current prison sentence. In my own situation, this was especially easily accomplished by the "smear-technique", what in childhood we called "name-calling". It is a myth that one is innocent until proven guilty. Consider the example of the McCarthy era and the witch-hunt and destruction of lives that ensued by merely calling people "communists". Because I am an "animal rights activist", a legally dismissed and expunged case was allowed into evidence in a court of law in order to show the jury my "intent of previous crimes" or political ideology. Because I am an animal rights activist the States' Attorney called me a "terrorist" in court, after the judge had ruled that this prejudicial word could not be used; however, the judge did not reprove him in any way when he used it. Because I am an animal rights activist (or "terrorist" as they would have you believe to be synonymous) I was sentenced to four years in prison for making lanterns (or "candles" as the explosives/electrostatics consultant for the military called them in his expert opinion) that did not injury or property damage nor were intended to. This was to make an "example" of me. Having succeeded so well in their political agenda, backed up by the Department of Corrections while in prison (remember denial of good time and denial of transfers based upon the allegations of potential endangerment in the omnipotent Official Statement, supported by the fictitious charge "Possession of Explosives" in the computer), further situations can be exploited to further the "terrorist" libel. Even situations that are meant to be mitigating to the prisoner, such as a clemency hearing based upon claims that the sentence was grossly disproportionate to the crime, can be used to augment the "terrorist" image, beloved of media as well as by government. In order to make a clemency hearing as much as a travesty as the original trial, several simple rules can be followed: 1. do not read the petition 2. do not read the letter of character testimony and support 3. do not read the evaluation of the actual nature of the candle by the explosives expert 4. DO interrogate supporters about their "terrorist" affiliations and/or arrest records.

Most taxpayers, like the general population in Nazi Germany are feeling safer and more protected [now] that "terrorists" are in prison. In China they are called "capitalist roaders", in the former Soviet Union "intellectuals". Now, having tagged an activist a terrorist, it is a simple matter to scapegoat this person with another charge BEFORE SHE EVEN LEAVES PRISON ON THE FIRST UNJUST CONVICTION AND INCARCERATION. This is the ultimate recidivism: arrange for the whole gamut of arrest by deceptive practice, fabrication/manipulation of evidence, conviction and imprisonment before she even gets done with her first sentence. Then she will receive another prison sentence, this time doing 85% of the sentence under the new crime bill, denied the Pell Grant to go to school under the new crime bill, and the taxpayers will be paying another $25,000 per year into the pockets of the government for many more years to come.

How can this be arranged when the accused person is wholly innocent? Well she isn't "innocent", in fact she's a convict, no matter how unjustly. The best way to fabricate another case when there is no evidence to convict a person is to find probably cause to arrest before a Grand Jury. In this secret proceeding (no attorney can attend to witness it) 23 innocent main-stream people are presented with a slanted scenario that invariably leads to indictment. Case in point: being imprisoned for being an animal rights activist leads irresistably to being arrested for anything and everything that has the word "animal" in it. Unable to find actual suspects for smokebombs discovered in Chicago department stores in November '93, the FBI has been fingerprinting by deceptive means friends of mine in order to try, seemingly, to match us with the gadgets. None match. Hence, implied evidence is necessary in order to achieve an indictment. This can be done in three ways: soliciting bank statements and implying that any amount that seems unusually large, such as a bequest from a dying relation as in my case, came from a mysterious and illegal source, a sort of "hit-man" implication. Another method is to state that the accused person worked near one of the department stores in question (of course, in the downtown area of a major city, so did thousands of other people, but that common-sense reality is not presented). The last means is the use of paid informers, not those who overheard secret plots and then tell (that cannot be when no plots were hatched), but those who fabricate completely invented testimony for cash.

The tremendous majority of cases, however, do bear some link to the "offense" for which a person is imprisoned, although the prisoners are innocent of any crime. A minor example of this is the divorced mother who removed her own belongings from the house where she had been renting, then was charged with residential burglary. I say "minor" because the sentence, after plea-bargaining, was "only" 2 1/2 years. The situation becomes deadly serious, though, when the "offense" involves self-defense of a woman's person or that of her children. Twenty year sentences for murder involving self-defense are common in Illinois and throughout the United States. Case in point: the mother discovered that her long-term boyfriend had raped her baby daughter. In a flash she remembered how this had happened to another woman who had, like a dutiful citizen, called the police. The rapist received a three-year sentence and all his good time. In fact, he spent a mere nine months in prison. So, knowing that justice would not be served by the "criminal-justice system", she took a butcher knife and stabbed him -- once. He died. Then she called the police. Once at the hospital, as the doctors were examining her baby, screaming and calling for her mother, she was handcuffed, separated from the screaming child as well as her two older sons (whom she lost to the Department of Children and Family Services), and taken to jail. Her arrest for murder resulted in a twenty-year sentence: no extra good time, no school days. She has never gone back home again. Her baby is now seven years old.

Self-defense and the battery of women and children is not considered a defense in Illinois. Illinois has the lowest clemency rate in the United States. Of the eight women who presented a clemency appeal under the Illinois Battered Women's Clemency Project, only four received clemency. The governor, Jim Edgar, however, stated on television that yet another, Vickie, "should have received clemency". Since he is the one to bestow it, the question arises: why didn't he?

Vickie is, therefore, in prison. So is Fran, who, unlike Vickie, is serving a life sentence for murder -- a murder that was also an act of self-defense. This occurred in Texas, in a rural community. A rejected suitor broke in Fran's farmhouse and attacked her, threatening to kill her. She shot him. Unfortunately, Fran's situation was complicated by the fact that she happened to be an animal rights activist, opposing the cruelty of the meat industry in an area that depended largely on factory farming. The political agenda and local prejudice against Fran led to her being taken out of commission -- forever.

The United States, under the guise of a democracy, has the highest rate of imprisonment in the world. We are the most imprisoning nation, according to Citizens United for the Rehabilitation of Errants. As the government in its "war on crime" allows channels for drugs to enter the country, it also has a multi-million dollar industry on the receiving end in arresting addicts, small-time dealers and middlepersons; then, in collaboration with the current trend in tabloid media which is always happy to exaggerate, magnify and sensationalize any case in order to market their titillating product, all these people are put in prison, presented to the middle-class taxpayer as important and threatening drug kingpins. As in a wartime economy where jobs are generated in munitions factories, the prison industry is our current substitute for the factory. In Florida, the legislature approved building 14,000 new prison beds in 1994. According to the Coalition for Prisoners' Rights Newsletter, author unknown of Bonifay, Fl., ***"UNCLE SAM NEEDS YOU...to fill his prison bed! Who's gonna fill these beds? Someone will have to fill them. Whether guilty of a crime or not! By the time you get out of court with your P.D. (Public Defender) you will be guilty of things you've never heard of. Cause Uncle Sam needs you..."***

The prison industry, like any other big business, has audits, accountants and quotas. Before election time a certain quota has to be met for judges to be re-elected and considered tough on crime by the naive and unaware taxpayer who votes for him -- little dreaming that his own demise from taxpayer to prisoner is just around the corner. Judges publish how many convictions they achieved in order to get votes. How many black, how many white, how many Hispanic....This quota must be met. Sentenced prior to an election, I received four years for an "offense" that did not property damage nor injury nor was intended to. Even any accidental potential for damage or injury was refuted by a nationally renowned explosives-electrostatics specialist who has designed an

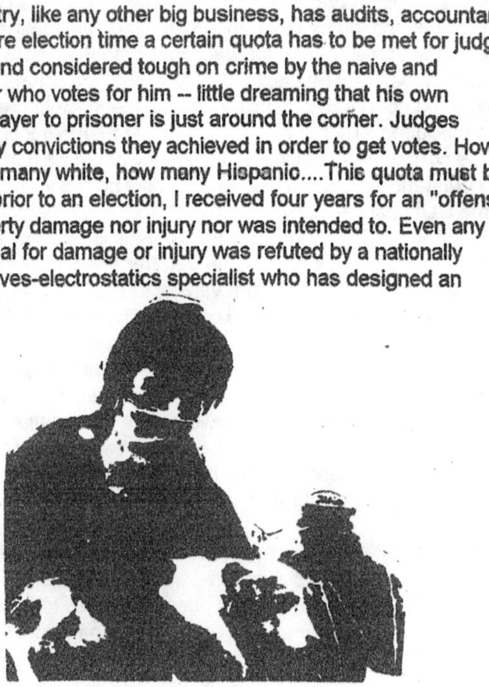

explosives dispersal system for a submissile warhead for the Department of Defense -- and who testified that my "configurations" were "candles" with no danger to the public whatsoever. After the election, I met another prisoner with a two year sentence, sentenced by the same judge. Her crime? Aggravated Battery with Armed Violence with a Weapon (she stabbed a man in the chest and punctured his lung three times), Class X.

Denied the extra good time I am eligible to as a Class 2 prisoner, extra good time awarded to Class X prisoners charged with Armed Robbery, Armed Violence and Aggravated Arson solely to make an example of me as a political prisoner, denied transfer to a minimum-security prison solely because of Possession of Explosives being entered in the computer against me in defiance of an Appellate Court Order to remove it (five prisoners with the charge of Murder live there), denied work-release or home monitoring due to the slanderous allegations of potential danger inherent in my lanterns, I wish my experience to serve as a warning for others. The United States, far from being a "free" society, is in fact a totalitarian regime profiting on the destruction and enslavement of its own people. Although the United States has the routine of elections, thereby creating an image to the world of "democracy" or freedom to choose by voting, in actual fact the two-party system is dead as it relates to the ordinary citizen. What is in operation in reality is a king, replaced at intervals, and a court of wealthy protected courtiers. Instead of replacing the king (president, prime minister, call him what you like) by coup d'état, we do it in a "civilized" way, by a ritual called elections. But the end result is the same: a privileged minority and a slave class in prison, funded by a mainstream Americana who is full of fear at having their traditional way of life threatened and therefore supportive of the prison industry, which they are taught by the media to believe contains those violent criminals who would jeopardize their way of life. Little do they know that they are next, the future grist for the prison mill. Make one tiny error: unresolved traffic tickets, removing one's belongings from a former house or apartment, riding a bike in a neighborhood where police know that you have been arrested before, being an animal rights activist, defending your life or the life of your children -- and you will find that your illusion of middle-class American freedom was only that, a dream. You too will cross over to the other side, into the land of imprisonment that is a living hell and which you never imagined that you could possibly ever enter.

One fellow prisoner at Dixon Prison was waiting for a taxi one snowy night. A police car pulled up. The officer asked her if she was alright, did she want to sit inside his car. Bitter experience had taught her never to trust police, as she had suffered through the whole arrest-and-court system previously on a DUI (Driving Under the Influence) charge, on which she was found "not guilty". She told the stress of her trial on that charge was so intense that she burst out crying after the ordeal was over. Now, remembering the deceptive practices perpetrated on her by the police before, she declined to sit in a police car out of the snow. The officer did not like this. So he asked for identification, which of course she produced, like any normal citizen. He then proceeded to check his police computer (checking an innocent woman waiting for a taxi) for any outstanding warrants for her arrest. And found one! For the very same DUI case, all concluded, which had never been removed from the computer. She found herself inside his police car, all right, in handcuffs. Five days later, separated from her children and having lost her job, she was taken, after a vaginal exam, TB test and multiple strip-searches, before a judge. And of course he saw that the warrant was invalid, she had been found not guilty, the case concluded. No apologies offered. No compensation advanced. But "justice" had been served, the "law" had been followed. Citizens are obliged to walk a tightrope of good behavior, following rules and regulations one could not even predict would be required, such as not attracting police attention while waiting for taxis in the snow. But government is held to no accountability whatsoever. Is this America?

To quote another "voice from inside", this one from Anamosa IA (Coalition for Prisoners' Rights Newsletter, Vol. 19, No. 12, December 1994), "For the privately owned prison business to expand and profit, it will become increasingly appealing to induce failure into every effort at reforming society's mistakes. As in any livestock operation, the rancher will always seek to enlarge his herd...Without support for social and economic programs needed to repair the moral and financial fabric of our communities, our country will naively continue to believe in this failed system until every citizen is either a rancher or owned by one

-Lise Olsen is now free after having served the prison sentence given to her by the courts. Lise's case serves as an example to all of us of ho the government will do what ever it can in its attempt to destroy the animal liberation movement.

ANIMAL LIBERATION PRISONERS

ENGLAND

Melanie Arnold GJ0940
HMP Pucklechurch, Pucklechurch, bristol, BS17 3QJ, England.

On remand charged with Section 2 o f the explosives ac t in realtion to attack on a bottoir in Gloucester.

Gurjeet Aujla HV2047
HMP Leicester, 118 Welford Road, Leicester, LE2 7AJ.

On remand for alleged Justice Department Actions

Greg Avery HV3313
HMP Birmingham, Winston Green Road, Birmingham, B18 4AS

Remand prisoner charged with conspiracy to commit criminal damage.

Dave Callender HV3314
HMP Birmingham, Winston Green Road, Birmingham, B18 4AS

Remand prisoner charged with conspiracy to commit criminal damage.

Michael Green VA2923
HMP Gloucester, Barrack Square, Gloucester, GL1 2JN, England.

On remand charged with Section 2 of the explosives act in realtion to attack on abottoir in Gloucester.

Angie Hamp TW1687
HMP Askham Grange, Askham Richard, York, YO2 3PT, England

Sentenced to 4 years for conspiracy to commit arson. The actual raid in question caused 3/4 million pounds worth of damage.

Niel Hanson HF3184
HMP The Mount, Bovingdon, Hemel Hempstead, Herts, HP3 0NZ, England.

Sentenced to 3 for Conspiracy to dispatch a hoax bomb and criminal damage to the property of the public relation officers of Glaxos (vivisectors).

Keith Mann EE3588
HMP Full Sutton, Nr Stamford Bridge, York, YO4 1PS, England.

Sentenced to 14 years for Arson attack on meat vehicles, inciting others to cause criminal damage, escape from jail and conspiracy to cause explosions.

Michelle Ratcliffe RL1456
HMP Holloway, Parkhurst Road, Holloway, London, N7 0NU, England.

On remand on charges of an arson attack on a lairage connected with Shoreham harbour.

Geoff Sheppard MD1030
HMP Wandsworth, PO Box 757, Heathfield Road, London, SW18 3HS, England.

Sentenced to 7 years for possession of items with intent to make incendiary devices and possession of a shotgun. Geoff has already served a four year sentence in the 1980s for incendiary actions against the fur trade in department stores.

Note: Gillian Peachey is to be sentenced on the 20th October for conspiracy to plant incendiary devices, and is expecting in the regions of two years.

Laura Nicol
HMP Low Newton, Brasside, Durham, DH! 5SD
Laura was sent down for 98 days for non-payment of fines relating to hunt sab and live export activity. She's expected to do about 7 weeks.

GOOD NEWS - Several prisoners released!

Allison McKeon, Max Watson, and **Terry Helsby** (serving 2 years, 3 years, and 3 1/2 years respectively for damage caused to butchers' shops and a zoo) have all been released. Allison was released in late 1994, Max was released in February 1995, and Terry was released in March 1995.

Colin Chatfield, who was doing 4 months for sending a hoax bomb call to Boots, was released on November 25/94.

Jeannette McCallum, Gillian Peachey's co-defendant in the Tesco's egg hoax contamination, was released on strict bail conditions.

Anette Tibbles, serving 4 years for conspiracy to commit arson in relation to two arson attacks on meat vehicles, wasreleased on parole in April.

Justin Wright was released on bail on Oct 27.

Robin Webb was on remand on Section 38 of the Public Orderact (conspiracyto incite), in relation to the release of a press statement concerning a contamination hoax. Robin was released from HMP Winchester where he had been enjoying (ha ha) the security of his one man cell, an unusual item in the UK.He's back in court in Dec., and it's possible he may end up back inside.

*POLICE GRASS*POLICE GRASS *

(from the Liberator)

JEANETTE McCLUNAN: Due to suspicions about this activists behaviour and an increase in police activity, the decision was taken to set this person up with information that only she was privy to. A time and date was arranged with her for an "action", and activists sat back and watched 14 police units (including 4 inspectors, 2 riot vans, 2 dog units and 2 undercover detectives swarm in. Just to be sure, they set her up a second time with false info, again to watch police swoop down searching for activists. It came to light that at her trial for ALF activities, she implicated 2 activists openly in court, naming names. She had also made statements to the police implicating 3 local activists and her co-defendent. It has been suggested that people may want to contact Jeanette and tell her what you think about those who grass on friends to save their own skin.
Jeanette McClunan, 4 the Butts, Warnford Rd. Corhampton, Hants. S032 3ND. tel: 01489-877807

SWEDEN

Djurens Befrielse Front
Box 179
S-265 22 Astorp, Sweden
Tel +46 42 576 93

According to Swedish media, during the evening of June 18, 1995, an unidentified 18 year old woman was arrested in central Uppsala and charged with arson. The woman allegedly set fire to a meat lorry. In a report from the Djurens Befrielse Front (Swedish ALF) the young woman was unknown by them. She faces up to two years in prison. **Please write the DBF for more details about support for this activist.**

USA

please see page 65 for information on the various hunting and trapping organizations that contributed to a fund that PAID an anonymous tipster

for info on Rod Coronado...
Rod Coronado #03895000
FCI RR#2, Box 9000, Safford, AZ 85546, USA.

Authorities wanted to link Rod to a series of A.L.F. arsons connected to the A.L.F.'s "Operation Bite Back" which caused well over $1.5 million damage, but were unable to make the charges stick.However, Rod was recently sentenced to 47 months for offenses relation to his actions as spokesperson for the ALF in the USA. (see pg 64 for Rod's Support Committee's address).

Captain Paul Watson Serves 30 Days

October 9, 1995

Paul Watson of the Sea Shepherd has been sentenced to serve 30 days in a maximum security prison, on top of the six days previously served in pre-arraignment detention, and to pay a fine of $35. On October 9 Watson was convicted on one count of felonious criminal mischief in connection with harassing the Cuban dragnetting trawler Rio Las Cases off Newfoundland in international waters in August 1993. Watson was cleared of two more serious charges in connection with the same incident, which could have carried life prison sentences.

Watson reportedly said that while he was disappointed in the outcome, still believing himself to be innocent, it was a matter of satisfaction to him that the Canadian government had spent $4 million to secure the conviction; had emulated his tactics this year against Spanish trawlers; and has in convicting him, ironically establishing a legal precedent for Spain's case against the Canadian government for alleged piracy, which will be heard in a Canadian court.

MEMPHIS EMERGES AS ANIMAL RIGHTS HOTBED: 39 ARRESTED IN PROTEST

(from FUR AGE WEEKLY, Aug 14, 1995)

Thirty-nine animal rights activists were jailed July 23 after they stormed department stores selling furs in 10 cities. This possibly unprecedented number of arrests during one coordinated protest was due to the militant style of Coalition to Abolish the Fur Trade (CAFT), which coordinated the event. Mostly young (many teenaged) protesters aggressively blockaded store entrances and chaining themselves to clothes racks.

As reported here July 17, the Memphis-based CAFT announced in advance its intention to "declare war" on Federated Department Stores Inc. in order to "convince the retailer to stop selling animal furs."

CAFT said more than a dozen cities were targeted but Federated reported disturbances in six of its chains in 10 cities: Goldsmith's in Memphis, TN; Bloomingdale's in Chicago; Macy's in Minneapolis and Oxford, PA; Lazarus in Dayton, Columbus and Cincinnati, OH, and Indianapolis, Indiana; and Bullock's in Torrance and Newport Beach, CA.

CAFT said arrests totaled 10 in the Los Angeles area (Newport Beach six, and Torrance four), seven in Chicago, seven in Syracuse, four in Memphis, and 11 in Minneapolis.

Media coverage of the event was minimal. The Fur Information Council of America (FICA) found stories the Chicago Sun-Times, the Minneapolis Star-Tribune and scant television attention.

CAFT threatens, "This is only the first salvo in the campaign," but contacted in advance of the protest by Fur Age, Federated appeared unfazed. "We reserve the right to sell the merchandise in our stores that our customers indicate by their purchases that they want. This is the essence of the free market system in which we participate," said a spokesperson.

Federated increased security to prepare for the protest. "My hat's off to them," Carol Wynne, executive director of FICA, praised the department store chain. "They did a great job securing the environment. Security acted quickly, there was no violence or vandalism, and arrests were made."

The timing of the protest was perplexing to the trade. During mid- summer, they had little effect on consumers or the media. Fur salons in Bloomingdale's stores were even closed that day. During the summer, the Maximilian salons are closed every Sunday.

The fact, however, that CAFT was able to generate enough grassroots supporters willing to go to jail for their cause is another sign that the group may be generating a more unapologetically militant version of animal rights activism. The Fur Commission USA (FCUSA) announced that Memphis emerged in 1994 as a veritable hotbed of Animal Liberation Front (ALF) activity directed against the fur industry.

According to documents obtained by FCUSA, nine of 13 ALF attacks which occurred in the Midwest since Jan 1, 1994 took place in Memphis. Two more ALF incidents occurred in or near Indianapolis, where CAFT operates a second office. Another 25-30 ALF attacks occurred at fur stores in California and New York. The list was compiled by a private company which monitors and keeps computer records on animal rights incidents.

Between March and November of 1994, records reveal, one fur farm and four fur retail outlets in Memphis were hit by the ALF in nine separate incidents. They involved broken windows, paint bombing, glued locks, damaged merchandise and other unspecified damages.

CAFT established operations in Memphis in 1994, according to the organization's literature. In its statement of purpose, CAFT endorses the methods of the Animal Liberation Front and states its intent to "carry on" the work of the Coalition Against Fur Farming (CAFF). CAFF was founded by admitted arsonist Rod Coronado, who pled guilty in May to one count of arson in connection with an ALF firebombing at Michigan State University laboratory where research was being conducted using mink. Coronado will be sentenced Aug. 10 in Michigan federal court.

Although records show little activity by CAFT before 1994, the organization stepped up its attack on the fur trade in 1994. FCUSA found the following among CAFT actions since Jan. 1, 1994.

A Jan 7, 1994 incident at the International Mink Show in Madison, WI, where two protesters infiltrated the meeting and chained themselves to the podium before being removed by police. This incident is believed to have been the first major CAFT action against the fur trade; A Jan 8 1994 protest at Goldsmith's Department Store in Memphis, TN, where activists rushed the store with skinned fox carcasses, which they displayed to customers and tv cameras, resulting in three arrests; A Nov. 25 1994 blockade at Neiman Marcus in Newport Beach, CA where 48 protesters from CAFT and other animal rights groups blocked the entrance to the fur salon for 30 minutes before the police arrived; A Jan. 7 1994 demonstration at the International Mink Show in Madison, where one activist confronted in an elevator the 10-year- old daughter of a Wisconsin fur farmer and 75 protesters stormed the meeting, disrupting proceedings and overturned display tables, leading to four arrests.

FCUSA Chairman Skip Lea said, "many businesses today face harassment from one extremist group or another, our industry is no different. We can't prevent extremist organizations from taking illegal or violent action against the fur trade, but we can minimize their impact by using common sense. The best way to defeat our adversaries is to stay fully informed about their activities, understand their goals and tactics, make thorough preparations when incidents are expected, and be prepared to press charges against any individual who breaks the law in the name of animal liberation."

* * *

Congratulations go out to CAFT for all their efforts and successes, and especially for scaring the shit out of the fur industry. Now if every anti-fur activist followed CAFT's lead ... Here's an update on CAFT's actions:

UPDATE ON COALITION AGAINST THE FUR TRADE (CAFT) DEMO IN CHICAGO

Oct 8, 1995

Four animal rights activists were arrested in Chicago for chaining themselves to the entrance to Bloomingdale's in mid-July. An additional three activists were arrested for simply being present at the event. All were charged with violation of Illinois' Disorderly Conduct Statute. Coverage of the incident went exceedingly well -- all major television channels gave neutral reporting. And although some smaller, progressive Chicago print media gave us very favourable coverage, major print media wasn't extensive. Six arrestee's appeared in Cook County Court on the 15th of August. At the end of the day, NOT A SINGLE ARRESTEE was fined nor did anyone receive additional sentencing! Four of the six, were told to not get arrested at that site again and were let off. The remaining two accepted the offer of a public defender and their court date looms in the near future. The seventh sent in an attorney to appear for them, but the case was dismissed as the arresting officer did not appear.

All activists were shocked at the major turmoil such a small demonstration caused among Chicago's Finest and the various judiciary. Starting with formal arrest proceedings, each activist spent a great deal of time in "holding" with a female arrestee clocking in at nine hours in Women's Lock-up.

The arresting police varied in their reaction to the demonstration. One individual, presumably a Bloomie's handyman/employee took a frightening amount of pleasure in injuring demonstrator's wrists with the bolt-cutter. Another individual took delight in telling a male demonstrator wearing an ACT-UP! t-shirt "The "Boys" in holding are gonna love you!" Several officers discussed issues such as hunting during our detention. We were shocked to have female officers come in and tell us they were members of animal rights groups! Another officer even took an anti-fur pin and attached it to her uniform! Finally the incident took a surreal turn as one of female warders told us she has a vegetarian daughter and through the cell bars we discussed recipes!

Presumably, the event was complicated by the eventual "two-prong" approach that demonstrators utilized. The first group of activists held their event at noon. Individuals were arrested by 12:15 and were in their first of two "paddy-wagon" rides across town. The arrestees were being processed when another group of activists, having just left the Shedd Aquarium demo, spontaniously took it upon themselves to join in the fun at Bloomie's on the Magnificent Mile! Detained at the 8th Precinct, demonstraters heard as late as 3:00 P.M. that the demo was still going on!

-edited from a post from AR News

For more information of CAFT write:
Coalition To Abolish the Fur Trade
Po Box 40641
Memphis, TN 38174
USA

...AND MORE GOOD NEWS ABOUT FUR!

EF! August: "... the US House of Representatives deleted subsidies to the mink fur industry from the Agriculture Appropriations Bill, HR 1976. A substantial majority of congressmembers voted for an amendment removing $2 million that would have contributed to the unconscionable cruelty of the mink industry.

Representatves Peter Deutsch of Florida and Christopher Shays of Connecticut were sponsors of the amendment to remove the funding. It is highly unlikely that the money will be reinserted into the Appropriations Bill by the Senate."

IMMEDIATE ACTION REQUIRED AGAINST SALE OF OSTRICH MEAT

In the United States Emu meat is now on sale at least one Giant store and ostrich meat is on sale at a Graul's store.

PLEASE LET GIANT AND GRAUL'S KNOW HOW YOU FEEL ABOUT THIS:

Mr. Israel Cohen, President
Giant Foods
P.O. Box 1804
Washington, DC 20013 USA

Mr. Harold Graul
Graul's Market
7713 Bellona Avenue
Baltimore, MD 21204 USA

The commercial exploitation of emus and ostriches is a tragedy. Wildlife should never be treated as a commodity to be bought, sold, used up and thrown away.

Emus and ostriches are living creatures who are capable of feeling pain and pleasure. In the United States there are no federal laws regulating the humane treatment of poultry at any stage of operation. The idea of introducing another class of birds into a system that does not extend basic welfare protection to birds is indefensible.

Emus and ostriches belong to the oldest living family of birds on earth, the ratites, or flightless fowl. They are nomads, designed by 90 million years of evolution to roam over vast tracts of land. With their long powerful legs and camel-like feet adapted for speed, they can run up to 40 miles an hour, emus covering 12 feet in a single stride. It is particularly cruel to confine nomadic wildlife.

Ostriches grow to be 7 to 9 feet tall, weigh up to 350 pounds and live for 40 to 70 years. Emus grow to be 5 to 6 feet tall, weigh up to 140 pounds, and live for 25 to 30 years.

VIC: ANIMAL RIGHTS PROTESTORS BLAST HEART FOUNDATION

MELBOURNE, Sept 2 AAP - Animal rights protesters today branded the Heart Foundation of Australia as "heartless" over its support for kangaroo meat.

The Australian Wildlife Protection Council said the Foundation was aiding commercial wildlife exploitation by giving kangaroo its tick of approval as a healthy meat. Professor Peter Singer, the Council's patron, said he was concerned at the level of cruelty involved in kangaroo killing. "A lot of the kangaroos that are shot are not killed outright. A lot of female kangaroos have joeys either in the pouch or at their feet," he said at the launch of a leaflet protesting the Heart Foundation's approval of the meat.

"Ones in the pouch will get bashed to death, the ones at their feet will hop off into the bush and be unable to survive," he told reporters outside the Foundation's King Street offices. "I think for the Heart Foundation to just give a tick to kangaroo meat is really heartless."

Prof Singer, a Senate candidate for the Greens, said he wanted the Heart Foundation to reconsider the tick. "We are also saying to them that you've got to think about more than whether something is high or low fat before giving it a tick," he said. "You've got to think about the cruelty and the suffering and the effect that it's having on Australia's image of its wildlife to do this sort of thing."

KFC in India ordered to shut down

By RAVI PRASAD

BANGALORE, India, Sept. 13 (UPI) -- International fast food giant Kentucky Fried Chicken was ordered Wednesday to shut down its only outlet in India after a municipal government revoked the restaurant chain's operating license.

KFC's outlet in Bangalore had come under attack from municipal authorities in the southern Indian city for allegedly serving food containing too much monosodium glutamate.

Municipal health officer V.G. Shetty said the city government's decision was based on the analysis of food samples taken from the restaurant last month.

"We are seeking legal action for misbranding," Shetty said. "KFC has not declared the presence of monosodium glutamate in capital letters as a warning clause and they don't have a proper warranty clause from whom the monosodium glutamate has been brought."

Bangalore health officials had earlier charged KFC's food was "adulterated, misbranded and unfit for human consumption." Laboratory analysis showed the seasoning KFC used for its chicken contained nearly three times the amount of monosodium glutamate allowed under India's Prevention of Food Adulteration Act.

The international food chain -- the first to enter India -- was used by politicians opposed to economic liberalization as an example of the country's "economic colonization" by multinational companies.

A local farmers' group had been campaigning against the restaurant since it opened for allegedly depleting the region's food grains. Even after initial warnings from Bangalore's municipal authorities, KFC had maintained it would continue its expansion plans in India to open two new restaurant outlets by the end of the year -- in Delhi and in Bombay.

DEAD COW BLOCKS McDONALD'S DRIVE-THRU IN GRAPHIC ANTI-MEAT PROTEST BY MILITANT ACTIVISTS

Oct 1, Huntington Beach, CA -- Militant animal rights activists blocked the drive-thru lane at a McDonald's restaurant here Sunday, October first, with the corpse of a dead cow in what is probably the most graphic anti-meat demonstration ever held in southern California.

The direct action, sponsered by Orange County People for Animals, is in conjunction with national demonstrations for "World Farm Animals Day," which marks the birthday of Mahatma Gandhi, the world's foremost advocate for farm animals.

"This aggressive action is designed to jolt the public out of denial and painfully smack two realities up against each other...the everyday reality of hamburger eating and the behind-the-scenes reality of the real source of those hamburgers," said Jerry Friedman, spokesperson for OCPA, the largest animal rights group in Orange County.

"For those who find this shocking, we must ask, WHY? Technically, this is simply yet-to-be processed 'food.' If this is horrifying, it is surely because, after seeing a dead body, people immediately recognize the tremendous suffering involved in the process...a hideous process from which most people prefer to be shielded," he added.

"We cannot shield ourselves any longer, but must face the truth of the triple whammy of meat eating: animal suffering, preventable human disease from the eating of animal products and the tremendous environmental damage our meat habit wreaks upon the planet," he said.

Nearly 1.5 million Americans are crippled and killed prematurely each year by heart failure, stroke, cancer and other killer diseases linked conclusively to the consumption of animal products. Meanwhile, nearly all of our irreplaceable ancient forests have been leveled to create more grazing and cropland for farm animals, while intensive cultivation and irrigation of these lands has depleted topsoil and ground water supplies and contributed more pollution to our waterways than all other human activities combined.

NEW FROM THE NA-ALFSG

Two Great T-Shirt designs, fabric patches and stickers!

X03-Stickers. 50cents each, $2.00 for six (Actual size shown)

Support the A.L.F.

The Animal Liberation Front
Saves Animals Lives

TS01- above design on T-shirt. XL only. Black ink on White, Gray, Red. $15

X04- Fabric Patches, great for stitching on bags, jackets, etc. $2.
(Actual size shown)

WHO GRASSED ON ROD CORONADO?

Someone did, and they were paid for their troubles. The November issue of Michigan Out-Of-Doors (special Deer Hunting Issue) magazine lists those groups that contributed to a fund that paid an anonymous tipster for info on Rod Coronado. A reward totaling $22,000 was put out by these groups:

Michigan United Conservation Clubs: $5000
Michigan big Game Hunter's Assoc.: $5000
Incurable Ill for Animal Research: $5000
Michigan Trappers Assoc.: $1000
Michigan Fur Conservation Assoc: $1000
National Rifle Association: $1000
Fur Information Council: $1000
Americans for Medical Progress: $1000
Safari Club International: $1000
Ohio Big Bucks Club: $1000

North American

A
L
F

Supporters Group

TS02- Above design on T-Shirt. XL only. Black on White, Grey, Red. $15

Milk 'bomb' scare called unfortunate

BY DESMOND BILL
STAFF REPORTER

A milk sales promotion that sparked an explosive burst of publicity has embarrassed rather than pleased its sponsors.

A prize milk carton used in the campaign caused a bomb scare and ruined business for hundreds of merchants at the Eaton Centre Sunday afternoon.

It was an unfortunate incident, said a spokesperson for the Dairy Farmers of Ontario, but it won't stop the milk promotion.

The carton was wired so it emitted a mooing sound when opened and a sign on its side said: If this carton goes MOOOO you win. The carton was one of hundreds of thousands distributed since the campaign started Oct. 1.

But when it was found by an employee in Cultures restaurant, she saw the wires inside it but didn't read the message on the side. She called mall security officials.

They called Metro police who took one look at the carton and ordered the immediate evacuation of half the mall and the closing of a section of Queen and Yonge Sts.

An expert on the police bomb squad X-rayed the carton, saw the wiring and a microchip and blew up the package.

Staff Sergeant Garry Silliker, said yesterday police didn't know about the contest. All they saw was a milk carton with wires and a device inside it.

"Things that look innocuous may be dangerous and this was perceived as a package of a possibly explosive nature," he said.

"Our people were not sure of what they had and obviously they were taking no chances."

Bill Mitchell, an official of the Dairy Farmers organization — formerly known as the Ontario Milk Marketing Board — said it was obvious that whoever had left the carton in Cultures didn't know they had a winning carton.

"Maybe the restaurant was noisy and they didn't hear the carton moo," he said in a phone interview. He called it "an unfortunate incident, a misunderstanding."

But it won't stop the promotion, which he said is one of the most popular in the history of the industry.

Milk drinkers have a chance to win prizes such as cars, ski vacations and snowboard gear.

When they open a prize carton, it emits a mooing sound and there is a ticket inside with a phone number to claim their prize.

TORONTO STAR Tuesday, October 31, 1995

Send orders to :NA-ALFSG DISTRO, BOX 241532, MEMPHIS, TN 38124 Please make cheques and money orders out to:"NA-ALFSG." Allow a couple of weeks for delivery, etc etc!

UNDERGROUND

$3 FREE TO PRISONERS

THE MAGAZINE OF THE NORTH AMERICAN ANIMAL LIBERATION FRONT SUPPORTERS GROUP

#4
ANIMAL LIBERATION
DON'T JUST TALK ABOUT IT...

GOT SOMETHING TO SAY? GIVE US A SHOUT!

We welcome letters, articles, artwork, action reports or anything else for publication in *Underground*. Please be sure to write "FOR PUBLICATION" on anything you send us for the newsletter, so that we know what should and should not be published. Also please make it clear whether or not you will accept editing of your contribution.

We do not believe in censorship. If we have serious concerns about printing something that is sent to us, we will make every effort to discuss our concerns with the author. As part of our taking responsibility for *Undergound*, we will let readers know if we have a serious problem with something we end up printing. Keep in mind that this is a magazine by and for people who support the A.L.F. and please strive to keep your letters/articles respectful.

SUPPORT THE A.L.F: BECOME A MEMBER OF THE NORTH AMERICAN A.L.F. SUPPORTERS GROUP

Suggested costs for a membership to the North American ALFSG, including a year's subscription to "Underground", are on a $20 - $30 sliding scale. Canadian subscribers can pay in Canadian currency; we ask that US and overseas subscribers pay in US currency (US cheques or money orders). All money, EXCEPT that going towards merchandise and distribution should be sent to:

NA-ALFSG
Box 69597
5845 Yonge St.
Willowdale, Ontario
Canada. M2M 4K3
<an246614@anon.penet.fi.>

Cheques and money orders should be made out to: NAALFSG.

For a catalogue of NA-ALFSG merchandise, for distribution information and/or to order products, write to:

NA-ALFSG Distro
Box 241532
Memphis, TN
38124 USA

DISCLAIMER: The information in *Underground* is not intended to encourage or discourage anyone to do anything illegal; it is for entertainment only. Material within *Underground* is not necessarily that of the A.L.F. or the North American ALFSG.

ALF GUIDELINES

TO liberate animals from places of abuse, ie laboratories, factory farms, fur farms, etc, and when ever possible, place them in good homes where they may live out their natural lives, free from suffering.

TO inflict economic damage to those who profit from the misery and exploitation of animals.

TO reveal the horror and atrocities committed against animals behind locked doors, by performing non-violent direct actions and liberations.

TO take all necessary precautions against harming any animal, human and non-human.

Any individual or group of people who are vegetarians or vegans and who carry out actions according to the A.L.F. guidelines have the right to regard themselves as part of the Animal Liberation Front.

The NORTH AMERICAN A.L.F. SUPPORTERS GROUP is a 100% volunteer organization. All money raised goes directly to the work of supporting animal liberation and assisting imprisoned activists. Supporters can help raise money by: making personal contributions; promoting our magazine *Underground* and our other merchandise; organizing fundraising events; designing merchandise; and suggesting strategies for our fundraising efforts. Supporters can also become involved in our other projects:

PRISONER SUPPORT

* Letter writing: prisoners rely on letters as their link to the outside world. Letters to newspapers help inform the public about the plight of imprisoned activists.
* Publicity: articles for magazines, letters to the editor, public speaking, and other media work such as radio broadcasts help fundraise and raise awareness. Of course any press work that is done under the name of the North American ALFSG must be approved by the North American ALFSG.
* Distribution/Subscription drive: if you can help us distribute the newsletter or increase subscriptions, that helps us educate about animal liberation.

If you have any other ideas, please let us know. We welcome your feedback and participation.

MAIL SECURITY

If you are a member of an active A.L.F. cell, send us any clippings, or your own report, with date, time, place, and a few details about the action. Send your reports on plain paper, using block capital letters, or a public typewriter that many people have access to. Wear gloves at all times so your fingerprints are not on the paper, envelope, or stamp. Do not give your address, and don't lick the stamp or envelope; wet it with a sponge. Remember you should expect that all of our mail and any other support groups' mail is opened and read by the authorities. DO NOT inform us of upcoming actions BEFORE they happen.

NA-ALFSG NOTES

First off, a huge round of thank you's to everyone who has provided us with support over the last few months. Our gratitude is extended to everyone who had a hand in compiling the information you'll find within this issue, with special thanks to Darren, R@bbix, the UK ALFSG, Animal Info from New Zealand, Rod Coronado, the folks in Memphis, Lise Olsen, and Zab for her work on prisoner issues. We are, however, most indebted to all of you who showed your support through subscriptions and donations - What can we say? We were overwhelmed by the generosity and kindness exhibited by so many of you (and you know who you are!). We're happy to announce that the $300.00 debt owed to the old SG crew has been completely paid off, and money set aside for ALF prisoner support has been building steadily since November, leaving us in an excellent position for the publication of *Underground #4*. Coupled with financial support has been the outpouring of letters of support. Thanks for all the positive feedback with regards to Underground #3. Ok, on to other things...

In terms of animal liberation, early indications are that 1996 is shaping up to be Year of the Mink, with well over 7000 mink freed by January alone, in a series of daring raids across North America by A.L.F. activists. At the same time, fur farms around the world are being struck in similar actions, and these actions continue even as we write about it within these pages. The cumulative effect of these liberations and hits against the fur industry is very apparent. The desperation they're experiencing is reflected for all to see in the outrages jumps of the fur lobby's "reward" money, offered for any information on A.L.F. raids against fur farms. Already we've seen the blood money offered hit $50,000, only to leap to $70,000 as hundreds more mink escape to freedom in the latest round of liberations in Washington.

The past few months since *Underground #3* was published are also notable not only for the increase in A.L.F activity, but for the definite increase in support shown across Canada and the United States for the Animal Liberation Front and the actions it carries out. People choose to support the A.L.F. and the Supporters Group in a variety of ways, all of which are greatly appreciated. Magazines, web sites, and hand copied zines focusing on animal liberation have sprung up seemingly everywhere. Several months ago the Supporters Group was contacted by an enterprising supporter from British Columbia who had managed to pull together a series of benefit concerts, out of which came a tape of 17 Canadian bands and over 30 songs. Over 500 tapes were produced, with several hundred donated to the NA ALFSG to use to raise funds for imprisoned ALF activists and their families.

More and more people seem to be aware that, as the editors of *No Compromise* put it, *"Not only is it legal to argue in support of the ALF's tactics, it is also perfectly legal to write letters of support to imprisoned ALF activists, and to send money to the ALF Supporters Group, to wear pro-ALF t-shirts, buttons, and bumper stickers ..."* (No Compromise #1, 11)

Of course, it's not all good news out there. As the support for animal liberation take root and grows, animal abusers dig in their heals and try to fight back. The recent series of raids against activists in the United Kingdom and Finland should serve as a warning to everyone involved in animal liberation activities (above ground or otherwise), that none of us are invulnerable when it comes to harassment from the State. Within a week or two of my return from a stay with the ALF SG (UK) coordinators over Christmas/New Years, we learned that the UK SG headquarters had been raid by Hampshire police. Six people in total were arrested in a series of coordinated raids that took place hundreds of miles apart, all targeting animal activists. Those arrested included the ALF Supporters Group newsletter editor, four activists connected to *Green Anarchist Magazine* and the ALF Press Officer, Robin Webb. The ALF SG's computer was temporarily held by police, forcing the SG temporarily offline (no fear, they're back online and business continues as usual). See page 36 for an update from the ALFSG (UK). As we go to print, nothing further has developed with regards to their charges. Stay tuned for more details.

Right then. Once again, we'd like to thank everyone for their amazing show of support. Please enjoy *Underground #4*. Hopefully you'll find it both informative and inspiring.

yer editor,
t.
NA-ALFSG

LETTERS TO UNDERGROUND

DEATH ROW VEGETARIAN SEEKS INFO

To Whom it May Concern,

I appreciate you sending me your publication. I am a death row prisoner. I have always been considered odd by my family because from the time I figured out where meat came from I refused to eat meat. At age 17 when I became a Buddhist, I realized being a vegetarian was the right thing to do. In here I'm also considered odd because I don't eat meat and I am a Buddhist, so I seldom speak to anyone. Anyone in the freeworld who can help me in the way of friendship and information - how to get a proper diet in prison - would be greatly appreciated. Any vegetarian who is in here and does not eat beans is in big trouble. The prison system really screws us around. I would greatly appreciate any help I could get on this.

Thank you!

Burley Gilliam
097234 A1-41-1091
Box 221 Raiford, Florida
32083, USA

WHO PAYS OUT PRISONER SUPPORT?

Dear NA-ALFSG:

Please find enclosed $10, to be used for prisoner support. Actually, this brings to mind something that's been bothering me for a while...Why is it that your organization and other Supporters Groups are always having to scrounge up whatever donations people can send you for prisoner support and certain larger and well known animal rights organizations which has raised MILLIONS over the years for activist defense, never seem to shell out any money to help prisoners in for ALF activities? Has any ALF prisoner in North America EVER received any financial support from PETA or similar groups? I mention PETA by name since it seems to me that PETA spends money for bail and fines to help THEIR activists when arrested on simple misdemeanor counts. Is this an accurate view? The last thing I want to do is to add to the bickering and infighting that seems to occasionally take place within our movement, but I have serious concerns that money that could be going directly to prisoners in jail who have put their lives on the line for animals is being diverted instead to pay off basic civil disobedience fines. What's going on?

E. from Boston.

EARTH LIBERATION PRISONERS

Anyone who has had the opportunity to read any of the last three issues of *Underground* will have seen the NA ALFSG's attempt to expand the mandate of prisoner support, especially regarding political prisoners and prison issues. While we believe it's a step in the right direction, there is always room for improvement, and certainly more can be done. The following is an excerpt from a letter from a UK supporter, addressing the very important links between ecodefence and animal liberation, as well as the general lack of listings of imprisoned ecodefenders within our pages. This issue of *Underground* does not list ecoprisoners, but that's not to say that future issues won't:

... One criticism I do have though is that you don't mention any ecodefence prisoners. And I'm sure you're aware of the links between animal lib and ecodefence ... For example, I am sure you know that in 1995, EF!ers carried out an action against pollution in Cape Cod, Massachusetts, USA. Over recent years pollution in the Cape has resulted in the decline of whales and turtle populations. I don't think I know of any animal libber who would disagree with fighting against pollution of the seas, because we can all recognize pollution creates animal suffering and threatens the survival of many animal species.

I am also sure you are aware that the Brit Government is obsessed with building roads. To lower the costs of these building schemes they build their roads through woods, sites of special scientific interest (SSSI's) and things like that. Basically anywhere that developments are restricted the land is 'cheep'. By building in these ecologically important spots the animals 'homes' are being destroyed, animals ARE being killed and animal abuse is happening. For example, back in 1994 the government built a road outside the city of Bath. They put the road straight through a wood as the land was cheep. The destruction of the wood led to ancient badger sets being destroyed and worse to come. When the contractors turned up it was during the 'nesting season' for birds. Ignoring the nesting birds the contractors cut down all the trees. After the trees had been cut injured birds lay on the ground. The anti-roads activists naturally wanted to help the birds and pleaded with the security guards who were holding them back to let them help the birds. To rescue them. The guards ignored the requests. As the injured birds lay on the woodland floor the contractors set the woodland floor alight. All the birds were burnt to death.

I have many more examples of how animal lib and ecodefence are basically one and the same, but I'm sure you're getting the picture. So, in recognition that the animal lib and ecodefence are one and the same I feel ecodefence prisoners should be listed alongside the animal lib prisoners.

-R

STILL INTERESTED IN COMMUNICATING

Greetings, endangered species...

Hopefully these words find you and your colleagues in the very best of health and determined spirits.

Just a few words to maintain contact and let you know that i am still interested in communicating. Indeed, a question occurred to me that i thought perhaps you might find useful ... What are the current numbers regarding near or extinct animals or species? With spring and the current state of deforestation it may be instructive to monitor the declining number, area of habitat and reason why each individual animal species is being murdered and/or exterminated...

Otherwise thank you for sending me the *Underground* A.L.F. - do please continue to do so - and any other information or publication that you think i should be made aware of.

Lots of movement down here - this summer should be very interesting. Especially since it means the construction of more camps and prisons - and population thereof...

Nevertheless, thank you, take care

Onward (until it is done)

J. Frazier
California State Prison
Sacramento A-4107/B38808
Box-290066
Repressa, Ca 95671-0066

JUSTICE DEPT. HOW-TO BOOKLET?

I am writing this letter in the hope that a member of the Justice Department in England will get to read it.

For many years now people "in the know" have compiled various how-to booklets describing to potential activists how to make incendiary devices and giving tips on other forms of direct action. These booklets have undoubtedly saved thousands of animals lives directly as a result of the necessary information contained within. However, these have all been put together by A.L.F. members in accordance with A.L.F. policy and as such do not include information on making letter bombs, for example.

Now with the emergence of groups like the Justice Department, who go further than A.L.F. policy, isn't it about time someone from the J.D. put together a "how-to" manual including the information missed out in A.L.F. manuals?

Many people would like to participate in J.D. activity but can't as they don't know the required information. Just think how many more animal abusers could be targeted if only more people knew how to construct a letter bomb!

So PLEASE will someone out there do the decent thing and put together a Justice Department manual!

Yours in Hope,
Ian Sendury

FREEDOM OF INFORMATION ACT YOURS TO USE!

FOIA FILES KIT - INSTRUCTIONS

As posted to alt.activism, June 30, 1994
USING THE FREEDOM OF INFORMATION ACT REVISED EDITION Fund for Open Information and Accountability, Inc.
339 Lafayette Street, New York, NY 10012
(212) 477-3188

INSTRUCTIONS

The Freedom of Information Act entitles you to request any record maintained by a federal Executive branch agency. The agency must release the requested matieral unless it falls into one of nine exempt categores, such as "national security," "privacy," "confidential source" and the like, in which case the agency may but is not compelled to refuse to disclose the records.

This kit contains all the material needed to make FOIA requests for records on an individual, an orgnaization or on a particular subject matter or event.

HOW TO MAKE A COMPLETE REQUEST

Step 1: Select the appropriate smaple letter. Fill in the blanks in the body of the letter. Read the directions printed to the right of each letter in conjunction with the following instructions:

For organizational files: In the first blank space insert the full and formal name of the organization whose files you are requesting. In the second blank space insert any other names, acronyms or shortened forms by which the organization is or has ever been known or referred to by itself or others. If some of the organization's work is conducted by sub-groups such as clubs, committees, special programs or through coalitions known by other names, these should be listed.

For individual files: Insert the person's full name in the first blank space and any vaiations in spelling, nicknames, stage names, marriage names, titles and the like in the second blank space. Unlike other requests, the signatures of an individual requesting her/his own file must be notarized.

For subject matter or event files: In the first blank space state the formal title of the subject matter or event including relevant dates and locations. In the second blank space provide the names of individuals or group sponsors or participants and/or any other information that would assist the agency in locating the material you are requesting.

Step 2: The completed sample letter may be removed, photocopies and mailed as is or retyped on your own stationary. Be sure to keep a copy of each letter.

Step 3: Addressing the letters: Consult list of agency addresses.

FBI: A complete request requires a minimum of two

letters. Send one letter to FBI Headquarters and separate letter to each FBI field office nearest the location of the individual, the organization or the subject matter/ event. Consdier the location of residences, schools, work and other activities.

INS: Send a request letter to each district office nearest the location of the individual, the organization or the subject matter/event.

Address each letter to the FOIA/ PA office of the appropraite agency. Be sure to make clearly on the envelope: ATTENTION--FOIA REQUEST.

FEE WAIVER

You will notice that the sample letters include a request for fee waiver. Many agencies automatically waive fees if a request results in the release of only a small number of documents, e.g. 250 pages or less. Under the Act, you are entitled to a waiver of all search and copy fees associated with your request if the release of the information would primarily benefit the general public. However, in January 1983, the Justice Department issued a memo to all federal agencies listing five criteria which requesters must meet before they are deemed entitled to a fee waiver. Under these criteria, a requester must show that the material sought to be released is already the subject of "genuine public interest" and "meaningfully contributes to the public development or understanding of the subject"; and that she/he has the qualifications to understand and evaluate the materials and the ability to interpret and disseminate the information to the public and is not motivated by any "personal interest." Finally, if the requested information is already "in the public domain," such as in the agency's reading room, no fee waiver will be granted.

You should always request a waiver of fees if you believe the information you are seeking will benefit the public. If your request for a waiver is denied, you should appeal that denial, citing the ways in which your request meets the standards set out above.

MONITORING THE PROGRESS OF YOUR REQUEST

Customarily, you will receive a letter from each agency within 10 days stating that your request has been received and is being processed. You may be asked to be patient and told that requests are handled cafeteria style. You have no alternative but to be somewhat patient. but there is no reason to be complacent and simply sit and wait.

A good strategy is to telephone the FOIA office in each agency after about a month if nothing of substance has been received. Ask for a progress report. The name of the person you talk with and the gist of the converstaion should be recorded. try to take notes during the conversation focusing especially on what is said by the agency official. Write down all the details you can recall after the call is completed. Continue to call every 4 to 6 weeks.

Good recordkeeping helps avoid time-consuming and frustrating confusion. A looseleaf notebook with a section devoted to each request simplifies this task. Intervening correspondence to and from the agency can be inserted bewteen the notes on phone calls so that all relevant material will be at hand for the various tasks: phone consultations, writing the newsletter, correspondence, articles, preparation for media appearances, congressional testimony or litigation, if that course is adopted.

HOW TO MAKE SURE YOU GET EVERYTHING YOU ARE ENTITLED TO ... AND WHAT TO DO IF YOU DO NOT

After each agency has searched and processed your request, you will receive a letter that announces the outcome, encloses the released documents, if any, and explains where to direct an appeal if any material has been withheld. There are four possible outcomes:

1. Request granted in full: This response indicates that the agency has released all records pertinent to your request, with no exclusions or withholdings. The documents may be enclosed or, if bulky, may be mailed under separate cover. This is a very rare outcome.

Next Step: Check documents for completeness (see instructions below).

2. Requested granted in part and denied in part: This response indicates that the agency is releasing some material but has withheld some documents entirely or excized some passages from the documents released. The released documents may be enclosed or, if bulky, mailed under separate cover.

Next step: Check documents released for completeness (see instructions below) and make an administrative appeal of denials or incompleteness (see instructions below).

3. Request denied in full: This response indicates that the agency is asserting that all material in its files pertaining to your request falls under one or the nine FOIA exemptions. These are categories of information that the agency may, at its discretion, refuse to release.

Next step: Make an administrative appeal (see instructions below). Since FOIA exemptions are not mandatory, even a complete denial of your request can and should be appeals.

4. No records: This response will state that a search of the agency's files indicates that it has no records corresponding to those you requested.

Next step: Check your original request to be sure you have not overlooked anything. If you receive documents from other agencies, review them for indications that there is matieral in teh files of the agency claiming it has none. For example, look for correspondence, or references to correspondence, to or from that agency. If you determine that there are reasonable grounds, file an administrative appeal (see instructions below).

HOW TO CHECK FOR COMPLETENESS

Step 1: Before reading the documents, turn them over and

number the back of each page sequentilaly. The packet may contain documents from the agency's headquarters as well as several field office files. Separate the documents into their reqpective office packets. Each of these offices will have assigned the investigation a separate file number. Try to find the numbering system. Usually the lower righthand corner of the first page carries a handwritten file and document number. For instance, an FBI document might be marked "100-7142-22". This would indicate that it is the 22nd document in the 7142nd file in the 100 classification. As you inspect the documents, make a list of these file numbers and which office they represent. In this way you will be able to determine which office created and which office received the document you have in your hand. Often there is a block stamp affixed with the name of the office from whose files this copy was retrieved. the "To/From" heading on a document may also give you corresponding file numbers and will help you puzzle out the origin of the document.

When you have finally identified eahc document's file and serial number and separated the documents into their proper office batches, make a list of all the serial numbers in each batch to see if there any any missing numbers. If there are missing serial numbers and some documents have been withheld, try to determine if teh missing numbers might reasonably correspond to the withheld documents. If not, the realease may be incomplete and an administrative appeal should be made. *(cont. on page 32)*

NEWS BRIEFS FROM ALL OVER

Animal Advocates Targeted in Arson Attack

On Friday 20th October at 8pm arsonists targeted Mike and Maureen Taylor's animal rescue at Mistley Place Park, Nr Manningtree. Mike and Maureen are both regular anti live export protesters at Brightlingsea. Mercifully, none of the 1700 animals and birds were injured but hay, which should have lasted the horses until Christmas, has all been burnt. The rescue is situated near Manningtree on the A137 north of Colchester.
-ar-news

Anti - Hunters Bay For Leader's Blood

Taken from Friday November 3 Electronic Telegraph

The head of the League Against Cruel Sports has been urged to resign after he called fox-hunters 'respectable' and allegedly suggested a compromise to give hunting ' a new lease of life'. James Barrington, executive director of the League for the past seven years, was accused of 'treachery' by a senior colleague after his remarks (appeared) in The Field magazine. Mr. Barrington said: "Fox hunting has culture, tradition, and there are many pillars of society involved in the sport".

If terrier work, when a fox that has gone to ground is chased or dug out of a hole for it to be shot, were stopped "the League would fell less antagonistic towards hunting", he said. "It would have a new lease of life". He added "I don't want to see tens of thousands of respectable fox-hunting people classified as a disaffected class".

A former member of the Hunt Saboteurs' Association, Mr. Barrington's views have become increasingly moderate and some fear a 'defection' to the hunting fraternity.

Mr. Barrington, 42, survived a vote of no confidence at a League meeting shortly after his comments became public, but a number of members have resigned and he is likely to face disciplinary action. Janet Smart, the League's North-West representative, said "I was disgusted at the stupid comments. Members are seething about this. We feel betrayed".

EU FUR BAN POSTPONED

November 22

The European Union Commission announced a postponement of EU Regulation #3254/91 better known as the EU Fur Ban. This is the second one year postponement of the regulation that was originally due to take effect January 1, 1995.

Irate MEPs challenged European Commission Vice-President Leon Brittan to come and explain why he wants to delay for a year the introduction of a ban on imports of furs from animals caught in leghold traps. British MEP, Ken Collins, who chairs the European Parliament's environment committee, was furious that "Mr Mestopheles" had declined to tell MEPs why he thought the ban on pelts from countries still using the steel-jawed traps might be incompatible with World Trade Organization rules, as Canada and the U.S. are claiming.

The ban on trade in 13 types of fur, was due to start on January 1, 1996, after being delayed for five years to allow fur trappers to adapt. Leghold traps are condemned by animal welfare activists and MEPs as one of the most inhumane ways of snaring animals like beavers, otters and lynxes, biting deep into their flesh. Creatures are often held in their jaws for days and frequently resort to gnawing off their own limbs to escape. North America trappers have fought a bitter battle to continue using them, with support from the Canadian and U.S. governments.

ANIMAL DEFENDERS FORCE BANKRUPT ORANGE COUNTY DA TO DROP CHARGES;TAXPAYERS SAVED THOUSANDS OF DOLLARS

NEWPORT BEACH November-- Animal rights advocates are claiming a major victory after all charges were dropped against them for protesting the mutilation killings of animals for their fur skins.

The Orange County District Attorney's office agreed to dismiss charges only minutes before jury selection was to begin in Harbor Municipal Court. The trial of 5 animal defenders arrested July 23 at Bullock's during an anti-fur protest could have cost the bankrupt county as much as $20,000.

FBI Outlines Expanded Wiretap Plan

Thursday November 2

NEW YORK (Reuter) - The Federal Bureau of Investigation has proposed a national wiretapping system that would give law enforcement officials the capacity to monitor as many as one out of every 100 phone lines in high crime areas, the New York Times reported Thursday.

The plan, as outlined in the October 16 issue of the Federal Register, would exceed the current average number of wiretaps of fewer than 850 in a year, or one in every 174,000 phone lines, the Times said. The paper said law enforcement officials would still need court approval to conduct the taps and the plan would need congressional approval for the money to finance it.

Although the FBI would not comment on the proposal, the Times said the agency argues that more of modern life, business and crime is taking place as voice or computer conversations over digital phone lines.

Telephone industry executives have questioned the agency's need for access to such a large portion of the phone network and privacy-rights advocates have said the access could lead to abuses of power, according to the Times.

The proposal is the first comprehensive outline by the FBI of the surveillance requirements it will require under the controversial Digital Telephony Act signed into law in 1994; Congress has yet to appropriate funds to enact the law.

Baltimore opens high-tech police booking center

BALTIMORE (Reuter) - The 1990s version of prison stripes is the supermarket-type bar code. Baltimore officials unveiled a new central police booking center Wednesday they said was the most advanced in the United States.

The center, which aims to cut booking time and get police officers back on the streets, has video conference facilities for bail hearings, electronic fingerprinting devices and bracelets with supermarket-style bar codes to track prisoners' movements through the system.

"Once I get used to the system I should be able to make the arrest, book him or her, process the statements and be back on the street in 45 minutes," Baltimore Police Sergeant J.R. Sharpe said at a preview of the facility. That compares with current times of 90 minutes to four hours, he said.

The $54 million booking center will process its first suspect Nov. 28. It is as big as two and a half football fields, and may eventually serve other counties in Maryland.

SAS Won't Ship Research Animals

November 28, ar-news

COPENHAGEN, Denmark - Fearing threats from animal rights activists, Scandinavian Airlines Systems has imposed an immediate ban on transporting all research animals between Britain and Scandinavia. The decision was taken because SAS feared attacks by British animals rights activists known to be violent, spokesman Jens Peter Skaarup said. He emphasized that SAS had not received any specific threats. Skaarup added that should the Scandinavian carrier meet problems elsewhere, the ban would likely be extended to other routes.

The ban applies to all animals out of Britain. Since May, SAS - owned by Sweden, Norway and Denmark - has refused to fly cats and dogs used in medical experiments. According to Associated Press, British Airways also recently ended shipments of research animals in Britain.

NRA president dead

December 5: The president of the National Rifle Association died of a heart attack while hunting. -Sniff-

McLibel Trial becomes the longest civil case in British history

Dec. 11
Monday, December 11 marked the day when the McLibel trial became the longest civil case of any kind in British history. Monday was the record-breaking 199th day that the court has sat since the start of the trial in June 1994. (The 199 days does not include the many pre-trial hearings.)

U.S. McLibel Support Campaign
Press Office
PO Box 62
Phone/Fax 802-586-9628
Craftsbury VT 05826-0062
Email dbriars@world.std.com
http://www.interlog.com/eye/Misc/McLibel
http://student.uq.edu.au:80/~s002434/mcl.html

26 ACTIVISTS ARRESTED IN MILITANT FFF PROTESTS

Twenty-six activists were arrested Friday, Nov. 24 in coordinated disruptions in a dozen cities from San Francisco to Syracuse of department stores that continue to sell fur. The militant direct actions were sponsored by Coalition to Abolish the Fur Trade (CAFT), and other grassroots groups as part of a campaign to put economic pressure on stores who sell fur.
The arrest totals included San Francisco (9), Seattle (2), Syracuse (8), Minneapolis (3), Indianapolis (3) and Memphis (1). Other disruptions and store blockades took place in Albany, Canton, Los Angeles, Atlanta and Buffalo. It was the third direct action since July by the grassroots coalition. In July 39 activists were arrested in several cities, and October 23, 20 activists were jailed in San Francisco. The demonstrations and arrest numbers are the largest in years for Fur Free Friday, which was created in 1986 for direct action on behalf of the fight to end fur. In recent years, most groups have focused on less militant forms of demonstrating.

33 ARRESTED IN NEW ROUND OF ANTI-FUR PROTESTS DEC. 17

In another lightning-quick action, anti-fur activists occupied and blocked entrances to department stores Sunday, Dec. 17 as part of a campaign to convince the retailers to stop selling animal furs. This time, 32 protestors, and one bystander were arrested in 5 cities -- with support demonstrations held in several other cities. The action was carried out by grassroots groups as part of the anti-fur campaign now underway by Memphis-based Coalition to Abolish the Fur Trade. Some were jailed as long as 3 days in an attempt to harass and discourage the activism. Instead the tactic backfired on the stores and police because of additional media coverage.
LOS ANGELES: Sixteen Animal Rights Direct Action (ARDAC) activists, and one bystander, were arrested after they blocked the main entrance and shut down escalators to the Bullock's (Federated Dept. Stores) at the plush, downtown Beverly Center. Dozens of police, and security personnel were called in to end the blockade, which lasted nearly 2 hours. Activists locked themselves to each other, and railings to prolong the peaceful takeover. Some activists were slightly injured by overzealous security guards. But, the action was covered by 7 different television stations, radio and the LA Times, along with numerous other smaller news media. Activists were charged with felony burglary and conspiracy and bail set originally at $30,000 -- which even arresting officers thought was uncalled for. Activists went on an immediate hunger strike, and did not eat until they were released Tuesday night, more than 50 hours later.

ATLANTA: Five CAFT activists were arrested, and held incommunicado, at Rich's as they blocked the doors. Activists are considering a lawsuit because Rich's personnel held them for more than an hour without giving them an attorney, and necessary medication.

MINNEAPOLIS: Four Student Organization for Animal Rights (SOAR) activists were arrested after they locked themselves together with kryptonite locks in a circle, blocking the entrance to Dayton-Hudson for more than 3 hours. They also locked onto a Santa Bear, the mascot of the store, which apparently decided to defect and join the anti-fur action.

DALLAS: In reportedly the first civil disobedience ever in Dallas, 3 CAFT activists were arrested at a Macy's, and held overnight before being released.
The action received massive coverage days before it happened, and the day of the protest.

BUFFALO: Four activists from Animal Defense League were arrested after blockading the entrance to Bonwit Teller.

Jacksonville ABC raided by FL SWAT team

At 1 PM Friday, January 12, 1996, 22+ tactical SWAT unit and police intelligence officers with evidence technician vans raided the residence of Jacksonville Anarchist Black Cross SG and Youth Action Movement.

During the 3 hour raid police took into custody Rob Cluesman, confiscated 2 legally owned shotguns, a police scanner, spray paint, stencils, political literature and computer disks.

Police quarantined the 3 remaining collective members in one room of the house while other officers searched the house, took photographs of the house and members. Members of police intelligence attempted to interrogate collective members about their political activities and affiliations. Collective members refused to sign consent forms to allow a legal search.

Robert M. Cluesman, Youth Action Movement / Jacksonville Anarchist Black Cross activist, writes:

"We are seeking an attorney to help us contest the illegal search of our home. The illegal seizure of our private property. And the blatant violation of our civil and human rights!

The purpose of this raid was a petty attempt by the power structure to terrorize us out of existence. It is amazing the lengths these pigs will go to. And even more amazing is their stupidity. Do they really think that by raiding our homes and taking our things that they will calm a mighty storm that rages in the consciousness of the people? If they do then they are sadly mistaken. This petty attempt has served only to make us stronger in our determination and desire to see a better life for all of the people. To see a better life for my mother, who has been busting her butt all of her life simply to survive. Like so many other mothers. Like all those fathers out there and brothers wondering where their gonna get a paycheck. Wondering how their gonna feed their babies. YOU and I, as activists, must put the petty aside, must put our individual egos aside and re-dedicate ourselves to this struggle. Re-dedicate ourselves to educating all those out there who are sick, shooting up, cracking out, losing their minds. This, People, is the kind of struggle we must dedicate ourselves to. We must realize that WE ALL are responsible for the justice and injustice that happens in this world. That we must choose a side to fight on. And that neutrality is just another word for SELL-OUT! Power to the People, yall....."

The situation took a turn for the worse when on January 24 at about 8:15 pm, about 8 Jacksonville Police officers raided the home of Jacksonville Anarchist Black Cross and Youth Action Movement again. No less that three officers were also at the January 12th raid of the same home. Unlike the first raid, officers this time came with warrants for the arrests of three Jacksonville ABC members, Rob Cluesman, Justin Tichy and Chris Herndon. Police arrested Rob Cluesman at their home and arrested Justin and Chris at their workplaces. All three have been charged with Criminal Mischief which is a felony in Florida. They face over $3,500 in fines and 2 years in prison each. Their bail has been set at $10,000 each or 10% of that amount cash each. After the first police raid, the television news media ran several supportive interviews of Jax. ABC and YAM and their work in the community such as free food/literature distribution. It needs to stressed that this is a serious situation not to be taken lightly. This repression comes as a direct result of their political activity and efforts in the community. Most of Jax. ABC are now being held by the state so all inquiries and funds for now should be directed toward NJ ABC at:

New Jersey Anarchist Black Cross
Post Office Box 8532
Paterson, NJ 07508-8532
office phone: 201-357-0994
email: pacnjabc@aol.com

All ABC affiliated groups and supporters should be cautious and prepared in the event of similar occurrences.

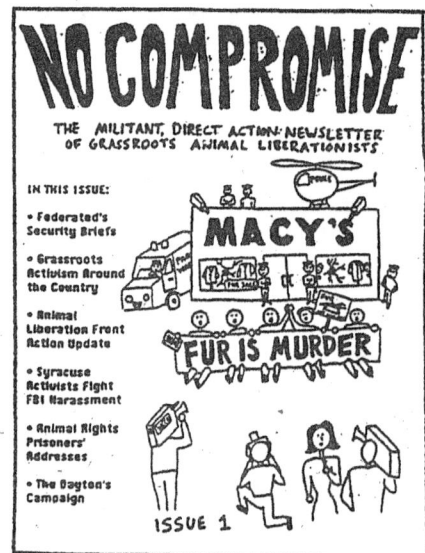

Chicken Rescuer Runs "Fowl" of Local Bylaw

posted to ar-news, Jan 1, 96

A Port Coquitlam, (nr. Vancouver), BC resident has been ordered to find a new home for his 4 chickens. The chickens, which are amongst 15 that Mike Bohnert rescued following their fall off the back of trucks, or escape from the local processing plant, are in violation of a local bylaw that prohibits the keeping of poultry in a residential area. Bohnert plans on appearing before Port Coquitlam council in two weeks, in an effort to appeal the decision of city staff that he get rid of them.

Dutch Ban Fur Imports from Leghold-trapped Animals

ar-news

THE HAGUE, Jan 11 (Reuter) - The Dutch government said on Thursday it had banned with immediate effect the import of all furs from animals caught in leghold traps.

"The move takes effect from January 1," a ministry of agriculture spokesman said.

The European Union said in 1991 it would bring in the ban this year, but last month the European Commission decided on a 12-month delay to allow humane trapping standards to be agreed internationally.

The Commission left the way open for individual members to adopt the measure and the Dutch decided not to wait. "We didn't feel like postponing the ban," said the spokesman.

Leghold traps are condemned by animal welfare activists as one of the most inhumane ways of snaring animals such as the beaver, otter and lynx.

DOLPHINS FROM OCEAN WORLD ESCAPE RESORT INTO ATLANTIC

The Miami Herald, Sat. Jan. 20, 1996
by staff writer Ron Ishoy

For everyone who fought to keep Ocean World's 12 dolphins from being sold and transported from Fort Lauderdale to a Honduran resort 16 months ago, news that eight of the dolphins have escaped into the Atlantic Ocean was bittersweet.

"I'll be honest, my first reaction was, 'I told you so,'" said Naomi Rose, a marine mammal scientist with the Humane Society of the United States. The society filed an unsuccessful federal suit in September 1994 to pre-vent the exportation of the dolphins from the closed Fort Lauderdale marine park to Honduras.

"I'm glad to hear it. I'm only sorry that four were left behind," said Russ Rector, an activist with the Dolphin Freedom Foundation.

The dolphins have been missing from Anthony's Key Resort in the islands off Honduras' northern coast for more than 10 days. Resort owner Julio Galindo said that strong winds destroyed the natural barriers that form the sea pen where the dolphins lived. Resort workers, diligently looking for days for the dolphins, have seen no sign of them.

"The dolphins will die if we don't find them quickly," Galindo said. Six of the dolphins were born in captivity and may not know how to hunt for food themselves, he said. However, if the dolphins haven't been seen by boaters in the area nor shown up dead, then there's a good chance they're OK, says Rose.

"If they're alive, and they're active, and no one has seen them begging after this long, then they don't want to be found."

$70,000 REWARD FOR MINK LIBERATORS 'INSULT' TO REAL VICTIMS

SHEBOYGAN, WI -- A huge reward being offered by the fur industry for the apprehension of animal rights activists who freed thousands of mink here and in Canada is being characterized as "totally absurd" by an anti-fur industry group.

"The $70,000 reward is totally absurd, and should be an insult to anyone victimized by true criminal activity," said J.P. Goodwin, executive director for the Coalition to Abolish the Fur Trade (CAFT), a national animal advocacy group based in Memphis.

The massive reward fund was established after hundreds of mink were freed by the clandestine Animal Liberation Front (ALF) from a mink farm in Sheboygan, and thousands liberated from similar farms in Canada and the state of Washington over the past few months.

"People should ask themselves what kind of reward is being offered for real criminals, like those who rape and murder," said Goodwin. "The answer is that nothing close to this $70,000 is being offered for crimes against people. Apparently, the fur industry cares more about their property then people victimized by murderers and rapists."

A message from the ALF released this week to CAFT noted that mink "spend their entire lives in tiny cages, breeding offspring for the fur trade. (They) are taken and raised in intensive confinement, and then gassed...their lives destroyed for a mere luxury item."

And, contrary to reports by fur farmers, most, if not all, of the released mink will survive in the wild, said Goodwin.

"No one can convince me there won't be survivors," said British Columbia government wildlife technician Mark Pimlott. He has cited Newfoundland, Iceland, Britain, Scandinavia and the former Soviet Union as among the areas in which escapes from mink farms have resulted in viable wild populations.

For more information, contact: Coalition to Abolish the Fur Trade (901)725-7595

ANTI-FUR ACTIVISTS HARASSED BY SYRACUSE POLICE,

YOUTH, MOTHER,ARRESTED AT 'FREE SPEECH' PROTEST

-ar news

SYRACUSE (Wednesday, 2/21/96) -- Police incited a near riot here when they arrested a youth and his mother -- who was asking why her 15-year-old son was handcuffed -- at a demonstration that, ironically, claimed Syracuse police are guilty of brutality and unlawful arrest of political activists.

James Light, 15, and his mother Avril -- who went to the peaceful demonstration to make sure he was not abused -- were apparently arrested on unspecified charges after James began passing out flyers. They were released later but face trespass charges Thursday.

In addition, at least one other activist was arrested when she went to the Public Safety Building to file abuse charges against police. Activists had been asked to go into the PSB one at a time, rather than as a group, but when the first 2 individuals entered, Denise Lynn of Syracuse was handcuffed and led away.

"There is a pattern of misconduct here by police that cannot be ignored," said Crescenzo Vellucci, executive director of the Activist Civil Liberties Committee, a non-profit legal defense group sponsored by the National Activist Network.

"There is a pattern of misconduct here. Anti-fur activists in Syracuse have been slandered, and abused physically and emotionally by Syracuse police. Now they arrest them, and even a parent, for simply passing out flyers critical of the police. The arrests are, without any doubt, self-serving, and unconstitutional," he added.

The activists are volunteers with Animal Defense League, which has been protesting the sale of animals furs by Syracuse retailers for several years. There were 3 arrests at a demonstration this Saturday protesting fur at Georgio's Furs in Syracuse.

PENTAGON WATCHING THE 'NET'

Feb 15, 1996

According to an article from *The Nation* magazine (March 4, 1996) a Pentagon study discusses ways in which the military can exploit the Internet. The Pentagon paper suggests using the Internet for the routine interception of global e-mail, for covert operations and propaganda campaigns, and for tracking domestic political activity, particularly that of the left. Author David Corn writes: "Last summer, Charles Swett, a policy assistant in the Office of the Assistant Secretary of Defense for Special Operations and Low-Intensity Conflict, produced a report that assessed the intelligence value of the Internet for the Defense Department. His study discovered the obvious: By monitoring computer message traffic and alternative news sources from around the world, the military might

catch 'early warning of impending significant developments.'

"Swett reports that the "Internet could also be used offensively as an additional medium in psychological operations campaigns and to help achieve unconventional warfare objectives."

A striking aspect of his study is that there is one sort of Internet user who attracts a large amount of attention from Swett: cyber-smart lefties." [The Pentagon paper specifically mentions Earth First! and People for the Ethical Treatment of Animals by name -ed] Corn's article also discusses how "[t]he Pentagon and intelligence services will conduct 'routine monitoring of messages originating in other countries' in the search for information on 'developing security threats.' That means overseas e-mail, like overseas phonecalls, will be intercepted by the electronic eavesdroppers of the National Security Agency or some other outfit. The data will be fed into filtering computers and then, if it contains any hot-button words, forwarded to the appropriate analyst. 'Networks of human sources with access to the Internet could be developed in areas of security concern to the U.S.' ... Another growth area is the dirty tracks department. Noting that government officials, military officials, business people, and journalists all around the world are online, Swett envisions "Psychological Operations" campaigns in which U.S. propaganda could be rapidly disseminated to a wide audience. He adds, 'The U.S. might be able to employ the Internet offensively to help achieve unconventional warfare objectives.'

JUDGE SENTENCES COLLEGE ACTIVIST TO 90 DAYS IN JAIL FOR PEACEFUL PROTEST

March 11, 1996

MINNEAPOLIS -- A University of Minnesota political activist -- with no prior convictions -- was sentenced Monday to 90 days in jail, the maximum under state law, for his participation in a peaceful demonstration at the university last year.

The sentence is being condemned as a miscarriage of justice, and a flagrant attempt to stifle the activist's free speech rights by a national civil liberties group.

Freeman Wicklund, student organizer with Student Organization for Animal Rights (SOAR), was found guilty last month of disorderly conduct when he attempted to meet with UofM President Nils Hasselmo to discuss research at the university that involves addicting monkeys and rats to cocaine, PCP and other drugs.

Hennepin County Judge Joan Lancaster Monday morning initially sentenced Wicklund to 1 day in jail, time-served. But, as a condition of probation, insisted he accept guidelines that would have prohibited his participation in protests for 3 months.

"I cannot, in good conscience, accept that prohibition," said Wicklund, who said the terms of probation violated his constitutional rights to free speech. "The threat of prison will not deter me from continuing my activity as an activist," he said.

"The sentence is outrageous, and absurd," said Crescenzo Vellucci, executive director of the Activist Civil Liberties Committee (ACLC), a national legal defense organization based in California.

"The length of sentence, coupled with the court's attempt to stifle his free speech rights, makes it apparent that the goal of the court is not to serve any public safety purpose, but to chill Mr. Wicklund's free speech rights," added Vellucci.

Wicklund, who represented himself at the trial, will be free pending appeal.

Contact:
SOAR: 612/626-5566 or ACLC 916/452-7179

END-OF-SEASON MADNESS STRIKES ESSEX AND KETTERING POLICE

ENGLAND: As the foxhunting season draws to a close, two of the most notoriously biased police forces in the country seemed determined to have a "final fling" at oppressive policing of sabs. At the Essex Foxhunt meet at Hatfield Broadoak, 10 sabs were arrested for aggravated trespass, while at the Fitzwilliam Hunt near Corby Kettering police made 11 entirely arbitrary arrests.

At the Fitzwilliam Hunt 11 sabs were blocked in on a public road by hunt supporters and were astonished when the police arrived to be told "there's nothing we can do". In fact, such behaviour, encompasses about half a dozen public order and road traffic offenses. A Sgt. Eaton from Corby police then announced he had been told that sabs had been trespassing so that he could "probably arrest you all under S.69 of the Criminal Justice Act". When it was pointed out to him that he was just making this up, he replied "Right, that's it, I'm arresting you all to prevent a breach of the peace", presumably conceding the point that he had in fact been making it up. It is difficult to see how such arrests can be justified when the 11 sabs in question were sat in a van on a public road. All 11 were held until the hunt had finished and then released without charge. This amounts to an unofficial (and unlawful) "internment" policy. It is a tactic we have seen before elsewhere in the country, most notably Cheshire, where 15 arrests were made under similar circumstances last weekend. Similar unlawful arrests in the late 1980s cost various police forces millions in damages after sabs sued. Unfortunately for the taxpayers of Kettering, their local police haven't got enough sense to be biased properly - six sabs already in the field on foot continued to sab the hunt successfully, ensuring no kills.

Meanwhile, at the Essex Hunt taxpayers' money was being thrown about with wild abandon as 50 officers and the force helicopter were called in to deal with about 40 sabs. Again the police were not quite so interested in dealing with offenses committed by hunt members as with harassing sabs - the officers, from Braintree, took no action against a hunt rider who deliberately rode his horse over a woman protester while busying themselves with illegal searches of sab vehicles and confiscation of equipment. One van alone was searched four times, an obvious abuse of power as a delaying tactic. Staves and baseball bats were found in the hunt stewards' vehicle and these were confiscated but despite the obviously violent intention of anyone carrying such items, none of the stewards were so much as cautioned. In contrast, the highlight of the day for the inaptly named Braintree Police came when sabs entered a field some distance away from the hunt. Despite the fact that they were doing nothing more criminal than walking across a field, a task force of police Land Rovers skidded across the field from all sides and officers leapt on anyone they could grab, making 10 arrests for "aggravated trespass". As yet, it is not known if anyone has been charged.

.Hunt Saboteurs Association <hsa@gn.apc.org>

CLANDESTINE RESCUE REUNITES WOMAN, CAT

ar-news

WEYAUWEGA, WIS (AP) -- Susan Weiss sat in a church and wept with worry: Her cat, Kynda, was home alone after the derailment of propane tankers forced an evacuation of Weiss' community.

ON the 12th day of the evacuation Friday, Weiss shed tears of joy. She and Kynda were reunited, thanks to strangers who snuck past safetylines and risked arrest to reach Weiss' home.

"I don't know who did it. I don't know first names or anything. It was like a cloak-and-dagger operation. But I got her with me," Weiss said in a telephone interview from the motel where she is staying. Kynda was "very, very thirsty" but otherwise OK, Weiss said. The National Guard continued draining the derailed tank cars through the weekend in hopes of allowing the 1,700 inhabitants of the central Wisconsin community of Weyauwega to return home.

Two day earlier, on March 8, the National Guard let 132 people don helmets and flak jackets and enter the town in tank-like personnel carriers to rescue pets. Weiss was told her home was too near the wreckage to be included in the rescue. The news devastated Weiss, who is disabled. The 10-year-old cat is her sole companion.

Wednesday night, Weiss' 52nd birthday, she got a call. She was told if she wanted Kynda rescued, she was to meet a guy with a ski cap at a designated place. She said she made the rendezvous and handed the keys to her home to strangers.

"Four hours later, they came back with my cat. What can I say?" Weiss said. "It is totally bizarre. I know. ... I felt like I was on 'Mission Impossible.' To come up with my precious cat, it was like 'Wow, I don't believe it.'"

NOW AVAILABLE!

NORTH AMERICAN A.L.F. SUPPORTERS GROUP

working towards animal liberation & freedom for all political prisoners

Animal Liberation Front Supporters Group BENEFIT COMPILATION TAPE

34 Songs by:

**** BLACK KRONSTADT * MAX * NINTH HOUR * FORGOTTON * THIRD WORLD PLANET * HERMIT * ULTRA VIRES * PLASTIC * SENSORY CROSSOVER * SUB-MISSION HOLD * MEXICAN POWER AUTHORITY * SUB-GENIUS * OFFAL CONSUMPTION * ENFA/LAK * DISASTER AREA * INSURRECTION * LET'S PUT THE ''X'' IN SEX ****

Each A.L.F.S.G. BENEFIT COMPILATION TAPE comes with a **24 paged booklet and sticker [''A.L.F. Supporter'']** This kick-ass tape is a collaboration of efforts from Vancouver Island and area musicians, who came together for the common cause of **animal liberation.** Recordings were made during benefit shows held May 5 & 6 and June 10 & 11 of 1995. This tape is a **non-profit project** and all proceeds from the sale of the tapes will be used to further the cause of animal liberation and **directly benefit imprisoned Animal Liberation Front activists and their families.**

To order:
Send cheque or money order [made out to ''NA ALFSG''] for $7.50 to:

NA-ALFSG DISTRO
Box 241532
Memphis, TN
38124, USA

Canadian residents may pay in CDN funds, US and international orders, please pay in US funds. **(Tapes are $6, plus .25% for shipping and handling costs = $7.50)**

COMMUNITY & PIRATE RADIO STATIONS interested in receiving a free copy of this tape, **please write** for more details, **or email: <an246614@anon.penet.fi>**

[*TAPES also available from **CARPE DEIM DISTRO, 218 Kingfisher Pl, Nanimo, B.C. U9U 1A9, Canada** - do NOT send NA ALFSG cheques to this address!]

Diary of Actions

PLEASE NOTE: THE DIARY OF ACTIONS IS INTENDED TO REPORT THE NEWS OF DIRECT ACTIONS TO SAVE ANIMALS, NOT TO ENCOURAGE CRIME. THE FOLLOWING LIST DOES INCLUDE SOME ACTIONS THAT TOOK PLACE IN THE TIME PERIOD COVERED IN UNDERGROUND #3, BUT WERE NOT REPORTED UNTIL RECENTLY. ALL REPORTS COME FROM OTHER PUBLICATIONS, THE INTERNET, OR COMMUNIQUES SENT ANONYMOUSLY TO THE NA ALFSG.

CANADA

SEPT 15/95: Guelph, Ont - A McDonald's billboard was altered so the Big Mac looked like a skull and the slogans now read "*Murder* Deluxe" and "*Cancer* has a great new taste."

OCT 24/95: Near Chilliwack, B.C. - 2400 mink released at Reg and Lydia Dargatz's fur farm in the early morning hours, breeding information also destroyed. - A.L.F.

NOV 14/95: Aldergrove, B.C. - 5000 mink released at Fred Rippin's fur farm. In the early morning shortly after security guards had made their regular rounds, someone using bolt cutters cut through fences, opened every cage and destroyed 70 years of breeding information. The mink were due to be killed in a couple weeks by carbon monoxide gassing -A.L.F.

FROM THE COMMUNIQUE:
"Man's inhumanity to man is only surpassed by his cruelty to animals."
On the evening of October 26, a cell of the Animal Liberation Front visited Dargatz Mink Ranch (10282 Reeves Rd, Chilliwack, B.C.) and on November 13 we visited Rippin Fur Farm (27413 8th Avenue, Aldergrove, B.C.). To verify the authenticity of this notice, allow us to describe the occasions. Mr. Dargatz has nine and one half mink barns (8 in use) and Mr. Rippin has nine mink barns (all in use). Each barn generally has four rows of cages - two inner and two outer. At Mr. Dargatz's farm, a full barn contains about 64 cages in each outer row and 81 cages per inner row, while at Mr. Rippin's farm a full barn contains 288 cages per outer row and about that many for each inner row. About one cage in ten was already empty. Mr. Dargatz also has goats inside his mink compound.

We were disappointed but not surprised with the one-sided media coverage. As purveyors of the status quo, they say our actions were careless and futile. They broadcast the words of Mr. Rippin and Mr. Engh (Canadian Mink Breeders Association - Chris Engh, (30030 Burgess Mt. Rd. Langley, B.C.) as though it were plain fact. They say our friends are domesticated. We in the A.L.F. say they are wild animals placed in cages ... They say we are terrorists and criminals with no respect for property. We aren't out to terrorize anybody, we simply want to save lives and end this terrible trade. While trespassing and minor barn damage my violate B.C. law, their notion of sentient creatures as "property" violates Natural Law ... These farmers don't care about the welfare of these animals - they would have been slaughtered and skinned in a matter of weeks. Their sole concern is the damage we have done to their profits. All we did was give our friends a fighting chance to escape from that scheduled slaughter ... Releasing our 2,000 friends at Mr. Dargatz's farm and 4,000 friends at Mr. Rippin's farm were two of the most satisfying things that we have ever done. Some of them were rather friendly; others were curious with their new found freedom; some were terrified by our presence, while many just showed signs of dementia caused by their living (loosely defined) conditions - pacing back and forth, tailbiting, cannibalizing, etc. After their jailbreak, many of our friends took off and never looked back, many wandered around exploring the new world, while many simply played a little too loud at Mr. Rippin's ranch as this seems to have woken our kind farmer and his neighbours. We would have freed all 10,000 of our friends had not farmer Fred's arrival necessitated our departure. We regret that many of our friends have been enslaved once again, especially now that they have had a taste of freedom. While we recognize that our actions will financially damaged Mr. Rippin and Mr. Dargatz, their employees and their families, we have come to realize that this concern is secondary compared to the amount of pain and suffering that they would cause if left alone. They reap profits from that which simply should not be. We hope that someday they will see how truly wrong the things are that they do.

From the Vancouver Sun - November 24th:

Contrary to the view of mink farmers, mink released from their cages by animal-rights activists in Chilliwack and Aldergrove are capable of surviving in the wild, a BC wildlife branch official says.

"Mink are wild animals raised in captivity" wildlife technician Mark Pimlott said from his regional office in Surrey. "They will suffer high mortality in the first few weeks. But no one can convince me that there won't be survivors"

Newfoundland, Iceland, Britain, Scandinavia and the former Soviet Union are among the areas in which escapes from mink farms have resulted in viable wild populations, Pimlott said. "Newfoundland and Iceland are a lot more inhospitable than the Fraser Valley in terms of food", he said. Fur farmers have suggested that the mink, as domesticated animals, face certain starvation in the wild.

"I take those claims with a grain of salt" said Pimlott, noting that the breeding of mink in captivity, in North America has occurred only this century. "To say that because they've been fed a predictable diet and because they've had no chance to forage they'll starve, I find that a little self-serving."

Asked to comment Thursday on Pimlott's remarks, Carrol Rippin (wife of one of the farm owners) said " I really don't know. He's obviously the expert and we're not. We felt that they were not raised as wild animals."

NOV 22/95: Guelph, Ontario - Guelph Fashion Furs was hit TWICE over the weekend by activists. The front display window was smashed. This shut off the alarm system for the evening and forced the replacement of both window and alarm tape system. "Fur is Dead" was spray painted on the walls of the building in two places and several "Fur: It's DEAD simple" posters were pasted to doors.The walls required repainting.

JAN/96: British Columbia/Alberta - Razor-sharp blades dipped in rat poison have been mailed to at least 65 B.C. and Alberta guide outfitters, designed to slice open the fingers of anyone opening the letter. JUSTICE DEPT. Examples of the device were sent to a number of media outlets. According to one newspaper report, the "... package received at the Times Colonist included a sealed envelope within a second envelope. the former contained a razor sharp utility knife blade about 7 1/2 centimeters long, positioned where it could easily cut the hand of anyone opening the envelope. the package contained two written messages. One included in the envelope with the blade, was addressed to the outfitters and said *"Dear animal killing scum! Hope we sliced your finger wide open and that you now die from the rat poison we smeared on the razor blade. Murdering scum that kill defenseless animals in the thousands every year across B.C. for fun and profit do not deserve to live. We will continue to wage war on animal abusers across the world. Beware scum, better watch out, you might be next! Justice Department strikes again"*

The second note, which read like a new release, said 65 rat-poison smeared blades were sent to outfitters. *"With luck may all there (sic) fingers be sliced open and die from poisoning. The world would be a better place."*

JAN/96: Victoria - A Rockland man involved in the fur industry came home to find the words "murderer", "death", "fur" and "killer" spray-painted in red on his front door and garage door."ALF" was painted on the side of his truck. Activists also slashed tires on his truck and trailer. ALF

From the Campbell River Mirror January 17, 1996 - No. 5 Vol. 26

-ECO TERRORISM

Hunter Forced To Quit

By Matthew Plumtree

A local hunting guide is calling it quits after being mailed a booby-trapped letter last week.

David Fyfe said receiving the letter, which RCMP confirmed Monday contained a razor blade designed to cut an unsuspecting letter opener, was the final straw.

"I love a good fight," Fyfe said Monday, "But I'm no longer willing to subject my family to continued threats and harassment from ... animal rights terrorists."

The razor blades, supposedly dipped in rat poison, were mailed to a number of guides in B.C., including at least three on Vancouver Island. Vancouver RCMP Sgt. Peter Montague confirmed Fyfe's envelope contained a razor blade.

"A few of them have been received," he said, "It's being investigated out of headquarters here: it's being co-ordinated on a provincial basis."

Montague said he knew of no suspects.

Fyfe said he informed the province on Friday that he will no longer using the guiding license he's had slightly more than a year.

"Some of the more radical of these eco-terrorists are in the Campbell River area and my family being an easy target made it an easy decisions to quit.

"They're becoming more and more brazen" he said, pointing to recent incidents that frightened his wife and children.

Some of the incidents documented by Fyfe:

- bear hides stolen:
- followed on hunting exhibitions: vehicles blocked in and ditches dug behind their parked vehicles;
- Fyfe's name and number put on the Internet for environment groups to target
- family followed so frequently that at he approached local RCMP to enforce stalking law;
- local residents shouted obscenities to him and his family; followed by "drive-bys" and writing on his truck;
- the latest threat through the mail.

"Hunting in B.C. is under serious threat," he said, "and with out some sort of accountability, groups ... will intensify their actions. I see an acceleration in their campaign. They're gaining ground."

He reiterated that while his "retirement" will be construed as a victory, he would be taking the group on if it wasn't for his family.

"It's a relief to be out of guiding and this is my way of telling them to leave me -- to leave my family -- alone.

FEB 9/96: Toronto, Ont - marking Canada's National Anti-Fur Day, six different fur shops had doors glued shut in Toronto's rapidly dissappering fur district.

FEB 9/96: Guelph, Ont - Guelph Fashion Furs vandalized with slogans. "FUR IS DEAD" was spraypainted several times on the walls of the building. The walls have been repainted several times in the past year because of repeated 'grafitti' attacks. ALF.

MAR 1/96: Newfoundland - A Victoria man, David Francis Arnold was arrested in Newfoundland with a vehicle full of incendiary devices. He had allegedly set out to target the Whitbourne seal processing plant. At this point in time we do not know if this was an animal liberation action. We are also lacking any details on where Arnold is currently being held.

MAR/96: Toronto, Ont - Two young female animal lib activists just happened to be parked across from a 24hr pig slaughter house (Niagara & King), watching a macho pig "handler" show off with his "long electro-shock prod" as he unloaded a shipment of pigs. At one point the handler set the shock prod down and took an electric "tickle" whip to the pigs inside the transport truck. Sick of hearing the pigs screaming, one of the two women dashed over and grabbed the shock rod from the side of truck and then drove away before the animal abuser even knew what happened!

MAR 5/96: Guelph, Ont - Garden Brothers Circus vehicles sloganized. Messages included "Let the animals live," "Animal Liberation" and "Free Us."

MAR 6/96: Guelph, Ont - Bomb hoax called in to Memorial Gardens where the Garden Brothers Circus was set up to perform. According to newspaper reports, a large crowd was forced to flee and the circus was delayed for nearly two hours as bomb-sniffing dogs combed the building. Animal Rights Milita

MAR 8/96: Vancouver, B.C. - The Justice Department mailed out at least 87 razor letters to Canadian furriers across Canada. The razor blades were allegedly dipped in tainted blood, and threatened the retailers with death if they did not shut down their businesses within six months. According to a Vancouver Sun report, a letter they received stated:

"Enclosed you will find a booby-trapped envelope ... ours does not contain the infected blood, so if you use your brain you should avoid problems ... It is unfortunate such drastic actions must be taken but in war, people die, And we haven't even started yet."

The letter addressed to the furriers read:

"Fur is dead. And hopefully so are you. We placed these razor blades (coated with AIDS infected blood, by the way) in the hopes of eliminating scum like yourself from the earth. There is no excuse for the fur trade. This is war and in war, people die. Enough animals have been killed, now it's your turn ... You have been marked. You have six months to shut down your business. After that you will start receiving explosive devices which WILL kill you. "This is not a joke."

The letter also stated that groups such as theirs might not be needed if the news media took a greater interest in printing the facts about industries that profit from animal exploitation. So far, we are aware of at least one letter being received in Toronto and two in Montreal.

USA

Date unknown: St. Pete, FL - fur shop vandalized, with the entire store front washed in red paint. "Shame" and "ALF" was spraypainted all over the building, awning and windows. ALF

Date unknown: Pasco County, FL - bomb threat was sent to the Pasco County Sheriff's Dept, regarding a bomb planted in the Clyde-Beatty Cole Brothers circus. Newspapers were tipped off when the sheriff's dept failed to act, potentially endangering peoples lives. The sheriff's dept was the one sponsering the circus, but the report says "there won't be a circus back for a while in Pasco County because 'it wasn't worth all the hassle.'"

JUNE 10/95: Memphis, TN - Micheal Frankel, vice president of King Furs had paint poured over his car while it was parked at his house. ALF

JUNE 10/95: Memphis, TN - King Furs delivery van had its locks glued. ALF

JULY 11/95: Edina, MN - locks glued at the Leather entre.

ALF

JULY 11/95: Hopkins, MN - Simeks Meats billboard was paint bombed. ALF

AUG 2/95: Minneapolis, MN - McDonald's billboard paint bombed. ALF

AUG 13/95: Annedale, MN - 1 coyote released from Davidson Fur Farm, a sign was spray painted. ALF

SEPT 29/95: Eden Prairie, MN - Heavenly Ham locks glued. ALF

OCT 5/95: Minneapolis, MN - Mandevill butchers supply 2 windows broken, door spray painted. ALF

OCT 18/95: Memphis, TN - Jean Benham Furs paint bombed. ALF

NOV 12/95: Minnetonka, MN - North American Outdoor Adventures, a hunting outfitter, had locks glued and slogans painted. ALF

NOV 16/95: Minnetonka, MN - Pleasant View, TN - Mac Ellis fox farm raided for the second year in a row. 30 cages were opened before a disturbance forced the ALF to evacuate. ALF

COMMUNIQUE:
Friends, comrades and armchair liberationists,

In the early hours of Thursday, November 16th 1995 The A.L.F. carried out a raid against Clarence Jordan's mink farm. Three to four hundred minks were released and an attempt at burning down his storerooms, refrigeration unit and killing shed was aborted because he came out. This action was an attempt to shut down his operation down permanently and we regret that we failed at this mission though many minks got to taste freedom. Clarence has recently secured his cages with extra wire I suspect as a response to earlier attacks in British Columbia.

In continuing struggle we fight for the animals,
A.L.F.

And According to news reports from the Olympian, WA newspapers;

The owner of the mink farm Clarence Jordan, called 9-1-1 after hearing his dogs barking just after 2:15 a.m. He reported to dispatch officers that his cattle and mink were set loose.

Thurston County Sheriff's Detective Lt. Dan Kimball said writing was painted on a fence at the farm on Mink Street Northwest near Steamboat Island Road. The marking said: "mink liberation" and "release mink now."

Thurston county detectives are contacting Canadian officials to compare notes.

He said he was not sure whether those responsible for the Canadian releases were behind Thursday's incident or whether activists saw the media coverage and copied them. Damage estimates in one newspaper was listed at over $75,000.

NOV 18/95:Memphis, TN - Jean Benham Furs paint bombed big time. Media reports stated that the locks had been glued on several occasions (apparently severalcells are active) and that the furrier was out $8000 after multiple attacks. ALF

NOV 23/95: St. Paul, MN - For thanksgiving the ALF broke out windows at the offices of the Minnesota Turkey Growers Assn. ALF

NOV 24/95: Eugene, OR - On Fur Free Friday Kaufman's in the Valley River Center Mall was hit, and 25 fur coats were sprayed with red permanent fabric paint, rendering them valueless. An estimated $75,000 worth of animal skins were instantly unmarketable. ALF

FROM THE COMMUNIQUE: "Please call Kaufmans at 1-800-452-2617 and let them know that you are boycotting their store ... If any stores in your area sell furs (see "Fur" in your yellow pages) take appropriate action to see that they change their policy. YOU have the power to make postitive changes in this world!"

DEC/95: Indiapolis - Kincaid's has three windows

smashed, aprox. $1200 damage.

DEC/95: Indiapolis - Long John Silver's windows were smashed.

DEC/95: New York, NY - Furs New York billboard damaged.

DEC/95: Memphis, TN - Road spikes left under a furriers car at King furs. ALF

DEC/95: Detroit, MI - Dittrich Furs Billboard paintbombed. ALF

DEC/95: Memphis, TN - Goldsmith's dept store (sells furs) delivery van had it's windows smashed. ALF

DEC 3/95: Washington, DC - 2 fur shops, Millers Furs and Rosendorf Evans, had their windows smashed. Paint Panthers

DEC 3/95: Bethesda, MD - Millers Furs, windows smashed. Paint Panthers

DEC 24/95-Eugene, OR; Dutch Girl Ice Cream had three trucks spray painted with slogans "Go.Vegan!", "Dairy=Death" and "A.L.F.", three incendiary devices were also left under the trucks, one went out, the second damaged the tires and the third spread to the interior causing extensive damage totaling at least $15,500. ALF

JAN 2/96: Memphis, TN - The home of Kevin Hoslinger, manager of the Goldsmith's fur salon was paint bombed and his locks were glued. ALF

JAN 16/96: Memphis, TN - Goldsmith's dept. store security van had it's windshield smashed. ALF

The Minnesota ALF claims that more actions have happened, but they aren't all listed. Apparently, according to media reports, this is the case in Memphis as well. It has been reported that the DC locations of Millers Furs was paint bombed in November. We don't have a specific date on that.

JAN 19/96: Mclean VA - Furs of Kiszely windows shot out. ALF

JAN/96: Sheboygan, WI - ALF activists release between 200 and 400 mink from a fur farm outside Sheboygan, making it the sixth liberation by the ALF in the past four months, resulting in nearly 7,000 animals freed from fur farms in Canada and the U.S. According to a communique issued by the ALF, the Wisconsin mink were released from their cages during the early morning hours. The farm is owned by Bob Zimbal, and is located on Washington Road. Reportedly, more than 20,000 mink were on the farm at the time of the raid. ALF

A spokeswoman for the Fur Commission USA, a national organization representing domestic fur farmers, said protests against mink farmers were increasing across the United States, and Wisconsin, the nation's leading mink producer, may be targeted more often.

FROM THE COMMUNIQUE:

"(We) opened the cages and released these wild creatures into their natural habitat," said the ALF in their message. "They spend their entire lives in tiny cages, breeding offspring for the fur trade...the offspring are taken, and raised in intensive confinement, and then gassed. Their lives are destroyed for a mere luxury item. Now these mink have a chance at life. Beforehand, death was certain. More (actions are) coming."

JAN 22/96: Memphis, TN - jean Benham Furs paint bombed. ALF

JAN 24/96: Memphis, TN - King Furs billboard paint bombed. ALF

JAN 25/96: New York, NY - Fur promotional billboard altered.

JAN 29/96: Memphis TN- Residents have been warned that if they wear furcoats, they may be subject to "paint attacks." The warnings were issued in the form of posters blanketing neighborhoods near stores that sell animal furs, including Goldsmith's. The posters read:

"WARNING: Spray paint attacks on fur wearers known to occur in this area.If you are wearing a fur coat, remain calm but be on the alert for red spray paint."

FEB 2/96: Washington, DC - Millers Furs front door and window shot out.

FEB 2/96: Chevy Chase, MD - Adrianna Furs window shot out.

FEB 9/96: Syracuse, NY - Sam's Chickenland locks were glued, the sign was paintbombed, front picture window smashed, neon sign destroyed. ALF

MAR 25/96: Ballard Locks, Seattle - in an effort to stop the killing of sea lions, ALF activists sank a gigantic float cage used to trap the animals. The action was done to protest the shooting of sea lions, animals often wrongly blamed for declining fish stocks.

AUSTRALIA

NOV 23/95: Melbourne/Hawthorn [an inner-city suburb of Melbourne]: bricks were thrown through three butcher shop windows in Glenferrie Road about 3.30 a.m. Graffiti left behind said: "This is the ALF." The manager of University Meats, Mr Frank Maher, told the media the ALF had left him with a damage bill of $2000. The words "Meat is murder" had been sprayed in white paint outside his shop. Damage to another shop was estimated at $2500. The owner of Butch's Bangers, Mr Rob Kelly, reported damage totalling $1600.

NEW ZEALAND/AOTEAROA

JULY/95: Dunedin - Reports of butcher shops getting smashed up. ALF

AUG/95: Christchurch - Several McDonalds signs get redecorated with appropriate slogans.

AUG/95: Auckland - A Cancer Society banner is redecorated and relocated to Grafton St bridge just before Daffodil Day sept.

AUG/95: Wellington - Prestons Meats, Hopper St. Tyres slashed on two meat trucks. ALF

AUG/95: Wellington - Vivsectors turn up to a conference in the Town Hall to discover the ALF had glued the locks.

AUG/95: Wellington - 15 masked animal libbers attempted to "gate crash" a vivisectors converence dinner at the Skyline resturant. The activists banged on doors and windows, chanted and threw things.

AUG/95: Auckland - Auckland Zoo given a new paint-job. ALF

OCT/95: Wellington - Tyres slashed again and slogans painted on meat trucks parked in Hopper St. Activists returned a week later to find that the trucks were no longer being parked at the depot overnight so used a slingshot to break windows at Prestons meats in Hopper St and at Charcoal Chicken in Cuba St. ALF

OCT/95: Christchurch - Three butcher shops lose large plate glass windows to ALF slingshots in Cashmere and Riccarton. ALF

NOV/95: Christchurch - Nov 1 (World Vegan Day). Activists use slingshots to smash windows at several butcher shops and redecorate KFC in Sydenham with anti meat slogans. Linwood McDeaths got ALF anti-meat slogans painted on it. ALF

NOV/95: Christchurch - Nov 5 (Earth Night) "All the little pixies came out to play - Love and Slingshots, ALF". Windows smashed at Charcoal Chicken in Riccarton Rd and butcher shops in Lincoln Rd, Richmond shopping centre, Colombo St, Blenheim Rd and one other unspecified location (Total of 6). KFC in Papanui Rd was covered in grafitti, including "KENTUCKY FRIED CORPSE" and "SMASH FACTORY FARMING", and finally Merivale McDonald's has "MURDER" painted on a Big Mac sign. Not bad for a single night! ALF

NOV/95: Auckland - Six butchers in Papatoetoe, Pt. Chevalier and Westmere have their windows smashed and slogans painted on them. Pork market shop vandalized. Ingham chicken plant covered in slogans. Activists then visited the home of Lois Armiger, vivisector, and paint slogans. Laura Mumaw, director of the Auckland jZoo gets house and car paint stripped and grafittied. ALF

NOV/95: Auckland - Several butcher shops painted and superglued. Cancer Society HQ painted with slogans. Inghams Chicken processing plant covered in slogans. Dunnighams meat suppliers get painted and two windows smashed.

ANIMAL RIGHTS ACTIVISTS ATTACK SHOPS ANONYMOUS CALLER TELLS OF SABOTAGE

by Hans Petrovic 'The Press' November 14 1995

Radical animal-rights activists have been sabotaging butcher shops and other meat-associated firms in the Christchurch area in recent weeks, possibly causing as much as $25,000 damage.

A check yesterday of butcher shops, meat processors and KFC and McDonald's fast-food outlets revealed that many had their front windows smashed, red paint daubed on the premises, or locks filled with superglue.

Many of the most-recent known incidents occurred last week in an area extending from Cashmere to Riccarton and Richmond.

'The Press' was alerted to the sabotage in a call from a public telephone box by a man who wished to remain anonymous. He claimed the sabotage was done at Moots Meats in Riccarton, Peter Timbs Meats in Cashmere, various butcheries, McDonald's and KFC outlets, causing about $25,000 of damage to windows alone.

The man described the protest campaign as "economic sabotage" and said it would continue. "It is being done because these people make a lot of money off the murder of animals. Legal means don't work, so you have to break things."

Rob Moot, the manager of Moot's Meats, said the front window of his Riccarton Road shop was broken three times - about two weeks, four weeks, and six months ago. Each time a lead No. 2 fishing sinker was used to smash the window, each of which cost about $400 to replace. There was no indication left why the windows were broken.

Brent Milner, the manager of Peter Timbs Meats, said a lead sinker smashed through the front window of his Cashmere shop last week. "I believe it was the animal rights people, but they didn't write anything on the windows. Unfortunately, we have no control over it".

Trevor Rhodes, owner of Hibbards Butchery in Stanmore Road, said the shop's front window was broken last week for the fourth or fifth time. "This has been going on for a couple of years. We've had the locks filled with superglue and the place covered with buckets of red paint. They wrote ALF, presumably for Animal Liberation Front, and other messages, like 'Meat is Murder'." Although the windows were insured, the cost of other damage came to about $1000.

Arthur Grieves, owner of another butchery in Stanmore Road, said he found the front window smashed twice in the past 18 months. Animal rights messages were also painted in red on the window.

The market manager of KFC, Nick Sealey, said from Auckland yesterday he was aware of this activity in Christchurch.

Graffiti has been written on KFC's Papanui and Colombo Street shops, another outlet had glue put in the locks.

"This kind of activity is not confined to New Zealand, but occurs also in Australia. It appears now and again, but this is the first time it has affected KFC," Mr Sealey said.

"It's done by a fringe element that is out to create a nuisance against those who process meat and eat meat. Besides always reporting cases to the police, we are at a loss what to do," he said.

Although incidents were also claimed to have occurred at McDonald's outlets, no company spokesman could be found to comment yesterday.

The national coordinator of Save Animals From Exploitation, Anthony Terry, said yesterday his organisations was aware of the sabotage activities, but did not condone them.

"I sympathize with the people who are doing it because they are frustrated over stopping the killings. But it's a negative reaction because it causes a lot of damage and loss to property."

Detective Senior Sergeant John Rae, of the Christchurch Police, said he was not aware of the sabotage. This probably was because it had occurred in different areas and the activities had not been connected yet.

NOV/95: Wellington - fish delivery van tyres slashed in Adelaide Road.

NOV/95: Auckland - Chicken delivery truck totally re-painted with slogans and superglued. Leather and skin shop sign removed. ALF.

DEC/95: Auckland - Several seafood billboard/signs removed and destroyed. Seafood Shop in Albany covered in painted slogans. Livestock truck painted and glued in Browns Bay. ALF.

DEC/95: Auckland - 3000 hoax leaflets distributed offering free ham and turkey to supermarket customers. Several supermarkets inconvenienced by this. Leaflets signed by 'Auckland Livestock Federation.' ALF.

DEC 25/95: Christchurch - Windows smashed at four butcher shops. ALF.

DEC 25/95: Christchurch - Sydenham KFC painted with slogans and locks glued. Two butchers shops painted and glued. Two leather shops get superglued locks. Cancer Society Shop (pro-vivisection) gets glued locks. Verkerks Butcher shop superglued. ALF.

DEC/95: Dunedin - Butcher shop gets a brick through the window. Slogans painted and super glue in locks at McDonalds, a fur shop, a shooters shop, and a leather shop.

JAN/96: Auckland - Northcote KFC gets four plateglass windows smashed and decorated with graffiti. Windows smashed at two butchers. Onehunga butcher shop covered in paint, slogans and glue in locks. Lois Armiger, vivisector, gets her house painted with ALF slogans. ALF.

JAN/96: Auckland - Rabbit rescued from cage as 'owners' were neglecting him. Taken to a new and better home by ALF.

JAN/96: Auckland - Windows smashed at two butcher shops. Beef restaurant painted and window smashed. ALF.

JAN/96: Hamilton - Construction site of future McDonald's vandalised and painted with "McDonalds destroys rainforests".

JAN/96: Wellington - Two meat trucks owned by Prestons Meats get tyres slashed and slogans painted on them after they are foolishly left parked on roadside even though the company had been visited by ALF three times previously in recent months.

ENGLAND

MAY/95: Essex - Roger Mills, a farmer involved with live animal exports, has his landrover damaged for the third time.

MAY/95: Sussex - Two shops in Brighton have their locks glued after they sponsor the county (animal abuse) fair.

MAY/95: Sussex - McDonald's in Brighton have their locks glued.

JUNE/95: Hampshire - Five chickens from Webbs Poultry Products, Winchester liberated by the ALF.

JUNE/95: Hampshire - Hoax bomb left under the vehicle of Paul Dowsett, owner of Garetmar Kennels.

JUNE/95: Hampshire - The car of William Cartmell of Wickham Labs is blown up whilst parked in his garage. Prior to the explosion the car had been paint stripped three times in three months by the ALF.

JUNE/95: Hampshire - ALF torch empty stable at Torbay Farm, lab animal suppliers.

JUNE/95: Kent - Three animal lib hoax letter bombs sent to John Carter in two days.

JUNE/95: Meon Valley - Fake bomb planted in pro-blood sports pub, The Bucks Head.

JUNE/95: Somerset - letterbomb sent to the MAFF Minister and live exports farmer, William Waldergrave MP. -Justice Deptartment.

JUNE/95: Walsall - Former abattoir worker Victor Golding rallies other ex-employees to release 15 cows from Harlescott abottoir. When arrested by police, Golding claimed he was connected with the ALF. the police didn't believe him and released him without charge.

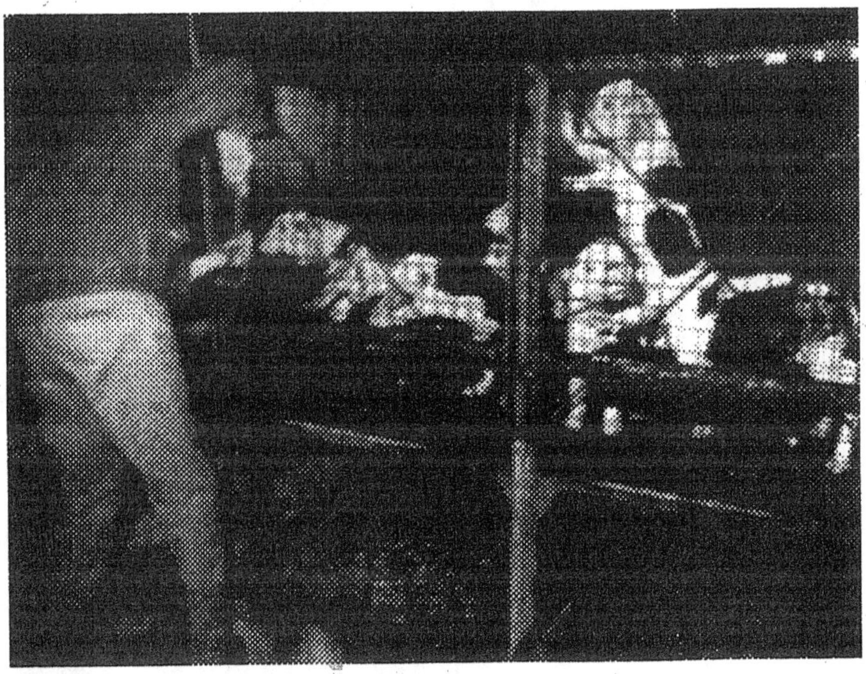

JUNE 11/95: Gloucestshire - 30 incendiary devices were planted at the A.F. Ensor abattoir in Cinderford, Gloucestshire. Some of the devices ignited and caused about $80,000 damage. This included the destruction of a lorry tractor unit and the damaging of 4 other lorries. (Sadly, two people were arrested for this action: Melanie Arnold and Micheal Green [see pg for prisoner info]).

JUNE/95: Bedfordshire - Sonya Egan, the landlady of the Cock Inn at Broom receives warning letters from the ALF because her pub includes crocodile on the menu. The letters warned her pub would be "visited" if she did not change the menu. Bening a sensible woman, she changed the menu. Tim Webb of "Jontis Bistro" in Ampthill, also receives warnings because his resturant serves ostrich meat, frogs legs and crocodile. Unfortunately Tim Webb was not a sensible man, and in July...

JULY/95: Bedfordshire - ALF cause over L1000 when they redecorate "Jontis Bistro" in Ampthill. In June, Tim Webb, the owner of Jontis was given warning that his resturant would be targetted if he didn't change his menu. Perhaps next time he'll listen to good advice!

JULY/95: Cornwall - four incendiary devices were planted in a poultry farm. All four were discovered, however, before they ignited.

JULY/95: Berkshire - Razorblade device sent to Thames Valley Eggs. Justice Department.

JULY/95: Cambridge - Razorblade device sent to V. Harrison of Interfauna rabbits. JD.

JULY/95: Cornwall - Razorblade device to Ian Hodge, blood-sports equipment supplier. JD.
JULY/95: Devon - Razorblade device sent to Jean Indian calf exporter and Autor Carter, sponsor of the Waterloo Cup. JD.

JULY/95: Gosport - A fish and chip shop, a Littlewoods and two medical charity shops all lose their windows. ALF.

JULY/95: Hampshire - Windows broken at the homes of Wickham Lab scum David Walker and Paddy Edwards.

JULY/95: Hampshire - Razorblade devices sent to blood-junky Peter Loyd MP, W. Cartmell, owner of Wickham labs; Croften Manor Farm, who allow circuses on their land; D. Walker, lab supplier; Paul Dowsett; Deborah Dowsett and Nicola Scarr all of Garetmar Kennels; Stonegate Farm Eggs; Peter Humphries, Caroline Humphries and Curtis Thompson all of H&H Hunts; Paddy Edwards and Chris Biship of Wickham labs; Kevin Coker, hunt terrier thug and Chitty Group slaughterhouse. Justice Department.

JULY/95: Razorblade device sent to C. Smales, supplier of Farose produce.

JULY/95: Lancahsire - Razorblade device sent to Colin Sheddon, BASC blood-junkie. JD.

JULY/95: London - Razorblade devices sent to Coutryside

Business group sponsors of blood-sports, J. Taylor of Brookers Cash & Carry. Brookers supply Farose island products and Lord Donahue blood-junkie Labour peer. JD.

JULY/95: London - ALF fire bullets at windows of Imperial Cancer Research charity shops in both Richmond and Twickenham. In both Barnes and Chiswick ICR shops, locks were glued and windows broken. Warnings were issued of future actions.

JULY/95: Oxford - JD send razorblade devices to David Muir, Animal exporter, Prof P.J. Morris vivisector and Penny Mortimer of Leave Country Sports Alone. JD.

JULY/95: Somerset - razorblade devices sent to Richard Coate, sheep exporter; John Dryden BASC blood junkie; and W.Waldergrave MAFF Minister and veal calf exporter. JD.

JULY/95: Shoreham - Razor devices sent to Don Barrett of Wyeth Labs, Alland Revell live exports agent, N.Fawcett blood-junkie, and Philip Lacey port manager at Shoreham.

JULY/95: Brighton - ALF paintstrip five vans belonging to Brighton University (vivisectiors). In a seperate action six university minibuses were paintstripped. Also 9 shops, including Cancer Research, Heart Foundation, a leather shop, KFC, Whimpey and Burger King all have their locks glued. Also a butchers van is paintstripped. Same thing again four days later two more vans, then the next night the butchers locks are glued.

JULY/95: Sussex - A small terrier bitch, used for breeding, is rescued from Hursley & Hambledon hunt kennels.
JULY/95: Yorkshire - Razorblade devices sent to Geoffry Hall, animal exporter. JD.

JULY/95: Warwickshire - Razorblade devices sent to C. Barret-Jolley, live animals exporter. JD.

JULY/95: Wiltshire - Foxhound puppies are rescued from hunt kennels at Newton Tony. At least one puppy is located by the police. One person arrested.

JULY/95: Woodridge - Razorblade device sent to Roger Mills, animal exporter. JD.

JULY 4/95: Chichester - an angling shop had it's windows bricked and ALF slogans painted.

JULY 7/95: Chichester - 5 lorries and a storage barn at a feed merchants were torched, causing L750,000 damage.

JULY 8/95: Chichester - Boots the Vivisectors was bomb hoaxed and closed for three hours.

JULY 13/95: Chichester - a Boots truck was sloganised with "SCUM" and "ALF" (sadly, one person arrested). Also N. Fawcett of Chiddingflold Hunt had his landrover sloganised and two windows broken.

AUG/95: Hampshire - Windows broken at Torbay Farm (lab animal supplier) and Garetmar (puppy farm). Also during a candle light vigil outside Torbay Farm, someone destroyed TF's advertising signs.

AUG/95: Hampshire - Signs at Marwell Zoo redesigned. ALF.

AUG/95: Hampshire - Whilst David Walker, lab animal supplier, was resting in his back garden, ALF activists were around the front smashing windows. ALF.

AUG/95: Hampshire - animal lib activists paint slogans on Wicham Labs, two people arrested.

AUG/95: Manchester - McDonald's signs are redesigned in Bolton. ALF.

AUG/95: Wickham - Wickham Labs targetted by animal lib
activists. $4000 damage after signs broken, locks glued, slogans painted, vehicles damaged and a large Wheelie Bin turned over. Two people arrested.

AUG/95: Sussex - the home of one of the joint masters of East Sussex & Rommey Marsh fox hunt is raided, and a four month old Jack Russell terrier is liberated. ALF.

AUG 4/95: Chichester - the angling shop lost its window and was spraypainted again. An angling shop owner in Bognor had his car doors glued and tires slashed.

AUG 10/95: Sussex - signs for the Sussex "Game & Country Show" were removed or painted. A vehicle advertising the event had its windows smashed and was sloganized.
AUG 14/95: Webb's Country Foods was closed for four hours due to bomb hoax. Later two Webb's vehicles were spraypainted with "Murder" and "ALF"

SEPT/95: Devon - Anonymous telephone callers harrass a local MAFF employed vet involved with the live animal export trade.

SEPT/95: East Anglia - Youths in Redditch set fire to a joyrided car. The fire quickly spreads to a nearby building owned by "Clarkes," a fishing tackle distributor. 95% of Clarke's stock is destroyed in the fire.

SEPT/95: Hampshire - security conscious ALF activists help secure Wickham Labs against burglars by glueing locks. They also give the walls a new coat of paint.

SEPT/95: Hampshire - Hoax bomb left on Garetmar Kennels doorstep is "made safe" (blown up) by bomb disposal.

SEPT/95: HMP New Hall - ALF prisoner Angie Hamp, helped by some Life sentence prisoners, rescue a budgie and cokertiel off an inmate who was seriously neglecting the birds. Sadly, due to the neglect, the cockertiel has since died. The budgie, named Tinkerbell, was in a serious state but with plenty of care and attention has been getting a lot better.

OCT/95: Cornwall - unnamed farmer accidentally contaminates thousands of bottles of milk with cleaning product.

OCT/95: Devon - Animal liberation activists torch two barns at Choakford Farm, Smithaleigh. The farm was involved with live exports and has been the sight of many protests in recent months.

OCT/95: Essex - Lorries were attacked durring a mass protest against live animal exports at Brightlingsea. One lorry had its windscreen smashed.

OCT/95: Northampton - ALF incendaries ignite inside Genus Breeding company building, Moulton. Building destroyed.

OCT/95: Cumbria - a group of animal libbers held down three anglers whilst other activists cut an anglers line to release a 'hooked' fish. The animal libbers then stole the angler's rod!

NOV/3 95: A press release and a contaminated carton of Ribean are sent to several media groups, including *Green Anarchist Magazine*. The press release claimed that hundreds of cartons of Ribena, a drink produced by Simthkline Beecham, one of the bigest animal exploiters in the UK, was contaminated with 20mls of Surgical Spirit. People buying Ribena are directly funding the unnecessary inliction of pain, suffering, torture and deaths of millions of animals by this company. The press release was signed "BUAV"(Bugger up All Vivisection).

NOV/95: HMP Exeter - ALF Remand prisoner Darren Cole is kept "banged up" because he refuses to wear prison issue leather shoes.

NOV/95: HMP The Mount, Bovingdon - Animal Rights Militia prisoner Neil Hansen rescues his third cockatiel whilst in prison. Despite the bird only being 8 week sold, 3/4ths of its wings had been cut off with scissors. Although the bird obviously can't fly, Neil reports its wings do appear to be growing back.

NOV/95: Sussex - A Crawley & Horsham Hunt huntsman is injured when the Hunt Retribution Squad (HRS) drop a rock on his head. Also the HRS trash several vehicles belonging to members of Crawley & Horsham Hunt.

NOV/95: Sussex - Barry Turner of Chiddingfold Hunt is attacked by HRS. HRS also trash his vehicle. The attack was in retaliation for a hunt sab being battered the previous week. According to an anonymous note, the Hunt Retribution Squad has a philosopy in which "*...for every wild animal killed by a hunt on a chosen day, a hunt rider will be dealt with and/or a vehicle trashed. This philosophy has been used on several occassions with satisfying results.*"

DEC/95: Avon - ALF rescue 60 hens from School Time Eggs, Myrtle Farm, Siston. A press release stated: *"Most of the hens were severely de-feathered, a typical sign of a lifetime in a cage that is so small that they cannot even spread their wings. Their feet were swollen and sore from never being able to perch - constantly on the wire mesh floor, and their beaks were semi-amputated ... Those removed are now all living comfortably in their new homes. They are able to scratch earth, dust bathe, breath fresh air, experience daylight and make a nest..."*

DEC/95: Somerset - Residents in Yeovil, who evict badgers from a set that runs under gardens have received death threats. The residents have hired a badger trapper who intends to sell the badgers to MAFF vivsection labs.

DEC/95: Sussex - arson attack on Webbs Country Foods, Chischester.

DEC/95: Surrey - HRS activists smashed up pheasent rearing pens and equipment at a farm near Edenbridge. The HRS went onto attack members of a shooting party and set alight a grain store.

DEC 26/95: A parcel bomb, wrapped in Christmas paper, was left at the Chiddingfold, Leconfield & Cowdray hunt kennels on Boxing Day. The bomb squad was called in and the device defused. A second similar device, left on the doorstep of a Chiddingford etc hunt steward, was 'made safe' by being blown up by the bomb squad. The devices were described as "most alarming and dangerous."

SCOTLAND

MAY/95: Edinburgh - Staff at Roslin Institute, a Government funded genetic breeding lab, are put on alert for fear of ALF actions. Staff are also warned about JD letter bombs.

JULY/95: Musselburgh - Razorblade devices sent to Inversek Research Int. Ltd. Justice Dept.

NORTHERN IRELAND

JULY/95: Razorblade device sent to Michael McKeekin, BASC blood-junkie. JD.

JULY/95: Crossgar - A hoax bomb is sent to Sam Smith, a farmer involved with live animal exports.

JULY/95: Police issue a warning to animal abusers to be suspicious of all packages received in the post.

IRELAND

JULY/95: Razorblade device sent to the Secretary of World Greyhound racing Federation.

OCT/95: Stockholm - Pals-Bruno (a large department store) is closed for several hours after being bomb hoaxed. People from all over Sweden visit Pals-Bruno and because of the hoax, several coach loads of people were turned away.

From the Djurens Hamnare (Animal Avengers) report: over the past year, Animal Avengers have produced "a magazine, The Liberator, with news, advise about how to destroy shops, burn lorries and how to get useful info. Issues were spread to animal rights activists all over Sweden. Also produced was a list of names, addresses and telephone numbers of vivisectors and fur-farms."

NOV/95: Umea - To celebrate the anniversary of the first arson against Scan meat co. property, two Scan offices were torched. One office was totally gutted. Additional offices were also damaged from smoke. In a separate celebration, three Scan trucks were destroyed.

SCANDANAVIA

NOV/95: Scandanavian Airlines ban shipments of live animals detined for vivisection from Britian, for fear of sabotage actions by British animal libbers.

FINLAND

In 1993 there were 25 EVR (ALF) actions in Finland. In 1994 there were 174. In 1995 there have been over 300 EVR actions. What does this mean for 1996...? According to a report in ECO-VEGAN 6 (UK), the Finnish A.L.F. - Elainten Vapautus Rintama, (EVR) have carried out over a two month period, from the start of April 95 to the end of May 95 the following actions:

*smashed at least 22 McDonalds windows
*vandalised 2 McDonalds
*blocked the toilet of a McDonalds
*carried out two paint attacks against McDonalds
*damaged 2 McDonalds signs
*glued at least 14 fur store locks
*smashed 41 fur store windows
*paint attacked 29 fur stores
*glued up 2 butchers/meat factory locks
*smashed 23 butcher/meat factory windows
*paint attacked 6 butchers
*damaged meat factory vehicles
*sloganized a fast food resturant
*glued the locks of 3 hunting stores
*paint attacked 2 hunting stores
*smashed a hunting store window
*glued the locks/sloganized a leather shop
*twice sloganized a University involved with vivisection,
smashing 8 of its windows
*targeted a L'Oreal studio
*turned off the refrigeration unit of a milk truck and spraypainted an ice cream bar.
*Plus, of course, 650 foxes were liberated from fur farms (see *Underground* #3 for details on the two activists arrested for this action)

JUNE/95: Helsinki - Two fur stores targeted. One has its locks glued, the other has its windows smashed. EVR.

JUNE/95: Kuopio - Meat shop painted. EVR

JUNE/95: Oulu - EVR is suspected to be behind the release of fur farm animals into the wild.

JULY/95: Turku - EVR visit a vivisection lab. Slogans painted. Also EVR glue the locks of four fur stores.

JULY/95: Helsinki - Fur store has its window smashed. EVR.

AUG/95: Hameelinna - Fur store targeted for vandalism. Windows etched, locks glued. EVR.

AUG/95: Turku - Fur store spraypinted. EVR.

AUG/95: Helsinki - Several fur stores targeted, with windows smashed, walls painted, locks glued. EVR.

AUG/95: Oulu - Windows smashed at fur stores.

AUG/95: Helsinki - Ten more fur stores have their locks glued. an eleventh has two windows smashed.

SEPT/95: Pheasants from a farm owned by a blood-sports group are released. EVR.

SEPT/95: Helsinki - Several fur stores come in for a "major vandalism attack." EVR.

SEPT/95: Helsinki - on International Anti-Gillette Day, EVR paint slogans on the HQ of the Finnish Gillette importer. EVR also target offices of Braun and Oreal-B which are subsideries of Gillette. Slogans include "Vivisection is Murder," "Elainten Vapautus Rintama fights," "Gillette has blood on its hands" and "Boycott Gillette."

SEPT/95: Kupio - Three fur shops have windows broken. A meat company has its locks glued. EVR.

SEPT/95: Porvoo - 110 foxes released from a fur farm. EVR.

SEPT/95: Riihimaki - a leather factory is trashed. EVR.

OCT/95: Helsinki - the same fur store is targetted three times in one week. Each time, windows are smashed. EVR.

OCT/95: Kuopio - Earth Night - a fur shop is attacked, windows smashed, the walls are paint-bombed, slogans painted, including "War continues..." A second fur shop had its windows smashed and "Deathstore" slogans painted. EVR.

OCT/95: Helsinki - two more fur shops are hit with spraypaint. A third recieves slogans and then has its windows broken twice over the following two nights.

SPAIN

JULY/95: A bull manages to injur four people durring a "bull run" festival.

SEPT/95: Anti-bullfighting slogans appear on bullrings.

NORWAY

JAN/95: on two different occasions, two butchers shops had windows smashed.

MAY/95: between 30 and 40 mink liberated from a fur farm.

AUG/95: 25 foxes on a fur farm were painted with cruelty-free, non harmful red Henna colour, rendering their coats valueless.

SEPT/95: Gillette's Norwegian HQ enterance was painted with slogans: "Stopp torturen -NA!" [Stop the torture - NOW!], etc.

OCT/95: slogans painted in area around Circus Merano: "Boikott Sirkus -frigjor dyrene!" [Boycott Circus - free the animals!]

NOV/95: at least 110 foxes were painted with cruelty-free red Henna on a fur farm. Breeding books were stolen, slogans painted and the farmer's combine harvester had its wires cut. Action performed by the Norweigan ALF, Dyrenes Frigjorings Front (DDF)

NOV/95: "Pels Inform" [Fur Inform], the fur industry's main organization (located in a building amongst others related to the Norwegian fur industry) had four windows shashed and slogans painted on the enterance. DDF

From the update sent by the Dyrenes Frigjorings Front: *"Things are starting to happen in Norway TOO! We can only hope for these actions to continue and increase! ANIMAL LIBERATION NOW -AND FOREVER!!!!!!!"*

SWEDEN

[Some updates care of Animal Avengers, c/o DBF, Box 179, s-265 22 Astorp, Sweden]

SPRING/95: Umea - The building to a hot-dog bar was vandalised, windows smashed. A leather store had its windows smashed.

APRIL/95: DH torch Slona Korv meat truck. The truck was completely destroyed. Vivisector's home windows were smashed. Hot dog bar had its windows smashed. Leather furnature shop's windows smashed and a van vandalised, slogans painted. Several Hot-dog bars vandalised, slogans painted. Leather shops also vandalized, windows smashed.

JUNE/95: Uppsala - Meat vehical at Charlman burned and slogans painted, including "Murderers," "Meat is Murder," and "Nazi." Activist freed after 3 months on remand.

SUMMER/95: Umea - a hamburger and hot dog bar had windows smashed on three separate occasions. A leather shop was hit twice, smashed windows.

LATE SUMMER/95: Uema - Hamburger bar burned for the third time, smashed windows.

AUTUMN/95: Hamburger bar was hit, windows smashed, roof burned. Two weeks later, smashed windows and slogans.

AUTUMN/95: Umea - Dairy company has lorry burned, damage for 750,000 Swedish krona. Leather shop's windows smashed.

SEPT/95: Exactly 1 year after the arson attack when 3 meat-lorries were destroyed, Scan receives 2 fire-bombs through windows in two offices. Large amount of damage.

SEPT/95: Umea - Arson attack on two fish company offices.

AUTUMN: Hamburger-bar burned, causing 3000,000 Swedish krona in damage (was not insured). 3 activists arrested, but are free now, but still under suspection.

NOV/95: Kuopio - EVR damaged two fur truck wind-screens. A third had its windows smashed and slogans painted. Also a fur shop attacked in October is hit again, with widows smashed. Later in the month a rock was sent through yet another fur shop window.

NOV/95: Helsinki - Whilst fur traders were inside a huge fur auction house, 'Fur Centre,' having a party, the EVR were outside redecorating the walls. Also, two fur shops had windows broken.

NOV/95: Helsinki - Ees-turkis fur store had locks glued by EVR. The same cell attacked 5 more fur shops. Two had windows "kicked in," one had nine windows smashed, while another had two windows broken. The last had its locks glued up.

DEC/95: Helsinki - EVR target Junotex fur store. Six windows are smashed. As a result of the action Junotex closed down. EVR also smashed 3 windows at Tuganay fur store. A third fur store has 6 windows taken out and a fourth gets two smashed. A butcher shop is hit with three windows smashed and "Meat is Murder" painted on it.

DEC 21/95: arson attack against a university which has a fur farm. EVR burned a storage building which usually holds fur pelts. Damages estimated several hundred thousand Finnish Marks (one Finnish Mark is roughly 1/4 USD). Two hours later about 100 kilometers away from the first site, the EVR struck again. This time the target was a feed company that sells feed to fur farms. According to the report, damages were estimated at a couple of hundred thousand Finnish Marks.

DEC/95: Helsinki - Tuganay fur store has its windows smashed (again) by the EVR. Saukko fur store also has its windows smashed, plus the glass door is shattered and a paint bomb thrown through one of the windows into the shop. the cell claiming responsibility stated "Our EVR cell has been targetting fur stores in Helsinki. In this year at least five fur stores have closed in Helsinki. We're going to get them all!"

DEC/95: Helsinki - the EVR targeted two meat trucks, slashing tires, smashing windows and painting slogans. Sugar was also poured into one of the truck's fuel tanks. The next day the truck with the sugar in the fuel tank was spotted, (still covered in slogans) having engine problems!

DEC/95: Helsinki - another cell of the EVR decided to leave meat trucks alone and instead set out to rescue guniea pigs from a vivisection lab. Sadly, they were interupted during the raid and had to flee empty handed. Frustrated that the animal rescue had failed, the cell went out and smashed windows at 14 different furriers, a McDonalds and a military magazine office.

POLAND

JULY/95: Hajowka - Punks, throwing stones and fire-bombs, attack circus.
JULY/95: Poznan - Two stinkbomb attacks inside McDonald's.

SLOVAK

AUG/95: Bratislava - Six HYKO advertising signs destoryed (mass producers of turkeys). Slogans painted on a fur shop "Liska." A Meathouse was closed all day when its locks were glued, and another Meathouse had its locks glued six times.

SEPT/95: Bratislava - Fur shop has windows smashed and slogans painted. Three other fur stores subjected to paint attack. Advertisment board on Slovak Hunting Assoc. building is destroyed. Four big hunting platforms are destroyed.

OCT/95: Bratislava - Slovak Hunting Assoc. building targetted, slogans painted, bells destroyed, mail box is removed and a new advertisement board (replacing the one destroyed in Sept.) is destroyed. Three fur shops receive slogans. The hunting company, ZVEREX has its locks glued, walls painted with slogans. A forth fur shop is sloganized and 40 advertisements for Arles Circus are destroyed.

SOUTH AFRICA

FEB 28/96: An ALF styled direct action animal liberation group called "Umkhonto Yesizwe" has formed in South Africa. The name comes from the Xhosa tribe, meaning "The Spear of the Leopard," similar to the name that the armed wing of the ANC went by, "Umkhonto We Sizwe" meaning the "Spear of the Nation." According to one Umkhonto Yesizwe member, "by choosing a name that sounds almost the same we want to emphasise the message that the struggle for animal liberation is part and parcel of the struggle for human liberation. The Leopard is also an animal that is feared and respected in our folk-lore."
Umkhonto Yesizwe participates in direct action against poachers and other animal abusers who wants to exploit members of Africa's animal kingdom. The Umkhonto Yesizwe has already been engaged in direct action, and we look forward to hearing details in the future.

SOUTH EAST ASIA: SINGAPORE

NOV/95: Animal libbers vandalize a McDonald's restaurant.

INDIA

Jan 31/96: Bangalore - Over 100 Indian farmers ransacked a Kentucky Fried Chicken outlet, wanting the chain to leave India for serving unhealthy and un-Indian food.

KFC

The FBI Domestic Counterterrorism Program

Down--loaded from:
http://www.cdt.org/policy/terrorism/cnss.FBI.auth.html

Recent news commentary has suggested that the FBI is hamstrung in its efforts to combat domestic terrorism. One former FBI official was quoted as saying that "you have to wait until you have blood on the street before the Bureau can act." Steven Emerson has asserted that the FBI is severely restricted in infiltrating known extremist groups, that it has no terrorism data base like the CIA's, and that it is powerless to stop extremist groups from masquerading as "religious" groups.

All of these claims are incorrect. Persons concerned about addressing the threat of terrorism need to begin with a clear understanding of current FBI capabilities, which are in fact broad.

Attorney General Guidelines

The FBI currently operates under a set of guidelines issued in 1983 by Ronald Reagan's Attorney General, William French Smith. The Smith guidelines were a modification of guidelines issued by Gerald Ford's Attorney General Edward Levi in 1976. The Levi guidelines were criticized as being too restrictive and cumbersome. Indeed, many of the criticisms of the current guidelines are really the same criticisms lodged against the Levi guidelines, which the Smith guidelines were intended to rectify.

The Smith guidelines make it absolutely clear that the FBI does not have to wait for blood in the streets before it can investigate a "terrorist" group. The guidelines expressly state: "In its efforts to anticipate or prevent crimes, the FBI must at times initiate investigations in advance of criminal conduct."

The threshold for opening a full investigation is low: a domestic security/terrorism investigation may be opened whenever "facts or circumstances reasonably indicate that two or more persons are engaged in an enterprise for the purpose of furthering political or social goals wholly or in part through activities that involve force or violence and a violation of the criminal laws of the United States."

Indeed, the FBI is also authorized to open a preliminary inquiry on an even lower threshold: The Bureau can begin investigating when it receives any information or allegation "whose responsible handling requires some further scrutiny." Preliminary inquiries can be conducted without headquarters approval for 90 days, during which the FBI can conduct interviews, contact confidential sources and previously established informants, and carry out physical surveillance. Preliminary inquiries can be extended with Headquarters approval.

Advocacy

One of the main purposes of the Smith guidelines was to make it clear that the FBI could open an investigation based on advocacy of violence. While urging respect for the First Amendment, the guidelines state: "When, however, statements advocate criminal activity or indicate an apparent intent to engage in crime, particularly crimes of violence, an investigation under these guidelines may be warranted ...." *(cont on pg 30)*

TACTICS FOR SABBING ANGLING

by Pisces

What's Wrong with Angling

Angling is said to be Britain's most popular participation pastime, but just like other bloodsports it causes pain, stress and often death to the quarry, (fish), as well as the thousands of swans, ducks and other animals killed and injured by lost and discarded fishing tackle.

Angling does cause pain and suffering to fish, even if they are returned to the water after capture, this fact being backed up by a number of scientific studies. When a fish is caught, it is deceived into impaling itself on a usually barbed hook resulting in an injury to the lip, or another part of the body if it is foulhooked. The fish is 'played' on the line to tire it, then removed from the water, entering an alien environment in which it begins to * suffocate. Handling, removes the outer mucous covering which provides waterproofing and protects from disease. If a hook has been swallowed, retrieval causes more pain and can damage internal organs, leading to death. In addition, stress is caused by the sudden change in noise, temperature, vibration and light intensity. If the fish is confined in a keepnet, it may receive injuries from the mesh, from being squashed together with other fish, depletion of oxygen and the build-up of waste products.

There are 3 main types of angling:

* Coarse fishing is the most popular form of angling. In the UK there is a 'close season' on rivers and most canals (when no angling is allowed) 15th March to 15th June. Anglers must have a National Rod License and charges are made at many fisheries. Coarse fish include barbel, bream, carp, chub, perch, pike and roach and are mostly inedible. Coarse fishing can be sub-divided into specimen angling (catching large fish of a particular species), pleasure angling (supposedly for relaxation) and match fishing where anglers compete to catch the most weight of fish in a given time. During the match the fish are confined in a keepnet.

* Sea fishing is practised from piers, beaches, rocks, harbour walls and boats. Most of the fish caught are edible and are rarely released. In matches sea fish are weighed at dead weight. Fish targeted include shark, cod, conger eel, turbot, plaice and dogfish. Licences are not required though charges may be made for the use of the pier, etc. There is no close season for sea fishing.

* Game fishing. Freshwater game anglers aim to catch salmon, trout and grayling. Game fish are usually killed, using a stick, stone or 'priest' (a specially designed club), with which they are smashed on the head. Only under-sized non-migratory trout and salmon parr are spared. Artificial flies are used to deceive the fish into impaling itself on the hook. Game fishing can be expensive as many waters are privately-owned or belong to water authorities, so a day ticket is required as well as a game fishing licence. The close season for game fishing differs between fish species.

Why Sab Angling?

Anglers are unfortunately famous for denying the wealth of scientific evidence showing that fish suffer when caught with rod, line and hook. Although an increasing number of people are realising the barbarity of this popular blood-sport, it will take a long time before angling ceases. The only way to stop suffering being inflicted on fish now, is to use non-violent tactics to directly intervene to stop angling. The tactics given below have been developed primarily for coarse fishing, although many of them would work equally well for sea or game fishing.

The Tactics

MATCH ANGLING - How to find out about matches:

* In angling magazines.

* Fishing tackle shops may have posters/noticeboards and lists of local club fixtures, usually given out on request.

* Some local newspapers and radio stations have angling features. At matches, the section of bankside to be fished is divided into 'pegs', at least 15 yards apart. Some waters have permanent pegs. Others are marked out and numbered the night before or the morning of the match. The anglers arrive 1-2 hours before the match to draw for peg numbers then go to their allocated peg to set up. The match is started and ended by a signal, usually a whistle. The anglers fish for 3-5 hours to catch the highest weight of fish which are retained in a keepnet. At the end of the match the fish are weighed then released. The winner receives a prize - money and possibly a trophy.

Before the match, do the following:

* Ring up the organiser (see above for how to get the phone number) and book a peg. You could ask for directions to the venue or, to sound more convincing, ask about bait bans (e.g. bloodworm,joker,wasp grub).
* Removing or changing around the peg numbers on the morning or the night before the match will cause confusion and maybe confrontation amongst the anglers.
* Wire up access gates to the water.
* Talk to local anglers on the same water or in tackle shops to find out the best day, weather conditions and stretch of water to fish from so you will know when and where to concentrate your sabbing.

During the match, do the following:

* Blow a whistle 10-15 minutes before the start of the match is due to begin. Some anglers may start fishing and be disqualified. Blow a whistle again near the end of the match. Some anglers may pack up early.
* Row up and down the river in a canoe or boat to prevent the anglers from casting or make them reel in. Go near to the line/float and disturb the surface of the water with the paddle to scare fish away.
* Swimming, wading or splashing your feet in the water (wetsuits, waders, wellies advisable depending on weather conditions!) to stop anglers casting and to scare away the fish. If you can, remove line from water, but be very careful not to break it or damage any other tackle.
* Making noise in the water by submerging metal objects (e.g., dustbin lid and spanner) and banging them together will scare away fish. Equally, make noise above the water with whistles, shouting, airhorns, hunting horns, etc. This has the added bonus of annoying the angler and detracting from the enjoyment of the "sport".
* Talking to anglers may disturb their concentration. Get information to be able to argue against them. (Not difficult!)
* Standing behind anglers can make casting more difficult and your shadow on the water may scare away the fish, especially when the water is clear and still.

Use poles, (e.g., long bamboo canes), to disturb the float and/or line. Try to lift the float and/or line out of the water, but again be careful not to break the line or damage the float.

* Use high powered water pistols aimed at the anglers float/line to encourage him/her to remove the tackle from the water.

* Empty keepnets. Ideally with 2 people who are in the water. Some keepnets have removable bottoms held on with clips. Others have only one way in or out - at the top. Ensure that the fish will exit the net downstream. Keep the net submerged at all times and do not touch the fish. Move the keepnet in such a way as to encourage the fish to swim out without touching the mesh. If in doubt do not attempt it, as keepnets can do a great deal of damage to fish.

SPECIMEN AND PLEASURE ANGLING

Pleasure anglers are easier to sab as they may be present in smaller numbers and are more likely to pack up, as they are out for relaxation, peace and quiet. Use the tactics shown above plus when you first arrive, explain to the anglers why you are there to made them aware of your purpose:- Erect "No Fishing - Contaminated Water" signs or similar. Make them look as professional as possible with the name and address of the regional river authority.

ALSO: Clean up any litter and discarded fishing tackle. If left, this could injure or kill fish, birds and animals. We are the conservationists not the anglers who leave all this mess behind them.

ALSO: Take a camera with you to get pictures of dead fish, poor handling of fish, tackle victims, discarded tackle in the river, trees, etc, poor emptying of keepnets.

WARNING!!

DO NOT take dogs/pets to the bankside. They are in danger from hooks, line and discarded tackle.

DO NOT pre-feed. Putting food in the water attracts the fish. Furthermore, any food not eaten would rot and pollute the water.

DO NOT throw tackle in the water. It is a danger to fish, birds and animals. Maggots will drown in the water.

DO NOT break fishing line for the same reasons.

DO NOT throw large stones in the water as there is the tiny risk of actually hitting a fish. Small pebbles also shouldn't be used as fish may confuse them with the ground bait anglers use to attract fish.

for more info:Pisces, P.O. Box 90, Bristol, BS99 1ND, UK.

FBI DOMESTIC COUNTERTERRORISM *cont:from pg 28*

How do the Guidelines work in practice?

In any given year, the FBI engages in approximately two dozen full domestic terrorism investigations. Over the years since the Smith guidelines were adopted, nearly two thirds of these full investigations were opened before a crime had been committed. Nothing in law or logic prohibits the FBI from opening investigations based on public source material or reports from private civil rights groups like the Southern Poverty Law Center. The FBI opens investigations based on any credible source, including news reports.

Terrorist Information System

The FBI has a state of the art, on-line computer database known as the Terrorist Information System containing information on suspected terrorist groups and individuals. The system has over 200,000 individuals and over 3000 organizations or enterprises. The individuals indexed include not only subjects of investigations but also known or suspected members of terrorist groups, associates, contacts, victims and witnesses. The organizations or enterprises include not only terrorist groups but also affiliated organizations or enterprises. TIS allows the FBI to rapidly retrieve information and to make links between persons, groups or events.

...Be aware and take care...

Up Coming Events and Gatherings

April 27th-May 2nd

The Freedmenstown Squatter Festival: This Festival will feature a massive housing takeover/occupation of Allen Parkway Village, workshops, live music, IWW/FNB/EF! direct actions against corporate assholes who seek to profit of the suffering of the people and the earth, guerilla theater, Anarchy Ale, FM micro Radio, self determination,and whatever else we collectively decide to do!!!!

APV has hundreds of empty apartment units available for squatting,and large open spaces for massive "tent cities". We also have access to the community center (which has a large concert space,several smaller meeting rooms and a kitchen). We've also secured the use of the mini amphitheater (perfect for out door concerts and improv theater, etc. Local bands have already agreed to play at the festival and concert collective is being formed. The local Food Not Bombs group has begun to secure food for people attending.

For more info on the APV community campus plan or to get involve write to Lynwood Johnson po box 21371 Houston ,Tx 77226

June 26-30 Eugene, Oregon: Resist and Exist

Resist and Exist will be held either in downtown eugene or on land just outside of town. There are over 20 bands confirmed to play and 20 or more workshops planned on topics like Food Not Bombs and Earth First! tactics.
Resist andExist is "intended to be a large, eclectic gathering of punks from all different 'scenes' and walks of life. the focus of this event is on unifying the punk communicty for positive change through music, cooperation, and activism"

the antipathy collective: 503-302-1838. po box 11703, eugene, OR 97440 .<tac@efn.org>

ACTIVE RESISTANCE: A COUNTER-CONVENTION

AUGUST 21-31, 1996
CHICAGO, IL

ACTIVE RESISTANCE is both a convention and a gathering, bringing together individuals and collectives to create sustainable communities of resistance. This union will engage intensive work on long term goals, high spirited activism, as well as share in the challenge and fun involved in putting this all together. We hope to accomplish a great deal. And we know we'll have fun. The Counter-Convention is scheduled to take place in Chicago for 10 days -- before, during, and after the 1996 Democratic National Convention. For more information email the AUtonomous Zone at <ugwiller@uxa.ecn.bgu.edu> or
1573 N Milwaukee #420
Chicago IL 60622

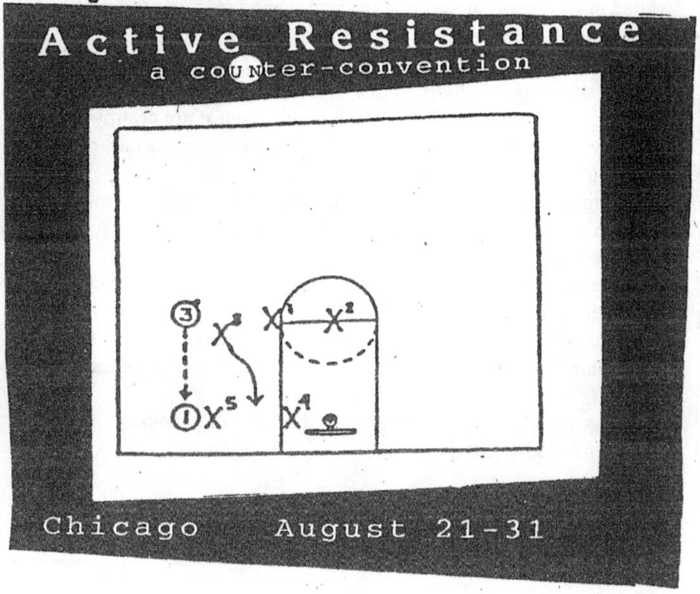
Active Resistance
a counter-convention
Chicago August 21-31

Do You Speak Vegetarian?

While in travelling around the world to pull off various liberations and direct actions, the hungry A.L.F. activist sometimes needs to communicate her/his meatless preferences come dinner time. Here are a few translations that ought to cover a lot of ground:

I am a vegetarian.

Ana la akul laham (Arabic)
Jeg er vegetar (Danish)
Ik ben vegetarier (Flemish)
Je suis vegetarien/vegetarienne (Frence masculine/ feminine)
Ich bin Vegetarier (German)
Eimai hortofagos (Greek)
Ani tzimhoni (Hebrew)
Main shakahari hoon (Hindi)
Sono vegetariano/vegetariana (Italian)
Watakushi wa saishoku shugisha desu (Japanese)
Jeg er vegetarianer (Norwegian)
Eu sou vegetariano/vegetariana (Portuguese)
Ya tolko yedu ovoshchi (Russian)
Yo soy vegetariano/vegetariana (Spanish)
Sili nyama (Swahili)
Jag ar vegetarian (Swedish)
Ben vejeryanim (Turkish)

FREEDOM OF INFORMATION CONTINUED:

(cont. from page 7) Step 2: Read all the document released to you. Keep a list of all document referred to the text--letters, memos, teletypes, reports, etc. Each of these "referred to" documents should turn up in the packet released to you. If any are not in the packet, it is possible they may be among those document withheld; a direct inquiry should be made. In an administrative appeal, ask that each of these "referred to" documents be produced or that the agency state plainly that they are among those withheld. Of course, the totals of unproduced vs. withheld must be within reasons; that is, if the total number of unproduced documents you find referred to the text of the documents produced exceeds the total number of documents withheld, the agency cannot claim that all the referred to documents are accounted for by the withheld category. You will soon get the hand of making logical conclusions from discrepancies in the totals and missing document numbers.

Another thing to look for when reading the released documents if the names of persons or agencies to whom the document has been disseminated. the lower left-hadn corncer is a common location for the typed list of agencies or offices to whom the document has been directed. In addition, there may be additional distribution recorded by hand, there or elsewhere on the cover page. There are published glossaries for some agencies that will help in deciphering these notaitons when they are not clear. Contact FOIA, Inc., if you need assistance in deciphering the text.

Finally, any other file numbers that appear on the document should be noted, particularaly in the subject of the file is of interest and is one you have not requested. You may want to make an additional request for some of these files.

HOW TO MAKE AN ADMINISTRATIVE APPEAL

Under the FOIA, a dissatified requester has the right of administrative appeal. the name and address of the proper appeal office will be given to you by each agency in its final response letter.

This kit contains a sample appeal letter with suggesting for adapting it to various circumstances. However, you need not make such an elaborate appeal; in fact, you need not offer any reasons at all but rather simply write a letter to the appeals unit stating that "this letter constitutes an appeal of the agency's decision." Of course, if you have identified some real discrepanices, you will want to set them for fully, but even if you have not found any, you may simply ask that the release be reviewed. If you are still dissatisfied after the administrative appeal process, the FOIA gives you the right to bring a lawsuit in federal district court on an expedited basis.

SAMPLE FBI REQUEST LETTER

Date:

To: FOIA/PA Unit

Federal Bureau of Investigation

This is a request under the Freedom of Information Act. I request a complete and thorough search of all filing systems and locations for all records maintained by your agency pertaining to and/or captioned: ______________________

[describe records desired and/or insert full and

____

formal name]

____

including, without limitations, files and documents captioned, or

whose captions include

____

[insert changes in name, commonly used names,

____

acronyms, sub-groups, and the like]

____

____

This request specifically includes "main" files and "see references," including, but not limited to numbered and lettered sub files, "DO NOT FILE" files, and control files. I also request a search of the ELSUR Index, and the COINTELPRO Index. I request that all records be produced with the administrative pges.

I wish to be sent copies of "see reference" cards, abstracts, search slips, including search slips used to process this request, file covers, multiple copies of the same documents if they appear in a file, and tapes of any electronic surveillances.

I wish to make it clear that I want all records in your office "identifiable with my request," even though reports on those records have been sent to Headquarters and even though there may be duplication between the two sets of fils. I do not want just "interim" documents. I want all documents as they appear in the "main" files and "see references" of all units of your agency. If documents are denied in whole or in part, please specify which exemption(s) is(are) claimed for each passage or whole document denied. Please provide a complete itemized inventory and a detailed factual justification of total or partial denial of documents. Give the number of pages in each document and the total number of pages pertaining to this request. For "classified" material denied pleae include the following information: the classification (confidential, secret or top secret); identity of the classifer; date or event for automatic declassification, classification review, or down-grading; if applicable, identity of official authorizing extension of automatic declassification or review; and if applicable, the reason for extended classification.

I request that excized material be "blacked out" rather thatn "whited out" or cut out and that the remaining non-exempt portions of documents will be released as provided under the Freedom of Information Act.

Please send a memo (copy to me) to the appropriate units in your office to assure that no records related to this request are destroyed. Please advise of any destruction of records and include the date of and authority for such destruction.

As I expect to appeal any denials, please specify the office and address to which an appeal should be directed.

I believe my request qualifies for a waiver of fees since the release of the requested information would primarily benefit the general public and be "in the public interest."

I can be reached at the phone listed below. Please call rather than write if there are any questions or if you need additional information from me.

I expect a response to this request within ten (10) working days, as provided for in the Freedom of Information Act.

Sincerely, name:

address: telephone:

signature

SAMPLE AGENCY REQUEST LETTER
DATE:
TO: FOIA/PA Unit

This is a request under the Freedom of Information Act.

I request a complete and thorough search of all filing systems and locations for all records maintained by your agency pertaining to and/or captioned

____

[describe records desired and/or insert full and

____

formal name]

____

including, without limitation, files and documents captioned, or whose captions include:

____

[insert changes in name, commonly used names,

____

acronyms, sub-groups and the like]

____

I also request all "see references" to these names, a search of the ELSUR Index or any similar technique for locating records of electronic surveillance.

This request is also a request for any corresponding files in INS Headquarters or regional offices.

Please place any "missing" files pertaining to this request on "special locate" and advise that you have done this. If documents are denied in part or whole, please specify which exemption(s) is(are) claimed for each passage or whole document denied. Please provide a complete itemized inventory and detialed factual justification of total or partial denial of documents. Specify th^ number of pates in each document and the total number of pages pertaining to this request. For classified material denied, please include the following information: the classification rating (confidential, secret, or top secret); identify the classifier; date or event for automatic declassification, classification review or downgrading; if applicable, identify the official authorizing extension of automatic declassification or reviw; and, if applicable, give the reason for extended classification.

I request that excised material be "blacked out" rather than "whited out" or cut out. I expect, as provided by the Freedom of Information Act, that the remaining non-exempt portions of documents will be released.

Please send a memo (copy to me) to the appropriate units in your office or agency to assure that no records related to this request are destroyed. Please advise of any destruction of records and include the date of and authority for such destruction As I expect to appeal any denials, please specify the office and address to which an appeal should be directed.

I believe my request qualifies for a waiver of fees since the release of the requested information would primarily benefit the general public and be "in the public interest."

I can be reached at the phone listed below. Please call rather than write if there are any questions or if you need additional information from me. I expect a response to this request within ten (10) working days, as provided for in the Freedom of Information Act.

Sincerely,
name:
address: telephone:
signature:

SAMPLE ADMINISTRATIVE APPEAL LETTER
Date:
To: FOIA/PA Appeals Office
RE: Request number [Add this if the agency has given your request a number]

This is an appeal pursuant to subsection (a)(6) of the Freedom of Information Act as amended (5U.S.C. 552).

On [date], I received a letter from [name of official] of your agency denying my request for [describe briefly the information you are after]. This reply indicated that an appeal letter could be sent to you. I am enclosing a copy of my exchange of correspondence with your agency so that you can see exactly what files I have requested and the insubstantial grounds on which my request has been denied.

[Optional paragraph, to be used if the agency has withheld all or nearly all the material which has been requested]: You will note that your agency has withheld the entire (or nearly the entire) document (or file, or report, or whatever) that I requested. Since the FOIA provides that "any reasonably secregable portion of a record shall be provided to any eprson requesting such record after deletion of the portions which are exempt," I believe that your agency has not complied with the FOIA. I believe that there must be (additional) segregble portions which do not fall wihtin FOIA exemptions and which must be released.

[Optional paragraph, to be used in the agency has used the (b)(1) exemption for national security, to withhold information] Your agency has used the (b)(1) exemption to withhold information [I question whether files relating to events that took place over twenty years ago could realistically harm the national security.] [Because I am familiar with my own activities during the period in question, and know that none of these activities in any way posed a significant threat to the national security, I question the designation of my files or portions of my file as classified and exempt from disclosure because of national security considerations.]

[Sample optional argument to be used if the exemption which is claimed does not seem to make sense; you should cite as many specific instances as you care to of items withheld from the documents that you ahve received. We provide two exarhples which you might want to adampt to your own case.]

"On the memo dated ____________ the second paragraph withheld under the (b)(1) exemption appears to be describing a conversation at an open meeting. If this is the case, it is impossible that the substance of this converation could be properly classified." Or, "The memo dated _____ refers to a meeting which I attended, but a substantial portion is deleted because of the (b)(6) and (b)(7)(c) exemptions for unwarranted invasions of personal privacy. Since I already know who attended this meeting, no privacy interest is served by the withholding."

I trust that upon examination of my request, you will conclude that the records I requested are not properly covered by exemption(s) [here repeat the exemptions which the agency's denial letter claimed applied to your request] of the amended FOIA, and that you will overrule the decision to withhold the information.

[Use if an itemized inventory is not supplied originally]

If you choose instead to continue to withhold some or all of the material which was denied in my initial request to your agency, I ask that you give me an index of such matieral, together with the justification for the denial of each item which is still withheld.

As provided in the Act, I will expect to receive a reply to this administrative appeal letter within twenty working days. If you deny this appeal and do not adequately explain why the material withheld is properly exempt, I intend to initial a lawsuit to compel its disclosure. [You can say that you intend to sue, if that is your present inclination; you may still decide ultimately not to file suit.]

Sincerely yours,
name:
address:
signature:

North American A.L.F. Supporters Group Animal Liberation Prisoner Support Policy

The NA ALFSG will:

* provide financial support, to the best of our abilities, to people incarcerated for actions that fall under A.L.F. guidelines. We shall also endevour, on a case by case basis, to offer support to activists imprisoned for actions that may not necessarily fall under A.L.F. guidelines, but are clearly animal liberation actions (ie: activists charged with Justice Department or Animal Rights Militia actions, etc). This is to ensure that all imprisoned animal activists have access to support.

* provide publicity and letter-writing appeals for political prisoners who ask for our assistance, and work on setting clear guidelines for who we will assist in this way (i.e. what do we mean by "political prisoner"?)

* continuing prison justice education work in *Underground* so that people within the animal liberation movement are more aware of what is happening in North American prisons, with the assistance of the **Prison Justice Project** and other prison abolition groups.

* in cases where we are contacted/make contact with prisoners who appear to be incarcerated for actions that fall under our Animal Liberation Prisoner Support guidelines but are unknown to the SG, we will endevour to confirm their status as animal lib prisoners. We believe that not only does the NA ALFSG has a duty to provide support to animal liberation prisoners, but to also ensure that freeworld SG members/readers know exactly who they are dealing with when providing support.

UNDERGROUND AND NON-ALF PRISONERS: Beginning with issue #2 [Nov 94], *Underground* has included an expanded "Prisoner Support" section that includes general prison justice issues and support for political prisoners who are incarcerated for actions that fall outside A.L.F. guidelines. Prisoners are being provided space to write about the many struggles for freedom and dignity, to work on general prison abolition/prison justice issues, and much more. This section of *Underground* is designed by activists and prisoners working in cooperation with, but independently of, the NA ALFSG. Some basic limits do exist. We don't have the resources to provide information on every political prisoner/prisoner of war within North America. We don't want to cover ground that is being covered by specific defense committees for certain prisoners (eg. the Leonard Peltier Defense Committee). Please see pages 42-47 for more details on the **Prison Justice Project.**

WHAT YOU CAN DO TO SUPPORT PRISONERS

* Prisoners REALLY appreciate mail. It is often the only link they have to the outside world.
* Prisoners also appreciate money. Some prisoners can receive money sent directly to the jail; others cannot. Your best bet is to send money to one of the SGs, *clearly* marked "for (name of prisoner)". The SG can then pass it on to the prisoner in whatever form is necessary.
* Some prisoners can get other items sent to them in jail, eg. postcards, stamps, letter paper, envelopes, photos, books, clothing. Write the prisoner and ask what they can be mailed. Regulations vary from jail to jail.
* Buy magazine subscriptions so prisoners have reading material. In most cases, the magazine will get through if it is sent directly from the publisher.
* At certain times, in certain cases, letter-writing appeals may be requested. Often prisoners ask that letters be written to newspapers, state officials, or prison officials, to protest treatment of the prisoner or to protest a sentence. Again, the SGs are the best way to find out what letter-writing campaigns are currently happening.

This is only a general list. Individual prisoners may have needs above and beyond the points listed here. Your best bet is to write the prisoners themselves and ask what you can do for them.

Prisoners are frequently moved, occasionally released, and there are often people going in and out of jail on short sentences. It is best to contact the prisoner support groups that exist for up-to-date information.
For more information on Animal Lib prisoners, write: UK-ALFSG: BCM 1160, London, WC1N 3XX, England /NA-ALFSG: PO Box 69597, 5845 Yonge St. Willowdale, Ont. Canada, M2M 4K3

NEWS FROM THE ALF SG (UK)

ALF SUPPORTERS GROUP

BCM 1160 LONDON WCIN 3XX

Dear members and supporters

Once again, the Supporters Group is the subject of police investigations. On 16 January, Hampshire Police carried our a series of raids, including the homes of SG magazine editor, Simon Russell, as well as Robin Webb from the ALF Press Office. In all, six people have been charged with conspiracy to incite others to commit criminal damage over a 5 year period. This is the same charge which Ronnie Lee faced in 1987, and for which he was sentenced to 10 years. All six have been released on conditional bail, but the arrests have again disrupted the SG.

Firstly, Simon has had to give up editing the SG magazine, partly due to the pressure of the case, but he will remain on hand to give help and advice to those taking over. The police also confiscated much of the SG's equipment, including the main computer, which at present they are refusing to release, claiming it is needed as evidence.

For these reasons, this mail-out will replace the scheduled Winter edition of the SG magazine, but we expect to be back in business in time for the Spring edition, which is due out in the middle of April. The deadline for articles in March 25.

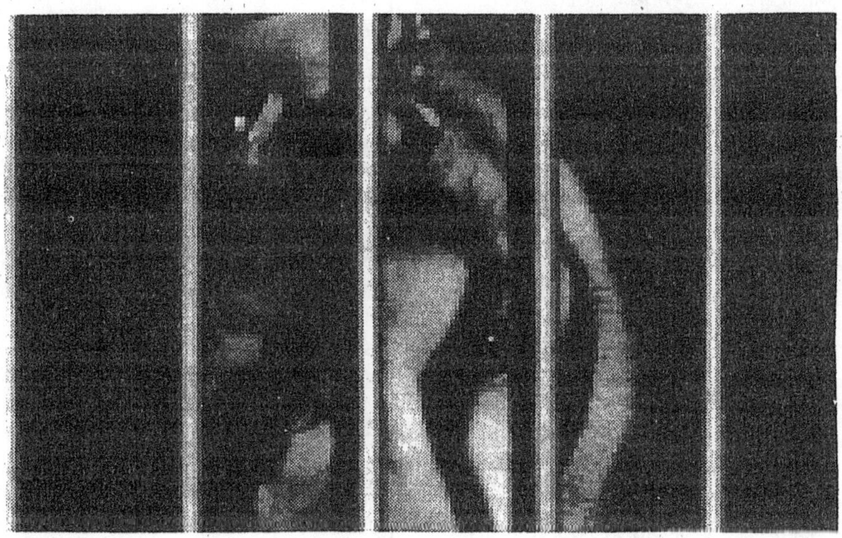

The vital work of supporting animal liberation prisoners has not been affected in any way, as contingency plans had been put in to cover exactly this kind of emergency. There are currently 16 prisoners on the SG list, nearly all of whom receive regular financial as well as moral support from the SG. Ensuring the welfare of prisoners has always been the main role of the SG, so we hope that members will be patient and supportive during this difficult period.

PRESS OFFICE REOPENS

After its recent problems, the Press Office is now back in business, and already interviews have been given, and, talks are planned. This follows Robin Webb's acquittal in December at Winchester Crown Court, where he was facing charges in connection with alleged contamination hoaxes. The Judge threw the case half way through, after hearing the prosecution evidence, or rather, lack of it. Although Robin has been re-arrested on the conspiracy charges mentioned above, his bail conditions no longer include a ban on press talks, meetings etc. For further details contact the press office. Anyone with information about new prisoners should phone the Press Office with full details and a contact number if possible for verification.

ALF PRESS OFFICE

Bm 4400, London WC1N 3XX

tel: 01954 230542 or 0850 96761 (mobile)

[overseas callers: Country code for England is 44]

NEWS ABOUT THE PRISONERS

On Christmas Eve three animal liberation activists from Hampshire were arrested in a car. They were held over the Christmas period and then returned to police custody by a magistrate decision for another three days of questioning.

On the 29th of December they were all formally charged with conspiracy to possess explosives and cause criminal damage by arson on a unspecified target. They were also charged with arson at Webbs Poultry farm on the 5th of December.

The three are Sandra White, Gaynor Ford and Gillian Peachey. Gillian was recently convicted of conspiracy to plant incendiary devices at a hotel hosting a hunt meeting and if convicted will be in breach of a 21 months sentence, suspended for two years.

In court Sandra was released on bail with strict curfew conditions, but Gaynor and Gillian have been remanded to Holloway. *Please see page 50 for addresses to send support.*

On the 6th of March Dave Callender was sentenced to 10 years imprisonment. His co-defendent, Greg Avery, who had been on remand for over 18 months was found not guilty.

Dave was convicted of Conspiracy to commit arson, although no actual fires ever took place. he was convicted of being in possession of a number of timers, theatrical maroons and a list of targets.

Dave is a well known and respected activist of many years standing here in England and has served on the Hunt Saboteurs Association (HSA) committee. *Please see page 50 for an address to send letters of support.*

Finland Police Crackdown on Activists

According to a report we received from an animal activist in Finland, police have been working overtime to make arrests related to two EVR arson hits that took place just before Christmas last year. Police have raided over 10 homes in the last year searching for evidence, and two activists were arrested in early Febuary police paid them a visit. A third activist refused to tell police anything beyond "No Comment!" and was held in jail for ten days. The activist in question apparently had nothing to do with the arson being investigated, but knew better than to co-operate with the police.

The two arrested activists spent some time in jail, also refusing to provide information. One eventually gave police an alibi, but the other refused and continued his "no comment" answers. After 10 days in jail, police were finally forced to release him due to lack of evidence.

In late Feburary a second series of raids followed, resulting in the arrests of three activists. One person provided police with an alibi while the other two refused to say anything. Of those arrested, one was a minor and was released after 2 days in police custody. The other, a 23 year old activist, Mika Marenk, was jailed for 33 days for refusing to co-operate with police. Marenk has been arrested twice before for alleged involvement in animal liberation actions. In 1994 he was arrested for vandalizing a fur shop, coca-cola billboard and a Shell gas station. The second time he was arrested with two others for smashing up windows from a meat factory. He has been charged for a series of arsons last December (he has pleaded not guilty). Marenk and co-defendant Miika Saukkonen will face trial on the 3rd of May. We hope to have more information on their case in the near future.

Two Dutch Activists Arrested Under Suspicion of Arson

March 24: Two vegan activists living in Amsterdam were arrested during the early hours of the morning under suspicion of arson. Their home was invaded and searched for over 3 hours by a 15 strong police task force. Numerous personal items, including shoes, 200 cassettes and letters were taken during the raid.
Two activists, Frank Kocera (25) and Eric van de Lann (20) are being held seperately in Alkmaar and Den Helder. Reports state that Eric is being denied vegan meals by police. More details to come.

Wayne Cody -Not Who He Says He Is?

BACKGROUND

For many SG supporters, Wayne Cody Lassell was first heard of when a prisoner listing for him appeared in *Underground #2*, which included the passage, *"Let Cody know that he IS remembered by kindred spirits. He has never made any pretensions to be incarcerated for animal liberation charges (unlike Anthony Miller, for example) and we are certain from our correspondence that he is not looking to milk the movement (unlike Anthony Miller)."* (30) As readers know, the NA ALFSG has made a decision to support ALL political prisoners and takes a prison abolition position. We do of course have a mandate to prioritized support by focussing on prisoners that fall within our Prisoners Support Guidelines [see page 35].

So far, so good.

The Supporters Group listed Wayne Cody Lassell in with the understanding that he was not an ALF activist, but was seeking correspondences from like minded, politically active freeworld pen pals, and that *Underground* could alert people to Lassell's presence. From the outset the SG has been willing to support Cody, regardless of what he is behind bars for. This same support is offered to other prisoners seeking letters or help from the freeworld (again as defined by our prisoner policy). In fact, Lassell's convictions have not been an issue in terms of the SG supporting or not supporting him. If Wayne had a problem with being listed in *Underground #2* as someone who "has never made pretensions to be incarcerated for animal liberation charges," he certainly never took steps to inform and correct any "misinterpretations" of his position. Wayne has stressed to both the NA ALFSG and to the ALFSG (UK) that he is simply seeking contact with the outside world, and not financial support. To the best of our knowledge, Wayne has never asked for financial support from those who write him letters, and certainly the NA ALFSG has never received a request for any kind of financial support.

Concerns with Wayne began to develop when a number of contradictory reports regarding Wayne's activism and reasons for being in jail began to come to our attention. Nearly a year after *Underground #2* was printed, around the same time the NA ALFSG coordinators positions were changing over, we began seeing posts on internet [alt.prisons and talk.politics.animals] purportedly issued on Lassell's "behalf." These posts requested support for Lassell, describing him as incarcerated for animal liberation activities. Other accounts surfaced in which people mentioned having written him, but were not clear on why exactly he was in jail. Our attention was directed to a discussion on talk.politics.animals, by a SG supporter who wrote, *"As you can see by these post's I think some people think that W.C.L. is in for A.L.F. activities etc.*

and are obviously getting a false impression from somewhere (possibly their own heads a little)."

Another supporter wrote to the SG via email, stating, *"It is not clear what exactly he did, but he is considered a terrorist by the US authorities and is imprisoned for 18 years. I think he's been inside for two of those years. Why isn't he listed in Underground #3 as ALF?"*

So, who is Wayne Cody Lassell?

Why is there so much confusion around his case? Is he an ALF activist or not? Part of the confusion seems to come from Lassell's own description of himself to the various people/organizations that he has written to. The NA ALFSG has compiled a variety of writings by Lassell, to help illustrate our concerns. In his own words:

"A few months ago I wrote a letter to you that was printed in your paper. The letter explained that I was a long time ecological warrior who was currently imprisoned for acts against the state in the name of saving our earth..."
(Earth First! Journal Aug/Sept 94.31)

"I am an animal rights activist, imprisoned at Pelican Bay state prison. My actions for liberation are viewed as "terroristic" by my keepers my sentence is 18 years." **(ALF Supporters Group Newsletter (UK) - Autumn 1995. 32)** [with the postscript from the ALFSG: *"Note: To date we have no full details of what Wayne has been imprisoned for..."*]

"I understand the inability for the ALFSG to diverse so far as to support ALL prisoners, but I would strongly hope you continue to extend your support to those who have embraced the concepts of animal liberation. Undoubtedly some will falsely claim allegiance for purely self serving reasons ... but these few will be quickly found out, and the many who honestly support the animal rights agenda, will benefit by being embraced by the support of loving, caring, people within the movement.
My own confinement happens to fall within the guidelines of accepted ALF crimes..." **(Letter from Wayne Cody Lassell, Dec 13, 1995)** [no mention of what the "accepted ALF crimes" are, however.]

When pressed for details by the NA ALFSG on his ALF actions, Lassell wrote back,

"My break in and theft charges surrounding the DOCKTOR PET center that I used to work for, was ONE of the charges I am serving time for. I am also suspected of and was investigated for the liberation of animals at the Livermore Lab on Oct. 7th of 1990. I also was CONVICTED FOR the Oct 20th break in at the same facility." **(Letter from W.C.L. Feb 1, 1996** - letter in full below)

The above statement from Lassell is interesting when compared to what he wrote to the ALFSG (UK) regarding his conviction:

"The charges are surrounding two separate break-ins at the Livermore, Calif. primate testing center on Oct 3rd 1989 and Dec 24 1991. The charges are 2 counts of 1st degree burglary, one count of grand theft and one count of terrorist activity."

It is important to note the differences in dates given by Lassell to both SG's. The more we heard from Lassell, the easier it was to see contradictions in his numerous statements, to supporters, to the NA ALFSG and the ALFSG (UK), as well as writings too other activist organizations like Earth First!.

Questions, Questions, Questions.

What began as simple, non-financial support for an apparently lonely, isolated activist shifted when Wayne began claiming ALF status. Was Lassell someone who presented himself a particular way depending on where he was writing and depending on who would be providing support (as an earth activist to Earth First!ers and as ALF to the Supporters Group)? Why, if Lassell was an ALF activist as he was now claiming, had nothing been said before, even if he didn't wish to be listed or receive financial support? Why was there no known record, especially in the media (mainstream, animal lib or animal industry press) of any ALF action against the Livermore Lab, especially one that ended in a conviction that included one count of "terrorist activity?" Surely Putting People First or the Americans for Medical Progress wouldn't miss an opportunity to gloat...

We wrote Wayne in the hopes of receiving some kind of documentation to clear things up:

January 20, 1996

Wayne Cody Lassell D71733
Box 7500 SHU D4-104
Pelican Bay State Prison
Crescent City, Calif. USA
95532-7500

Dear Wayne,

Thank you for your letter (Dec 13/95). It's good to know that you've received Underground, and as a prisoner you are entitled to receive a copy for free when each issue comes out.

You state in your letter that your "own confinement happens to fall within the guidelines of accepted ALF crimes" - please specify EXACTLY why you are in jail. There has been some questions raised as to whether or not the NA-ALFSG should support you, stemming mainly from the contradictory nature of what little information we have concerning you and your imprisonment. We have been told everything from you've never claimed to be an activist but are sympathetic to animal liberation, to you're currently in jail for animal lib actions - (ie, at a pet shop break-in, and/or at a lab liberation). It is important that you know that there are ALF supporters, including some ex-ALF prisoners, who strongly suspect that you are trying to con support from the movement.

As it stands right now, it is nearly impossible to tell what exactly is true with regards to your case, and as the Supporters Group we are reluctant to act one way or the other until the facts have been cemented. On one hand, if you are a legitimate animal liberation prisoner, you need to be listed as such and are deserving of all the support that can be generated. However, without corroborative evidence illustrating this to be true, we cannot act in your favour. As you are likely well aware, a precedent was set regarding support after American prisoner Anthony Miller put forth claims to be in jail for animal liberation activities. He received widespread support from both the North American and UK Supporters Groups, until his (very intricate) con was discovered. By that time, however, he had already manipulated a great deal of money, personal items and favours from a number of people from the animal rights movement. As the North American A.L.F. Supporters Group, we have a duty to make sure this does not happen again, and are therefore much more cautious when faced with prisoners asking for support for which there are seemingly no records of their activism.

We are requesting from you any and all documentation regarding animal liberation convictions against you, including court documents, newspaper articles, testimonials from recognized animal liberation organizations, etc. including any documents pertaining to animal liberation actions/convictions from your past. We will be publishing Underground #4 by the mid to end of March, and hope to be able to have things cleared up by then. You are of course, entitled to respond to the issue of your "legitimacy" as an ALF activist, and in fact, we encourage you to do so. We would happily publish an article from you explaining your situation, if you are interested in putting forth a position paper. We will be discussing the problems that revolve around your case in Underground, and with your help in providing arrest and court records, we will be able to clear things up once and for all.

We hope you understand our position on all of this. It is our sincerest hope that things work out for the best and that you can be listed for prisoner support in the near future, but with the confusion and blatant contradictions revolving around your case, our hands are tied until we are able see the documentation requested.

North American A.L.F. Supporters Group

Wayne Cody Lassell's reply was as follows:

Feb 1, 1996

People at Interrogation headquarters;

After reading your letter, I have a new respect for what people must feel like under questioning and false accusation by the F.B. I. I find it ironic that I should need to document MY legitimacy to someone who doesn't even sign their letters! This is especially true since I have been in contact with NA ALFSG for well over a year, and have NEVER asked for, received, or would accept the sort of "help" $ you seem to have your mind set on believing I want. Just to be included in the same breath as Mr. A. Miller is a slap in the face to someone who, I assure you, doesn't deserve such treatment. Mr. Millers claims of theft of animal traps, to gain monetary support, is equally distasteful to ALL who struggle to end the needless torture of animals, but the disservice you have done to me, hardly will get you a medal for support and compassion of someone who listens to the same whispers of conscience (as I would HOPE) as yourself!

Just because someone is not of high profile (by choice or media result) does NOT mean their actions aren't perfectly in line with the ideas of your group. I don't PANDER for attention via articles and letters because I don't especially like the grade of people who answer such requests for hero worship. I'll leave such actions to Rod C., and the like. So, for this reason I am PURPOSELY slow to wave the banner of Animal Liberationist. I would much rather be accepted as a fellow activist (of which I am), who finds himself in a lonely situation and requests the gift of contact with people who think and believe as I do. Since this is my only objective, I take strong issue with the need to supply you, or anyone else, with more than my word that I am indeed what I have stated. I'll leave the Rolling Stone articles and letters pandering visits, money, etc. to those who WANT that sort of following. I'm sure this makes me an unpopular target for all the Rod. C. groupies, but so be it. None of this changes the fact that a group that is suppose to be there for activists in my situation has instead set themselves up as a clearing house for verification by means of accusation and interrogation! The person who said I never claimed to be an activist (in the sense of A.R. actions) was ZABAGLIONE who ASSUMED that, because I never discussed my reason for being in prison. This was by design, because I enjoyed the chance to get to know Z on a personal level for over a year before she wrote the article you speak about. My break in and theft charges surrounding the

DOCKTOR PET center that I used to work for, was ONE of the charges I am serving time for. I am also suspected of and was investigated for the liberation of animals at the Livermore Lab on Oct. 7th of 1990. I also was CONVICTED FOR the Oct 20th break in at the same facility. So, when you have the nerve to accuse me of CONTRADICTORY statements, this doesn't make your illusions, fact!

It seems the shadow that Mr. Miller cast, so long ago, truly did take it's toll, and continues to, to this day. I am not only deeply ashamed of his dishonesty, but also of YOUR inability to NOT assume every plea for contact is some sort of con "plot." People who seek money and gifts on the backs of those who support REAL AR warriors, are filth, at best ... but those people are always uncovered and discovered quickly because of their own illusions of wiseness ... NOT because YOU are setting yourself up as judge and jury to ANYONE and EVERYONE who asks for support. (via letters, NOT money)

Once again, I've never requested money support or expensive gifts. I never will. So, why would I spend over a year (and $20.00 in postage) to "con" you into writing me? Your foundation for accusation is built on paranoia from another person's actions.

Please withdraw my request for letters from my fellow activists via your publication. Each gain has its "worth" and the price of a few pen pals from the A.R. movement is not WORTH having to prove my convictions to someone who won't even sign their name while they tell ME I'm questionable!

You need to check yourself!

I remain,
Wayne Cody Lassell
ANIMAL ACTIVIST

We were disappointed by Wayne's response. As we go to press, no documentation regarding any of his charges have been received by the Supporters Group. His anger at our "nerve" to question his word regarding his "ALF status" only ended up making us even more suspicious, espcially considering Lassell's acknowledgement of concerns regarding "false claims" for support by the likes Anthony Miller. His general reluctance to provide any details around his conviction also made us question his motives. In any of the letters we've examined from Wayne Cody Lassell (over 8, dating from 7/24/94), he appears to go out of his way to avoid directly discussing why he is in prison, and only recently provided any kind of detail to a Supporters Group (UK), but then gives completely different dates regarding his supposed actions and convictions to the North American SG(!).

We made a series of telephone calls to activists in California to find out if anyone knew of any actions against Livermore Labs on (any of) the dates given by Lassell. No one we spoke to had, including one activist who has been a part of the animal liberation "scene" in California since the early 80's.

We also conferred with Zab, who had been running the NA ALFSG when initial contact with Lassell had been made, in the hopes of finding out more information. We explained the situation as it had developed, and asked about Lassell's claims to be ALF. She responded: *"I hate shit like this. It seems obvious that Cody is not telling the truth. I don't know how much of his story to believe ... It's bullshit for him to blame this on me, saying he claimed to be an activist - in his earlier correspondence he *did* claim he wasn't an ALF activist."*

We feel that we've done nearly everything we could to straighten things out with regards to Lassell's claims to ALF status. By refusing to help with our enquiries, Lassell has effectively cut himself out of a process of confirmation that, if he truly is an ALF activist, would have worked out 100% to his benefit, not the SG's. At this point in time, given the contradictory statements made by Lassell, the discrepancies in dates he has provided, his general reluctance to provide ANY supporting documentation, and given our inability to guarantee in any way Lassell's legitimacy as an activist (ALF or otherwise) the NA ALFSG is distancing itself from Wayne Cody Lassell. Our request for documentation of any kind that supports his claim still stands, but until proof of his conviction and claims are supplied, Lassell will not be listed in *Underground*.

We encourage anyone who has had contact with Lassell in the past to pass on any information that may prove useful in relation to this matter. Thank you.

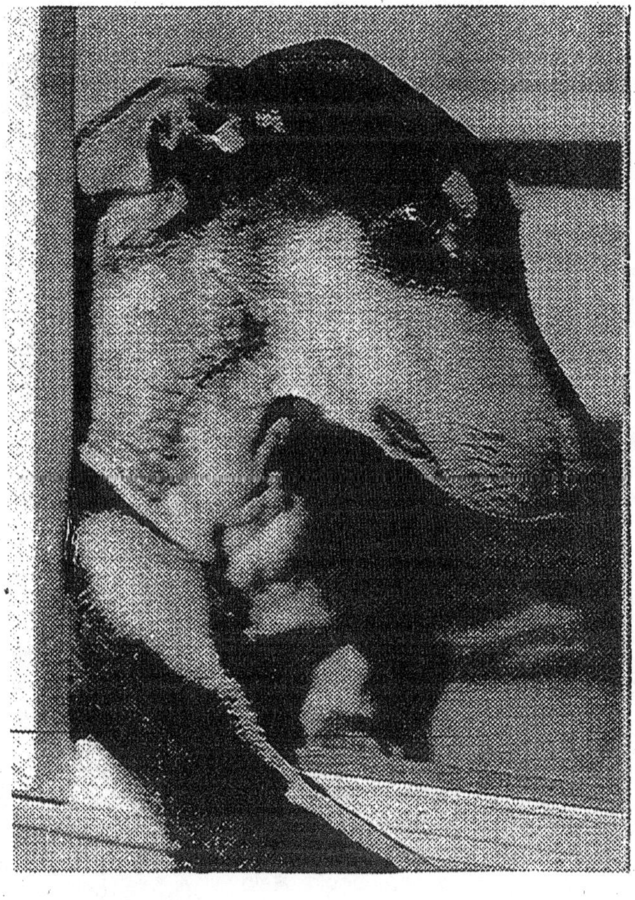

WHAT IS TO BE DONE?

For comrades who ask, "what is to be done?" during this particular historical juncture, a (partial) list of things to do.
Tim Blunk, political prisoner: June 1987, Marion Prison

throw a stone
throw another
fire a poem
slash a tire
raise a fist
raise your voice
raise a child
wear a mask
paint a slogan
paint a dream
honour the martyrs
build a barricade
build a network
claim your history
claim the streets
sing a message
shoot a bullet
sow a seed
set a fire
break a window
break a sweat
rent a safehouse
learn from workers
mark the time
free a p.o.w.
steal the files
steel your heart
hound a landlord

feed
the
homeless
squat a building
join a cell
learn a kata
memorize the code
cut the bars
vault the fence
clear the perimeter
swim the river
disarm a cop

disable a missile
create a diversion
tell a joke
secure a march
walk the picket
pick a lock
bait a trap
spring an ambush

blow a horn
make a plan
plan a back-up
cut the wires
wreck the tracks
lose a tail
find your hope
raise the stakes
change your name
wipe for prints
test a theory
challenge a dogma
change a diaper
print a leaflet
forge a document
shelter a fugitive
bind a wound
love a friend
hold a lantern
hold your ground
clean your weapon
practice your aim
strike a chord
strike a blow
tell the truth
trick the man
hold a meeting
take a beating

hold your tongue
watch your back
watch the sky
cut a trail
leave no traces
pick a target
launch a rocket
slip the noose
slip the checkpoint
use your fear
tighten the drum
plant a thought
tend the orchard
cherish a tear
commit it to memory
check your ego
study the map
deal with the traitors
silence the snitch
start from scratch
carry your weight
take on some more
fight to love
say it again
cross the line
take us with you
don't look back

SOME WAYS YOU CAN SUPPORT PRISONERS

INCREASE PRISONER VISIBILITY AND AWARENESS OF PRISON ISSUES

Bring up prisoner issues wherever possible. When you take part in political events, bring a placard or wear a t-shirt saying "remember our brothers and sisters inside", and hand out information on how prisoners can be supported. Write about the ongoing contributions prisoners make to political movements, and about prisoner struggles. Connect prison struggles with freeworld struggles - for better AIDS education, against racism, etc.

SHARE RESOURCES WITH PRISONERS

Send money to defense funds and prison support groups. Donate supplies to prisoners (ask each prisoner what the rulers are in her/his institution, and what is most needed). Share information: buy prisoners subscriptions to magazines or newspapers, or send books. Help prisoners get their information out by soliciting articles from prisoners, and helping distribute prisoner publications.

CONNECT WITH PRISONERS

Giving prisoners a way to connect with the outside world is essential in helping prisoners resist the violence, behavior modification techniques, and the isolation & boredom of jail. Non-prisoners can connect with prisoners by writing letters, visiting, or talking on the phone.

If you can't think of enough to write a full letter, just send a colorful postcard explaining who you are, how you heard of the prisoner, and that you are writing to let them know they are not forgotten. Remember that all letters to prisoners are opened and read by prison officials, so do not send anything that could jeopardize the prisoner. Don't expect a reply, as many prisons restrict the number of letters that can be sent, and prisoners may not have enough money to buy paper, envelopes, or stamps.

Most prisons limit the number of visitors allowed in, so make sure you check with any prisoner you want to visit to ensure you are not taking up a family member or friend's visiting time. Many prisons organize yearly "socials" or other large, structured activities for people who find it difficult to think of what to do during a visit.

LISE OLSEN: AN UPDATE

Lise Olsen was recently released from prison having been charged with the "possession of Incendiary Devices" - what were in actual fact lanterns created for an anti-fur Fourth of July protest that took place in 1992. The State's case against Lise relied heavily on lies and the fabrication of evidence against her. *(SEE UNDERGROUND 3 FOR MORE DETAILS)* Lise's case should stand as an example to all political activists of the extremes the FBI and other government authorities will go to suppress political activism and dissention. Be aware.

DEAR FRIENDS AND SUPPORTERS-

At last I am able to write you a letter thanking you for the letters of support you wrote for me and to me, without asking you for yet another protest letter on my behalf in return. It feels good just to be able to say "Thank you" for all your time and trouble and help. Let me tell you about my current situation. unbelievably, I am actually typing this in my own small apartment, with my two beloved cats, Hamlet and Aida, close by, enjoying the quiet and beauty and peace of my surroundings, decorated with objects spiritual and artistic. Just to experience the joy of normal beautiful things like white lace curtains and green plants is a wonderful privilege.

I bonded out of prison on October 10. My official release date from prison would have been October 13. As you know, IDOC continued to deny me approval for the electronic home monitor that would have counted on my sentence, even after my conviction was overturned by the Appellate Court 8/4/95.

Because the State is determined to reconvict me because I am an animal rights activist who they have a mania about inventing into a terrorist, I am now rearrested and facing trial all over again on the same case I was originally arrested for in 1992. With these differences: on my first arrest on this case, I was free on bond for almost two years (20 months) until unjustly (now determined illegally) convicted in a mock trial that employed the common methodologies of confes sion invention, perjury, fabrication of evidence and withholding of evidence that would have proved innocence. These are the routine techniques that also convicted Leonard Peltier (AIM) and Mumia Abu-Jamal (MOVE).

Now, I am "free" on bond again - only in the meantime I have become the target of a political conspiracy agenda to destroy the animal rights movement, strange when one recollects that I am not a leader nor ever was a prominent personality in animal rights. As a condition of my bond, I requested the protection of the electronic monitor so long denied me in prison. With it, I can hopefully defend my life against case fabrication bye the FBI (by being able to verify my whereabouts at all times), or even my life if they decided to attack me, as they did environmental activist Judi Bari.

To deflect their attempts to plant horrendous "evidence" in my apartment, which they tried by bribing my catsitter to enter it when I was still in prison, my attorney wrote them inviting them to search my apartment under his supervision, to tap my phone, to give me a polygraph test to rule me out as a suspect in any legitimate investigation they might have under way, and to monitor me electronically. So, on October 13, what would normally have been my "freedom day," I voluntarily re-entered Chicago's cook County Jail to be banded with my protective monitor. The "arresting offense,"* theoretically the same as it was originally in 1992, has now been augmented into something called BOMB (printed in my monitor ID card). There is no Illinois "bomb" statute, so I guess this is to prejudice people against me, as usual.

I now live in virtual isolation, unable to even go to the grocery store, subject to arrest at any moment if there is a monitor fault: but at least I am alive! My attorney (57 years experience) states that he has never seen the State have such a mania about retrying a "non-violent offender" who has done her entire sentence (they can't give me more prison time). They never retry cases short of murder, he says, not even rape or armed robbery. They "hate" me, he says.

So now I await retrial: for making lanterns. As my attorney says, it's "hard to believe." Please pray for me.
Lise.

*"arresting offence" was originally "attempt arson."

LISE OLSEN'S SITUATION AS IT NOW STANDS:

Lise's attorney, a very prominent and well known lawyer has suffered a recent heart-attack and undergone a leg amputation, leaving Lise attorney-less and vulnerable to arrest at any time.. Lise has been forced to spend over $40,000 of her retirement savings on her situation. She has recently applied for disability, and so is without any source of income. Lise is now facing another trial revolving around the release of smokebombs in a Chicago fur store in 1993,

an action Lise had nothing to do with. Despite a lack of evidence and the fact that the fingerprints on the smoke bomb do not match Lise's, the State is actively seeking to frame her and send her back to jail. Lise needs your support!

The NA-ALFSG is asking that concerned activists and animal rights/liberation organizations to come together in support of Lise, and to help with her financial situation. REMEMBER: Lise was not an A.L.F. activist. Her only "crime" was to create a banner and illuminate it with home-made lanterns. What ever your position may be on direct action and the A.L.F., we are asking that you set aside a dollar or two to help out someone who is clearly innocent of the charges against her. Please help support Lise Olsen. Any donations, large or small, for Lise can be sent to the **NA-ALFSG at Po Box 69597, 5845 Yonge St., Willowdale, Ont. M2M 4K3, Canada.**
Cheques or money orders should be clearly earmarked for Lise Olsen, and made out to either: Lise Olsen or NA-ALFSG. We will forward ALL money directly to Lise.
Thank you.

ROD CORONADO

SOME BACKGROUND ON ROD CORONADO FOR NEW READERS: Rod Coronado has been a longtime animal rights activist, having worked with a number of organizations concerned with animal issues, including the Sea Shepherd and In Defense of Animals. In the Faroe Islands in 1986 he was arrested and beaten and held for 5 days until Amnesty International Secured his release. Rod later helped disable one of Iceland's illegal whaling station and sank two of their four whaling ships. Rod has also been involved with the Hunt Saboteurs (UK), Earth First!, and in 1987 founded the Hunt Saboteurs of America. Rod also worked for a period of time with People for the Ethical Treatment of Animals and documented allegations of abuse on fur farms in America for Friends of Animals. The list goes on.

On Sept 27, 1994, Rod Coronado was arrested by officials of the FBI, BATF, and BIA at the Pascua Yaqui Reservation, where he had been working as a youth support worker with children from the reservation.

Rod accepted a plea agreement offered by prosecutors in which he pled to aiding and abetting the arson at Michigan State University's mink facilities. Rod accepted responsibility for receiving and sending a press release and items stolen during the raid and for acting as a spokesperson for the series of ALF raids from '91 to 92 (Operation Bite Back). Rod received a sentence of roughly 4 1/2 years (57 months). During this same period, Rod faced intense pressure from the US government to testify against other ALF activists, which he refused to do. The judge saw this as an obstruction of justice and came down hard on Rod for protecting others.

The NA-ALFSG supports Rod as someone who lived by the principles and beliefs of a member of the Yaqui Nation, and acted to save the lives of countless animals. Both the North American and UK Supporters Groups have been in regular contact with Rod since he was locked away. Rod is in good spirits and stands strong in his beliefs. He writes:

"I want it to be publicly known that I'm affiliated with your prisoner support work, because I support your views ex pressed in Underground*100%! ... Thanks again for all the work you have done on my and the Yoawam (animals) behalf. The ALF is truly, probably one of the only non-indigenous movements that have embraced the respect and reverence that my people have for the Yoawam and fought for them as hard as my ancestors tell me I should. What separates "us" from "them" as far as humans and animals go is our unwillingness to protect them as we would our own species if we witnessed the same atrocities committed against us..."*

-Rod Coronado, December 25, 1995

ROD NEEDS YOUR SUPPORT.

Rod can receive magazines, SOFTCOVER books and photos directly from those who write him Newspapers and hardcover books must come from the publisher or a bookstore.For activist interested in helping with general donations for Rod's support work, please earmark cheques/and or envelopes "for Rod." [Cheque or money orders made payable to NA ALFSG]. Currently, Rod has requested that money sent to the SG for his support work be added to the general ALF prisoner fund to help with any expenses with prisoner support or to help other ALF prisoners.
To write Rod directly with letters of support, please see page for his address.

ANIMAL LIBERATION PRISONERS

NORTH AMERICA

Rod Coronado #03895000: FC1, PO Box 23811, Tuscon, AZ 85706, USA.
Sentenced to 47 months for offenses relation to his actions as spokesperson for the ALF in the USA.

UNITED KINGDOM:

Melanie Arnold GJ0940: HMP Eastwood park, Falfield, Wotton under Edge, Gloucester, GL12 8DB, England.
Charged with arson, possessing articles with intent to cause criminal damage for an attack on a abattoir in Gloucester. Arson for the attack against livestock transporters in Northampton and a general conspiracy to cause explosions charge.

Gurjeet Aujla HV2047: HMP Birmingham, Winson Green Road, Birmingham, B18 4AS. England.
Sentenced to 6 years for alleged Justice Department Actions against numerous animal abusers.

Dave Callender HV3314: HMP Birmingham, Winson Green Road, Birmingham, B18 4AS. England.
Sentanced to 10 years for conspiracy to cause criminal damage by arson.

Darren Cole HD2301: HMP Exeter, New North Road, Exeter. EX4 4ex, England.
On remand charged with conspiracy to cause criminal damage.

Michael Green VA2923: HMP Bristol, Cambridge Road, Bristol, BS7 8PS, England.
Charged with arson, possessing articles with intent to cause criminal damage for an attack on abattoir in Gloucester. Arson for the attack against livestock transporters in Northampton and a general conspiracy to cause explosions charge.

Angie Hamp TW1687: HMP Askham Grange, Askham Richard, York, YO2 3PT, England
Sentenced to 4 years for conspiracy to commit arson. The actual raid in question caused 3/4 million pounds worth of damage.

Niel Hanson HF3184: HMP The Mount, Bovingdon, Hemel Hempstead, Herts, HP3 0NZ, England.
Sentenced to 3 for Conspiracy to dispatch a hoax bomb and criminal damage to the property of the public relation officers of Glaxo's (vivisectors).

Keith Mann EE3588: HMP Full Sutton, Nr Stamford Bridge, York, YO4 1PS, England.
Sentenced to 14 years for causing L6000 worth of criminal damage to lorries, attempted incitement, possession of explosive substances, escape and attempted arson.

Gillian Peachey RL3415: HMP Holloway, Parkhurst Road, London, N7 0NU, England.
On remand charged with causing criminal damage.

Dominic Peaty XD1642: HMP Exeter, New North Road, Exeter. EX4 4ex, England.
On remand charged with causing criminal damage.

Micheal Roberts GE3743: HMP Lewes, Brighton Road, Lewes, E. Sussex, BN7 1EA, England.
On remand charged with conspiracy to commit arson.

Geoff Sheppard MD1030: HMP Wormwood Scrubs, po Box 757, Du cane Road, London, W12 0AE, England.
Sentenced to 7 years for possession of items with intent to make incendiary devices and possession of a shotgun. Geoff has already served a four year sentence in the 1980's for incendiary actions against the fur trade in department stores.

Charles Skinner No24250: HMP La Moye St, Beades,Jersey, Channel Isles.
Imprisoned for starting a fire at Jersey to visitors centre which caused over 322,000 pounds worth of damage and to letting off a smokebomb inside an artificial insemination centre causing L6,000 of damage. He was given 4 and 2 years to run concurrently.

Barbara Trenholm RL1292: HMP Holloway, Parkhurst Road, London, N7 0NU, England.
On remand charged with conspiracy to commit arson

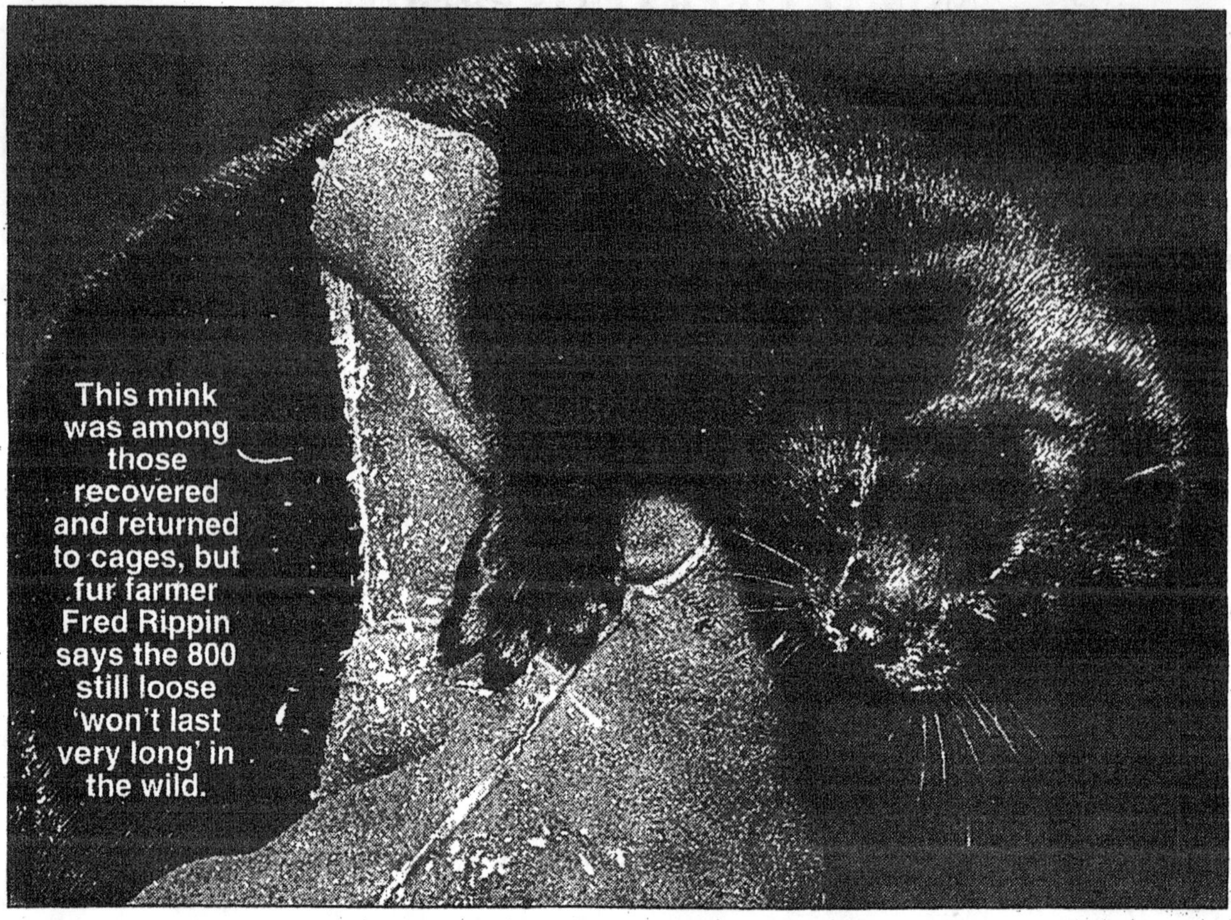

This mink was among those recovered and returned to cages, but fur farmer Fred Rippin says the 800 still loose 'won't last very long' in the wild.

IN FAVOR? FUR SURE

Vandals' minky business wins activists' nod

By John Colebourn
Staff Reporter

An animal rights group called Animal Allies said yesterday it supports the vandals who released about 5,000 mink from their cages in Aldergrove.

"Fur is a totally unnecessary product," the group said in a statement.

"It panders to humans' worst traits — vanity and greed."

Robert Noding of Animal Allies asked in the statement: "Who are the real terrorists? People who release some mink from an animal concentration camp, or the people who keep animals cooped up their whole lives in unbearable conditions for no other reason than to make lots of money?"

Fur farmer Fred Rippin said he had not heard of Animal Allies.

"They're copying material I've read before," he said of the group's statement.

About 3,000 mink have been rounded up since their cages were opened on Tuesday night. Another 50 were rounded up yesterday, leaving about 800 on the loose.

Rippin is not sure how many will survive. "They won't last very long in the wild."

Rippin said each mink pelt was expected to fetch $50 at an auction next month in Seattle.

He was not insured.

And, he said, releasing the mink destroyed his breeding lines because the mink are all mixed up.

The attack at Rippin's farm comes three weeks after several thousand mink were released at fur farmer Reg Dargatz's Chilliwack farm.

No arrests have been made in either case.

VANCOUVER PROVINCE NOV. 15/95

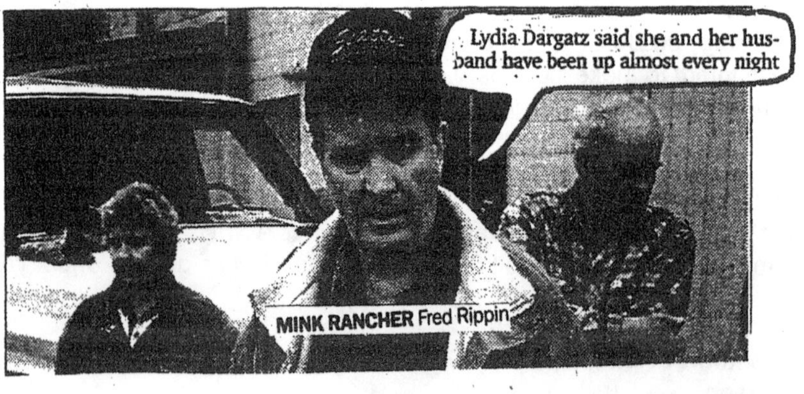

Lydia Dargatz said she and her husband have been up almost every night
MINK RANCHER Fred Rippin

..Aldergrove fur farmers are extreme and stupid.

neighbors and other mink farmers
spent the day catching the animals —
but Next to hunting humans this is the
worst. It really tarnishes the whole
Mink Breeders Association, said
every farmer in the area
"Apparently the [security] guy was
here at midnight and he said he saw
Other farmers in the area running free all over
breeding throughout the night. animal-rights
groups have condemned the acts.
"fur farmers are really stupid", Rippin said.

Get Caught Up On All the Action...

NA-ALFSG: Box 69597, 5845 Yonge St., Willowdale, Ont. Canada. M2M 4K3

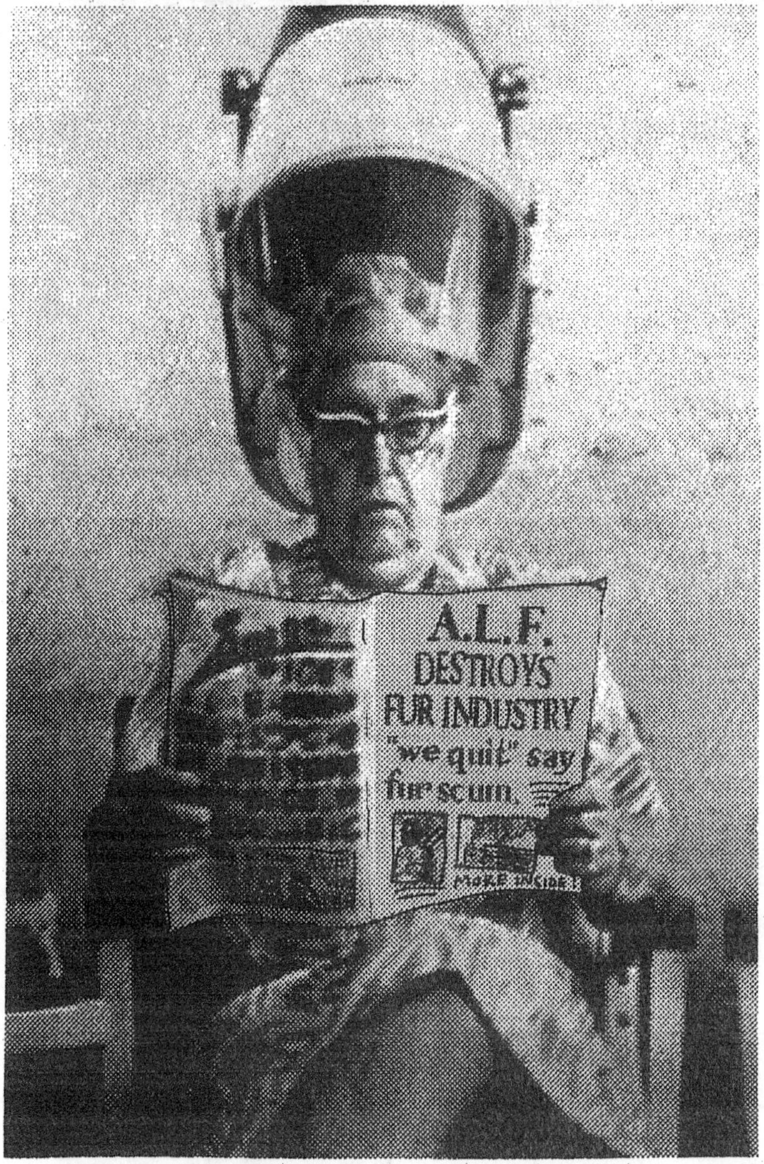

SUBSCRIBE

NOW TO *UNDERGROUND*

The Magazine of the North American A.L.F. Supporters Group

Help support the Animal Liberation Front by picking up your copy of *UNDERGROUND.* All money sent to the North American A.L.F. Supporters Group goes directly towards support of imprisoned A.L.F. activists, educational activites, and the support and defence of the A.L.F. So join the Animal Liberation Front in the battle against animal abuse and exploitation by supporting their efforts - either by buying a copy of *UNDERGROUND*- or by becoming a member of the NA-ALFSG!

The NA-ALFSG is for those who wish to support A.L.F. without breaking the law. We encourage the input and participation of all activists - including those who are unable to, or who do not wish to, take part in direct action.

"Smash it, Spray it, Break it, Burn it - What ever you do, Just DO IT!"

-the thoughts of one active A.L.F. cell.

Remember! The information published in UNDERGOUND is for educational and entertainment purposes only!

YES! I want my copy of *UNDERGROUND* rushed to my door today! Please find enclosed $....... in either US or Canadian funds (made out to: NA-ALFSG). I can barely wait to receive my descretely wrapped copy of the NA-ALFSG's official newsletter, so hurry up and mail it to:

____

____

____

☐ Enclosed is an additional $______ to go directly to A.L.F. prisoner support.

You've convinced me! Here's my $20 - $25 cheque or money order (US or Can. payable to NA-ALFSG) for a membership in the North American A.L.F. Supporters Group. I can hardly wait to start receiving 4 issues of *UNDERGROUND* a year, along with updates on prisoners, actions, A.L.F. victories, etc. between issues. Send *UNDERGROUND* (and anything else the SG mails out to members) to:

____

____

____

☐ Enclosed is an additional $______ to go directly to A.L.F. prisoner support.

copy and distribute this page

MERCHANDISE DISTRIBUTION

THIS YOUNG MAN
HELPED RESCUE BEAGLES
FROM A TORTURE LAB....
....HIS REWARD WAS PRISON

POSTCARDS

<-- P02 **$2/SET OF 4** P03 -->

(not shown: P05: chickens deep fry Colonel Sanders)

P04

coming soon: t-shirts, notepaper, stickers, buttons...
designs & other merchandise ideas appreciated

O R D E R F O R M

CODE	ITEM TITLE/DESCRIPTION	PRICE PER	QUANTITY	COST

NAME		SUBTOTAL	
ADDRESS		-10% (ALFSG MEMBERS)	
		+25% OVERSEAS POSTAGE	
PHONE		TOTAL	

Mail to NA-ALFSG, PO BOX 241532, Memphis, TN 38124

TOWARDS ANIMAL LIBERATION & FREEDOM FOR ALL POLITICAL PRISONERS

BOOKLETS

B101 Keep Fighting: 64pgs, 1/2 size, $3 - interviews with UK ALF Press Officers.

B02 An Animal Liberation Primer. 2nd Edition. Compiled and edited by @nu: 32pgs, 1/2 size, $2.50 - A DIY booklet of direct action tactics: how to stake out an action site, breaking into buildings, vandalism, arson, how to react to police interrogation, etc.

B03 As long as there are slaughterhouses ... then there shall be battlefields: 30pgs, $3 - An historical look at the actions against animal abuse, from 1991 onwards and a critique of the branch upon which we're sitting. An invaluable look at the A.L.F. in Britain, and some interesting analyses of the A.L.F.

B04 Explosives Manual: 84pgs, 1/2 size, $7 - Guide to building explosives and incendiaries from easily acquired materials. Similar to CIA-type manuals.

B05 Grand Jury Comix. 1978: 13pgs, 8x14 size, $3 - Although put out almost 20 years ago, this booklet provides useful information for our movement today - and is a great tool for public education as it is far more readable than the usual legal articles.

B06 Huddersfield:4, the State:0 - 36pgs, 1/2 size, $3 - The story of a 1992 trial of four people accused of being A.L.F. activists in England. The trial "did not produce sensationalized lies in the papers, did not make threatening examples of the defendants and did not produce harsh prison sentences..."

B07 Interviews with Animal Liberation Front Activists: 52pgs, $6 - Compiled in England from interviews with many different A.L.F. cells, covers most aspects of the A.L.F.

B08 Into the 1990's with Animal Liberation Front Activists: 18pgs, $3 - A how to book from England on A.L.F. tactics.

B09 The Power Is Ours: A Manual on Saving the Earth and the Animals: 15pgs, $2 - An updated version of Into the 1990's with slightly different layout and tactical info.

B10 Without a Trace: A Forensic Manual for You and Me - 36pgs, 1/2 size, (1987), $2 - A good reality check on how the police actually work. Good tips on not leaving behind clues.

B11 This is the ALF #2: 20pgs, 1/2 size, $1.50 - Primer from Australia. Clippings as well as DIY directions.

B12 Animal Liberation Primer 3rd Edition: 20pgs, 1/2 size, $2 - How to guide, similar to previous primers. Covers some different ground.

B13 Press Clippings: 49pgs, 8 1/2x11, $3 - News clippings from U.S. actions dating back to the 80's.

B14 On the Road Again. Direct Action Underground: 8pgs, 8 1/2x11, $1 - a guide to living underground, info on acquiring fake ID's, transportation, funds, communication, etc.

B15 Interview with California ALF Activists: 6pgs, 8 1/2 x 11, $1 - Answers to basic questions asked by beginning ALF activists.

LEAFLETS (50 cents)

L01 Direct Action for the Animals: A member of the ALF tells why she broke the law for animals.

L02 Information about Djurens Hamnare/Diary of Animal Avengers Actions (from Sweden)

L03 Wake up! Strategy, addresses, musings and artwork in this 4 page centre spread from a 1994 issue of Earth First! Journal.

MAGAZINES

North America

M01 Dressed in Black #1: 20pgs, 1/2 size, (1994), $1.50. **#2**: 24pgs, 1/2 size, (late 1994), $2. **#3**: 20pgs, 8 1/2x11, (march 1995), $2.

M02 Out of the Cages: #7: (Fall 1993), 24pgs. **#8**: (1994), 24pgs. **#9**: (1994), 24pgs, $3 each

M03 The Militant Vegan: #1: (1993), 20pgs, $3. **#2-7**: (from 1993 to late 1994), all 12pgs and $2 each.

M04 Underground: #1: August 1994, 28pgs, $3. **#2**: November 1994, 48pgs, $4. **#3**:Dec94-Nov95, 65pgs, $3. **#4**: Spring 96, 56pgs, $3.

FOREIGN

M011 ALF Supporters Group Newsletter (UK): current and back issues,$4 each.

M012 Arkangel (UK): #12 (Fall 94), 56pgs, $3. #13 (spring 95), 68pgs $4. plus current issues $4.

M013 HOWL - English Hunt Saboteurs Magazine: #55, Fall'94. #56, Winter'94. #57, Spring'95. #58, Summer'95. $3 each.

M014 Liberator (UK) $3 each (back issues and current)

M015 Annimal Info (New Zealand) #3 June'95, 8pgs, $1.

NO LONGER IN PRINT

M016 COMBAT; published by the old Canadian SG, #1 1990, 16pgs, $2. #2 1992, 8pgs, $1.

M017 Homo Milk: 12pgs, 1/2 size. $1. Animal Liberation from a gay perspective.

MISCELLANEOUS

X01 Yet Still Comes the Rain: Benefit tape. A collection of punk/hardcore music to raise money for the NA ALFSG. $5.

X02 Vivisectors are Scum: buttons $1

X03 Stickers: "Support the ALF" Masked activist with tool. 50 cents each, $2.00 for six.

X04 Fabric patches, featuring circled "A" - North American ALF Supporters Group. Great for stitching on bags, jackets, etc. $2 each

X05 ALF Supporters Group Benefit Compilation Tape. 17 Canadian punk/hardcore bands. High quality. Comes with 24pg 1/2 size booklet with information etc. Sticker: "ALF Supporter" included. $7.50

TS01 T shirt: Masked activist, "Support the A.L.F." "Animal Liberation Front Saves Animals Lives" XL. Dark Blue, Green, Off White with black ink. $15. Limited number of grey long sleeve: $18

TS02 T shirt: Circled "A" North American ALF Supporters Group. XL Dark Blue with white ink. Green, Off White with Black ink, $15. Limited number of grey and black long sleeve: $18.

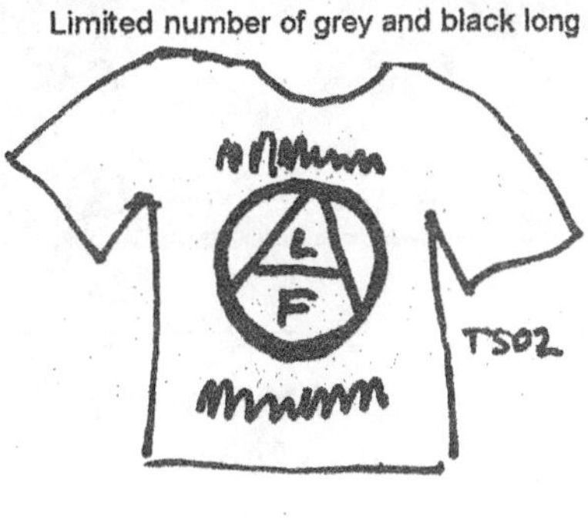

ANIMAL LIBERATION

THE TIME IS NOW

NA-ALFSG: Box 69597, 5845 Yonge St., Willowdale, Ontario, Canada. M2M 4K3
<an246614@anon.penet.fi.>

UNDERGROUND

$3 THE MAGAZINE OF THE NORTH AMERICAN ANIMAL LIBERATION FRONT SUPPORTERS GROUP #5

FREE TO PRISONERS

Animal Lib Prisoner, Rod Coronado

WANTED BY FBI

INSIDE: Special Supplement -- Rod Coronado & the U.S. Animal Liberation Movement, page **20. ALSO:** Interview with Darren Thurston. Diary of Action. Fur Farms feel the Heat, and much more!

Animal Liberation Front Supporters Group BENEFIT COMPILATION TAPE

Each A.L.F.S.G. BENEFIT COMPILATION TAPE comes with a **24 paged booklet and sticker [''A.L.F. Supporter'']** This kick-ass tape is a collaboration of efforts from Vancouver Island and area punk bands, playing for the common cause of **animal liberation.** All proceeds will be used to further the cause of animal liberation and **directly benefit imprisoned Animal Liberation Front activists and their families.**

To order:
Send cheque or money order [made out to ''NA ALFSG''] for $7.50 to:

NA-ALFSG DISTRO
Box 767295
Roswell, GA,
30076, USA

Canadian residents may pay in CDN funds, US and international orders, please pay in US funds. **(Tapes are $6, plus .25% for shipping and handling costs = $7.50)**

COMMUNITY & PIRATE RADIO STATIONS interested in receiving a free copy of this tape, **please write** for more details.

LETTERS TO UNDERGROUND

WHO PAYS OUT PRISONER SUPPORT -- A REPLY

Dear Liberationist friends,

Thank you for the latest *Underground.*

To answer your reader's question re: "Does PETA pay for activists' defence over and above civil disobedience?"

Under the charities laws, PETA cannot pay fines, although our Grassroots Department raises money separately to help activists pay fines, by selling vegetarian food and junk they collect, etc. However, we argue that we are allowed to pay for legal defence in a system that accepts the right to a fair trial (in principle, anyway!) and the tenet that a person is innocent until proven guilty. With that in view, although the FBI and ATF threatened to invoke RICO to shut us down, PETA paid for such defenses as those of Roger Troen (Uninversity of Oregon raid) and Rodny Coronado (University of Michigan mink farms raid).

We take each case separately and do not pay for every defense. For example, we paid a great deal in trial and defense-related costs to assist over two dozen people called before Grand Jury witchhunts in Pennsylvania, California, Oregon, Maryland, New York, and Louisiana and have supported other liberationists financially and in other ways.

As you may know, PETA also funded a successful lawsuit against Pennsylvanian authorities for failure to provide medical care, beds andfor harrassment endured during the two-week stints PETA, Fund for Animals and other activists spent in that not-so-fine Pottsville Prison (where the Molly McGuires were executed for political activities) as a result of pigeon liberations and disruptions at the Higins Pigeon Shoot.

We raise money for all our programs, from obtaining undercover footage from slaughterhouses and labs, to printing pamphlets, going into the schools, demonstrations, grassroots support, video-making, media blitzes and so on, but people give sparsely, if at all, for activist defense and that will probably always be so. Historically, we have had to spend tens of thousands of dollars more in each of various cases than the amount specifically donated for activist defense. It is a hard fact that if anyone out there decides to break an unjust law to help save man or mouse from unnecessary suffering (which PETA cannot advocate but which we will defend and support as allowed by the First Amendment to the U.S. Constitution), they must do so expecting nothing but the satisfaction of having done something useful that few have the courage to do. Anything tangible received, whether money, a book or a letter, is a gift, so it is better to start off expecting nothing than to live disappointed! Such is revolution.

With every good wish for your success and safety, I am very truly yours,

Ingrid E. Newkirk
Cofounder
PETA

FROM THE BELLY OF THE BEAST -- LETTERS FROM UK PRISONERS

Dear NA ALFSG

Many thanks for the letter and Underground - it was a truly brilliant read, a real morale booster! It's more than most of our "respectable" Nationals manage to put out over here! I'd really like to see future editions if that would be possible.

Sorry it's taken so long to get back to you, but I've been revising for exams which finally finished this morning, so I can now catch up on letter writing!

I am not exactly flavour of the month amongst the authorities here. Apart from the fact that they caught me brewing booze (again!), I've started a campaign to get caged birds banned from British jails. I've rescued 6 and arranged for them to be taken to outside sanctuaries, and some of the cruelty is incredible. I've issued a press release which was taken up by at least six newspapers and several radio stations. It's against the regulations to contact the media, so they weren't best pleased here and

I've had non-stop aggravation ever since! Someone "upstairs" seems to have taken it seriously, though, as an investigation into my claims has been started and I've been interviewed at length. They've also had a vet to inspect every bird, so who knows, the campaign may succeed. I'm getting a leaflet together now.

Before all this blew up, they did let me out for 3 days for home-leave, which was great. Loads of petty conditions attached to the licence, including "no animal welfare activities" but freedom none the less! Hard work getting it, mind, they had refused, saying to release me would pose an "unacceptable risk to public order." Fine...

I've written all the material for a new National Anti-Hunt Campaign mailout, but as we mail to 10,000 people, we can't afford to post it - I haven't been able to get out and do many fund-raising stalls lately! It can be bloody frustrating not being able to do the things that need to be done, but not long now ...

The government are having one of their periodic "get tough on law and order and win a few extra votes" clampdowns at the moment, resulting in loads of petty new rules and regulations in jails all over the country. They're also hugely increasing the number of prisons while reducing the number of prison staff, which can only lead to a loss of facilities for prisoners. Looks as though I'll be getting out just in time. I just feel sorry for all those starting, and probably about to start, long sentences.

Some major trials are coming up as I'm sure you're aware - Robin, Mel, Michael, Barbara ... lets hope for some decent results for a change!

Well, loads of letters to catch up on, so I'd better close for now.

Take care, keep in touch, and keep fighting,

Neil Hansen HF 3184
HMP the Mount,
Bovingdon, Hemel Hempstead
Herts, HP3 ONZ, England.

[We 're happy to say that we've received word that Neil has been released, and can now have a pint any time he wants without fear of being nicked!]

Hi There,

Thanks for writing, really good to hear from you. Letters are your life-line inside, hearing news of what's happening out there and knowing that someone does really care; for that I thank you.

Let me tell you a little about what's happened to me in the last 2 1/2 years since I've been inside.

I originally came to prison in 1991, and was remanded for 6 weeks before being granted bail, the main advantage of my short stay (if you can call it that) was the fact that I had now experienced prison, knew what to expect, and most of all knew that there was nothing to be frightened of. You often fear what is unknown, and afterwards wonder what all the fuss was about, although nobody loves prison, it's certainly not the worst experience in the world.

I was re-arrested in April of 1994 after being on the "run" for two years, I breached my bail on World Day for Laboratory Animals 1992 after deciding that I wasn't going to walk into court to be sent to prison by the same system that we are fighting against. I was fed up of seeing so many friends walking into court only to be locked away for many years.

Keith Mann and myself were eventually re-arrested at an Animal sanctuary we were both working at, and after being questioned by Hastings police, Keith was taken to Manchester and I to Northampton to be interrogated yet again by our dear old friends in blue. I was then remanded and sent to HMP Holloway and Keith to HMP Strangeways.

From Holloway I went to a prison in the north of England for a trial against an incident at a fur farm, nothing became of that so back to Holloway for me. the next 6 months I felt like a yo-yo, back to Newhall and then to Holloway, appearing in court in Northampton, Oxford and Birmingham. Eventually on September 30 I was sentenced to 4 years in prison.

After a year in Holloway, working doing re-cycling and eventually being on the same wing with a fellow activist, I was shipped back to Newhall.

Both my time in Holloway and Newhall was spent as constructively as possible and the time really went quite quickly for me. I became a qualified life guard and took a Community Sports Leaders Award as well as a BAWLA weight training instructor, I worked in the gym as well. The only mishap was when I was nicked for refusing to deliver a meat sandwich to a screw.

I finally ended up here in Askham Grange, again it's in the North, just 18 miles from Keith's prison. It's an open prison for short termers, less serious offences or if you are coming to the end of your sentence, like me.

It was here that my parole was refused, not by this prison, but by a panel that hasn't even met me before and has just read reports that our friends in blue wrote about me. The reasons for my refusal were 1) the incident with the meat sandwich and 2) because of my strong commitment to animal rights. Did you know that it is an offence to be vegan, and to have a job at an animal sanctuary when you're released from prison?

Anyway, I've just got on with it, you have to, no use being bitter, it just eats you up. So I've made the most of my time here.

Because it's an open prison you get a lot more privileges, I work in the gym here as well. Twice a week I go out and help autistic children to learn water safety and how to swim. I also help at a sports centre once a week working with adults with learning difficulties and special needs. I love doing this work and get a lot out of it.

I also get two town visits a month, that's when you can leave the prison between 10am and 6pm. I go and visit Keith once a month cause he is only down the road, that's really good, we hadn't seen each other for a year before I came here so it's certainly made it easier for us. My other town visit is spent with my three dogs; my best friends Winnie, Witch and Patch. I hadn't seen them for well over two years but after my parole refusal we decided to see them so they could get used to me being around again. It was a really hard decision to make but I think it was the right one, they are so beautiful, I wish you could meet them, they are all really grey now and showing their ages.

I've just got under three months left to serve, I can not wait to get out of this place and go home and be re-united with the animals and my friends at the sanctuary.

Receiving letters really do help you so much, it brings a smile to your face, knowing someone cares, it also shows the authorities that you're not forgotten and certainly are not alone. Thankyou for writing and bringing a smile to my day.

Take care out there,
Love, Peace & Liberation

Angie Hamp TW1687
HMP Askham Grange
Askham Richard, York
Y02 3PT, England

Dear NA ALFSG,

Hi ya,
It's only me, Darren Cole at HMP Exeter. Thank you so very much for your letter - it was really cool to hear from you, and thank you for the copy of *Underground #4* it was was an extremly good read. Thanks. Well, I think I'd better tell you a bit about myself. I've been on remand since November 95 charged with ason on a live export's depo (Choakford Farm). It's a total stitch up -- I've been to court 10 times now for this action and there is no direct evidence against me at all. My solicitors have been trying their very best to get me released but to no avail. The police have continually lied in court. My trial date is some time in December! As for conditions here, they're not all that bad. My vegan diet is extremely good.

Before I carry on, please can I thank everyone for the support I've received so far. It really does mean a lot to me and I'm sure I speak for other Prisoners of War when I say that. So, a BIG thank you to you all -- keep it coming (cheers!) Hey, could I ask you a big favour? Has anyone got any pictures of whales? If so, if you could spare one or two it would be great. Thanks. Anyway, my solicitor is coming to see me tomorrow, so I should learn more about my case. Don't worry, I'll keep you updated, have no fear. Anyway, I'm really crap at writing letters, so I'm going to sign off, but I will write again soon. Until then, take care and write soon!

Lots of love and liberation,
Daz (Darren Cole) XD2301

[FORMERLY AT: HMP Exeter, New North Road,
Bristol, BS7 8PS, England]

NEW ADDRESS:
HMP Feather Stone
New Rd, Feather Stone
Wolverhampton
West Midlands WV10 7PU

[ed note: Darren wrote us back later to say that he was sentenced on the 23rd of July, where he received a prison sentence of 3 1/2 years. Darren faced anywhere from 8 to 10 years, and with time
served, he should be out in 12 months. Congratulations Darren!]

CORRECTIONS TO "LISE OLSEN: AN UPDATE
(UNDERGROUND #4, pg 47/48)

Dear SG et al --

I want to give you heartfelt thanks for publishing my letter in the last issue of Underground. I felt that your support and text made a big difference to me ... I must also commend Underground on the quality of its journalism too. In an era of corporate censorship, good alternative media is rare.

May I correct two things you wrote about my situation, though? You didn't make a mistake in the last issue on purpose, I know, because my situation is so rare it is hard to really grasp. Point #1 is: I am not facing trial on a second case (the '93 Chicago smokebombs allegedly "claimed" by the A.L.F.). The FBI Grand Jury failed to indict me since my fingerprints, and no fingerprints of any friend or distant aquaintance obtained by the FBI by illegal means, matched those on the smokebombs. I am facing a second trial on my own lantern project case from '92, for which I have already completed an entire prison sentence, with only parole to do if reconvicted. This is unique in the history of the U.S. No other person has had more than one trial for the same "offense" other than very serious murder/homicide cases. It has never happened to anyone before who has done ALL their prison time. Fancy getting your trial AFTER the prison sentence. That is what happened to me.

Point #2: it was not the STATE trying to stitch me up for the smokebomb case indictment, based entirely on my conviction on the lantern case (now decided as illegal by the appellate court 8/4/95). It was the FBI.

God bless you for your hard work, and for caring.

Lise

ALF Actions Send Fur Industry Reeling -- Mink Liberations Reach All-Time High

After 7 years of struggling to break even, the fur farm industry is finally starting to get back on it's feet. Unfortunately, many animal rights groups turned away from the fur issue assuming that the industry was finished off. This was not the case, and now the market has bottomed out. With the number of North American fur farms down by as much as half from 1989, the remaining farmers are doing quite well. It is a simple example of what happens when supply goes down while demand stays relatively stable as it has for the past four years.

To make matters worse, new markets have opened for fur producers. Many former communist nations are turning to capitalism. Now many people in Russia, China, and South Korea are finding disposable income as their economies become westernized. this upswing in these nations' economies is leading to a massive increase in fur sales. With the exception of Russia, these countries have very limited fur production. This means that North American and European fur farmers and trappers stand to gain. the average mink pelt that went for $30 in 1994 (just a little above the cost of raising a mink to maturity), is now going for $68. the fur farming industry has become profitable again because we didn't finish them off when we had the chance.

The news isn't all bad though. The Animal Liberation Front is the one group in the position to hurt the fur farmers the most. The ALF knows this, and has responded. In late 1994, an ALF cell broke into the Mac Ellis Fox Farm in Pleasant View, TN. 25 fox were liberated before the coming day light forced the ALF to evacuate. This was the first known U.S. fur farm action since the Western Wildlife Cell had gone into hiding several years previous.

1995 started off slow with no North American fur farm actions. ALF activists in Finland were not going to sit by though! Four fox farms were raided and 700 fox were liberated. Two women, Mia Salli and Minna Salonen, were turned in by traitor Krisi Kultalahti. These brave young women made the best of their situation by making a media circus out of it. This led to major national exposure on fur farming in a nation which produces 70% of the world's fox. More farm raids occurred and a fur feed supplier and a pelt storage barn were burnt to the ground. Over 300 acts of economic sabotage occurred and scores of fur stores were driven out of business. All in 1995!

In the fall of '95, the North American ALF decided it was time for war! Two major raids occurred in British Columbia. The first occurred in October, with 2,400 mink released into their natural habitat in Chilliwack, BC. The following month saw 5,000 released from the Rippin fur farm in Aldergrove, BC. This caught the media's attention in a major way. Fur farmers went all out in a misinformation campaign designed to make the public believe that rance raised mink would die if released into the wild. A British Columbia wildlife technician refuted these claims by pointing out that mink had escaped from fur farms all over the world and survived. Countries such as Iceland and England never had native mink populations. In these countries mink would occasionally escape from farms. Evidently these few escapees did so well, and reproduced so well, that these countries now have viable mink populations. So much for the claims that they would starve to death!

The Canadian Mink Breeders Association responded by putting out a $50,000 reward for anyone who would turn over information leading to the arrest and conviction of an ALF activist responsible for saving mink an fox. The ALF was not intimidated. Just three days after the Aldergrove raid, on November 16th, the ALF raided two U.S. farms. In Olympia, WA, a cell broke into the Clarence Jordan mink farm and released 400 of the furry prisoners into what is excellent mink habitat. In a press release the group said that they wanted to burn the processing barns down, but Jordan came out and they had to quickly leave. On the other side of the country the ALF was back in Tennessee. Mac Ellis fox farm was raided once again with 30 fox spirited away to freedom. This would be the last raid the Ellis Fox Farm could take. The farm went out of business just weeks later.

The ALF followed up on this victory with a trip to the Zimbal Minkery in Sheboygan, WI in January of 1996. The Zimbal mink farm could be the largest in North America. ALF activists found one of two facilities and hopped the fence. 200 to 400 cages were opened and the breeder mink walked out to taste freedom for the first time. Conservative animal welfarists threw a fit, repeating the fur industry propaganda that the mink wouldn't survive. After this myth was debunked they went on to claim that releasing a large number of mink into one area would be bad for the ecosystem. The WI Department of natural Resources told one activist that this would not be a problem as the mink could travel many miles in a single day and would disperse along the waterways. Ironically, the Sheboygan newspaper ran an article shortly after which discussed how the area rivers were short of mink. Pollution had decimated the local population and they needed more mink for a healthy river ecosystem. Apparently the ALF had done the environment a big favour by releasing those mink.

At this point the Fur Commission USA raised the reward fund to $70,000. The Coalition to Abolish the Fur Trade sent out press releases calling this reward fund absurd, and pointed out that this was easily 14 times more money than was offered for the average rapist or murderer. Of course, in America, corporate property is more important than life.

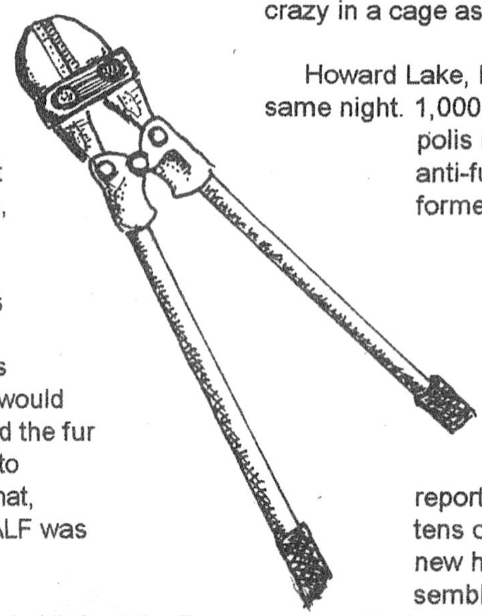

The ALF would next surface in Victor, NY, at the L.W. Bennett fur farm in April. Under the cover of a heavy blizzard, the group cut through the perimeter fence of the farm, evading guard dogs, and released 3,000 breeder females. Each of these females would later have about five kits each, so you can see how devastating this raid was. The farmer stated that his survival was questionable, and that he would have to lay off workers. The reward fund the fur industry was offering would now go up to $100,000. This kind of money proved that, despite an upswing in the market, the ALF was devastating the fur farmers.

After a quite May, the ALF turned up in Utah at the Fur Breeders Agriculture CoOp in Sandy, on June 7th. This feed supplier kept 100 mink for research. The research was designed to find cheep feed mixes that would provide a quality pelt. ALF activists opened a gate and let 75 of the mink go. Sadly, they had to leave the other 25 for fear of waking a sleeping security guard.

North American Fur Auctions began to fear that their producers would start to go out of business despite the fact that the market was picking up. This proved how devastating the ALF attacks were to the fur trade. NAFA brought out a blanket insurance policy to try and offer some protection for the farmers that shipped through them. This insurance still had a $25,000 deductible and only covered losses up to $250,000. It began to appear as if this was only a cheap ploy to get fur farmers to ship through them, so that they would receive some limited protection, instead of through the competing Seattle Fur Exchange.

On June 21st, the ALF raided a true hell hole in Riverton, UT. The group found dead and cannibalized mink rotting in their cages, with other corpses lying in the feces building up under the cages. The ALF freed 1000 of the survivors and warned that even more raids were to come.

During the same month 80 mink were liberated from a WA fur farm. Unfortunately, we have no information on this particular raid. The important thing is that 80 more mink are enjoying freedom as opposed to intensive confinement and then death by neck breaking or a gas chamber.

On July 4th, the ALF struck twice for an Independence Day for animals. In Langley, BC, the Akagami farm was raided and 400 mink liberated. The wife of the farmer stated that the mink couldn't hunt for food and would starve. She then contradicted herself and complained that the escaped mink had eaten 12 of her geese. Once again, the mink had proven that they still maintain their natural instincts, and are much better off running free than going crazy in a cage as death draws near.

Howard Lake, MN was the site of another raid on the same night. 1,000 more mink were liberated. The Minneapolis media took great interest and militant anti-fur activists from CAFT and the newly formed Animal Liberation League presented the ALF's side of things to the general public.

The ALF was not ready to rest yet. The next thing you know, they're back in Utah, this time freeing 3,000 mink from Holt Mink Ranch, in South Jordan. The ALF reported that Utah fur farmers have spent tens of thousands in security. this farm had a new heavy duty fence which the ALF disassembled and rolled up, as well as wire wrapped locks on the cages, which were quickly destroyed. The group caused $35,000 in damage by destroying breeding records alone. the message was sent, get out of the fur trade or pay!

So, what happens now? Mink pelts are fetching top dollar, but the ALF is making the business a risky place to be. Above ground activists need to increase the pressure on the fur trade in a major way. Meanwhile, it is quite obvious that the ALF is far from finished with this campaign. If you want to help with the above ground campaigning, then contact Coalition to Abolish the Fur Trade at PO Box 822411, Dallas, TX, 75382. CAFT also sells a booklet called the Final Nail for $2. this booklet lists all of the known fur farms in North America. These addresses are great for research and investigations.

Our hat is off to the ALF. They are doing a fantastic job and may be hitting the jugular veins of this morally bankrupt industry. Only time and persistence will tell.

J.P. Goodwin
CAFT
Box 822411
Dallas, TX 75382

OPENING THE CAGES --
A LOOK AT MINK LIBERATIONS

BY ROD CORONADO

On October 23, 1995 the Animal Liberation Front (ALF) opened the cages on the Dargatz Mink Farm in British Columbia, Canada freeing 2,400 mink into the surrounding countryside. The liberation from Dargatz Mink Farm was the first in what now has become 12 liberation raids by the ALF of fur farms in North America in less than a year. The result has been the release of approximately 11,000 mink, 30 fox, and one coyote from the intensive confinement that would have lead to death for all prisoners. The release of animals from fur farms is nothing new. In the former Soviet Union, Iceland, mainland Scandinavia, Western Europe, Britain and Newfoundland,animal liberation raids as well as accidental and intentional escapes from fur farms have resulted in mink and some fox being introduced successfully into the natural environment. In Britain, the ecological impact of these releases has been measured, and as liberated mink conveniently fill the ecological niche left by Britain's now extinct native otter population, the negative impact has been minimal. In Iceland's island ecosystem, and in parts of Scandinavia, mink have been slightly more destructive to the ecological balance. Never has the question of formerly captive minks survivability been questioned by those in the know, only the level of impact these beautifully fierce predators have as the successfully readapt to a wild life.

In North America, it's a whole different story. Although there is a Eurasian species, mink are believed to be native to North America with the theory that the Eurasian species originated from North American ancestors who crossed the ice bridge between this continent and Asia. Previous to the "discovery" of the "New World", mink were one of many aquatic animals that flourished in virtually every lake and waterway in North America except the desert regions. The war against the mink nation that continues today, began when the first Europeans invaded their homeland. When the Mayflower first rounded Cape Cod, Massachusetts in 1620, already Jamestown, Virginia was the hub of an extensive fur trade. A price list from 1621 records mink among other animals fetching up to ten shillings apiece on the market to which modern day fur farmers can claim as their bloody lineage. To their credit, the fur trade can also accept responsibility for causing the extinction of the native mink salt water cousin, the sea-mink. Nearly twice the size of their freshwater relations, and recorded as Inhabiting the whole Northeastern North American Seaboard, all that remains of this being are two skins and a number of bones. That and of course the memory of one furrier who before the American Revolution recalls the pelt of the sea-mink selling for five guineas. And so it is, by the end of the 19th century, fresh-water mink were severely depleted from their former range in all of North America by a fur industry thirsty for the blood of this continents fur animals.

...all captive mink should be released one way or another from their prisons we call fur farms. Highly intelligent, fierce and very adaptive, mink are anything but successfully domesticated.

Unlike their European and Scandinavian counterparts, mink farmers in the United States and Canada began the attempted domestication and economic exploitation of mink often from live captured wild mink populations. In the 1920's this new element to the fur trade began. In 1925 Kent Vernon's family in Northern Utah (now president of the Utah Fur Breeders Co-Op) live-trapped chicken-killing mink from the wild and began breeding them in captivity. In 1927 the U.S. Government opened its Experimental Furbearer Research Station in Corvallis, Oregon (shutdown by an ALF raid in 1991) and began experimentation in different techniques to breed wild mink in captivity. With overexploited wild mink populations unable to satisfy the demands of an increasing demand for fur, trappers across North America began to captive-raise wild mink, and in the 1930's discovered fur mutations that altered the minks fur color.

Now just 70 short years later, mink farmers are still battling the still dominant wild DNA of captive mink that causes these normally free-roaming solitary animals to contract diseases from close confinement, self-mutilate and even cannibalize their own kind. All for the price of a fur coat.

Beginning in 1990, I researched mink farms by visiting over 25 in Oregon, Washington, Utah, Idaho, Montana, and Michigan. What began as a quest to document conditions and killing techniques on fur farms quickly turned into the study of the first ever attempted domestication of a North American predator. What I learned both by my research and by the rescue rehabilitation, and release of sixty mink from a Montana mink farm leads me to conclude that all captive mink should be released one way or another from their prisons we call fur farms. Highly intelligent, fierce and very adaptive, mink are anything but successfully domesticated. Arguments by the fur industry that mink are domesticated are ludicrous. Like all wild animals held in captivity, some mink when released from their cages will fare better than others. Many factors contribute to successful mink reintroduction as does the impact they will have on their surrounding eco-system. These are issues I will address in this article.

In 1990-91, I spoke with many mink farmers and researchers who, believing I was a mink farmer, instructed me in ways to avoid my mink from losing their recessive genetic structure that gave them the fur quality and color variations that separated them from their wild relations. Captive mink are genetically 95% similar to their wild counterparts, the only difference besides behavior being fur color and quality which is solely maintained by a scientifically controlled diet. This is the key to maintaining their genetic difference from wild mink, black and dark mink being the closest genetically to wild mink. Jim Leischow, a second generation mink farmer from Kenosha, Wisconsin in a discussion at the 1991 Seattle Fur Exchange auctions described to me how without a scientifically controlled diet mink on any fur farm would lose their recessive genes, and overpowered by their dominant wild genetic structure, return to their wild roots in a few generations. Leischow also detailed how a mink escapee that breeds with a wild mink would produce offspring that in one more generation would have lost all traces of any altered genetic structure. The difference between mink and other animals raised in intensive confinement is totally incomparable as not only are all other domesticated livestock ungulates and herbevorous but also having been domesticated for well over a thousand years. The closest comparison which is hardly applicable but for the sake of argument will be used is the domestication of the common house cat. Originating in ancient Egypt, the cat has had over two thousand years of domestication, yet still this feline predator is proven capable of surviving in the wild as feral populations in the U.S. and Britain will attest to. Once again, survivability is not the issue but impact on their native species. Captive mink are so far away from successful domestication that they rarely are caged together unless with their own off-spring, and then only before they reach sexual maturity. Self-mutilation and cannibalism, which is not uncommon on mink farms is yet further proof of a wild animal's behavior as it attempts to deal with the neurosis caused by intensive confinement. Anyone who has ever been on a mink farm has heard the incessant scratching mink will make as they attempt to escape or attack their captive neighbors, separated only by a plastic or metal divider. This also is common behavior of a wild predator unfamiliar with close proximity to others of its own species. The psychological as well as physical torture associated with the confinement of mink naturally accustomed to solitary wandering is beyond our comprehension. Genetically speaking, mink are predominantly still wild, separated only by a controlled diet from their wild ancestors. Physiologically they are identical. What remains as the greatest division between wild and captive mink is predatory instincts and natural behavior that dictates how they hunt, find shelter, build nests, and forage. Fear of other animals is minimal as mink are renowned for their fearlessness.

Captive mink are genetically 95% similar to their wild counterparts, the only difference besides behavior being fur color and quality which is solely maintained by a scientifically controlled diet.

These separations were the basis of personal research into the potential for rehabilitation and release of the 60 mink I had purchased in Montana in 1990. The Coalition Against Fur Farms (CAFF) began as a rehabilitation project, the objective being to determine the feasibility to reintroduce native mink from fur farms back into their natural habitat. In January of 1991 the trials began as CAFF volunteers placed mink in cages four times as large as their previous enclosures and introduced natural objects such as logs, rocks, plants and gallon baths. Fur farmers had assured me that escaped captive mink already had at least a 50% chance of survival, and CAFF hoped to increase that figure as much as possible. The introduction of 12"x6" bathtubs allowed the mink their first opportunity to acquaint themselves with water besides that that came from a small water nozzle or dish. Their response was to fully submerge themselves and spin in a cycle that quickly splashed all water out of their baths. This would be followed by grooming sessions in which the mink dried themselves and maintained utmost cleanliness, yet another sign of a healthy wild animal. Once the mink had built up muscular strength after their time in a fur farms cramped conditions, we began to nurture hunting instincts. Though morally opposed to the killing of animals CAFF felt the survival of our captive mink could not be guaranteed without a minimal amount of live-animal feeding. We knew that our project would later be used by others to determine the potential for successful reintroduction of fur farm prisoners, and so chose to do everything possible to ensure not only their survival but also their survival without human dependency. This also meant live-feeding which would teach them how to hunt rather than scrounge near or where humans were. This would ensure greater independence and less likelihood of human/mink encounters. Then mink in our rehabilitation project dug into their instinctual memory to remind themselves how to first seize the prey with one bite, then without releasing it, crush down until the skull or neck was broken. Then the mink would release its prey and scour the logs and rocks for others that might have gone unnoticed. Once assured of no other present prey, the mink would return to the kill and eat everything or place the remainder in its nest just like wild mink. Once the mink had learned to kill and had tasted live food, they refused to eat the scientific diet we had been supplied by National Fur Feeds.

Finally, we released the mink to natural waterways across the Northwest's many forest lands. Always far from human habitations,and never within a 5-mile radius of another captive released mink of the opposite sex. We wanted to ensure the breeding only with wild mink. We also waited until the natural breeding season had passed so as not to burden the mink with the upbringing of offspring in their first season of freedom. Our mink releases were filled with encouraging signs that the mink would survive. On one release a mink quickly found an abandoned animals burrow, and as we left we could see its head peeking out watching our departure. Another release had a young female mink burrowing under a log, gathering twigs and grass building a nest. Still another mink quickly found a mouse hole, and burying its nose in it began to dig frantically. On many releases near streams the mink were quick to explore the shore of the water, eventually plunging in and swimming completely submerged playing with pebbles and rocks with their forepaws. Returning to one release site weeks later I quickly found mink droppings and tracks near the creek and the dropping contained hair from a preyed upon animal. Most of the behavior exhibited by our mink was not learned, but simply returned to them as they found themselves in their natural element.

It is my belief that the liberator becomes responsible for the lives of the liberated when she/he endeavors to free them. Ideally the liberated will become truly independent of human needs and achieve complete liberation. But until then there are a number of factors that liberators can influence and by doing so increase the possibilities of a liberated mink's survival. The priority being the time of year liberations take place. The best time being between May and January, the worst being during the breeding and kit-bearing season. Releasing an impregnated mink increases the needs of the liberated mink for food and shelter, female mink naturally raise their kits alone. Releasing mink once they have given birth to a litter will also mean abandonment of kits which sometimes can be foster-raised by another mink mother. Of course it cannot be overlooked that all captive mink are destined for death, and there is room for debate as to what kind of death is most desirable, a mink being the only one to surly know. Still I have hesitated to release mink from fur farms near heavily travelled roads knowing a large number would become roadkills. This is yet another moral dilemma the liberator must face when they decide to open the cages. Personally, I have seen mink watching as the gas-chambers are wheeled down the rows of cages and seen them screech frantically and attempt all manner of last minute escape as it becomes painfully evident that they will die.

There is also the very compelling argument that even with the recapture of 100% of all released mink from a targeted farm, that still the breeding has been completely disrupted as farmers have no way of separately identifying their breeder mink from their pelter mink. A mink raised to be pelted will often be in a much smaller cage than a breeder mink. For this reason liberators would do best by releasing mink from both large and small mink cages so as to confuse the two. As of yet mink farmers have not devised methods of tagging, branding or tattooing individual animals except for labeling on the cage. For this reason it is always advantageous to remove all record-keeping cards from cages when releasing mink. Transportation of mink either a short distance from cage to guard fence of a larger distance is best achieved by securing the mink individually in its nestbox. A small flat piece of sheet metal is often used to divide and block the hole leading from the nestbox to cage at which point the nestbox can then be removed and the hole blocked with a gloved hand or more permanent means for long transportation. Despite the average liberators aversion to leather, nothing protects human skin better than a thick pair of leather welding gloves which usually can be found lying around a mink farm. With criminal DNA testing liberators should take every precaution not to leave a blood trail of their own. Remember, you are dealing with a wild predator unfamiliar to kind human hands.

It is not uncommon for a mink to travel 5 miles in one night (they are mostly nocturnal) and a large number of mink released in one area will not stay concentrated but will travel until they establish a territory all their own...

Often given the choice, a mink will leave the immediate area once outside of the guard fence, which usually is a 5-6 foot fence lined with sheet metal to prevent escape should a mink get out of its cage. If left inside the guard fence often a mink will linger simply because of the smell of food or other mink cages, and also because of the familiarity of its own nestbox which is all it has ever known. Once a large number of mink have left the guard fence area the quickest method of natural distribution is waterways. Without interference from the irate mink farmers attempting to recapture his furry investments, mink will not overcrowd themselves in the wild. It is not uncommon for a mink to travel 5 miles in one night (they are mostly nocturnal) and a large number of mink released in one area will not stay concentrated but will travel until they establish a territory all their own, searching out other mink only to breed. This leads us to the issue of ecological impact caused by mass mink liberations on their new environment. There will be a noticeable impact on local prey populations and for this reason liberators should research target areas to guarantee that the sensitive habitat of a vulnerable endangered species is not nearby. Mink will attack almost anything. I've seen mink chasing large dogs and heard a story of one seen flying through the air attached to the leg of a large heron, the mink unwilling to release its targeted prey.

Mink will kill beyond their need, and for this reason caution should be taken when releasing mink near large concentrations of small animals. Mink are ferocious. Long persecuted at the hands of man native predators are continually routinely killed by ranchers and other gun-toting humans. Much like the coyote has filled the ecological niche the wolf has left behind and by doing so extended its own historic range, so also do mink have the potential to fit nicely into the niche otters and other predators have left as their numbers are continually reduced by humans. Native mink populations are still drastically reduced, and given large-scale mink liberations, individual mink are sure to redistribute themselves to their former habitat with a little help from their two-legged friends.

There should be not hesitation to reintroduce captive mink into their native habitat. The ideal environment being undeveloped areas with a nearby water source and infrequently used roads. As ALF liberators open the cages, they not only liberate an individual animal but the whole species. Mink, fox, bobcat, and lynx farm liberations are not only a blow to a fur farmers profit margin but also a boost to North America's ravaged environment. With an absence of natural predators, prey populations often explode causing undue harm to their environment and are also known to spread disease. By releasing fur farm prisoners, liberators are guardians of healthy eco-systems. Before one single animal abuser can argue the merits of a captive fur animals impact on the natural environment, they must first address the overall impact the whole domestic livestock industry has had on the earth. It is no coincidence that the number one reason behind predator eradication is the protection of politically powerful livestock interests. Still it remains that for the mink nations of North America the shortest path on the road to animal liberation lies from the opened cage to the outlying guard fence.

Now it is time for liberators across the continent to follow the lead of the ALF in British Columbia, Washington, Utah, Wisconsin, Tennessee, New York, and Minnesota and take action to liberate the four-legged prisoners from the war on nature.

Until all fur farm prisoners are free...Open the cages!!!

And while on the subject of mink and mink liberation, what better time to introduce readers of *Underground* to a new publication that arrived recently in our mailbox: *THE FINAL NAIL*, a guided tour to destroying the fur industry. With 24 pages of information, including state by state listings of fur farmers, suppliers, etc, *THE FINAL NAIL* is a an informative booklet and a must read for all animal activists. The following four pages are just an example of what you'll find inside ... (see our Distro listing at the back of *Underground* for details on how to order a copy of your own.)

THE FINAL NAIL
DESTROYING THE FUR INDUSTRY
- A GUIDED TOUR -
Written and Compiled by
M. Clifton / B. Clausen Enterprises
- Summer 1996 - 1st Edition -

TRACKING DOWN A PRISONER

by Rabbix

In *Underground No.4* you'll have read a short article on page two entitled "Prisoner Support." This article encourages people to write letters of support to those people listed on the prisoner lists. But have you ever wondered how those lists are compiled?

When I first started out in the animal lib movement I just assumed that every activist knew about the Animal Liberation Front Supporters Group and so I assumed the ALF-SG would automatically know when an animal lib activist was jailed. How wrong I was!

Now, don't get me wrong. Of course a lot of people who are arrested know exactly who to contact, but some don't at that is the key point. some people who are jailed for animal liberation and Ecodefence actions have no idea that there is a support network waiting to support them. Without YOUR help these people may serve their ENTIRE sentence without receiving any support what so ever. Yet is so easy to help these jailed activists. All it takes on YOUR behalf is a little bit of initiative and research. The following account is what one person did when they heard of a person being arrested.

On 20.10.95, two barns belonging to an English farmer in Devon were set on fire. The farmer had his property attacked because he is involved with the trade in live animal exports.

On 11.11.95, "Jevon from Devon" heard on their local TV news that a man had been arrested and accused of the arson.

On the 12.11.95, "Jevon" watched the main local TV news where it was revealed the man who can been arrested was called Darren Cole and he had been remanded by Magistrates in Ivybridge, Devon.

On the 13.12.95, "Jevon" visited his local library and found out the main address for the Magistrates who operate in Ivybridge. He then contacted the Magistrates and asked in where had Darren been Remanded to? Although the Magistrates were not keen to give a definite answer, they suggested Darren might be in HMP Exeter.

As soon as "Jevon" had a possible prison address he quickly wrote a letter to Darren. In his letter "Jevon" explained a little bit about himself, asked Darren if he knew about the ALF-SG, explained a bit about the ALF-SG and then gave some general interest direct action news. "Jevon" also wrote to the British ALF-SG saying what he knew about Darren and his case (this information was just bits and pieces "Jevon" had picked up from the local news).

Darren was (and still is) at HMP Exeter. He was very greatful for "Jevon's" letter and as soon as he received it he wrote to both "Jevon" and the British ALF-SG.

Less than a week after his Remanding Darren's details were being circulated around the prisoner support network and both the British ALF-SG and Earth Liberation Prisoners Support Network (ELP) had been able to make personal contact with Darren. Prior to "Jevon's" letter, Darren was unaware that either the ALF-SG or ELP existed.

If YOU hear about a person being arrested, DON'T assume that a person will automatically get bail or that they will know who to get in contact with. If YOU hear about a person being arrested do everything YOU possibly can to find out if they have been charged and if so, have they been jailed? Both the ALF-SG and ELP networks would much rather be told about the same prisoner twenty times, than not at all. You will also, by your actions, give encouragement to the prisoner because, even if they already know about the prisoner support network, they will appreciate what you have done on their behalf.

This article is dedicated to Carl Robinson who in the late eighties was jailed for setting fire to a butchers shop. Carl never received any support whilst in prison. Not because he wasn't entitled to support from the ALF-SG, but because he didn't know about the ALF-SG and they didn't know about him.

PLEASE HELP TRACK DOWN THE ANIMAL/EARTH LIBERATION PRISONERS.

(a version of this article first appeared in Eco-Vegan No.7)

Doing time with the Animal Liberation Front

An Interview with Darren Thurston

How did you get involved in animal rights?

• I started getting involved in the hard-core/alternative/straight-edge music scene in 1985/6 and through that got involved in animal rights/liberation. I stopped eating meat, and, shortly after, stopped eating dairy and eggs. I formed an Animal Rights group called Citizens Organized for Animal Liberation because none of the local AR groups wanted to do civil disobedience actions or even demonstrations. They would do their annual anti-fur pickets and the odd anti-rodeo and anti-circus pickets and sit on the fence the rest of the time.

What led you take a more militant approach to animal liberation and join the A.L.F.?

• First off, animal rights organizing was very frustrating. I saw animals every day getting killed and tortured for human greed, vanity and food, while people wanted to write letters and talk to vivisectors about the 'problem'.

Secondly, you can't join the Animal Liberation Front. It has no central command, address, or membership list. The A.L.F. is everywhere. It's composed of dedicated people who take the first step and do something — smash a window, glue a lock, spray paint a butcher shop, free some mink, burn a meat truck, liberate some animals from a laboratory. Remember, YOU ARE THE A.L.F.! and the animals need you NOW.

How did you learn to do A.L.F. actions?

Post raid photos at the Ellerslie motel.

• I never really learned from anywhere or anyone. But I do remember an old adage that "practice makes perfect" or something along those lines. For those that would like to learn the finer details of how to do certain things, they are available in numerous booklets.

The morning after; Ellerslie cat & dog facility laboratory.

Recommended reading; An Animal Liberation Primer 2nd edition, Interviews with A.L.F. Activists, The Power is Ours, and The Final Nail.

What security precautions did you see activists take while involved in the A.L.F.?

• Physical security was a major concern of everyone as it always should be. You have to assume that every word you say over a telephone is being heard, pay telephones included. Never talk inside anyone's home or vehicle, both can and are bugged very easily.

...crowbar, large ball-peen hammer, portable electric drill, radios, radio frequency-scanners...

The best cover of course is to have never been involved in above-ground animal rights organizing at all. Animal Rights groups are the first place the police will start looking for suspects. Police regularly video tape demonstrations so they know who is active. More and more activists are forming small tight knit groups of close friends that they can work with. We are also seeing activists both here in North America and in England go underground so that they may continue direct action against the animal abusers and/or avoid arrest.

Recommended reading; Without A Trace, the entire Security section of EcoDefense.

What was the University of Alberta doing to the animals?

• I had done some research in the University library and found information about the ongoing experiments at the University of Alberta such as the testing of drugs on primates, spinal cord research on cats, smoking experiments on dogs, etc. A lot of the cats that were liberated would have ended up having their spinal cords broken and drugs tested on them.

How did you obtain that information?

• A lot of it came from lab animal research journals and other University publications at the University libraries. The vivisectors love publishing papers of how they torture and mutilate animals in order to get further research grants. It doesn't take that long to figure out how to use any University's computer search functions and check out ongoing experiments and specific researchers.

What did you do to prepare for the raid?

• I watched the entire facility for numerous days and nights familiarizing myself with the normal routine of the facility; the time the staff came and left work, when staff that lived on the farm/facility were at home and when they went to sleep, at what time University security did their routine checks. I also obtained both road and aerial maps of the area from local libraries.

The facility was quite large - it has approx. a dozen buildings including breeding facilities for mice, cows, pigs, sheep, dogs and cats. Two caretakers (both vivisectors) lived in separate houses on the facility.

Any other planning?

• I picked a night that I knew would be quiet, a new moon when there would be very little moonlight. We also made a visit to the facility the night before the raid to make sure everything was in place and to familiarize everyone of what the facility looked like and what their roles were.

What equipment was necessary to do the raid?

• hmm...... well, let's see; crowbar, large ball-peen hammer, portable electric drill, radios, radio frequency-scanners (so we could listen to both University Security and the Police), pick-up truck, cat carriers, paint, large bags.

How did you carry all of the equipment inside?

• There wasn't all that much equipment needed, a duffel bag and back-pack worked fine.

Hallway of the Ellerslie cat & dog facility.

How did you handle the security systems and enter the building?

• The facility had a security system including an ADT card entry system at the front door, and an intrusion alarm system - the vast majority of the facility was totally insecure though. There were numerous windows that it would have been very easy to break and enter through including windows directly into the large cat colony cages. There were many doors that could have been opened in a variety of different ways; pushing hinge pins out, drilling large holes right through, drilling or picking locks, or forcing the locks with a crowbar. Mysteriously though, the door we went to, which opened directly into the cat kennel room, was left unlocked?!

What did you do when you entered the building?

• Immediately went to work getting the cats out. The most important part of the action was getting the animals out safely. Once that was done the other tasks could be completed; finding and taking important files and of course economic damage.

There was approx. $100,000 in damage done to the facility could you tell us what equipment you damaged and why?

• There was only one small laboratory in the dog and cat kennel we were in. We damaged as much as we could in the entire building after all the cats were safely away from the facility. Damaging torture devices and other equipment makes them inoperable to torture and kill animals anymore - otherwise they could go back to torturing animals the very next day. Destroying the actual instruments of torture is practical. It ensures that the sadism will be stopped at least temporarily. It also ensures that they will be wasting money (which would have otherwise gone to vivisection) to hire extra security and install expensive alarm systems.

How did you damage it?

• Inside the laboratory itself, we forced open every locked storage cabinet dumping the contents on the floor, smashed sterilizers and other equipment and splashed red paint everywhere. In their office, boxes of files pertaining to illegal sources of the dogs they used and research were taken, everything else was scattered on the floor and then soaked in muriatic acid. Throughout the facility, slogans were spray painted, red paint splashed on walls, electrical cords cut, toilets and sinks smashed.

There was also one delivery truck outside used to transport animals from the facility back and forth to the main University lab, it had paint stripper dumped all over and the tires slashed and was also spray painted with slogans.

How did you leave the "blood" marks on the wall?

Extensive damage inside the laboratory room.

• Red paint that had been thinned a little and placed into several plastic 2 liter soda bottles, which made it very easy to splash anywhere and everywhere.

What did you wear during the raid?

• Coveralls to keep clothes underneath paint free, gloves, inexpensive throwaway shoes and balaclavas (in case of video security cameras.)

How did you get the animals out and how many were there?

• The cats were originally going to be placed in large cloth bags and then carried to an awaiting vehicle and placed into cardboard cat carriers. Upon putting the first cat into a bag it was promptly shredded. So much for that plan - plan two went into effect as the cardboard cat carriers were carried two at a time across a long field, two cats placed in each box and then carried all the way back to the awaiting vehicle. 29 cats were liberated all together.

How long did the University raid take?

• The entire time inside the facility probably took 3 hours or so, mostly because it took so long transporting the cats across a field to the truck.

How did you re-home the animals?

• I did not take part in the re-homing of the animals. The cats were supposed to go to a home that would hold them for a while and then send them off to other homes where they could live out their lives free. The homes didn't get set in advance as they were supposed to. With a lot of hard work and stress, homes were finally found.

Is there anything you would have done differently?

• The film and video footage taken and sent to the media had too many traces of where they were taken and helped police to track down the motel we used after words. More thought definitely needed to be put into not leaving any trace of location as to where the photos were taken.

How did you get caught?

• An informant named Jessica Sandham. She was a woman who had rented a motel room where the cats were to be taken after the raid (where video and still photographs for the media were taken). Jessica who rented the room didn't have to show any identification at all but instead showed her own and did not tell anyone else that she had done this. Investigators, who started checking every motel/hotel in the entire city looking for similarities to the media, video and still photographs, quickly tracked down the motel we used. The room was rented by Jessica who was already in the National Crime Index Computer (unknown to me or her at that time) as a suspected animal liberation radical which of course rang big warning bells. After placing her under physical surveillance for over a week, on June 19th members of the Integrated Intelligence Unit knocked on her door and asked her to answer questions. Instead of saying "NO COMMENT", or "call my lawyers" or "fuck off", she went with them to answer questions.

She was questioned for 4 1/2 hours on video-tape (unknown to her). Where the police tried all the typical police tricks and traps and she went for them all and talked freely about all she knew including rumors about the UofA raid. The police led her questions and tried to scare her by mentioning the so-called increasing "violence" in the animal liberation movement and my completely legal possession of several firearms.

Recommended reading; War at Home by Brian Glick, If An Agent Knocks, Agents of Repression by Ward Churchill.

What happened to Jessica Sandham?

• Jessica Michelle Charlotte Sandham (DOB Jan. 31/1973) is free, has always been free and was never arrested, we know immediately after the arrests she moved to another city and has since moved back to Edmonton and lives with her parents (12033-41 St., Edmonton, AB, Canada 403-479-1898). She was immediately disowned by the animal liberation community in which she was active, she has been labelled a traitor and informant in Canada.

Can you tell us about your initial arrest experience?

• I was arrested Friday June 19th at approx. 5:30 pm. I had just finished working at a small store where I was the manager. The police, who had placed me under 24 hour physical surveillance since June 3 (two days after the action), knew where I was. I was standing at a transit stop when I heard a car screech to a stop behind me. As I glanced over my shoulder I saw two large men, obviously cops, jumping out with guns drawn.

I was originally charged with 4 counts (Break and Enter, Mischief over $1000, Theft over $1000 and including a conspiracy charge that was later dropped) related to the UofA liberation, after I was taken to the police station. I was then put in a holding tank and finally brought into an interview room with one of the cops. He proceeded to ask me a huge list of questions, to which I responded with little except that I would like to talk to a lawyer.

As I was being arrested, the police were also executing search warrants on my partner's and my apartment and a friend's home. A warrant was also issued for the arrest of a friend of mine, Grant.

Can you explain your experience with the courts and jail?

I was finally processed after about 5 hours at the police station and 12 hours sitting in a holding tank at the Remand Center and moved to a really dirty and cold dormitory with 80+ other men. Next I was called out again and taken over to the police station to be charged with another 3 charges (arson and two mischief's). These charges were in regards to two actions at Billingsgate Fish Market.

One was in December '91 when the store and 4 large fish delivery trucks were spray painted with slogans, tires slashed and incendiary devices left on their front seats. Three of the incendiaries

Burned out trucks at Billingsgate Fish Market.

ignited causing approx.. $75,000 damage. The other action (also at Billingsgate Fish Company) was the following month when their store and three replacement rental trucks were spray painted with slogans and tires slashed.

After a few days, I finally got moved into a unit in the Remand Center, bunked up with a hyper-active 18 year old car thief, and another 56 'children' on one of two units called "the zoo" (so-called because of all the fights and craziness in general).

I saw two large men, obviously cops, jumping out with guns drawn.

I finally obtained a good lawyer, one of the top lawyers in Alberta, who took the case for a very low expense. He did his best and more a lot of the time. I would have much rather had an animal activist lawyer, but there's just not that many around in Canada.

Oullette Meat Packers after an A.L.F attack.

About four days after my arrest late one night just after lock-up, I got called out again and was brought over to the police station to be charged with yet more charges. This time I was charged with another 7 charges related to damage done to three billboards carrying advertisements for the Fur Council of Canada "Fur Our Choice Naturally". At one of the signs a note was left for Hook Outdoor Advertising telling them to stop running the ad's or it would be there most expensive advertisement campaign ever. At the end of December the A.L.F. entered Hook's yard and wrote a long message on the side of one of their vans telling about the horror's of fur production and one of the boom trucks was gutted by fire, another charge of arson. On Jan. 1, 1992 at Oullette Meat Packers a van had it's tires slashed, side window smashed and a timed incendiary device was left on the seat. Both the building and van were painted with slogans. The incense sticks had gone out (according to court testimony) for some reason - extreme cold, wind? And so one more attempted arson charge and another mischief charge. The police were telling me they want six years in prison.

Approximately June 29, 1992 a Canada-wide arrest warrant was issued for David Barbarash and photos of David were circulated to television stations and newspapers.

David was wanted for three charges related to the UofA liberation (Break and Enter, Mischief over $1000, Theft over $1000). The Royal Canadian Mounted Police visited several activist's homes in B.C. looking for David. David disappeared underground.

My attorney had seven separate bail hearings to try and get me released on bail, even with numerous conditions, to no avail. I was refused on the grounds that I 'was a threat to society' and that 'I may not appear for trial'. Even after my family offered to put up property and $50,000 cash for my bail. At the bail hearing before mine one day, the same judge granted bail for a person convicted of murder that was facing a trial for manslaughter.

Early September 1993, I finally got my 4 day preliminary trial, after I'd been inside for over 14 months. Jessica Sandham took the stand and testified about her role in the U of A liberation — renting a motel room, buying paint and meeting with several people from 'out of town'. She also talked about the Billingsgate arson and how I had allegedly said that it looked like it would have been easy or was easy. The police testified all about the actions that I was charged with. My attorney got the police to answer questions about the surveillance they undertook and we learned that they had me and my residence under 24 hour physical surveillance in December 1992 for three weeks. June 3rd two days after the UofA liberation they had set up 24 hour physical surveillance on me and Grant, both our residence's, Jessica, and several 'targets' that they hoped might get 'hit'. They had placed legal 'bugs' on both mine and

Grants phones and also a 'bug' in my residence. We also got the police to testify about involvement in the case from the FBI, BATF and Michigan University Police. Members from all three had actually traveled to Edmonton to take part in a second search of my residence, looking for more 'evidence'. Police also testified that the FBI took photocopies of all of my files, an entire filing cabinet. So four days later it was over and now it was time to wait for a two week trial.

After a few weeks I finally heard that my trial date was not going to be for another 8-12 months, and I would be in jail the whole time. The situation re: the UofA and the Billingsgate arson charges wasn't looking all that good because of evidence against me. My attorney had been trying to get me a deal where I would plead guilty to the UofA and the Billingsgate arson charges and I would get out with time served, the other charges would be dropped. On Oct. 12, 1993 I plead guilty to three charges - Break and Enter to Commit Theft and Mischief (UofA liberation) and arson (Billingsgate fire). I was acquitted of all the other charges against me. Later that day I walked out a free man after 15 1/2 months inside.

Within one week after I was out, I got a visit from the chief investigator, serving me with appeal papers. The police and prosecution didn't think that my 15 1/2 months locked up was enough. They wanted me to serve several more years. On March 8th 1994, five months after I got out, the appeal was heard at the Alberta Court of Appeals (the highest court in Alberta). The Appeals Court reserved their decision. Their decision came several weeks later; they sentenced me to another two years, less a day inside. I was taken into custody immediately and shipped back to the Edmonton Remand Center.

From Edmonton Remand I was transferred and spent 4 1/2 months in Calgary Correctional Facility (Spy Hill) and then 5 months at Fort Saskatchewan Correction Facility (The Fort). A lot of my time was spent on the phone helping out with other prisoners' support including Rod's (who had just been arrested) and working towards an early release. I spent my spare time reading, writing, playing cards, and working out. Time went by a lot quicker than in the Remand Center because there was a little more to do.

Finally out Jan., 1995 I was granted an early release under probation and partial house arrest. I accepted it and was out yet again. For 4 months I was to be home from 6pm till 6 am, parole workers would call every night to make sure I was home and also knock on the door every other day or so. I also had to see my probation officer every week. After aprox. 5 months, I was finally finished with the house arrest portion of my probation and now just had to visit every two weeks. Two days before completing it, my probation office ordered me over the phone to attend a meeting at his office on one hour's notice - I refused. The next morning when I called him, he told me to turn myself in - he had pulled my probation because I was allegedly seen at the airport boarding a plane (I was not allowed to leave Edmonton without permission as part of my probation conditions). After contacting my attorney for advice on what to do, he told me that they could pull it at will and that I would likely have to serve another two weeks until my sentence expiration. Three days later I turned myself in and served another 10 days.

What happened to your co-defendant in this case?

• Grant was arrested the day after me on June 20th on nothing other than complete speculation. He was charged with the same four counts related to the U of A liberation that I was. Aprox. ten, days later he was released on $4000 cash bail and stiff conditions including moving 3 hours away to another city to live with his parents, a curfew and report once a week until his trial. Grant did not have a criminal record and was 29 at the time. At Grant's trial several months later the prosecutor gave him a stay of charges because they had no evidence at all.

How long were you in jail?

• All together, just under two years.

What was prison like?

• It was the first time I had been to jail in my life so it was quite eye opening in the beginning. I didn't know what to expect really. You got used to the routine really quick - you don't have much of a choice. Overall it really wasn't that bad though.

Work with as few people as you need to, make sure you know them all very well and KEEP YOUR MOUTH SHUT!

Did you fear for your personal safety while in prison?

• No. Things were a little crazy at times, I got into several fights over my beliefs.

Timed incendiary devices inside Oullette Meat Packers van.

Did prison have any effects on you?

• Being imprisoned strengthened my resolve even more. It gave me the chance to improve my mind and body. I got involved in weight training and jogging which strengthened my body. It made me

Gutted inside of a Hook OutDoor Advertising truck.

realize even more that we need to keep up the pressure on animal abusers around the world on every level, both above-ground and the underground. We can win this war! I certainly knew that if I was caught doing A.L.F. activity, I could end up serving time in jail. But those are the risks we take. Every A.L.F. activist must be ready to go to jail rather than incriminate other A.L.F. activists or do anything that would put the animals' freedom at risk.

Do you have any regrets?

• I wish we could have taken every animal there.

What words of wisdom do you have for other activists?

• Don't let anything get you down, there's a lot of bad stuff happening out there, and things are pretty tough sometimes. Actions can still be done and NEED to happen. Work with as few people as you need to, make sure you know them all VERY well and KEEP YOUR MOUTH SHUT! You don't need to spread rumors or gossip about other activists and actions or about your own. I'm in this for the animals - if you're not, get the fuck out.

Thank you for your time and for all that you have done for the animals. The personal sacrifices you made for animals are truly inspiring and needed if we ever want to see animal liberation become a reality. Best wishes to you Darren.

All recommended reading booklets can be obtained from the North American A.L.F.S.G. Distribution, send a SASE to P.O. Box 767295, Roswell, GA 30076, USA (New Address)

SPECIAL SUPPLEMENT TO UNDERGROUND

ROD CORONADO AND THE U.S. ANIMAL LIBERATION MOVEMENT

Tracking the Rumours, Tackling the Truth

A NOTE FROM THE EDITOR

Welcome to Underground #5. In a slight break from the format we've been using for the past couple of issues, we've decided to skip the Editor's introduction at the start of this issue and simply put everything we have to say together, here, at the start of this special supplement. We hope that the following background info can explain a bit about how this focus on Rod Coronado and the U.S. grassroots animal rights movement came about, so that readers of Underground have a context within which to place these writings.

BACKGROUND

In March of 1996 the NA-A.L.F.S.G. began to hear a number disturbing rumours about Rod Coronado, rumours that had apparently been circulating amongst animal activists soon after Rod received his sentence of 57 months (August 1995) for his participation in the A.L.F.'s Operation Biteback. We began to receive angry letters from a few U.S. activists demanding to know why we were still supporting Rod, especially since he "had turned his back on us."

As spring turned into summer, we heard from a variety of people, all quite certain in the validity of their information, that Rod was now a meat eater, that maybe Rod had named names in court, that he killed animals. People felt that Rod had denounced the A.L.F. and animal rights in general and was thus no longer deserving of support. When pressed for more information as to the proof of these allegations, the majority of those asked simply said that they had heard this from people they trusted. Some of the rumours could be directly linked to a press release put out on the internet by the Americans For Medical Progress, a spindoctor agency for the biomedical community, which contained quotations allegedly from Rod Coronado's sentencing statements in which he distanced himself from the animal liberation movement. Few of the people we spoke to about the rumours circulating had been in contact with Rod or had made an attempt to verify the rumours with him. Instead, we found that all too many people had been quick to believe and condemn Rod on the basis of what they heard third and fourth hand over the telephone and in person at rallies and demos.

With the help of several concerned supporters, the NA A.L.F.S.G. directly contacted activists who seemed to be the source of many "rumours" (or at the very least were indicated as having passed on information about Rod to others). A letter was sent out asking for details, sources, etc regarding Rod and the question of meat eating, "betrayal of the movement," the wearing of fur, etc. Out of ten people sent this letter, only two people chose to reply. Otherwise, silence. This took place over 5 months ago.

Meanwhile, the letters condemning Rod continued to be written, only this time they were being sent directly to Rod and not the NA-A.L.F.S.G.. Copies of Rod's sentencing statements began to circulate through the grassroots movement, and activists angry at Rod's apparent withdrawal from the animal liberation movement threatened to withdraw their support from both him and the NA-A.L.F.S.G. Aware that his sentencing statements were floating around, but unaware of the motivation behind the circulation of these pages, Rod had his entire court documents sent to the NA-A.L.F.S.G. for our inspection. We have spent what now amounts to a huge chunk of the past few months reading through hundreds and hundreds of pages of court documents, including the entire day long sentencing report (not just Rod's statements) looking for anything that may indicate that Rod should not be receiving support from the S.G.. We found nothing that indicated Rod broke the Supporters Group's stipulations for support **[1. Was the action for the animals? 2. Don't name names.]** We wrote to both the A.L.F.S.G. (UK) and to Zab, who ran the NA-A.L.F.S.G. before us, for their thoughts on what was happening. Both letters are to be found at the start of this section.

As things seemed to be going from bad to worse and the rumours continued to spread, and since no one involved was ready to stand up and stand behind the things being said (either directly to Rod or in response to the S.G.'s enquirers), Rod decided it was time to bring everything into the open himself. The focus of this supplement is an open letter that Rod has written for *Underground* in which he outlines his history in the movement, his position with regards to animal liberation, his reasons for saying what he did in court, and some of the reasons he feels he has been losing support from the grassroots movement. Any person who has been mentioned in Rod's letter in any way has been given the opportunity to respond in kind. These responses follow Rod's letter and address a variety of concerns raised. We ask that readers look beyond the sometimes emotional, often accusatory aspects of some of the things said within the letters printed in this supplement, and focus instead on the important issues raised by everyone concerned -- issues of prisoner support, activist networking, court strategies, etc.

NA-A.L.F.S.G.'S POLICY ON SUBMISSIONS

Perhaps it is important to once again state our policy with regards to submissions/letters to *Underground.* As it states quite clearly on page 2, we do not believe in censorship. While we have serious concerns about the nature of the following series of letters, we are also very much aware of the destructive nature of the silence that this issue has existed in. Up to this point, there has been no attempt to address any of the concerns raised about Rod Coronado and the issue of support. As we see it, *Underground* and the North American A.L.F. Supporters Group exists because A.L.F. prisoners exist. Unable to directly address the things being said about him or to confront activists whom he feels may be responsible for undermining support, *Underground* allows Rod Coronado the chance to have a voice in this matter. At the same time, those mentioned in Rod's letter have every right to say what ever they feel is necessary in response to Rod's letter. As it stands, the NA-A.L.F.S.G. is not interested in taking sides on this issue. We support Rod for a variety of reasons as outlined at the end of this article. By printing Rod's article and the series of replies, we are in no way trying to say "we support A's position and not B's." No submission has been edited or re-worded. The replies to Rod's letter are ordered as we received them. It is also important to mention that Rod has had direct input in this matter every step of the way and fully endorses the publication of these letters.

THE NA-A.L.F.S.G. AND PRISONER SUPPORT

The North American A.L.F. Supporters Group fully supports Rod Coronado, and has done so from the start. Let me repeat that. We support Rod. To us, the issue is not whether Rod ate a vegetarian burrito with cheese on it, or whether Rod told a US court that he has forever ended his involvement with the A.L.F. and wants to move on -- the issue is whether Rod Coronado, as an A.L.F. activist jailed for participating in an operation that cost the fur industry over $2 million dollars, should be left to rot in a jail for 57 months, or should he receive any and all support we can provide? A.L.F. Supporters Groups around the world have very simple criteria for who receives support. First, was the person's actions done for the animals? Secondly, did the person at any time grass on fellow activists? Support from the NA-A.L.F.S.G. is not determined by personal politics, what the activist is like as a person, whether they are vegetarian vs. vegan or whether the co-ordinators of the S.G. like the person in question. From its humble beginning out of the Band of Mercy in the early '70's, A.L.F. activists themselves have stipulated the support policy that the UK Supporters Group (started in 1982) and the Canadian/North American S.G. (1984) has followed since then.

The original Canadian A.L.F. Supporters Group was formed in 1984, three years after the first A.L.F. action where 1 cat, 5 rabbits, 1 rat and 14 guinea pigs were liberated from a laboratory at the Hospital for Sick Kids in Toronto, Ontario. In the late 1980's a U.S. A.L.F.S.G. briefly started up, did some good press work, sold a lot of merchandise and then after a lot of police pressure and internal problems, disappeared. The Canadian A.L.F.S.G. stayed in Eastern Canada until 1990, when it was transferred to activists in Edmonton, Alberta. With the arrest of A.L.F. activist Darren Thurston in June of 1992, the S.G. moved again, to Victoria, British Columbia. In 1993 it was decided by several former A.L.F. prisoners and animal activists in the United States and Canada that it was time that the US was covered again by an active Supporters Group. At the time things in the U.S. were pretty crazy with Jonathan Paul, Deb Stout, Kim Trimiew, and Rik Scarce all being jailed for refusing to testify to Grand Jury investigations into the A.L.F. Anyone helping to run a Supporters Group in the U.S. would face a lot of heat, and just no one wanted that kind of attention at the time. Fortunately Canada does not yet have anything similar to the Grand Jury. It was decided that the North American A.L.F.S.G. should be created, and things have taken off from there.

A.L.F. Supporters Groups are here for the prisoners. What ever our personal feelings may be, as co-ordinators of a Supporters Group, it is our job to make sure that anyone and everyone imprisoned for animal liberation actions receives the support they deserve. They've sacrificed their freedom for the animals, and that needs to be respected.

Active A.L.F. cells should not be primarily concerning themselves about the potential media their actions may or may not receive. Quite simply, the action itself is what is most important. Once an action or liberation has occurred, that should be it as far as the A.L.F. activists involved are concerned. Events like "A.L.F. Appreciation Day" as organized by groups like SOAR are wonderful and we encourage any "above-ground" activist or organization out there to take full advantage of any press coverage they can muster. However, naive, uncritical and sacrificial engagement between A.L.F. cells and the media can often turn the focus from the act of animal liberation into the pursuit of newsbites and media events, separate and isolated from the reality of an A.L.F. action. The Animal Liberation Front has flourished outside the reach of the media. It did not need the media for the construction of its structures (or lack of!). Media coverage has never been the main motivator for an action, and never should be. Similarily, for "above-ground" activists or groups to use A.L.F. prisoners and trials simply as a means of generating media means that A.L.F. prisoners are forced to behave in a way that coincides with the code for correct media performance -- a code of behaviour that the media controls, not us. Political and media trials have their place and their use -- that's not at issue here. However, when our own concerns about "good" and "bad" press (or the potential media "damage" Rod's defense strategy might have) overrule our concerns for Rod himself (facing at the time as much as 22 years in prison), something is wrong. By insisting that OUR approach is the only one, by imposing our desires on activist facing prison, by insisting on media trials over any attempt to reduce a prisoner's sentence (even if it means telling the court that an activist has "reformed"), we are potentially condemning future activists to harsh and unreasonable prison sentences. As the U.S. government talks more about fighting terrorism and invokes new "maximum sentence" legislation in court cases, prosecutors may in the future be able to send young activists down for 10 to 20 years for A.L.F. actions. Who are we to say to jailed activists that they are "selfish" for trying to reduce their sentences if at all possible? A.L.F. martyrs may make good press, but how can the loss of their actions and dedication be in any way good for the "movement?"

As far as we are concerned, A.L.F. activists have an obligation to those that they work with within their cell, and to the animals that they are acting on behalf of. The A.L.F. belongs to no one, and activists putting their lives and freedom on the line have no obligation to fit any set of criteria beyond the A.L.F. Guidelines. If organizations or individuals feel they are unable to support someone because they're not vegan (or are queer, or are a woman or whatever) then that's their choice. No one is under any obligation to support any animal liberation prisoner they are uncomfortable with. Are we honestly saying that we're more than happy to celebrate and publicize all the liberations, the fur shop closures, the mink releases and the smashing of the labs, but once an activist is arrested, we may shut the door in their face if they've ever worn leather boots, if they try to reduce their jail time in ways we don't approve of, or if they've only been vegetarian for a few weeks?

ATTENTION ACTIVE A.L.F. CELLS/INDIVIDUALS:

We want you to know that the NA-A.L.F.S.G. will do everything in its power to ensure that those arrested for animal liberation actions are supported during their time in prison.
-NA-A.L.F.S.G.

In Defense of Rod Coronado

by the A.L.F.S.G. (U.K.)

The A.L.F.S.G. in the UK has been approached by a number of people from the US indicating that they are unhappy with our support of Rod Coronado. Their reasons for wishing us to stop supporting him revolve solely around court statements and other statements he has made distancing himself from the animal liberation movement in the USA.

In respect of the court statements, there have been a number of court cases in relation to A.L.F. and other animal activists where the people involved have denounced their actions and repented. The A.L.F.S.G.(UK) has a clear policy that what is said in court is the defendant's own business, as long as it does not endanger the liberty of another activist. It is obvious to us that what may be said in court by the defendant or their representatives may not be their true feelings, but could be the correct way to proceed at that time.

We have been in communication with Rod for a long time, before and after his arrest,and we feel his record as a dedicated activist speaks for itself. We have neither heard nor seen anything which leads us to believe that Rod has changed his beliefs in a fashion which would lead us to withdraw support. Rod's comment on withdrawing from the USA animal liberation movement is understood to be a personal decision he has made due to the way he feels he was treated while on the run, and us such we do not feel concerns us in any way.

What has been said about Rod and his actions is indicative of the fact that the USA movement has been fortunate enough not to have to deal with many prisoners over a long period. Rod's worth is as a human being who took great risks to save and protect animals, not as a vehicle to gain information from the state or as a symbol of martyrdom. We support him not for his unfortunate imprisonment but for his brave and selfless actions for the well-being of all living creatures.

We wish him a painless time inside and a speedy release.

A.L.F.S.G. (UK)
Personally Signed by:
Simon Russell

LEARNING FROM THE MISTAKES OF THE PAST

by ZAB, former Coordinator, NA-A.L.F.S.G.

Although I have been putting most of my energy to prison justice and native sovereignty movements lately, I am still involved in animal liberation circles enough to have heard that, for whatever reasons, people have been spending a lot of energy discussing rumours about Rod Coronado lately. This is having a heavy impact on Rod and on other people who should be putting their energy to better use than dealing with rumour and innuendo.

As someone who's been in and around activism for 25 years -- as a child in an activist family, and in my participation in animal liberation, environmental, and social justice movements as a teenager and an adult - I've seen a lot of mistakes made in the name of "animal liberation", "earth liberation", "social justice", etc. A lot of the time, I've been the one making some of these mistakes. So it's not as if any of us are perfect, or as if any of us are above criticism. That includes Rod Coronado. What disturbs me is not that Rod is being questioned, but that the way people are gossiping is really harmful. And, in my opinion, the questions being asked are not helpful ones - they're old rehashings of other movements' mistakes.

In the 1970s, the slogan "feminism is the theory, lesbianism is A practice" was quickly misquoted to "feminism is the theory, lesbianism is THE practice". What I'm hearing now amongst animal rights activists seems to be "animal liberation is the theory, veganism is the practice". Veganism, like lesbianism, is a part of liberation from oppression. But it is not the only contribution people can make to animal liberation -- nor is being vegan enough to end animal exploitation (just like licking clit is not enough to end women's oppression - I only wish it were!). All power to those people who make lifestyle choices that minimize their economic support of the animal exploitation industries. But just as it's not important to me whether or not someone jailed for burning bulldozers has ever used styrofoam, it's not important to me whether or not someone jailed for animal liberation actions has ever eaten eggs. We all contribute, in various ways, to industries based on exploitation. All of us in this movement contribute, in various ways, to animal liberation.

Rod is in jail because he was identified by the state as someone who has made a hell of a contribution to animal liberation. Whatever has happened since Rod's imprisonment, why is one aspect of animal liberation considered an important criterion for judging Rod's commitment? And why are people feeling the need to judge Rod's commitment? It would seem to me that anyone who has studied history would understand that even if Rod never lifts a finger for animal liberation again, he is in jail for his commitment to animal liberation. He is an animal liberation prisoner.

The A.L.F. guidelines lay out structure for what can or can't be called an A.L.F. action; they do not define who is or isn't an animal liberation prisoner. Veganism -- or any other lifestyle criterion -- is not a prerequisite for anyone wanting to take action against animal abuse and exploitation. And why should it be? Lifestyle is not just a matter of animal liberation ethics. It's tied in to class, cultural practices, sexual orientation, and every other aspect of our lives. I make choices about how I will live based on a complex set of commitments I have, commitments that sometimes conflict, resources that limit my choices in varying degrees. I have my own sense of what's right and wrong in different situations, and I don't expect that everyone in the animal liberation movement will agree. I also don't assume I have the right to any moral high ground, that I have the right to judge other activists based on where their own sense of "right and wrong" isn't the same as mine.

What I do expect is that there be room for me in this movement, that if I end up in jail for animal liberation activism that people will take care of me just as I would (and do) take care of them. We can all ask ourselves - if we were in Rod's shoes, how would we want to be treated by other animal liberation activists? What would we want from this movement? And then we can ask ourselves, are we treating Rod as we would want to be treated? If not, why? And if we know we won't be supported by the movement when we go to jail, how much will we really be willing to risk imprisonment ourselves? How can we promote direct action in one breath and then shit on a prisoner in another?

When we don't look after our own and embrace them 100%, we do the work of the F.B.I. When we demand that people be vegan to be considered a part of our movement, we send a message to people that there is nothing they can do for animal liberation unless they follow our rules, and we prove ourselves willfully ignorant of peoples' resistance to cultural and economic assimilation. When we tear apart a prisoner's legal strategy, when we set ourselves up as judges, when we slap each other down instead of help each other up, when we spend our time on gossip rather than on the work of liberation -- WHAT THE FUCK ARE WE DOING? Please, let's not repeat the mistakes of the past over and over again. Let's move on, to create a movement that can actually end animal exploitation and free all political prisoners.

Zab.

OPEN LETTER FROM ROD CORONADO

In Spring of 1985 a friend and I hopped the fence of a small zoo and clipped holes in a wire enclosure housing two small mammals who were later released outside of the animal prison. Red paint was used to spell out the letters A.L.F. next to the empty cage and thus began my involvement with the Animal Liberation Front. Now, eleven years later I'm sitting in federal prison serving a 57-month sentence for aiding the A.L.F.'s destruction of Fur Animal Research for the fur farm industry at Michigan State University in February 1992.

I've seen a lot in the last eleven years of my involvement with the animal liberation and radical environmental movements, ended up in jail more than a few times, been beaten up, threatened, and still have warrants in three other countries for A.L.F. and Sea Shepherd direct actions. Not all of what I have seen is a proud reflection on the struggle for animal, earth and human liberation. I've seen fistfights between activists who claimed to be advocates of peace, the promotion of animal rights actions with no other intent than to make money, A.L.F. activists who were more concerned with media coverage than the animals they helped to rescue. With all that I have seen behind the scenes of the animal liberation movement over the last ten years, I feel it is important that young activists know the truth about the often media maintained image of the animal rights movement. The truth shall set you free, and it is imperative that as a movement we recognize our faults as well as our strengths if we are to deal with them and continue growing in a positive way.

I believe that if A.L.F. prisoners are to be put on trial by their own movement as I have been by some, and support withheld unless certain criteria established by non-A.L.F. activists in the animal liberation movement is met, then I as an A.L.F. prisoner also have the right to bring into question the condemnation, lack of support and betrayal that I have witnessed as an A.L.F. activist by the animal rights movement. These questions are not intended to create yet another division amongst our ranks, but hopefully contribute to the mature resolution of faults within our movement that lead to the prevention of growth and foundation of a structure to support and create A.L.F. activity and prisoner support. And most importantly to help insure that the A.L.F. is never again met with tactics that drive a wedge between them and the above-ground animal liberation movement, a tactic that is purely and clearly a goal of Federal law enforcement in the past, present and future.

In 1992 when I rode away from the animal liberation movement and back into the indigenous communities of my ancestors, it wasn't because of an abandonment of a previously held philosophy, but a question of security and physical support. Since December of 1990, when I broke away from my employment from Friends of Animals as a private investigator, I began to receive criticism from the animal rights movement. This first came when the Coalition Against Fur Farms was formed with the buy out of a Montana Fur Farm. As outlined in the December '91 issue of the Earth First! Journal, the buy out of the fur farm was in response to what was felt as a failure of the animal rights movement to challenge the fur trade with anything but moral arguments. Our year-long investigation of the fur farm industry revealed the on-going challenge to domesticate native wildlife that could still easily be returned to their natural habitat. The animal rights movement had not supported a strategy using these arguments and chose instead to only see our investigation as a source of graphic video and photographic evidence of physical abuse of fur farm animals. The knowledge uncovered of economic weaknesses and vulnerabilities was ignored. The movement was quick to capitalize on our risks and efforts but completely unwilling to help us attack the fur industry with our new found knowledge of its weak spots.

Friends of Animals in Norwalk, Connecticut refused to endorse the fur farm rehabilitation project, and my former partner in the undercover investigation contributed by charging CAFF for his services to assist in the relocation of the lynx, bobcats and mink from the farm knowing that every penny of CAFF's money was going towards simply feeding the animals and building rehabilitative housing. During this time the only organizations to offer their support were the California Anti-Vivisection and Animal Defense League, the Good Shepherd Foundation, and Ingrid Newkirk who contributed personally despite PETA's differences with the project.

The rehabilitation project was a 100% success thanks to the tireless efforts of a handful of dedicated activists who often dumpster-dived their own meals so the animals would be able to afford their next meal. As animal liberationists and earth defenders CAFF believed it was essential that we prove to the fur industry and others that fur farm prisoners rightfully belonged and could survive in their natural habitat, rather than just philosophically argue for animal liberation. The proof of such an action would lead to the justification of massive mink liberations like we see today. It was then also that I solicited my undercover investigation information to the A.L.F. who did not ignore it and listened attentively to all the evidence obtained by CAFF.

In June 1991 when the A.L.F. began its Operation Bite Back, once again no animal rights organizations came out publicly to support the A.L.F. except CAFF and PETA. Following the MSU raid CAFF attempted to organize press conferences to counter fur industry press conferences condemning the A.L.F., but no animal rights organizations were willing to go public with support for the A.L.F. Thus it was CAFF alone who circulated A.L.F. press releases and videotapes and did numerous interviews with media regarding Operation Bite Back. So it was with little surprise to either CAFF or PETA that they became the target of Federal grand juries between 1991 and 1994. Following the Operation Bite Back raids in the Northwest only a handful of CAFF activists and supporters offered legal assistance and support to my involvement as a spokesperson for the A.L.F., JP Goodwin being one of the few who remains active in the movement today.

In April of 92 I received a copy of an FBI affidavit that named me as the sole party responsible for the A.L.F. raid on Washington State University in 1991. This and recent death threats from fur farmers helped me make the decision to go underground. In 1992 when I left my volunteer position with the Sea Shepherd Conservation Society after narrowly escaping an ATF helicopter assault on my home and CAFF headquarters in Oregon, I literally had to beg for financial support from animal rights activists and groups as most were fearful of FBI repression or just plain unwilling to support the underground animal liberation resistance. That is when I accepted the offer of others outside of the animal liberation community to take shelter amongst them where I would be fully protected.

In July of 1993 at a press conference in the Western District of Michigan Federal Building, U.S. Attorney Brian Smietanka announced the First federal indictment of an animal rights activists in the U.S. I was indicted on five counts ranging from arson to conspiracy all of which added up to a maximum of 50 years that I faced in prison. No co-defendants were named. Within days my face was in every post office in the country, published in USA Today and many hunting and fur industry publications. U.S. Attorney's announced their intention to use my indictment to help obtain evidence that would lead to further indictments of A.L.F. members. During this time, virtually no one in the animal rights movement responded in my absence to defend me or the A.L.F. and so the hunt began. Thankfully, a small network of activists welcomed me, themselves hardened veterans of FBI and U.S. government repression. They provided me with everything the animal liberation movement was unable or unwilling to. If its one lesson the animal liberation movement can learn from the underground existence of A.L.F. activists David Barbarash and myself in the US and Canada, it should be that we need to build an infrastructure of physical support that can financially and morally support A.L.F. activists who choose to live and fight from the underground. If we as a movement fail to do this, we remain nothing more than another special interest group. Its ironic that my loudest critics now were silent or absent when I was assisting A.L.F. actions and running from federal law enforcement.

People could have contacted me if they wanted to donate money or offer support but the FBI was sure to make an example to the animal rights movement of friends who had previously supported CAFF. CAFF volunteers were threatened or imprisoned, threatened with having their children taken away, and offered money for information. Had it not been for support from people outside the animal rights movement I would have been captured within weeks of my going underground.

In October of 1994 after my arrest, I was approached by many in the animal rights and radical environmental movements who were willing to support the fight for my own freedom. I willingly accepted all help offered, and to accommodate the diversity of the activists formed the Rod Coronado Support Committee. The committee was composed of indigenous women and men, animal rights and environmental activists and people of color from the social justice movements. The only problems faced by the committee were continued threats by the National Activist Network's Cres Velucci to pull out of the committee due to the refusal to accept the media strategy proposed by NAN. Though not represented in the committee, PETA was willing to cover over 80% of the legal expenses of my case without demanding any influence in the decision-making. This point was addressed repeatedly as NAN repeatedly accused me of caving into demands by PETA whenever I strayed from their own direction.

In November of 1994, I agreed to allow Larry Weiss, an attorney provided by NAN to be a member of my defense team. At that time I believed that my case would develop into a political trial addressing FBI and ATF misconduct as well as the targeting of the animal liberation movement for federal harassment. At the same time my defense lawyers received evidence lists from the prosecution and I was not surprised to discover that the FBI had obtained physical evidence connecting me to more than one A.L.F. raid. A type written letter by myself asking for funds to strike three separate fur farms that were later attacked and included as charges in my seven-count superseding indictment was the most incriminating. The prosecution also had DNA evidence linking my saliva to that of a cigarette used in a incendiary device that malfunctioned in a Utah fur farm. The FBI also produced fingerprints and handwriting analysis evidence found on a package of records stolen from a fur researchers office at MSU. Other evidence included letters, receipts, and phone records that placed me near many A.L.F. targets during Operation Bite Back. The FBI's coup de grace was fingerprints of mine found on an empty museum case at the Little Bighorn Battlefield Monument in Montana where a seventh cavalryman's journal was stolen in February 1992. The FBI also had phone evidence placing me near Denver, Colorado where a press release was issued demanding the return of

sacred indigenous religious objects in the same museum before the journal would be returned.

In December of '94 I was offered a plea agreement whereby if I testified to who sent me to Michigan to act as an A.L.F. conduit I would be given a maximum 18 month sentence. When I refused the government increased the pressure. Threatening to indict me separately in Montana for felony theft of a historical artifact which carries a maximum ten year sentence, the U.S. Attorney's also issued a superseding indictment adding an additional two counts of misprision of a felony and a racketeering charge for interstate organization of criminal acts which upped my maximum possible prison years to 70. I began to doubt that my upcoming trial would be anything but criminal in nature. The FBI was thorough in guaranteeing the possibility of imprisonment when they indicted me. That is why once I was apprehended a superseding indictment was issued with seven counts as the possibilities were greater that if I beat one charge another would impose an equal amount of prison time. From the start I knew I'd be found guilty of at least two charges.

Following my December '94 bond hearing where my pretrial freedom was priced at a $650,000 bond, my Michigan defense team met with me and Larry Weiss in the Kalamazoo County Jail where I was being held. My Michigan lawyers explained that due to concerns based on the changing agenda of my case from political to criminal, that they did not want to retain Larry Weiss as a defense team lawyer. They stated that they had no problems with Weiss being retained as a consultant and contributing lawyer but their firm had never and was unwilling to include an outside attorney in a criminal defense case. In the company of myself and Weiss my Michigan lawyers clearly stated that their decision was in no way influenced by PETA or outside sources but was one purely their own. They felt that my freedom might be compromised by others in political movements who were interested more in a platform for politics rather than a focus on getting me out of a tight legal situation in which I realistically faced about 22 years in prison. I asked Weiss if he would mind his legal advice coming to me, and then I would channel it to my lawyers directly. He agreed to this only to tell me days later when I contacted him that he didn't want anything to do with my case unless he was retained on equal standing with my Michigan defense team. In a phone conversation Weiss stated that if he couldn't make important legal decisions he did not want to help me. I told him I valued his opinions, and he still refused to work with me, even as a consultant.

Immediately following this, NAN pulled out all of their support for me and Cres Velucci angrily accused me on the phone of once again caving into PETA's interests and denying the animal liberation movement its day in court. I told him I was more interested in my avoiding over 20 years in prison than giving him and others a political platform at my expense. What influenced my decision most was that NAN and others who advocated me facing 20 years by going to trial, had never offered their support previous to my arrest. Either when I was an active A.L.F.

member in Operation Bite Back, when I was on the run from law enforcement, and fur farmers or when my indictment was issued in my absence. At these times anyone who claims to support the A.L.F. should do just that, yet almost no one in the animal liberation movement did. Yet now they were more than willing to tell me what I should do. Repeatedly over the years I have experienced criticism from activists who were eager to tell direct action activists what their focus should be, but unwilling to make the sacrifices themselves or support any strategy other than their own. Another major factor in the decision-making process of how to fight my indictment was what my potential co-conspirators felt I should do. The US Attorney, FBI, and ATF agents had always indicated their intent to call fellow CAFF activists into the case to testify. Their testimony might unintentionally contribute to further indictments as well as implicate those already indicted further before a judge and jury.

Some CAFF volunteers reassured me that they would sooner go to jail then testify in my trial. Contempt charges have imprisoned activists for as long as two years in some political trials, and I did not want others to pay for the criminal actions I was more than willing to assist with. The US Attorneys office readily admitted that they believed me to be only a contributor to A.L.F. actions and intended to use my trial to obtain information as to the identity of remaining A.L.F. members. My decision to avoid trial was not only to avoid a longer prison sentence for myself, but also to avoid dragging other activists into my case as well as endanger my free remaining A.L.F. comrades.

In February of 1995 I began plea negotiations with the US Government after having consulted at length with Earth First!ers Peg Millet and Mark Davis, who had both been incarcerated in federal prison after a lengthy legal battle that ended for them in a plea agreement also. No animal liberationist previous to my indictment has ever been charged in the U.S. with federal offenses. It is impossible for the NAN or other activists to claim experience and knowledge in a field never tread by animal liberationists in the U.S. Ultimately in any A.L.F. criminal case to come the actual defendant should be supported in any decisions they chose to make as long as those decisions do not include testimony which endangers other A.L.F. activists. Pressuring A.L.F. defendants to adhere to someone else's agenda is being no less manipulative than the U.S. Government. Fighting grand jury subpoenas is one thing, fighting a seven-count federal indictment in a four-year nation wide investigation is another issue all together. Especially when the prosecution holds physical evidence connecting the defendant to the indicted offenses. I always knew that my political actions involved committing serious federal offenses and chose to face the consequences once captured. In my opinion, that is the warrior's responsibility: do the deed but be proud enough of your actions to accept the consequences should you be caught. I was in no rush to enter into a legal process that I knew all along I was destined to lose in. Anyone who has ever known me or indigenous history knows how little faith we should hod for the U.S. justice system. I've never believed that crimes against the earth and animals would ever be seen in the same light as crimes against those committing them. The justice system is one that we can never win in. When representing earth and animals the government and businessmen always prevail. Originally it was widely reported that I faced between 25-50 years for the "crimes" alleged in my indictment. The fact that I was able to bargain only a 4-1/2 year sentence should be seen as a small price to pay for actions that cost the U.S. fur farm industry irreplaceable research that would have led to the further exploitation of literally millions of animals. It's a nice thought to think that an A.L.F. member would be acquitted by a sympathetic jury, but such fantasies for political movements labelled as terrorists rarely if ever become reality. Earth defense and animal liberations is a crime in the U.S. Governments eyes plain and simple.

In March 1995 I signed a plea agreement that not only ended a seven year FBI campaign against me but also resulted in the cessation of five grand juries investigation A.L.F. actions in Washington, Utah, Oregon, Michigan and Louisiana, investigations all of which I was a target for prosecution in, not to mention many other grassroots activists. This brought to an end the harassment of many activists the FBI knew all along had nothing to do with the A.L.F. A.L.F. actions will always be used by law enforcement as a justification to harass innocent parties. It's part of the strategy to divide those who participate in illegal direct action from those who might support them. Before I was even out of the airport from Michigan NAN member Jonathan Paul had left a scathing message of non-support and criticism on my answering machine accusing me of selling out the movement and asking me why didn't I fight my case like Leonard Peltier and other political prisoners. The answer? Simply because I don't want to sit in prison like Peltier who has been in prison for almost 20 years and counting. I refuse to sacrifice my freedom to provide NAN or others in the movement with a useless martyr. Any activist who wishes to be a martyr is free to commit the crimes I did and turn their trial into a political one, but I see no one rushing to the courtroom to battle the opposition on their own turf. My obligation is to the earth and I do her no good if behind bars for twenty years.

Jonathan Paul's phone call was the beginning of NAN's campaign to isolate support between the animal liberation movement and myself. Luckily, PETA never questioned any of my legal decisions and continued to support me even when my strategy did not reflect their own opinions. For as long as I have been in the movement PETA has supported the A.L.F. and any prisoners who do not slander their organization. Though PETA's tactics may not reflect those of many in the grassroots movements, they have always been willing to walk the talk of A.L.F. support.

On August 11, 1995 my prosecution culminated in my sentencing. As has been clearly documented in my legal proceedings, the prosecution was determined to make me pay for refusing to testify against other A.L.F. activists. Already I had been offered a reduced sentence of as little as 18 months if I only revealed who directed me to await the package of stolen research records from MSU. My refusal to do so was the greatest obstacle in receiving a light sentence and the prosecution was sure to make me aware of that, since my refusal to cooperate meant a criminal investigation of the A.L.F. would end with me. With no physical evidence connecting others to the A.L.F., law enforcement relies on coerced testimony from other activists, to lead them to additional criminal indictments in a conspiracy case like the A.L.F. investigation.

I am not ashamed of my statements to the judge with the hopes that I might receive a crucial three point reduction in my sentencing guidelines for acceptance of responsibility and expression of remorse. These three points translated into an additional 18 months on my sentence. Also, at my sentencing, the judge could have rejected the plea agreement forcing me to go to trial which is exactly what the biomedical, sportsman's and fur industry wanted to happen. In over thirty letters to the judge these special interests asked that the plea bargain be rejected on the basis that it was too lenient for the U.S.'s first captured A.L.F. activist.

The opposition knew in a trial I stood to lose where "victims" of A.L.F. actions could be paraded before a jury, yet if the past was any indication, I knew I could count on almost no one in the animal liberation movement to stand up on my behalf. Needless to say, the judge was not influenced by my admonishments and clearly stated that he could not give me the crucial three point reduction as my refusal to testify was not acceptance of responsibility, but obstruction of justice. Also he could not himself believe the sincerity of all my statements renouncing my illegal acts, stating that they contradicted numerous statements I made to the media in particular to Dean Kuipers of the *Rolling Stone* and Ken Olsen of the *Moscow Pullman Daily News* who had written numerous articles on my case beginning with the Washington State University A.L.F. raid in August 1991. The most damaging aspect of my sentencing was statements I had made to the media. The very same type of statements that NAN and other activists would have liked me to make at my sentencing had cost me 18 months, and to think that I would risk anymore time in prison for news print is egotistical and ludicrous. The only people who didn't want me to plea bargain were the opposition and the NAN.

Operation Bite Back's intent was to cripple the research and development base of the U.S. fur farm industry. Beyond the obvious dollar damage and liberated prisoners, the five raids on research institutions and fur farms cost the industry many millions more in profits, had the increased efficiency of university research been implemented into modern mink farming and predator control. The Animal Liberation Front is a strategic guerrilla force. As a guerrilla force its objective while I was a member was to neutralize its targets and disappear. That was the reason I chose to participate in Operation Bite Back. In the early 1990's I saw a movement unwilling to provide for above-ground follow-through of a effective illegal direct action campaign, without others willing to risk their own safety to support the A.L.F.'s actions so I gave up on that

---

U.S. Department of Justice

United States Attorney
Western District of Michigan

RECEIVED
AUG 16 1995
FREDERICK D. DILLEY
ATTORNEY AT LAW

The Law Building
330 Ionia Avenue, N.W.
5th Floor
Grand Rapids, Michigan 49503

Mailing Address:
United States Attorneys Office
Post Office Box 208
Grand Rapids, Michigan 49501-0208

(616) 456-240
Facsimile (616) 456-240

August 15, 1995

Frederick D. Dilley
Boyden, Waddell, Timmons & Dilley
5000 Riverfront Plaza Building
55 Campau, N.W.
Grand Rapids, MI 49503

RE: United States v. Rodney Coronado

Dear Mr. Dilley:

There were two things at Friday's sentencing that disturbed me, and I want to share them with you. First, I was impressed with what I believe is your client's genuine commitment to the Pasqua Yaqui community, and that community's affection for him. I thought Anselmo Valencia's statements and the presence of several members of the tribe in court spoke very persuasively about the good works your client has begun to set in motion. It bothered me, and I believe it bothered Judge Enslen, to think that your client was being taken out of this community at such a crucial time.

I also was disturbed by the absence of any show of support by any member of the animal rights movement. Your client has sacrificed a lot for those people, and I thought it was a shame that none of them thought enough of his sacrifice to show respect by appearing in the courtroom.

Your client has apparently concluded that it would be honorable for him not to assist us in bringing to justice the others responsible for the ALF arsons. I think it would be far more honorable for him to help those who need him most. It would be a tragedy for Mr. Coronado to be taken away from his community now, because he believes he owes allegiance to others who have turned their backs on him.

As we have discussed before, we are not interested in making your client the scapegoat for these actions, which we both know were perpetrated by others who were equally (if not more) responsible. If Mr. Coronado would assist us now, I would readily file a motion for a reduction in his sentence. Although Judge Enslen gave a fair sentence on Friday, I believe he would carefully consider a motion for a reduction in sentence under these circumstances.

Your client owes nothing to the animal rights community, and he can do a lot for the Pasqua Yaqui community. I hope you urge him to carefully consider this offer.

Sincerely,

MICHAEL H. DETTMER
United States Attorney
TIMOTHY P. VERHEY
Assistant United States Attorney

State prosecutors offered Rod a deal to grass on other activists. Rod refused.

avenue and chose a more active role in the A.L.F. I accepted that prison was imminent and that if arrested would not go through a trial where I attempted to prove my innocence from crimes I was morally obligated to commit. A.L.F. prisoners should be expected to do nothing more than remaining tight-lipped about other A.L.F. operatives when captured which is what I have done. Any other actions taken that increase the likelihood of a lessened sentence should be supported and encouraged. Our movement does not grow with prisoner posterboys, it grows with more action, and visible evidence to others in the movement that if you are captured for A.L.F. actions, the animal liberation movement will support you 100%.

What the animal rights and liberation movements do with publicity generated by A.L.F. actions is up to them not the A.L.F. or its members. A.L.F. members should not be expected to sacrifice more than they already have just to further the political and public image that others are unwilling to sacrifice for. The animal rights and liberation movements had over three years to capitalize on the actions of the A.L.F. since the beginning of Operation Bite Back, and did not. Neither did NAN or any other group attempt to build a support network for the A.L.F. while we were being hunted by the U.S. Marshals, FBI, ATF, state and university police. Nor did they respond publicly on our behalf when I was indicted in absende in July 1993. We were abandoned plain and simple. There is an important lesson to be learned from all of this. To now criticize the A.L.F.'s only captured U.S. member for not prioritizing the political or media importance of the animal rights movement instead of his own freedom is a disgrace to a movement that should mature to the degree of its counterparts in Canada and the UK which have built strong establishments of prisoner support based on nothing more than whether the prisoner is imprisoned for acts of liberation and their unwillingness to testify against other activists.

Following my incarceration I never once was approached or contacted by NAN or the Students Organization for Animal Rights despite both these organizations claims of supporting the A.L.F. and its prisoners. In April of 1996 another inmate told me of seeing the A.L.F. on the local news. That same week I received from CAFT (one of the only grassroots organizations that has never wavered in my support since imprisonment) a copy of "No Compromise" which detailed the past "A.L.F. Appreciation Day" which called for, among other things, support and freedom for A.L.F. prisoners. Yet none of the organizers of this event had or has ever written to me to voice their support. It is only rhetoric to promote yet again a media image of our movement's support for A.L.F. prisoners while the organizers themselves of the national "A.L.F. Appreciation Day" fail to do so. Its beginning to look once again like the days in the '80's when the U.S. animal rights movement's most vocal grassroots organizers issued press releases that mattered more to them then the actual reality of the movement and its treatment of activists.

There is nothing wrong with not wanting to support Rod Coronado as an A.L.F. prisoner, but if that is the intent of groups like NAN and SOAR, then they need to clearly state why they will not and not stand on their soap boxes and deceive people to believe that they support A.L.F. prisoners, when they do not.

At the same time an animal rights organizer here in Tucson, Arizona contacted me asking why I was not aware of the A.L.F. Appreciation Day and why my imprisonment was not included in the press materials provided to their Tucson animal rights group. I said I did not know and suggested that she contact the organizers herself to find out. After her conversation with Cres Velucci she informed me that Velucci said I was not an A.L.F. prisoner but imprisoned for the theft of the Cavalryman's Journal alone, had sacrificed animals in "Indian ceremonies," eaten dead animals, wore fur, and how could we know for certain I hadn't been cooperating with law enforcement authorities? These and a host of other rumors were given to an animal rights group with Velucci knowing from his own past experience that they would cost me support from the grassroots animal rights movement. It was also Velucci who went out of his way to obtain only the portion of my court documents that he knew would cost me support and who then distributed them to grassroots activists with the planned intent of severing my support from the animal liberation movement. All this, without any explanation that what they were seeing was less than 1% of all my court transcripts, the rest clearly detailing my refusal to testify and jeopardize others in the animal liberation movement.

Are these the actions of an A.L.F. supporter? Why did Velucci obtain and distribute a portion of my court records AFTER I was in prison and unable to defend myself? He or anyone else could have asked me for court documents rather than just taking out of context fragments that have in no way presented the depth of my prosecution which every interested activists should be aware of. And why did he and Jonathan Paul or others not attend my sentencing hearing if they were so concerned with my case in the first place? Never has either NAN or SOAR contacted me directly to address their grievances with my case. Instead they chose to initiate a campaign intended to isolate me from support.

As soon as I heard of Velucci's distribution of my sentencing statement, I made available all my legal papers to the S.G. to attempt to minimize the damage done by NAN's actions. If anyone in the animal rights movement was concerned about my strategy of fighting the government, all they had to do was ask -- and none did. Instead, I had to hunt down the source of rumors and disinformation before anyone was willing to acknowledge to me that the rumors even existed, and that, my friends is fucked.

The intent of this letter is not to launch into a time and energy wasting feud that diverts our attention from the real goals of animal liberation, but to face full on the undeniable detrimental actions by some grassroots leaders against the A.L.F. and prisoner support. If the uncomfortableness of dealing with such issues allows it to be unresolved, then we can be assured that it will continue to happen. The last thing I've wanted to do from inside a prison cell is initiate in-fighting but I fear if these issues are not addressed what happened to Deb Stout, Kim Trimiew, and Rod Coronado will happen to any other animal liberation prisoner who does not measure up to other people's standards. Cres Velucci and Jonathan Paul have been friends of mine, but their actions since my arrest have been those of anyone but a friend. Not only do they represent NAN, a grassroots organization with respect within the movement, but also the movement we all have been a part of for the last 10 years. If vocal grassroots activists have issue with any of my actions they should take them up with me personally before disseminating misinformation in a way that allows for our ranks to be further fragmented. To kick someone when he's down and unable to defend himself is not the example longtime veterans of the animal liberation movement should be setting for people new to the movement. And it's behavior far removed from what I would call friendship.

Anyone is free to criticize me for my actions, but to voice that criticism to anyone but me only allows for a one-sided uniformed discussion that shows potential A.L.F. members that the animal liberation movement is unable to support A.L.F. prisoners unless they mirror the opinions and views of themselves. If the actions of those who have spoken out against me are motivated by facts, then they should be direct with their criticism rather than spreading it to only those who can be influenced and who are not encouraged to solicit the truth that only I know, as a result of being the subject of that criticism. Over the years our movement's most radical fringe has often been a favorite target of criticism. I personally believe this is a tactic by activists who would rather discredit individuals in the illegal direct action movement then admit that they themselves should participate in such actions if they truly believe in the rhetoric they spout. Otherwise those who do take action are a living example of other activists' own hypocrisy. If NAN's criticism is founded in my traditions or lifestyles as an indigenous person then perhaps the animal liberation movement needs to begin a discussion as to whether traditional use of animals by native peoples constitutes oppression.

I am not a philosophically-based animal liberationist. My foundations for fighting against animal and earth abuse is my culture's religious teachings, my very DNA -- lessons that have taught my people for thousands of years to respect and protect animals and the earth. Prior to 1533, the Yaqui Nation subsisted on a plant-based diet and lived a pacifist existence. Only when the European conquerors arrived did we begin to hunt, though since then it has been done only after due ceremony or death could befall the hunter. When I returned to my indigenous community for my own survival I returned to a culture that does not separate any of creation from respect and reverence. All things are sacred, land, animals, water, air, and plants. Living on the handouts of others in my community meant that I haven't been as adherent to a strict vegan diet, and for those reasons I don't call myself vegan any longer, despite 99% of the time living what animal liberationists would call a vegan lifestyle.

I am an animal liberationist and an indigenous traditional, and I do not view my ceremonial use of animal parts derived from roadkills as exploitation or abuse. If the animal liberation movement is to label traditional indigenous use of animals in religious ceremonies as oppression, then it not only is severing the potential for a strong alliance, but also establishing behavior which is nothing more than a thin guise to keep the animal rights movement as it is, predominately white and promoting cultural racism. And if the question is actions that cause animal suffering, than what shall be our stance on the everyday consumption of fossil fuels, paper, plastics and agricultural produce that are directly derived from the destruction of wildlife habitat and the direct cause of animal deaths and earth destruction as a result of resource extraction, pollution and pesticide use?

As an indigenous animal liberationist I do not limit my measurement of my impact on earth strictly to what I put in my mouth but also by how much I drive, how much paper and plastics I use and what taxes I pay. I believe in a return to the lifestyles that supported human life on this continent for thousands of years, already tried and proven. Personally, this means the plant-based diet of my ancestors as well as less dependence on all environmentally destructive products and practices. A lifestyle that does not rely on ozone destroying computer manufacturing, financial support of anti-earth/animal/human corporations or any of the poisons of techNO-LOGIC society including animal and earth exploitation.

If these beliefs of mine call into question whether the animal liberation movement should support my eleven years as an A.L.F. activist and my present imprisonment, then by all means let us enter into a mature level of discussion and debate, and not limit criticism to whispered rumors about activists behind their backs while they are behind bars. And let's also address the issue of whether victory is measured in press releases and TV coverage or actual lives saved, live animal liberations vs maximum destruction economic sabotage. To limit our debates and discussions within our movement to whether someone is as vegan as others in the movement who use criticism as a substitute for their own action and constructive self-evaluation. Because truly if we all lived closer to our ideals of animal liberation and earth defense, many more would and will be imprisoned.

More than anything, the reason I have chosen to address the questions and issues raised in this letter is because the actions of some within the animal liberation movement serve the U.S. government's continued war against those who would defend earth and animals. We are doing the FBI's job for them when we disseminate rumors and misinformation that results in fragmented support for imprisoned activists. None of us are perfect, yet our diversity and level of commitment should not be used to isolate us from the one fight for animal liberation and earth preservation. The American Medical Association and Americans for Medical Profits (progress) must be laughing as they see their press releases and battle plans used to isolate support from an A.L.F. prisoner, as they have in my case.

As NAN states in an excellent article written in *Underground #2:*

"The animal rights movement can minimize the effectiveness of covert agents and informants by refusing to spread lies and rumors about dedicated activists - who are the subject of the government campaign - and tracing those rumors back to their source, where government informants can usually be found. Activists can wholeheartedly support other activists, especially those who are the targets of break-ins, grand jury harassment and defendants in political trials."

Only by confronting our differences head-on can we continue to mature as well as broaden our support base to include more than just a small segment of society that has been the tradition of the animal rights movement.

There are many ready to oppose the institutions of animal and earth abuse and in that opposition diversity can be strength as well as a bridge to unify the oppressed of other nations and struggles. To continually address the familiar and already converted we begin to lose touch with political reality and our hopes for a true struggle for peace and liberation, become lost.

I will spend the rest of my life fighting for earth and animals as will countless others across the nation in various struggles and movements. Let us fulfil our opposition's worst fears by uniting together to fight for our earth and her animal nations.

Rod Coronado
#389500
FCI 8901 South Wilmot Rd.,
Tuscon, AZ. 85706, USA

RESPONSE TO ROD CORONADO'S LETTER:

By Cres Vellucci
National Activist Network

I have been asked to respond to allegations printed elsewhere in this issue of *Underground* by Rod Coronado, a former friend and comrade in the struggle for liberation of all animals, human and non-human.

Before I continue, let me state, for the record, that this is a sad day for me to have to counter lies and innuendo by a former earth warrior. For, that is what Rod Coronado was. Make no mistake about it. Rod sacrificed much for the planet and the animals.

Sadly, all that has changed, my friends.

I have thought long and hard on how to respond to Rod's wild untruths. Frankly, I did not want to respond at all, but his lies about some of the most energetic people in the movement today cannot be left unchallenged. So, as difficult as this is -- and please believe me when I say it is among the most difficult decisions I have faced in 14 years in the liberation movement -- this is the truth, a story that must be told only because Rod Coronado seemingly wants it told.

And, while Rod sits in his cell -- initially because of his brave actions to save animals, but now as a result of a morally bankrupt philosophy -- it saddens me to think how all of this may isolate him further from the grassroots liberation movement. I take no pride in writing this piece for *Underground*, which many of us believe should have waited to print all of this. Because this can only strengthen our enemy, and weaken the resolve of some of our own.

But, that appears to be Rod's plan. To divide us, and to cause friction where there is none, and more friction where there is some already. Why he is doing this is a mystery. One theory is that he is just mad at being in jail. The other is that he has given up on the cause, and the struggle.

I choose the latter. The man I once knew is no more. The spirit in Rod Coronado has died. And, to give him credit, I believe it is the result of his trials and tribulations, his run for freedom and the pressures of the system on him. If anything, Rod should stand as an example of what can happen to any of us -- even the strongest -- if we lose our way, if we forget why we arestruggling.

In my heart, I hope that Rod Coronado finds his way back from the dark path he has chosen. I will welcome him then, as the brother I have always considered him to be.

The Network's Support for Rod

Rod has suggested that the National Activist Network and/or me personally caused "problems" with his defense. And, suggests further that we were "silent" or "absent" during his run from law enforcement. That is totally untrue. This is, in fact, what happened:

Rod called me immediately after his arrest, begging for help, legal and political. Attorney Larry Weiss and myself had to borrow the money to fly to Arizona to meet with Rod. But, we did what we had to do for a fellow warrior. Rod insisted to us that he wanted a political trial and would spend, in his words, a "100 years in jail to help the cause if that is what it takes." He added that "I will do it the right way, Cres, you won't have to worry about it this time."

Rod was talking about 1990-91 in California when a series of federal grand juries -- the first ones ever convened in this movement to look for the ALF -- frightened activists, some of them very good ones, so much that they sold each other out, took deals and helped destroy the real liberation movement in California at the time -- where, coincidentally, the majority of ALF actions were taking place in the U.S.

Certainly, as his friend, I did not want Rod to spend any time in jail. But, his spirit lived, and he believed in fighting the system that enslaves people and other animals. It was invigorating to talk with Rod, and plan a strategy of defense and freedom. Let me make it perfectly clear that this was ROD'S IDEA -- a political defense, a martyrdom, if that is what it took, to save the animals and the planet. I personally pledged to Rod that we would organize activists nationwide for him, and the cause. That law enforcement, and animal abusers alike would look back on Rod's arrest as a major mistake.

But, then, something went drastically wrong.

Although we worked for months on a plan, Rod and his new friends -- many of whom were not animal rights activists -- suggested they did not want to use the animal rights angle. In the end, they decided to not use a political defense, which Rod has originally suggested. In the end, Rod was co-opted, he was used....not by me, or the grassroots liberation movement, but by money of the nationals and the club of fear wielded by the government.

PETA's Pressure:

Rod was pressured by PETA to fire Larry Weiss, who as a nearly indigent activist attorney (he usually works for nothing) had already dropped his few clients, on my recommendation, to devote his entire time to Rod. Why PETA chose this action is up to speculation, but we do know in the grassroots movement that several PETA, or former PETA, staffers cooperated with the Justice Dept. in its attack on Rod. That would give PETA every reason to encourage Rod to NOT go to trial, which would have produced full discovery that some PETA activists are acting in traitorous ways.

Why Rod is covering for PETA at this time is also up for speculation --

my guess would be that they promised to pay his legal bills. Money talks, and for Rod, money apparently meant more to him than friendship with people like me and Jonathan Paul, the animals, the planet and the future of this cause.

Ingrid Newkirk even instituted her own plan, suggesting to many that I was an "FBI agent," something Rod and I laughed about (as did others in the movement who know I have been in the forefront of attacking abusive federal grand juries since 1987). But, these are the games that people play in this movement to get their way, to preserve their "image" and...to make money. Some of us DO NOT play those games, and as a result we don't have money, or an "image." But, we would like to think we help the animals, which is the bottom line.

The Network's History of Support

Rod has suggested the Network didn't support him hile he was on the run. First of all, we did not exist until late 1993. And, Rod knows full well that the LAST person he should come to would be me or Jonathan Paul. Because, as he knows, Jonathan and I (along with Bill Keogh) were, in fact, the FIRST activists to ever be indicted in the U.S. for ALF activity. Not Rod Coronado, but us. As a result, we were prime targets, and key people to watch. Rod would have been foolish to try to contact us.

Rod also knows that many did support him financially and otherwise. But, if they speak up, they could be charged with aiding a wanted felon. So, his claims of a lack of support are patently untrue...and he makes those claims knowing people and groups cannot come forward to say he is wrong because they would be subject to arrest.

Jonathan Paul and I had our own troubles. At the time of Operation Bite Back, we were facing 19 years in jail for our alleged involvement in ALF activities. Ultimately, despite the FBI and ATF claiming they had more than a half a dozen witnesses who had seen us break into a lab, the charges were dropped. Why? Because we fought them, for the animals, and for ourselves. We knew we were innocent of any wrong doing, and we would not give in to the government's threats.

Rod did. And, while he claims "non-support," those of us who were first indicted had virtually no support, except from a handful of supporters. Virtually no national groups helped us at all -- especially PETA. But, we didn't attack the movement, or other activists because of it -- as Rod is doing. We just held our ground, and fought. In the end, this strategy worked.

Rod says only PETA supports ALF activists. Why does he lie? Because he's getting his bills paid by PETA? Rod knows that the I have led the fight against abusive grand juries since 1987, coming to the aid of grassroots activists in California, Oregon, New York and other areas where the government has attacked suspected ALF activists. PETA hasn't helped, except for a few "special" activists they found lawyers for. The rest of the grassroots movement has gone wanting. And as stated earlier, some PETA members have cooperated with the government's "investigation" of the ALF.

Rod also acts like he doesn't really know who the Network is, or the individuals involved. Rod, we were your close friends, remember? In fact, the Network is....myself, Sheila Laracy, Henry Hutto and Jonathan Paul. Sheila, Henry and I organized the first-ever civil disobedience and arrests for animals in the U.S. We co-organized dozens of other actions. Henry and Sheila were the first activists to refuse to cooperate with federal grand juries investigating the ALF in 1990. Henry went to jail for 45 days (the longest time ever spent in jail by an activist at that time). Jonathan is a longtime environmental and animal activist with plenty of credentials and his 5 months in jail for refusing to cooperate with the grand jury in Washington stands as a victory against such tribunals.

That's who we are. And, Rod knows it.

Additionally, the Network is dedicated to providing legal assistance to grassroots activists. NO ONE ELSE is doing this in the U.S. Dozens of groups from New York to California and many places in between can attest to our help. We help do media, and provide legal expertise for needy activists in many states.

We help coordinate national actions, and co-produce *No Compromise*, the only direct action newspaper in the movement. We get arrested, go to jail, support others who go to jail from coast-to-coast, as long as they remain loyal to the cause.

We have little or no money, but we do what we can for our brothers and sisters in this movement. For Rod to say, to suggest, we do otherwise is an outright lie, and something I personally cannot believe he has said. But, he has.

ALF Appreciation Day

Rod criticizes this day, held first this year, that organizes support for the nonviolent ALF and their actions to free animals. His main reason for criticism? Because he wasn't the main focus. Someone should inform Rod that there are hundreds, maybe thousands of ALF activists in the U.S. And, only one is in jail -- him. And, only one is criticizing other ALF activists -- him. The Network and SOAR support ALF prisoners, if those prisoners still support animal liberation. Rod clearly does not (see his comments below). And, besides of all of this, the ALF (whether jailed or not) should not be doing actions for personal gratification. Apparently, many ALF, if not all, know that. Rod appears to have forgotten that, if he ever knew it in the first place....ego has no place in a war of liberation.

Morally Bankrupt Defense

Rod has said that "NAN pulled out...support" for him. That is patently untrue. Rod called us as often as 2-3 times daily during the early days of his defense. When he fired Larry Weiss (because PETA's attorney suggested he do so), Rod NEVER talked to us again. Not once. He has never written, and made it clear that he prefers financial help, to moral support of animal activists. Despite this, we have never gone public with Rod's lies because we still believed he had earned the respect of the movement, even if he now does not believe in the true freedom of animals from exploitation and torture. I personally believe Rod was embarrassed by his decisions, and was just afraid to call. He need not have been.

Our eventual disagreement -- one we never had up until PETA interfered by insisting on firing Larry Weiss -- was that we believed he had a political defense to his alleged participation in illegal activities. If Rod had taken the opportunity to talk about the injustice against animals, and the planet, and his native people, then, although he may not have won in court (but then again, he may have), the world would have known more about how animals are brutalized in this society.

Instead, Rod took the easy way out. Instead, Rod stopped talking with us. It was not the other way around. Rod cut off communication....and since he was in jail, we had NO way to get to him. He had made it clear it did not want liberation activists any where near him.

Further, Rod mistakes the intent of the U.S. government. He says that he took a deal, not only to get himself less time in jail (which didn't work), but because he wanted to save other activists from scrutiny. He fails to understand that the government's desire is to NOT jail activists, but to frighten them into leaving, or disbelieving in their cause.

That is exactly what has happened to Rod Coronado. He was broken, his spirit was destroyed and now we have a former activist sitting in jail lying about other still active activists because he, possibly, cannot live with what he has done. It is a very, very sad situation.

Rod's defense was morally bankrupt. While we understand that some in the U.K. believe in telling the court anything it wants to hear in order to get a better sentence, that tactic has not worked here. It didn't work for Rod, or others. Besides that, how ethical is it to denigrate your own movement in open court to get a better deal for yourself?

Some argue that it means nothing because you don't mean what you tell the court. I would say it means everything. It says much about our resolve, on whether we cooperate or not with an obscene system. It also shows the other side we can be broken. That is not something we need to advertise.

Rod says he could have had his sentence dropped to 18 months if he would have "snitched" on ALF activists. Hey, Rod, I could have had my charges eliminated if I had told authorities everything I knew in 1990-91, when I was facing 19 years in jail (and that was only state charges, the feds were also in line) and in jail on $250,000 bail. But, I did not cooperate in any way, refused all deals and eventually won.

Rod makes reference to Leonard Peltier, an American Indian who has been jailed for 20 years by an unjust legal system. I have better things to do with my life, Rod says, rather than be a "useless martyr" for animal rights. By making such a statement, Rod makes a mockery of Peltier, and other political prisoners like Nelson Mandela, who many times during his long imprisonment had a chance for freedom if only he would say the "right" things, whether he meant them or not.

For us to believe that we must bow down, and say we don't believe animals have a right not to be tortured and killed, and that those who do so are "victims" and not the animals, is a repugnant tactic - whether we mean what we say or not.

Where is our integrity, our respect for political prisoners before us, and the animals and the planet that we have pledged to help. Rod could have done a lot of good for the animals during his stay in jail -- now, he appears to just attack other activists.

What Rod and many in this movement do not yet understand is that we cannot lose. As long as we maintain our integrity and our belief that animals should be free. As long as that remains, they cannot defeat us.
They can jail our bodies, but they cannot take our freedom.

Rod's Statements:

Rod has said he is "not ashamed" of what he said to the sentencing judge last year in order to get a better deal for himself. But, he does not advertise what he said. Here are a few samples:

"... you need to be punished when you misbehave in society. When you cannot follow the law of society, you deserve punishment ... I want to retrace my steps first and go to the victims (of ALF actions) and I think that I ... can erase the intimidation and fear that some of these victims still feel ... I want to offer my hand in friendship to all of these people I have hurt ... I will no longer view any of these people as opponents or enemies..." **[Ed note: All the quotations as presented in this section have all had material edited out by the author of this article, (hence the "..."). For example, the above excerpts have been edited from over 4 pages of Rod's sentencing statement.]**

Think about this comment. He is telling the judge, and the government that the ALF should be punished. And, he is saying that he wants to apologize, and that ALF activists should apologize to animal killers.

"What I feel that I can do to the victims is to prove to them ... that what I have done is wrong, and to diffuse and take away whatever (sort) of people who would support the ALF by showing them their most vocal proponent is now an opponent ... I do want to serve as a deterrent to other people who might contribute to criminal activity such as I have been a part of."

Again, Rod is saying that the victims are not animals, in his mind, but those who brutalize animals. Further, he says he wants to act as a "deterrent" to other people who may consider being ALF activists. How can anyone support some one who believes this?

"I don't know that I can do that sitting in prison, where other people are going to be circulating free Rodney Coronado t-shirts and nag magazines and writing articles about me and holding me up as an ALF prisoner ... in England with the ALF a lot of times that it only served to inspire the wrong element of people."

Rod is admitting that he did not want our help. His claim now that he had no support is false. He refused to accept our help, because as he says, he would rather be shaking the hands of animal torturers than have people organizing around his jailing. Further, he added that the ALF support in England has inspired the "wrong" people. What people are those? Ones who care?

"I am not the Rod Coronado that the animal rights created and not the Rod Coronado that some people in the law enforcement agency might have created ... I started abandoning the movement completely, just as if it were old clothes that no longer fit me. Very comfortably, I abandoned it ..." **[Ed Note: For accuracy's sake, it should be noted tat this excerpt combines two statements separated by 21 pages, and has switched the order in which they were said.]**

Rod again points out that he is NOT an activist, and has shed the movement. And, he wonders why people were not at his sentencing hearing. This is the character he took on long before sentencing, one of a native American but not an animal rights liberationist.

"...as a political activist ... you don't admit wrong. You don't give up the fight. You keep justifying it ... (But) I found elders ...they told me I was wrong... And, I thought, wait a minute, they're right. How can I justify something that causes people pain just because of what they've done." **[Ed Note: the edited lines "(But) I found elders ... they told me I was wrong" has been inserted by the author in place of material removed between "You keep justifying it" and "And, I thought..." We have also inserted "..." in several places to show where the author has edited text but neglected to make note of it.]**

Here is the new Rod. He has given up the fight because (he believes) he has found peace with his elders, who tell him not to struggle for justice for those oppressed. Does this mean Rod would "forgive" those who, through acts of genocide, destroyed the great American Indian nations? Or, does he only forgive those who torture non-human animals?

From a tactical point of view, not only did his statements not work, but Rod, in effect, gave aid and comfort to the animals' enemies. He let them believe the great Rod Coronado had been beaten, and that if he could be beaten, so could other animal liberation activists. Rod showed his weakness, and that of the movement.....a weakness that only encourages our enemies to continue to fight us longer and harder. We will not know for years just how much Rod's comments and actions have affected activists in this country.

Finally, Rod wonders why we obtained only part of a transcript of his trial. It was simple. We had only enough money to get a portion, and the portion we were interested in was that in which he purportedly criticized the movement, and said he has "shed" it like old clothes. Many of his best friends could not believe Rod would say those things...we set out (since Rod has stopped contacting us) to prove Rod had NOT said those things.

In fact, he did say those things.

Now, since we have the transcripts, Rod is not denying his statements (of course, neither is he printing them). Instead he attacks us for obtaining them.

This has NEVER been an issue of a betrayal of Rod Coronado by fellow animal liberationist -- including those of us who Rod knows to be ALF spokespeople and supporters and activists.

This is an issue of Rod Coronado betraying the animals, the planet and his ideals.

Sure, he may sit in jail. And, he may not have "in formed" on other activists. But, he has, sadly, given in to the pressure of the system, and of the big, monied national groups. He has helped continue the oppression by apologizing to animal abusers. He has helped keep the covert government attack on activists a secret by refusing to fight in open court a battle that must be fought.

Some would say Rod has done many good things, so he still deserves our support. That may be, but Rod has changed. While we can appreciate what he may have done in years past, that does not excuse these attacks on activists, the ALF and the very idea of animal "rights."

Rod's hypocrisy is repugnant to many animal liberationists. He admittedly eats animal parts when before he was a staunch vegan. In fact, he has laughed in the face of another activist who complained about Rod eating animals, and then bit into a burrito filled with animal parts.

Rod, by his own admission, uses animal skins (fur) in religious ceremonies. Is that not hypocrisy? Rod suggests in his letter that the Network should not consider the "traditional use of animals by native peoples" as oppression. That native peoples "respect" animals before killing them. Who does that sound like, Rod? A hunter, or trapper? How can you buy into that philosophy of unnecessary cruelty? And, although we were all friends, how can we now support you without question when you, yourself, are a supporter of avoidable animal killing.

Rod, just a few years ago, would have told all of us that oppression is oppression, and that caused in the name of religion is only so much hypocrisy. In fact, he would have been right. For anyone to attempt to justify the killing of any animals, human or non-human, through religion is hypocritical and sickening.

Finally, Rod quoted and praised, ironically, the Network story in *Underground* where we explain that activists should not spread lies and innuendo, and that we should support those involved in political trials. In Rod's case, the stories about him, as you see here, are true. Therefore they are not lies. And, Rod, by his own admission, was never involved in a "political" trial. He gave up long before that.

No, if people are looking for heroes, Rod is not one. Many of us touted him as one not too long ago. That was our mistake. If you're looking for heroes, look, instead, in the mirror. And, look to your few close comrades. Work together in REAL unity. Do what you can do TODAY to free animals, and this planet from human oppression.

And, always, always, remember that you are doing it not for yourself, or for glory, or for money, but for the animals. If you truly believe that, you will accomplish great things. And, you will never find yourself on the dark path now travelled by one Rodney Coronado....

May peace someday be with him.

OPEN LETTER FROM LAWRENCE E. WEISS

Attorney at Law

To Rod:

I wanted to reply to your letter and explain why it is that you no longer have the unreserved support of many within the movement. It is because you abandoned your principles during the court proceedings. I didn't know you from your activist days, but I understood from many people that you were a true earth warrior, and I will always respect you for this and for what you have done on behalf of the animals. At court, however, you proved to be anything but principled in the face of pressure, and I cannot support that.

Much of what you say in your letter is true, and yet at crucial points you state untruths. Let me be specific.

First, you say in your letter that your "Michigan lawyers clearly stated that their decision was in no way influenced by PETA or outside sources but was purely their own." Why are you being dishonest about this? The first thing that Fred Dilley stated to me when he came into the attorneys room at the sail was that he had received a call or fax the previous night from Phil Hirschkop, PETA's attorney, who said that he would not participate in the case in any way so long as I was on the defense team. You were there when he said that. Such a statement from PETA's attorney has to be taken as a statement from PETA and clearly implied a withdraw or reduced level of vital financial support from PETA. That's not pressure?

Second, after I returned from Michigan I told you on the phone that I could no longer be a part of your defense team. That was because you had abandoned any reference to the animals in your defense. You made clear to me that your only priority was getting you the best "deal." If you had brought in another political attorney, or even expressed an interest in raising issues that helped the animals or the movement, I could have continued to be part of the defense team. But I could not support a "me first" defense. Your case, to me, was always more than a criminal case.

I also made it clear that I would continue to help you in ways that did not involve such compromises. I would help, but not as a member of the defense team. In fact, are you aware that Fred Dilley called me three weeks after our last talk and sought my advice on matters of grad jury tactics? I gave him the best advice I could based on my experiences. Does that indicate a refusal to help "even as a consultant" as you state in your letter?

What you call a political defense is what I call a principled defense, in which things are done in such a way as to help the animals of the movement. It wasn't me personally that you turned your back on, but the idea of helping the cause through your case. Here is what Nelson Mandela, in his book, *Long Walk to Freedom* says about his treason trial in South Africa, in which he was facing the death penalty: *"Right from the start we had made it clear that we intended to use the trail not as a test of the law but as a platform for our beliefs ... We saw the trail as a continuation of the struggle by other means."*

That is not what you did. You were out to get yourself the best deal and did not consider what your choices would do to the movement or how you could help the animals. You had the media's attention. The essence of a political defense is to see and utilize the possibilities inherent in the criminal law system without compromising your criminal defense. You could have effectively publicized the horrendous conditions of animals in "fur farms" or uncovered important information about grand jury informants through the discovery process. But you did neither.

I came to see you twice in Tucson and once in Michigan to offer you a certain kind of defense. You told me then that you wanted a political defense. I have always felt that a political defense will not lose your case or get you more jail time. It will help your defense and help the animals too. The other side has treated this a s a political (read media) case from the beginning, and you can dither fight them in that arena or give up. If you choose to negotiate a deal, that is ultimately up to you. It's your life and you have to do the sentence. But while the case is still going on you should do things in such a way as to help the movement, get publicity for the plight of animals in fur farms, and obtain discovery materials that are helpful to the cause. You did not choose to do this and that's why I could no longer be a part of your defense team. I do not regret taking such a position, and I'm glad that I was not part of what came afterwards.

What I see you doing now is backing away from positions that you took during the case. Rod, you made many statements during the course of your sentencing that are now returning to haunt you. But you did this to yourself. Either you meant what you said at the sentencing, in which case you have little in common with those who continue to believe in nonviolent direct action, or you made those statements for expediency's sake, to get a reduced sentence. But I don't respect that either. A person has to stand up for his/her principles even while under pressure.

Here's what you said to the judge at sentencing on Aug 11, 1995. Do you stand behind these judgements or were they made purely for the sake of expediency?

"When you cannot follow the laws of society, you deserve punishment. And as I said before, I have been, I have done disrespect to my elders, I have hurt my family by making them go through this, and I stand to hurt my community by what I have done in the past, and I, I have hurt animals by participating in actions that destroyed research that might have benefited animals, and in that way, I would do anything that I could to help reconstruct that research, help reconstruct anything that I have contributed to the constructs (sic) destruction of.

... I do want to retrace my steps first and go to the victims and I think that I am the only individual in this room who can erase the intimidation and fear that some of these victims still feel. I don't know that I can do that sitting in a prison, where other people are going to be circulating free Rodney Coronado t-shirts and nag magazines and writing articles about me and holding me up as an ALF prisoner. I feel like I have seen in England with the ALF a lot of times that is (sic) only served to inspire the wrong elements of people. What I feel that I can do to the victims is to prove to them as I say whether it than (sic) financially or through my behavior that what I have done is wrong, and to diffuse and take away whatever sales of people who would support the ALF by slowing (sic) them their most vocal proponent is now an opponent and somebody who is retracing their steps to right a wrong, and to recognize the victims's legitimate fear and intimidation and try to heal that and erase that."

What was ordered from the clerk was the full transcript of what you said to the court at your sentencing. Not what other people said, but what you said. It is a public record, but you seem uncomfortable with the idea that anybody as ordered your transcript and I can understand that. Given what you said, it must be embarrassing. Who are the victims, the animals or the fur farmers?

I've made my position as clear as I can. I feel really bad that you are in prison, Rod. I don't dislike you, but I simply cannot be a part of the flip-flop or positions that are outlined above. Maybe our differences can be resolved some day. I hope so, because you have done much that is honorable.

Larry Weiss

OPEN LETTER TO ROD FROM HIS LAWYER

BOYDEN, WADDELL, TIMMONS & DILLEY
ATTORNEYS AT LAW

Dear Rod;

You have asked that I confirm your understanding that PETA's financial support of your legal defence was unconditional. That is true. At no time were any conditions placed on you or your defense for the support that PETA provided

With regard to the involvement of attorney Larry Weiss in your case, it was my requirement that there be no co-counsel that was unacceptable to me in your case. Larry Weiss was unacceptable as co-counsel.

It was for that reason that I indicated to you that if you wished Larry Weiss to be a formal part of your defense team as co-counsel, that I would withdraw. I think that you also had concluded that some of Mr. Weiss' actions were not appropriate and not in your best interests.

At no time did PETA attempt to influence that decision. In fact, PETA's attorney made it plain to me that, while he had personal reservations about working with Larry Weiss, it would not affect PETA's financial support of your defense in the event that you chose to hire Larry Weiss.

Very Truly yours,
Frederick D. Dilley

OPEN LETTER TO ROD CORONADO

by Freeman Wicklund, SOAR, Organizer of A.L.F. Appreciation Day

Dear Rod,

Thank you for your recent letter. I hope by discussing its contents, we can clear up some misunderstandings, and at the same time help our movement learn from its mistakes and grow into a strong, unconquerable force for animals.

First, I deeply regret that the letters I have written you have either been returned to me, have not been sent, or were in transit when your letter arrived. If I had known how much distress these delays in contacting you would have caused, I would have been more vigilant in reaching you. I apologize for any problems my laxity created.

Now I would like to clear up a few misconceptions. First, I take full responsibility for ALF Appreciation Day. Certainly the Student Organization for Animal Rights was essential in organizing our local ALF Appreciation Day and in producing and distributing the ALF-related merchandise, but SOAR should not be blamed for any of the organizational faults regarding the nation-wide ALF Appreciation Day because organizing it was my full responsibility.

Unfortunately, I must not have been clear in explaining the primary focus of ALF Appreciation Day, which caused you some confusion. It's main purpose was not to generate media coverage. Activists definitely tried to get media coverage, but ALF Appreciation Day's primary purpose was to educate other activists on the importance of the ALF for the animals and our movement.

As your letter testifies, support for the ALF and ALF prisoners have been lacking within the movement. I figured that in order to help create an effective ALF Prisoner Support network, people first needed to know who the ALF are! This was the main purpose of ALF Appreciation Day: introducing activists to the ALF and its underlying philosophies. I hoped that an increased understanding of the ALF by the movement would result in increased support for the ALF and animal rights prisoners.

ALF Appreciation Day also wanted to teach by example that public support of the ALF does not translate into immediate grand jury subpoenas, arrests, convictions, etc. Many ALF supporters fear government harassment, leading them to publicly denounce the ALF in the hopes of avoiding it. What they fail to realize is that government harassment targets EFFECTIVE activists, regardless of their stance on the ALF. We hoped to dispel activists' fears and give them the courage they needed to exit the closet and publicly support the ALF.

Beyond ALF Appreciation Day, your letter brings up many issues. However, it all seems to be saying one thing: We need better prisoner support. In an attempt to make this discussion a positive one, I would like to suggest some ways we could improve prisoner support:

1. UNIFORM EXPECTATIONS FOR A.L.F. ACTIVISTS. ALF activists need to know what is expected of them. Currently the ALF are expected to ensure their actions do not harm humans or animals, that they take appropriate security precautions, and that they never give evidence that would incriminate other activists or themselves. **[Ed Note: self-incrimination is not at issue with regards to receiving support]** These are all reasonable expectations for ALF activists. But should their be more? Is it reasonable to expect them to be vegan? Is it reasonable to expect them to not condemn the animal rights movement? or should ALF activists be expected to do whatever it takes to reduce their sentence so they can get out of prison and get back into action? These are questions that need to be discussed and answered by former and current ALF prisoners and ALF supporters so a clear policy can be in place on these issues and we can avoid further problems like this one.

2. CLEAR EXPECTATIONS OF A.L.F. SUPPORTERS. Of course all of the responsibility must not lie with the ALF activists. ALF supporters must help imprisoned activists by demanding vegan food, linen, and toiletries for them; ensuring they are not mistreated or placed in dangerous situations; and provide them with the things that will make their prison stay more comfortable -- be it requested books or money to purchase paper, envelopes, and stamps, etc.

3. IMPROVED COMMUNICATION. Communication between ALF prisoners and the movement are essential. I think a break-down in that communication helped facilitate the current misunderstandings and allowed our opponents to effectively exploit the situation to their advantage. Had ALF Supporters known prior to your sentencing of your plan to denounce the animal rights movement and the ALF in an attempt to lessen your sentence, it could have prevented much of the confusion and anger that resulted when your statements were published in the popular press. Both *No Compromise* and *Underground* would be willing to publish articles by prisoners to help facilitate this communication.

4. PRISONERS FIRST. At the end of the day, I think it is important to place the prisoner's concerns first. They took the risks that many of us are unwilling to take, and now their suffering the consequences of their actions. It is a trying time for them, and we need to be there for them to help them through it. Their burdens should be eased by our support. Certainly I think ALF Supporters should counsel ALF activists on the best strategy to fight their charges and expose government harassment and animal exploitation. But ALF activists should ultimately make their own decision on how to handle their situation and we should respect that decision as long as it does not incriminate other activists, or hurt the animals and the movement that is fighting for them.

Rod, you have done many great things for animals, and I respect you for that. However, I have also worked closely with Cres Vellucci, Jonathan Paul, and Larry Wise -- three of the activists whom you criticize in your letter. I know they are good activists who are totally committed to the animals. I hope all of you can work through these misunderstandings so that TOGETHER we can continue our non-violent war for animal liberation.

For Total Liberation!

Freeman Wicklund

OPEN LETTER IN REPLY TO ROD CORONADO

by Jonathan Paul

This letter from Rod Coronado has come at a very bad time for it came the day that the China Left timber sale blockade was taken down by the U.S. government.

I have put some time aside to respond to Rod's ludicrous letter and I will be as clear as I can. I am amazed that Rod would even write lies like these and it seems to me more and more that Rod's warrior spirit has been broken by the government and he has succumbed to not believe in the grass roots but in the mainstream movement of compromising, wealthy animal welfare groups.

I will correct and respond to the direct lies Rod has said about me and about the National Activist Network. I would like to say that these issues should not be brought out in the public for the enemy will use it against us in the future but the North American ALF-SG wants to do it and I cannot stop them. All this stuff that Rod is saying is petty whining and untrue. If the movement chooses to focus on this instead of the earth and the animals then so be it.

I want to state that I know Rod probably better that anyone else in this movement. We met in 1987 and were best friends, shared a house together, were active in animal rights together and had a business together, Global Investigations. Since his arrest Rod is a totally different person than the Rod I used to know.

In case people do not know who I am I have been an activist since 1987 involved in animal rights, Hunt Saboteurs, Earth First!, Siskiyou Forest Defenders, Sea Defense Alliance, Global Investigations and the National Activist Network. I was indicted in 1990 for allegedly participating in the UofO raid in 1986 by the ALF(but I was not convicted) and spent 5 months in jail in 1992-93 for refusing to testify to a grand jury about other activists. I am also a committed vegan for the past 13 years of my life.

1. Why is Rod blaming everyone and not owning up to his own issues? How can Rod say no one else supported him while underground? That is a lie. But Rod is smart. He knows that we cannot have the actual supporters come forward for they will get in trouble for their actions.

2.Rod does not mention me by name but I was his partner in the fur farm investigations which he accuses me of being bitter and charging Caff for my services. The reality Rod and I were both being paid for the investigation by Friends Of Animals for just under a year. You see, when the relocation of the fur farm was in process I put $1600 on my credit card paying for gas, hotel etc. with Rod's assurances that I would be reimbursed by FoA. FoA told me later that I would not be reimbursed for they had never committed to the rehabilitation project in the first place. Was I upset with Rod for lying to me? Of course! Did I charge Caff? No. Rod and I made a personal deal and we walked away from this without any issues. Did I get paid to relocate the animals? No. Did I ask? No. All I wanted was to be reimbursed. This is a funny accusation Rod made about me from someone who used to jetset all over the country and get paid to hang banners for mainstream groups. I would like to also mention that I did decide to not be involved with the rehabilitation project because I was not comfortable with the feeding of live animals to mink and bobcats and I also could not put my whole life aside and move to Washington state for the amount of time it would take to finish the project. I was also the primary organizer of the Hunt Saboteurs and I was not willing to give up that commitment.

3. Rod is upset about the fact that the National Activist Network obtained the court minutes only pertaining to Rod's statements. We had heard rumors of Rod discrediting the movement so we wanted to see. The reason we only obtained his statements was purely financial. To obtain the whole court hearing would of cost us thousands where only obtaining Rod's statements cost us $120 which I paid out of my own pocket. It is as simple as that.

4. Did the National Activist Network support Rod after his arrest? Of course we did! Did he take it? No. He wanted the support of the mainstream (PETA) and non-political lawyer. Did we agree with him? Of course not so we backed off. We did fly to Tucson a couple of times and up to Michigan to his bail hearing. Why did we not go to the sentencing hearing? We had exhausted our funds. We are grass roots, not PETA. Did we give Rod financial help? I personally handed Rod a $2000 check from the Nat. Activist Network even after PETA was giving thousands to Rod. Two thousand dollars to us is equivalent to twenty thousand dollars to PETA. **[Ed Note: Rod acknowledges receving $2000.00 from Jonathon]**

5. I would like to point out that one of the main reasons Rod was in a corner during his case was the liberating of the diary from the Wounded Knee monument. Leaving fingerprints on glass is got to be the most stupid thing one could do.

6. Did Rod work out a plea agreement? Yes he did, but only after the government offered him the plea bargain. If the government had all this evidence why would they offer him a plea bargain in the first place? I believe the government did not want to release discovery so they offered him a plea agreement instead.

7. Rod called me a "NAN member". This is incorrect. I am the president of the National Activist Network. He said I called him and told him that I said he was "selling out" the movement. I believe he was and I still believe that today. Rod claims no one from the National Activist Network

contacted him after he was in jail. That is untrue. We asked others to ask him to call our office and I personally contacted him last spring and offered to put our differences aside so we could start supporting him. He refused.

8. Rod makes it ok to exploit animals in the name of religion. I disagree. This attitude is speciest and anthropocentric. Many different religions have made it ok to kill.The planet is dying in the name of religion and human dominance. Just because Rod has some Yaqui blood in him does not make it ok to kill animals. No matter what background you come from you are still simply a human being. There was a rumor that Rod was hunting again but I cannot back that up.

9. The biggest issue to me is whether Rod is or was eating animals. I know for a fact he was while underground. He ate meat based food as so not to offend the Native Americans he was around. When I went to visit Rod in Tucson after he made bail we went to a Mexican diner for breakfast. I asked him what was vegan and he ordered for me. When I got the food I found it had cheese, sour cream, and lard in the beans. When I pointed this out Rod just shrugged his head and ate his meal which was exactly the same as mine. I was shocked. Why was he not concerned that he was offending me? Is it because I am white? What about the animals and the earth? Are they not native? When I last asked Rod to tell the truth to the animal movement that he was not even a vegetarian anymore he would not. In the most recent letter he does admit some of it. Rod also was wearing a leather belt and shoes when I saw him last.

10. Rod accuses the animal movement of cultural racism. How can we expect "minority" people to help the animal movement when they themselves are struggling to survive? It is unfair but the reality is that white people in this country have the resources to expand their beliefs beyond themselves for we are not being as directly oppressed as African Americans, Native Americans etc. Rod himself grew up in a middle class family in middle America and lived an easy life. Rod talks like he grew up in the reservation all his life. He did not. Do not get me wrong, I am fine that Rod has found his roots within the Yaqui culture. If Rod wants to do that, fine, but just do not take everyone else down with him so he may feel ok with his decisions.

11. Where was Rod when I was arrested along with Cres Vellucci and Bill Keogh for allegedly liberating 275 animals from the University of Oregon? After Cres was arrested and the cops were coming for me what did Rod do? He shrugged his shoulders and said "oh well". We were looking at 19 years apiece. The state had four witnesses who claimed to be at the action were testifying against us. Did PETA support us? No. Who did PETA support? Roger Troen, who ended up becoming an informant against Cres, Bill and I. Did we win? Yes. We did because we demanded discovery and the feds refused countless times until the judge dropped the whole case. When did the feds offer Rod the plea agreement? After his lawyers demanded discovery.

12. Last but not least...Rod accuses us of spreading rumors. That is not true. Actually I wanted to make public that Rod was eating animals but Cres Vellucci talked me out of it for he did not want to see Rod get isolated. When people asked me about the case I told them the truth. Rod is upset that I told the truth. The truth hurts in this case and Rod is on the defensive. After Rod got sentenced we had a party for him in Santa Cruz, CA. We walked off and chatted and he admitted to me that he should not have taken the deal and should have fought it all the way for the feds admitted that they did not have as much evidence as they claimed to have. I told him I would be waiting for him when he walked out prison. Sadly, I guess that will not happen.

Rod should not be squashing the ALF and just because you liberate animals does not make it ok to eat their flesh or secretions. Would it be ok for someone to liberate people from the concentration camps while at the same time the liberators were making money by making the gas that killed the prisoners? I think not. Maybe Rod should read up on William Wallace ("Braveheart").

I personally do not support Rod anymore and many people I know are upset and disappointed in him. I am sorry Rod has to be in jail for the time he is in. But, Rod could have avoided all of this if he had good security, was not so obvious and careless, and allowed to put his ego aside and maybe looked at the fact that there are a lot of great activists out there ... the big difference is that they are there for the animals not for ego

I feel the animals would be very disappointed in Rod.

I also want those out there to know that I do not think I am perfect ... and I do make mistakes for I am human like everyone else.

Animal liberation!
Earth First!

Jonathan Paul

LETTER OF CLARIFICATION

by JP Goodwin, CAFT

Let me being by saying that I do support Rod Coronado. Both Rod and myself have a particular passion for mink, and that is a bond that will always draw us together. At the same time, I am a strong supporter and a friend of Cres Vellucci as well. I believe that the National Activist Network is a fine organization which has been a major asset for the new generation of militant animal rights groups that have been popping up in the last few years. Without NAN, the new grassroots groups would never have become the force that they are becoming today. At the same time, the coalition to Abolish the Fur Trade can be linked to Rod's now defunct Coalition Against Fur Farms. Both men have given a lot and this feud should be settled so as not to stir up any more division in the animal lib movement.

As I said, I do support Rod. This does not mean that I agree with every move he made during the course of his legal proceedings. I think there is no question that the animal rights movement could have benefited from a political, media oriented trail. Rod decided he did not want that for fear that it might mean more time in jail. I think Cres would have been more supportive of Rod, had Rod wanted that. It is my impression, however, that Rod decided he did not want the type of support Cres and NAN had to offer. He felt it would hurt his chances in court. Either way, I think Cres and NAN did make an effort to help.

I am writing this because I do not want to see the integrity of the individuals involved to be dragged through the mud any longer. All involved are hard workers who have an intense drive that makes them a major threat to the animal abusers. The abusers must be loving this as we fight each other with abusive language and hard feelings. Rod was victimized by an unjust legal system. though some friendships are now damaged, possibly beyond repair, I think we should turn our energies in other directions. All parties should focus on the here and now, and destroy the furriers, etc. instead of each other. Mistakes were made, no doubt about it. For the animals and the earth, let's forgive and take the bastards out.

Ok, that's it. Now on with the rest of Underground!

A single act of defiance is worth more than a thousand angry words.

MEMORIES of FREEDOM
by the WESTERN WILDLIFE UNIT of the ANIMAL LIBERATION FRONT

Join the Earth Warriors of the Animal Liberation Front in a first hand account of Operation Bite Back, the A.L.F. battle against the U.S. fur industry that resulted in over $2 million dollars in damages to fur research and development.

"This is a story. The story of a handful of people who cared enough to risk their lives and freedom for what they believe. For Earth and for the release of the prisoners of the war on nature. It hasn't been without its costs. though we are all here tonight, one of us is sitting in an 11 by 17 foot cell in a Federal Prison for the next four years. He isn't the first and he sure as hell won't be the last. In this story there are many chapters. We are but one. The rest is up to you." **--Memories of Freedom**

Now available for the first time.

100pages, 1/2 size. Only $3
To Order, send cheque or money order (U.S.)
to NA-A.L.F.S.G. Distro, Box 767295, Roswell, GA. 30076
Canadian orders can be made in CDN funds.

Diary of Actions

PLEASE NOTE: THE DIARY OF ACTIONS IS INTENDED TO REPORT THE NEWS OF DIRECT ACTIONS TO SAVE ANIMALS, NOT TO ENCOURAGE CRIME.

CANADA

FEB/96: Vancouver, BC - Activists liberated several chickens from a processing plant. *"The animals are now in loving homes where they won't be killed for the table."* A.L.F.

MARCH/96: Vancouver, BC - A fur and leather cleaning company had several tires slashed on a delivery van. A.L.F.

APRIL 3/96: Guelph, Ont - Guelph Fashion Furs was vandalized again by anti-fur activists. The action involved the breaking of the car window of one of the owners of the fur store. This is the latest in a series of attacks on Guelph Fashion Furs in downtown Guelph, in the last year.

MAY 5/96: Cambell River, B.C. - A group of bear advocates were charged under Section 82 of the Wildlife Act for "interfering with a legal hunt" on Vancouver Island logging roads. According to the Conservation Officers, the six were allegedly involved in successful hunt sabotage actions on the previous day, (Saturday, May 4). The six activists were following Outfitter Brian Swift of Trophy West Guide Outfitting on what they believed to be a bear trophy hunt. Three armed Conservation Officers were dispatched the following day to arrest the six bear advocates. *"Bear Watch supports the peaceful and non-violent actions of concerned individuals who wish to protect B.C. bears from trophy hunters"* says Bear Watch Spokesperson, Jana Thomas. *"The Wildlife Act should protect B.C.'s wildlife, not prosecute its defenders!"*

JUNE 27/96: Abbotsford, BC - For the fourth time in two years, fire broke out in the now abandoned Coaspack Meats warehouse. Two fires, one in the barn area in 1994 and 1995 closed the plant down. This blaze destroyed what remained of the buildings.

JULY 7/96: Vancouver BC - 400 mink were released from Akagami Mink Ranch in Langley as part of an "Independence Day" operation conducted by the A.L.F.. According to the communique:

"We liberated these mink to save them from a life of torture, enslavement and eventual death. If we would have left them behind, these innocent animals would have been grotesquely killed, through neck-breaking, gassing or anal

electrocution."

JULY 10/96: Abbotsford, BC - An empty pig barn was set on fire, $10,000 damages. Unclaimed.

UNITED STATES

1995-1996: The following is a report from the A.L.F. Southland Unit, Southern California, detailing their activites:

Dear SG, - It's been a while since we've corresponded, but we've been busy. We extend our gratitude to all activists fighting for our precious animals. We wholeheartedly support your effort to pay special attention to our fellow warriors who have the misfortune to be incarcerated - we must let them know that they are in our hearts and our thoughts at all times! Here is a report on actions that occurred between 1995 and 1996 to date.

POPEYE'S (fast-food operation selling chicken) was targeted three times. They were spraypainted with slogans expressing our feelings about their meat-peddling business. They were also treated to glued locks.

KENTUCKY FRIED CHICKEN (more scum like the above) was twice the recipient of our redecorating talents; slogans were painted all over their walls and block fencing, and their locks were rendered inoperable in the usual manner.

BURGER KING was beautified with slogans such as MEAT IS MURDER; they were hit twice. Their carnivorous customers were unable to enter the next morning because of non-functioning locks, courtesy of superglue.

Another object of our outrage and artistic endevors was an Italian Restaurant featuring SIX different veal dishes on the menu. Their back walls, side walls, fences, parking lot, and porch were refurbished with slogans such as VEAL IS CHILD ABUSE and SCUM. Front and back locks were also glued. Hit #2.

RED LOBSTER was sloganized and glued -- they had to replace several locks as well as clean up their walls, (hopefully having to repaint). Hit #3.

LEATHER STORES (2) were hit, painted with slogans (WEAR YOUR OWN SKIN) and superglued.

McDONALD'S had their doors, walls, parking lot, and menu spraypainted with MEAT IS MURDER as well as comments on their practice of supporting deforestation. Locks were glued.

WINNICK'S FURS was painted with FUR IS DEAD and had their front locks glued; the back lock was already glued -- someone was there before we were! Hit #3.

WOODLAND HILLS FURRIER, a particularily resistant bunch, were treated to glued locks once again. Hit #10

A BABY PIGLET was liberated from an institution intending on turning her into sausages. She was placed in a loving home and is doing fine.

A HEN AND A DOG were liberated separately from abusive owners. The hen was half-starved and had a wound on her neck. She was placed in a loving home and is now the beautiful, happy bird she deserves to be. Her new human companion reports that she loves to be held and petted. Likewise for our canine friend!

TWO RABBITS were rescued from owners who were planning on killing them. They were placed in loving homes where they are now doing fine.

The above took place in Southern California. We are doing what we can when opportunity presents itself. We hope we are making a difference, however small. Whether you write letters, contribute money, or participate in an active A.L.F. cell, all of your efforts are needed and appreciated in our battle to liberate our animal friends. A.L.F.SU (A.L.F. Southland Unit)

AUGUST/95: Madison, WI - Fur shop in Madison was hit and locks were glued. Less then a month later the store was shut down dure to repeated actions of this nature. **VICTORY**. Only one fur shop remains in Madison. A.L.F.

DATE UNKOWN/96: Memphis, TN - a number of Derby Lane Greyhound Track's billboards were vandalized with red paint. 50,000 DEAD DOGS and A.L.F. were painted on many of them.

JAN/96: Mankato, MN -Several animal transport trailers spray-painted. -A.L.F.

JAN 24/96: Syracuse, NY - Syracuse Northern Sports Show exhibitors paint bombed, furs slashed, cars gouged in parking lot. -A.L.F.

FEB/96: Memphis, TN - A column of small windows were smashed at Especially Leathers. A.L.F.

FEB/96: Memphis, TN - meat market on Brooks Rd. had slogans painted and locks glued. A.L.F.

FEB 9/96: Solvay, NY - Chicken restaurant spray-painted, windows destroyed. -A.L.F.

MARCH/96: Memphis, TN - Windows shot out with a slingshot on two occasions at Hataway Taxidermy. A.L.F.

MARCH/96: Salt Lake City, UT - Meiers Chicken had seven windows smashed with rocks. The same treatment was given to a leather factory. Cell 4, A.L.F.

MARCH 7/96: Duluth, MN - Lake superior Furs and USA Foxx & Furs had their locks glued. A.L.F.

MARCH 15/96: Syracuse, NY - Hickory House BBQ's store front was paint bombed, 5 picture windows smashed, all sides of the building were covered in A.L.F. slogans, all locks filled with super glue, 3 large neon signs destroyed. The store remained closed for at least 2 days. A.L.F.

MARCH 17/96: Cicero, NY - Plainsville Turkey Farms Restaurant - 5 picture windows completely smashed, all locks filled with super glue, all sides of the building spray painted with A.L.F. slogans, front sign paint bombed. This action received intense media coverage. A.L.F.

MARCH 17/96: Memphis, TN - Jean Benham Furs sustained a massive paint attack with the awning, store front, sign, sidewalk, outside carpet, and brick wall covered in red paint. The owner has since installed video equipment costing thousands of dollars. The Memphis A.L.F. state that they wear masks, so this equipment is worthless. A.L.F.

MARCH 17/96: Syracuse, NY - Syracuse Mustards, a hotdog restaurant, suffered 7 smashed windows, had 3 locks glued, all sides of the building spray painted with A.L.F. slogans, outside lights smashed and several other fixtures disposed of. The store front was also paintbombed. A.L.F.

APRIL/96: Mankato, MN: Several animal transport trailers spray-painted. -A.L.F.

APRIL/96: Atlanta, GA: Atlanta Furs windows smashed out. A.L.F.

APRIL 2/96: Salt Lake City, UT - A.L.F. APPRECIATION NIGHT, Egg Products had two trucks burned out, as well as their store, which burned to the ground. Over $100,000 damage. The same night, Sniders had two huge windows smashed out. Cell 4 A.L.F.

APRIL 3/96: Victor, NY - Sometime between 9pm, Wed April 3 and 6am Thursday morning, A.L.F. activists struck L.W. Bennett & Sons' Fur Farm (Strong Rd, Victor, N.Y. 14564, USA 716-924-2460) and released over 3000 mink. According to the Sheriff's Office, each mink was worth $8, meaning that over $240,00 "worth of pelts" were set free.

Officers mentioned that tracks left in the snow indicated that several individuals took part in the liberation, and the investigation was broadened when local media received a fax entitled "A.L.F. Communique." The communique included the following statements: "The A.L.F. operates under the policy that life is more important than property," and in relation to the actual raid, that the animals set free were "coated in excretement and filth."

The raid took place to prevent the mink from "being murdered for the bloody fur trade."

"It's going to be a real tough one," said Keith Bennett, who manages L.W. Bennett and Sons' Fur Farm. "We were in bad trouble anyway." While declining to mention how big his work force is [8 employees] he predicted layoffs on the farm, which has already lost staff because of stiffening government regulations for labour, and a shrinking market for fur.

During the 1970's, L.W. Bennett's Fur Farm was the largest mink farm east of Wisconsin, then just a few years ago the farm had less than 12000 female mink on it. Before the raid by A.L.F. activists, the mink stocks had been reduced to roughly 5000.

APRIL 7/96: Eden Prairie, MN - Locks glued at the following shops: Heavenly Ham, Bentley's Outfitters (fishing store), Baker's Ribs, Ken's Fresh Meats. A.L.F.

APRIL 7/96: Mankato, MN - R.Craig's Leatherworks had locks glued and a window broken. -A.L.F.

APRIL 8/96: Mankato, MN - Chip Steak had slogans spray-painted -A.L.F.

APRIL 8/96: Mankato, MN - Hilltop Meat Market had slogans painted -A.L.F.

APRIL 13/96: Richfield, MN - Locks glued at Simek's Meat & Seafood and at Tandy Leather. A.L.F.

APRIL 13/96: Syracuse, NY - Shriner Circus locks glued and slogans painted at show place. A.L.F.

APRIL 13/96: Syracuse, NY - NY home of Murray Deitchman, CEO of Bonwit Teller Dept. Store (fur retailer) spray painted. A.L.F.

APRIL 14/96: St Paul, MN - Locks glued at City Meat Market and Pioneer Sausage Co. A.L.F.

APRIL 14/96: South St. Paul, MN - Heger Co., a fur farm feed supplier had locks glued and slogans painted. A.L.F.

APRIL 14/96: Moundsview, MN - Best Steak House was visited and locks were glued. A.L.F.

APRIL 16/96: Minneapolis, MN - The following businesses had locks glued: Brothers Halal Meat Market, Mandeville Co. (butcher's supply co.), Crown of MN. Inc. (fur farm cage/fence supplier), and Albrechts (fur retailer). A.L.F.
APRIL/96: Atlanta, GA - Atlanta Furs windows smashed out. A.L.F.

LATE APRIL/96: Atlanta, GA - Atlanta Furs locks glued. A.L.F.

APRIL thru JUNE/96: Madison WI - according to active A.L.F. in the area, a series of actions have taken place. On several occasions the local McDonald's was hit with glued locks, and the drive through windows were sealed shut. Other attacks included more locks glued and service signs were hit with spraypaint. Also spraypainted was the cement all around the service line drive through. A.L.F.

MAY/96: Pheonix, AZ - Bomb threat phoned into the national headquarters of the "Make a Wish" Foundation. The Foundation granted a wish for a terminally-ill Minnesota youth to kill an Alaskan brown bear. -Unclaimed

MAY/96: Buffalo, NY - The A.L.F. has had about 14 actions over the last few months. Included in these 14 actions are the following. Pallanker's Fur Store was paint bombed and had its lock's glued. Pollack's Furs has its windows smashed and locks glued. Federal Meats has its windows smashed and locks glued. -A.L.F.

MAY 5/96: Mankato, MN - R.Craig's Leatherworks had window broken, again. -A.L.F.

MAY 10/96: Salt Lake City, UT - La Blanc furs had windows smashed. Cell 4 A.L.F.

MAY 18-19/96: Chesapeake, VA - $60,000 damage to Central Meat Packing, cut refrigeration equipment, freon lines, electrical lines and two natural gas lines, spray painted the building with "Meat is murder", "Killers." and "A.L.F." According to media reports there have been at least 6 actions against them in the last 15 months including having a cinder block thrown through a window and slashed tires on trucks, they have also received telephone calls from people who refer to the owner and his employees as murderers in a high-pitched scream and then hang up.-A.L.F.

MAY 24/96: Memphis, TN - Jean Berham Furs locks glued. Store was to be paint bombed but the group had to leave quickly due to a disturbance. A.L.F.

JUNE/96: Washington State - 80 mink liberated from an unknown fur farm. We received word of this late, with littel detail as to location of the farm. A.L.F.

JUNE 7/96: Sandy, UT - Utah Fur Breeders Agriculture CoOp (feed supplier) raided and 75 mink used in nutritional research liberated. According to the communique, the A.L.F. broke in to the Fur Breeders Agriculture Coop at 8700 South 700 West in the early morning hours of June 7th. Two sheds were half full with mink, and one of them was completely emptied out.

JUNE 10/96: Salt Lake City, UT - La Blanc furs had locks glued. Cell 4 A.L.F.

JUNE 11/96: Huntington Beach - Two burger restaurants, Bun & Burger and a Jack In The Box were covered with anti-meat messages. Signpost at Bun & Burger were sprayed with "Where's the beef?" "War declared on animal killers," "Meat is Murder," "Next time fire."
The 24-hour Jack In The Box at Bolsa Avenue and Edwards Street received the same anti-meat slogans, This is the 3rd hit at this restaurant.

JUNE 13/96: Memphis, TN - 3 Goldsmith's delivery trucks spray painted, one windshield shot out, retaliation fro this department store's continued sale of fur. A.L.F.

JUNE 21/96: Riverton, UT - 1,000 mink liberated from fur farm. A.L.F. found dead mink lying in cages, under the cages in piles of feces, with many half eaten by other mink. "More actions are coming. Murderers beware."

JUNE 28/96: Memphis, TN - Goldsmith's dept. store advertising banner at a festival was paint bombed. A.L.F.

JUNE 30/96: Memphis, TN - Goldsmith's dept. store paint bombed. A.L.F.

JULY 4/96: Howard Lake, MN - A.L.F. raiders liberated 1000 of mink at Latzig Mink Ranch in Howard Lake, Minn. as part of an Independence Day action, coinsiding with a similar raid on another fur farm in Vancouver, Canada. This is the 12th mink release in the last 10 months -- 5 in the past month -- at U.S. and Canadian mink farms. More than 11,000 animals have been freed in actions at fur farms in Canada, Washington, Wisconsin, Minnesota, New York, Tennessee and Utah.

JULY 4/96: Nashville, TN - A.L.F. found that J. Jacklyn Furs was still closed for renovations after an arson attack in early Febuary. The group went ahead and glued the locks and painted slogans anyway. The the Fur Vault in Nashville was hit. All accessible windows were smashed, locks glued and the front of the building and their sign was spraypainted. A.L.F.

JULY 4/96: Memphis, TN - 2 windows shot at with CO2 powered pellet gun. A.L.F.

JULY 4/96: Pleasant View, TN - The A.L.F. visit Mack Ellis Fox Farm in hopes of raiding it for the 3rd time in as many years. The group discovered that the second raid (Nov 95) had put the fur farmer out of business. **VICTORY!** A.L.F.

JULY 15/96: Memphis, TN - Motes Furs and Dixie Meats paint bombed and slogans painted including "A.L.F. IS WATCHING YOU" and "MEAT IS MURDER" A.L.F.

JULY 20/96: Memphis, TN - A.L.F. attempted to burn 8 trailers at Goldsmith's Dept store as retribution for their continued sale of fur. Lots of slogans painted and a fire was started. Police arrived immediately and put the fire out. Some damage done, and a strong message was sent: THIS IS WAR! A.L.F.

JULY 17/96: South Jordan, UT - 3000 mink libereated from Holt Mink Ranch. The communique read:

In the early morning of July 17 well over 1000 mink were released from their prisons into the wild where they belong. (Holt Mink Ranch at 10291 South 1230 West South Jordan, UT 84065) The fur farmers are scared. They are all stepping up security. Mr. Holt had just installed a new fence and used wire to lock each and every cage; but as you can see this proved to be useless. This new fence was simply cut down and rolled up leaving the animals plenty of room to escape. The locks were cut or ripped open, causing plenty of damage to the cages. What Mr. Holt did not or does not understand is that nothing will stop us. Original plans were to open every cage, but a cop arriving on the scene forced us to leave. Breeder cards were also destroyed. Once again, more actions are coming. The time is now for animal liberation. A.L.F. till next time.

LATE JULY/96: Boston, MA - A sign advertising "Fresh Killed Poultry" was smashed. A.L.F.

AUGUST 2/96: Boston, MA - Macy's dept. store (sells fur) had a window smashed out. A.L.F.

AUGUST 4/96: Syracuse, NY - The Skanaetlas Fur Exchange was trashed. The store front was covered in red paint, large windows were smashed to pieces, a full length fur on display was destroyed as was a glass chandalier, and the interior of the store was paint bombed. A.L.F. was painted on the sidewalk. The Syracuse A.L.F. announced in the same release that a hit on Mustards Hot Dogs from a few months ago put the place out of business. A.L.F.

AUGUST 5/96: Memphis, TN - American Association for Laboratory Animal Science, which is an industry front group, had 5 windows smashed, the door shot out, slogans painted and the locks glued. A.L.F.

AUGUST 5/96: Memphis, TN - Nancy Kelso, the head manager at Goldsmith's department store had her home targeted. Both of her cars were totally covered in paint stripper. A.L.F.

VICTORY!: A shop in Salt Lake City has stopped selling fur as a result of an A.L.F. campaign against them. A sign appeared in their window which says: "We no longer sell fur or fur products on these premises." Congratulations go out to Salt Lake City A.L.F.!

AUGUST 9/96: Hinsdale, MA - thousands of mink were liberated from a fur ranch near here, according to a communique released by the A.L.F.. This is the first ever raid in Massachusetts by the A.L.F. The Carmel Mink Ranch, off Rt. 143 in Hinsdale, was reportedly attacked by the A.L.F. in the early morning of Aug 9 according to the communique. *"Most cages were opened .. and [we] painted A.L.F. on the shed."* A.L.F.

AUGUST 12/96: Alliance, OH - A.L.F. liberated 2500 mink from Justice Jorney's Fur Ranch in Alliance, Ohio.

"As the cages were ripped open we were amazed at how quietly and patiently each mink waited for its turn to be liberated. They felt mud beneath their feet for the first time and splashed playfully through the rain puddles.

As we skulked our way through the corn and saw the ranch for the first time, one word jumped into all of our minds ... Auschweitz. The mink were crammed five to a cage with no apparent source of food or water.

We refused to allow the barbaric imprisonment and murder of innocent creatures for the vanity of selfish humans. As long as there are animals suffering at the hands of humans, there will be the A.L.F."

AUGUST 16/96: Boston, MA - The home of furrier Arnold Rosenkrantz was paint bombed. The newspaper ran a photo of his house with paint all over it after the A.L.F. called in the hit. Rosenkrantz was the target of a CAFT demo several months ago. The media mistakenly referred to him as retired. Though he closed his own storefront, he merged his company with another furrier and still works full time with fur. A.L.F.

AUGUST 16/96: Washington Crossing, PA - Kudra Furs received the normal treatment (smashed windows, glued locks, painted slogans, etc) A.L.F.

TO ANIMAL LIBERATION FRONT SUPPORT GROUP

On the night prior to the "Fur Fashion Week" activities in New York, A.L.F. members were busy causing a small mess in downtown Manhattan. Two locations were targeted. One was a future fur salon which is actually attempting to open its bloody doors in Greenwich Village, the "bohemian" heart of Manhattan, albeit a very touristy heart. The second was a steakhouse in soho hosting a dinner party for furriers the next evening as part of "Fur Fashion Week." Both locations had their locks super-glued, were thoroughly splattered with paint, and had many animal lib. slogans wheatpasted to their outer walls. As expected, the restaurant was quickly cleaned, but the soon-to-open fur salon was a mess for 24 hours. Security was beefed up for the dinner party. total dage costs unknown.

ENGLAND

AUGUST/95: Metro News reports "there is a strong A.L.F. network operating in the North West" of England.

DECEMBER/95: Sussex - Hunt sabs visit Chiddingfold Hunt Kennels. A window was smashed and photographs taken of the appalling conditions inside the kennels.

DECEMBER/95: Sussex - 'The Swan' pub in Chichester is bomb hoaxed twice on New Years Eve. The Swan was host to the Chiddingfold Foxhunt Boxing Day celebrations.

[The Chiddingfold Foxhunt is close to ceasing hunting activity on Saturdays due to a continual sab presence and a spate of A.L.F. and Hunt Retribution Squad actions. Local sabs were told by a reliable source that if the hunt continues to be targeted the hunt would have to stop all weekend hunts.]

JANUARY/96: Surrey - five masked animal libbers assault Christopher and Virginia Elliott, blood-junkies with the Surrey Union Foxhunt. One person was arrested.

JAN/96: Buckinghamshire - A.L.F. warn that a number of "Sunday Roasts" on sale in Tescos, Saindburys, Safeway, Asda and Waitrose have been contaminated.

JAN/96: Sussex - Five butchers in Brighton have their walls painted and windows smashed.

JAN/96: Sussex - The bognor branch of Boots is bomb hoaxed.

JAN/96: Sussex - Hunt Retribution Squad (HRS) smash the window of a Crawley & Horsham blood-junkie. the blood-junkie was inside the vehicle at the time of the attack.

JAN/96: Surrey - Hund Retribution Squad attack Christopher and Virginia Elliot, blood-junkies with the Surrey Union Foxhunt. One person arrested.

JAN/96: Yorkshire - HRS attack blood-junkie scum.

FEB/96: Dorset - Around 70 sabs manage to prevent any kills in a mass action against Cattistock Foxhunt. Also hunt supporters discovered the back of their jackets were covered in horse-shit.

FEB/96: Shropshire - At the end of a good days sabbing of the South Shropshire Hunt, the sabs decided to take away with them a couple of hounds. Sadly, the police made them return the dogs.

FEB/96: Sussex - Large plate glass window of a cancer research shop in Brighton was smashed.

FEB/96: Wiltshire - over 100 sabs and HRS activists attended the Beufort FH hunt. Whilst the sabs did their bit, the Hunt Retribution Squad attacked hunt supporter's vehicles and assaulted blood-junkies. At one point over 20 HRS activists all attacked the same Land Rover! Because of the action, two blood-junkies were hospitalised that day with many more receiving lessor injuries. Over 20 vehicles needed new windows, headlights, etc.

MARCH/96: Argos is warned to withdraw fishing tackle from their catalogues or else their stores will be bombed.

MARCH/96: Avon - JD posts a razorblade to the Countryside Movement.

MARCH/96: Avon - Bristol port is bomb hoaxed and sloganised after it puts in a bid to transport live animals.

MARCH/96: Gloucestershire - 40 animal libbers visit the home of Gordon Gilder (live animal exporter) and repaint his walls, free of charge.

MARCH/96: Hampshire - JD post razorblades to Paddy Edwards (Wickham Labs), Sir Andrew Lloyd Webber (wants to start up an ostrich farm), Prof. D. Walker (vivisector), Simon Day (Torbay Farm) Chris Bishop (Wickham Labs) and Joan Cartmell.

MARCH/96: Kent - JD send out two razorblades to animal abusers.

MARCH/96: Lancashire - 15 armed men trash Pedigree Pups shop in Tarleton.

MARCH/96: London - Notorious blood-junkie Charly Windsor, Prince of Wales, receives a Justice Dept. bomb threat.

MARCH/96: London- JD post razorblades to the British Field Sports Society (hunters), J. Cole (chicken murderer), The Research Defence Society (Pro-vivisection), British Fur Trade Assoc., Fur Education Council and the Ivy pub (serves ostrich meat).

MARCH/96: London - Activists spray LEAVE THOSE OSTRICHES ALONE ANDREW on the walls of Andrew Lloyd Webbers "The Really Useful Group Ltd" building. Action to protest Webbers decision to become an ostrich farmer.

MARCH/96: Hampshire - HRS attack New Forest Fox Hounds blood- junkies. Also two vehicles trashed. Five arrested.

MARCH/96: Norfolk - McDonald's in Norwich bomb hoaxed.

MARCH/96: Nottingham - JD post a razorblade to the Ostrich Farming Corporation.

MARCH/96: THE SOUTH - Various prominent blood-junkies are sent obscene, threatening poems.

MARCH/96: Sainsbury's is warned to stop selling all blood-sports magazines in all their supermarkets or else the stores will be firebombed.

MARCH/96: Seal - Butcher Chris Martin has bullets fired through his shop window. The local paper suggests the action may have been taken by an armed posse of turkeys who previously escaped from the shop!

MARCH/96: Sussex - a news agents in Lancing is warned to stop selling "Petersens Hunting Annual" by April 5th or they will be subjected to ever increasing damage attacks, starting with smashed windows and glued locks, but if they continue to sell the mag, then arson.

MARCH/96: Sussex - the home of Avril Warren-Williams is covered in red paint, after she orders a vet to kill a perfectly healthy horse.

JUSTICE DEPARTMENT PRESS RELEASE

On July 30 1996 100 (One hundred) letters booby trapped with razor blades were sent to the enclosed list of scum. A slip of paper explaining why they had been targetted was enclosed with the booby trapped letter.

COSTAIN, COSTAIN HOUSE, NICHOLSON WALK, MAIDENHEAD, SL6 1LN
COSTAIN GROUP PLC, HEAD OFFICE, 111 WESTMINSTER BRIDGE ROAD, LONDON SE1 7UE
COSTAIN (CONSTRUCTION DIVISION), 6-8 PHOENIX CHAMBERS, MARKET BUILDINGS, MAIDSTONE, KENT ME14 1HP
DAVID RENDEL MP, HOUSE OF COMMONS, LONDON SW1A 0AA (SUPPORTS NEWBURY BYPASS)
McDONALDS RESTAURANTS, 11-59 HIGH ROAD, EAST FINCHLEY, LONDON N2 8AW
THE MD, BURGER KING LTD, 20 KEW ROAD, RICHMOND, SURREY TW9 2NA
A.ENGEL (MD), KENTUCKY FRIED CHICKEN, COLONEL SANDERS HOUSE, 88-97 HIGH ST BRENTFORD, MIDDX TW8 8BG
STONEGATE FARMERS LTD, 15 NORTH ST, HAILSHAM, EAST SUSSEX BN27 1DH
D.WATTS (MD), THAMES VALLEY EGGS LTD, MEMBURY, NEWBURY RG16 7TX
CHITTY GROUP, UNIT 1, SLYFIELD IND ESTATE, GUILDFORD (ABBATOIR)
M. YATES LIVESTOCK TRANSPORT, FRIDAY THORPE, HUMBERSIDE
RICHARD OATLEY, NEW LODGE, SUDBOROUGH, KETTERING NN14 3AU (LIVE EXPORTER)
MR C SMALES, SMALES LTD, WEST DOCK STREET, HULL HU3 4HL (FAROESE FISH)
PETER BRYNE, 53a MOSTYN AVE, WEMBLEY, LONDON (SLAUGHTERMAN)
J COLE POULTERERS, 10b LEYDEN ST, LONDON E1 7LE
SHAFTESBURY LIVESTOCK MARKET, CHRISTYS LANE, SHAFTESBURY, DORSET
SALISBURY LIVESTOCK MARKET, ASHLEY RD, SALISBURY, WILTSHIRE SP2 7TH
SIR ANDREW LLOYD WEBBER, SYDMONTON COURT ESTATE, ECCHINSWELL, HAMPSHIRE
REALLY USEFUL GROUP LTD, 19 TOWER ST, LONDON WC2 (WEBBERS COMPANY)
TESCO STORES LTD, TESCO HOUSE, DELAMARE RD, CHESHUNT, HERTS EN8 9SL (SENT TO J GILDERSLEEVE, GROUP BUYING DIRECTOR) (SELLS OSTRICH)
NATIONAL FED OF MEAT TRADERS, 1 BELGROVE, TUNBRIDGE WELLS, KENT TN1 1YW
LONDON FISH & POULTRY RETAILERS ASSOC, 66 ABERDOUR RD, GOODMAYES, ESSEX IG33PG
THE MD, WORLD OF LEATHER PLC, NORTH CIRCULAR RD, LONDON NW10 7SX
LEAVE COUNTRY SPORTS ALONE, PO BOX 4402, HENLEY ON THAMES, OXON
COUNTRYSIDE MOVEMENT, FREEPOST, ROOM GUA3, BRISTOL BS38 7HL
COUNTRYSIDE BUSINESS GROUP, 32 BRENTON ST, LONDON W1X 8JS
KNIGHTS, REGENCY HOUSE, 25 HIGH ST, TUNBRIDGE, KENT (BLOODSPORT SOLICITORS)
BFSS, 59 KENNINGTON RD, LONDON SE1 5BR
BASC, MARFORD MILL, ROSSETT, WREXHAM, CLYWD LL12 0HL
THE FIELD, KINGS REACH TOWER, STAMFORD ST, LONDON SE1 9LS (HUNTING RAG)
CLIVE ASLETT, EDITOR, COUNTRY LIFE, address as above, (PRO HUNT RAG)
STEVEN LOVERIDGE, ARKWRIGHT RD, LONDON NW3 (HOME ADDRESS OF HUNT RAG EDITOR)
ROXTON BAILEY ROBINSON, FIELD SPORTS & SAFARIS, 25 HIGH ST, HUNGERFORD, BERKSHIRE RG17 0NF
FOX & HOUNDS, EGGESFORD HOUSE HOTEL, EGGESFORD, MID DEVON EX18 7JZ
THE TREASURER, MUSEUM OF HUNTING TRUST, THE ROWANS, COLLEGE ST, LEICESTER LE2
COUNTRYSIDE AUDIO & VISUAL, PO BOX 7206, TADLEY, BASINGSTOKE, HANTS RG26 5YR (SELLS HUNTING VIDEOS)
BAILYS, CHESTERTON MILL, FRENCH'S RD, CAMBRIDGE, CB4 3NP (HUNT DIRECTORY)
HOBSBURN HOUSE, HOBSBURN, BONCHESTER BRIDGE, ROXBURGHSHIRE (HUNT HOTEL)
PATEY (LONDON) LTD, 1 AMELIA ST, LONDON SE17 3PY (HUNT CO.)
COUNTRY LANDOWNERS ASSOC, 16 BELGRAVE SQUARE, LONDON SW1X 8PQ
HOUNDS MAGAZINE, ROSE COTTAGE, HUGHLEY, SHREWSBURY, SHROPSHIRE
FIELD SPORT PUBLICATIONS LTD, 48 QUEEN ST, EXETER, DEVON EX4 3SR
FARLOW'S, 5 PALL MALL, LONDON SW1 (SHOOTING SHOP)
DAVID BARNES, 1-3 DOGS HEAD ST, IPSWICH IP4 1AF (HUNT SOLICITORS)
KEVIN COKER, ROUGHAY FARM, COLDEN COMMON, HANTS (HUNT TERRIERMAN)
Mrs D OWEN, THE OLD RECTORY, TEIGH, OAKHAM, LEICS LE15 7RT (HUNTER)
Mr P HILL-WALKER, MAUNBY HALL, MAUNBY, THIRSK, N YORKS YO7 4HA (HUNTER)

This list continues on the second sheet enclosed...

MARCH/96: Sussex - at least ten empty trucks used in live animal exports have their windows smashed durring a demo at Dover.

MARCH/96: Sussex - Window shashed at chiddingfold hunt kennels. Also the hunt ball was disrupted by sabs.

MARCH/96: West Midlands - Over 100 demonstrators attended the annual Horse and Hound Ball, held in Birmingham. The private security firm hired to protect the blood-junkies couldn't cope with the sheer numbers of sabs and gave up, letting the demonstrators run freely through the car park. Several vehicles were damaged. The Blood-junkies were also flour-bombed.

MARCH/96: THE SOUTH - The Justice Department soak eggs in urine and then leave them on the shelves of supermarkets. The J.D. also posted 18 razor-blades, allegedly smeared in HIV infected blood to vivisectors.

MARCH 16/96: London - One of London's top furriers, Michael Hockley of the Philip Hockley fur shop in central London, has resigned from his job as manager due to pressure from animal rights activists who visited his shop and home during a day of action against fur. A letter from Michael Hockley's solicitors, Davenport Lyons, was hand-delivered to the office of London Animal Action.
It stated:

"Dear Sirs,
Our client, Michael Hockley, has instructed us to inform you that having given consideration to the overall position, your campaign and your recent activities have left him with no alternative but to resign his position as manager of Philip Hockley, No 20 Conduit Street, W1 and to give up any connections and interests whatsoever in and with the fur industry.

You should know that although our client is the manager of Philip Hockley of Conduit Street, he and his family have no beneficial interests of any nature or sort in the firm, he being merely an employee.

Mr J SNOWBALL, NEW HOUSE, NURSERY FARM, RICHMOND, N YORKS DL10 6ER (HUNTER)
Mr J FURNESS, KNOWLE HOUSE, KIRKBY, THIRSK, N YORKS (HUNTER)
WH SMITH, STRAND HOUSE, 7 HOLBEIN PL, LONDON SW1W 8NR (MAJOR HUNT RAG STOCKIST)
PETER HUMPHRYS, ASHTON MANOR, ASHTON, BISHOPS WALTHAM, HANTS (HUNTER)
ARTHUR CARTER, BARTON GATE, PANCRASWEEK, HOLSWORTHY, DEVON (WATERLOO CUP)
IAN HODGE, PENGELLY, WADEBRIDGE, CORNWALL PL27 7LA (HUNT FANATIC)
RW BIRD, PASTON RIDINGS, PETERBOROUGH PE4 7UY (HUNTER)
Dr J PECK, BILBOA HOUSE, DOLVERTON, SOMERSET TA22 9DW (HUNTER)
A HART, PARSLOES COTTAGE, BAGENDON, CIRENCESTER, GL7 7DU (HUNTER)
SIR DAVID STEEL MP, HOUSE OF COMMONS, LONDON (PRO HUNT MP)
BULLET PUBLISHING LTD, PO BOX 1383, WINDSOR SL4 3LG (HUNT PUBLISHERS)
ACEVILLE PUB. LTD, 89 EAST HILL, COLCHESTER, ESSEX CO1 2QN (HUNT PUBLISHERS)
RAVENHILL PUB. Co LTD, STANDARD HOUSE, BONHILL ST, LONDON EC2A 4DA (HUNT PUB.)
ST MARTINS PUBLISHING, PO BOX 4041, LONDON W9 0ZH (HUNT PUBLISHERS)
G MOWBRAY LTD, 21 BRIGHTON RD, CROYDON CR2 6UL (HUNT PUB.)
EMAP PURSUIT PUB. LTD, BRETTON COURT, BRETTON, PETERBOROUGH, CAMBS PE3 8DZ
COUNTRYWIDE PERIODICAL PUB. LTD, YELVERTON, DEVON, PL20 7PE
HARMSWORTH ACTIVE, ASTLEY HOUSE, 33 NOTTINGHILL, LONDON W11 3JQ (HUNT PUB.)
BPG (BOURNE) LTD, 2 WEST ST, BOURNE, LINCS, PE10 9NE
CLIFFORD SMARTS ANGLING HOLIDAYS, 29 BRIDLE RD, BURTON LATIMER, NORTHANTS, NN15 5QP
KINGS ANGLING HOLIDAYS, 27 MINSTER WAY, HORNCHURCH, ESSEX RM11 3TH
ANGLERS WORLD HOLIDAYS, 46 KNIFESMITHGATE, CHESTERFIELD, DERBYSHIRE S40 1RG
ANGLERS ABROAD, 14 HIGH ST, WOMBWELL, BARNSLEY S73 0AA
CAST AWAY, IRISH ANGLING HOLIDAYS, IRISH TRAVEL BUREAU, 1 MARSLAND RD, SALE MOOR, MANCHESTER M33 3HP
ARTHUR OGLESBY, 9 OATLANDS DRIVE, HARROWGATE HG2 8JT
THE SALMON & TROUT ASSOC, FISHMONGERS HALL, LONDON BRIDGE, LONDON EC4R 9EL
POLAR FURS LTD, BELLSIDE HOUSE, 4 ELTHORPE RD, LONDON N19 4AG
EKER FURS LTD, 19-29 REDCHURCH ST, LONDON E2 7DJ
M MICHAELS LTD, 38 TRIANGLE WEST, BRISTOL BS8 1ER (FUR SHOP)
PARISIAN TAILOR LTD, 29 HULME ST, SOUTHPORT, MERSEYSIDE PR8 1PQ (FUR SHOP)
Dr K ALEXANDER, DIRECTOR, THE LEATHER TECHNOLOGY CENTRE, LEATHER TRADE HOUSE, KINGS PARK RD, MOULTON PARK, NORTHAMPTON NN3 1JD
FUR EDUCATION COUNCIL, PO BOX 1EW, LONDON W1A 1EW
THE RESEARCH DEFENCE SOCIETY, 58 GREAT MARLBOROUGH ST, LONDON W1
SCHUCO INT, LYNDHURST AVE, LONDON N12 0NE (VIV EQUIPMENT MAKER)
ANDREW JAMES REDPATH, 79 ELMS RD, LONDON SW4 9EP (GILLETTE DIRECTOR UK)
DR A LANSDOWN, DEPT OF COMPARATIVE BIOLOGY, CHARING CROSS HOSPITAL, FULHAM PALACE RD, LONDON W6 (VIV)
INSTITUTE OF NEUROLOGY, THE NATIONAL HOSPITAL, QUEEN SQUARE, LONDON WC1
DEPT OF MEDICAL MICROBIOLOGY, WESTMINSTER HOSPITAL, HORSEFERRY RD, LONDON SW1
PADDY EDWARDS, 13 TANFIELD PARK, WICKHAM, HANTS
WILLIAM CARTMELL, BINGHAMS, MISLINGFORD RD, WICKHAM, HANTS
SIMON DAY, TORBAY FARM, SCIEVERS LANE, LOWER UPHAM, HANTS
CHRIS BISHOP, BLAGDEN FARM, CLANFIELD, HANTS
DON BARRET, WYETH LABS, HUNTERCOOMBE LANE, TAPLOW, MAIDENHEAD SL6 0PH
JUDY McARTHUR-CLARK, 12 AYNSLEY COURT, SANDWICH, KENT (VIV)
DAVID WALKER, OLD HAWTHORN FARM, HAWTHORN LANE, FOUR MARKS, HANTS
Dr D BARRY, GROUP DIRECTOR OF R & D AND MEDICAL AFFAIRS, WELLCOME PLC, PO BOX 129, UNICORN HOUSE, LONDON NW1 2BP
THE DIRECTOR, ICRF, PO BOX 123, LINCOLN'S INN FIELDS, LONDON WC2A 3PX
THE DIRECTOR, CANCER RESEARCH CAMPAIGN, 10 CAMBRIDGE TERRACE, LONDON NW1 4JL
THE DIRECTOR, BRITISH HEART FOUNDATION, 14 FITZHARDINGE ST, LONDON W1H 4DH
JASON AMESBURY, 32 ELDER ST, LONDON E1 (SELLS SHARKSKIN SHOES)
MISS ALICE MARY PASCOE, 995 GREENFORD RD, GREENFORD, MIDDX UB6 0NN (VIV)
PP TRAVEL, 16 HAMILTON RD, LONDON NW10 1NY (BULLFIGHTING TRAVEL AGENTS)
THE BACKPACKER Co, 2 ADELAIDE GROVE, LONDON W12 0JJ (as above)

and as if we would forget;
JEREMY PHILLIPS, LWTP, LONDON TELEVISION CENTRE, UPPER GROUND, LONDON SE1 9LT

Yours faithfully,
Davenport Lyons"

The Daily Telegraph reported that his wife's car had been sprayed with paint a few weeks previously, and it could have been this coupled with the home demo which made him decide to resign.

APRIL/96: Petworth, Sussex - A.L.F. liberate 9 hounds from Chiddingfold hunt kennels. Sadly, two arrests.

APRIL/96: Barlavington, Sussex - A.L.F. liberate two birds imprisoned by blood-junkie games keeper. Cages were trashed.

APRIL/96: Sunderland - A.L.F. warn chemists to stop stocking products tested on animals.

APRIL/96: THE SOUTH - The Earth Liberation Front (ELF) damages the inside pages of shooting magazines on sale in W.H. Smiths.

APRIL 28/96: Avon - A.L.F. activists liberated 21 hens from a battery unit at School Time Eggs, Myrtle Farm, Syston. All hens were in extremely poor condition - all were pecked bare, all had foot sores, some had foot deformities. However, now all the liberated hens are in safe, loving homes and able to live out normal lives without abuse.

MAY/96: Barkingside, Essex - A.L.F. glue and spraypaint a Butchers.

MAY/96: Seven Kings, Essex - A.L.F. brick Halal butcher's window.

MAY/96: Lancaster - Animal Rights Militia (ARM) torch Rentokill van.

MAY/96: London - A.L.F. smash a butchers window in Hackney.

MAY/96: Sussex - Animal Libbers bomb hoax Hastings Council to protest tree cutting. The loss of habitat inevitably leads to animal suffering.

JUNE/96: Liverpool - McDonald's restaurant is sloganized, locks were glued and paint splashed on walls.

JUNE/96: Liverpool - Boot Chemist shop on Smithdown Road was hit with the slogan VIVISECTORS and all windows were broken, two nights running.

JUNE/96: Liverpool - Several shops on Lark Lane were hit by busy activists, including L'Allouette, a restaurant that sells veal had its windows smashed. As a result, veal has been pulled from the menu! Other actions were taken against a betting shop and a fish shop, where windows were smashed out.

JUNE/96: Kent - Incendiary devices discovered on a railway line. Police believe they may have been left by anti-live export activists.

JUNE/96: Liverpool - A.L.F. glue and paint a McDonald's. Slogans are painted and windows are smashed at the Boots Chemist on Smithdown Rd two nights in a row. Also smashed were the windows of L'Allouette, a reasturant that sells veal (the veal was shortly after deleted from the menu!). Also, a betting shop and a fish shop in Lark Lane both had their windows smashed.

JUNE 24/96: Cambridgeshire - Firebomb attacks hit cattle trucks in the yard of a cattle hauliers In Cambridgeshire. Michael Speechley, 42, arrived at his yard at Dry Drayton, Cambs, at night to find two of his five lorries ablaze. He moved another truck out of the way and only later found that an incendiary device had been placed on top of the front off-side wheel. It failed to explode.

JUNE 24/96: Minsterworth, Glocestershire - two lorries and a barn were destroyed by incendiary devices in H Lyes and Son's abattoir yard. Damage was estimated $300,000. The owner said police found three petrol bombs - two of which failed to go off.

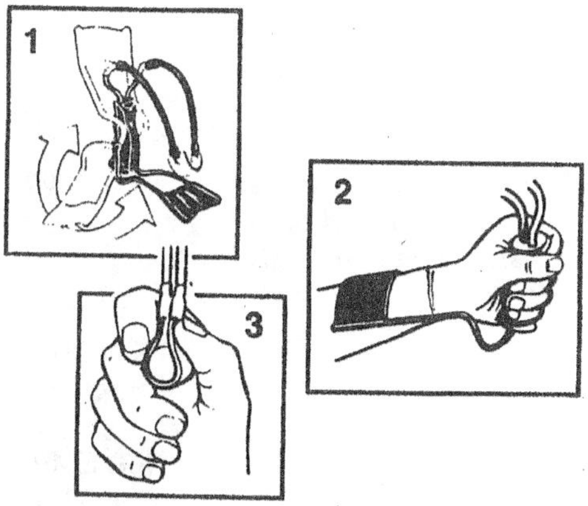

3. *Loading:* Center ammo in the middle of the pouch, pinching the ends of the pouch over the ammo, using thumb an index finger.

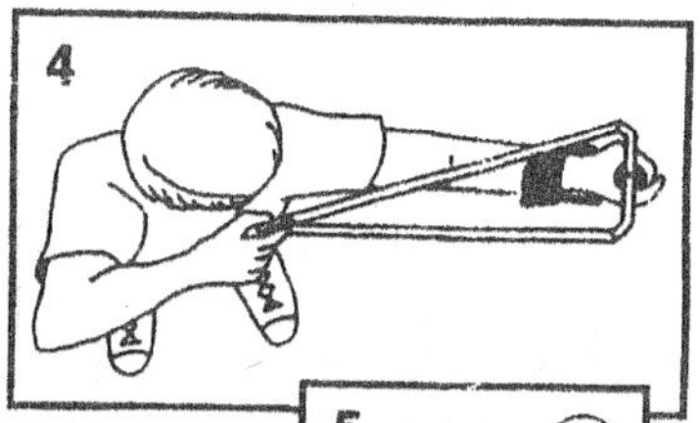

4. *Stance:* Point your left foot and shoulder directly at the target, while turning body to the right. Distribute weight evenly on both feet, spacing approximately shoulder width apart. Turn head directly towards target.

5. *Aiming:* Hold slingshot handle parallel to the ground. Use top prong of yoke as aiming reference. Move yoke up or down, adjusting for distance.

6. *Drawing Bands Back:* Hold left arm straight and firm. Draw right hand back level with right side of chin, holding ammo pouch firmly between thumb and index finger.

***Accuracy Tip:* Always pull ammo so that bands are not twisted and remain level, centered between the slingshot yoke.**

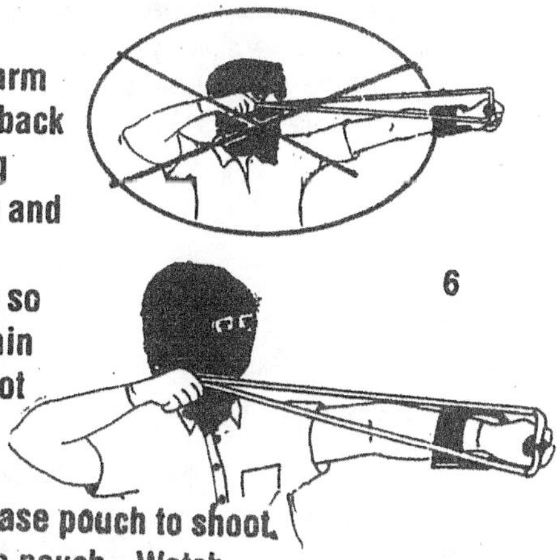

7. *Firing and Follow Through:* Release pouch to shoot. Hold position until ammo has left the pouch. Watch where ammo has left the pouch. Watch where shot hits and adjust aim for next shot.

Army bomb disposal experts made safe one device which was being examined by police.

JUNE 28/96: Avon - A.L.F. activists return and liberated 50 hens from a battery unit at School Time Eggs, Myrtle Farm, Syston. From the Press Release: *"50 hens were liberated from a life times incarceration in the barbaric and outdated "battery hen" system. All hens removed were of an appauling condition, showing the common signs of suffring these birds endure. Many were severely defeathered, de-beaked, had ulcerated feet and showed signs of injuries due to fights which break out due to the stress of never being able to walk, spead their wings, with five birds in each individual cage ... This is at least the fourth time this "farm" has been raided by the A.L.F. ... in the last two years over 200 chickens have been given a life far removed from what School Time Eggs had planned for them!"*

JULY/96: Liverpool - For the Earth Liberation Front's (ELF) "Animal's Revenge" Earth Nights BONA PETS on Bold St. was paint attacked. Also, a slogan was written on the pavement outside the shop, a big mirror was smashed and flyers circulated calling for a boycott of the shop. Elsewhere in

Liverpool for Earth Night an aquarium, a veal restaurant, a butchers and a betting shop all had their locks glued.

JULY 26/96 Bristol - 2 explosive devices were placed in high Street shops, including the Imperial Cancer Research Fund (vivisectors) and British Home Stores. Unfortunately an arrest was made, and the activist reportedly had four more devices on his person. According to papers, the 44-year-old man had four explosive devices strapped to his body when captured by officers in a struggle in Halfords store in Bristol's central Broadmead shopping centre. It is understood they had tracked the suspect from the west Midlands and followed him into stores where devices were planted.

Newspaper reports describe the incendiary devices. They were "all of similar construction, involving a 20-pack of Superking cigarettes attached to small white-taped packages, one of which incorporated a watch as an apparent timing device.Wires connected the cigarette packet to two white-taped smaller packages. The wires were attached in every case with similar blue tape."

What, like the diagram on page 14?

AUGUST/96: A.L.F. PRESS RELEASE
"Enclosed is a letter sent to Sir Andrew Lloyd Webber at his home address on August 1, 1996.
To Andrew Lloyd Webber, Ostrich Killer.
the Animal Liberation Front is FUMING MAD at you, you lowlife animal abusing wretch. What the fuck have ostriches ever done to you? From now on it's full scale war. Theatres playing your musicals will be targetted with incediary devices and other packages. Windows will be smashed, record shops selling your soundtracks will be targetted and we will leave them in do doubt as to WHY they were targetted. The A.L.F. is going to break you just like we did the entire fur trade. We HATE scum like you.
Final warning. A group called the JUSTICE DEPARTMENT have been known to plant car bombs and mail out high explosive parcel bombs to animal abusers like you. So unless you want your hands blown off we suggest you stop your little exercise in ostrich murder and LEAVE THEM WELL ALONE.
YOU HAVE BEEN WARNED!!!"

WALES

MARCH/95: Clywd - JD post a razorblade to the British Assoc. for Shooting and Conservation.

MAY/95: Police confirm that a number of A.L.F. actions take place in Wales every month.

NORTHERN IRELAND

FEBRUARY/96: Belfast - Several butchers loose their windows. Also, Ian Buchanan, the Master of the Co.Down Staghounds had a rock thrown through his fron window late one night. Letters of "sympathy" to Ian Buchanan, 21 Fort Rd, Drumbo, Belfast, N. Ireland. Tel: 01232 826795.

GREECE

FEBRUARY/96: Athens - Arson attack against a McDonald's in Sytagma Square. Sadly, one arrest.

HOLLAND

NOVEMBER/95: Amsterdam - A.L.F. hit several meat trucks. Tires are slashed.

NOVEMBER/95: Groninger - A.L.F. target meat trucks. Tires slashed.

DECEMBER/95: Oostzaan - Animal Justice Front (A.J.F.) arson attack on a meat truck.

JANUARY/96: Castricum - A.J.F. arson attack on meat truck and meat processing plant.

FEBUARY/96: Halfweg - A.J.F. arson attack against Hot Dog King truck. Elsewhere the A.J.F. painted anti-meat slogans on a training school for butchers.

MARCH/96: Amstelveen - A.J.F. arson attack on several meat trucks.

MARCH/96: Den Helder - A.J.F. arson attack against a butchery, slaughterhouse and meat truck.

MARCH/96: Hilversum - A.J.F. arson attack on meat trucks.

MARCH/96: Rotterdam - A.J.F. arson attack on meat trucks and a meat company building, causing hundreds of thousands of guilders worth of damage.

GERMANY

MAY/95: Selm - Animal libbers torch poultry breeders. Over $2,000,000 damage!

JULY/95: Anton Pohlmann - Animal libbers torch another poultry breeders with resulting damage reaching as high as $17,000,000!

Date unknown, (OCT?): Westerheim - activists from Germany and Switzerland worked together to destroy a slaughterhouse. $60,000 damage done, but sadly, five people arrested, all from Switzerland.

JUNE 25/96: Offenbach (Hesse) - the Anti-Jager Front (Anti-Hunter Front) destroyed over 23 hunting towers in the forests near Offenbach/ A flyer was left on each tower : "Wie die Dinge liegen, liegen sie richtig - ANTI-JAGER FRONT" ("How these things lay, they lay right - ANTI-HUNTER FRONT")

NORWAY

MARCH/96: Oslo, Dyrenes Frigjorings Front (DFF) smashed 28 windows, threw in a stink bomb, glued the locks, spraypainted slogans and paint attacked the Norweigan Fur Animal Breeders Assoc. 300,000 NOK damage. This was the second time this building was targeted.

MARCH/96: Tonsberg - DDF smashed windows, glued locks and painted slogans at Pels atelier Knut Poverud (furrier). After smashing the windows a paintbomb was thrown in, wrecking 60,000 NOK worth of fur.

MAY 3/96: Sennesvik - An attempt to sink a Norwegian whaling vessel took place. Water was allowed to flow into the engine room when activists tampered with a pipe. The whaling vessel was in the port of Sennesvik by Mortsund when the sabotage took place. One of the owners discovered the damage friday morning. If it had passed unnoticed, the vessel would probably have sunk, according to the police at the Lofoten and Vester-len PD.

FINLAND

JANUARY/96: Helsinki - Elainten Vapautus Rintama (E.V.R. -- the Finnish A.L.F.) spraypaint a butchers, smash the windows of Tuagany fur store, similar treatment given to two other furriers. A bloodsports shop had its windows smashed and "HUNT SCUM" and "BLOODSPORTS" slogans painted. E.V.R.

JANUARY/96: Tampere - E.V.R. smash two windows at a furriers.

FEBRUARY/96: Helsinki - Several meat ads vandalized. The furrier Taganay is attacked twice. First time they lost a window, the second time "WORST NIGHTMARE" slogan was painted over the new window. Similar treatment dealt to Valtonen fur shop. A bloodsports shop was hit and painted with "HUNTING IS MURDER." "McHUNGER" was painted on a McDonald's and the furrier Saukko lost three windows. E.V.R.

MARCH/96: Helsinki - E.V.R. vandalize several furriers and bloodsports shops.

MARCH/96: Lappeenranta - E.V.R. smash a fur store window.

MARCH/96: Oulu - E.V.R. hit a McDonald's, smashing a window.

APRIL/96: Helsinki - E.V.R. hit several furriers and bloodsport shops.

APRIL/96: Jyvaskyla - A fur shop loses a window. E.V.R.

APRIL 5/96: Lappeenrata - E.V.R. attacked McDonald's - two windows smashed and slogans painted to nearest tunnel. E.V.R.

MAY/96: Helsinki - E.V.R. hit a circus and several furriers and bloodsport stores with slogans.

MAY/96: Kauniainen - E.V.R. hits a McDonald's.

MAY/96: Lahti - E.V.R. put cancelled stickers on advertisments for an animal circus.

MAY 20/96: Helsinki - Anti-fur protesters clashed with police Monday outside one of Finland's largest fur auctions. Police detained about two dozen of the 100 demonstrators after they tried to force their way into the auction grounds in Vantaa, 12 miles north of Helsinki, the capital.

MAY 31/96: Lappeenranta - E.V.R. in action: Meat truck vandalized, windows smashed, locks glued and slogans painted. A fur store gets its locks glued. McDonald's tunnel receives more anti-McDonald's slogans. E.V.R.
JUNE/96: Imatra - A McDonald's window smashed a few weeks before opening.

JUNE/96: Espoo - E.V.R. glue locks and sloganise a furrier.

JUNE/96: Helsinki - Two McDonald's get their windows smashed out. Also, numerous meat ads have "GO VEGAN!" spraypainted on them.

AUGUST 6/96: Imatra - E.V.R. gets very angry with a new McDonald's, and painted all over the building over 15 slogans, including "THERE IS NO PEACE BEFORE JUSTICE," "McTORTURE," "WE'LL BE BACK," and "E.V.R.." Six locks glued and painted. Security number system was glued and painted. Doorbell glued and painted. Building next to McDonald's (owned by McD.) also received attention: Slogans painted all over and 2 locks glued. Some McD's signs painted. E.V.R.

AUGUST 8/96: Lappenranta - McDonald's was targeted. Three windows smashed and "ELF" [Earth Liberation Front] painted on the walls. ELF

AUGUST 11/96: Lappeenranta - 2 fur stores hit, locks were glued. E.V.R.

AUGUST 12/96: Lappeenranta - McMurder gets 5 windows smashed out. ELF

SLOVAKIA

JAN/96: Bratislava - A.L.F. target Liska (fur trade company) stealing their postbox, advertisement board and some rings. A Liska shop also had slogans painted and its locks glued. Similar treatment was given to several other fur shops. Two billboards belonging to HYKO (turkey farmers) were destroyed. Four butchers had their walls painted and slogans painted.

FEB/96: Bratislava - A.L.F. destroy a hunting platform, glue and paint six furriers. Also destroyed were two HYKO and a zoo billboard. Locks were glued at the Atrakt (fur trade) building.

SWEDEN

APRIL 7/96: An egg factory was attacked by arsonists in Umea. As well as torching the building the activists wrote on a metal door HAPPY EASTER YOU BLOODY MURDERERS.

MAY 7/96: Gothenburg - A meat truck from Scan (Sweden's largest meat producer) was burned out. MEAT STINKS, ANIMAL LIBERATION, and MURDERERS was spraypainted. -Militant Vegans

MAY 9/96: Obbola - A closed down fur farm had its empty animal sheds burned out, as well as the killing shed.

JUNE/96: Lulea - Militant Vegans (MV) attack a group of Nazi skinheads.

JUNE/96: Umea - Animal libbers torch SCAN truck used to take animals to the slaughterhouse.

JUNE/96: Umea - Militant Vegans suspected to be behind the leaving of an incendiary device on the back doorstep of a vivisector.

JULY/96: Umea - Animal libbers rescue five cats from a University vivisection lab. Slogans on the walls read "NO MORE AUSCHWITZ."

JULY/96: Stockholm - DH paint and stick stickers on three animal abuse shops.

AUGUST/96: Stockholm - DH target several animal abuser shops. Locks are glued, windows were smashed and stickers pasted everywhere.

POLAND

MARCH/96: Bialystok - A.L.F. glue and spraypaint two furriers.

APRIL/96: Bialystok - Zieloni Anarchisci (Polish Green Anarchist) organized a mass demo against McDonald's.

APRIL/96: Warsaw - A warthog, en route to California's San Diego Zoo takes matters into its own hands and escapes from quarantine. It is now living in a suburban woodland. All attempts to capture the pig have failed.

BELGIUM

JAN/96: Gent - Fifty activists blockaded a McDonald's. Action in solidarity with the McLibel Two.

JUNE/96: A.L.F. activists destroyed two hunt lodges.

SWITZERLAND

LATE 1995: Zurich - activists torched a McDonald's on its opening day, causing $80,000 damage.

HUNGARY

MAY 3/96: An autonomous animal liberation group, "Nagerfront" (Rodent-Front) destroyed over 13 hunting towers. A letter to a Hungarian newspaper promised further actins, until such times as hunting is recognized as "real" murder.

LEBANON

SEPTEMBER/95: A hunting ban was imposed just before the season was to begin.

AUSTRALIA

DECEMBER/95: Hawthorn - Three butchers have their windows bricked by the A.L.F. "This is the A.L.F." and "Meat is Murder" slogans painted. A.L.F.

JANUARY/96: Melbourne - A.L.F. smashed six windows and painted slogans at a McDonald's in Doncaster St. They then went next door and did the same to KFC. In nearby Tunstall Square a butchers and a chicken shop had their windows bricked.

JUNE/96: Perth - A.L.F. cover circus posters in paint. Also Hungry Jacks and a KFC are sloganised.

NEW ZEALAND

JANUARY/96: Hamilton - KFC walls painted and windows were smashed.

FEBUARY/96: Dunedin - Three butchers and a McDonald's were painted with animal rights slogans.

MARCH/96: Christchurch: Opening day of Sydenham McDonald's delayed as A.L.F. glued all the locks and left a hoax bomb by the door.

MARCH/96: Christchurch: Windows broken at Hunting shop in Montreal St as well as at a Leathergoods shop in Fitzgerald Ave by A.L.F. slingshots.

APRIL 24/96: (World Day for Laboratory Animals), the A.L.F. claimed it had contaminated Sunsilk Shampoo and put them on supermarket shelves. Sunsilk is made by Lever-Rexona, a subsidiary of Unilever who test their products on animals. Hundreds of thousands of bottles have been recalled by the manufacturer. In a statement delivered to 'The Press' (a Christchurch newspaper), the South Island Animal Liberation Front claimed it had put bleach into some shampoo bottles. The same group sent a letter from Auckland on Tuesday to the manufacturers claiming to have added red food colouring to bottles throughout the country.

APRIL/96: Christchurch - GunCity hunting and fishing shop painted with slogans, superglued and GunCity car splashed with red paint.

MAY/96: Auckland - Four butcher shops lose their windows, KFC in Dominion Rd loses window, Laura Mumaw, Director of Auckland Zoo has her car paintstripped in her driveway. A.L.F.

MAY/96: Auckland - KFC and three butchers in Ponsonby Rd all get locks glued. A.L.F.

MAY/96: Wellington - Prestons Meats in Hopper St get windows smashed and completely covered in anti-meat slogans (Hit #5 in just six months). Charcoal Chicken in Cuba St. had its windows smashed and a free repaint from the A.L.F.

MAY/96: Wellington - Slogans painted at KFC in Courtney Place and Georgie Pie in Adelaide Rd.

MAY/96: Auckland - Five butcher shops get their windows smashed including Perfection Meats, Great North Road for the second time in a week. Also, Deidre Goatley, and ostrich farm investment promoter has her driveway painted with animal lib slogans.

MAY/96: Auckland - Four butcher shops get holes in their windows, indluding Puhinui butchers, Blockhouse Bay and Westend Road. One milk delivery truck was covered in red paint.

MAY/96: Auckland - A McDonald's and several butchers were painted with animal lib slogans.

MAY/96: Christchurch - A.L.F. destroy 15 duck shooting platforms on Lake Ellesmere a few days before hunting season was to begin.

JUNE/96: Christchurch - Hibbards Butcher shop in Stanmore Rd had its windows smashed and walls covered in red paint. A fish shop round the corner had its locks glued.

JUNE/96: Christchurch - GunCity was hit with red paint and animal rights slogans. Two windows were also smashed out, locks were glued. Unfortunately, two people were arrested in connection to this action.

JUNE/96: Christchurch - Three butchers on Colombo St. were superglued and paint bombed. A.L.F.

JUNE/96: Dunedin - McDonald's gets its locks superglued with the A.L.F.'s secret-sauce.

JAPAN

JULY/96: Osaka - Animal Lib group ALIVE along with British group ANIMAL CRUELTY INVESTIGATION GROUP (ACIG) help to expose the National Cardiovascular Research Centre in Osaka, as carrying out horrific animal tests. For more info, contact ALIVE, 2-5-12, 2F Hongo, Bunkyo-ku, Tokyo 113, Japan.

SOUTH AFRICA

APRIL 19/96: Steytlerville - Game reserves for wealthy tourists shoot lions, leopards and Springbock were hit by the South African A.L.F. (Spear of the Tigers). The following message was sent to a south african press agency:

"In the early hours of Wedensday morning the barbed wire fences of 2 huge concentration camp 'farms' in the Steytlerville district have been cut by activists from a shadowy new, animal liberation movement- the Spear of the Tigers. Just as we as a proud African people did not want to be interned by apartheid, so Spear of the Tigers give expression to our animal brothers and sisters desire to be free from oppression. Spear of the Tigers boldly claims equality & freedom, justice & peace for all!
This is the beginning of total animal liberation in Africa. This is the beginning of an African reinassance where all Africans, human and animal, will live as one with our Mother Africa. Beware trophy hunters, poachers, all oppressors! This is only the beginning!

The cutting of the fences is thought to have allowed hundreds of animals to return to a natural habitat free from the danger of becoming a trophy hunter's wall ornament.

NEWS BRIEFS

ALF APPRECIATION DAY

April 2, 1996

SEATTLE -- The first ever "A.L.F. Appreciation Day" took place April 2 in front of the Magnuson Health Sciences Centre, on Northeast Pacific Street, on the University of Washington Campus. Supporters conducted a press conference and encouraged the A.L.F. to visit the facility. Other events took place in Minneapolis, San Francisco, Honolulu, Memphis, Washington DC, Bloomington, Syracuse, Buffalo, Atlanta and Rochester.

The A.L.F., which has caused tens of millions of dollars in damage to U.S. research labs, factory farms and fur farms in 15 years of existence, has been branded a "terrorist" organization by the justice department and the FBI. However, no one has ever been injured or killed in A.L.F. actions, which are designed to rescue abused animals and sabotage animal abuse industries.

April 2 has been declared "A.L.F. Appreciation Day" in honour of the 1989 raid at the University of Arizona (Tucson), where an estimated 1,200 animals were freed and more than $250,000 in damage was done to the labs.

April is also the anniversary of the costliest attack ever by A.L.F. -- the destruction of an animal diagnostics research lab at the University of California, Davis in April, 1987 (total damage estimates: $4.5 million).

SYSTEM OF JUSTICE IS OUTRAGEOUS -- TIME FOR TOTAL NON-COMPLIANCE

-name withheld by request

Once more I have been totally shocked by the completely unjust nature of our "system of justice", as it is called. Yesterday a hunt sab and friend of mine was convicted of assault at Corby magistrates.

No police person has seen anything. No evidence of injury was provided at any stage, not even immediately after the incident. Only 3 huntspeople 'witnessed' what happened, but no-one of them actually saw the defendant do the alleged assault. One said, he felt the assault, and two others said, they saw the defendant with a raised arm.

As a matter of fact there was NO assault on a hunter, as has been witnessed by 6 other protesters. On the contrary, 2 hunters lost their temper and attacked a protester by riding at the defendant and squashing him between their horses. He managed to escape and was then followed on foot by the 2 hunters and assaulted. The sabs who witnessed that, threatened to inform the police, which led to the hunters claiming an assault against them had happened in turn. While the complaint of the protesters left the police unmoved, they took the defendant's details only because some hunters said so.

The two female and one male judge, all probably hunters or shooters or at least affiliated to such, had the audacity to smile at us and then, without much deliberation, just said "we find the defendant guilty". The sab faces now even potential prison, as he is in breach of a conditional discharge and has a number of earlier 'convictions' against him. The sentencing has been adjourned.

I think that this 'system of justice' does not deserve our respect. It is a farce, a joke, really. I think we, in Britain at least, should adopt a policy of total non-cooperation with police and courts. We should from now on, in the event of an arrest, refuse absolutely everything, refuse to move, to talk, to eat, to drink, to even open our eyes and acknowledge the presence of anyone and anything until this 'system' has set us free again. Let them carry you into the police cell, and let them carry you out again later, if they want to. Refuse to go to court, refuse to acknowledge their correspondence, refuse to sign anything, refuse to address the magistrates, refuse to pay any fines, refuse refuse refuse.

This type of "justice" does not deserve anything else.

We should seriously talk about the implementation of such an approach for ALL animal rights related cases, especially mass arrests. Imagine 200 protesters being arrested and going completely limp and not regaining consciousness until they are dumped outside a police station. I can't imagine how they would deal with that.

TERRORISM BILL PASSES - RIGHTS TO DISSENT, FIRST AMENDMENT, PRIVACY LOSE

The President of the United States signed the terrorism bill into law Wednesday, April 24, 1996, Public Law #P.L. 104132. With its passing, US citizens lost some key safeguards to free expression and the right to dissent.

THE DANGERS IN THE TERRORISM LAW

In sum, P.L. 104132:

GUTS STATE PRISONERS' CONSTITUTIONAL RIGHTS TO APPEAL

The habeas corpus right of state prisoners to appeal their cases to federal court has been effectively cut -- even when they have good evidence of their innocence or having been wrongly jailed. Now prisoners will have to prove the state has acted "unreasonably" - a very tough standard. Further, prisoners have only a short time - a year usually - to request their one round of federal review. The federal courts can't overrule state courts' interpretations of federal constitutional law - an amazing headstand of precedent. People who need this provision most are the poor and people of colour who are more likely to have had inadequate representation in their original cases. This provision includes everyone convicted under state jurisdiction , not just those who are on death row - EVERYONE. Those in jail on "terrorism" offenses are in federal prisons and so are unaffected entirely by these habeas changes.

DEFINES TERRORISM OVER-BROADLY

The definition of terrorist activity is so broad (encompassing even threats to do property damage as long as they involve conduct in the U.S. and abroad). The provision would make state and federal laws including murder and kidnapping but also illegal property damage now federal terrorism offenses with higher sentences. In practice, the label inevitably will be used selectively and in a political way.

CRIMINALIZES HUMANITARIAN FUNDRAISING

The new law allows the Executive Branch great latitude to label groups "terrorist". The law bars fundraising even for acknowledged humanitarian assistance for groups even remotely affiliated with labelled "terrorist" groups, again inviting selective use, and violating First Amendment activity.

ANIMAL LIBERATION PRISONER NEWS:

NEW ZEALAND ANIMAL ACTIVISTS ARRESTED

New Zealand Animal activists Ben Griffiths and Mark Eden were arrested at gun point early in the morning of Tuesday 11 June by police for alleged involvement on an A.L.F. attack at Gun City, one of the biggest hunting shooting and angling shops in the South Island. The two were arrested only blocks away from the shop, which had two large shattered plate glass windows, glued up locks and had animal rights and anti-hunting slogans in bright red paint on it's walls. Graffiti from a previous A.L.F. attack in May was also still visible.

The two activists were made to stand facing a fence with their hands in the air while police searched them and their bag for evidence, and afterwards the two were arrested and charged with wilful damage and possession of offensive weapons (slingshots).

On July 1, Ben and Mark both pleaded guilty to intentional damage to Gun City and a second shop, The Complete Angler, located in Christchurch. Police agreed to drop the more serious weapons charge when they plead guilty to the damage. Both men have been ordered to pay reparations of $955 each and to do 100 hours community services each.

Money is needed to cover legal costs, and any help would be appreciated. Please send funds (made out to ACTIVIST LEGAL FUND) to:
BUST FUND
c/o Box 6387
Te Aro, Wellington
New Zealand

POLICE POUNCE ON SUSPECT BOMBER

Date: Jul 25, 1996

An animal rights activist Barry Horne was recently arrested when undercover police officers pounced on him in Bristol's downtown shopping centre.

The 44-year-old man had four explosive devices strapped to his body when captured by officers in a struggle in Halfords store in Bristol's central Broadmead shopping centre. The devices were made safe later by army bomb disposal experts. They also dealt with two other suspect explosive devices found in a main chain store and neighbouring cancer charity shop.

The arrest is understood to have followed a lengthy surveillance operation by officers of the South East Regional Crime Squad. They had been involved in a five-week long intensive surveillance operation which had taken officers throughout the country. It is understood they had tracked the suspect from the west Midlands and followed him into stores where devices were planted.

Det Chief Insp Roy Lambert, of the regional crime squad, said: "The devices were all live, armed and ready to go."

He said that although only one person was arrested inquiries were continuing. He said the suspect, who was from the west Midlands, was believed to have connections with the Animal Liberation Front.

"The devices appeared to have been designed to cause the maximum damage where they had been placed."

See page 66 for Barry's address to write letters of support to.

TWO DUTCH ACTIVISTS ARRESTED UNDER SUSPICION OF ARSON

In the early hours of the morning of 24 March, two Vegan activists living in Amsterdam were arrested under suspicion of carrying out arson attacks on three meat transport trucks in Zaandam, Castricum and Den Helder, as well as one or more arson attacks, attempted arson and the placing of anti-meat slogans on a Butcher's School and a slaughterhouse. Their house was searched for over 3 hours by a 15 strong task force.

The investigation was started last year by the police in Den Helder, after attacks on slaughterhouses in that area. In December 1995, the investigation broadened to include members of the Regionaal Recherche Team (Regional Investigation Team) of North Holland and police from the Kennermerland area, after there had been more arson attacks in those areas. The two men used the initials RAT (Right Animal Treatment) and later AJF (Animal Justice Front).

Both men have since confessed to the following:

- arson on 23 December 1996 in Oostzaan on a meat transport truck;
- arson, on the night of 20 and 21 January 1996 on a meat transport truck and surrounding meat processing plant in Castricum.
- attempted arson in Halfweg on meat transport trucks of Hot Dog King, early February 1996.
- attempted arson on a butchery in Den Helder, attempted arson on a slaughterhouse and a meat transport truck both in Den Helder on 30 March 1995.
- arson on meat transport trucks in Amstelveen, Hilversum and Rotterdam. The damage caused to 4 meat transport trucks in Rotterdam totals hundreds of thousands of guilders, because the fire spread to a surrounding "meat company" (the press release does not specify if it was a slaughterhouse or processing plant).
- placing the slogans "meat is murder" and "murderers" on a school for butchers in Amsterdam on 11 February 1995.

The two activists Frank Kocera (25) and Eric van de Laan (20) were being held without trial -- as we go to print we have had no word on any new developments -- a trial was supposedly set for July. They stated that they carried out these actions because they are passionately opposed to every form of animal use/abuse. Their actions were an

attempt to mobilise /shut down butcheries and meat processing plants, and to cause meat-eaters to pause and think about the fate of the animals who end up on their plates.
Please drop them both a line to show your solidarity and support. See page 67 for their addresses.

PRISONER UPDATE

Anarchist Dimos Hristofidis was arrested and charged with the attempted arson at a McDonald's in Athens, Greece. No address is known at this time regarding where Dimos is being held.

Swedish animal libber Erika Schriever-Abeln was found guilty in August of another two arson attacks. She was given a $40,000 fine and is undergoing "rehabilitation" into society. (ie they are trying to brainwash her).

Gurjeet Aujla HV2047
HMP Birmingham, Winson Green Road, Birmingham, B18 4AS. England.

Sentenced to 6 years in connection with postal devices sent to various companies and individuals involved in the meat and livestock export trade.

Dave Callender HV3314
HMP Birmingham, Winson Green Road, Birmingham, B18 4AS. England.

Currently appealing against a 10 year sentence for conspiracy to cause criminal damage by arson.

Darren Cole HD2301
HMP Featherstone, Wolverhampton, WV10 7PU England.

On remand charged with arson on farm buildings used in the live export trade.

Michael Green VA2923
HMP Bristol, Cambridge Road, Bristol, BS7 8PS, England.

Co-defendant of Melanie Arnold, charged with arson on abattoir in Gloucester and conspiracy to commit arson at various meat and lairage companies, etc.

ANIMAL LIBERATION PRISONERS

NORTH AMERICA

Rod Coronado #03895000
FC1, South Wilmot Rd., Tuscon, AZ 85706, USA.

Sentenced to 57 months for aiding and abetting arson and handling stolen property in connection with acting as spokesperson for the North American ALF, and for damaging government property as a protest against the treatment of native Aericans (Rod is a member of the Yaqui Nation).

UNITED KINGDOM

Melanie Arnold GJ0940
HMP Eastwood park, Falfield, Wotton under Edge, Gloucester, GL12 8DB, England.

On remand charged with arson at an abattoir in Gloucester and at two Milk Depots in Cheshire, and on conspiracy to commit arson at various meat wholesalers, lairage companies, etc.

Angie Hamp TW1687
HMP Askham Grange, Askham Richard, York, YO2 3PT, England

Serving 4 years for conspiracy to commit arson. Angie has recently been turned down for parole, and is now due for release in Oct. 96.

Barry Horne VC 2141
HMP Bristol, Cambridge Rd, Horfield, Bristol, BS7 8PS

On remand charged with possession of explosive material with intent to cause damage.

Keith Mann EE3588
HMP Full Sutton, Nr Stamford Bridge, York, YO4 1PS, England.

Sentenced to 11 years for criminal damage, attempted incitement, possession of explosive substances, escape and attempted arson and escaping from custody.

Gillian Peachey RL3415
HMP Holloway, Parkhurst Road, London, N7 0NU, England.

On remand charged with conspiracy to use incendiary devices to cause criminal damage and arson.

Micheal Roberts GE3743
HMP Lewes, Brighton Road, Lewes, E. Sussex, BN7 1EA, England.

On remand charged with conspiracy to commit damage.

Geoff Sheppard MD1030
HMP Wormwood Scrubs, po Box 757, Du cane Road, London, W12 0AE,
England.

Sentenced to 7 years for possession of items with intent to make incendiary devices and possession of a shotgun.

Charles Skinner No24250
HMP La Moye St, Beades,Jersey, Channel Isles.

Imprisoned for starting a fire at Jersey to visitors centre which caused 322,000 pounds worth of damage.

Barbara Trenholm RL1292
HMP Holloway, Parkhurst Road, London, N7 0NU, England.

Found guilty of committing arson along with Justin Wright, due to be sentenced Sept 6.

Justin Wright CE3046
HMP Lewes, East Sussex, BN7 1E4

Found guilty of committing arson along with Barbara Trenholm, due to be sentenced Sept 6.

HOLLAND

**Eric van de Laan Reg No. 1648819
**
Bijlmer, Demersluis, Postbus 41901, 1009 CE Amsterdam, Holland

Awaiting trial on various charges of arson against the meat industry in Holland.

**Frank Kocera Reg No. 1648820
**
Bijlmer, Demersluis, Postbus 41901, 1009 CE Amsterdam, Holland

Awaiting trial on various charges of arson against the meat industry in Holland.

Animal Liberation Frontline Information Service <http://envirolink.org/ALF/alf.html>

MISSION

These pages at intended to provide an on-line information service dedicated to the activities of the animal liberation movement in Europe, North America and World-Wide. Its aim to provide an uncensored clearing house for information and news about animal liberation activities and activists. This service is needed because many actions go unreported by the mainstream media leaving people in the dark regarding what is really going on.

SCOPE

The service does not aim to supply news on the activities of the main stream animal rights groups since this is being done brilliantly by the Animal Rights Resource Site. What the service does is provide information about the 'underground' groups and individuals that are labelled by the mainstream as; 'extreme', 'terrorist', etc.

SOURCES

The vast majority of the information found here has been provided by various Animal Liberation Front Supporters Groups; such as the North American A.L.F.S.G. and the UK-A.L.F.S.G., and the UK's A.L.F. Press Office.
Some of the information is from national media sources or various on-line sources such as newgroups and mailing lists. Some of it has been sent to us anonymously.

DISCLAIMER

The Animal Liberation Frontline Information Service is not itself part of any existing Animal Liberation Front Supporters Group and is not intended to replace their work. The Information Service exists in the interest of free speech, freedom or information and public interest. The Information Service does not exist to incite people to commit any immoral and illegal acts.

EARTH LIBERATION PRISONERS

E.L.P. prisoners have been imprisoned for actions against the destrcution of the environment. For more info contact EF! Action Update, Box 9656, London N4 4YJ, England.

Clive Dairymple, PB 2529,
HMP Pentonville, London N7 8TT
Tim Barford, LW 1062
HMP Elmley, Isle of Sheppey, Kent
Posco Boscovitch, Casuarino Prison, Locked Bag 1, Kwinana, WA 6167, Australia
Helen Woodson, c/o C. Dixen, 3559 County Highway 6, Wisconson Dells, WLI 53905, USA

NA-ALFSG...merchandise distribution...NA-ALFSG

po box 767295 roswell, ga 30076

❖BOOKLETS❖

•**B01 Keep Fighting. 64 pgs 1/2 size $3** Interviews with UK ALF Press Officers.

•**B02 An Animal Liberation Primer. 2nd edition. Compiled and edited by @nu. 32 pgs 1/2 size $2.50** A DIY booklet of direct action tactics: how to stake out an action site, breaking into buildings, vandalism, arson, how to react to police interrogation, etc.

•**B03 As long as there are slaughter houses..then there shall be battlefields. 30 pgs $3** A historical look at actions against animal abuse, from 1991 onwards, and some interesting analyses of the ALF. An invaluable look at the ALF in Britain.

•**B04 Explosives Manual. 84 pgs 1/2 size $4** Guide to building explosives and incendiaries from easily acquired materials. Similar to CIA-type manuals.

•**B05 Grand Jury Comix. 1978. 13 pgs 8x14 size. $3** Although put out almost 20 years ago, it provides useful information for our movement today - and is a great tool for public education concerning the evils of grand juries.

•**B06 Huddersfield:4 The State:0. 36 pgs 1/2 size $3** The story of a 1992 trial of four people accused of being ALF activists in England. The trial that "did not make threatening examples out of the defendants and did not produce harsh prison sentences..." Invaluable info regarding defense strategy.

•**B07 Interviews with Animal Liberation Front activists. 52 pgs $3** Compiled in England from interviews with numerous ALF cells. Covers most aspects of the ALF.

•**B08 Into the 1990's with ALF Activists. 18 pgs $2** A how to book from England on ALF tactics.

•**B09 The Power Is Ours: A Manual on Saving the Earth and the Animals. 15 pgs $2** An updated version of Into the 1990's with a slightly different layout and tactical info.

•**B10 Without a Trace: A Forensics Manual for You and Me. 36 pgs 1/2 size 1987 $2** Details the police department's capabilities on tracking activists.

•**B11 This is the ALf. #2 20 pgs 1/2 size $1.50** An Australian primer. Clippings as well as DIY directions.

•**B12 Animal Liberation Primer. 3rd edition. 20 pgs 1/2 size $2** How to guide. Covers some different ground than the previous primers.

•**B13 Press Clippings. 49 pgs 8 1/2 x 11 $3** News clippings from U.S. actions dating back to the 1980s.

•**B14 On The Road Again: Direct Action Underground. 8 pgs 8 1/2x11 $1** A guide to living underground: acquiring fake IDs, transportation, funds, communication, etc.

•**B15 Interviews with California ALF Activists. 6 pgs 8 1/2 x11 size $1** Answers to basic questions asked by beginning ALF activists.

•**B16 Their Lives Are In Your Hands. 16 pgs 1/2 size $1** Summary of actions for '94 ALF attacks.

•**B17 History of the American ALF: Diary of Actions. 1977-1995. 12 pgs 8 1/2x 11 $2** Everything the North American ALF has been up to since 1977.

•**B18 The Final Nail: Destroying the Fur Industry. 24 pgs 8 1/2x 11 $2** Manual for defeating the fur industry. Contains a state by state listing of fur farms, suppliers, etc.

•**B19 Memories of Freedom. 90 pgs 1/2 size $3** A first hand account of the Operation Biteback campaign engaged by the Western Wildlife Unit of the ALF.

❖MAGAZINES❖

north american

•**M01 Underground** #3 Winter '95 **65 pgs $3, #4** Spring '96 **56 pgs $3**

•**M02 No Compromise** #2 Spring '96 $3, #3 Summer '96 $3 Covers militant animal rights groups (CAFT, SOAR, etc.) as well as the ALF. A necessity for all activists!!!

foreign

•**M11 ALF Supporters Group Newsletter from the UK** Spring '95 **32 pgs $2.50,** Summer '95 **28 pgs $2**

•**M12 Arkangel** (UK) **#13** Spring '95 **68 pgs $4, #14** Fall '95 **60 pgs $4**

•**M13 Liberator** (UK) #2 Summer '95 **40 pgs $3,** #3 Fall '95 $2, #4 Winter '95 $2

•**M14 Animal Info** (New Zealand) #5 Dec. '95 **8 pgs $1**

no longer in print

•**M16 Combat (published by the old Canadian SG) #1 1990 16 pgs $2**

❖MISCELLANEOUS❖

•**X01 Stickers: "Support the ALF" Masked activist with bolt cutters OR "ALFSG" with shackled hands breaking free.** 50 cents ea./6 for $2

•**X02 Bumpersticker: "No Blood For Vanity" (Coalition to Abolish the Fur Trade)** Full-sized, professional vinyl bumpersticker. $2

•**X03 Fabric Patches, with circled "A" and NA-ALFSG around it.** Perfect for jackets, backpacks, etc. **$2**

•**X04 ALFSG Benefit Compilation.** 17 Canadian punk and hardcore bands. High quality tape. Comes with a 24-page booklet and "ALF Supporter" sticker. **$7.50**

all prices include postage for north america. overseas orders please add 25% for postage.

WANTED:

ANY NORTH AMERICAN A.L.F. VIDEO FOOTAGE

The **North American A.L.F.S.G.** is colaborating with some small film producers to put together a full length North American A.L.F. Documentary/History. **We want your video clips from television news, any action big or small** -- from fur store that got their locks glued all the way up to footage of the Penn State Head Injury raid.

Any quality tapes would be appreciated. We will return tapes after copying and if needed will reimburse people their postage for sending tapes to us.

North American Animal Liberation Front Supporters Group

Box 69597, 5845 Yonge St. Willowdale, Ont. M2M 4K3, Canada.

UNDERGROUND

THE MAGAZINE OF THE NORTH AMERICAN ANIMAL LIBERATION FRONT SUPPORTERS GROUP

$3

ISSUE #6 WINTER'96 Free to Prisoners

LETTERS TO UNDERGROUND

(remember to put "FOR PUBLICATION" on 'em when you want to see them printed!]

FROM HOLLOWAY WITH LOVE

Firstly, my personal vote of thanks to all of you out there who continue to take the fight for our friends directly to the abusers in such a varied and imaginative fashion. So many of you somehow still make the time to support those of us lazing around in enforced inactivity! There is nothing that gladdens the heart more than hearing of all the actions taking place and there was plenty of that in the latest "*Underground*." Brilliant stuff.

Animal rights has such a high public profile now and we must none of us let the opportunity to capitalize on this escape us. We've seen what we can achieve but we've still only scratched the surface of abuse. Keep on kicking them in the economic balls and eventually we can bring all the lousy businesses that profit from blatant misery and suffering to their knees. Do whatever you can, fight in whichever way your conscience dictates, but above all, PLEASE keep fighting. There has to be an end to all abuse, to the idea of man placing himself above other species to their detriment, to this horrendous concept that other species are there for man to do with as he pleases.

My respect and love goes out to all of you who are fighting for our friends and we are all out there with you in spirit every inch of the way. Never forget that animals have no voice but ours and we must not allow our voices to be silenced where ever we may be. Rather, we must raise our voices together until we deafen the abusers and the rights of all species are recognized. Together we can halt the abuse and put an end to the appalling suffering that our friends endure every minute of every day.

Keep fighting, stay free
Love and Liberation always
Gillian Peachey RL3415
HMP Holloway, Parkhurst Rd, London
N7 ONU, England.

Gillian adds in another letter, "My congratulations, love and total support for the many brilliant actions that have been going down over there. It really does do you a power of good reading about it when you're stuck in enforced inactivity. Good on those activists. Keep it up. We'll all be back to join you, that's for sure!"

DUTCH ACTIVIST UPDATE

Dear people of the NA-A.L.F.S.G.

Many thanks for the magazine. Before I was in prison I didn't realize so much actions were going on in America, England, etc. It's nice to know so many people have decided to take up direct action against the animal abusers.

You asked me for some updates about Frank's and my case. Well, we've been to court and Frank will be out in +/- 12 months, and I about 6 months. I guess you already know about all of the case
because it was in the NO COMPROMISE which I also received, and I read that you are in contact with them.

Well, just to say hello and thanks for the support!
Greeting, Eric. R.A.T.

Eric van der Laan, Reg No. 1648819
Bijlmer, Demersluis,
Postbus 41901, 1009 CE
Amsterdam, Holland

THOUGHTS ON PRISONER STRATEGIES

Hi Guys,
Two things. Firstly, to let you know of our case. On the 9th September 1996, after 15 months on remand, I was sentenced to 3 1/2 years imprisonment for an A.L.F. firebomb attack on a Gloucestershire slaughterhouse building and its fleet of refrigerated lorries. My co-defendant, Michael Green, received 5 years for this and an attempted arson at a lairage company associated with live exports in Northamptonshire, UK. The police had been highly hopeful, confident even of our both getting 8 years (more wishful thinking on their part than having any basis in fair legality) and had already stated that anything less was appealable by them as being too lenient. So, understandably, as the sentences were handed out, there was a lot of heavy nail biting (not to mention breathing) and mutters of "appeal ... appeal ..." by the police.

Originally, when I knew a "guilty" plea from myself would be evident, I was determined that no "mitigation" would be brought forward. Having not even acknowledged my name to my interrogators, let alone anything else, I had no intention of speaking to the courts either to put forward an apology or put forward a defence. The attack, after all, spoke for itself. I did not recognize nor accept the distribution of "justice" from a male carnivorous stranger and I fully accepted and expected my silence to be indicative of a remorseless and unapologetic stance, which is what I had and still have. I conditioned myself to accept 6-10 year, I prepared long-term plans and achievable goals for myself and my pride was the dominating factor in everything I said, done and thought about. Pride!

Over those 15 months I naturally still had a great deal to do with activists who kept up regular correspondence and visits, and inevitably, the question of "mitigation" or damage limitation arose during various conversations. Although I originally rejected any hint of such a thing, I couldn't help but notice, that those who insisted I should make a political speech out of the court process (which would reach the ears of a judge, the police and a room full of supporting and already converted animal activists -- the media not really prone to doing our propaganda for us) thereby ensuring at best a paragraph or two, at worst an extra year or two, were the self same people whom there was very little, if any evidence of activism in themselves. On the other hand, the people who insisted the opposite, were those who worked round the clock and not just on animal lib issues either, and were usually so exhausted with the amount of work they had been doing that to see a fellow activist wasting valuable time in prison, the length of which was, to an extent, controllable, was little short of criminal (if you'll pardon the pun). I was forced to re-examine a very personal part of myself, a part that very nearly made me forsake extra productive years in the struggle for claps in the courtroom, paragraphs in papers and for all the armchair activists to jerk off on. When did the most stirring political speech ever save lives? Have you ever saved a life after a courtroom speech of two minutes of interruptions? Have you ever saved a life -- period? And perhaps, more to the point -- would you deliberately inflict upon yourself extra time away from your loved ones and the fight at hand for nothing but a few moments of personal infamy? In fact, would you do anything which had the risk of imprisonment attached to it at all?

"It's a note from the Animal Liberation Front"

One activist in jail for one year amounts to a massacre in unsaved lives; one activist in jail for one year is a lifeline to the animals suspended until that activist is free. One activist in jail for one year is a thousand and one opportunities to enlighten, educate and inspire others -- missed! One activist in jail for one year is a necessary casualty of war sometimes, but 4 years? 6 years? 14 years? And when I stopped thinking about MYSELF, I remembered what I was doing in prison in the first place -- I didn't think of myself when I blew the building up, why should I start now? What made me so important that I was putting my own "political" status and pride before the cause I'd "sacrificed" myself to earlier? Me? I'm stubborn. But the thought of appearing beaten didn't appeal to me at all, not one little bit. Yet, when I listened, I heard the whispers of the animal spirits who had died during my inactivity; and when I remembered, I saw the faces of the 7 day old calves, wrenched from their mothers, and staring at me with accusing eyes through the slats of a lorry enroute to a continental veal system, I saw primates with broken arms and noses, bloodied from a beating by a lab "technician"... There are things that all of us end up doing that we don't like. Who likes to bring themselves to watch films like "Hidden Crimes"? Who likes trying to convince the public to part with their cash on a raining and cold weekend? Who likes trying to wean a pack of hounds off the scent of a fox when an assortment of heavies are assaulting us with whips and cudgels? Who likes facing up to the fact that our own happiness, our own survival is entrenched in doing not necessarily what we want to do but what we HAVE to do? I'm not interested in pandering to the press or pandering to the public. I do what I do because it has a proven success rate in spite of, not because of public support.

Knowledge bears responsibility and once we recognise that, we have the responsibility to acto and we have the responsibility not to get caught, but if we are, we also have the responsibility to be free as soon as possible to carry on the work. And, with this in mind, I entered the courts, not as the police had hoped, donning a paramilitary uniform and with an attitude to match with which to provide visual evidence of the sinister terrorist description they gave of me, but looking classy and demure in a suit and blouse to negate that image. The police know who I am and what I'm capable of, but their opinion, unless corroborated with evidence, is disallowed. The police may well see a scheming, devious, manipulative, unrepentant "femme fatale," but the judge sees a young, presentable, first time offender whose citizenship is not altogether lost and he has to take into account the level of mitigation; the guilty plea, the fact we'd taken innumerable precautions to ensure life would not be harmed, our academic and professional backgrounds, our promise to stay within the law in future (yeah, but who's law? -- Ours of course!!). We used and abused the system we knew we couldn't win by argument alone, we played along with them, told them what they wanted to hear, fed them the fodder and generally played dead. The sentencing reflected the fact that we were believed. Currently, I have six months left to serve but I have 3 1/2 years to make up for.

Which brings me onto my second point. Here in the U.K., albeit each and every person has their own viewpoint on these things; at the end of the day I was and am supported for my decision. It's MY time, MY life, MY choice and MY responsibility to the animals which hangs in the balance.

I've always known that whatever the decision, whatever the outcome, I have a hardcore support network that does just that -- it supports. There aren't conditions attached, it doesn't exist for some prisoners but not for others and we have a good association with prisoners and support networks abroad. Which is why I particularly cannot understand why there are individuals in the United States who have gone out of their way to attempt to diminish the noble spirit of one of their own prisoners, including taking his own mitigation papers and using his words, out of context, as a rebuttal of the movement. What they intended to achieve by sending them to the A.L.F.S.G. UK, God only knows. But suffice it to say that we, in the UK, are in total solidarity with the A.L.F./E.L.F. prisoner Rod Coronado, and always will be for as long as he continues on that path (which, if my knowledge is anything to go by, is forever).

What can be happening, I wonder? Why would the apparent proponents of animal liberation be slagging off a one-in-a-million activist desperate to get back to his tribe, home and the people and animals he has served and represented for so long? Why does the prospect of a prisoner who has already sacrificed so much who is now itching to get out and resume the work that so few are prepared to do with the same vigour, commitment and disregard for personal consequences, bother them so much? Is this level of devotion so terribly threatening to their own fragile standards of activism? Are they jealous? Are they hurt because a member of an indigenous people can not only fight and work for his own people but can organize, initiate and see through various plans of his own without the predominantly white, middle class movement in the States?

We in the UK deplore and pity the people who sent those documents in the pathetic attempt at denying a tremendous and imprisoned man the support he deserves. If the same energy and funds were spent on alienating an abuser of animals, we may have seen some progress by now. A movement like ours will always have its fair share of cranks and free-loaders, or wasters and parasites, of informers and egoists, of sad, pitiful, helpless, actionless, gutless morons, whose prejudices and low self-esteem is only matched by their low level of activism; the law of averages demands it. The further fact that a few individuals can encompass ALL these qualities is also something to ponder.

Anyone with a modicum of sense, however, will be able to weed out the slime and not get dragged into their defeat-minded depths. To those of you who are genuine, I say -- Keep the faith, overcome your fears and support ALL our prisoners, for one day you may be in need of support yourself.
To those of you who propagated the infighting, I say: Get a life, or even better -- GO SAVE ONE!
For the Earth
Mel

Melanie Arnold, GJ0940
HMP Eastwood Park, Falfield,
Wotton under Edge
Gloucester, GL12 8DB, England.

MORE ON ROD

Thank you so much for printing Rod Coronado's letter -- I agree with him 100% and if ever the NA-A.L.F.S.G. declines to support Rod or joins in the vicious character attack on him, then the NA- A.L.F.S.G. will be a sham and a shame. I wish we could all stick to discussing the plight of the animals and quit talking about people.

Why are we so willing to dissect fellow activists? No one is truly cruelty-free, no one walks on water, and while we fight amongst ourselves we promote animal suffering by weakening our own forces and by fractionalizing our movement. The energy and time spent in tearing down fellow activists should be spent in tearing down fences, on emptying cages, on liberating animals and supporting each other.
Beware the ego!
P.

Hello. I am new to the animal liberation circles. I super-glued some McDonald's locks and did some hunt sab stuff when I was studying at the London School of Economics (1989-1990), but I have been doing mostly faith-based anti-militarism, anti-colonialism stuff since then. I have done a few years in jail, all told, for my belief in nonviolence. I have been a devout vegan since 1987.

Allow me to make an observation or two, simply because I haven't seen them here before, a reality check perhaps:
1) ROD CORONADO IS DOING 57 MONTHS IN PRISON FOR ANIMAL LIBERATION!
2) PRISON SUCKS! As all who have spent more than a few weeks behind bars know, it's not fun.
3) No one else in the U.S. is doing significant time for animal liberation.
4) Division is what the (extremely well-funded and totally "legal") opposition wants.
5) No matter what our differences are, we should love and support one another, at least and especially in jail.

I believe, based on my limited correspondence with Rod, that he will be back in the struggle for animal liberation once he is released from the state's dungeons.

We love you Rod. Thank you for your sacrifice.
For the animals,
B.F., Virginia

Dear t. and the S.G. --

I want to thank you for your most recent Underground and your heroic attempt to separate accusation from truth in the animal rights court-martial of Rod Coronado. The problem seems to be that he has abdicated his original role as warrior-hero-martyr, which some took ill, perceiving his revised trial strategy as unpopularizable media material. Since he did not violate the two criteria of a resistance fighter (he betrayed no-one, he harmed no-one) he deserves all our support. The criteria of support of an activist is not that he/she is popular hero material, nor even that their resistance action succeeded, nor yet that they were known and applauded by other activists. No. The standard by which they are evaluated and supported is their MOTIVATION TO HELP. For example, many anti-Nazi Resistance Movement activists walked into traps, made stupid errors out of panic or ignorance or inexperience -- some even informed under torture, and it was expected by the Resistance Movement that this could occur. These activists were ordinary persons like ourselves, and their heroism lies in that very fact, not that they were media figures brilliant enough to publicize a cause. Nor were they ignored and disowned because their actions were sometimes not successful, that they were caught and arrested and imprisoned.

We need to humble ourselves and learn from the sincerity of some of the resistance movements of yesteryear. The greatest activist may be the one nobody has heard about, BECAUSE they are anonymous. Dutch farmers concealed Jews in their homes for years, without their neighbours being aware. Yet, if they made one mistake and were arrested themselves, should we then turn our backs on them, because their efforts were not corporate successes?

The corporate, media-accessed animal rights movement and even many grassroots individuals are influenced, often unconsciously, by the corporate national values, where successes are praised and failures disowned. We are just as hasty as any mainstream person to judge and criticize, jumping on the political demagoguery grandstand of detraction, and using the same techniques prosecutors do: quoting out of context, rumour, character assassination, discarding certain individuals for a greater "political good." We need to excise such corporate values from our minds and replace them, not with agendas of "compassion" and "ethics," but with spiritual values that teach us that we are servants of all, not egos, and not publicity figures. The greatest is the one who tries to serve, whether his efforts were an apparent, calculable success or not. The case of Jesus Christ, a political prisoner fabricated on the crime of treason, is a classic example of this.

I urge every animal person to spend five minutes daily, or equal time to that which we spend detracting and being irritated at the shortcomings of our fellows, in prayer and meditation for their benefit, in order to develop the spiritual perspective that is the foundation of helping other beings. We do not wish it said of us, by the corporate government which thrives on our dissension: "With supporters like those, who needs prosecutors?" No matter to what creed or denomination you belong, or even if you are not in touch with any of the wisdom traditions -- spiritual values need to be nurtured, they are not inherent. Only potential is inherent, and it needs to be cultivated through the formal practice of focusing on loving kindness. Only thus can unity in effective action be achieved.

Lise Olsen

MOWING THE GRASS

Dear North American A.L.F.S.G./Animal Activists

When we read the letter from Ingrid Newkirk in Underground #5, regarding prisoner support which mentioned that PETA supported Roger Troen and paid his legal defense, "What?" we said, "didn't Roger inform on the A.L.F.", why was PETA supporting him or did they not know?

So we went to work and did some research. And as we thought, Roger Troen testified at least once, most likely several times, against animal activists on the west coast. (We've enclosed copies of one of Roger's statements, minus the people he named, for the A.L.F.S.G. to reprint).

Roger is still active in Portland, going to demonstrations and telling stories to young activists about how he was arrested. We don't think Roger has anything to brag about after what he said about other animal activists.

Traitors to the animals should be banished from the animal liberation movement and dealt with accordingly. We suggest that you give Roger Smith Troen a call and see what he has to say 503-287-7894 or maybe say hello to him in person 4226 N. Montana, Portland, Oregon 97217.
We don't need friends like Roger and neither do the animals.
Anonymous for the Animals.

The following page contains the statement made by Roger to the FBI:

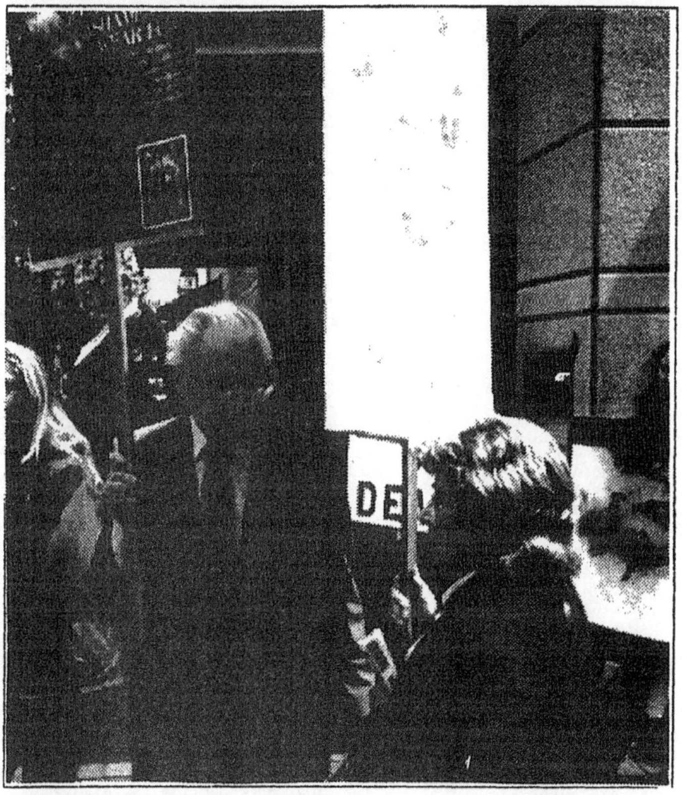

ABOVE: Roger Smith Troen at a recent (96) anti-fur demonstration.

FEDERAL BUREAU OF INVESTIGATION

Date of transcription 6/20/90

ROGER SMITH TROEN, 4226 North Montana Avenue, Portland, Oregon, was interviewed by Special Agents KAREN A. SABOL and FRANCIS M. HICKEY and Assistant U.S. Attorney R. STEPHEN LAPHAM at the United States Attorney's Office in Sacramento, California. The identities of the interviewing agents and AUSA were made known to TROEN, as was the purpose of the interview. Also present during the interview was TROEN's attorney, STEPHEN A. HOUZE, of Portland, Oregon

TROEN was preinterviewed relative to his consenting to the interview as a result of his acceptance of a "Use Immunity Agreement" between the AUSA, Eastern District of California, Sacramento, and TROEN's attorney, with regards to his ANIMAL LIBERATION FRONT activities at the University of Oregon. This immunity agreement required TROEN to fully cooperate and testify before the Federal Grand Jury or any future court proceedings.

TROEN provided the following information prior to his grand jury appearance:

TROEN became involved in the animal rights movement in 1976 by assisting a group called ANIMAL AID in Portland, Oregon. The group focused on neutering and spaying of area animals.

By 1983, TROEN became involved with a new group called MOBILIZATION FOR ANIMALS (MFA). TROEN attended a rally sponsored by MFA in Davis, California.

In 1984, chapters for a group called PEOPLE FOR ETHICAL TREATMENT OF ANIMALS (PETA) were being formed in Oregon and California, in which TROEN subsequently became involved. Thereafter, TROEN created a new group called RAT ALLIES because of his love of rodents.

In late summer 1986, TROEN first heard about a possible break-in at the University of Oregon from an individual identified as [redacted]. [redacted] contacted TROEN and showed him a five minute video tape of a man wearing a mask holding a rabbit supposedly at the University of Oregon. [redacted] advised TROEN that

Investigation on 6/6/90 at Sacramento, California File # 266F-SC-13666

by SA FRANCIS M. HICKEY & SA KAREN A. SABOL/kml Date dictated 6/8/90

he had access to the University of Oregon and it was possible to remove approximately 70 research rats from the laboratories. [redacted] knew of TROEN's interest in rats and thought he would like to become involved.

Approximately two to four weeks before the actual break-in October, 1986, [redacted] telephoned TROEN in Portland and asked him to come down to Eugene. While in Eugene, he and [redacted] looked for rabbit cages to be used to house the stolen rabbits.

Later that day, TROEN and [redacted] drove to the Eugene Airport in TROEN's aunt's vehicle, a 1973 brown Ford. There they met two male individuals who just arrived. TROEN advised he had previously met one of these individuals in [redacted] and knew his name as [redacted]. The four then drove from the airport to the University of Oregon campus to look the facilities over and locate a place to park vehicles to be used in the break-in. TROEN advised no one entered the buildings while they were on campus. He further noted that while on campus, the four broke up into two pairs to walk around the area. TROEN and [redacted] were one pair and [redacted] and the other male individual were the second pair. The four stayed approximately one hour on campus.

TROEN recalled on one of his three visits to Eugene prior to the break-in, his role was to obtain a telephone number from a pay phone located at a rest stop south of Eugene on Interstate 5. This telephone number was to be called after the animals had been stolen from the University of Oregon. It was on one of these prior trips to Eugene that TROEN learned of the date and time of the actual break-in.

On the day of the break-in in October, 1986, TROEN recalled driving to Eugene in his aunt's 1973 Ford vehicle and arriving at a predetermined motel on the south end of Franklin Boulevard approximately at 7:00 p.m. At the motel, he observed approximately one-half dozen individuals, all males except for one female. TROEN could only identify [redacted] and [redacted] in the motel room. TROEN could not recall [redacted] role in the break-in.

TROEN waited in the motel room until just after dark and then left with an unknown male individual he described as having a large build and a beard. The two drove to several locations to place getaway vehicles for after the break-in. TROEN then made his prearranged telephone call to a designated rest stop and spoke with a female whose voice he recognized as [redacted].

At the completion of the call, TROEN slept in his vehicle until time to carry out the break-in, not socializing with the other participants.

Just before the break-in, TROEN rode in a van with several participants to one of the break-in sites on campus. TROEN remained in the van while the others entered the facility. TROEN described the other participants as wearing normal clothing and not wearing masks or hoods. TROEN assisted the participants in loading the van with the stolen animals. The participants then re-entered the van and drove to a prearranged site where the animals were to be distributed. TROEN recalled the large male with the beard driving the van to this location.

At the distribution point, approximately three-quarters of a mile east of the University of Oregon campus, near Interstate 5, the animals were transferred into waiting vehicles.

Subsequently, TROEN contacted [redacted] and arranged for her to take possession of three rabbits. TROEN noted that he still had in his possession several rats that had not been given away to homes.

TROEN advised the next time he had contact with [redacted] was at his trial for the burglary of the University of Oregon.

TROEN contacted the local PETA Chapter for legal referral and was given the name of GARY FRANCIONE, Law Professor, University of Pennsylvania. FRANCIONE arranged for representation by local attorney, STEVE HOUZE. TROEN advised PETA paid for his legal defense for the university break-in.

TROEN, ROGER SMITH

animal liberation: *if not you, who?*

by The Todd

In today's society, those who rescue animals from places of abuse and cause economic damage to institutions of earth and animal exploitation while revealing the horror that is committed against them, are terrorists. In today's society those who burn, maim, electrocute, shoot, trap, poison and torture animals are sportsman, scientist, farmers, and businessmen and women. We live in a society where these convoluted perceptions of good and bad are force-fed to us as the value-system that the government claims makes us the most free society in the world today. In school, work and family we are sometimes brutally reminded that to stray from the accepted norms of society is to be ostracized from it, which all too often is followed by police repression of us social deviants and potential "domestic terrorists."
Many authoritarians in this society speak of our "war for independence" and pride themselves on their heritage of building a democratic society out of a harsh and forbidding wilderness. In North America, the dominant world views (both moral and legal) that we are intimidated into accepting is nothing short of the forced indoctrination of a foreign value system from a invading force occupying our homelands which has historically sought to destroy all human cultures that strengthen and maintain our connection to earth and animals.

6/4/86-Hartley, DE; Sydell's Egg Farm, 25 hensliberated by the Farm Freedom Fighters

Each of us in our own hearts knows it is wrong to force-feed poisons to rabbits, rats and mice or any animal for that matter, but how many of us are willing to violate the "laws" of our society and commit the "crime" of breaking and entering, grand theft, and destruction of property to stop it? Once we cross that line, it takes us form peaceful protesters to alleged felons in our pursuit of the bond to earth and animals. Animal Liberation Front activists face many years in prison, huge fines and restitution, long periods of probation where violations mean more years in prison, loss of certain constitutional rights such as the right to keep and bear arms, to vote and the bearing of a "scarlet letter" which prevents employment, international travel and almost always guarantees government harassment for the rest of their lives. Such is the price for taking our opposition to animal abuse and earth exploitation beyond the accepted perimeters of protest.
So why risk all in order to save a few animals and lesson the profit margin of the government sanctioned vested interests who destroy nature? Because we're tired of waiting for others to stop unquestionable evil in this world. We're tired of being dragged from the picket line and watching truckloads of animals going to slaughter, of bulldozers rolling toward the destruction of wilderness animal homes. Where civil disobedience in our movement mostly centers around drawing attention to the abuse and exploitation of animals and earth, A.L.F. actions seek to rescue the prisoners of that abuse and hinder if not cease that abuse by destroying the machines and tools of life's destruction. Through sharing the very same goal, the difference in tactic and regard for mans law matters greatly in the eyes of the slanted scales of justice. Legal strategies that might be proven effective in one realm may not apply in another, the only similarity being the motive behind the action. So why does the A.L.F. continue to participate and advocate tactics and strategies that seriously threaten their personal liberty and physical freedom? Because what we endure in a prison cell or at the wrong end of a fur farmer or law enforcement officers gun is minuscule when compared to what our governments have allowed to happen on this continent to animals in the last 5 centuries. Though the A.L.F. may never receive the support or participation of as many who support or participate in civil disobedience and protests, these are some of the reasons A.L.F. activists have chosen to sacrifice certain unnecessary liberties to ensure fundamental liberties for animals.

Anyone who has ever seen video or photographic documentation of animal abuse (often obtained by the A.L.F.) can relate to the feelings of powerlessness and inability to stop the torture. Screaming your lungs out on a protest line and even getting arrested in acts of civil disobedience are ways that we manifest our rage and anger, but often the feelings of impotence return and we are left facing the continued torture and abuse of literally billions of animals. For A.L.F. members a life of obedience to laws and values that sanction the destruction of all we love is no life at all. How can we as fellow members of the same species responsible for such cruelty and global destruction, as we now witness today, not do all that is humanely possible to stop it? One need only rescue one individual from the fate of the vivisection laboratory or fur or factory farm to experience the satisfaction and peace that comes with knowing that at least one prisoner has escaped. Any feelings of insignificance from such an action when compared to the thousand not liberated are erased as you witness the joy and love for life that all animals are capable of expressing when released from their misery. I will never forget the reward of watching a little female guinea pig I once knew being received with such gentle love and compassion by an elderly women who warned me of animal dealers who kidnap pets for vivisection. Little did she know (or need to know) of the impending fate of our little animal relation had the A.L.F. not rescued her from the vivisection supplier who had already sold her to a lab for LD50 testing. Thousands of guinea pigs are tortured in vivisection laboratories every year, but at least this one wouldn't be.

Fighting factory farming can also leave the average activist feeling overwhelmed when simply being vegan doesn't stop millions of chickens from being forced to live a cramped existence on an egg farms. Yet it doesn't take more than even the smallest backyard to build a chicken coop that would be heaven to 6 or 7 laying hens. Many times I have broken into egg farms to help rescue a few chickens who were precariously clinging to life in their squalid conditions, and it has been a true blessing and beacon of hope to see these intelligent animals recover from their confinement. Within days, even chickens are capable of some how remembering how to dust-bathe, scratch for bugs and worms, and roost at night. Social structure and individual personality returns to all animals when given the opportunity.

When one liberates any animal from a certain death with the guarantee of life incredibly better than any other in its intended fate, a victory is achieved for all who believe in the rights of animals. We remind ourselves and others of the inherent worth of all life and how the values and laws of the society we oppose deny not only animals but also ourselves true freedom.

So open up your home to rescued animals and assist others in finding homes for the liberated. Let it be known to fellow activists that you can support certain types of animals and maybe the A.L.F.'s Underground Railroad will come knocking on your door. And if you know of some-one who would feed and care for animals if a coop or other facilities were built on their property then get out there with hammer, nails and recycled lumber and build it. And when its built don't wait for the A.L.F. to find tenants, get out there and get em out yourself.

For the urban guerilla or activist who wants to really impact the cycle of animal abuse, economic sabotage is the A.L.F.'s salvation. How often we all have stood in front of university torture chambers on that one day a year we dedicate to laboratory animals, only to go away at the end of the day knowing that for the 364 other days that year the animals will be used and abused as if they weren't the living, breathing, and feeling sentient beings that they are. Yet in one night animal research laboratories have been shutdown, hundreds of animals liberated and research experiments ruined by A.L.F. attacks. Though the tactics may appear extreme to the uneducated or unaware, the A.L.F. has always countered that the true extremists and terrorists are those who in the light of day and fully within the bounds of the law, conduct painful experiments on animals. Many above-ground activists find it easier to support live animal liberations with their happy endings, but for the animals left behind there is no happy ending when the torture chambers are emptied but not destroyed.

To this day, the greatest impact caused in vivisection laboratories and other A.L.F. targets has been through arson. In June of 1991 when the A.L.F. torched Oregon State Universities Experimental Fur Farm a handful of activist no different from yourself, accomplished every anti-vivisectionists dream. Not only was the 65 year old laboratory shutdown and every research project de-stroyed, but information obtained from the vivisectors own records helped contribute to numerous raids on other fur farms and laboratories. Most often animal rights activists are mistakenly led to believe that animal research labora-tories are secured fortresses, but such is not always the case. All it takes to find out is for every animal liberation activist to adopt a vivisection center in their area and spend late nights observing the nightly habits and routines of maintenance and security staff if any. After a few weeks you may be surprised to discover that a window of opportunity is available, enough to allow liberationists the opportunity to strike. Once you have balanced the scales of true justice by making your own rules in the fight to defend animals and the earth through illegal direct action, you will have discovered what our enemies fear most, the unleashed fury that is the A.L.F.

Federal investigators, bio medical researchers, fur Industry officials and other pro-animal abuse forces rarely talk of their fears of a demonstration, protest, or civil disobedience. What really keeps them awake at night are the lightning strike raids of the A.L.F. The current $1000,000 reward for the capture of an A.L.F. activist speaks the truth of what animal abusers fear the most.

So why not try pursuing the shortest path to animal liberation? Think of all the risks you would take if your very own dog or cat was being tortured in a vivisection laboratory and then try to explain the difference between you own companion animal and the millions of animals in research lab, factory and fur farms today. Remember, animals are our brothers and sisters in this world. They are innocent beings who know not why they are being punished at the hands of man. Lets not forsake them and leave them to the fate of the merciless. The A.L.F. will not forget our connection to the natural world and the animal people and will continue to strive towards a harmonic relationship with all life. We do this because of love not hate. Governments can imprison us, but they cannot break our spirit. Please join us in our quest for immediate and total animal liberation. @

A BLAST FROM THE PAST

This interview is reprinted from *Without A Trace* originally printed in *Interviews with A.L.F. Activists.* Both are great booklets and are available from the North American A.L.F.S.G. Distribution.

This interview, although it is with a UK A.L.F. activist, is still very relevant to North American animal abusers.

How do you go about carrying out actions?

There are a number of aspects that one has to take into consideration. First and foremost it's important to look round the region at all the targets, laboratories, and as many of the factory farms as one can find, hunt kennels, fur shops, abattoirs, etc. If actions have taken place already in your home area it's a good idea to go for the most straightforward, squirting paint stripper from a lemon juice squeeze or a washing up liquid squeeze bottle over the van(s) of an animal exploiter, gluing up fur shop locks to start with, then progress to factory farms which generally are not alarmed (there is the odd one that is particularly those that belong to the large chain stores). If no actions, or only one or two small actions have taken place, it may be beneficial to go for a laboratory, the reasoning being that once things start in your area the labs will start investing in more security measures. There are still labs with only minimal security. The animals are not necessarily in the labs at all times. There is usually an animal house in a separate building where animals are held until needed, or in some cases are bred there. We can usually gain access to the grounds, (we're not put off by the usual security fence with strands of barbed wire, these can be climbed with practice - we use the concrete posts as a support and wear 2-3 pairs of gloves when learning. N.B. Razor wire is much more tricky/dangerous - be careful!) we usually find the buildings with animals have fans operating, pumping out the stale air and the fresh in. We can smell which one has them (the animals) within.

With factory farm units we can tell what kind of animals, if any, are in the units, simply by placing our ears against an air duct on the side of the unit or at the door, listening and smelling. Or we try shining a pencil torch, with coloured plastic held over the end by an elastic band, through any openings. In fact, we double or triple the layers of plastic so that only the minimum of light gets through, not only reducing the chance of anyone else seeing, but shine a bright light onto battery hens and they may well make a lot of noise. We always try the door handle, etc. and have been pleasantly surprised a couple of times to find it is unlocked. With experience one can often tell what animals are held in a particular unit by its shape, size and building materials used.

When looking at potential targets, we don't take balaclavas, etc. We also make a point of emptying our pockets of everything including door keys, discarding matching jewelry etc. before setting out, in case we drop anything. If we need to cover our faces a scarf is fine and we wear gloves of course We also carry bird watching books and binoculars. Usually a lad and a girl will go by public transport or be dropped off at a prearranged time. We avoid parking a car in an area where a future target is being looked over, unless it's hidden. We try to limit our visits to any target to one or two and we do not leave any trace of our visit. We find we can make a totally silent look round by removing our shoes, though this is usually unnecessary. During the day we explore the approaches to the target with the help of an Ordnance Survey (O.S.) map, looking for a suitable dropping off point/place to stash the vehicle(s), emergency meeting point if necessary, noting any guard dogs at the target or in the gardens of homes along the route in. After dark we walk the route to ensure there are no guard dogs, go in and examine the units, check if there are any animals in them, can we climb in through an air duct, if not, what types of locks will we have to deal with.

If it's a lab, and not straightforward, we need to know the times of security patrols, then we'd do a spot of camping nearby.

In our group there are four people and over a period of time we have equipped ourselves with ordinary scarves for covering our heads and faces, gloves, two crowbars (one small roughly a foot long, the other roughly a yard) a large screwdriver, a well oiled brace and 1" auger bit (it's a wood boring drill the type used to make the hole in your door for the Yale lock), two mortar drills (one being extra long), two sledgehammers (a 14'lb one with a full handle and a 10'lb one with the handle cut to 20" for working in a confined space), a pair of boltcutters, two 35mm SLR cameras with flashgun (with diffuser and tilt - occasionally we can bounce off the ceiling to get natural shadow). Duracell batteries are used in the flashgun - recharge is then much quicker. We use 400 ASA B&W film in one, and 100 ASA colour slides in the other. When we carried out our first raid there were three people with scarves, gloves and large screwdriver. We rescued 36 hens. Four sacks each, one carried on each shoulder by their draw strings and one in each hand, 3 hens in each sack.

We have since found that cardboard boxes are fine for chicks, etc., if the 'items' involved are rodents we sometimes find the cages in which they are housed are portable and we place the lot in our boxes or rucksacks. For hens and rabbits we use fairly large sacks (approx. 24" wide X 36" long) with rope nylon drawstrings in the middle. The rope is threaded in and out of the sack at 6" to 8" intervals and the length, when knotted together is the same as the circumference of the sack. We seal the double knot of the rope by using a match and literally lighting the two ends. As the nylon melts we blow out the flames and the resulting black blobs keep the strands together.

Another useful item that we make from a sack is a guard sack. Two brush poles are sprayed a dark colour, then placed inside the sack, one either side, and stitched securely into place. Roughly 6 - 8" of the handles protrude. One or two of these act as good barriers when you have to deal with a guard dog. The protruding poles are placed under the armpits and are held as high as possible. If anyone asks what they are they would be told that they are hides for photographing wildlife.

A brace and 1" auger drill have been used to make a series of overlapping holes allowing entry into this laboratory animal house.

The actual day chosen for the raid is considered well in advance. A full moon and no clouds means a well-lit night which is undesirable, as are hot muggy nights when people find it hard to get to sleep. Overcast nights are good, and any rain is very welcome. With a particularly difficult target, everyone is made aware that we are expecting 'bad' weather and to expect very short notice. It is also important not to work to a pattern (e.g. actions every Friday/Saturday night). Weekends evenings are good because of the amount of people travelling to and from pubs/clubs, but for night raids weekdays are more appropriate because of the amount of early morning traffic. Saturday nights are the worst possible, the roads early Sunday are dead. On the day of the raid a planning meeting takes place and a thorough briefing/ discussion takes place. Details dealt with include the transport of equipment and activists, time of raid and departure, while studying a plan of the target - who will be responsible for being a lookout breaking in, taking the animals, holding the sacks/boxes, where to meet up if things go wrong, who will be acting as back up by sitting at a phone, ensuring everyone has a few ten pences and some emergency money - while the raid may go OK, a car could break down. Everyone empties their pockets. We do take a container of water if the raid is likely to take a long time - wearing a mask for lengthy periods results in dry throat and coughing .

Before the tools are transported everything is wiped first with a rag soaked in warm soapy water and then again with a dry rag. This also goes for the cameras (and battery), flashgun (and batteries), everything, even glasses if worn. A further refinement is to cover our clothes with something like a boiler suit or old baggy clothes over our normal clothes and have a spare set of footwear. These items virtually eliminate the risk of us carrying traces home. These items can be discarded when we return to the vehicle(s), placed in a black bin bag it all looks like jumble. Someone has the responsibility of thoroughly washing the scarves, gloves, boiler suits/old clothes and shoes immediately upon returning after a raid. This person is not directly involved in the action and stores the clothes and equipment. In other words we use a 'safe house'. Generally speaking, the arrangements for events after the action are just as important as the precautions beforehand.

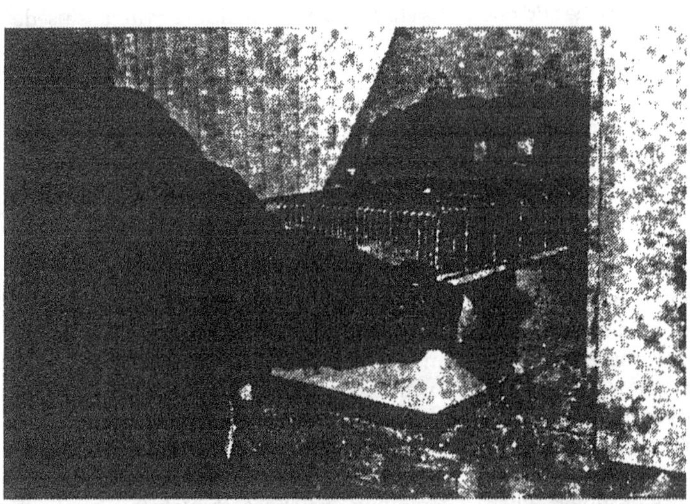

The end result after a nice size hole was drilled out. Over 100 animals are now in good homes.

Before setting off we make sure that everyone has a plausible reason for travelling in that direction or homewards, we consult the music press to see if there are any concerts applicable. If a male activist is driving, a female member will sit behind him. The police have a habit of glancing into cars and mixed company is far less likely to be stopped.

Choosing the day for the raid can be crucial. If possible we carry out the raid mid-evening so that we are home before 10:30-11:30 pm. Once the pubs close, and particularly after midnight there is always the chance of a spot check by the police looking for burglars. If travelling by car (we avoid hired vans, hired cars are OK, the police take less notice of new cars) we try to arrange for the tools, and hoods if used, to be well hidden in the target area by mid-evening by just two people - a girl and a lad using public transport if possible. We take only the minimum amount of equipment.

The raid may need to be at night. Battery hens often make quite a din, though we are not put off by this. Unless we carry out the action while the house is unoccupied or is some distance away we raid the unit at 3-4 am while everyone is fast asleep. We never travel between 12 midnight and 6-7 am there or back. We arrive in the evening and hide out in a wood (we avoid the local pubs for the obvious reason) and time the raid so that we arrive back at the transport after the raid shortly before dawn. Generally speaking, by planning well ahead we tend to concentrate on late evening raids during the summer and night-time raids during the long nights of autumn and winter. The transport will often be minimum of one mile away from the target and probably two or three miles away hidden in a field or wood (we carry a good quality compass in case we have to leave in a hurry, though it's generally not required). Vehicles are never parked in country lanes as the police will generally treat them as stolen vehicles that have been dumped, or certainly suspicious. Anyone sitting in such a vehicle will certainly be questioned. We push the car(s) down a track into a wood or similar. Pushing does away with driving with lights on and resultant noise and thus dealing any locals out walking the dog. We have parked in a nearby housing estate, leaving the vehicle(s) locked and empty, the drivers returning in couples to pick up the vehicles, and later the raiders. If the target is in an awkward area the raider can be picked up by vehicles returning at a prearranged time or called in by portable C.B.'s (again Duracell batteries are used).

If there are a number of cars hidden in a field/wood for an evening raid, depending on circumstances, it may be prudent for driver(s) to remain hidden nearby and watch that no dog walkers/courting couples stumble across them. If this were to happen and the dog walker/couple take a lot of notice, the vehicle(s) are moved to the emergency meeting place. When the raid is over one person travels ahead and checks that the transport is o.k.

The first thing we do during an actual raid is for the look out(s) to get into position. Binoculars are a very useful addition that can be used at night. They may take a little getting used to, focusing and time for ones eyes to adjust but it's work worth persevering. We find the usual, long, thin straps on binoculars are unsuitable. They not only leave them dangling, and thus banging on fences being climbed, etc. but they're also uncomfortable to wear after a time. We substitute wide camera straps, suitably shortened. If portable C.B.'s are being used they are tested beforehand to make sure they are in working order and tuned in. Because of the noisy static when both units are switched on, the raiders will have their C.B.'s switched on all the time while the look-out(s) will have theirs switched off. This gives total silence; if the look-out needs to reach the raiders, a flick of the switch and it's on and ready to use. However, we do not rely on the C.B.'s alone as sometimes we may be working in a spot that gives poor reception. The look-outs should be positioned so that they can also warn the raiders directly and quickly. Usually bleeps are used rather than voices on the C.B.'s, two bleeps to keep still and quiet, four for 'all clear' and continuous bleeping if it is time to run for it, though we've not had to use the last sequence so far.

We have once or twice locked a gate using a plastic covered bike lock. This method is both quick and silent and ensures security vehicles cannot pursue us.

Usually we do not cut the telephone wires but occasionally this is necessary. Either they are cut near the house or office, if this is not possible, a piece of brick is tied to a nylon rope and is thrown over the wire between two poles and two people will pull the wire down. It's usually a struggle and requires two people to use all their weight to yank it down. Wires are not cut at the big commercial labs as they are likely to have alarms connected via the phone lines to the nearest police station. *(note: Most business intrusion alarms these days are wired into the phone line. Cutting the phone lines may trip either an audible or silent alarm)*

When entering the target area we usually have to deal with a fence of some sort, two people go forward and deal with it. The ordinary 3 strand barbed wire farm fences have the bottom 2 strands cut only. The top one prevents cows or horses following us or straying in the road. On the other hand, anyone pursuing us will be in for a shock. If it's a chain link fence we cut a strand at the very top, following that strand down through the others to about thigh height from the ground and cut it again. Then, holding the strand where it is cut at the bottom we force it to twist and corkscrew it out. We can then part the fence and climb through the gap. We leave the bottom part uncut if there are guard dogs, if disturbed it would be harder for them to get out after us, particularly if the top half is also blocked by one of the guard sacks with the poles jammed in the netting. The same two people then check out the unit and immediate area.

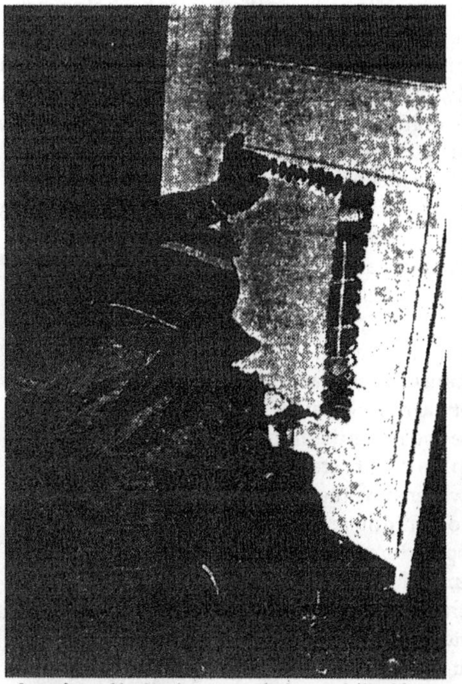

A series of holes have again been drilled in a door that is alarmed. Where 1 or 2 holes hadn't quite overlapped the wire cutters finish the job.

Having drilled through the mortar around 1 or 2 bricks and removed them, a pad saw is used to cut around the others.

When actually breaking in to (say) a factory farm unit, usually all that is required is a large screwdriver and a couple of crowbars to deal with a Yale lock on the front door (straightforward) or to deal with the inside bolt(s) on the back door. In the case of the back door, if it's a tight fitting one we first pull it from the bottom, we can then judge where the inside bolt or first bolt is. We force the first screwdriver roughly 12" from the bolt and force the opening until the small crowbar can be inserted. Further force is exerted until the large crowbar can be put in by a second person, who puts their full weight behind it and rocks it to and fro, forcefully yet gently. The idea is to make the screws which hold the lock/bolt eventually pop out, not to take the door off its hinges.

For padlocks, we may need to use boltcutters, we ignore the lock and go for the hasp which is often mild steel. With the cutters in place, a wet towel is wrapped round the cutter and hasp. This helps to deaden the sharp crack noise. If we are unsure about a door being alarmed, the two people who dealt with the fence will also break in and then rejoin the rest of the group for 30-40 minutes to watch for any reaction, from a couple of fields away.

If the animals being liberated are battery hens, all the group enters very quietly, then closes the door. A torch covered with coloured plastic is switched on. The cages are opened. A variety of different types of cages are used, common sense tells us if they unclip, slide up or across. A last resort is simply to tear them apart with our hands. We are not put off by the noise the hens will be making by now. Due to the barbaric conditions it's not unusual for fighting to break out, so factory farmers are used to outbreaks of noise. Having closed the door most of the noise is absorbed by the usual wooden building.

Working in twos, one person clasps a hen (remembering their wings are quite strong) so that the head is facing away from us, while the other holds the sack which is rolled down to the drawstring beforehand which helps to keep the neck open. The hen goes in head first, we don't let go until the bird is sitting comfortably at the bottom of the sack - two more follow. To try and simply drop them into the sack just does not work, they will get their feet caught up in the sacking and nap their wings about. If this happens, it's taken out and the procedure repeated properly. We are very careful not to injure the hen. The three hens safely in, the drawstring in the middle of the sack is drawn closed and the resulting loop goes over the shoulder. We take as many hens etc. as we have good homes for.

With experience it's possible to work in total darkness which usually reduces the amount of noise the hens make. When working in a broiler unit with full grown birds we move more slowly, otherwise 10-15,000 hens may start off. We don't panic if they do though, it may sound loud in the unit but outside it's surprising how much the wooden units deaden the noise.

With rabbits we select single mothers with well-developed young. Large rabbits on their own often indicates a pregnant female, and for obvious reasons rabbits with small young are not disturbed. Rabbits go into the sack back end first because of their large rear feet. Sacks are ideal carriers because the material is comfortable and keeps the animals warm, and with plenty of fresh air. Following the raid we ensure the door is closed so that the cold night air doesn't result in a sharp drop in temperature and discomfort for the animals left behind.

For buildings that are alarmed we try to gain direct access into the room holding the animals by going through a wall. Using a well oiled brace and mortar drill long enough to drill out the mortar from around one or two bricks, we then lever them out with a large screwdriver or small crowbar. We then simply cut bricks along the mortar with a padsaw (keyhole saw) and literally cut bricks out. Squirting water from a squeeze bottle onto the padsaw reduces the noise of cutting the mortar (3-4 squeeze bottles are usually required).

To go through a door that may be alarmed we use our brace to drill a series of overlapping holes using a 1" auger bit until a square can be removed big enough for us to get in and out of with our boxes etc. We have also been able to remove a window from an animal house by taking out the putty using one of those screwdriver sets that has a pointed implement. On another occasion we gained access to an animal house during the day when the alarms were switched off. During the lunch break we gained access using a skeleton key. We had already established on a previous visit at night that it worked, by unlocking the door, but not opening it, then relocking it.

Old type alarms can be dealt with by removing the bell with a screwdriver or forcing it to one side with a crowbar so that the hammer can be cut off or bent so that it cannot possibly strike the bell. Another method with the klaxan-horn type is to spray cavity wall insulation fluid (the type that sets in 15 minutes) into the horn and through the vents into the alarm box.

Once enough time has elapsed for the animals to be got away it's time to deal with the labs and offices. As these premises may also have alarms we crawl along the floor. The aim is to quickly smash up enough equipment to put it out of action or plant incendiary materials to burn it down once satisfied there are no people or animals in there and, if possible, to obtain any documents relating to the experiments, who supplied the animals, names and home addresses of the vivisectors/

One of the 40 rabbits liberated from E-Y Laboratories on March 11 1989 in Soquel, CA by the A.L.F.

animal technicians etc.

With the big commercial labs, there is always the chance of a silent alarm connected to the local police station. By going through a wall into a room with animals we usually find this is no problem, but later when entering the actual labs, to destroy it or rescue animals undergoing experiments we prefer to go for a smash and grab effort. Sledgehammers then come into their own. A 14'lb hammer is aimed at the mortise lock repeatedly. We save vital time by going through the outside wall first or smashing in through a window and then dealing with the internal doors with the sledgehammer. In a confined space a 10'lb hammer with the handle cut down to about 20" is the answer. Crowbars are also of use.

In planning this type of action we have to be totally practical. Those fit enough to run some distance after the raid carrying dogs, etc. and rucksacks full of documents will be responsible for taking the animals, papers, for destroying equipment and if possible, the lab itself. For the most part, raiding labs is straightforward, only a handful of the very big labs have more elaborate security equipment. ***(note: unfortunately all University labs these days have security systems, look around and with a little luck and lots of hard work you will find one that can be done.)***

We never paint the letters A.L.F. on a unit or lab, at most we will spray 'Animal Liberation' or 'Animal Belsen'. We paint slogans in dark colours and where they are visible to any reporters following up the story — this helps confirm the action has taken place when the owner or manager denies it ***(note: things have been very different over here in North America)***. Where the noise of a spray can may alert a guard dog a large felt tip pen is sufficient.

If everything goes well, we do, of course, mention it was an A.L.F. group to the media so that everyone concerned is aware who was responsible.

If we have to carry potentially noisy animals, e.g. dogs, a long distance over fields, etc. particularly after a smash and grab, we carry some anti-mate (as used by hunt sabs to put hounds off the scent of foxes). We give a good squirt after crossing a stream, road, etc. for obvious reasons.

When returning to the vehicles on no account do we walk along roads at night. If something went wrong we would, at most, walk in the fields parallel with roads to help direct us to the meeting up place.

Much of what I've said may appear to be processes that would take some getting used to but we found after a while that they became second nature. We've never been discovered carrying out a raid and the four of us had no previous experience. It is simply down to common sense.

Further reading; *An Animal Liberation Primer, Interviews With California A.L.F. Activists, Into the 1990's with the A.L.F., Without A Trace, Interviews with A.L.F. Activists.*

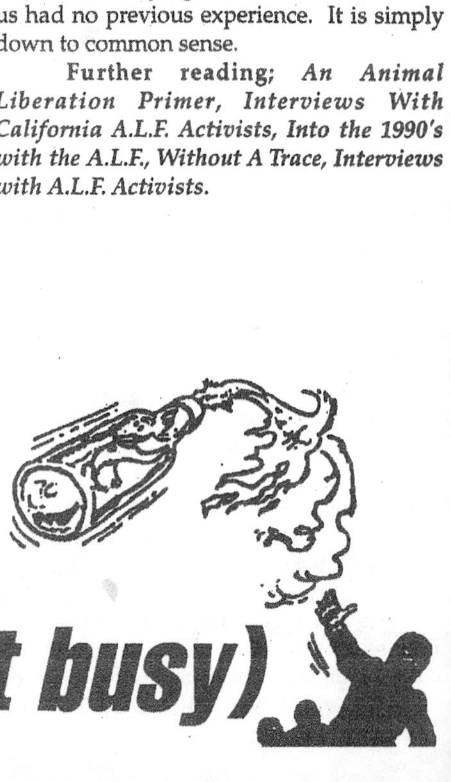

Talk - Action = Zero *(get busy)*

Preparing Ourselve For Action

by Freebird

Hunt sabotage in today's world is a dangerous activity. Perhaps it has always been that way. Sabotage of hunt campaigns is, by it's very nature a very precarious prospect. Coming into contact with armed men immediately prepared for inflicting and imposing their violence onto animals in the wild, in the context of working against them, creates prime conditions for conflict and violence.

The conditions under which a hunt sabber will find themselves in during a campaign or action is very often extremely stressful and emotionally exhausting. Preparing ourselves is vital to our health, not only in the more obvious ways, but more importantly, in our emotional health. Being prepared means that we might be as effective as possible.

We must be prepared in many different ways - physically, mentally, psychologically, emotionally, and spiritually in order to deal with sometimes large angry men. And still nothing you do or know may have any effect on a violent situation.

Field conditions

Have the conditions which make hunt sabbing so dangerous really changed all that much over the past decade or two? They have in terms of new laws which have come into effect; laws which have been created to protect the hunter's interests, and against the interests of us or the animals. In the UK we now have the Criminal Justice Act which has spelled out specific anti-sabbing laws, and in the U.S. most states have specific Hunter Harassment laws on the books.

These laws have not had the desired effect of decreasing hunt sabotage activity, but they have potentially increased hunt sabber/police contact which could, and very often does, lead to more violence, arrest, and/or incarceration.

Conditions have improved in terms of increased public awareness and consciousness about hunting issues. But the gain of compassion in the public mind has not had any noticeable effect on the incidents of hunter-initiated violence against sabbers. Indeed, the only change in sabber/hunter conflict which I've noticed has been an increase in violence.

In the recent past we've seen sabbers beaten up and put in the hospital, particularly in the UK where that reality of sabbing has always been a constant. We've also had two deaths in that country. It's no different today, except that sometimes now the violence comes from the police as well.

From the Hunt Saboteurs Assoc. fact sheet on hunt violence:

"There is a very real problem of violence at hunts - it overwhelmingly consists of assaults by hunt thugs against saboteurs. In the first 3 months of 1993 alone, some 75 saboteurs were victims of violent attacks by hunts, 13 of them

requiring hospital attention as a result. In recent years saboteurs have been kicked, whipped, beaten with staves, spades and other weapons, ridden down by horses and vehicles, throttled, threatened with knives and shotguns, knocked unconscious and sexually assaulted in a range of attacks all across the country. There has also been an alarming rise in the use of vehicles as weapons despite the deaths of two saboteurs in recent years under the wheels of hunt vehicles."

Here in N. America, we have not had to deal with violence anywhere near the levels which we see in the UK, but physical violence is on the increase. Although the two situations are not really that comparable, perhaps due only to the lack of numerous and continuous hunt sab actions in this part of the world, it is worth noting and tracking the developments.

In one of the first organized hunt sab actions in California in 1990 (against the bighorn sheep kill in the Mojave Desert), a sabber was beaten resulting in a broken nose, and held hostage in a trailer by the hunting guide. Today, we continue to witness beatings in North America, at varying types of campaigns, such as the pigeon shoot in Hegins, or the woman hit and punched on the 1995 Bear Watch campaign.

In the 1996 BW campaign, an ambush on a sabber's vehicle led only to damage to the minivan, and the line between property damage and physical violence (thin as it was while the windshield was being smashed and shattered across the laps and faces of the occupants inside) was not crossed perhaps only because the sabbers were all women.

In today's reality we have to deal with vandalism and property damage actions against us by hunters and their allies. If nothing else, those events are simply retaliatory in nature, against us either because of who we are and what we represent, or because of the increase in similar economic sabotage campaigns being waged against them by activists and groups such as the Animal Liberation Front, the Earth Liberation Front, or the Earth Liberation Army, amongst others.

In addition to the increase in violence from hunters, we also have an increase in violence from the state in the way of jail terms. In Chicago recently, an activist was handed a six month term for his participation in hunt sabotage, of which he will have to complete the entire term (because he was convicted of criminal contempt of court for violating a court injunction - an increasingly-used tool by hunters and guides).

Dealing with stress

As with most direct actions, there is a high level of stress which seems only to build during the course of a campaign or action, until a release valve opens. During these stressful times you may find other issues coming to the surface. These might include: personal matters which have not been dealt with between comrades might flare up; power issues which might arise as activists begin to feel that their voice is not being heard in decision making; others might find that under the pretence of continuing a solidarity amongst sabbers that some peer pressure may come into play.

How can we expect to deal with personal conflicts and/or differences of strategy and ways of working when you might not even know all your comrades very well? In the field, decisions need to be made very quickly. The solutions might be found in figuring out and deciding who you want to work with in your immediate affinity group, and sticking together. Or perhaps we need to swallow a bit of pride and acknowledge that another's choices might be more effective and better thought out. There is the inevitable give-and-take between comrades on any campaign.

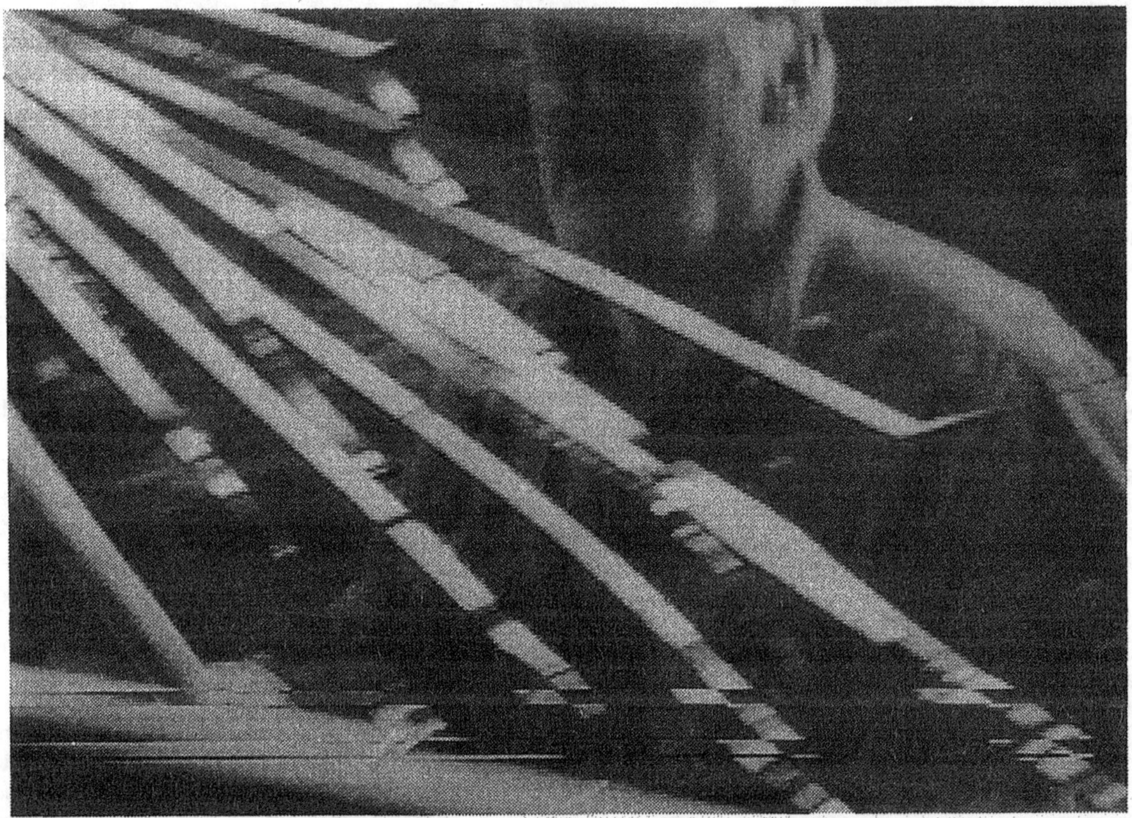

With the state of hunt sabbing as it is, and if we are to continue to engage in these types of campaigns, we will need to prepare ourselves in every way possible to effectively deal with not only the hunters and police, but also with each other.

A strong community bond is crucial to a campaign, but it is difficult as activists come and go. A high level of trust is required in these situations, and that is asking a lot of most of us. The least we can do, for ourselves and for the benefit of our comrades, but most importantly, for the ultimate benefit of the animals we are trying to save, is to be as prepared as possible. Besides, whether you're a hunt sabber or not, it's a good idea to be prepared for anything in this day and age!

Physically - It's important to actively participate in self defence courses, and continually keep ourselves in good physical shape. At the very least, we need to know key points on a human body to strike at, to create a moment of possible escape from a dangerous situation.

Intellectually - Conflict resolution skills are an asset to have, and hopefully someone in your group will have some experience to share. We need to have the verbal skills necessary to try and calm down angry hunters, as futile as it might seem to be.

Psychologically - Understand clearly, and before you enter into a sab situation, that there is a good chance of physical danger to yourself. Avoid creating surprises for yourself; understand the hunter mentality and mindset. In other words: Know Your Enemy!

Emotionally - We need to remain grounded and calm, and we need to avoid being reactionary; learn to stop for a moment to think and analyze situations and to develop appropriate responses. But more importantly, we need to support our fellow hunt sabbers - know your comrades, spend time socially. Know your own, and other's weaknesses and strengths. We are who we have for support, so let's treat each other well!

Spiritually - Trust and have faith in Gaia, in the Earth, in the positive energy of the animal spirits. Know fully that what you are doing is right, and remember to come back to this knowledge in times of chaos and stress.

Finally, remember to eat well, and above all else, remember to breathe!

As direct action against hunting continues and increases in North America, activists need to understand the differences between this type of campaign and others. A better understanding of the dynamic, and of ourselves, can only lead to more effective sabbing. @

Now get out there and SAB THE BASTARDS!!

Fur Farm Liberations Continue, Most Intense A.L.F. Campaign in Years

The A.L.F. is continuing its hard hitting campaign against the North American fur farm industry. As we go to print over 30,000 animals have been released from their cages. We have confirmed that several farms are going out of business, and others, including those never raided, are spending tens of thousand on extra security.

On August 9th an A.L.F. cell raided the Carmel Mink Ranch in Hinsdale, MA. 1,000 mink were liberated. This action led to national news coverage on CNN and National Public Radio. It was a devastating blow to the farmer, as was reported in several news publications. Just days the later the A.L.F. was in Alliance, OH. This time they were targeting the president of the Ohio Mink Breeders Association. The Jorney mink ranch was raided and 2,500 mink released. Both of these farms would hear from the A.L.F. again!

On September 28th the A.L.F. followed up on a promise to return to the Jorney Mink ranch in Alliance, OH. This time they opened 8,000 cages and released most of the 15,000 incarcerated mink. Newspaper articles had headlines like "Fur Farm Struggles to Survive After Second Raid" and so on.

On October 2nd the A.L.F. carried out their fourth raid on a UT fur farm.The Paul Westwood farm in Salem, UT was hit and 1,500 animals liberated. It was beginning to look like a tough year for Utah ranchers. Now, in addition to releasing animals, the A.L.F. was destroying the fur farmers breeding records as well. While the breeding records become worthless for the released mink because they escape, or can't be traced back to the right cage, the A.L.F. still ripped the cards up for the still captive mink so that the farmer would have no pedigree background, and would be hesitant to breed any of them.
Utah has more fur farms than any other state. Utah has also seen more A.L.F. raids on fur farms than any other state.

October 5th saw the A.L.F. moving into New Hampshire for the first time. Gauthier Fur Farm was hit and 35 fox and 10 mink released. One TV station did an interview with a masked A.L.F. member, voice disguised etc. The interview was shown along with killing footage from fur farms. This was one of the few times that this type of footage has been shown on the news. This was a major victory for the A.L.F. in terms of educating the public about why they do what they do.

On October 11 they struck again in Hinsdale, MA. This time they struck the Carmel Mink Ranch for the second time. Devastated by the previous raid, Carmel had put in an advanced, expensive security system. In a communique to CAFT the A.L.F. stated that infra red beams were going across the tops of the cages. No cage could be opened without breaking the current. The A.L.F. went to work anyway, and had opened 75 cages by the time the farmer came out screaming and yelling. The A.L.F. escaped, and it will be interesting to see what they do to this ranch next.

October 23rd saw the A.L.F. back in Oregon. The first major strike against the U.S. fur farm industry was in June of 1991 in Corvallis, OR. The A.L.F. completely shut down the Oregon State University Experimental Fur Farm. It was quite fitting for them to return to this state. The Krohl Fur Farm was hit in Lebanon, OR. 2,000 mink were released. This became big news in OR and the A.L.F. received some pretty decent coverage as well. CAFT members did many interviews to explain why the raids were necessary.

The A.L.F. struck next in Utah. This was the fifth raid on a UT fur farm in 6 months. The Reese Fur Farm in Coalville, UT was raided and 2,000 mink, as well as 200 fox liberated. Breeding cards were destroyed as well. As it became increasingly obvious that the A.L.F. would not stop, it was reported in the UT media that edgy ranchers were sleeping outside with shotguns cradled in their arms. The ranchers in UT are getting desperate, but no more desperate than the mink who will soon see the gas chamber wheeled down through the shed towards their cage.

Showing that Oct. was their month, the A.L.F. struck once again. This time it was a repeat performance on the Bennett Fur Farm in Victor, NY that had been nearly cleared out in April. The A.L.F. cut through 3 fences that surrounded the compound. After searching through 40 or 50 empty sheds they found a few fox at the front of the facility. 46 fox were released and breeding cards for the rest destroyed. The A.L.F. had to evacuate as a security truck interrupted the action.

At this time 22 fur farms have been raided by the A.L.F. in North America. The idea is catching on and a cell in Austria recently broke into a mink farm and released 100 animals. An empty Swedish farm was burnt to the ground and the offices of a Norwegian trade group were trashed with scores of windows smashed, etc. As new Asian markets make fur farming more lucrative, the A.L.F. makes the cost of business increase like never before. Sheriffs patrols are increasing in areas with high concentra tions of fur farms. Others are putting up electric fences, letting packs of dogs loose, hiring security guards, etc. Many have flood lights sweeping their compound or infra red beams shooting across the tops of the cages.

Despite expensive security measures and a $100,000 reward over their heads, it is clear that the A.L.F. will continue to attack the fur farm industry. There are many states which have not seen action yet. Judging by the recent spate of actions, they will all be hit soon. Until every gas chamber is smashed, and all of the cages are empty, GO A.L.F.!!

J.P. Goodwin
Coalition to Abolish the Fur Trade
PO Box 822411
Dallas, TX 75382

Diary of Actions

Please Note: The Diary of Actions is intended to report the news of direct action to save animals, not to encourage crime. [That would be bad!] All reports come from other publications, the internet, or anon. communiques sent to the NA-A.L.F.S.G. and other animal rights groups. As usual, the following list includes actions that took place in the time period covered in *Underground #5*, but were not reported until recently. Better late than never!

CANADA

September/96: Toronto, Ont - A Swiss Chalet restaurant (Bloor & Bathurst) had locks glued and windows sloganized. A.L.F.

October/96: Toronto, Ont - Furs by Nicolas & Lous Kallinikos And Sons Furs were both hit, locks were glued and front windows and walls spray painted and sloganized. Six more fur shops were spray painted and sloganized with "Fur is Dead," and "Scum." A.L.F.

October/96: Toronto, Ont - St. Andrew Poultry, a slaughterhouse in the heart of downtown, had locks glued and was spraypainted with slogans. A.L.F.

October/96: Toronto, Ont - Two butcher shops were spray painted and sloganized with "Meat is Murder." A KFC on College St. had its locks glued and windows painted with slogans. A.L.F.

October 11/96: Lower Mainland, BC - Animal Avengers announced in a news release to local media outlets that it had contaminated several turkeys in three of the Lower Mainland's major supermarket chains. The group claimed to have poisoned turkeys at local Safeway, IGA, and Save-On-Foods stores. From the communique: *"Every year hundreds of thousands of turkeys are murdered for food and sold in neatly wrapped packages to the public, while the butchers and meat industry pockets the blood money. The Meat industry over the last several decades have poisoned people with growth hormones, additives and chemicals. At least we're being honest about it. Wake up or die.*
Only the beginning -- animal avengers"
The poisoning claim is similar to one in the same area made just prior to Xmas 1994.

October 22-28/96: Vancouver, BC - Several McDonald's billboards spraypainted with "Go Vegan," "McDeath," and "Resist." - Unclaimed.

UNITED STATES

March 23/96: Mercier Island, WA - "Milk is torture" was painted on an R&R Espresso building, and four other businesses were hit with animal liberation slogans.

April 29/96: Mercier Island, WA - activists poured glue into the front and back door locks at Subway Shop, and spraypainted "Meat is Murder" and "A.L.F." on the walls. A window was smashed out with a brick. Damages estimated at $1600.

June/96: Minneapolis, MN - Marigold Foods (Kemp's Dairy Products), had two trucks hit with spraypainted vegan slogans. A.L.F.

June/96: St. Pauls, MN - Steak House restaurant had locks glued. A.L.F.

June/96: Wayzata, MN - Wayzata Bait & Tackle had locks glued, a brick through the window and a live-bait vending machine overturned. Damages estimated at over $2000. A.L.F.

June 25/96: Mercier Island, WA - A McDonald's on 77th Ave S.E. was hit with a brick through the window and "meat is murder" and "A.L.F." painted on the building's north and south sides. Also hit was a Baskin Robbins which had locks glued and animal liberation slogans painted on the walls. Subway Subs also had a window broken and graffiti painted on a rear wall. A.L.F.

July 25/96: West Fargo, ND - A fire extinguisher with Animal Liberation note attached was thrown through the front window of Quality Meats. Slogans such as "Animal Liberation" and "Meat is Murder" were also written on trucks. A.L.F.

August/96: Newport Beach, OR - A crab, momentarily left unattended in an empty 5-gallon bucket, was liberated and returned to the Pacific Ocean. *"It made a difference for that one."* Crustacean Liberation Front.

August 25/96: Dallas, Tx -Bifano Furs Downtown delivery van was paint stripped. A.L.F.

August 25/96: Richardson, Tx - Richardson Fur Center had a window shot out. A.L.F.

August 25/96: Plamo, Tx - Alaskan Fur Exchange had it's window smashed. A.L.F.

August 27/96: Boston, MA - Michael Hawley, president of Gillette Co. has his home soaked in red paint. A.L.F.

August 31/96: Collierville, TN - RusDun Farms Inc., a large egg farm had incendiary devices planted in four semi-trucks and in the loading dock area. Warehouse air-conditioning units were also sabotaged. A.L.F.

September/96: Atlanta, GA - In the past month, Atlanta Furs has been hit again (at least once), "McDonald's = murder and greed" and "A.L.F." were painted across one of McDeath's Atlanta stores and a local supermarket was spraypainted with "Vegan Revolution". A.L.F.

September/96: The Poultry Liberation Organization claimed credit for an action in which "a small billboard advertising an annual chicken bar-b-q was completely removed." P.L.O.

September/96: Atlanta, GA - Atlanta Furs gets their locks glued. A.L.F.

September 1/96: Dallas, Tx - Morris Kaye and Sons Fur shop had locks glued and slogans painted. A.L.F.
September 2/96: Richardson, Tx - Richardson Fur Center windows smashed, paint bombed, slogans painted and locks were glued. A.L.F.

September 2/96: Dallas, Tx - Bifano Furs in North Dallas was paintbombed, acid was sprayed into the office through the mail slot, locks were glued and slogans painted. A.L.F.

September 2/96: Dallas, Tx - Valentine Furs was paint bombed and slogans were painted. A.L.F.

September 2/96: Dallas, Tx - Macy's Dept. Store: steel balls were shot at the windows, it was unclear, however if the windows broke. A.L.F.

September 9/96: South St. Paul, MN - An attempt was made to burn down a building at Heger Co., a major fur feed supplier. A.L.F.

September 20/96: Atlanta, GA - Atlanta Furs is hit, three large windows are smashed. A.L.F.

September 28/96: Provo, UT - 8000 mink released from Paul Westwood's mink farm, breeding cards were destroyed. Huge holes were cut into two surrounding fences. *"Many animals were left behind and for that we are sorry, but this war is far from over..."* from the communique. Over $20,000 in damages.

October/96: Olympia, WA - The Clarance Jordan Mink Ranch in Olympia, WA is now out of business. This facility was raided on Nov. 16th, 1995 by the A.L.F. 400 mink were released, and equipment was sabotaged. A CAFT investigator spoke with Jordans son, who admitted that it was the A.L.F. that caused the farm to go out of business. Another raid that same night led to the liberation of 30 fox from a TN fur farm. That farm closed as well.

October/96: Atlanta, GA - Atlanta Furs is hit and once again several windows are smashed. A.L.F.

October 3/96: Syracuse, NY - Georgio Politis, owner of Georgio Furs in Syracuse, said his home had been paint "bombed" -- slogans were written and red paint dumped over his property, including "You can't hide." Two automobiles were severely damaged, slashed with paint and windows smashed. The damage was estimated in the thousands of dollars. A.L.F.

October 5/96: Alliance, UT - The A.L.F. struck Justice Jorney's fur farm for the second time in less than two months, 8000 mink were liberated. A.L.F.

October 5/96: Redmond, WA - A Kentucky Fried Chicken is spraypainted with "All meat is murder" and "Sadist." A.L.F.

October 5/96: Lyndeborough, NH - A.L.F. activists liberate 35 fox and 10 mink, slogans were painted and extensive damage was done to farm equipment at the Gauthier Fur Farm. A.L.F.

October 8/96: Bellevue, WA - Honey Bee Hams, 700 108th Ave. N.E., had seven large windows smashed. Graffiti sprayed on the sidewalk read, "Animal Killers" and "A.L.F." Total damage was about $8,500. It was the third and most damaging incident at Honey Bee Hams. [Meanwhile, 11 similar incidents have been reported on Mercer Island since March, said Sgt. Alan Lacy. Windows at several fast-food outlets were broken, Lacy said. In one case, the vandals used an indelible pen to write "Meat is murder" on an awning at Cucina Presto. At a McDonald's, the words "McDeath" were spray-painted on a wall. And at a Baskin-Robbins store, "Dairy equals death" was painted on the building.] A.L.F.

October 11/96: Hinsdale, MA - The A.L.F. revisited the Carmel Mink Ranch as a follow up to the August raid at the same farm. They found that infra red beams were being transmitted over the tops of the cages, so that none could be opened without breaking the current. The A.L.F. still managed to get 75 mink out before the farmer came out screaming and yelling.

October 11/96: Bellevue - Three more businesses report being hit by the A.L.F., including an action in which four 10-by-6 foot windows and a glass door at Golden Steer Meats were taken out, with damages estimated at over $2000.

Gauthier Fur Farm in Lyndeborough, NH
35 fox and 10 mink liberated 10/5/96
Animal Liberation Front

October 14/96: (Columbus Day) Eugene, OR - The 26th and Willamette Chevron Gas Station locks glued and painted with the slogan "504 years of genocide." E.L.F.

October 14/96: (Columbus Day) Eugene, OR - The IZ and Pearl public relations office of Weyerhauser and Hyundai locks glued, spraypainted "504 years of genocide" and "Fuck Corporations" E.L.F.

October 14/96: (Columbus Day) Eugene, OR - Hwy 99 and Garfield Mcdonalds locks glued and spray painted. E.L.F.

October 16/96: Grants Pass, OR - McDonalds locks glued and spray painted for the McLibel Two. E.L.F.

October 16/96: Ithaca, NY - An early morning "attack" on a McDonald's Restaurant on Route 13 in Ithaca, NY was carried out by The Band of Mercy, and sabotage consisted of damaged locks and other equipment, and a huge banner had been dropped from the top of the restaurant, reading: "McDeath: Killing Animals, the Earth and You!" According to their communique: *"This is part of a nationwide attack on McDonalds, which sells body parts of tortured animals, destroys the environment and sells unhealthy foods....We are sending a message that this will not be tolerated...we will continue our actions until the atrocities stop."*

October 16/1996 (Anti-McDonald's Day): Eugene, OR - the following stores had their men's and women's restrooms toilets plugged with sponges, walls covered with slogans and walls, ceilings, floors and fixtures sprayed with "blood." 5 McDonalds, 1 Taco Bell, 1 Taco Time, 1 Arby's, 1 Burger King, 1 Carl Jr's, 1 Wendy's. A.L.F.

October 17/96: Cottage Grove, OR - McDonalds locks glued and slogans painted. E.L.F.

October 17/1996 "Exit 104 on I-5", OR - McDonalds receives same treatment as listed before. E.L.F.

October 23/96: Lebanon, OR: Arnold Kroll's mink farm raided and 2000 mink were liberated. *"As long as there are animal concentration camps there will be an Animal Liberation Front! We'll be back."*

October 24/96: Coalville, UT - At the ranch of Devar Vernon (1155 SW Hoytsville Rd.) 2,000 mink and 200 fox were liberated. Breeder cards were also destroyed. At the end of their communique, the A.L.F. claimed that *"This is not the end, this is a war, and we will continue to fight it."*

October 25-31/96: Portland, OR - Two bus stop benches corrected ... instead of "Eat more Rabbit" with a rabbit foot keychain, they now read "Meat is Murder" and "Animal liberation now!"

October 26/96: Philadelphia, PA - a Flemington Furs billboard on Interstate 95 in was paint bombed.

October 27/96: Texas - the A.L.F. blockaded the toilet pipes in a McDonalds in rural Texas and wrote slogans in the bathroom including Meat is Murder, A.L.F., and Tell Your Corporate Masters That the Pipes Were Blocked for the McLibel Two. When the A.L.F. left the toilets were already flooding both bathrooms.

October 27/96: Detroit, MI - Activists set a truck on fire and spray-painted "Earth Liberation Front," "Forest Rapers," and other anti-logging graffiti on buildings and vehicles at a U.S. Forest Service Rangers Station. E.L.F.

October 29, 1996: Victor, NY - Yet another mink raid! The A.L.F. entered the Bennett Fur Farm by cutting through a series of 3 different fences. *"We saw remnants of older fences that had possibly been cut down on previous raids. The fence nearest to the sheds had metal sheets on the top of it so as to make noise if they were being tampered with, but this proved a frivolous security precaution as they were easily by-passed. Once inside the actual fur farm, we came across countless empty sheds, possibly 40 or 50, which each shed could have housed several hundred animals each, but all were empty. This could have been because of previous successful raids on the farm, or we may have been to late as the killing season may have already claimed the lives of our animal friends.*

We continued onward hoping to find at least a few sheds with animals still in them. Nearing the front of the farm, we heard animal noises and followed them to a shed. Inside were dozens and dozens of silver foxes. They were making a tremendous amount of noise as we searched the shed. We opened a total of at least 46 cages and destroyed the breeding cards on all of the cages inside that particular shed. Liberation for all of the foxes would have been possible if we had not been interrupted by a security truck that forced us to evacuate.

This is the second known raid on this particular fur farm. All in all, forty six foxes were liberated, fencing was cut through and torn down, and A.L.F. slogans were spraypainted on various sheds throughout the farm.

We will be back-as long as there are animals trapped inside that concentration camp- we will fight for their release...
Much more to come from A.L.F.!!"

***NOTE: 22 raids in the U.S. and Canada have so far led to the release of 38,000 mink, 410 fox and 1 coyote . Farms are closing as a result of these raids, despite the fact that fur pelts are bringing decade high prices. The A.L.F. has proven that when they say they'll be back, THEY WILL BE BACK!**

October 30/96: Oakridge, OR - The Forest Service office was burned to the ground by a molotav. This follows a similar attack on the office in the Detroit Ranger District where vehicles were damaged. Both incidents were in the Willamette National Forest, which plans to sell about 14 million board feet of timber. Unclaimed.

October 31/96: Richardson, TX - Richardson Fur Center windows smashed. A.L.F.

November 8/96: Benson, UT - 1,000 ring-necked pheasants were released from the Wild Ringneck Ranch -- a canned hunting operation -- in Benson, Utah. Three sheds of pheasants were completely emptied. The owner said that once the birds are out of their cages, they are almost impossible to capture. He estimated a $10,000 loss by the release of the birds. Unclaimed.

November 9/96: Charlotte - Montaldo's Furs had the front of their building (windows & walls) spraypainted red with the slogan "FUR KILLS" & "A.L.F.". Montaldo's is the second fur store to open in the last two months in Charlotte.

November 10/96: NYC, NY - Revillon Furs window smashed. A.L.F.

November 11/96: Chevy Chase, Maryland - A.L.F. activists paid a visit to two Fur stores located in Chevy Chase, Maryland. Miller's Furs had the side of their building decorated in red paint in very large letters with the slogan "FUR IS FOR ANIMALS NOT FOR COATS". The A L and F were underlined. Miller's Furs parking signs were crossed out with red paint also. Local animal activists were paid a visit but were unable to help police with their enquiries. Also hit was Gartenhaus furs, two doors down from Miller's. Red paint splattered over all of the awnings as well as the sidewalk. A.L.F.

November 12/96: Bloomington, MN - Alaskan Furs Co. was gutted in an arson which reportedly caused more than $2 million in damages to furs and other merchandise. The building sustained another $250,000 in damages. An incendiary device was thrown through the front window of the shop. As of yet the action is unclaimed.

November 15/96: Atlanta, GA - Atlanta Furs has three windows taken out. A.L.F.

November 19/96: Boston - A group calling themselves Vegan Supremacy called in a bomb threat to the World Trade Center in Boston. The Filenes Basement dept. store was holding a fur sale, and the place was emptied out for an hour and a half as the building was secured. Filenes Basement leases salon space to Evans Furs, which is the largest fur company in North America.

ENGLAND

October/96: The A.L.F. bomb hoaxed six tesco supermarkets throughout England because they are selling ostrich and kangaroo meat. A.L.F.

[Of course we know that piles of animal liberation related actions have been occurring throughout England over the past few months – we'll just have to wait 'til the reports come in...]

IRELAND

April/1996 - 250,000 salmon were set free from a salmon farm in Ireland, costing the owners 1,000,000 pounds in lost profit.

AUSTRIA

June/96: Six A.L.F. activists raid a mink farm, liberating 50 mink and damaging some equipment. This action received great media coverage.

September 21/96: The storing units of a chicken battery farm were burned down by A.L.F. activists. Additionally, the activists had tried to connect the petrol tanks of the three transport lorries parked at the place to the main fire, but this apparently failed. Result: 10 million shillings damage.

GERMANY

April 12/96: Zirtow, Mecklenburg-Vorpommern - A.L.F. activists target a fur farm and set buildings on fire. A non-lethal acidic substance was smeared in an accommodation building used by farm workers. Various slogans were also painted.

August 24-25/96: Wesseling (near Cologne) - 151 minks were set free by animal rights-activists in one of the biggest mink-farms in Germany. The farm is in Wesseling (a small town near Cologne). was owned by breeder and furrier, Eberhard Huthmacher. The activists also destroyed his collection of furs with the help of butyric acid. Huthmacher told the newspapers and police that the animal activists not only destroyed the furs but also his 30-year-old business because his "best breeding-minks" had been set free. Huthmacher was also one of the first German farmers to start breeding chickens in small cages (batteries). One of these old (today empty) sheds still exists. Eberhard Huthmacher's mink farm has 500-600 minks and about 20 polecats. The minks cages measure 0.36 square-meters and are 38cm high. In addition the minks have something like a nesting box (33x22x23cm). Many of the mink had visible injuries, especially around the tails. The minks' diet consisted of "mash", made from the garbage of a pig-slaughterhouse. The farm workers lay the mash on the topmost roof of the cages, so that the minks in the lower cages have to wait and hope for the rest of the muck to fall to them. The German Pro-A.L.F. magazine, *VOICE* received a letter from the activists stating, *"We wanna make a change for the animals NOW - not in a hundred years!"* and, *"Solidarity with all animal rights-prisoners - our thoughts are with you!"* Over 100,000 DM in damages.

September 9/96: Hamm (near Dortmund) - One or more animal rights-activists sprayed butyric-acid through the door-lining into the interior of six butcher-shops in Hamm. The acid spray destroyed also a large number of the dead animals carcasses and shop furnishings. *"For animal liberation! No peace for animal abusers!"* the animal rights-activist(s) wrote in their letter to *VOICE*.

NEW ZEALAND:

July/96: Wellington - two Butcher shops get superglue in locks. A.L.F..

July/96: Auckland - More than forty butcher shops get threats in the mail warning them to close down or face vandalism attacks.

July/96: Auckland - two butcher shops in West Auckland smashed up.

July/96: Auckland - West End Road Fish shop windows smashed twice in July.

July/96: Auckland - Ponsonby Road Butcher shops get windows smashed.

July/96: Auckland - West Coast Road butcher shop gets windows broken three times in July. Now has a steel shutter protecting them.

July/96: Auckland - an unknown group delivers letters containing mousetraps to four Auckland vivisectors (Bruce Baguley, Robert Faull, Peter Gluckman, Lois Armiger). Faull and Gluckman also get their cars covered in paintstripper.

August/96: Auckland - Cot Death Society Building graffittied as a warning against using animals in experiments. Shirley Tonkin of the Cot Death Society who has defended the use of piglets in suffocation experiments, gets her car covered in A.L.F. slogans and paint stripper.
August/96: Auckland - Happy Hen egg truck paint stripped, two milk trucks paint stripped and graffittied, "Sensational Sausage" truck smashed up and five butcher shops get windows broken. All in one night!

August/96: Christchurch - Media reports of A.L.F. attacks on Cancer Society buildings on Daffodil Day.

August/96: Auckland - Cancer Society building painted with "Murderers" on Daffodil day.

August/96: Wellington - A.L.F. splashes red paint over the entrance to the Wellington Cancer Society Building on Daffodil day.

August/96: Auckland - Leather Shop (Hunters and Collectors) graffitied with A.L.F. slogans.

August/96: Auckland - Zoo entrance and signs graffitied with A.L.F. slogans.

September/96: Auckland - McDeaths at AIT campus gets windows smashed. Newmarket McDeaths window and sign smashed. Shop displaying cow skins gets windows smashed.

October/96: Southland - Vegan activists found and destroyed four leghold traps (gin traps). These are illegal but still widely used by trappers.

October/96: Wellington - Preston's Meats in Hopper St was spraypainted with A.L.F. etc slogans. This is hit #6 for Preston's since late last year. Also on same night a fish processing factory in Cuba St was painted with animal rights and A.L.F. slogans.

November 1/96: Christchurch - (World Vegan Day). Four leather shops, one fur shop, one hunting shop, one butcher, one Cancer Society shop get superglued.

SWEDEN

January/96: Umea - A stall was set up on the streets selling fox and mink products. Some seconds after it was set up 5-10 activists approached it and took it down. Police came and chased away the activists, but the furrier packed up and never returned.

May/96: Orik - A fur shop was sloganized and its locks were glued.

May 10/96: Obbola, Umea - An empty fur farm was burned (5 buildings of 8). The farm had no insurance and damages came to over $660,000 US dollars. The processing plant was destroyed as well and the farmers car was spraypainted.

* All fur shops in Umea have closed because of daily direct action. Victory!

July/96: Umea, an angling shop that sold various fur products,
including polar bear, had its windows smashed. The same thing happened twice in August.

A Quick Guide to MOVE.

by Rabbix.

As I guess a lot of Underground readers will know, both the British Animal Liberation Front Supporters Group Newsletter and (more recently) the American *Earth First! Journal* have started to publish the names and prison addresses of the MOVE prisoners. But who are the MOVE prisoners? What is MOVE? Why are nine of their activists in prison? And why was their family home bombed May 13th 1985? The following article has been written to help answer those questions.

"MOVE's work is to stop industry from poisoning the air, the water, the soil, and to put an end to the enslavement of life -- People, animals, any form of life." (Quote MOVE)

MOVE (short for MOVEMENT) was born in the USA in the early 1970s. Right from its beginning it was a radical ecological, mainly (but not exclusively) black, no compromise, strict vegetarian, communal living group who only ate raw organic food, watched no TV, educated their own children, shared a common surname, wore dreadlock hair and composted all their waste.

Under the teachings of their founder, John Africa, MOVE opposes all exploitation and oppression. Everything from motorway construction to vivisection. Animal Circuses to State oppression. Violence against women to child pornography. *"Every problem in the world."*

During the early 1970s MOVE was based in Powelton Village, Philadelphia. MOVE members worked hard helping out around their own house and within the neighbourhood. They swept streets, helped homeless people find accommodation, assisted the elderly with home repairs, intervened in gang violence, helped prisoners meet parole requirements, etc. One of the fundraising activities MOVE performed to support themselves was carwashing, this proved very popular. MOVE also ran regular study sessions for people interested in John Africa's teachings. They welcomed dissenting views as a chance to test their oratory skills.

By 1974 MOVE was regularly appearing in public, demonstrating at zoos, pet shops, political rallies, public forums and media offices. On these demos they used nonviolent protest to expose injustice. However, during their demos MOVE was met with much police violence. According to their vocal supporter (and fellow prisoner) Mumia Abu Jamal, *"In 1973 they were in Philadelphia Zoo protesting caged exploitation of animals, and they were beaten for it, they were jailed for it, and the got ridiculously high bails for it."*

Throughout the 1970s, Frank Rizzo was a key figure in Philadelphia's Government. A former cop, Rizzo controlled the streets with a heavy handed police force that won national notoriety for brutality. MOVE's response was to run a series of street demonstrations focusing on police abuses. Other groups agreeing with MOVE started their own demos, seeking MOVE's advice in setting them up. This angered the police which started a concerted campaign of harassment against MOVE. MOVE members found themselves being arrested and beaten, on whatever trumped up charges the police could think of.

Police brutality against MOVE members soon reached alarming levels of violence. On 18.5.74, Leesing and Janet Africa were stopped by the police and roughhandled, despite both women telling the police they were pregnant. Both suffered miscarriages. On 29.4.75 during a demonstration against ill treatment by the police against MOVE members, Alberta Africa, who was pregnant, was arrested and taken to a police station. At the station she was dragged into a holding cell, held down 'spread eagled' by four cops whilst a matron repeatedly kicked her in the stomach and vagina. Alberta suffered a miscarriage.

On 28.3.76, after seven MOVE members were released from jail, the police turned up at the MOVE home claiming MOVE was creating a disturbance. Without provocation the police turned on the MOVE members, beating them so hard they received fractured skulls, chipped and broken bones and concussions. During this attack Janine Africa was grabbed, thrown to the ground and stomped on. In her arms was three week old Life Africa. Life Africa's skull was crushed. No police officer has ever been prosecuted for the murder of baby Life Africa.

Because of the police harassment MOVE was dragged into the legal system. MOVE readily took on the courts and eventually overwhelmed them by clogging up the system with paperwork. Many MOVE cases were dropped to help clear the backlog and this angered the police even more who quickly planned revenge.

On 5.11.76, twenty MOVE members were summoned to court. Several were taken into custody. On the way to the holding cells Sheriff Jerry Saunders started to beat one young handcuffed MOVE member, Dennis Africa. As the police hoped, other MOVE members rushed to Dennis's side and a scuffle ensued. After the scuffle the MOVE members involved were locked up and the police then went in search of other MOVE members. Three more members were arrested and brutalised. This included Rhonda Africa who was nine months pregnant. Rhonda went into labour the next day and gave birth to a bruised and injured baby that died soon after. As a result of the police set up, three MOVE members were given prison sentences.

The setting up of three MOVE members led MOVE to hold a demonstration demanding the release of their three political prisoners. The demonstration started on 20.5.77 and was held on MOVE property. The MOVE members carried firearms to defend themselves against police attack. MOVE was determined there should be no more undercover deaths. If the police wanted to murder MOVE people they would have to do so in full view of the public. The response of the police was to issue arrest warrants for eleven MOVE members on riot charges and "possession of an instrument of crime." The police then began a 24 hour surveillance to make their arrests. This surveillance continued for many months and eventually included a failed attempt to try and starve the MOVE members out of the house.

Eventually, with no other way of getting MOVE out of the house, on 8.8.78 the police launched a full scale invasion of the MOVE house on the grounds MOVE weren't keeping to an agreement MOVE never agreed to. During the storming of the house MOVE members took refuge in the basement. The fire brigade, in league with the police, flooded the basement with water forcing the adults to hold onto children and animals to prevent them from being drowned. Some dogs did drown. As the water flooded in, tear gas canisters were activated and gun shots rang out as the police opened fire on the building. During this police assault the police managed to shoot one of their own officers, James Ramp. Ramp was killed with a single shot. Three other police officers and three firemen were also injured.

With tear gas, water and bullets, MOVE was forced to come out of their house. 12 adults were arrested, all were beaten by the police. Delbert Africa was smashed in the face with a police helmet and hit with a shotgun butt. Delbert fell to the ground and was dragged across the street by the hair. Other officers then set about him, kicking him in the head, kidneys and groin. As soon as the MOVE members were taken away, the police set about destroying the house, flattening it completely.

Out of the twelve people arrested, there were three who were not well known MOVE members. These three were told if they disavowed themselves from MOVE they could walk free. Consuewella Dotson Africa refused to distance herself from MOVE and was later tried and sentenced to 10-20 years in prison.

Having tried the first three people arrested who were not known MOVE members, the police then turned to the nine who were all well known MOVE activists. Desperate to lock them up, the nine were accused of murdering the cop who the police themselves had shot. After a farcical trial, with planted evidence, all nine were found guilty of murder and sentenced to 30-100 years. the next day, whilst appearing on a talk show, the sentencing Judged was asked "Who shot James Ramp?" He replied, "I have no idea." The man who phoned the radio station and asked the question was Mumia Abu Jamal.

During the next seven years the persecution of MOVE continued. This included another nine MOVE members being accused of terrorist activities; charges that were later proven totally bogus. Despite the harassment MOVE continued to exist and continued to demand the release of their political prisoners. By this time MOVE had a new communal house in Osage Avenue and fearing more police assaults, they decided to fortify the building.

On 11.5.85, arrest warrants were signed for four MOVE members on terrorist charges. A fifth person's warrant was signed for gun violations. On 12.5.85 police evacuated Osage Ave and towed away cars. On 13.5.85, at 06:00hrs, over 600 police launched a military style assault on the MOVE home. The police were armed with tear gas, water cannons, shotguns, Uzi's, M-16s, silenced weapons, Browning Automatic Riffles, M-60 machine guns, a 20mm anti-tank gun, a .50-calibre machine gun and 37 pounds of C-4, a powerful military explosive.

Between 06:00-07:30 hrs, the police fired 10,000 rounds of ammunition at the house. They also tried to blast through the walls using the C-4 explosive. When these measures failed, a state helicopter was used to drop a bomb onto the roof of the building. A fire started which was allowed to blaze out of control, eventually destroying 60 buildings.

With their home ablaze the MOVE members tried to flee. But as they did so they were shot at by police and forced back into the burning house. Those that chose not to be burnt to death were gunned down outside the house. Six adults and five children were inside the house at the time of the assault. Only one adult (Ramona Africa) and one child (Birdy Africa) survived. Both were taken into custody. Birdy was subjected to a "normalisation" program which included being force fed McDonald's burgers. Ramona went to jail for seven years charged with conspiracy, riot and multiple counts of assault.

The bombing was intended to end MOVE once and for all. However, this has failed. MOVE continues to exist and in 1991 they purchased a new communal house on Kingsessing Ave. Several months passed before the police learnt about this new house. Once the police knew of the new house media slurs started against MOVE and there is genuine fear MOVE may be attacked again ... @

There are currently nine MOVE members in prison in AmeriKKKa. All nine are serving life for the murder of the cop shot on 8.8.78. All nine are innocent.

MICHEAL DAVIS AFRICA, AM4984
CHARLES SIMS AFRICA, AM4975
Both at: SCI Gratersford, Box 244, Gratersford, PA, 19426-0244, USA.

DEBBIE SIMS AFRICA, 006307
JANET HOLLOWAY AFFRICA, 006308
JANINE PHILLIPS AFRICA, 006309
MERLE AUSTIN AFRICA, 006306
all at: SCI Cambridge Springs, 451 Fullerton Ave, Cambridge Springs, PA 16403-1238, USA.

WILLIAM PHILLIPS AFFRICA, AM4984
DELBERT ORR AFRICA, AM4985
Both at: SCI-Dallas, Drawer K, Dallas, PA 18612, USA

EDWARD GOODMAN AFRICA, AM4974,
SCI Camp Hill, Box 200, Camp Hill,
PA 17001-0200, USA.

MOVE PRISONERS OF WAR

Alberta Africa – served 7 years.
Alfonso Africa – served 5 years.
Carlos Africa – served 13 years.
Charles (Chuck) Africa – served 18 years. Still in prison.
Conrad Africa – served 1 1/2 years.
Consuewella Africa – served 15 years.
Debbie Africa – has served 18 years. Still in prison.
Delbert Africa –has served 18 years. Still in prison.
Edward Africa – has served 18 years. Still in prison.
Janine Africa – has served 18 years. Still in prison.
Janet Africa – has served 18 years. Still in prison.
Jerry Africa – served 1 1/2 years.
Merle Africa – has served 18 years. Still in prison.
Michael Africa – has served 18 years. Still in prison.
Ramona Africa – served 7 years.
Robert Africa – served 1 1/2 years
Sue Africa – served 12 years.
William (Phil) Africa – has served 18 years. Still in prison.

"As long as we are alive, we will never abandon our innocent brothers and sisters in jail, and they know we will never abandon them, and this city gonna always have a problem until every last one of our brothers and sisters is home." (Quote MOVE).

This article has been written in memory of:
Vincent Leapheart, aged 54, Raymond Africa, aged 50, Rod Africa, aged 36, Rhonda Africa, aged 30, Theresa Africa, aged 26, Frank James Africa, aged 26, Tree Africa, aged 13 Zenetta Africa, aged 12, Delica Africa, aged 11, Phil Africa, aged 11, Tomaso Africa, aged 9, all murdered May 13th, 1985.

For more information about MOVE contact either:
The MOVE Organisation, Box 19709, Philadelphia, PA 19143, USA. Friends of Move, Box 3069, London, SW9 8LU, England. Or better still, write to any of the MOVE prisoners. They welcome letters and are more than willing to answer questions.

Are You A True Animal Liberation Activist? Now You Can Find Out!

We all want to do something to help the animals. It's likely that we've all opened our homes to stray dogs, cats and field mice at one time or another, picketed a research lab or two and cut the eating of flesh out of our diets. But how active are you? There's more to being an animal liberation activist than chanting "Hey Hey, Ho Ho," or wearing your favourite Green Peace t-shirt.

Here's a fun to answer quiz that will reveal whether you are committed to the cause of animal liberation, or merely looking to pick up members of the opposite sex by attaching yourself to a "hip" cause. Answer all the questions, a b or c, then add up your final score.

1. You are a member of an animal rights organization and discover that a local research lab was broken into and vandalized. What do you do?
a. Go to any and all local media willing to listen and sternly state that "this sort of thing puts the cause of animal rights back 20 years."
b. Tell reporters that while your organization does not participate in those kinds of actions, you "understand the underlying reasons why someone would choose to carry out such an action."
c. Hold a press conference in full support of the activists who broke into the lab, telling the reporters that "more of these actions are necessary" as well as publishing a list of addresses of local labs, fur farms, slaughter houses and factory farms all needing targeting.

2. You have just left your local animal rights group meeting when the newest member (the 6'2 fellow with the crew cut, short mustache and strange habit of saluting you) asks you if you want to help him "break into a few labs, maybe blow up a vivisector's car or two." You hardly know the fellow, but decide
a. What the hell, you've forgotten your gloves and mask and had a few drinks, but what could go wrong? You let him know you have a few friends who are also into this sort of thing and happily write down their names and phone numbers for him to contact later.
b. Perhaps not this evening. You politely decline his invitation but have a nice time telling him about all the times you've put a brick or two through fur shop windows yourself.
c. Something's strange about this fellow. You can't put your finger on it but decide it might be wise to watch what you say and do in his presence. Who knows, the way he keeps badgering everyone to do something illegal may just indicate he's tactless, but...

3. An extremely dedicated animal liberation activist is eventually arrested and sentenced to prison time. You've come into personal conflict with him in the past and still hold a grudge. You decide
a. To denounce him publicly at rallies and demos and privately to any activist who listens in order to undermine his support. When this tactic fails, you publicly claim to have always supported him and can't understand why anyone could have doubted your intentions.
b. That while you feel yourself unable to support this activist for personal reasons, you recognize others may feel differently and do your best to stay out of things.
c. To put aside any personal problems that may exist between the two of you and decide to fully support the imprisoned activist in any and all ways possible.

4. While out shopping one day downtown, you notice a shop that is selling expensive mink and fox fur coats. How do you react? Would you
a. Go in and purchase a few of the most expensive coats.
b. Ask to try on a few of the coats, but postpone any decision to purchase in order to think it over.
c. Put superglue into all of the shop's locks and return later that evening to firebomb the premises.

5. A balaclava is
a. a rich pastry dessert containing almonds and smothered in honey
b. a Romanian folk tune
c. an essential piece of head gear for those evening walks through the fur district.

6. While out tabling one morning for the local animal liberation group, a belligerent passerby eating a hamburger identifies herself as the owner of a large slaughterhouse. An argument between you ensues at which point you
a. Decide she's right, God did indeed put chickens cows and horses on this earth for us to eat. Feeling a bit peckish you join her for a large plate of steak and kidney pie.
b. Stay calm, argue your points, do your best to speak for the animals and convince her to take home some information about animal rights to read later.
c. Stay calm, argue your points, do your best to speak for the animals and convince her to take home some information about animal rights to read later. You then follow her to work, spend a week observing the site and security measures and return late one evening to cause thousands of dollars worth of damage to several delivery trucks and windows.

7. Several activists at a demo are overheard speculating about who may have spraypainted the McDonald's last evening. You
a. jump into the middle of their conversation, bragging about your participation in the action in an attempt to gain personal credibility. You even show everyone the spraycan, which you've been carrying around for just such an opportunity.
b. Realize that their conversation serves only to spread rumours and could be dangerous for the activists who did do the action. You begin to chant "Hey Hey, Ho Ho" at top volume in an attempt to drown them out.
c. Take the activists aside and inform them that the fact the action occurred is more important than who did it. You point out the fact that there are uniformed and undercover cops everywhere who love hearing this kind of speculation.

8. While out one morning on a nature hike through the woods you come across a trapper in the process of hooking up several wires to his truck's battery. You realize he is about to anally electrocute several beaver and mink that he's caught in his steel-jawed leghold traps. You
a. offer to hold the squirming critters down for him in return for a fur hat or pencil case
b. take down his license plate numbers and run quickly to the nearest Ministry of Natural Resources to report what you've seen. After all, there is an incredibly slim chance that this guy was illegally trapping and killing animals as opposed to being licensed and sanctioned to do so by the state.
c. quickly pull on your balaclava, bonk the guy on the head with a improvised cudgel, hook the bastard up to his wires and give him a taste of his own medicine. You then leave a communique behind on the behalf of the Justice Dept. The animals of course are taken to a sympathetic vet.

How did you do?

Give yourself 3 points for every C, 2 points for a B, and 1 point for each A. Then add up your score and see how you rate!

20 to 24 Congratulations! You have the stuff of a true animal liberationist. Get yourself down to your local A.L.F. recruiting office immediately and sign on! You'll be out liberating mink and taking out research labs in no time (once you've completed the A.L.F.'s rigorous training course at their hidden mountain fortress).

13to 19 There's hope for yet, pick yourself up a copy of Singer's Animal Liberation and drop us $20-30 for a subscription to Underground. You'll soon come to know the difference between animal welfare and animal rights (and the difference between animal rights and animal liberation). Good luck!

12 or less: You heartless bastard! You probably run a bloody fur farm or spend your day dripping acid into the eyes of bunnies for your kicks. Well guess what, pal, you're days are numbered. The world will be a better place when the likes of you are permanently put out of business.

* NEWS * NEWS * NEWS * NEWS *

9 Arrests, Injuries, Sabotage Reported in U.S. Anti-McDonald's Protests

Nine arrests, injuries were reported -- and one McDonald's was sabotaged -- nationally Wednesday as anti-McDonald's activists blocked drive-thrus, disrupted business and hung banners calling the multi-million dollar fast food giant a "murderer."

The demonstrations were carried out by environmental and animal rights organizations as part of a "World Day of Action Against McDonald's," held Wednesday in 25 countries, including the United Kingdom, Australia, Canada, and many other locations in Asia, Europe and U.S., where nearly 50 McDonald's' were targeted.

There were five arrests near San Francisco at a Santa Cruz McDonald's when activists scaled the store's roof to drop a banner. One activist was hospitalized for a concussion after police ran her head into a air-conditioning duct. All were cited for trespassing and released.

There were also four arrests in Minneapolis, where activists also took over the roof of a McDonald's. They were maced, and sent to the hospital before being jailed for trespassing. They are being held on bail until a court hearing Thursday morning in St. Paul.

And, in Ithaca, NY, the Band of Mercy damaged locks and hung the banner: "McDeath: Killing Animals, the Earth and You" during an pre-dawn raid.

In Muncie, IN activists hung a banner from the local McDonald's reading, in part: "Special Today: McMurder Deluxe." And, in Chicago, Bloomington and several other American cities activists also disrupted sales at the drive-thru for up to several hours.

McDonald's has been the focus of intense protests by environmentalists and animal rights activists, who say the $30 billion food giant is responsible for feeding people disease-ridden meat, which could be laced with E-Coli, or Mad Cow's Disease, and destroying the environment, including the world's rainforests, which are being ripped down to make way for grazing land for cattle -- and future Big Macs.

U.S. McLibel Support Campaign Press Office
PO Box 62 Craftsbury VT 05826-0062
Phone/Fax 802-586-9628 Email <dbriars@world.std.com>
http://www.mcspotlight.org/

UK A.L.F.S.G. Newsletter Now on the Net

We are pleased to announce that A.L.F.S.G. News on the Net can now be received by e-mail. The Animal Liberation Front Supporters Group in the UK has been producing A.L.F.S.G. News since 1982, making it the oldest animal rights direct action newsletters in the world. A.L.F.S.G. News on the Net is an e-mail version of the material in each quarterly issue of A.L.F.S.G. News. The Summer 1996 issue is now available, including: Prisoners and Court News, Prisoners List, International News, Manchester Conspiracy Trial, Interfauna Raid.

To subscribe to A.L.F.S.G. News on the Net send an e-mail to <alfsgnews@gn.apc.org> with the message: <subscribe alfsg> and the word <subscribe> in the subject line. Be warned - A.L.F.S.G. News on the Net is no light-weight. It is sent out in four separate messages, to avoid overloading some of the more feeble e-mail software.

15 PEOPLE CHARGED, 6 PEOPLE MACED, 12 PEOPLE OCCUPYING THE MNR HEADQUARTERS IN PETERBOROUGH

Oct 15: Over 100 demonstrators gathered outside Ministry of Natural Resources head office in Peterborough [Ont. Canada] to protest the continued logging of Northern Ontario's Temagami region.

15 people managed to enter the lobby of the MNR. During a confrontation with the police inside the MNR 3 people were charged with assault police. One person was released two were taken to the police station. Later on one protestor outside the building was chased by police officers. He was arrested for an unknown reason.

6 outside protesters supporting the people inside the building were maced by the police without warning. According to one woman maced "they [the police] gave no warning, we were pushing on the revolving door one of the police officers reached around from behind me and maced me. The police officer then prevented me from leaving the front of the protest to get medical attention."

Citizens of Peterborough were joined by people from Kingston, Guelph, and Toronto in expressing their outrage at the prospect of the destruction of the unique Temagami region. Temagami's Owain Lake region, home of North America's third largest old growth red and white pine stand, will be completely logged by December of this year, if logging is not stopped now. The MNR, under the Harris government, currently threatens 48% of North America's remaining old growth red and white pine forests, all of them on unceded Native land.

This summer, Chris Hodgson (Minister of Natural Resources) rejected the recommendations of the Comprehensive Planning Council and unilaterally withdrew from treaty negotiations with the Teme-Augama Anishnabai. The MNR has now approved 77% of Temagami for mining and 71% for logging. Only 24% of the old growth forest is protected. Presently, Ontario's old growth forests cover less than 1% of their original range.

12 more arrests were made against activists who had occupied the building, bringing the total number of arrests up to 15.

ACTIVISTS SET SIEGE TO SLAUGHTERHOUSE

October 2, Petaluma, Ca. - Several dozen demonstrators surrounded a slaughterhouse and shut it down by barricading all entrances with cement-filled barrels, kryptonite bike locks and other locking devices. The slaughterhouse siege began about 5:20 a.m. Wednesday morning when activists blocked all driveways into the "Rãncho" (located at 1522 North Petaluma Blvd/Petaluma exit off Hwy 101). The slaughterhouse kills mostly veal calves and dairy cows. The protest was part of "World Farm Animals Day," a national observance of the rights of farm animals. Four activists were arrested and charged with misdemeanour counts trespassing and failure to obey a police officer.

"He doesn't want to leave — he's

Trio arrested for McDonald's Arson No Charges Laid

November 9: Two men and a juvenile were arrested and released in relation to an investigation of arson at a West Jordan McDonald's restaurant in August that caused an estimated $400,000 damage.

The adults, both 19, were from South Jordan and Salt Lake City, and the juvenile, 17, was from West Jordan. The three could face second-degree felony charges of arson, with additional counts of possession of explosive devices, theft, burglary and contributing to a minor. The trio had not been formally charged as of yet.

The two-alarm, 2 a.m. blaze at the restaurant wiped out nearly 80 percent of the building, which was under construction near 1250 West and 9000 South. Investigators with West Jordan Public Safety, Salt Lake Fire Department, Salt Lake County Fire Department and the Salt Lake County Sheriff's Office and agents with Alcohol, Tobacco and Firearms determined accelerants caused the blaze.

Snooks said footprints, tire impressions, accelerant samples and other evidence were found in and around the charred building. The restaurant was supposed to open Sept. 5 but was reduced to a blackened structure of bare drywall, roofing frames and scorched windows. Investigators are still identifying other suspects as well as looking into related incidents in the Salt Lake Valley.

Swedish/German Activists Released

As reported in the Diary of Actions from *Underground #5*, five activists were arrested for their part in damaging an abattoir near Ulm in South-west Germany last October. Three Swiss activists and two Germans spent 10 days in jail under very poor conditions until being released on a bail of 123,000 DM. A total of 20,000 DM in fines has been added to the bail deposit. Activists in Germany and Sweden have been helping with costs by holding benefit shows, but a large sum is still needing to be paid.

Environmentalists Ordered to Pay $1 Million in Idaho

Nov 8/96 OISE, Idaho -- A state court jury has ordered 12 members of the environmental group Earth First! to pay $1.15 million in damages to a contractor for damaged equipment and work delays as the result of protests in the virgin forests of northern Idaho.

The plaintiff, Highland Enterprises of Grangeville, Idaho, was awarded about $150,000 in compensatory damages and $1 million in punitive damages in the civil case. The defendants will be required to share the cost of the punitive damages by paying $83,333 each, court officials said, while compensatory damages were spread among the defendants in different amounts.

Leslie Hemstreet, 31, co-editor of *The Earth First! Journal* in Eugene, Ore., said of the decision: "The magnitude is so huge I can't even conceive of it. But you can't squeeze blood out of a bee." Most of the defendants do not have jobs and will have trouble making any payments, Ms. Hemstreet said. Don Blewett, owner of Highland Enterprises, said he expected to see some payment over time because the jury's award -- if upheld -- would remain in effect for the defendants' lifetimes.

"If their Great-Aunt Matilda buys a Volkswagen van and she dies and gives it to one of them, that baby's mine," Blewett said. Highland filed the lawsuit in late 1993 after three pieces of heavy equipment sustained total damages put at $20,000 by the company.

Police Arrest 8 Anti-Fur Activists After Sak's Fur Show Protest

SAN FRANCISCO Nov 13 -- Eight anti-fur activists were arrested at a non-violent but noisy demonstration inside the fur department of Sak's at Union Square. Four activists locked themselves together with heavy bike locks to blockade the fur department where Hana K, a fur designer, was scheduled to give a special presentation at Sak's on furs starting at 10 a.m. The designer has been met by animal rights pickets in several U.S. locations the past 2 weeks.

Those arrested were being held at the Vallejo Substation on trespassing and resisting arrest charges. Numerous police, including several police vans, and the fire dept. were called in to quell the disturbance. The protest was organized by the Animal Rights Direct Action Coalition (ARDAC).

HORSES STOLEN FROM ABATTOIR

(New Zealand, Nov. 15): Rosalie Ann Jones, 51, pleaded guilty in the Christchurch District court to stealing three horses worth $600, from a petfood abattoir. She was convicted and ordered to come up for sentence if called on in the next 12 months. Sergeant Halligan said Jones and two associates had gone to the abbatoir about 10pm on November 3. They led three horses to a waiting horse float, but could not load the animals and had to return them.

Defence counsel Kirsty Wilson said the theft was an offence of conscience. Jones wanted to save the horses from the certain death that awaited them. Judge Erber said that he had to bear in mind the motive for the offence, which could attract sympathy from many quarters.

SABBING NEWS FROM GERMANY

(translated from VOICE) November, 9: Seventeen animal rights activists recently met at Weickertshhain, a small village near Giessen (in the State of Hesse), with plans to sab a hunt on deer, wild boars, foxes, hares and so called "beasts of prey".

It wasn't long before the activists had tracked down the hunters, and supplied with bright vests and alarm whistles, the sabbers ran to the hunters in order to keep them away from the animals. When activists noticed the animals were being pushed by hunters to a nearby clearing, they arrived there first and started to make noise between the hunters and hunted. Shortly there after, a hunter appeared and tried to catch one of the sabs. The activist was much faster and easily took refuge amongst two friends who were actually engaging another hunter in a calm discussion. The same hunter even defended the three activists when his hunting colleagues tried to attack them. Unfortunately, this hardly had an effect on the aggressiveness of the beaters and hunters; they separated the three sabs from the others by pushing them up a hill through the thicket. The three managed to escape and meet up with four other activists that had been preventing, in couples, two hunters from killing deer.

The hunt was called off after around four hours sabbing. According to the law, it should have been stopped for the whole day as soon as civilians showed up in the hunt area. Eleven of the seventeen sabs were caught by the police. They will be facing charges. In the states of North-Rhine Westfalia, Bavaria and Hesse, hunt sabbing is now dealt as an offense and severely punished. In Hesse, the fine can come up to 50,000 DM.

Just say No to the FBI, RCMP and the Police

1. YOU DON'T HAVE TO TALK TO FBI AGENTS, RCMP, POLICE OR INVESTIGATORS. You do not have to talk to them on the street, it you've been arrested, or even if you're in jail. Only a judge has legal authority to order you to answer questions.

2. YOU DO NOT HAVE TO LET THE FBI, RCMP OR POLICE INTO YOUR HOME OR OFFICE UNLESS THEY HAVE A SEARCH OR ARREST WARRANT. Demand to see the warrant. It must specifically describe the place to be searched and things to be seized.

3. IF THEY DO PRESENT A WARRANT, YOU DO NOT HAVE TO TELL THEM ANYTHING OTHER THAN YOUR NAME AND ADDRESS. You have a right to observe what they do. You should take written notes of what they do, their names, badge numbers, and what agency they're from. Have friends who are present act as witnesses.

4. IF THE POLICE, RCMP OR FBI TRY TO QUESTION YOU OR TRY TO ENTER YOUR HOME WITHOUT A WARRANT, JUST SAY NO. The police are very skilled at getting information from people, so attempting to outwit them is very risky. You can never tell how a seemingly harmless bit of information can hurt you or someone else.

5. ANYTHING YOU SAY TO A FBI AGENT OR COP MAY BE USED AGAINST YOU AND OTHER PEOPLE. Once you've been arrested, you can't talk your way out of it. Don't try to engage cops in a dialogue or respond to accusations.

6. YOU DO NOT HAVE TO REVEAL YOUR HIV STATUS TO THE POLICE, JAIL PERSONNEL, RCMP OR FBI. If you've been arrested, you should refuse to take a blood test until you've been brought before a judge and have a lawyer.

7. YOU HAVE A RIGHT TO MAKE THREE TELEPHONE CALLS if you've been arrested on state charges and booked into jail. Within three hours of your arrest, you have a right to free local calls to a lawyer, a bail bondsman, and a friend or relative. Demand this right .

8. LYING TO A FEDERAL INVESTIGATOR (FBI OR OTHER,) IS A CRIME.

9. THE FBI MAY THREATEN YOU WITH A GRAND JURY SUBPOENA IF YOU DON'T TALK TO THEM. They may give you a subpoena anyway, so anything you tell them may permit them to ask you more detailed questions later. If you're given a subpoena, you should call a lawyer immediately or contact the National Lawyers Guild. Tell movement groups and your friends about the subpoena. Don' try to deal with it alone.

10. IF YOU ARE NERVOUS ABOUT SIMPLY REFUSING TO TALK, YOU MAY FIND IT EASIER TO TELL THEM TO CONTACT YOUR LAWYER. Once a lawyer is involved, the FBI and police usually back off because they've lost their power to intimidate.

THE ENEMY HAS
BIG EARS
Avoid loose talk on the phone and in public
stop needless speculation about underground actions
and keep sensitive materials secure

North American Animal Liberation Front Supporters Group
Box 69597, 5845 Yonge St. Willowdale, Ont. M2M 4K3, Canada
email: <naalfsg@envirolink.org>

UNDERGROUND

THE MAGAZINE OF THE NORTH AMERICAN ANIMAL LIBERATION FRONT SUPPORTERS GROUP

ISSUE #7

SPRING '97

FREE TO PRISONERS

$3

IN THIS ISSUE:

Greetings to all our readers!

Welcome to issue #7 of *Underground*. It's been roughly three months since the last issue went out, and in that short period of time we've seen some pretty dramatic occurrences in the war against animal abuse and abusers. One only has to take a glance at the current Diary of Action to get a sense of the huge increase in animal liberation activity, not only in North America, but world wide that has occurred. Not only has there been an increase in activity, but the nature of the actions has developed to a more serious level. Every lock glued at a fur store and every window broken at a butchers shop increases the frustrations of the shop owner and sends insurance costs soaring, but along side these actions we've witnessed some incredibly damaging acts of sabotage. Fur shops and hamburger joints are burning to the ground around America. Mink raids continue unabated despite the fur industries feeble security measures. In Brazil, activists entered a research lab destroying equipment and freeing over 50 monkeys. On the home front raids have spelled freedom for 50,000 salmon on the Canadian Pacific coast, have cost the fur industry over $1 million in damages due to the arson attack at America's second largest fur farm feed company, and caused Cornell University potentially tens of thousands of dollars in damages due to a recent Band of Mercy lab break in. The list continues...

Other notable developments over the last three months include the increase in police surveillance and harassment of animal liberation activists. The police and industry are desperate to bring an end to the A.L.F. and similar groups, and are striking out anywhere they can, which usually means raiding, arresting and harassing activists who have done little more than vocally support direct action for animal liberation.

In Canada, the Royal Canadian Mounted Police's (RCMP) National Security Investigations Section (NSIS) has been "interviewing" activists across Canada for information, and has lead raids on the homes and families of several innocent activists in B.C. In the United States, the FBI and police have conducted a covert campaign of harassment and intimidation of local animal rights activists most notably in Salt Lake City, Utah. The authorities' campaign against animal activists started as early as November of 1994 but appears to be coming to a head now, with over 40 animal rights supporters in the area reporting some form of police harassment. Federal agents and police have stalked, threatened, and slandered animal rights supporters on a massive scale. Authorities have fabricated court evidence to obtain false criminal charges, entered people's homes without a warrant or permission, conducted grand jury-witch hunts, and have harassed activists at their homes and workplaces.

It is also worth noting the increased presence of willing informers and grasses in the American direct action scene. Much of the trouble in Utah can be traced back to specific individuals who chose to cooperate with the police, spreading rumours, innuendos and undermining the activist community. Trouble within some A.L.F. cells has also occurred when arrests have been carried out and (some) activists have chosen to give evidence to the police that implicate others. The recent A.L.F./E.L.F. raid on the Eberts Fur Farm **(R.R. 4, Blenheim, ON, N0P 1A0, co-owner: Tom McLellan (519) 676-4969)** should stand as a good example to others to pick your cell-members carefully. Already we have seen one participant make statements to the police that were read in court, including a blow by blow account of everyone's alleged activities that night. A second participant, under pressure by family and police also appears to have made statements, and even implicated the other defendants in a previous raid.

So what's to be done? One step may be to pick up the latest *No Compromise* (issue #6) and read the article, **"Creating a Security Culture"** for basic tips on how to prevent your activities from becoming known by everyone from your landlord to the local P.C.Plod walking the beat. It's also time that people stopped trying to earn "scene points" by bragging about what they've done or what they know about "----" action. As the principles of animal liberation are embraced within various scenes and communities, particular individuals always appear that want to show how "hardcore" they are by bragging about their own and other people's involvement in A.L.F. actions. It is our collective responsibility when encountering these people to be up front and tell them this behaviour is intolerable. Far from being "cool" or "admirable," this kind of boasting and rumour-milling is a sign of weakness and these folk should be avoided at all cost, especially if you plan to break the law in any way. As activists face daily police harassment and surveillance and animal abusers vow revenge, it's about time people realized that illegal direct action is not a game. The lives of animals and the freedom of A.L.F. warriors are at stake, and we all play a part in making sure the liberations safely continue.

Ok, on with the rest of Underground. *Thanks again to everyone who sent action reports, newspaper clippings, articles, cartoons and graphics. Special thanks to Andreas, Freeman, JP, D, Weena Mercator (Roach) for tat flash and cartoons, Gina, Rod, Catherine, and everyone who has been so generous with their support. You are appreciated!* @

Letters to Underground

A.L.F. and E.L.F. Fight Together Against A Common Enemy

In 1995 the Earth Liberation Army (E.L.A.) in Canada targeted outfitters, trashing hunting lodges and burning a "Wildlife Museum" (a museum full of stuffed animals). Inspired by our transatlantic cousins, the Earth Liberation Front (E.L.F.) in Britain initiated a campaign against W.H. Smiths, Britain's largest newsagents chain and biggest retailer of blood-sports magazines, the hunting of wildlife being an attack on nature. My own cell has targeted W.H. Smith stores all over the South of England, damaging the inside pages of blood-sports magazines before placing the magazines back on the shelves.

Just recently reports are starting to emerge that the Animal Liberation Front (A.L.F.) has joined in the E.L.F. campaign against W.H. Smiths. Across the South of England a number of W.H. Smiths stores have been bomb hoaxed by the A.L.F. The A.L.F. have specifically said their actions against W.H. Smiths are because the newsagent chain is the largest stockist of blood-sports magazines in Britain. Exactly the same reason the E.L.F. targets W.H. Smiths.

The Earth Liberation Front welcomes and encourages the Animal Liberation Front joining in our campaigns and we look forward to hearing of many more cross over actions being carried out by both movements, such as the bomb hoaxing of Hastings Town Council by the English A.L.F., to protest the destruction of woodland which resulted in animal homes being destroyed; or the action in Holland where the Dutch Earth Liberation Front destroyed meat lorries to highlight the links between the meat trade and eco- destruction.

Earth Liberation and Animal Liberation are essentially the same struggle. Working together we can achieve our common goals.

Piklon,
Earth Liberation Front

CAFT Activists Wrongly Charged

Dear Supporters,
Greetings from your fellow activists, Jaime Roth, Alex Smolak, Grant Upson, and Warren Upson. The four of us are members of the Boston chapter of CAFT (Coalition to Abolish the Fur Trade). We as CAFT activists organize legal, above-ground, campaigns to abolish the bloody slaughter that is the fur trade. We also act as spokespeople for the clandestine Animal Liberation Front and publicize their actions.

In misunderstanding the very large differences between CAFT and the A.L.F., the state of Massachusetts has charged us with committing an alleged raid on a fur farm. On November 28, 1996, we were arrested and charged with breaking and entering in the night time with intent to commit a felony, larceny of property above $250, malicious destruction of property above $250, and trespassing. Of these charges, the first three are felonies and the fourth is a misdemeanor.

This fur farm, Berkshire Furs of Hinsdale, MA, was raided by the ALF in August of 1996 and again in October. In these raids, over one thousand mink were liberated. No arrests were made. Out of frustration stemming from their inability to stop the A.L.F., the Hinsdale police got desperate. The Fur Commission USA's offer of a $100,000 reward for the conviction of an A.L.F. activist probably contributed to their motivation. We as above-ground activists have been wrongly accused. For this, we may face more than nine years in prison.

The Hinsdale chief of police, Mark Green, has been quoted as saying, *"these are not people interested in animals, they are terrorists. My boys should have just shot them."* His attitude reflects a blatant disregard for justice and the concept of "innocent until proven guilty." While the police and prosecution have been busy framing us for the alleged raid, we have had to hire four attorneys to represent us in this case. At this point, it is impossible to tell how much money will be needed, but we have already exhausted our funds. We are urging our fellow activists to stand behind us and support us in any way they can. After our trial, for which no date has been set yet, any remaining funds will go into the Direct Action Defense Fund maintained by the Animal Liberation League, the Rod Coronado Support Committee, and the North American A.L.F. Supporters Group. Your help is greatly appreciated. For more information, please contact the Mass Four Support Committee at **<mass4SC@waste.org>**.

Much needed contributions and/or letters of support may be sent to: **MASS4 Support Committee PO Box 80632 Mpls, MN 55408**

Sincerely,

Jaime Roth
Alex Smolak
Grant Upson
Warren Upson

Letter From Keith Mann

Dear NA-A.L.F.S.G.

Many thanks for sending the magazine again. Its always a good read, a right good read! Shame this one had so much space taken up with internal problems [Issue #5], I hope you can resolve them without there being any negative long term effects. That aside -- I shall cop out on passing comment -- its good stuff. Much respect to all U.S. activists. Thanks also to everyone who has written to me or the other prisoners listed, I'll be trying as I always am to acknowledge any letters -- always remember, its better late than never, apparently!

This here letter I've just started to send out and it already needs updating with another. Firstly, the powers-that-be have now conceded I don't have to be kept in this end of the system for another year and I can if I so choose to apply for a transfer. They also now say I will be allowed to go and visit my dad under escort. This has come about because of the hassle people outside the prison have been kicking up: letters and phone calls, and questions they wanted answers to that just weren't there. It's easy to fob a prisoner off but not so the public, public figures and MP's. Also, the Ombudsman's report I mentioned has now been accepted by the Director General, so all vegans with a principled objection to vivisection should soon get free issue vegan toiletries. This is a result! Lets do a deal -- if you good people out there keep having yours we'll keep having ours, then we'll put them all together and what will we get -- Animal Liberation!

Well, stop reading about it and go get it...
Love and Respect,

Keith Mann

CALL FOR ACTION -- INTERNATIONAL EARTH NIGHT

April 1st-7th, 1997
Bite Back Against the Fur Industry

The Earth Liberation Front (Last Tiger Clan) calls for the annual April (Fools Day) Earth Nights to commence. This year we are asking all groups wherever possible to target the international Fur industry. This is as much an ecological as an animal issue, and the industry is now on the increase with many species facing total extinction, either from fur farms, hunters, developers, international exporters and importers, etc. As always, the aim of this diabolical business is to make a profit out of others suffering. We ask all E.L.F., A.L.F., eco-teur groups, etc., to target all the above aspects of the Fur Industry, and make this a night when the animals of all nations are given a voice, but also importantly a voice that acts with actions as much as words.

Governments have made promises to save our planet's wildlife, but the extermination still continues. Let us now act where others have failed to do so. Of course, for those who want to focus on other planet destroyers, or who don't have access to any of the above but want to take part, please do! Together we can unite, planting yet another mortal wound into the multi-national profit machine.

As always, we ask that there be no injury to life, only injury to property or profit.

E.L.F.

WAYNE CODY LASSELL -- REMEMBER HIM?

To Whom it May Concern,
I saw the e-mail post you put out back in the Spring regarding the Wayne Cody Lassell mystery [see issue #4]. I found it very interesting because he straight-up told me he was a member of the A.L.F. and that his current jail sentence was connected to a 1992 Livermore break-in. I began questioning him after his 2nd letter and wondering why the SG was not helping him get support, or the EF! Journal. My concerned lawyer/friend called Pelican Bay and they told him Wayne Cody Lassell was in with a long list of assault and batter charges and guaranteed him that his imprisonment was not for animal rights activism. I'm not sure how much they should be trusted either though, but that's what they told us. Also Pelican Bay is a pretty serious place to be -- and why would he wait until he was in his 3rd year of imprisonment to begin asking for support (just a thought). Also, his 3rd letter to me was asking for $. I have cautioned folks against writing
him.
Hope this letter helps out.
J.O.

The NA-A.L.F.S.G. has received a number of letters from people who have had contact with W.C.L. and have been suspicious of his claims to be an A.L.F. activist. The NA-A.L.F.S.G. does not support Wayne Cody Lassell or his claims to be an A.L.F. activist.

LETTER FROM GEOFF SHEPPARD

Dear NA-A.L.F.S.G.,

Just a note to thank you for sending me issues 5 and 6 of *Underground*. It's an impressive read, and I think I can say that the direct action movement for animal liberation in North America is really coming of age.

Please note my address. I've been here at Parkhurst since the middle of July. It's not too bad as prisons go, though security is very tight -- strip-search after every visit, for example.

I've done 18 months now, so that's something in the bank at least. We'll get there eventually. Anyway, thanks for your support. Take care.
Individuality and animal liberation,
Geoff

RAZE THE WALLS

Dearest Comrades of *Underground*/NA-A.L.F.S.G.
Greetings from minimum custody here in Seattle, WA. How are things in your yard? As a way of continuing this letter please allow me to introduce myself. My name is Michael Lee, the Seattle section facilitator for RAZE THE WALLS!

I'm writing today first of all to thank you for mention of our comrade Anarchist Political Prisoner, Harrold Thompson, on page 64 of issue #5. I'm also writing concerning Rod Coronado. I found the debate over Rod interesting and sad. Sad because of the fact that if anyone deserves support, I publicly state Rod does. Yes, I can understand there have been some criticisms levelled at him. Valid or not, Rod's doing time for actions and he didn't grass on anyone including those that assisted him while underground. Because of this, there still remains an underground support network for those on the run from the Feds. I'm sure the next person who goes under will be thankful for Rod's silence.

To those persons who think withdrawal of support from Rod is justified -- I have only one thing to say -- hang your head in shame. Yes, my friend, when you and I are in the cage I'll smile at you and reminded you of Rod's example.

Until all are free,
Mike Lee

VEGETARIAN DEATH-ROW INMATE SEEKS PENPALS

Greetings NA-A.L.F.S.G.
In the name of Allah, Most Gracious, Most Merciful. I am a Florida death row inmate, I have been confined for the past fourteen years struggling to stay alive & fighting hard against these prisoncrats & their

inhumane conditions that we're forced to live under.

I am a Muslim and I don't eat meat at all. I am not communicating with anyone at this time in my life, therefore, I am not receiving any mail. I was just wondering can *Underground* help me get introduced to a or some mature pen-pals to communicate with? Appreciate anything Underground can do for me.

Peace,
Amiyn!

Mr. Amiyn Mahdi Abdush-Shahid #046651
41-1086 A-1
Box 221
Union Correctional Institution
Raiford, FL 32083

UPDATE ON FRANK AND ERIC

Hi there,
Many thanks for the *Underground* you sent me a while ago. Everything is O.K. here, I've done more then half of my sentence at this moment. As you probably know, they gave me a sentence of 3 years from which 8 months are probation. This means that I'm free in October this year. Eric has got 30 months, 10 of which are probation. He's free in April. So this is not so bad if you compare it to the sentences they give in other countries. Prison-life is not so very bad in Holland. Everyone has his own cell. I have my own radio and music here. I even have a T.V. in my cell (you can rent them here for 10 Guilders -- don't know how many dollars that is). I've also asked for a weekend off, you can here if you've done half of your sentence. They let you go for 60 hours. My first change was on January 4, but they turned it down. The reasons they gave were the things [A.L.F. actions] happened to short ago, there was a lot of media attention created by us, and naturally society was still too shocked! Well, my second chance is on March 3. We will see what happens.

I finally managed to get soya-milk in here. They first didn't give it to me, but on a doctor's prescription I managed to get it. The food here is really horrible. We can do some shopping here once a week so I can buy some food there. I've also got a waterboiler and with that I can cook pretty good, so I manage to get some normal food. But the prisons aren't so bad in Holland so I end my sentence with a smile and they can't get me down. And one of these days they're gonna move me to an even better prison.

Well, in Germany they found a calf with B.S.E. so now everybody is getting crazy here again. They're trying to trace the parents (from England) but now they found a fraud with the registration. So the trust of people in the meat industry is getting worse, good news, but unfortunately they think of their own healt and not the animals.

Well, that's it for now, thanks everybody, for your support.
Love & liberation,
Frank

NEW FOCUS FOR PRISON NEWS SERVICE

Greetings:
It is with deep regret that *Prison News Service* is announcing that we are having to pull back from our commitment to the American prison struggle. We've been doing this work in one form or another since 1980. Our own political and personal growth, has been intimately connected to our comrades and friends locked down in American dungeons. But we can not keep up with the massive volume of mail that we get from American prisoners, nor can we continue to pay for the more than 3,000 free subs that we were sending across the border.

The paper will continue as is, but with a primarily Canadian focus. It will provide good radical journalism covering Justice-related issues in Canada from a grassroots perspective. We realize that as a specifically Canadian paper, it may not appeal as much to you. But the political and social issues are similar enough in both countries that hopefully you will find it interesting and useful. The recent riots and disturbances in jails and prisons across the country show how timely and necessary this work is. We want to expand our coverage to include immigration and refugee detention centres. We will continue to make coverage of the First Nations' struggle a top priority, to reflect the crucial importance of that struggle within Canada. Because of the mounting level of resistance and repression in Ontario particularly, we feel that we need to put our limited resources closer to home.

Subs will remain $10.00 for five issues. (American prisoner subs will be $3. or ten stamps.) If you wish to receive the paper, please send a check or money order (made out to PSC Publishers) to the address below. We need help to spread the word about *Prison News Service.*

So please tell friends, comrades or whoever might be interested in struggles within Canada.

Thanks for your support in the past. And to all those doing prisoner support work -luck, love and strength. The american prison struggle will remain closely intertwined with our own, one we keep always inside our hearts.

Prison News Service
P.O. Box 5502, Stn A
Toronto, Ont M5W 1W4
pns@pathcom.com

CONCERNS ABOUT ROGER TROEN LETTER (Issue #6)

Dear Friends at *Underground,*

A few points regarding "Mowing the Grass," in which you print a message from "Anonymous" and a statement made by Roger Troen to the FBI. First, since when do we take FBI documents as truth? Look what that lying agency did to Martin Luther King and the SDS! Secondly, do we know what the blacked out names are (I'm not asking for them, obviously)? Could they be people who had agreed to be named (this happens when one or two people try to outwit the feds by working together to protect others)? Could they be names Troen made up? Thirdly, shouldn't we always ask for the story "from the horse's mouth?" I called the number listed and spoke to Troen. He said he did not name names to the FBI. I don't know whether to believe him or not, how can you know? However, the FBI does set people up and good activists can be torn down on the strength of rubbish, so let' s not act as if we know.

Fourthly, what is the motive of Anonymous in asking *"why was PETA supporting (Troen) or did they not know?"* Say it's true. Of course we didn't know! How can you? The implication can't be that PETA, for god's sake, would knowingly support someone who would implicate others? I hope no one is as daft as to believe that. Unless you are clairvoyant, it is impossible to know exactly what anyone will say when they meet behind closed doors with the police or go before the panel in a Grand Jury witchhunt. All you can do is a) refuse to help anyone (I don't think Anonymous is suggesting that, but what is s/he suggesting?) or b) take a chance and try to help people you believe are in real trouble for doing good things and who don't seen likely to harm others.

The original Troen trial put the University of Oregon on trial. PETA paid for Troen's defense (Attorney Steve Houze tried "the greater good, lesser evil" defense, which the judge eventually rejected). We flew in expert witnesses who took the experiments apart piece by piece. The University' s dirty laundry was in the papers every day. I debated the vivisectors on radio and made sure everyone heard every gruesome detail of 14 hour surgeries from which primates did not survive, kittens with their eyes rotated in their skulls made to balance on planks above water-filled tanks, etc. As a result of all this, the community changed its opinion, the head of Animal Care packed his bags, and even the judge said, at sentencing, that he was ashamed of his alma mater. Troen was hit with a big fine and "retribution" costs, but the University lost its reputation and more.

Yes, absolutely, let's say we think Roger may have "grassed." It is vital to let people know that such a possibility exists and seems to be supported by FBI documents, because we must warn people it is unwise to approach him about any illegal act. However, even if we give him no benefit of the doubt, aren't our energies wasted targeting a liberationist who may have cracked under pressure rather than people who make money daily from torturing and slaughtering animals? I still count as a friend someone else who admitted breaking down under Grand Jury questioning probably because of pressures from family, stress, and ill health, and who gave the feds a name that lead directly into the PETA office. Luckily, the next victim was strong and the ball stopped there, but things could have turned very ugly. We paid all the expenses of the person who gave the name.

Finally, it hasn't just been a few times that I have received desperate calls from big tough activists who opened the door and found police officers standing there and immediately committed foolish and dangerous errors that jeopardized others. They didn't mean to, they aren't evil bastards who set out to hurt other people they cared about, they always thought they would behave just right. But they panicked, lost their nerve, or miscalculated and thought they could or should say a little something.

What can we do? In my book, **Free the Animals!** the A.L.F. instructs every newcomer to really act out in their own heads how it will be if they draw the short straw. Every actor must be personally prepared to take the heat, do the time, whatever, without involving others. Ask yourself that question every day if you are a liberationist. This is America. We can use the system. We mustn't be afraid to exercise our right to remain silent and never try to outwit law enforcement by saying a little something, no matter what they tell us. The right to remain silent is, of course, technically waived before the Grand Jury. Then we have to hope that people will be strong, even if it means they go to jail and stay there for a long time.

Best wishes,

Ingrid E. Newkirk,
President [PETA]

BLACK PANTHER PARTY PRESS

Dear NA-ALFSG,

I would like to announce to your former **Prisoner Justice Project** readers and writers that I will help publish their articles, Art and poetry. We are on the internet, in college campuses, libraries, and would be glad to help them.
Prisoners can write to:

Black Panther Press
POB 135, Daly City, CA
94016-1305, USA

Thank you for your time and consideration.
Cordially,

Malikia Sharifa

THEIR STRUGGLE CONTINUES

IN MEMORY OF FALLEN COMRADES

A.L.F. Spokesperson Dies – Remembering Steven Simmons

On January 12, 1997, Steven Simmons, 27, crossed over to the spirit world. I never knew Steve, but I knew of him and his passing saddens me as I realize what a great brother to our diverse movement and to the Animal People that Steve was. Steve was a victim of AIDS, and was a fervent believer that animal research was not the answer to his illness - Steve was one of the few who bravely stood up to pro-vivisection AIDS activists at the March on Washington. How strong a heart, that an individual suffering from a painful disease can stand up and say he does not want others to suffer for his benefit.
But how I best remember Steve is from his courageous role as spokesperson for the A.L.F. when we raided Michigan State Universities Fur Research Station in 1992. In light of rabid federal investigations eager to entrap anyone in their search for A.L.F. activists, Steve took up our flag and adamantly defended our arson attack On M.S.U' s laboratories. Steve paid the price for his actions and was hauled before the Michigan Grand Jury where he continually frustrated federal investigators with his uncooperativeness. Steve never knew the faces behind the masks he spoke for nor did he ever see the animals in M.S.U's labs he defended, but we both knew who he was, and we salute him for his selfless risk and sacrifice he has made on all of our behalf. We will miss you, and your memory shall live on in future actions against the vivisection industry we all despise.
--Rod Coronado

Judith Beatrice Bari – November 7, 1949 - March 2, 1997

Judi Bari died peacefully at home on March 2nd, at 6:45 am of the effects of breast cancer which had metastasized to her liver. She was 47. At her side were her 16-year-old daughter Lisa Bari, her companion and assistant Alicia Littletree, and fellow Earth First! organizer and close friend Karen Pickett. A leader of the environmental group Earth First!, Bari was seriously injured in an Oakland, Calif., car explosion, which also hurt a fellow activist. Bari at the time was involved in organizing protests against logging in northern California redwood forests.

Bari later sued the Oakland police and the FBI, alleging they tried to portray her as a suspect in order to smear Earth First!. She also alleged they failed to investigate the bombing and destroyed evidence, her attorney said. Bari's lawsuit against the Oakland police and the FBI will still be pursued despite her death.

``She'll be sorely missed," said Gary Ball, a fellow Earth First! activist. ``But I think her passing will be cause for doubling and redoubling our determination and effort." @

UNDERGROUND EXCLUSIVE

RAIDING ARIZONA

How The A.L.F. Carried out the University of Arizona Raid

by the A.L.F.

In the summer of 1988 we were alerted to animal experimentation conducted at the University of Arizona in Tucson. We were told that pound-seized dogs from the Sierra Vista Animal Shelter and greyhounds from local racetracks were only a few of the thousands of animals used in vivisection on campus. Other animals including rabbits, rats, guinea pigs, frogs and primates were used in primarily cancer and diet research with the majority of the experiments being a variety of grant-funded disease research and basic repetitive vivisection such as skin irritancy experiments to teach the medical students and, of course, the notorious LD-50 testing.

The raid in progress.
Activists leave their mark.

Whereas many Animal Liberation Front (A.L.F.) targets are chosen to target specific experiments of the work of a controversial vivisector, the UofA was chosen simply because it was one of the nation's top ten animal research campuses funded by both the federal government and the pharmaceutical industry. Annually, thousands of animals were ground up in the institutional mechanism of animal research that generates millions of dollars for universities in this country and billions for the pharmaceutical corporations that use educational institutions to develop the drugs that will make them filthy rich. All at the expense of innocent animal life while animal-based diets, environmental contamination, substance abuse and the true causes of most deadly illness and disease remain unaddressed by the very same people who profit from vivisection with one hand while the other encourages the lifestyle that creates the illness and disease.

We began our reconnaissance by disguising our members as college students who would walk the halls of university buildings searching out the vivariums where the laboratory animals were housed between and during experiments. Campus maps detailed the biological and psychological sciences buildings where we knew we would find animal research, the rest of our search was focused on the research wing of the nearby university hospital renowned as one of the best in the world. Once it was determined where vivisection was conducted, the next goal was simply using our noses to lead us to the animal rooms themselves which are usually kept either at the basement level or at rooftop. The scent of pine shavings and urine emitting from underneath doors and through extractor fans and vents lead us to our target.

Once it was established which buildings we would target, we began nighttime surveillance of the outside areas surrounding the labs. This meant spending countless hours hunched low in cars parked in filled parking lots where all comings and goings by staff, students and security patrols were recorded in our notebooks. After the first few weeks an obvious routine began to become apparent. Before long we could correlate the late night visits by students with lights that were turned on and off that were visible from the parking lot. Custodial activity was very predictable as these employees followed a meticulous routine. Security patrols were equally predictable and we learned the times of shift changes for the nearby university police by surveying their campus station. Of course, there were completely unpredictable events, which are always a factor, but the majority of activity was the day in day out mundane habits of a university during a school year. We chose the school year as our time for action, as it was expected that there would be late night activity on campus and in the targeted buildings and "students" coming and going would not draw unwanted attention.

Next, we obtained the frequencies of university police and began to monitor their transmissions with police scanners to gather intelligence on the periods of greatest police activity and their appropriate responses. This way we were able to learn response times and familiarize ourselves to common police communications and codes. The equipment and frequencies are commonly available from Radio Shack-type electronic stores.

Now it was time for us to begin physical infiltration. Our first actions were simple walks around the target buildings, visibly inspecting doors and windows for possible entry. During daylight hours the target buildings exterior doors remained unlocked which allowed us the opportunity to inspect locks on doors and windows. This gave us an idea of what kind of tools we would need to gain late night entry. Our next objective was to search the trashbins and wastepaper receptacles outside of the targeted buildings where we discovered a wealth of information on what type of animals were housed in the buildings and the names of researchers and their individual experiments. This allowed us to reference the Index Medicus at the campus library for more information on particular published works by the targeted vivisectors. What was more important to us was when we struck a goldmine by finding in the trash physical descriptions of the buildings construction. This saved us having to draw up our own maps for the different units of A.L.F. members that would be called in for the raid.

The night finally came when we began to enter the targeted buildings at night surveying firsthand the interior traffic and conditions we would encounter on the night of our action. By this time we felt fairly confident that the targeted vivariums and labs would be empty due to our exterior surveillance and our interior observations confirmed this. Our only problems would be encountered should we run into anyone in halls, stairways or elevators the night of the action. We would only be able to liberate rabbits, rats, mice, guinea pigs and frogs from the biological sciences, psychology and microbiology buildings while inflicting economic damage to equipment and the buildings themselves at the microbiology labs and the off-campus headquarters of the animal sciences department which was located in a house in a residential area.

We did everything but enter the targeted rooms during our reconnaissance mission and recorded the times it took to enter and leave the buildings. Once we knew how long it would take to carry out the action, we then took on the task of choosing a window of opportunity that would correlate with our outside recon. We needed not only enough time to enter, break-in to the individual rooms, load the animals and transport them to the ground floor, but also a safe time to literally drive a vehicle to the door to load the animals without any witnesses whatsoever. Here lay our greatest risk. No amount of preparation could help us deal with having to explain to anyone why we were taking animals out of the buildings late at night on a weekend.

Finally, the word went out to the individual specialists that would be required for an action we knew would be North America's largest laboratory animal liberation ever. All unit members would have to fit into the visible role of students should they encounter another person, as well as have the skills to carry out the raid. Homes had to be arranged for the rescued victims of vivisection and a safehouse established where a sympathetic veterinarian could inspect the animals before they could go on to safe homes to live out their natural lives. We also had to prepare for the unfortunate circumstance should any animals be deemed too far gone to survive whereby they would be humanely euthanized. No healthy animals or any with a fighting chance would be killed. Vehicles for transportation of both the animals and A.L.F. members had to be tuned up and inspected for no signs of mechanical or legal failure and cages constructed for transportation. Most of the animals would be transported in the cages they were already in. Tools were purchased far away that would be needed for the break-in and our technological division had to develop and build incendiary devices that would allow enough time to escape, while at the same time ignite at a synchronized time. Disguises were constructed for each individual member including wigs, false beards and eye-wear and clothing that would be expected of college students.

Shoes to be worn during the action would either be too small or large, depending on the wearer so that any footprints would not match the feet of A.L.F. members. All tools, clothing and equipment for the raid were kept in plastic bags where it could not collect fingerprints or even the minutest fragment of forensic evidence such as hair or lint. This precaution was taken in the case that any item should be inadvertently left behind during the operation.

A day was chosen for the action that would fit the safest window of inactivity for the four targeted buildings. April 4th, which also happened to be the anniversary of Martin Luther King's assassination. All unit members were assembled and some told for the first time what their target was. The next 48 hours were spent meticulously going over each individual unit member's role and conducting final surveillance on the campus. Meanwhile, the "handlers" that is the people charged with caring for and transporting the rescued animals once they were safely out of the labs prepared boxes, cages, water bottles and feed in the transport vehicles. Now all that remained to be done was perhaps the hardest part of any A.L.F. action. The waiting.

University of Arizona
the aftermath

On the day of April 3rd, while the majority of the A.L.F.'s active service unit tested and recharged radios and the incendiary devices to be used in the Microbiology laboratories and the animal sciences department offices, another team was on campus where they walked out a "dry run" of the action insuring that all doors and windows were just as they were supposed to be. This team also was charged with the responsibility of estimating just how many animals could be safely liberated in the time allotted for the action. The break-in unit would be given a cut-off time after which they would have to be out of the building to ensure that their entry and exit would not coincide with one of the regular police patrols or cut into the time needed to allow the demolition unit entry and exit to plant the incendiary devices.

As the dusk turned to darkness, over eight A.L.F. members began to load their daypacks with tools, radios, spraypaint and ski-masks which would be worn once inside the buildings. Lastly, the whole operation was reviewed with each team repeating its role and objective and the time they would take to carry it out. If all went well, not only would hundreds of lab animals be rescued, but also two animal research facilities would be set ablaze thereby destroying the equipment used to torture animals and countless records for research experiments that were kept in the off-campus offices of the animal sciences department.

At approximately 2100hrs. a man and woman holding hands passed two male students walking towards the biological sciences building. Neither couple were students and while the two men headed in one direction the man and woman approached the bottom floor doors of the Microbiology Building. Not far away in a campus parking lot, a surveillance member watched carefully the surrounding area should the need arise to radio either team to alert them to the occurrence of anything out of the ordinary. The man and woman reached the door and quickly gained entry with the aid of a few small hand tools which left no telltale

(Continued on page 17)

CRACKDOWNS ON THE FRONTLINES

What if you get arrested?

Ingrid Newkirk, PETA President

Dear Young Warriors, Wonderful People,

Below is an unimportant-seeming little extract from the part in my book, Free the Animals!, in which liberationists are advised by an old hand. I ask you to read it because, right now, as the crackdowns begin again and new warriors put themselves on the front lines, good people are finding themselves unprepared for the confusion, stress, fears, uncertainty, loneliness, disruption, isolation, separation and insecurity that their arrest can bring.

If you are arrested, you must be prepared to go it alone. Communications may be strained or impossible (they should be as limited as possible for everyone's safety), people may run from you in fear, or be warned away from you (for their good and/or yours): there will be rumors, lies, misunderstandings, miscommunications, disappointments, and pressures. The key is to already have accepted the fact, before you act, that you, and you alone, may have to go to jail for acting on your conscience. All energy must go into protecting others and the collective fight for animal justice.

"We're not building flash-in-the-pan heroes here," said M, "but a long-term army of committed people who accept that they may end up in prison. Don't think for one moment that you're too smart to be caught. You're not. The best-laid plans can go out the window with one fluke occurrence you could never possibly have planned for. It happens. Before you as much as think about being part of one of our (raids), you must be prepared to rot in jail rather than implicate others. The time to think about what your mom and dad will say, what will become of your job, who's going to walk your dog, how you'll stand up to all this, is now and here, not one sunny day when you are being depended upon by other people in the same boat. You shouldn't have to doubt your friends' commitment if they're caught, and your arrest shouldn't give them any loss of sleep, either. Without that trust, that pact, everything can being to crumble."

M had spent three months in prison for her part in the rescue of pregnant beagles from a lab breeder's farm. She spoke of her initial fears. "Then I read Solzhenitsyn's Gulag Archipelago," she said. "I read how the authorities would take a prisoner and put a strip of towelling through his mouth like a bit, pulling the ends over the man's shoulders, and tying them to his heels. They'd leave him like that for days. It was called 'the swan dive.' Or they would take a prisoner out into the hot sun and make him dig a trench to lie in with no shade or water. Sometimes prisoners would be forced to sit on the edge of a chair or stand without being able to move or stretch all day or night. The cells were so crowded five men would have to lie on their sides and then turn over as one. The usual sentence was called 'a quarter,'meaning twenty-five years. Men would cry with joy to hear they had only received ten or eight years at hard labor. Never were they able to write to their families or receive letters.

"Everything Solzhenitsyn wrote really happened to people like me, so how could I be depressed when I would be home within a few months, I was not beaten, I had food to eat, shelter, and my own bed?"

I urge all direct activists to practice, even role-play, being questioned by the police. It's not nerdy to be prepared. The fact is that we are lucky enough to live in a land which affords constitutional protection to our right not to have to answer any questions (unless we are before the grand jury, then off to jail we may go). Yet people get nervous or think they are smart enough to outwit a questioning officer or to divert his/her attention, and so they dig holes for themselves and others. They throw away their right to silence and become a prosecutor's dream, inadvertently scuttling any later defense strategy.

The right to privacy is also sacred in this country. So, it is up to you whether or not to let the police or FBI through your door. They're hoping you'll mistakenly think the correct response to "We'd like to come in and ask you a few questions" is "Okay, come on in" rather than "Sorry, I have nothing to say, so lease leave now or I'll have to have you arrested for trespassing," followed by a politely shut door. (You can do the same with their phone calls). And, yes, they all say, "If you don't let us in, we'll just come back with a warrant." Well, they may be able to get a warrant in the time it takes you to swallow some Rescue Remedy, but, chances are, they're bluffing: if they could get a warrant, they'd have been waving it at you. What have you got to lose by waiting to see?

The police lie (that's legal) and they sometimes break the law (that's not), but despite all their assurances to the contrary, they will never, ever go "easier on you" if you cooperate with them in their quest to get you. Later, if you need an attorney, you can decide what deals there are to be made (involving only you, of course), but not before.

Many of us will be lucky enough not to draw the short straw, but we should all be fully prepared to do so. Therein lies our strength. My best wishes for courage, strength, and good luck (upon which we are all somewhat dependent) to every liberationist!

UK PRISONER, ENDS HUNGER STRIKE ON A POSITIVE NOTE

Originally arrested in July of 1996 for allegedly planting explosive devices as part of a campaign against vivisection, U.K. A.L.F. activist Barry Horne has continued in waging a battle against animal abuse while behind bars. Part of that battle included a dramatic hungerstrike that touched the hearts and fueled the anger of animal activists world wide. Five full weeks after beginning his hunger strike, Barry Horne announced that he would consider his dramatic protest resolved on February 9. Three main reasons were given for deciding to end the hunger strike -

1) POLITICAL- Barry's demand was that the government withdrew it's support from vivisection. He knew from the outset that this demand would not be met by the then present Tory government. Recently elected Labour have committed themselves to ending cosmetic testing together with tobacco, alcohol and weapons research using animals. We are told that a Royal Commission will consider the area of the use of animals in 'medical research'. This is, obviously, not to say that all will be sweetness and light - far from it - because we know how 'economical with the truth' politicians can be but there is a degree of hope upon which we can build.

2) VIVISECTION AS A PRIORITY CAMPAIGN - The animal protection movement as a whole had, perhaps, somewhat neglected the subject of vivisection

H.O.F.

THE HOUSE ON FIRE PRISONER SUPPORT PROJECT is seeking prisoner opinion and first-hand accounts of dealings with the (in)justice system of any state.

Also needed are contact with radio & print activists for the coordination of an international prisoner support media network.

Send queries or submissions to:
HOUSE ON FIRE
BOX 29056
55 WYNDHAM ST. NORTH
GUELPH, ONTARIO, CANADA
N1H 8J4

Don't Let The Bastards Grind You Down!

during the past few years. Barry's actions, and those actions by others in support of his demands, has put vivisection back as a firm priority on the animal liberation agenda. Barry knew what he was doing by embarking on a hunger strike - he knew that it would force us into acting against vivisection - and that's what happened!

3) RECHARGING THE BATTERIES - Last, but by no means least, the animal liberation movement has been fired by a renewed determination and enthusiasm. From political campaigning to direct action an intensity of effort has galvanised us into action, once again - so let's keep the kettle boiling! One of the recurring themes of many conversations over the past few weeks has been that it is sad that it took someone to go on hunger strike, in order for this upsurge in activity to happen, but there you go. The important thing is that it's happened! It's better to light a candle than curse the darkness. Barry said, when announcing the end of his hunger strike, "We

must now pursue this evil, this obscenity, this black art called vivisection to it's final destruction".

All 18 prisoners in the UK participated in a 48 hour fast to mark the anniversary of Jill's death and to show solidarity for Barry and were joined by Rod Coronado in the US. On Monday Feb 3rd activists in San Francisco blockaded the British Consulate and burnt the Union Jack as part of a series of actions planned in support of Barry. On Thurs Feb 6th the British Tourist and the British Consulate in New York City were blockaded and the Union Jack was burnt. On the same day the British Embassy in Amsterdam was blockaded by angry Dutch activists. A day of Action has been called for next Wednesday, Feb 12th, in Amsterdam to support Barry. There is a new feeling of international solidarity.

4 DAYLIGHT RAIDS IN SUPPORT OF BARRY'S HUNGERSTRIKE

In between the start of Barry's hunger strike on 6th January, and when he stopped 36 days later, a large number of actions took place across Britain, but also in other European and North American countries. The most remarkable of those actions will surely be those daylight raids on animal breeders for vivisection.

What was a much more common thing in the 1980s had not happened for quite a while as the police did a crack down and arrested and imprisoned a number of activists, essentially closing down the Animal Liberation Leagues, who were then mostly responsible for this type of activity.

However, there were occasional exceptions, like when in 1991 Laundry Farm in Cambridge was raided in broad daylight by about 40 activists and a number of mongrel dogs were saved. Unfortunately, though, most of those dogs were retrieved by police later on, but only one arrest was made at the time.

RAID ON A RODENT BREEDER

Saturday 18th January saw a demonstration outside Bullingdon prison, near Bicester in Oxfordshire in support of Barry Horne's hunger strike. At the end of the demo, a few hundred protesters went down the road to a rodent breeding centre at Blackthorn owned by Harlan.

About a dozen police officers were guarding the premises. Undeterred, the protesters just pushed their way through, tore down the fences and stormed into the place. Doors were broken down and all windows smashed, and all instruments in reach were totally destroyed.

Those police trying to intervene were greeted with a number of rocks hurled at them, keeping them at bay. So, police just waited for re-inforcements to arrive. But they still filmed everything that was going on from a safe distance.

When more police arrived, including a helicopter, the angry protesters retreated into their vehicles. No arrests were made by then. A wide cross-section of people had been present, though, with everyone totally supportive of the action.

RAID ON A CAT BREEDER

Next some 50 protesters left the immediate area and converged on Hill Grove Family Farm near Witney in Oxfordshire, Britain's only breeder of 'Specific Pathogen Free' (SPF) cats for laboratory use. The owner, Christopher Brown, had just left the premises before the protesters arrived.

While some people stayed outside the farm, others went on to smash every single window and lots of farm equipment and a tractor. At the same time others broke through the doors into the housing area of the cats and liberated 14 of them. This caused an alarm system to go off and call the police.

When some police officers had already arrived, trying to control the demo outside the farm, activists were still busy inside the farm smashing it up. Some time later reinforcements arrived and also a helicopter with thermal cameras searching the area. 5 cats were recaptured and put down as they had lost their use for the breeder being not 'pathogen free' anymore. Amongst the cats who made it to freedom were 2 kittens and 2 pregnant females.

Several vans were pulled leaving the area and all in all 26 people were arrested. Only 8 of those were kept inside and were investigated for burglary, theft and criminal damage; the rest were soon released without charge.

RAID ON A BEAGLE DOG BREEDER

On the following Saturday 25th January, Consort beagle breeders at Harewood End, Ross-on-Wye, Herefordshire were targeted. At their premises, hidden from the road, they breed hundreds of beagles for use in vivisection.

On arrival, protesters were greeted by heavy police presence. Consort kennels had been a target of an ongoing campaign for quite a while and police were fully aware of the plans for a demo this Saturday as well. After some fluffy demo-ing, people left the area and drove 70 miles away. There they gathered and decided to return.

Back at the breeder no police were present and hundreds of people entered the sinister looking kennels protected by rolls of barbed wire. Numerous activists managed to gain access to the housing area of the beagles and 8 beagle puppies were smuggled to safety, despite police having arrived already by that time. Again, people of all walks of life were involved and unified in their attitude to this type of action.

Even police helicopter and vehicle searches did not lead to any beagles being retrieved by police. No arrests were made. Later that day it was reported that A.L.F. activists had torched 7 Buxted poultry lorries at Brackley in Northamptonshire.

ACTIVITIES IN DOVER TO COMMEMORATE JILL'S DEATH 2 YEARS PRIOR

The next Saturday, 1st February, was the second anniversary of the death of Jill Phipps, run over and killed by a live export lorry at Coventry Airport. There were demonstrations to commemorate the event at Dover docks - the last port involved in live exports - and Yorkshire.

Over 300 protesters converged in Dover. Despite a large police presence, the roads leading to the docks were blocked for about 2 hours. The crowd was large and determined enough to ensure attempts to clear the road were unsuccessfull.

An impromptu march was held to Dover town centre to take the message to the locals. Hundreds of masked-up activists suddenly found themselves outside a McDonald's with no police at all in sight. Leather shops nearby were observed hastily winding down their shutters.

This was too good an opportunity to be missed, so several of McDonald's windows got smashed. One have-a-go hero eating at McDonald's was foolish enough to come out and hit a demonstrator round the head. This proved to be a big mistake as the unfortunate gentleman was dragged into the crowd and received a good kicking.

Police eventually caught up and one police inspector made an attempt to arrest someone. He was unsuccessfull due to a crowd de-arresting, during which the inspector found himself on the ground being booted. Also, a butcher shop was invaded and trashed, with many bits of dead bodies being removed from the shelves to be burried with respect later on. At the same time a Kentucky Fried Chicken place was trashed.

Later on people made their way in vehicles to Capel lairage where animals are rested before their boat trip. A farmer who lived nearby had previously been seen on televison being filmed secretly beating calves using a heavy rubber pipe. Hundreds of people converged on his bungalow and farm and lots of damage was done to his property.

RAID ON A RABBIT BREEDER

The next stop was Homestead Rabbit Farm at Wingham, about 20 minutes drive away. At this place the owner Malcolm Rogers is breeding rabbits, apparently both for vivisection at the Pfizer laboratories and for their flesh for human consumption.

When the protesters arrived, the owner came out of his house wielding a pick axe handle. Six men overpowered him and used his own tool to beat him up severly, also breaking one of his legs in the process. The ambulance later confirmed that this was indeed his injury. Also, his mobile phone was removed and trashed before it could have been used to jeopardize the safety of the rabbits being liberated.

Another man from the farm used a tractor to drive into protesters. 4 protesters managed to jump onto the vehicle and remove the driver. The breeding place was thoroughly trashed and 10 rabbits were liberated, some of them right under the noses of arriving police. Three people werearrested for theft and one rabbit retrieved.

Later on the same day, 6 calves were liberated from a farm at Barnsby, near Leicester. They have all been rehomed, safe and free from the threat of live export and slaughter.

(Continued from page 12)

sign of a forced entry. Next they climbed the stairwell to the top floor where they first pulled on their ski masks before swinging open the doors that lead to the vivarium where it was known over 100 mice were being used ir cryptosporidium experiments. While one member stood watch, the other carefully transferred the mice into small boxes which were then placed in two separate long duffel bags. With this completed, the two A.L.F. members each picked up a bag and exited separately out of different doors minutes apart. Before they left the Microbiology Building there had been no radio transmissions which translated into everything appearing normal to the surveillance unit. The two team members walked towards a van where waiting inside for both of them was a driver and handler to receive and transfer the mice to larger cages for their journey to freedom. The two A.L.F. members then returned to their own vehicle and drove away; their role completed with total success.

At about the same time as the Microbiology Building was being entered, the A.L.F. team that had passed the other A.L.F. members reached the basement loading dock of the Psychology Building. Here they were somewhat hidden, as only a pedestrian walkway passed the adjacent doorway where the unit members would gain entry through an extractor fan that led to the vivarium of the Psychology Building where hundreds of rats used in experiments were housed. While one member stood watch, the other began cutting through the sheetmetal ventilation cover with tin snips. Next came the removal of the fan itself which took all of the twenty minutes allowed for this stage of the action. With precious minutes ticking away (which would translate into more lives saved, should any time be saved) the break-in team member entered the vivarium while the watchperson replaced the slightly bent and cut vent cover which would only appear tampered with at close inspection.

Next the A.L.F. member on the inside opened the adjacent door allowing in the other team member. Quickly the two began to remove individual rat cages from their tall racks and place them on rolling tables which could then be rolled to the loading area. Once 150 rats were ready for transport, the two-person team called in the transport vehicle which was awaiting their call with anticipation. In the time it took for the vehicle to arrive, one of the A.L.F. members began to smash the small electroshock boxes that were used in the psychology experiments and spraypainting demands that all vivisection be ceased. With the transport vehicle now at the loading area and the driver serving as a lookout, the two A.L.F. members began wheeling out the carts full of rat cages. Unfortunately, there was limited space in the vehicle allowing only a certain amount of rats all of which were standing on their hind legs sniffing at the cool night air as they were taken away from the sterile smells of the vivarium. Looking back at the hundreds of rats that would be left behind to a certain painful death, both team members rushed back in to grab one cage each which they carried on their laps as the transport vehicle ferried the animals to freedom.

Phase two of the operation was now complete with no unexpected developments. With radio-communicated word that both the mice and rats were safely off campus and both strike teams equally safe and secure, now came the most dangerous and largest stage of the five- pronged attack. Between timed police patrols a vehicle drove up to the five-story Biological Sciences Building and dropped off one unit member who was to gain entry through a bottom-floor door. Once that was accomplished, two separate teams entered the building bringing the number of A.L.F. members in the building to five. Meeting in a stairwell, the unit members donned ski-masks and white labcoats and, pulling a five pound sledgehammer from one of their packs, charged to the fifth floor where hundreds of animals awaited their freedom.

Days later police and media would still be talking about the brazen attitude of the "A.L.F. Commandos" who, not only carried out the lightning strike raid, but also videotaped their crime. In the video, A.L.F. members, many of whom were obviously women, are seen smashing through vivarium doors and rushing in to spirit the animals away. When the team reached the fifth floor, one member approached each locked animal room and with the sledgehammer smashed a hole through the reinforced glass and then reached in unlocking the door from the inside. Immediately after, each room was entered where first a small colony of guinea pigs were transferred to smaller cages.

Many of the animals were without food and water and sank to the back of their cages, many with shaved fur awaiting exposure to toxic substances which would inflame their skin. The A.L.F. had arrived in time to prevent such cruelty. Slowly, rolling carts were filled with guinea pigs, then more rats, hundreds of mice and finally six African frogs used for breeding, their offspring sacrificed for dissection. A separate cart was filled with over a dozen rabbits in cloth sacks. Now the elevator was brought to the floor by an A.L.F. member who was in it. The carts full of animals were carefully rolled into the elevator with two unit members while another two spaypainted our greetings to the animals' executioners.

Now travelling downward in the elevator, the A.L.F. team held their breath, hoping no one else in the building would call the elevator. If they did, the doors would open to reveal not only two masked members but hundreds of mice, rats, frogs, guinea pigs and rabbits. When the elevator full of animals left the fifth floor, a radio call was made to the pick-up vehicle which was to receive the over 900 animals. At the ground floor the two A.L.F. members wheeled the animals to double doors where the transport vehicle was reversed directly to the building. Any student or police officer who saw this would immediately become suspicious, but here the weeks of nighttime surveillance paid off. The unit knew that as long as it stayed within the window of opportunity they would evade the regular police cruiser patrols.

Backing up to the Biological Sciences Building, a handler swung open the rear doors of the vehicle and was met immediately with the break-in team who quickly began to load the many cages. Within minutes the animals were safely loaded and the vehicle drove away at a normal pace. The break-in team rendezvoused with the other unit members in the stairwell where clothes and tools were neatly packed back into their daypacks and the team split up to leave the campus on foot. The surveillance watchperson would later report that not three minutes after the vehicle full of animals departed from the doorway, a student would exit from the very same doors.

When the A.L.F. watchperson received word that all animals and unit members were safely out of the buildings, a radio call was made and with a one word prearranged message called in the demolitions unit.

Minutes later a solitary "student" entered the Microbiology Building carrying in their daypack an incendiary device. Climbing the stairs to the rooftop laboratory where the cryptosporidium mice had earlier been liberated from, the demolition member pulled on their ski-mask and set the device in the center of the laboratory. Carefully setting the timer for 0400 hrs., the A.L.F. member then built a pyramid of dissection boards and desk drawers around the device to fuel the fire once it ignited. As the member left the building, they took one last look at the torture chamber where literally thousands of animals had lost their lives, their eyes being the last to ever see it standing.

Exiting the building the demolition member met with their driver who next drove them to the quiet residential neighborhood where the Animal Sciences Department headquarters was located. Previous reconnaissance had revealed a weakly constructed basement vent which entered into a crawlspace beneath the house filled with computers and file records which contained vital information and data necessary to every animal experiment on the UofA campus. The same unit member now walked casually to the basement and crawled beneath the building and set the second incendiary device also for 0400 hrs. Completing this, they returned to the vehicle and departed towards the interstate, their mission completed.

At approximately 0438hrs university district residents were awakened to the sounds of multiple sirens responding to a blaze on the rooftop of the Microbiology Building. Before the fire could be brought under control it had destroyed not only the complete animal research laboratory, but water doused on the flames had caused hundreds of thousands of dollars damage to the labs beneath the targeted lab.

No sooner had the fire at the Microbiology Building been brought under control when the Tucson Fire Department received the call the Animal Sciences headquarters was also ablaze. Though damage caused by the fire at the residential offices was first thought to be minimal, later news reports would detail that the heat had caused irreparable damage to the complete computer systems and since the fire caused serious structural damage to the very foundations of the building, it would later have to be demolished.

Meanwhile, in the network of safe homes established as the A.L.F.'s Underground Railroad, the 1,231 rescued lab animals were beginning a new life -- one that would quickly erase the nightmarish memories of the laboratories of the University of Arizona. Though federal investigators and local police pursued over 150 leads in the A.L.F.'S raid at the UofA, investigators would later report in law enforcement journals of the virtual lack of evidence that might lead to any arrests. Michael Cusonivich, head of research for the UofA later conceded that not only had the A.L.F.'s raid caused the cessation of over a dozen experiments, but also the university was forced to spend over half a million dollars on an improved security system for all animal research on campus. University officials would also admit how the raid had placed such attention on their animal research program, that they were left with no alternative but to clean up their act to ensure that not even the slightest violation of weak federal animal welfare guidelines were violated.

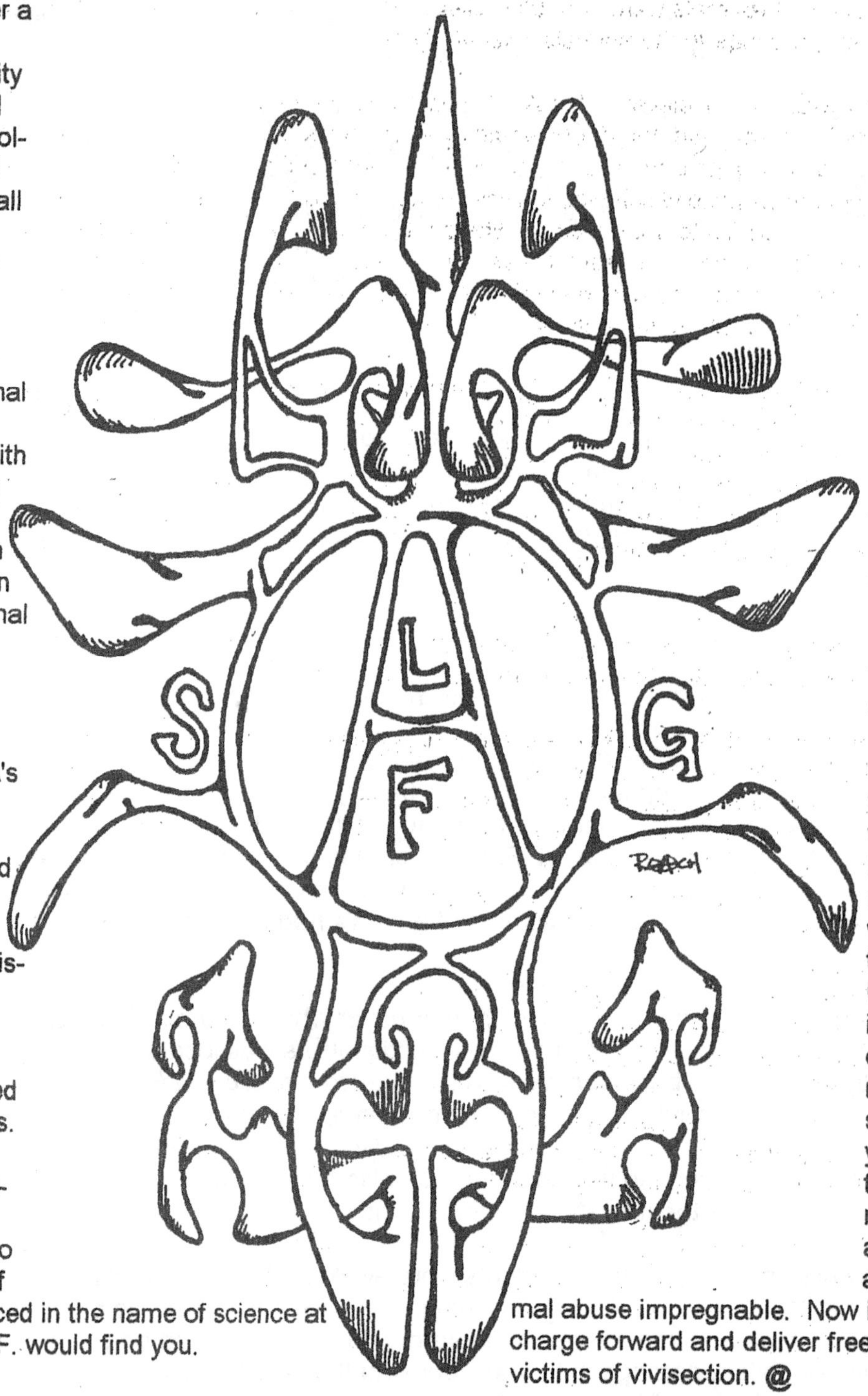

While attention was focused on the UofA's animal research, a small A.L.F. active service unit infiltrated Tucson once again that year. This time the Veteran's Administration Hospital was targeted where four former racing greyhounds were liberated from outdoor kennels. The message was painfully clear to vivisectors in Arizona. Wherever you are, no matter how hidden, if animals were sacrificed in the name of science at your hands, the A.L.F. would find you.

Now it is up to you. The A.L.F. active service unit which carried out the raid on the University of Arizona may not have been caught, but without the young blood of the next generation they may not survive. Though this action was highly organized, it was carried out by simple people who never imagined they would be labelled as domestic terrorists by the U.S. Government. They are people just like you and me, men and women, young and old. They were not career criminals, veterans of military operations, but simply people who cared enough to stand by their beliefs even when it meant breaking the law. For many, the UofA raid was their first laboratory action. But as the UofA proved, with vigilant surveillance, a lot of common sense and most importantly, the self-confidence that you can achieve anything you put your mind and heart into, anything is possible and no target of animal abuse impregnable. Now it is time for you to charge forward and deliver freedom to millions of victims of vivisection. @

DIRECT ACTION DEFENSE FUND

Are you, or is someone you know, an activist recently arrested for illegal animal liberation activites? The DADF is here for you! A cooperative effort by the NA-A.L.F.S.G., the Animal Liberation League and the Rod Coronado Support Committee, the DADF will assist arrested activists during their times of immediate need, helping activists to post bond, assisting with lawyer expenses, etc. Decisions are made on a case by case basis. *DONATIONS ARE WELCOME!*

DADF: BOX 57357, Tucson, AZ, 85732-7357, USA

Diary Of Action

Please Note: The Diary of Action is intended to report the news of direct action to save animals, not to encourage crime. All reports come from other publications, the internet, or anonymous communiqués sent the NA-A.L.F.S.G. and other animal liberation groups. As usual, the following list includes actions that took place in the time period covered in *Underground #6*, but were not reported until recently.

CANADA

NOVEMBER 26/96: Pacific Coast - the "Poultry Liberation Organization" and "Animal Avengers" has claimed credit for poisoning turkey carcasses in grocery stores along the pacific coast of the United States and southwestern Canada (from Los Angeles, CA to Vancouver, Canada). The stores targeted most were large grocery chains including (but not limited to) Albertsons, Safeways, and Fred Meyers. The turkey brands most targeted (but not limited to) were Butterball, Norbest, Heartland, Jeannie-O, and Honeysuckle White.

JANUARY 15/97: Cloverdale, BC - Wayside Farms (a large chicken farm) has a fire started in a pile of debris stacked outside a barn door destroying the entire barn. -Unclaimed

FEBRUARY/97: Guelph, ONT - Vase, an expensive restaurant selling veal, etc. has huge side windows broken on several occasions. -Unclaimed

MARCH 8/97: Clayoquot Sound, ONT - Activists cut nets and released about 50,000 farmed fish into the wild, at the Pacific National Group in Cypress Bay. The fish were healthy, early juvenile chinook [salmon] The lost 500-gram chinooks would have fetched the farmer an estimated $1.2 million at maturity in about 18 months. The Ahousaht native bands claim the farm had threatened wild salmon stocks and shellfish and herring habitats in their traditional territories.

MARCH 15/97: Belhiem, ONT - "Greetings from the Great Lakes Earth Liberation Front. Furriers beware the ides of March! Like the evil Roman empire before you, your kingdom of cash and cruelty will fall by the weight of its own iniquity (or with a little help from our friends). On March 15, our band of eco-anarchists paid a visit to the Eberts fur farm in Blenheim, Ontario on Mink Lane Rd. We were amazed at the openness of the operation. The sheds were practically next to the main road, with no attempts being made to hide the farm from the public. This made our work somewhat more difficult, as traffic constantly passed us while we were on site. There were some 12 sheds, though at least a few were empty. We cut several holes in the perimeter fence, but also opened the driveway gate leaving plenty of exit routes for our friends to choose from. We entered the first shed and had some trouble opening the cages. Once we figured out the latches, we started opening the cages and collecting the breeding cards. When possible, we damaged the cages. The mink were ready to party, rushing past us to the nearby safety of wooded farmland. We also knew that Rondeau Provincial Park was not far away, offering plenty of suitable habitat for our sleek brown buddies.
One of our group left a spray paint autograph on the feed shed, just to let them know that we care. When we had released about 240 of our captive comrades, a truck pulled up to the front gate that we had already pried open. Saddened to leave without finishing our intended business, we managed to escape detection by hopping the back fence and meeting our driver up the road. Though it is maddening to have been so close to freeing so many, we are somewhat comforted by Mother Jones' words: 'Mourn the dead and work like hell for the living!'"

MARCH 31/97: Belhiem, ONT - Ebert's Fur Farm hit for the second time. 1,800 mink were freed from their cages at the Belheim fur farm before 5 American activists were caught and arrested. Mink cages had been opened and at least four holes were cut in the perimeter fence. Breeding cards were also removed. Damage estimates range between $90,000-$500,000. Two men and three women from the Detroit area were charged with mischief over $1000, theft over $1000, possession of stolen property and possession of burglary tools.

UNITED STATES

JUNE/96: Snohomish, WA - Brainard Fur Farm: Daylight raid by A.L.F. resulted in the release of 80 mink. (not in Duvall). -A.L.F.

SEPTEMBER/96: Shoreline, WA - meat storage locks glued. -A.L.F.

SEPTEMBER/96: Seattle, WA - Ruddy's Meats locks glued. -A.L.F.

SEPTEMBER/96: North Seattle, WA - Butcher store had a large window and one door window smashed. -A.L.F.

OCTOBER/96: Shoreline WA, 2nd hit on meat storage building. 1 large window smashed, 1 small window bashed. -A.L.F.

NOVEMBER 10/96: Mercer Island, WA - A carload of people threw a bucket of rocks at the windows of McDonald's - but the business had installed shatter-proof glass.

NOVEMBER 16/96: Cleveland,OH - 7 animal abusers hit.3 Arby's (1)painted in the past. smashed window and drive thru sign.(2)painted walls "A.L.F.","killing is wrong" smashed drive thru sign (3) painted walls 1 Wendy's smashed window painted walls "A.L.F." "murder" "Meat Is Murder" 1 unknown butcher shop glued locks painted walls 1 red lobster painted walls "Killers of the Sea" 1 K.F.C smashed windows painted walls.-A.L.F.

NOVEMBER 17/96: Charlotte, NC - Douglas Furs and The Carriage (sells fur) had their windows, doors, walls and sidewalks spraypainted with "A.L.F." and "Fur Kills". A Belk department store was also spraypainted with the same slogans. Four McDonald's spraypainted with slogans saying "Meat Is Murder", "Meat Kills", "McDeath" and "A.L.F." -A.L.F.

This fur shop received a lovely new paint job, care of the A.L.F.

NOVEMBER 22/96: St. Louis, Missouri - A.L.F. activists hit the Fur and Leather Centre, spraypainting "A.L.F." on the building entrance and two trailers used for transporting fur. Using a strong acid, the axles of one truck were melted off. Doors were also spraypainted, stickers and license plates were ruined on two trailers. Damage: $5,000. Increased security at all St. Louis fur locations has cost over $250,000. -A.L.F.

NOVEMBER 23/96: Cleveland,OH - Blue Ribbon Meats has trucks painted and an attempted arson. -A.L.F.

NOVEMBER 27/96: Charlotte, NC - 2 Honeybaked Ham stores had their locks glued and were spraypainted with "A.L.F.", "Meat Kills", "Meat Is Murder". Carolina Country BBQ - two catering vans, locks glued and spraypainted with "A.L.F.", "Animal Killers", "Meat Kills". A steak house restaurant was painted with slogans everywhere "A.L.F.", "Meat Kills", etc. -A.L.F.

NOVEMBER 28/96: Hinsdale, MA - Four activists arrested near Carmel Mink Ranch charged with Breaking and Entering with intent to commit a felony, Trespassing, Larceny over $250, and Malicious destruction of property.

NOVEMBER 28/96: Suffield Township, OH - Goodyear Hunting and Fishing Club lodge and surrounding buildings covered in spraypainted anti-hunting slogans. Hartville, Ohio: Butcher store window smashed. -A.L.F.

NOVEMBER 30/96: Cleveland, OH - Ohio Farmers Inc.(egg distributer) trucks painted one truck completely burnt. -A.L.F.

NOVEMBER 30/96: Cleveland, OH - K.F.C (hit before) walls painted window broken and small fire set (not a lot of damage done). -A.L.F.

NOVEMBER 30/96: Solon, OH - Boston Market (chicken fast food) window smashed and "Meat is Murder" painted. -A.L.F.

NOVEMBER 30/96: Aurora, OH - McDonald's "Billions Slaughtered" painted. -A.L.F.

NOVEMBER 30/96: near Akron, OH - Dumas Meats truck window smashed slogans painted. -A.L.F.

NOVEMBER 30/96: ?, OH - Sea World sign changed to read "Sea Prison". -A.L.F.
NOVEMBER 30/96: ?, OH - Pro-hunting signs spray painted for the animals. -A.L.F.

DECEMBER/96: New York City, NY - Alexandros Furs in the heart of the NYC fur district, found it's locks filled with Krazy Glue, and it's windows covered with anti fur posters. -A.L.F.

DECEMBER 6/96: Ithaca, NY - Wendy's Old Fashioned Hamburgers, one front and one side double-paned window were smashed and spray-painted slogans including "Killers" and "Free the Earth". Also, the restaurant's front door lock had been filled with a compound making the lock inoperable. -A.L.F.

DECEMBER 8/96: Eugene, OR - Kaufman's Clothing Store in the Valley River Shopping Mall had approx. $75,000 worth of fur coats sprayed with permanent red fabric paint. -A.L.F.

DECEMBER 14/96: Snohomish, WA - 2nd raid on the Brainard Fur Farm. Activists returned to find most cages empty. By the lights from the farmer's house, activists liberated approx 50 mink, smashed cages and left messages like "SCUM," "A.L.F." and "stop or be stopped."-A.L.F.

DECEMBER 15/96: Oak Park, MI - Blood-red paint bombs splattered on front and side of El-Mars Furs, locks glued and jammed, slogans painted on side of building. -A.L.F.

DECEMBER 15/96: West Bloomfield, MI - Bricker-Tunis Furs bombarded with red paint bombs. -A.L.F.

DECEMBER 15/96: West Bloomfield, MI - Cohen's Kosher Meats splattered with red paint bombs, "Meat is Murder" written on building. -A.L.F.

DECEMBER 19/96: Birmingham, MI - the front door, brick alcove and brick window ledges at Ceresnie & Offen Furs were drenched in blood-red paint and the locks glued and jammed with toothpicks. Ceresnie & Offen is located on Woodward Ave. in downtown Birmingham and was not cleaned up for two days. It was a great statement for them to have a "blood"-soaked store front and sidewalk for two days! -A.L.F.

DECEMBER 21/96: Seattle, WA - Markethouse Corned Beef hit with "MURDERER" on front and "CLOSED" painted on sign. -A.L.F.

DECEMBER 21/96: Seattle, WA - Ruddy's Meat's 2nd hit. 6 meat trucks painted with "murderer" & "scum." -A.L.F.

DECEMBER 22/96: Philadelphia, PA - Grill Master Deli (sells veal) had their locks glued. -A.L.F.

DECEMBER 21/96: Troy, MI - Nordstrom's fur department at Somerset Mall-North hit with butyric acid during the busy Christmas rush. The odour permeated the entire 2-floor store. The next day, the odour was still detectable but Nordstrom's was open for business. All the fur coats, however, had been removed! -A.L.F.

DECEMBER 23/96: Sterling Heights, MI - Sana Furs at Lakeside Mall had butyric acid thrown on carpeting under fur garments during one of the busiest pre-Christmas shopping days. The store had to be closed for the duration of the shopping season. It is believed the carpeting probably had to be replaced and the garments cleaned. Sana's also carries a large number of leather items. -A.L.F.

DECEMBER 25/1996: Bath, MI - A small group of Great Lakes ELFers traveled MI to pay a holiday visit to Jack Brower Fur Farm. From the communique: "Our intent was to throw a special Christmas party for the mink held captive there. Upon arriving, we discovered that we were unexpected guests. To our surprise and delight, there were no surveillance cameras and no guard dogs to greet us or announce our arrival. We set to work immediately with our handy-dandy tin snips. We cut several openings through both the inner and outer fences surrounding the 6 sheds housing the mink. When we entered the shed area, we found that three of the sheds were empty pelting stock housings. The other three were filled with anxious white mink restless to be free. After the rear door of each shed was removed (so that the mink could run out without having to run past their rescuers), each cage was opened. Those that didn't climb out immediately (most practically threw themselves out of those tiny wire cages!) were lifted out and released. One ferocious little guy would not let go of the glove of one human helper and had to be carried outside the perimeter hanging from a glove. Once laid on the ground (glove still gripped in his teeth), the mink took a look around and realizing that he was at last free, finally released the mitt and bounded across the snow to a nearby woods and away. We wish him and the others (some 150 mink we estimate) very happy lives. There was no better Christmas present that we could have received than the sight of all those beautiful creatures playing about, chasing each other, and finally running away. But no party would be complete without "decorations", so we liberally decorated the structures with festive green paint wishing all a Merry Christmas from the ELF! And just think, less than $30 worth of gas, tools, and paint was all we needed to throw our mink party!"

DECEMBER 26/96: Eden Prairie, MN - Incendiary devices left on a truck at the Haertel Co. (15151 Technology Dr.), they ignited causing destroying the truck $18,000 damage. The Haertel Co. produces Fursheen Liquid, a pelt cleaner used on fur farms. -A.L.F.

JANUARY/97: Kirkland, WA - 7 of 8 trucks at Meat Distributers had their windshields smashed out and messages left: "ANIMAL KILLERS! -A.L.F" Local TV reports put the damages at $5000. -A.L.F.

JANUARY/97:(either Greenbrook and East Brunswick),NJ - Furs by Guarino in NJ was spray painted with "Fur Hurts" on the roll down metal door and "Fur Is Dead" was painted on the side of the building. -A.L.F.

JANUARY/97: Bellvue, WA - 4 large windows at Golden Steer Meats were smashed. A previous hit where the same 4 windows were smashed had damages reported at $2,000 by local media. -A.L.F.

JANUARY/97: Salt Lake City, UT - Over 20 stores had their windows shot out or smashed, including, but not limited too Burger king, Mcdonald's, Arby's, and Kentucky fried chicken. Jim Bridger trapping supplies had their windows broken or etched with A.L.F. All the cars in the parking lot had their tires slashed and A.L.F. Etched in their windows. A leather store had their windows smashed and their cars got the same Treatment as a Jim Bridger. 4 "got milk" trailers were broken up. -Northern Utah A.L.F.

JANUARY 1/97: Ithaca, NY - Cornell University's Poultry Research Station broken into, documents taken. Photo's of the chickens and conditions taken. According to researchers, the break-in will likely force the university to scuttle several major research projects. "The cost of this could run into the hundreds of thousands, maybe millions of dollars," vivsector Fred Quimby, director of Cornell's Center for Research Animal Resources. -Band of Mercy

JANUARY 1/97: Dallas, TX - Oshmans Sporting Goods fur trimmed coats sprayed with red paint. -A.L.F.

JANUARY 3/97: Bloomfield Hills, MI - Dittrich Furs had windows smashed. -A.L.F.

JANUARY 3/97: Westbury, NY - The Fur Vault had "FUR IS DEAD" spraypainted over the front wall and plaque. -A.L.F.

JANUARY 5/97: Dallas, TX - Bifano Furs North Dallas location highly corrosive acid sprayed through mail slot; paint bombed, locks glued. -A.L.F.

JANUARY 5/97: Richardson, TX - Richardson Fur Center windows shot out, paint bombed, locks glued. -A.L.F.

JANUARY 5/97: Dallas, TX - Valentines Furs paint bombed and locks glued. -A.L.F.

JANUARY 5/97: Dallas, TX - Macy's window shot at with a slingshot (unknown damage) and paint poured on sidewalk. Done in haste because of security guards present. -A.L.F.

JANUARY 5/97: Dallas, TX - Morris Kaye Furs paint bombed and locks glued. -A.L.F.

JANUARY 5/97: Dallas, TX - Koslows Furs locks glued. - A.L.F.

JANUARY 8/97: Philadelphia, PA - Jacque Ferber Furs had paint sprayed into store through mail slot, and all locks glued. - A.L.F.

JANUARY 8/97: Philadelphia, PA - Grill Master Deli (sells veal) had their locks glued. -A.L.F.

JANUARY 9/97: Towson, MD - A.L.F. strike "Ravers Discount Meat." Meat trucks were painted with slogans like "meat is murder" and "A.L.F." -Maryland Cell, A.L.F.

JANUARY 9/97: Baltimore, MD - Fell's Point Wholesale Meats had locks glued and slogans painted on the store front and on the company's meat trucks. -Maryland Cell, A.L.F.

JANUARY 9/97: Winthrop, WA - An explosion and fire destroyed The Outdoorsman hunter/outfitter shop and blew a mounted moose head out the window and across the street into a toy store. Federal agents from the Bureau of Alcohol, Tobacco, and Firearms were called to investigate. -Unclaimed

JANUARY 10-13/97: Dallas, TX - Andrianna Fur Sale (A travelling fur sale) has over 100 coats sliced with razor blades. The communique stated that the most expensive coats were targeted, and the cuts were done at a diagonal angle under the armpit so that they damage was maximized. The cuts went through the whole coat according to the A.L.F. -A.L.F.

JANUARY 11-12/97: New York City, NY - Le Chien pet supply store at Trump Plaza to protest owner Lisa Gilford's use of wild cat fur to make coats for dogs. "Lisa is Cruella" and "Fur Scum" were spray painted on the front doors and the locks were glued shut. -Paint Panthers

JANUARY 11-12/97: New York City, NY - Throughout the weekend, the backs of more than 75 fur wearers were covered with red paint. "Thousands of foxes, lynx,rabbits, beavers, raccoons, sables, and mink were avenged this weekend. Fur wearers who continue to show a disgusting disrespect for animals beware," say the Panthers. -Paint Panthers

JANUARY 11/97: Woodmere, NY - Alexandros Furs had "FUR IS DEAD" spraypainted on the side wall. -A.L.F.

JANUARY 11/97: Woodmere, NY - Laurette Couturier had "FUR IS MURDER" spraypainted on the rear doors and wall. A hole was also punctured in the front window. -A.L.F.

JANUARY 11/97: Cedarhurst, NY - Fur Galleria had a hole punctured in the front window. -A.L.F.

JANUARY 11/97: Seattle, WA - Ruddy's Meat's 3rd hit. 6 meat trucks painted with "murderer" & "scum" and "A.L.F." and "we're back." - A.L.F.

JANUARY 11/97: Seattle, WA - meat storage building hit for 3rd time. 2 large windows smashed. -A.L.F.

JANUARY 11/97: Ballard, WA - The Butcher Shoppe was hit 2 large windows smashed and one extra large neon sign destroyed. -A.L.F.

JANUARY 11/97: North Seattle, WA - activists went back to the butcher store to find security patrolling = "more $$$ spent!"-A.L.F.

JANUARY 12/97: Woodmere, NY - Alexandros Furs had the front window smashed. -A.L.F.

JANUARY 13/97: New York, NY - Alexandros Furs locks superglued, store stickered and graffitied with "FUR IS DEAD," and "A.L.F." - A.L.F.

JANUARY 13/97: New York, NY - Adar Leather graffitied with "LEATHER IS DEAD" -A.L.F.

JANUARY 13/97: New York, NY - Corn furs and B&N Furs graffitied with "FUR SHAME," "A.L.F.," and "FUR HURTS." -A.L.F.

JANUARY 14/97: Flemington, NJ - Three Flemington Furs billboards spraypainted with "Fur is Dead," "A.L.F." etc. -A.L.F.

JANUARY 15/97: New York, NY - Alexandros Furs stickered, McDonalds redecorated with "Meat is Murder". Majestic Furs locks superglued, Fashion Institute of Technology "Evita" display stickered and "fur hurts" was written on window. -A.L.F.

JANUARY 16/97: West Hamstead, NY - Strathmore Furs had three holes punctured in the front window. -A.L.F.

JANUARY 16/97: Woodmere, NY - Alexandros Furs had the front door window smashed. -A.L.F.

JANUARY 16/97: Oceanside, NY - Leslie Aaron Furs had two punctures in the front windows. An attempt was also made to break the neon sign. -A.L.F.

JANUARY 16/97: Oceanside, NY - Burger King had the rear door window smashed. -A.L.F.

JANUARY 18/97: Baldwin, NY - Metropolitan Argo Furs, Ltd. had a hole punctured in the front window. -A.L.F.

JANUARY 18/97: Woodmere, NY - Laurette Couturier's rear window was cracked. -A.L.F.

JANUARY 19/97: New York, NY - Zamir Furs graffitied with "FUR IS DEAD." Kenny Rogers Roasters graffitied with

"MEAT IS MURDER." Lamb and beef packing graffitied with "ANIMAL LIBERATION," and at least a half dozen meat packers vans graffitied with "MEAT IS MURDER." Wendy's redecorated with "MEAT IS MURDER," "GO VEGAN," and "A.L.F." -A.L.F.

JANUARY 22/97: Virginia Beach - A McDonald's had its drive through and windows spraypainted.

JANUARY 26/97: DesMoines, IA - Cownie Furs and Furs by Manolidis had smashed windows, slogans such as "Fur Scum" and "Fur Is Dead" painted on the sidewalk, doors and walls of the stores, and glued locks. -Paint Panthers

JANUARY 27/97: Salt Lake City, UT - Producers Meats in North Salt Lake had 3 incendiary devices placed at the back entrance. A Simpsons Milk billboard was set on fire. Unfortunately the fire was soon put out by the wind. -Northern UT A.L.F.

JANUARY 28/97: Dallas, TX - Petco Pet Supplies cat toys made out of rabbit fur sprayed with red paint, several fur wearers sprayed as well. -A.L.F.

JANUARY 28/97: New York, NY - Kenny Roger's Roasters on 6th Ave were tagged twice and had the side lock glued. 12 windows were smeared with etching fluid. -A.L.F.

Fur Free Friday/97: New York, NY - the day after FFF, two large Fifth Avenue fur stores -- Fendi's and Revillon -- were informed that explosive devices had been planted in their stores as "revenge for the animals." Associated Press was also contacted. -A.L.F.

FEBRUARY/97: Seattle, WA - Eilers Furs storefront spraypainted. -A.L.F.

FEBRUARY/97: Cincinnati, OH - Window smashed at Fettner Freidman Furs.

FEBRUARY/97: Cincinnati, OH - Window broken and "A.L.F." painted on wall at New York Fur and Leather.

FEBRUARY/97: Cincinnati, OH - Locks glued and window damaged at Katsatos Fur Store.

FEBRUARY/97: Cincinnati, OH - Several fast food restaurants (Hardee's, McDonald's, KFC) covered in spray painted slogans. Bathrooms damaged at Burger King.

FEBRUARY/97: Near Akron, OH - Several windows and lights smashed, locks glued, and slogans painted at Goodyear Hunting and Fishing Club.

FEBRUARY/97: Akron, OH - Locks glued at Honeybaked Hams.

FEBRUARY/97: Near Akron,OH - Locks glued at Butcher Boy Meats.

FEBRUARY/97: NYC, NY - in early Feb. over 30 fur coats in NYC were sprayed with either red paint or red fabric paint.

FEBRUARY 1/97: Detroit, MI - A.L.F. activists made it inside Hudson's "Gigantic Fur Sale" at Cobo Hall, despite heavy security presence. From the communique: "...[S]ecurity was so tight at this fur sale that women's handbags were being searched, pockets emptied and coats taken and hung behind long tables before one could enter ... Customers were followed on a nearly one-to-one basis everywhere." The A.L.F. made it inside and managed to release butyric acid in a $10,000 fur coat pocket, scattering customers from the sale. -A.L.F.

FEBRUARY 1/97: Dearborn, MI - Saks Fifth Ave Fur Salon at Fairlane Town Center hit with butyric acid in coat pocket. -A.L.F.

FEBRUARY 1/97: Dearborn, MI - Sana Furs at Fairlane Town Centre also hit and butyric acid was put in fur coat pockets. -A.L.F.

FEBRUARY 2/97: Lansing, MI - Two McDonalds in Macomb County had all of their locks cemented. -A.L.F.

FEBUARY 4/97: Philadelphia, PA - Ferber Furs windows etched and locks glued. -A.L.F.

FEBRUARY 6/97: West Bloomfield, MI - Bricker-Tunis Furs windows smashed and set on fire. Extent of damage not known. Windows boarded up for 2 days. This is the fur store that was selling "Barbie" fur outfits. -A.L.F.

FEBRUARY 9/97: Charlotte, NC - Slogans spraypainted including "A.L.F.", "Fur Kills", "Fur Is Murder", and "We Are WatchingYou". Sidewalk was also sprayed with red paint & slogans. -A.L.F.

FEBRUARY 10/97: East Lansing, MI - Jacobsons Fur Store hit (517-351-2250), three huge front windows smashed. The windows have been stickered hundreds of times in the last month or so, "No big deal but its really pissin' them off!" Window smashing and paintbombing came the night after a statewide protest of Jacobson's stores. Police estimate damages at over $9000. -A.L.F.

FEBRUARY 12/97: Virgina Beach - Meat market was hit, locks glued, paint was splashed on the front of the store, slogans "meat is murder" and "Blood money" was sprayed on the back. A PETA anti-meat poster was also wheat pasted on the back door.

FEBRUARY 13/97: Virginia Beach - A McDonalds was spraypainted with the slogans "Murderers," "Meat is murder," and "The killing must end." Three locks glued. PETA anti-meat posters were glued up. A can of red paint was dumped on the drive- thru sign.

FEBRUARY 13/97: Virginia Beach - Three milk billboards were attacked with christmas orniments filled with red paint. One billboard was perminently removed.

FEBRUARY 16/97: Baltimore MD - activist struck the Seleh's De Federal Hills Furrier. Locks were glued and slogans painted. -Maryland Cell, A.L.F.

FEBRUARY 17/97: Baltimore, MD - A.L.F. activists find and destroy traps used to catch and kill furbearing animals. -Maryland Cell, A.L.F.

FEBRUARY 19/97: Petaluma, CA - The Rancho Slaughterhouse (1522 North Petaluma Blvd) was attacked by activists of the Bay Area Cell of the A.L.F. At least one semi-trailer rig was heavily damaged by fire.

From the Communique: "We placed 4 incendiary devices in a double, semi-trailer truck used for live animal transportation. We used a total of 5 liters of flammable liquid, which we placed in the engine, the top of the cab and the connecting wheelbase. We had a direct link to the fuel tank. We confirmed that there was the fire ignited through visual confirmation ... This is just the beginning of a war...our war for your end has begun."

FEBRUARY 19/97: Salt Lake City, UT - A vacant Kentucky Fried Chicken restaurant, located at 250 W. North Temple,

sustained an undetermined amount of damage from an arson attack. When firefighters arrived, they reported heavy smoke shooting out of the two-story building. Twenty-three firefighters battled the blaze for more than four hours.

FEBRURARY 19/97: Rochester, NY - Berman's fur store had locks glued, slogans written on front and back. -A.L.F.

FEBRUARY 21/97: Virginia Beach, VA - A Red Lobster was spraypainted with "Stop Raping the Oceans" and "Lobster Liberation." A Hardee's was wheat pasted with anti-meat posters. Also postered was a Steakhouse, which was also spraypainted with the slogan "Avenge." A second Hardee's had anti-meat posters glued up and the slogan "Meat = Death" painted on it.

FEBRUARY 23/97: Cyberspace - The first ever Animal Liberation Action on the Internet took place when hackers changed the Kriegsman Fur's web site in Nov. '96 adding graphics of what people's fur coats look like before their killed and more! Take a look before and after <http://www.2600.com/fur_hacked/>

FEBRUARY 28/97: Washington, DC - Miller's Furs paint-bombed. -A.L.F.

FEBRUARY 28/97: Indianapolis, IN - The hunting shop, the Outdoorsman, had its windows broken, was torched and spraypainted with animal rights slogans (Stop the Murder -- A.L.F). From the Communique: "In the early morning Friday, February 28, the ALF hit a hunting and trapping store on the far south side of Indianapolis. The Outdoorsman promotes the murder of innocent life through the sale of hunting and trapping equipment and by selling magazines and other literature advocating the torture of animals. Windows were broken, slogans were painted, and the back of the wooden building was burned."

MARCH/97: NYC, NY - 7 fur stores and pelt sellers in NYC's fur district had their locks jammed with toothpicks, including a sheepskin dealer and one that advertised wild furs and chinchillas. Also hit was a Wendy's, a burger joint, a leather shoe shop, and a McDonalds. A number of these places had their locks jammed while OPEN, to increase costs by forcing someone to be paid to guard the store after closing until the locks were fixed.

MARCH/97: ?, New Jersey - Activists are likely responsible for a fire at Flemington Fur Co. The front entrance was damaged and sprinklers caused water damage throughout the store.

Coming Soon? Not any more thanks to the A.L.F. This "Jack In the Box" burger joint received over $80,000 damages...

MARCH 1/97: Washington DC - During the early morning, DC Miller's Furs store was paint bombed. A.L.F.

MARCH 5/97: Washington DC - DC Miller's Furs was hit for the second time, etching cream was used to decorate "FUR HURTS" on one of the windows. A road-kill deer that was "extremely" bloody was also placed in front of the doors.

MARCH 5/97: Virginia Beach, VA - Two milk billboards previously hit were replaced with new signs were once again redecorated with paint filled orniments. both signs removed the following day! Another milk sign was also hit.

MARCH 6/97: Murrieta, CA - An A.L.F. cell burned down a construction sight for a new Jack in the Box burger restaurant. The communique claimed they "quickly searched it for any living creatures. When the building was found clear two incindiary devices were placed and set." Reports list over $80,000 in damages. The entire building was destroyed.

MARCH 6/97: Lake Elsinore, CA - A Douglas Burgers, nearly finished with construction escaped destruction as an incindiary device failed to go off. The A.L.F. activists stated that they believed the base of the incense sticks used as a fuse were too moist from the kerosene they used as an accelerant.

MARCH 7/97: West Hartford, CT - Lloyd/Roberts Furs locks glued slogans painted. A.L.F.

MARCH 7/97: West Hartford, CT - Exclusive Furs locks glued.-A.L.F.

MARCH 10/97: New York, NY - Maggios Beef Corp and Moore Wholesale Meats trucks had a tire punctured. A Gerrback Beef truck had a tire punctured and paint splashed across the front of the truck. Zamir Fur (MacDougal and Houston) almost had their lock glued, but it was found still glued from the last attack. This would have been hit #3. Ben & Jerry's (3rd Ave. @ 10th St.) hit #2, East Village Meats (2nd Ave. @ St. Marks) hit #2, McDonalds (1st Ave. @ 6th St.) hit #5, East Village Cheese (3rd Ave. @ 9th St.), Dallas BBQ (2nd Ave. @ St. Marks), The Village Tannery (broadway @ Astor P1.), Faicco Sausage (260 Bleeker), Leather & Suede (268 Bleeker), and Guerra, Anthony, and Joe Fish Market (265 Bleeker) all had their locks glued. -A.L.F.

MARCH 11/97: New York, NY - Maggios Beef Corp and two other meat company trucks had a tire punctured. Burger Kig (6th Ave. @ 14th St.) had their locks glued, hit #2. Balducci's, a food store specializing in meat and cheese, who proudly display large chunks of animal carcasses in their window, had their security gates locked in a down position by locks and chains. McDonalds (6th Ave. @ 28th St.) was tagged, had their locks glued, and had "MURDER" etched into six enourmous windows, one two-foot high letter in each window. - A.L.F.

MARCH 11/97: Salt Lake City, UT - A.L.F. activists carried out a firebomb attack in Sandy, Utah (just outside of SLC) that leveled the offices, and destroyed at least four trucks, at the second largest fur feed company in the U.S. Early estimates suggest damages exceeding $1 million. No injuries were reported. From the communique: "In the early morning hours of March 11, we attacked the Agricultural Fur Breeders Co-Op in Sandy, Utah...firebombs were set in four trucks and the main offices." The activists dedicated the attack to four Syracuse anti-fur activists in prison hungerstriking.

MARCH 12/97: Springfield, IL - Burlington Coat Factory targeted by A.L.F. The store sells fur-lined coats and accessories as well as leather products. Display windows were spray painted with "Fur is Dead," and "A.L.F." The front door lock was glued. -A.L.F. ABRAHAM LINCOLN FACTION

MARCH 12/97: Millstone, NJ -Jack's Prime Meats had locks glued, A.L.F. slogans spray-painted & windows etched.

MARCH 12/97: Howell, NJ - "Cowards" spray-painted on floor of the Sportsmans shop, locks glued.

MARCH 12/97: Jackson, NJ - Jackson Taxidermist had locks glued, spray-paint.

MARCH 12/97: Freehold, NJ - Roy Rogers had locks glued, A.L.F. slogans spray-painted, windows etched.

MARCH 12/97: Howell, NJ - McDonalds hit, locks glued, "McShit" and "A.L.F." spray-painted. Also hit was a Burger King and a KFC, each had locks glued, spray-painted.

MARCH 13/97: South Windsor, CT - Activists glued the locks on the door of an animal abuse shop, painted slogans on the building, and on the 5 trucks. They also paint bombed the sign in front of the store as well as the windows on every truck. They then smashed every window in the building.- A.L.F.

MARCH 13/97: New York, NY - Kenny Rogers Roasters (6th Ave. @ 14th St.) had their locks glued, and paint splattered along the entire side of the building, hit #5. The Village Tannery (Broadway @ Astor Pl.) hit #2, and Kentucky Fried Chicken (2nd Ave. @ 14th St.) had their locks glued. Wendy's (14th St. @ University Ave.) had "MEAT IS DEAD" etched into their window, hit #2. Tad's Steaks (14th St. @ 4th Ave.) had "MEAT IS DEAD" etched into their window, and had their lock glued. Ben & Jerry's (3rd Ave. @ 10th St.) had "DAIRY IS RAPE" etched into their window, and had their window, and had their lock glued, hit #3. Zamir Fur (MacDougal and Houston) had "A.L.F." etched into their window, hit #3. -A.L.F.

MARCH 14/97: Robinson Scott Clearcut, near the McKenzie was the site a solidarity action between The Animal Liberation Front and the Earth Liberation Front.From the communique: "47 trees were spiked either with quartz rock spikes or metal rails. In addition, an incendiary device was placed in a forest service vehicle, however it failed to ignite and was removed by activists for fear of harming any operator of the vehicle.
The action was to protest and stop the clearcutting of habitat that is important for owls, voles, and woodpeckers, as well as many other species including humans. The clearcut area is near the McKenzie river, and siltation caused by logging would harm drinking water and kill fish.
The Spiking was done by a cell of the Animal Liberation Front known as the Eco-Animal Defense Unit, and will be followed by actions from the Earth Liberation Front. Solidarity between these two movements is the worst nightmare of those who would abuse the earth and it's citizens.
Two of the trees spiked with rock are flagged with red paint. All spiking was done at high levels in an effort to avoid any harm to humans. Leave the forest alone, and no one gets hurt.

For the animals, and for the earth,
A.L.F. Eco-Animal Defense Unit."

MARCH 18/97: Ogden, UT - A.L.F. activists doused Montgomery Fur Co.(trap supplier) with gasoline, but didn't light it as they realized a night watchman was inside the building.

MARCH 20/97: Davis, CA - A.L.F. activists firebombed an animal research lab at the University of California, Davis. The "Bay Area Cell of the Earth X Animal Liberation Front" said it "set fire" to the Center for comparative medicine, now under construction adjacent to the Regional Primate Research Laboratory at UC Davis after ensuring that no one was in the area and in danger of injury. Ten years ago (April 1987) the ALF firebombed another UC Davis lab, causing $4.5 million in damages.

MARCH 22/97: St. Louis, MO - Hardee's on Olive St. in Olivette was hit, spraypaint and slogans left on the walls. Activists also poured paint thinner and other flammable liquids on the windows. From the Communique: "WE DID NOT LIGHT THE THINNERS BECAUSE WE ARE SENDING A WARNING. WE ARE OUT HERE READY TO COMMIT JUSTICE AGAINST THE ABUSERS OF THE WORLD.

We demand the Nicole Rogers and Jeff Watkins be released from Prison NOW! If this is not done then more actions will follow. This time the flames will be seen!" -A.L.F.

MARCH 23/97: Seattle, WA - A.L.F. activists raid the Acme Chicken Slaughterhouse (1024 S. King St.). Activists entered the killing rooms and sabotaged forklifts and other machinery. They also entered two offices and destroyed all the paperwork by pouring acid and paint over everything. 3 chickens left for dead on the killing room floor were rescued. The chickens have been placed in loving homes "where they will be able to live out their lives free from torture, something (human and non-humans) deserve." A.L.F.

MARCH 25/97: Annapolis, MD - A.L.F. strike a fur and leather shop. The store front was hit with paint-bombs. Also hit was Maryland Meats. Slogans and paintbombs caused extensive damage to the store front. -Maryland Cell, A.L.F.

MARCH 29/97: Ithaca, NY - McDonald's, route 13, rock hurled through window with decal. Locks glued on corporate office across street. Envelope removed from mailbox containing check was ripped up.

MARCH 29/97: Ithaca, NY - Two rocks sent through route 13 Wendy's windows, one kept going and smashed another window inside. Slogans spraypainted. All locks glued.

MARCH 30/97: Minneapolis, MN - A.L.F. damaged the unfinished house of a Dayton's Fur Store owner Sunday morning. Construction equipment was vandalized, tires were slashed, power tools were destroyed, power cords were cut, walls and windows were painted and smashed and the house blueprints were destroyed.

MARCH 30/97: Minneapolis, MN - A blank billboard on East Highway 94 was painted with "pro A.L.F. action" to celebrate A.L.F. Appreciation week.

APRIL 1/97: Seattle, WA - Isernio's Sausage hit. All three trucks hit with heavy spraypaint, locks sealed with Liquid Steel, and etched windshields. Tires were also slashed. -A.L.F.

APRIL 6/97: Seattle, WA - 8 windows etched at Markethouse Corned Beef. Ruth's Chris Steakhouse billboard hit with "meat is murder." -A.L.F.

APRIL 6/97: Seattle, WA - Eilers furs hit again, storefront was heavily spraypainted. -A.L.F.

APRIL 9/97: Indianapolis, - A.L.F. visit the home of John Marcopolis, owner of Elan Furs. To vehicles in the driveway were completely covered in paint stripper. The house was doused on all sides with red paint. Slogans left included "Justice for your victims, A.L.F."

APRIL 9/97: Deberry, TX - Ten chinchilla were freed in a raid on the Don Kelly Chinchilla Farm, (border of Texas and Louisiana) by A.L.F. activists.

BRAZIL

FEBUARY 2/97: Florianopolis - A university Experimental Psychology Lab was raided by animal liberation activists. A number of slogans were painted on internal walls, including "Free the animals", "science or hypocrisy?", "respect to the animals," and "death to vivisectors."

From the communique: "80 monkeys were liberated from the labs .The raid has been focused upon in both national and local TV, and in some newspapers. The Federal Police is looking for the "vandals". The media says that the raid was an "Eco Terrorist" act. The scientists at the Lab says that those who did the act are merely vandals, not ecologists, and that in the lab there is 'no torture on animals.' Some of the monkeys liberated were eventually recaptured, but many did manage to escape."

The activist(s) entered and left the lab through the rail roof, and left this as an escape for the freed monkeys to escape through.

"Freedom to the Animals!" and "Death to Torturers!" painted beside opened monkey cages.

ENGLAND

APRIL 24/96 (World Day for Lab Animals): West End, London - "Zwirns" fur shop windows smashed, causing 4,500 pounds damage.

MAY/96: Eastnor Castle - Over 60 Hunt Retribution Squad (H.R.S.) activists weilding clubs and throwing rocks damaged cars belonging to blood-junkies attending the 150th Anniversary Ball of the Ledbury Hunt. Over $2000 damage caused to cars. Sadly, several people arrested.

JULY/96: Surry - activists smash the window of a tour operator offering shooting holidays in Africa.

AUGUST/96: Cambridgeshire - A.L.F. raid Trinity Foot Beagles Hunt Kennels and rescue five 11 month old beagles.

AUGUST/96: Durham - Hunt Retribution Squad (H.R.S.) mingle with sabs disrupting a shooting party at Stanhope Common. While the sabs did their thing the H.R.S. attacked a gameskeeper and trashed vehicles belonging to the blood-junkies. -H.R.S.

AUGUST/96: Hampshire - Two pet shops in Southhampton have their windows smashed and slogans painted.

AUGUST/96: Newbury - During the "Flim-Flam Festival" the E.L.F. launch a mass raid on the road-bypass security. A bus, a generator and security lights were all smashed. -E.L.F.

AUGUST/96: Sussex - During the Brighton "Reclaim the Streets" party the E.L.F. dismantle traffic lights.

OCTOBER/96: London - Bookies on Crafton Rd have their windows smashed.

OCTOBER/96: 12 branches of W.H. Smiths were bomb-hoaxed by the A.L.F. due to the chains's stocking of pro-hunt magazines.

NOVEMBER/96: Public libraries warned to pull all copies of Country Life Magazine permanently from branches or face an incendiary device campaign. From the communique: "This magazine can often be found trying to promote all kinds of bloodsports including the hunting and shooting of animals. By stocking it in libraries it acts as free, accessible pro-hunt propaganda." If the magazine is not removed, the activists threaten to place incendiary devices under shelves and behind books in libraries.

NOVEMBER/96: E.L.F. COMMUNIQUE: "To celebrate National Tree Week, the Earth Liberation Front removed & destroyed every Welsh Mountain Zoo leaflet we could find. Although the E.L.F. supports conservation work we say all conservation work should be directed at saving and defending natural habitat -- not imprisoning animals. Where the animals' habitat has already been destroyed, conservationists should work to recreate the lost habitat ... Once the traditional British forests have been recreated we call for the reintroduction of the lost British wildlife species such as the bear, the boar and wolf." -E.L.F.

NOVEMBER/96: Six Tesco Supermarkets were bomb-hoaxed for the second time by the A.L.F. Each branch was phoned and told a device had been planted in the store. Tescos is targeted due to the sale of kangaroo and ostrich meat. -A.L.F.

NOVEMBER/96: Six branches of WH Smith were bomb hoaxed because they sell blood-sports magazines. -A.L.F.

NOVEMBER/96: Brixton, Hackney, Notting Hill - Three branches of McDonald's were bomb hoaxed. -A.L.F.

JANUARY 24/97: Headquarters of Waitrose Supermarkets received a bomb hoax due to their plans to sell live lobsters for people to boil alive. Three days later they announced they had dropped their sick plans. Another A.L.F. VICTORY!

JANUARY 24/97: London - Harrolds was bomb hoaxed due to their decision to start selling fur again. -A.L.F.

JANUARY 25/97: Brackley - Several fire bombs were hidden underneath seven trucks loaded with frozen chickens, parked outside Buxsted Fresh Quality Poultry. The devices caused thousands of dollars of damage to the vehicles. -A.L.F.

FEBRUARY/97: Preston - An A.L.F. cell raiding a research lab at the University of Lancashire during the early hours of the morning found (to their amazement) a few hundred earthworms who were being experimented on. They released them all and wrecked computer equipment and daubed slogans on walls. This raid was part of the campaign against vivisection and in support of Barry Horne's demand that the government end its support for vivisection within five years.

FEBRUARY 3/97: Andrew Lloyd Webber yields JUSTICE DEPARTMENT demands to end his ostrich farm venture. A year ago Sir Andrew announced his intention to build an ostrich farm at his grand Sydmonton Court estate in Hampshire. Said a member of Webber's staff regarding the JD campaign against him, "We've been sworn to absolute secrecy." VICTORY!

FEBRUARY 16/97: Devon -- The E.L.F. spiked a number of trees in a private woodland owned by the Forestry Commission in Devon. This action marked a start of a week long spiking action hitting woodland all over the English Westcountry. From the communique: "Our Earth Liberation Front cell have a policy of randomly spiking any tree we feel needs to be spiked regardless of whether the tree is under threat or not. By doing so we will ensure that by the time a woodland area is under threat some of the trees in the threatened area will have been spiked ... By spiking the trees we hope to ensure that the Forestry Commission and their ilk will soon discover their is no profit in chainsaw massacres." -E.L.F. Westcountry Wildlife Cell

FEBRUARY 20/97: Devon - E.L.F. return to the woodland owned by the Forestry Commission, this time gluing five padlocks shut on gates leading into the woodlands. -E.L.F. Westcountry Wildlife Cell

FEBRUARY 21/97: Devon - E.L.F. Westcountry Wildlife Cell strike again, spiking trees in Hannicombe Wood.

FEBRUARY 21/97: Devon - arsonists struck at a sandblasting works causing over $100,000 damage. - Unclaimed.

FEBRUARY 22/97: Devon - The Fernworthy Reservoir is hit by the E.L.F. -- locks were glued at a self-service Fishing Licence building. Angling is a blood-sport "and like all blood-sports, angling is an attack on wildlife." -E.L.F. Westcountry Wildlife Cell

FEBRUARY 23/97: Devon - A number of felled trees destined for the saw mill are spiked in Charles Wood. Activists then moved on to Hannicombe Wood where the gate leading in was permanently closed. Also locked up tight with glue were padlocks securing the gates to the Willingstone Plantation and Hitchcombe Wood. From the communique: "Our cell would of liked to have done more. We intend to do more. Stay tuned. We will do more..."

MARCH 15/97: Sussex - The Sussex-based Chiddingfold, Lecontree and Cowdray Foxhunt had their hunt ball at a hotel at Walberton near Arundel in Sussex, and the 150 guests were attacked by almost the same number of demonstrators. One blood-junkie told press: "Our car was surrouded by 50 or more, banging on the roof. They smashed the back windscreen and the side window and the glass went all over my daughter- in-law. THen one jumped on the bonnet and smashed the windscreen. Then they yanked open the door and tried to pull me out. My driver is only a young chap and he was petrified."
Protesters wore balaclavas, and bricks and eggs were thrown at guests and car windows were smashed. Damage was estimated at thousands of pounds.

MARCH 29/97: Cambridgeshire - about 50 protesters converged on the Cambridgeshire hunt kennels at around 10am. One policeman was already present guarding the place. Protesters invaded the kennels and all windows of the hound-van were smashed. Tires were punctured and at least two windows of the house of the huntsman were broken. Police arrived soon in force and protesters left swiftly. No immediate arrests. However, there were some road blocks and car searches, but without any outcome.

MARCH 30/97: Oxford - about 30 activists protested outside a cat breeder (sells them for vivisection). Despite police efforts to prevent protesters from moving closer to the building, activists stormed into the place smashing a number of windows and doing a lot of damage. No arrests.

APRIL/97: Razor blade devices were posted to Anne McIntosh, Tory MEP for Essex North and Suffolk South and Prospective Parliamentary Candidate for the Vale of York, a bloodsports supporter. Included was a letter that said "murdering bastard" and "animal murderer". Police said the letter was Another envelope stuffed with razor blades was received by a second unnamed Tory candidate in the North of England.

APRIL 5/97: Liverpool - The Grand National Steeplechase, along with races at Aintree racecourse, was called offbecause of a bomb threat. All 60,000 spectators, including Princess Anne, were evacuated because of two coded warnings received by police. Although there were suspicions that the warnings may have come from IRA terrorists, trainer Jenny Pitman believed the threats were the work of animal rights activists, who have tried to disrupt the race in the past. The 38 horses were already parading when police told organizers that two coded bomb warnings had been received.

APRIL 28/97: Warwickshire - A depot belonging to the livestock haulage firm Spiers Haulage in Claverdon, Warwickshire, was firebombed. A lorry tractor unit was destroyed by flames and bomb dispoal experts defused a number of other devices.

GERMANY

*****CORRECTION to Issue #6,Page 28: "Swedish/German Activists Released". The headline and sentence reporting on German and SWEDISH activists is incorrect. Those involved in this case are German and SWISS activists. Our appologies to those involved!**

DECEMBER 8/96: Hamburg - A group of five animal rights activists attacked six shops with butyric acid: Shoe-shop "Blanke" (because of leather), the leather-shop "Alladin", one fish-restaurant, one angling-shop and the fur-shop "Samrei". The damage at the fur-shop: 15,000 Marks (about 10,000 US-$). After several weeks the windows of the angling-shop were wide open and parts of the carpet in the shoe-shop have been dragged out.

On February 11th (7 o'clock) the police raided two animal rights activists in Hamburg. Police took possession of several letters and flyers, adresses, videos and destroyed a box of unused photo paper. The police took photographs and fingerprints of both animal rights activists.

DECEMBER 19-20/96: Mannheim - "Aktion gewaltfreier Dezember" ("Action nonviolent December") liberated 22 geese of the geese-farm of Richard Karl, Marderweg 60, 68229 Mannheim in Germany, telephone (Germany+) 621-47 14 26. The geese were due to be slaughtered but are now with people who don't want to eat 'em. 22 families had no goose on christmas (it's a German tradition like turkey in the USA)... Financial damage to the farm came to about 2,250 DM (about $1,500 US).

JANUARY/97: Bavaria - 16 hunting towers destroyed! According to a German hunting magazine, "Die Pirsch," damages came to 80,000DM (about $53,300 US).

JANUARY/97: near Rothenstein (Bavaria) - A group of animal rights activists destroyed 12 "hunting towers". Damage: 70-80,000 Marks (about $47-53,000 US).

JANUARY 25-26/97: Karlsruhe/Stuttgart - 23 hunter's towers have been destroyed by animal rights activists. Those involved worked in four groups between 1am and 6am.

JANUARY 26/97: Nothern Blackforest - A group of animal rights activists destroyed 23 "hunting towers" until the early morning.

MARCH 29/97: Rodermark (State of Hessen) - Animal rights activists burned up a wagon of "Pelz Beetz", a local fur shop. It has been a advertisment-tag with the fur shop's name and adress on the hood. Damage: About 5,000 DM (about $3,340 US).

ITALY

MARCH 18/96: Pisan - A.L.F. torch two cars belonging to vivisectors. -A.L.F.
MARCH 31/96: Venice - activists released ten Thrushes caught by blood-junkies. Cages were also trashed causing 1,000,000 Lira damage. -A.L.F.

MARCH 31/96: Venice - Two fur shops and a butchers were vandalized. -A.L.F.

APRIL 11/96: Venice - the Padoan A.L.F. targeted a battery farm and rescued 35 hens. Over 1000 cages were opened, equipment was destroyed, a truck was badly damaged, a conveyor belt was destroyed and over 3000 eggs were contaminated. Damages were over 10,000,000 Lira.

APRIL 17/96: Boloona - activists rescue a pig and two Dorenmice from a vivisection lab. they also caused a great deal of damage to the lab, trashing several rooms and causing hundreds of million Lira damage. -A.L.F.

MAY 5/96: Reggio Emilia - over 2,300 mink were released from a fur farm causing over 60,000,000 Lira in damage. -A.L.F.

JUNE 17/96: Mestre - Two Furriers had their shops hit by arsonists. A.L.F. slogans left at the scene. -A.L.F.

JULY 20/96: Venice - Activists visit an abattoir. Rooms were flooded, knives, machinery, and a refrigerator cell destroyed. An expensive compressor was stripped down and many documents removed. -A.L.F.

SEPTEMBER 5/96: Venelia - 150 cows and bulls rescued from a farm. A milk tanker was also trashed. -A.L.F.

OCTOBER 5/96: Cerignola - A butcher and a furrier were hit. Locks glued, slogans painted. -A.L.F.

OCTOBER 14/96: Milano - Two furriers hit, acid poured over the windows causing damage. -A.L.F.

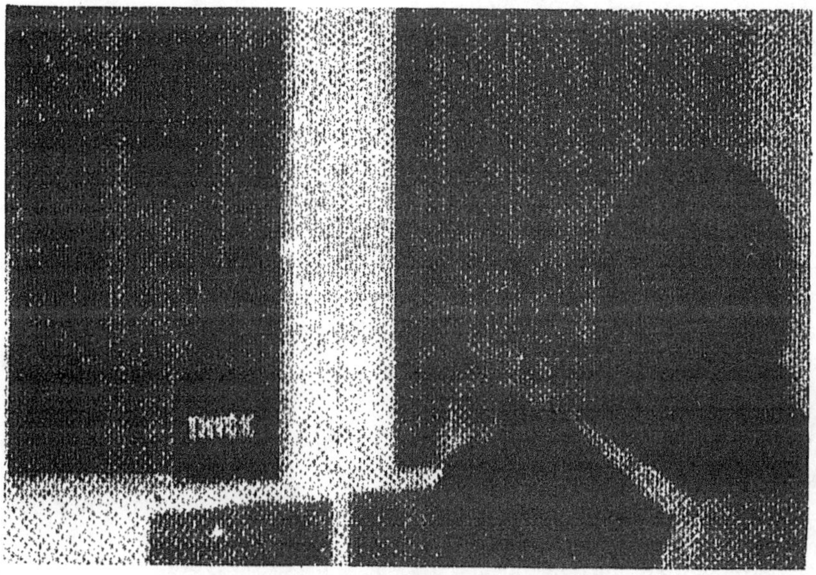

December D.B.F. raid and aftermath.

SWEDEN

DATE UNKNOWN: Sundsvall - A meat factory is painted with "Murderer" and two expensive advertisement boards are destroyed. The signs' value is 33,000 Swedish Crowns, and insurance will NOT cover damages.

OCTOBER/96: Karlskrona - a fur shop had several windows smashed, causing over $2000 (US) damage.

DECEMBER/96: Stockholm - 2 furs shop hit, first has windows smashed, the second is paint-bombed.

DECEMBER/96: Malmo - 3 fur shops and 1 meat shop spray-painted with anti-meat slogans and had locks glued.

DECEMBER/96: Stockholm - An owl was freed from the Skansen zoo. Best of luck to him!

DECEMBER/96: Stockholm - A meat delivery truck had its windows smashed.

DECEMBER 5/96: Gothenburgh - Djurens Befrielse Front (Swedish A.L.F.) carried out an early morning sabotage action against the University of Gothenburgh, Dept. of Anatomy and cell Biology's vivisection lab. Two rats were rescued and placed in a loving home. Several computers and a variety of equipment was destroyed to a value of nearly one million SEK (roughly $200,000). The visitors took some interesting information on the researchers with them.

DECEMBER 17/97: Stockholm - Nestors meat factory receives a visit from militant vegans. Slogans painted included "Meat is Murder." The activists set fire to the building causing huge damages. This it the 4th arson attack at this site.

JANUARY/97: Stockholm - Djurens Hamnare activists arson attack over 7 meat trucks two nights in a row at Scan (Sweden's largest meat company). Damage was over 3-4 millon SEK. Scan has had arson attacks directed against their vehicles and buildings in Stockholm, Gothenburg and Umea. Over 20 meat trucks have been completely destroyed.

FEBRUARY/97: Horsnas - The main building of a temporarily empty fur farm was hit and burned down by activists. -THE WILD MINK

FEBRUARY 2/97: location not given - a newly built meat factory belonging to Scan was hit. Electrical wires were burned and destroyed, preventing phones, computers and other electrical equipment from working. Intense damage caused by smoke. The building was to be opened the next day but was delayed several months by the attack.

FEBRUARY 23/97: Soderby (Osthammar) - A battary hen farm was raided and 8 hens were liberated. The hens were in bad condition but with love and care will heal. Slogans left behind included: "Liberate the Hens" and "DBF." -D.B.F.

FEBRUARY 24/97: Eksjo - An empty building belonging to a mink fur farm was burned. A feeding machine was also destroyed. - D.B.F.

FEBRUARY 26/97: Stockholm - A lab breeder, Mrs. Ann Hagstrom was visited. During 1993/94 Animal Avengers rescued rabbits and guinea-pigs from her during two different raids. This time, Animal libbers went through a window to her building. Rumours had it that she was back in business, but no guinea-pigs were found. Left behind by the activists was the message "Ann -- We See You!" in case she ever thinks of going back into business again.

MARCH 1/97: An anti-fur demo at a fur breeders meeting turned into a riot and several windows at the hotel hosting the meeting were smashed by masked activists.

MARCH 6/97: Stockholm - 2 meat-lorries at two different companies (100 meters away from each other) are burned out by animal activists.

MARCH 13/97: Gnasta - D.B.F. activists visited Ustarmalma's hunting school. Activist released between 400-500 birds, (geese, wild-duck, partridges, pheasants and other birds) from their cages and pens. The birds are bred and sold for hunts. Cages and pens were destroyed to a value of several hundred thousand dollars.

MARCH 30/97: Sundsvall - [Easter] a fur shop was spray-painted.

MARCH 30/97: Vetlanda - 2 meat trucks hit and windows and lights were smashed out. Slogans painted.

MARCH 30/97: Savsdo - A meat truck was hit with slogans.

MARCH 30/97: Boras - Three meat trucks burned and one more damaged by smoke. Damages were 3-4 million SEK.

DATE UNKNOWN - Sundsvall - A meat factory was painted with "Murderer" and two expensive billboard signs were destroyed (each valued at over 33,000 Swedish Crowns). Insurance refused to cover the damages.

MARCH 31/97: Horsnas: A fur farm was hit by a group called "THE WILD MINKS." The farm had room for 1500 mink, but at the time only had 500 breeding animals. Activists painted the main buidling outside and inside with slogans like "MURDERERS," "YOU ARE NEXT," "WE WILL BE BACK," "DIE," and "CLOSE DOWN." Everything in the main building was destroyed including clothing, medical supplies, the heating system, tools and equipment. 10 mink-traps were destroyed and the locking system of 600 cages were cut by boltcutters. All food supplies were destroyed. Waterpipes in two sheds were demolished and the breeding cards of 500 mink were stolen and destroyed. -THE WILD MINK

FINLAND

MAY/96: Lapeenranta - Fur store locks are glued. -E.V.R.

MAY/96: Lapeenranta - A number of meat truck had windows smashed and slogans painted on them. -E.V.R.

JUNE/96: Kuopio - Snelmann's meat office had a brick sent through the window.

JUNE/96: Imatra - A window of a McDonald's was smashed.

JUNE/96: Iittala - Several road construction vehicles had windows smashed and slogans painted on them. -E.V.R.

JULY/96: Kuopio - meat processor vandalized. 40,000 FIM damages. - E.V.R.

JULY/96: Tampere - Fur store visited and windows smashed.

JULY/96: Helsinki - Fur dressmakers windows smashed.

JULY/96: Turku - over 50,000 FIM damages done to a McDonald's, including a number of smashed windows.

JULY/96: Mikkeli - a McDonald's was vandalized.

JULY/96: Lohja - Owner of a local McDonald's complained to media about continued attacks and vandalism.

JULY/96: Tampere - Fur store vandalized.

AUGUST/96: Helsinki - Two fur stores (Tuganay and Valtonen) had their windows smashed in.

AUGUST/96: Lahti - Fur store windows smashed.

AUGUST/96: Hameenlinna - McDonald's windows smashed.

AUGUST/96: Jarvenpaa - A McDonald's and a Shell station were vandalized. -A.S.T.

AUGUST/96: Lappeenranta - Two fur stores had locks glued. -A.L.F.

AUGUST/96: Lappeenranta - McDonalds had 5 windows smashed. -E.L.F.

AUGUST/96: Lappeenranta - 3 McDonald's windows smashed, and "E.L.F." spraypainted on the walls. -E.L.F.

AUGUST/96: Imatra - McDonald's and their storage buildings were vandalized in "the usual way." -A.L.F.

AUGUST/96: Helsinki - McDonald's has 8 windows smashed and slogans painted, a second McDonald's was also visited and 18 windows were smashed and slogans were painted. - E.L.F.

SEPTEMBER/96: Kouvola - Fur store was vandalized.

SEPTEMBER/96: Kuopio - A window at a McDonald's was smashed out and 2 signs from a Shell station were destroyed. -E.L.F.

SEPTEMBER/96: Jyvaskyla - Fur store visited and 4 windows smashed.

SEPTEMBER/96: Ijala - 10 windows smashed on road construction machines, slogans also spraypainted. -E.L.F.

OCTOBER/96: Orimattila - 150 cages opened on a fox fur farm. A number of fox were eventually re-caught, but several did escape.

OCTOBER/96: Orimattila - One week after the first fox farm raid, over 300 foxes were dyed with red henna and breeding records were stolen. The farmer stated that damages were over 200,000FIM. A radical news-office received a claim from the group called "the Color of Autumn." The described the action in detail and gave instructions on how to do similar actions.

Out of commission! Finnish A.L.F. strikes again.

OCTOBER/96: Tampere - 3 fur stores were vandalized.

OCTOBER/96: Hyryla - A fur retailer was visited and vandalized, slogans painted.

OCTOBER/96: Tampere - Two fur shops visited, 5 windows and a sign smashed at one, one window smashed at the other.

OCTOBER/96: Loviisa - Fur factory - slogans painted and a huge sign destroyed.

OCTOBER/96: Salo area - 4 hunting platforms destroyed.

OCTOBER/96: Helsinki - 2 fur stores paintbombed and slogans painted.

OCTOBER/96: Naantali - hunting platforms destroyed.

OCTOBER [EARTH NIGHT]/97: E.V.R. raid Kuopio University's vivisection labs and rescued a beagle pup. The dog is now in a loving home and doing well. The activists dedicated the liberation to all the animals they could not rescue from the labs.

NOVEMBER/96: Espoo - Fur dressmaker visited, slogans painted.

NOVEMBER/96: Lahti - McDonald's ad redesigned. Now reads: "McMurder destroys rainforests."

NOVEMBER/96: Orivesi - Hunting platform destroyed.

NOVEMBER/96: Karttula - EVR raid a vivisection breeding centre, rescuing a beagle. this was the first liberation raid against vivisection in Finland. The dog was in bad condition and activists described the breeding centre as a horrible place. -E.V.R.

NOVEMBER/96: Vantaa - 2 McDonald's were vandalized.

NOVEMBER/96: Tampere - fur store windows were smashed.

NOVEMBER/96: Anarkistinen Suora Toiminta (AST) [Anarchist Direct Action] vandalized property belonging to the army.

DECEMBER/97: Vantaa (near Helsinki) - several meat trucks burnt out.

DECEMBER/97: Tampere - fur farm raided, 50 foxes painted with red Henna colour, making their coats unmarketable.

DECEMBER/97: Helsinki - over 15 fur stores and several McDonald's had windows smashed.

DECEMBER/97: location unknown - a huge pelt processing plant belonging to Finland's second largest Fur Farm burned down. The building contained over 20,000 polecat pelts and 2000 fox fur pelts inside, as well as lots of machinery. Millions of Finnish marks worth of damage caused!

DECEMBER 3/97: Vantaa - Huge anti-fur demo turns violent near Helsinki. Rich scumbags from around the world had plans to attend an international fur auction. Busses carrying the scum were ambushed by over 200 Finnish and Swedish activists. Protesters occupied the busses, climbed on the roofs, smashed windows, covered the busses in paint and terrified the scum. Gustav Smulter, one of the Finnish Fur industry's biggest animal abusers was hit with plenty of red paint bombs. Police used tear-gas and violence to break the demo up. Activists were attacked and arrested, dragged away to the police bus -- three activists made their escape by smashing out the windows and climbing onto the roof -- they jumped while the bus was moving. Over 40 people arrested and facing charges including rioting, obstruction of police, criminal damage, obstructing the highway, and violent disorder. One of the best protests ever seen in Finland!

DECEMBER 24/96: Turku - Three meat trucks were hit in

an arson attack. Over $200,000 damage. Slogans left included "EVR" and "Leave the Animals Alone." -E.V.R.

JANUARY/97: Helsinki - Fur store window smashed in.

JANUARY/97: Kupio - Billboard ad for McDonald's smashed totally. Also hypermarkets sign ecotaged.

JANUARY/97: Kupio - McDonald's street ads sabotaged several times. E.L.F.

JANUARY/97: Joensuu - fur shop paintbombed and slogans painted.-E.V.R.

JANUARY/97: Helsinki - McDonald's toilets blocked and damaged.

LATE JANUARY/97: Helsinki - 11 rabbits were liberated by the A.L.F. during a raid on a vivisection lab. All rabbits are now in good and caring homes free from the hands of the vivisectors. This raid is dedicated to Barry Horne and his courageos hungerstrike.

FEBRUARY/97: Helsinki - several fur shops lose their windows. E.V.R.

FEBRUARY/97: Kuopio - Fur store lost 4 windows and slogans painted. The hit was dedicated to the memory of Jill Phipps.

SLOVAK

DECEMBER/95: Modra - A meat shop and a pet shop had locks glued and animal liberation slogans painted on walls.-A.L.F.

DATE NOT GIVEN: Topolcany - meat shop and advertisement boards sloganized. Poultry meat shop sloganized and locks glued. Egg shop spraypainted. -A.L.F.

DATE NOT GIVEN: Prievidza - Circus Kludsky ads are destroyed. 1 meat shop sloganized, 4 meat and 1 fur shop had locks glued. Hunting shop advertisement board destroyed. 18 hunting platforms cut down. Meat delivery van sloganized. -A.L.F.

JANUARY/96: Bratislava - Hunting shop had its locks glued, windows sprayed with red paint and sloganized. -A.L.F.

FEBRUARY/96: Bratislava - Meat shop sprayed on two occasions with slogan "MEAT IS MURDER". -A.L.F.

MARCH/96: Bratislava - Fur shop sloganized. Liska fur shop hit with red paint and door locks glued. Also, advertisement board of Hyko (mass producer of turkeys) destroyed. -A.L.F.

MARCH/96: Zilina - 7 meat and one fur shop had windows smashed. - A.L.F.

APRIL/96: Bratislava - Hunting platform cut down. Bulbs filled with red paint thrown on Hyko billboard. Also, a meat shop was sloganized and two advertisements of Aquarium Terarium shop destroyed. A fur shop was also sloganized. -A.L.F.

APRIL/96: Bratislava - 46 advertisement boards of circus Arles destroyed. Posters pulled down or stickered with "Performance Cancelled." -A.L.F.

MAY/96: Bratislava - 14 advertisement boards of circus Arles destroyed. A meat shop and a McDonald's billboard sloganized. -A.L.F.

MAY/96: Modra - pet shop sloganized "TRADE WITH LIFE," windows sprayed with green coloured paint. A meat shop was also sloganized. -A.L.F.

JUNE/96: Bratislava - Lighting McDonald's advertisement destroyed. Also, McDonald's advertisement boards on road flyover sloganized. Another ad board was removed and smashed. A hunting platform was destroyed. -A.L.F.

JUNE/96: Zilina - 6 meat and 2 fur shops had windows smashed. -A.L.F.

JULY/96: Bratislava - Fur and meat shop sloganized. Stickers "MEAT HURTS" placed directly on meat products in Kmart supermarket. 2 McDonald's billboards sloganized. -A.L.F.

AUGUST/96: Bratislava - Fur shop sloganized, locks glued, advertisement board destroyed. Two McDonald's lighting advertisements were also smashed. Paint bombs thrown on Hyko turkey billboard. -A.L.F.

AUGUST/96: Zvolen - 31 advertisement boards of Circus Kludsky destroyed. -A.L.F.

SEPTEMBER/96: Bratislava - Circus Alex: over 250 advertisement boards destroyed, as well posters were pulled down and/or stickered with "PERFORMANCE CANCELLED" or animal liberation slogans. Meat industry advertisement posters were destroyed. -A.L.F.

SEPTEMBER/96: Bratislava - Circus Grant-Berousek: over 90 ad boards were destroyed. Circus Kludsky: posters pulled down and over 110 ad boards were destroyed. -A.L.F.

SEPTEMBER/96: Bratislava - Activists took part in a daylight lab raid liberating a dog from very bad conditions. Messages were left including "STOP ANIMAL TORTURE" and "A.L.F." on the walls. -A.L.F.

SEPTEMBER/96: Bratislava - on several different occasions hunting platforms were attacked. 2 hunting platforms destroyed, 2 partly destroyed, at least one platform burned. Windows and lights on a hunting cottage were smashed and a search light destroyed. - A.L.F.

OCTOBER/96: Bratislava - Meat industry ads heavily attacked. Hyko turkey billboard paintbombed, 20 meat advertisements destroyed or sloganized with "MEAT IS MURDER." Billboard promoting a poultry company sloganized. McDonald's billboard destroyed. Also, anti-zoo stickers and slogans placed on cages and information boards in the zoo. -A.L.F.

NOVEMBER/96: Bratislava - McDonald's lighting advertisement destroyed. -A.L.F.

DECEMBER/96: Bratislava - carp fish kiosk burned. -A.L.F.

YOUR SUPPORT IS NEEDED

The following activists have charged with alleged participation in mink farm raids and will shortly be facing trials. They desperately require financial support.:

CAFT ACTIVISTS FRAMED FOR A.L.F. ACTIONS

Four members of the Boston chapter of the Coalition to Abolish the Fur Trade have been charged with allegedly breaking in at Carmel Mink Ranch in Hinsdale MA,. Authorities charge that the activists destroyed cages and released a number of mink. *See **Letters to Underground, page 4**, for more details.*

Originally, bail for Jaime Roth, Warren Upsom, and Grant Upsom was set at $10,000, but they were later released on their own recognizance. Alex Smolak, identified by the prosecution as a "ringleader," was originally held on $25,000 bond, but it was later reduced to $1,000. All activists are currently out of jail. At this point in time, all four are still in need of money to cover legal costs. The Coalition to Abolish the Fur Trade is raising money for these activists as well as any others that may be accused of A.L.F. activity in relation to anti-fur campaigns.

Donations for legal and court costs can be mailed to:
CAFT
PO Box 822411
Dallas, TX 75382, USA
Please mark it for the "MASS. 4"

or:

MASS 4 SUPPORT COMMITTEE
BOX 80632
MPLS, MN, 55408-8632, USA

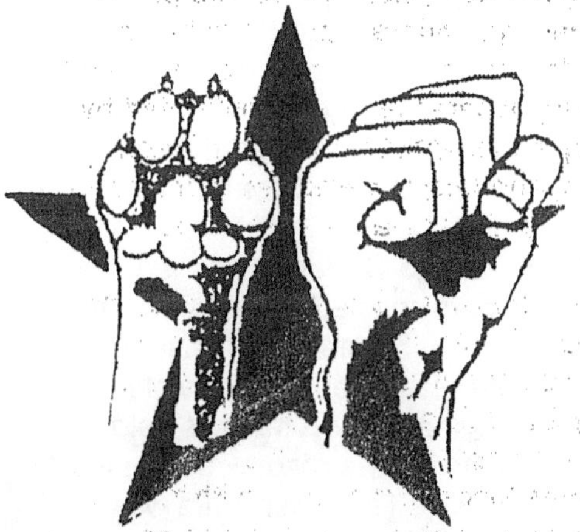

ONTARIO MINK RAIDS END IN ARRESTS

5 American activist were arrested Sunday, March 30, after 1,800 mink were freed from cages at a Beleheim fur farm, near Chatham Ontario. The three women and two men from the Detroit area were arrested outside Ebert's Fur Farm, which had been hit two weeks earlier by the Earth Liberation Front. Mink cages were opened at at least four holes were cut in the farm's perimeter fence. Breeding cards over each cage were also removed — damage estimates range between $90,000 to $500,000.

Unfortunately, it would appear that two of the activists have made damaging statements to the police whioh may implicate the other activists. Funds raised will go towards the support of the three remaining activists. Earmark any donations "Chatham 3." Please support Hilma Ruby, Pat Dodson and Gary Yourofsky

Funds can be sent to the NA-A.L.F.S.G. (payable to "NAALFSG)

Box 69597, 5845 Yonge St.
Willowdale, Ontario, Canada
M2M 4K3

or

DIRECT ACTION DEFENSE FUND (payable to "DADF"
Box 57357, Tucson, AZ
85732-7357

NEWS BRIEFS

ANTI-NUKE PROTESTS ROCK GERMANY

MARCH :The first week of March saw the biggest ever mobilisation of police in peacetime Germany to force through a shipment of nuclear waste containers to the storage depot at Gorleben, near Hamburg.

Over 30,000 Police were mobilised for the operation which began when 6 storage flasks (Castors) were moved from their base at Neckar Westheim in Southern Germany the previous Friday. Protests happened during the weekend, with 30,000 people marching in Luneburg, and transport links being sabotaged. The transports were moved by train as far as Dannenburg, where they were confronted by nearly 3000 people the night they arrived. Tracks were cut through, and people cemented themselves to the rails, delaying the arrival by over 8 hours.

For the last 15 kilometres to Gorleben by road, the Castors were loaded onto specially reinforced lorries. They were confronted by massive resistance. There were only 2 possible routes, and one of these was made impassable by 50 tractors belonging to local farmers blocking the road, with tunnels dug under the road as well. The other route was lined with Police virtually the whole way, and a new law was passed, making it illegal to go within 50 metres of the road.

At midnight on Monday the Police began moving over 4000 people who were sitting in front of the gates by the Castors, initially picking them up, then hosing them with water cannon, and finally drawing truncheons on them. Some people dangled from trees above the Castors. It took over 8 hours to remove them all. When the Castors were finally ready to move, thousands of people who had been staying in different camps near the route were mobilised, employing various tactics. They were confronted by 1000 Autonome (German anarchist types) in a field outside the village of Quickborn, who erected burning barricades. A full-scale battle ensued, with the German state employing helicopters, water cannon, and armoured cars to force the transports through.

Later, a group of 50 protesters managed to get to the Castors, with one man locking on to the trucks. At one point riot Police who had tried to slash the tires of tractors blocking the road, were chased away by a crowd of over 100 people, and then had to be rescued by helicopter! Because the route was so heavily policed, the Castors were hardly delayed once they had begun, but the got through at an estimated cost of 53m DM, and with accusations by opposition MPs of gross mismanagement. It is unlikely that there will be any more transports for 2 years, and with over 60% of Germans opposed to nuclear power, and thousands prepared to take direct action, it is questionable that the authorities will ever be able to repeat such an operation.

SEA SHEPHERD CAPTAIN ARRESTED IN NETHERLANDS

APRIL: Paul Watson, president of the Sea Shepherd Conservation Society and long-time proponent of direct-action environmentalism, was seized Wednesday by Netherlands police acting on behalf of the Norwegian government. Three days earlier, Watson had been arrested by German authorities and then released when they declined to extradite to Norway.

Norway wants Watson to serve a sentence handed down when he was convicted in absentia for anti-whaling protest activities in Norway. According to the Sea Shepherd's International Director, Lisa Distefano, "If Paul is imprisoned in Norway, we know he'll never leave alive."

Watson was arrested March 31st by German authorities in the port of Bremerhaven while supervising the transfer of a Sea Shepherd vessel in preparation for a campaign against illegal drift netting in the Mediterranean. He was seized by Dutch police in Amsterdam. At a preliminary hearing in The District of Haarlem Court, Judge Toeter ordered Watson held for 20 days to allow Norway to make a formal request for extradition.

"Since 1986 it has been illegal to kill whales, and Norway has defied that law," said Watson. "We have continued to focus our protest activities on Norway's illegal whaling. We will put Norway on trial in the Netherlands court and use this opportunity to further expose Norway's illegal activities to the world."

For further information contact the Sea Shepherd Conservation Society at Tel: (310) 301-7325. Fax: (310) 574-3161.

Support the Gandalf Six

"You'll say people can speak freely until the speech begins to threaten your idea of so-called freedom. then folks ain't free to speak, they're kicked, punched, clubbed,stomped, handcuffed, shot- jailed by the cops and jailed again by you the judges when the trial takes place." (John Africa, The Judges Letter).

"Free speech is a crime - punishable by State brutality and false arrests!" (Mumia Abu-Jamal, Free Speech = Police Riot, The Blast No.6)

On January 16, 1995 British police acting for Special Branch's "Animal Rights National Index" (ARNI) launched a series of 55 or more dawn raids throughout England, resulting in the arrests of four GREEN ANARCHIST magazine Editors, the Animal Liberation Front (A.L.F.) Press Officer and the then Animal Liberation Front Supporters Group newsletter Editor. The six were eventually charged with "conspiring together to incite persons unknown" and "to commit criminal damage." In reality, most of the six had never met each other and some had never even heard of each other, prior to their arrests.

The Gandalf (GA and A.L.F.)defendants' crimes are to have published animal liberation news in GREEN ANARCHIST magazine, to have spoken about Animal Liberation Front activity, or to be somehow to be connected to those that have. Police links between activists are as tenuous as individuals attending the same rally or perhaps receiving a letter sent out by another.

As British law now stands, the State does not have to prove that any actual criminal damage was committed, or that anyone was actually incited. Neither do they have to show that any "conspirator" had connections to anyone doing illegal actions -- only that the defendants intended others to be incited and that when illegal direct action occurred, the "defendant would have wished this to have happened."

The normal defence in cases of incitement is to argue that the alleged inciting material was not circulated -- obviously you can't incite someone with material they've not seen. However, in a "Conspiracy to Incite" case this defence does not hold. With a Conspiracy to Incite, anything ever written by the defendant can be used as evidence of intent. As well, a conspirators' associates or beliefs can also be used as evidence against the defendant. The burden of proof is on those facing prosecution to show that they did not intend to incite anyone.

Interestingly, when THE TIMES reports animal liberation actions, they are not deemed to be inciting similar actions since they are not seen as wanting the acts to occur. However, when GREEN ANARCHIST reports the exact same news, the State sees it as evidence of intent to incite since GREEN ANARCHIST "supports such actions and therefore would of wished them to occur."

Why Green Anarchist? Why now?

The case against the Gandalf Defendants is a culmination of ARNI's Operation Washington against the British A.L.F. Press Officer. For years ARNI have been trying to frame the A.L.F. Press Officer in order to silence him and remove a major voice of

A.L.F. Support.

During the course of operation Washington, the officers involved 'discovered' GREEN ANARCHIST magazine was also reporting animal lib direct action news. Although the reports came from sources entirely independent of the A.L.F. Press Office, the police hope to link the A.L.F. Press Office with GREEN ANARCHIST magazine and silence both. Conspiracy laws allow them to scuttle any effective defence . Similarily, the linking of the former A.L.F. Supporters Group Newsletter Editor with "the conspiracy" was also aimed at attacking another source of information about the Animal Liberation Front.

Another focus of the case is on the activities of the Earth Liberation Front (E.L.F.). Since the early 90's, militant green activity in Britain and across Europe has escalated dramatically. In 1993, ARNI extended its shadow over the militant green movement. Links between militant greens and animal liberation activists were established. For example, someone who might be seen demonstrating against live animal exports one day could also be a familiar figure fighting against road developments and the destruction of woodlands. One of the most spectacular E.L.F. actions to take place was when activists broke into the Department of Transport's central London offices and trashed more than one hundred computers, before making off with a number of hard drivcs. GREEN ANARCHIST has regularly reported the activity of the Earth Liberation Front and indeed at least one of its editors is well known to be involved with the Earth Liberation Prisoners Support network (E.L.P.), an international support group that circulates the details of people arrested/jailed for eco-defence reasons.

The attack on the Gandalf Defendants should not be seen in isolation. Right across Europe police are cracking down on militant publications and groups that support direct action. In Holland, the eco-zine RAVAGE was raided after they published an Earth Liberation Front press release claiming responsibility for a bomb attack on empty building owned by a German company linked with dumping toxic waste. In Germany, police used a series of arsons as their excuse to raid TIERBERFREIUNG AKTUELL, a radical animal liberation magazine that reports German A.L.F. activity. Meanwhile the Finnish A.L.F. Supporters Group was actually forced to close down after the police launched series of raids and continually harassed known animal liberation activists after two high profile Elainten Vapautus Rimtama (Finnish A.L.F.) actions.

What happens next?

The Gandalf Defendants have no intention of presenting themselves as victims. Such spectacles may please the State and gutless fluffies with no stomach for direct action, but such apologists do not help to create change. The fluffies who apologize for, and distance themselves from, A.L.F./E.L.F. activity are the enemies of the movement. This case is really not about the guilt or innocence of six individuals, but about making our movement strong enough to withstand police repression. If the police are allowed to outlaw support for the A.L.F./E.L.F. and can criminalize the reporting of illegal actions, then the police will have the power to shut down any group or publication they feel is a threat. The Gandalf Defendants are on the front-line fighting against legislation that will be used against the whole Animal/Earth liberation movement, not just in Britain but across Europe and possibly further afield. Defending the Gandalf Six is about defending yourselves. Should the Gandalf Defendants be found guilty they face a maximum ten years in prison.

Some Good News...

During the 9-13th December 1996 committal hearing in Portsmouth, the Special Branch officer for Operation Washington, DI Des Thomas, admitted the case was doomed unless A.L.F. press Officer Robin Webb was tried alongside the other five defendants. Unfortunately for ARNI, Robin Webb was able to walk away since the evidence presented against him was already used in an earlier case against him -- he can't be tried twice on the same evidence!

More to come...

For more information about the case and how you can help the defendants, contact:

THE GANDALF DEFENDANTS CAMPAIGN,
Box 66,
Stevenage,
SG1 2TR, England

ANIMAL LIBERATION PRISONERS

UNITED STATES

Rod Coronado #03895000,
FCI Unit SW,8901S Wilmot Rd,
Tuscon, AZ85706, USA
Sentenced to a total of 57 months for aiding and abetting arson and handling stolen property in connection with acting as spokesperson for the North American ALF, and for damaging government property as a protest against the treatment of native Americans.(Rod is a member of the Yaqui Nation)

UNITED KINGDOM

NEW
Kenny Gloster HG3042
HMP Bedford, St. Loyes St. Bedford, MK40 1HG
Charged with criminal damage against a butchers and theft from an animal lab.

Dave Callender HV 3314
HMP Birmingham, Winson Green Rd, Birmingham, B18 4AS
Currently appealing against a 10 year sentence for conspiracy to cause arson. Appeal due to be heard very soon.

Darren Cole XD2301,
HMP Cornhill, Shepton Mallet,
Somerset BA4 5LU
Serving 3 years for arson on farm buildings used in the live export trade.

Michael Green AV2923
HMP Ashwell, Oakham, LEICS LE15 7LF
Co-defendant of Melanie Arnold, who has been sentenced to 3 1/2 years for the Ensor's slaughterhouse arson attack and a further 1 1/2 years for an attempted arson attack at Padbury's cattle transporters, in Northampton.

Barry Horne
HMP Bristol, Cambridge Rd, Horfield,
Bristol BS7 8PS
On remand, awaiting trial, on charges of attempting to cause damage by arson.
Recently ended his hungerstrike.

Keith Mann EE3688,
HMP Full Sutton, Nr Stamford Bridge
York YO4 1PS
Sentenced to 11 years for criminal damage, attempted incitement, possession of explosive materials, attempted arson and escaping from custody.

Gillian Peachey RL3415
HMP Holloway, Parkhurst Road,
London, N7 ONU
On remand charged with conspiracy to use incendiary devices to cause criminal damage by arson.
New trial date : June 30th '97

Mick Roberts GE3743
HMP Lewes, Brighton Road, Lewes,
East Sussex. BN7 1EA
On remand charged with conspiracy to cause criminal damage.

Geoff Sheppard MD1030
HMP Parkhurst, Newport,
Isle of Wight
PO30 5NX.
Sentenced to 7 years for possession of a shotgun and possession of items for making incendiary devices.

PRISONER LIST CONTINUED:

Charles Skinner 24250,
HMP La Moye, St Beades, Jersey,
Channel Islands.
Sentenced to 4 years for causing over L322,000 worth of damage by arson to Jersey Zoo visitors centre.

Barbara Trenholm RL 1292
HMP Holloway, Parkhurst Road,
London. N7 ONU
Sentenced to 10 years for arson against the White Hart pub which the prosecution claim was in connection with the campaign against live exports. She maintains her innocence.

Justin Wright CE3046
HMP YOI, Portland,
Dorset DT5 1DL
Sentenced to 5 years for the same offence, as above. He maintains his innocence.

HOLLAND

Frank Kocera Reg. No 1648820
Penitentiaire Inrichtingen 'Over Amstel'
Postbus 41901, 1009 CE Amsterdam.
Frank was sentenced to 3 years, with 8 months probation for his part in various arson attacks against the meat industry and painting slogans on a butcher's.

U.S. CIVIL DISOBEDIENCE PRISONER INFO:

A number of US animal activists just been released from jail, serving time for their part in several anti-fur civil disobedience demonstrations. During their incarceration, activists participated in hungerstrike protests. The following demands were put forth by the activists:

1. A federal ban on the leg-hold trap. Lawmakers are attempting to introduce a bill to end this practice but the hunting/trapping lobby is holding it back.

2. The U.S. must end its opposition to the European Union wild fur ban. The U.S. has been threatening to sue the EU over its plans to impose a fur ban.

3. The State of New York must kill a "Beaver Butchery" bill. The legislation is now pending in New York, and it would legalize snares for beaver, causing them painful deaths.

Currently, only one anti-fur activist remains in prison:

Jeff Watkins
Box 143,
Jamesville
NY, 13078, USA

Serving a 7 month sentence for damaging a fur coat and for participating in non-violent protest against the fur industry.

Congratulations to Tony, Stacey and everyone else who made it through.
Keep up the good work.

NA-A.L.F.S.G DISTRO

INFORMATION FOR THE SERIOUS ANIMAL LIBERATIONIST

ANIMAL LIBERATION FRONT

Operation Biteback -NORTH AMERICAN TOUR
Coming to a Fur Farm Near You...

OPERATION BITEBACK CELEBRATION T-SHIRTS

The NA-A.L.F.S.G. has released a new t-shirt which celebrates the A.L.F.'s campaign against the fur industry — actions which have led to the release of over 35,000 animals in North America alone.

Shirts are available in red, olive green or white (all XL) for only $15.

LIMITED SUPPLY! ORDER YOURS NOW!

The NA-A.L.F.S.G DISTRO carries a wide range of excellent magazines, How-To Booklets, and must-read manuals for the serious animal liberation activist.
Titles include: An Animal Liberation Primer, 2nd edition * Explosives Manual * Interviews with Animal Liberation Front Activists * Into the 1990's with the A.L.F. * The Power is Our - A Manual on Saving the Earth and the Animals * Without a Trace: A Forensic Manual for You and Me * The Final Nail - Destroying the Fur Industry, A Guided Tour* **and much much more!**

For a full catalogue of merchandise, or for information on distribution, write:
NA-A.L.F.S.G DISTRO, Box 767295, Roswell, GA 30076, USA

NORTH AMERICAN ANIMAL LIBERATION FRONT
SUPPORTERS GROUP
BOX 69597, 5845 YONGE ST. WILLOWDALE, ONT. M2M 4K3, CANADA
EMAIL: <NAALFSG@ENVIROLINK.ORG

UNDERGROUND

THE MAGAZINE OF THE NORTH AMERICAN ANIMAL LIBERATION FRONT SUPPORTERS GROUP

ISSUE #8 FALL '97 $3

FREE TO PRISONERS

DIRECT ACTION WORKS

Waves of Destruction

All in the beginning
we have seemed to achieve
an uncontrollable mess
if though our minds
were set in motion
in advance
to wipe out the total existence
of every living molecule
Why the madness?
war
famine
genocide
only the start of the devasta-
tion process
chop the trees (so I could
write this poem)
pollute the air
increase the chance
that next generation
won't have an ozone layer
Three Mile Island
Chernobyl next
Hey, did some expert say
that "Nuclear power is safe"
leaving toxic caste
by the bundle
to kill all the insects
with DDT
only MOTHER NATURE
turn the tables
on mankind species Some
how we can't
get the shit under control
what's our problem?
Keep on producing
things never intended
millions of guns
chemical warfare

EDITOR's NOTE:

And here we go again, another issue of *Underground* — at long last! In the short period between each issue (roughly 3 months) so much seems to happen within the animal liberation movement that it sometimes seems impossible to keep up. But we do try. In this issue you'll find all sorts of interesting reading, including a special section in which A.L.F. and E.L.F. activists share their experiences and offer some tips to others considering actions of their own. Also inside is the Diary of Action (of course) with listings of liberations, economic sabotage and all round trouble-making activities. Always a good read and an inspiration...

Our thanks go out to everyone who has helped us put this issue of *Underground* together and who have passed on info, offered support, lent a hand and so much more. Special thanks to the A.L.F., Darren, A.L.F.S.G. (UK), Catherine, the DADF, Gina, Rod, JP Goodwin, David, the E.L.F., Rabbix, Simon, Roach, Barry and Sue (keep up the fight!), the dogs for scaring off the RCMP, No Compromise, Who's Emma, Profane Existence, Factsheet Five, Hilma, Pat and Gary (Chatham 3), and to all of you who continue to show such generous and selfless support for the SG and the A.L.F. in general. Without you, we couldn't pull it all together.

It is important to note that this is a rough time for many activists within the movement. Police investigations continue to focus on the upsurge in animal and earth liberation actions, and raids and arrests continue. It is so important each and every one of us offers our support to those facing hard times ahead. Write a prisoner a letter. Send a support committee a donation. Set up a collection, a benefit, an info booth, and raise awareness and funds. Contact any recently arrested/raided activists in your area and tell them you care, tell them their efforts were appreciated, lend them your support. Set aside your petty disputes and be there for them. It's the least any of us can do.

yer editor,
t.

bombs galore
nightstick bashing
lethal injection
we use those knives
a little too often
hoping that our problems
would be solved
within a moment's time
building ideas
on oppressive techniques
Only
Homelessness
unemployment
welfare cuts
koncentration kamps
Educational deductions
are being manufactured by
such
Reactionary Solution
what are we to do,
overthrow the criminals
into it for the Money?
Hell fucking yes!
way in advance
before annihilation of
the masses
turns into an incurable
reality.

By D.A. Sheldon

#807779A
Box 316, Ft. Madison,
Iowa 52627, USA

"We think the butler did it, Sarge"

Letters to Underground

SUPPORT NEEDED

A.L.F.S.G.:

I am writing to you to see if you can help me and my fiancee out. We were recently (about one month ago) arrested for a mink farm raid. One other person was arrested but he wrote damaging statements about us, so we don't include him in anything. We have some legal fees to pay plus some back pay we owe. It would be greatly appreciated if you could send us some *Underground*'s to distro to help us out.

We run the risk of losing our only car to the police (our only way to get to our jobs), so we are in need of funds badly. I heard the Mass 4 received $3,000 worth of fines each, we would be screwed if that was our case.

A little about our case: We were arrested on Wed. July 9th. I spent six days in jail and Stephanie spent eight. We have been charged with six felonies, two Break and Enters, two vandalisms, and two possession of criminal tools. An incident at the same "farm" happened two days earlier. We are also being charged for that incident. On this night spraypainting was done and breeding cards were destroyed. The 2nd night more spraypainting happened and 40 mink were released.

If you can't do anything, I understand. I'm aware 13 other people face felony charges for A.L.F. activities. Joshua Ellerman from SLC seems the most needful for funds and support since he's facing 16 charges. If you have contact with him, send him our best. He's in our hearts and our minds, along with all the brave warriors across the world.

Thank you very much!
Jesse & Stephanie Parsh

Please send Jesse and Stephanie your support, financial and otherwise. They can be reached by writing:

Cleaveland Animal Defense League
Box 29492, Parma, OH 44129, USA

JONNY MELVIN REED
VIVISECTION IS TORTURE!

VEGAN PRISONER WRITES

Greetings,

A friend of mine recently gave me your address. I'm in prison and I had asked him about receiving a vegan diet without professing to a Christian religion I don't believe in ... I was also interested in other things: being active while in prison, contacts, information, etc. Any info would be way cool or just write and say "hey" ...

I've been involved with the punk rock scene since the early 80's -- anarchist politics, zines, mail art all have been like a saviour to me during my time "down" -- I believe in respect for all creatures. I also believe in radical tactics in order to liberate both mind and body. As I said before, I've been told the only way I can receive a vegetarian diet is to have my religion changed to a Christian oriented belief system. If I were to claim I was a buddhist or something like that (which wouldn't be as bad) I would have to have a written letter from a registered monastery saying I was a part of their organization. At any rate, none of that should be necessary.

Thank you very much for any help you may be able to give me, I totally appreciate it and will be looking forward to hearing from you.
Yours in Liberation

Jonny Melvin Reed, #93033
Arizona State Prison
Box 3400, SMV II
Florence, Arizona, 85232

North American prisoners with similar concerns about accessing a proper vegan meal should consider contacting the Vegan Prisoners Supporters Group (see letter below). Also check out page 27 for information about class war prisoner Harold Thompson's legal proceedings for vegan meals.

VEGAN PRISONER SUPPORTERS GROUP (VPSG)

Hi All,

Mel here, doing a spot of volunteering with the VPSG. Have you seen any of our literature before? Do you know if any similar organizations exist within the US for imprisoned vegans/prisoners of conscience?

We introduce ourselves to any new prisoner as a support group who will intervene on their behalf in order to obtain vegan food/toiletries etc. directly with the governors and have had many successes in these areas, as the enclosed information shows.

We've been contacting US prisoners regularly and are willing to extend our practical assistance to these as and when requested to by the prisoner concerned. At the very least we can send in dietary and nutritional sheets of information, and when we become more acquainted with the US prison system we could perhaps achieve for prisoners there what we have done so far here.

We also produce an inter-prison newsletter which the prisoners contribute to. It all helps build up solidarity and moral support and keeps people in touch with each other on the inside.

We're also working on a new arrest leaflet as there's a huge new influx of young campaigners around who've never dealt with the sometimes heavy handed nature of the police at demonstrations before. This way, the guidelines are there on what to expect in the event of an arrest and our emergency helpline if remanded. It all increases our efficiency in helping.

Anyway, just really wanted to formally introduce ourselves and let you know of our position. If there are any similar groups set up in the US, do please let us know so we can extend our knowledge of working prisons and be better able to assist those inside.

Take care then,
Best Wishes,
Melanie Arnold

VEGAN PRISONERS SUPPORTERS GROUP
Box 194 Enfield, Middlesex,
EN1 3HD England

WORD FROM HOLLAND

Hello There,
Here's a little note from Holland. So, how are you all? I'm writing to let you know that I've moved. I'm here a week now and it's very, very boring here. I've got more freedom but there's simply nothing to do here. I'm glad I don't have to go that long anymore, otherwise I would go mad in this shit-place. Got to keep strong for 4 months and then I'm out! Time can't go too fast for me. Also, the summer has started for real, the weather is beautiful so when you see that you start to feel what you have to miss while behind bars. Ok, enough moaning already!

Well, I don't have much news to tell you. Only that the outbreak of swine-disease is still spreading. They're finally talking about a breeding ban. Farmers can't transport and murder "their" pigs so barns start to get really full. They started to kill baby-pigs already, 500,000 at the age 4-17 days. To make room! This already cost the government and farmers 700 million guilders -- I think that's about 350 million dollars! They expect that the disease will go on at least 'til September. Yes, it's not going that good with the meat industry, ha ha ha. They want to make a lot of advertising for meat this years, spend twice as much money on it. Thing they can use it better now, ha ha ha. Well, if they want an answer for all these problems, we can give it to them easily: GO VEGAN!

Too bad people won't listen or are too scared to change. Afraid they can't eat anything anymore, pathetic sick wankers. Alright, that's it for now, thanx for all the magazines you send me. It's going very good in your country and it warms my heart to see so many good things happening. Take care and keep up the good work!!
Love and respect,

Frank 1648820
Gev. Zuyder Bos
Copernicusstraat 10
1704 SV Heerhugowaard
Holland

ROGER TROEN RESPONDS TO INFORMER ALLEGATIONS

To the publisher of *Underground* Issue 6:

I can't find any names in your publication that would tell me who the editor or publisher is so how can you be held accountable for what you print? After reading over the FBI account and the comments by "anonymous" in *Underground #6* I wok up at 4am on morning with what could be an explanation of the source(s.) Knowing I was never interviewed by the FBI it is possible that at least five others would have had this basic information. One of those people dropped out of the movement right after my arrest but I would never say who! That person popped into my head that morning ... then others.

That said, here are some questions for the unnamed editor and/or publisher and then some for anonymous.":

1. Don't journalists usually interview both accused and accuser?
2. Isn't it somewhat unethical to print charges made by anonymous sources?
3. Since "anonymous" provided my address and phone number urging people to call me and visit and you printed them, couldn't you, yourself contact me for a more complete report?
4. In fact why even supply that information which was available in the phone book with the same phone number and address since 1936?!

Now some questions for anonymous:
1. When and where was I interviewed by the FBI?
2. What was I to gain by divulging anything?
3. Have you read the stipulated facts presented in court?
4. Are you aware I was not required to testify during the "trial?"
5. Three years after the sentencing, serving my house arrest, paying restitution, completing 350 hours of community service, etc. what was I offered for any information?
6. If I revealed anything why didn't it result in further arrests that could have spread the $35,000 restitution out among more participants?

By some accounts I transported 100 rats, 30 mice, 11 hamsters, and 20+ rabbits to:
a. Five rabbits to a farmhouse a mile off the highway,
b. Five rabbits along I-5
c. 20 rabbits released in some "hills."
d. Various rats, mice, and hamsters to Canada.
e. Three rabbits delivered to Nanette Benson on the Oregon coast.

7. Isn't this a bit much for one person to have done?
8. And why stop with those 168 animals?
9. Didn't I also have the 24 cats and kittens?
10. Did I dump them too?
11. How did I manage to cram 168-192 animals into a two door sedan?
12. Wouldn't I have had to have cages in there with me?
13. If I did all this alone shouldn't I be entitled to "brag" about this to children?
14. Where did I do this bragging?
15. Why was the report written using the grammatical third person?
16. Doesn't this suggest to you this account was cobbled together by someone besides me. Perhaps those who consider you terrorists? The FBI???!!!
17. Why don't you (whoever you are) and anonymous get together and write a screen play about this phenomenal event?
18. Better yet, why don't we both do this and see who can sell it to some movie producer? I'll bet my truth will be stranger than your fiction. In the meantime I have more serious things to do than refute anonymous allegations. In fact I am ashamed to have spent even the last couple of hours on this questionnaire.

VIVA THE ALF,
Roger Troen

VEGAN SALUTATIONS

Dear Comrades across the Pond Vegan Greetings! Many thanks for your letter of support and the very interesting issue 7 of *Underground*.

As you can see I've been moved to another perfectly crap jail, but aren't they all?!

In the middle of May I was sentenced to a total of eight months for completely trashing the centre of a dead and rotting animal flesh shop, causing an alleged 2,500 pounds of "criminal" damage. I was also convicted of theft -- though not unfortunately of any animals from the University of Cambridge's Dept. of Pathology. Here, in the UK, prisoners serving less then four years only have to do half their sentence with something called "good behaviour" (??). So, all going well, I'll be out in July!

I would describe my brief spell away as highly constructive, giving me a much needed rest -- and most importantly the time to catch up on some necessary reading and research. If "they" knew this, I'm sure they'd never have stuck me away!

The severe lack of like minded folk in these places has been more than made up for by the overwhelming letters of support and offers of practical support. The fear of isolation in prison is unfounded. It leaves the authorities quite bemused and somewhat more cautious about denying us our rights, and when they do, it most often back-fires as they are inundated with representations from our supporters and even their own bosses. We are stronger than them -- we are, after all on the right and winning side.
When I am released I shall be going out to a nation

rid of two less evils. Firstly, the hunting of red deer has virtually been outlawed and secondly the Tory govt was well and truly ousted. The new Labour govt has begun to tighten up on the legislation surrounding live animal exports with the view to make it become virtually unprofitable... we will have to wait and see how genuine they are.

In the meantime people are well motivated, so the animals will embrace their revolution one way or another. Anyway, take care of yourself, don't follow my example and get caught, keep at them!
Yours for,
love, peace, justice and all animal liberation
Kenny Gloster HG3042
HMP Pentonville
Caledonian Rd
London, N78TT
England

P.S. It has just been disclosed that new legislation comes into effect next month (July) -- live animal exports will now almost certainly be ended! YES!

A second letter arrived shortly after the first from Kenny:
Yet again the Powers-that-be --whilst considerably better than the tyrannical Tories -- have demonstrated that any faith people put in their so-called democratic process is unfounded.

The P.S. attached to my recent letter to you was a case example. Unfortunately, I wok up and heard that Labour was introducing legislation and tightening up on existing laws and I jumped to the conclusion they were honouring their promise to tighten up on live animal exports that (if conformed to) would make it too unprofitable and therefore live animal exporters would be driven out of business. WISHFUL THINKING!! As the day developed it transpired that the legislation was so full of loop holes that it will make little or no difference. Yet another example of the state pandering to commercial exploiters and abusers. Ah well, I thought I'd better inform you of my mistaken report. Hope things are going alright with you over there. Anarchy is the Answer!
Love, peace, justice and all animals liberated,
Kenny

YONGE RECIDIVISTS FOR THE A.L.F.

Hello A.L.F.!

Is been a month ago, I wrote to you to subscribe at *Underground* and you did it and it was free because I'm in jail. Now I'm writing to say thank you, I think this is very cool on your part. Because over here I don't have money to give you. I made a drawing to send to you. It is cool on your part that you didn't forget me. If you can publish this nice Anti-vivisection drawing in a next Underground issue, that should be very great. Anyway, this is the most I can do for you and our friend the animal ... for the moment! So I must leave you here. Take care,
Vincent Gauthier
3100 Bl. Lemire
Pav Laforest
Drummondville,
QUE
J2B 7R2

Please try to publish my drawing. Excuse my english, I just speak in french!

FRIENDS OF MOVE

Revolutionary Greetings from Friends of Move U.K.

Glad to see your article about Move and thought *Underground* was a good mag. Perhaps you would like to print the enclosed letter from Debbie Africa in the mag. Also, Our group in London has a new address and it would be very helpful if you could put in a notice of this. We have loads more information available if you want it -- just write to us.
Stay strong,
Blessings,
Sister Ruby

LONG LIVE JOHN AFRICA'S REVOLUTION!
ALL PRAISE TO THE ORDER OF LIFE!
THE POWER OF TRUTH IS FINAL!

On the Move
To all nuclear resisters, environmentalists, animal rights rebels, Earth liberators and freedom fighters for all of Life.

We of Move want to commend you for the extraordinary work you are doing for Life.

I've gotten your newsletters and news magazines but don't always respond to every issue; with the worldwide correspondence it is almost impossible to respond to everybody individually and maintain any regular schedule.

The stand you are taking against this system for the enslaving, torturing of animals; uprooting, raping of the Earth; the stand against nuclear tech and environmental danger is *right* to take and has not gone unnoticed. The dedication you are showing in your effort to protect Life is *not* in vain and is not taken for granted. This work is urgently important! This system is not taking your work lightly. You *are* making a difference.

On behalf of the Move 9 Political Prisoners I want to send a personal message of encouragement to *keep up the good work!* It might appear that everybody's fighting for individual causes and appear to be unattached, but the truth is that we are *all* very much attached, because *all* of Life is *connected, attached.* This is what John Africa teaches. *LONG LIVE JOHN AFRICA!*

When an Earth protector saves *one* tree, she or he is saving thousands of animals as well -- for the tree is not *just* the mate to the Earth, the natural boundary of the land or the protector from disasters. The trees are shelters that feed, rest and house the creatures of Life, making the Earth liberator indeed an animal protector too. When an animal activist saves *one* animal, the animal activist is indeed promoting the saving of entire species of Life, whether it be animal life, plant or marine life or saving the soil from erosion. The nuclear resister who stops the making of just *one* nuclear piece of technology is saving human, animal, plant life, marine life, saving the air, water and soil from poison.

The nuclear resister is an environmental protection ally without question. So you see just as all of life is connected, *we* are all connected. *LONG LIVE JOHN AFRICA!*

For the past 25 years, the above-ground Philadelphia chapter of Move Organization has taken Our fight directly to the perpetrators of *all* this madness -- to the courts, judges, the legislators of these crimes and this is the real issue behind the Move 9 being in prison, because move tells the truth about this system, how it's *killing* Life for the sake of industry, money.

Move talked to these judges about Life and they talked to us about court procedures; we talked to these judges about Life's freedom and they talked to us about court procedures; we talked to these judges about Life's order and they talked to us about court procedures as if Life don't mean nothin'. This system is full of these kind of people like these judges who think they're somebody, think they ain't got to *account to life* for nothin', people who will ravish a *whole forrest* and when we tell them it's wrong, they act like we are *crazy; dump poison* in the ocean that belongs to Life and when we tell them we got the right to *stop* them from dumping poison *in* the ocean, but they ain't got no right to *dump poison* in the ocean, they look at us like *we're crazy* and threaten to but us in jail, but the crazy person is the person that is wrong, and it is *wrong* to *poison the ocean, the air, the soil, life,* , and *right* to *confront anybody* that *poisons life*. These are people that poison the air *unceasingly, 24 hours a day,* , which is *wrong*, and when we *tell* them that we don't want them putting poison in our air, which is *right*, they look at us like there is something *wrong* with us, because we want to *protect* the *breath of life* from their *insanity*, want to *protect* the air they got to breathe from that *godaming poison* they can't breath, and these *judges damn the law of God* in the *same* way as these idiots just described are damning *God's* air, *God's* water, *God's* soil, *God's* life. It is *right* to be safe; Move is constantly talking to these judges about *safety*, danger is *wrong*, these judges involve themselves in danger, get mad 'cause Move won't involve *ourselves* in danger, put us in prison for *resisting* this danger and give the public the impression that we are wrong, this is what the *syphilitic ravished* judge Malmed did ... *John Africa* explains very clearly that these judges think they got power because they can legislate these laws that hurt, cripple, maim, kill, Life treating Life like they know more about how to treat the lives of people than *Life*, yet without the force of Life, they couldn't even lift that damn gavel; these judges have spit their sickness on the *health of Move*, they have spit their sickness on *all of Life* and they are payin' for it, with weakness and sickness, bad health, weak lungs, retardation -- and the list goes on because remember, to blockade Life's plan is cruel, fatal, blind, deadly to those that imprison the force to be
free... *LONG LIVE JOHN AFRICA!* Nobody can tamper with any one form of Life without upsetting the entire balance of all of Life, because all of Life is connected. To quote *John Africa*, Move's coordinator (quote):

In Natural law we trust, all praises to the order of life, the presence of truth is the power of god, long LIVE God's power, the force we relate to, the power, the source the life force of Move, long live the rabbits, the beetles, the frogs, snakes, lizards, snails, buzzards, wolves, jackal, fox, cougar, the birds in the field that without Life is dead, the voice they obey when their young chirps, for balance, the worm in the field that connects birds' existence, the fruits of the orchards of life THEY are kin to, the tree that springs pregnant with fruit for all subjects, from soil that drinks in the rain it relates to, the breeze that skip 'cross the family of wheat fields with meaning that's gentle and smooth as united, long live the sun that forever must shine, the oceans that rise up full force when Life's threatened, the wind that distributes Life's seed of existence as rivers, brooks, streams, springs of life it is linked to, the Thunder that shakes free the germ of stagnation, the lightning that plucks out the weak in Life's presence, long live our mama who suckles, feeds, cuddles all subjects of Life with no notion of RACE, no exceptions of color, of creed, rank, POSITION, no commitment to anything breeding division, the force of our power is mama, the source, the force of God's law that's as mighty as thunder, mom's strong as lightnin' bolt, swift as the wind, stout as the ocean that beats at man's door, mama's reaching as rain, broad as her snow, outstretched as sunshine that blankets ALL subjects, rich as her dirt, tough as iron-oak, bold as the mountain that cuddles the valley, she is the blizzard before Move, the quake at our flank, the gale at our back as we rid Life of sickness, mama's all that we need to turn 'round this intruder, so long as we all Move together as one there can be no divisions to pull us apart ... No matter how hopeless Life's work may yet seem, the power that's needed will NEVER betray us, remember how water seems pent-in and trapped til the dam breaks and crumbles and dies like its maker, remember to blockade Life's plan is CRUEL, FATAL, BLIND, DEADLY to ANYBODY that imprisons the force to be free!! LONG LIVE JOHN AFRICA!!

On the Move,

Debbie Africa
Minister of Education
The Move
Organization.

Let this be clear that the information you have just read is coming from the wisdom of *John Africa* and only *John Africa*. I am just a student of this wise and brilliant teacher.

LONG LIVE JOHN AFRICA THE COORDINATOR OF MOVE!

Friends of Move
Box 14129
London, W12, 8GR,
England

NEWS BRIEFS

LONDON POLICE RUN OFF THEIR FEET

From the *POLICE REVIEW* (March 21/97): *"In the last five years, the Metropolitan Police has had to deal with 510 separate policing operations classified as being concerned with enviromental groups -- and the trend is upwards."*

The MET police force is for London alone. British police do make a differentiation between Animal rights and Environmental groups (recognizing about a 50% cross over). So, according to this report, London cops are called out to an environment related action every three to four days "and the trend is upwards!" -thanks to Ecovegan

AUSTRALIAN ACTIVISTS STAMP THOUSANDS OF BATTERY EGGS!!

March/97
In the early hours of the morning the Animal Liberation Action Rescue Team inspected Victoria's largest battery hen factory HAPPY HENS EGG WORLD for the 16th time! Thousands of battery eggs were individually stamped with the words *"made with cruelty"*. The egg industry consistently misleads consumers with false advertising. The time has come to tell the truth. The health of Victorian people is seriously at risk. The appalling, filthy and cruel conditions in egg factories is a disease outbreak just waiting to happen. A minimum of 30 dead rotting green decomposing bodies were pulled out of the cages in a short time by the rescue team. Living hens were forced to live and lay their eggs on these corpses. Mice were seen running through the cages. Many violations to the State's Prevention Of Cruelty To Animals Act and Code of Practice were videotaped and photographed. Four very ill hens were rescued and taken to a veterinary surgeon, one had to be euthanased (she was severely emaciated, only had one eye and suffered a long-standing wound). Two of the hens rescued were half their normal body weight.

[UK] Cats liberated from Hill Grove Farm

April 26, 1997
ENGLAND - Hill Grove Family Cats in Minster Lovell, Witney, Oxfordshire is a farm/bed & breakfast business that also breeds cats for vivisection.
It is run by a Christopher "Farmer" Brown and has been the focus of demonstrations for some time.

On Saturday 26th April during the Day of Action in Oxford, Hill Grove Farm had to be protected by dozens of riot cops who only prevented more damage being done by sheer force of numbers. The breeder had been raided by activist the week before and at least 20 cats were rescued. Farmer Brown is rumoured to be suffering from panic attacks. As this is only a small family run business with no large companies behind it, it is particularly susceptible to pressure from activists and is an ideal candidate for closure.

3rd charged in Weber fur arson

April/97
The owner of the pickup truck allegedly used in the attempted firebombing of the Montgomery Fur Co. has become the third suspect charged in the case. Bret G. Walton, 18, of Bountiful, was charged in 2nd District Court with attempted aggravated arson, a second-degree felony.

Although the Animal Liberation Front has claimed credit for what it calls an aborted attack, Walton's attorney said his client has no links to radical animal-rights groups.

Walton waived his preliminary hearing and pleaded not guilty. Trev J. Poulson, one of two men arrested days after the March 19 arson attempt, also waived his preliminary hearing and pleaded not guilty to attempted aggravated arson. Also charged was Cameron Michael Kraus, 18, of Centerville, had his preliminary hearing on an attempted aggravated arson charge delayed until May 14.

Court documents show that police believe Poulson and Kraus used Walton's 1992 Toyota truck the night of the arson attempt.

NOOSE REBEL HALTS RUNWAY BAILIFFS (UK)

MAY/97:
ENGLAND - A protester with a noose around her neck halted bailiffs trying to clear the site of Manchester's proposed second runway.

The young woman, who attached the rope to a tunnel entrance, would be hanged if the trap door to the tunnel were opened, Randal Hibbert, the Under Sheriff of Cheshire, said. The device made opening the door "virtually impossible", he said.

The protester, one of four holed up in a tunnel at the Sir Cliff Richard OBE Vegan Revolution Camp, had also attached herself to reinforced concrete in an attempt to thwart the bailiffs. The activist had volunteered to put herself in this position "to stop the bailiffs entering the tunnel and to delay them as long as possible".

A diagram showing her position and that of the noose was pasted on the door to the tunnel and the woman was not expected to be in any immediate danger, a spokesman said. Authorities were also told that protesters had embedded butane gas cylinders into concrete blocks which could explode, injuring bailiffs and tunnellers. The "booby traps" around the camps, were said to include glass, barbed wire and nails.

The Cliff Richard camp, where up to 30 protesters in seven tree houses 50-60ft above ground were defying climbing specialists, and presented the worst obstacle for builders.

MASS 4 SENTENCED

July, 1997
PITTSFIELD -- Four CAFT activists accused of vandalizing a Hidsdale mink farm last year were ordered to pay $3,100 in restitution and stay out of trouble for one year. Prosecutors were hoping for at least 6 months in jail for the four animal liberation activists. Sentenced were Jaime Roth, 19, Alex Smolak, 20, Warren Upson, 18, and Grant Upson, 16.

Without entering a plea, the group admitted that the commonwealth had enough evidence to prove their guilt. The case was suspended without a finding.

The group had been arrested last November after a second release attempt at the Carmel Family Mink Farm. Charges included breaking and entering in the nighttime with intent to commit a felony, larceny over $250, malicious destruction of property over $250 and trespassing after notice.

DNA DATA BASE

ALBUQUERQUE, N.M -- Law enforcement agencies announced in May that New Mexico will start building a DNA data base over summer. Everybody who is convicted of a felony will be required to give police a DNA sample, said state Democratic Sen. Cisco McSorley of Albuquerque. DNA samples will be extracted through blood samples, he said.

DAM PUT ON HOLD -- NEW ARRESTS

ITOIZ RIVER, SPAIN -- Plans to dam the Itoiz River in the Basque Country in Spain were put on hold after acts of sabotage forced the authorites to abandon the project. Villagers in the area would have been flooded out by the dam waters, but in April of 1996 activists used circular saws and cut steel cables used to transport concrete to the dam wall. Eight people went to prison for the action, but after public pressure, all eight were releaed early.

Since then, however, two more people have been arrested and sentenced to three years, despite the fact that neither participated in the action. The two are Patxi Gorraiz and Daniel Unziti. Addresses for Patxi Gorraiz are unavaiable, but Daniel can be reached at:

Daniel Unziti
Iruneako Gartzela
San Roque Kalea z/g
Irunea-Pamplona
Spain

Any support for this environmental activist would be greatly appreciated!
-thanks to Ecovegan

US HUNGER STRIKE CONTINUES

September/97:
ATLANTA - Sentenced to jail for 45 days for her part in a peaceful picket at the residence of the chief of Yearkes Primate Research Center, animal rights activist Sue McCrosky has engaged in a hungerstrike from behind bars.

Jailed Sept. 3, Ms McCrosky has been refused life-saving medications, has been put in a cell without a bed, and housed in another cell with no running water. As her condition worsens, her jailers have moved Sue to isolation, restricting visits by family and supporters.

Animal rights activists continue to rally in support for Sue, and have been joined by longtime civil rights leader Hosea Williams in demanding humane care for McCrosky.

Contact: Jean Barnes (770) 719-1241 or (770) 242-4343

The DIRECT ACTION DEFENSE FUND

Animal and Earth liberation activists are on the rise and with them a renewed effort by local, state and federal authorities to capture and imprison those responsible. The support needed to sustain criminalization of environmental and animal defense requires much organization from our movements. Prisoner support, legal defense and consultation, fund-raising and public awareness all play an important role in ensuring that we do not let our warriors on the front-lines down.

The DIRECT ACTION DEFENSE FUND (DADF) was established as one small beginning of this vital network. But DADF is only one step in the foundation building of direct action prisoner support and it needs others to contribute if we are to successfully support and aid our imprisoned comrades in their sincerest times of need.

DADF is nothing more than a few activists from the animal, earth and indigenous liberation movements who believe that more is required to support direct action groups like the A.L.F. than just moral or vocal support. DADF's primary purpose is to raise funds to be used in a completely legal manner to help post bail for activists arrested for illegal direct action in defense of animals and earth.

DADF's advisory committee is made up of volunteers active in prisoner support and every donation is used 100% for activist defense. DADF has no overhead, we do not print a newsletter nor invest in expensive equipment. All of our resources are devoted to those behind bars fro animal and earth liberation.

Fundamentally, DADF believes the direct action warrior's decision to take action involves the acceptance of responsibility to never cause an injury or loss of life. That responsibility also entails the acceptance of the possibility of imprisonment without compromising information that endangers fellow warriors. If potential direct action warriors are unable to accept these responsibilities or believe that their freedom is more valuable than others, the DADF absolves itself of all involvement and association with such individuals. DADF's limited resources are
only available to those activists who adhere to these basic guidelines.

In recent months DADF has assisted imprisoned activists including posting $1,500 to bail out a mink liberator in Ohio and helping got fund raise fro the Chatham 3 in Ontario. Though DADF's primary purpose is to act as a bust fund, we also use our combined experience and resources to help arrested direct action warriors any way we can.

DADF is currently assisting Delyla Wilson of the Bison Action Group who was federally indicted on felony assault charges for her actions in defense of the free-roaming bison of theYellowstone ecosystem. Though our finances prevent us from covering legal expenses, DADF is helping Wilson with legal research in preparation for her federal trial.

Though Wilson's actions were more in the area of civil disobedience DADF believes her federal indictment warrants our support as the use of federal law enforcement, the grand jury process and the threat of a federal conviction for non-violent action all have far-reaching implications for both the animal liberation and the radical environmental movements. It will not be long before other activists find themselves the targets of federal prosecution and in violation of new federal "anti-terrorism" legislation such as the Animal Enterprises Protection Act.

DADF wants our movements to be prepared to fight this repression and in order to do that we need your help. If you are a paralegal or know one that is willing to donate their time and energy please contact us. If you can organize fund raisers for the DADF bust fund, let us know and we'll provide you with educational materials for distribution.

As other revolutionary struggles have learned, our worth as a movement is reflected by how we treat our prisoners. Please help us in our efforts to support direct action warriors.@

The Direct Action Defense Fund
Box 57357, Tucson, AZ, 85732-7357, USA

SPECIAL SECTION:
IN THEIR OWN WORDS:
A.L.F./E.L.F. ACTIVISTS TALK

YOU DESERVE A BRICK TODAY

Fun and Games at Your Local McDonald's care of the A.L.F.

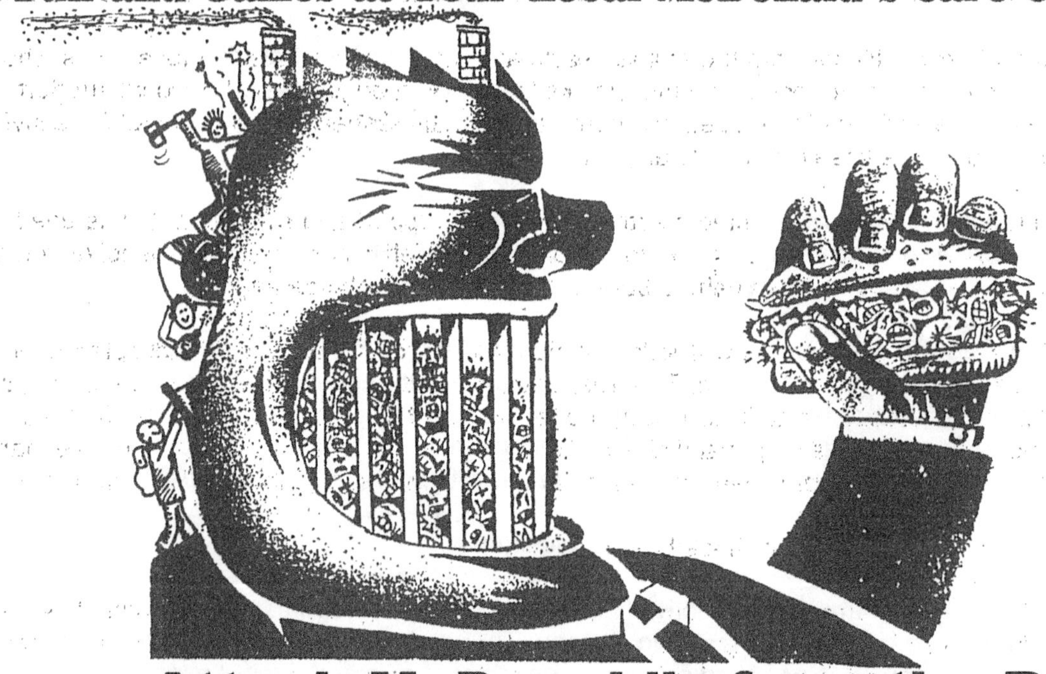

Attack McDonald's from the Roof!

One of the most effective ways to damage and interfere with regular operation of McDonald's is to directly attack the equipment they use to fry dead animals into food. Fortunately, you don't even have to go inside or make excessive noise to shut them down.

First, find a way onto the roof. We found a ladder that belonged to McDonald's sitting behind the dumpster. Some McDonald's have built-in ladders on the exterior that aren't locked or just have a padlock on them. All you really need on the roof is a dim flashlight, bolt-cutters, a socket wrench set and maybe a banner and cans of paint. Once on the roof, you will notice a series of steel domes and other equipment. Almost everything on the roof we were on had power switches at its base. First, turn everything off, then start removing the nuts on all the dome lids with your socket wrench or sometimes they come off by hand. When the fan belts stop moving, cut them with bolt-cutters and discard them. next, find any electrical cords from the domes and cut them. [USE CAUTION AND SOME RUBBER HANDLED GRIPS!] Cut the metal cords last because they explode. If you see other important looking wires then cut them too. To finish it off, you might want to warn any activists on ground level that you're dropping the bomb -- pour paint or drop paint grenades down the hatches if there is nobody inside. NOTE: Often times there are people inside even when the store is closed.

By disabling all this equipment on the roof there are different things that will result. You could cause short circuits and power-failure. You could cause smoke to fill up inside since the exhaust fans won't work. Hopefully enough smoke will force an evacuation. You might damage the air conditioning or heat units and make it unbearable inside. Our spy went in the next day to find out that they were only serving hotcakes and muffins at least until 11:00am.

I hope this works for you as well as it worked for us. There is probably different security at different McDonald's so be careful when you plan. Good Luck! @

A.L.F. Bulletin to all Fur Farm Raiders:

By now I'm sure you've all read the *Final Nail* and know of a bunch of fur farms in your area with animals eager to be liberated. Due to the recent continent-wide barrage against the animal torturers, you should expect security to be tightened. If you the would-be raiders, here are some tips:

1. Guard dogs may be an option but they probably won't be near the cages. Security guards may be hired. Cameras may be placed at some of the larger fur farms. Still undeterred? Read on. Always survey the area before-hand, possibly on a different night then the raid.

2. Tools: thick gloves (unfortunately leather is the only real option); common-brand shoes which will be thrown away later; flashlight with red cover over light, red attracts less attention and does not blind you or take away your night-vision (the red cover can be made of red grocery bags and tape if need be); razor/knife to cut the nets around each shed, bolt cutters for fences and locks etc.; small wrecking bar; walkie-talkies, perhaps if this is a team effort. Carry no ID or key sets or change. Individual keys, like the key to your getaway van, can be carried as long as they don't rustle. Emergency money bills should be carried.

3. Fur farms that imprison mink and fox hold between a hundred and a hundred thousand animals. They are made up of long sheds side-by-side with open sides. Inside are row upon row of cages about three feet off the ground. The sheds are always aligned north to south to make for even light distribution and proper pelt development. Sometimes there will be a wall surrounding all the sheds, sometimes each shed is individually enclosed in a net or fencing.

4. After a survey of the area decide on an escape route for your animals away from roads. Then decide on escape routes for yourself in case you wake the neighbours. You may wish to place a member of your troupe as "watch-dog."

5. Gloves at all times, no fingerprints. Do all the setup work first. Cut the bottom of the nets or fence around each shed. Open up sections of the fence around the perimeter, only a few will do.

6. Start at the shed farthest from the farmhouse. You'll figure out how to open the cages. Start opening at one end and work your way down. Don't worry about the animals, they'll find their way out. After you've finished the first row of cages, go onto the next. Some of the animals will fight or play. You can separate them or leave them alone. The noise can be unnerving, though. You'll notice sounds from the mink that they didn't make in their cages. The animals will coo as they run along when before all you've heard were hisses and shrieks in the cages.

7. After you have finished the last row of cages in the shed closet to the farmhouse go back and check on the other cages. If breeding cards are on top of the cages, you can take them. It will be an amusing scene of mayhem. Animals will be jumping out of cages and running about everywhere. They will be frolicking and darting through the exits you created beforehand. You can leave when all the cages are open -- the animals will find their own way out.

8. But your party may be disrupted early. If the farmer is awakened by you he will probably come running with a flashlight. Immediately leave quietly. He may know what is going on and call his neighbours and police before coming out to try and surprise you. CAREFUL!

9. At the very least, the priceless breeding info will be lost forever. And chances are the "lost" animals will not be insurable either. Each animal saved is about a $35(US) kick in the ass to the fur farmer. Multiply this by 1000 or 10,000 and we're talking major eco-tage.

10. Be careful if fur farm raids have occurred in your area. Be extra careful if you hit the same farm twice.@

Now get out there and have fun!

AN INTERVIEW WITH AN E.L.F. MEMBER

The following interview was sent anonymously to Underground, postmarked England.

INTERVIEWER: You say you are a member of the E.L.F. What does "E.L.F." stand for?
E.L.F.: E.L.F. stands for Earth Liberation Front. It's like an eco-A.L.F. In fact, most Elves [E.L.F. members] support the A.L.F. Animal Liberation and Ecodefense are all tied in together, you see. It's impossible to cause ecological and environmental damage without harming animals as well. Take road building for instance. Roads tend to cause a lot of ecological damage. They are built through woodlands and other important ecological sites.

What would be the point of a hunt sab, running around all day trying to save the life of say, a deer, but then allowing the same deer to die at the hands of a construction company that is destroying its natural habitat. It's crazy. Likewise, most animal abuse fucks up the environment.

INTERVIEWER: When did the Earth Liberation Front first form? How did it come about?

E.L.F.: That's easy. The E.L.F. was born in Britain in 1992. Back in 1991 the radical American ecology movement, Earth First!, came to Britain. EF! arrived at just the right time and became popular very quickly. With it's message of Deep Ecology it appealed to a large number of animal liberation activists, like myself. It also gave the power back to the people, allowing us to take control and defend our own local environment. It was all very inspiring.

Because EF! was so popular and had so many backing it, it became concerned about public appearance. At the first British EF! gathering it was suggested that if British Earth First! was lined with overt law breaking, (monkeywrenching, etc.) then it could loose some of its support. It was decided that Earth First! would strictly stick to the "Politically Correct" stuff. You know, civil disobedience and such. Meanwhile, other forms of action -- meaning monkeywrenching -- would be claimed under the banner of the Earth Liberation Front.

INTERVIEWER: You are a self-confessed Tree Spiker. Why do you spike trees?
E.L.F.: Tree spiking is carried out to stop the destruction of woodlands. The destruction of a woodland is a direct attack on nature. Chainsawing trees destroys ecological sites and deprives animals of their natural habitat. The reason the Red Squirrel is dying out in England isn't because of the introduction of the Grey Squirrel. It's because the natural habitat of the Red is being destroyed. Likewise, you can't save bears and wolves in North America if you allow all of their habitat to be destroyed. Across the world both animal and plant species are becoming endangered because their natural habitat is being destroyed. Tree spiking is a way to fight back and save natural habitat -- to preserve wildlife.

INTERVIEWER: But isn't tree spiking considered a "violent" act? Isn't the E.L.F. committed to nonviolence?
E.L.F.: The Earth Liberation Front is totally committed to nonviolence, and tree spiking is an act of nonviolence. Tree spiking is the hammering of pieces of metal, for example, headless six inch nails, into the trunks of trees. When a tree is chainsawed, it is then taken t a sawmill. If a tree has a spike in it, as soon as the sawmill blade hits the spike the blade is damaged. There was one "famous" incident in America where a sawmill blade shattered upon hitting a spike. The truth is this sawmill blade wasn't well maintained and it could have shattered if it hit anything hard. A bullet from a hunter's gun could have been in the tree. That was a one off. A well maintained sawmill blade will not shatter if it hits a tree spike and will not harm anyone.

(Continued from page 15)
INTERVIEWER: One of your main targets when spiking trees has been the Forestry Commission. Why?
E.L.F.: The Forestry Commission is obsessed with planting pine. They move into a natural woodland, chainsaw all the trees and then plant a mono-crop of pine to harvest later. With its acidic nature, pine pollutes the soil and kills off all other flora in the forest.

As well, as a vegan animal liberation activist, I have another reason to hate the Forestry Commission: they kill deer. Just recently, in Scotland, the Commission slaughtered a number of heavily pregnant deer outside of the hunting season. They did this to stop the deer from eating saplings. Most of the deer were only six weeks away from giving birth. After the does had been shot, the unborn fawns were cut from their mother's womb and left to die by her side. So horrific was this particular cull that even local hunters objected to its barbarism.

INTERVIEWER: Besides tree spiking, the E.L.F. is also known to target angling buildings. Why?
E.L.F.: Angling, like all blood-sports, is an attack on wildlife. The Earth Liberation Front is committed to defending all forms of wildlife, be it animal or plant.

The reason I personally choose to target anglers rather than any other sort of blood-junkies is simple. Angling is a neglected blood-sport. In England we have thousands of sabs out every weekend trying to save the lives of the cute and furry. But fish aren't cute, so they tend to be ignored. Yet, as a deep ecologist, I know that all life is equal and all life must be protected.

INTERVIEWER: Do you ever worry about being caught and going to jail?
E.L.F.: Of course. Doesn't everyone? But in the end I know I can't just sit back and watch as woodland areas are destroyed, as animals are terrorised and abused, as ecological destruction takes place and as the human race turns planet Earth into a rubbish heap. We must fight back. We can't wait for others to do it for us. We must do it ourselves -- and if that means ending up in prison, so be it. Besides, I've been arrested three times now, and it's not half as bad as you're led to believe. You do get kind of used to it after a while.

A song I used to listen to as a teenager had the words:
"Everyone is looking for a hero. Everyone is looking for the Preacher man. Everyone is looking for the hot shot, waiting for the person that can ... But what they don't know, They don't see, It all comes down to you and me."

And fucking too true that is. Don't sit on your arse all day waiting for someone else to trash the local Earth wreckers machinery or rescue the animals from the local lab. Go and do it yourself. Just get up, and get active!@

A FIGHTING chance

The following is the story of just one of the many mink farm raids that have taken place in North America in the past year and a half.

Late one night, I sat on a small patch of grass under the stars, listening to the dried leaves rustle in the wind. A few moments had passed when I saw the headlights of a small vehicle turn the corner and head towards me. After loading my gear into the trunk, I climbed into the front seat and exchanged anxious smiles with the driver. She gave my hand a quick squeeze before steering the care (rented in an untraceable manner) back onto the road. We were on our way.

As we drove, the sun came up. Stopping only to eat and refuel the car, we continued driving all day. A few hours after the sun disappeared, we met up with another man, well known to us and trusted wholeheartedly. Together we headed to a dark clearing near a small lake, and sat and discussed our plans.

Afterwards, taking special care to be sure we didn't have unwelcome company, we hit the road and headed for our final destination. Using detailed maps, we made many, many turns off the main road. We found the address we were looking for and quickly found some thick brush where we hid the car from sight.

We had brought with us a radio scanner which had already been programmed to monitor all the local and state law enforcement frequencies. One of my comrades double-checked that it was working and the controls were set appropriately, secured it in her jacket pocket and inserted the small earphone in her left ear, leaving the other ear unobstructed. Throughout the reconnaissance and the raid, she would listen carefully in case the farmer or a neighbour reported any suspicious activity or in case an undetected alarm caused an officer to be dispatched to the farm.

We also made sure that no one was carrying any loose articles, wearing jewellery or anything else that could inadvertently be left behind. The last thing we did was hide the door key near the car so one person would be carrying it (if that person should run into trouble, the others would have no mode of transportation). Our pockets were empty except for the scanner, flashlight and gloves. We were ready to go.

Our team knew how important it was to be familiar with the area, so we scouted around on foot for about an hour. Of course, while on or near roads, anytime we saw or heard a car in the distance we hit the ground or bush and made ourselves invisible. We located a creek which ran through the area nearby and out to open, wilder spaces. We also made note of the darkest areas for hiding and which side of the country road was least lit. We set up an emergency rendezvous point in case we were separated.

When the wind was just right, it carried the stench of the fur farm to us -- an overwhelming assault on our senses. When I inhaled I could taste the blood and filth, I could hear the cries of pain, I could see the suffering and I could feel the terror of this place. It was (and is) pure evil.

We cut across several large fields to get to the back fence of the mink farm. When walking in open spaces, we haunched over and let our arms hang down so that, if anyone was watching, we wouldn't look human. As we travelled we often had to pull strands of barbed wire apart and squeeze through to get past perimeter fences. We made friends with the many cows and other animals we passed on our way towards the farm.

After checking for alarms, trip wires and video cameras, we easily climbed the back fence and entered the concentration camp. Still watching carefully for alarms, etc., we hurried through he many sheds. Our presence brought the many thousands of mink to attention. They became very excited, rustling around in their tiny cages and "talking" to each other with short, high-pitched squeaks. With our small flashlights, we could see their curious little faces and inquisitive eyes -- truly beautiful creatures! I imagined the fate that would have awaited them if we had not come to intervene: their necks snapped or their lungs filled with gas after a few more months of enduring the psychological and physical torture of being imprisoned in this hell.

We took note of the cages: four rows in each shed. Filthy, corroded cages which provided no bedding for mink that normally nest in the wild. Simple latches held most cages shut, but some (the breeders) had a piece of heavy gauge wire twisted around the wires of the cage, securing the doors.

Our reconnaissance told us what we needed to know and we retreated to the back of the field that ran behind this farm. We sat under an old willow tree for a few hours, watching the compound to see if anyone was aware of our intrusion. On this evening we would leave the critters behind, but we would return. We hiked through the fields and creeks, back to the vehicle, and drove for about an hour. We then camped for the remainder of the morning.

At mid morning we rose and began to further discuss a plan of action, detailing tools we would need and delegating duties. We had brought with us a radio scanner, dark disposable clothing, flashlights, wire cutters, gloves, spray paint and ski masks. We would need to purchase packaged envelopes, paper and stamps (to send a communique after the action) as well as back up batteries. We fuelled up the car and drove by our target once (and only once) during the daylight to further familiarize ourselves with the surroundings.

The rest of the afternoon/evening was spent taking apart all our equipment, and wiping it down inside and out. We went over every detail of the plan in our heads and prepared ourselves mentally for whatever we might encounter, including any consequences we might face.

It began to rain. We double checked our inventory of equipment, and then set out. We made our way back to the concentration camp, again making sure we were not followed. Just like the night before, we checked and secured the scanner, emptied our pockets and hid the key to the vehicle. Again, we followed the road part way, diving to the ground with the coming of headlights, and then crept through the dark, still fields, towards the many mink awaiting their freedom.

We opened the cages. After opening roughly a dozen cages in the dark, I paused for a brief moment to shine my flashlight across them and caught sight of a shiny, sleek figure, hopping out of her hell-hole. The mink scurried across the ground and out of the barn. While I wanted to focus and appreciate each and every animal as they found their way to freedom, I knew I couldn't do so at the expense of those who would be left behind. I had to spend every moment on the farm opening cages to allow as many as possible a fighting chance at a natural life.

I continued my work, frantically unlatching and cutting wires. While I worked, several mink ran across the top of the cages while others scurried about my feet, squeaking with joy. Before long, these feisty critters were all over the place, running this way and that, playing and fighting with each other. Now and then I would briefly stop my work to separate two of the little guys and shoo them towards the outer fences, where they would find their freedom. RUN LITTLE GUYS, RUN!

Suddenly I heard -- or thought I heard -- a slamming noise. *"The mink have woken the farmers,"* I thought. *"Here he comes."* I looked to the end of the barn towards the farmer's house. Struggling to adjust my focus for such a distance in the darkness, I made out a light colored, upright figure. Were my eyes playing tricks on me, or was someone standing there? I grew very uneasy and almost nauseous, as I imagined 'Farmer John,' angry as a wasp evicted from her nest (but much more dangerous), standing in the doorway, holding a rifle. I prepared myself for the worst and tried again in vain to focus on the end of the shed.

Better safe than sorry, I reminded myself and quickly left the shed. I looked for my partners, and, not finding them, my anxiety increased. I moved across the adjacent field and hid in some thick, dark bushes, and watched the farm for about 20 minutes. I saw nothing out of the ordinary and no lights were turned on, so I eventually crept back and cautiously re-entered the compound. I ducked into the sheds where my friends were working, to be certain that all was well. I found them working away undeterred. I went back to my shed and continued opening the cages.

The work was exhausting and I could feel my bones ache with the monotony of the routine. But I kept going -- I could never live with myself if I didn't open as many cages as was humanly possible. I lost count at 500.

I finished my shed and checked on the others to see if they needed help. Finding their sheds empty, I moved on to the next one, and we finished that one off together. Sadly, we came to our pre-designated cut-off time. Though there were many more sheds full of prisoners, we had to leave -- the farmers would wake soon and the rise of the sun would provide no cover for ours and the minks' escape.

We marked some of the now empty sheds with spray-paint and then retreated. As we fled, we chased many mink to the holes cut in the fence. Once on the other side, we stopped for a moment to watch the many dark figures gliding and scampering through the fields towards the creek which would lead them to their new prospective homes.

Using the moon as our guide, we found our way back to our hidden vehicle. We briefly shared our experiences as we

(Continued on page 20)

RIOT at CONSORT

April 19, 1997

ENGLAND - Animal liberation campaigners protesting laboratory experiments gathered to march on Consort Kennels. There were 500 loud, angry, compassionate people prepared for anything there. And this is a force to reckon with.

Protesters gathered outside the premises. There were a number of police present, and many more police hiding in the area and also inside the compound. Protesters waited till the last ones had arrived and then, suddenly, moved off, down a track and around to the back of the beagle breeding place. There police had put up a fence, with barbed wire, and some 15 police officers, some with dogs, tried to keep the crowd off at this point. About 100 yards behind the police was the actual breeding place which was again surrounded by a wall with razor wire all around.

Suddenly, without much build up of emotion, people stormed passed the police to the razor wired wall and fence. Some tried to climb it (and a few managed), but most just got stuck outside. Two guys managed to enter the compound and take one beagle dog and flee up onto the roof of one of the buildings inside. At this stage riot police moved in (as people were seriously tearing on the fences outside). The riot police surrounded the building with the two men and the dog visible on the roof.

It was at this point, when all the people in the crowd saw the dog and the two men surrounded by police and barbed razor wire, that the protesters showed their true strength of feeling: they tried with all means to get into the place and to free the men and the dog.

First some fence on one side was torn down and people managed to get far enough inside to wreck two sheds and destroy everything inside it, and drag it out and set it on fire. This included a small tractor. However, riot police managed to stop the protesters from moving further inside the area, although they were showered with rocks.

Next some protesters tried it a bit further down and managed to overcome the fence by putting bits of an asbestos roof over the razor wire fence, but again riot police managed to beat people back.

One has to imagine the scenario at this stage. There are these two masked liberationists on the roof with the beagle dog. The house on which they are up on is surrounded by maybe 50 riot police in full gear, with helmets, shields, batons, the lot. Then there are some more 50 or so police buzzing around inside, with many police crews filming, and there is a helicopter above the scene, also filming I'm sure. And around all those police is a heavily protected fence with a rock wall on some parts, and razor wire and rolls fixed over it all the way. And all this is surrounded and besieged by an angry crowd of protesters, attacking from all sides, determined to get those men and the dog out.

Next, a large crowd of protesters attacked from the entrance gate side again, this time smashing up the windows of the cars of employees and of the manager of the place in the car park. Protesters were not aware of one arrest that had taken place earlier, with the arrestee sitting in the police van in this very car park. As I shared a police cell with him in the following night, he told me that he felt all those rocks raining onto them, but police had pushed him firmly to the ground so that he couldn't show himself to protesters. Otherwise he might as well have been de-arrested.

For those not used to such protests, in order to give you a full picture I would like to add that most protesters were totally masked up. Also, it was not just one or two throwing rocks, no, it was really everyone. And the people on megaphones shouted *"go on, do it, don't be afraid, smash the bastards"* etc. It was mayhem. And also, protesters constantly changed clothes with each other so that no particular protester could be pointed out. Protesters were constantly on the alert against police snatch squads, and effectively de-arrested immediately when such a squad tried their luck.

Next some protesters managed to break through the razor wire by dragging a bath tub to the fence, tearing the fence down and putting this tub over it. So within minutes, hundreds of protesters entered the inner area, surrounding the house with the two men and the dog on top. A line of police posed little resistance, and soon hundreds of people reached the side of the house, smashing up the garden fence and invading the front area. Police with batons stormed in from one side, and riot police from the other, but protesters resisted. A wall was broken down and split into handily sized rocks as missiles. Another fire was started in the garage and sheds just beside the house.

About five protesters were cut off by police inside the garden, as the police had managed by then to move protesters slightly backwards. At this stage the two men appeared on the roof just above protesters and lowered the beagle dog straight into the arms of the protesters. Then one of the men followed. I don't know what happened to the other. The protesters had managed to resist riot police attacks by then long enough so that one of the guys from the roof and the dog were safely hidden in the crowd.
Next, half the protesters moved off, broke through police lines and managed to get the beagle safely out of the immediate area. About 40 people made off with the beagle.

Unfortunately, they were spotted by two overenthusiastic police officers, one with a police dog, who gave chase. Also, the police helicopter was alerted and stayed above those protesters. At this stage all the 40 protesters took their jackets off and rolled them up and held them in front of their hands as if they had a beagle dog and made off in different direction. This confused police and the two officers chased different people in different directions. However, the people were not running fast enough, so more and more of those running off were caught and checked, and more and more police officers were getting involved in the chase, being drafted in from the roads. After a two mile chase the people with the beagle dog were discovered. The police dog was set on the people and two were severely bitten. 13 protesters then piled together onto a heap and hid and protected the beagle underneath their bodies. More and more police officers were drafted in and eventually they moved in and beat the 13 away and took the dog. All 13 were arrested under suspicion of theft.

In the mean time protesters continued to fight police in the area of the beagle breeding farm. It was then that CS gas was used, and many protesters ended up needing hospital treatment. Also, the road was blockaded in protest for a while, using equipment taken from a near road building site. Later on the day, three employees and the manager of the beagle breeder had home visits and got their houses thoroughly smashed up.

Altogether 24 people got arrested. One was immediately released as the arresting officer could not be found. The reasons for the arrest for the remaining 23 varied from theft to burglary, criminal damage and assault.

As far as I know, no-one was charged and everyone was released during the same night and the early hours of the morning.

I was arrested under suspicion of burglary and theft. Just prior to my arrest I was attacked by a police dog and severely bitten. The dog handling police officer encouraged the dog all the way through this attack and praised him/her afterwards. I had to remove the dog by stuffing my sweatshirt into his/her mouth and just removing him/her manually.

On the drive to the police station I had the beagle dog on my lap while I was hand-cuffed which made it impossible to comfort the poor soul in the way she would have needed it. The dog was a young female, and pregnant. Later during the night she was retrieved by an unknown man from the police station. Protesters who besieged the police station managed to drive him off at first, but eventually, with a heavy police escort, the dog was removed. Most likely, she will be dead by now.

I wish to say for myself that, apart from the sad end for the beagle, every second of this demo was worth it. It was such an empowering experience what 500 compassionate people with bare hands can do against an army of well-armoured riot police with batons and CS gas, and barbed razor wire.

I am humbled by the self-less determination those protesters showed. There was no fear, there was just simply no fear.@
M.

FIGHTING CHANCE *(Continued from page 18)*

walked -- one of our team had been bitten while attempting to open a cage. All of us had found several mink, dead and decaying in their cages.

We piled our soaked, sore, and muddied bodies into the car. We made frustrated faces at each other -- we were excited but knew we could not talk in the car. We drove silently back down the dark roads to our campsite, where we sorted out our things, throwing all clothes and shoes into the campfire and placing tools into bags to be discarded safely and immediately.

We talked a little more about our experiences, including what we could do better next time. We made plans to meet again, and shared warm hugs before embarking on our long journey home. During the following day's drive, we heard news reports of the raid on the radio. We smiled proudly with the satisfaction that many that many mink had a chance at freedom that day, that the fur trade had just become a little less profitable, and that 'Farmer John' just might go out of business.@

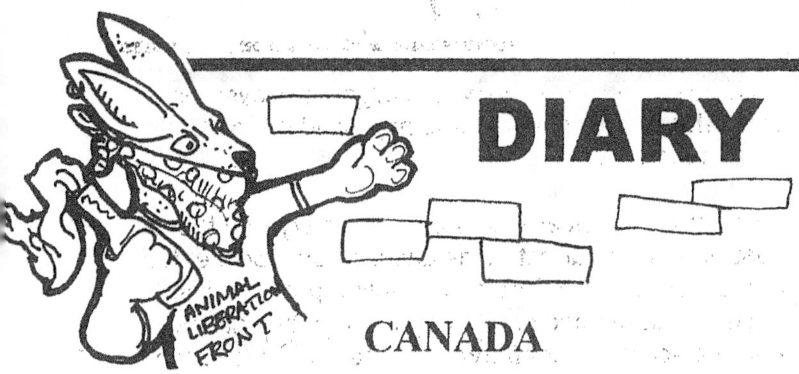

DIARY OF ACTION

CANADA

APRIL 19/97: Kitchener, ON - A bomb threat was phoned into the Kitchener Memorial Auditorium during the Garden Brothers Circus by someone representing the A.L.F. Local paper, *The Record,* also received an anonymous fax threatening "direct, militant action" against the circus because it continues to enslave, abuse and exploit animals for entertainment. A.L.F.

JUNE 20/97: Waterloo, ON - McDonald's at King and Columbia streets spraypainted and sabotaged from the roof. Electrical cords, exhaust fans and more were damaged to prevent regular operation of the restaurant. Spraypainted slogans included "McDeath," "Dead meat," "McFuck You" on walls and sidewalks. A.L.F.

JUNE 23/97: Waterloo, ON - McDonald's on King St. in Kitchener was spraypainted with "Eat Shit," "A.L.F.," and "McLibel." Windows were also smashed. A.L.F.

From the Communique: "*Both actions were executed in solidarity with the McLibel Two to commemorate the end of the six year court battle with McDonald's. We maintain that all statements made in the original pamphlet are true. Some statements were difficult for the two self-represented defendants to prove against the McDonald's law team. Regardless of our problems with the verdict, we are still considering this case a victory and McDonald's everywhere will be forced to face their human, environmental, and animal rights violations as long as they exist. McDonald's will see the justice they deserve.*"

SEE PAGE 13 for tips on having fun at McDonalds.

MAY 17/97: Scarborough, ON - butcher shop owner Tony McPherson called it quits after a visit to his shop from the A.L.F. Meat King Butcher Shop, at Kingston Rd. and Eglinton Ave. E., had been ransacked. In green and yellow spray paint vandals activists had plastered Animal Liberation Front slogans everywhere, including on both of the freezer doors in the kitchen. McPherson said about 25 similar messages were scattered throughout the restaurant, including one that read "I'll Be Back." Fear of further attacks and the higher insurance cost costs have made him decide to close his business down, he said. *"I don't know what else to do. It has turned me off completely,"* he told reporters. Even if he cleaned up the mess and re-opened, McPherson said he would still end up thinking about the vandalism every day, worried they would do it again. *"It's opened my eyes to how much animal rights there is out there."* -A.L.F. VICTORY!

UNITED STATES

MARCH 13/97:NYC, NY - Approximately 20-30 locks glued in the meat district, 25-35 locks glued in the fur district as well as the locks to the store security system. Anti-fur messages spray painted. To the surprise of activists doing the action, several locks had already been glued that night. -A.L.F.

MARCH 15/97: Huntington, LI- Huntington Furs', Village Furs, and a leather store have all locks glued. Several trucks belonging to a meat wholesaler received the following: locks glued, sugar poured into gas tank, freezer lines cut, and random wire cuts. *"We were prevented from doing more due to sparks shooting out of one of the cut wires."* -A.L.F.

MARCH 16/97: Westbury, LI- Long Island Fur Factory locks glued.

MARCH 20/97: NYC, NY - Many locks glued in the fur district.

APRIL 1/97: NYC, NY - Once again most of the store in manhattans fur district get their locks glued.

APRIL 17/97: Virginia Beach, VA - during the early morning hours the construction site of a partially built McDonalds was attacked by activists. Cell members gained access to the building through an unlocked back door. Nine windows smashed, boxes of screws dumped out, slogans left, including "A.L.F." and "For the Animals." Damages estimated at between $15,000 and $20,000. -A.L.F.

APRIL 17/97: Virginia Beach, VA - Construction site of a Golden Corral also hit by the same A.L.F. cell as above. Activists destroyed electrical system wiring, extension cords, power tools, lighting fixtures, manuals, five freezer doors, on freezer fan, and a water generator. Then bags of concrete and plaster were poured on the floor. 10 to 15 slogans painted, ranging from "meat is murder," to "Stop the Slaughter" and "Animal Liberation Front." -A.L.F.

Before leaving water hoses were turned on in hopes of flooding the building and mixing the concrete. 22 windows also smashed. Damage estimates near $20,000. A.L.F.

APRIL 20-MAY 8/97: Lakewood, OH - Novotny furs and Fashion was hit 3 times, 1st receiving two broken windows and painted walls (Fur is Dead), the 2nd having 6 windows smashed and again slogans left. The 3rd visit included a bucket of red paint on the walls and the sidewalks were painted. Also hit during this time was Sabu Furs, with painted walls, and two broken windows, and a leather outlet store that had "wear your own skin" painted on its walls, with two windows smashed out. A.L.F.

APRIL 29/97: Souteastern VT - 5-30 Doves liberated from cages.

MAY/97: Kirkland, WA - A.L.F. cut a hole in the fence of a meat distributor, painted the trucks and smashed the windshields. The owner of the meat distributor was a former Seattle Seahawk. News reports place damages at $1500+. -A.L.F.

MAY 2/97 -NYC, NY - McDonalds on 28th St & 6th Ave has "meat is murder" and "ALF" etched into 3 windows. Banana Express (a meat market) has "ALF" etched into the window. -A.L.F.

MAY 3/97: Eugene, OR - McDonald's office at 1471 Pearl St. had its windows shot out. A.L.F.

MAY 10/97: San Diego, CA - A.L.F. attacked Kentucky Fried Chicken - windows were broken, glues were locked, and "ALF Meat is Murder" was spray painted. - A.L.F.

MAY 11/97: Parsons Fur Farm in Maryland raided. Approximately 500 mink were released. This is the same farm where a few years ago PETA got undercover footage of the furrier using Blackleaf 40 -- a nicotine-based insecticide -- to kill the mink. This insecticide causes the lungs to stop, and the victim to suffocate.

MAY 11/97: Lakewood, OH - A.L.F. activists celebrated mothers day by painting trucks at Blue Ribbon Meats. Trucks hit with slogans, including "Meat is Murder," "Blood money," "Vegan Power,"and "A.L.F." Windows were etched and one truck cab was doused in gasoline and set ablaze. WE WILL CONTINUE FOR THE EARTH AND ALL HER CREATURES!!! -Northern Ohio A.L.F.

MAY 15/97: Jensen Beach, ? - A.L.F. activists hit Scoozi's Italian Restaurant causing an estimated $200,000 in damages after an arson attack. At least 6 fires were set inside the restaurant. Twice last year activists visited the restaurant, writing "Veal is an innocent meal" and "Veal is dead." Activists warned the owners "next time it burns to the ground." Obviously Owner Bob Muzzo didn't pay enough attention to the warnings about removing veal from the menu. A.L.F.

MAY 17-18/97: Chevy Chase, MD - An artistic masterpiece was created at the Miller's Furs. The front of the store was covered with the following slogans: "STOP OR BE STOPPED," "MURDERERS," and "ALF"(3 times). The art continued onto to the side of the building with "FUR IS DEAD," "ALF," "STOP NOW!" and "KILLERS." -A.L.F.

MAY 20/97: South Florida - A truck at Anderson's Meats in Palm Springs was spray-painted with slogans, and had its windshield covered with etching fluid. A.L.F.

MAY 20/97: West Palm, FL - Tandy Leather had locks glued and slogans written on windows. A.L.F.

MAY 21/967: Kirkland, WA - meat distributers (715 8th St.) Activists returned for 3rd time to find a fence surrounding Meat Distributers seven trucks. Access gained with boltcutters. All trucks received painted slogans and windshields smashed on six trucks. Media reports $30,000 damage. Also reported is the formation of a special taskforce by local authorities to address A.L.F. attacks in East King county. A.L.F.

MAY 21/97: Seattle, WA - E&E Meats (3922 6th Ave S.) has holes cut in fence and four trucks painted and windshields smashed. A.L.F.

JUNE 1/97: Mount Angel, OR - Activists released thousands of minks from their cages on a fur ranch. An estimated 8,000 to 9,000 animals were freed in what may have been the largest A.L.F. attack on the U.S. mink industry according to the Fur Commission of U.S.A. Marion County Sgt. David Hussey said Friday's loss could amount to several hundred thousand dollars. Arritola said the intruders got past his alarm system. *"They were professionals. It took a lot of people to do what they did,"* he said.

JUNE 28/97: Seattle, WA - Macdonald Meat Co. (2709 Airport Way S.) access to lot gained by hole in fence. All five trucks recieved painted slogans and smashed windshields. A.L.F.

JUNE 29/97: Seattle, WA - Vitamilk Dairy Products (427 NE 72 St.) 19 trucks received painted slogans and smashed windshields. Better Meat Inc (305 NW 82 St.) 2 trucks painted and windshields smashed. A.L.F.

JUNE 30/97: Seattle, WA - A&J Meats and Seafood (2401 Queen Anne Ave N) 20 windows smashed. Varlamos Brothers seafood (8279 Lake City Way NE) 3 trucks hit with painted slogans and smashed windshields. A.L.F.

JULY 2/97: Tukwilla, WA - Petschls Quality Mats (1150 Andover Park E) three trucks receive painted slogans and smashed windshields. A.L.F.

JULY 3/97: Burlington, WA - Galbreth Packing Co. Slaughterhouse raided during the early morning hours. Masked activists broke into the killing room where millions of pigs met the end of a miserable life with a bloody death. Using boltcutters, the sole killing mechanism, a captive bolt air gun was taken, assuring at least one blood free day in the slaughterhouse. Once outside, the meat transportation truck was put out of commission. Muriatic acid was poured into the refrigeration unit, slogans painted ("Animal Liberation Now!!!" "A.L.F."), and the windshield smashed. A.L.F.

JULY 4/97: Mt. Hood, OR -- from the communique:

"the morning dew is erased by the heat of the sun
as another workday has almost begun
men arrive eager to clearcut Mt Hood
to destroy the wild for profit from wood

only this day is different as they find work done at night
by elves who sab machines and disappear from sight
remove six valve covers and oil caps
add sand and the monsters are scraps

so next time you bid for a sale on public land
remember elves are everywhere
and there is plenty of sand..."

Mt. Hood: 1 feller buncher, 1 dozer, 1 articulated loader ruined. E.L.F.

JULY 13/97: Cougar Hot Springs, OR - three dumptrucks (Eugene Sand & Gravel), 2 hydraulic excavators, 2 front loaders, 1 dozer destroyed. E.L.F.

July 21/97: Redmond, OR -- A.L.F. paid a visit to the Cavel West Horse Murdering Plant at 1607 SE Railroad Ave. About 35 gallons of flammable "vegan jello" was brought with the team, who drilled a number of large holes into the rear wall of the slaughterhouse, bypassing any alarms on the doors or windows. The "jello" was poured into the numerous holes near the refrigeration units and three electrically-timed incendiary devises were assembled and activated. Other team members left 10 gallons of jello in a storage shed/office. Two gallons of muriatic acid was poured into the air conditioning vents to destroy any horse flesh that might survive the fire.

As the devices were being set a spark from a battery started the entire area on fire. At least $1,000,000 damage had been done and the entire plant is out of operation. - A.L.F. Equine & Zebra Liberation Network (EZLN)

JULY 23/97: Murrieta, CA -- An under-construction International House of Pancakes restaurant on Radison Ave was destroyed by an arson attack. Damage estimates range from $150,000 to $250,000. From an A.L.F. communique, *"Cliff, I'll have my tofu scrambled now. A.L.F."*

SEPTEMBER 13/97: Indianapolis, IN — R & M Leathers is visited and has three windows smashed out, locks glued and slogans painted. The action was done in solidarity with Barry Horne and Sue McCrosky's hungerstrikes.

ENGLAND

Hunt Retribution Squad 96-97. Sussex:
1. August/96: Eight shooters' vehicles trashed.
2. August/96: Huntsman's cheque-book "acquired" and account wiped out on bondage and fetish gear. Three months later he was dead (not sure if he was wearing nipple clamps at the time)
3. August/96: Hunt Supporter's bank account emptied
4. September/96: Six shooting pens demolished and birds released.
5. September/96: Hunt supporter's car tires slashed.
6. May/97: "Toby Stone," a hunter, has his grave smashed.
7. July/97: Over 600 pounds damage done to anglers' cars.
-- Don't normally claim stuff but though you might be interested. H.R.S.

APRIL 19/97: Ross-On-Wye: Animal Rights campaigners broken into kennels which breed beagles for laboratory experiments. Around 500 people came to the kennels in Ross-On-Wye and some broke through a police cordon and entered the area where the dogs are kept. One dog was temporarily rescued before police discovered the dog's whereabouts. Activists laid wreaths outside for all the animals killed in laboratories. The protest was held to coincide with "World Day For Laboratory Animals". Police used CS spray to disperse the crowd. At least 27 people were arrested. **(see page 19 for a first-hand account of this action).**

APRIL 19/97: Oxfordshire: Hill Grove Family Cats in Minster Lovell, Witney, was raided by activists. Over 20 cats were liberated and cages and doors were left open to allow the rest (roughly 250) to wander outside. Several of these were picked up over the next few days and taken to safe homes but the rest were recaptured by Chris Brown and presumably "destroyed". The cats are "Specific Pathogen Free (SPF)" so have to be raised in sterile conditions otherwise they can't be used in research.

MAY 13/97: Ross-On-Wye - Consort Beagle Breeders at Harewood End Ross-on-Wye, Herefordshire raided and 25 dogs were liberated.

SWEDEN

EARLY 1997: Activists burned the main building of an empty fur farm, damaged a second building and the Swedish A.L.F. released two red fox from a fur farm.

MARCH 16/97: Alunda - tranbyns fur farm is visited by animal libbers and two red foxes are released into the wild. Action dedicated to U.S. prisoners on hunger strike as well as in solidarity with Rod Coronado.

MARCH/APRIL/97: Ostersund - Fur shops get slogans painted on their windows.

APRIL/97: Malmo - Advertising signs for McDonalds spraypainted.

APRIL/97: Umea - The department of Zoophysology at Umea University is attacked and one security camera is smashed, three searchlights and one window smashed, and three litres of yellow paint was thrown on walls.

APRIL 4/97: Vingaker - two hunting towers destroyed.

APRIL 18/97: Eksjo - Ugglekarrs fur farm is hit by the group "The Wild Minks" and all breeding cards (300) are destroyed. The office was also destroyed, important papers stolen, a feeding machine is destroyed. The fence around the farm is cut and 46 black mink, all breeding males, are freed from their cages.
Slogans such as "bloody scum" and "die" were painted.

APRIL 18/97: Nassjo - a fur/leather shop is attacked and shit from a fur farm is thrown on the building. Slogans painted and three windows smashed. Estimated damage is $10,000 US.

APRIL 24/97: Norratlje - Swedish A.L.F. (DJURENS BEFRIELSE FRONT) rescued 25 rabbits (among them were eight rabbit-children) from a breeder for vivisection. The rabbits were in poor shape: inflammation in the eyes, one rabbit's back leg was paralyzed and another rabbit's claws had grown into its feet, causing bleeding. Thanks to professional and loving care, all rabbits are expected to be healthy and safe. This action is dedicated to all animal rights prisoners all over the world. D.B.F.

MAY/97: Huddinge - the only fur shop in Huddinge is attacked several times and windows are smashed, slogans sprayed. The owner of the fur shop had her car smashed and destroyed at her home.

MAY 1/97: Hokarangen - Polar-Pals fur Shop has five windows smashed and "Fur is Dead" and "Murderers" sprayed.

MAY 1/97: Klomarden - The Wild Mink attack another fur farm. 750 breeding cards are destroyed, slogans painted and 8 male mink are released. - The Wild Mink

MAY 3/97: Eskilistuna - Fur shop locks glued and slogans painted, including "fur is murder."

MAY 4/97: Oskarshamn - Fox farm is attacked and 50 foxes are released. 10 cages destroyed, breeding cards stolen, slogans painted and a killing device stolen. THIS FOX FARM IS NOW CLOSED! VICTORY!

MAY 4-5/97: Lund - two leather shops, one meat shop had slogans sprayed, including: "ALF," "SCUM," "Murderers," "Meat/Leather is murder."

MAY 8/97: Strangnas - a breeder of birds for hunts is visited and 550 pheasants are released into the wild. Damage is done to cages and pens and other equipment. A new group, ANIMAL LIBERATORS, claim responsibility. - Animal Liberators

MAY 10/97: Eskilstuna - Trangsas Fur Farm was hit by the Wild Minks and 600 breeding cards are stolen (destroying four years of breeding information), slogans sprayed and 70 mink breeding males are freed. - The Wild Mink

MAY 13/97: Kumla - Skyberga mink fur farm is attacked by the Wild Minks. 1000 breeding cards destroyed, fences taken down, slogans such as "auschwitz," "stop the torture Now!" and "The Wild Mink" are painted before 68 breeding males are released into the wild. -The Wild Mink

MAY 19/97: Horsnas: This fur farm receives a second visit by the Wild Minks. This time, 30 minks are released and the slogan "Hello again bloody murderers" is sprayed on a newly painted wall. - Wild Minks

JUNE/97: Karlstad - a furs shop is sprayed with slogans like "ALF" and "Fur is murder." -A.L.F.

JUNE 29/97: Hofors - Sweden's largest fox farm is attacked and 1200 breeding cards stolen, a car is redecorated on the inside and the engine is destroyed, damage is done to several buildings and torture equipment is destroyed. Slogans also spray-painted.

JULY/97: Huddinge - The fur shop in Huddinge lost all five windows as soon as they had been replaced from a previous attack. Slogans painted as well.

JULY 8-9/97: Lund - two pet shops and one fur shop get slogans painted, including "Animal Liberation Now!" "ALF," "Murderers" and "fur is murder." -A.L.F.

AUGUST/97: Karlstad - a butcher shop is sprayed with slogans such as "ALF was Here" and "We see you." - A.L.F.

AUGUST/97: Lulea - two meat lorries are burned out for the first time in this part of Sweden.

AUGUST 13/97: Horsnas - the largest fur farm raid ever is Sweden is carried out against Horsnas Fur Farm (third attack). Over 1200 mink are released into the wild. - The Wild Mink

AUGUST 21/97: Wrigsad - Local fur farmers were set to have a meeting when a bomb hoax was called into the local media, claiming to have placed 3 bombs at the meeting place. The meeting was cancelled!

SEPTEMBER 11/97: Hultsfred - Wild Minks strike again, visiting the Linde Magnussons fur farm. Foxes were found to be in very bad health. Over 100 foxes were painted with harmless henna-colouring making the fur worthless to the idustry. Cages for other foxes were opened and roughly 80 fled into the forest. - Wild Mink

These are only a few of the actions that have occurred in Sweden. Almost every day, fur shops get slogans painted, locks glued and windows smashed out in Stockholm. Hundreds of circus posters have been taken down all over Sweden and lots of hunting towers have been destroyed during the summer of '97.

FINLAND

SEPTEMBER 4/97: Riihimaki - raid attempted at a fox fur farm. Farmers spent at least two weeks guarding the farm 24hrs a day, but decided to go to sleep — activists struck and opened at least one cage and stole breeding cards. A guard dog woke the farmer, who passed within one meter of a hidden activist. No arrests made.

SEPTEMBER 15/97: Kaustinen - several hundred mink and a dozen foxes were released. Fences destroyed by activists. Action claimed by "Kaustinen Yopelimannit" (meaning Night Musicians of Kaustinen), playing on the fact the Kaustinen is known for its music festivals.

STAND BY ME.

by Rabbix: A defendant in the Gandalf Trial

In the animal lib movement we pride ourselves on the fact that if an activist goes into prison they will receive the support of the movement. Whilst as a remand prisoner, Keith Mann once wrote:

"Most people in prison tend to find out the hard way who their real friends are. Its a different story for A.L.F. prisoners. The amount of support I've had from friends and people I don't know is heartwarming. Its easy to forget or ignore people in prison, but be assured if you end up off the streets you won't be forgotten." (TURNING POINT, July-Sept 1992)

But what about before the activist goes to prison? What happens whilst they are on bail awaiting trial? How much support does the Animal/Earth liberation movement offer then?

On April 4, 1995, I was arrested by members of Hampshire CID who accused me of "Conspiracy to Incite Criminal Damage." On that occasion I was held a few hours, interviewed and then released without charge. Following my arrest, over the next few days, I worked up the courage to tell my friends that I had been arrested. At that time I had a number of friends, most of whom were either vegan or vegetarian Animal and Earth libbers. To my horror, rather than receiving support from my friends, most of my friends decided they wanted nothing more to do with me. This included a very dear vegan friend, who only months before had told me that my friendship meant a great deal to her.

Out of all the friends I had before my arrest, excluding my then girlfriend, her family and my family, only two people stood by me. One vegetarian friend and a meat eating friend. NONE OF MY VEGAN FRIENDS STOOD BY ME. I can honestly say that if it hadn't been for people like Gillian Peachy (herself a remand prisoner at the time) and Zab, the then coordinator of the North American Animal Liberation Front Supporters Group, I don't think I would have got through the shock of my initial arrest. And it was a shock for me. I lost two stone in weight in just three days because of the stress.

I felt really afraid and alone after my arrest. This was made all the worse for the fact I knew that people I used to call friends no longer wanted anything more to do with me. Since my arrest, I have found out a number of other activists have had exactly the same thing happen to them. I have heard tales of people in both Britain and America loosing all their friends after their arrests. This has led to at least one person committing suicide.

Obviously, not everyone who is arrested finds their friends leaving them. A number of the animal rights prisoners I have spoken to about this have said their friends have stuck by them. This is excellent. However, as this article shows, this is not always the case. What I am trying to say with this article is if you know of someone who has been arrested, please do get in contact with them. Offer them support and friendship. **BE A FRIEND.** It might be what they are looking for.

Nine months after my initial arrest I was re-arrested and formally charged with Conspiracy to Incite Criminal Damage. After I was formally charged I was gutted made worse by the fact no one wanted to know me. I tried to make new friends, but as soon as they learnt I was on Police Bail charged with a criminal offense, people just didn't want to know. For two months my confidence hit rock bottom, and I admit I did consider suicide. However, luckily for me, I started doing things outside of the Animal/Earth Liberation movement. I started doing voluntary work for a homeless charity. Here, I discovered that people outside of the Animal/Earth liberation movement were much more supportive to me than the people from within the movement ever were, and I was able to develop new friendships.

As the date of my trial approaches, I have started getting some support from people within the Animal/Earth liberation movement. I think about five or six people have written to say good luck with the trial. So, I am now getting some support, and I would like to thank everyone who has offered me their support. To everyone else, I say, **IF YOU KNOW OF A PERSON WHO HAS BEEN ARRESTED AND IS AWAITING TRIAL, CONTACT THAT PERSON AND MAKE SURE THEY ARE OKAY.** Be supportive towards them, but above all, be a friend. You may literally be the only friend they have.

Chatham 3 - The Story So-Far

In the early morning hours of Sunday, March 30th, five Michigan animal rights activists were arrested for allegedly raiding a Canadian mink farm. According to media reports, 1,500 mink were released from Ebert's Fur Farm owned by Tom McLellan, fences were cut and breeding cards were removed from the cages, effectively costing the fur farmer half a million dollars!

It is believed that McLellan will collect this sum in insurance money but that he will not be insured again. Further, it is probable that this action has put him out of business for good! (The Earth Liberation Front took credit for a similar action at Ebert's Fur Farm two weeks earlier when 250 to 300 mink were released.)

Those charged in the mink raid are Patricia Dodson, 48; Hilma Ruby, (now 60); Robyn Weiner, 25; Gary Yourofsky, 26; and Alan Hoffman, 47; all of whom live in Michigan. All are charged with breaking and entering and mischief. Robyn and Alan are also charged with possession of stolen property (breeding cards). Patricia is additionally charged with possession of burglary tools.

The five had several court hearings and several delays before they were finally released almost two weeks later, each on $10,000 bail. By this time, two of the defendants -- Alan Anthony Hoffman and Robyn Rachel Weiner -- had made damaging statements to the police which were read in court. Alan gave an alleged blow-by-blow account of everyone's actions (including the scouting out of farms in the U.S.), and Robyn's statement included the implication of one of the other activists in a previous raid.

Robyn claims her informing was in the best interests of everyone. However, her co-defendants' legal cases have been seriously compromised by her statements and it has left them feeling betrayed. These "activists" have turned against their own and expressed their willingness to work with the authorities against their fellow defendants. This is NOT OK and must not be tolerated within a direct action movement. Once activists make statements which incriminate others or compromise the defense of others, they are excluded from support. Thus, the Chatham 3.

All five returned to court in Chatham, Ontario, three weeks later, where they were served with a $3.5 million civil suit by Ebert's Fur Farms, Inc. The owners of the farm are seeking:

$2,000,000 in general damages
$1,000,000 in specific damages
$500,000 in punitive damages
plus legal costs.

The suit claims that 20 years of breeding information was lost; 1,542 minks were released (1,500 female, 42 male); 95 percent of females were pregnant with an average expected litter of six kits each; 1,500 females would have produced 7,125 pelts at $70 per male pelt and $50 per female pelt. The defendants are accused of cutting a hole in the fence, damaging or destroying 100 pens, damaging or destroying 400 drop-in nest-boxes, and damaging or destroying 2 gates. The legal fees and other costs yet to be incurred will undoubtedly be enormous – any help raising funds would be greatly appreciated! Information on where to send donations and letters of support is in the box to the right of this article.

Robyn has pled guilty to the charges and waived her right to a trial. She was sentenced on June 30th to 400 hours of community service to be served in Canada on weekends and her $10,000 bail was forfeited to McLellan with an apology to him for the "suffering she had caused". She also said that she was going to have to live with what she had done for the rest of her life.

This deal was worked out as she has cooperated with the authorities and promised to testify against the others at trial. The Crown's attorney (prosecuting attorney) said he will NOT show the Chatham 3 the same leniency because they "have not shown any remorse". The remaining activists face a possible 2 year prison sentence on each count.

In early August, a warrant was issued for Hilma's arrest as a result of Robyn and Alan's statements regarding their belief that she was one of the people who was involved in the earlier raid at the same farm. They said Hilma knew all about it and who else was involved. Hilma is expected to turn herself in on September 5 to be placed under arrest again. She may have to stand a separate trial for the new charges, cover double the lawyer's costs and possibly come up with another $10,000 bail.

CHATHAM 3 LEGAL FUND:

This ordeal has been financially devastating for those involved. They are burdened with enormous legal fees and don't have enough for separate representation for some of the activists, which they desperately seek. Good people who are accused of taking action to alleviate the suffering of innocent animals and whose lives have been subsequently turned upside down should not have to worry about how to pay for their lawyers of choice. The Chatham 3 have endured enough.

Please find it in your heart to contribute as generously as you can to the fund to help cover their legal costs. Donations will not be used to pay fines or to pay the mink murderers. If money is left over when the case has been resolved, it will be donated to the North American A.L.F. Supporters Group's prisoner support fund so that it can be used to help others who face serious charges for crimes of compassion.

WHAT YOU CAN DO TO HELP

Donate - Funds for the Chatham 3 legal defense are desperately needed and much appreciated. Please make checks payable to the NA-ALFSG and earmarked "for the Chatham 3".

Write a Letter - Let the Chatham 3 know that you support them. Write letters of solidarity to see them through this difficult time. Send a letter or card today!

Raise Funds - Help raise funds by organizing a benefit concert or other fundraiser. Let us know and we'll send you flyers to distribute at your event.

Spread the Word - Contact us for Chatham 3 flyers to distribute far and wide or for a prepared article to publish in your animal rights magazine or newsletter.

Protest - Plan to organize and/or attend a national demonstration in support of the Chatham 3 upon the release of the verdict. Continue to protest against the bloody fur trade and doing whatever you do for animals.

Stand Up - Take a moment to let Tom McLellan and his co-owner/son, Bill, know what a wretched mistake they are making by pursuing a lawsuit against accused freedom fighters: Ebert's Fur Farm, R.R. 4, Blenheim, Ontario, N0P 1A0 Canada, (519) 676-4969.

Letters of support, donations, requests for flyers and articles can be sent to:
Chatham 3 Support Committee
c/o NA-ALFSG: Box 69597, 5845 Yonge St. Willowdale, Ont. M2M 4K3, Canada
e-mail: chatham3@envirolink.org

UNDERGROUND

THE MAGAZINE OF THE NORTH AMERICAN ANIMAL LIBERATION FRONT SUPPORTERS GROUP

SSUE #9 | Winter '97 | FREE TO PRISONERS | $3

FUR FARM RAIDS CONTINUE...

lso inside: End the Canadian Seal Hunt * Gandalf Trial Concludes * Diary of Action * Mink Release Myths and Facts * Prisoner Justice Project: Year in Review * Animal Lib Prisoner Updates AND PLENTY MORE!

Notes from the NA-A.L.F.S.G.

Greetings! Welcome to issue #9 of Underground. We hope you all are in the best of health and your spirits are strong (unless you're a vivsector, fur farmer, butcher or all round animal abuser, in which case we hope your research grants dry up, your farm collapses into bankruptcy and you wake up to find your shop fitted with "air conditioning" care of an A.L.F. brick.) At any rate, it has been a busy year over all for animal liberationists of all caliber, and we're pleased to say that 1998 shows no sign of slowing down. As the Swedish activist on our cover shows, fur farm raids are still happening with overwhelming frequency around the world, although for some the debate on tactics continues. We received a letter from the Swedish group, Djurens Befrielse Front, condemning the actions of Swedish fur-farm raiders like the Wild Mink, who have struck numerous times throughout Sweden, releasing thousands of mink. Our intention is not to step into the debate or take sides, but we do recommend for those concerned about the issues surrounding mink liberations to review Rod Coronado's piece, *"Opening the Cages — A Look at Mink Liberations"* **(Underground #5)** to understand more about mink survivability, appropriate and inappropriate release times/seasons, environmental impact, etc. Another good resource for mink liberation information is the Coalition to Abolish the Fur Trade (CAFT) :
Box 822411, Dallas, TX 75382, USA.

In other news, we regret to announce the closing of the NA-A.L.F.SG's Roswell GA Distro group. Merchandise is still available for you to order, but those interested should write our Willowdale Ontario address from now on. Unfortunately, there remains a huge mess to clear up with the old distro — we are still waiting to receive records of unfilled orders — many of you have been waiting as long as six months for shirts, magazines and leaflets, and for this we can only apologize. At this moment there are dedicated activists within Canada who have taken over the Distro and will work hard to fill those outstanding orders. However, we are also still waiting for folks in the U.S. to ship us a number of merchandise items that we don't have stocked here. At any rate, without boring you all with the details of our quest to be reunited with our merchandise, suffice to say we will do our best to make it up to everyone who has been waiting.

One final note: for several weeks Canadian postal workers have been on strike, and hence many of your letters and updates have not reached us in time for this issue. There is however, a pile of very interesting stuff between the pages of this magazine, and we hope you all enjoy!

yer Editor,
t.

Letters to Underground

ACTIVIST NEEDS OUR SUPPORT

About a month or so ago two persons from the Worcester (central Mass.) area, Vern Flynn and Chat(?), were arrested and charged with one felony, "possession of a incendiary machine". Allegedly going to be used to burn a veal crate lot. Chat talked, but did not admit and got a deal, one year probation and 55 hours community service. Vern did not talk, and is going to pre-trial Nov.10. Vern has two other open mis. Civil Disobedience charges.

So far no one has put the word out about this and no one seems to know about it. So, in turn Vern has not seen any support. He has a public defender, but does not seem to have much faith in him.

Letters of support can be emailed to **<MASSHardline@juno.com> or sent to:**

Vern Flynn
PO BOX 381855
Cambridge, MA 02238

Alex from Boston

Letter From Lise Olsen and Harold Thompson

Dear NA-A.L.F.S.G.

I send my warm @ greetings from the belly of the beast!

I hope this letter finds you and all at NA-A.L.F.S.G. in good health and spirits with everything going well. At this time I am in fair health and low morale with things going in typical chaotic fashion here. Still no news on our forced double cell or the lack of vegetarian diet lines lawsuits. One positive note is I'm still alone in my cell with its limited, though cherished, privacy.

I have been asked by Lise Olsen to send you a statement about her present situation/circumstances which is below:

I have been asked by my very dear friend, supporter, and former AR prisoner, Lise Olsen, to contact you with an current update of her situation. After having served her entire prison sentence at Lise's second trial she was acquitted of the four felonies and received a sentence of "time served" on the last remaining felony charge of "unauthorized use of a weapon" charge so is legally free at this time. In reality the felony she was convicted of at her second trial was the "crime" of possessing in excess of three tablespoons of gasoline under Illinois state law. The only reason Lise Olsen was convicted on this felony at all was the Grand Jury had indicted her on the first half of the statute but left off the second part of the statute pertaining to weaponry. Her conviction is on appeal at this time and Lise Olsen has informed me she has spent thus far approximately five thousand dollars on this appeal.

Recently Lise Olsen relocated from Chicago to another state, which she prefers not be disclosed at this time in order to lessen chances of her being framed on additional bogus charges by law enforcement, and she is doing well. She is working to rebuild her life after her legal ordeal, to recuperate spiritually and physically following her period of incarceration and later Lise's electronic monitored house arrest. Lise Olsen requested I thank all who supported her during her time of suffering, plus all who cared enough to communicate during it. Lise Olsen requested I express her gratitude, love and admiration for all good people struggling in behalf of the animals worldwide.

Take care, stay strong and continue to struggle against the monsters of the earth for the animals and for a better day for all!
In struggle & Solidarity,

Harold H. Thompson, #93992
Turney Center Industrial Prison
Route 1, Only, Tennessee 37140-9709, USA

FROM PARTISANS TO FIRE ELVES

For those who never read the *EF! Journal*, or bother to keep abreast with some actions, then one would not be guilty if they had not heard of the Earth Liberation Front. But the Earth Liberation Front is now becoming quite a name amongst the radical movement, plus an annoyance to the security services. So just what is the ELF?

The ELF was established after the first EF! gathering in Brighton UK, in 1992, as a method in protecting the sabotage side of EF!, and also to protect the surface direct action movement from infiltration similar to what has happened in the US. But more importantly the ELF rose from an inspiration of the A.L.F., plus previous radical revolutionary groups such as Autonom and the Angry Brigade. It was these decentralised, confrontational based movements that to many in the ELF showed the way forward, especially as mainstream environmentalism had failed, and even the EF! approach was limited. It was decided at the gathering that the two groups would publicize each other, with the ELF as the underground wing of EF!.

Sadly, this never really happened, as some sections of the movement were trying to link up with the mainstream, and saw the elves as an embarrassment. Those in the EF! movement who supported the ELF were isolated and frowned upon. Naturally, this didn't stop the ELF, who saw themselves as much more homogenous than EF!, and had originated through a struggle for earth/animal liberation, rather than as a bunch of red-necks ... The ELF philosophy was also totally different, in that it immediately formed a link with animal liberation, something that took EF! ten years to do. In Britain, when EF! had need of person-power on the protest line, they would utilised hunt sabs. The ELF saw a holistic link between earth, animal and human liberation, and focused on issues such as anti-fascism (round River ELF being responsible for targeting green fascist papers such as *Nexus)*, and eco-feminism.

What was important to the ELF was the whole aspect of revolutionary means to overcome the common enemy, multi-nationals and big business. Instead of getting into endless discussions of deep Vs social ecology, it praised revolutionary ecology, which says, "lets hit the bastards with a well organised eco-resistance movement, rather than prating around with intellectual gobblygoop." Underground zines like *Partizan* and the *terra-ist* were produced, that openly printed a "scum directory," causing heavy security to be placed around directors, etc. Some elves, seeing the need for prisoner support, set up the *ELP*, which featured A.L.F. and eco-prisoners. Not content with this,the ELF began travelling the globe, setting up units in europe and elsewhere, doing interviews, pushing the annual earth nights.

Internationalism was vital in taking on the transnationals, playing them at their own gain. One only has to remember the "Send Shell to Hell (SSHA)," a sister groups of ELF, who focused purely on SHell.

The ELF is now active in 10-15 countries, with some daring actions taking place in the Netherlands, Finland, Poland and now Canada and the US. Of course, as said above, we do have a problem with some element of EF! in Britain, the most recent being the Manchester EF!'s "Action Update" to Eco-vegan, which said the ELF never existed and was just a joke. Such scumbags are a disgrace to the movement, and are a joke themselves. Hard work and an activist risking their freedom is forgotten about.

We need solidarity not refusal, the Gandalf 6 - with three *Green Anarchists* going down saw more support from the Animal lib activists then the green movement. It's alright to wear a monkey wrench on your T-Shirt and to shout "no compromise," but if you're not prepared to use it, then what's the point?

An ELF group recently said that the biggest worry for the security services will be when the earth & animal liberation movements get together. Well, they have -- world watch out , 'cause we've got a big planet to save, plus millions of species depending on us. United we can begin to claw back the territory we've lost. With Earth Night just around the corner, we now have the ultimate chance to do that. Lets get serious and use the best weapon we have: "imagination".

There is now a web site sit up where folks can send news etc. (use security at all times) at http.www.fortunecity.com/skyscraper/sterling/58,/index.html, or write <E.L.F@exitemail.com which has prisoner news etc on it.

Earth Liberation Front

Right Lads, who's up for a bit of fun?

NEWS BRIEFS

Finnish activists shot by fur farmer

December 6/97
Orimattila - During what appears to have been an early morning raid against a Finnish fur farm, one woman and four men were shot down by the farm owner. The five were hit by shotgun blasts after alarms alerted the farmer to their presence. One activist remains in hospital, while the remaining four were arrested by police. The farmer, Markku Kuisma, was also arrested.

According to reports, the farmer opened fire without warning. After his initial shot the farmer charged the activists, shooting at least ten more times, hitting several activists in the legs, arms and in the back.

The Finnish activist community was outraged when news of the shooting was released. Over 150 people attended demonstrations in Lathi outside the police station, showing support for the activists. When the demo ended, protesters peacefully rallied outside the farm where the activists were shot.

Finnish animal rights activists have vowed to step up the direct action in the war to end the fur trade.
Contact the Finnish ALF-SG (P.O. box 403,00121 Hki, Finland)

Demo at Huntingdon: rooftop demo & Several arrests

ENGLAND - On Sunday 21 Sept. there was a national Animal Rights Coalition meeting at the protest camp outside Huntingdon Life Sciences. About 100-200 people were present, and took the opportunity to demonstrate to the few workers on the premises.

Although it was a Sunday, a few staff come in to feed the animals, etc. These were delayed from leaving by several hours by crowds blocking the gate, and it was gone 8pm by the time police reinforcements arrived to escort them out.

The Group 4 security guards had been joined by other private security with dogs (from Crimeshield?). An inner perimeter fence has been constructed across the site facing the camp and triple rolls of razor wire have been laid all round the place. Despite all this security, motion sensors on the fence have been repeatedly cut in several places, and three activists managed to scale the fence and gain access to the roof of one of the labs.

They had a banner highlighting Barry's demands. Local press turned up eventually, from the local TV, radio and newspapers. The three people on the roof announced they were on hunger strike for as long as they were up there and as night set in blankets were allowed to be passed up to them.

There were nine arrests outside the gate, mainly for obstructing the police.

Two activists were knocked down by cars speeding from HRC. Ambulances arrived and carted them off to hospital, but not surprisingly the police did nothing.

Later that night there were reports of a home visit to an employee of HRC who got about 20 windows smashed. There were no arrests that we know of.

There have been reports in the local media, TV, radio and papers, generally good coverage.

Swedish Demo Trashes Fur Shops

Stockholm, Sweden - September. Roughly 30 activists gathered in protest against a busload of furscum planning a trip to a huge Swedish fur store in another city. Activists delayed the bus by blocking the road until police arrived. Eventually the bus was able to leave.

Activists met again at noon in the central of Stockholm where two

SIMPLE THINGS YOU CAN DO TO SAVE THE EARTH
ESTABLISH A ZERO GROWTH POLICY FOR THE WORLD'S POPULATION...
HEY BUDDY!.. IF I LOVE KIDS, THATS MY BUSINESS!
DISMANTLE THE MILITARY INDUSTRIAL COMPLEX...
HEY BUDDY! I NEED THIS JOB!!. I GOT A FAMILY TO SUPPORT
NEW FOR 1993 CHILD NAPALM! BABY SHREDDER GRENADES!
END OUR DEPENDENCY ON FOSSIL FUELS...
HEY BUDDY! @*%$ OFF!
RECYCLE YOUR OLD NEWSPAPERS...
SURE IT'S A LITTLE EXTRA WORK, BUT ISN'T OUR PLANET WORTH IT?

demos were planned, one against a fascist organization and the second one against fur shops. Over 100 activist had gathered for the first demo, but the fascists never turned up, so the activists went to a nearby fur store and blocked entrances. Protest chants filled the air as one activist poured red paint over fur coats and leather jackets. Paint bombs rained down on the shop walls and windows. A fur store owner was also covered with paint.

Events escalated quickly and undercover cops started to try and make arrests, starting with an activist in a balaclava and pro-A.L.F. shirt. Attempts were made to "de-arrest" as cops were pushed and beaten, but were unsuccessful. Incredibly, the activist broke free and ran through the streets, but was sadly arrested again.

Over 14 police vehicles arrived, and officers placed themselves between the store and the angry crowd. Two other activists were quickly arrested. As police cordoned off the street, the activists dispersed and headed for another fur store.

The next fur shop targeted was Amores, a large fur retailer that had been targeted in the past. Police were already at the shop when activist arrived, and despite the huge police presence a bottle of red paint flew right through one of the shop windows, covering some very expensive chinchilla coats in red paint.

As activists cheered the broken window police attacked the crowd and arrested at least 24 activists, including one who had only just been released from an arrest at the other demo. Activists were charged with rioting, one for "maltreatment" and one for "criminal damage."

Damages at the two shops were heavy, with the first suffering over 70,000 SKR ($10,000 US) while the second was hit with an estimated 1,000,000 SKR (roughly $150,000 US).

NIEMAN MARCUS EXEC. JAILED FOR ASSAULT ON PROTESTOR

Sept 27/97
Dallas, TX - Police arrested and jailed a top security executive with Nieman Marcus Headquarters for assault and battery after he attacked and choked an anti-fur demonstrator as she was driving away from a protest at the Dallas downtown store.

Activist Lydia Nichols, founder of the Dallas animal rights group Animal Liberation of Texas, was thrown to the ground and her head rammed into the pavement. She was also chocked.

Other Nieman Marcus security personnel joined the fracas, beating J.P. Goodwin, director of the national anti-fur organization Coalition to Abolish the Fur Trade as he attempted to defend Nichols.

Nichols was rushed to Baylor Hospital after she sustained major contusions, and blacked out from the attack. Goodwin was also taken to the hospital for numerous cuts and bruises.

Activist Gets Prison for Illegal Gun Buy

Nov 6/97

SLC, Utah - Jacob Lymon Kenison, an animal rights activist accused of setting a Tandy Leather store on fire was sentenced to 16 months in prison for illegally acquiring an assault rifle.

Jacob was charged in February with one count of aggravated arson for allegedly starting a June 15, 1995, blaze at the Murray store. Damage was estimated at more than $300,000. In March, one month after the arson charge was filed in state court, Kenison bought an assault rifle at Golden Spike Firearms. As part of the transaction, Kenison was asked whether he was facing charges for any crime for which he could be imprisoned for more than one year. Kenison was indicted on a federal count of acquiring a firearm by false statement a month later. He pleaded guilty to the charge in August.

At sentencing, defense attorney Deirdre Gorman asked U.S. Chief District Judge David Sam to consider probation. Kenison bought the gun as a birthday present for a friend, Gorman said. The friend pawned the gun and did not commit any crimes with it. ``It's a situation where there is no harm done," she said.

Kenison faced 10 to 16 months of incarceration under federal sentencing guidelines. Sam ordered Kenison to serve 16 months, noting the teenager has been in custody and has credit for three months. Sam said he would recommend Kenison for a boot-camp program, and ordered 36 months of supervision after his release. Kenison also must serve 100 hours of community service. The state arson case against Kenison is pending.

NEW ZEALAND ACTIVISTS CHARGES DROPPED

Oct 2/97 Auckland, New Zealand - Five activists facing trespass and intimidation charges stemming from a demonstration on the property of Auckland Medical School Dean Dr Peter Gluckman, were happy to hear their charges had been dropped.

Gluckman and his wife refused to appear in court to present evidence, at which point police asked that the matter be adjourned, but were turned down. According to the judge, the case had "already languished for too long in the courts," and the matter proceeded.

Prosecutors were without any primary witnesses and were forced to admit they had no evidence to offer. The trial judge then dismissed all charges against an elated five activists.

McDonald's Arsonist Jailed

Sept/97 SLC, UT - A 19-year-old man who last year helped firebomb a West Jordan McDonald's restaurant to protest the slaughter of cattle, chickens and fish was sentenced to a year in jail. Mark Klein's sentence is similar to two other teens-- Ryan Zacharie Durfee, 20, and Jason Troff, 19-- who were sent to jail in August by other judges for the same arson fire. A fourth defendant, age 17, was given probation by juvenile-court authorities. Prosecutor Ernie Jones had urged 1-to-15-year prison terms to send a strong message to other animal rights activists. Discouraged, Jones said he may file future arson cases in federal court, where the teens could have faced a minimum of 35 years behind bars.

Judge Timothy Hanson said Klein's youth and an absence of any prior criminal record justified probation. And it made a difference that the building was under construction and unoccupied. **See our prisoner listings for addresses to write to!**

Oh, Too Bad! Fur Feed Supplier Burns to Ground

Oct/97 Finland - One of the largest fur feed suppliers in Finland burned to the ground due to an electric malfunction. The damages were estimated at between $5-7 million US.

2 face charges in '96 release of 3,000 minks

October/97 Two men have been charged in connection with releasing minks from two South Jordan farms last year.

In the early morning of July 17, 1996, two people entered the Holt Mink Ranch and released more than 3,000 minks from their cages, according to 3rd District Court charges filed Friday.

The release caused more than $200,000 in damage to the mink farm, the charges state. The loss included damage to fencing, genetic records and a truck motor. Agents from the Salt Lake Area Gang Project and Utah Criminal Investigation Bureau arrested Kevin Dexter Clark, 21, and Clinton Colby Ellerman, 20, hours apart and at different places. Police state the two admitted to police that they were ``involved in the Holt Mink Ranch release and destruction of property," the charges state.

The 20-year-old also admitted that on June 22, 1996, he was involved in another vandalism at the Beckstead Mink Ranch, also in South Jordan. During that incident, the release of minks and vandalism to the farm cost more than $50,000 in damage, the charges state.

Both men have been charged with criminal mischief, a second-degree felony; release of fur-bearing animals, a third-degree felony; and burglary, a third-degree felony.

Police said Ellerman is related to Douglas Joshua Ellerman, 19, who has been charged with the March 11 bombing at the Fur Breeders Agricultural Co-op in Midvale. Six pipe bombs were detonated at the Midvale mink feed plant under trucks, causing about $750,000 damage.

West Haven Fur Arson now at Trial

October 97
OGDEN -- Trev J. Poulson, who is accused of attempted aggravated arson at a West Haven fur company went to trial in October. Prosecution said Poulson gave them a detailed confession for the incident March 19th at the Montgomery Fur Co., 1678 S. 1900 West.

Deputy Weber County Attorney Gary Heward said two accomplices were ready to testify against Poulson. He faces up to 15 years in prison if found guilty.

Agents from the federal Bureau of Alcohol, Tobacco and Firearms joined the Weber County Sheriff's Office in investigating the foiled arson, meant as protest of harvesting animals for fur or meat.

"We're not trying Mr. Poulson on his beliefs," Clark reminded the eight-person jury. "Keep that dear to your heart...this young man is different. He's not normal...he subscribes to an online service for animal rights activists. He is anti-government. He is paranoid about law enforcement. He is paranoid about big bureaucracies. He subscribes to a magazine that accuses the ATF and the FBI of abuses, of planting evidence."

According to the prosecution, Poulson, 19, of Layton, and an alleged accomplice were identified by a security guard at Montgomery Fur, who told police that he watched the two men pour an estimated 25 gallons of gasoline around the base of the building early the morning of March 19.

As the suspects were preparing a one-gallon milk carton to use as a fuse, the night watchman yelled at the two men and they fled in a pickup truck.

Terry Montgomery, the owner of the fur company, testified Thursday about two other "terroristic" incidents at the business. He said he sells hunting and trapping gear, plus "raw furs."

Last November, Montgomery said he went to the office one night to discover the place had been broken into and gasoline had been splashed around the office.

In January 1997, tires were slashed on several vehicles at the fur company. One vehicle had the letters ALF scratched on the body, which Montgomery said he took to stand for "Animal Liberation Front." After that, he said, he hired a security guard.In news reports the ALF took credit for planning the abortive March 19 incident.

Clark said a witness will testify that Poulson was in Logan visiting her at the time of the crime. But Heward said that convicted co-conspirators Cameron M. Kraus, 18, of Centerville, and Bret G. Walton, 18, of Bountiful, will testify against Poulson.

Clashes at animal rally

England- An animal rights protest at a farm that breeds cats for scientific research erupted in angry clashes between demonstrators and police.

Eight people were arrested and several suffered minor injuries as 300 protesters gathered outside Hillgrove Farm near Witney, Oxon. Activists pelted the police with stones and other missiles. Officers, some mounted and many with protective gear and shields, tried to push back the crowd and disperse the demonstrators. About 150 police, backed by a helicopter and dogs, tried to prevent the demonstrators breaking down the farm's perimeter fence but were later accused of using "heavy-handed" tactics. One woman campaigner, who suffered an ankle injury when she fell as the crowd was being pushed back, was taken to hospital. A woman police officer suffered a wrist injury and other demonstrators, including children, sustained cuts as they fell into barbed wire fences.

Hillgrove Farm has been a focal point for animal rights demonstrations following revelations that cats are bred there for medical experiments. Earlier this year, activists broke in and released 14 cats. Thames Valley Police described the incident as "serious" but rejected the suggestion that officers had been heavy-handed and said that every effort had been made to facilitate the protest. A spokesman said: "We fully support people's right to peaceful protest but we cannot stand by and allow people to commit criminal acts." The eight held during the protest were arrested for public order offenses and were in custody at a police station in Oxford.

A spokesman for the protesters said: "The point of the campaign is that Hillgrove breeds cats for vivisection in laboratories and we feel that both lawful campaigning, regular demonstrations and direct action can help close them down."

"We had to let the animals go. No one informed them of their rights when they were arrested."

FOOD FOR THOUGHT

SWEDISH GROUPS CRITICISM RAISES DEBATE ON MINK RELEASES

A recent press release sent to radical animal liberation organizations has sparked off some serious debate over tactics used in mink farm raids. Originating from the Sedish A.L.F.'s (DJURENS BEFRIELSE FRONT) ress officer, Emilie E:son, the release has stirred up plenty of emotion on both sides of the issue. Cutting through all the name calling and back stabbing that all to often accompanies this sort of debate, we've decided to publish Emilie E:son's original release, and the Swedish direct action group The Wild Mink's response. Also accompanying the two letters is some straight forward information provided by the Coalition Against the Fur Trade about mink releases. Back issues of *Underground* contain information on both the history of the DJURENS BEFRIELSE FRONT (issue #3) and expert mink liberation advice (issue #5).

THE RELEASE:

The Swedish ALF
DJURENS BEFRIELSE FRONT
BOX 179
5-265 22 ASTORP
S W E D E N

AN ANIMAL- AND ECOLOGICAL DISASTER

A nameless, unknown group or individual have released eight thousand (8000) minks from two fur farms in Svenljunga, Boras in southern Sweden on Oct 12-13, 1997. Minks are not a natural Swedish animal and to let out 8000 is nothing else than animal abuse and an ecological disaster. Already a lot of the minks has been run over and killed by cars and soon, in a couple of weeks, the minks won't find anything to eat.

According to ALFs/DBFs guidelines "activists must take all necessary precautions against harming any animal, human and non-human"!! The people responsible for these mink releases can not be serious animal-rights activists, but people who doesn't care for animals and who wants to destroy the serious animal rights movement.
The Swedish ALF, DBF who have over 12 years experience in the business have a policy saying :

- not more than 20-25 minks from each fur farm
- only minks with dark fur
- if the fur farm is located close to roads and traffic, bring the minks to safe areas and release them there.

At many occations in Sweden non-ALF/DBF actions has taken place, carried out by people without knowledge nor respect for animals and who cowardly have used ALFs/DBFs name. The Swedish ALF/DBF strongly condemn these kind of actions

Emilie E:son
(Press Officer)

THE REPLY:

DBF-REALLY FRIENDS OF THE ANIMALS?

After the direct action group "The Wild Minks" raided 2 mink farms in Svenljunga, southern Sweden, and released all together about 7-8,000 mink, lots of animal rights groups condemned the actions claiming it caused pain and death for the animals.

We expected it from the legal ones, but not from the DBF, a group similar to the ALF, though they don't use arson. Another difference is that you have to apply to their press officer Emilie E:son to become a "member". Emilie E:son, press officer for the DBF, went out in the media after the attacks, totally condemning the actions.

We, the Wild Minks, do not publicize this to cause in-fighting in the movement, but to open the eyes for many people abroad that have no idea what is happening in Sweden.

Emilie E:son condemned the activists and called them STUPID, UNPROFESSIONAL, AND NOT SERIOUS. She also accused the activists of causing the animals pain and a secure death. She also said if DBF releases animals they only release 20-25 because they can destroy the eco-system.

We ask us the question-what's the point in going to the media and condemning the Wild Minks and not the fur industry? In what way will that help the animals tortured on fur farms? The Wild Minks feel sad about her comments, but really we don't care, WE CARE ABOUT THE ANIMALS, but we feel it necessary to say what she has done, because it is betrayal.

The release of all mink has been criticized a lot, but we will continue because mink can survive in the wild, even though they kill other animals, they will spread, they might kill each other, they will be re-captured. One day in freedom, one day with grass under their paws is much better than a life in a barren cage. On only one of the mink farms in Svenljunga the owner claimed 2 million SEK in damages, 5,000 mink lost and many years of breeding work destroyed.
WAS IT WORTH IT? IT'S UP TO YOU TO DECIDE.
The Wild Minks
Sweden, October 26th, 1997
end-----

MYTHS AND MINK RELEASES: A CLARIFICATION.

by CAFT.

As the Animal Liberation Front, the Wild Minks, and other direct action groups have carried out their campaigns, there has been an element of our movements that has criticized their liberation efforts. Specifically, more conservative groups and "activists" have claimed that liberated mink would somehow pose a threat to the ecosystem that they are released into.

The Coalition Against the Fur Trade is convinced that mink liberations are a good thing. We have studied the works of various mink biologists, and have concluded that mink releases are good for the animals and the earth.

One must be especially glad that these liberations have led to the closing of fur farm death camps which are destroying water systems from the tons and tons of waste that they produce each year.

(Continued on page 12)

MYTHS AND FACTS ABOUT MINK RELEASES

The following will address the most common arguments that the fur industry, and conservative activists, have used to discredit mink liberations on ecological grounds.

Myth: Liberated mink will destroy native wildlife, causing irreparable harm.

Fact: It is interesting that this argument is usually preceded by the claim that the mink will starve to death because they haven't been taught to kill. If this were true and they don't know how to hunt, then they certainly won't be killing any wildlife. The truth is, however, that mink kill out of instinct, much as the domestic cat does. No training or rehabilitation is necessary.

So do liberated mink destroy wildlife? Of course they destroy some wildlife. They are predators, and they help maintain the balance of nature by killing and eating prey animals. But, at the same time, they do not pose a threat to any particular species as a whole. Mink are not specialized predators. Certain predators, like lynx, will have a principal prey that they rely on. Lynx will usually only eat snowshoe hare, otter normally eat fish, etc. On the other hand, the mink have a varried diet.

Examination of mink scat shows that this animal will eat mammals, fish, birds, reptiles, and amphibians. They do not specialize, but rather eat whatever is most readily available. Furthermore, the mink is a very solitary animal. The only time one will see mink together is when they are mating, or in the weeks immediately following their birth, when the mother is still caring for her kits.

When released mink go in search of their own habitat, they will not tolerate the presence of other mink. Mink normally have a range of just under 3 square kilometers. Being so spaced apart it is unrealistic to assume that the mink could have enough of an impact on any particular species to make any noticeable difference at all.

Myth: Because ranch raised mink are often bred for mutant color genes, mink liberations can damage the environment by polluting the wild gene pool.

Fact: The standard mink genes found in wild populations are dominant over most mutant color genes that have been exploited by fur farmers. Studies indicate that these mutant color genes are bred out of existence in just a few short generations.

In England the entire mink population is the offspring of animals that escaped from fur farms. Despite the fact that there were no wild mink to breed with, the recessive mutant color genes have been virtually diminished by the more dominant standard genes that most ranch mink carry. A 1986 study in Devon, England found that only 3% of the mink population was showing any sign of these mutant genes. A similar study in Scotland showed nearly the same results.

Myth: Mink in England have decimated the otter and the water vole.

Fact: Sadly, the mink became the scapegoat for the decline of the otter. Otter populations were decimated by pesticides and hunting. In recent years the otter has made a comeback, and examination of their scats has shown that contrary to claims made by mink hunters and the fur trade, otter actually kill and eat mink. Mink do not kill otters.

The water vole is another species whose numbers have been decimated by man, yet we continue to blame the mink for their problems. Studies show that in areas with the water vole, this animal still only accounts for about 2% of the minks diet. It is doubtful that feral mink could have any noticeable impact on the number of water voles when they are not in any way a principal source of food for mink.

Those are the most common anti liberation arguments used by those that would rather see predators confined to cages, instead of out in the wild, serving the purpose nature intended. There have been 35 fur farm raids in North America, in a time span of 2 years. Approximately 75,000 fur farm prisoners have been released into the wild. If any of these arguments had any merit, then why aren't we seeing some evidence in areas were mink have been released? This doesn't have to be a hypothetical argument based on interpretations of scientific literature Mink have been released in large numbers, so where is the damage? The fact is, there hasn't been any.

We know that the mink have survived. One chicken farmer wrote a letter to a Utah newspaper complaining that a mink released from a farm months before had eaten some of his chickens. And yet, we aren't seeing this ecological damage the fur trade has predicted.

In many ways the ALF has done the earth a favor by raiding these farms. In addition to stopping the mass accumulation of animal wastes by shutting these places down, they have re-introduced mink to areas where they had been nearly wiped out. For example, the ALF freed 400 mink from a fur farm in Sheboygan, WI. At roughly the same time there was concern about the lack of mink along the Sheboygan River.

It is estimated that as few as 150 lynx may still exist in Montana, yet the state still allows a trapping season. Montana is the home of several lynx fur farms, and there could very well be more lynx in captivity than in the wild.

The lynx is only a few short generations out of the wild, and even the Forest Service has considered using ranch lynx for reintroduction (see Lynx, Wolverine, and Fisher in the Western United States, Research Assessment and Agenda by John Weaver, 1993). Imagine what direct action groups could do without all of the red tape and bureaucracy.

The Coalition to Abolish the Fur Trade has always supported the release of fur animals, and always will. Direct action groups have sent us anonymous communiques which we have publicized, so as to generate attention on fur animal death camps. We will always be willing to act as the spokesgroup for those that risk their freedom for the benefit of others.

In the meantime, please use the evidence presented here to show people that the fur industry, and conservative activists, lie when they claim mink liberations are a bad thing.
Until the last cage is empty,
Coalition to Abolish the Fur Trade
PO Box 822411 Dallas, TX 75382
MINKLIB@aol.com

GANDALF TRIAL CONCLUDED

Portsmouth Crown Court: Judge David Selwood, 66, finished his four-day summing-up in the case of Steve Booth, 38, Simon Russell, 33, Sax Wood, 24, and Noel Molland, 24 on November 11. The four have been on trial since 26th August 1997 for editing *Green Anarchist* and the *Animal Liberation Front Supporters Group Newsletter* (hence GA-aND-ALF), a supposed conspiracy to incite criminal damage. The jury returned the next day with their verdict, finding Booth, Wood and Molland guilty of "being part of a conspiracy to incite criminal damage." Noel Molland's publication *Eco-Vegan*, which also lists animal/earth direct actions, was said to encourage others to carry out similar actions. The three were sentenced to serve three years in jail.

Simon Russell, the former editor of the ALFSG UK newsletter, was happily found not guilty and was released.

The Gandalf trial went on twice as long as it should have. Defence solicitor Tim Greene estimates it has so far cost 2 million pounds. The two year long Operation Washington that preceded it cost 2 million more and involved 60 cops at its height. When the defendants were all finally arrested on 20th January 1997, Limington and Lyndhurst police stations were set aside exclusively to process them. At one stage Sgt. Gunner, one of the Operation Washington team, was sent on an all- expenses paid 'fact finding' trip to Italy. Operation Washington may also have cost the life of kidnapped French student Celine Figar, as Hampshire police (who should have been searching for her) were instead seizing alternative newspapers from bookshops and homes. The Gandalf Defendants Campaign consider the 4 million pounds spent a gross waste of public resources: it would have been cheaper for the cops to buy up *Green Anarchist* at 1,000 pounds a copy!

By convicting three of the defendants, basic freedoms of expression, association and conscience have undermined by this case. If people can't report direct action news or express opinions, receive unsolicited phone calls, write innocent letters or attend rallies with thousands of others without risking imprisonment, England is no longer a democracy. Much has been made of 'how to' advice defendants are accused of publishing but this is a smokescreen. The vast majority of the 6,000 pages of evidence discussed in the Gandalf trial were just political opinions that the State wishes to criminalise.

What also became apparent during the trial was the prosecution's hit-list hierarchy, revealing who they wanted to jail most. As was no surprise to anyone, Robin Webb was their number one target. The general Editor of Green Anarchist was second, and Noel Molland, who compiled diary of actions and sold Black Widow slingshots to activist in Europe was third. The two folks involved with the distribution and mail order side of *Green Anarchist* were four and five, while the former editor of the ALFSG Newsletter was in sixth place.

JUDGE SELWOOD

Judge Selwood agreed originally to exclude jurors with a military background 'to ensure a fair trial'. Not only did he fail to do this -- one juror served 17 years in the Royal Navy, while another's father was an RAF cop -- but he holds the rank of major general himself, having served all but the last five years of his career officiating over military courts with NATO. Selwood also failed to exclude a juror who said he knew the victim of an A.L.F. attack on a dairy in Fareham who's statement was in evidence! During half-time legal arguments, Selwood refused to listen to defence submissions. Sax Wood's barrister, Steve Kamlish had to threaten to refuse to present further evidence and go straight to appeal to get Selwood to even give reasons why his arguments were being unheeded! The reason given was that "he thought the defendants guilty." He then went on to indirectly tell the jury that one defendant, Sax Wood, was guilty. Consequently, the defence team have denounced the Gandalf trial as a 'travesty' and 'farce.'

During the first afternoon of his summing up, judge Selwood was clearly drunk. Even sober, he was unable to remember the names of defendants he's spent the last three months in the same courtroom with, referring to 'Saxon Webb', 'Saxon Booth', 'Simon Robin' and 'Simon Rogers' and calling the publication at the centre of this prosecution '*Green Activist*.' He was similarly confused as to evidence, attributing publications to defendants who hadn't written them until even prosecutor Dick OnSlow had to intervene and set Selwood straight. The judge had clearly acted as a second prosecutor throughout the trial, drawing the jury's attention to stuff OnSlow has missed, but his summing-up even included reference to arguments and evidence he'd previously ruled inadmissible!

DARREN THURSTON

Anyone doubting this is apolitical prosecution should check out the case of Simon Russell's witness, Darren Thurston. Simon was accused of the 'crime' of putting a report about Justice Department activities on the Internet. In fact, North American A.L.F.S.G member, Darren Thurston, did. The court agreed legal aid to fly him in from Vancouver, Canada, and he was due to arrive 10th October 1997. On arrival at Heathrow, Darren was immediately deported as an undesirable alien on advice from the Royal Canadian Mounted Police (RCMP) that he had firearm charges outstanding against him.

Not only was the RCMP's allegation untrue, it should have been no reason to bar him from the UK as a visitor, let alone as a witness in an important trial. The involvement of the RCMP, a foreign security service, shows the lengths the State went to twist the trial to secure a conviction.

THE PRESS

Given that the Gandalf case will have profound implications for the freedom of the press in the UK, the reaction of the media deserves particular mention here.

The solidarity shown by the alternative press has been marvellous. The majority of animal liberation publications have affiliated to the Gandalf Defendants Campaign, all publications distributed by INK have agreed to a motion in support of the defendants and over 100 publications and individuals (including four college professors) have signed an Alternative Media solidarity statement. They realize that any restriction of free expression that applies to Green Anarchist will also apply to them.

The mainstream media's reaction, by contrast, has been almost universally disgraceful. The silent collaboration with Special Branch's attempt to stifle free press is clear. Green Anarchist is on trial for carrying the direct action news that they wouldn't. The timid conformity of the mainstream media is epitomised by Portsmouth News reporter Graham Keeley, who appeared to be wholly at the beck-and-call of the state. Coming to court only when invited by OnSlow, and talking only to the police, Keeley refused to correct even the simplest errors in his pro-prosecution propaganda despite repeated requests to do so.

STILL TO COME

It now turns out that Robin Webb, will have his case put back to trial, for much of the same charges as the other defendants faced. Expect his trial to begin sometime in the new year, possibly at the same time Paul Rogers, Green Anarchist's general editor, goes back to court. Rogers was severed from the Gandalf trial when his barrister Ken McDonald resigned.

For addresses of the three defendants convicted through this farce, please refer to our prisoner section at the back of the magazine.

DIARY OF ACTIONS

CANADA

NOV 24/97: Montreal, QU - Four bombs exploded at buildings owned by the company that invented a popular anti-AIDS drug. No Injuries were reported and damage was minor. Two bombs rocked the headquarters of BioChem Pharma Inc. in Laval, just north of Montreal, and two more blasts went off at the company's plant in Montreal. The bombs exploded within a 70 minutes of each other. Police defused two other bombs at the headquarters building. The blasts there were preceded by a telephone warning but authorities provided no details. Spokespeople confirmed that the company conducts tests on animals. A further bomb threat was called in to the pharmaceutical plant the next morning and the plant was evacuated by police, but no further devices were found. There was also speculation that AIDS activists might have been responsible, as a way of protesting the high cost of AIDS/HIV medication. CTV News reports later stated that Laval police state they believe the Animal Liberation Front was responsible for the four bombs. Police said an anonymous call had been placed to a Quebec newspaper, claiming the bombs were planted by members of the A.L.F.'s Quebec cell. The bombs were of a high-explosive type usually used in mining operations. The name of the manufacturers was found on the two devices defused by police. The manufacturers say they have checked their inventory and have not found any explosives missing.

Quebec police are probing a possible link between these explosions two bombings in Alberta, in which one blast destroyed $5 million worth of equipment at a logging camp a week earlier. The other, a month earlier, damaged the concrete base of a public waterslide, leading Calgary police to believe the bomber "was practising." The RCMP in Alberta are working on the assumption that "eco-terrorists" destroyed logging machines at the Water Valley timber project, 90 kilometres northwest of Calgary. Police said, "the conclusion 90 per cent of us would make" is that 'tree huggers' planted the bombs."

UNITED STATES

JUNE/97: Indianapolis, IN - Picking a warm summer evening the A.L.F. toured the city defiling some of the biggest oppressors in the nation--fast food restaurants. Windows were broken in eight or nine different fast food restaurants this fine night. The restaurants included two McDonald's (with nice, large plate glass windows with the big "M"), a Wendy's, Kentucky Fried Chicken, Dairy Queen, Hardy's, Burger King, and an Arby's. From the communique: *"While many times more significant targets can be found, fast food restaurants will be aware that, as some of the largest abusers of the animals and the earth, they will not escape the tide of action against oppression.* ANIMAL LIBERATION"

JULY 16/97: West Palm Beach, FL - locks glued at the Revillion and Valentino boutiques. -A.L.F.

AUGUST 19/97: Fort Collins, CO - the premises of Wildlife Pharmaceuticals Suite 600, 1401 Duff Dr., Fort Collins, CO 80524 (970) 484-6267 was raided. After holes were drilled and incendiary attack was made. Unfortunately only minimum damage was sustained.Wildlife Pharmaceuticals is the solitary manufacturer of Prime-X melatonin implants for the fur farm industry in North America. The implants are used by mink and fox farmers to unnaturally speed up the fur growth process allowing the animals to be killed 4-6 weeks earlier. Pounding the final nails into the fur industry. Animal Liberation Front

SEPT/97: Washington, D.C. - The A.L.F. struck Andriana Furs in Northwest Washington, in which etching-cream-filled lightbulb "bombs" exploded on two of the store's display windows. In an attempt to cover up the huge splotches (right at head-level of the mannequins) without replacing the windows, the fur store decided to put up an autumn-leaf-collage-type window display, plastering several leaves on top of each other over the etching cream, in the center of the two windows that had been hit. Needless to say, the cover up job looked--and still looks--ridiculous. As well, "FUR HURTS" was etched in big, thick, beautiful letters in a second hit. Again, Andriana's tried to cover the message with a few leaves, but the words are still very visible.

SEPT 7/97: Hollywood, FL - locks glued at Jordan's furs for the second time this summer. -A.L.F

SEPT 7/97: Pompano Beach, FL - locks glued at the International Game Fish Association (IGFA) headquarters. -A.L.F

SEPT 12/97: Oviedo, FL - Boys Town research centre hit by activists. Damage inflicted included a resident passenger van (all 4 locks glued, body paint-stripped, all tires slashed, slogans painted, engine monkey-wrenched). The facility was also hit and had 3 windows shattered by a sledgehammer, as was the front door. The A.L.F. warned, "Actions will escalate as long as kittens die at Boys Town. Time for the killer$ to pay. -A.L.F.

SEPT 20/97: Anderson, IN - On the early morning the A.L.F. raided Adam's Fox Farm. Unknown number of animals released.

Upon reaching the house of the fur farmer, the liberators snook around the property hiking through a field. It was necessary to cut one of three fences in between the clearing and the actual cages. After cutting the first barbed wire fence, and trekking through the thick woods for some time, another barbed wire fence faced the A.L.F., which were easily cut in various places with large wire cutters and peeled back.

Upon reaching the cages, another fence, about two to three feet tall was encountered which was stomped to the ground almost in it entirety to allow the fox escape to freedom. Several cages were empty, but there were eight full rows of twenty cages found. From the communique: *"Each cage had one or two fox in imprisoned within. The cages were about fix feet long mesh wire with wooden boxes on the end with metal tops on them that merely had to be pulled off or pushed up to allow the fox to jump out. The fox never made a sound once we began opening cages. They were all quite timid, and most would look at the liberator for a second before turning its back until we were safely out of their sight. As we opened the cages very few were jumping out immediately, but as they are quite timid creatures, they began to jump out as we were leaving."* About 200 fox were liberated that night.

SEPT 23/97:Hillsborough, NJ- Milk billboard on Rt. 206 vandalized with slogans "Animal Liberation", "Milk = Pain", and "Stop Hurting Cows". -A.L.F.

SEPT 24/97: Bridgewater, NJ - Hind and Fore Quality Meats and Seafood on Rt. 28 has one of its two front windows broken, and "Meat is Dead" spray painted on its back wall. -A.L.F.

Late SEPT/97 Rockville, Maryland - Two bottles of fox urine were opened and the contents were poured onto the carpets and merchandise of a Sports Authority store.The urine, collected on fur farms, is sold by the national retailer for use by hunt scum attempting to cover their foul odour while out killing innocent animals. From the communique: *"The urine has quite a smell and sends customers running for the door. Activists are urged to visit their local Sports Authority and open a bottle in memory of the animals killed fro their fur and urine."*

OCT 2/97: Oviedo, FL - The local branch of BOYS TOWN (research facility) windows were broken and 'A.L.F.' was spraypianted along with the warning "NEXT TIME THERE WILL BE FIRE."

OCT 5/97: McHenry County, IL - 5000 mink released by activists on a raid against fur farmer Larry Frye [Frye Fur Farm, 2222 Benham Rd., Crystal Lake, IL 60014-2632 (815-455-4862)]. Roughly 5000 of Frye's mink escaped after the A.L.F. cut through chicken wire and opened pen doors early Sunday morning. Industry experts say Frye's losses could reach $800,000 because the activists also stole all the farm's pedigree records. Without the pedigree records, Frye cannot verify the lineage and quality of his mink. Some are of such "high quality" that a single pelt can sell for $1,000. According to the papers, Frye was quoted as saying: "I don't know if we'll be able to go on. It takes years to breed in the best qualities. I'm sure I'm going to lose breeder sales for at least the next three years. I recently sold four males for $10,000. Now I'll be lucky to get $100 for an animal." Frye is a member of the Illinois Mink Breeders Association Board of Directors. From the communique: *"The farm has approximately 40 sheds. Surrounding the concentration camp was a chicken wire fence 4 feet high. Attached to the top of the fence were strips of sheet metal suspected to deter mink from climbing over or to make noise if any unwanted guests attempted to climb over. Above the fence was one electrical wire. For unknown reasons there was no electrical current running through it. We were prevented from rolling the fence up because it was buried in the ground at the bottom. Instead we cut holes 2 feet high and 15 feet or more across in 3 sections. The chicken wire was folded down along the ground so as to allow the mink to run away. We cleared 8 regular stock breeding sheds each containing 400 cages with measurements 18" x 12" x 6" (l x h x w). The wooden nesting boxes were lifted from each cage. The mink would climb out if not already in the boxes when lifted out. 5 sheds with breeding stock mink were cleared along with the breeding stock of 3 sheds filled half with regular stock and half with breeding stock. Each full shed contained 200 cages each measuring 18" x 12" x 12" (l x h x w). Some cages confined two mink in each. The nesting boxes were unattached from the front leaving an exposed opening for the animals to jump out of. The breeding cards in each cleared shed were torn from the beams above the cages and thrown mixed together in the excrement below the cages. Cables to a tractor were cut, the electrical system's wires slashed, and the water pumping system sabotaged. An estimated 5,000 mink were liberated. Stores will be attacked and farms raided until the whole industry is destroyed and all animals are free. Millions of animals are slaughtered each year at the hands of the fur industry and by their support from callous and selfish humans. This is the season of blood. Fur farmers and animal murderers beware! THE ANIMAL LIBERATION FRONT VISITS YOU NEXT!"*

OCT 6/97: Preston, ID - The A.L.F. paid a visit to an Idaho mink and fox farm where thousands of breeding cards were removed from both mink and fox cages. Next, the cages were opened and nesting boxes removed. From the communique: *"The mink quickly climbed out of their prison cells, jumped to the earth, and excitedly ran through the fields, enjoying their first taste of freedom, ever. The foxes, being much more shy and cautious (and a bit neurotic after spending their entire existence in small, filthy cages) did not exit their cages as anxiously as the mink. Nevertheless, we did witness a handful of foxes leave their cages and one sprint away from the farm, never slowing down or looking back! A water pipe in one of the sheds was also broken."* -A.L.F.

OCT 7/97: Downers Grove, WI - activists released 4,000 minks from the Charlie Ide Fur Farm.

OCT 17/97: Watertown SD - activists struck mink farms in Iowa and South Dakota, releasing a 5000 mink in one action and a further 4000 in the second.

OCT 18/97: Bridgewater, NJ - Hind and Fore Quality Meats and Seafood hit a second time. The words "Meat is Murder" spraypainted on the back wall, along with "A.L.F." in numerous spots once with "Ed", the death shop owner's name). Both front windows broken. -A.L.F.

OCT 19/97: Elizabeth, NJ - Three leather couches, valued at $2000 a piece, were slashed in an IKEA furniture store. -A.L.F.

OCT 24/97: East Millstone, NJ - Huntington Life Sciences had two spotlights smashed, and a window broken on its medical building. -A.L.F.

OCT 25/97: Bridgewater, NJ - Hind and Fore Quality Meats and Seafood has one front window damaged, but not broken. On this third attack of the meat market, it is noted that the invested in thicker glass, and 5 or 6 spotlights in a weak attempt to protect his area. -A.L.F.

OCT 26/97: Medford, WI -Three raids against mink farms took place over the weekend with approximately 800 mink released from the Smieha fur farm in Independance, and more than 300 from a second mink ranch near Tomahawk. Over 3000 mink were freed from the Jack Dittrich farm.

OCT 29/97: Hebo, OR - The A.L.F. has claimed credit for a raid that led to freedom for 6 rabbits that were being held at a former mink farm. The group claimed that the mink farm was closed down, but that the owner seemed to be getting into the rabbit fur and meat business.

OCT 31/97: Berkeley, CA - Nearly 30 activists dressed as A.L.F. members payed a late night visit to a UCB vivisector. A tire jack from his garage was applied to the lights of his sports car.

NOV 5/97: NJ - Marianne Fur in Highland Park had a rock with "A.L.F." painted on it thrown through its front window. -A.L.F.

NOV 5/97: Ft. Wayne, IN - In the early morning hours of Wednesday, November 5th, the A.L.F. raided the Lair Fox Farm on Shoaff Rd. (owner Blaine Leffers). From the communique: *"As we approached the farm we noticed a bright flashing light and heard loud music blasting from a radio. This was an obviously weak attempt to deter liberators from breaking in and setting the prisoners free. The cover of the loud noise from the radio allowed us to cut two 8 foot long and 3 foot high holes in the surrounding fence. Once inside, we opened the cages. A total of 125 foxes were liberated. "Free the Enslaved-ALF" was painted on a wall. All of this was accomplished in full view of a security camera on a nearby barn. As we left, we saw many of these bluish-silver foxes run to freedom. -A.L.F."*

NOV 5/97: Highland Park, NJ - Marianne's Furs on Woodbridge Ave. had 2 windows broken with two rocks. The rocks had "ALF" written on them, along with "Fur is Dead", and "Stop or be Stopped". -A.L.F.

NOV 5/97: Bridgewater, NJ - Hind and Fore Quality Meats and Seafood had its front window broken with rocks exclaiming "ALF", "Meat is Dead", and "Animal Liberation". -A.L.F

NOV 8/97: Metuchen, NJ - Lowey Designer Furs has two front display windows, and a glass door broken. - A.L.F

NOV 8/97: Hillsborough, NJ - McDeath's on Rt. 206 has it's drive through speakers broken. -A.L.F.

NOV 8/97: Flemington, NJ - McDeath's on Rt. 202 has

it's drive thru speaker broken, and glass broken on the drive thru menu. -A.L.F.

NOV 25/97: Mission Bay, CA -activists with spray paint and marker pens did more than $5,000 damage to signs and buildings at Sea World. Police believe the vandalism occurred sometime between midnight and 2 a.m., said San Diego police spokesman Bill Robinson. He said the graffiti referred to the capture of animals for display at the park. Police had no suspects.

NOV 29/97: Portland, OR - The Animal Liberation Front (A.L.F.) and the Earth Liberation Front (E.L.F.) claimed responsibility for the release of 500 wild horses and a fire that destroyed a BLM corral on November 29 near the town of Burns, Oregon. This latest action was designed "to help halt the BLM's illegal and immoral business of rounding up wild horses from public lands and funnelling them to slaughter." From the communique: *"The Bureau of Land Management (BLM) claims they are removing non-native species from public lands (aren't white Europeans also non-native) but then they turn around and subsidize the cattle industry and place thousands of non-native domestic cattle on these same lands. This hypocrisy and genocide against the horse nation will not go unchallenged! The practice of rounding up and auctioning wild horses must be stopped. The practice of grazing cattle on public lands must be stopped. The time to take action is now. From an investigation like the Associated Press' to writing the BLM to an action like ours, you can help stop the horse slaughter and save our Mother Earth,"* said both the A.L.F. & ELF.

ENGLAND

APRIL/97: Warwickshire - Activists attacked a Midland livestock transport firm and caused over 20,000 pounds damage. Spiers Haulage had an HGV tractor unit destroyed, and a device attached to another vehicle went off while fire crews were at the scene. Two further bombs were defused by army bomb disposal experts. Activists have threatened to launch a firebomb blitz across the UK. -A.L.F.

APRIL 9-11/97: Exeter - Exeter University hosted a vivisectors conference, but every night the Science Dept was visited and had windows smashed, as was the sleeping quarters of the vivisectors. The conference also was bomb hoaxed on the last day.

APRIL 28/97: Oxfordshire - Windows smashed at OLAC, a lab animal breeders.

MAY/97: Banbury - badger baiters were beaten up outside the magistrates when they came out of court following their first hearing.

MAY/97: Dorchester - the Dorset Meat Co. was visited by activists and had 1,300 pounds worth of windows smashed. The owner told media, "I moved down from London four years ago to get away from all that vandalism -- now look what happened."

MAY/97: Isleworth - The A.L.F. visited Spreo Pets painting the front of the shop and leaving a threatening letter, telling the owner to get out of the business of selling animals.

MAY 29/97: Stukely Meadow - Eight guinea pigs, all heavily pregnant were liberated from Interfauna. This was the first raid on this particular site. The raid took place in broad daylight, when activists took advantage of the fact that decorators were in and had left the doors open.

JUNE/97: McDonald's all over the UK had windows smashed, locks glued and toilets blocked up following the verdict of the McLibel case.

JUNE 10/97: all the windows at the home of Hobbs, a director of Consort, smashed.

JULY/97: Stevenage - Animal rights activists walked through the main gates of GlaxoWellcome, a research facility, barricaded themselves in an office and accessed computer files for over two hours before being discovered. The two activists were seeking evidence of animal testing. Sledgehammers were needed to break down the door, as the pair had piled furniture against it, refusing to come out. They were eventually arrested on suspicion of criminal damage.

JULY/97: Activists happened upon a trailer full of fully grown chicks, parked beside the entrance to a batter unit. In the few minutes the driver was gone, 47 chicks were liberated and are now safe and sound, happy and free.

JULY/97: 150 hens liberated from Leyton St. Slaughterhouse.

AUGUST 16/97: Oxford - The Animal Liberation Front claimed responsibility for several weekend attacks on the homes of five notorious Oxford University animal torturerers. In a statement to the press, the activists said they were "trying to draw attention to a fellow activist, Barry Horne," who was on hunger strike in jail at the time. The vivisectors, including Colin Blakemore, had their homes and vehicles redecorated with slogans and paint-stripper, locks glued and tires slashed, causing thousands of pounds worth of damage. An A.L.F. spokesperson warned, "The severity of actions can be escalated." In a bizarre twist Colin Blakemore later offered the A.L.F. a "place at the negotiating table", a euphemism for the whitewash which passes as the Scientific Procedures Committee. -A.L.F.

AUGUST/97: E. Sussex - 200 battery hens liberated from a unit in Polegate.

SEPT 8/97: Huntingdon - One of the Huntingdon Research Centre employees in court on cruelty charges had his car redecorated by A.L.F. activists. Andrew J Mash, 4 Grainger Ave, Godmanchester, Huntingdon, Cambs, who was filmed last year by an undercover investigator shaking and hitting beagle dogs undergoing experiments, had blue paint poured all over his car. At a later date his house was attacked by activists who used bricks and iron bars to smash every window. In what appears to have been a sustained attack, reinforced doors prevented entry to the property. Mash and four or five 'friends' inside the house who had armed themselves with various implements to ward off a beating. Apparently on leaving, activists warned Mash that they would return before too long to ensure he "receives real justice for his crimes."

SEPT 22/97: Labour Party HQ bomb hoaxed because of government unwillingness to implement animal welfare policies. -A.L.F.

OCT 27/97: WH Smith HQ bomb hoaxed again as they sell bloodsport magazines. WH Smith have now had 25 known bomb hoaxes. -A.L.F.

OCT 27/97: John Lewis HQ bomb hoaxed since they own a shooting estate where their directors and guests shoot hundreds of animals every year. [John Lewis is a newsagents chain in the UK]. -A.L.F

OCT 27/97: The HQ of Sainsbury's supermarket was bomb hoaxed because they sell ostrich meat. The campaign against supermarkets selling "exotic meats" has recently had good results, as Tesco stopped selling ostrich and kangaroo meat recently. Somerfield supermarkets announced they were also dropping plans to sell crocodile meat as well. -A.L.F.

SWEDEN

Following fur farms has closed down during 1997:

Uggelsta Fur farm, Uppsala * Vimmerby fox farm, Oskarshamn * Kristdala Fox farm, Oskarshamn * Madsens Fur farm, Alvangen * Mink farm, Habo * Nordic Fur farm, Perners

Closed down fur stores 1997:
Pals-Bruno, Lulea * Polar Pals, Hokarngen * Goran Korsnar, Dstersund * Orion Furs, Stockholm * Palsbutik, Halmstad

SEPT/97: Stockholm - After a fur farm raid, several fur store owners went out in media to the media to complain about the trouble the A.L.F. has caused during the last year. Here follows some quotes taken from CNN Sweden: "The vegans vandalism has increased. To our store I estimate that they have vandalized for over 1 million skr all together. The insurance companies do no longer want us as customers..." - Fur store owner, Stockholm.

"This year they have smashed my windows 8 times. Every time it costs me 10,000 SKR. Soon I can't take it anymore...."
- Another fur store owner in Stockholm

"They(The insurance companies) don't want to do business with us anymore. The vegans cost to much!" Surprise, a fur store owner, Stockholm

SEPT/97: Karlstad - A sustained A.L.F. campaign against a meat company was successful in completely closing it down. Activists hit the company four times smashing windows, gluing locks and painting slogans. Owners of the company refused to comment to the media for fear "of reprisal."

SEPT/97: Ume - A vivisection company called Biopol got their windows smashed and animal liberation slogans were spraypainted. The action was dedicated to Barry Horne.

SEPT 9/97: Overhornas --A fur farm in the north of Sweden was raided by the A.L.F., with over 30 foxes liberated before several vehicles arrived and interrupted the raid. The activists fled through the forrest, to their nearby parked car, and drove away. No arrests. The same farm had been raided around a month ago. -A.L.F.

SEPT 18/97: Vingaker - Kasta fox farm raided and several foxes released. -Wild Mink

SEPT 30/97: Alunda - During a day light raid on Monday 29, Sept. the direct action group 'The Wild Minks' raided another fox farm. Tranbyns Fur Farm in Alunda, was raided in the past by the Swedish A.L.F. at which time they found six foxes, releasing two of them (Red Foxes) into the wild. On this visit the activists found five foxes (one red and four silver), possibly the same four silver foxes seen on the previous raid, with one red recaptured. Two of the silver foxes had missing tails. All five foxes were liberated by the activists and carried out from the farm and released into the nearby forest. This farm looks like it was closing down and cages had been taken down by the farmer.

OCT 6/97: Vingaker - The direct action group, The Wild Minks, hit a fur farm, for the second time. Kasta fox farm had been raided previously on Sept 18. This time the activists were determined to free all the foxes. This farm is a breeding farm that breeds foxes and sells breeding foxes to other fox farms throughout Sweden, so it was chosen as a good target. When we entered the farm we were happy to see that the animals released last time had not been recaptured. The remaining 13 foxes (mostly red and silver, some arctic marble) were carried out from the farm and released into the woods where they quickly disappeared to a new life- a life of freedom, free from abuse. Every year 20,000 foxes are killed for fur in Sweden. We will continue to fight the evil fur trade until it is gone, whatever means necessary... SMASH THE FUR TRADE. The Wild Minks

OCT 11/97: Karlstad - A new opened butcher shop and a skin-store gets it windows smashed and slogans painted.

OCT 12/97: Karlstad - The same butcher shop is attacked again. Activists empty two spraycans on the store. They sent out an communique, which was covered by local papers and tv.

OCT 13/97: Svenljunga - Hulan mink farm was raided and holes were cut in the fence surrounding the farm and all the gates left open. Activists opened the cages and freed about 4,000 minks (media and farmer claim 5-6,000). The mink quickly made their escape. Breeding cards and some mink traps were destroyed as well. -Wild Mink

OCT 13/97: Svenljunga - Bloms mink farm also raided. The farm had both polecats and mink. The fence was cut down and activists opened the cages for 2,000 mink. Breeding cards destroyed. -Wild Mink

OCT 14/97: Fargelanda - Bjorkebo mink farm was the next farm to get a visit from the Wild Minks. This farm has 14,000 mink captive and about 1,000 of them were released.

OCT 18/97: Karlstad - A meat company was hit again by activists: slogans painted and several big windows smashed. And the crushed glass flew into the machines so they was damaged! The company's boss said this to local media: "This can mean the death for our company!" The same night a hunting-firm had windows smashed and slogans painted: "For all the dead elks"

OCT 21/97:Falun - the Wild Minks attacks mink farm - 200 free. Hemmingsbo mink farm had the surrounding fence and cages trashed. According to local media the farm owner lost his newly bought breeding animals, which makes this raid even more expensive.

OCT 21/97: Hofors - Sweden's biggest fur farm was attacked. Activists cut several holes in the surrounding fence before they entered this massive concentration-camp, with over 11,000 foxes imprisoned within. The activists destroyed the skinning-machine, a tanner-machine, all the interiors, dressing room and the employees personal stuff/lockers, and poured oil over the clothes, floors and ceiling. Then the activists started to carry out blue-foxes. After around 25 blue-foxes had been carried out a car came up and stopped around 5 metres from the activists. The activists were able to escape to safety and no one was arrested. On the farm the activists found corpses of dead animals, victims of cannibalism. An unworthy death after an unworthy life.

OCT 13/97: Ullunda - 13 rabbits saved from vivisection by the newly founded group Djurrattsmilisen (Animal Rights Militia) from a vivisection breeder in Enkping (Gunnar Hagdahl, Ullunda 5462, 199 91 Enkping, Sweden). The activists broke into one building where they found 40 rabbits. They were able to take 13 with them and placed them in loving homes. The Breeding records of the rest of the rabbits were also stolen. "Djurrattsmilisen" was spraypainted on the building. Gunnar Hagdahl has bred animals destined for animal testing since the early '80s.

Nov 18/97: Eskilstuna - DE VILDA MINKARNA (The Wild Minks) raided Kungsor mink farm in Eskilstuna. This farm was attacked previously in May when 70 breeding males were released and all breeding cards stolen and slogans sprayed. This time, 7 holes was cut in the fence and the activists released well over 1000 minks. -Wild Mink

FINLAND

APRIL/97: Lappeenranta - 11 containers belonging to the largest milk producer, Valio, sloganized. -EVR

APRIL/97: Tampere - Fur store has a window smashed.

APRIL/97: Lappeenranta - Fur store has window smashed and slogans spraypainted. -EVR

APRIL/97: Helsinki - Fur shop has windows smashed.

MAY/97: Tampere - Fur shop has two windows smashed, another fur store and a leather shop each lose a window.

MAY/97: Varkaus - Two hunting towers destroyed.

MAY/97: Tampere - ad signs for McDonalds is destroyed. -ELF

MAY/97: Helsinki - several fur shops have windows smashed.

JUNE/97: Tuuslua - a hunting tower is destroyed.

JUNE/97: Tampere - A digger was sabotaged. -ELF

JUNE/97: Tuusula - Five hunting platforms were wrecked.

JUNE/97: Hameenlinna - A fur store has its walls sloganized. -EVR

JUNE/97: Lappeenranta - two fur shops have windows smashed. EVR

JUNE/97: Mellila - several tires of slaughterhouse vehicles got
slashed.

JUNE/97: Pieksamaki - 9 hunting platforms destroyed.

JUNE/97: Hameenlinna - meat processors truck sabotaged and slogans spraypainted.

JUNE/97: Lappeenranta - Slaughterhouse was attacked: windows smashed, slogans spraypainted and two vehicles damaged. -EVR

JUNE/97: Ylojarvi - Six hunting platforms destroyed.

JULY/97: Vihti - Fur farm raided and 300 breeding cards taken. 50 mink were released. -EVR

JULY/97: Helsinki - A huge fur store lost one of it's windows.

AUGUST/97: Vihti - Second raid a fur farm, and over 100 mink cages opened.

AUGUST/97: Karttula - One beagle rescued from a vivisection breeding house.

AUGUST/97: Pohja - Shell station sabotaged. Also painted was a Shell ad and a Meat advertisement. -ELF

AUGUST/97: Parkano - about 500 mink set free from a fur farm. An estimated 6000 breeding cards were destroyed.

AUGUST/97: Helsinki - a road construction machine loses windows. -ELF

AUGUST/97: Orimattila - About 50 fox cages opened in a fur farm (raided twice in the last year). Activist fled when owner Markku Kuisma woke up. (The same owner who has shot several activists in December '97)

AUGUST/97: Lahti - Jarvenpaa road construction site has road survey sticks removed on several occasions. -ELF

SEPT/97: Korsnas - over 700 mink released from a fur farm by EVR activists. Slogans included "EVR" and "concentration camp." -EVR

SEPT/97: Maalahti - roughly 350 foxes set free from their cages. A large number of breeding cards destroyed. Many fox remain free.

SEPT/97: Vassa - Hundreds of mink and foxes liberated from a fur farm.

SEPT/97: Riihimaki - attempted fur farm raid, unfortu-

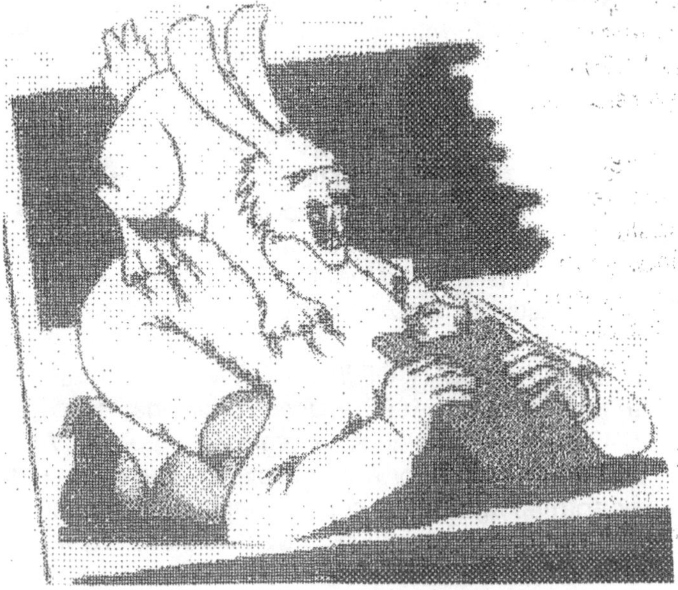

nately the farmer awoke due to his restless guard dog. No arrests made. Minimal damage.

SEPT/97: Lahti - Jarvenpaa road construction site visited several times and many survey stakes removed.

SEPT 21/97: Tampere - A Tampere university laboratory was raided by activists: 30 rats were rescued, green paint sprayed everywhere, the glass of a washing machine broken and the messages "Vapaus. Lopettakaa el inten kidutus. EVR." was painted on the wall (Freedom. Stop the torturing of animals. A.L.F.). Activists raided the lab on a Sunday knowing staff were away, sometime between 2:30 p.m. and 7:30 a.m. -EVR

SEPT 22/97: Kuopio - Raids took place at the university animal breeder's building in Karttula. Four beagle dogs were rescued. Karttula has been raided three times within one year, six beagles in total have been rescued. -EVR

SEPT/97 Korsholma - EVR activists raided another fur farm where several hundred mink were released and breeding cards were destroyed. -EVR

SEPT 28/7: Forssa - Two meat trucks belonging to the large meat company, LSO-Food burned to the ground. The trucks were used by the company to transport animals.

OCT 4/97: Linkping - An unknown number of meat trucks belonging to Farmek (a cooperative with Scan meats) were set on fire by activists. -A.L.F.

NOV 14/97: According to media sources, over the weekend unknown persons dyed at least 400 foxes in Porvoo farm. This far has about 1500 foxes and it has been raided 3 times already (1995: 110 cages were opened and 20 foxes remained free, 1996: some breeding cards were stolen), This raid resulted about 200,000 FIM in damages (about $45,000 US).

NORWAY

NOV 11/97: A Norwegian fishing vessel owned by Steinar Bastensen, a well known whaler and fisherman and leader of the whalers own organization in Norway. It is believed that the action had been carried out by activists opposed to Norwegian whaling.

A BRIEF HISTORY OF THE NORWEGIAN A.L.F.
In late December 1996, Dyrenes Frigjrings Front (DFF), the Norwegian A.L.F., formed a group in the city of Bergen in Norway. Multiple small actions were performed against the commercial fur and meat industry. At least 10 actions have take place so far in 1997.

AN OVERVIEW:

January 4th, 1997, the DFF attacked the largest corporation in Norway selling eggs from battery chickens, Prior.Slogans like "Ban Battery Farming" and "Hens out of Cages," were spraypainted on the building. Windows were smashed and locks glued. Three trucks were also painted and windows were smashed, locks glued. Total damage is estimated to be 15,000. The largest sabotage action by DFF was done the 16th of July 1997. The attack was against the largest slaughterhouse in the area, Fatland. At the slaughterhouse the buildings were spraypainted, windows smashed, locks glued and a manifest was pasted on a door. One large truck and a van, were first spraypainted, before they both were torched and burnt to the ground. Total damage has been estimated at 65,000. The following week the press informed that the slaughterhouse owner had received a death threat on his and his family's life, signed DFF. DFF claimed no responsibility for this, and spoke out against these kinds of tactics in the press. Later, it has been revealed that the police investigators, in conspiracy with the slaughterhouse owners, sent this death treat in an attempt to discredit DFF and their means.

Unfortunately, 5 DFF activists have now been caught by the police after extensive investigations and media hysteria. They are all pending trial in early 1998. At the same time, couple of members of the legal animal rights group, NOAH, were also arrested and charged with DFF actions. However, charges have now been dropped, and NOAH's name has been cleared. Two DFF activists were held in police custody, but have since been released. One activist sat in jail for 55 days. Being a vegan, he rarely given anything he could eat, but is now doing ok now...

AUSTRIA

According to articles in Austrian news papers, several fur shops recently attacked by activists with butyric acid claim 4 million schillings damages in Salzburg and more than 60 million schillings damages in Vienna. Police have raided homes and arrested at least two people and the animal rights group Animal Peace's office in Salzburg has also been raided.
By the way, 65 million Austrian schillings is roughly 9 million German marks, 3.25 million British pounds.

BRAZIL

NOV 17/997: Santa Catrina Federal University - A dog was liberated from a dissection class in which he was scheduled to be killed so his lungs could be studied. The rescue took place in the middle of the day, when three biology students took the dog and placed it in a home where he is being well cared for. The Lab registered theft and "invasion" charges against the three with the university police, but they are standing strong. This is the same university that the A.L.F. hit in February '97, liberating more than 80 monkeys.

AUSTRALIA

NOV 7/97: Victoria - A number of women activists rescued hens and labelled eggs as "cruelly produced" at Montalto Poultry Farm 12 McDonalds Road Epping Victoria Australia 61-(0)3-9404-1524. In a daring night raid on one of Victoria's notoriously cruel battery hen farms seven women from AWA successfully rescued eight seriously ill battery hens. It was the sixth rescue at the Montalto Poultry Farm in Epping and the women also managed to correctly label over 1,000 battery eggs with an ink stamp reading MADE WITH CRUELTY.

Montalto Poultry, known for its rat and lice infestations, was once again exposed in dramatic video footage to be a virtual hell for the hens imprisoned in dilapidated and run down old cages. The women were forced to leave the sick hens behind because they couldn't carry any more. Three of the hens had to be humanely euthanased by a vet with three others seriously ill. Many were infested with lice. One hen was so badly trapped under the food trough it took three people to pry her free.

Another tiny hen was so weak she couldn't stand and her head hung limp. On vet examination she weighed a mere 850 grams (normal weight 2.2 kilos). Two had enormous tumours on their heads preventing them from eating. All these hens were being badly trampled and attacked by other hens gone mad in the small cages.

While the women rescued, others stamped over 1,000 eggs with the words "MADE WITH CRUELTY" which is the correct definition of battery eggs.

The rescue team has been involved on over 100 peaceful and non-violent undercover rescues and inspections in Australia during the last three years. The team feel forced to go and rescue factory farmed animals who are so brutally and callously ignored by the authorities. This was the second rescue during the weekend, with a further twelve hens rescued from another property the night before. GRAPHIC VIDEO FOOTAGE AVAILABLE Further Information Contact: Patty Mark 61-(0)3-9531-4367 or Debra Tranter 61-019-181-573

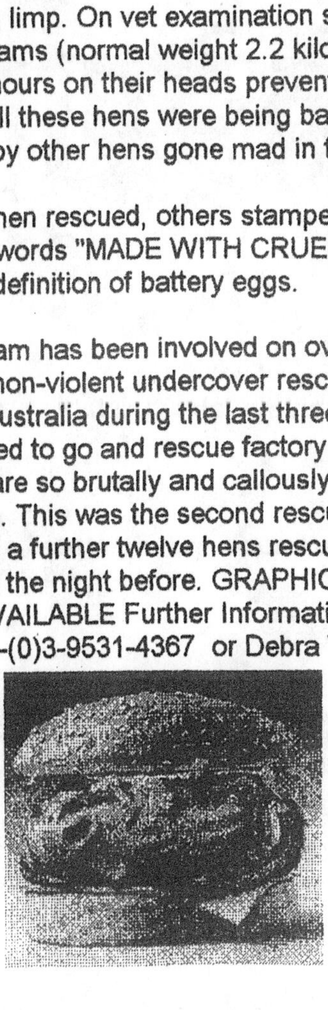

DIRECT ACTION DEFENSE FUND

The DADF has been established to assist activists facing charges for illegal direct action.

100% of all donations go directly towards activist defense. The DADF has no overhead, does not print a newsletter or invest in expensive equipment. All our resources are devoted to those behind bars for animal and earth liberation.

TO CONTACT THE DIRECT ACTION DEFENSE FUND, OR TO MAKE A DONATION, write:

Direct Action Defense Fund, Box 57357, Tucson, AZ, 85732-7357, USA

ANIMAL LIBERATION PRISONERS

UNITED STATES

Rod Coronado #03895-000
FCI Unit SW, 8901 S. Wilmot Rd, Tucson, AZ 85706, USA.
Sentenced to 57 months for aiding and abetting arson and destruction of government property in the USA.

NEW ADDITION
Ryan Z. Durfee BA03
c/o Oxbow Jail, Inmate Mail, 3148 South 1100 West, Salt Lake City, UT 84119
Serving a one year sentence for his part in an arson against a Mcdonald's. Convicted of 2nd degree felony arson or criminal mischief.

NEW ADDITION
Mark S. Klein AA45
c/o Oxbow Jail, Inmate Mail, 3148 South 1100 West, Salt Lake City, UT 84119
Serving a one year sentence for his part in an arson against a Mcdonald's. Convicted of 2nd degree felony arson or criminal mischief.

NEW ADDITION
Jason D. Troff
c/o S.L. County Jail, 450 South 300 East, Salt Lake City, UT 84111-3207
Serving a one year sentence for his part in an arson against a Mcdonald's. Convicted of 2nd degree felony arson or criminal mischief.

NEW ADDITION
Jacob Kenison
c/o S.L. County Jail, 450 South 300 East, Salt Lake City, UT 84111-3207
Accused of burning down the Tandy Leather shop. Jake is waiting for trial.

UNITED KINGDOM

Dave Callender HV3314
HMP Birmingham, Winson Green Rd, Birmingham. B18 4AS
Sentenced to 10 years for conspiracy to commit arson to assorted animal abuse establishments.

Michael Green AV2923
HMP Ashwell, Oakham, Leicestershire. LE15 7LF
Sentenced to 5 years for conspiracy to commit arson on a slaughterhouse and attempted arson to cattle transporters.

Barry Horne VC2141
HMP Bristol, Cambridge Rd, Horfield, Bristol. BS7 8PS
Sentenced to an incredible 18 years for the attempted use of incendiary devices in Bristol and the successful use of incendiary devices on the Isle of Wight.

Keith Mann EE3588
HMP Long Lartin, South Littleton, Evesham, Worcs. WR11 5TZ
Sentenced to 11 years for criminal damage to meat vehicles, attempted incitement, possession of explosive materials, attempted arson and escaping from custody

Gillian Peachey RL3415
HMP Holloway, Parkhurst Road, London. N7 0NU
On remand charged with conspiracy to use incendiary devices to cause criminal damage, and arson on a poultry farm.

Geoff Sheppard MD1030
HMP Parkhurst, Newport, Isle of Wight. PO30 5NX
Sentenced to 7 years for possession of a shotgun and possession of items for making incendiary devices.

Barbara Trenholm RL1292
HMP Durham, Old Elvet, Co Durham. DH1 3HU
Sentenced to 10 years for arson with intent to endanger life.

Justin Wright GE3046
HM Young Offenders Institution, Easton, Portland, Dorset. DT5 1DL
Sentenced to 5 years for arson with recklessness.

Dru Benson ME2494
HMP Eastwood Park, Wootton-Under-Edge, Gloucestershire. GL12 8DB
Sentenced to 3 months on 10th October for Assault on a police officer at the Consort Beagle Kennels demo in May.

NEW ADDITION

Noel Molland
HMP Winchester Romsey Rd. Winchester SO22 5HY
Sentenced to 3 years for incitement as his part in the "Gandalf" trial.

Shoreham Campaigners Walk Free

The four animal rights activists involved in the Shoreham live animal export protests were finally released from jail. Mike Roberts, John Taylor and Geoff Chapman had their convictions for 'conspirarcy to cause criminal damage' quashed by the Court of Appeal who called the case "fatally flawed". A fourth man, Tony Daly had his sentence reduced but still walked free. They had all been jailed in May of this year in a six month 2 million pound trial which even the Judge at the time advised the jury to acquit.

The GANDALF Defendants

The three convicted GANDALF folk are now into their three year prison sentences. While Noel Molland is the only one of the three directly involved in the struggle for animal liberation (address listed above), Green Anarchist is an outstanding magazine and both Saxon and Steve should receive our support.

Saxon Burchnall-Wood CK4322,HMP Winchester, Romsey Rd. Winchester, S022 5Hy England

Steve Booth CK4323, HMP Preston, Ribbleton Lane, Preston Pr1 5AB, England.

Gustafsen Lake prisoner support

We do not have all the details for all the prisoners sentenced as a result of the Gustafsen Lake (B.C.) shoot out (see *Underground #8* for details), we have addresses for 3 people needing letters, books, subscriptions, stamps, etc. If you can, please write:

Robert Flemming: Bear Creek Correctional Centre, Box 1761, RR 1 Clearwater, B.C. V0B 1N0, CANADA
Sentenced to seven months.
Suniva Bronson: B.C.C.W., 7900 Fraser Park Drive, Burnaby, B.C. VJ5 5H1, CANADA
Sentenced to three years (she was photographed with a gun).

UNDERGROUND

THE MAGAZINE OF THE NORTH AMERICAN ANIMAL LIBERATION FRONT SUPPORTERS GROUP

ISSUE #10 Spring 98 $3

FREE TO PRISONERS

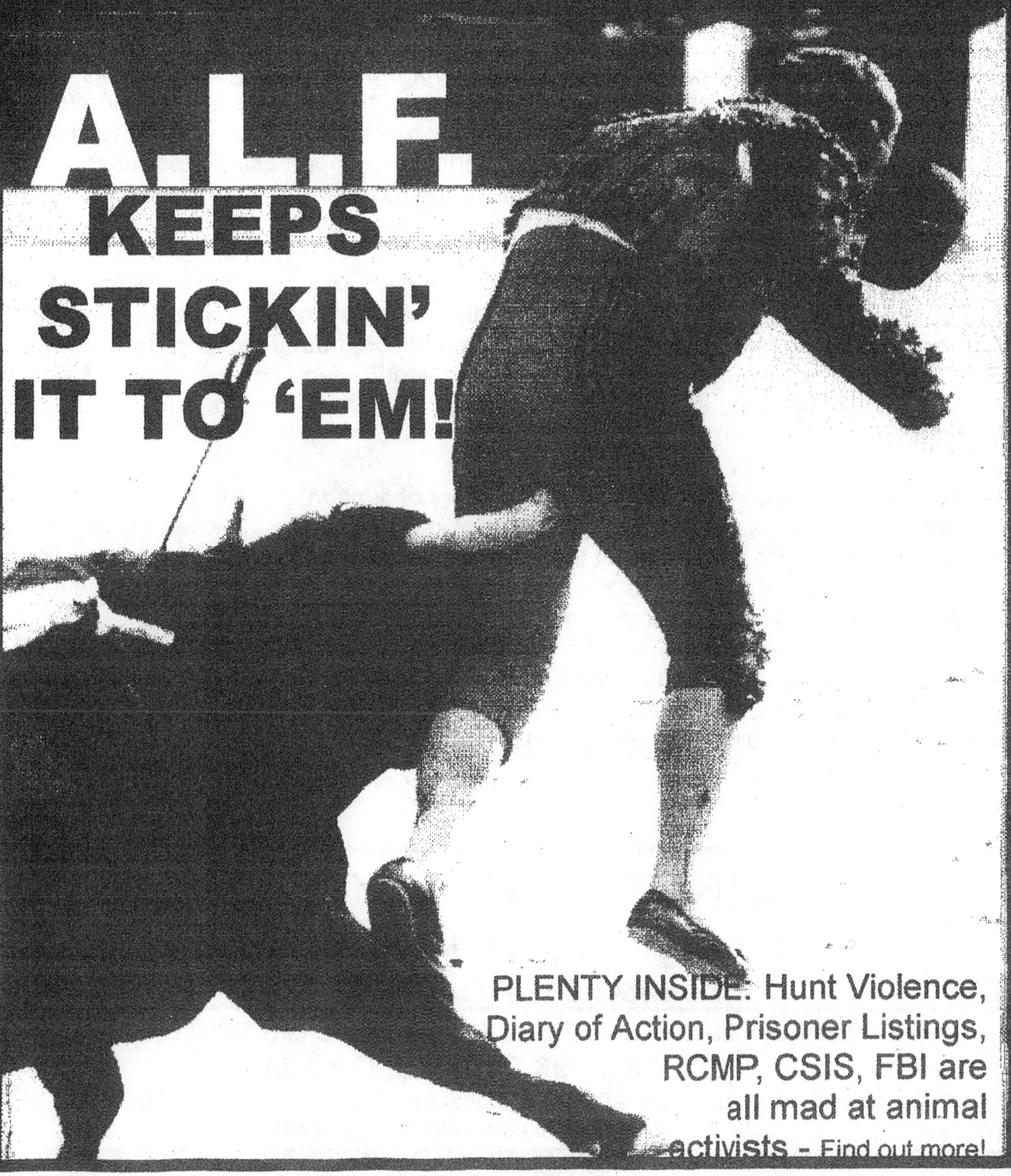

A.L.F. KEEPS STICKIN' IT TO 'EM!

PLENTY INSIDE: Hunt Violence, Diary of Action, Prisoner Listings, RCMP, CSIS, FBI are all mad at animal activists - Find out more!

OK folks, just a brief introduction from the desk of yer Editor, before we get dug into the rest of the magazine. Mainly, I wish to take this time to give thanks to everyone out there who has shown such incredible support and generosity, not only to the NA-A.L.F.S.G., but to all the various support campaigns and defense funds currently set up and running in North America. Many of those who have given us support cannot be named, but we'd like to thank a few of you that can — Thanks go out to Darren, Gina, and David for all your efforts, to Catherine and EVERYTHING you've done, to Consolidated and Propaghandi for spreading the word and asking us to table, to the kids in Hamilton, Roach, Nikki, Katie (the new Press Officer), J.P. and other CAFT folk, Who's Emma, No Compromise!, EF!, and everyone who does a zine on Animal Liberation. There are so many more who deserve acknowledgment and I'm sorry you can't all be listed, but you know who you are!

We are at a point in our movement's growth where for the first time a large number of dedicated activists are facing jail time or have already been thrown in prison for their efforts on behalf of the animals. While admittedly, it can be confusing, frustrating and disheartening to see so many warriors taken out of action, your continued support acknowledges the sacrifices they've made and lets others know they will be supported if ever they're caught. Too many times we've seen above ground activists (who should know better) offer their support ONLY if they get something out of it. We've seen activists put their names at the bottom of A.L.F. communiqués sent to the media, happy to get their names known as A.L.F. "Supporters," who then cut loose those same A.L.F. activists once they've been caught, because they're not happy with the activist's trial strategies. We've seen above ground "supporters" spread rumours, undermine support for jailed activists, and outrightly sabotage the efforts of animal liberation activists because they weren't getting their own way — thanks guys, the Feds couldn't do better.

To everyone who has donated to a fund, sent letters of support, put on shows, distributed flyers, attended court cases, made calls to jails, or asked a prisoner, "How can I help you?" — thank you. And to those who have put their freedom and even their very lives on the line to save an animal's life, to destroy machines that torture and kill, who have sabotaged the profits of earth and animal abusers, from the bottom of our hearts — thank you.

Some have ended up in jail, and as likely as not others will join you there in the future, but every liberation, every act of sabotage, brings this battle that much closer to the end, and will spell total liberation for all. Keep on fighting.

Love and Liberation,
t.

Letters to Underground

INTRODUCING THE PROVISIONAL ALF

We are long-standing Animal Liberation Front activists who have become impatient with the painfully slow progress towards a better world. This lack of progress is due in part, so we believe, to the policy of non-violence pursued for so long by the ALF.

Although we continue to fully support the sacrifices and successes of the ALF - both animal liberation and economic sabotage - we align ourselves firmly with the Animal Rights Militia and Justice Department by feeling that animal abusers should be made to pay directly for their crimes.

We could have acted under the umbrella of the ARM or JD but, having been active within the ALF for so long, are reluctant to deny our roots. We therefore declare ourselves to be the logical radicalisation of the Animal Liberation Front; renouncing non-violence against individuals in common with many other just liberation struggles both past and present. We are the Provisional ALF.

Unlike some areas of the animal liberation movement we do not accept that it is wrong to endanger secretaries and others who may be perceived by some as "innocent". We argue that anyone who profits in any way from animal abuse is as guilty as those who actually perpetrate the obscenities. The abusers at the "sharp end" could not continue in isolation. They shall all pay. None who receives rewards from evil deeds shall be exempt from vengeance until they renounce animal torture.

Our targets will not only be animal abusers and those who profit from their work but also those infiltrators and turncoats who claim to represent the animals while selling them down the river.

To announce our existence we have mailed out hoax devices - video cassette boxes containing packets of cat litter. These packages also contain detailed instruction on constructing a viable incendiary device (copy attached). We intend these hoaxes to act as a warning so that both animal abusers and traitors may have the opportunity to change their ways before our unashamedly violent campaign begins in earnest.

We have designs for many types of devices with capabilities to attack both people and property. Our period of warning will end in April this year. Animal torturers - you still have time to end your abuse of the innocent before it's too late.

We wish the ALF, ARM, JD and all similarly active units continued success. That said, we have torn up the rules. The animals have suffered far too long already... now it's the turn of their tormentors.

The Provisional ALF accepts completely that if non-human animals could fight for themselves then there would have been a lot of dead animal abusers already. We are here to achieve what our non-human comrades cannot achieve for themselves - ANIMAL LIBERATION.

"We cannot wait for the world to turn, for times to change that we might change with them, for the revolution to come and carry us around in the new course. We ourselves are the future. We are the revolution."
(Beatrice Fruteau)

SWEDISH UPDATE

Hi!
I did spend some time in "jail" (about 17 days I think), but now I'm free and fighting. Henrik (the other guy who was caught together with me, was on a Swedish radio show some days ago and had a debate about fur farm liberations/fur farming. A scum called Gsta Larsson, who is "president"(?) for the Swedish fur industry was also there, but he got kicked by both Henrik and an ecologist, who said that liberations of minks aren't bad for the environment etc, so Gsta was all crazy ... The third guy, David, isn't all that good. I heard from Henrik that he had given our names to the police in the hearings, and said that we were the ones who planned everything, so I think he's not gonna get any support if we get to prison. But the police love him, so I also heard that they are going hardest on us two. The support, by the way, has been very good. On the first days we got 72 letters, and that really made me wanna keep fighting. I don't think that it's decided when the trial is gonna be, but I think it's going to be in late April; and all supporter-demos etc is already planned. I and Henrik has also decided to go out to the media, with names and everything and talk about what's happened, and explain about our philosophy. There hasn't really been anything like that before in Sweden, so it is going to be really good, cause the newspapers are always writing stuff like "Oh, how can undemocratic groups like this exist in a democratic country like Sweden?", and always that all minks starve to death and shit like that. I hope it will

turn out good. Well, now I have to go.
Take care, Kristofer

HURRAH SWEDISH ACTIVISTS

First there was the traditional animal welfare organizations in Sweden, then nothing. Nothing ... for a LOOOOONG while. Then, suddenly, on June 16th 1985 the Swedish ALF (Djurens Befrielse Front) carried out the first animal rights action in Sweden. Two "lab" dogs were rescued from a lab in southern Sweden. Action after action took place, but unfortunately the Swedish ALF operated alone.

Late 1994, to our big (but happy) surprise, something happened and it was done by others. Great, there were others operating! In Umea (North Sweden) meat trucks had been set fire to. Of course, the media went crazy. Hour after hour I spent on the phone with the media. They believed it was the Swedish ALF who was behind the action -- well, we were not. More fire attacks were carried out by nameless groups, against meat trucks and slaughterhouses, all in Umea.

We, the Swedish ALF were very happy. Finally, more groups were in business and that would really confuse the police and SAPO (the Security Police). Meanwhile, of course, the Swedish ALF was in business as usual. Work, work and more work. Because of the Umea actions the police had increased their interest in us. Also our enemies began to take and interest in us -- more threats against the Swedish ALF Press Officer over the phone, and an increase in surveillance by whom?

These last years we have seen more new animal rights groups in business. Especially in 1997, with many new groups on the move -- some very serious and dedicated but unfortunately a few less serious when it comes to animal's rights. Hopefully they'll learn. Take note of the ALFs guidelines, specifically "To take all necessary precautions against harming any animal, human and non-humans." There are also ALF groups in Norway and Finland, but as far as we know, not in Denmark.

The Swedish ALF are happy to see new serious groups in business and we wish them good luck. Work hard and stay away from the police. The Swedish ALF will have its 13th birthday in June -- and still no activist in prison.

We wish all imprisoned A/R activists good luck!

To contact the Swedish ALF:
DJURENS BEFRIELSE FRONT,
Emilie E:son, Box 179
S-265 22 Astorp, Sweden.
Tel: +46 42 576 93

We have always made an effort to support imprisoned animal-rights people all over the world by letters. Lately we haven't been living up to our intentions. Why? Well, animals come first and there has been a lot of work lately. The Press Office and the Supporters Group is run by one person with some extra help by one more. There is not enough time to do all we want to do. We hope you can forgive us and understand. Rest assured, you are not forgotten. Not at all. We wish you good health, success and good luck.

Emilie E:son (Press Officer)

DEATH ROW VEGAN NEEDS LETTERS

Underground,
First of all I want to thank you for sending me your paper. It is very informative and one of the best I have ever read.

I am Buddhist, a vegan and on Death Row in Florida. I am interested in hearing from anyone who is an activist, and who may be able to tell me how to get a proper vegan diet.

Thank you
Burley Gilliam
097234-AI-P11098
Box 221, Raiford, FL
32083, U.S.A.

LETTER FROM BARRY HORNE

Dear Comrades,

Greetings from England, and a happy new year to one and all. Many thanks to the North American A.L.F.S.G. for the newsletters and all the support over the past 1 1/2 years that I've spent in prison. And many thanks to all the comrades in North America for support, love and solidarity through the long months that have passed. Needless to say, my thoughts and love are with you all. My solidarity with your actions for the animals, and my support for your fight for liberation, is 100%, and it always will be.

As you'll know, I finally came to trial in Nov.'97, on a whole list of charges that have little relation to reality. The main charges against me, and the ones that the police were desperate to convict me of, were for incendiary device attacks allegedly by the ARM on the Isle of Wight in August 1994. Despite the fact there was no direct evidence to link me with these attacks, I was found guilty on all charges and sentenced to 18 years in jail. To say the trial was a farce would be to understate the case somewhat. The whole point of the prosecution's case seemed to be to blacken my name as much as possible, with the view to convincing the jury that I was a dangerous person with no regards for the safety and lives of the public at large. The judge, for the most part, acted as a second prosecutor. He even directed the jury that because my defense team had failed to indicate who was responsible for the Isle of Wight attacks, it therefore followed that I must be and they should find me guilty accordingly! And they clearly did. In the three weeks between the end of the trial and my sentencing, the police gave numerous interviews to the press in which I was described as all manner of things -- such as "dangerous and ruthless," "a dangerous extremist," and "prepared to kill, having no consideration for innocent members of the public," to name but a few. The press gleefully printed all these things, plus a few that they seem to have made up themselves! Even the probation office, who compiled a pre-sentence report based on one short interview with me, joined in with it all. They produced a report on me that bore little relation to anything I had actually said to them. So it was no surprise when the judge brought the whole sorry process to its inevitable conclusion by sentencing me to 18 years. In fact, the only surprise was that, considering how dangerous I apparently am (!), they didn't immediately order me out the back to be executed by a firing squad!

You may have noticed by now that, despite getting lumbered with 18 years, I'm tending to take it all a bit light-heartedly. And why not, ME, dangerous? I think not. Where are the bodies of the people I have killed? Where are the people I have injured? Where are the innocent members of the public who have been terrorized by any actions I've ever been involved in? There are none. A statement was read on my behalf outside the court building after I was sentenced, it contained the most truthful words about me that had been spoken throughout the whole proceedings. They were that I "had not, and would never, harm anyone." And that is the truth. The police, the security services, and all those who conspired to convict me, know it as well. I will be appealing against a lot of the convictions, and against the sentence. Who knows, maybe a little bit of justice may filter through then.

all animals
prefere liberation
over
vivisection

So, is there anything we can learn from this whole sorry business? Seems to me there is, and it involves the whole Animal Liberation movement in Britain, and quite possibly North America as well. To explain what it all means, I'll give you a few background details to the whole case against me.

In July of 1996, I was arrested in Bristol on an action to firebomb animal abuse stores in the city centre. As always with this type of action, I was using incendiary devices timed to activate around 1am in the morning, when no members of the public would be around and no-one would get hurt. At the time of my arrest, the police themselves issued a statement admitting that the action was obviously an attack on property and not people. As the months went by, the prosecution settled for a number of charges against me of attempted arson with intent to cause criminal damage. All fine and good, I had no problem with that. I indicated my intention to plead guilty to these charges. On sentencing I would then have been looking at a maximum of around 10 years in jail. A date was agreed, in November '96, for me to attend court, plead guilty, and be sentenced. Two days before this court appearance, the prosecution suddenly dropped all theses charges and in their place substituted a whole new set of charges of, basically, endangering peoples safety and lives. These new charges were nonsense, and they knew it. But it meant that I now had no alternative but to plead "not guilty" to all the charges, as they knew I would. It was obvious that a decision had been taken, for political reasons, that I was not to be allowed to "get away with" a 10 year sentence, but that I was to be made an example of. that decision could only have been taken by a person or persons much higher up the ladder then the police or prosecution service. What other explanation could there be, considering that at no time had the police or prosecution indicated any interest in, or desire to, send me down for anything other than attempted criminal damage by arson?

As the saying goes, the rest is history. With a "not guilty" plea entered, it meant that the date of a trial could be delayed for months and months, giving the police and prosecution time to "fit me up" for the Isle of Wight action, and ensure that I would ultimately go down for much longer than 10 years. I believe this was all done under political pressure by those faceless people much higher up the ladder.

In the 6 months or so before my trial, several other people appeared in court on relatively minor charges connected with arrests on demonstrations and suchlike -- the sort of charges that would, in the normal course of things, result in fines and/or community service orders. Unexpectedly, some of these people were sent down for short prison sentences. One has to wonder why. On January 9 this year, 12 people attended court to answer section 3 and section 4 public order charges in connection with a demonstration at a live export depot. A deal had been struck with the prosecution prior to this, that if all 12 pleaded guilty then only 2 or 3 would be in danger of a short prison sentence, the rest facing fines or something similar. The judge ignored this deal and imprisoned ALL TWELVE of the defendants. Again, one has to wonder why. There have been other unusual events over the last 8-9 months that seem to link in with all this as well, all this sudden hardline sentencing of AR people. And believe me, I think there is a definite link between all these events. When the courts begin displaying bias that is so blatant that it even takes MY breath away (and I thought I'd seen it ALL over the years!), then it can only mean that pressure from "high-up" is being brought to bear on the courts. And that pressure can only originate from one source - big business animal abusers.

Over the last year in Britain, we have enjoyed a definite and unprecedented upturn in activity against animal abuse. New tactics have been used and found to be effective, the commitment of our people has been heightened to new and unseen-before levels. Not just with the "front line" activists, but with the Animal Rights movement as a whole. The result of all this has been that many areas of animal abuse are under attack as never before. As a movement, we have advanced as the abusers have retreated, and all of this new activity has hit the profits of the abusers and had them running scared. So, I believe that the big business animal abusers have pressured the British government into doing something about it. the orders have been passed down to the courts to slow us down by imprisoning people on the smallest pretext, and (of course) handing out a record sentence to me as an attempt at a deterrent to other people.

So, who are these big business animal abusers? They're the multinationals who operate in many countries of the world, and in many cases, in both Britain and North America. For Animal Rights and Animal Liberation, things are going well in North America, as I read all the time in publications such as *Underground* and in letters I receive. If its not already happening there, then how much longer before you encounter a similar situation to us in Britain? A situation where the courts are pressured, on behalf of big business animal abusers, into "slowing" you down? Not long, I would think.

I could say a lot more about this, but I'm sure you get the message. Obviously this is all a theory of mine, I have no proof, so I may be wrong -- but I don't think so. Britain in 1998, since the "New Labour" government took office, is increasingly big business oriented at the expense of the working class and those on the lower rings of society. Nothing is too much trouble where the rich and powerful are concerned, with New Labour bending over backwards to protect their interests. By comparison, New Labour have shown time and time again that the interests of the animals come nowhere when profit is at stake. They've even admitted this, so we should be under no illusions about that. Bearing that in mind, it becomes all too easy to see that New Labour would not hesitate to stifle opposition to their big business friends by instructing the courts accordingly. WE are that opposition, and we are now under attack because of our successes against the animal abusers.

So what should our answer be to all this? Seems to me there is only the one answer. The strength of Animal Liberation is that we never give up. We go on and on until we wear down our opponents, wearing down their resistance until they give in. We must now continue to do just that. The strategy of defeating us by imprisoning all and any can only work if we let it. The Animal Liberation movement is made of better stuff than that though. keep on fighting brothers and sisters, wear down their resistance as never before. Show them that we can not be defeated, and we will not be intimidated. Sooner or later this current strategy by our enemies will collapse as all of their previous strategies have done. Until then, and until ALL animals are free, we continue, we fight on, we do not surrender!

Take good care my brothers and sisters, in love and solidarity I send my thoughts to you. One day we shall all be free, and this world shall be one of justice and peace. This will be our achievement for we shall succeed, never doubt it.

For the cause,

Barry Horne

NEWS BRIEFS

CSIS IS WATCHING

Canada's spy agency, The Canadian Security Intelligence Service (CSIS)is trying to keep a close eye on radical animal liberation activists.

CSIS is responsible for advising the government or police of security threats, including the possibility of political violence, sabotage of vital property, foreign espionage and subversion of "democratic" institutions.

Recently released documents reveal how CSIS sees the potential for "serious violence" by animal-rights activists as "a threat to the security of Canada." It is believed to be the first explicit indication from the intelligence service that it believes some militant animal-rights activists are potential political terrorists.

David Harris, a former director of strategic planning for CSIS, says, "I'm confident that CSIS has an active animal rights-related program under way. Certainly the service is very interested, to put it mildly."

The evidence of CSIS's concern comes in the wake of bombings at BioChem Pharma Inc. in Laval, Que., that might be linked to the company's use of rodents in drug and vaccine testing.

In the last five years, Canadian activists have released animals from farms and laboratories, claimed to have contaminated meat and food tested on animals and sent a bomb to a genetics laboratory.

A July memo prepared by the service addresses the "potential for serious violence related to animal-rights extremism. The activities of this subject of investigation may on reasonable grounds be suspected of constituting a threat to the security of Canada ..."

JOSH ELLERMAN UPDATE

U.S. District Senior Judge J. Thomas Greene issued that ruling in denying a motion to dismiss the federal charges against Douglas Joshua Ellerman. Ellerman, 19, was indicted last year on 16 counts of using destructive devices (pipe bombs) to destroy the co-op and delivery vehicles at 8700 S. 700 West on March 11, 1997. The Animal Liberation Front claimed responsibility for the bombing. Authorities contend Ellerman was a member of that organization.

Defense attorney Ronald Y. Yengich asked Greene in December to dismiss the charges, arguing that a criminal act must substantially affect interstate commerce to be subject to federal prosecution. According to Yengich, the U.S. Supreme Court in recent rulings "stepped back" from interpretations that allowed a broad application of the Interstate Commerce Act.

U.S. Attorney David J. Schwendiman insisted federal charges were appropriate because the co-op served mink farmers in Idaho and Utah, traded extensively with out-of-state feed producers and distributed mink furs throughout the nation with a fleet of long-haul trucks, some of which were destroyed by the bombs.

The issue is important to Ellerman because if he's convicted under federal law, he could be sentenced to life in prison.

The March 11 (1997) bombing was one of a rash of attacks by animal-rights activists in Utah beginning in 1995. More than 40 incidents of broken windows, vandalism and arson fires followed.

CAVEL WEST LAND SOLD - A.L.F. VICTORY!

The Cavel West Slaughterhouse which was recently burned to the ground by underground animal and earth liberationists has been sold. According to media sources the zoning regulations prohibit any slaughterhouse from being built on that property. What this means is that the Animal Liberation Front, in burning down the slaughterhouse causing $1 million in damages, shut that slaughterhouse completely down and prevented another from being built in its place.

NYC FURRIER JAILED FOR DEATH THREATS AGAINST DALLAS FUR GROUP

NEW YORK: A New York City furrier and board member of a prominent fur trade organization was arrested for making death threats against a representative of a Dallas-based anti-fur group.

J.P. Goodwin, director of CAFT, said his office has been vandalized twice in the past 2 years, and he and another Dallas activist sued Neiman Marcus after the store's security attacked them sending the other activist to the hospital with a concussion last October.

Goodwin said he was not surprised to hear about the threats, noting that "an industry that gasses, electrocutes and breaks the necks of animals certainly wouldn't have qualms about making death threats."

Police nabbed Fur New York treasurer Steve Cowit after an undercover operation found Cowit was making threatening phone calls to Mike Nicosia, a Long Island representative of the Coalition to Abolish the Fur Trade, based in Dallas.

Cowit, who was arrested on Aggravated Harassment charges, also works for Henry Cowit Furs, a major NYC fur manufacturer, whose retail division, Madison Avenue Furs, has annual sales estimated at about $2.5 million.

Nicosia said he alerted police after he began receiving death threats months ago. Cowit apparently was making the calls from a pay phone, and was arrested Thursday morning when police caught him making one of the calls to Nicosia.

JILL PHIPPS DAY

A variety of events were held in memory of Jill Phipps, a dedicated animal liberation activist, killed three years ago during a live export demonstration.

The day started of in Reddich where the live exporter Woods lives. The police blocked off the road leading to his house and were out in force though hidden from view. There was about 100 to 150 people there including some Hare Krishnas. There was a march through the town intending to go to his house, but the police would only let a few people through at a time to lay flowers. There were a few scuffles with the police being heavy handed. Two people were arrested and one was seen being punched by a copper while in custody.

At 2.30 people left to go to Guilders, another live exporter, for a second demonstration. There was a heavy police presence there with a helicopter out in full. A short prayer and silence was held for Jill.

Finally people returned to Reddich to pay a surprise visit on a huge turkey/poultry farm there. This time the police were behind and the protestors managed to close the area down and got a huge response from the filth with a helicopter and many police called there to deal with it. There was a lot of anger as at a previous demo one of the owners threatened the 10 year old daughter of a protestor with explicit detail of the sexual acts he was going to do to her and her mother. When a complaint was made to the police they refused to do anything about it. A worker was also said to have boasted in the pub that he put cigarettes out in the eyes of turkeys.

On the night a worker was seen carrying around a baseball bat, and the son of the owner came out to taunt the protestors but was escorted away by the police for his own safety. A few nice spits landed on him.

ANTI-FUR VICTORY IN AUSTRIA

Feb/98

It's official: the provincial government of Lower Austria, Austria, had a vote on banning fur farming. The vote went UNANIMOUSLY AGAINST fur farming. Hence, Lower Austria is now the next province banning fur farming outright, and Austria is now fur farm free. It remains to be seen whether the last Austrian fur farm can do their ugly business this year for the last time, or whether it has to close down immediately.

5 long years of intense campaigning are over. The Austrian ar movement has managed to finish off the fur farming business starting from scratch (with a couple of hundred fur farms in the 1970s, to 43 when the campaign started in earnest, to a complete ban 5 years later). However, a number of fur shops still operate in Austria, and the fur trade is still active here, although it is completely illegal to produce fur in Austria at all now.

15 ARRESTS IN CAT FARM PROTEST

Feb 22/98

Anti-vivisection campaigners tore down metal fencing around a cat breading farm in Oxfordshire and clashed with mounted police as over a dozen people were arrested. In the largest demonstration so far at Hillgrove Farm, near Witney, around 600 protesters, many disguised in balaclava helmets, tried to break in to free kittens. At least 280 officers with riot shields, backed up by tracker dogs and a helicopter, prevented animal rights activists from reaching the buildings. There were no injuries reported. Hillgrove, which has bred cats for medical research for nearly 30 years, has become a national focus for protests. Protecting the farm has cost Thames Valley Police $8,000,000.

The demonstration began peacefully, with families singing and holding placards showing cats being dissected. The site around the farm's perimeter was cordoned off, and those entering were searched for weapons. As mounted police rode in to stop protesters from pulling down fence, rocks were thrown Sergeant Helen Roberts said "We have a duty to protect the property and the farmer's family from these activities." The farms owner, Christopher Brown, called the protesters an "anarchic mob" who enjoyed causing trouble. He was also one of several targets for hoax bombs sent by a splinter section of the Animal Liberation Front.

An ALF spokesman said: "We are trying to stop them from breeding animals for vivisection. Anyone who saw these cats during the experiments would be horrified." Those arrests were for alleged criminal damage and public order offenses.

GANDALF THREE FREED

from: SchNEWSflash 31/3/98

In a shock move on Friday lunchtime (27/3/98) the GANDALF 3, Saxon Wood, Noel Molland & Steve Booth were told they could pack their bags and were free to go. Their lawyers had put in a standard bail application to push for an appeal date [still unknown]. Mr Justice Sedley signed the papers for their immediate release after they'd served four and a half months of a three year sentence.

The three UK editors were jailed for reporting the facts of direct action protests. They were sentenced under a catch-all 'conspiracy' law and found guilty of inciting 'persons unknown' by disseminating environmental and animal rights literature over a five year period - akin to a gagging order on journalists working in similar fields. This clear case of denial of free speech was not lost on *Index on Censorship* which reprints samples of the 'offending' copy, from the radical journal *Green Anarchist* (GA) and the Animal Liberation Front (ALF) supporters newsletter, on its website.

The move has led to hope that their convictions may be quashed. In the meantime, the trial on the same charges of Robin Webb with possibly Paul Rogers is going ahead, starting on 27th April at Portsmouth Crown Court. A demonstration will be taking place outside the court on the first day of the trial (Mon 27th Apr, 10am, Winston Churchill Plaza).

Steve Booth told *SchNEWS*: "When I was told I could go the lads in the cells were cheering. People inside have a defeatist attitude - but this time it was like 'Yes! You've fought the system!'. I'm completely shocked and stunned by the whole thing. The guard said he'd never heard of this happening before. We've heard a rumour that the reason we've been let out was Amnesty in the US was about to list us as political prisoners."

"I went into prison with bar of soap, biro and toothpaste. I came out with four huge binbags of letters and books - I couldn't carry them! It shows that the campaign must have been having some success. It's not over yet. We don't know when the appeal is and its even possible there'll be a retrial. We can't let them get away with this. The conspiracy law is so bad, it's a licence to nick people. I was disappointed at lack of coverage of the case in the mainstream. Absolutely pathetic. The grassroots came through with the goods - and thank goodness for the internet."

"They've not heard the last from me - jail is no deterrent. Don't do it folks! The next *Lancaster Bomber*, Issue 20, will be out as soon as I can do it! Thanks for all the support, letters and books. It really cheered me up and helped me through it all. "

Saxon Wood told *SchNEWS*: "It's very bizarre being out. I went clubbing on Saturday which startled a few friends who thought I was still locked up. I think it had become too much of a hot potato - so thanks to *SchNEWS* and everyone who supported me. I'm writing lots of thankyou notes - if anyone needs a spare organ they can have one of mine! Public pressure what goes us out."

Noel Molland told *SchNEWS:* "Within half an hour of being told I was standing outside the prison gates, totally stunned and amazed. The first person I phoned burst into tears. "Prison was not hard, just dull and boring. My main hassle was three neo-nazi skinheads singing: `You're Red, you're Scum, you're public enemy Number One!' I had around two hundred supporters and I'd like to say thanks to all - it was really appreciated. Although we are physically out there are other people inside who would also appreciate letters of support. ...Maybe our release is the whole case starting to unravel and hopefully Robin will walk."

The freed men will now join the Liberation Tour, a speaking tour of the two outstanding defendants, Paul & Robin.

LONDON GANDALF SUPPORT CAMPAIGN c/o London Greenpeace, Panther House, 38 Mount Pleasant, London WC1X 0AP
E-mail:<lgp@envirolink.org>
Also see the SchNEWS GANDALF Web Pages: http://www.cbuzz.co.uk/SchNEWS/

ANIMAL RIGHTS GROUP FILES MULTI-MILLION DOLLAR SUIT AGAINST POLICE

March 31/98
A civil rights action was filed in federal court on behalf of the Animal Defense League, charging the Syracuse police department with multiple violations of their constitutionally protected rights.

For more than 2 years, the Syracuse police deliberately and systematically interfered with the activists ability to protest animal abuse by harassing them, subjecting them to unreasonable search and seizure, false arrest, and denying them their rights to free speech and due process.

"This suit is our way of saying that we will not let the Syracuse police trample the rights of activists in our area", states activist Sean White. "There are animals being exploited in our society and we cannot waste any more time sitting in jail cells on trumped-up charges."

The suit, which is being filed by Richard Marris, of Marris and Bartholomae in Syracuse, will ask for damages of $1 million dollars for the ADL, $500,000 for each activist wrongfully arrested and $100,000 for each activist subjected to police misconduct.

DEATH ON THE HUNT

ENGLAND A Huntsman died on the Chiddingfold, Lecontree and Cowdry hunt on Monday 2nd February after falling from his horse and suffering head injuries. The police helicopter had to be called out in order to air lift him from a field. Michael Taylor (60) from Surrey was a former master of the Surrey Union hunt.
The hunts were out again two days later and a minutes silence was observed for Mr Taylor.
What can One say! What goes around comes around.

FOUR CHARGED OVER CHICKEN DEATHS

feb98, AUSTRALIA THE deaths of about 2000 chickens in sweltering heat in one day at a poultry factory has led to the first animal cruelty prosecution under the chicken industry code of practice.

Georgina Sabaliotis and Andrew, Anna and Anastasious Christopolous, proprietors of the Adelaide Poultry Service at Wingfield, are charged with handling poultry at a slaughterhouse in a manner which failed to comply with the model code of practice for the welfare of animals at slaughtering establishments.

The allegations forming the basis of the charges, which are being prosecuted by the RSPCA, include that they failed to:

PROVIDE protection from direct sunlight, radiant and reflective heat and adverse weather.
ENCLOSE the shackling areas adequately.
PROVIDE a cool holding area.
The model code of practice states that holding areas should be cooled with strategically placed fans, fine water-misting sprays, water reticulated over the roof cover areas or blinds or tarpaulins hung from the roof.

It is alleged birds were dying from heat exhaustion in cramped crates between January 13 and February 23 last year, while a large number died in one day when the temperature reached about 40C.

The alleged regulation breaches were discovered by the South Australian branch of Animal Liberation, which said it had had the Wingfield slaughterhouse under observation for several weeks after a tip-off by industry sources.

MOVE PRISONER DIES IN PRISON

On March 13th, Merle Africa died in Cambridge Springs prison in Pennsylvania, of "natural causes." Although Ramona Africa of the MOVE family said that Merle was a physically & mentally strong 40 year-old woman, no other explanation was given for her death. The first reports said she died of tumours, but that was changed to natural causes. Merle had a stomach virus, but it is not known for how long. Although she felt ill, she was said to be still very strong.
On March 13th, her cellmate says she alerted prison officials that Merle was sick; her pulse was still very strong, & she was breathing well. The prison doctors removed Merle's cellmate. After 40 minutes, a CPR crew arrived; within minutes they came out & said that Merle was dead.

Merle Africa was a strong-minded & strong-bodied woman. She had done 7 hunger strikes, as long as 40 days, & was still doing pushups late into the hunger strikes. She was known to run 5 miles a day and, in keeping with MOVE beliefs, to eat well, & to be very careful of her health. It is very suspicious that she would die like this.

2 Courageous Activists Under Fire

GINA LYNN

A year ago, we reported on the harassment experienced by activists in Canada. David Barbarash and Darren Thurston have, over the past three years, undergone intense police scrutiny, including foot, vehicle and aerial surveillance; monitoring devices placed in both vehicles and homes; had thousands of email, fax and voice communications intercepted; and had vast amounts of files and property seized in raids. The Royal Canadian Mounted Police (RCMP) even surreptitiously seized my truck under false pretences to place a bug.

The RCMP had named Darren and David as their prime targets in their investigation of four mail bombs sent to racists and a geneticist in 1995, and razor blade booby trap letters sent to 27 guide outfitters in 1995-96. The mail bombs were claimed by the Militant Direct Action Task Force and the razor blade letters by the Justice Dept.

On March 20, 1997, almost immediately after listening devices were found in and removed from my truck and the apartment Darren and I were living in, the RCMP executed five search warrants on the homes of Darren and David, as well as other places where some of their belongings were stored. Tons of property was seized under the guise that it may be relevant to their investigation.

Since then, the Crown has successfully applied to further detain the seized property several times. We have opposed their applications and, over time, had a few items returned. In the meantime, these unscrupulous federal agents have unveiled an arsenal of dirty tricks in their attempt to destroy these freedom fighters.

The RCMP have now laid charges against both men in relation to the Justice Dept. actions, as well as a couple more resulting from the raids. One year had passed since their property was seized, during which time the Crown, on two occasions, had successfully applied to further detain it all (save a few items). On March 19, 1998 the feds had to make a choice whether to fight in B.C. Supreme Court to continue to keep it all, which they probably would have lost, or to lay charges. They chose the latter.

Last summer, they launched a media smear campaign by making the information used to obtain the search warrants available to a slimy reporter who could be counted on to paint an inaccurate picture of non-violent activists as "violent terrorists" which will surely taint a potential jury pool in the event of a trial. The headlines read, "Stalked by Eco-Bombers," and Barry Clausen, infiltrator, was interviewed on the radio as a self-appointed "expert on domestic terrorism."

Since that first media onslaught (not the first in the overall media disinformation campaign) since the raids, a sealing order was sought and successfully obtained by lawyers for Darren and David. After charges were laid in late March the media attack began anew. Now both the Vancouver Sun and Province will be brought to court to answer to contempt of court charges.

The National Security Investigative Section (NSIS) and the Canadian Security and Intelligence Service (CSIS) have both contacted and visited dozens of people (some numerous times) across Canada, probably the United States, and also England to question friends and associates of Darren and David. They have attempted to coerce activists to turn against their peers by making up ridiculous stories that would get anyone else sued for defamation.

On June 16, Warren Leigh Ryan, head investigator on the case, sunk to new lows in his disgusting, twisted and pathetic attempts to destroy the lives of Darren, David and anyone close to them. He came to our apartment and told me that Darren killed my dog - my precious Whiskey, who died the day after the raid on our home while I was in California - and that they have it on tape (um, yeah, Darren spent two years in prison for freeing cats from a lab but he beats dogs.....whatever).

He was clearly trying to get me to turn against Darren and make statements as he insisted that I come down to Headquarters to listen to the tape for my "own benefit". Shortly after this visit, our lawyer attempted to get a copy of this tape but, since it obviously doesn't exist, it was never made available.

I entertained this demented excuse for a human being much longer than I should have and I hope that this is a lesson to all about what not to do. When cops are at your door, do NOT open it PERIOD! No matter how nice they seem and no matter how innocent their line of questioning is and no matter how close to your heart the topic they bring up is, don't let yourself get sucked in! Tell them IMMEDIATELY to contact your lawyer and say NOTHING more.

Later on, in September, I was kicked out of Canada because of my criminal record back home in California (for protest-related trespassing). I guess when Leigh's sick little story about Whiskey didn't succeed in splitting Darren and me up, they decided to take the easiest and most brutal measure: selectively use the law in an attempt to remove me from the picture.

In October, Darren attempted to visit England where he was supposed to testify in the GandALF trial, as mandated and approved by the court, but was denied entry. Reportedly, the RCMP told British authorities there that he had outstanding weapons charges, which is ridiculous as he has never had any weapons related violations nor did he have any outstanding charges at all.

On January 28 of this year, Darren was visiting me in California and was arrested at gunpoint by at least 15 thugs from Immigration and Naturalization Services (INS), FBI and the Anaheim Police Department. After being searched, he was immediately taken to the Public Library where they had a command post set up and about 20 more federal agents in suits waiting for him. There, he was shackled and caravanned to LA to be processed as an "undesirable alien".

Darren was held in custody for about 2 weeks without bail based on his "criminal" convictions in Canada (freeing cats from a lab and burning meat trucks 5 years ago). During his deportation hearing, the DA said that he was being investigated by the FBI as a "threat to national security" but she wasn't sure why. That wasn't good enough for the judge - she issued him a "voluntary departure order", which is not as bad as the deportation we feared would be ordered. Darren was escorted by INS officers to a plane bound for Canada, with no opportunity for goodbyes, on February 7th.

David was arrested on March 27, 1998 on a warrant sworn out on the one year anniversary of the raids, and spent 23 hours in jail awaiting paperwork that should have taken no longer than a few hours. Darren arrived back in Vancouver and turned himself in a couple days later. They are jointly charged with 27 counts of "sending an explosive or dangerous thing in the mail". David is additionally charged with "possession of an explosive substance" and "possession of a prohibited weapon" (stun gun). Darren is additionally charged with "impersonation". No charges have been laid in connection with the mail bombs.

Both have been released on bail on their own recognizance with strict conditions - they are not allowed to leave B.C., had to surrender their passports, are not allowed to have contact with each other and must report to RCMP headquarters once a week. Any violation means being sent back to jail to face a harder bail hearing, and they can also be sued for $10,000.

David will be proceeding, on April 16 in B.C. Supreme Court, with a motion to quash the search warrants.

The increasingly uphill battle just got a little steeper. But Darren and David are not your everyday activists - they are lifelong soldiers, they are tough, and they will march on and overcome whatever ordeal is put before them. That is just one of the many qualities that makes them special to those who know and love them and invaluable as advocates for the animals and the environment.

Please support our fellow warriors during this most trying time. Send letters of support and donations for their legal defense *(earmarked "for Darren and David")* to:

North American A.L.F. Supporters Group
Box 69597,
5845 Yonge St., Willowdale,
Ontario, M2M 4K3 CANADA

INTRODUCING:

THE NORTH AMERICAN A.L.F. PRESS OFFICE

Since the recent formation of the North American ALF Press Office, things have been very busy! The first media interview for the Press Office was to explain a bomb hoax in Rochester, New York. Channel 9 (24 hour cable news show) and channel 13 conducted phone interviews. The bomb hoax was a pipe bomb with the initials "ALF" spraypainted on it and left in a county park. A warning was also sent to the County Park Supervisor. The park is considering a deer bait and shoot massacre. The Press Officer highlighted the fact that no one was injured (or even close to being injured) in the hoax, and therefore fell within ALF guidelines.

Many students and reporters have been in contact for general ALF information and future news stories, because word is spreading fast about the Press Office. You can certainly help by passing on our address etc. to everyone you know. Also, check out our web page at the always exciting Frontline Information Service!

Be sure to tune into the Toronto based animal rights show "Animal Views" on Thur. April 16, 1998 at 10:30am Eastern time. The Press Officer will be interviewed about the ALF. Previous guests include Rod Coronado and the NA A.L.F. Supporters Group. Remember that you are the eyes and ears of the movement, so whenever you see the Press Officer speaking, be sure tape any interviews and send any news clippings to the Press Office, (don't worry, you will be reimbursed for expenses.)

Currently, a Press Office leaflet is in the works, and we are raising funds for buying a computer (in preparation for all those wonderful actions taking place in North America!) Much, much more to come, as the Press Officer is on call 24 hours a day.

Finally, this is the time to renew your support of direct action for the animals. Remember that the animals, ALF, and prisoners are counting on each of us to stay strong in support of direct action, especially when it's easier not to. You know that the ALF works, you know it's the right thing to do.

Katie Fedor
NA-A.L.F. PRESS OFFICER

What does the Press Office Do?

Similar to the ALF Press Office (UK), the NA-ALF Press Office has several basic functions, all of which are designed to explain why the A.L.F. carries out actions, how it does, and how non-human animals are treated by our species.

Any anonymous information received by the press Office which details ALF-style actions will be communicated to the media. The Press Office will be available as part of the network of contacts for the media, able to confirm actions that fall within ALF policy and explaining the suffering that necessitates such actions.

The Press Officer, as a public face for the A.L.F. is available for interviews, phone-ins, news reports, etc. The group is 100% volunteer run. Any reporters or interested parties may contact the NA-ALF Press Office at:

NA-ALF Press Office
Box 103,
Osseo, MN
55369, USA
<NAALFPO@waste.org>
phone: 612-601-0978

The NA-ALF Press Office is an independent pro-ALF organization working closely with the NA-ALFSG and other above-ground animal liberation groups.

READING THE LABEL

IN TODAY'S WAR AGAINST PEOPLE, THE EARTH AND THE ANIMALS, JUST WHO ARE THE TERRORISTS?

by A.L.F. Information Services

In the 45 day 1990 Gulf War, the U.S. military and allied forces bombed Iraq with an estimated 40,000 tons of explosives killing an estimated 200,000 Iraqi citizens including women and children and other innocent civilians hiding in bomb shelters. In 1994, agents from the U.S. Bureau of Alcohol, Tobacco and Firearms (BATF) and the F.B.I. using U.S. manufactured CS gas and other military hardware burned down a religious community in Waco, Texas killing 86 people including 24 children. And in the southern Arizona desert, employees of Raytheon Corporation, one of America's top three bomb factories, recorded record-breaking profits in 1997 assembling $750,000 Tomahawk missiles which once again are threatened to be used against Iraq in a U.S. military recommended 4-day round-the-clock bombing campaign.

These are just a few examples of the duplicity of U.S. government policy that labels the use of deadly force against innocent women, men and children by its own police and military equipped with U.S. manufactured explosives as legally-sanctioned and justified activity while calling the isolated use of homemade explosives against property, not people used in the death and destruction of innocent life as "terrorist activity" punishable with decades in prison. Not one soldier or policeman responsible for the indisputable death forementioned has or will spend a day in prison, on the contrary some of those responsible have received promotions and been recognized for their "valor" with one U.S. Gulf War veteran using his military training to bring human death and destruction to the Oklahoma City Federal Building in 1995. Somehow, we are supposed to believe that U.S. government sanctioned murder is not a crime punishable with prison while the strategic targeting of inanimate objects intended for life's destruction for economic gain is.

March 11, 1997 Sandy, Utah; In the early morning hours, a series of small explosions destroy tractor-trailers and administrative offices at the Utah Fur-Breeders Co-operative injuring no one, but causing over $1 million in damages in a courageous attack on the nerve center of Utah's fur farm industry. The Fur-Breeders supplies Utah's fur farms, which comprise the nation's largest captive-bred mink pelt trade killing over 300,000 animals a year for the luxury fur trade. The Fur-Breeders also serves as one of the U.S. fur farm industry's last remaining research facilities which develop the scientific diets necessary for the domestication of a wild North American predator, the mink, and to create the fur quality that will guarantee millions in profits to the U.S.'s 500 fur farms. It was in Utah in the 1920's that fur trappers first captured live wild mink and began to raise them in captivity for their fur.

When Josh stands before his sentencing judge in May, his action will be called extreme and it was, but it was an extreme response to an even more extreme crime, the rape, commodification and harnessing of a life force that no human has a right to extort or demand from our peaceable animal sisters and brothers.

The Fur-Breeders bombing was a successful attempt to sabotage an industry's efforts to transform one of this nation's last remaining wild predators into a factory farmable fur machine with no consideration or regard to the physical and psychological torture they will endure to produce a product no on really needs. The bombing also represents the first U.S. action by animal liberationists using explosives to strike a long-time target of animal defenders on this continent, the fur trade which for the last 400-plus years has delivered devastation and extinction to wildlife with full U.S. government cooperation and assistance.

Unlike the U.S. government's aforementioned slaughter of innocent people, 19yr. old Josh Ellerman who has pled guilty to the Fur-Breeders action was not motivated by a willingness to use deadly force to secure an economic monopoly or political power and control. Josh's action was motivated by a desire to end the commercial exploitation and senseless suffering of an animal species whose only crime was to be born with a fur coat that some humans believe appears more attractively on their own backs rather than on that of its original owner. Growing up in Utah, Josh probably saw mink in their natural environment and maybe even saw the escaped mink from the Fur-Breeders who have taken up residence in the creek that passes behind the Co-operative. Josh's brave action was motivated by something the U.S. government has failed to understand despite generations of resistance against its destruction and taming of the natural world in North America, that is a great feeling of love, compassion and empathy for the other-than-human life we share earth with.

When Josh stands before his sentencing judge in May, his action will be called extreme and it was, but it was an extreme response to an even more extreme crime, the rape, commodification and harnessing of a life force that no human has a right to extort or demand from our peaceable animal sisters and brothers. Josh simply is the first warrior of our time who was willing to risk and pay the ultimate price to launch an opening salvo that must ultimately end the war against nature that the fur industry has waged on the animal nations for centuries. Josh represents America's new generation of youth who believe differently from their forefathers, who themselves believe it is time we ended the war on wildlife waged by the fur trade. Unlike the mass of people his age lost in their own self-centered existence, Josh was willing to sacrifice his own freedom to achieve peace for the mink nation. For his action, Josh faces a mandatory minimum of 35 years in prison due to his use of an "unregistered explosive device" and as a result of recently legislated "anti-terrorism" laws which mandate life imprisonment and the death penalty for the use of explosives which the U.S. government only allows if you wear their uniform and represent their own selfish interests.

Though the Fur-Breeders bombing has been labelled by the U.S. government as a terrorist act, we must remember that historically so have the actions of runaway slaves, indigenous warriors and others brave enough to thwart violent acts of war waged by the U.S. government against the earth and her people. Terrorism is simply a convenient buzzword long used by those most guilty of its committance to cast a dark shadow over those whose only goal is true freedom from oppression. It was not Africans who chose to be slaves, it was not the indigenous peoples of this continent who chose to have their lands stolen and it was not all animalkind and the natural world that volunteered to abandon their pursuit of peaceful existence and ecological worth to serve the greed of the U.S. power structure and its ruling classes. It was the U.S. government that first sanctioned such activity and began the war against the people of the world and all animal life and the earth we all live on that continues today. And though our actions may be criminal in the government's eyes, they are not in the perspective of those who choose to preserve our planets life nor are they even extreme when compared to the much greater acts of violence which they aim to prevent.

The bombing of the Fur-Breeders was a just act of defense in an attempt to maintain the resistance to economic practices that continue to spell danger for earth and continue the war against animals and nature. The actions of Josh Ellerman in Utah are simply the latest in a battle that must continue if we are to carry the torch of resistance that many have died for in this country and many continue to die for in other countries. Aggressive defense of the natural world that targets the fur industry in this country is nothing new, just ask the descendants of the Plains Indians whose ancestors went to war against the U.S. government and buffalo hide-hunters who exterminated the great buffalo culture that existed in this country a little over a hundred years ago. In their day, those warriors too were accused of terrorizing the "law-abiding" interests of U.S. citizens and industry but now we see them as the heroes that they were. The question that Josh's action demands an answer to is whether we as 21st Century generational warriors can do our part to ensure that such a resistance survives in our own time with its own increasingly repressive climate towards the same undying resistance.

Victory against the fur trade is a possibility. Already in Britain a multi-faceted strategy including A.L.F.-type direct action has forced that country's fur farmers closer to their final days of operation, but here in the U.S. where a large percentage of the world fur markets pelts come from we still have our work cut out for us before we can see such a victory on the horizon. The A.L.F.'s direct action campaign against the fur trade has proven the success of guerilla tactics. Operation Bite Back's attacks against the research and development wing of the fur farm industry in 1991-92 was just the beginning of our movement's renewed assault against an old enemy. The A.L.F.'s mink liberation campaign as phase two of OBB that began in 1995 has since pushed many a fur farmer to the brink of bankruptcy while giving tens of thousands of mink the opportunity of freedom in their natural environment.
The Fur-Breeders action was also an important strike in the continuing campaign against a vulnerable industry

that was already feeling the bite of the A.L.F.,and its timing showed the valuable potential of an A.L.F.-type direct action campaign to cripple an already weak enemy. And that is why Josh will be sent to prison, not because he endangered human life, a laughable condemnation from a blood-stained and guilt-ridden accuser but because his actions and others of the A.L.F. threaten something much more dear to the black hearts of our opponents that the sanctity of life and that is profit margins.

The U.S. government cares not about what is done to the natural world or innocent life, but an opponent who values life over property and who strikes at an industry which profits from its destruction and exploitation is a threat that must be crushed. And with history as our teacher, we should learn that such government repression as Josh now faces must be met with a renewed and resilient effort to maintain our movement's pressure on the fur trade. If our targets did not sincerely feel threatened by our present strategy, they would not be responding with such repressive actions.

Now it is time to show Josh, the animal nations, our ancestors and our enemies of all wild and free life that resistance will flourish not falter in light of the U.S. governments attempts to destroy it. To do this we must not let Josh's sacrifice intimidate us into inaction. We must not let it plant the seed of fear within our hearts that maybe if we follow the warrior path it will be us who next goes to prison. That is the strategy and intent of the U.S. government and its earth rapist and animal abusing allies, to publicly display captured and persecuted warriors for all to witness the price of resisting their deadly regime. A practice that the anti-nature patriarchal forces have always used to discourage earth-centered and life-respecting peoples resistance. Before it was a wild Celt warriors head displayed on a pike, or a Pueblo Indians foot or hand severed for the act of resistance, now it's many years of brutal imprisonment for refusing to kiss the boot of the very same Imperial Empire.

The sacrifice of Josh should be seen for what it really is, the recognition that every individual can still rise above the oppression of humans, earth and animals and empower him/herself to strike deep into the core of the evil institutions built on the blood and bones of all life and nature.

As Josh is led off to Leavenworth, we must show him that not only is he not forgotten, but neither will be his struggle. We must register our anger and dissatisfaction with his prosecution, not only on a street corner holding a sign but in the night where our power is strong and ungovernable, where we are able to thrust our sword of direct action deep into the heart of our enemies in the fur industry. We must show Joshua that his resistance was not in vain and for it we will act with renewed determination to stop once and for all the war that the fur trade has waged on this continent, and we must show Joshua and our animal brethren that the spirit of resistance is far from being crushed and we must show them by screaming our support for the A.L.F. and his actions from the top of the crumbled remains of what once was the source of every fur animals fear, the defeated fur trade. Whether each of us in our individual battles against our often larger and stronger enemy win or lose is beside the point. What matters most is that we simply keep alive our resistance with or movements particular target if the defeat of the fur industry as a goal. Against you local fur retailer, fur farmer, state licensed trapper, fur auction house or department store that deals in fur, make your voice heard. And always remember the prisoners, both human and animal of the fur trades war on nature. Joshua Ellerman may be the first to be stolen from our ranks, and he wont be the last. Do not leave this struggle in the hands of other activists to fight. Take responsibility for defending the animal nations and the earth they call home. Increase the pressure.

VICTORY TO THE A.L.F.!!!

UPDATE ON FRANK ALLEN

Frank Allen, a southern California animal liberation activist, was arrested on September 13th 1998. He was charged with the attempted arson of a high school slaughterhouse in Mission Viejo, California. Students at this high school receive extra credit in a 4-H program which includes watching their teacher slaughter cows.

After serving five days in Orange County Jail, Frank was released on $50,000 bail. He then pled guilty on January 8th, and was subsequently sentenced on April 2nd to 90 days of "psychiatric evaluation" at Ohino State Prison.

Frank surrendered to prison on Thursday, April 9th to begin his sentence. At the end of the 90 day term Frank will be re-evaluated by the judge to determine whether he is suitably "remorseful" and ready to be released.

THE EVIDENCE OF ESCALATING HUNT VIOLENCE

Here follows a brief summary of some of the more serious attacks on hunt saboteurs so far this season in the United Kingdom:

Late August 1997: Saboteur Neil B from Dorchester visited at home by Portman FH terrierman Nick Stephens who tried to kick the front door down, warning the saboteur that if he or any of his group try to disrupt Stephens' hunt, they will pay for it. Issued threats to kill Neil, his wife and their pets. Reported to police - no formal action taken by police.

Early September: Nick Stephens (as above)attacks the Dorset sabs' transit van with a pickaxe handle while at the Portman FH, trying to smash the bodywork and windows. Foresight on the sabs part meant that the windows were grilled with mesh, stopping the glass from shattering. However, the van was damaged in an ensuing chase as Stephens tried to ram the van off the road, driving recklessly without lights at night, and then with full beam lights to blind the driver. A 999 call to police elicited no response from Dorset Constabulary.

Early September: A single saboteur out trying to stop the Western FH from killing fox cubs in Western Cornwall was attacked by several jeering hunt followers. He was battered about the head and had his head and neck wrenched severely, was knocked unconscious and dragged around. He was then thrown into a huge patch of stinging nettles. The sab walked 4 miles home. This was an appallingly cowardly and sad attack on one of the only saboteurs in the area of this hunt.

Mid September: More than 20 hunt supporters chased and threatened with pick-axe handles a group of less than 8 saboteurs who turned up at an evening cub-hunt of the Ashford Valley FH. Police attending the incident turned on the saboteurs and used extendible batons to hit them with. Later the police attacked the saboteurs in the Ashford Police station when the saboteurs attempted to make a formal complaint about the policing.

The police's actions were caught on video, as were the hunt supporters actions, but the tape was then confiscated by the police. A video also exists of the police actions within the police station.

Late September: Two saboteurs were injured when run over by an All-Terrain Vehicle (ATV) - one was run over in a field, the other was hit and carried along on the ATV for over 50m before being punched and kicked by hunt supporters of the Ashford Valley FH. While this was occurring, another lone saboteur was set upon by up to 6 hunt supporters who punched, kicked and beat him around the body with lumps of wood. The sab was left semi-conscious in the field after being hit across the head with an iron bar. Upon arrival, Ashford police arrested the dazed saboteur for assault, before eventually taking him to a hospital in Ashford.

Mid October: Middle aged female saboteur attacked by a hunt supporter of the Cattistock FH who was armed with a shovel. She narrowly avoided serious head injuries by raising her arms in defense, but was injured on the hand. In the same incident, a saboteur has his face rammed into the front grill of a transit van as hunt supporters try to wrestle his camera from him. Meanwhile a duo of hunt supporters had climbed into the back of the transit van, containing 5 terrified saboteurs and set about punching several of them in the face, and jabbing the driver of the van in the face with a stick. Three members of the same family (the notorious Martin family) have been arrested for this series of incidents and are currently on police bail.

Early November: Saboteur from Bettering is kicked unconscious by hunt supporters of the Oakley FH in North Bedfordshire. At the time the saboteur was accompanying a young female saboteur on her first protest. The two were having difficulty keeping up with the rest of the group (7 sabs)and were separated from it at the time of the attack.

(Continued on page 21)

THE SOUTHERN ANTI-BLOOD SPORTS CAMPAIGN
SUPPORT THE PORTSMOUTH THREE

The Hursley Hambledon Hunt is a vicious hunt notorious for violence against sabs. Because of this it's unsafe for a small group of sabs to attend this hunt. However hunt saboteurs are not prepared to allow hunts to terrorize them into not sabbing and so, every so often, a mass hit is organised against the Hursley Hambledon. Experience has shown that there is safety in numbers.

Just recently there has been a lot of extreme violence shown towards hunt saboteurs across Britain. This has included sab vans being rammed & windows broken and sabs being hospitalised after assaults by hunt members. Sabs have been threatened with guns and in one incident, the home of a leading Dorsad hunt sab, who has been issued with death threats warning him not to sab, was visited by a gang of hunt supporters who were wielding machete type blades. It is in recognition of the fact that no hunt must be allowed to terrorize sabs away from attending it, but with acknowledgement of a very real threat of violence from the Hursley Hambledon hunt thugs that a mass hunt sab was organised - this hunt sab was very well publicised. People openly discussed this sab over a month before it actually happened.

On the day of the hit (Saturday 13th December 1997) it was decided that everyone would meet up at a common meeting point and go in convoy to the Meet. It was feared if lone vans were spotted by the hunt they would be vulnerable to attack. Well publicised, at the meeting point there were between 9 to 14 sab vans, a police Range Rover and a police spotter plane in the sky above. Most of the vans contained sabs from the South Coast, groups from Dorsett to Sussex. However a few of them were from outside of the region and were people unknown to the South Coast sabs. The vans set off in convoy, followed by the police Range Rover with the spotter plane flying over head. For some unknown reason, just before getting to the Hunt Meet, the police vehicle turned off and went down a side road. There was not a single police officer present at the hunt when the sabs arrived! At the Hunt Meet, the sabs parked and headed towards the hunters. According to one sab, "We all started walking towards the hunt when suddenly we heard a fracas going on behind us. We turned around and saw people smashing up the hunt vehicles."

Although most attending were hunt sabs intent on lawful hunt sabotage, some of those who came from outside of the region were Hunt

(Continued from page 20)

The assault took place an a footpath and was apparently witnessed and videoed by Bedfordshire police (although why they didn't intervene is a mystery). No police action on this one either.

Early - Mid November: Mass ridings down by mounted hunt-followers of the Chiddingfold, Leconfield and Cowdray FH, resulting in many injuries to saboteurs, and in one case, a cameraman from Nippon TV was rode into and over by one of the masters of the hunt. Miraculously, he was shaken but uninjured. These assaults were also caught on video by two saboteur cameras! Dismounted riders had to be restrained by W. Sussex police when they whipped and attacked several female sabs with upturned bone-handled whips -- again caught on video. Also, a saboteur was lucky to escape serious injury when a whipper from the hunt charged his horse over the top of him. The hooves smashed a scent-spray lying next to the head of the saboteur - a couple of inches either way and this could have been the third dead saboteur of the 1990's.

Mid November: A female saboteur was held down by hunt supporters and repeatedly punched by a male follower of the Garth and South Berks FH.

End November: Several sabs ambushed and attacked by well-known hunt followers in balaclavas using pickaxe handles and metal piping. The two worst injured taken to Salisbury hospital with head injuries. The sab van was rammed by hunt follower's Land Rover. Several hunt staff got involved in the clashes, one of the red coated riders pulled out a cut-down axe handle from his saddle to smash sabs in the field. Video and Photo evidence of the attacks.

Early December: Dorset sab contact was threatened at his place of work by man with machete! The sab had to leave his work site as his workmates restrained the assailant. The attacker was a part of a gang of poachers linked with the army of hunt followers of the Portman, south West Wilts, South Dorset and Hursely Hambledon hunts in Southern England. They have now threatened to shoot or 'chop' any sabs that turn up in the Dorset area. The CID are currently investigating these death threats, and have installed a panic button in the home of the local saboteur.

Mid December: Ashford Valley, Kent -- a lone saboteur returning from a fundraising stall in town found the hunt trespassing over land near his house from which they have been barred. His vehicle was blocked by hurt followers and all the windows were smashed with axe handles and iron bars. The sab was pulled out the smashed driver's window and given a severe beating and repeated kicks to the head. When the police finally arrived they (as usual) arrest the saboteur and impounded his car. He was released from the police station at 3am, after which he went to hospital to have his injuries treated.

End December: Several sabs injured at the Essex Farmers Union Hunt at their Boxing Day meet in Maldon, Essex. As usual, the press, TV cameras (and

Retribution Squad activists. The HRS headed straight for the hunters vehicles which they proceeded to smash up. The intention of the HRS appears to be mainly criminal damage with no premeditation to injure or harm the hunt and their supporters. Where 'assaults' took place, it was the fox hunters trying to stop their vehicles being attacked and they were forcefully pushed aside. The HRS activists did not stop until every hunt vehicle had its windows and lights smashed, they then jumped back into their vans and fled. The hunt sabs, realising that the Hursley Hambledon hunt was likely to take revenge on any sabs in the area decided that this was also an ideal time for them to leave.

The Hunt Retribution Squad action was obviously well planned and professionally executed. The HRS activists have obviously never revealed theiridentity, but they clearly had an escape route organised and were able to leave the county as planned before the police were able to react to what had happened. Sadly, as the South Coast hunt sabs had not been privilege to any knowledge about what was going to happen they did not have any 'escape routes' planned out.

The police set up a number of road blocks which failed to capture any of the HRS activists but instead caught the innocent hunt sabs who were travelling across Hampshire to return to their respective homes.

The police road blocks caught a total of five of the sab vehicles. All of the vehicles they caught were South Coast hunt sabs, from the Dorchester, Southampton, Portsmouth and Dover, none of whom had taken part in the Hunt Retribution Squad action. In total the police arrested forty-two people. All forty-two were taken to police cells, subjected to strip searches and had their clothes confiscated. They were held for 36 hours, had their homes raided and vehicles impounded. The police even decided to raid the homes of some people who weren't even on the hit!

Having been held for 36 hours all of the sabs were eventually released on Police Bail to return in February 1998 where they were told they could face possible charges of 'Conspiracy to commit criminal damage, ABH and violent disorder".

In the middle of February 1998 the hunt sabs surrendered themselves into police custody. When they did so they found that the police in-

(Continued on page 22)

(Continued from page 21)
most of the demonstrators) left after the initial demonstration against the hunt. When the saboteurs left their vehicle to follow the hunt on foot, they suffered several violent attacks from hunt followers and riders. In the worst attack, a sab was knocked to the ground and repeatedly punched in the head, leaving him with a broken nose and head injuries. A female sab who came to his aid was punched in the face, resulting in a black eye. Also on this hunt, two sabs narrowly avoided being run over by demented hunt followers in vehicles. A sab was run over by a lunatic rider on horseback, sustaining back injuries. This incident was apparently caught by Essex police an video, and resulted in an arrest. There were also a couple of arrests for the earlier unprovoked assault, and we await any outcome with interest.

There have been many more incidents around the country than those detailed above, but this is a fair selection! What has seemed to be an unusual feature of the violence so far this season (apart from the stuff we expect from the foot followers and terriermen!) is the amount of riders who are charging down sabs and either whipping them or trying to ride over them. We are taking this as a sign that the 'average' mounted followers of hunts are increasingly desperate after the Foster Bill on November 28 and are taking their frustration and anger out on those in the front line - i.e. the saboteurs.@

(Continued from page 21)
tended to single out three long-standing members of the Portsmouth sab group who they accuse of 'masterminding' the sab. Out of a total of 42 sabs arrested these three individuals are the only one's facing charges, they are being made scapegoats by the police for everything that happened on the day. They have all been charged with 'conspiracy to commit violent disorder'.

As a result of the police laying charges against the three defendants a Support Campaign has been set up to help them. This campaign is made up of friends and supporters of those arrested. We ask for as many people as possible to join the campaign and show your support with the defendants by;

1) Sabbing the hunts. All those arrested are dedicated hunt sabs who are committed to defending wildlife. Carrying out hunt sabotage on a regular basis will both directly help to save animal lives and show the police and hunts that we will not be intimidated by their tactics.

2) If you are unable to sab, then another way to show your support for both the defendants and the animals is to do everything possible to help make sure the 'Wild Mammals (Hunting with Dogs)' Bill becomes law.

3) Waiting for trial can be a traumatic time. Send letters of support to the defendants c/o;

The Defence Campaign: Portsmouth HSA, Box H, 167 Fawcett Road, Southsea, Hants. P04

5) Send a donation to the Support Campaign to enable us to support the defendants and produce more mailouts. If you would like to receive more mailouts please do contact us at:

Support Campaign, South Dorset Anti-Bloodsports, Box 1119, Dorchester, Dorset, England

DIARY OF ACTIONS

Ok, kids, you know how it goes. The Diary of Actions is intended to report the news of direct action to save the earth and animals, not to encourage crime. All reports come from communiques, other publications, the internet and the news. Some actions took place in time periods covered by other issues of Underground but were not reported until recently.

CANADA

FEBRUARY 24/98: Abbotsford, BC - A fire at a mink farm destroyed a house, but the residents managed to escape unharmed, and the minks on the farm also were unharmed. Twenty-four fire-fighters were dispatched to the blaze at the 28300-block Townshipline Road. Damage from fire, smoke and water is estimated at $49,500. Cause of the fire is still under investigation.

MARCH 6/98: Montreal, PQ - The Quebec headquarters of Canadian AIDS drug maker BioChem Pharma Inc. (BCH.TO) near Montreal was evacuated as bomb disposal experts inspected a "suspicious package" found outside the vivisection complex. The pharmaceutical company, which was rocked by four small bomb blasts last November, had not received any threatening message or warning, police said. Trading in BioChem Pharma's stock was halted on Nasdaq and the Toronto Stock Exchange shortly after 11a.m.

UNITED STATES

OCTOBER 29/97: Neligh, Nebraska - activists caused over $100,000 damage to the construction site of a controversial hog farm, in an attempt to protect the local environment. Unclaimed.

NOVEMBER 17/97: Justice Dept. contaminated supermarket turkeys up and down the east coast of N.America, including at Acme Shoprite, Superfresh, Pathmark Food, Stop 'N Shop, with a lethal substance. This contamination occurred when the consumption of turkey flesh is at its highest, but the group vowed the contaminations would continue long after the "Thanksgiving" holidays were over. -Justice Dept.

DECEMBER 4/97: Lake Worth, FL - Locks glued, and slogans spray-painted at Intra-Coastal Packing Inc. ("Wholesale Poultry"). A truck was also spray-painted and had its windows broken. -A.L.F.

DECEMBER 9/97: Boca Raton, FL - Slogans spray-painted at The Leather Center and the windshield of a delivery truck was broken. -A.L.F.

DECEMBER 10/97: N.Y.C., NY - A.L.F. activist(s) raided the Astora Live Chicken Market (31-37 20th Ave, N.Y.C. 718-777-7249/718-278- 8915), releasing a dozen pigeons and four rabbits. Dozens of hens, roosters, turkeys and ducks are also housed and slaughtered at this Market. More NYC liberations to come, and in greater numbers. -A.L.F.

JANUARY 18/98: Los Angeles County, CA - from the communique: *"Hello, SG and fellow activists! It's been a while, but we have a couple of things to report ... We liberated 18 rabbits, 1 duck, 3 hens, and 5 quail from a slaughterhouse which kills the animals by beheading them. They also leave the animals out, in small cages, in the 100-degree heat in the summer. Among the 18 rabbits was a tiny baby girl who was severely malnourished. All the animals were immediately rehomed. Sadly, the baby girl bunny passed away during the night. Her starvation was too advanced already at that point. We were heartbroken, but tried to console ourselves thinking about the other animals who would live the rest of their lives in loving homes ... In addition to the above, we have also treated several animal-abusing businesses to the standard lock-gluing and slogan-painting forays. One thrift store, whom we have targeted countless times, has separated from its "parent," the City of Hope (VIVISECTION SCUM)! I guess we don't know for certain, but it seems like our ministrations (gluing and painting) could have been a factor in their "divorce"! Until our next communication, we thank all activists fighting for our brothers and sisters. We do what little we can to make this world a little better for the animals."* -A.L.F. Southland Unit

FEBRUARY 2/98: North Brunswick, NJ - Police believe that a group of environmental activists is responsible for recent damage to facilities and equipment at a Sutters Avenue construction site off Route 27. A trailer office and several work vehicles were vandalized. Extensive damage was done to property owned by Forest Gate Associates Inc., North Brunswick, and O & S Landscaping. "Eco-Defense" was written across a vandalized vehicle. Windows were smashed and tires were flattened on the same vehicle. Police also found mothballs in the fuel tank. Other writings found on vehicles include: "End this murder of all life" and "Earth Liberation."

FEBRUARY 11/98: Chevy Chase, MD - The A.L.F. struck at Miller's Furs, covering three windows with etching cream. -A.L.F.

LOOSE LIPS
PREVENT LIBERATION!

FEBRUARY 23/98: Rochester NY - Durand Eastman Park was bomb-hoaxed to protest a deer-bait-and-shoot program. For at least the last 5 or 6 years the park closes early for one month and off-duty police officers shoot deer that are baited to certain areas with piles of corn. So far they've killed about 700 deer since the inception of the program. A bomb warning was painted on the pavement near the start of a hiking trail and realistic looking bombs with copper wires sticking into ground were hidden in the park. County Parks Supervisor Alan Cassidy received a suspicious envelope in his mailbox. That too turned out to be harmless but contained a note warning what might happen if deer bait and shoot program was not halted. -A.L.F.

MARCH 4/98: Spencer, N.Y. - Animal activists sabotaged a vehicle belonging to organizers of a "donkey basketball" game sponsored by Spencer Van Etten High School as a fundraiser. Observers at the event say students were playing basketball while riding donkeys, and they often punched, kicked and screamed at the animals to force them to "cooperate." The activists say they slashed tires and may have damaged other parts of a blue, remodelled school bus owned by Shaw Brothers, the providers of the donkeys. The animals are apparently transported in this poorly equipped, non-insulated vehicle.

MARCH 6/98: Washington, D.C. - activists struck Miller's Furs in downtown D.C. Two large show windows, each sporting huge "Drastic Reductions" signs, now have the following messages written in etching cream: MANNIE KILLS (Manny Miller, owner of both Miller's Furs stores) and FUR STILL HURTS.

ENGLAND

MONTH UNKNOWN/97: Kingbury, Staffordshire - A field of genetically modified rape-seed was destroyed by local residents. They said, *"Our natural world is being tampered with for private profit, and its only a matter of time before something goes seriously wrong."*

NOVEMBER/97: Portsmouth/Hampshire - In support of the Gandalf 3, A.L.F. activists smashed a number of butcher shop windows. Trucks were also torched in Chichester. -A.L.F.

NOVEMBER 20/97 - Portsmouth/Hampshire - Animal libbers demonstrating at a Sainsburys Supermarket protested the sale of kangaroo, crocodile and ostrich meat by conducting a "trolley run" -- in which meat was removed from the freezers and left in shopping trollies in a warm part of the supermarket. Bleach was also poured over the "exotic meat." This is the third such protest of its kind in Portsmouth during November. Sadly, nine activists were arrested and have been threatened with a conspiracy charge.

EARLY DECEMBER: Wanstead - (West London) A McDonald's had its window taken out using some sort of explosive device, possibly a kind of firework that was taped to the window. When it went off, it cracked the whole window. -A.L.F.

DECEMBER/97: Oxfordshire - A.L.F. activists gained access to Christopher Brown's Oxfordshire cat breeding farm. Despite filth swarming all round the area (Home Secretary Jack Straw lives less than a mile away), they leave having smashed 17 windows.

DECEMBER/97: Oxfordshire - In a similar action, Farmer Brown loses 26 windows to the A.L.F.

DECEMBER/97: Oxfordshire - Two workers employed at the vivisection cat breeders receive home visits from the A.L.F. They both get most of the windows in their houses put through, and their vehicles get similarly trashed. Also: A worker returning to their vehicle having parked it in a car park finds it in a considerably worse state to that in which they left it.

DECEMBER 13/97: Wheely Down - Three hunt supporters were injured and 44 protesters were arrested during an attack on a hunt meeting by saboteurs. About 70 masked activists set on the Hampshire Hursley and Hambledon Hunt. Car windows and headlights were smashed and several people were injured in the clash. The Hunt Retribution Squad claimed that it had carried out the attack in revenge for assaults by members of the hunt.

JANUARY 9/98: Dorset - 50 mink were liberated from a UK fur farm.

JANUARY 6/98: Carterton - masked animal rights raiders targeted the home of a breeding farm worker by daubing paint on the walls. In the latest in a series of attacks on the homes of employees at Hillgrove Farm, corrosive liquid was also poured over the employee's car and the windows smashed.

JANUARY 15/98:Oxford Professor Colin Blakemore was presenting the 72nd Conway Memorial Lecture to 150 members of the South Place Ethical Society when a bottle was thrown and two women jumped on the stage, a witness said. Prof Blakemore, Waynflete Professor of Physiology at Oxford, was describing experiments on rat brains when he was attacked. A witness described how "They rushed the stage, threw the lectern over and caused a lot of damage. They smashed glasses and threw flowers to the floor." One woman was arrested on suspicion of assault, criminal damage and threatening behaviour after kicking a car door closed on the academic as he climbed into the vehicle after the lecture ended at 9pm.

FEBRUARY 9/98: London - the North London Angling Centre in Finsbury Park had all its front windows smashed by A.L.F. activists, before it was even able to open for business. The shop had signs up but the inside was not yet fitted out. A few days later a heavy duty security shutter was installed.

FEBRUARY 11/98: Stevenage - A.L.F. activists broke into the John Lewis Partnership (pro-bloodsports) storage depot and caused $20,000 damage to several trucks. -A.L.F.

MID FEBRUARY/98: London - Stall holders at car boot sales in the West London area had recently been spotted selling new fur coats. The coats being sold were apparently mostly mink. A.L.F. activists carried out an arson attack and destroyed the vehicle used by the furriers. -A.L.F.

FEBRUARY 17/98: UK - The Provisional Animal Liberation Front announces its launch by sending out 20 hoax devices to animal abuse targets while clearly showing that it could easily have assembled viable anti-personnel letter bombs.

Packages were sent to:

VIVISECTION

Roslin Institute, Edinburgh: Dolly the sheep and similar obscenities

Huntingdon Life Sciences, Suffolk: Contract testing laboratory

L Powell, Cambridgeshire Rodent studies director at **HLS, Huntingdon D Cameron,** Cambridgeshire Small shareholder in HLS

C Brown, Oxfordshire Breeds cats for vivisection

MEAT INDUSTRY

Meat City, London Dead Animals City!

Bernard Matthews, Norfolk Major animal murderers

Crawshaw Pigs, Humberside Breeds pigs

Sandyford Hides & Skins, Strathclyde By-products of murder

LIVE EXPORTS AND THE DAIRY INDUSTRY

Gilders Transport, Gloucestershire Long a target for protests

Dover Harbour Board, Kent Refuses to stop live exports

Wensleydale Creameries, North Yorkshire No dairy industry no veal calves

FISHING INDUSTRY

Midland Fish, Lancashire Left to drown slowly in alien atmosphere

FUR TRADE

Peter Ley, Dorset Part of the obscene fur industry

CAPTIVE ANIMALS

Colchester Zoo, Essex Life imprisonment without trial

INFILTRATORS, ETC

M Jennings, West Sussex Pro-vivisectors' lackey at RSPCA HQ

D Hammond, West Sussex Stole from animal lib PoW's defence fund

"PET" TRADE

Sengora Toy Poodles, Mid Glamorgan Breeds for profit while strays are killed

BLOODSPORTS

County Down Stag Hounds Properties, Belfast Even the National Trust have seen sense!

Leckford Abbas Estate, Hampshire Pheasant shoots for John Lewis employees

Attached is our introductory statement and the message/diagram which was enclosed with each hoax device. Please check out whether it's a viable design! Had the devices been genuine then stronger cassette boxes would have been used to avoid detonation by the contacts meeting if the box were crushed in the post.

ATTACHED DIAGRAM:
WITH THE COMPLIMENTS OF THE PROVISIONAL A.L.F. - IT COULD SO EASILY HAVE BEEN FOR REAL!! YOU'VE BEEN LUCKY THIS TIME -
[Diagram drawn showing:
Sodium Chlorate weedkiller / sugar mixture
Car bulb or maroon
Battery (PP3)
Contact inside lid
Contact inside body of cassette box]
CIRCUIT COMPLETED AS CONTACTS ENGAGE WHEN CASSETTE BOX IS OPENED
BOOM!! Bye-bye!

ATTACHED LIST OF ADDRESSES

Senior Animal Technician
Roslin Institute ,Blythbank Farm WEST LINTON
EH45 7DF

Purchasing Officer
Huntingdon Life Science Research, Barrie Lane EYE IP23 7PX

Linsay Powell
52 Welland Close
HUNTINGDON PE17 6FL

David Cameron esq
59 Hollow Lane
HUNTINGDON PE17 1DQ

Christopher Brown esq
Hillgrove Farm Crawley Dry Lane, WITNEY OX8 5NA

Accounts Dept
Meat City Ltd, 507 Central Market LONDON EC1A 9NL

Plant Manager
Bernard Matthews Ltd
North Pickenham
SWAFFHAM PE37 8LL

Crawshaw Pigs
Crawshaw Farm
Lowfield Lane, HULL HU12 9AH

Personnel Officer
Sandyford Hides and Skins
Sandyford Road PAISLEY
PA3 4HP

Accounts Dept
Gilders Transport Ltd
Gretto Fields CHELTENHAM .
GL45 5HH

Dover Harbour Board
Harbour House DOVER
CT17 9BU

Managing Director
Wensleydale Creameries Ltd
Gayle Lane HAWES DL8 3RN

Managing Director
Midland Fish Company
Herring Arm Road FLEETWOOD FY7 6NB

Peter Ley
104 Lower Ashley Road
NEW MILTON BH25 5QG

Head Keeper
Colchester Zoo, Maldon Road
COLCHESTER CO3 5SL

Dr Maggies Jennings
Research Animal Dept
RSPCA Causeway
HORSHAM RG1 1HG

David Hammond esq
37 North Court HASSOCKS
BN6 8JS

Sengora Toy Poodles
Maendy Farm Llantrisant Road
PONTYCLUN CF72 8NJ

County Down Stag
Hounds Properties Ltd
Stokes House
BELFAST BT1 6DE

Estate Manager
Leckford Abbas Estate
Leckford STOCKBRIDGE SO20 6JF

MARCH/98: Berkshire - The Vine & Craven foxhunt held their annual hunt ball at Greenham, near Newbury. Whilst the blood junkies were inside enjoying themselves, A.L.F. activists did several thousand pounds worth of damage to their vehicles. Paint-stripper was liberally applied to the bodywork and tires were slashed, as well as windscreen wipers being snapped off. -A.L.F.

MARCH 16/98: A.L.F. activists smashed several windows of the Waitrose supermarket on Holloway Rd, north London. Waitrose are owned by the department store chain John Lewis plc, currently the target of a campaign by the National Anti-Hunt Campaign. John Lewis own a pheasant shooting estate in Hampshire where their staff go on weekend killing sprees. -A.L.F.

MARCH 19/98: Oxfordshire - Billy Butler (Farmer Brown of Hillgrove Cat Farm fame) had his windows smashed, in response to Kevin Hickey's 12 month sentence.

IRELAND

SEPTEMBER 28/97: Carlow - The Gaelic Earth Liberation Front destroyed an entire crop of genetically engineered cereal grain owned by US based biotech corp. Monsanto. The Gaelic E.L.F. have said "This was the first genetically engineered crop in Ireland, and hopefully will be the last." -G.ELF

HOLLAND

JANUARY 4/98: Barneveldt - Nine meat lorries at a poultry slaughterhouse were burned to the ground, causing 4 million guilders damage (1,5 million pounds or so). Responsibility has been claimed by an A.L.F. cell the Rode Haan (Red Rooster). Their communique stated the action was "a good start for 1998". The media reported extensively on the arsons. -Rode Haan A.L.F.

Spanish A.L.F. hard at work.

SPAIN

FEBRUARY 1/98: Bilbao (Bizkaia, Basque Country) - Three shops run by animal abusers were targeted by activists, resulting in windows and walls being severely hit with red paint-bombs. The targets were Peleterias Delmar (Furrier), Caza Y Pesca Ollagorra (Ollagorra Hunting and Fishing), and an important bullfighting bar called La Taberna. The actions were in protest of any activity that harms the dignity and life of any animal, and to show solidarity with all A.L.F. prisoners, as well as those killed for defending the earth and all its creatures. The communique states more actions will be forthcoming! -ACCION Y JUSTICIA POR LA LIBERACION ANIMAL Y ECOLOGICA (Justice and Action for Animal and Ecological Liberation)

GREECE

FEBRUARY/98: Athens - Fire-bombers struck at two McDonald's restaurants in a northern suburb of the Greek capital. What police said were home-made devices went off outside the fast-food outlets in the suburb of Halandri within two miles and ten minutes of each other. Both branches suffered damage, but nobody was injured as they were closed. No organization took responsibility for the blasts, which shattered windows in nearby flats. -unclaimed.

SWITZERLAND

DECEMBER 31/98: Bellruzoue - A.L.F. activists attacked several fur and butcher shops, smashing windows and doors and spraying slogans. -A.L.F.

SWEDEN

OCTOBER 25/97: Enkping - During the early morning of the October the 25th the new-found group Djurrattsmilisen (Animal Rights Militia) liberated 13 rabbits from a vivisection-breeder in Enkping (Gunnar Hagdahl, Ullunda 5462, 199 91 Enkping, Sweden). The activists broke into one building in which they found 40 rabbits of which 13 were rescued and placed in loving homes. The Breeding records of the rest of the rabbits were also stolen. "Djurrattsmilisen" was spraypainted on the building Gunnar Hagdahl has bred animals designated for animal testing all the way back from the 80s.

NOVEMBER 18/97: Eskilstuna - the underground direct action group "De Vilda Minkarna" (The Wild Minks) struck again, freeing 1000 mink from a fur farm. 7 holes was cut in the fence surrounding Kungsor mink farm, and we opened the cages for over 1000 minks, (most of them black), and set them free. This is the second raid this year on this farm and since February 1997, and at least 25 raids has been carried out against fur farms resulting in 12,000 minks and 260 foxes being set free. UNTIL THE BLOODY FUR TRADE IS GONE, THE WILD MINKS

NOVEMBER 25/97: Enkoping - The DJURRATTSMILISEN (Animal Rights Militia) made its first appearance on the Swedish scene in a raid against rabbit breeder, Gunnar Hagdal. 13 rabbits were freed and are all now in loving homes. DJURRATTSMILISEN" was painted on the building. -DJURRATTSMILISEN

DECEMBER/97: Varberg - A.L.F. raiders trashed 16 wheels on trucks belonging to a fish company, and 10 windows were smashed at an egg-factory. -A.L.F.

Swedish A.L.F. strike!

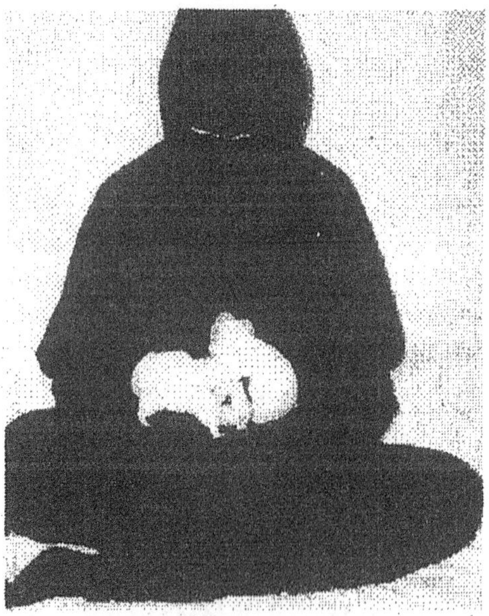

DECEMBER 10/97: Urea - Activists attacked a skinstore, spraypainting slogans, and a fire-extinguisher was used to fill the store with powder. The fire extinguisher were afterwards thrown through a large sign, shattering it. The store is nowadays shielded off by an steel gate which they must role down every evening.

DECEMBER 11/97: Stockholm - An early morning raid by the direct action group Djurattsmilisen (Animal Rights Militia) against a breeding unit belonging to Brothers Eklund in Vallentuna, just outside Stockholm. They breed rats and mice for vivisection. A total of 57 animals (48 rats and 9 mice) were liberated. Two of the mice were pregnant so many more mice was saved from vivisection. From the communique: *"All animals has now been placed in loving, caring homes. This action is dedicated to united Kingdom prisoner of war Barry Horne, who recently was sentenced to an 18 year prison sentence for his acts of compassion. Long prison sentences like that don't make us afraid, it's just makes us even more determent to get an end to all animal abuse."* - Djurrattsmilisen (Animal Rights Militia)

DECEMBER 12/97:Urea - Biopol (vivisection) gets 5 windows smashed by santa who got mad when he heard what Biopol was up to!

LATE DECEMBER/97: Urea -A meat truck is severely vandalized; all windows and spotlights were smashed, all tires were slashed and slogans spreypainted.

DECEMBER 31/97: Urea - Biopol gets 15 windows smashed and electronic equipment destroyed.

JANUARY 15/98: Uppsala - Activists of DJUR-RATTSMILISEN (Animal Rights militia) raided labs belonging to Bio Jet Service, rescuing 92 guinea pigs. Bio Jet Service is owned by Ghote Olofsson, a vivisector at Uppsala University. Bio Jet Service breeds guinea pigs for vivisection. The activists went in through open doors and had planned to liberate about 50 guinea pigs, but when there was "only" 92 guinea pigs in the Premises, it was decided to rescue them all. Most of the 92 guinea pigs has now been placed in good homes after being checked by a vet. Several of the females were pregnant, so an estimated 120 guinea pigs were rescued, if you count the unborn ones. When leaving the Premises the activists were lucky. One minute after their disappearance, a security car drove up to the labs. The owner of Bio Jet Services told the newspapers that he will probably close down after this attack. Djurrattsmilisen will continue it's action until all animal abuse is only a memory in the Past. -DJURRATTSMILISEN

FEBRUARY 6/98: Karlstad - the activist group Djurens Hamnare (Animal Avengers)attempted to burn a meat factory down. Unfortunately, the activists were seen and the fire department was called, but it was on fire in at least three places and the building was damaged by fire and smoke.

FEBRUARY 14/98: Bredared -activists from the Wild Minks visited the Segerstorps mink farm. Damages unknown. -The Wild Minks

FEBRUARY 14/98: Boras - A fur farm in the south of Sweden was raided by activists and all breeding minks on the farm, (300 minks) were set free.

FEBRUARY 21/98:location unknown -- A fishing company had one of their vehicles vandalized: windows were smashed, slogans such as "go vegan" were painted and the interior of the car was vandalized.

FEBRUARY 25/98: The group The Wild Minks made a second visit to Ugglekarrs mink farm, a place well known for it's breeding work. The last attack on this farm was in april-97 so this time the farmer was prepared. In the woods and on small roads around the farm he had placed barb wire at stumbling height. Also, several scare-crows had been made to look like farmers with sticks in their hands that should look like guns. On the farm the activists was met by a sign reading "WARNING! mines!" Activists checked it out and found that the gate had been rigged with some kind of explosive crackers that would have made a lot of noise if they were set off, so the activists decided on another way in. Several holes were cut in the fence around the farm and after that all minks on the farm (breeding animals) was released. The result was 650 minks released into freedom, and a farmer without breeding animals. Hopefully he understands our message; CLOSE DOWN, if not - see you! NO COMPROMISE! -The Wild Minks"

FEBRUARY 26/98: Hagshult - a mink farm had a visit from the Wild Minks. Holes were cut in the fence and 550 black minks (breeding animals) were released from their cages. DESTROY THE FUR INDUSTRY! - The Wild Minks"

FEBRUARY 28/98: Bredared -activists from the Wild Minks was going to free some minks from Segerstorps mink farm. "The Wild Minks" had been sprayed on a building and the activists went in the farm, unfortunately triggering a motion-detector and spotlights went on. A few minutes later cars arrived to the farm. Fortunately, the activists from The Wild Minks made a quick escape and no one was arrested. This is the same farm that was attacked on february 14 this year.

MARCH 15/98: Dstersund - A number of animal rights activists raided the Brunflo fox farm. The activists open the cages to the foxes(70) and took every breeding card. The activists carried out as many foxes as possible from their cages. The foxes were given something never given before in their tragic lives - freedom! Some of the foxes ran out in the woods without looking back once. Slogans such as "A.L.F.", "Treblinka", "Close down" and "Freedom" were sprayed on some of the sheds. All the animals released was breeding animals. The action is dedicated to the 3 activists on remand in Sweden. -A.L.F.

MARCH 17/98: Stockholm - A group called "The Avengers of Fur-Bearing Animals" attacked 11 fur shops throughout the city. Several windows were smashed at each store, slogans sprayed, paint poured over walls and locks glued. The actions were in support of the 3 activists on remand in Sweden, and to show the abusers that nothing will stop animal liberation.

MARCH 22/98: In the early hours over 200-300 breeding minks were released from Forsheda mink/fox farm in Sweden. The action is dedicated to Kristofer Aberg, on remand for releasing minks. NO COMPROMISE! - The Wild Minks

FINLAND

JANUARY 26/98: Helsinki - Two meat trucks were attacked and burnt out by animal activists. A third truck was also targeted, but the fire failed to ignite.

POLAND

FEBRUARY/98: Bialystok - "Eco-punx" paintbombed three McDonalds billboards.

AUSTRALIA

MARCH 13/98: Victoria - Friday 13th turned out to be a 'lucky' day for 16 battery hens rescued from one of Victoria's larger and most notorious battery hen farms. Activists raided the farm in the evening. The hens that were lifted from the tiny cages were dehydrated, and suffering from the initial stages of feather loss, caused by overcrowding where boredom and stress lead to severe mutilations. The 16 hens are now being rewarded by living out the rest of their lives at secluded hen sanctuaries. The farm is presently under surveillance. Further actions are expected.

ISSN 1483-5258

THERE AIN'T NO JUSTICE.
JUST US.

NA-A.L.F.S.G Box 69597, 5845 Yonge St. Willowdale, Ont. M2M 4K3, CANADA
<naalfsg@envirolink.org>

UNDERGROUND

THE MAGAZINE OF THE NORTH AMERICAN ANIMAL LIBERATION FRONT SUPPORTERS GROUP

ISSUE #11

Summer 98

FREE TO PRISONERS

$3

Inside:

and much more...

JOSH ELLERMAN BACK IN CAPTIVITY

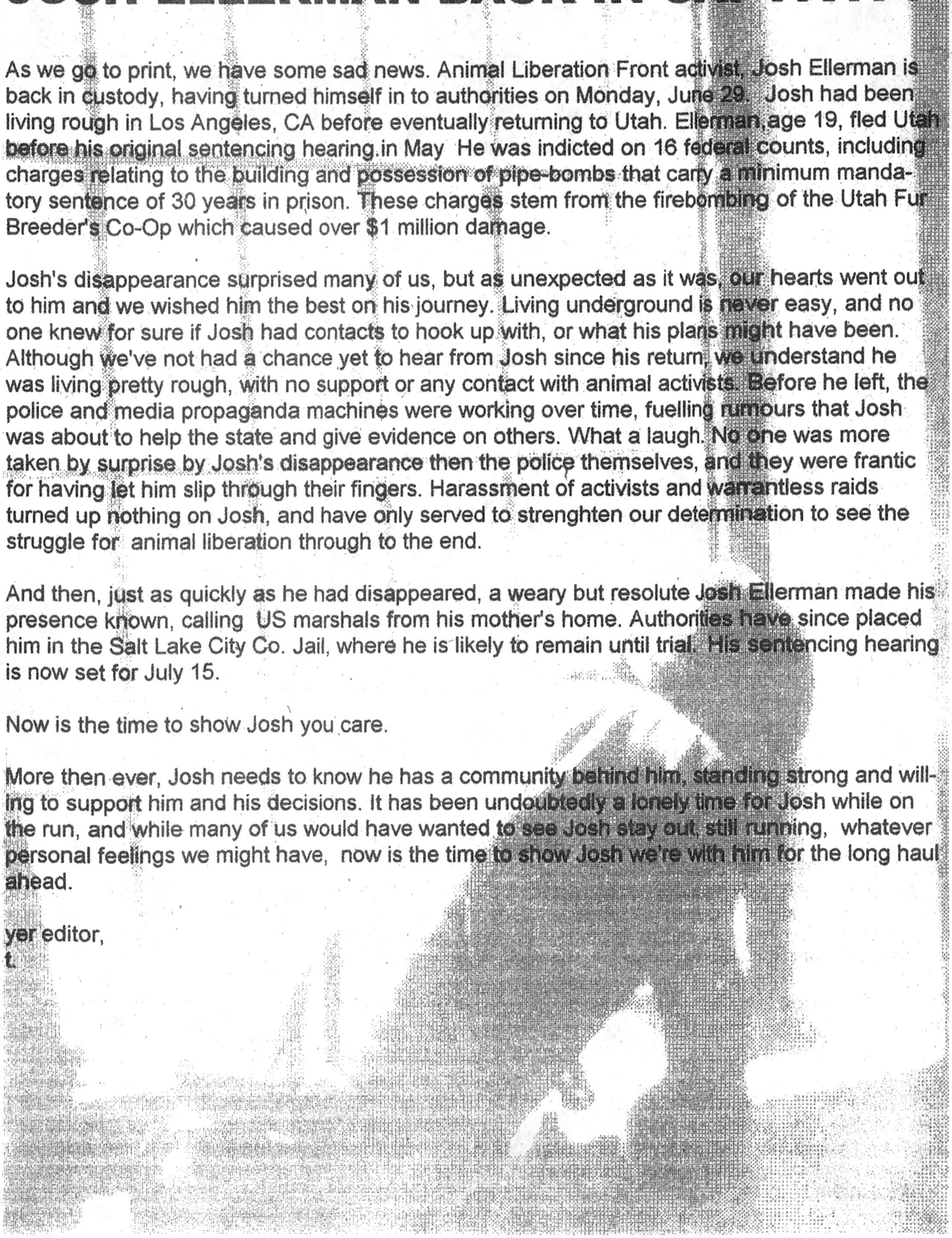

As we go to print, we have some sad news. Animal Liberation Front activist, Josh Ellerman is back in custody, having turned himself in to authorities on Monday, June 29. Josh had been living rough in Los Angeles, CA before eventually returning to Utah. Ellerman,age 19, fled Utah before his original sentencing hearing.in May He was indicted on 16 federal counts, including charges relating to the building and possession of pipe-bombs that carry a minimum mandatory sentence of 30 years in prison. These charges stem from the firebombing of the Utah Fur Breeder's Co-Op which caused over $1 million damage.

Josh's disappearance surprised many of us, but as unexpected as it was, our hearts went out to him and we wished him the best on his journey. Living underground is never easy, and no one knew for sure if Josh had contacts to hook up with, or what his plans might have been. Although we've not had a chance yet to hear from Josh since his return, we understand he was living pretty rough, with no support or any contact with animal activists. Before he left, the police and media propaganda machines were working over time, fuelling rumours that Josh was about to help the state and give evidence on others. What a laugh. No one was more taken by surprise by Josh's disappearance then the police themselves, and they were frantic for having let him slip through their fingers. Harassment of activists and warrantless raids turned up nothing on Josh, and have only served to strenghten our determination to see the struggle for animal liberation through to the end.

And then, just as quickly as he had disappeared, a weary but resolute Josh Ellerman made his presence known, calling US marshals from his mother's home. Authorities have since placed him in the Salt Lake City Co. Jail, where he is likely to remain until trial. His sentencing hearing is now set for July 15.

Now is the time to show Josh you care.

More then ever, Josh needs to know he has a community behind him, standing strong and willing to support him and his decisions. It has been undoubtedly a lonely time for Josh while on the run, and while many of us would have wanted to see Josh stay out, still running, whatever personal feelings we might have, now is the time to show Josh we're with him for the long haul ahead.

yer editor,
t.

Letters to Underground

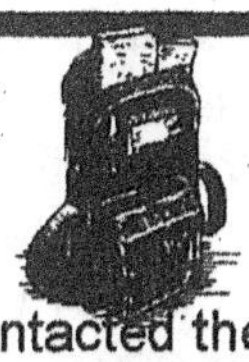

ECO-ACTION FRANCE INFILTRATOR REVEALED

Dear friends,
It has been brought to our attention through various sources that Adrian Franks of Eco-Action France is an infiltrator selling information on activist groups to corporate clients.

Adrian Franks has made himself known to various organisations and movements in Europe as one of the central members of a small direct-action group, Eco-Action, (also known as Earth First! France) which has its base in Equihen-Plage. Adrian Franks has presented himself as an activist focussed on the oil and arms industries and animal liberation. In this guise, he has attempted to weave himself into the European movement active on these issues. He has become involved in ENAAT (the European Network Against the Arms Trade), A-SEED Europe, Earth First! and People's Global Action. In some cases, he has claimed to be working very closely with organisations and networks (such as Corporate Watch UK), but is almost unknown to these organisations/movements.

To his corporate clients, Adrian acts under the surnames Mayer and Lechene. His intelligence agency, Risk Crisis Analysis, is registered in both France and the UK under Adrian Lechene. According to sources, he has created a corporate- oriented information- market on the activities of European activists. He has sought to convince corporate clients of the necessity of his services by way of dangerous exaggeration and misrepresentation of the aims and action-philosophies of movements/organisations he has infiltrated. He has apparently presented these networks as violent, 'extremist opposition' which plan to harm the families of corporate executives. While all of our movements/ organisations Adrian Franks/Mayer/Lechene has infiltrated are very clear in our commitment to impede if not stop the activities of certain corporations, we are all committed to non-violence. Mr Franks/Mayer/ Lechene's portrayal is therefore not only a lie, but exposes our movements to possibly more aggressive, violent strategies by corporations to counter our activities.

We are aware that such a denunciation has very serious implications for the person accused. We have been very careful not to accuse without substantiation, and to act upon information rather than speculation. We have confronted Adrian Franks/Mayer/Lechene with the information we have about his activities. He was unable to refute the evidence we found against him. Further, we have contacted the companies he has approached (as well as those we suspect he has approached) to make clear that while we oppose and will continue to oppose their ecologically and socially destructive activities- we are non-violent. We have also made clear to them that they will no longer receive valuable information from him. In so doing, we hope to break the working relations between Mr. Franks/Mayer/Lechene's and these companies.

We strongly recommend you and your organization, to cut all ties with Adrian Franks/Mayer/Lechene. Take him off mailing lists (95, rue de la Marine, 62 224 Equihen-Plage, France,
email: <eco-action.ef.mala@wanadoo.fr>) and prohibit his participation in gatherings. We ask you to forward this warning to any groups or individuals within your networks so that they do not unwittingly encourage his involvement in their activities. We would be interested to know any further information others might have on his activities within the environmental and social justice movements.

AMOK, A SEED Europe office, Corporate Watch UK
Jansen & Janssen, Oilwatch Europe

For further information, contact:
Janssen and Janssen <respub@xs4all.nl>,
AMOK <amokmar@antenna.nl>, or
A SEED Europe <aseedeur@antenna.nl>.

THEY CAN KILL US BUT THEY CAN'T STOP US

REMEMBERING SISTER MERLE OF MOVE

This isn't the first time we have suffered the lost of our family. The May 13th 1985 bombing of our family was devastating, not only to us but the world! The death of our sister Merle is no different -- The System killed our family May 13th, The System killed Merle march 13th. MOVE people know who the real enemy is, THIS SYSTEM, and because of John Africa we've never been under any illusion about the treachery of this enemy. For over 20 years, officials, politicians, those running this System have tried to stop the MOVE organization from putting out the truth about their crimes against all of Life. They tried to silence us with bribery, when that didn't work they cam at us with blackjacks and false arrests, when that didn't work they cam at us with guns and when that didn't work they dropped a bomb on our family. As y'all can see by the strong, consistent example of MOVE people in prison and on the streets, that this System's bomb didn't work either! but just like the May 13th bombing of our children, sisters and brothers didn't stop MOVE, the death of our sister Merle ain't gonna stop us now. it's doin' just the OPPOSITE, it's making us STRONGER and even more determined to be right.

LONG LIVE REVOLUTION! It should be clear to people at this point how this government feels about ANYONE who dares to stand up against this System and it should be clear after the examples with MOVE that this government will stop at NOTHING to get rid of people who fight this system. This System tried to kill the MOVE 9 on August 8, 1978 with automatic weapons, deluge guns, gas and other explosives, and when they didn't succeed, they continued trying to kill us while in these prisons. The courts gave us 100 years each in prison, knowing we're innocent, we've done 20 years already and in these 20 years we've been attacked by guards with firehoses, pipes, ice picks and dogs; we've been locked in solidarity confinement for three, four, five years at a time, we've been raped of our blood and had something injected into us that made us sick while on a 50 day hunger strike; some of us were almost killed in the camp hill riots, we've been shipped from prison to prison across the States, we've been separated and at times held incommunicado from each other and our family. We've been denied our natural raw food diet and threatened with misconduct if we have more than one piece of fruit in our possession. This is why there is no doubt in our minds that THIS SYSTEM killed Merle. This System is doing all it can to make sure the MOVE 9 don't come out of these prisons alive, because they see they can't break us, can't make us turn traitor against our belief, against revolution! JOHN AFRICA's teaching, our belief is the most important thing to us, we will NEVER leave MOVE! We are going to stay strong and keep fighting for what is right, to do anything LESS would be to make the deaths of our family May 13th and Merle's death to have been in vain and we will NEVER let that happen. We're here to tell y'all not to get discouraged or hopeless because the strong example MOVE has sent is still here and will ALWAYS be here. The seed of revolution has been planted and there is nothing this system can do to stop it! To quote John Africa, the Coordinator, *"The MOVE Organization is not a martyrdom example, we are not suicidal, sacrificial, scapegoats, self-destructive, we're revolutionaries, strategic revolutionaries with expertise in every facet of systematic confrontation, MOVE is strong willed, clear visioned, one minded, true in dedication, MOVE don't stagger, waver, stumble or fall short, with the MOVE organization a step forward is a step gained and a step lost for the System because the MOVE Organization will not take a step backwards, our aim is revolution, our trust is momma, our drive is consistency, our target this System and we will not be stopped for we have the courage of Life, the understanding of True Law and the power of god in both fists."*

John Africa, long live John Africa, long live revolution and DOWN WITH THIS ROTTEN SYSTEM!

ON THE MOVE
JANINE, JANET AND DEBBIE OF THE MOVE 9

SPIRIT OF CHANGE

I write to you on behalf of the editorial of the magazine *Muutoksen keviit* (*Spring of Change*). *Muutoksen keviit* is an eco-revolutionary publication, which tries to gather a wide spectrum of visions and actors of change. We deal with many issues ranging from energy, transport, biodiversity, labour and welfare to food and animal issues. The combining principle is to weave a loose web of ideological connections between these seemingly separate questions. Actually we believe that perceiving these issues as separate ones may be harmful to the movements of change. In short, we deal on Earth Liberation. A great deal of people ranging from ecoteurs to sanctuary keepers, politicians, activists of legal and civil disobedience leaning etc. have been writing in our magazine. This is our eight issue, so our second year is closing. It is not closing quietly. In the last few months Finland has been a hotbed of action. A lot of things have been happening, not all of them good.

We have thus translated a few of our articles for your use. You may already know of some/all of these things, but we hope these articles will deepen your knowledge. Finnish activists urgently need your attention and support. Without too much exaggeration one might say, that the future of the alternative movements in Finland is hanging on the edge. The future seems very insecure, at least to me... The police searched our office, which disrupted our activities almost catastrophicly. Only now, when I'm writing this, I am sure that *Muutoksen kevdt* will go on. This was a close shave economically, for security reasons (e.g. subscribers) and for our ability to just plain WRITE the damn zine.

The latest news however are even worse. During the Orimattila investigation (which seems to be delayed, the police tries to get ballistics results that would vindicate the farmer of attempted killing charges... fat chance) the police stumbled upon a beagle that had been liberated from the Karttula breeding facility. It seems that the process was started by a snoopy neighbour... sometimes all the work seems hardly worth it. HOW can a person willingly send a pup to torture chamber? The police has been making several arrests, and it seems 100% certain that a few activists will be convicted of a series of liberation raids to laboratories around Finland. This is a sad chain of events including dirty elements that I don't wish even to recall here. Loose lips DID sink ships... The chief investigator of the criminal police Tero Haapala has been bragging on the media, that "the hard core" of the EVR (Finnish equivalent of the ALF) has been pierced and most of the actions will be solved. This is clearly a bluff (if you believe the defence attorney who has specialised in these cases, and has taken a strong political stance on the issue), and a part of Tero Haapala's quest for glory. In any case a repetition of the notorious "terrorist trial" is expected, where all cases even remotely dealing with political action will be lumped, and the jury will be confused with loads of circumstantial evidence. The last time a person was convicted of breaking a fur shop window, even though the SECURITY CAMERA showed him walking peacefully before the shop, doing nothing! So, all of the activists need you help very much. Please keep in touch with us, publicize the news on these events and send support to the prisoners who might be coming (hope not).

See you in May. By that time our Web pages should be ready, and we will try to translate some articles there. What kind of issues would you be interested in? Lets keep in touch. And good luck to you all.

The Editor of *Muutoksen Kevdt*

DEFINING NON-VIOLENCE

Dear Editor
I have been informed that there is a rumour going around certain parts of North America at the moment which claim I have renounced the use of economic sabotage as a legitimate tactic for the Animal/Earth Liberation movement. This is not true. What I have done is renounce the use of premeditated violent direct action. However, economic sabotage, including tree spiking and arson, is nonviolent and therefore still something I totally support.

Throughout the history of the Animal/Earth Liberation movement there are numerous examples where it has only been because of economic sabotage (which has always included arson) that has produced positive change and results.

For example, in Britain there use to be a seal cull on The Wash along the Norfolk coast. This slaughter happened every year up until, in the early 1970's, the Band of Mercy set fire to the boats used in the killing. The fire resulted in the organiser of the massacre going out of business and no one else dared start up a similar business in case their boats met the same fiery fate. Since the Band of Mercy action there have been no seal culls on The Wash. Nonviolent direct action works.

In Britain department stores use to sell fur coats. Then throughout the mid to late 80's the Animal Liberation Front ran their incendiary device campaign targeting any department store that sold fur. The result was the department stores stopped selling fur. The protests and the pickets did not stop the sale of fur in British department stores. It was the Animal Liberation Front who can claim sole credit for that. Nonviolent direct action works.

In May 1989 the British fur trade magazine *FUR REVIEW* published the following statement
FUR REVIEW - THE FINAL EDITION . This is the final issue of Fur Review. After more than a quarter of a century serving the Fur Trade, the magazine is closing down. As publishers of Fur Review for the last 15 years we though long and hard before taking the decision to finally cease publication. That decision had nothing to do with its success or profitability. In spite of its now trimmed down appearance compared with the heady days of ten years or more ago, Fur Review *has continued to be a success in its own field and to contribute to the overall well-being of our publishing group. Our decision resulted wholly from our own experiences of the actions of those extremists who planted a fire bomb on our premises before Christmas and have made other threats since.*

As that article clearly shows, nonviolent direct action works.

Also, if you look at some of the actions happening in North America at the moment you can clearly see that nonviolent direct action works. Rod Coronado is serving two concurrent 57 month sentences. One of these sentences directly relates to the fact Rod aided and abetted an A.L.F. raid on a fur research centre which saw the release of two mink and the torching of the lab. That action was nonviolent. It saved the lives of the animals and it caused massive financial damage to those who would have butchered those animals. If the A.L.F. had merely gone in and rescued the animals without causing any damage, the research centre would of just had to go out and buy a couple more mink. As it was their entire building was destroyed. Nonviolent direct action works.

At the end of last year a joint action by the Animal Liberation Front and the Earth Liberation Front saw the release of 500 wild horses caught by the BLM and then the torching of the corral used to confine the horses. If the horse prison had been left standing the BLM could of just rounded up more horses. As it was, they didn't have anything to put the horses in and the BLM announced it was cancelling its horse kill program. Nonviolent direct action works.

Arson and criminal damage has always been two tools of the nonviolent Animal/Earth Liberation activist. Damaging property does not constitute violence even if that damage is caused by fire. As this letter has shown, the use of arson has, in the past, had very dramatic, positive effect in the advancement of Animal/ Earth Liberation.

If people would like to know what my arguments are against the use of Violent Direct Action then I encourage them to read my article 'Violence is Wrong' published in the leading British animal liberation magazine ARKANGEL number 19 (available on subscription from BCM 9240, London, WCLN 3XX, England).

I hope that this letter has helped clear up the misunderstanding people may have about my views on the use of the nonviolent direct action tool of economic sabotage (or rnonkeywrenching as some folks like to call it). It has been proven time and time again that economic sabotage (including arson) works. Economic sabotage (including arson & tree spiking) is ethical. I totally support and applaud all forms Nonviolent Direct Action including economic sabotage.

For Animal/Earth Liberation
RABBIX.

MAKING IT COUNT

Greetings Comrades,

In the interest of speeding the process of animal liberation, I want to throw out some strategic comments to help people better direct their energies.

These comments are related to the United States and Canada solely. the current political climate as it relates to animals, and economic considerations, are entirely different in other countries. Some of this may be relative to England, Sweden, or where ever else, but this is primarily meant for North American readers.

To get right to the point, our cell believes that actions against fast food restaurants and small butcher shops are, at this time, a waste of time. Notice that I said "at this time." We are concerned about activists risking arrest at a place where the impact from the action is going to be rather insignificant.

Actions against the meat industry can be highly beneficial. But smashing a window at McDonalds isn't even a drop in the bucket. Live liberations of farm animals, on the other hand, is always great for the individual animal and can be a great propaganda tool. The lab liberations of the 80's were highly successful in publicizing vivisection, especially when videos were given to the press after the raids. Similar actions today against factory farming would be priceless.

Acts of economic sabotage would have much more impact against an actual factory farm, than against a multi-billion dollar corporation. KFC and Burger King won't even feel the loss of a couple of windows -- but a factory farm can be shut down if all the equipment is damaged. This is especially true if their particular product is suffering from a low market value at the time of the hit.

Putting a fast food restaurant or small butcher shop out of business doesn't save any animals. People will still buy meat, just somewhere else. These places deserve to get smashed up, but is this what we want to risk long jail sentences with? Meat trucks, however, are good targets. This way the distribution of the product itself is affected. if done on a large scale, it can have an impact directly on meat consumption. We are simply asking activists to think their actions out and to go for larger objectives, instead of acting with little forethought.

With the fur industry, it is conceivable the whole thing can be brought down by ALF attacks. Any fur target is strategic since we can put the whole industry under. Fur farms are suffering big time and the continuation of the current campaign will shut the remaining farms down, no matter how high Russian demand pushes the pelt prices.

For vivisection any property owned by a vivisection university is fair game, but cells need to finish campaigns that they have begun. Don't stop with one action, follow through. Just think your actions out and go for real change. Our cell does not sympathize with McDonalds at all -- we just think that we need to avoid arrests when the action that led to the bust doesn't have a chance of producing any tangible results.

An A.L.F. Cell

NEWS BRIEFS

EUROPEAN ACTIVIST GATHERING WENT WELL

The European activists' gathering took place in April in the Netherlands. With well over 200 activists present from all over Europe, including: Germany, UK, Holland, Ireland, Sweden, Finland, Norway, Belgium, Spain, Greece, Poland, the gathering offered a chance to exchange ideas and tactics and to connect with like-minded individuals.

Over the weekend there were workshops on various issues involving animal liberation, as well as discussions, networking, games of football, demonstrations, fund raising gigs and so on. A demo at the local McDonald's had over 150 people invade the premises and throw rubbish around while the police stood by looking helpless. One window got smashed and a Swedish activist was arrested. People moved on to the other McDonald's which was closed down for several hours. The demo received national news coverage in Holland, and also appeared on German TV.

That same night over 100 activists besieged the police station and make a lot of noise to let the arrested person know everyone was out there for them. According to reports, there were only 2 police officers felt brave enough to leave the station at that time. Police had to radio for riot cops from Amsterdam because they were worried activists would smash up the police station and liberate our 'comrade'.

There was also a demo at the last dolphinarium left in Holland.

The food was done by Rampenplan, a vegan organic caterers, which was inexpensive as well as being tasty & nutritious.

The event took place at 'Eurodusdie', a spotlessly clean squatted school in Leiden, whose residents put up with the visiting activists admirably.

PREDATOR HUNT EXTREME 98 CANCELLED.

American anti-bloodsports campaigners have successfully managed to get the 'Predator Hunt Extreme 98' cancelled. The hunt is a two day killing frenzy where hunters are awarded points for killing animals. The person who accumulates in the most points wins $10,000. In this competition different animals are given different values. A Bobcat is worth 60 points. A Mountain Lion 100 points. A Fox 15 points. Following anti-bloodsports protests and the resulting public outcry, this year's competition his been cancelled.

2 SWEDISH ACTIVISTS REMANDED

On April 19, two female animal liberation activists was arrested for allegedly driving a car without a license, and which police claimed may be stolen. Both women attended their court hearings where they were also charged with conspiracy to commit arson/conspiracy to do criminal damage.

The two arrested are Jeanette Hansson, 19, and Sara Raberg, 20, from Sweden.

The police have allegedly found two firebombs in the car after they were arrested, and speculate that the target could have been Allmans chark," a meat place attacked once already last year (three meat trucks burned down).

£10,000 AWARDED TO ACTIVIST

May 14/98

A 53-year-old woman was awarded £10,000 damages by Kent police in the latest payout to animal rights' demonstrators arrested trying to stop live exports to Europe. Angela Petro is being paid the money, plus legal expenses, after claiming officers unlawfully arrested and imprisoned her three times, strip searched her, and damaged her wrists. David Philips, the Chief Constable of Kent, has denied the allegations but agreed to the award. The police face at least twelve more claims, having already paid small sums of £900 to £2,500 to at least three animal-welfare protesters.

ENVIRONMENTAL PROTEST RESULTS IN CHARGES

May 19/98

PRAGUE, Czech Republic - Nine young people were charged with "hooliganism" after an environmental protest in Prague ended in looting and clashes with police.

Police with batons broke up a crowd of 2,000 stone-throwing youths after a peaceful protest on the impact that multinational corporations have on the environment turned violent. Twenty-two police officers were injured in the melee. The protesters overturned a police car, looted several shops and damaged two fast-food restaurants. A judge ruled the nine young people, who were charged with hooliganism and attacking public officials, would remain in custody during the investigation. They face up to three years in prison if convicted. The Czechoslovak Anarchist Federation, the U.S.-based radical environmental group Earth First!, and the Moscow-based Rainbow Keepers were among those organizing the demonstration.

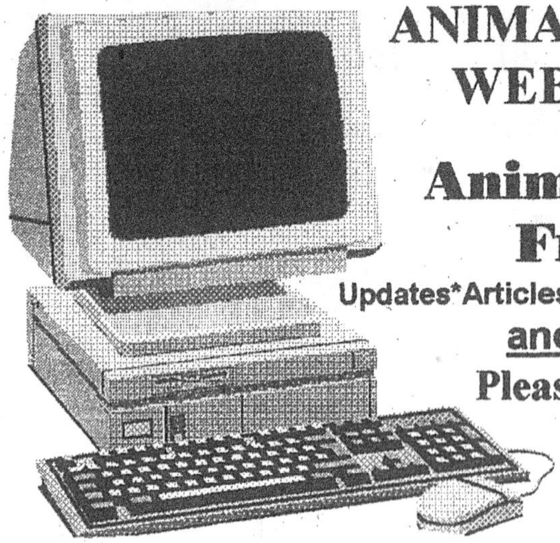

ANIMAL LIBERATION WEB PAGE INFO:

Animal Liberation Frontline News

Updates*Articles*Prisoner Support*Security

and much more....

Please note that our url has recently changed.

The new url is:

http://host.envirolink.org/ALFIS/

Frontline Information Service<frontline@rocketmail.com>

FINLAND ALFSG! EVRTR

Elinten Vapautusrintaman Tukiryhm
Web Site

http://www.sci.fi/~blindeye/evrtr/englsh.htm

EVRTR is a Supporters Group for Animal Liberation Front activists who have been charged with carrying out illegal actions for animal liberation. Information on the EVRTR web pages are mostly in Finnish, however, at the end of each article and/or interview you will find a brief English summary.

SUPPORT ANIMAL LIBERATION PRISONERS!

Thank You!
FINLAND ALFSG!

AUSTRIAN BLOCKADE OF TURKEY CHICK TRANSPORT

19 Turkeys Liberated

May 26/98

BELGRADE - Over 50 Austrian animal liberation activists stormed an airport loading section for the Dutch airline, KLM, at Linz airport. Workers were in the process of loading 20,000 few days old turkey chicks from an airplane onto a truck. The activists surrounded the chicks that were packed in cardboard boxes, and blocked the loading process.

Initially aggressive workers left and came back with police. Two hours later enough police had arrived to start moving the activists. Activists then tactically retreated out of the loading hall to the airport entrance. A little later the truck came out and was blocked by activists, who did a lock-on with d-locks in an octopus position. After a stand-off of another hour or so, the truck retreated into the airport area again. People unlocked themselves.

Eventually, a state vet arrived to inspect the chicks. He never actually looked at them, but declared them fit for travel. They had come from Toronto, Canada, and had come down from Amsterdam, to continue by truck to Belgrade. They had been travelling for 46 hours when activists started their action, obviously without ever getting fed or watered. About 10% were found dead during the inspection by activists. After a delay of another hour, police managed to evade the blockade of the protesters by bringing the truck - without lights on - of the runway towards another exit before protesters could catch up. Apart from that, protesters were a bit reluctant to act firmly, as it was obvious that every minute of delay meant more chicks dying of hunger and thirst. 19 chicks had decided to join the protesters and are now in good hands.

HARPOONED WHALE TURNS ON BOAT

June 2, 1998

OSLO, Norway -- A harpooned whale fighting for its life rammed the Norwegian boat that shot it, breaking the vessel's mast and hurling two crewmen into the icy waters.

The whale escaped, but it was unclear if it survived, the Oslo newspaper Verdens Gang reported Tuesday. The two crewmen, one of whom suffered cracked ribs, were rescued.

According to the paper, the whaling boat, the Bolga, was off Norway's northern tip on Monday when it harpooned a minke whale, which can grow up to 30 feet in length. The whale then rammed the 53-foot-long wooden boat. The two crewmen, who had been spotting whales from the crow's nest near the tip of the mast, were thrown into the ocean, about 425 miles north of the Arctic Circle.

Norway resumed commercial whaling in 1993, despite a ban imposed by the International Whaling Commission.

MINK PROTEST LEADS TO JAIL

June 12/98
ENGLAND - AN animal rights campaigner has been jailed for seven days following a protest at a mink farm.

Liz Crocker, 35, of Sandyford, Newcastle, was jailed by the city's magistrates after failing to pay £3100 in court costs, imposed when she was convicted under the Protection from Harassment Act.

Crocker was found guilty of harassing the owners of Cornyhaugh Mink Farm in Ponteland in February during a campaign to try to close the farm.

A warrant was issued for her arrest in May after she wrote to the court saying she would not "contribute towards a legal system that criminalises peaceful protesters". She was jailed despite her claims that she had not harassed farmer, Peter Harrison, but had "simply tried to publicize what she believes are cruel animal husbandry practices".

Last September Mr Harrison took out a court injunction banning protests under the Protection from Harassment Act 1997, legislation designed primarily to protect women from stalkers.

Under the terms of the injunction the Newcastle Animal Rights Coalition - including Crocker - were banned from demonstrating and protesting near the farm. They were also banned from using the road alongside it or telephoning or writing to Mr Harrison.

MORE MINK ARRESTS IN UTAH

SALT LAKE CITY, UTAH:
Three men are facing two second-degree felonies and four third-degree felonies for vandalizing and releasing minks at two West Jordan mink farms in 1996. Charged in 3rd District Court are Brandon James Mitchener, Alexander David Slack and Sean Albert Gautsch, all 22 years old.

The three activists were arrested Fri. June 19 after twenty police with guns drawn stormed an apartment building. Without search warrants police took pictures of companion animals, and searched through files and personal belongings. The arrests were made by officers from the Department of Public Safety, Criminal Investigations Bureau; the Salt Lake Metro gang unit; the U.S. Marshal's office, the Utah Highway Patrol and the Salt Lake police department.

All three are charged with 6 felony counts for allegedly liberating animals from two Utah fur farms. Alex Slack was held for seven hours while being interrogated as to the location of A.L.F. activist Josh Ellerman. Alex, a paraplegic, was finally released for medical reasons, without ever having his rights read to him.

The other two activists, Brandon Mitchener and Sean Gautschy were being held on $100,000 bail for allegedly taking part in two fur farm liberations in Utah. They are charged with two counts burglary (2nd degree felony), two counts criminal mischief (2nd degree felony), and two counts releasing fur bearing animals (3rd degree felony). Brandon Mitchener has since been released from Salt Lake City Co. Jail on $10,000 bail, ($1,000 actually paid), after a bail reduction hearing.

Sean Gautschy remains in Salt Lake City Co. Jail on $50,000 bail. He is considered a flight risk since he is originally from California. Police had originally offered to drop all charges for information on Josh Ellerman's location.

Clint Marvin was also arrested for an assault charge (not animal rights related) and also was told that charges would be dropped for information on Ellerman's location. Marvin is currently free on bail.

Ellerman, age 19, fled Utah before his sentencing hearing. Josh has since been recaptured and is being held until trial.

Also facing charges is animal liberation prisoner, Jacob Kennison, who was only about one hour away from being released from prison when he was detained on 6 felony counts. Jacob faces the same six counts as Brando and Sean. Jacob was about to be released to a halfway house 90 days early for good behaviour.

Sean's address can be found in our prisoner listings.

CANADIAN ARRESTS

On June 29th in Edmonton, Alberta, two activists aged 19 and 20 were arrested by the Edmonton City Police. Police arrested the two in relation to vandalism at ACME Meats, which was covered in anti-meat and "ALF" slogans. We have no further information at this time.

SEEING THE LIGHT OF DAY

U.S Activists Carry Out Their First Daylight Raid. 19 Rabbits Liberated!

June 20th 1998 marked a first for animal liberationists in North America. We may now proudly celebrate our first ever daylight raid!

For years now, Lance Patton and his father, Oregon State University vivisector Nephi Patton, have bred rabbits for research on a small farm in Philomath, Oregon. The Western Oregon Rabbit Supply's address was unknown, until now.

The action started when about 25 activists from 3 states descended on 2475 Rosecrest Drive around noon on a quiet Saturday. Neighbours sat in their lawns sipping tea, others rode around on big green lawn mowers. After the last activists rounded a bend in the road that took them out of the neighbours sight, they had quite a surprise in store. Masked activists began jumping the fences and running towards the breeding sheds. Soon the activists returned with rabbits in hand, directing the other activists to take them to safety. In total, 15- 19 were rescued.

One anonymous activist had this to say:
"It was phenomenal. I ran down the road and peered inside the sheds. As far as I could see there were white rabbits. A stream of urine and feces ran for hundreds of yards. I began to cry, all I could think about was rescuing these creatures. I opened a cage and gently lifted one out. We began to run back up the road, not fully knowing how the less militant protesters would respond., but to our delight they helped us spirit the rabbits to freedom. It was a life changing moment. I saw 60 year olds running as fast as they could, nearly out of breath trying to get these wonderful beings to safety. I saw younger kids, holding banners so that others may hide behind them to continue working opening the cages. Even those who didn't help remained calm. Somewhere inside we knew that this was the last chance for these rabbits. We just did what needed to be done."

Reports place all of the rescued rabbits out of state and in safe hands. Four of the rabbits required medical attention for stress and heat related anxiety. One had a slight infection in its eye.

Due to the nature of this action, and current FBI / ATF investigations in the Northwest, activists expect harassment and lawsuits. Whatever the outcome of such government repression, activists will not forget the victory they had that sunny day. "I've been arrested tons of times," said one activist, "But I never felt like I was saving anyone. This time, I have tangible proof that my efforts made a difference. I've tasted success, and I want more!" Another activist cheerfully said, "I've never been so happy, and I imagine that the rabbits haven't either. Lets keep this up! Nephi Patton, no where is safe for you!"

This action was organized by the Western Regional Animal Liberation Coalition, just one of four new organizations dedicated to holding militant regional demos. More actions have been planned, stay tuned for updates. For more information, contact Animal Defense League Eugene at adleugene@yahoo.com. @

NOW YOU'RE COOKIN WITH GAS!

How to Grab Ronald McDonald by the Balls

Reprinted from Earth First! Journal, June/July'98

by Jebidiah

This little gem of a trick is a quick way to really fuck up a fast-food joint for awhile. The beauty is that it only takes a second, can be performed with no real preparation and is totally safe. You can do it on your way to grandma's, the store, work or church. The only tool you need is a 12-inch crescent wrench.

Walk up to the fast-food slop-shop with your crescent wrench. Locate the gas meter behind the building (usually near the back door). It looks like R2D2's little brother. It will be a medium grey color and will have either a few gauges or digital readout in a plastic case on top. There will be one pipe coming in and one going out. Examine the pipes, and on the incoming one (usually the left one) there will be a little valve. It looks just like any other fitting except there is a circle about the size of a 50 cent piece in it. Coming off this circle is a rectangular tab with a hole drilled in it. That's your baby. Just grab the tab with your Stanley drop-forged crescent wrench, turn it 90 degrees and watch greasy tears roll down the faces of all those sad people in the drive-thru. Orders will quit going out within five minutes.

Since I know, I'll give you a quick rundown on what is going on inside. Jim Bob just dropped his last load of fish sticks into the fryer for today's lunch rush. the safety valves on all the fryers and grills just closed, and the grease is quickly coagulating. The manager is having chest pains as her labor-to-profit ratio plummets before her eyes. One honor student gives a shit. And the rest of the crew snicker and give each other looks while they get a well deserved break. Dozens of sorry souls are denied their chickenmickwhopperwithfrize. For you tree huggers, that means a ream or two of paper bags, napkins, boxes and shit doesn't walk out the door. For you animal lovers, that means that Bambi's cow cousin stays on ice for another day with the chicken parts and fish pieces.

The best part is it's just plain fun to grab a corporate fast-food joint by the nuts and twist. I like to wait until the lunch rush is hopping and the drive thru is full, then coolly cruise up and shut off the gas while tying my shoe or whatever. No One will notice, No one notices anything. Then walk to a good hide-out to watch as the drivers screech away pissed off. You can laugh over a sprout sandwich or a jug of Jim Beam. The fun will be over in 40 minutes when the gas repair guy comes rolling in and figures it out. But by then lunch is over, three or four hundred bucks in profit are gone, lots of customers are pissed, and McSchmuck owes Jebediah the gas repairman $60. So all in all, it's got pretty good result-to-effort ratio. Plus, it's funny as all hell!

Here's a quick rundown on most of the vulnerable chain restaurants: **Boston Market, McDonalds, Burger King, Taco Bell, Skippers, Jack Off in the Box, Kentucky Fried Chicken, supermarkets with delis and any pizza joint.** Tjese places not only rely on gas equipment, they intentionally hire employees who will never figure out how to fix it. @

TROUBLE AT THE BORDER

Canadian Customs Detain U.S. Activist

When Nik Hensey leisurely drove across the U.S. border into Canada during a camping trip in Blaine, Washington, the last thing he expected was to be pulled over, have his belongings stolen by Canadian boarder authorities, and to be interrogated for hours about what his political beliefs are. Unfortunately, this is exactly what happened in an outrageous and blatant abuse of authority by Canadian boarder guards.

While travelling on US 5-North, Nik and a travelling companion soon discovered the road turned into a huge divided highway leading straight to the border. With no place to stop or turn around, no sooner had he reached the border when he was asked to pull over and a female immigration officer took possession of his driver's license, photocopied it, and kept it. The car was searched by a customs officer "searching for weapons" amongst the camping gear. Two other officers joined in the search and Nik and his friend were 'patted down,' and told they were being detained.

Four customs officers tore through the truck, and upon finding animal rights related books and literature, the mood quickly went from bad to worse. Throwing the books to the other officers, one stated, *"This is what they're here for ... ecodefense, animal liberation, timber wars. they're here to start a war!"* The two were immediately arrested and taken to a holding cell where their personal belongings were confiscated.

According to Nik, *"About an hour later we were supposedly read some rights but never told we had the right to remain silent. When we asked for a lawyer they brought us a phone with some lady claiming to be a lawyer, as the authorities listened in on another phone. They came in from time to time and asked us stupid questions."*

The car had been impounded and the two were told it would cost $700 US to get it back. They were never once told why they were arrested and at one point, when told they were free to go, they were in fact locked in a room so another unknown person could ask where they worked, etc. Many hours later they were again lead to believe they were being released, when two more men from immigration 'escorted' them to an interrogation room. The two were separated and Nik was questioned by a woman from immigration for two hours. According to Nik, *"She claimed she was just asking basic personal information because she 'deals with the people and they deal with the property' and that she 'didn't know what went on in customs.'"* An obvious lie. *"They took digital photographs of me while she asked questions ranging from my political viewpoints on animal testing to my involvement with Earth First!. She asked about a demo I attended at Yerkes in Atlanta and what groups I belonged to. "She then accused me of being in the A.L.F. and wanted to know who my 'friends' were."*

> **"We were carrying nothing illegal and as soon as the animal rights material was discovered we instantly became referred to as the 'eco-terrorists' and treated accordingly."**

After two hours of ridiculous questions, Nik was accused of being involved in the arson of Washington University and was asked about any association he might have with Canadian activists Darren Thurston and David Barbaresh. To top it all off, the customs officer hinted to the possibility that his friend made bombs *"because he had a book on Albert Einstein and we were carrying gas oven propane containers."* At no time did either of the two answer any question regarding political and personal affiliations, or any question not directly connected with the impounding of Nik's car. At long last, the two were "allowed" to pay for the truck's release. The truck's contents were torn to pieces and lay strewn everywhere, but Nik was able to locate his camera, and. since the customs authorities refused to give their names or badge numbers, he took a few pictures of the area and people. When the female immigration officer saw him taking a picture she *"hit me in the face and took my camera."*

(Continued on page 15)

One of Our Own

U.S. Prisoner Fran L. Thompson: Fallen Through the Cracks?

Fran L. Thompson, at one time a highly visible and vocal opponent of factory farming and large-scale, environmentally destructive poluters in Knox County, now sits in prison — not for any animal liberation actions — but for killing her fiance-turned stalker, having shot him out of defense during a home invasion. Unfortunately for Fran, U.S. courts do not recognize acts of self-defense in cases where battered women have killed known attackers, and she was sentenced to life in prison. Since then, life has been very lonely for Fran, cut off from the things she oved, and from the local animal and environmental community she once was an active part of. Until very recently, Fran's situation was largely unknown within the larger networks of animal/earth liberation support, and while it is clear that she is not an animal liberation prisoner, our hopes are that readers will take the time to contact Fran, and let her know she is not alone.

HER STORY: In 1976, Fran's husband was killed in a construction accident, leaving her with a 7-year-old son to raise on Social Security survivor's benefits. She was active within the community, helping the animals and people around her, any way she could. Having long been involved in local environmental and animal issues, Fran at one time had been considering a career in Environmental Law.

In 1979, Fran fell in love again. She thought he was too good to be true, and he was. Ron Thompson turned out to be a man given to paranoid fantasies and jealous rages. When Fran tried to sever the relationship, she was kidnapped, bound and gagged, threatened and tortured psychologically, and repeatedly raped over a period of two days. She barely escaped with her life. Fran had no other meaningful relationship with a man until Dean Frank came along.

Dean Frank, a local in Knox County, had lost two farms to bankruptcy. Fran's mother hired him to work on the farm the family had bought, and where Fran was living. Dean Frank liked what he saw -- both in the farm and in Fran. He became her friend, but when he also tried to become her husband, Fran wavered in her interest. As Dean Frank became more demanding, Fran looked into his past relationships to discover he had an outstanding history of violence towards women. Fran called the relationship off and focused on her activism

Fran was a prominent organizer in a number of local fights against environmentally destructive projects in her area, many of which eventually brought her into direct conflict with John Thomas, the Knox County Attorney and chief proponent of these industrial agendas. In October of 1986, John Thomas, in concert with the Knox County Board, removed vital zoning laws from the county charter. Four months later, Knox County was the leader in the Dames and Moore Survey for proposed and preferred sites for nuclear waste burial. Soon, too, the Waldbaum project, factory farming at its worst, was built in Knox County, and a hazardous waste incinerator was targeted for the Santee Sioux Indian Reservation by John Tomas, Knox County Attorney.

In the fight to stop all of these, and to reinstate the zoning laws, Fran was always prominent. She frequently attended and spoke at public meetings. She initiated and organized petition drives and had researched and documented Waldbaum's lack of environmental safeguards at their existing facility in Wakefield, Nebraska. She had proven mis-statements of fact in Waldbaum's Environmental Assessment. Needless to say, John Thomas and

Fran Thompson did not become close friends.

Meanwhile, in August of 1991, Dean Frank had begun to phone Fran, making threatening statements, and was becoming increasingly irrational. She was told by the Sheriff's Department that there was nothing they could do until he acted, and they refused her protection. It was too reminiscent of her kidnap, torture, and rape in 1983. The police refused to intervene in what they considered a "domestic dispute," so Fran began keeping her deceased husband's .3 57 magnum with her at all times. To top it off, Fran also began to received death threats from "friends of Waldbaum", the factory-farm, adding an additional ingredient of fear.

On Sunday, August 18, 1991, Dean Frank entered the residence of Fran Thompson, uninvited and unannounced. Because of a hearing deficiency, Fran did not become aware of his presence until he was in the next room, again declaring that he was going to kill her. She produced the pistol from next to the chair where she had been working at her computer, and said, "No, you're not." When he launched himself at her, she fired, and fired again. She fired until he went down, striking him three times, and then continued to fire into the floor until the gun was empty, seized by sheer terror and the instinct to survive.

In the kitchen where the phone was - and a box of ammunition - she called the Sheriff's Department to ask for help, even as she reloaded her gun in desperate haste, shaking with fear. Fifty minutes later, help arrived - the sheriff and an ambulance. The sheriff was apologetic that he was unable to do nothing more for her before tragedy struck, and took her back to the station with him, saying that it was obviously self defense, and she would be released after a coroner's inquest. But the next morning, John Thomas, Knox County Attorney, charged Frances L. Thompson with first degree murder and commission of a felony using a firearm. Despite everything showing this was an act of self defense by a woman terrified for here life, things did not go well in the Knox County court, and Fran was found guilty as charged.

Fran L. Thompson was placed in jail garb, handcuffed, and taken to the women's prison in York, Nebraska, where she was held in solitary confinement, with inadequate food, clothing, and blankets in an unheated concrete cell with a metal bed. Fran is currently among the general prison population, but after two months of solitary, the transition is almost as difficult as the higher incarceration.Fran was sentenced to life in prison, and remanded back into custody. She will be eligible for parole in 2022.

Fran Thompson is recognized by the British Vegan Prisoners' Support Group as a prisoner requiring (but not receiving) vegan/vegetarian meals.

Fran wants to hear from you. No, she is not in jail for animal liberation activities, having focused her activities more on welfare and rights issues. But she is a part of our community, and needs to know she has not been forgotten. Fran is not in any way claiming A.L.F. prisoner status, nor is she requesting financial support -- simply a kind word. Please write Fran at the following address:

FRAN THOMPSON 93341: Nebraska Center For Women, Route 1, Box 33 York, Nebraska 68467, USA
Prison rules: No letters from prisoners are allowed. Envelopes must have return address, no enclosures, no stickers, write on one side of page only*

(Continued from page 13)
TROUBLE AT THE BORDER cont.... Things did not end with their eventual release from Canadian customs. Upon reaching the US border, the pair were met by more authorities, and it wasn't until they reached Oregon that they were able to check their belongings. The Highway Patrol had followed them the whole way in the distance. Besides the theft of legal camping gear ("weapons"), much of the animal liberation literature Nik carried for tabling was missing, as well as a bunch of pamphlets, animal rights magazines, membership cards, and personal items.Damages were documented with a video camera. Everything was trashed, stolen, or 'confiscated' and after 8- 9 hours of imprisonment and interrogation neither of the two were ever formally charged. *"We were carrying nothing illegal and as soon as the animal rights material was discovered we instantly became referred to as the 'eco-terrorists' and treated accordingly."*

Welcome to Canada folks, we love your US tourist dollars, but if you are in any way politically motivated, outraged by injustice, active for positive change, questing for a new and better world, you'd be better to stay the hell away, because Canada Customs wants to make your life a living hell, and will trample over any and all basic "rights" you might have thought you had... @

STOP, GODDAMN IT!

Orimattila, Finland, December 6 1997
by Elina Salonen

On the night before the Finnish Independence Day a group of five activists headed for a fox farm with plans to dye the animals with henna, rendering the animals coats useless to the fur industry. They also had a camera for photographing the animals and their living conditions. Unfortunately, when the activists reached the edge of the field surrounding the fur farm, they triggered an alarm and the farmer got himself ready to stop the intruders. In two minutes, he fired his first shots in the air. He had planned for this event, making sure that his pockets were filled with buckshot. After the first shots, the farmer shifted his aim lower. As the activists ran for their car, they were chased by the farmer and his shotgun blasts. It was 200 meters to the car, and the farmer fired ten shots, hitting three of the activists with a total of 15 pellets, before they got out sight.

From the dark came the shout: *"Stop, goddamn it!"* and we ran. Shots were flying all around us, and the only thing we could think of was to get out fast. Once in the car, we almost drove into a ditch, but then a police patrol stopped us. The next thing I knew we were heading for a hospital in an ambulance. *"I would have shot at you, too, if you had come to my fur farm"*, was the nurse's comment at the hospital. I was transferred from the hospital to a jail, arrested for being suspected for trespassing. The next day the interrogations began. The meaning was to find out what had happened. After three days I heard that there had been demands to imprison us all.

Three days later, Tuesday, December 9 Helsingin Sanomat, the leading Finnish newspaper, discussed the event in an editorial. The paper claimed that *"Eco-terrorists have taken the law to their own hands and the farmer responded in kind..."* It seems strangely unfair to compare the use of henna and camera to the use of deadly force, e.g. a shotgun. The editorial continued "The reaction of the farmer can be understood, as he is practising a legal trade which is under repeated criminal assaults." Sure, we all understand the actions of the farmer: here's a man who practices a trade in which he violently kills living beings year after year after year, and with it any respect for life and the rights of the living has disappeared. There is no justifying his actions. Although a trade is legal, it does not mean it is acceptable. This reaction cannot be justified simply because the farm has been the focus of mischief or nuisance actions. There is no excuse for attempted manslaughter or grievous bodily harm.

The fur farmer Markku Kuisma has received the status of a hero by the media. He plainly had no regret for his actions, and in the TV-interviews he gave he told how there was nothing else left to do. Nothing but to shoot people. Defending one's private property with a gun is not allowed by Finnish law, but it seemed to be more acceptable than defending animal rights. Newspapers were filled with columns sympathetic to the farmer, and concerned citizens expressed their support for this poor man. The Justice Minister, Kari Hdkiimies (National Coalition Party), defended the actions of the farmer, and fantasised about a future Finland without the freedom of expression. The Minister of the Interior, Jan Erik Enestam (Swedish People's Party) compared animal rights activists to Satan worshippers, and concluded that activists are much more dangerous. All that remained was that the Chief Inspector of the Central Criminal Police, Tero Haapala, leaked rumours about an animal rights activists' base filled with explosives and plans for further actions. The smear campaign had begun in earnest.

As the debate heated up, the media and the public tended to forget the real issue at stake. The farmer had seven guns, the activists a camera and some dye. Not only that, the activists had not actually committed any actions at the farm.

At the first hearing I was imprisoned for a week for suspected vandalism. I would be going to Lahti jail. The thought of being locked up in a cell felt strange, and for the first days I tried getting used the idea of being imprisoned. Staying in a cell is not that bad, if you know how to deal with it mentally. Before this happened I had thought it would be much worse than it actually was.

The cell was small and made of concrete, the guard brought me porridge in the morning and some food in the after-

noon. In the evening I got some tea and was even allowed to go outside on the grounds. Time passed slowly, I spent it reading the same magazines over and over again, I was looking forward to every event, even the interrogations, which meant repeating the same things over and over. At first I could not receive any mail, because, as they told me: "That might make you feel better...". In other words, during the first days they tried to make the isolation as distressing as possible. After a few days I started receiving mail and was allowed to see my mother a lot.

There was no shortage of arbitrary police actions and arrests on the grounds of opinion in this case. After the incident, one activist was interrogated, then released. The others were jailed for three days, arrested for trespassing, which normally in Finland is not grounds for arrest. These people were animal rights activists and thereby treated very differently. One activist remained imprisoned for 27 days. The day she was released, another activist was arrested, this time for two weeks. These arrest periods were uncommonly long compared to the seriousness of the crimes. By comparison, several skinheads were arrested for assault just before Christmas, but were then released, as it would be "too cruel" to keep them in jail during Christmas. Meanwhile, one of the activists was held in jail during both Christmas and the New Year.

After one week the Lahti District Court decided to continue the imprisonment by two weeks.

That hearing was short and it seemed to me that the decision had been prearranged. The next day I was transferred to Vantaa, which meant that I would be spending Christmas in jail. That Christmas was very lonely. I had some Christmas food and my mother brought me presents. The third hearing was held December 30 in Vantaa, where I travelled by plane, just to hear again the same things the two previous judges had said. I was sent to prison for two more weeks. Later that day we drove back to Vantaa. The jail in Vantaa was more comfortable than that in Lahti. The guards were friendlier and the food was better.

The interrogations took place less often during the Christmas holidays, about every three days, if not less often. They dealt with the same things than before, apparently my answers did not satisfy the police. The pages of the tactics manual were turning, and the most amusing comment was: *"Let's go for a beer when you're free. The one good thing in all this is that we have become friends."* In other words, one of the goals of the interrogator was to strike a friendship in order to get satisfactory answers. In between the interrogations, there were sometimes "conversations", in which the policeman presented his own ideas and views on ethics, trying to make me share my thoughts. The last two weeks went slowly. he last eight days I was on hunger strike, during which I received more support mail than ever. It was really great to receive all that mail and I read some letters many times over. The first day of my hunger strike I phoned my mother after the interrogation and I heard about the demonstration outside the jail. Of course I did not know what was going on outside and I can't find the words to describe how amazing it was to hear the demonstrators. Without all of your support it would have been very difficult for me, so I want to thank you for all the mail, the food, the books, the magazines, the posters and all the other support I got.

On January 7 the Vaasa Court of Appeal released me. This was just a few days before the next hearing. The decision came as a surprise to the police and they kept telling me that we had not had enough time to deal with everything and that we would meet again. Thinking about it afterwards, compared to the sentences other animal rights activists have received, a month seems like a short time, even though it felt very long inside. Receiving support is very important to anyone who has to spend time in prison, so do not forget our foreign friends who are imprisoned.

While the activists were imprisoned, they received support from all around the world. The support demonstrations outside the jail were the first of their kind in Finland. There were also support groups in other countries, activists from Poland, Sweden, Britain, the USA, and in other countries raised their voices in protest. The event awakened many people to support the activists in prisons all over the world. The situation these activists faced in Finland should act as both an example and a warning to others in the field. Given half a chance, those involved in animal abuse would gladly try to kill those of us trying to end it -- and the system will reward them for their blood lust. Let's not give them a chance to try again. Be safe, stay strong, destroy the fur industry! @

World Day was a Riot

By Noel Molland.
The Eco-Journalist who writes with Conviction.

The 18th of April, 1998, was the annual international World Day for Laboratory Animals. On this particular World Day, in England, a demonstration was held outside the lab animal suppliers Hillgrove Farm in Witney, Oxfordshire. People started to gather for the demo at just before midday. As people arrived they discovered two different police check points. At both checkpoints you were photographed, searched and had your details taken down which included your name, address and a physical description of what you look like, what your wearing, etc.

Having been searched twice everyone made their way towards Hillgrove Farm only to find a large military style security fence complete with observation turrets. The first people to arrive made their way to the security fence without any problems. But after about half an hour of a constant stream of people the police tried to block the protesters way and prevent them from getting to the main demonstration. Initially this seemed to work. At least until one or two activists spotted alternative routes to the 'farm' and walked around the police block.

Once people reached the 'farm' the security fence was quickly inspected for any weak links. The mood of the crowd at this point was one of expectation. People wanted to rip the fence down and get to the farm. There was a sense of both anger at the suffering of the animals, but also of hope as people predicted there was going to be a big kick off. In hushed whispers people discussed where they thought the weak spots of the fence were. Then the demonstrators got to work ...

It started with people either picking up rocks and banging the fence or hurling abuse at the riot clad police behind the fence. After a short while people stopped banging the rocks on the fence and instead chose to throw them over the fence instead, both damaging the roof of the property the fence protected and bombarding the riot police. Others busily used sticks to try and dig their way under the fence. Crowds gathered around the diggers protecting them from the view of the police. Suddenly a cry went up. A group of activists had managed to force open a large gate in the fence. The crowd, which numbered about 800 to 1,000 people, surged around and tried to force their way inside. At this point a wall of riot officers with shields blocked the gate entrance. By now the crowd was whipped up into a frenzy and people were determined to get inside. Even two charges by the mounted police failed to remove the

crowd. Instead the cops themselves became the targets as people hurled rocks and mud at them. One cop, with a video camera appeared at the top of a turret and was forced to retreat as he came under a barrage of missiles. He only returned when he had a colleague with a riot-shield to protect him. The fact they were being filmed did not seem to worry the crowd who were busily hurling rocks, mud and insults at the police.

Elsewhere on the fence a group of demonstrators found a large log which took four of them to pick up. This log soon became a battering ram which pounded against the security fence. Others continued to dig at the very foundations of the security fence.

It was literally only because the police had a proper military security fence they were able to prevent the demonstrators from gaining access to the farm. However, according to the national evening news, the roof of the family home of Chris Brown (owner of Hillgrove Farm) sustained considerable damage from all the rocks that bounced off it. The demonstrators may not of been able to rip the buildings apart brick by brick, but the volley of rocks pounding the roof was certainly the next best thing.

On the day of the demonstration ten people were arrested and charged with Violent Disorder. Over the next month or so the police are bound to go through their video surveillance footage and more arrests are inevitable.

The demonstration caused much media interest. There was live radio commentary. Film footage on the TV news broadcasts and column inches in the national Sunday newspapers.

Regardless of whether people feel the tactics of the demonstrators were right of wrong, the protests that day achieved national media attention. It forced the media to debate the rights and wrongs of vivisection (even if the debate was very one sided) and it will of certainly forced Chris Brown to seriously consider if he really does want to put up with this sort of thing every couple of months.

Life's a riot folks. Enjoy the party.

RAGE AND REASON

By Michael Tobias
The ultimate animal rights novel of revenge!

REVIEW

Rage and Reason is Michael Tobias' most recent work of fiction. Well known as a film director and producer, _Rage and Reason_ explores the mind-set behind an outraged ex-US soldier who has turned to violent retribution in defense of the earth and its animals.

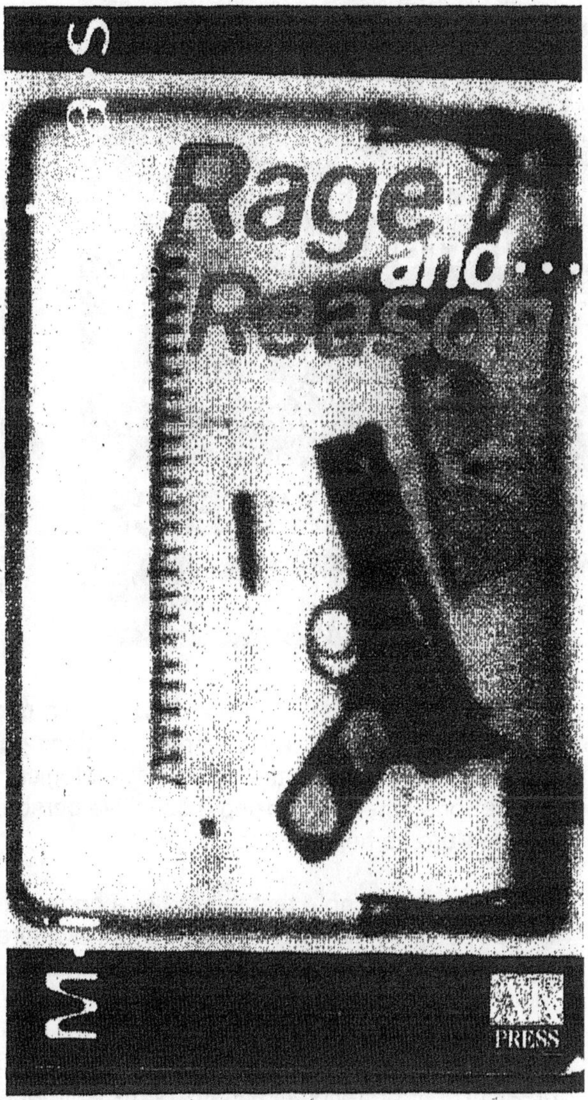

Rage and Reason was a different book then I first expected, perhaps as I'm use to thinking of animal liberation literature as consisting of primers, how-to manuals, or even, for example, in the case of *Memories of Freedom*, anonymous tales of sabotage and victory, in which the participants disappear, unknown into the night. Rage and Reason, in contrast, sometimes reads more as a blockbuster action film, full of gun fire, car chases and explosions. We see the hero extract justice and revenge on a plethora of animal abusers: a chief executive's severed head is served up at a stockholder's luncheon ... a furrier is skinned alive ... hunting season in the Maine woods is turned into a human massacre. The conditions under which various animals in captivity are kept are graphicly and accurately described.

The novel is narrated by the younger brother of the protagonist, Felham. On the run and living underground from both the FBI and Thai animal poachers, Felham confesses to his brother a number of brutal murders recently committed in the name of animal liberation. Confused, shocked and at the same time protective of Felham, the younger brother tries to make sense of how any of this could have happened. The more he comes to know, the more he spirals dangerously closer to joining his brother in extracting the "ultimate revenge" on animal abusers.

Rage and Reason is shocking, brutal, entertaining, and believe it or not, thoughtful about its subject matter. The novel looks at a subject that is taboo for most of us within the animal liberation movement, even amongst supporters of so-called "extreme" tactics: the deliberate killing of animal abusers. What are we supposed to think of Felham and Muppet, the two activist/assassins who make their way across four continents with no compunction against killing humans who play a major role in the suffering of animals? Are they simply psychopaths as we first might think if this were not a work of fiction but taken from today's headlines -- or is something more at work?

What held my interest with *Rage and Reason* was the attention given to this very issue. Very soon into the novel you realize that the people involved are caring, dedicated, sensitive beings. The motivations behind the killings are explored in detail, and while outsiders may find the portrayal of the activists far too sympathetic, Tobias' writing provides the readers with important insights and that make these actions understandable to the rest of us. Far from

A NEW SPECTRE?

By Noel Molland

The British 1997-1998 fox hunting season has seen a marked increase in the use of direct action against the hunt. In fact so many actions have taken place, hunt journalist Elizabeth Peplow, writing in the HORSE & HOUND (16th of April 1998), suggested there is "a new spectre, the Hunt terrorist."

Within Peplow's list of what she classifies as "the new spectre" is a sab of the Crawley & Horsham Fox Hunt on the 27th of September 1997 which saw about 60 hunt sabs hurling abuse at the hunters attending a Meet. One hunter, who admitted locking themselves inside their car to escape the sabs, told Peplow the event was "terrifying."

Other 'new spectre' actions include a Hunt Retribution Squad action against the Portman Fox Hunt. Peplow does not go into great details about the events on the 30th of November 1997, but other sources have said approximately six vans pulled up at the Portman Meet. Masked activists, armed with clubs and chains, jumped out of the vehicles proceeded to smash up some hunt vehicles before piling back inside their vans and fleeing.

A similar Hunt Retribution Squad action occurred on the 13th of December 1997, when HRS activists damaged about sixteen vehicles belonging to members of the Hursley Hambledon Fox Hunt. Three hunters were also injured in this attack. Sadly 42 innocent hunt sabs arrested, 3 of whom were later charged with 'Conspiracy to Commit Violent Disorder'

On the 21st of March 1998, the Hunt Retribution Squad struck yet again. This time at a Meet near Aylesbury. Once again vehicles were attacked and hunters assaulted. One man, a forestry worker

(Continued on page 22)

(Continued from page 20)

RAGE AND REASON cont ... being a manual on how to kill vivisectors, *Rage and Reason* was written, in the author's words: "...as a warning of things gone wrong, terribly wrong, in our society, and for purposes of throwing some dark light on the tragic, psychological forces at work that compel people to kill...of venting the inevitable frustrations inherent to being a sensitive person..." In the end, we may not agree with the tactics used by Felham, but we sure as hell can see his point.

It is important to note that this is not a book reflecting upon any existing animal liberation group, including the Justice Dept. or similar organizations that have directly targeted individual animal abusers. The characters in *Rage and Reason*, while sharing our goal for total animal liberation clearly fall outside of the animal liberation movement." At the same time readers will share in the characters outrage, understand their motivation and empathise with their pain. Some may be disheartened by the acts of violence, having actively worked to try and dispel the myth that animal liberationists are violent, raving terrorists. If anything, *Rage and Reason* serves to put the lawbreaking but non-violent actions of the Animal Liberation Front in proper perspective. In fact, vivisectors, fur farmers and others of their ilk should be GLAD when visited by A.L.F. activists given some of the alternatives presented with the *pages of R*age and Reason...

For information on how to order copies of Rage and Reason, please check out our merchandise page.

(Continued from page 21)
named Roderick Wilson, was beaten unconscious sustaining a broken nose and jaw in the attack. A few hours after the incident, Wilson's mother (another hunter) died from a stroke. The police made 22 indiscriminate arrests of innocent hunt saboteurs after the incident.

A week after the Aylesbury incident the HRS was at it again. This time in the Cotswolds when Joint-Master of the Cotswold Vale Farmers Hunt was dragged off his horse and clubbed unconscious.

However the targeting of the hunt is not just confined to the HRS. A new group calling itself The Provisional ALF, in February 1998, sent out a series of hoax bombs some of which went to blood-sports targets. The Provisional ALF have warned that a real bombing campaign will start shortly.

Taking a nonviolent root to the hunt problem, the Animal Liberation Front have also been very active, both targeting the hunts directly by damaging their property, rescuing hounds, etc. and also by targeting companies and organisations that support hunting. On the day Tony Blair made it clear New Labour would renege on its pre-election promises to ban hunting, the Labour Party HQ was bomb hoaxed. W.H.Smiths stores have received a number of bomb hoaxes, including on the 27th of October its Headquarters, because of W.H.Smiths involvement with the selling of blood-sports magazines. Meanwhile Earth Liberation Front activists have been sneaking into W.H.Smiths stores, damaging the inside pages of the hunt magazines, before placing them back on the shelves.

The Animal Liberation Front have also been incredibly active with the anti-John Lewis Partnership campaign (John Lewis run a shooting estate in Hampshire for their staff). The John Lewis Partnership HQ has been bomb hoaxed, businesses belonging to John Lewis have started to loose their windows. On the 7th of February 1998, an estimated E20,000 damage was caused to lorries parked at the John Lewis depot in Stevenage. Etc etc.

The result of all this action has been to create a lot of fear within the hunting community. Peplows concerns of "a new spectre, the Hunt terrorist" have been confirmed by Alison Hawes of the Countryside Alliance (formally known as the British Field Sports Society). In early May 1998, Hawes told the DORSET EVENING ECHO *"These groups of vehemently aggressive hunt saboteurs don't necessarily intend to disrupt a hunt. They are only interested in damaging property and people. They dress in black balaclavas and are almost like an army. They use staves, iron bars and baseball bats with nails on. We are worried that with the hunting bill having failed, this group will take the law into their own handseven more."* The DORSET EVENING ECHO informed its readers that Hunt Retribution Squad groups are targeting hunts throughout the South of England including Dorset. As if to confirm how widespread and how common Hunt Retribution Squad actions have become, Mrs J. Davidge, in a letter to HORSE & HOUND magazine (30th April 1998), informs us: *"this brand of thuggery is a weekly ritual."* Davidge stated that for the Hunt Retribution Squad *"destroying hunting has become their 'blood sport'."*

(The author wishes to make it clear that he is totally against the use of Violent Direct Action and he does not condone the Hunt Retribution Squad's use of assault tactics - This article was written to keep UNDERGROUND readers informed as to what is happening in Britain).

Ok Fox — We've got the bastards riding in circles over in that thicket. Now's your chance to make a break for it!

DIARY OF ACTIONS

Ok, kids, you know how it goes. The Diary of Actions is intended to report the news of direct action to save the earth and animals, not to encourage crime. All reports come from communiques, other publications, the internet and the news. Some actions took place in time periods covered by other issues of Underground but were not reported until recently.

CANADA

APRIL 10/98: Guelph, ON -- "Fur is Dead," "A.L.F." and "Meat is Murder" were among the messages spraypainted in red on Guelph Fashion Furs and several fast food restaurants, including Kentucky Fried Chicken and Wendy's. --A.L.F.

JUNE 7/98: Guelph, ON - Members of the A.L.F. slashed all four tires of the car of known vivisector, Keith Linder, operating out of the University of Guelph. The car was parked outside of the vivisector's residence. As well, several slogans / signatures were spraypainted on surrounding roads , including "Animal Rights Now," and "A.L.F."

JUNE 21/98: Tobermory, ON -- a breeder (female) rabbit was liberated from a roadside covenience store/ gas station. The owners of the station operated a breeding farm for rabbits on their property. The rabbit in question was locked into a 1' by 1' cage with a wire bottom. Feces had piled up to the extent where the rabbit was lying in them. The rabbit is now living in a caring household filled with toys, yummy food, clean living spaces and another rabbit companion.

JULY 5/98: Guelph, ON -- Vivisector, Keith Linder, operating out of the University of Guelph had his car "attacked" again. The University Of Guelph is one of the largest users and abusers of animals in Canada. The car had its tires slashed, windshield broken and the word "A.L.F." painted on the hood of the car. This demonstration is only latest in a series of actions against the known vivisector, who operates on dogs at the university. -- A.L.F.

UNITED STATES

NOVEMEBER 9/97: Philadelphia, PA.-- Phil Leather Man's Leather Manufactures had all of their security gate locks filled with liquid steel. -A.L.F.

NOVEMBER 9/97: Philadelphia, PA. -- A McDonald's/ Taco Bell eatery had 2 large windows destroyed. The slogan "MEAT IS DEAD" was etched. VICTORY!! NOW CLOSED!!!

NOVEMBER 9/97:Philadelphia, PA: Bassett's Original Turkey, had three windows destroyed, locks were filled with liquid steel. This is the second attack.

DECEMBER 2/97: New York: The "Paint Panthers" claimed responsibility for attacking the Soho home of Vogue editor Anna Wintour, at 172 Sullivan St. "Bloody" paw prints were painted on the sidewalk leading to the house, where a pool of red paint was left on the doorstep. The words "Fur Hag" were also spray painted on the sidewalk. Anna Wintour has been the target of other direct protests for her advocacy of killing all kinds of animals, including Russian steppe ponies, for their coats. In January, an animal rights activist threw a dead raccoon on Ms. Wintours plate as she dined at the Royalton. --Paint Panthers

MARCH 4/98: Tucson, AZ -- The A.L.F. destroyed two refrigerated trucks with incendiary devices and vandalized five others with spray paint at the Shamrock Dairy Distribution Center. This action was taken in the name of spreading awareness about the suffering of animals at the hands of the dairy industry.

MARCH 30/98: San Jose, CA -- a Safeway (West Coast supermarket chain that was targeted because of open butcher viewing rooms in the deli) at the corner of Union Ave. & Los Gatos Almaden Rd. had "Meat is Murder, Stop Killing Innocent Animals, A.L.F. and End the Police State" spray painted on it.

APRIL 7/98: Philadelphia, PA -- Bassett's Original Turkey: Windows were destroyed and locks filled with glue. NOW CLOSED!

APRIL 7/98: Philadelphia, PA --Taco Bell and McDonald's eatery had two windows destroyed. NOW CLOSED!

APRIL 14/98: San Jose, CA -- KFC in the Sunrise Shopping Center had one window broken out and "Meat is Murder, Stop Murdering Chickens, and A.L.F. spray painted on the drive thru.

APRIL 16/98: Pennsylvania -- A McDonalds was fire bombed, destroying the bathroom totally. "McMurder spray painted on walls."
APRIL 18/98: Palm Beach -- A.L.F. activists smashed windshields and spray-painted anti-circus slogans on

three vans belonging to local Shriners. "Circus Cruelty," "Stop Animal Abuse," and "No circus!" were painted on the vans. Graffiti on one van said "A.L.F."

MAY 4/98: Wimauma, FL -- Activists burnt a veal processing plant to the ground. "A.L.F." was painted on the building. The plant claimed $ 2.5 million profit annually. Estimated damages are half a million dollars. Witnesses say the plant is completely destroyed! The fire at Florida Veal Processors Inc., 6712 State Road 674, was set at two places; upstairs in an employee locker area and in a first floor office. The same cell claimed responsibity for an earlier arson in October/97, at Palm Coast Veal Corp. (3698 NW 16th St) in Lauderhill, FL."

MAY 10/98: Sacrameto, CA - The city's only fur store, an old house downtown, has sustained $10,000 in structural damage, $10,000 in damage to goods (not including, the story said, the money to clean the fur coats which had major smoke damage) after an early morning fire. Police reported someone threw acceller-ant on the front entrance and took off. No one has claimed credit.

MAY 27/98: Seattle, WA: Cascioppo Brothers Meats had two dozen glass panes, and two glass doors broken. Three parked vans had windows destroyed. A.L.F. did not leave any spray paint or message. One year ago there was another similar action claimed by the A.L.F.

JUNE 3/98: Cincinnati, OH - Home of Joel A. Belsky (11643 Almahurst), Vice President of Federated Department Stores, had 11 windows etched, all scReens of screened porch slashed. "FUR OUT OF FEDERATED" and "A.L.F." spraypainted on garage door, and blood red paint splattered on front door, porch, walkway, and driveway.

JUNE 3/98: Cincinnati, OH - Home of Dennis J. Broderick (8617 Twighlight Tear), Senior Vice President of Federated Department Stores, had 20 windows etched, "FUR OUT OF FEDERATED" and "A.L.F." spraypainted on garage door, and blood red paint splattered on front door, porch and walkway.

JUNE 5/98: Cincinnait, OH - Bomb threat phoned in to 911 claiming bombs placed in Federated Department Stores' Headquarters (7 W. 7th Street).

JUNE 13/98: DC -- activists visited Andriana Furs:
*front glass door (in etching cream): "FASHION DOES NOT REQUIRE CRUELTY"
*side wall (in paint): "FUR IS DEAD"
*other wall (in paint): "END THE BLOODY FUR TRADE"

JUNE 13/98: MD --Saks Fifth Avenue also visited by the A.L.F.: *on wall by reserved parking spaces (in paint): "RESERVED PARKING FOR KILLERS"
*on loading dock door (in paint): "FUR HURTS" and "STOP KILLING ANIMALS"
*on wall (in paint): "VIOLENCE AGAINST ANIMALS IS VIOLENCE AGAINST ALL"
*on display window (in etching cream and paint, respectively): "FUR HURTS" and "STOP!"
*on other wall (in paint): "FUR HURTS!"
*on sidewalk (in paint): "STOP THE SUFFERING"
*along bottom of wall (in paint): "STOP THE MADNESS IN THE NAME OF FASHION!"
*on other display window (in etching cream): "STOP THE CRUELTY"
*on wall (in paint): "FUR IS DEAD"
*first glass door (in etching cream): "FUR HURTS"
*second glass door (in etching cream): "FUR HURTS"
*third glass door (in etching cream): "FUR IS CRUEL"
*fourth glass door (in etching cream): "COMPASSION"
*fifth glass door (in etching cream): "STOP THE CRUELTY OF FUR"
*sixth glass door (in etching cream: "FUR HURTS"

JUNE 19/98: Eugene, OR -- activists liberated 19 rabbits from the Western Oregon Rabbit Co., during a daring daylight raid. Conditions within the breeding centre, which raises domestic New Zealand white rabbits for research throughout the United States, were horrific - - thousands of rabbits in outside cages, unprotected from heat or cold, many laying in their own feces. No police, no opposition, no arrests. All rabbits were safely taken out of state and are now in loving homes.

JUNE 21/98: Olympia, WA -- A.L.F. and E.L.F. activsts joined forces and destroyed two U.S. Department of Agriculture animal research operations with well planned arson fires. The U.S. Forest Service wildlife research center near Littlerock and the smaller animal damage control building were hit, causing an estimated at $400,000 in damage.

JUNE 21/98: -- The A.L.F. and E.L.F. had a bonfire (or two) at facilities which make it a daily routine to kill and destroy wildlife. This war against Nature has lasted over 500 years and must stop! This genocide against Mother Eartri and her children MUST STOP! Activists targeted the nerve center of these wildlife destruction facilities to provide some REAL WILDLIFE SERVICES. Between 25 and 30 gallons of a 50% unleaded fuel 50% diesel fuel combination was brought to the research facility on Blomberg Road. Slightly less was required for the smaller Animal Damage Control building on O'leary Road. The buckets were placed at key points and left open so the flames could climb up the walls and shoot underneath the eaves and ventilation holes of the building beginning

its great cleansing process. This war on wildlife and nature must end! We will not stop until it does.
-The Animal Liberation Front and Earth Liberation Front -the real Wildlife Services-

JUNE 25/97: Philadelphia, PA.-- The following animal abusers had their locks filled with glue. Burger King, 2 steak houses, Bassett's Original Turkey (15th St.), Kentucky Fried Chicken, Corn Beef Academy, Leather Man's Leather Manufactures and Grill Masters Deli (specialty meats).

JUNE 28/98: Boston, MA -- Earth Liberation Front activists struck at the Mexican Consulate, in an action showing solidarity with the people of Chiapas. From the communique: "The unjust government of Mexico is complicit in murdering the Indigenous population of Chiapas. Red hand prints, symbolizing the blood on the hands of the Mexican government, were painted on the walls and spilled on the ground. "Viva EZLN" was spraypainted on the entrance. Earth Liberation Front disappeared into the night but the blood on the hands of the Mexican government won't easily disappear." "TODOS SOMOS MARCOS"
"REMEMBER GUADALUPE"

JUNE 28/98: Atlanta, GA -- "The home of Helen Frushtick (Owner of Helen Frushtick Furs), 5581 Arundel Dr. (404) 255-1025, was visited. One gallon of red paint was left on her outside lawn furniture, on the side and front of her garage, on a lampost in the front yard, and on the sidewalk leading to her front door. 'Fur is death' was painted on her driveway and one stone pillar in front of her house with red spraypaint. 'A.L.F' was spraypainted five times on other stone pillars in front of her home. As a final note, a kryptonite bike lock in the form of a cord, was locked around an electric gate that was at the foot of the driveway, effectively locking her in.

JUNE 28/98: Atlanta, GA -- activists visited "Atlanta Furs, 1099 Ponce De Leon Ave. (404) 875-3335. A sign on the side of the building that read 'fur Sale' was altered with red spraypaint to read 'Death Sale', "A.L.F." was also spraypainted on the side of the building. Also, one gallon of red paint was poured down the front of the store from the roof of the building, splashing over the front of the store, the sidewalk, and a wooden sign suspended over the storefront.

JUNE 28/98: Atlanta, GA -- "Macy's on Peachtree St. (404) 221-7221. 'Fur is Death' was spraypainted at the main entrance. 'A.L.F.' was also spraypainted on a stone surface in front of the store. Around ten shots were fired from an air pistol with at least one plate glass window being destroyed. Other results from other shots are unknown.

JULY 3/98: Madison, WI — A.L.F. and E.L.F. forces carried out a daylight raid on the United Vaccines experimental research fur farm. All cages containing animals were opened, some requiring cage doors to be bent to allow for escape. All prisoners were seen climbing out of cages. 310 animals liberated. Each cage in the fenced in area was numbered and each mink had small black tags on both ears. Light bulbs smashed out in all sheds and a weighing scale smashed. "INDEPENDENCE DAY FOR FUR FARM PRISONERS" spraypainted on storage barn. 3 windows smashed causing alarm to go off and force liberators to evacuate before causing more damage.

The experiments conducted at the United Vaccines' laboratories and research farms are solely to decrease "profit-losses" incurred by premature deaths on fur farms. The cause of these deaths can be attributed to the widespread diseases on farms due to close confinement, malnurishment, poor sanitation and the pschological stress of captivity. The blatant disregard for the mink and fox nations' well-being is apparent in this industry which cares only about fur quality and maximum "production" and death.

This action commemorates the worldwide struggle for independence from occupation and freedom from domination and is dedicated to Josh Ellerman for his dedication to defend Mother Earth and her animal nations. Returning the prisoners back home, the Fur War continues. A.L.F. and E.L.F.

JULY 4/98: Dryden, NY -- activists from the A.L.F. entered the Marmotech facility to liberate over 150 woodchucks from experimentation. Approximately 50 cages were opened, containing an average of three woodchucks each, and left the door ajar to permit the animals escape. When the A.L.F. departed, most of the woodchucks were moving toward the door. Three who happened to be in carriers were brought outside directly and released. According to data cards on the cages, these animals were all disease free. Unfortunately, the A.L.F. had to leave behind several hundred more who had been infected with woodchuck hepatitis virus and other diseases. The A.L.F. took and destroyed the data cards on these cages, as an act of sabotage against this callous treatment of fellow creatures. All log books and other information were also confiscated and disposed of, and vials of infectious serum were removed from a refrigerator to spoil. The liberation was timed to coincide with the time of year in which young woodchucks leave their family unit and begin fending for themselves. Since some of the woodchucks at this facility were wild caught, it is hoped that they will readily return to life in the wild. Those who have always lived in cages may have a harder time of it, but surely it will be better than being killed by "intravenous injection of excess pentobarbital," as would be their fate otherwise. Since the facility was in an area surrounded by fields and woodlands, the now free woodchucks should be able to find plenty of vegetation to feed on.Until this tyrannical and obscene use of our tax dollars stops, the Animal Liberation Front will be there to correct such injustices.

We will never forget looking into the eyes of creatures doomed to a horrible death and not being able to save them. More actions will be forthcoming.

ENGLAND

NOVEMBER/97:Dorset: Hunt Retribution Squad attack Portman Hunt. Hunt vehicles firebombed and hunters threatened by masked HRS activists. -HRS

FEBRUARY/98: Hampshire: Anti-Bloodsports activists hold a noisy demo outside the home of the John Lewish Partnership chairman. The activists, believed to be members of the Hunt Retribution Squad, in a press release announced "it would of taken us two minutes to trash the house compeletely and unless we hear very soon that the shoots are not to continue that is exactly what we'll do."

MARCH 21/98: Buckinghamshire -- Hunt Retribution Squad attacks the Wendover Hunt. Masked activists weilding iron bars, sticks and clubs ambush hunters. Two hunters were seriously injured. 22 innocent sabs are arrested as a result of this action.

APRIL 17/98: Stockbridge, Hants -- The A.L.F. claimed responsibility attacking an estate belonging to the John Lewis Partnership. Thousands of birds were released and 1,500 worth of damage was caused to breeding pens at Leckford Abbas, where the department store chain has pheasant and duck shoots. - A.L.F.

APRIL 18/98: Oxfordshire -- The largest demo yet against Hillgrove Farm is held. Some people are saying that up to 2,500 people gathered at the lab animal supplier and then tried to tear the place apart. Thousands of pounds worth of damage was caused to the farm roof as it came under a volly of rocks thrown over a military style security fence that the police had erected. Elsewhere sections of the fence were damaged when repeatedly charged with a makeshift battering ram, had rocks banged on it and had its foundations undermined by determined diggers using their bare hands.

MAY 1/98: Cornwall: Animal activists are beleived to be behind the removal of seven newly born sharks from the Newquay Sealife Centre. All the sharks are native to British waters and could easily be reintroduced into the wild.

MAY 20/98: Hackney -- in Brenthouse Rd a meat van was the victim of a devastating arson attack by the A.L.F. The cabin and engine was completely destroyed in the blaze. The heat also smashed the windows and headlights, and the tyres were burnt out. The van was left "looking slightly darker than usual".The owner of the van attacked has since got a new vehicle. This time, perhaps wisely, they have left it unmarked.

MAY 28/98: Oxford -- four 6 week old kittens were rescued from Hillgrove Farm. The cats were in a carrying box in a vehicle ready for dispatch to a lab, when intrepid activist(s) entered Hillgrove Farm undetected and rescued them.

MAY 30-31/98: London -- Activists smashed the windows of the Philip Hockley fur shop, located at 20 Conduit St. This action represents an escalation in the campaign against the largest of the ten or so fur shops left in London. (Although the shop is still very small by other country's standards!). With police arresting peaceful protesters en masse for leafleting outside the shop, actions like this look set to occur more often.

JUNE 1/98: Somerset -- A bomb disposal team and police searched an animal transport firm after up to 40 firebombs were discovered under company trucks. The devices were discovered after firecrews were called to a blazing lorry at George's Yard, Bruton.. At least three of the devices-placed under trucks are said to have gone off. The premises had been locked at 9pm
on Sunday night. When a driver arrived for work at 3.30am yesterday he noticed a glow under one of the trucks which then burst into flames. The second lorry [illegible] as fire crews fought to contain flames [illegible] the first vehicle.

JUNE 4/98: Derbyshire, Gloucestershire, Lincolnshire, Nottinghamshire, Worcestershire -- In an escalation of popular action against 'frankenstein food', at least seven separate crops of genetically engineered rapeseed were destroyed across the UK. The fields appear to have been strategically chosen and these attacks brings the total number of known genetic field 'decontaminations' in the UK to 19. It may be that these nighttime activities could prevent this particular controversial crop coming to market.

The deliberate release sites, part of at least 300 nationwide, were being trialed by the following transnational companies, Agrevo, Monsanto, Pioneer Genetique and Plant Genetics Systems. The crops which together cover approximately 10,000 sq metres were cut down using common gardening tools and bare hands. It is likely that hundreds of thousands of pounds worth of damage will have been sustained.

This is a significant blow to companies already feeling the effects of public distrust and crop failures. It may be that the commercialisation process for genetically engineered oilseed rape has been slowed down because necessary data is now destroyed. The sites visited were -

* Thorn Farm, Inkberrow, Worcstershire 95/R24/2. Pioneer Genetique.
* Dryleaze Farm, Siddington, Cirencester, Gloucester 97/R15/22. Plant Genetics Systems
* Hall Farm, Kneeton, Nottinghamshire 97/R19/17. Agrevo.
* Nickerson Farm, Rothwell, Lincolnshire 97/R27/1. Perryhall Holdings.
* East Lodge Farm, Kings Newton, Derby - 3 sites: 98/R22/13, 97/R22/9 plus one 'fast-track site' not listed on GMO public register of deliberate releases. Monsanto.

JUNE 5/98: Plymouth -- A suspicious fire set at a McDonald's restaurant caused an estimated £85,000 worth of damage.The premises in New George Street were evacuated after the blaze was discovered in a stock room on the third floor at the top of the building.

JUNE 12/98: Oxford -- Letter bombs have been sent by animal activists to an Oxford professor and the owner of a farm which breeds cats for experiments. Colin Blakemore and Chris Brown escaped injury when the devices failed to go off and army bomb disposal experts were brought in to make them safe. They were sent only weeks after Mr Brown received a bomb threat from a group calling itself the Provisional A.L.F. Two more devices were sent to two workers at Hillgrove Farm in Minster Lovell, Oxfordshire, which has been a target of animal welfare protests for several years. They also failed to go off.

JUNE 17/98: Hackney -- another meat van was the recipient of an arson action. The vehicle, in Frampton Rd, was also totally gutted. In an anonymous message, the activists warned that the other meat vans will be targets whenever spotted. The communique concluded: "They cannot stop us! - A.L.F."

JUNE 29/98: London -- A.L.F. activists smash window of Calman Links fur shop, the Queen's own furriers, of 36 Knightsbridge SW1.The communique said that the action was done "in solidarity with the woman jailed for leafleting a fur shop". They also warned that more attacks on fur shops would follow.

SWEDEN

MARCH/98: Ume - the site of a future McDonalds had its windows smashed. The restaurant, to be located inside a large supermarket, advertised it's plans with large ads in the window. It wasn't long before activists replied and gave them a first warning; huge windows were smashed and eviromental slogans was spray-painted.

MARCH 25/98:Taljestad -- 22 hens were liberated from the Taljestads Egg battery farm, all of which were in very poor condition. The hens were taken to a vet and then transported to their new, loving homes, "were they not will be treated like money-machines without any fellings". The raid was carried out by Commando Astrid Lindgren, (named after an imprisoned Swedish Writer) and the "actions will continue untill the Goverment fulfil the promise they have given Astrid and the hens!" "BAN BATTERYFARMING 1999!"

MARCH 29/98: Stockholm -- Animal research vet, Krister Iwarsson, from the Karolinska Institute had his car redecorated at his home address;Hagavagen 20, Bromma, with red paint. The locks on the car were glued.

MARCH 30/98: Stockholm -- Two windows were smashed at a fur shop and a paint bomb was throwed inside, damaging merchandise.

APRIL/98: Timo Nevalainen, a headman of Karttula beagle breeding centre, received a letter which inclued two bullets. The message was: "a month time to give the beagles back, two months time to close the place or..." (three liberated beagles were found at their new homes and returned to the breeder by the police).

APRIL 3/98: Solna -- Vivisector Viktor Mutt, (Jungfrudansen 18, Solna), who's work tortures cats and guinea pigs for " research," had the door to his apartment filled with public information, "CAT ABUSER" and red paint was splashed all over the door and in the letter-box.

APRIL 5/98: Stockholm -- Four fur shops had their windows smashed and red paint poured over furs on display.

APRIL 5/98: Kil -- A mink farm with space for 1000 minks received a visit from the Wild Minks (DVM). The farm was empty at this time, but traces showed that it was used last season and could be used in the near future again. The DVM decides to trash the farm. All cages and traps were destroyed, slogans sprayed, a feeding machine was destroyed and water-system destroyed. -- Wild Mink

APRIL 6/98: Enskededalen -- A small fire burned a meat lorrie at Eriksson kott. According to local newspapers, an incendiary device was the source of the flames..

APRIL 18/98: Uppsala -- One beagle was liberated from the veterinary school in Uppsala. It was rescued by the new DBF, a group which operates under the same policies as international A.L.F. activists, and has no connection with the "old" DBF or Emilie E:son.

APRIL 23/98: Vallentuna -- Activists from the animal liberation group "djurrattsmilisen" (Animal Rights Militia) made a visit to lab animal breeders "The Eklund Brothers" outside Stockholm. 121 rats was liberated from their cages and carefully removed to loving and caring homes all over Sweden.This action was to rescue the rats but also to mark the world day for laboratory animals on april 24. This was the second raid at this place. In december 1997 57 rats and mice was rescued from there. The Eklund Brothers are expanding their operations, and the activists involved urge all animal rights activists in Sweden to start up an campaign to close the place down.

MAY 2/98: Karlstad -- a total of 28 hens were liberated from their cages at Kils battery hen unit. All hens have now been placed in good homes. The action was carried out by the new Djurens Befrielse Front (DBF).

MAY 20/98: Molndal/Gothenburg -- A furshop has been forced to close down due to a series of devastating sabotage actions. The A.L.F. activists say that their most effective weapon was a powder fire extinguisher emptied into the store through a mail delivery slot.

JUNE/98: Karlstad --Milk company had several trucks sloganized.

JUNE/98: Umea -- A scan meat truck was vandalized.

JUNE/98: Umea -- Windows smashed at one of the only two skin-stores left in the city. The same store closed down totally later that week! A.L.F. VICTORY!

JUNE 19/98: Bjarshog -- The Wild Minks struck a mink farm, destroying at least 75 breeding cards before having to flee.

JUNE 1/98: Stockholm -- two lorries belonging to ARLA (a large dairy company in Sweden) in Kallhall, north Stockholm, were set on fire and totally destroyed. Slogans left at the scene included "Murderers" and "symbols connected to anarchism."

JUNE 9/98: A owner of several closed down fur farms, mostly fox farms, Soren Svensson, was met by spray-painted slogans such as "Soren - this is the 1st warning" "Start the farm and you will die!" when he arrived to one of his fox farms he is thinking about starting up again.

JUNE 10/98: Stockholm -- McDonalds got their windows smashed in.
JUNE 10/98: Umea -- McDonalds had at least one huge window trashed in a restaurant which THEY HOPE will open in Sept.

JUNE 10/98: Bisam institution (UN animal house) had one large window smashed, 2-3 lamps destroyed, and an office trashed (two computers totally destroyed, phones broken). A security car arrived on the scene in about 40 seconds, and chased the activists who fled on bikes. One activist fell, but managed flee on foot to saftey. The other activist eluded the security car and also made it to safety. Important data and valuable property was destroyed in the action.

JUNE 11/98: Amal -- A DBF (A.L.F.) inspection on an old mink farm became a daylight raid when DBF-activists checking to see if the mink farm had closed down found 20 rabbits trapped in cages, most likely being bred for their fur and meat. The rabbits were in bad shape and poorly treated. The activists destroyed the empty cages, took breeding cards and liberated two rabbits.

JUNE 17/98: Avesta -- the direct-action group,"The Wild Minks" raided Karl Bengs chinchilla farm, liberating animals and destroying breeding cards. Karls Bengs has been an active breeder for over 20 years and breeds chinchilla both for their fur and to sell for vivisection. The activists broke into the farm and found hundreds of chinchillas in small cages. 6 chinchillas were removed from the farm and are now in safe hands. An estimated 100 breeding cards were removed from cages and later destroyed. Over 10 year of breeding information was ruined. About 60 chinchillas was also released on the floor inside the farm, tasting freedom from their small cages for the first time -- breeding and pelting animals mixed freely, effectively destroying the farm's breeding work. This is the first chinchilla farm raid for many years in Sweden, but rest assured, it won't be the last one. "It does not matter what they farm; mink, fox, ferret or chinchilla ...we are coming after them all, one after one... The Wild Minks"

JUNE 30/98: Gothenburg - The Wild Minks struck again, this time at a combined mink and ferret farm in Rya Hed. An estimated 200-250 minks was found and also 15-20 ferrets. All mink cages was opened and the minks released, but as the minks might kill the ferrets, they was not released, but instead all breeding cards for the ferrets were taken.

JULY 1/98:Norrtalje -- activists from the Djurens Befrielse Front (DBF/ALF) cut a fence to the premises of Estuna animal farm, a place that profits mainly from breeding rabbits for vivisection labs in Sweden. Conditions were bad. The activists carefully removed 15 rabbits from the farm. The activists sprayed the new rabbit house with slogans such as "SCUM", "DBF" and "ENOUGH" before leaving the farm. All the rabbits has now been placed in good homes were they will be able to live out they natural life. Several of the rabbits had shown signs of neglect, with overgrowned claws and teeth causing them problems.. "Be aware, animal

abusers, we're everywere and there's no place to hide!"
DJURENS BEFRIELSE FRONT (new)

JULY 5/98: Vetlanda - activists set fire to 5 lorries at ARLA, a Dairy company. Two of the lorries was totally destroyed and the others were heavily damaged.

FINLAND

JANUARY/98: Tampere -- A fur shop lost all windows, the third time in three months.

JANUARY/98: Helsinki -- Three animal export trucks were firebombed at a meat company. One specially equipped truck and a van were destroyed, the third vehicle was badly damaged.

JANUARY/98: Tampere -- Three McDonald's attacked by the E.L.F., and a fur shop lost its windows.

LATE JUNE/98: Konnevesi -- A wildlife research lab owned by Jyvaskyla university was raided by activists.Animals liberated included moles and birds captured from the wild. While most of the animals were released to the surrounding area which puts them at some risk for recapture, the birds have a very good chance of escape. The exact number of liberated animals is still uncertain, but information at the researcher's doctor thesis were destroyed as a result of the raid.

JUNE/98: Tampere - The Earth Liberation Front has been active in Finland, attacking three road construction machines and destroying a partially constructed bridge.

JULY/98: Outokumpu --EVR saved 12 hens from a battery unit. The hens were then placed to a good home where they will be taken care of the rest of their lives. This was the first chicken liberation in Finland.

POLAND

APRIL/98: Bialystok -- Just a few days after it was erected, a McDonalds billboard gets paintbombed.

APRIL/98: Warsaw -- For Earth Night, in the mountains just outside Warsaw, Polish Earth Liberation Front activists cut the cables and blocked the tracks of a mountain 'ski' lift development which is causing massive logging and deforestation.

AUSTRIA

MAY 26/98: Belgrade -- 19 turkeys were liberated by protesting activists at the Linz airport. Activists stormed the loading docks to the Dutch airline, KLM, blockading entrances and keeping workers at bay.

LATE MAY/98: Vienna -- Activists liberated several pigs and an unknown number of battery chickens from a factory farm. 4 fur shop windows broken in one night. Also, an exotic meat fair venue was attacked with butric acid the night before the event. Rocks were thrown through the windows and little bottles filled with butric acid followed.

JUNE/98: Vienna -- 9 fur shops had glass fixed to their windows with a paper slipped in between reading "fur is animal abuse". To remove these glasses, the whole windows had to be changed.

JUNE 1/98: Vienna -- 16 fur shops had their display windows smashed. This marks the 3rd attack in as many weeks of that kind. Other actions have included 15 shops being attacked with butric acid in one night, and almost every fur shop in the city has at least once had their locks glued and slogans sprayed on the windows.

GREECE

MAY/98: Athens -- on an almost nightly occurance, politicians, police, U.S. businesses and cars belonging to the rich have been targeted in a wave of fire-bomb attacks.So far, there are no suspects, but a number of sophisticated bombs were used to blow up three American car dealerships, two McDonald's and a Citibank branch. At first, most attacks fit no visible pattern, but in recent weeks they have been going after specific, protected targets. ``It started as a social phenomenon," said one offical. ``This is terrorism." The Conscientious Arsonists appear to be the most organized group, sending written claims of responsibility to newspapers. Their message is simple: "Unemployment, high prices, austerity, and oppression is the future that that the European Union has in store for us."

ITALY

MAY 10/98: Florence -- 6 firebombs exploded at a Nestle warehouse, which the A.L.F. took credit for.

NEW ZEALAND

MAY 19/98: Christchurch - A central meat and seafood wholesalers building was destroyed by fire. According to firefighters who attended, 60% of the Lichfield St building was destroyed and all stock (meat) is unusable. No one was hurt and police are investigating to determine the cause of the fire.

ANIMAL LIBERATION PRISONERS

UNITED STATES

Frank Allen - 1809138 L-20-14, 550 N. Flower, Santa Ana, CA 92703, USA - NEW ADDRESS
Jailed for the attempted arson of a highschool slaughterhouse in southern California.

Rod Coronado #3895000, FCI Unit SW, 8901 S. Wilmot Rd., Tucson, AZ 85706, USA
Sentenced to a total of 57 months for aiding and abetting arson and handling stolen property in connection with acting as spokesperson for the North American ALF, and for damaging government property as a protest against the treatment of native Americans (Rod is a member of the Yaqui Nation).

Clinton Colby Ellerman, c/o Salt Lake County Jail, 450 S. 300 E., Salt Lake City, UT 84111-3207, USA
Colby Ellerman, Josh's brother, chargeed with burglary and theft for freeing thousands of mink from the Holt Fur Farm in Utah. Sentenced to two years for mink releases. Also sentenced for $300,000 arson damage caused to Tandy Leather store.

Douglas Joshua Ellerman, Salt Lake County Jail, 450 S. 300 E., Salt Lake City, UT 84111, USA
Josh's sentencing hearing is set for July 15. He is being held as a federal prisoner without possible bail. His charges stem from the firebombing of the Utah Fur Breeder's Co-Op which caused over $1 million damage.

Sean Gautschy 2C3 s/o#0229294, S.L. City Co. Jail, 450 South 300 East, Salt Lake City, UT 84111, USA
Alleged to have taken part in two fur farm liberations in Utah. Considered a flight risk since he is originally from California. Charges: 2 counts burglary (2nd degree felony), 2 counts criminal mischif (2nd degree felony), 2 counts releasing fur bearing animals (3rd degree felony).

Jacob Kenison #06329-081, Yuma Unit, 37900 N. 45th Ave., Dept. 1700, Phoenix, AZ 85027-7004, USA
Only one hour away from being released from prison, Jacob was detained on 6 new felony counts related to Utah fur raids. Convicted of an arson attack on a Tandy Leather store in Murray, Utah. Jake is also serving a 16 month sentence for violating federal firearms laws for buying an rifle he later gave as a gift to a friend.

Mark S. Klein AA45, Oxbow Jail, Inmate Mail, 3148 S. 1100 W., Salt Lake City, UT 84119, USA
Convicted of 2nd degree felony arson (McDonald's) sentenced to 36 months of probation upon the conditions that he serve 1 year in jail.Mark is due to be released July 28.(Do not send news clippings or other items or letters will be returned to sender.)

ENGLAND

Darren Cole - CX4137, HMP Longport, Canterbury, Kent, CT11PJ, England
Currently on Hungerstrike (as of May 1). On remand charged with sending 7 bomb hoaxes to protest the live export of animals used in ritual slaughter at Dover Docks.

Kievan Hickey AP7904, HMP Springhill, Grendon, Underwood, Aylesbury, Bucks., England - New Address
Sentenced to 12 months for receiving stolen property (a cat) in connection with a demonstration January 1997 when activists broke into Hillgrove Farm vivisection breeders and attempted to rescue some cats.

Barry Horne VC2141, HMP Full Sutton, Moor Lane, York, YO41PS, England
Recently Moved to HMP Full Sutton after he was found guilty of charges relating to the attempted incendiary devices in Bristol and the successful incendiary devices on the Isle of Wight. Sentenced to 18 years.He is in the process of appealing both sentences.

Keith Mann EE3588, HMP Parkhurst, Newport, Isle of Wight PO30 5N, England - NEW ADDRESS
Sentenced to 11 years for criminal damage to meat vehicles, attempted incitement, possession of explosive materials, attempted arson and escaping from custody.

Gillian Peachey RL3415, HMP Winchester, Romsey Rd., Winchester, SO22 5HY, England -- New Address
Sentenced in late Feb. to 6 years 9 months - 5 years for conspiracy to commit arson plus 21 months for being in breach of a previous suspended sentence.

Geoff Sheppard MD1030, HMP Parkhurst, Newport, Isle of Wight, PO30 5NX, England
Sentenced to 7 years for possession of a shotgun and possession of items for making incendiary devices. Due to be released soon.

Barbara Trenholm RL1292, HMP Bullwood Hall, High Rd, Hockley, Essex, England - New Address
Sentenced to 10 years for arson against the White Hart pub which the prosecution claim was in connection with the campaign against live exports. She maintains her innocence.

Justin Wright GE3046, HM Young Offenders Institution, Easton, Portland, Dorset, DT5 1DL, England
Sentenced to 5 years for the same offence, as Barbara Trenholm. He maintains his innocence.

ONE DAY PEOPLE WON'T HAVE TO RESCUE ANIMALS FROM PRISON....

...ONLY TO END UP THERE THEMSELVES

Support Animal Liberation Prisoners.

N. American A.L.F. Supporters Group,
Box 69597, 5845 Yonge St. Willowdale, Ont.
Canada M2M 4K3
<naalfsg@envirolink.org>

ISSN 1483-5258

UNDERGROUND

THE MAGAZINE OF THE NORTH AMERICAN ANIMAL LIBERATION FRONT SUPPORTERS GROUP

ISSUE #12 Fall 98 $3

FREE TO PRISONERS

INFORMERS!

Utah Snitching Result in More Arrests

Clinton Colby Ellerman: ALF activist turned police informer — And who else?

PAGE 9

Dairy of Actions

Prisoner Listings

SNV: A Response

and much more...

A few thank-yous from the editor:

I'd like to take a moment thank everyone for their patient wait for this issue of *Underground*. Due to a number of recent events, in particular those revolving around Clinton Colby Ellerman and the arrests that resulted from his statements, *Underground* had been on hold until all the information that passed our desks could be digested. As readers know, the NA-A.L.F.S.G. has a strict policy of reviewing all available documents that deal with police stooges/grassing before releasing statements condemning anyone as an informer. We'll not get into it much here, but every reader should take a moment and review the article on the Utah situation that follows this editorial.

Also to be found in this issue is a lengthy and detailed piece by U.S. A.L.F. prisoner, Rod Coronado, addressing a recent trend amongst some U.S. activists who, as one-time A.L.F. supporters, now make it a major focus in their campaigns to attack the A.L.F. and its methods. The purpose of this article is not to give unnecessary attention to critics of militant direct action, but more to examine the very necessary role of the A.L.F. and like-minded groups within the animal/earth liberation movement today. Love it or lump it, the A.L.F. has had a direct hand in many of the victories we celebrate in the war against animal abuse. Rod's article provides insights into the mindset of both the militant activists taking the war to the abusers doorsteps, and those activists who spend their time running to the media shouting, "This puts the movement back twenty years!"

Our ***"You ROCK!"*** award without question has to go to activists busy causing mayhem in picturesque Sweden. Nearly every day we receive word about a new Swedish mink farm raid or a well planned attack against an animal abuser -- and while there still seems to be some internal politics working themselves out amongst activists in Sweden -- the folk there must be amongst the most active in the world at this moment. A recent report leaked by the Swedish security police, SAPO, states that animal liberation related "crimes" jumped from 84 in 1996 to 340 in 1997. If the pages of our Diary of Action are any indication, we can't wait to see the numbers for 1998 and beyond. Inspired by the work being performed by their American cousins, fur farm raids continue at an unprecedented rate, showing no sign of abating. Well, no matter what country you're active in, it's important you know that we love you and thank you everything you're doing for the animals. Stick it to the bastards!

On a more local note, we'd like to thank a number of groups and individuals who have shown us so much support. Firstly, there are a number of long-term contributors who have been so generous with funds -- without all of your support, the work we do could never have happened. You know who you are -- thank you. Also, our thanks to the fine folk at Toronto's anarchist info shop, Who's Emma, for stocking the complete line of NA-A.L.F.S.G. merchandise (visit the shop if you're ever in Toronto!), and to the organizers of **Active Resistance '98**, who kindly allowed us to host a workshop on animal liberation and prisoner support during their 5-day gathering. We met a number of activists from across North America, and we appreciate your support and dedication. Love and lib to Darren, *No Compromise*, Gina, Katie, A.L.F.S.G. UK, M/M & X for contributing to the new buttons, Josh, *Profane Existence, FactSheet 5* and other zines that have shown support and spread the word

RCMP, CISIS, FBI, ATF, vivisectors, multi-nationals, fur shop owners, animal abusers and police informers everywhere: Go suck a lemon.

Yer Editor,

t.

Letters to Underground

Chatham 3 update...
MORE DELAYS

The Chatham 3 appeared in court on Monday, September 28, where a trial date was once again suppose to be set for October or November. However, for the umpteenth time, we were delayed once again. The judge rescheduled our assignment court date for November 16. So, now it looks like our trial won't be set until late December or early January of 1999. Nevertheless my good vegans, the trial will go on and, if convicted, the 40-day hunger strike WILL go on as well.

Incidentally, traitor Alan Hoffman, was suppose to be sentenced on September 8. However, his lawyer, Frank Miller, never showed up. He is scheduled once again to be sentenced on November 2. FYI, the Crown Attorney wants to keep Hoffman around for our trial so he can testify on the stand against us. Technically, his statement implicating The Chatham 3 is inadmissable until he takes the stand. Therefore, our lawyers want him sentenced and done with because once Hoffman is in the U.S., Canada cannot force him back to testify. I will keep everybody apprised of the situation as details become available.

Liberation Now,
Gary Yourofsky

UK PRISONER,
DARREN COLE WRITES

Hello Everyone, it's me, Daz!
Well, firstly I'd like to say I'm very sorry for not writing for what seems like a life time, but this was due to conditions placed on me for my release -- and tonight I thought to hell with the conditions and to hell with the system that has so many of our brothers and sisters imprisoned. I very much hope everyone is Okay and looking after themselves. I'm Okay. I'm hoping to come to the states some time next year, as I'm free February -- Wey Hey!

I'm looking forward to getting back into action which is one of the reasons I'm writing: Just to say a big thank you all, not only for the support I've received, but to say a big "well done" for everything we've managed to do as a team and family. We've all been through a lot, but we've stuck together through thick and thin, i.e.: If we all look back, we've been laughed at by governments and by certain members of the public, but I don't see many people laughing any more... all I see is good, caring people who have stuck by the cause and fought hard and long for what we all want: Humanity and compassion. We may have to fight that little bit longer, but we are so close to winning and I myself am very proud to be a part of it. I'm not too good with words, but I just thought as we never realize what good we are doing I'd like to say a big thank you and well done. No matter what the system (government) throws at us to try and stop us, it will never work. Some of us may live thousands of miles away from each other, but we are all united as one. God bless you all.
No Compromise!

Daz CX4137
HMP Longport,
Canterbury, Kent CT11PJ
England

Mail Bombs, etc. Cross the Line

Dear *Underground* letters,
The English action report about the letter bombs in issue #11 is very troubling. Your own guidelines insist that *human life* be respected too, so how can these people be considered part of the A.L.F.?

I also think sending bombs thru the mail is the worst form of cowardice! These people don't even have the guts to take their anger and passion directly to the source and confront their targets or bomb their offices with them not present. Consider yourself scorned, you idiots!

I am sympathetic, but attempted murder and death threats (there as one elsewhere in the issue) cross the line for me. If some members of the A.L.F. want to cross that line, then form a separate organization and go for it. *Underground* is probably inhaled by people who want you in jail, and they will be quite happy to tar and feather ALL A.L.F. people with the blood of anyone who is bombed or shot successfully.
T.K., California

UK PRISONER UPDATE:
GEOFF SHEPPARD

Dear NA-A.L.F.S.G.
Just a note to thank you for sending me issues 10 and 11 of *Underground*. It's really good, and is quickly consumed!

As for my release -- well, my first possible parole date is this November. November 98. However, I'm sorry to say that it is extremely unlikely that I will get parole My second chance at parole will be in November 99, but I'm not expecting to get it even then. Without parole, my release date is in January 2000, and that's the date I'm working towards. Since this is my second sentence for the animal liberation cause, and since I still hold to my beliefs, it's just highly unlikely that they will let me out any sooner than they have to. I hope I'm wrong!

So, life grinds on as usual here, and I'm O.K. I've managed to have a few brief conversations with Keith since he's been here, and (despite everything) he's as irrepressible as ever! You've got to admire the bloke.

I was really sorry to hear that Josh is in custody now. He is much in my thoughts, and I wish him (and all Animal Liberation prisoners) all the inner strength they need, to face what may lie ahead.

Many thanks for your support.
Best Wishes,
Individuality, Solidarity and animal liberation.

Geoff Sheppard, MD1030
HMP Parkhurst, Newport
Isle of Wight, P030 5NX
England

LIBERATORS NEEDED: THERE'S WORK TO BE DONE

To the A.L.F.:
I read what you are doing to save animals, and feel so thankful there are people like you around.

Is there any chance of some of you animal liberators liberating the pigeons to be tortured and killed in the annual Hegins Pigeon Shoot in Hegins Pennsylvania on Labor Day (1st Monday in September)? Maybe some of your McDonald's fire-bombers could come bomb that plaque in the park honoring a leader of the shoot (the originator, I think) as well as the items in the park bought with the pigeon's blood.

Thank you for your time.
A supporter

NEWS BRIEFS

GENETICALLY ENGINEERED CROP ACTIONS: UNITED KINGDOM

The UK Government has been asked to stop disclosing the locations of test sites of genetically engineered crops to prevent attacks by a new breed of "eco-terrorist".

Companies developing the controversial crops are worried by the growing number of guerrilla-style attacks aimed at preventing the plants being grown commercially in Britain. The first such crop, an engineered variety of oilseed rape, is close to receiving official approval, and farmers could be free to plant it as soon as next spring. It has been made resistant to herbicide, so that farmers can spray weeds in the crop without damaging it.

Over the past two months militant opponents of the new technology have damaged plants at a score of sites in England and Scotland. AgrEvo, a German biotechnology company with a base at East Winch, near King's Lynn, in Norfolk, has 40 trial plots around Britain growing genetically modified oilseed rape, sugar beet, maize and potatoes.

"During the past few months five of the 40 sites have been attacked, and we fear that many more will be damaged," Des D'Souza, a company product manager, said.

"VIGILANTES' TARGET CAT-KILLING SUSPECT

July 29/98 MONTREAL -- Posters screaming an accused cat-killer's name, address and phone Number were plastered on every mailbox and telephone pole in the Mile End district of the city.

The neighbourhood, in the city's east end, has been covered with signs about missing cats for months. Last month city workers found a garbage bag filled with mutilated cats. A search of the area turned up 10 dead felines in total.

The signs read "Cat Killer" in French and listed the suspect's name, address and phone number and instructed residents to call a Montreal police station for more information.

Police don't know who made the signs but warned the perpetrator could be charged with mischief, Sgt. Sylvain Bissonnette said.

"People were surprised the suspect was released," Bissonnette said. The suspect was arrested and released July 16 and the Quebec attorney general took over the investigation. No court date has been set.

Neysa Murray's cat Pousseline disappeared three months ago. Murray's mother, Jan, formed the Mile End Animal Advocacy Group to lobby the city and the police to do something about the disappearing cats.

Neysa Murray said she didn't see the posters, which police have taken down now, but she thinks they were a good idea. "If the cops aren't going to do anything and we can't go clobber the guy, what are we going to do?"

Montreal police will not release the suspect's name in this specific case because they are worried about the suspect's safety and endangering the attorney general's investigation.

OILPATCH HIT BY PAIR OF BOMBINGS

August 4, 1998 Beaverlodge, Canada - Police are blaming a group of militant environmentalists for two weekend bomb attacks on natural gas installations near Beaverlodge, 560 km northwest of Edmonton.

A sweet gas well was destroyed Friday and a sour gas pipeline was damaged in separate bomb attacks. Both the well and the pipeline are owned by Alberta Energy Co.

The gas well was not operating when Friday's explosion occurred and an automatic valve shut off the pipeline late Sunday.

Beaverlodge RCMP Sgt. Don MacKay told reporters, "The kind of people who do this kind of thing -- how do you know when they're going to strike next?"

Based on evidence collected so far, MacKay believes the bombers are a small group of militant environmentalists trying to protect the Peace River area's natural resources.

He avoids using the term "eco-terrorists," saying he doesn't want to "glamorize these people. We call it 'criminal vandalism.' "

There have been more than 100 acts of industrial vandalism in the Beaverlodge area -- including damage to wells, nails spread on roads and pipes punctured by drills -- over the past two years, says MacKay. A Telus propane tank was punctured by a high-powered rifle bullet. An employee found an explosive device attached to a Rife Resources pipeline in July, and in June a bomb exploded at another Alberta Energy pipeline.

Alberta Energy posted a $50,000 reward which still stands after its office at Hythe northwest of Beaverlodge was hit by a high-powered bullet Oct 27, 1997.

Alberta Energy spokesperson Dick Wilson said extra security, damage and lost production has cost his company more than $1 million over the past two years.

Local environmentalists deny any responsibility for the attacks. Spokesperson Henry Pirker says oil industry pollutants are rapidly destroying the Peace River's renowned agricultural potential. "Nature can't handle it anymore, and people are losing patience. I wish there was some other way to get through to the government, but there isn't."

"These are desperate people."

INTERNET DIVISION OF A.L.F.: Activists to Hack Animal Abusers

In a communique released on the world-wide-web, the Internet Division of the Animal Liberation Front announced that the Internet will no longer be a safe haven for animal abusers to push their bloody trades.

"We will take offensive actions to damage animal abusers on the Internet in any way possible. This may include Denial of Service attacks, Virii attacks, e-mail bombing, hacking web servers. We have already cracked numerous computer systems and borrowed useful data, in the future we will also destroy data."

According to the group, all animal abusers and animal abusing establishments on the Internet are valid targets.

"In this day and age when most large animal abuse establishments have a presence on the Internet they use the world wide web for selling their blood products and for pushing their warped ideals to the masses. As other warriors free animals from concentration camp around the world, we will take the war to the Internet.

"Our cell has already been active for one year and has under taken many actions against animal abusers. Recently other A.L.F.I.D. volunteers have formed autonomous cells."

LOGGERS KILL HEADWATERS EARTH FIRST! PROTESTER

Humboldt Co. California — David Chain, an Earth First! Headwaters Forest activist also known as Gypsy, from Texas, was killed Sept. 17, while trying to protect trees from being cut down. Loggers were felling trees in an area close to a publicly known protest near Grizzly Creek, an area just

Introducing:

ANIMAL-LIBERATION.NET

We are pleased to present animal-liberation.net, the new home of the ***Animal Liberation Frontline Information Service.*** We have completely revamped the entire web site and added many new sections, publications, articles and more.

Our new url is http://www.animal-liberation.net/

Bringing you uncensored news from around the world since 1994.

The web site now receives hundreds of visits a day from over 30 different countries. If you can help us out in any way, or have any comments, suggestion, criticisms, etc., please feel free to contact us at: **<frontline@rocketmail.com>**

A huge thank-you to several anonymous donators who helped us pay for our domain name and cover our ISP costs, and to the handful of people that have helped with the new site.

For the Animals,
animal-liberation.net administrators
<frontline@rocketmail.com>

outside the Headwaters Deal acquisition area, but considered vital to the integrity of the forest by ecologists. A tree felled by the loggers hit another tree which fell on Chain, causing severe head injuries. He died in a helicopter en route to the hospital.

A video taken by Earth First! activists in Grizzly Creek captured the hostile voice of a PL faller threatening their lives less than an hour before David "Gypsy" Chain was killed by a falling tree. The video blatantly contradicts Pacific Lumber's claim that the company "had no knowledge" that Chain and others were nearby in Grizzly Creek. In fact, the logger who later cut the tree that killed David Chain can be heard furiously shouting obscenities and vowing to get his "pistol." Several other Earth First! activists were just six feet away from Chain when the tree came crashing down.

Contrary to Pacific Lumber's public statements, David Chain's death was the inevitable result of the timber company's deliberate campaign of violence toward environmental activists. In the last year, Earth First! protesters have been hog-tied and lowered from tree top perches and had their tree sit safety lines cut by PL climbers. Loggers have cut trees in the direction of tree sitters, and have threatened lives by cutting trees with activists in them. Logging helicopters have been used to harass and endanger treesitters, such Julia Butterfly, flying within feet of their platforms and whipping up forceful winds. Recently, activists encountered a "goon squad" of PL employees in the Mattole watershed who chased, threatened and assaulted community members who were trying to stop illegal logging in their home. The escalating use of violence by Pacific Lumber has been ignored by Humboldt County law enforcement.

This vigilantism in the woods also threatens the safety of PL employees. Logging rates as one of the most dangerous occupations in the country. PL's policy requiring logging crews to also act as company thugs only adds more risk to employees in the woods. The tragic death of David Chain under these circumstances shows clearly that to PL, profits are more important than human life. Earth First! activists who witnessed the tragic death of their comrade David Chain will cooperate with a full investigation into the incident and its causes. Earth First! will continue to protest Pacific Lumber's illegal logging in Grizzly Creek in David's name.

For more information on this, or other Earth First! demos/projects/publications, e-mail or phone:
Earth First! Media Center
707/923-2114
efmc@asis.com
http://www.geocities.com/RainForest/Vines/9901/

MAIL-BOMB GAS ATTACK ON UK PRESS OFFICER

ALF Press Officer Robin Webb and his wife Margaret needed medical treatment shortly after Robin opened an envelope addressed to him c/o Cambridge Animal Rights.

The envelope was white and had P.O. Box No. 114, London E1 8HL printed on the front in the top left hand corner. The address on the envelope was also typed or printed.

The envelope contained a second envelope, within which was a white powder.

Robin and Margaret began to feel the effects even before he opened the second envelope. Their eyes and noses began to run and their eyes became sore. Robin described the symptoms as being similar to those caused by CS gas, so it is quite possible that the substance was CS gas crystals. It has been passed to the police who are having it analyzed.

At this point, similar letters have NOT been received by any other animal campaigners, so this may be an isolated incident. Nevertheless all animal liberation campaigners should be careful at all times when opening mail. It is inevitable that as the animal abusers get more and more pushed up against the wall, some of them will fight back - and our mail is an obvious avenue for this.

POLICE GUARD SWEDISH MCDONALD'S TO FEND OFF ATTACKS

Sept 25/98 STOCKHOLM, Sweden - Police surrounded a new McDonald's in northern Sweden to prevent an attack on the fast-food restaurant by protesters ahead of its grand opening.

Some 50 students were demonstrating outside the restaurant in the northern university town of Umea under the watchful eyes of about 15 police after vandals broke windows and threw red paint on its outside walls earlier this week.

The restaurant was set to open later Friday and would be the fast-food giant's first outlet in Umea.

"Young people here have started an anti-McDonald's campaign," McDonald's spokeswoman Birgitta Mossberg told reporters in Stockholm.

She said the students were against multinational companies, but the Umea McDonald's would open regardless.

Signs the protesters made accused

McDonald's trademark character Ronald McDonald of being an animal killer.

Mossberg said 22 fur shops had been forced to close in Umea after harassment and threats from youths.

``There are a lot of strong feelings up there," she said.

180 PIG SAVED -- SUPPORT NEEDED

Poolesville, MD -- On the evening of October 1, DC police found an abandoned truck containing 180 five-month-old pigs who were going to slaughter. No owner could be found, so the truck was towed to Poplar Spring Animal Sanctuary in Poolesville, MD. Several volunteers worked all night and most of Friday unloading the pigs into a four-acre pasture at the sanctuary.

The pigs' owner (a North Carolina factory farmer) found out about the botched transport and demanded that we turn his property back over to him. At this point, a press release was sent out and basically every media outlet in DC was at the Sanctuary, showing the gross abuse suffered by these pigs.

The pigs, who had never touched dirt before, were covered in urine and feces, and had burn marks from electric prodding. Several were found dead in the truck upon arriving at the sanctuary. Needless to say, they didn't really know how to react to fresh veggies, mud, and positive attention. The story was on the cover of the Washington Post's Metro section and was feature story of almost every major news station that evening.

By Saturday, the veterinary, food, and rent bill incurred during the pigs' stay grew larger than the pigs' financial worth ($12,000). Instead of losing money by paying the bill, the farmer simply signed over custody of all 180 pigs to Poplar Spring. Again, a release was sent out and the story was shown on every major news station that evening, some even doing live segments from the sanctuary. Several radio shows covered it as well.

Now that the sanctuary has about 180 new, extremely fortunate residents, it would be nice if people could help out with financial contributions to help feed and care for them.

Poplar Spring Animal Sanctuary
15200 Mt. Nebo Rd.
Poolesville, MD 20837
301-428-8128

UTAH: HOME OF THE SUPERGRASS

Activists turned informers wreak havoc. New arrests result.

POLICE INFORMER #1: CLINTON COLBY ELLERMAN

As many within the animal liberation movement are already painfully aware, an already abysmal situation in Utah has taken a turn for the worse. Five activists were indicted on Thursday, Sept. 10, 1998 for militant non-violent animal liberation actions. Facing charges connected to the destruction of the Utah Fur Breeder's Co-op ($1 million + in damages), evidence is beginning to show that the charges stem from information provided to police by convicted A.L.F. activist, Clinton Colby Ellerman, who is serving time for his participation in mink liberations and an attack on a leather store. Those charged with the Utah Fur Breeder's arson are:

Clinton Colby Ellerman, 21; Andrew N. Bishop, 24, of Ithaca, N.Y.; Alexander David Slack, 23, of Sandy (also facing charges from 2 '96 mink farm raids); Adam Troy Peace, 20, of Huntington Beach, CA (also facing charges from 2 '96 mink farm raids); Sean Albert Gautschy, 23, of SLC (also facing charges from 2 '96 mink farm raids).

All are currently facing the same 16 charges that Douglas Joshua Ellerman had been facing for the Co-op arson. Adam, Alex and Sean have all been charged in state court in connection with the release of mink and $200,000 in damage at two West Jordan mink farms in 1996. These charges stem from voluntary interviews given by **Clinton Colby Ellerman** to police April 19 and 20, 1997. Also implicated as an informer is **Kevin Clark,** who participated in two mink raid farms, but willingly and even eagerly grassed out alleged companions on the raid. Those accused of being

(Continued on page 10)

(Continued from page 9)
participants in the mink raids and the arson attack strongly maintain their innocence.

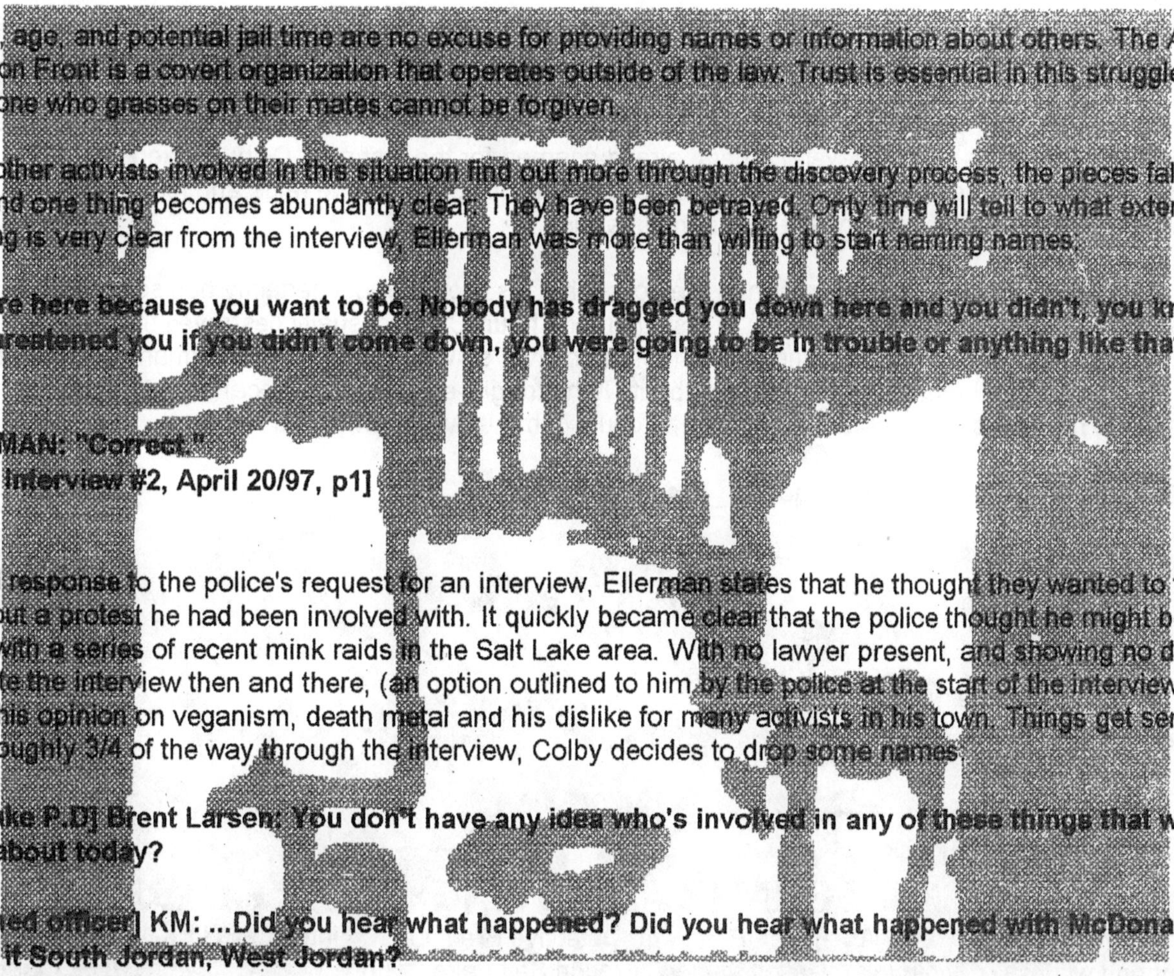

Naivety, age, and potential jail time are no excuse for providing names or information about others. The Animal Liberation Front is a covert organization that operates outside of the law. Trust is essential in this struggle. Above all, anyone who grasses on their mates cannot be forgiven.

As the other activists involved in this situation find out more through the discovery process, the pieces fall into place and one thing becomes abundantly clear: They have been betrayed. Only time will tell to what extent, but one thing is very clear from the interview, Ellerman was more than willing to start naming names.

"...you're here because you want to be. Nobody has dragged you down here and you didn't, you know, nobody threatened you if you didn't come down, you were going to be in trouble or anything like that, correct?"

ELLERMAN: "Correct."
[C.C.E. Interview #2, April 20/97, p1]

In initial response to the police's request for an interview, Ellerman states that he thought they wanted to talk to him about a protest he had been involved with. It quickly became clear that the police thought he might be involved with a series of recent mink raids in the Salt Lake area. With no lawyer present, and showing no desire to terminate the interview then and there, (an option outlined to him by the police at the start of the interview) Colby shares his opinion on veganism, death metal and his dislike for many activists in his town. Things get serious when, roughly 3/4 of the way through the interview, Colby decides to drop some names.

[Salt Lake P.D] Brent Larsen: You don't have any idea who's involved in any of these things that we've talked about today?

[Unnamed officer] KM: ...Did you hear what happened? Did you hear what happened with McDonald's up in, was it South Jordan, West Jordan?

C.Ellerman: I heard DURFEY did something to it, when I heard that he had gone to a show and started bragging around everybody, to everybody, 'hey, I did that,' or something."
[C.C.E. Interview #1, April 19/97, pg 46]

(Ryan Durfee served one year in jail after being convicted of burning down a McDonalds restaurant under construction in West Jordan.) As the first interview ends, Colby has said very little else that directly implicates others, beyond his statement about Ryan, but he indicates to the officers his willingness to start grassing. As he prepares to leave the interview room, Officer Lee Perry, from the Utah Division Department of Investigations, gives Colby his card:

LP: "...You hear something on the street and you want to talk to me, want to talk to any of us, you, all three of us are communicating all the time. We all work for different agencies, but we're all talkin' getting together trying to compile this information."

C.Ellerman: "If I hear something, I'll definitely give you guys a call."

...[Special Agent Maknamora, Bureau Alcohol, Tobacco and Fire Arms] KM: "Give me a buzz."

C.Ellerman: "If I, if I do hear something, like I say, I'll let you guys know."

LP: "That'd be Great."

C.Ellerman: "A.S.A.P."

[C.C.E. Interview #1, April 19/97, pg 50-51]

True to his words, Clinton Colby Ellerman was back in touch with Utah authorities the very next day, where he willingly gave information on two mink raids he participated in. With little delay, Ellerman begins to implicate others in the raids. His told police that Brandon Mitchener, Jacob Kenison, Kevin Clark, Sean Gautchy, Troy Peace and Alex Slack were all accomplices. For the second mink raid he participated in, he also named Ang Bishop and his brother, Josh Ellerman, as well as several others, already named for the first raid. Colby walked the police step by step through the raids, careful to blame his alleged accomplices for planning the raids and for most of the property damage and animal liberation slogans left at the mink farms.

And hey, why stop there? Next, Colby informed the police that his brother most certainly had something to do with the arson attack at the mink breeders Co-op. In less than one hour, Colby casually destroyed the lives of seven innocent people and gave evidence against his own brother. Ever so willing to please, Ellerman then shared with the cops every half-baked rumour he ever heard about Utah straight-edge kids and local animal rights campaigners. Even those he's not so sure about, he figured he could come up with something:

Saranacki : But what about, do you know a _[Name deleted]_?

C.Ellerman: _[Name Deleted]_, you know, I think I know who that is but if you had a picture for me I could tell you..."
[C.C.E. Interview #2, April 20/97, pg42]

Clinton Colby Ellerman INFORMER
Salt Lake City Jail, 450 South 300 East, Salt Lake City, Utah, 84111-3207, USA
Date of Birth:11/27/76
SS#: 529-55-4538 Drivers License: 159245713

POLICE INFORMER #2: KEVIN DEXTER CLARK

On Wednesday, March 11, 1998, Agent Lee Perry and Detective Brent Larson interviewed Kevin Dexter Clark as a participant and witness of two mink releases that occurred in Salt Lake County. Clark told authorities that he would be willing to testify against the others involved. He spoke with the police in detail about the raids he participated in. Clark had already provided the police with signed statements that provided the names of several alleged participants in the mink farm raids as early as July 7, 1997. In his March 11 interview, Clark on at least three separate occasions gives a list of names of those he says helped on the raid, and at one even offers to repeat the list again: **"...just everyone I named. Do you want me to name them again?" [Kevin Clark Interview, March 11/98, pg9].** Like Ellerman, Clark seemed happy to place most of the blame for the raid on others, citing one person in particular as the leader, and the rest for doing the majority of the damage. Hard-core animal activist to the end, Kevin explains to police why he was committed to animal liberation:

LP: "Why did you decide to go raid these mink farms?

K.Clark: "Um."

LP: "Why did you get involved?"

K.Clark: "Uh, I thought it was a good cause, I guess."
[Kevin Clark Interview, March 11/98, pg27]

Kevin Dexter Clark INFORMER
Salt Lake City Jail, 450 South 300 East, Salt Lake City Utah, 84111-3207 USA

Date of Birth/29/76
SS# 529-51-5414 Drivers License: 153518540

(Continued on page 14)

STRATEGIC NONVIOLENCE:
DISSENT FROM THE COMFORT ZONE

by Rod Coronado
A Response to "Strategic Nonviolence"

In the July/August 1998 issue of Animals' Agenda, former Animal Liberation Front (A.L.F.) supporter, Freeman Wicklund authored an article entitled, "Direct Action: Progress, Peril or Both?" in which he evaluates the role of direct action in the animal rights movement. Recently Wicklund held a press conference where he distanced himself from his former stance and condemned the tactics and strategy of the A.L.F.

As an A.L.F. volunteer serving a 57 month sentence in federal prison for my participation in the 1992 raid on Michigan State University's Experimental Fur Farm, and as a long time believer and practitioner in the power and effectiveness of nonviolent -- albeit illegal -- direct action, I am compelled to respond to Wicklund's recent statements.

Since 1984 I have been actively involved in the struggles for animal, human and earth liberation, and it is not unusual when various activists choose to re-evaluate their personal contributions and roles within these movements. Such questioning is something we all must do to validate our current strategies and tactics, so as to maximize the efficient use of our limited resources and energy. Nothing unhealthy about that.

What is disappointing however, is the criticism some activists seem all too eager to heap on those of us who still adhere to the strategy and tactics they so recently believed in. It is almost as if they need to rationalize the reasons why they have opted out of a commitment that truly puts them on equal ground with the oppressed that they've appointed themselves to represent.

After years of observing this phenomena within our ranks among what are now some of the A.L.F.'s most vocal critics, I am led to the conclusion that inevitably those who condemn the A.L.F. are largely separated from a life where suffering and oppression is a daily occurrence. While claiming to believe in equality for animals and all life, such critics fail to see that with their chosen "nonviolent" philosophy, they maintain a greater allegiance to the rules of the oppressor than to the lives of the oppressed.

Monkey-wrenching? Why, that's illegal isn't it?

To criticize those in the same struggle who adhere to a code of aggressive rather than passive nonviolence -- which still respects the sanctity of all life -- pacifists like Wicklund practice a kind of moral imperialism. They separate themselves from the majority of life on earth, oppressed by our own species, while promoting their own narrow strategic agenda. An agenda that not only fails to recognize the effectiveness of an aggressive nonviolent strategy to achieve human, animal and earth liberation, but an agenda that fails to empathize with those forced to take, what some might consider, drastic measures.

These measures, as many clearly understand, are necessary for the oppressed's survival. It's also recognized that the majority of us in the animal rights and environmental movements in America know little or nothing of what it is like to be ruthlessly tortured and murdered, simply for trying to live a way of life that ancestors, be they human or nonhuman, have lived for the thousands of years previous to the "advance" of modern human "civilization".

By condemning those who readily defend the oppressed of the earth through tactics that violate the laws of man, and not those of humanity or nature, we push animals and earth away from the circle of equality we claim to believe in. Instead, we reinforce the societal belief that they are not worthy of our challenge to, and violation of human enacted laws.

Hens rescued by the Animal Liberation Front now live their lives free from abuse ... Setting the movement back twenty years...

There has never been a practitioner of non-violence, be they Martin Luther King Jr., or Jesus Christ himself, who condemned the destruction of the tools of oppression or the liberation of the oppressed as acts "of violence." Even the greatest philosophers and moral models of humankind have been able to separate the sanctity of life from the individual rights of private property. They recognized that the prevention of violence through the breaking of society's laws is indeed in adherence to the highest principles and rules of nonviolence.

By promoting a strategy for the just struggles of human, animal and earth liberation that excludes and condemns the nonviolent tactic of liberating the oppressed and destroying the implements of their torture, we are adhering more to the laws of our oppressors than those of nature or morality. Whether to avoid the repression that accompanies such a spiritual and political belief, or to avoid alienation from the dominant society that still places a greater value on property than life, those who condemn the actions of illegal direct action practitioners are betraying the majority of life on this planet — lives which depend on such tactics for their very survival.

Over the years I have seen many Americans who claim to align themselves with Earth First! or the animal liberation movement, who then opt out for a less personally endangering association, rather than face the threats, police harassment, and the violation of civil rights and imprisonment which my philosophical allies and myself have faced. While such repression by law enforcement agencies is nothing to brag about, it is most definitely an indicator that your chosen strategy and tactics truly create fear among those oppressors you are challenging.

Those who argue that illegal direct action endangers rather than benefits the struggle for liberty, fail to see that such has never been the case historically with any of the movements that were forced to engage in what was then considered illegal activity -- a time when basic human rights and freedoms were deemed criminal.

Associating oneself with a movement or strategy that freely accepts the necessity of breaking arbitrary laws in the pursuit of true justice and freedom has been the mandate of many resistors seeking to improve the lives of the oppressed. We see it in the very foundation of the United States' own history, which began as a settler's revolt against British imperialism. It can be seen in the recent history of Northern Ireland, where the occupying British forces have recognized the legitimacy of the outlawed Irish Republican Army which engaged in guerilla warfare against their oppressors for almost thirty years.

While we cannot ask American revolutionaries whether they believe their strategy against British oppression was justified, we can look towards the Irish Republicans of today and see that their present achievements towards liberty could not have come without the willingness to challenge unjust laws with illegal direct action. The fact remains that no oppressor has ever given liberty to its victims without the latter's willingness to fight for it by all means necessary and available. Some might say that there is a unique separation in the quest for human

(Continued on page 18)

(Continued from page 11)

NA-A.L.F.S.G. PRISONER SUPPORT -- AND INFORMERS

The North American A.L.F. Supporters Group, like Supporters Groups around the world, have a very clear policy in place that deals with grassing. Only those activists who refuse to give evidence on others will receive any support. This applies not only to giving names of those who are A.L.F. activists, but also to giving ANY name and alleging their involvement. It is, of course, not up to the Supporters Group to impose court strategies or lines of defense on an activist facing prison time. Legal strategies will vary on a case by case basis, and individual activists have the right to decide what defense is best for them. This can also include an activist acknowledging their own participation in an action -- but NO activist has the right to endanger the lives and liberty of others in a strategy to save their own hides.

On a final disturbing note, evidence is growing that **Josh Ellerman** has started to give evidence against others for the Fur Breeder's Co-op arson. Douglas Joshua Ellerman, 20, pleaded guilty to the March 11, 1997 bombing and arson at the Cooperative in Sandy, Utah. The co-op, which provides materials and mink to hundreds of farmers in the West, sustained nearly $1 million in damage. Josh was sentenced to seven years in prison, after working out a deal with the prosecution that spared him from a sentence of 35 years. The lesser sentence hinged on Ellerman's cooperation and contrition, The NA-A.L.F.S.G. is still awaiting documentation, but defendant Alex Slack has informed us that his lawyer has indeed confirmed that Josh Ellerman has made statements to police that name others as alleged participants. More will become known as the Discovery process continues. **Josh Ellerman has therefore also been removed from the NA-A.L.F.S.G's prisoner support list.**

The North American A.L.F. Supporters Group will do everything in its power to generate support for all activists facing jail time for animal liberation actions. We call on you to help with the support for Alex, Adam, Sean, Jacob, Brandon and Andrew, financial, or otherwise. Updates on their situation will be posted immediately on the Frontline Information Service (www.animal-liberation.net) web page as more becomes known. Financial donations for prisoner support can be sent directly to the Supporters Group, ear-marked "Utah Support." Please make any donations payable to "NA-A.L.F.S.G."

As government crackdowns on animal activists continue, we run the risk of seeing more activists ending up in prison, unless as a movement, we learn from this situation. Illegal direct action for animal liberation is not a game, and does not earn you scene points or bragging rights. All too often in recent memory we've seen apparently "dedicated" activists turn traitor at the drop of a hat, grassing out friends and comrades in a desperate attempt to kiss up to the state. One year, two years, seven years later these informers may again join the freeworld -- but their actions will never be forgotten or forgiven. @

Two Indicted For Mink Release

Men Face Commerce, Terrorism Charges

MADISON, Wis. September 22, 1998 -- Two men accused of releasing thousands of mink last fall face federal charges of interfering with interstate commerce and participating in animal enterprise terrorism.

Peggy Lautenschlager is a U.S. Attorney in Wisconsin. She says the six-count indictment unsealed today charges Peter Young and Justin Samuel with conducting surveillance on numerous farms and releasing breeding stock mink from fur farms in Independence, Medford and Tomahawk.

A federal grand jury returned the indictment against the men. The indictment says Young, of Mercer Island, Washington, and Samuel, of Snohomish, Washington, raided fur farms last October in Wisconsin, South Dakota and Iowa in an effort to get fur farmers to close their businesses.

About 3,600 mink were released. In the meantime, mink release are taking place at a phenomenal rate around the world. Fur farms in Sweden, Finland, England and the United States continue to be raided on an almost weekly basis. Check out the Diary of Actions for cell reports from around the world. Also to be found in this issue are communiques from several U.S. A.L.F. cells that share their experiences with us all...@

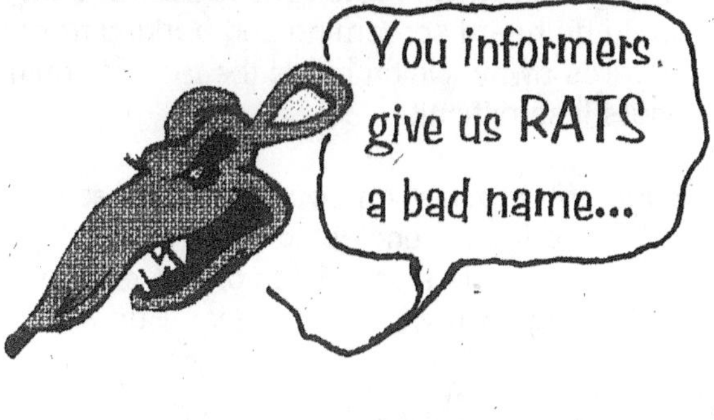
You informers, give us RATS a bad name...

ORANGE COUNTY JAIL PUTS ANIMAL LIB PRISONER AT RISK

Orange County, CA -- For some time now, Frank Allen (serving a one year sentence for attempted arson on a high school slaughterhouse) has been abused and put at risk by guards at the Orange County Jail here in California. Frank is a diabetic and his health is at serious risk because he is not being properly cared for or given vegetarian food (he's lost a lot of weight because of this). Frank, his family and his fiancee have tried to resolve the problems without calling on outside activists and taking us away from other important work but their efforts (and Frank DeG's writ) have been ignored. So, he's decided its time for national pressure from fellow activists.

Please call the jail today:
(714) 647-6015
ask to speak with the watch commander (most likely Lt. Coots or Nearing)

Here's all the info:
Frank Allen
Booking #1809138
Mod L (all grievances apply to all of Mod L where 6-7 other diabetics are housed and having the same problems)

Grievances:
*** non-adequate medical staff (little or no knowledge of diabetes)**
*** receiving incorrect dosage of insulin**
*** all locked down (which he believes is a violation of the *Americans with Disabilities Act*)**
*** no "early kicks" for medical ward (also ADA violation?) - most prisoners get at least a 10 % kick not available to inmates in the medical ward.**
*** vegetarian food should be given for religious reasons as well as medical reasons (they don't recognize religious diets AT ALL)**
*** denied regular exercise**
*** locked down to eat (inconsistent with other prisoners)**
*** denied access to church**
*** day room privileges not consistent with other prisoners)**
*** general harassment from guards (example: when they go for their shots, their commissary is thrown away, beds thrown on the floor and rooms messed up)**
*** strip searched anytime and told the only reason is "because they can"**

Our thanks to everyone who gets involved on Franks behalf. Show our prisoners they are not forgotten and will never be neglected! @

REPORTS FROM THE FRONTLINE:

MINK RAID COMMUNIQUES

AUGUST 20/98: Guttenburg, Iowa -- eco-animal warriors raided Steve Hansel's Hidden Valley Fur Farm. After following a sign indicating the location of the fur farm, liberators travelled miles of gravel road to reach this fox concentration camp: The fox could be heard screaming and barking from hundreds of yards away, which made the task of finding the prisoners less difficult.

Upon entry to the compound, operatives were surprised to find no fences enclosing the area. On the grounds, two large sheds stood. Each of these were capable of containing six rows of fox cages. Further inspection revealed one empty shed and one shed with two rows of cages. This second shed imprisoned about thirty fox. The area behind these sheds appeared to have once been used for more sheds. Old wooden frames littered the ground in this area. Reportedly this farm also contained members of the mink and ferret nations; however, none of these were found. We suspect Hansel's stock has decreased in recent years.

Near the sheds six long rows of individual breeders cages stood. Most of these cages contained two fox each. The cages measured about six feet long by two

(Continued on page 16

(Continued from page 15)
and a half feet wide. The rear of each cage was separated into a nesting box. The nesting box doors were concealed under a layer of sheet metal that could simply be lifted up. Each of the nesting box doors underneath were secured with unlocked clips. Although these could be opened, another exit was necessary for the prisoners' escape because in most cages the nesting areas were closed off to the animals inside. Therefore, operatives opened cage doors located on the top. The doors on the top required liberators to pull back a metal latch and lift up the hinged wire mesh door.

All thirty cages containing fox in the shed were opened and some of the imprisoned fox were lifted out to freedom. Approximately 150 breeder's cages, all that were found, were opened. Some of the fox were seen running around the compound. An estimated 330 members of the fox nation were liberated in all. This concentration camp imprisoned many kinds of fox. Coat colours varied from white to red to dark brown and black.

In addition to the release of prisoners, two feed machines, one in the shed and one in a nearby barn, were sabotaged and had wires cut. In a large building near the barn, operatives peered through windows to discover large amounts of tools and processing equipment.

This was all done in view of the farmer's house.

Gaia's blood has been spilled for far too long. We took it upon ourselves to reclaim justice for our Earth Mother and all of her children. The time has come for the two-footed animals to reestablish their link with the four-footed animal nations and the earth of which we are all a part.

This action was done in solidarity with the warriors of the Chatham 3. We will not forget our comrades. Our brothers' and sisters' forced inactivity will not abate the A.L.F.'s resistance against the capitalist death machine.

Smashing the fur industry piece by piece,
Animal Liberation Front

MIDWESTERN WILDLIFE UNIT COMMUNIQUE:

In the early morning hours of August 28, 1998 the Midwestern Wildlife Unit of the Animal Liberation Front raided the Zumbro River Mink Concentration Camp. Breeding information for over ten thousand mink was torn from above cages and trashed on the ground. An estimated 3,000 mink nation prisoners were released from cages.

A portion of fence was rolled over away from the road to decrease the risk of released animals crossing the road. Surrounding the compound on both sides were houses. The sheds were clearly visible from the road. This prevented liberators from freeing more prisoners. The total number of captives in the camp is an estimated 15,000 in seven sheds.

The placement of this concentration camp is highly beneficial to the release of wildlife such as the mink. Nearby the camp is large forest area and across the street is the Zumbro River which runs far north of town. These mink will now have a chance to establish themselves in the local ecosystem and regain the natural instincts which the confinement of fur farm imprisonment had all but destroyed.

Operation Bite Back will be continued through the efforts of the Animal Liberation Front, Earth Liberation Front, and the Wild Minks. Nothing will deter us Guardians of Mother Earth. The animal nations will be set free to live again as one with the forest.

Animal Liberation Front, Midwestern Wildlife Unit

MINNESOTA COMMUNIQUE:

On the 22nd of Aug. the A.L.F. payed a visit to Would Mink Farm (Route 1, Box 144, Hinkley, MN 55037) owned by Ronald Would. This visit was in hopes of liberating more prisoners from their life of hell in small, filthy, dirt ridden concentration camps. They would have been returned to their natural habitat in the forests of Minnesota. Since mink are native to North America, they would be at home in rural, northern Minnesota.

In approaching the sheds on the fur farm, the distinct smell of excrement and suffering was missing. When entering the sheds, it was noticed that they were empty of both animals and cages. This is a notice to all compassionate activists for animals that this fur farm in now seemingly vacated. May the few, dedicated, brave, committed, activists who are truly working for total animal liberation remain strong, when others collapse and take easier paths, while denouncing those who risk their freedom. After all, there is not an easy route for the animals.

It's now their time-or never!

A.L.F.

BARRY HORNE RESUMES HUNGER STRIKE!

At exactly midnight, October 6/98, Animal Liberation Front activist Barry began his third prison hungerstrike to protest government inaction on the issue of vivisection. Proceeding the hungerstrike, the British Home Office has been contacted on several occasions to remind Labour party of pre-election pledges to address pressing animal issues. The government's initial reply ignored the questions and issues put to them, in what has become the typically arrogant manner of the Home Office. Their reply after being contacted for a second time clearly shows the Labour government's contempt and disregard for the Animal Liberation movement, as exemplified in the final paragraph of their response: *The Home Office "will not allow this programme of work to be dictated (in timing or content) by the protest action of the Animal Liberation movement."* This has left Barry with no other option but to resume his hunger strike. Barry had this to say:

AN OPEN LETTER FROM BARRY HORNE

I think it is now necessary to update everybody on what has happened since the end of the second hunger strike (re: vivisection) and my thoughts on it all. That second hunger strike ended because the Labour Govt. agreed to meet with representatives of the Barry Horne Support Campaign (BHSC) as a means of resolving the differences between us, differences which had led to the escalation of the protest campaign and the second hunger strike. That the Labour Govt. negotiated with the BHSC, and agreed to a meeting, was very significant. It could be viewed as the Govt. affording the Animal Liberation movement official recognition, and as a precedent that could not be undone. After that one meeting had taken place, the BHSC no longer felt able to hold further talks with the Labour Govt. and all contact between us was broken. At the same time, it is possible the wider movement didn't understand that decision by the BHSC, but in view of the lack of action by the labour Govt. on vivisection since then, the reasons for it must now be clear. In the year since the end of the second hunger strike, no significant action has been taken by the Labour Govt. to limit or decrease the activities of the vivisection industry. Despite all the fine words at the time of the election, New Labour have displayed complete indifference to the plight of the animals suffering and dying in the labs. In the last year that indifference has been matched only by the increased scale of animal suffering. While the Animal Rights movement organises legally to overcome the horrors of vivisection it has to be said that the Labour Govt. has sought to block all progress towards a rightful and just solution to the problem. In all dealings between Animal Rights / Liberation activists and the Govt., we are treated with contempt and fobbed off with further lies, while behind the scenes the Govt. approves the further increased use of animals for vivisection. While we, the movement, have acted in good faith, the Govt. have responded with contempt and indifference. That situation cannot be allowed to continue.

Recently, communication from the Animal Liberation movement was delivered to the Labour Govt. detailing our feelings on the matter, and expressing our dismay at the bad faith displayed by them since the end of the second hunger strike. That communication calls on the Labour Govt. to make a significant and positive response on the issue of vivisection, to avert the possibility of a complete breakdown of trust between ourselves and the Govt. At midnight on September 26th 1998, exactly one year since the end of the second hunger strike, the deadline for the Govt to respond elapsed. Sadly, there was no response, so it will not be possible for any further negotiation, and further action in support of the ongoing campaign against vivisection has become inevitable.

The situation as outlined above has arisen solely because of the arrogant and indifferent attitude of the Labour Govt., and at their door must be laid the blame for any situation that arises as a result. It is inevitable that we, the movement, shall drive back and defeat the vivisection industry. The actions of the Labour Govt. merely delay the inevitable and prolong the suffering of the animals. I would ask everyone to fully support the ongoing campaign to end vivisection in this country, and to fully support any and all actions taken as part of that campaign. At all times we should remember just what we have achieved so far, make no mistake that since the beginning of the present campaign we have driven the vivisection industry back and weakened their position. Now is the time to strike a major blow against them. With the second hunger strike the Animal Liberation movement showed it has the strength and commitment to fight and to resist, and to suffer in that resistance. AtConsort, Hill grove and HDS we have shown our determination to overcome, no matter what the odds, those who torture and murder animals. It is now necessary for us all to show this Govt.(and all Govt.s) that we, the movement, cannot be ignored or defeated, and that we will fight until we win.

The fight is not for us, not for our personal wants or needs. It is for every animal that has ever suffered and died in the vivisection labs, and for every animal that will suffer and die in those same labs unless we end this evil business now! The souls of the tortured dead cry out for justice, the cry of the living is for freedom. We can create that justice and we can deliver that freedom. The animals have no-one but us, we will not fail them.

For the cause,
BARRY

(Continued from page 13) *SNV: Dissent from the Comfort Zone*

liberation and the struggle that will bring greater rights for our fellow beings and the earth we share with them; those involved in the animal and earth liberation struggle are fighting for the sake of those who cannot fight for themselves. However, be it human, animal or earth liberation that we fight for, we inevitably come up against the same system responsible for the oppression of us all.

Regardless of who we fight for, when we challenge the very principles of the society most responsible for the oppression of humans, animals and earth, we find ourselves open to state-sponsored repression. This has been the case for hundreds of years and it will probably be the case for hundreds of years to come. Those in positions of power and control benefit most from oppressing others. They are directly and negatively affected by anyone who

Proponents of Strategic Non-Violence are quick to celebrate the accomplishments of Dr. King (left), but completely ignore any contributions by those who chose to fight their oppressors by other means. Some of the people SNV spokespeople might wish you'd forget about: Angela Davis (middle) and the Black Panther Party (right) .

engages in tactics and strategies that threaten their oppressive behavior, and worse, who set an example that others might follow.

It is for this reason that the condemnation of past allies, like Wicklund, who disagree with the strategy and tactics of the A.L.F., contribute more towards stifling the struggle for animal liberation then helping it. Condemnation from within our ranks is always capitalized upon by our opponents, to be repeatedly used by those who wish to discredit groups like the A.L.F. -- groups engaged in effective campaigns against them. Meanwhile, within our own ranks, the condemnation of the A.L.F.'s effective strategy is followed by pleas "to restrict" our tactics to only those which do not "isolate the public." or its support. While such pleas place incredible faith in the power of the media establishment, they fail to acknowledge that the media is nothing more than the voice of special interests that equally profits from exploitation and abuse.

Measuring the success of our movement in media presentations condemns it to be controlled by the very power structure we need to overthrow. Again, history is replete with examples where the media establishment has served the interests of the oppressor more than the oppressed. Whether the media, governments, corporations or pacifists like Wicklund label the actions of the A.L.F. as "violence" or "terrorism," we cannot subscribe to their collective illusion and disregard the truth we have in our own hearts. We know the face of real terrorism in our society. To say that the actions of the A.L.F. "are violent," especially when voiced by those with real blood on their hands, is not only hypocritical, but has nothing to do with preserving human morality and everything to do with them trying to alter our perception of violence itself.

How are we supposed to believe that a bomb that explodes in Omagh, Northern Ireland, that killed innocent people is the work of terrorists when bombs exploded by the US just days later in Sudan and Afghanistan are not? Equally, why should we believe that the act of burning of a building is violent while the physical torture inflicted within its walls is not? Why should we accept that actions of the A.L.F., which injure no living being, are unacceptable acts of violence and terrorism while the actions committed daily by industries awash in the blood of their non-human victims, are not?

Such is the rationale of a society unable to accept responsibility for the violence its values and lifestyle demand. Such is the twisted perspective of a society determined to keep its citizens in denial regarding the violence that has become part of day to day existence. This is a society that has lost all concept of the laws of morality and humanity, adhering instead to laws established by those most responsible for bringing institutionalized violence into our daily lives.

A.L.F. action against a dairy company. Financial ruin will ensure this company never profits again from animal exploitation. SNV calls this bad publicity.

It is this distorted view of violence that Wicklund and some pacifists unknowingly reinforce when they accuse the A.L.F. of violating codes of nonviolence. This misfocus ignores and overshadows the real acts of violence within our society. By condemning the actions of the A.L.F. (who value living, sentient beings much more than the machines used to destroy them), these critics fall in step with our opponents, those who would sooner label A.L.F. volunteers as terrorists while continuing to legitimize their own physical violence and terror everyday. No allowance of credibility should be given to the media in defining the level of our morality. We should all know that successful movements focused on positive change and peace are not created by the media, but by the sincere commitments of our members. It is their ability to define what is right and wrong with their own heart, and not the questioning of what is "legal" and "illegal" that gives them favorable media coverage.

Much of Wicklund's argument for what he calls "strategic nonviolence" is based on the Gandhian principles of nonviolence, developed during Gandhi's campaign of civil disobedience against British colonialism and applied more recently by Martin Luther King Jr. in his fight for civil rights in America. Principles that Wicklund and others believe the A.L.F. violate in its campaign of aggressive nonviolent direct action.

Missing from Wicklund's argument is the fact that neither Gandhi or King ever condemned the more aggressive tactics of their allies. In British occupied India the armed struggle of Indian nationalists lasted far beyond Gandhi's own campaign and undoubtedly influenced Britain's decision to pull out of India as much, if not more, than the nonviolent tactics Gandhi personally adhered to. Similarly, the limited accomplishments of the civil rights movement in America cannot be solely accredited to King, but also to African American nationalists like Malcolm X, Angela Davis, the Nation of Islam and the rioters in the Los Angeles community of Watts. All played a part in forcing the U.S. government to make concessions to those opposed to racism.

This is not to say that the A.L.F. or others in this struggle need to advance to a level of armed struggle or violent self-defense, but merely to demonstrate that even Gandhi and King understood the legitimate ranks of their movements included diverse tactics. Condemning the tactics of others only help the oppressors to divide our ranks.

This is why Wicklund's (and other pacifists) desire to see us surrender tactics that have won indisputable victories is morally and strategically weak. The contemporary forces of oppression which plague this earth today have no respect for either the morality of their opponents or the lives of those they oppress. The majority of oppressors are fuelled by an insatiable greed that will see our planet reduced to an uninhabitable wasteland in their never-ending quest for wealth and power.

Like Wicklund and other pacifists, I too desire to live in a world where even our opponents respect our adherence to peaceful means and our willingness to engage only in activity that will not offend members of the public. But, as Ice-T said about the reality of the role of police in his South-Central Los Angeles community, "Shit ain't like that."

Hoping for a moral awakening among those most responsible for the violence in today's world is a pipe dream, dreamt by those most isolated from the struggle and resistance of the forces currently destroying the earth, animals and indigenous peoples. History is filled with the failures of purely pacifistic approaches to stoping violent oppression, as noble as those attempts might be. A good example is the democracy movement in China. While this movement has survived extreme acts of repression, no one can deny the failure of passive nonviolence as a tactic which culminated in the slaughter of pro-democracy forces at Tianenmen Square in 1989.

The writing on the wall, Belfast. Agressive, grassroots resistance has played a large part in the struggle in Northern Ireland.

In British-occupied-India, nonviolent protesters were gunned down in Amistar. In apartheid-era-South Africa, peaceful marchers were murdered in the Sharpesville Massacre. In Derry, Northern Ireland, civil rights marchers were shot dead in what is now known as Bloody Sunday. In each case, the lack of respect by the oppressors for the strategy of passive nonviolence led to the oppressed's wider acceptance of more aggressive tactics. Tactics that quickly became legitimate elements of their struggles.

The struggles for earth, animal and human liberation shouldn't wait for a similar demonstration of the oppressor's disrespect for our own passive nonviolence before we fully appreciate and recognize the importance of the tactics and strategies of organizations like the A.L.F. How many Judi Bari's and David Chain's must there be before we recognize that there is actually a greater likelihood of violence through our practice of passive nonviolence, then there is in our execution of strategic, aggressive nonviolence against the mechanical monsters that destroy all we love?

We live in a time when greater rights and protection are given to multinational corporations than to the humans, animals and the earth which they ruthlessly exploit. We live in a society where power in our supposed representative democracy" is determined, not by citizen constituents, but by special interests that contribute heavily to the campaigns of politicians. We live in a world where it is legitimate behavior for a government to protect business interests through military action, economic embargoes, and by the funding and supplying of paramilitary death squads.

In such extreme social, political and ecological conditions -- where the worldview of a few powerful nations justifies the irreversible exploitation and destruction of all life on earth -- resistance by all means possible is less a choice than an obligation for those seeking peace in our modern world.

Given the incredible amount of death and destruction caused by the corporate and governmental forces we target in our struggle for liberation, the tactics and strategy of the A.L.F. and other like-minded groups should be commended, not condemned.

In over 15 years of operation in the U.S., the A.L.F. has yet to cause even one human injury, let alone loss of life while rescuing literally tens of thousands of animals and destroying millions of dollars worth of the equipment used to torture them. This contribution to freedom for beings of the earth is a demonstration of the principles of nonviolence equal to any demonstrated by Gandhi or King.

Since its inception, the A.L.F. has strictly targeted only the machines and material used to commit atrocious act of terrorism rather than the humans committing these acts. This demonstrates a moral high ground rarely seen in the history of any struggle for liberation, be it human, earth or animal. If people like Wicklund think it's better to condemn those who have risked their very lives and freedom to save the lives of others, they are wrong.

The actions of the A.L.F. are far from violent, as alleged by critics. This attitude -- that the just defense of the defenceless is an act of violence -- is one shared by our oppressor, and its proponents fail to recognize the inherent violence their own class and privilege was built by. An example: it is moral arrogance for anyone in our country to condemn those victimized by the U.S. government and its policies who then engage in aggressive and even armed defense to protect their lives. Such condemnation fails to acknowledge that the lifestyles of most people in this country contribute to the oppression of people in countries such as Mexico, Columbia, East Timor, Peru and Palestine, all places where the people are engaged in armed resistance to this oppression.

As our movement is quick to argue: the struggles for human, animal and earth liberation are inextricably connected. So to is our contribution to and support of greater acts of violence than any of the actions for which the A.L.F. has been condemned by pacifists like Wicklund. Even the vegan activist is not free from supporting petroleum, mining, chemical and arms industries, as well as other multinational corporations that exploit the earth, animals and humans. These are the same corporations that have created a situation where people have been forced to violence to defend themselves. Such is the reality behind the purchase and consumption of even the most (apparently) innocuous product.

This is the society for which activists like Wicklund would have us sacrifice our effective strategy for. Their hope is to demonstrate moral purity while not offending those most responsible for oppression; of offending a society built on the blood and bones of millions of indigenous peoples and the bodies of others forced into slavery to build it. The economy of this country has from its inception relied on the exploitation and abuse of the environment and animals. Ours is a moral-less society where economic wealth is concentrated amongst those who will smash any who resist it, even through genocide.

This is why I have no desire, nor I believe does the A.L.F., to try to passively reform the lifestyles and values of what is the most destructive civilization on earth. While we support the efforts of those that do, we ourselves are focused on preventing the needless destruction of innocent nonhuman life through all nonviolent means available. Our greatest consideration is for those forced to endure a living hell rather than those who might consider our actions violent.

A.L.F. volunteers recognizes that the oppression of animals is directly connected to the oppression of all life, and representative of the larger problems threatening our existence on earth. Militarism, racism, sexism, imperialism, they are all indicative of the problems created when we separate ourselves from nature and the laws of humanity. Our personal contributions to a remedy requires a code of behavior that recognizes that when peaceful, passive, democratic means fail to achieve liberation of the oppressed, "illegal" direct action is not only morally justified, but required. Since 1991, the A.L.F.'s code of aggressive nonviolence has successfully contributed to the continuing decline of the fur industry, in particular. Since 1995, over 50 fur farms and numerous fur retailers have felt the bite of the A.L.F.'s campaign. These actions have not only liberated tens of thousands of mink and fox who would have otherwise died, but have led to the bankruptcy of many fur farms and retailers. It would be strategically foolish to ease the pressure now.

The A.L.F. has never endorsed or participated in physical violence, nor will we ever. The A.L.F. does not support actions with the intent of causing physical injury or loss of life. Our ability to avoid such violence during years of operations is no coincidence. We are not fighting a violent war, but fighting with aggressive nonviolence to end the war on other-than-human life.

Each member of my past A.L.F. cells who have carried out raids on laboratories, fur and factory farms and other institutions of animal abuse over the last 13 years, has been motivated not by hate or a willingness to rationalize of use violence, but by love. They have a tremendous sense of compassion for the other races of life we share earth with. My fellow A.L.F. volunteers have always been grounded in a reverence and respect for life and freedom, so much so that together in the course of every A.L.F. action we ever participated in, we were willing to risk losing our own freedom while liberating our victimized animal relations. Far from compromising the principles of nonviolence, the A.L.F.'s actions are those of a highly moral, disciplined group of caring humans, whose efforts would be hypocritical if they ever sanctioned physical violence. The A.L.F. exists in part to provide an avenue of freedom for those innocent beings the animal rights movement is unable at this time to rescuing legally. The A.L.F. brings hope when others feel hopeless. For the peaceful warriors of the A.L.F., nonviolent direct action to save lives remains not our choice, but every enlightened human beings obligation. @

NORTH AMERICAN PRESS OFFICE

...view was given about ..."al" Animal Liberation

REPORT

It's been a busy time for the NA-A.L.F. Press Office over the past few months. Here's a sampling of some of what Katie Fedor, the Press Officer, has been up to...

MORE INTERVIEWS:

A via satellite interview was given about the "unusual" Animal Liberation Frontline Information Service Web Site. Since that interview, the web site has a brand new domain and has more information about The A.L.F. than anyone could imagine. If you have any questions about The A.L.F., they will be answered on this wonderful resource for activists of all movements. The new url is: **http://www.animal-liberation.net/**

The Animal Liberation Collective at the University of Guelph, Canada, hosted the Press Office as a guest for an hour long radio interview. The "Voice of the Voiceless" radio show is an excellent weekly program devoted solely to animal rights. Broadcast: Fridays, CFRU 93.3fm

Another radio program featuring animal rights topics is The Animals Forum heard on the cable radio network. You can listen around the country on your computer by contacting http://www.blusalley.com/animal_forum.htm. The Press Office has been a guest for three consecutive weeks along with a PETA campaign coordinator. This show seeks to have guests from all sides of the animal rights debate which includes animal welfarists, and animal abusers. A direct challenge to animal abusers to appear on the show has remained unaccepted...not a surprise!

KEEPING BUSY IN NEW JERSEY

On July 16 in Paramus New Jersey, the Animal Liberation Front firebombed a truck belonging to Steven Corn Furs. According to a communique sent by The A.L.F, the damage caused to the truck in unknown. Associated Press did an interview about this action. The Animal Defence League issued a news release in support of the action with a newspaper article quoting the supportive activists.

A Flemington Furs billboard was paintbombed by possible Animal Liberation Front activists. This action remains unclaimed but certainly bears the hallmark of an A.L.F. action. For this reason, the Press Office considers it to be an A.L.F. action. Courier News called for an interview which again shows that smaller actions are still receiving media attention.

Six different fur stores had seven nonviolent actions carried out against them. Steven Corn Furs is becoming very popular for actions. An example of an action is tire puncturing devices placed at the entrance, which worked! A car tire was shredded by the devices. Other actions include etching messages into just about anything that has glass on the store. As most of you know, there's usually tons of glass, which amounts to a lot of messages.

Media totals Associated Press Newspaper and radio. The AP story was covered all the way in MN where the Press Office is located. Three radio stations had ran the story with a live talk show debate with a fur industry representative.

FIVE LIBERATIONS IN ELEVEN DAYS!

Starting with almost 4,000 mink released on Aug. 18 near St. Cloud, Minnesota, the A.L.F. show no signs of letting up on continuous, powerful actions. Charles Mueller's Fur Farm was selected and media went wild. A grand total of four radio interviews, two in-person television interviews and two newpapers. Follow up stories were printed from the Associated Press when more actions continued in New Jersey.

(Continued on page 28)

DIARY OF ACTIONS

The Diary of Actions is intended to report the news of direct action for earth and animal liberation, not to encourage crime, etc. All reports come from communiques, other publications, the internet and news reports. Some actions took place in time periods covered by other issues of *Underground*, but were not reported until recently.

CANADA

OCTOBER 8/95: Grand Prairie, AB -- Arsonists torch six railway cars at the Weyerhaeuser mill. About 400 bales of pulp were in each car, with damages estimated up to $750,000.

JULY 14/97: Grand Prairie, AB -- eco-activists used a loader to tear up 115 metres of railway track just past a switch that directs cars from CN's main line to the Weyerhaeuse mill. The culprits also ram the loader into a power pole, taking out the main power line.

OCTOBER 27/97: Hythe, AB -- Someone fired a high-powered rifle at the office of the Alberta Energy Co. plant manager. The bullet pierced the window, two walls, a water pipe, and then lodged into a second pipe. No injuries.

DECEMBER 29/97: Grand Prairie, AB -- activists use chainsaw to down 17 power poles, which deliver electricity to oil wells. More than $20,000 damage.

FEBUARY 1/98: Grand Prairie, AB -- A skidder, belonging to Vidar Forestry Technology of Hythe, set ablaze. No injuries.

JULY 19/98: Saskatoon, SK -- Prairie Meats has 1 van painted and 1 truck paint stripped. -A.L.F.

JULY 31-AUGUST 1/98: Beaverlodge, AB -- Explosions at two separate Alberta Energy Co. well sites. No injuries but nearby farms had to be evacuated after Aug. 1 blast.

AUGUST 24/98: Hinton, AB -- Blast destroys equipment shed at Suncor Energy well. Four people arrested but Crown drops charges.

UNITED STATES

JULY/98: Branchburg, NJ -- Flemington Furs billboard paint-bombed. -Unclaimed

JULY 16/98: Paramus, NJ -- Truck belonging to Steven Corn Furs was firebombed. The damage is unknown. - A.L.F.

JULY 16/98: Woodbridge, NJ -- members of the A.L.F. took action and Woodbridge Furs had its two main display windows and glass door damaged by rocks proclaiming, "Stop or be Stopped" and "Close Now." "A.L.F." was spraypainted on the front of the death shop. "Such actions will continue until all living beings roam free." -A.L.F.

JULY 21/98: Philomath, OR -- The Animal Liberation Front claim responsibility for rescuing three female rabbits destined for breeding from the Western Oregon Rabbit Supply (2475 Rosecrest Dr., Philomath). This breeding facility sells animals to laboratories to be used in research for household products, and other painful experiments. From the communique: "The rabbits are now safe in a good home. This is in no way a victory for those still imprisoned-we will keep fighting ..." -A.L.F.

JULY 26/98: Woodbridge, NJ -- A.L.F. glued the locks of Woodbridge Furs. -A.L.F.

JULY 26/98: Location not given -- Kemps Dairy Corporate Headquarters hit with red paint: "Kemps=Death", "A.L.F.", etc. One ice cream delivery truck also painted with skull and crossbones and "Death". -A.L.F.

AUGUST/98: Germantown. MD -- four turkeys who had been "living" at a roadside petting zoo were rescued by the Animal Liberation Front. While the turkeys would have eventually been slaughtered for their flesh, all four have been placed in homes where they will not be treated as a source of mere food or entertainment, but rather as individualswho deserve the right to live free of exploitation. Until all are free, A.L.F.

AUGUST 1/98: Honolulu -- the Honolulu Zoo was evacuated (of human visitors) due to a bomb threat. No bomb was discovered. - Unclaimed

AUGUST 12/98: Rockville, MD -- Murry's Meat Wholesale had its locks glued. --A.L.F.

AUGUST 11/98: Paramus, NJ -- Ten tire puncturing devices placed across the driveway of Steven Corn Furs. -A.L.F.

AUGUST 12/98: Teaneck, NJ -- Large air conditioning unit at Cedar Lane Furs damaged. -A.L.F.

AUGUST 12/98: Rockville, MD -- A meat store and a neighboring restaurant on Rockville Pike were targeted by animal rights activists. The doors at the Murry's Steaks store at 1550 Rockville Pike had been glued, preventing employees from getting inside. While police were on the scene, they were approached by an employee from the Phineas restaurant at 1580 Rockville Pike who said that the restaurant's locks had been glued shut as well.

AUGUST 13/98: Montclair, NJ -- "FUR IS DEAD" etched into the front display window at Bergen Fur Company. -A.L.F.
AUGUST 15/98: Paramus, NJ -- Ten tire puncturing devices placed across the driveway of Steven Corn Furs. -A.L.F.

AUGUST 15/98: Englewood, NJ -- The letters "ALF" etched into the three front display windows at Fleischman Furs. -A.L.F.

AUGUST 15/98: Ledgewood, NJ -- "FUR IS DEAD" and "ALF" etched into two front display windows and a glass door at Nicholson Furs. -A.L.F.

AUGUST 18/98: Teaneck, NJ -- "MURDER" etched into three front display windows, two glass doors, and a glass display case at Queen Anne Furs. -A.L.F.

AUGUST 18/98: St. Cloud, MN -- 4,000 (aprox.) mink were released from Charles Mueller's Fur Farm. - A.L.F.

AUGUST 20/98: Guttenburg, Iowa -- eco-animal warriors raided Steve Hansel's Hidden Valley Fur Farm -- 300 fox liberated. *"This action was done in solidarity with the warriors of the Chatham 3. We will not forget our comrades. Our brothers' and sisters' forced inactivity will not abate the ALF's resistance against the capitalist death machine."* -A.L.F.

AUGUST 21/98: Jewell, Iowa -- the Animal Liberation Front struck the Isebrands Mink Ranch (3221 Queens Ave in Jewell, Iowa), setting free 1500-3000 mink. From the communique: *"Let this raid be a call to action. It is time for all those who oppose needless suffering to start the attack. This is the third fur farm raid in the Midwest this week, let's make this only the beginning. By brick, boltcutters, or fire, this is the dawn of liberation."* - A.L.F.

AUGUST 23/98: Philadelphia, PA -- 3 glass panels in front door and front display window at Jacques Ferber Furs etched with "FUR KILLS". - A.L.F.

AUGUST 26/98: Beloit, WI -- The Brown Mink Ranch was hit by activists, and over 3,000 mink were released. The ranch has 13,000 total captive mink and is across the street from a river which makes it great mink habitat.

AUGUST 28/98: Rochester, MN -- Close to 3,000 animals were released from Zumbro River Fur Farm (4625 West River Rd. NW.) This is the second fur farm liberation in Minnesota in 11 days.

SEPTEMBER 8/98: Westfield, NJ. La Marque Furs had "ALF" etched into three front display windows, and "DEAD" etched into four glass doors. -A.L.F.

SEPTEMBER 11/98: New York, NY -- animal rights activists are behind a hoax against NYU Medical School Dean David Scotch because of his support of animal research. Dr. Scotch is at NYU Medical Center for back surgery. Someone apparently called the nursing station and ordered that he be prepped for circumcision and prostate surgery instead. The hoax was spotted in time and the orders were not carried out.

SEPTEMBER 19/98: Burlington, Wa -- eleven chickens were liberated from Broadview Egg Farms by the Animal Liberation Front (A.L.F.). A videotape and communique was released to the public by the activists. From the communique: *"The meat, dairy, & egg industries are responsible for suffering and murder on an epic scale. Veganism is the answer to end this holocaust. Unfortunately, education of the public is a slow process, and the animals confined for our greed do not have time. The Animal Liberation Front rises to their call to end their suffering and save their lives. Animal abuse industries wish to keep the public ignorant to the suffering involved in their products."* The videotape clearly shows A.L.F. volunteers removing animals from their cages and placing them in carriers. The video also shows the deplorable conditions that activist's report in the communique. This includes four to five animals living in 11" x 17" cages. Unfortunately, not all the animals could be rescued because of limited homes. Activists also stress that the immense suffering of these animals is completely preventable by avoiding all animal products in a diet.

SEPTEMBER 20/98: Davis, CA -- The E.L.F. sabotaged seven large yellow machines of death. Gas tanks were filled with sand, chest-high tires were slashed, and wires were cut. -E.L.F.

ENGLAND

MAY 20/98: Hackney -- meat van set on fire. The cabin was destroyed, windows shattered and tires melted from the heat. - A.L.F.

MAY 28/98: Oxfordshire -- Four 6-week old kittens were rescued from Hillgrove Farm by intrepid activists. All four kittens were in carrying boxes waiting to go off to vivisection labs, but no longer!

JUNE 11/98: Oxfordshire -- Four letter bombs were posted to targets involved with vivisection. Two of the targets were COLIN BLAKEMORE (infamous vivisector who stitched up kitten eyelids) and CHRIS BROWN (ower of Hillgrove Farm, supplier of cats for vivisection). The other two devices went to two Hillgrove employees. No group as of yet has claimed responsibility, but some speculate in might be the work of the Provisional A.L.F.

JUNE 17/98: Hackney -- meat van set on fire. -A.L.F.

JULY/98: London -- On the night of the big England World Cup match (football) a butchers in Walthamstow, east London had its window smashed by A.L.F. activists.-A.L.F.

JULY/98: Stamford Hill -- Butchers window smashed. Butchers window smashed: Hackney, east London, Exotic Chinese restaurant has window smashed: Walthamstow, east London. -A.L.F.

JULY 26/98: Devon -- eco-activists from the Devon branch of the Ethical Consumers Association destroyed a field of Maize owned by a farm involved with genetic engineering. While the field itself was not genetically engineered, they caused a financial loss to the farm totalling over £18,000.

AUGUST/98: Hampshire -- Animal activists claim responsibility for the release of up to 6,000 mink from a fur farm. The animals escaped when intruders cut the fence at a farm in Ringwood which has been at the centre of cruelty allegations.

AUGUST 4/98: Walthamstow -- a butchers in East London had its locks glued and slogans painted. -A.L.F.

AUGUST 5/98: London -- Locks were superglued at 1 angling shop, 3 butchers, 1 burger restaurant, 1 William Hill betting shop. One of the butchers shops had "A.L.F." sprayed on it.

AUGUST 6/98: London --Locks were superglued at 2 burger restaurants, 1 chicken restaurant, 2 William Hill betting shops, 1 pet shop, 1 butchers shop.

AUGUST 7/98: London -- The headquarters of the Countryside Alliance (formerly the British Field Sports Society) was graffitied. The words "SCUM" were daubed in large red letters all over one wall and "CLASS WAR" was written on a nearby wall. The address of the Countryside Alliance (hunt scum) is 367 Kennington Rd, London SE11. Tel: 0171 582 5432

AUGUST 17/98: New Forest -- 1000 more mink were set free from the same fur farm hit one week earlier, in which 6,000 mink were released. A section of the perimeter fence was cut and 40 cages opened. The A.L.F. claimed responsibility for the first raid.

According to the BBC Website story on this, the ALF-SG UK have said this latest raid was not the work of the A.L.F.

SEPTEMBER 2/98: London -- An angling shop on Tollington Park Rd, Finsbury Park, was attacked by A.L.F. activists. The shopfront was protected by a steel shutter but this was kicked in with such force that the window underneath was shattered. The premises has been attacked several times before since it opened earlier this year.

SEPTEMBER 12/98: London -- An angling shop in Leytonstone has closed down after repeated A.L.F. attacks. VICTORY!

SEPTEMBER 17/98: Staffordshire -- Up to 8,000 mink were released from a mink fur farm near Stoke on Trent. Reports suggest that most remain in the farm compound but around 2000 made it loose. The farm is owned by Len Kelsall, Chair of the Fur Breeders Assn UK. Kelsall has been on national radio, almost in tears, saying he can't explain what this raid has done to him! Kelsall has also said on radio that the raid is the fault of the govt as they pledged to ban fur farming but have done nothing and animal liberation activists are responding to that. He basically suggested that the govt should just hurry up and get on with the ban or this thing will continue!

SEPTEMBER 18/98: Staffordshire -- Suspected animal rights activists attacked a fur farmer's car less than 24 hours after releasing 8,000 of his mink into the wild. They poured acid over the Audi A4, causing extensive damage to the paintwork, and slashed both rear tyres while the car was parked outside Len Kelsall's home. The activists also damaged Kelsall's work van and punctured two tyres.

SEPTEMBER 23/98: West Sussex -- the Animal Liberation Front rescued 80 hens from a battery egg unit. The unit raided was part of the Kinswood eggs farm in Brooks Green near Horsham. When activists enterd the unit they discoverd birds in appauling condition. Many of them were crammed 5 to a cage and had almost no feathers left. The A.L.F. call upon all those compassionate people out there to take a stand against all animal torture. It is now time to consider radical direct action as the next step against the crimes of the animal abuse industry. This raid was not carried out by elite "shock troops" just normal every day vegan activists who are determined to achieve animal liberation. The raid took less than one hour and needless to say all the hens rescued now have the rest of their lives to relax scratch the earth and enjoy a life free of exploitation.-A.L.F.

SEPTEMBER 10/98: Oxfordshire -- Death threats have been issued to workers at the Occold research lab as part of a campaign of the Provisional A.L.F. Anonymous letters were sent to Huntingdon Life Sciences staff at their homes threatening to kill them unless they give up their jobs. Signed simply "the Provisional Animal Liberation Front" the message on a typed A4 sheet reads: *"Not only do we know who you are but also where you live and work. No one, as yet, has been 'killed' by 'animal protectors' as yet."* It continues: *"It's now your turn to experience exactly what the innocent animals have had to endure. Our advice is to withdraw from your animal abusing connections now... before it is too late."*
The research complex has been hit hard financially by the negative publicity caused by an increasing number of protests by animal rights groups and the letter campaign coincides with an announcement by the company that it is withdrawing its appeal to build a new dog breeding centre at Occold.

SCOTLAND

JULY/98: Tayside -- Tayside fields of genetically engineered crops have been the popular stomping grounds of nocturnal eco-activists. So many actions have occured that the police decided to stakeout a field in the hopes of catching activists at work. An observation hideout was setup in a nearby barn. However, things did not go well for the police ... The police drove their cop car into the barn to hide it, but the car's exhaust pipe was very hot at the time, and when the car was parked beside some hay, the hot exhaust pipe set it all on fire! The entire barn, along with the cop's Vauxhall Astra car and all the police observation equipment went up in flames. The damage has been estimated at over £30,000!

SWEDEN

JUNE 29/98: Savsjostrom -- The Swedish A.L.F. (D.B.F.) visited Rudolf Johansson's wildlife station. All cages were cut open so the birds could fly to freedom. Some were carried out of the cages. Pheasants, wild ducks, quails and capercillies were rescued. Also, Rudolf Johansson's porch had chemical butter-acid poured over it. -D.B.F.

JUNE 30/98: Kalmar -- 3 fur shops had their locks glued, slogans painted and chemical butter-acid poured on to them (smells horrible!) -D.B.F.

JULY 3/98: D.B.F. raided Sevsas wildlife farm, where wild boars and birds were kept. The bird cages were inside the wild boar fence -- attempts were made to free the birds, but due to safety issues (boars are large, aggressive animals) only the boars were set free. Two large openings were cut in the fence, allowing them freedom. -D.B.F.

Wild boars set free by the D.B.F.

JULY 4/98: Vetlanda -- D.B.F. set fire to five milk trucks belonging to Arla, Sweden's largest dairy company. All five trucks were totally destroyed. -D.B.F.

JULY 8/98: Funbo-Lovsta -- members of the Djurens Befrielse Front (DBF/ALF) raided the closed down research fur farm outside Uppsala. All kinds of research is based at this farm, as well as general agricultural research (they have pigs and hens, plus a chicken slaughterhouse in the research area). A building with four native wild birds was found. The birds were removed from the building and released in the wild.--Djurens Befrielse Front (new) Working under the international ALF policy

JULY 17/98: Linkoping -- the roof of a new build McDonalds was set on fire when someone threw a fire-bomb through the window of it. Damage was done, but the fire department says that if the fire had continued the place would have totally burnt down in 10 to 20 minutes. -Unclaimed

Turning up the heat, A.L.F.

JULY 22/98: Enanger -- D.B.F. visited Boda hunting and fishing centre, and released ducks and wild boars. The centre is owned by the Swedish hunting association.

JULY 24/98: Uppsala -- D.B.F. cut up the fence at an ostrich farm where 40-50 ostriches was kept. -D.B.F.

JULY 26/98: Varberg -- three lorrries at Kronagg (egg producer) had all windows smashed and the slogans "ALF" "Animal suffering" and "Murderers" sprayed on them. --DBF

JULY 31/98: Stockholm -- Ploughshare activists liberated 5 hens from a battery farm in Karby gard. The activists later turned themselves in to police to "take their punishment" to get publicity for the plight of battery animals.

AUGUST 2/98: Eskilstuna -- Between 500 and 1,000 mink were released by The Wild Minks from the Trangsas mink farm. Also, Vingaker fox breeding farm was raided, but unfortunately the activists did not manage to release them. Breeding cards were taken.

AUGUST 6/98: Orebro -- circus posters destoyed.

AUGUST 8/98: Vingakar -- two farms raided by activists: One foxfarm (Kasta Silverrav) in Vingakar and one minkfarm (Trangsas Minkard) outside eskilstuna. There were about 20 foxes at the foxfarm. The cages were opened so the foxes could find their way to freedom thru the holes that had been cut in the fence. Breeding cards were destroyed. In Eskilstuna 500 minks were liberated. This was the third time these farms were raided. -D.V.M.

AUGUST 9/98: Orebro -- circus posters destroyed.

AUGUST 10/98: ? -- Lulea chark (meat) had windows smashed.

AUGUST 11/98: Rimbo -- Thousands of eggs were destroyed and 30 hens were reported "stolen" after a D.B.F. raid on Smedsmora Research. Slogans were also spraypainted at the site. Also, research papers was destroyed and they say that 10 years research is now destroyed because of that. They do research with farm animals feeding and that kind of research. "It's devastating", commented an employee who wished to remain anonomous for fear of retaliation.

AUGUST 14/98: Orebro -- locks glued at hunting and angling shop.

AUGUST 16/98: Karlstad -- A milk truck was totally burned out in an arson attack. Police stated this was the eighth milk truck burned out in Sweden this summer.

AUGUST 17/98: Halmstad -- Lonestigs fur farm is raided and 150 minks are released by the Wild Minks.

AUGUST 22/98: Landa -- a fur farm was raided by activists. The fence was cut at several place and 500 minks and 30 foxes were set free.

AUGUST 22/98: Orebro -- two windows smashed and locks glued at hunting shop.

AUGUST 26/98: Sundsvall -- at least 1,000 minks was liberated from their cages at a mink farm in the northern Sweden.

AUGUST 27/98: Storuman -- A hunting house has been totally destroyed. One of the hunters woke up in the middle of the night and saw that the house was on fire. The house burned to the ground. The same hunters had their hunting house burned down last year as well. Earlier this year a hunting tractor (used for shipping killed elks) was burned out. -A.L.F.

SEPTEMBER/98: Fargelanda -- During an daylight inspection on Bjorkebo mink farm, animal rights activists heard the sound of a shotgun being fired at or near them. All activists managed to escape to safety. The Bjorkebo mink farm was raided by The Wild Minks last year in october when 800 minks were released.

SEPTEMBER 4/98: Harryda -- a mink farm was raided for a second time by activists from the direct action group THE WILD MINKS. The farmer had put up fake alarms and signs about security guards. An estimated 200-250 minks was set free. During the previous raid, the ferrets held on the farm had to be left behind. This time all ferrets (6) were put in bags for release. -- THE WILD MINKS

SEPTEMBER 5/98: During the night to September the 5th, activists from the Swedish A.L.F., Djurens Befrielse Front, smashed all 5 windows on B:sons fur shop in Boras, Sweden. -- D.B.F.

SEPTEMBER 19/98: Ormaryd -- Larssons mink farm was raided by The Wild Minks. Holes was cut in the fence and an estimated 180 cages was opened and approx. 400 minks were set free. The Wild Minks wants to give our support to the people arrested recently in USA for the fur farm raids.
We never give up...

SEPTEMBER 26/98: Kunsngen -- What is to believed bomb was placed under a lorrie belonging to an egg company. The driver noticed a device made up of a bottle, some wires and a battery. The truck was full of eggs. Bomb specialists were called in and the device was blowed up. Police suspect animal rights activists were behind the attack.

SEPTEMBER 28/98: Sundsvall -- over 2,000 minks was released from a mink farm. This is the same farm that was attacked some month ago when 1,000 minks were freed. The letters D.B.F. were found painted on a shed.

FINLAND

APRIL/98: Tampere - A fur store has 3 windows broken.

APRIL/98: Toijala - Road construction site: 3 windows of a machine broken.

APRIL/98: Toijala - Group called "The voice of the forest" ignited a bridge under construction, damaging the wooden intermediate structure. The group also removed 60 survey stakes to teach a lesson to the Earth rapists.

APRIL/98: Riihimki - A McDonalds has windows broken.

APRIL/98: Yljrvi (?) - 7 hunting platforms demolished.

APRIL/98: Juupajoki - 10 hunting platforms broken. The remains of one has a large abount of elk shit on it and the text "BLACK ELK"

MAY/98: Helsinki - A fur store has windows broken and spraypainted.

MAY/98: Espoo - Furcrafter has the windows broken.

MAY/98: Helsinki - Furrier's van is covered with spraypainted slogans and the wall has the words "animal abuser" spray-painted.

MAY/98: Tuusula - 7 hunting platforms demolished.

MAY/98: Helsinki - Several fur stores have windows broken.

MAY/98: Tampere - A McDonalds has 4 windows and a sign broken. The text "War begins..." spraypainted" --E.L.F.

MAY/98: Tampere - Road administration depot: a machine and barracks torched. --E.L.F.

MAY/98: Kangasala - Shell has 4 windows broken. -E.L.F.

MAY/98: Tampere - A fur retailer has 6 windows broken and two large EVR-texts spraypainted on the wall. -E.V.R.

MAY/98: Tampere - A fur store has 4 windows broken, another one 5 windows. -E.V.R.

MAY/98: Kangasala - Shell has 4 windows broken and slogans spraypainted. -E.L.F.

MAY/98: Iittala - Shell, 6 windows broken. -E.L.F.

MAY/98: Helsinki - Three fur stores have 2 windows broken each.

JUNE/98: Tampere - Two fur stores have a window broken twice.

JUNE/98: Tampere - F1-races sabotaged: cars broken and spraypainted at the depot, beer tent sloganised, adverts sabotaged, and logs dropped into water (the logs were notified to the authorities by the activists before the race started to avoid injury).

JUNE/98: Nivala - Shell visited three nights in a row: sloganised and locks glued. -E.L.F.

MID JUNE/98: Vihti -- A fur farm's warehouse was burnt to ground by activists.

JUNE 27/98: At the Konnevesi recearch center, moles (about 50) and birds (14 of the common Finnish bird, Turdus iliacus) were released to nature.

JULY/98: Toijala - Road construction site: one truck burned, another damaged by fire.

JULY/98: Tampere - A fur retailer has 3 windows broken and butric acid thrown inside plus a text spraypainted: "EVR here again!"

JULY/98: Toijala - Road construction site: a transport vehicle plus a machine it was carrying were torched. Also one tractor burned to ground and one digger has sand put in the tank. Dozends of survey stakes removed and a bridge under construction vandalised.

JULY/98: Valkeakoski - the locks of a meat store glued.

JULY/98: Helsinki - A fur store loses its display window.

JULY/98: Helsinki - Junotex fur store lost windows. -E.V.R.

JULY 2/98: Outokumpu -- 12 hens rescued from the battery unit.

JULY 21/98: Karttula -- A beagle and rabbit breeder suffered economic damage when windows and motion detectors were trashed in what seems to be a spontaneous hit. One person was arrested in connection to the action, and they are being charged with criminal damage. The owner of the breeding centre has been targetted in the past. A letter was received from "The Animal Court" included in which was several bullets. The letter stated that Nevalainen has three months to close the breeder or else... The owner's home has been repeatedly vandalized with slogans, and his workplace has had windows smashed, as well as a van used to transport lab animals was slashed, paintstripped and had windows smashed.

JULY 30/98: Kuopio -- 31 rats were rescued from the National Health Bureau vivisection laboratory.

AUGUST/98: Loviisa - 2 hunting platforms demolished.

AUGUST/98: Toijala - A road construction machine spraypainted with the text "Who cares about the world?"

AUGUST/98: Turku - Two fur stores have their windoes broken.

AUGUST/98: Tampere - McDonalds: 4 windows broken, Furrier: 3 windows broken, A fur retailer: 3 windows broken (According to our knowledge the retailer has been attacked 7 times this years, with 32 windows broken).

AUGUST/98: Teisko - 2 hunting platforms broken, a road construction machine sabotaged. -E.L.F.

(Continued on page 29)

(Continued from page 22)**PRESS OFFICE REPORT**

Two days later, Aug. 20, 330 foxes were liberated from Steve Hansel's Hidden Valley Fur Farm in Guttenberg, Iowa. Three newspapers, and one television station conducted interviews. In a communique, the action was dedicated to the Chatham 3.

The following day, Aug. 21, at Isebrands Fur Farm in Jewell, Iowa 3,000 mink were set free. A communique for each of the 3 raids has been received claiming full responsibility. The communique for Isebrands speaks directly to all of us:

"Let this raid be a call to action. It is time for all those who oppose needless suffering to start the attack. This is the third fur farm raid in the Midwest this week, let's make this only the beginning. By brick, boltcutters, or fire, this is the dawn of liberation," We are called to question our comfortable lifestyles as well: *"Many will wear an A.L.F. t-shirt, but will not jeopardize their middle class lifestyle to end the suffering of others."* Security is described as "non-existent" and the raid itself is said to be a "simple low risk operation." The liberators are able to challenge each of us directly with the statement: *"The only things separating life from death for the mink in these dens of suffering are a latch on a cage and your own fear."*

Another liberation on Aug. 27 at Bown's Mink Ranch had 3,000 mink rescued in Beloit, WI. A communique is yet to be received. Two media outlets in Illinois carried stories as well as three Wisconsin newspapers. The fifth liberation happened Aug. 28 in Rochester, MN where almost 3,000 mink were released from Zumbro River Fur Farm. More media including Associated Press, two other newspapers, and two radio stations carried stories. Several media sites have directly linked with Frontline Information Service web site, which educates even more people about the A.L.F. The grand total of animals saved comes to 13,000 mink, and 330 foxes.

VARIOUS THINGS

Four turkeys were rescued from a roadside petting zoo in Germantown Maryland. The communique described the animals placed in loving caring homes where "they will not be treated as a source of mere food or entertainment, but rather as individuals who deserve the right to live free of exploitation." The Gazette Newspaper conducted a thorough interview.

In Oregon, on July 21, the A.L.F. claimed responsibility for rescuing three female rabbits destined for breeding from the Western Oregon Rabbit Supply. If you remember, just over a month ago at the same location, over 15 rabbits were liberated in the first daylight raid for North America. KMTR-TV and the Albany Democrat Herald are waiting for larger actions, they seem to have the idea that there is much more to come in the future....

In a very bizarre story, the Press Office reported that an activist from Guelph, Canada was arrested for spitting on Guelph Fashion Furs. Animal Liberation Collective sent a release which caused a flurry of front page stories about the activist. Apparently an arrest warrant was issued, so the activist turned himself in. He is charged with Criminal Mischief which carries a 2 year sentence and maximum fine of $2000. He immediately was on hunger strike and eventually signed a statement agreeing not to come within 20 meters of the store. He was released after 24 hours. Police didn't even witness the spitting. It was caught on video while the activist rode on a bicycle past the store. If arrest warrants are issued for spitting on a fur store, what's next? Indictments for frowning at a fur store?

Media for the most part continues to be receptive and positive. Stay tuned for many more exciting actions courtesy of The A.L.F. And remember, whenever you hear about a possible A.L.F. action, don't assume we know about it--please contact the Press Office immediately. "Now is the time for activists who are unwilling to risk their freedom for the animals to question their own dedication and conviction," from Isebrands Fur Farm Communique.

Katie Fedor
North American A.L.F. Press Office: P.O. Box 103, Osseo MN 55369 USA

612-601-0978
http://host.envirolink.org/ALFIS
naalfpo@waste.org

(Continued from page 27)

AUGUST/98: Kangasala - Shell, 5 windows broken. -E.L.F.

AUGUST/98: Tampere - A fur store has 2 windows broken. -E.V.R.

AUGUST/98: Valkeakoski - Road construction site: machines spraypainted and signs removed. -E.L.F.

AUGUST/98: Valkeakoski - Road construction site: sand poured into the tanks of two construction machines. Third one has windows broken and slogans spraypainted. -E.L.F.

AUGUST/98: Tampere - 4 fur stores get glue in their locks and walls spraypainted with the text "E.V.R. A sticker glued on the door: "Closed because of bad conscience." -E.V.R.

AUGUST/98: Tampere - McDonald=B4s: lock glued, window spraypainted, and the "Closed..." sticker glued to the door.

AUGUST/98: Tampere - A road construction engineer's house spraypainted: "Shame on you, Jorma Jokilehto!" -E.L.F.

AUGUST/98: Helsinki - A fur store spraypainted with anti-rust spray which forces the store to buy new windows. Info on the spray widely distributed (Carosol F-40)

AUGUST/98: Tuusula - 6 hunting platforms demolished.

AUGUST/98: Espoo - A furcrafter has windows stoned. -E.V.R.

AUGUST/98: Helsinki - A fur store has windows broken.

AUGUST/98: Helsinki - A fur and a leather store both have windows broken.

AUGUST/98: Helsinki - A fur store has windows broken.

AUGUST 1/98: Vihti -- over 500 minks were liberated from a fur farm. Several escape routes were cut to the surrounding fence. The same fur farm had been targeted in June when a storagebuilding was torched.

SEPTEMBER/98: Joroinen -- activists liberated mink from a fur farm releasing an estimated 2000 mink from their cages after making holes in the fence through which they could escape. The farm is owned by Eero Joensuu from Himanka, whose Gold Safir company owns other mink farms. They have also started farming sable in Finland. *"If we hadn't made this raid, the animals that now escaped would have been killed. Unfortunately the farmer has recaptured some of the animals to his death camp. On farms of the same kind around Finland there are 5 million fur animals suffering. The raids will continue until the last cage is open. We invite everyone to join the struggle - tonight!"* - E.V.R.-T.R.

SEPTEMBER/98: Joroinen - A fur farm raided and 2000 mink liberated and other facilities sabotaged. Fence cut.

SEPTEMBER 8/98: Kirkkonummi -- activists raided a farm and 4000 minks were liberated.

BELGUIM

MID JULY/98: Kontich -- Arson attack at Quick (fast-food joint): Ballbath destroyed, outside furniture little bit much black and smokey. -A.L.F.

AUGUST 3/98: Antwerp --McDonald's hit in an arson attack: walls and inside furniture destroyed,water and smoke damage. - A.L.F.

AUGUST 6/98: Merksem -- Arson attack at McDonald's, resulting in damage to the outside of the building. -A.L.F.

AUGUST 9/98: Antwerp -- activists destroyed the outside furniture at McDonald's in the centre of the city. -A.L.F.

AUGUST 11/98: Antwerp -- McDonald's Teniersplaats (centre of city) had windows smashed out and slogans like "Smash the Mac" and "Meat means Murder" sprayed on the wall.-A.L.F.

AUGUST 13/98: Antwerp -- Arson attack on Quick at Grotesteenweg Berchem, resulting in outside damage to the building, including smoke damage. Slogans included "Meat industry = Death" and "A.L.F." --A.L.F.

AUGUST 29/98: Purrs -- Arson attack at McDonald's, which totally destroyed the building. Damage costs: between 35 and 50 million Belgian francs. Belgian State Security Service spokesman Jan-Baptiste De Smet told VTM television, "For a number of years we have some information on the A.L.F. Since the 1970s they have committed attacks in Great Britain and United States, but until now we did not know that they were active in Belgium too."

HOLLAND

MARCH 22/98: Oirlo -- Two battery farms in North Limburg were sabotaged. In one battery unit of 30 000 chickens, pallets with a total of 200 000 eggs were pushed over and sprayed with paint and fire extinguishers. Electrical equipment was damaged. A conveyer belt of 100m was cut up. Damage is estimated at 125 000 dfl. "Dierenbevrijdingsfront" (Animal Liberation Front) was written on the walls. In what the police believe is a related attack a nearby mink farm suffered some damage when 10 empty cages were trashed. --A.L.F.

Activists help renovate a McDonalds...

ISSN 1483-5258

INTERNATIONAL EARTH NIGHT
OCT. 31 — NOV. 7, 1998
THE HALLOWEEN SMASH

The EARTH LIBERATION FRONT (E.L.F.) invites you all to join with them in celebrating its annual International Earth Liberation Nights. This is a chance for all radical groups — be they Earth Liberation, Animal Liberation, anti-nuclear, indigenous land rights, women's, anti-fascist or revolutionary — to join together and target those who are destroying this planet and our lives. No matter what the target, be it road contractors, oil companies, vivisection labs, genetics/biotechnology labs, repressive governments, whaling nations, logging companies, nuclear offices, trans-nationals, etc. etc., the E.L.F. asks that you use the night constructively. The time for words is over! Only direct action can put the fear into the enemy's heart. The E.L.F. also asks that this Earth Night be celebrated as an act of solidarity with the Zapatistas (EZLN) who are presently being forced off their land by the Mexican Government.

One Earth, One Chance to Save It!

(As always, we call for no loss to life — only property)

NORTH AMERICAN A.L.F. SUPPORTERS GROUP
Box 69597, 5845 Yonge St. Willowdale, Ont.
Canada M2M 4K3
<NAALFSG@ENVIROLINK.ORG>

UNDERGROUND

THE MAGAZINE OF THE NORTH AMERICAN ANIMAL LIBERATION FRONT SUPPORTERS GROUP

ISSUE #13

WINTER '98

FREE TO PRISONERS

$3

SUPPORT
ARRY
RNE
HUN
STRI
END VIVI
SAVES
IMALS
IVES!
Words are cheap. Only actions really count.
is is not for me, it is for every animal
n every torture lab. We are creating a
urnin ment in history that will be
remembered. Never doubt this.
we will see an end to this
evil...

MATTERS OF LIFE AND DEATH

68 days on Hunger Strike with Barry Horne

plus:

CHATHAM 3 UPDATE*DESTROYING THE FUR TRADE*DIARY OF ACTIONS*MORE!

From yer Editor:

An update on the Utah Snitching situation: it's official, Douglas Joshua Ellerman has been assisting authorities in their investigations of ALF activities in Utah, and has named others as participants. As more details become available, we will share them with you, but needless to say how disappointing this situation is for us all. The arson at the Mink Feed Co-operative in Sandy Utah struck a real blow against the fur industry, causing nearly $1 million in damages, and we're saddened to see some-one who's actions spoke so loudly for animals everywhere turn so com-pletely against the struggle for animal liberation. No matter how much we can applaud the ALF actions Josh participated in, we can never ac-cept the fact that he has turned on his comrades and his grassing can never be forgiven, or forgotten.

On a different note, right off the bat we'd like to thank everyone for their patience in waiting for this issue of *Underground*. A number of things have kept us busy and delayed the release of this issue (normally out by late December) — like everyone else following Barry Horne's hunger strike, we've been waiting with breath baited and stomachs knotted, wondering if we were about to lose a dedicated and courageous warrior. Deadlines came and went, but we didn't dare wrap things up with so much hanging in the balance — Well, 68 days later, Barry Horne re-joined the land of the living, but even as we finally go to print it's unclear what kind of lasting damage his hunger strike may have caused him, physically and mentally. We've managed to put together an over-view of Barry's hunger strike for readers who may not have been able to follow it on a day by day basis. One thing was made very clear through all of this: our movement is one of compassion. The strength of Barry's con-victions and his determination to put it all on the line brought people from around the world together. Actions erupted everywhere that were dedicated to Barry and the animals he was trying to save. On a more personal level, we saw how the energy generated by Barry's struggle was able to both recharge the batteries of the "war weary" within our ranks, and give courage to those acting for the first time. With love, courage and rage the struggle for animal liberation continues.

Let me take a moment to thank everyone who has helped with this issue of Underground, and who has continued to show their support for the ALF and the Supporters Group. A huge thank you goes out to the folk who sponsored an ad for the SG in Animals Agenda, also to Darren, Gina, Katie, David No Compromise, the ALFSG UK, folks at Frontline, everyone who writes a prisoner, Craig Burton for donating signed copies of his book to the SG to raise funds for ALF prisoners (is that cool or what?), and of course, a big round of applause to YOU for reading this and supporting us!

yer editor,
t.

Letters to Underground

INFORMERS DESERVE NO SYMPATHY

Dear Underground,
Thankyou for writing about the Utah Snitching situation. Its important for our movement to be made aware of informers and the damage they can do, so we can take steps to prevent these situations from arising in the future (if only!). Why is it so many within the animal rights movement are willing to chum around with known informers? Robyn Weiner from the Chatham situation is one that comes to mind but unfortunately there are all to many out there -- too often activists want to say "Aww, forgive and forget" well you know what? These people have fucked over their closest friends and in many cases provide the only evidence there is to connect them to actions -- actions that were to save the animals! Grasses, snitches and informers, take careful note, there are those of us who are not prepared to forgive you for sending our warriors to jail. If you don't even have the backbone to stand up for what you believe, you deserve nothing but contempt from the rest of us. Animals have died because you wanted to save your own pathetic skin. Shame on you.

Stand tall,
Crescent Wrench Collective

Prisoner seeks Animal rights friends

Dear *Underground,*
For sometime now, someone here has shared *Underground* with me and I enjoy the publication and hearing about all the work everyone is doing. I don't know anyone from the outside world who is into animal rights. I would appreciate it if you would publish this letter. I am in hopes someone into animal rights will read this and write to me.

Thank you!
Manuel Pardo #111983
P1112 box 221 Raiford FL
32083, USA

Fran Thompson Update

Dear *Underground,*
Regarding Fran Thompson, animal/environmental activist who received a life sentence when she fatally shot a suitor-turned-stalker in self-defense, AFTER having informed the authoritiesthat she was receiving death threats from him, upon which they failed to take any action: letters are requested in an urgent action to obtain legal help on appeal. They are to be directed to:
Gerry Spence
Attorney at Law
15 S. Jackson, Jackson Wyoming
83001, USA

Please urge Mr. Spence (the most renowned defense attorney in the U.S. today with multi-state legal licensure, second in reputation only to the deceased William Kunstler) to undertake Fran's appeal. Please point out that it has merit because 1) Self-defense was disallowed as a mitigating factor 2) the case was upgraded with the direct intention to silence Fran as an activist 3) of fabrication of evidence/police perjury

Fran's new address (same prison) is:
Fran Thompson 93341
Nebraska Center For Women
1107 Recharge Rd. York, NE
68467-8003, USA

Thank you!

RE: Mail Bombs, etc. Cross the Line

Dear NA-A.L.F.S.G.
In response to T.K.'s letter from CALIF *re: Cross the Line* [issue #12] -- Are they not crossing the line [in reference to graphic pictures of lab animals sent with letter] -- these animals did not have a chance to confront their tormentors and murderers! We support ALL means to get these and other atrocities STOPPED. Our members are in jail for nothing. It's PAY-BACK TIME -- the only language they understand.
--anon.

Dear Underground,
If TK bothered to read #11's action report properly, s/he'd realize it referred to the "Provisional ALF," not the actual ALF. If TK had half the sense of humour they have, s/he'd realize this nom de guerre was chosen as a skit on those other well-known freedom fighters over here, the Provisional IRA. If TK had half the intelligence of the pALF, s/he'd realize it takes a lot more guts to take on the State's whole repressive apparatus with the rest of your life inside as possible penalty than it does to counsel nonviolence to the oppressed. And if TK was less hooked on moral indignation, s/he'd realize pALF are through with sacrificial Gandhian toss as tried and failed. After years of

their sanctimonious self-righteousness, I also now take Gandhians no more seriously than any other religious cult. I accept many people have problems with letter bombs -- mine is that they're not deadly enough, given their targets. Maybe pALF should take lessons from TK's namesake, Ted Kaczynski.

Yours for the destruction of Civilisation,
Oxford GA's

Aw, Shucks!

Dear *Underground,*
I am 17 years old and into the punk rock scene. I've been vegan since I was born, thanks to my mom and dad, both activists for animals and peace. I've been reading your magazine for over a year and wanted to let you know it is great! Some of your covers are amazing, and it's cool to see such good drawing/artwork. I also read a magazine from England, called **ARKANGEL**, that has cool covers. Any chance that issue #8's cover will become a t-shirt? Any way, I work very hard at spreading the word to anyone who will listen about animal liberation. I've made photocopies of your magazine, and spread them around and even if some kids aren't completely into animal rights, *Underground* sure does open their eyes. Good work everyone!

xTobyx

SKIING THE ASHES OF VAIL

To Whom Ever it may concern,
I condone and commend anyone and everyone associated with the fires committed in Vail, Colorado.

I agree 100% that there is no need to expand-the already largest ski resort in America. As an avid skier and environmentalist, I would like to send my best wishes and good-luck to everyone associated with this act and hope that all is well with the organization.

As a skier, I appreciate everything ski resorts have to offer for me. I understand that trees need to be cut down, roads need to be constructed and lodges need to be built. But there MUST BE a limit to what these humongus corporations can do, and I think that what you do is very commendable. The partners and shareholders of these corporations should know what their holding and what their company actually approves. As a former ski instructor for Stowe Mountain Resort, in Stowe, VT (owned by another environmentally notorious corporation --AIG), I know what goes on behind the scenes. I know that they felt no remorse in proposing to cut down over 200 more acres of land to build upon Stowe's already vast terrain. Luckily, the state of Vermont felt it unnecessary and thusly rejected the idea (thank God).

Keep up the good work and godspeed. Sincerely,
Joe Okubo
Ski Instructor/Sales Asst/Environmentalist

Swedish ALF and Emelie E:son

Dear *Underground,*
The latest months I have had some correspondence with Emelie E:son, the person behind what she calls DBF, Djurens Befrielse Front (Swedish Animal Liberation Front). According to her, her so called DBF is the Swedish ALF, but she is far away from following the international guidelines. The largest differences are that her DBF isn't organized in the same way, and that the methods of working not have been the same.

According to ALF's guidelines, anyone who is at least vegetarian and who carry out actions according to the guidelines have the right to regard themselves as a part of the ALF. Though Emelie E:son thinks that she has some kind of patent for working under the name ALF in Sweden. Therefore she has said that if anyone wants to work under the name DBF, then they must contact her to get approval to do so.

For that reason one can also say that she is breaking to another one of the ALF guidelines - that the ALF doesn't have any centralized organization, address etc. Emelie E:son's DBF both have a postbox and a phone number, and the media is always contacting her when larger actions happened, and there have been a lot of those the latest years. However, Emelie E:son has not taken the opportunity to explain why these actions happened, and to me she said that she doesn't respond to "fascist-newspapers", and I wonder what she means by that... I think that she is missing a lot of opportunities to focus on the animals situation, and though she said to me that the media contacts her a couple of times a week, she has only been seen in media a couple of times a year. By that, one can also say that Emelie E:son not has worked as a Swedish ALF press officer.

Besides that she hasn't done the job as a Swedish ALF supporters group. Maybe she has sent letters to prisoners outside Sweden, but when I and two other Swedish activists were caught earlier this year at a fur farm, we didn't hear a word from her. When I asked her about this she just said that "no Swedish ALF-activists ever had been caught", and she also made it clear that she didn't support those fur farm liberations that have taken place the latest years.

In Sweden there have been more than 30 fur farm raids where altogether thousands of animals have been released into the wild, and Emelie E:son has condemned everyone of them. I myself think that all the fur farm raids are one of the largest threat to the Swedish fur industry, but apparently Emelie E:son thinks it better to fight the fur industry by sitting at home watching TV. Emelie E:son has bought everyone of the fur industry's myths about the minks capability to survive in the wild, how the ecology is effected etc., and she has gone out in the media with the only purpose to condemn the liberations. I don't want to take up too much space explaining the facts to you here, because I hope you all know about it, and as far as I know fur farm liberations have taken place in a number of countries worldwide, and are supported by CAFT, NA-ALF SG, UK-ALF SG etc.

As I said to Emelie, she is responsible for more deaths to minks than I am, because if you don't do anything then 100 % of the minks will die. Now at least some will have a chance to live a life in freedom, and besides that the farmer loses a lot of money.

Now, in the latest years there have been a remarkable increase in direct action against animal abuse in Sweden, by all different kind of groups (except by Emelie E:son's DBF who has been very passive). Because of Emelie E:son's behaviour there have been started other groups like "Animal Rights Militia", "Animal Avengers", "The Wild Minks" etc, who all have done very successful actions.

Because of Emelie's "patent" for the name DBF, some actions have also been claimed by (international) ALF. But since an English name isn't very effective in Sweden, some activists decided to "take the name DBF back". The first action happened on April 18, where a dog was liberated from vivisection. The communique said that from now on the Swedish ALF was to work according to the international guidelines, and they urged everyone (following the guidelines) to work under the name DBF from then on.

Since then there have taken place lots of actions claimed by the new DBF, including as well liberations as sabotage and arson. On July 5, five dairy trucks were burned down in Vetlanda, and the new DBF claimed responsibility for the action. The problem is that when the media wanted to write about it, they contacted Emelie E:son to get more information. Now, if we would have a good press office in Sweden a lot could have been won in the articles which were published all over Sweden the days after the action. But in Sweden we don't have a good press office, in Sweden we have Emelie E:son.

In the articles, interviews etc, she had all the chance in the world to explain about what the dairy industry is responsible for, but she didn't say a word about the animals. All that she cared to talk about was to say that "this action wasn't done by DBF", and that "those who have done this have used our name without our approval". She also said that it was "cowardly" to do so by the persons behind the action. The worst thing she said in one of the interviews was; and I quote "We are tired of condemning/denying actions we haven't done. What's it gonna be next time - murder?" In the same interview, she also said that she dissociated o.s. from using arson as a method of working, because she said that "life could be hurt". Of course this action harmed no one, and I hardly have to say that under all ALF-actions that have taken place during the last 20+ years, no one has ever been hurt.

I have tried to explain all this, about the ALF guidelines etc to Emelie herself, and I have also recommended her to shut down her postbox and stop her contact with the media, so that other people can start working seriously with a Swedish ALF SG, PO etc. - but she just don't understand! I know that more people have talked and written to her, and in fact I don t know any Swedish activist who thinks that what Emelie E:son is doing is good, but she just refuses to face facts.

Because of that she refuses to listen to us, then maybe some international pressure can have her to evaluate her situation. Please observe that I don't care if she wants to continue work as just one ALF-cell among all others, that s totally ok - the thing is that I (and many others) want her to shut down her postbox and contact with the media.

Kristofer Aberg
SWEDEN

This letter was sent to Underground a little while ago, but we held off printing it in the hopes that Emelie E:son would have a chance to reply in the same issue -- something we felt was only fair given some of the accusations made against her -- a copy of Kristofer's letter was sent to her (with his permission) but unfortunately we have not heard back from Emilie. However, we'll be glad to print anything she might send that addresses Kristofer's concerns. We are not interested in turning **Underground** ***into a forum for activists to air their dirty-laundry against each other, and have no intention of getting embroiled in a situation that does not directly involve us. Our hopes are that the folks in Sweden will finally have it all worked out -- so many actions are taking place in Sweden these days that inspire us all, and we hope they continue...***

NEWS BRIEFS

Bird Watchers arrested for Raid

Oct. Finland -- Two people were arrested by Finish police, accused of taking part in a fur farm raid in Kirkkonummi, where 3800 mink were liberated. The two were soon freed due to lack of evidence, however, police are attempting to gather more evidence against them. Local activists contacted the accused, who said they were simply local kids who were bird-watching in the area when the raid happened. The two have never had any contact to the animal rights movement, never been to demos and never been charged for any actions before.

£310M CASE AGAINST ACTIVISTS DROPPED

Charges have been dropped against the remaining two campaigners connected to the Gandalf trials, a case which has dragged on for almost 18 months at an estimated cost of £310 million.

Robin Webb, the Press Officer for the Animal Liberation Front (ALF) and Paul Rogers, editor of Green Anarchist magazine are both free from prosecution following an extraordinary decision made at Portsmouth Crown court. The two men had been charged with several counts of inciting persons unknown to commit various illegal acts on unspecified dates over a five-year period. Known as the Gandalf case (from GA and ALF), it was widely seen by campaigners as a crude attempt to 'gag' the entire UK protest movement. Three others, named as their co-conspirators, had earlier been jailed for three years on similar charges but were cleared following a Court of Appeal hearing and released after four months.

The decision to abandon the charges against Webb and Rogers came following a complicated legal decision from the Court of Appeal. It ruled that the case against the first three animal rights and environmental activists, Noel Molland, Sax Wood and Steve Booth was nullified. Judge Selwood, who was presiding over the case ruled that by extension the case of Robin Webb and Paul Rogers was nullified and therefore there was no case to answer. Tim Green, Robin Web's solicitor welcomed the judgement:: "This is a welcome end to a ludicrously drawn out prosecution which should never have been brought in the first place."

(Continued on page 8)

Belgium Activists Need Support

Dec. Antwerp, Belgium -- two activists, Anja Hermans and Lindsey Van Keer - both 19 - were arrested by police and had their homes in Antwerp and St Amands Belgium searched. The two are charged with arson and conspiracy. If found guilty, they risk 20 to 30 years in jail. A third activist, Peter Terryn was also arrested by police, and later freed when charges were dropped.

Between July '98 and November '98 over 60 attacks in Belgium (ranging from graffitti's to arson and from butchers to McDonalds) were claimed by the ALF, but so far it is not clear wether Anja and Lindsey were involved in any way. Police press releases say both admitted taking part in a televised interview that claimed 8 raids on fast food restaurants. One is said to have admitted participating in an arson attack on a fast food restaurant near her home.

The arrests are the result of a collaboration between local police, state security and Scotland Yard. Scotland Yard was supposedly called in when a debate on animal liberation took place in Antwerp. A Belgian senator of the green party (Eddy Boutmans), a local politician of the Socialist Workers Party (Vincent Scheltiens), an animal rights activist of GAIA (Michel Vandenbosch) and a spokesperson for the ALFSG-UK (John Curtin) took part in de debate before an audience of over 120 people.

Anja - who just celebrated her 19th birthday - has been the victim of police harassment and violence since she was 16. She is the cofounder of 'Wordt Vervolgd...' (to be continued/prosecuted) a policewatch organization, monitoring police brutality since 1997. She has since been arrested about 50 times (often violently) and had to endure over 10 police raids on her house, 8 of them long before the ALF was active in Belgium. Anja, she was released on 29/12 (on parole) after an imprisonment of one month. She is still facing charges related to an interview she allegedly gave to the TV-program "Terzake" on the CANVAS-station, as a spokesperson of the ALF.

Anja states that she's has not been personally involved in the A.L.F. and that she has received information about the claimed fire attacks by e-mail.

The second woman that was arrested, Lindsey Van Keer, remains in jail. She has allegedly confessed to the fire attack in Puurs (where a McDeath-restaurant was completely destroyed). She however denies involvement with any of the other arson attacks. You can write them and show support:

You can contact the support groups:
ZALF (political support)
voice: ++/32/(0)3/232 53 10
email: resist@earthling.com
mail: ZALF
Paardenmarkt 18
2000 A'penstad
Belgium

Animal Rights Office Hit by Gunfire

Dec 6. Santa Fe, New Mexico -- The office of Animal Protection of New Mexico, Inc. was sprayed with gunfire sometime during the night of Dec. 6. A shotgun blast through the front window of the office resulted in extensive damage to an interior room. Fortunately, none of the women who work in the Santa Fe office were there at the time.

Animal Protection of New Mexico, Inc. is the state's largest animal rights organization. It is unknown if a particular person or issue was being targeted or if the gunfire was aimed at the organization as a whole. The incident was reported to Santa Fe Police, who are now investigating.

Lisa Jennings, the executive director of APNM, has received two threatening anonymous letters in recent months. One letter stated: "Ms. Jennings, you are approaching a point where we will have to hurt you. We are going to make a concerted effort to kill any wolf reintroduced in to the wild and poison bison as long as you interfere with wildlife issues." The second letter said: "We are a group that will not put up with your anti-hunting agenda. If you initiate any proposal next year to hurt the New Mexico hunter, you will witness the systematic destruction of N.M. endangered and threatened species. If you hurt us you hurt yourself. We are willing to use any means to preserve our heritage. Species can be eliminated without firing a shot. If we can't hunt them, you can't see them. Your choice."

Other women associated with the group have also been threatened or harassed in recent months, but all are solidly committed to continue their work on behalf of animals and will not be silenced or intimidated by this cowardly attack.

GOVERNMENT INTEND TO TIGHTEN MINK FARM SECURITY

England -- As a direct result of the ALF raids on UK fur farms in 1998 the Ministry of Agriculture (MAFF) have announced plans to force fur farmers to significantly increase security in a move that may well force some of them out of business.

In late December MAFF issued a consultation letter on amending legislation and "introducing a requirement to maintain adequate security installations and equipment for the purpose of: **a.** detecting any unauthorised entry on to the premises and any act of sabotage aimed at releasing the farmed mink, and so far as reasonably practicable withstanding any such act of sabotage; and **b.** ensuring that all reasonably practicable precautions are taken that are reasonably sufficient to deter and impede any such unauthorised entry or sabotage."

Current legislation requires farmers to carry out certain precautions to prevent mink escaping, but "are not aimed at preventing unauthorised entry on to the premises or any act of sabotage leading to the release of farmed mink into the wild." The alleged effects of mink releases on wildlife and domestic animals, and the cost to the local councils, government and local people in dealing with mink appear to be the reasons behind this proposed legislation.

The consultation letter states that estimates suggest that the total breeding stock in fur farms in the UK is around 50,000, with around 160,000 mink pelted each year. The letter also states that the number of mink held on each farm varies between 100 and over 1,000.

The letter admits that "a physical barrier alone is unlikely to keep determined intruders out for long in an isolated situation" and lists other security measures along with their costs.

The recurring costs (per farm per year) could range from £300 to £20,000 ; the non-recurring costs from £350 to £12,000. "The security measures will be required to be maintained in place and in full operation until fur farming is prohibited." It also appears that the more 'targeted' a farm is the more pressure there will be for greater security measures.

We are aware that some mink farms are only still operating in the hope that they will receive compensation when they are banned. Having to now pay extremely large amounts of money, particularly at a time when pelt prices have dra-

(Continued on page 10)

UPDATES FROM THE ELECTRONIC FRONTLINES

Animal-Liberation.net Goes Global

Over the past several months animal-liberation.net and the Frontline Information Service has become the host to 5 new web sites. We now have animal liberation news and information available in Finnish, Swedish, Danish and Norwegian. The fifth the belonging to the group Tactical Internet Response Network a electronic civil disobedience group who recently held the first animal liberation virtual sit-in at SMI's web site in Sweden, which resulted in them shutting down their computer network. A major renovation of the Frontline Information Service is underway and is due to complete and online by mid February.

http://www.animal-liberation.net

The Email 2 Prisoners Project

The Email 2 Prisoners project allows anyone who has access to the internet to send email to animal liberation prisoners -- its easy, and anyone can do it! Email 2 Prisoners is simple: compose and send your letter to <alf-pows@envirolink.org> with the prisoner that you would like it directed to in the subject line. A.L.F.S.G. members will forward your messages on to the respective prisoners!

Important considerations before you write:

-All Email 2 Prisoners letters will be confidential, but please realize email is not secure and can possibly be read by third parties.

-All incoming mail to prisons is read and inspected by prison authorities.

-Please be sure to include a regular postal address in your letter if you want a prisoner to reply -- the prisoners are not on email! Please do not expect a reply through the internet.

Up to date prisoner listings can be found on www.animal-liberation.net.

What are you waiting for? send some Email 2 Prisoners today!

matically fallen, may well encourage some farmers to pull out now. However, increased security would also impede legal inspections by groups such as CAFT. These inspections are used to gain footage for either prosecutions against the farm or to keep the issue of fur farming in the public eye.

If anyone would like more info on all this please contact us at:
caft@caft.demon.co.uk

ROYAL FUR SHOPPERS SLEEP UNEASY AFTER LIST THEFT

Animal rights' activists have warned of a campaign of violence against members of the aristocracy following the theft of a Royal furrier's list of customers.

The Animal Liberation Front warned of attacks on the property of "well-known" customers of Calman Links, whose client list includes lords, ladies and countesses, according to anti-fur protesters.

The company said campaigners had obtained a list of about 50 of its customers and senior staff were having meetings with police to try to find the source of any leak.

A.L.F. Press Officer (UK) Robin Webb said: "Anyone who would be perceived as a high profile fur wearer would be seen as a legitimate target for the ALF in as much as their property and equipment would be possibly targeted. As far as personal attacks, that would be out of the question."

Some customers have already received a hoax letter in which the company, which holds Royal warrants for the Queen and Queen Mother, appears to make a grovelling apology and says it is about to cease trading.

Police survey damage at the Vail Ski Resort caused by the E.L.F.

Hearing Set for Anti-Oil Company Activists

Jan 26, Grand Prairie AB -- Wiebo Ludwig, 57 and Richard Boonstra, 53 who each face nine vandalism-related charges, including destroying or damaging oil-company property over $5000, will have a preliminary hearing in May.; The two have chosen a judge and jury trial. Since being re-arrested by police (Ludwig was arrested earlier last month by police but released due to lack of evidence) the two have begun a hunger strike.

Farmers and community members in the Grand Prairie area have been fighting the oil company's presence, claiming the company is responsible for illness and death of farm animals, crops and for higher incidents of illness within the community. There have been over 160 documented acts of sabotage and vandalism against the oil company and its property, dating back to at least 1995.

Grand Jury to Probe Vail Fires

Jan 27, Denver, CO -- A federal grand jury will investigate the fires that destroyed seven structures atop Vail Mountain last fall, officials said.

Vail Associates, which owns Vail and Beaver Creek resorts, was told late last week that subpoenas were being issued to compel witnesses to testify before a federal grand jury in Denver.

No one has been arrested in the Oct. 19 fires, which caused $12 million damage, destroying Two Elk Lodge and a ski patrol headquarters along with smaller buildings. The Earth Liberation Front later claimed responsibility for the fires. The group, in faxes to news organizations, claimed it set the blazes on "behalf of the lynx."

The reference was to Vail's planned Category III expansion into an area that environmentalists call vital habitat for the lynx.

Agents of the federal Bureau of Alcohol, Tobacco and Firearms said the arsonists stuffed sponges into plastic jugs filled with gasoline, then lit them. No one was injured in the fires, which mainstream environmental groups denounced.

The Earth Liberation Front has been linked to last month's fire at an Oregon timber products company.

CHATHAM 3 UPDATE

During the early hours of March 30th, 1997, five Americans were arrested for allegedly raiding a Canadian mink farm. Over 1500 mink were released from Ebert's Fur Farm, one of two mink farms owned by Tom and Bill Mc-Clellan. Fences were cut, breeding cards destroyed and mink released. Those charged were Patricia Dodson, Hilma Ruby, Robyn Weiner, Gary Yourofsky and Allan Hoffman, all of whom live in Michigan. Both Alan Hoffman and Robyn Weiner made damaging statements to the police, implicating others in the raid.

photo credit: ALF

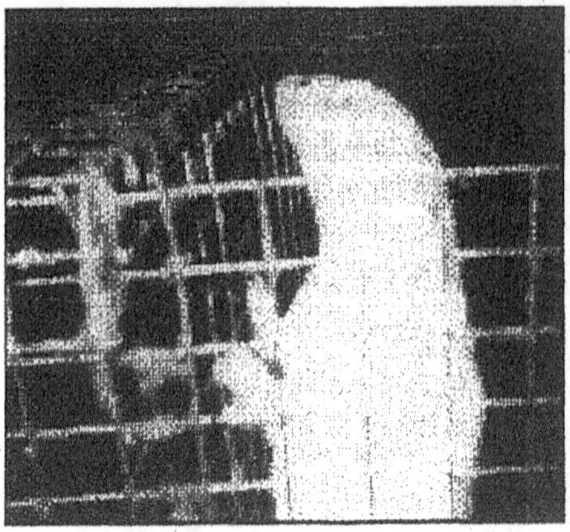

On January 18, 1999, Hilma Ruby and Patricia Dodson were brought before the Canadian court, where both activists plead guilty to charges of breaking and entering an enclosure containing fur bearing animals, and theft. Ontario crown attorneys were seeking 18 to 24 month prison terms for Ruby and Dodson. The Crown made it clear the wanted to make examples of the metro Detroiters to stop a rash of Canadian fur farm attacks.

Testimony from the owners of the fur farm, Tom and Bill McClellan (Tom's father) outlined the physical layout of the farm and gave details regarding the 21 sheds housing mink. On March 16, 1997, in an unconnected raid, unknown activists liberated at least 180 mink from shed #8. Breeding cards were destroyed during the raid. A communique from the Earth Liberation Front claimed responsibility for the raid, and promised more to come. On March 30th, a chevy van with Michigan plates was observed near the farm by farmers guarding the property. Police were informed, and the van was soon stopped. According to evidence from the crown, Pat Dodson was the driver, and police observed suspicious equipment and materials in the back, but allowed the van to drive on.

Word came to the police that the farm had just been raided. Robyn Weiner was arrested on site, and shortly there after implicated both herself and others for the raid. Police again stopped Pat and the van, arresting her.

Police later came across Hilma Ruby walking along a road, and arrested her. A taxi destined for the US/ Canadian boarder containing Alan and Gary was intercepted on highway 401. Almost immediately after arrest, Alan confessed to the raid and named others as participants.

During Pat and Hilma's trial, witness for the prosecution, **Brian Tapscott**, a Minister of Agriculture (rural division) testified about the financial loss the raid caused the Ebert Fur Farm. Tapscott, a "live-stock specialist" provided assistance to the McClellan's for two days following the raid. According to Tapscott, the loss of production of kits, plus the loss of breeding females totalled at least $7924. Replacing the liberated female breeding mink would have cost $60912.94 The total costs of the 42 male mink liberated plus the destroyed breeding cards came to $23463.76, with a total net loss reaching well over $163801.30

Owner Bill McClellan took the stand and testified how the raid had effectively closed the fur farm for good. Due to the raid and poor mink prices the farm was shut down and three employees let go. It was revealed that McClellan still operates the Aberage Fur Farm, but that they now face huge expenses for higher security. Describing the tactics used by fur farm liberators, McClellan explained the effectiveness of destroying breeding cards: "When you have no breeding cards, you have nothing. Breeding cards contain all the records, pedigrees, everything. Breeding cards are the backbone of fur farming." When breeding cards are destroyed fur farmers must "...start all over, they have to be replaced with new stock which you can't afford." With every raid, insurance rates also go up, and for many farmers, it has become difficult to even get insurance due to the threat of massive losses during raids.

McClellan also described the anxiety and fear generated by communiques issued on the internet by activists threatening to hit fur farms. According to McClellan, the fur farmers couldn't sleep at night for fear of attack, and were often forced to stay awake on 24 hour shifts for weeks on end, guarding farms in case they were targeted. McClellan made it clear that the monitoring animal liberation web sites is a past-time many fur farmers partake in, partially to stay abreast of new raids and tactics, but also out of fear that their farm may be next. Communiques threatening attack apparently send the fur farming community into a frenzy of sleepless nights, paranoid all-night patrols of farms, and creates a (might we say satisfactory) climate of fear and anxiety.

Tom McClellan also took the stand, and between bouts of onion-induced tears and dramatic fits of boo-hooing, described the costs of repairs and extra security precautions at their farms. (Cost breakdown: Two security guards hired for 3 month: $7130.00, Two cell phones for security: $559.00, Repairs to farm: $4500.00, legal fees: $10,000.00, interruption of business: $10,000.00)

Finally, Gary Hazlewood, Director of the Canadian Mink Breeders Association described the impact of the Ebert Fur Farm raid on other mink farmers. Feeling picked on, fur farmers have been forced to hire extra staff, security, etc. at costs that begin at $20,000 and up. New fences cost between $10-$12 a foot, meaning a fenced farm can cost well over $20,000. Sensors, monitors, additional insurance and other related expenses are forcing fur farmers out of the business, and is certainly discouraging others from entering. Additionally, fur farmers find it a bit disconcerting to find their farms listed on the internet, creating "a great deal of stress."

"When you have no breeding cards, you have nothing. Breeding cards contain all the records, pedigrees, everything. Breeding cards are the backbone of fur farming." When breeding cards are destroyed fur farmers must "...start all over, they have to be replaced with new stock which you can't afford." — Bill McClellan, Mink Farmer

Witnesses for the defense took the stand to explain to the court the abysmal conditions on mink farms in North America. While other nations introduce legislation to force fur farms to clean up their acts, or ban fur farming outright, North American fur farms refuse any kind of animal welfare reform that cuts into the bottom line profit for the farmer. Colleagues and family members also took the stand and described the courage, dedication and compassion both Pat and Hilma exhibited in their daily lives for people and animals.

On the stand Pat echoed what she had told media previously, "This is not a personal attack on Mr. McClellan, It's what he does that we don't like. Everyone does have a right to a job, but not a job that hurts people or animals. The animals can't speak for themselves. They don't want to be gassed or skinned alive... It's our obligation to speak for them."

Hilma released a statement explaining her position: "What I did was in defense of voiceless, defenceless, sentient creatures that faced death for the vanity of fur garments. My compassion and concern for these animals was no less than the concern and desperation I'd have felt for a child, dog or cat or any other living creature locked in a burning house -- I would have risked my life to save them. If someone breaks into a house to rescue a trapped child or animal, under the law, they would have committed a Break and Enter, but who would question their motive? To imprison a companion animal in a small cage until it becomes insane and hill it in a cruel way is punishable by imprisonment in a vast majority of states. Why we are allowed to expose animals on fur farms to the same cruelties is a question I have been asking myself for many years.

"A truly humane society should protect every sentient creature, human or non-human, from exploitation and from suffering and pain. This is why all 15 nations of the European Union outlawed the cruel leghold traps in 1996; this is why fur farming was banned in all provinces in Austria last year. A bill which would outlaw fur farms in the United Kingdom will soon be voted on the British Parliament. We should follow these civilized countries.

"I have broken the law in desperation. There is a law higher than man's and that is God's law. There is so much cruelty towards animals that goes unheeded, I could no longer sit by idly and not intervene. I simply wish that, as human beings, we could work towards a kinder, more compassionate world."

Sentencing for Pat and Hilma will take place on February 22, 1999. While it initially appeared that both Pat and Hilma might be going down for 18 months or more, the activists were encouraged by the way the judge laid into the crown prosecution for their blatant attempt to have the court "lynch" the two women. The crown has already made deals with informers Robyn Weiner and Alan Hoffman, effectively allowing the two to escape jail time, but the judge questioned how the prosecution could expect him to sentence Hilma and Pat to a year or more in jail instead. Accusing the prosecution of looking for the "lowest common denominator" and refusing to give the prosecution the "lynching" they were seeking, it would appear that if Pat and Hilma are to indeed receive jail time, it will not likely be for any substantial time.

The third member of the Chatham 3, Gary Yourofsky, faces trial on March 1, 1999, where it is expected he will plead not guilty. We will do our best to keep readers abreast of any new developments. This ordeal has been financially devastating for those involved (and we don't mean the mink farmers!) The Chatham 3 are burdened with enormous legal fees and we ask that you find it in your heart to contribute as generously as you can to the Chatham 3 Defense Fund to help cover their legal costs. Donations will not be used to pay fines or to pay the mink murderers. Please send any cheques or money orders earmarked **"CHATHAM 3"** to the NA- ALFSG.

Smashing

The Fur Trade *Quickly* And *Efficiently*

The North American fur farming industry is on the verge of collapse. In 1998, Russia experienced an economic crises that brought their fur trade to a halt. This is significant because in 1997 Russia consumed half the worlds fur skins. To make matters worse for American mink farmers, the usual disease became more widespread. Distemper killed many caged fur animals, damaging the fur farming industries profit margin even more.

The third major factor that has devastated the fur farming industry is the Animal Liberation Front (ALF).

Since late 1995, the ALF has raided approximately 50 North American fur farms, releasing close to 100,000 animals. This has cost the industry millions of dollars and provided a shot at life for countless mink and fox.

If these raids continue, the industry will collapse completely. The question is will these liberations continue?

In 1997, 21 North American fur farms were raided by the ALF freedom fighters, people just like you and me. Unfortunately, some people were arrested and this has had a chilling effect on the animal liberation movement. In 1998, less than 10 fur farms were raided in North America. Internationally the fur farm raids increased dramatically with Poland and Ireland seeing their first ever. North America saw a decline in direct action against the fur trade. Despite the decline, fur farmers are as paranoid as ever.

Leo Weisdorfer, the owner of the largest fur farm in Oregon, admitted to having spent $38,000 on security in 1996 alone. Fur farmers have put in flood lights, guard dogs, infra red beams, live security patrols and video cameras. This demonstrates the long term value of ALF mink liberations. By attacking a handful of farms, the ALF has forced the entire industry to spend millions of dollars on security. Fur farmers are very concerned about being raided and the pressure is pushing some out of the business. Pelt prices are dropping because of the Russian economic crises and mainstream anti fur campaigns. If ALF raids continue into 1999 it will be too much for the industry to handle. Farmers are already leaving the industry in droves. The industry has been cut by 2/3 since 1989.

The question is, will the raids continue? That depends on you!

The Animal Liberation Front is not a structured organization with a membership list. The ALF is nothing more than people who get together with their most trusted friends and fight back for the animals. Any regular person who carries out a non-violent direct action for the animals can consider themselves part of the ALF.

Will the fur farming industry collapse? The answer depends on the commitment of people who don't want mink gassed and fox anally electrocuted. We have an opportunity to completely finish off an industry built on the systematic torture of furbearing animals. Economic and social factors have given us an advantage. The majority of fur farmers are at retirement age and want to protect the money they have left. Times are tough for mink killers. A major campaign, carried out now, would be the final nail in the fur industries coffin. Between now and February many mink farmers will make a decision about whether or not to stay in the business for another year. Now is the time to strike. There are less than 400 mink farms left in the United States. At the end of the year their should be none.

IF YOU BELIEVE THAT FUR IS MURDER,

THEN ACT LIKE IT!

MATTERS OF LIFE AND DEATH

Barry Horne's 68 days on hunger strike

'It is not a question of dying. It's a question of fighting. If I die, so be it. We have tried to negotiate with the Government. They have condemned me to death.'

-- Barry Horne

Midnight October 6, 1998, UK animal liberation prisoner Barry Horne began a hungerstike that as time progressed seemed certain would kill him. Barry began his fast from a jail cell in Full Sutton prison, determined to see the recently elected Labour government carry out it's promise to set up a royal commisson on vivisection. During the 68 day hungerstrike, Barry's only comfort was a glass of ice-cold water by the side of his bed. No stranger to hunger strikes in the past, Barry made it clear that this time, if the government would not act, he'd see it through to the end.

Barry Horne, who is currently serving 18 years in jail for causing £33million damage in an arson attack at an Isle of Wight shopping centre and trying to target stores that used/abused animals in Bristol. Depite his massive jail sentence, Barry has continued to campaign for animal liberation from behind bars, inspiring activists around the world with his determination.

Barry began his hungerstike with one goal in mind: for Ministers to order a Royal Commission into vivisection. Not a huge request by any means. Prime Minister Tony Blair promised one to the electorate before the general election, but broke his word once the Labour Party was elected. 'Why is it impossible to agree an inquiry?' Barry asked. 'Politicians promise but why do we put up with them not keeping their commitments? Why do people laugh at politicians being liars all the time? We should be angry instead.'

On Day 44 of the hunger strike talks between a group of four of Barry's supporters and the government took place (19th November). The government was represented by Tony Clarke MP, two Home Office officials responsible for licensing vivisection, Rick Evans and Steve Wilkes from the Animals Procedures Section. The meeting was tape recorded and Barry received a copy of the tapes the following day. The Home Office meeting offered nothing new, other than a vague promise of an independent forum to investigate animal experiments and a wish from both sides for further dialogue.

As time quickly wore on and Barry's plea to the goverment went unanswered, support for Barry's stuggle grew. Animal liberation activists targeted fur farms, butcher shops, research labs and more, liberating animals, destroying equipment and dedicating the actions to Barry. Letters of support from the public poured in. Barry's spirits remained high, convinced the government would set up their promised Royal Commisson. Days passed, Barry grew weaker, and we all became aware that government was more than happy to see Barry die.

After 48 days on just water, Barry had suffered a week of constant and violent vomiting in the hospital wing of Full Sutton prison. He was rushed to hospital the following day suffering from dehydration.

The move to hospital caused a massive upsurge in publicity, and things began to move on the political front, or so it appeared. Two days later on day 51, Labour MP Kerry Pollard faxed a letter to Barry at the hospital which appeared to suggest that the Animals Procedures Committee review had recommended an independent high level committee to examine animal

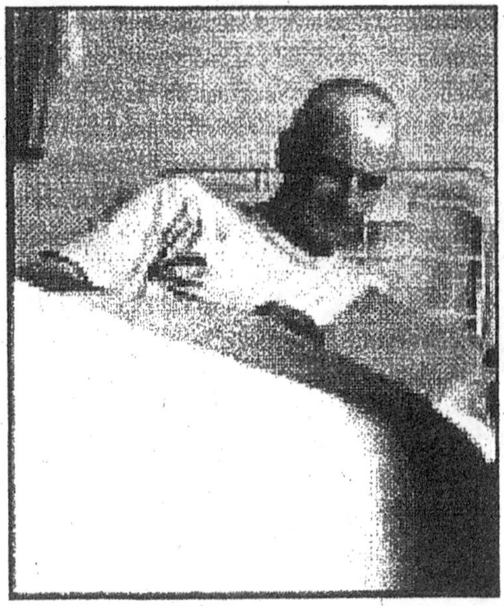

Barry Horne in prison hospital, reading letters of support.

experiments. The fax was headed: "In-depth research into whether benefits of animal experiments outweigh the suffering to animals is to be carried out". This was alleged to be a new development, and the letter ended with a personal plea to Barry from Kerry Pollard MP to end the hunger strike now. On the same day, a report on Channel 4 Teletext suggested similar Government proposals. Further explanation was promised over the weekend, and an eight page Home Office fax was received the following day.

At this point Barry, who was close to a coma, was faced with a large pile of documents to examine. He decided he needed to stabilise his condition in order to concentrate and began taking a small amount of fruit juice and tea with sugar, though he had problems keeping this down. However, after 3 days Barry decided that there was nothing in the government proposals that would help the animals he was fighting for. On day 54, Barry resumed the water only fast.

On December 2, as Barry slowly wasted away in his prison bed, the Animal Rights Militia upped the anty by releasing a list of 10 animal vivisectors they promised they'd target if Barry died. Only four on the assassination list were named by ARM -- two are university professors involved with vivisection, one works at the Research Defence Society and another runs a cat breeding farm. Reactions were swift -- many within the animal liberation movement were divided on where they stood with the ARM release, but one thing was clear -- animal abusers everywhere were looking over their shoulders in fear.

As the hunger stike wore on and the government still did not act, it looked certain that we'd lose Barry forever. Determined not to give up, Barry made preparations for his eventual death. Barry made out his will, arranged for a pagan funeral in his home town of Northampton and signed a declaration that he would not receive any medical treatment. If he were to lapse into a coma, he was to be left to die peacefully. Frantic activists worked around the clock on Barry's behalf. The Animals Betrayed Coalition held numerous meeting with government officials and put the word out to anyone who would listen. Despite the world's attention focusing on Barry and the plight of animals in UK labs, the government refused to act, seemingly cementing Barry's fate. By day 60 smuggled messages to the press read: 'I am fading, sinking, going down. Words are cheap. Only actions really count. This is not for me, it is for every animal in every torture lab. We are creating a turning point - a moment in history that will be remembered. Never doubt this. We will see an end to this evil.'

From the December 6 issue of the Observer: "Horne, a Category A prisoner serving 18 years for a firebombing campaign, is now so weak that nurses at York District hospital fear he could die at any moment. Desperate for protein, his body has started consuming his internal organs. He is blind in one eye, has almost lost sight in the other and is deaf in one ear. His weight has fallen from 14st to nine.

"He can only talk in short sentences, pausing for breath between each phrase, but yesterday he agreed to speak for the first time. Prison officials have banned interviews but The Observer smuggled in questions. Horne answered each one and also handed friends his last letter, written in spidery capitals on the back of one of the dozens of letters of support he receives each morning - and asked them to hand it to The Observer.

In the press and on TV and radio, the whole issue of vivisection and government policy became one of the top news items. Government ministers and MP's were grilled about broken pre-election promises. Finally, on the night of the 9th December, 64 days into the hunger strike, there were several important developments which came to light by way of a go-between (a solicitor used by the Home Office), and faxes forwarded to Horne supporters from various sources. Taken together, they appeared to show some movement on the part of the government.

The head of the "Associate Parliamentary Group for Animal Welfare", Ian Cawsey MP, issued a press release asking for his group to make independent recommendations on vivisection, discussed at the group's next meeting in January. This all-party group consists of "over 100 MPs and Peers with an interest in animal welfare, as well as 40 associate members from the animal welfare world, and from both ends of the spectrum of the debate". Ian Cawsey stated in this letter "I believe that the associate group can make a real and independent impact".

This same evening supporters learned that the Animals Procedures Committee had met earlier that day to discuss the hunger strike. The usually secretive APC issued a press release confirming that from now on, the APC would report directly to the Associate Parliamentary Group for Animal Welfare. The statement quoted the head of the APC, Prof. Banner, as saying "This is a very positive move, clearly it makes good sense". In an article in the Guardian about Barry's hunger strike, Prof. Banner further stated "...things cannot go on as they are".

The following day, Barry was visited in York hospital by supporters and was given copies of all the relevant faxes. Unfortunately, Barry's condition had deteriorated so badly that he was unable to take in all of the information. He could not focus mentally in the afternoons or see properly with his one working eye. Supporters explained to the consultant that a visit was necessary the following morning to fully clarify the faxes to Barry, to which the consultant agreed.

One hour after supporters left the hospital, Barry was moved back to prison, a move that had a hugely negative impact on his mental and physical health. We

Barry supports rally outside the hospital

may never know, due to the lack of information from the hospital, whether or not it was Barry's rapid deterioration that finally pushed them into taking this action.

For three days friends and relatives of Barry waited for Barry to become lucid enough to understand the documents. They repeated over and over the following summary of what was on the faxes. Finally, after hours of reviewing the information, on day 68, Barry felt that the hunger strike should end. Whether the apparent movement on the government's behalf will amount to anything substancial is still to be seen, but activists everywhere rejoiced when word went out that Barry would live to see another day. Despite the government propaganda machine kicking in full force (media claimed that activists wished Barry would become the movement's first martyr -- others stated the hunger strike was a hoax), Barry has shown us all that the human spirit's struggle for justice can never be smothered, no matter how many bars and chains lock the body down.

The massive show of support for Barry Horne continues, and letters of love and solidarity continue to pour in. Please write Barry and let him know how his struggle has touched you. Barry continues to fight for his life despite eating again, and the full damage from the hunger strike is not yet known.

Barry Horne VC 2141
HMP Full Sutton
Moor Lane,York YO4 1PS

If you wish to receive Animals Betryed Coalition (ABC) mailouts please write to ABC at the address at the start of the email. Donations or stamps to cover mailing costs would be appreciated. Cheques can be made payable to "Animals Betrayed Coalition."

Animals Betrayed Coalition
PO Box 21339, London WC1X 0NJ
Tel: 0171 278 3068 or (mobile) 0961 988575 or (mobile) 0589 026435

ARM LIST

The militant Animal Rights Militia has announced a list of ten vivisectors who, in the event that Barry Horne dies throught government broken promises. Keeping six of the names secret the ARM revealed that four targets would be:

- **Christopher Brown of Hillgrove Farm in Oxfordshire**
- **Colin Blakemore of Oxford University**
- **Clive Page of King's College, Chelsea in London**
- **Mark Matfield of the Research Defence Society**

Near the end of Barry's first hunger strike during February 1997 the ARM claimed to have a list of five vivisectors who would be killed if he died. When it appeared that Barry was fast approaching a seemingly inevitable death the ARM warning list appeared to intensify media interest in Barry's struggle.

Hunt Violence

By Noel Molland

In *Underground* (Summer 98) I wrote an article entitled 'A New Spectre?' where I looked at the dramatic increase in Britain of Hunt Retribution Squad (HRS) style actions against the hunt and their supporters. However, in this second, follow up article, I would like to look at the violence of the hunts against anti-blood sports activists. Every week Hunt Saboteurs and other anti-hunt protesters use lawful means to either disrupt and/or monitor the hunts. These anti-blood sports campaigners use tactics which are both lawful and non-violent. However too often the response they get from the hunts and their supporters is anything but lawful or non-violent.

In February, 1998, Christopher Owen, a League Against Cruel Sports hunt monitor was attacked by a supporter of the Cheshire Foxhounds. As Owen photographed the hunt he was spotted by a red coated huntsman who pointed him out to hunt supporter Anthony Kirkham. Kirkham chased Owen across a field and hit him with a bottle. He then pushed Owen to the ground and started to kick him in the head. Due to the attack Owen suffered severe bruising and a dislocated jaw. He also had a camera, valued at £31,300 stolen. The camera was later recovered, but the film was missing. When this case came to court Kirkham was found guilty of robbery and sentenced to 15 months imprisonment.

This was not the first time Kirkham had been found guilty of assaulting an anti-hunt protester. In 1995 he was convicted of violent disorder after attacking a hunt saboteur with a pick axe handle, for which he received a 12 month suspended sentence.

Acts of violence against anti-hunt protesters are quite common. On the 21st of November 1998 a hunt saboteur was left semi-conscious after an incident involving the Old Surrey and Burstow Foxhunt. Trouble flared as a group of saboteurs attempted to disrupt the hunt near Hartfield in East Sussex. As the saboteurs walked down a disused railway track three vehicles drove past them, stopped, and a group of armed people jumped out. Hunt saboteur, John Davis, described what happened. "We jumped out of the way (of the vans) but then their thugs got out armed with pick axe handles and one of them hit a sab in the head with a golf club so hard it (the club) broke in half."

In a press statement the Press Officer for the Hunt Saboteurs Association later said "Saboteurs find that this hunt resort to violence almost at the flick of a switch." Indeed in the early 1990s the Old Surrey and Burstow Huntsman, Mark Bycroft, and several hunt supporters were prosecuted for assaulting a saboteur in what the Judge at the time described as "a cowardly and premeditated attack."

Other incidents of hunt violence have included intimidation, threats of violence, criminal damage and arson attacks. In March 1998 a severed deer's head was found on the front lawn of Simon and Jaine Wilde, two high profile members of the West Sussex Wild life Protection group. Jaine Wilde said on the incident "Obviously, this has been done as some kind of threat to us." The police certainly see this as more than just a prank and have carried out tests on the head to try and determine the culprits.

One month after the incident with the deer's head, the Wilde's were targeted again when their garden shed was set alight, causing thousands of pounds worth of damage to the contents inside. However despite the intimidation the Wilde's remain determined in their campaigning vowing they will not be put off. "All these kinds of things spur us on to greater deeds. If anything, what's happened is a sign of flattery. It shows we are doing our job properly" said Simon Wilde.

Receiving an equal, if not greater amount, of intimidation is a Dorset hunt saboteur who wishes only to be known as Neil. In August 1997 Neil's home was visited by a terrierman of the Portman Hunt, Nick Stephens, who tried to kick down the front door. Stephens also threatened to kill Neil, his wife and his pets. The following month Neil's van was attacked by a person armed with a pickaxe handle. Later the van was nearly rammed off the road.

A few months after that, in December 1997, a man armed with a machete threatened Neil at his work place. Threats were also made to shoot or "chop" any hunt saboteur who turned up in the Dorset area. The police have taken this incident so seriously they have installed a panic button in Neil's house. Yet despite the police interest, the intimidation has not stopped.

Every week Hunt Saboteurs and other anti-hunt protesters use lawful means to either disrupt and/or monitor the hunts. These anti-blood sports campaigners use tactics which are both lawful and non-violent. However too often the response they get from the hunts and their supporters is anything but lawful or non-violent.

In the early summer of 1998 Neil had his van tyres slashed and glue placed in his locks. This incident was shortly followed by the discovery of a poisoned pregnant vixen which had been dumped in the garden of Neil's parents. Neil suspects his parents house was targeted because they were away on holiday at the time and so the house was empty. Speaking about the poisoned fox Neil stated "The way she was lying shows she was planted by somebody. A poisoned fox left to die will curl up in a ball." Neil's friends believe that the fox was meant as some sort of warning, but no one expected what was to occur next.

A week after the discovery of the poisoned fox somebody broke into Neil's parents house. Once inside the intruder cut through the gas pipes and attempted to start a fire. "They obviously tried to light it (the gas) because there were matches and pieces of paper on the ground," said Neil. Again police are investigating the incident.

It is widely believed by Neil and other anti-hunt protesters that the attempted arson was carried out by hunt supporters. However when asked about this and other acts of violence and intimidation, Paul Latham, the Press Officer for the pro-hunt Countryside Alliance, declined to comment. Neil, on the other hand, stated, "They are trying very hard to intimidate us but I want them to know that it is not going to work."

According to figures supplied by the National Anti-Hunt Campaign, over a three month period, between September and December 1997, there were fifteen separate acts of violence against anti-hunt protesters. Meaning that on average there was one attack every single week. In the past some of these attacks have proven fatal. In 1976, William Sweet from the League Against Cruel Sports was shot dead after an argument with a man shooting birds. In 1991, hunt saboteur Mike Hill was deliberately run down and killed whilst he disrupted the Cheshire Beagles. In 1993, hunt saboteur Tom Worby was deliberately run down and killed whilst he disrupted the Cambridgeshire Foxhunt. Some anti-hunt campaigners believe it is just a matter of time before the next anti-bloodsports activist is killed.

(Authors Note: It is not just anti-blood sports activists who have been killed by animal and earth abusers. In 1985 Greenpeace activist Fernando Pereira was killed when French Secret Service agents used explosives to since the boat The Rainbow Warrior. Also in 1985 Philadelphia Police bombed the communal home of the eco-revolutionary group MOVE, murdering 6 adults and 5 children. In 1994 two butchers from Ambarati, in India, hacked to death a leading vegetarian activist who they blamed for the fall in the sale of mutton. In 1995 British animal rights activist Jill Phipps was run over and killed whilst protesting against live animal exports. In 1997 a Finnish fur farmer shot at and attempted to murder five Animal Liberation Front activists who raided his farm. In 1998 American Earth First! activist David Chain was killed when a contractor deliberately fell a tree near to here he was protesting against the destruction of a forest. However the most shocking death list of all is that in the next minute 11,500 animals will be killed for their flesh. In the next hour 700,000 will die. 16 million animals will be killed today. Six billion deaths every year. Remember, it is for the animals we keep fighting. They are dying as we speak).

DIARY OF ACTIONS

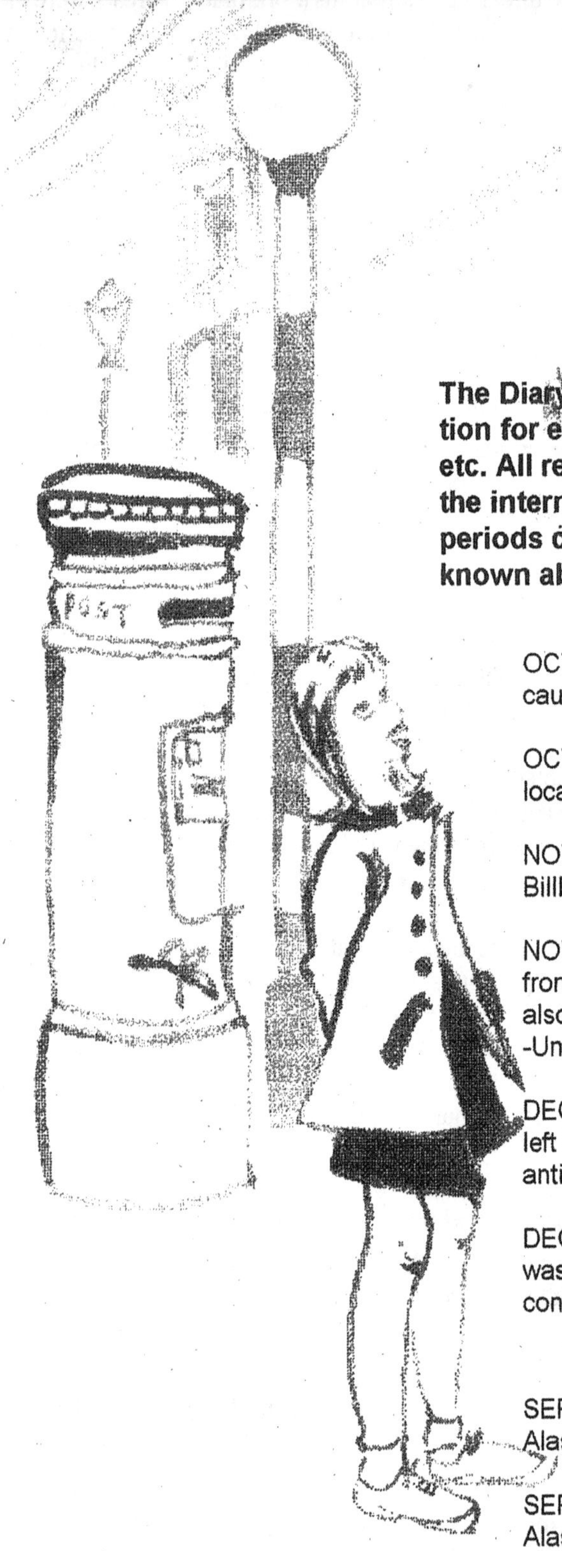

The Diary of Action is intended to report the news of direct action for earth and animal liberation, not to encourage crime, etc. etc. All reports come from communiques, other publications, the internet and news reports. Some actions took place in time periods covered by other issues of *Underground,* but were not known about until recently.

CANADA

OCTOBER/98: Hythe, AB - A bomb damaged an unstaffed oil well causing approx. $10,000 in damages. -Unclaimed

OCTOBER/98: Saskatoon, SK -- Locks glued at two McDonald's locations. -ALF Prairie Unit

NOVEMBER/98: Saskatoon, SK -- Four "Heartland Livestock" Billboards paint bombed. -ALF Prairie Unit

NOVEMBER 14/98: Edmonton, AB - A fur and hide tannery had a front window smashed and was set on fire. The letters "PETA" were also spray painted on the door. Damage estimated at $100,000. -Unclaimed

DECEMBER/98: Edmonton, AB - A bottle of a noxious chemical was left in the fur dept. of The Hudson's Bay Company along with an anti-fur message. -Unclaimed

DECEMBER/98: Edmonton, AB - A parcel addressed to a politician was intercepted in the post office and opened by the bomb squad. It contained an animal rights message. -Unclaimed

UNITED STATES

SEPTEMBER/98: Plano, TX -- ALF shot out several windows at the Alaskan Fur Center.

SEPTEMBER/98: Plano, TX -- ALF shoot out another window at Alaskan Fur Center.

SEPTEMBER/98: Dallas, TX -- ALF paint bombed and etched windows at Valentine Furs, paint bombed and etched windows at Bifeno Furs,

SEPTEMBER/98: Rockwell, TX -- ALF paint bombed and etched windows at Baumann Furs.

SEPTEMBER 1/98: CO - Gates opened at a BLM holding pen and 60 wild horses were released. -Unclaimed

SEPTEMBER 19/98: Burlington, WA - Broadview Egg Farms was raided and 11 chickens liberated. Video footage taken of the disgusting conditions. Messages spray painted including "freed by A.L.F.", "torture will end", had windows etched. "THERE IS NOWHERE TO HIDE. ANIMAL MURDERERS BEWARE. THERE IS JUSTICE COMING..." from the communique. -A.L.F.

MID-SEPTEMBER/98: Rock Springs, WY -- ALF and ELF have claimed responsibility for liberating almost 100 wild horses from Bureau of Land Management (B.L.M) wild-horse corrals.

SEPTEMBER 24/98: Trenton, NJ. Flemington Furs billboard was paintbombed.

SEPTEMBER 24/98: Yardley, PA. Flemington Furs billboard was paintbombed.

SEPTEMBER 27/98: Roselle Park, NJ -- Gold Furs' storefront was paintbombed. -A.L.F.

SEPTEMBER 27/98: Bayonne, NJ -- Famous Furs had three front display windows etched with the letters "ALF". The glass door was also etched.
-A.L.F.

SEPTEMBER 30/98: Paramus, NJ -- Ten tire-puncturing devices were placed across the driveway of Steven Corn Furs. -A.L.F.

OCTOBER/98: Duluth, GA -- McDonalds on Duluth Highway hit, slogans spraypainted included "Meat Is Murder," "A.L.F.," "Go Vegan," and "100 Billion Killed." McDonalds stated the damage likely will cost more than $500 to repair.

OCTOBER/98: Fort Worth, TX - Heino Furs had locks glued and were paint bombed. David Hunt Furs was paint bombed, had locks glued, and windows etched. Gavrel Furs was paint bombed and had windows etched. Then Stripling and Cox department store had many locks glued. --ALF

OCTOBER/98: Dallas, TX -- At Valentine Furs ALF etched the windows, glued locks, and spray painted slogans. At Bifano Furs ALF glued locks and etched the windows.

OCTOBER/98: Pluto, TX -- Activists shot out a window at Alaskan Fur Center. -ALF

OCTOBER 1/98: Caldwell, NJ -- Terzako Furs had "DEAD" etched into three front display windows and a glass door. -A.L.F.

OCTOBER 11/98: Chevy Chase, MD -- Miller's Furs had its locks glued. -A.L.F.

OCTOBER 11/98: Tenleytown, DC- A McDonald's under construction had the inside of the stores spray painted with anti-meat slogans. -A.L.F.

OCTOBER 13/98: Atlanta, GA -- A bomb threat caused the evacuation of thousands of people attending the Bass Pro Shops Buck Madness hunting show at the outdoors superstore in Duluth. The store and local tv stations received the threats. The caller said something like: "You murder animals.We're going to murder hunters. There's a bomb in the building." -unclaimed

OCTOBER 15/98: Duluth, GA - A McDonald's was painted with slogans including "Meat Is Murder", "A.L.F.", "Go Vegan" and "100 Billion Killed."-A.L.F.

OCTOBER 18/98: Farragut North, DC - Rosendorf/Evans fur store had 4 display windows covered with etching cream. -A.L.F.

OCTOBER 18/98: McLean, VA - Furs of Kiszely had 6 display windows covered with etching cream. -A.L.F.

OCTOBER 18/98: Vail, CO - "On behalf of the lynx," incendiary devices were placed at 5 buildings and 4 ski lifts which all ignited reducing them to ashes. 14 million dollars in damage. -ELF

HEARD ABOUT AN ACTION?

Some simple tips to make our work easier:

So your local animal rights group has learned of an ALF action in your area, and you want to pass it on. Great! But please make it easier on the people compiling Diary of Action lists — be sure to include the following: **DATE** (try to be as exact as possible) **PLACE** (country, state/province/city — this is important for internet postings, since many folk posting thru email and internet lists seem to assume the rest of us automatically know what country is being talked about!) **INCIDENT** —again, try to be exact — what happened, who did it (if claimed), damages, arrests, etc.

Following the general format of the Diary of Actions (DATE/PLACE /INCIDENT) will stop our chronic swearing and endear you to us forever!

OCTOBER 23/98: Passaic, NJ - Locks glued at Garber's Furs. -A.L.F.

OCTOBER 23/98: Cliffside Park, NJ - Evelyn's Furs paint-bombed. -A.L.F.

OCTOBER 24/98: Ventnor City, NJ - "ALF" etched into the front display window at Cohen's Furs. The glass door was etched as well. -A.L.F.

OCTOBER 26/98: Hermansville, MI - Pipkorn Inc. Mink Ranch was raided. Seven large holes were cut in their fence and approx. 5000 mink were released. -ELF

Members of the Mink Nation begin their journey to freedom.

OCTOBER/98: Dallas, TX - Valentine Furs had windows etched, glued locks and spray painted slogans. Bifano Furs had glued locks and etched windows. -A.L.F.

OCTOBER/98: Pluto, TX - Alaskan Fur Center had window smashed. -A.L.F.

NOVEMBER/98: CA -- "Traditional gardeners" known as the California Croppers held a tackle football match early Thanksgiving morning at the "Gill Tract" gardens, and in the process destroyed a crop of genetically-engineered corn. The Croppers plan to take similar actions against any future biotech experiments.

NOVEMBER 2/98: Bayonne, NJ - Window damaged at Furs by John Keffas. -A.L.F.

NOVEMBER 2/98: Bayonne, NJ - Window damaged at Famous Furs. -A.L.F.

NOVEMBER 2/98: South Orange, NJ - Window damaged at the Fur Salon. -A.L.F.

NOVEMBER 2/98: Woodbridge, NJ - Window damaged at Woodbridge Furs. -A.L.F.

NOVEMBER 2/98: Teaneck, NJ - Window damaged at Queen Anne Furs. -A.L.F.

NOVEMBER 2/98: Englewood, NJ - Window damaged at Fleischman Furs. -A.L.F.

NOVEMBER 2/98: Englewood Cliffs, NJ - Glass door damaged at Castor Furs. -A.L.F.

NOVEMBER 2/98: Linden, NJ - Window damaged at Furs by Severyn. -A.L.F.

NOVEMBER 2/98: Passaic, NJ - Garber's Furs window damaged. -A.L.F.

NOVEMBER 3/98: Atlanta, GA - Atlanta Furs was splattered with 1 gallon of red paint, a sign was completely destroyed by the red paint. Slogans were spray painted on the shop and the store's plexiglass windows were also punctured and cracked. -A.L.F.

NOVEMBER 5/98: Pine Plains, NY - Almost 100 pheasants and quail were liberated from a "canned hunt" where they were to be killed. This action was done in solidarity with the political prisoner Barry Horne. -A.L.F.

NOVEMBER 5/98: Harris Township, MI - Attempted raid at Jander Mink Ranch.

NOVEMBER 8/98: Ithica, NY -- activist sealed shut Comstock Hall at Cornell University. The Band of Mercy used bicycle locks and super-glue to prevent biology professors from entering the building and killing frogs for a morning class dissection.
NOVEMER 13/98: Chevy Chase, MD -- Miller's Furs had two display windows covered with etching cream.

NOVEMBER 16/98: Manalapan, NJ - The Leather and Fur Ranch store's van was fire-bombed. -A.L.F.

NOVEMBER 21/98: Greenfield, MI - 3 turkeys due to be killed in 2 days were liberated. -Unclaimed

NOVEMBER 24/98: Ridgewood, NJ - Bon-Ton Furs'

truck was heavily damaged. Tires slashed, locks glued, wires, cables and hoses cut. It was also painted with slogans such as "Fur is Dead", "Murder" and "A.L.F." "A.L.F." was also spray painted twice on the back of the building. -A.L.F.

NOVEMBER 26/98: Volo (near Ingleside), IL - Daniel Frey's mink farm was visited. Upon inspection it was believed that this farm has pelted out and is no longer in business. Numerous cages were destroyed to prevent further use. -A.L.F.

DECEMBER 13/98: Chevy Chase, MD - Miller's Furs; windows etched -A.L.F.

DECEMBER 13/98: Washington, DC - Andriana Furs; windows etched -A.L.F.

DECEMBER 24/98: Paramus, NJ -- Approximately one ounce of butyric acid was released into the Macy's department store at Garden State Plaza during the middle of one of the busiest shopping days of the year. Such actions will continue until Macy's stops their sale of fur. - A.L.F.

DECEMBER 24/98: Freehold, NJ -- Approximately one ounce of butyric acid, a harmless but powerfully foul-smelling substance, was released into the Macy's department store at Freehold Raceway Mall. - A.L.F.

DECEMBER 24/98: New York, NY -- butyric acid was released into the Macy's department store at Herald Square during Christmas shopping. - A.L.F.

DECEMBER 25/98: Medford, OR -- ELF celebrate their favorite season with a bonfire -- at the U.S. Forest Industrie's Corporate HQ. Two five gallon buckets filled with an unleaded/diesel mix proved to be more than enough punch for the party to get going right! The action was a retribution and a warning. People like Jerry Bramwell (U.S. Forest Industries president) who think they can continue to pillage the earth will pay. This is payback for your fucking greed. What cost santa's ELFs fifty dollars now cost you greedy bastards half a million. We won't quit until the earth and all relations are free. -ELF

JANUARY 4/99: Woodlawn Hills, CA -- Woodland Hills Furriers Inc. was visited by the ALF. "40 dead animals=1 fur coat" and "ALF" were painted across the entire entrance in red paint. windows were etched with "killers", "scum" , "stop now" and "alf". no windows were left unmarked. All locks were glued in front and back. two rocks marked with "killers beware... ALF" and "the ALF is watching" found their way through two windows followed by smoking devices that left the store engulfed in smoke. 1999 will not be a good year for those who profit off the blood and suffering of innocent animals... -ALF

JANUARY 4/99: Woodland Hills, CA -- fashion furs inc at 22941 Ventura blvd. celebrated their new year with anti fur slogans and etching cream smeared on their windows. All locks were glued in front and back and the following slogans were written in red paint: "fur is murder," "killers," "blood $$$." All windows were etched: "torturers," "scum" and "ALF." More actions to follow. --A.L.F.

JANUARY 6/99: Lake Wylie, CA -- animal rights activists set fire to a McDonald's restaurant and painted graffiti outside the building, including "ALF" and "McMurder."

ENGLAND

AUGUST 19/98: N. London - A small device which had been placed inside a package containing a cassette box, exploded at Mount Pleasant sorting postal office. The police say no-one was injured by the explosion. Anti-Terrorist officers were investigating and it was stated that animal rights activists were suspected. -Unclaimed

SEPTEMBER/98: - Workers at the Occold research lab of Huntingdon Life Sciences have received warn-

ing letters at their homes telling them they should quit their jobs. "Not only do we know who you are but also where you live and work. No one, as yet, has been 'killed' by 'animal protectors'." It continued "It's now your turn to experience exactly what the innocent animals have had to endure. Our advice is to withdraw from your animal abusing connections now... before it is too late." -Provisional A.L.F.

SEPTEMBER 2/98: London - An angling shop that has a shop front protected by a steel shutter, was kicked in with such force that the window underneath was shattered. The premises has been attacked several times before since it opened earlier this year. - A.L.F.

SEPTEMBER 16/98: Staffordshire - More than 3500 cages opened and 8000 mink released at a farm owned by Len Kelsall, Chair of the Fur Breeders Assn UK.

SEPTEMBER 23/98: - 80 hens liberated from a battery farm. -A.L.F.

OCTOBER 15/98: London - Numerous paint attacks on shops and hoardings in east London. 47 "Meat is Murder" and 27 "Go Veggie" slogans were daubed around the Dalston, Hackney, Clapton and Homerton areas. -A.L.F.

OCTOBER 17/98: Justice Department sent ten hoax packages out to a number of animal abusers, including Sainsburys HQ, Hillgrove Family Farm Ltd, Huntingdon Research Centre and Downley Common (a games keeper who has shot 39,234 animals including 50 cats, 154 badgers, 1838 ducks and 31,853 pheasants. The devices consisted of a video cassette box with coloured wires protruding. The box was sealed shut with glue and filled with cat litter. -JD

NOVEMBER 8/98: Brighton - Four lorries of a meat market were damaged by incendiary devices.

NOVEMBER 13/98: London -- 79 walls were sprayed in Dalston, Hackney central, Homerton and Clapton areas with slogans like "Support Barry Horne hunger-strike" , "stop vivisection ", "animal rights prisoner on hunger strike" , etc The action has been done in less than 1 1/2 hours , which shows how effective activist can be. This action is dedicated to Barry Horne with all
our love and support , and obviously to all the animals that suffer from human exploitation. RESPECT. THEY CAN'T STOP US!!! ALF

NOVEMBER 15/98: London -- Two butchers' shops in Palmers Green, north London had their windows smashed by ALF activists.

NOVEMBER/98: Crawly - Several lorries of an animal hauling company had their windows smashed and other damage.

NOVEMBER 29/98: Hounslow --McDonald's in west London had all its windows smashed by the ALF. Some if the interior was also damaged in the attack.

DECEMBER 2/98: England - In response to the UK Labour government's inaction to Barry Horne's hunger strike, a communique was sent out announcing a list of ten vivisectors who would be killed if Barry died. Four of the 10 were named: Christopher Brown of Hillgrove Farm, Colin Blakemore of Oxford University, Clive Page of King's College and Mark Matfield of the Research Defence Society. -Animal Rights Militia

DECEMBER 5/98: Leeds - A hoax bomb package was left in the washroom of a McDonald's. The action was dedicate to Barry Horne.

DECEMBER 5/98: Whitton - A hunting, shooting and fishing shop was attacked and had their locks glued and windows smashed. It was also dedicated to Barry Horne.

DECEMBER 6/98: Crawton - A chicken processing plant had 7 vehicles set on fire causing hundreds of thousands of pounds in damage.

DECEMBER 13/98; Wanstead - AG Dennis butchers was attacked for the second time this year. A small device attached to their window exploded.

DECEMBER 15/98: Ilford, East London - 2 butcher's shops and 1 McDonald's had their windows smashed. - A.L.F.

DECEMBER 17/98: Five Waitrose supermarkets bomb hoaxed because they are owned by pro-bloodsports John Lewis Partnership. -ALF

DECEMBER 17/98: Luton -- HQ of Whitbread Beer Co. was bomb hoaxed as they use a live export company to transport their beverages around the UK. -ALF

DECEMBER 17/98: London -- Head Office of Mirror Group Newspapers was hoaxed because they employ pro-animal abuse columnist Carol Sarler, who wished Barry Horne to "rot in hell." -ALF

JANUARY 4/99: London -- windows were smashed at the "Kennedy Fried Chicken" on Leytonstone High Rd. Also, a fish shop had door panels smashed and a pet shop had its window smashed.

JANUARY 6/99: London -- a fish/halal meat shop in Whitechapel had its windows smashed.

IRELAND

OCTOBER 26/98: Shanbally, Ring, Dungarvan - A large amount (number unknown) of mink were released from a fur farm in what may be Ireland's first ever mink liberation. Cages were opened and a perimeter fence was also damaged allowing mink to escape into the country side. -Unclaimed

GERMANY

OCTOBER 6/98: Fladderlohausen -- Animal rights activists destroyed a fence at a fur farm and releasing 2,500 mink. The farm's owner estimates the damage at 250,000 marks (about $150,000).

OCTOBER 8/98: Niedersachsen -- Militants raided a fur farm released at least 1000 river polecats into the nearby woodlands.The liberators tore down a fence making an escape route for the animals.

AUSTRIA

JUNE/98: Lower Austria - 9 hunting platforms cut down.

JUNE/98: Vienna - 4 butcher shop display windows broken.

JUNE 4/98: Vienna - 9 fur shop windows broken.

JULY/98: Live animal transporter attacked on lay-by on motorway. All tires slashed and windows smashed.

JULY 6/98: Vienna - 4 butcher shop windows smashed.

JULY 28/98: Lower Austria - 44 battery chicken liberated.

JULY 29/98: Vienna - 4 butcher shops display windows smashed.

AUGUST 6/98: Vienna - 1 butcher, 1 McDonald's, 4 fur shop, poultry shop and another animal abusing shop all had their windows smashed.

AUGUST 10/98: Lower Austria - 21 battery chickens liberated.

AUGUST 24/98: 5 shops that sell dead animals had their locks glued.

AUGUST 26/98: Vienna - 13 display windows of shops smashed. Shops include furriers, butchers and McDonald's.

SEPTEMBER/98: 4 animal abuse shops were damaged.

SEPTEMBER 9/98: Vienna - Meat lorry and display windows and doors of 2 butchers locks glued and spray painted with messages.

SEPTEMBER/98: Vienna - 6 fur shops had their windows smashed. -the "furious minks".

SEPTEMBER 24/98: Locks were glued of the following shops: 1 egg shop, 1 poultry shop, 1 butcher shop and 4 fur shops.

SEPTEMBER 24/98: Vienna - 3 lorry locks and a door lock of a butcher in Vienna superglued.

SEPTEMBER/98: Vienna - 5 shops have display windows smashed. Shops include hunters, butchers and furriers.

OCTOBER 3/98: Vienna - Animal abuse shops had 15 locks glued. Spraypainted messages were left "The fight against the animal exploiters does not make a difference between sex, age, religion or nationality, because for the animals it does not make a difference, who murders it".

OCTOBER 10/98: Vienna - 12 shops, butchers and furriers, have locks glued.

OCTOBER 13/98: Vienna - Butyric acid attack on restaurant that serves exotic meat.

OCTOBER 14/98: Vienna - "Stasta", a hotel restaurant that slaughters and serves wild pigs, was attacked with butyric acid.

NOVEMBER/98: Vienna - 6 fur shops attacked with butyric acid in Vienna.

NOVEMBER 5/98: Veinna - Fur shop window smashed.

NOVEMBER 10/98: Vienna - 8 restaurants selling pate fois gras in Vienna are attacked with butyric acid. Some claim big damage. A restaurant owner says in an interview that geese love being force fed. Force feeding any animal is illegal in Austria.

NOVEMBER 13/98: Locks of 3 fur shops were glued. -A.L.F.

DECEMBER 9/98: Austria - Six animal abuse shops got attacked with butyric acid. Action dedicated to Barry Horne.

JANUARY 11/99: Lower Austria - 120 battery hens were liberated. They are all well in loving homes now.

SPAIN

NOVEMBER 29/98: Bilbao - Activists attacked a bull-fighting club with stones and paint bombs to show, "their deepest solidarity" for Barry Horne.

NORWAY

DECEMBER 22/98: Sandefjord - a fur store was the object of an animal rights action. Slogans were painted and locks glued.

POLAND

APRIL 22/98: Poznan - Front windows of a big Butcher's shop smashed, signs damaged and locks glued in. Locks of 2 fur shops glued and 1 window smashed. -FWZ (A.L.F.)

MAY 8/98: Poznan - Front windows of meat shop smashed, sign damaged and locks glued. Front windows of 2 fur shops smashed, locks glued. Hunter's shop locks glued. -FWZ

MAY 23/98: Poznan - A big circus tent damaged. -FWZ

JUNE 14/98: Poznan - A few meat shops windows smashed and locks glued. -FWZ

JULY/98: Janow near Szczytno (Northern Poland) - A fox farm was raided and a few hundred fox were released. -FWZ

SEPTEMBER 16/98: Poznan - Front windows of 1 fur shop smashed. -FWZ

OCTOBER 25/98: Pozan - Circus vehicle damaged. -FWZ

OCTOBER 26/98: Janow near Szczytno (Northern Poland) - Fox farm raided and about 250 fox were painted with harmless dye. It was a second raid on this farm.-FWZ

OCTOBER 28/98: Ponzan - 3 fur shops painted with anti-fur/A.L.F. slogans and a big meat shop painted with A.L.F./vegan slogans. -FWZ

NOVEMBER 6/98: Poznan - 3 meat shops, 1 meat restaurant and 1 fur shop painted with more slogans.

NOVEMBER 10/98: Poznan - Front windows, the doors and shop signs of 2 of the largest meat shops smashed. Front window, the door and shop sign of 1 fur shop smashed. -FWZ

NOVEMBER 16/98: Jeziory Wielkie - 5 hunter's platforms destroyed. -FWZ

NOVEMBER 30/98: Jeziory Wielkie - Fox farm raided and over 330 red fox and 400 polar foxes were painted with harmless dye. Cages were also opened. Slogans including "For Barry Horne", "We dedicated this action to Barry Horne", "NO FOR FUR", "Enough Cruelty For Luxury" and "Fur Is Shame" were sprayed on the wall and sheds. The foxes were not insured and the farm is in serious financial trouble. A security guard, who was on the farm during the action lost his job. Dedicated to Barry Horne. -"Brygada R.R."(Rescue Rangers)

ITALY

DECEMBER/98: Two brands of "Panettone" Christmas cakes made by Nestle were sent to the Ansa news agency with a communique claiming that cakes in stores across Italy had been poisoned. Stores

across Italy and even Switzerland pulled all cakes from their shelves. Tests were ran and found that no poison was present in any cakes on store shelves. The communique stated the action was because of Nestle's genetic engineering. Damages have been estimated at over $30 million. -A.L.F.

DECEMBER 31/98: The ANSA news agency received a package of hamburger meat that had been tainted with rat poison. They also received a communique claiming responsibility from the "Animal Human Liberation Front".

NETHERLANDS

OCTOBER/98: Watergraafsmeer, Amsterdam - Several trucks belonging to a butcher were set on fire. - Unclaimed

JANUARY 3/99: The Dutch ELF sent five bomb warnings to McDonald's in Groningen, Den Haag, Zeist, Waardenburg en Best. McDonald's was targeted because, says the ELF, of "their filthy practices".

JANUARY 5/99: Rotterdam -- Bomb threat made to a McDonald's. -- unclaimed

JANUARY 6/99: activists told McDonalds a bomb was set to go off somewhere in a store in South Holland, forcing McDonalds to evacuate 9 shops.

JANUARY 9/99: Geleen -- arson at a McDonald's drive-thru resulted in substantial damages.

FINLAND

SEPTEMBER/98: Vihti - Fur farmer Leena Pitkanen's van was attacked and had tires slashed and it was covered with slogans.

SEPTEMBER 27/98: Laukaa - Tiituspohja fur farm raided and 200 foxes liberated.

SEPTEMBER 27/98: Jamsa - Antero Pelkonen fur farm raided and 500 mink liberated.

SEPTEMBER/98: Kerisalo Island, Joroinen - Approx. 2000 mink were released from their cages and holes were cut in the fence through which they could escape. -EVR

OCTOBER 2-3/98: Lappaj„rvi - A fur farm was raided and 300 foxes were dyed with henna dye and 20 cages were opened. -EVR

OCTOBER 11/98: Pyharanta - Terho Inkinen's fur farm was raided and 400 fox and 200 raccoon dog were released. Also destroyed was an electrocution style killing machine. "The raid is dedicated to Barry Horne, an English animal activist who is on a hunger strike in prison for the third time to end vivisection." -EVR

OCTOBER/98: Helsinki - A woman who was trying on a fur coat at Stockmann hurt her hand on a razor blade that was in the pocket of the coat. She got minor wounds. -Unclaimed

OCTOBER/98: Overmark, Narpes - An estimated 1000 mink were liberated from the largest fur farm in the area. There was no fence and the mink escaped the area fast. This raid was an answer to the Finnish fur farmer's declaration against anti-fur activists. "Your threatening will not scare us, because it's nothing compared to the suffering of the animals. You don't know us, you won't see us in TV or in newspapers. You will hear of us only when we hit your farms. You will see us only in your nightmares. We will burn the maps of your farms only after we have raided the farms. Now it's time for fur farmers to look for another way of living. The resistance against fur farming won't cease as long as the animals have to suffer on the farms. Stop now and leave the animals alone." from the communique. - The Black Mink Front

OCTOBER 20/98: Luum„ki - A fur shop suffered hundreds of thousands of marks damage from an incendiary attack.

OCTOBER 24-25/98: Rehula, Taipalsaari - A fur farm was raided and 300-400 foxes were dyed with henna and most of the breeding records were destroyed. -the Colour of Autumn

OCTOBER 25/98: Sipari, Lappeenranta - During an inspection of a fur farm, about 30 animals were found: fox and racoon dog. Their fur was dyed with henna and cages of the animals left open. Equipment was also destroyed. -EVR

NOVEMBER/98: Ristiina, near Mikkeli - Kauko Leskinen's fur farm had approx. 400 foxes dyed with red henna colour. -Colour of Autumn (Ruskanvari)

NOVEMBER 19/98: A car belonging to a laboratory worker of Karttula breeder was damaged. The action was dedicated to Barry Horne. -EVR

NOVEMBER 23-24/98: Helsinki - The windows of 8 different fur stores were smashed. The action was dedicated to Barry Horne and his demands. -EVR

NOVEMBER 27/98: Kil (Varmland) - Skarebols mink farm was visited and had empty sheds set on fire. Equipment was also damaged. The action was dedicated to Barry Horne -The Wild Minks

SWEDEN

AUGUST/98: Glommen -- 300 minks on the run.

AUGUST 6/98: Orebro - Circus posters destoyed.

AUGUST 9/98: Orebro - Circus posters destroyed.

AUGUST 10/98: Lulea - chark (meat) had windows smashed.

AUGUST 14/98: Orebro - Locks glued at hunting and angling shop.

AUGUST 22/98: Orebro - Two windows smashed and locks glued at hunting shop.

AUGUST 27/98: Storuman - A hunting house was totally destroyed. One of the hunters woke up in the middle of the night and saw that the house was on fire. The house burned to the ground. The house burned down last year too. Earlier this year a hunting tractor (used for shipping killed elks) has been burned down. -Unclaimed

SEPTEMBER/98: Sundsvall -- 2000 more minks are liberated from a fur farm.

SEPTEMBER 4/98: Harryda, Ryahed - A fur farm was raided a second time by activists. The farmer had put up fake alarms and signs about security guards. An estimated 200-250 minks was set free. The ferrets on the farm, only 6, were put from the farm. -The Wild Minks

SEPTEMBER 5/98: Varobacka - During an inspection at a fur farm, it was discovered the farm was closed down. The farmer was still involved in other animal abuse industries and damage was done to equipment on the farm. -The Wild Minks

SEPTEMBER 5/98: Boras - All 5 windows of B:sons fur shop smashed. -DBF

SEPTEMBER 19/98: Sm†land, Ormaryd - G"sta Larssons mink farm was raided, holes was cut in the fence and an estimated 180 cages were opened and approx. 400 minks was set free. "The Wild Minks... give our support to the people arrested recently in USA for the fur farm raids..." from the communique. -The Wild Minks

SEPTEMBER 23/98: The night of the 23rd of September the DBF (Swedish ALF) rescued twelve baby pigs from a pig farm in Southern Sweden. It seems as if a pig farm of this size does not notice pigs missing. We will be back! For all pigs, DBF

SEPTEMBER 25/98 An incendiary device was placed under a truck and trailer fully loaded with eggs at KronEgg, one of Sweden's biggest egg companies. Unfortunately, the bomb did not ignite. The police shut down the area and it took them 5 hours after they had found the bomb until they had disarmed it. -DBF

SEPTEMBER/98: Froso Zoo - A hole was cut in the fence allowing a one 4 month old female wolf to escape. -Unclaimed

SEPTEMBER 28/98: Sundavall - Over 2,000 minks was released from a mink farm . This is the same farm that was attacked some month ago when 1,000 minks were freed. -DBF

OCTOBER/98: Amal - During a daylight raid at the small rabbit farm, all rabbits on the farm (around 20) were liberated. Unfortunately a van was stopped a short distance away from the farm, 3 activists and several rabbits were arrested by the police. One activist and 8 rabbits managed to get away and were not caught.

OCTOBER 4/98: Goman (meat product factory) had windows smashed and the power cut off to one fish cold store and also smashed their outdoor lighting. Further smashing happened at an angling store that lost 2 windows and one leather and fur shop got 2 windows smashed and another leather & fur shop got 1 window smashed and finally one more fur shop got 1 broken window. -DBF

OCTOBER 4/98: Umea -- animal rights activists attacked an rabbit breeder. The breeding is a school project which includes massive inbreeding and slaughter of rabbits. All this only for the value of their furs and meat. The activists coloured the furs of all the rabbits (over 60 rabbits) in harmless henna colour, as an act of economic sabotage.

OCTOBER 5/98 - SMI gets 2000 e-mails. -A.L.F. (Internet Division)

OCTOBER 6/98 - 3000 e-mails were sent to SMI. Resulting in system crash. The Swedish media says that "the information war has begun". -A.L.F. (Internet Division)

OCTOBER 10/98 - Karolinska Institute gets 8000 e-mails because of it's collaboration with SMI. -A.L.F. (Internet Division)

OCTOBER 14/ 98: Brunflo - Fox farm raided for the second time. All of the animals there, 20 blue fox, were painted with henna dye and released. Cages were also destroyed. -A.L.F.

OCTOBER 16/98 - 20,000 e-mails were sent to SMI and KI, each. Operation Close-Down has started. -A.L.F. (Internet Division)

OCTOBER 17/98 - 25,000 e-mails to SMI. -A.L.F. (Internet Division)

OCTOBER 22/98: Bralanda - Approx. 5700 mink were set free from a mink farm. -DBF

OCTOBER 30/98: Nordmaling - A mink farm had their fence destroyed and 20,000 mink released. -The Wild Minks

OCTOBER 31/98 - Bisam University was spray painted with slogans.

NOVEMBER/98 - The Justice Department issued a communique responding to death threats issued to non-violent, anti-fur activists by fur farmers. It stated in part "The farmer of who threats any activist will have to live by the threats of repression; the farmer who injures any activist will be injured; the farmer who murders any activists will be murdered. We won't passively observe any further acts of violence towards animal rights activists, we will attack them who attacks us." -Justice Department

NOVEMBER 4/98: Karlstad - A horse slaugherhouse had 6 windows smashed and was spray painted with slogans. The owners car was also painted with slogans. The action was dedicated to Barry Horne. -DBF

NOVEMBER 11/98: - A further 20,000 e-mails has been sent to SMI in Stockholm, as a protest against their animal torture. 20,000 mails were also sent to the Department of agriculture. -A.L.F. (Internet Division)

NOVEMBER 30/98: - 2 vivisectors had their cars damaged and slogans painted in support of Barry and his demands. -A.L.F.

DECEMBER 15/98: Stockholm --during a demo at SMI, a car arrived and stopped at the gate waiting for the guard to open the gate. Activists spotted animals inside the car and managed escape with a box of 4 guinea-pigs, meant to be used for vivisection. They are all living a good life now.

LATE DECEMBER/98: Stockholm -- SMI has a window smashed and is doused in red paint.

JANUARY 1/99: Stockholm -- An arson attack was carried out at a meat factory in Charkman. The roof and lots of machinery were destroyed by the fire. Damages estimated at 1 million sek. -unclaimed

JANUARY 2/99: Kil -- One animal transporter was burn out and another was damaged by the fire at Scans slaughterhouse. Activists from Djurens Befrielse Front (Swedish ALF) were responsible. Activists placed one fire bomb at each front wheel of the trucks. The activists has 3 minutes delays to disappear before the bottles began to burn. The action was carried out as a protest against Scan. -DBF

NEW ZEALAND

OCTOBER 8/98: Hawkes Bay -- A.L.F. hits two butcher shops. Slogans were painted on the two shops and on the footpaths outside them.

WILLS AND LEGACIES

If you would like to remember the NA-A.L.F. Supporters Group in your will, the following words are suggested:

I bequeath to the North American Animal Liberation Front Supporters Group, presently at Box 69597, Yonge St. Willowdale, Ont. M2M 4K3, Canada, the sum of ________________, and declare that the receipt of the Treasurer or other authorized officer of said Society shall be good and sufficient discharge of such legacy.

If you are considering leaving property or land, we would suggest you consult your solicitor.

UNDERGROUND

THE MAGAZINE OF THE NORTH AMERICAN ANIMAL LIBERATION FRONT SUPPORTERS GROUP

ISSUE # 14 SUMMER 99 $ 3.50
FREE TO PRISONERS

Inside:

A.L.F. Spokesperson raided...

Anti-A.L.F. legislation introduced in U.S...

Prisoner Updates...

Common Sense Security for Animal Liberation Activists...

And of course, much much more...

In Memory of Alex Slack

On Tuesday, June 29, 1999 the animal rights movement lost a great warrior. Alex Slack, of Salt Lake City, UT, ended his life after several years of extreme pain and suffering. Alex was well known in the Utah animal rights movement and had been an FBI target for some time.

Years ago Alex was a major suspect in a case involving the firebombing of a Tandy Leather store. Alex was eventually charged with several mink farm raids that led to the liberation of thousands of animals, and for an attack on a major mink feed plant.

Alex had a serious liver illness and was waiting for a transplant. To make matters worse, he had been involved in a serious car wreck and was forced to spend the rest of his life in a wheel chair. Between the liver illness, paralysis, and the prospect of spending years and years in jail, Alex decided to say good bye. Alex was a true hero for animal rights, and he will be missed. I am lucky in that I got to know him during his short time on Earth.

He will be missed.

JP Goodwin

A Word From yer Editor

Regular readers of *Underground* will likely have noticed the absence of the Spring issue of the magazine - ever since the Supporters Group moved to Toronto in 94/95, we've been pleased to consistently bring *Underground* out on a regular schedule, so apologies go out to anyone left waiting and wondering whether issue 14 would ever arrive. The main reason this issue of *Underground* was delayed was because of recent developments in Minnesota, where blatantly anti-ALF legislation was introduced into the Senate in April. The bill directly attacked A.L.F. activists and their supporters, and appeared to be aimed at silencing the A.L.F. Press Office, headquartered in Minneapolis, Minnesota. Not content to simply try to silence A.L.F. support in MN, authorities raided the home of one A.L.F. Spokesperson and convened a Grand Jury in the same state in the wake of an A.L.F. raid against the University of Minnesota. Deadlines for our Spring issue came and went as we lent our assistance to the A.L.F. Press Officer and other supporters facing overt repression at the hands of the US government. Here's the situation in a nut-shell:

The government takes aim at the A.L.F. Press Office...

ANTI-A.L.F. LEGISLATION

Just two weeks after animal-rights activists destroyed laboratory equipment and made off with research animals at the University of Minnesota, Senators voted to make merely taking responsibility for such acts a crime punishable by up to a year in jail plus civil damages. Senators unanimously endorsed an amendment sponsored by Sen. Dave Kleis, R-St. Cloud, levelling triple damages and other new civil sanctions specifically against animal-rights raiders and their spokespeople. In addition, the amendment would be retroactive to Jan. 1, well before the April 5 raid on university labs at the UofM. Upon initial reading of the proposed legislation, it appeared that anyone coming forward in support of A.L.F. actions faced prosecution if authorities deemed that they "promote, advocate and assumes responsibility" for a criminal act. Reminiscent of the recent Gandalf Trial in the UK, in which police arrested and charged editors of *Green Anarchist* and the UK A.L.F. Press Office for conspiracy to incite others, the Minnesota legislation appeared to target groups and individuals who come forward to support A.L.F. actions publicly, even when these individuals have nothing to do with the A.L.F. action itself.

The section that, depending on how it was to be enforced, could impact the operation of the Press Office was as follows:

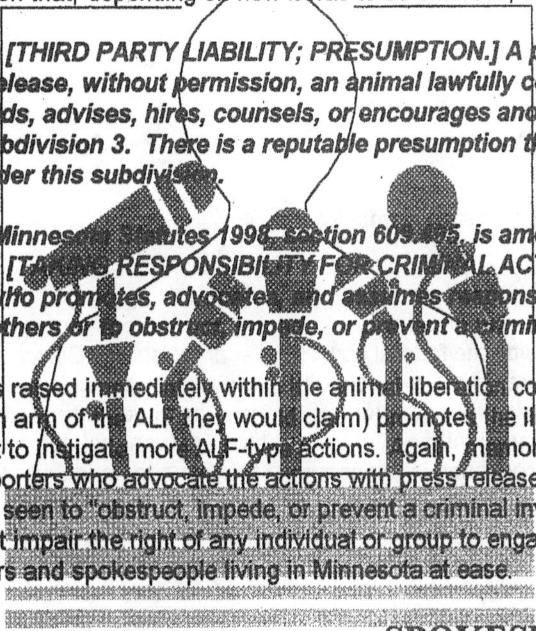

Subd. 4. [THIRD PARTY LIABILITY; PRESUMPTION.] A person or organisation who plans or assists in the development of a plan to release, without permission, an animal lawfully confined for science, research, commerce, or education, or who otherwise aids, advises, hires, counsels, or encourages another to commit the act is jointly and severally liable for all damages under subdivision 3. There is a reputable presumption that a person or organisation who claims responsibility for the act is liable under this subdivision.

Sec. 2. Minnesota Statutes 1998, section 609.495, is amended by adding a subdivision to read:
Subd. 4. [TAKING RESPONSIBILITY FOR CRIMINAL ACTS.] (a) Unless the person is convicted of the underlying crime, a person who promotes, advocates, and assumes responsibility for a criminal act with the intent to instigate the unlawful conduct of others or to obstruct, impede, or prevent a criminal investigation is guilty of a gross misdemeanour.

Concerns raised immediately within the animal liberation community was that the prosecution might argue that the NA-A.L.F. Press Office (an arm of the ALF they would claim) promotes the illegal activities of the A.L.F. through web pages, press releases, etc. with the intent to instigate more ALF-type actions. Again, memories of the Gandalf trail spring to mind immediately. Other concerns were that supporters who advocate the actions with press releases and then destroy the original communiqués received from A.L.F. cells might be seen to "obstruct, impede, or prevent a criminal investigation." The bill included a section which added that the new act would not impair the right of any individual or group to engage in speech protected by the US Constitution, but this did little to put supporters and spokespeople living in Minnesota at ease.

SPOKESPERSON RAIDED

If anyone was still in doubt about the State's plans to target the Press Office and the work it does, that changed May 5 when Federal agents raided the home of Kevin Kjonaas, who acted as the spokesperson for the A.L.F. after the liberations at the University of Minnesota in Mpls. Kevin was not at home at the time, but his housemate was and was made to witness the raid, which lasted many hours. Nine agents (one even in bullet proof gear) took three boxes of personal belongings, including computers, disks, personal effects, animal rights notebooks, videotapes, all documents and files related to the Press Office, all press clippings Kevin had gathered, phone numbers off his caller id box, an A.L.F. t-shirt, a hooded jacket, masking tape, etc.

Meanwhile, the omnibus criminal prevention and judiciary finance bill (that included the provisions that increase civil penalties for liberating animals and make third parties also liable for damages) passed both houses of the criminal section stricken out, and the retroactive effect of the remaining part removed.

OTHER ANTI-A.L.F. LEGISLATION INTRODUCED IN AMERICA

Government legislators in the US appeared to be on a role, and in late May an amendment to the Juvenile Justice Bill (S254) was introduced. Basically, the amendment would amongst other things:

1. Make it a federal crime to distribute info on how to "make bombs" (over the internet or otherwise) or other weapons of mass destruction if the "instructor" *intends* for the info to be used to commit a federal violent crime, or knows that the recipient will use the info to commit such a crime. The "A.L.F. website" and the "Final Nail 2" were specifically cited as examples of what would be targeted by the sponsor of the amendment.

2. Enhance penalties under the Animal Enterprise Terrorism Act - changing a minimum sentence to five years instead of one.

3. Create a "National Animal Terrorism and Ecoterrorism Incident Clearinghouse" to maintain records of such incidents to be made available to participating law enforcement agencies.

4. "Crack down on gangs" (with Utah straight edge animal rights "gangs" being used as an example).This includes only requiring three people to call it a gang, enhanced sentences, etc.

GRAND JURY HITS MINNESOTA

In June, things heated up again for spokesperson Kevin Kjonaas, when he was called before a federal grand jury regarding A.L.F. activity in Minnesota. Kevin was represented by the immediate past-President of the National Lawyers Guild. After giving only his name and address, Kevin, on the advice of counsel asserted his 1st amendment right to freedom of association and his fifth amendment right to be free from a compelled testimony. He refused to give any answers to any questions. After numerous questions Kevin requested permission to speak with his attorney. This and his refusal to answer questions irritated the federal prosecutor. After an hour and a half the prosecutor decided she had had enough and took from Kevin the notebook in which he was recording each question asked (to make consultation with counsel more fruitful). Kevin was dismissed and supposedly litigation about his right to counsel and notes are being challenged.. As of right now it is uncertain as to whether or not Kevin will be subpoenaed again.

Some of the questions Kevin was asked pertained to:

-his relationship to the university as a student and employee
-when "he got involved with the press office"
-how long had he been serving as the press officer
-how the A.L.F. sent communiqués to the press office
-if he had any part in the A.L.F. action at the University of M.
-was he in town during the action
-questions pertaining to his activist resume which they took off the harddrive of his computer

NOW WE WAIT

While Kevin was inside sitting silent, a large demonstration gathered outside the federal court house, organised by Citizens for Free Speech. The demo was well covered by all local media. At this point there is little more to tell. Kevin is still waiting to see what will happen with regards to the Grand Jury, and has petitioned to have all of his property returned. In the mean time, Katie Fedor, the NA-A.L.F. Press Officer since it's inception almost two years ago, has handed things over to long time earth/animal activist David Barbarash, so she can better focus her energies fighting the Grand Jury convened in Minneapolis. More on the handover of the Press Office elsewhere in *Underground.*

So folks, there you have it. Since issue #13 quite a bit has been happening in the good ol' U.S. of A, though it remains to be seen exactly how this will affect supporters of militant direct action. As you'll be able to see from our Diary of Actions, the A.L.F. continues to strike at animal abusers everywhere, with actions taking place nearly every day of the month. Despite the potential hardships above-ground A.L.F. supporters face from frustrated and ineffectual government legislation, one thing is very clear: the more the authorities waste resources and time attacking above-ground supporters, the less they have to focus on A.L.F cells and those carrying out actions and liberations.

At any rate, enjoy the rest of the magazine — better late than never!
yer editor,
t.

Letters to Underground

FAMILIES OF ANIMAL RIGHTS PRISONERS SUPPORT

Dear *Underground*,

This is to let you know about FAMILIES OF AR PRISONERS SUPPORT, a self-help network designed to support the families of Animal Rights prisoners. The network is open to the families & concerned friends of current prisoners, the families of ex-prisoners and to ex-prisoners themselves.

Basically the network will introduce families to each other so the families of AR prisoners can talk to other people who are in the same boat as themselves. It will also give the chance for concerned family members to talk to ex-prisoners to find out what prison is really like.

Sadly FAMILIES OF AR PRISONERS SUPPORT can not offer financial support.

For more information contact

FAMILIES OF AR PRISONERS SUPPORT
BM Box 2407
London
WC1N 3XX
Tel: 0797 955 2448
E.Mail: family.support@iname.com

MESSAGE FOR JUSTIN SAMUEL

Hello NA-A.L.F.S.G,

My son is Justin Samuel. He is currently a federal fugitive for letting some minks go. You can read about him in the article I found on the web and pasted below. I'm sure that you have seen this before.

"A federal grand jury in Madison, Wisconsin has returned an indictment charging Peter Young and Justin Samuel, both from Washington State, with animal enterprise terrorism and unlawful interference with interstate commerce.

The indictment alleges that in October '97 the two attacked fur farms and released livestock with the intent to cause significant economic damage to the farms. In addition, it alleges overt acts in three states as part of a conspiracy to engage in extortion by attempting to coerce the farmers to close their businesses rather than face the threat of further economic losses as a result of their attacks.

The overt acts alleged in the six-count indictment include conducting surveillance on numerous farms and the release of breeding stock. Young and Samuel face a maximum penalty of 20 years on each of four counts, and one year on each of the other two counts. A statement issued by the U.S. Attorney's office stated, "This indictment reflects the determination of the law enforcement community and my office to address criminal activity designed to curtail or shut down a lawful industry, such as the conduct alleged in this indictment." -Peggy Lautenschlager.

Anyway, as it turns out Justin has not communicated with his family for over a year. And we (Mom, Dad, and brother) are very worried about him. If you have any ideas about ways to put the word out to him to just let any of us know that he is ok it would be greatly appreciated. We love and miss him very much.

Thanks, Bob Samuel

Justin's father also informs us that not a day goes by that he doesn't think, dream, and sometimes cry about Justin. He writes, "Justin will be 21 on December 31, 1999, and at this point in time it looks like we won't be able to share this important event. It was always something the family had looked forward to, with the century change and all it will be a tough time for our family.

"It is very sad for all of us that we are not sharing our lives. At 52 years old I have come to appreciate this more than ever. We miss him and are very worried about him. What ever help and support he may need or want he can rely on us for it."

To Justin, from all of us at the Supporters Group: we wish you well, where ever you are! Stay safe, take care!

YOUNG RECIDIVIST'S FOR THE A.L.F.

The countdown has started...

Allo A.L.F.S.G.

My name is Catherine, I receive the *Underground* and I would like to say thanks. I did a drawing for publication if you want. I'm not very talented but I did my utmost. I speak French and I hope you understand what I want to say. For two years you didn't forget me and I'm very grateful. I'm in jail for the young, and the time is very long. I hate to draw but I want to do something for you and I don't have any money. Thanks a lot and take care!

Catherine Leblanc
Quebec

COME ON FOLKS! SUPPORT THE PRESS OFFICE!

Dear *Underground*,
As most readers of *Underground* know, the ALF now has an eloquent spokesperson in Katie Fedor, North American ALF Press Officer. The service Katie provides is invaluable, explaining ALF actions widely and cogently to a media who distributes her words to a public ready to hear and consider animal liberation arguments.

ALF actions are arguably the most effective method of gaining media attention for animal rights issues. But if media accounts simply relate actions, a chance to explain and gain public support has been lost. For example, a news account which says simply, "A veal slaughterhouse burned to the ground," or worse "A veal slaughterhouse burned to the ground and now little Jimmy won't get his operation," is perhaps worse than no media report at all. However, a media report which explains WHY anyone, animal liberationist or homemaker next door who is sick of the screaming animals, would burn a veal slaughterhouse to the ground-now that is a useful media report.

A small advertisement in a medium sized paper costs thousands of dollars. An article which raises issues does a better job than an advertisement of raising animal issues in the public consciousness. An Associated Press article has a media value of tens of thousands of dollars, or millions of dollars if it hits national news television programs, in terms of its ability to get the public talking about animal rights issues. The voice of animal liberation should be a part of every one of those articles.
Every ALF action has national media potential. The question is, will the article simply report the action; or will it, through the grace of Katie Fedor, tell readers WHY animal liberationists put their freedom on the line for animal rights?

I am writing to ask people to sponsor the ALF Press Office. Right now, Katie has to hold a full-time, non-animal rights job to pay her bills. Our movement should be able to fund one person to work on ALF publicity full-time. We should be able to buy her the equipment she needs, a clipping service, and media guidebooks.

I don't make a lot of money, but I have pledged to send Katie a check monthly. If enough of us with a bit of disposable income (and I know that many readers have no disposable income) took Katie's role seriously, we could allow her to quit her non-animal rights job and focus on animal issues with all her energies. The possibilities are endless, from a mailing to every major paper and talk-show in the country to a media database of sympathetic journalists and a letter writing alert for all articles which do appear.

The animal exploiters have literally thousands of generously funded media and public relations officials. Shouldn't the ALF have one full-time media representative?

A Supporter

Send donations to the new Press Office address: P.O.Box 21598, Little Italy Postal Outlet, Vancouver, B.C. V5N 5T5 Canada

Oh--and of course, don't forget to send your anonymous alerts

Ed note: there have been a few changes with the Press Office - Katie is still very active with it, but with recent Grand Jury developments taking place in MN (more on this elsewhere in the magazine), Katie has passed things on to the new Press Officer, David Barbarash. The writer is correct that the Press Office needs your support. Without it, the P.O. cannot continue to function. The Press Office has moved to the address above, and can also be contacted at: 604-805-5479 or emailed at naalfpo@tao.ca

THANK YOU FOR SUPPORT

Dear NAALFSG,
Oh, I thank you! I read my very first issue of *Underground* last summer and what a neat surprise to see your article about ME on page 14! To read, after all these years that I am NOT ALONE! When I was falsely imprisoned in '92 I tried with all my energy to connect with other animal activists ... I failed. By '98 I'd given up. I was the only vegan activist left on the prison, I'd been buried alive and no-one had even noticed. But now I see I was wrong! I feel so much less alone now, here in this hell of sadistic, sick, sociopathic, ethically-challenged, power-mad and disgusting meat eaters.

My time in InsaneWorld, alone, has been long indeed ... but now I'm not alone anymore!. There are all the super people I read about in Underground who help the animals like I wish I still could, and the lovely, kind readers who wrote so many supportive letters to me! Readers sent stamped envelopes and offer so much more - vitamins, vegan food, books, anything I might ask for - so nice! Animal activists are the best people. I have some new friends, good ones!

Now that I've received your Winter '98 issue of *Underground*, I wish also to express my boundless gratitude for your "Fran Thompson Update!" But all I can do is say THANK YOU for the ink!

For the animals,
Fran Thompson 93341
Nebrska Center for Women
1107 Recharge Rd., York
NE 68467-8003 USA

Fran Thompson is an animal welfare/rights activist in jail for the self-defence killing of a suitor-turned-stalker.

ALF DOCUMENTARY IN THE WORKS

Dear, NAALFSG,
In May, I will begin shooting a feature-length (2 hour) ALF documentary, "MAKE EVERY DAY COUNT FOR FREEDOM: The Story of the Animal Liberation Front in Their Own Words." The film is to cover the ENTIRE history of the ALF, from 1978 to the present. The entire project will be filmed on broadcast-quality, high resolution digital media.

Myself and the other activists working on this project posses the equipment, the energy, and the time necessary to make this the best ALF film yet. We are working hard to have this film featured in the Sundance Film Festival -- the largest independent film festival in the world.

Unfortunately, we have almost no ALF video footage at all -- video footage that is ESSENTIAL for making this groundbreaking documentary. Would it be possible for any readers of *UNDERGROUND* Magazine willing to share available video footage, photos, or press clippings to mail them to me?
My address is:
David Wilson
Director of Media Relations, Utah Animal Rights Coalition
PO Box 1681 Layton, UT 84040
Thank you for your support. For the animals,David Wilson
(See the back page of Underground for an ad for this movie project)

AROUND THE WORLD - AND GROWING!

Greetings Friends!
Sorry it took so long to advise you all I got my Winter 98-99 issue: Boy the fur farms are getting hit all over the WORLD! Its great to have the A.L.F., E.L.F., Earth First! And not just in my USA but your Canada, Finland, England, Ireland, Germany, Austria - my Grandfather and Grandmother's Spain - I wish they were alive to read your newsletter - it would bring joy to their stressed out minds (its always Kill, Kill all over - either human or animals!). With all the people around the world who can't stand this any more - from Norway, Poland, Italy, Sweden, Netherlands, Finland and New Zealand (Ok, I wrote Finland twice), but that's still 14 NATIONS, not 14 People against the ugly practice of destroying life. Stay Strong, and for all you people do - thank you!

PS: I've got a wait of 5 months before the Supreme Court of California, waiting for a response for this innocent man - it's coming. Later!
Sincerely,
Victor Trevino #J18382-D2-108
Salinas Valley St. Prison, Box 1060, Soledad, Cal. 93960-1060 USA

LOOKING FOR CONTACTS

To the NAALFSG
My name is Jarrod Coffill. Right now I am an inmate in a Mass. prison, serving a 6 month sentence for an assault and battery charge. This is a long story but basically I was protecting my grandfather's land.

One evening last fall I was visiting my grandfather, who lives alone at his house. He owns a good piece of land is western MA. He cannot walk that well so I acted as a guide for him so that he could go out into the forest for a walk. We noticed two men in a truck dumping what turned out to be asbestos shingles into a shallow ditch. After confronting the two men about the incident a fight broke out and because of their ignorance, here I am, and the men go unpunished.

I am a big supporter of E.F! but I have no addresses or contacts while I am here. I would appreciate some correspondence if you could work this for me I would be very grateful.

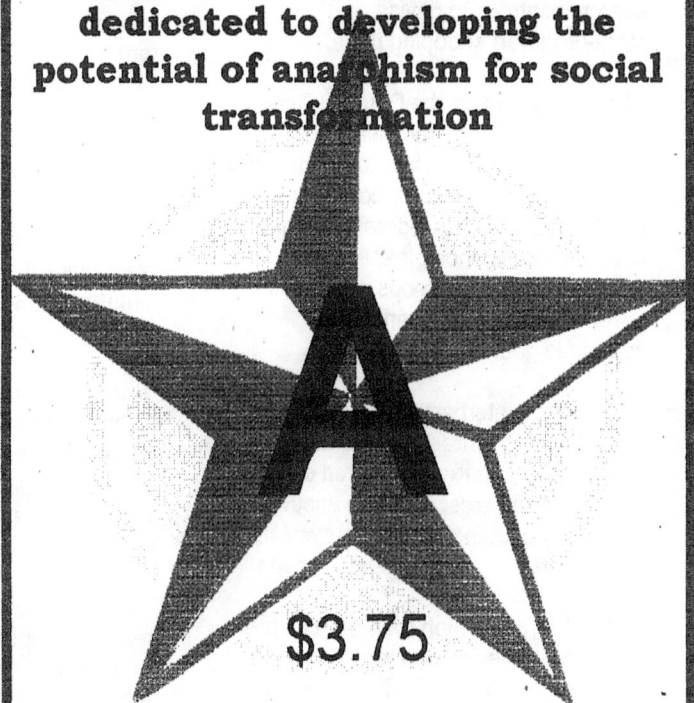

That's all for now,
Jarrod Coffill
269 Treble Cove Rd., Billerica MA, 01862 USA

News Briefs

POWERFUL NEW TOOLS FOR SPYING ON YOU

OTTAWA - Canada's electronic spy agency is quietly bankrolling the development of cutting-edge systems that can identify voices, analyse printed documents and zero in on conversations about specific topics. Documents show the Communications Security Establishment has enlisted the help of several leading Canadian research institutes to devise state-of-the-art snooping tools.

CSE, an agency of the Defence Department, collects and processes telephone, fax and computer communications of foreign states, corporations and individuals. The federal government uses the intelligence gleaned from the data to support troops abroad, catch terrorists and further Canada's economic goals.

CSE and counterpart agencies in the United States, Britain, Australia and New Zealand share intercepted communications of interest with one another, effectively creating a global surveillance web, according to intelligence experts.

CSE's interest in high-tech devices that help locate specific conversations and documents is a clear indication the five-member alliance collects and sifts large volumes of civilian traffic, said Bill Robinson, a researcher in Waterloo, Ont., who has long studied the spy agencies.

"This technology is needed to process vast communications streams when you're hunting for nuggets within it."

Robinson said the devices have legitimate uses, but hold "potentially frightening" implications for people's privacy as the technology advances.

"They'll be able to do things they never could've done in the past."

The Centre for Pattern Recognition and Machine Intelligence, located at Concordia University in Montreal, received $355,000 to develop two systems
for CSE that automatically analyse printed documents, such as faxes, once they are digitally captured in a computer data bank.

The first system, completed early last year, quickly determines the language of a document, said the centre's C. Y. Suen.

"Some humans may have problems in distinguishing Spanish from Portuguese, for example, or Spanish from Italian," he said. "So what we have developed is a system that can do it automatically."

The second device electronically searches captured documents for distinct features, including logos, photos, text or signatures.

Combining the two systems enables a user, for example, to search a data bank for Japanese documents containing photos, or Russian faxes with signatures.

can you tell me what this is all about, sergent?
Be reasonable at first...

Records obtained by media sources under the Access to Information Act show CSE commissioned several other projects during the last two years. They include:

(*) An $84,981 contract with the University of Waterloo in Ontario for the "development of multilingual computer speech recognition systems."

(*) A $115,000 agreement with the University of Quebec at Chicoutimi toresearch "speaker identification" procedures.

(*) Work by the Centre de Recherche Informatique de Montreal on "topic spotting" - a means of identifying the subject of a conversation. The $150,393 contract was the most recent of several awarded to CRIM.

CSE spokesman Kevin Mills did not provide information on specific goals of the projects, but allowed: "In general, any research that we're funding has some kind of interest for CSE."

The agency has been working on voice- and phrase-detection systems for at least a decade. The documents, however, show the research continues, with some devices yet to be perfected.

CSE and its four international partner agencies use computers capable of recognising intercepted messages containing specified names, addresses, telephone numbers and other key words or numbers, says a new report on surveillance technology, by Scottish researcher Duncan Campbell.

In addition, intelligence agencies are using systems that recognise the "voiceprint" or speech pattern of targeted individuals, though the technology is not yet fully reliable.

DUTCH EARTH LIB ACTIVIST SENTENCED TO 15 MONTHS

MAY/99
UTRECHT - A 37 year old earth lib activist was sentenced to 15 months prison sentence, with 5 months of the sentence to be served on probation. As part of the "Earth Liberation Team" (MBT in Dutch) the activist was charged with the sabotage of large numbers of expensive new cars, in a protest of their impact on the environment. The damages totalled half a million Dutch guilders.

LAST OF CHATHAM 3 NOW FREE

Gary Yourofsky, the last of the Chatham 3 to go before the courts for his part in a March 30th 1997 raid against the Ebert's Fur Farm, was sent to jail on April 27. Yourosfsky was sentenced to six months in jail after being convicted of helping free 1,500 mink from the Chatham fur farm.

Highlights of the trial included the cross-examination of Alan Hoffman, Gary's perfidious uncle who has testified against him. Steve Rogin, Gary's attorney, damaged Hoffman's credibility by highlighting numerous contradictory statements that he made in his written, videotaped and on-the-stand testimony. For instance, Hoffman claimed that there was a meeting - two weeks prior to the raid - that took place between all of the co-accused. Yet, when Det. Maddocks asked Hoffman during his written confession if he had ever met Pat and Hilma before this incident, Hoffman replied, "Never." Rogin also got Hoffman to admit further details about the deal between him and the Crown Attorney to testify against me in exchange for a $5,000 fine.

Moreover, when the Crown Attorney re-examined Hoffman, both made a huge blunder. It appeared that they had a scripted Q & A about the deal ... but Hoffman answered his part incorrectly. She queried him about the deal and Hoffman accidentally said that if he was sentenced before the trial, he would NOT come back to testify ... which completely contradicts his earlier statements about wanting to tell the truth and being veracious and upstanding.

The owner of Eberts Farm, Roger McClellan, also took the stand. He spoke of how the minks enjoyed their little prisons on his farm and NOT the freedom that was doled out on March 31, 1997. He made the following torpid comments:

1) When 1,018 of the 1,542 minks were recaptured, he said he had to take the chance of mating some of them over again in order "to get the best production out of the minks."

2) When he saw hundreds of liberated minks, he said it was "wrong for minks to be running on the ground. They belong in cages."

3) When referring to the light deception on the farm, i.e., bright lights being turned on from 4 a.m. - 8 a.m. everyday in order to trick the minks into believing days are longer so they will go into their mating season quicker, he said the lights "help the animals during their gestation period. And they seem to like it."

Before receiving his sentence, Gary made the following speech to the court:

I stand before this court without trepidation, without timidity, because the truth cannot be suppressed today and the truth will not be compromised. Mohandas Gandhi, one of the most benevolent people to ever grace this earth, once said, "Even if you are only one person ... the truth is still the truth."

The dilemma we face today is whether this court chooses to acknowledge the truth. The following statement is for everyone's edification. One day every enslaved animal will obtain their freedom and the animal rights movement will succeed because Gandhi also proclaimed that "All throughout history the way of truth and love has always won. There have been murderers and tyrants -- and at times they have seemed invincible -- but in the end they always fall ... always."

The true devoted humanitarians who are working towards the magnanimous goal of achieving freedom for animals cannot be stopped by unjust laws. As long as humans are placed on a pedestal above non-humans, injustice to animals will fester because without universal equality one type of equality will always create another type of inequality. There will be no compromise here to-day because the truth cannot be compromised. My presence in this courtroom today is paradoxical. I ask this court ... If it is NOT a crime to torture, enslave and murder animals, then how can it be a crime to free tortured, enslaved and soon-to-be-murdered ani-mals? Humankind must climb out of its abyss of callousness, its abyss of apathy and its abyss of greed. Enslaving and killing ani-mals for human satisfaction can never be justified. And the fur industry must understand that the millions of manual neck-breakings, anal and genital electrocutions, mass gassings, drowning and toxic chemical injections can never be justified. And, the snaring of millions of free-roaming animals in steel jaw leghold traps, who die slow, horrific deaths is unjustifiable, as well.

There will be no compromise ... for the truth cannot be compromised. The schism that this court has created between the five co-accused has been sealed.

If I am convicted through my volition and in a symbolic protest of the unjust conditions hat animals endure ... a hunger strike will begin tomorrow at 7:30 a.m.

For every mink that ever languished in a tiny cage and was savagely murdered at The Eberts Fur Farm ... I will go hungry. And for the 40 million other animals world-wide that have the skin ripped off their backs in a disgusting display of barbarity, in the name of vanity ... I will go hungry And if this court expects me to experience an apostasy -- meaning an abandoning of my beliefs ... it's sadly mistaken. In April of '97 ... when I was incarcerated for 10 days in a Chatham jail ... I briefly experienced ... vicariously ... what a caged animal goes through. And thanks to that 10-day bail hearing ... my empathy for every mistreated animal intensified.

No matter what I go through during my incarceration and hunger strike ... will be nothing compared to the everlasting torture that innocent animals endure on a daily basis.

And if this court is alarmed by my honesty, let me close with a quote from slave abolitionist William Lloyd Garrison. "I will be as harsh as the truth and as uncompromising as justice. On this subject, I do not wish to think or speak or write with moderation, I am in earnest. I will not equivocate. I will not excuse. I will not retreat a single inch. And I will be heard. The apathy of the people is enough to make every statue leap from its pedestal and hasten the resurrection of the dead. My influence shall be felt in coming years, not perniciously but beneficially, not as a curse, but as a blessing and posterity will bear testimony that I was right."

There will be no compromise here today because the truth cannot be compromised.

Ten days into his announced 40-day liquid-only hunger strike at the Elgin Middlesex Detention Center, Gary faced threats from prison guards concerned that other inmates were joining him on the strike. Guards threw him into solitary confinement/isolation and no visitors, phone calls or reading material were allowed. He was told he would have 30-60 days added to his stay and that he faced doing the rest of his time (nearly 6 months) in isolation if he didn't begin eating. Gary only agreed to eat a specially prepared vegan meal after guards threatened to retaliate against other pris-oners (identities unknown) who joined the strike by adding time to their sentences, and throwing them into isolation.

Gary was granted early parole and was back amongst his activist friends in the free-world on July 12. With his humour and deter-mination still intact, Gary spoke before his release about the antisipation of the moment he could join his dog for a nice (long) run in the open fields.

From all of us, welcome back, Gary!

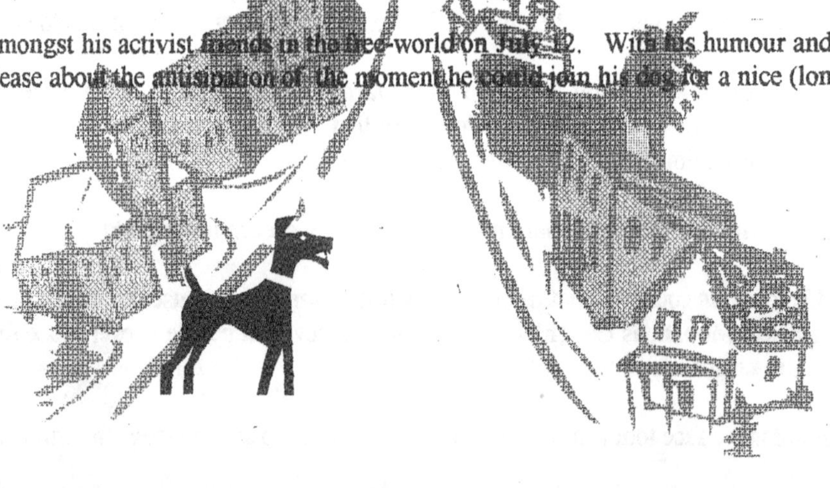

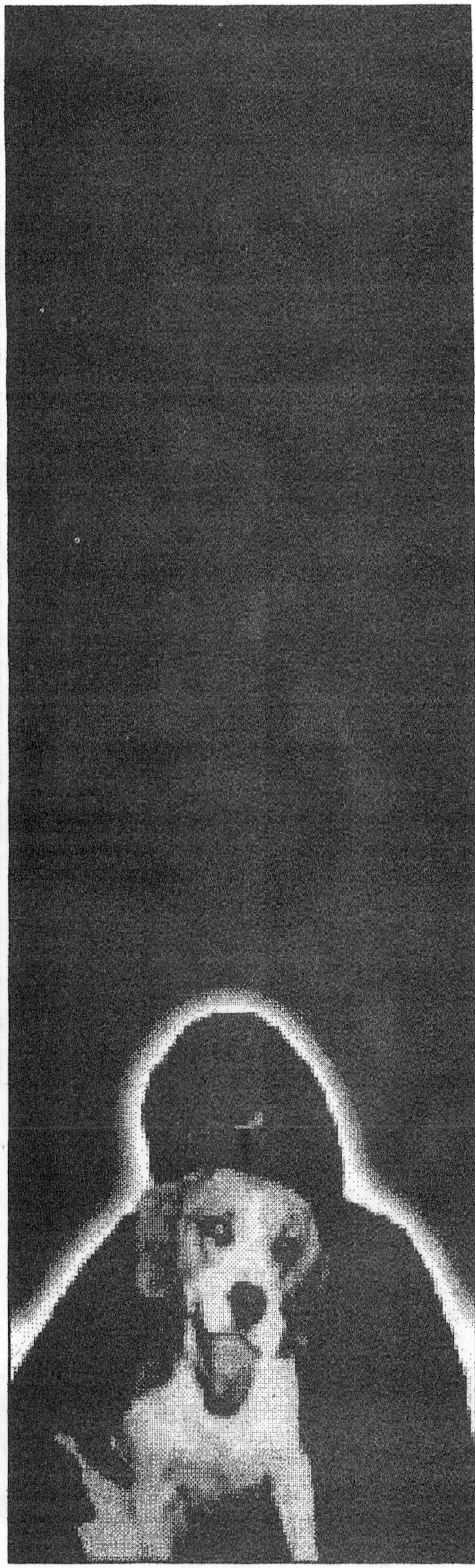

Finnish animal liberation trials

MARCH/99

During the week of 15-19 March, a total of 10 activists and one snitch went on trial for three separate beagle liberations, one alleged breach of the domestic peace on a Finnish fur farm and two counts aiding and abetting in two separate fur farms raids and handling stolen goods (giving a home to a liberated beagle).

Day one saw the trial of three activists who were on trial for breach of the domestic peace after they had been caught 200 m from a fur farm in Kuhmo, north Finland. The farmer alleges that the activists caused "cub losses" and was asking about 30 000 marks ($6000 US) compensation. However, after the testimony given by the farmer, it was clearly shown that there were no cub losses and that particular year the cub result was higher than the year before.

On day two, nine people (including the snitch) on trial for liberation and handling stolen goods. In these raids a total of five beagles were given their freedom. One person was accused of participating in three raids, one in two raids and the other three for the third raid.

The first trial was for the liberation of one beagle who was one of 6 being used in bone experiments. The beagle's thigh bones were sawed in half and then allowed to heal. Timo Nevalainen, who is director of the breeder took the stand and in true style and high drama eloquently told the court how this groundbreaking research would save people from great pain etc. In one sense, vivisection was on trial and the activists' lawyers gave Nevelainen quite a grilling. He also talked about xylitol experiments he was doing on beagles.

Witness for the activists was a well-known biologist who specialises in dogs and wild animals. He spoke about how the conditions at the breeder cannot satisfy the needs of any dog. He spoke mainly about the need for exercise and the lack of stimulus in the confined space they were kept in. He also stated that although the breeder is built according to the regulations, it is still against the spirit of the animal protection law.

Aiding and abetting three fur farms raids in Pohjanmaa in September 1997 was the theme of the last day. A 21 year old woman was charged for renting a car which was allegedly used in these raids. But the prosecution had to admit that there was no real evidence to prove the case and all the evidence was purely circumstantial.

The prosecution was seeking unconditional jail sentences while the defence was asking for fines or small probation sentences. Four of the defendants were also in the Orimattila trial and were serving four months probation. Also, two of the accused have promotional sentences from a couple years back from criminal damage to a fur store and a civil disobedience action against fur selling de-

A Liberation To Be Remembered

By: Katie Fedor and Kevin Kjonaas

World Week for Laboratory Animals for the year of 1999 started early with a surprise visit by the Animal Liberation Front. On April 5 the A.L.F. liberated 116 animals from two University of Minnesota vivisection laboratories. A communiqué was sent by the A.L.F. claiming full responsibility for the strategic non-violent action stating that "27 pigeons, 48 mice, 36 rats, and 5 salamanders will never be harmed again at the hands of vivisectors."

Along with the animals being liberated, economic sabotage was employed to decrease profits to the animal abusers in both Elliot Hall (Psychology Building) and Lions Research Building. The communiqué states that cages and equipment were damaged, research documents were taken and are being reviewed, and walls were painted with animal liberation messages.

Almost all equipment on the 4th and 2nd floors of Lions Research Building was severely damaged. "Vivisectors' own video footage of experiments were taken along with computer files and research notebooks...this shows that lab raids can still be successfully completed," states the communiqué.

The University of Minnesota is known for torturing 130,000 animals every year with wasted taxpayer money. Four medical doctors from around the country denounced vivisection as harmful to humans and animals and exposed the U of MN in the process. These doctors issued statements to the media via news releases to correct the many false claims from Vivisectors. In one such statement, Dr. Ray Greek openly challenged any vivisector to a debate on the University campus. Not surprisingly, this challenge remains unanswered. Earlier this year on Feb. 18, Dr. Greek lectured at the University of Minnesota on the scientific invalidity of animal research. After repeated attempts to find someone to defend vivisection, Dr. Greek lectured for almost two hours before 200 people against animal research.

In addition to the medical doctors, some of whom are former vivisectors themselves, a national animal research investigator also released a statement that scrutinised vivisectors' claims and found contradictions between earlier statements given in CRISP reports. In Defence of Animals also stepped forward to question erroneous statements made by animal researchers.

With the increased pressure from medical doctors coming forward to dispute the public relations department at the University, the U of MN started scrambling for cover by retracting their false claims in newspapers. Originally, the public relations department said that non animal research was also destroyed in the A.L.F. action. This was completely false and later retracted by the University of Minnesota in the media.

(Continued on page 14)

partment store. In the end, despite this, it was generally all good news for the activists when sentencing was made.

Case 1: "attempted fur farm raid" or breach of domestic peace at a fur farm up north in Kuhmo. Charges against three fellows were dropped because there was no case. The "attempted raid" was only in the prosecutions head and nothing illegal happened. Three men were spotted hanging out near a mink and fox farm and police was called in. But it was broad daylight, no one was masked etc. There was no evidence on the prosecutions claim that the activists were attempting to raid the fur farm.

Case 2: Three liberations of beagles from karttula vivisection center between November 1996 and September 1997. The case was clear against one accused who admitted all three raids. One person was done for two raids and three for the last raid where four beagles were liberated. So the outcome was pretty much what was expected: one man, 29, received 5 months probation for his part of three raids, another man, 24, got 4 months probation and three others, a man, 23, woman, 22, man, 25, all received three months probation for liberating four dogs and criminal damage. Due to the grass with outstanding memory, a bunch of people were charged with possession of stolen goods, in other words, giving a home to a liberated dog or transporting dogs from a "safe house" to a permanent home, got fines of 500 FIM (about $100 US).

Case 3: Aiding and abetting in three fur farm raids in Pohjanmaa area. The same woman who was on trial for taking part to one of the liberations was also charged for renting a car which was allegedly used in raiding three fur farms in September 1997. Hundreds of foxes and minks were liberated on that night from three different fur farms in fur farm intensive Pohjanmaa area. The case was shaky to begin with so the charges were dropped due to the lack of evidence. @

A LIBERATION TO REMEMBER cont: Along with countering the fallacies from the Universities public relations department and vivisectors, we had another problem to contend with. Freeman Wicklund from the Minneapolis based Animal Liberation League joined vivisectors in denouncing the liberation of 116 animals from their prisons. Wicklund was quoted in newspapers as saying "people who are concerned about animals are upset about this action...it closes a lot of doors, hopefully people realise the actions on Monday only represent a small fraction of the animal rights community."

On Minnesota Public Radio, a Press Office spokesperson was followed on air by Wicklund who was joined by vivisectors condemning the liberation. Wicklund said he wanted to reassure his contributors that he did not support this action. He has also informed local activists that he is able to denounce the A.L.F. on a full time basis after receiving a $12,500 six month grant from the Center for Compassionate Living. This is to be expected after the original 1998 press conference where Wicklund condemned the A.L.F. and the Alaskan Furs destruction.

The Press Office continued with the important work at hand when a videotape of the action taken by the A.L.F. was sent to animal rights organisations.

While inside the laboratories the A.L.F. videotaped their courageous rescue of the caged animals, the destruction of the cages and equipment used in the abusive research process, and the painted A.L.F. slogans on the walls. The video lasted approximately eleven minutes and was without any sound. It showed approximately five individuals all dressed identical, from flashlight headbands down to matching sneakers. On particularly horrid detail the A.L.F. focused in on with the video were the "no food" signs placed on the cages of the rats and pigeons that were freed. Of course the University tried to explain the these signs were their to discourage researchers from feeding the animals twice, and signified a "special" diet of the animals, but we all know of the notorious kinds of deprivation experiments that goes on in psychiatric laboratories.

The original A.L.F. tape was sent to the old A.L.F. Press Office PO Box, and was subsequently confiscated by the police, supposedly after it was received and viewed by the renter of the old PO Box. The Press Office has found this story to be quite suspicious considering this is the only time that A.L.F. PO mail has not been forwarded to the new address. Currently the Press Office is encouraging that mail fraud charges be pressed against the citizen who supposedly opened and viewed mail not addressed to him.

The A.L.F. sent the same video to a couple animal rights groups across the country. They in turn rushed delivered a copy of the A.L.F. video to the Press Office. The video was duplicated and a press conference was called for its public release. The A.L.F. Press Office held the press conference on the University of Minnesota Campus, and invited all local media representatives. Also attending were two University Police officers. During the Press Conference the video was shown and media packs were distributed that included all press releases for the action, and statements from a number of Physicians from across the country that supported the action and countered all University claims about the validity of animal research. The media, of course, ignored all conduct of journalistic professionalism and hurled biased questions and personal insults at an A.L.F. spokesperson. At one point, the police officer present sparred with the spokesperson over the use of direct action, but was quickly silenced when he could not explain intelligently how this action is different from that of other "criminals" like Harriet Tubman, whom time has vindicated. The coverage of the press conference, as with all mainstream coverage of the event thus far, was biased towards the University, but did use quite a few of the Press Office's quotes.

Exactly two weeks after the A.L.F. raid, the Minnesota State Senate ignored the Constitution and passed a bill increasing the jail time and fine for anyone convicted on such a crime. This bill went beyond the standard political knee jerking this time, and also targeted the Press Office. The bill, if made into law, intends also to prosecute any supporter of the A.L.F., who claims responsibility for the anonymous group and explains their actions, as a gross misdemeanour. This bill was also originally denoted as retroactive so that the Press Office could be prosecuted for speaking out on this last action, and leaves open the possibility that the University of Minnesota could sue the two Press Officers for triple the damages caused by the A.L.F..

Fortunately several aspects of the final bill were removed by a conference committee before being passed by the Senate and House of Representatives. It is not retroactive and the criminal section was removed. Thankfully it has been watered down considerably from the original intent and awaits being signed into law by the Governor.

Shortly after the Anti-Press Office bill was introduced, Kevin Kjonaas who was a Press Office Spokesperson for the A.L.F. liberation had his house raided by nine FBI agents on May 5.

For two hours the FBI searched through and stole personal belongings such as journals, notebooks, school homework, and clothing while his roommate was forced to sit in a corner of their home.

Just two days later, on May 7 he was also served a subpoena to attend a MN Grand Jury on June 14, 1999 that is "investigating" the University of Minnesota liberation. The Press Office has retained a lawyer who is the immediate past president of the National Lawyers Guild and a professor of constitutional law and first amendment rights at a local law school. We have developed a solid legal strategy to fight the Grand Jury and he is assembling a legal team.

The communiqué from the A.L.F. ends "our hearts go out to our friends that could not be taken, their futures depend on you...Act now." Thanks to all who have given such unconditional support during these times of severe government harassment for the Press Office. Thanks especially to the North American A.L.F. Supporters' Group, Darren Thurston, and Frontline Info. Service for their enormous continued support.

Please support the Press Office in the following ways:

A legal defence fund has been established by the North American A.L.F. Supporters' Group to continue the vital work of explaining A.L.F. actions to the public via the media and to fight the government harassment.

Please send donations to:

North American A.L.F. Supporters' Group
Box 69597, 5845 Yonge St., Willowdale,
Ontario, M2M 4K3, Canada
(Please mark donations for A.L.F. Press Office)

Please write to the Center for Compassionate Living who has given Freeman Wicklund a $12,500 grant which is renewable on a six month basis, and ask that they reconsider funding him. Through this grant, Wicklund joins vivisectors in denouncing A.L.F. actions on a full time basis.

Center for Compassionate Living
Zoe Weil and Rae Sikora
207-374-8808 phone
297-374-8851 fax
email: CCL@acadia.net
PO Box 1209
Blue Hill ME 04614

SUSPECTS IN SLC BOMBINGS WON'T FACE LIFE IN JAIL

Activists accused of animal-rights "terrorism" will not face mandatory life prison sentences if convicted. U.S. District Judge Thomas Greene has ruled that Andrew N. Bishop, 24, Ithaca, N.Y. and Sean Albert Gauschy, 23, Salt Lake City; cannot be sentenced to life for their part in five separate bombings of the Fur Breeders Agricultural Co-operative in 1997. Alexander David Slack, 23, of Sandy was also accused in the bombings, but tragically Alex has taken his own life.

The bombings did not result in any injuries. However, a federal law allows enhanced prison sentences when explosives are used. In cases involving one bomb, the enhancement calls for a minimum mandatory 30-year prison term. If the additional sentence involves two or more instances, the extra term is for life. But Judge Greene called the late-night bombing "one violent episode" for which the men could be charged with one count each under the enhancement statutes. However, Greene rejected a defence motion to merge the bombing charges into just one crime.

Federal prosecutor David Schwendiman said his office will ask Justice Department officials whether they should appeal Greene's consolidation of the enhancement charges. Schwendiman said there are special considerations within the U.S. 10th Circuit, which includes Utah and Oklahoma, because of the deadly bombing of the federal building in Oklahoma City.

Another Fur Breeders defendant, INFORMANT Douglas Joshua Ellerman, 20, Salt Lake City, pleaded guilty last year to helping plant the bombs. He was sentenced to seven years and two months in prison and ordered to pay $750,000 in restitution. Ellerman has given evidence against others he says were participants in A.L.F. actions.

Ellerman's older brother, 22-year-old INFORMANT Clinton Colby Ellerman, is expected to plead guilty to allegations he made the bombs, Schwendiman said. A sixth suspect, Adam Troy Peace, 21, Huntington Beach, Calif. is charged with attempting to bomb the co-operative six days earlier.

ANIMAL RIGHTS ACTIVISTS FREE MINK IN PROTEST TURNED RAID

SEATTLE FUR EXCHANGE RATTLED, MINK FARMERS RACE HOME

FEBUARY/99:

MONROE, Wash. -- Dozens of mink were briefly freed when animal rights activists took their anger to a Seattle area fur farm. Protesters attending the Seattle Fur Exchange drove up to the farm, about 25 miles northeast of Seattle, and five people jumped a fence and opened cages, Snohomish County sheriff's spokeswoman Jan Jorgensen told media.

Some 150 to 200 animals, worth about $250 each, were released. Five people in their teens and early 20s were held for investigation of burglary and theft. A day earlier, two protesters were arrested in a demonstration outside the Seattle Fur Exchange in suburban Renton. The exchange, the largest fur auction house in the nation and third-largest in the world, was conducting its four-day semi-annual auction that week. Snohomish County ranks eighth nation-wide in mink production with 63,420 pelts in 1997, Farm Census figures show.

The day before the auction began, 80 protesters gathered at the hotel that the furriers were staying in. As news cameras rolled, a coffin full of furs was set on fire. As the crowd became more energised, protesters stormed the front of the hotel and several expensive planters were smashed. Police threatened to pepper spray and club protesters, but the group moved away just in time. As the first protest ended at least one van load of activists was followed out of town by multiple police cars. The protesters were not pulled over, and apparently the police just wanted to make sure nothing else was going to happen.

Day two saw the first day of the auction with trapped skins going on the block. Two protesters were arrested early on as activists surrounded furriers cars that were coming into the auction. One protester was accused of beating on a vehicle, while another was grabbed by the neck and thrown to the ground by police. This vicious assault led to an angry response by the crowd, with lots of pushing and shoving by police.

Day three saw the first set of ranched mink skins going up for bid. On this day some buyers were going to bid through the Seattle Fur Exchange web page. These buyers lost out when the web page was brought down as the result of a virtual sit in by animal rights activists from around the world. Using a software called Flood Net, activists were able to bombard the web page with hits, bringing it to a halt. Morale among the industry was low, and their spokesperson Teressa Platt even left and went home.

That afternoon another protest took place at a nearby fur farm. As protesters arrived they learned that a teenage girl had been hit with a shovel and held at gun point by the fur farmer. Four others were in custody as well.

The fur industry claims that a mob of activists stormed the farm and released 200 mink in broad daylight. Many fur farmers attending the SXE left the auction in a panic to go home and guard their farms as a result. While many farmers have put in extensive security to protect their farms at night, they are unprepared for daytime assaults. Now they will have to take that into consideration when they put in $25,000 security systems.

While police held activists arrested at the farm, supporters carried out a well co-ordinated phone blockade of the Seattle Fur Exchange. This led to their phone being off the hook for hours at a time. Between the protests at the hotel, the auction house, and the fur farm, as well as the virtual sit in and the phone blockade, the fur industry took a beating they will not soon forget.

Skin prices were low, and many farms will not even break even. On top of that, the farmers are discouraged from having to drive threw a crowds of protesters to get to the auction, only to turn around to go home and guard their farms.

One member of the industry is being investigated for striking a member of the activists legal team with his car. More information will become available as that is investigated.

This was a very successful set of demo's and a round of thank you's go to everyone who took part. This includes the activists that were arrested, the Seattle locals that helped make this possible, the organisers and participants of the virtual sit in and the phone blockade and every person that showed up and spent days in the cold and rain fighting for animals.

Coalition to Abolish the Fur Trade
PO Box 822411
Dallas, TX 75382
CAFT13@aol.com

DIARY OF ACTIONS

The Diary of Action is intended to report the news of direct action for earth and animal liberation, not to encourage crime, etc. etc. All reports come from communiques, other publications, the internet and news reports. Some actions took place in time periods covered by other issues of *Underground*, but were not known about until recently.

CANADA

JANUARY/99: Toronto, ON -- McDonald's spray-painted with anti-meat slogans, including "McMurder," "McTorture," and "McDeath." -A.L.F.

JANUARY/99: Toronto, ON -- KFC spray-painted with red paint ("KFC=Death") and two KFC's had their double front doors locked together with thick chains and padlocks. -A.L.F.

JANUARY/99: Toronto, ON -- Pig slaughterhouse had slogans spray-painted on it, including "Pigs Die Here," "Murder House" and "Death!" - A.L.F.

JANUARY/99: Toronto, ON -- Four butcher shops were spray-painted and locks glued. -A.L.F.

JANUARY/99: Richmond Hill, ON -- Butcher shop hit by the A.L.F., walls were painted as was the store van. -A.L.F.

JANUARY/99: Toronto, ON -- Two meat packer trucks were spray-painted in the back parking lot of a Toronto slaughter-house. -A.L.F.

JANUARY/99: Toronto, ON -- A leather store mural was spattered with red paint. -A.L.F.

JANUARY/99: Toronto, ON -- Ten fur stores (Spadina Rd. and Bathurst St.) spray-painted and had locks glued. -A.L.F.

JANUARY/99: Toronto, ON -- Fur store on Adelaide St. was spray-painted three nights in a row. -A.L.F.

JANUARY/99: Aurora, ON -- A billboard for a duck slaughter-house (King Cole Ducks) was splattered with paint. -A.L.F.

JANUARY/99: Aurora, ON -- A chincilla fur farm sign was spay-painted. -A.L.F.

JANUARY/99: Location Undisclosed, ON -- A rabbit, duck and a chicken were all liberated from the brink of slaughter, from an animal auction/fair in Ontario. The A.L.F. cell involved does not want to say where from exactly because of the possibility of more animals being liberated in the future.

UNITED STATES

NOVEMBER 20/99: Dearborn, MI -- One male and two female turkeys were liberated from Greenfield Village (a museum/mock village complex owned by Capitalist/racist/fascist Ford Family). The turkeys were slated for dinner for the holidays. Local animal rights activists tried to negotiate release of the turkeys, but failed. The A.L.F. stepped in and they are now living in loving homes, enjoying happy lives without fear. This action was dedicated to Barry Horne. -A.L.F.

DECEMBER 2/98: Anerdson, IN - A.L.F. free 150+ breeding foxes from a fur farm.

DECEMBER 21/98: Southampton, PA - Hubert Furs has 3 windows and a glass door etched with "FUR KILLS" and "FUR IS DEAD" -A.L.F.

DECEMBER 26/98: Medford, OR - Communiqué from the ELF: "Happy fucking new year from the Earth Liberation Front! To celebrate the holidays we decided on a bonfire. Unfortunately for U.S. Forest Industries it was at their corporate headquarters office in Medford, Oregon. On the foggy night after Christmas when everyone was digesting their turkey and pie, Santa's ELFs dropped two five gallon buckets of diesel/unleaded mix and a one gallon jug with cigarette delays; which proved to be more than enough to get this party started. And after forty to fifty firefighters showed up to our party, they were unable to salvage anything, costing these greedy bastards half a million dollars. This was done in retribution for all the wild forests and animals lost to feed the wallets of greedy fucks like Jerry Bramwell, U.S.F.I. president. This action is payback and it is a warning, to all others responsible we do not sleep and we wont quit. For the future generations we will fight back! - E.L.F.

DECEMBER 30/98: Los Angeles, CA: A fur billboard on the corner of la Cienaga and Santa Monica blvd. was paint-bombed with organic bellpeppers filled with red paint. -A.L.F.

JANUARY 4/99: Woodland Hills, CA -- Woodland Hills Furriers Inc. (22941 Ventura Blvd.)was visited by the A.L.F. Slogans painted across the entire entrance included "40 dead animals = 1 fur coat" and "A.L.F. Windows were etched with "killers," "scum," "stop now" and "A.L.F.". No window was left unmarked. All locks were glued, in front and back. Two rocks marked with "killers beware... ALF" and "the ALF is watching" found their way through two windows followed by smoking devices that left the store engulfed in smoke. -A.L.F.

JANUARY 8/99: Teaneck, NJ - Locks glued at Cedar Lane Furs. - A.L.F.

JANUARY 8/99: Ridgewood, NJ -- Over a dozen 3/8" holes were drilled in the roof of Bon-Ton Furs to allow water from a heavy rain and snow melt to flow inside, hopefully damaging merchandise, equipment, etc. Approximately two ounces of butyric acid was poured through one of the holes. -A.L.F.

JANUARY 16/99: Wash., DC -- Rosendorf Evans Furs - 4 display windows etched.-A.L.F

JANUARY 16/99: Chevy Chase, MD -- Saks Jandel - 3 display windows etched. -A.L.F.

JANUARY 29/99: Chevy Chase, MD - Saks Jandel - butyric acid dispensed. -A.L.F.

JANUARY 30/99: Rockville, MD - Arby's Fast Food - locks glued. -A.L.F.

JANUARY 30/99: Gaithersburg, MD - Bares Bones Rib Joint - locks glued. -A.L.F.

JANUARY 30/99: Gaithersburg, MD - Chicken Out Restaurant - locks glued. -A.L.F.

JANUARY 30/99: Rockville, MD - Kentucky Fried Chicken - locks glued. -A.L.F.

JANUARY 30/99: Montgomery Village, MD - McDonald's - locks glued. -A.L.F.

JANUARY 30/99: Rockville, MD - Popeyes - locks glued. - A.L.F.

FEBRUARY 11/99: East Brunswick, NJ- Furs By Guarino's, 339 Rt. 18, was hit, activists left the words "Fur Is Murder" sprawled out in red paint across the store front.

FEBRUARY 13/99: Annandale, MN - A.L.F. visited Davidson's Fur Farm and released 6 fox (all that could be found). Mink sheds were empty and abandoned, and there were visible traces of cyotee and wolf having been kept at some point on the farm. Several fur farms have been discovered abandoned over the past few months, including:
KEITH FORTUNES, ATWATER MN
JOHNS RANCH, HAMIL MN
CANNON FALLS RANCH, CANNON FALLS MN

FEBRUARY 13/99: Philomath, OR -- The ALF attempted to raid the rabbit breeding facility owned by Lance and Nephi Patton, but unfortunately the owners have installed new security and a dog was roaming the premises. Activists discovered, however, the home and vehicle of Nephi Patton are still unprotected.

FEBRUARY 16/99: Warren, NJ -- Furs By Guarino van firebombed while parked in store owner's driveway (John Guarino, 45 Hillcrest Boulevard, Warren, NJ 07059, (908) 754-4394). - A.L.F.

FEBRUARY 24/99: Red Bank, NJ -- Winter's Furs had its front display window cracked and front door smashed with bricks, sounding an external alarm. - A.L.F.

FEBRUARY 24/99: Englishtown, NJ -- Classic Furs had numerous holes punched through display windows. Door and several windows completely shattered. - A.L.F.

FEBRUARY 24/99: Manalapan, NJ -- Fur and Leather Ranch had numerous holes punched through display windows. Door completely shattered. - A.L.F.

MARCH 2/99: Philadelphia, PA -- Bargain Furs has their security gate locks filled with glue. - A.L.F.

MARCH 3/99: Chevy Chase, MD -- Butyric acid dispensed in Miller's Furs.-A.L.F.

MARCH 3/99: Chevy Chase, MD -- Butyric acid dispensed in Gardenhaus Furs. -A.L.F.

MARCH 8/99: Burlington, NJ -- Burlington Coat Factory has 6 glass panels in their vestibule destroyed. One window etched

with "FUR KILLS." Slogans "KILLERS" "FUR IS DEAD" and "STOP SELLING FUR" were spray painted on the store walls. Until Burlington Coat Factory stops selling all fur and fur trim actions like these will continue. -A.L.F.

MARCH 9/99: Seattle, WA -- The A.L.F. attacked cars belonging to four furriers parked at the Embassy Suites Hotel during the Seattle Fur Exchange. Over four gallons of paint stripper was used, and the cars were then scraped down with steel wool. One vehicle had its tires punctured. The following morning a bomb hoax was phoned in to SFX.

MARCH 11/99: Minneapolis, MN -- the A.L.F paid visits to the following stores:
NEIMAN MARCUS, downtown, windows etched.
DAYTONS, downtown, windows etched.
SAKS FIFTH AVE, downtown, windows etched.
LA ROCKLER FUR COMPANY, downtown, windows etched and locks glued.
RIBNICKS FURS, downtown, windows etched
ALBRECHS FURS EDINA, downtown, windows etched and locks glued.

MARCH 12/99: Eatontown, NJ -- Macy's had all outside locks glued, four large windows smashed, and FUR KILLS spray painted in large, red letters visible from the highway. -A.L.F.

MARCH 12/99: Red Bank, NJ -- Winters Furs had their locks glued, and their door and front display window smashed. -A.L.F.

MARCH 17/99: Philadelphia, PA -- Meglio & Sons Furs has their locks filled with glue. -A.L.F.

MARCH 18/99: Philadelphia, PA -- Bargain Furs has their locks filled with glue. -A.L.F.

MARCH 27/99: Franklin, NJ - Six vehicles were firebombed at the Big Apple Circus, including two cabs connected to trailers carrying equipment which were completely destroyed. Also severely damaged were three flatbeds carrying equipment and one small vehicle. An establishment which enslaves others and causes them pain and suffering to perform degrading acts as a sick form of entertainment will not be tolerated. Until the Big Apple Circus decides not to profit from the exploitation of innocent animals, these actions will continue in each town they stop in. This action is dedicated to the Seattle 6.
NOTE: Firebombs were made of 1 gallon bottles filled with gasoline. Holes were drilled into the caps and candles (joke candles that can't be blown out) were inserted into the top of the containers. This method proved completely effective. A.L.F.

MARCH 29/99: Philadelphia, PA - Meglio & Sons Furs has 13 windows destroyed. The following slogans were etched into the windows: "FUR KILLS," "FUR IS DEAD," and "ALF." - A.L.F.

APRIL 1/99: Pine Brook, NJ -- Burlington Coat Factory paint-bombed. Actions will continue until Burlington stops supporting the bloody fur trade. -A.L.F.

APRIL 2/99: Teaneck, NJ -- Locks glued at Cedar Lane Furs. -A.L.F.

APRIL 5/99: Minneapolis, MN - A.L.F. started Lab Week early this year by raiding labs at the University of Minnesota. The following animals will never be harmed again at the hands of vivisectors: 48 MICE, 36 RATS, 25 PIGEONS, 5 SALAMANDERS.

From the communiqué: "ELLIOT HALL, THE PSYCHOLOGY RESEARCH BUILDING, WHERE THE ANIMALS WERE RESCUED FROM, HAD THE WALLS PAINTED WITH SLOGANS, CAGES AND EQUIPMENT DAMAGED, DOORS BROKEN AND RESEARCH DOCUMENTS WERE ALSO TAKEN AND ARE CURRENTLY BEING REVIEWED. LIONS RESEARCH BUILDING WAS ALSO VISITED AND HAD VIRTUALLY ALL EQUIPMENT ON THE 4TH AND 2ND FLOORS SEVERELY DAMAGED. VIVISECTORS OWN VIDEO FOOTAGE OF EXPERIMENTS WERE TAKEN ALONG WITH COMPUTER FILES AND RESEARCH NOTEBOOKS. THIS SHOWS THAT LAB RAIDS CAN STILL BE SUCCESSFULLY COMPLETED. A VIDEO ALONG WITH STILL PICTURES WILL BE ARRIVING TO SELECTED GROUPS WHICH SHOULD BE IMMEDIATELY RELEASED TO THE PUBLIC. OUR HEARTS GO OUT TO OUR FRIENDS THAT COULD NOT BE TAKEN THEIR FUTURES DEPEND ON YOU ...ACT NOW"

In addition to property damage and the loss of the animals, countless hours of research were destroyed in the action. University officials estimate the total cost of the damage will tally in the millions of dollars. Slogans were also left at the scene. Red spray paint reading "Vivisection is scientific fraud" and "A.L.F." greeted vivisectors the next morning. -A.L.F.

APRIL 5/99: Chevy Chase, MD -- three 3 display windows etched at fur shop -A.L.F.

APRIL 5/99: Washington, DC -- Rosendorf/Evans Furs, 5 display windows etched -A.L.F.

APRIL 5/99: Washington, DC -- Andriana's Furs, 4 display windows etched -A.L.F.

APRIL 21/99: Woodbridge, NJ -- Three display windows and front door smashed at Woodbridge Furs. -A.L.F.

APRIL 27/99: Woodbridge, NJ -- Three display windows and front door of Woodbridge Furs smashed with bricks bearing the message "Stop of Be Stopped" and signed A.L.F. The furriers seemed to be waiting in anticipation of the visit and rushed out to stop the activists, throwing a brick of their own. -A.L.F.

APRIL 23/99: San Francisco, CA -- Animal-rights demonstrators broke into three research labs at the University of California, shattering glass, overturning refrigerators and ruining at least one medical experiment, UCSF officials said. Four mice appeared to be missing from a neurology lab after a roaming group of demonstrators broke into the lab and confronted a UCSF researcher. Officials claim the disruption would mean "probably months" of scientific work lost.

APRIL 26/99: Bayonne, NJ -- Brick thrown through Gil's Furrier's display window. -A.L.F.

APRIL 26/99: Bayonne, NJ -- Bricks thrown through Famous Furs' center display window and glass door. -A.L.F.

APRIL 28/99: Philadelphia, PA -- Jacques Ferber Furs has their brand new window (in place less than 24hrs after being replaced from an attack on the 24th) etched with the word "DEAD." Also, the store front was covered with oil based red paint. -ALF.

MAY 2/99: Albequerque, NM-- Fur's by Michael has three windows etched, locks glued, and awning splattered with red paint.

MAY 2/99: Albequerque, NM-- Harper's Furs has five large display windows etched with "FUR IS MURDER" and "ALF". -A.L.F.

MAY 4/99: Washington, DC -- Andriana Furs hit: two display windows and two doors hit with etching cream.

MAY 5/99: Trenton, NJ -- Flemington Furs billboard paint-bombed. -A.L.F.

MAY 6/99: East Brunswick, NJ -- One display window at Furs by Guarino broken. A brick was thrown at the second display window, which did not break. -A.L.F.

MAY 8/99: Bayonne, NJ -- Gil's Furrier had their glass door, a small window above the door, and sign smashed out. The display window was damaged. -A.L.F.

MAY 8/99: East Brunswick, NJ -- Slogans painted at Furs by Guarino. Messages such as "FUR IS MURDER", "FUR KILLS", "STOP OR BE STOPPED", and "A.L.F." covered the walls. -A.L.F.

MAY 9/99: Eugene, OR -- A fire tore through a meat-packing business near the Eugene Airport, destroying a two-story office building, a shipping dock and a refrigeration unit. The A.L.F. claim responsibility. Police estimated $150,000 damage to Childers Meat Co. at 29476 Airport Road. Using 20 gallons of a diesel fuel/unleaded mixture, four 5-gallon buckets were strategically placed near the two-story office building containing the companies business records and along the main building near a natural gas line. Using two kitchen timer delays, with another two-timers as back up, there was plenty of time to leave town before the Mothers Day celebration really ignited. "As long as companies continue to operate and profit off of Mother Earth and Her sentient animal beings, the Animal Liberation Front will continue to target these operations and their insurance companies until they are all out of business. Happy Mothers Day." -A.L.F.

MAY 13/99: East Brunswick, NJ -- Furs By Guarino has two large rocks thrown at right display window, creating two holes which added to the hole already there from a previous attack. Two more large rocks were thrown at the left display window, shattering it completely. One more rock was thrown at the glass door, shattering it. -A.L.F.

MAY 15/99 : Manalapan, NJ -- Classic Furs had four bricks thrown through two front windows, shattering them both. Then one brick was thrown at the glass door, leaving a large hole. -A.L.F.

ENGLAND

DECEMBER 15/98: Ilford -- two butchers' shops and one McDonald's had their windows smashed by ALF activists.

DECEMBER 15/98: Wanstead -- The streets around AG Dennis were sealed off by police after an explosion at the butcher's shop caused by an incendiary device.

JANUARY/99: North London -- McDonald's at the Angel Islington had its windows smashed.

JANUARY 4/99: Leytonstone -- three shops on the High Road - Kennedy Fried Chicken, a fish shop and a pet shop - were sloganized.

JANUARY 6/99: Whitechapel -- windows were smashed at a fish and halal meat shop.

JANUARY 27/99: North London --"Meatland Butchers" in Green Lanes, Wood Green, had free ventilation installed thanks to a brick picked up from a local builders yard. The whole shop was smashed & spray-painted on tiles and pavement with "Murderers" and "ALF". A quick getaway was made and police arrived a few minutes later. -A.L.F.

JANUARY 27/99: London -- "Trust Meats" in Camden Road visited. Windows smashed and slogans were painted. However the alarm went off so a quick getaway was made. No arrests.

FEBRUARY/99: Wood Green - A.L.F. activists smashed up Meatlands, on High Road, A phone call to media warned that attacks would continue. An ALF spokesperson said: "We caused severe economic damage... and will continue to target this shop and all other shops in the area as retribution for all the animals which have been slaughtered." The shop sustained over 1,000 pounds damage from smashed windows and painted slogans. -- ALF

FEBRUARY 2/99: East London -- A mobile burger/meat stand in Homerton had its tires slashed and window smashed.

FEBRUARY 15/99: Shoreditch -- Fish shop windows smashed, east London.

FEBRUARY 15/99: Hounslow -- Butchers shutters painted with slogan.

FEBRUARY 15/99: New Cross --Butchers window smashed.

MID FEBRUARY/99: Mid London -- Simply Sausages Meat Van -all tyres slashed.

MID FEBRUARY/99: Mid London -- Russell & Hume Meat Van - 3 tyres slashed.

MID FEBRUARY/99: Mid London -- Meat Market Van - all tyres slashed twice, spray painted all over (van was hidden but found down a quiet road, the 2nd time, to have tyres re-slashed.

MID FEBRUARY/99: Mid London -- Smithfield van [famous London meat market] - 2 tyres slashed.

MID FEBRUARY/99: Mid London -- 5) "Meatland" Butchers, in Palmers Green was smashed again - the whole window was a write off. Second time in the same month

FEBRUARY 26/99: Hounslow -- Kebab shop window smashed, west London.

FEBRUARY 27/99: Shoreditch -- Butchers shop window smashed & graffitied.

FEBRUARY 27/99: Shoreditch -- Leather factory windows smashed & slogans painted, east London.

FEBRUARY 28/99: Leytonstone : Co-op windows smashed, east London. (Co-op Insurance Society own shares in Huntingdon Life Sciences).

MARCH 21/99: Towcester - A.L.F. activists claimed responsibility for an arson attack on a meat processing and packaging company. The three-storey offices used by Weddell Swift Ltd., Banbury Lane, Cold Higham, had the entrance of the building severely damaged as well as damages to the ground floor and stairwell.

MARCH 25/99: Surrey - A.L.F. activists raided the premises of Regal Rabbits, Great Bookham, Leatherhaed. Regal Rabbits breeds animals for cruel and useless animal experiments. Activists entered through a window on an outer wall and then through the ventilation system to reach the breeding cages. Around 60 rabbits were rescued from filthy, disease ridden conditions. The animals taken were breeding females with their litters, all now saved from the butchery of the vivisectors blade. The empty cages were trashed and slogans daubed all over the building.

These beautiful, playful rabbits are now able to live their natural lives in safe, loving homes. Animal liberation is easy, take control, just do it. Smash the labs. -A.L.F.

APRIL 19/99: London -- Metropolitan Meat Market - Lordship Lane - 2 tyres slashed.-A.L.F.

APRIL 19/99: London -- Simply Sausages van: 2 tyres slashed, window dented with brick.-A.L.F.

APRIL 19/99: London --W G Budd - butcher shop in Palmers Green triangle (opposite Safeways) - received brick through window. -A.L.F.

APRIL 19/99: London --Halal Meat Market - Cricklewood Broadway - also window caved in thanks to a brick - glass shattering over crates of eggs.-A.L.F.

APRIL 19/99: London --White meat van parked off Palmers Green - 2 tyres slashed.-A.L.F.

APRIL 19/99: London --Mr Bartfeld - Sheldon Avenue, Highgate (fur trader) his window was dented with a brick. -A.L.F.

APRIL 24/99: Edmonton, London -- Dixy Fried Chicken van had its windows smashed.-A.L.F.

APRIL 24/99: Edmonton, London -- Salisburys butchers on the A10 roundabout had a window smashed and 2 tyres on one of its vehicles slashed.-A.L.F.

MAY 5/99: Ilford -- Newstead the Butchers, in Aldborough Road South, Was hit by activists who exploded a bomb at the store. The device was taped to the window of the shop and shattered the glass.

MAY 7/99: Portobello Rd, W London -- Meat shop window smashed.

MAY 7/99: Maida Vale, W London -- Butcher's window smashed.

MAY 8/99: Stepney Green, E London -- Kennedy Fried Chicken windows and door smashed.

MAY 8/99: Whitechapel, E London -- Southern Fried Chicken and butcher's windows smashed.

MAY 10/99: London -- Wentworth St, E1. Cafe window smashed.

MAY 11/99: Devon -- A.L.F activists planted incendiary devices which exploded at a meat depot. Three lorries were destroyed in the incident at the Novacold premises.

MAY 11/99: Worcestershire -- a group calling itself AMBRIDGE AGAINST GENETIX has claimed responsibility for trashing five GM oil seed rape test sites. The name Ambridge Against Genetix is derived from the fictional rural town of Ambridge as featured in the long running British radio drama The Archers. Currently 'The Archers' are running a theme about GM crops and from this fictional story a very real direct action group has been born.

MAY 12/99: Angel, Islington, N London -- Kebab shop window smashed, Cafe signs smashed and slogans painted, Butchers signs smashed and slogans painted

MAY 12/99: Old St, E London-- Leather shop window smashed

MAY 12/99: Walthamstow, E London -- Kebab shop window smashed

HOLLAND

JANUARY 9/99: Geleen, Limburg - an attempted arson attack against a McDonalds was claimed by the Red Rooster, a cell responsible for several big arsons in the past three years against the meat (and in particular the poultry) industry. The McDonalds had been evacuated twice during the week prior to the arson. Staff came to work at around 8 on Sunday morning to find a jerrycan of petrol in front of the door. The activists had thrown petrol all over the entrance and set it alight. The same cell claimed responsibility for the following hits in Holland and Belgium:

1. Numerous bomb threats to McDonalds
2. Arson against poultry trucks in 1 April 1998
3. Arson at the Antwerp slaughterhouse Belgameat in Belgium 1-05-98: "liberation day."
4. Arsons against McDonalds in: Belgium Merksem, Berchem, Borsbeek, Antwerp, Brussels, Dendermonde and Deinze.
5. Paint-bomb attacks against McDonalds in St-Niklaas and Tongeren (both in Belgium).

MARCH 2/99: Meijel, Limburg - Holland's first mink raid occurred. 1500 mink were freed, and well over 3700 cages had been opened. The fence had been torn down in 4 places and the police do suspect activists of the liberation. The farmers were alerted at about 6 in the morning when the newspaper delivery boy told them he's seen some mink running around in the neighbourhood.

MARCH 2/99: Groningen -- McDonald's also received yet another bomb threat. The restaurant was closed down for several hours.

MARCH 18/99: Putten -- Activists from the 'Barry Horne Brigade' opened cages at a mink farm during an attempted liberation. Goeka Pelsfarming BV based in Putten was visited and 40 cages were opened. In their communiqué, just published in Holland's radical activist journal Ravage, the ALF cell's communiqué states "We encourage other activists to go and liberate mink, we have acquired a taste for this..."

APRIL 8/99: Putten -- During the second attempt at the Goeka Pelsfarming the Barry Horne Brigade cut a 4m hole in the fence around the farm and opened 500 cages. The mink ran straight into the woods. We know that not all of the released mink will survive this adventure, but many will. This is animal liberation."

BELGIUM

MAY/99: Lint -- Arson against meat truck at Lintor poultry slaughterhouse. - Red Rooster ALF

MAY/99: Sint-Niklaas -- The Belgium ALF set fire to a McDonald's restaurant after immobilising security cameras. Gasoline was poured through the ventilation ducts. Damage was limited to the storage area and the refrigeration area, there was also general smoke damage. The fire department claims that the fire would have gone out by itself eventually. The initials ALF were spray painted on the walls. - Red Rooster ALF

MAY 22/99: Wijnegem -- Police found what they claim are 5 bullet holes in the windows of a McDonalds. Cops say they found one bullet and 5 cartridge shells, at that the restaurant was targeted by the ALF. The day before, the manager claims to have received a threatening letter signed by the ALF.

MAY 23/99: Lint - A second arson attack occurred at a chicken slaughterhouse, in which a transport truck was the target. Damage is reported at 6 million Belgian franks. The front of the slaughterhouse was spray-painted with the slogan, which was in English: "Stop killing innocent animals".

SWEDEN

FEBRUARY 7/99: Listerlandet -- 400 minks and a tractor was smashed. -Unclaimed.

MARCH 6-8/99: Vimmerbym -- fur farmer Birger Alderbert was visited by DBF activists determined to cut short his plans to start up new fur farms. The DBF first visited the Aspenäsets fur farm. Several cages had been rebuilt and improved, but the DBF smashed over 300 of the cages that looked to be in the best condition, and also destroyed feeding machines. Next, the DBF visited Aldeberts fur farm in Sodra Vi where four new sheds with cages had been built. Two new was sheds were being built. The DBF trashed this farm and then visited Soren Svenssons fur farm in Kristdala, after a tip that there was animals on this farm. No animals were found but cages were destroyed and tools taken. An incendiary device was left in the main building, but unfortunately it did not go off. --DBF

MARCH 8/99: Kolboda -- Fliseryds sports-fishing club had a house damaged and boats were also destroyed. Also, 40 hunting platforms was destroyed in a area where foxes, elks and roe deer are being hunted.

MARCH 9/99: Skane - 1500 mink were given their freedom from the Mexico Mink Farm. -D.B.F.
MARCH 15/99: Falkenberg -- 500 minks set free at Lonestigs mink farm. This is the second hit against this farm. -D.B.F.

MARCH 16/99: Pitea -- A fish vehicle was set on fire. On the car's side the slogan "Murder of the fishes" was written. - unclaimed.

MARCH 17/99: Norrkoping -- a hot dog bar had the words "Meat is Murder" written on its windows. Arson was attempted but the fire was put out..

MARCH 18/99: Falkenberg -- Lonestigs fur farm outside was raided and approx. 500 minks were set free. The Swedish ALF has raided more farms than any other ALF in any other country.

MARCH 21/99: Skelleftea - two meat-companies have been attacked by animal activists. Damage unknown.

APRIL 1/99: Orbyhus -- During a daylight raid four beagle dogs were liberated from Wema-hund Ab. This places has bred dogs for vivisection for over 30 years. This was the first liberation ever at this facility. All the dogs have now been placed in new homes where they will be able to live the rest of their lives in peace. One of the liberated beagles had an injured eye. The breeders also claim that another one of the dogs has an eye that has just been operated upon. The breeder is privately owned and small, an easy target for grassroot animal rights campaigners to close, so we urge them to take action now and to save the WEMA-dogs. Djurens Befrielse Front.

APRIL 12/99: Stockholm - A DBF activist spotted a box with the text "live animals" being put on a train destined for a vivisection lab, sent from animal breeders Charles River. Liberated from the train was a rat mother and 14 baby rats. All are safe in new homes.

APRIL 14/99: Gothenburg -- 11 windows was smashed at a McDonalds. -DBF.

APRIL 14/99: West Sweden -- 14 chickens was liberated from a train. DBF activist watched boxes with the text "live ckickens" being loaded onto the train. When the coast was clear, the activists hopped on the train and open the boxes (they contained hundreds of chickens). The activists took as many as they could carry. The chickens are now in loving homes. The struggle continues. -D.B.F. (Swedish ALF)

APRIL 25/99: Aniagra -- nine hens were liberated from the largest egg production facility in the area. The DBF communiqué read: "The hens lives under horrible conditions in small cages where they hardly can move. The light is on almost all hours because the hens shall not be able to rest. Now they are living in loving homes where they can walk freely and do just what hens like to do." Swedish law prohibits these kinds of conditions for layer hens, and the DBF (Swedish A.L.F.) has acted to enforce those laws.

APRIL 24/99: Gothenburg -- One beagle was liberated from Salgrenska hospital by animal rights activists. A window was smashed, slogans sprayed and one beagle taken away. Three activists then sat down and called the police, to make a political point for getting arrested.

FINLAND

DECEMBER/98: Helsinki -- The fur store, Kokljuschkin, had 6 windows smashed.

DECEMBER/98: Vihti -- Fur farmers storage building: 4 windows broken and slogans spray-painted.

DECEMBER/98: Helsinki -- Leather store had several windows smashed, 3 other fur stores lost one window each.

DECEMBER/98: Espoo -- Fur dressmakers had all its windows smashed and slogans spray-painted.

DECEMBER/98: Tampere -- A new McDonald's was welcomed to town with 13 broken windows and two construction machines sabotaged. - E.L.F.

DECEMBER/98: Tampere -- A fur wholesale company had 4 windows broken, "Fur is Murder" spray-painted.

DECEMBER/98: Tampere -- A furs shop had three windows broken. This store is now closed after dozens of hits.

DECEMBER/98: Tampere -- Four windows smashed at a McDonalds, and smelly "potato goo" was thrown inside.

JANUARY/99: Helsinki -- Fur store had a window smashed and the fur store Kokljushkin lost 6 more windows.

JANUARY 14/99: Kuopio -- Eight windows were smashed at the vivisection center in Kuopio, and locks were glued. The action was dedicated to the activists jailed in Sweden.

FEBRUARY/99: Helsinki -- Fur store lost a window.

FEBRUARY 8/99: Uusikarrlepyy -- Fire severely damaged a fur feed centre, called Nyko Frys. This feed supplier is supposed to be the biggest one in Finland with about 250 customer fur farms. Damages were extensive. - Unclaimed.

MAY 2/99: Outokumpu -- 14 hens have been liberated from a battery unit in east Finland. The same place was raided last summer and 12 hens rescued.

AUSTRIA

MARCH 28/99: Vienna - animal activists were responsible for three butyric acid attacks on fur shops in the city.

GERMANY

SEPTEMBER 7-8/98: Aachen-Orsbach -- The windows of a farmer´s house on a mink farm in were smashed with stones (he lives on the farm). Animal liberation slogans were sprayed on the wall of the farm. -T.B.F.

OCTOBER 8/98: Vechta, Holdorf -- a mink farm was raided. The asbestos walls surrounding the farm were broken down, the fence was cut and 4000 mink were liberated. According to the farmer, the damage she sustained were around 250.000
DM (1US$ ~ 1,60 DM). -T.B.F.

NOVEMBER 8/98: Guestrow -- 300 mink were released at a farm. The main gates were opened and the mink escaped into the nearby woods. - T.B.F.

JANUARY 25/99: Borken -- a mink farm was raided. The asbestos wall surrounding the farm was broken down and 5000 mink used for breeding were released. The animals were all breeding stock held captive by Josef Brokamp, of Gemenwirthe 66, 46325, Borken (tel: 02862 2684). According to the speaker of the regional "Fur Breeders Association" damages reached between 40.000 DM and 100.000 DM. -T.B.F.

FEBRUARY/99: Gustrow -- Three hundred mink released from a fur farm.

AUSTRAILIA

FEBRUARY 17/99: Campbelltown, Sydney, NSW - A.L.F. activists set up a time delayed incindenary device outside a McDonalds store. Damage was not as extensive as was hoped as fire was discovered by passing motorist before it could take hold. These actions will continue.

MAY 23/99: Scone -- Animal rights activists broke into the Parkville Piggery, releasing the piggery's 4,000 pigs and spray-painted graffiti on the walls. Arrests were made.

AOTEAROA (NEW ZEALAND)

MARCH 11/99: Christchurch - at least a dozen activists launched an attack against genetic experimentation when a crop of GE potatoes was destroyed at Lincoln Crop and Food Research Institute. The $200,000 research project, which involved mixing the genes of potatoes with genetic material from toads and silkworms to make the potatoes rot resistant, was totally destroyed. "The Wild Greens" has claimed responsibility.

Common Sense Security For Animal Liberation Activists

As the tactics employed within the animal liberation movement become more sophisticated and effective, the techniques of the state, corporations and police that are used against us also become more sophisticated. It's up to all of us to make sure the efforts employed against us are not effective in hindering animal liberation. The use of caution in the face of the concerted effort to stop us is both prudent and necessary. Here are some useful suggestions:

VISITS FROM THE AUTHORITIES

DON'T talk to the FBI or any government investigator without your attorney present. Information gleaned during the visit can be used against you and your co-workers.

GET the names and addresses of the agents and tell them you will have your attorney get in touch with them. They rarely set up an interview under those circumstances.

DON'T invite agents into your home. Speak with the agents outside. Once inside they glean information about your perspective and life style.

DON'T let agents threaten you into talking. If the FBI intends to impanel a grad jury, a private talk with you will not change the strategy of the FBI.

LYING to the police is a criminal act. The best way to avoid criminal charges is to say nothing.

ANY information you give the authorities can and will be used against you. Don't try to outwit the cops, your arrogance could get you or others into serious trouble.

AGENTS of the state sometimes try to trick you into giving information "to help a friend." Don't believe them.

DON'T let them intimidate you. So what if they know where you live or work and what you do? This is still a democracy and you still have constitutional rights. They intend to frighten you; don't let them. They can only "neutralise" you if YOU let them.

GENERAL TIPS

If you wish to have a private conversation, leave your home or office and go outside and take a walk or go somewhere public and notice who is near you. Never say anything you don't want to hear repeated when there is any possibility of being recorded.

Don't use code of the phone. If you are being tapped and the transcript is used against you in court, the coded conversations can be alleged to be anything. From the very outset it is wise to assume that everything said on a telephone is totally public, and that everything can be overheard, so don't say anything on the phone you don't want to hear in open court. Also, do not gossip on the phone about other activists. Smut is valuable to anyone listening; it makes everyone vulnerable. Telephone records are also used to establish circles of contact between people - who knows who, etc. So be careful!

The above can also apply to e-mail and private electronic mail-lists. There is no such thing as a secure computer line: government agencies openly admit to collecting and processing telephone, fax and computer communications of groups and individuals. The federal government uses the intelligence gleaned from electronic communications to monitor "problem" groups, including animal liberation activists. Security agencies in Canada, the United States, Britain, Australia and New Zealand share intercepted communications of interest with one another, effectively creating a global surveillance web. Be careful! Learn to use effective encryption programs (like PGP) for all e-mail communications, not just sensitive ones, otherwise sensitive communications stand out like a sore thumb!

IF you are being followed, get the license tag number and description of the care and people inside it. Photograph people following you or have a friend do so. If you are followed or feel vulnerable, call a friend; don't "tough it out" alone. They are trying to frighten you. Debrief yourself after each incident. Write details down: time, date, occasion, incidents, characteristics of the person(s), impressions, anything odd about the situation.

Keep a "weirdo" file and keep notes from unsettling situations and see if a pattern emerges. Just because you're paranoid doesn't mean that they aren't watching!

Write for your government files under the FOIA and pursue the agencies until they give you all the documentation filed under your name.

AROUND THE OFFICE

Be sure to never leave one copy of an important document or list behind; take a minute to duplicate an irreplaceable document and keep the duplicate in a safe place. Back up, encrypt and store important computer disks off-site. Sensitive data and membership lists should be kept under lock and key.

Keep your mailing lists, donor lists and personal phone books away from light-fingered people. Always maintain a duplicate.

Sweeps for electronic surveillance are only effective for the time they are being done, and are only effective as they are being done if you are the person doing the sweep.

Remember to always assess your undertaking from a security point of view; understand your vulnerabilities; assess your allies and your adversaries as objectively as possible. Do not underestimate the opposition. Do not take chances. Plan for the worst, hope for the best.

Lastly, understand that these are some very basic security tips to help you live your life with minimum interference from the state - but this in no way cover everything you could do to protect yourself and your endeavours. Do not assume that if you have these basics covered you are untouchable. Prepare yourself ahead of time in case you are taken in by the police for interrogation. Know and trust your cell mates completely. When in doubt, walk away. The best way to prepare for run-ins with the law is to EDUCATE YOURSELF. Know your rights and take them seriously.!

PRISONER FRAUD DISCOVERED

Brian Ozzy Knecht trys to pull a fast one

In late August of 98, the animal liberation magazine, *No Compromise* received a letter from a Sayre, O.K. prisoner, Brian Ozzy Knecht, requesting a prisoner sub to the magazine. Knecht mentioned in his letter he was "*in for crimes dealing with the release of mink and the burning of the office*" at a mink farm in Wisconsin.(Knecht, 9/22/98) Knecht was apparently arrested and charged for a July 26/96 mink liberation and arson at Brn's Mink Ranch at Eagle Point, WI, for which he received a total of 15 years. Anne Crimaudo from *No Compromise* responded to Knecht's letter requesting supporting documentation to his claims, asking for press clippings, court documents, charge sheets, etc. Knecht's name was also forwarded on to the NA-A.L.F.S.G. and word went out that there may be another US prisoner entitled to support for animal liberation activities. We are disappointed to have to inform our supporters that after investigating his claims, it is clear that Brain Ozzy Knecht is NOT an animal liberation prisoner, but a fraud.

PRISONERS NEED SUPPORT

In the case of many arrested or imprisoned animal liberation activists, either the action in question or the activist arrested are known within the animal liberation movement. Communiqués for the action were received, or others saw news footage of the raid, or the activist arrested is known for their animal liberation views. However, this is not always the case - in the past there have been people in jail for animal liberation activities who are not aware of the network of support that exists for them. They may be unconnected to the animal liberation movement and acted out of their own conscience, or they might work within an isolated area or town, and not be connected up to the larger movement of activists, or their action went unpublicised and are relatively unknown. What ever the situation, it is important that any legitimate animal liberation prisoner receives support, whether they are well known or completely new. In cases where we are contacted or make contact with prisoners who appear to be incarcerated for action that fall under our animal liberation support guidelines, but are unknown to the Supporters Group or other activists, we endeavour to confirm their status as animal liberation prisoners. We believe that not only does the NA-A.L.F.S.G. have a duty to provide support to animal liberation prisoners, but to also ensure that freeworld SG members know who they are dealing with when providing support.

In Knecht's case, no one the SG contacted within the US animal liberation movement had heard about the mink raid action he claimed to have participated in. In a letter to the NA-A.L.F.S.G., Knecht wrote, *"There was absolutely no publicity about the mink farm itself that I know of, and I know that was hushed because the mink farm lied about how many mink were released and how much damage was done so they could collect big-time on insurance money. If there was any publication of my crime, my sentence, or my revocation at all, I know nothing of it because we were not allowed newspapers in the County jail."* (Knecht,12/23/98) Knecht sent court documents to *No Compromise* (who forwarded them on to the SG) which appeared to corroborate Knecht's claims. With Wayne Cody Lassell and Anthony Miller still fresh in all of our memories (two US prisoners who tried to pose as animal lib prisoners but were found out) it was decided that Knecht would be listed as a prisoner so Supporters could make contact with him. It was our feeling that everyone deserving of support should receive it, and that until such times as we were able to absolutely show Brain was NOT what he was claiming, freeworld activists should be made aware of his presence and make contact. That being said, it was strongly felt that further investigation of Brain's claim was needed since there were still so many questions about his situation. No financial assistance from the SG would be given to Knecht either, unless we were certain of who he was. Brain was listed in *No Compromise* and in *Underground #13*, but was not posted on the *animal-liberation.net* prisoner web page.

HUMMM...THAT'S ODD...

When word went out about Knecht and his alleged action, concerns were raised by activists who could find no record of the mink raid in any of their press clipping files, and there was absolutely no mention of the raid found in searches of mink industry data-bases. How was it that an activist could receive 15 years for mink liberations and the mink industry didn't jump all over it as an example to deter others? Brain mentioned in letters to No Compromise and to the SG that his prior convictions heavily influenced his sentencing, and that at least 10 years of his sentence was added due to breaching probation for unconnected crimes. In a letter to *No Compromise*, Knecht wrote, *"My prior [conviction] was not animal related, but a charge when I was 18 (16 years ago) for growing hemp, no hemp tax stamp, and possession of marijuana."* (Knecht, 10/20/98). However, in a letter to the Supporters Group, Knecht wrote, "*...to answer your questions concerning my crimes and the lengthy sentence I received, it was not all based on the crime concerning the mink farm. When I was young and stupid I got caught up in some big trouble running guns when I was 18 in a federal sting operation back in 1984. Most of the reason I got so much time was because I was revoked on parole violation and all my good time was taken away from me.*" (Knecht, 12/23/98). Perhaps it was a small thing, but later when we had a chance to compare his responses to exactly the same question, his explanation of drug charges affecting his sentencing to *No Compromise* and his claims of gun running problems in a letter to us made us wonder about the consistency of Knecht's claims in general.

Document sent by Knecht

STATE OF WISCONSIN — CIRCUIT COURT BRANCH — CHIPPEWA COUNTY

State vs Brian Clifford Knecht

JUDGMENT OF CONVICTION

Sentence to Wisconsin State Prisons

Date of Birth: 05-08-1965

Case No.: 96CF000116

The ☒ Court ☐ Jury found the defendant guilty of the following crime(s):

Ct.	Crime(s)	Wis Stat. Violated	Plea	Fel. or Misd.	Date(s) Crime Committed
1	1st-Degree Arson (Brn's Mink Ranch) [939.62 Habitual Criminality]	943.20(1)(a)	Guil.	MA	7-26-96
	Breaking & Entering [939.62]	940.23(1)	Guil.	MA	7-26-96

IT IS ADJUDGED that the defendant is convicted on 11-21-1996 as found guilty and is sentenced as follows:

Ct.	Sent. Date	Sentence	Length	Concurrent with/Consecutive to/Comments	Agency
1	11-21-1996	State Prisons	15 YR	Concurrent to Count 2 and Consecutive to sentence in 93CF000026	DOC
1	11-21-1996	Costs			
1		Restitution		Restitution to be determined. To include any and all mink which is still missing ordered	

FILED CHIPPEWA COUNTY, WI NOV 25 1996 JANET RUBENZER-KOKE CLERK OF CIRCUIT COURT

Conditions of Sentence/Probation

Obligations: (Total amounts only)

Fine	Court Costs	Attorney Fees	Restitution	Other	Mandatory Victim/Wit. Surcharge	5% Rest. Surcharge	DNA Anal. Surcharge
	20.00				70.00		

IT IS ADJUDGED that 116 days sentence credit are due pursuant to § 973.155 Wisconsin Statutes.

IT IS ORDERED that the Sheriff execute this sentence.

Thomas J Sazama, Judge
Roy La Barton Gay, District Attorney
Laurie Sazama Osberg, Defense Attorney

BY THE COURT:
Thomas Sazama
Circuit Court Judge/~~Clerk/Deputy Clerk~~
11-25-96
Date

State of Wisconsin }ss
County of Chippewa }
This document is a full, true and correct copy of the original on file and of record in my office and has been compared by me.
Attest 11-25, 19 96
Clerk
Deputy Clerk
SEAL

CR-212(a) 07/96 Judgment of Conviction
DOC-20 02/92

§§939.50, 939.51, 972.13, Chapter 973 Wisconsin Statutes
Page 1

Actual court document

STATE OF WISCONSIN — CIRCUIT COURT BRANCH — CHIPPEWA COUNTY

State vs Brian Clifford Knecht

JUDGMENT OF CONVICTION

Sentence to Wisconsin State Prisons

Date of Birth: 05-08-1965

Case No.: 96CF000116

The ☒ Court ☐ Jury found the defendant guilty of the following crime(s):

Ct.	Crime(s)	Wis Stat. Violated	Plea	Fel. or Misd.	Date(s) Crime Committed
1	1st-Degree Reckless Injury (939.63(1)(a)2 Use Dangerous Weapon (Felony > 5 Yrs))	940.23(1)	No Contest	FC	on or about 7/26/96

IT IS ADJUDGED that the defendant is convicted on 11-21-1996 as found guilty and is sentenced as follows:

Ct.	Sent. Date	Sentence	Length	Concurrent with/Consecutive to/Comments	Agency
1	11-21-1996	State Prisons	15 YR		DOC
1	11-21-1996	Costs			
1		Restitution		Restitution to be determined.	

FILED CHIPPEWA COUNTY, WI NOV 25 1996

Conditions of Sentence/Probation

Obligations: (Total amounts only)

Fine	Court Costs	Attorney Fees	Restitution	Other	Mandatory Victim/Wit. Surcharge	5% Rest. Surcharge	DNA Anal. Surcharge
	20.00				70.00		

IT IS ADJUDGED that 116 days sentence credit are due pursuant to § 973.155 Wisconsin Statutes.

IT IS ORDERED that the Sheriff execute this sentence.

Thomas J Sazama, Judge
Roy La Barton Gay, District Attorney
Laurie Sazama Osberg, Defense Attorney

BY THE COURT:
Thomas Sazama
Circuit Court Judge/~~Clerk/Deputy Clerk~~
11-25-96
Date

CR-212(a) 07/96 Judgment of Conviction
DOC-20 02/92

§§939.50, 939.51, 972.13, Chapter 973 Wisconsin Statutes
Page 1

CUT AND PASTE

The case against Knecht was cemented on July 6, when two members of the NA A.L.F. Press Office went to the Chippewa County Courthouse to look at the files of Brian Ozzy "Clifford" Knecht. What they found was very interesting and was very different from how Brian Knecht represented himself to animal activists.

Their investigation into Knecht started on the internet at http://ccap.courts.state.wi.us/internetcourtaccess and www.state.wi.us which turned up 27 case files for Knecht in three Wisconsin counties (14 in Chippewa, 12 in Eau Claire, and 1 in Dane County). From his original correspondences with animal activists at *No Compromise* and later the NA-ALFSG, Knecht stated that he had prior convictions for activities unrelated to animal activities, so the investigation focused on case numbers 93CF00026 and 96CF000116 in Chippewa County, covering the two documents that Knecht sent activists to prove he was ALF prisoner. Katie and Joe from the Press Office brought those two papers with them and read through the entire files for those case numbers.

Case #96CF000116 from Knecht says the crime is 1st Degree Arson (Brn's Mink Ranch) and Breaking and Entering. The actual court documents from his file says that case number 96CF000116 is a crime of 1st-Degree Reckless Injury, Felon in Possession of Firearm and Theft-Movable Property. Katie writes, *"We compared the exact pages and noticed everything was the same except for the charges. We read through the 27 page court transcript which has nothing to do with animal rights in any way. The transcript reveal that he shot a man in the left arm and kidnapped his wife."*

Case #93CF000026 from Knecht says the crime is Criminal Trespass (Brn's Mink Ranch) and Criminal Damage (Brn's Mink Ranch).

The actual court documents from his file says Interfere w/ Child Custody. Katie and Joe compared the exact pages from Knecht and the court and noticed everything was the same except the charges have been changed. There was a court statement that was copied that reads that Knecht and a Christopher Kurschner transported two 16 year old runaway girls to Texas. Both 16 year olds returned pregnant and were transported without permission from their families.

Brian Ozzy Knecht is NOT an A.L.F. activist. None of the charges against Knecht have anything to do with animal liberation, mink farm raids or arson as he claimed. Comparisons between documents Knecht sent to activists and documents retrieved from the court house show beyond a doubt that Knecht has forged and concocted a story in order to receive support from the animal liberation movement. We appreciate the efforts of everyone involved with bringing to light the con-job Knecht was attempting to pull, including those activists who so quickly voiced their distrust of Knecht's claims. We encourage anyone in contact with Knecht to cease corresponding, and anyone possessing any other relevant information to pass it our way. @

What Brian sent us...

STATE OF WISCONSIN — CIRCUIT COURT BRANCH — CHIPPEWA COUNTY

State vs Brian C. Knecht

Date of Birth: 05-08-1965 137710 L-49

JUDGMENT OF CONVICTION 30
PROBATION REVOCATION
Sentence to Wisconsin State Prisons
Case No.: 93CF000026

The [X] Court [ ] Jury found the defendant guilty of the following crime(s):

Ct.	Crime(s)	Wis Stat. Violated	Plea	Fel. or Misd.	Date(s) Crime Committed
1	Criminal Trespass (Brn's Mink Ranch) [939.62 Habitual Criminality]	948.31(2)	Guilt.	MA	7-26-96
2	Criminal Damage (Brn's Mink Ranch) (939.62)	946.32(3)	Guilt.	MA	7-26-96

IT IS ADJUDGED that the defendant is convicted on 08-10-1993 as found guilty and is sentenced as follows:

Ct.	Sent. Date	Sentence	Length	Concurrent with/Consecutive to/Comments	Agency
1	11-21-1996	State Prisons	2 YR	Concurrent with sentence in 96CF116 and 96CM458.	DOC
		Restitution		All damages to property $864.05 Read-in-for uncharged.	

Conditions of Sentence/Probation

FILED CHIPPEWA COUNTY, WI NOV 25 1996 JANET RUBENZER-PIKE CLERK OF CIRCUIT COURT

IT IS ADJUDGED that 0 days sentence credit are due pursuant to § 973.155 Wisconsin Statutes.

IT IS ORDERED that the Sheriff execute this sentence.

Thomas J Sazama, Judge
Roy La Barton Gay, District Attorney
Laurie Sazama Osberg, Defense Attorney

BY THE COURT:
Circuit Court Judge/Clerk/Deputy Clerk
11-25-96
Date

State of Wisconsin, County of Chippewa } ss
This document is a full, true and correct copy of the original on file and of record in my office and has been compared by me.
Attest 11-25, 1996
Clerk
Deputy Clerk
SEAL

CR-212(a) 07/92 Judgment of Conviction
DOC-39 92/92

...What was discovered.

STATE OF WISCONSIN — CIRCUIT COURT BRANCH

State vs Brian C. Knecht

Date of Birth: 05-08-1965

JUDGMENT OF CONVICTION
PROBATION REVOCATION
Sentence to Wisconsin State Prisons
Case No.: 93CF000026

The [X] Court [ ] Jury found the defendant guilty of the following crime(s):

Ct.	Crime(s)	Wis Stat. Violated	Plea	Fel. or Misd.	Date(s) Crime Committed
1	Interfere w/ Child Custody (939.05 Party to a Crime)	948.31(2)	Guilty	FE	11-04-1992

IT IS ADJUDGED that the defendant is convicted on 08-10-1993 as found guilty and is sentenced as follows:

Ct.	Sent. Date	Sentence	Length	Concurrent with/Consecutive to/Comments	Agency
1	11-21-1996	State Prisons	2 YR	Concurrent with sentence in 96CF116 and 96CM458.	DOC

Conditions of Sentence/Probation

FILED CHIPPEWA COUNTY, WI NOV 25 1996 JANET RUBENZER-PIKE CLERK OF CIRCUIT COURT

IT IS ADJUDGED that 0 days sentence credit are due pursuant to § 973.155 Wisconsin Statutes.

IT IS ORDERED that the Sheriff execute this sentence.

Thomas J Sazama, Judge
Roy La Barton Gay, District Attorney
Laurie Sazama Osberg, Defense Attorney

BY THE COURT:
Circuit Court Judge/Clerk/Deputy Clerk

CHIPPEWA COUNTY-9 CIRCUIT COURT — CRIMINAL COURT RECORD — 11-25-96 9:54am

Caption: State vs Brian Clifford Knecht
Responsible C.O.: Thomas J Sazama
Case Number: 96CF000116

Name: Brian Clifford Knecht
Address: 16765 Stillson Road Lot 20
City: Chippewa Falls
St: WI
Zip: 54729
DOB: 05-08-1965

Filing Date/C.O.: 07-29-1996 Thomas J Sazama
Disposition Date/C.O.: 11-21-1996 Thomas J Sazama
District Attorney: Roy La Barton Gay
Defense Attorney: Laurie Sazama Osberg
Next Action:

No.	Offense	Statute	Sev	Amend Offense	Amend Statute	A/Sev	Disposition	Sent
1	Attempt to cause death of another human [939.63 - Use of a Dangerous Weapon]	940.01	FB	1st-Degree Reckless Injury	940.23(1)	FC	Amend	
1	1st-Degree Reckless Injury [939.63 - Use of a Dangerous Weapon] [939.63(1)(a)2 - Use Dangerous Weapon (Felony > 5 Yrs)]	940.23(1)	FC				Guilty / No Contest	81
2	Kidnapping/Seize or Confine w/o Consent [939.63 - Use of a Dangerous Weapon]	940.31(1)(b)	FB				Dismissed /Pr Motion	
3	Possession of Firearm by Felon	941.29(2)	FE	Felon in Possession of Firearm	941.29(2)	FE	Amend	
3	Felon in Possession of Firearm [939.62 - Habitual Criminality]	941.29(2)	FE				Guilty / No Contest	72
4	Burglary-Armed w/ Dangerous Weapon	943.10(2)(a)	FB	Theft-Movable Property (Special Facts)	943.20(1)(a)	FD	Amend	
4	Theft-Movable Property (Special Facts) [939.62 - Habitual Criminality] [943.20(3)(d)5 - Penalty-Theft if Property is Firearm]	943.20(1)(a)	FD				Guilty / No Contest	72

Date	Court Record Entries		C.O.
07-29-1996	Complaint with warrant filed		Julie Anderl
08-02-1996	Amended complaint		
08-02-1996	Bail/bond hearing Court minutes filed		Steven Cray
08-02-1996	Bail bond cash No contact with: Lowell and Catherine Faukner if released. Not to leave Chippewa County if released unless notify Sheriff's Dept.	50000.00	Steven Cray
08-02-1996	Warrant cancelled/served		Julie Anderl
08-05-1996	Notice of hearing		
08-06-1996	Initial appearance Court minutes filed		Thomas J Sazama
08-08-1996	Other papers Public Defender order appointing Atty. Laurie Osberg.		

CR-300(a), 07/95 CRIMINAL COURT RECORD

Page 1

MEDCF IS NOW IN PRODUCTION AND WE NEED YOUR HELP!
WE NEED PRESS CLIPPINGS, PHOTOS, AND VIDEO FOOTAGE OF ALF RAIDS.
PLEASE MAIL THESE MATERIALS TO:
DAVID WILSON C/O UARC, PO BOX 1681, LAYTON, UT 84040, USA

uarc PRESENTS
MAKE EVERY DAY
COUNT FOR FREEDOM
THE STORY OF THE ANIMAL LIBERATION FRONT IN THEIR OWN WORDS

UNDERGROUND

THE MAGAZINE OF THE NORTH AMERICAN ANIMAL LIBERATION FRONT SUPPORTERS GROUP

ISSUE # 15 WINTER 99 $ 3.50

FREE TO PRISONERS

Genetic Food Crops Uprooted * Hillgrove Cat Breeder Closed * Utah Activists: NOT GUILTY! * Higgins's Pigeon Shoot Ends * Justin Samuel Faces Extradition * Gina Lynn vs. the Grand Jury * Diary of Action * Prisoner Listings ...and much more!

Into the New Millennium with the A.L.F.

Well folks, what can we say, it's been a scant 20 years or so since the Animal Liberation Front first appeared on the scene in England, and as we approach the new century, militant direct action for animals has become a world-wide phenomenon. Every single day of the year, non-stop, dedicated individuals risk life and liberty in a struggle to allow our animal brethren to live their lives unmolested and free of exploitation.

And what a struggle it is.

Horrors that only a few years ago belonged in the realm of distopian science fiction have become common place in today's world - genetically engineered Frankenstein foods are forced down our throats by governments and corporations; animals soaked in a bath of poisonous growth hormones are slaughtered in the name of a quick buck and increased profit; vast warehouses of "bio-machines" (better known to you and I as pigs) lie in darkness, ready to be harvested for their organs for human transplants; the country side is dotted with concrete bunkers where bloodied vivisectors tirelessly work their way through the guts and viscera of endless animal victims.

The horrors are seemingly endless, but they are not inevitable.

Despite the overwhelming odds stacked against them, each and every day individuals stand up to the abuse and exploitation of mother earth and her loved ones and, with a resounding "NO!" they choose to fight back.

As you read this issue of *Underground* you will meet some amazing people who are all fighting back in their own way. Many are anonymous, but their actions speak clearly enough. Others are known by name: like Gina Lynn, currently in prison for refusing to speak to a federal grand jury; like activists Sean Gautschy, Andrew Bishop, Adam Troy Peace who were cleared of all charges in a Utah mink feed bombing; like Justin Samuel, currently sitting in a Belgium prison awaiting extradition to the United States; and like Bob and Marlene Samuel, Justin's parents, who have stood by their son through this ordeal, providing unconditional love and support for their son and his beliefs.

As we worked our way through the news articles and the Diary of Action, it became very clear to us that this in this issue of *Underground* everything points to one thing: As we go forward into the new century, we go forward fighting.
Towards animal liberation, Yer editor, t.

Letters to Underground

BARRY HORNE UPDATE

Dear Underground,

This letter is to update Barry's many friends and supporters on his condition since his 68-day hunger strike ended last year. It is from the point of view of friends who have been visiting him regularly throughout his time in prison.

After the last mail-out, it was decided to wait for Barry to get better before mailing out again. Sadly he has still not recovered. In recent months his condition has worsened again and for this reason it was felt that an update was necessary.

The attitude of the prison authorities has been negative and unhelpful. There was a campaign of disinformation after the hunger strike. It was claimed that the hunger strike had been a hoax from the start, and that Barry was in good health. The reality was that he was gravely ill, with possible damage to his brain and some of his vital organs. Only after a long period of recovery would it have been possible to diagnose whether the damage was permanent. The actions of the prison staff have made this very difficult.

It was important for Barry's recovery that he had regular contact with his friends and family so that he could regain his memory and ease his obvious pain and confusion. He was and still is unable to write out forms for visiting orders to his friends and family. In the crucial first three weeks after the hunger strike the prison refused to help and he had no visits.

Eventually the prison staff began to help him to send out visiting orders, but only after persistent pressure from friends. Even then they were uncooperative and for a long time they only sent out a visiting order about once every 3 weeks.

When the visits became more frequent, he did begin to make a slow recovery, and his memory started to return. However the negative attitude of the prison staff continued. They were indifferent to Barry's health problems, and some prison staff even made remarks, accusing him of faking and saying he had taken up a valuable hospital bed. This encouraged other inmates to make similar remarks. This hostile environment was exactly the opposite of what Barry needed.

Early optimism about Barry's recovery was premature. He never fully recovered, and he is still in a poor physical condition. In the past few months his behaviour has caused concern among those visiting him. He has stopped eating on several occasions and told friends he was resuming the hunger strike, without explaining why or what his demands were. This has been a major setback in his recovery and has caused his condition to worsen even further.

It is time for the Prison Service and the Home Office to act. Barry is still a category 'A' prisoner after over 3 years in prison, which means he is regarded as dangerous and a threat to security.

This cannot be the case in his present condition. He has been in the hospital wing of the prison for over a year, apart from short spells in York Hospital. He has not written a letter or made a phone call for almost a year. His category 'A' status means that most of his friends are not allowed to visit him. Seeing old friends again may be just what he needs to recover. This would also make it easier for him to be transferred to another prison, where a change of environment would also be helpful.

There is a review of Barry's category 'A' status in the next few weeks. It will not be reviewed again for another year. Please take a few minutes to contact the Prison Service by letter or fax, and ask them to remove Barry's category 'A' status as a matter of urgency. This is a totally reasonable request, and would go a long way in helping him back to health. Point out that Barry has been ill for some time and cannot be considered a security risk.

Explain that being category 'A' is hindering his recovery. It is unusual for a prisoner to spend so long on category 'A'. Because he hasn't been able to reply, many people have stopped writing to Barry. If you used to write to him, it would help to write again, but don't expect a reply. It may be better to keep letters short or send cards with messages of support, as his concentration has been affected.

Write cards and letters of support to Barry;
Barry Horne VC2141
HMP Full Sutton,
Moor Lane,
York,
YO4 1PS.

Phone, write letters or/and send faxes to;
Martin Narey, Director General, HM Prison Service,
Clealand House, Page St, London,
SW1P 4LN.
FAX; 0207 217 6961.
Telephone; Home Office Switchboard, 0207 217 3000, ask for Martin Narey's office. Tell them to remove Barry's Category A status urgently. He is very ill and no threat to security

SPIRITED SUPPORT

Dear NA-A.L.F.S.G.,

Thank you for the work you are doing. In the spirit of "I'd rather die on my feet than continue to live on my knees." Some may criticise you for your tactics, but I am thankful to you. As an animal advocate, I've sniped at night -- putting up signs to deter people from buying tickets to a circus, I've protested and rallied but sometimes I feel like it's not enough. If we'd have had any huevos at all, we'd have charged the big top and created the media event the media requires when you are trying to educate the public and save an animal. I do support you and will send a donation soon. Please keep me informed as to what you are doing--I will monitor the web site.

Maxine

FREEMAN DEBATED - FRIEND OR FOE?

Dear NA-ALFSG,
It has come to our attention that the North American A.L.F. Supporters Group, in its issue of *Underground #14*, has requested that people write to us asking that we reconsider funding Freeman Wickman, who has received a grant to offer humane education programs in the Minneapolis region. The group states that "through this grant, Wickman joins vivisectors in denouncing A.L.F actions on a full-time basis."

Freeman, who is an extraordinary young activist and educator, received one of our grants in order to teach young people about animal issues, and to help build a more compassionate world through humane education. The grant enables Freeman to offer school programs on animal rights, compassionate living, vegetarianism, vivisection, hunting and trapping, and other issues free of charge. Freeman will by no means "join vivisectors in denouncing A.L.F. actions on a full-time basis." In fact, Freeman will do much toward ending vivisection through his powerful and inspiring presentations that not only promote kindness, but also teach critical thinking.

We are proud to support Freeman in his outstanding education work, and we hope that this letter answers any questions or concerns that you may have. Thanks for contacting us, and for caring about other species.

For the earth and all animals,
Zoe Weil and Rae Sikora
Co-Founders, Centre for Compassionate Living
P.O. Box 260 Surry, ME 04684 USA
fax/tel:(207) 667-1025

Dear NA-ALFSG,
[in reference to **A Liberation To Be Remembered**, *Underground #14]* I never like to discover a split dividing us on issues in the animal rights movement and therefore check out all allegations. Character assassination is a non-productive approach. Today, I received the summary of a conference held by United Poultry Inc. "Direct Action for Animals Forum." Among other facts and opinions, I learned that Freeman had founded *No Compromise"*and served as an ALF Spokesperson and was very active in organising and participating in protests. Apparently, his ideology has changed, but not his loyalty and commitment to animal rights.

There should be room in our movement for variant views without labelling those who don't follow our concepts as dissidents. I don't see any disparity in my beliefs by supporting all components of the spectrum championing animal rights. A conformist attitude would be counter productive. Organised religions, politics and cults require an allegiance that is counter productive to my nature.

In summary, do what you believe in, provided you maintain the ALF guidelines you have set, and I will continue to support the NA-ALFSG. Also, please don't demand that I give the NA-ALFSG sole allegiance. I trust you will re-examine the human tendency to disparage other individuals or groups that don't abide by your philosophy. As long as they are sincerely involved in pro-animal action, respect the different approach. We're more likely to attain our common goal through diverse efforts and accomplishments.

Sincerely, Jean Lauren.

-- Excellent concerns raised by your letter, which are exactly the same concerns Katie Fedor and Kevin Kjonaas address in their article when they question Freeman's repeated denouncing of the ALF's successful liberation of 116 animals from the University of Minnesota. Look, don't take our word for it, Freeman was interviewed extensively in print and televised media condemning this and other A.L.F. actions. The Supporters Group certainly accept that there are many roads towards the goal of animal liberation, and non-violent direct action is simply one such route, but Freeman has made it very clear that he does not. All of our readers/supporters are free to choose their own path towards animal liberation, (we've never suggested otherwise), but how can anyone claim that Freeman's very public stance against the A.L.F. can not be open to scrutiny or criticism?

THE BIBLE SAYS: ANIMALS CONTAIN GOOD VITAMINS

Dear ALF,
I would like to address the comments made by your group about the sport of rodeo. There is no animal on the face of this earth treated better than a rodeo animal. Our animals (in most cases) are our best friends. We do nothing to hurt them or jeopardise their health. WHY would we? In most cases we spend thousands of dollars of our hard earned money to keep them healthy and well maintained. Your accusations of us beating or being cruel to animals is down right ignorant.
We believe in animal welfare just as much as you do. But animal rights????

Why should an animal have the same rights as humans if they do not have the same responsibilities? We believe in being good and treating our animals decent. After all they are our best friends. But even in the bible it says that animals are on this earth for our use. The human body needs the essential vitamins and minerals that come from meat. God did not intend us to take protein supplements.

Even so you do have the right to voice your opinion, but I have the same right. And with that right I have the right to stand up for the great sport of rodeo. And the welfare of our animals
Sincerely,
Heiney6625@aol.com

JUSTICE DEPT. SEND FUR TRADERS WARNING

We are tired of asking for an end to the fur industry in North America while millions of defenceless animals are put to death. Animal rights activists have spent almost two decades writing letters, chanting, and holding pickets to end the slaughter of fur-bearing creatures. Yet even our sisters and brothers in the

(Continued on page 7)

HILLGROVE CAT BREEDER CLOSED - THANKS TO PROTESTERS EFFORTS!

ENGLAND -- The last establishment in the UK to breed cats for scientific research and testing closed early August. RSPCA inspectors worked throughout the night to remove more than 800 breeding cats and kittens from Hill Grove Farm in Witney, Oxfordshire, which closed due to immense pressure from public protests. Farmer Christopher Brown, 61, owner of the centre, claimed to be "retiring."

The animals, due to be sold for experimentation in laboratories around the world, were transported to an undisclosed RSPCA holding centre where they were being kept to await new homes.

The Home Office licensed farm has become one of the main focal points for animal rights protesters over the past two years and several demonstrations at the premises in Witney turned into violent clashes between police and protesters. Since March 1997 Thames Valley Police has spent 2.8 million pounds protecting the farmhouse and breeding pens, and policing the

(Continued on page 9)

LETTERS *(Continued from page 5)*

ALF have not always stopped fur farmers through live liberations and economic sabotage. Every year millions more animals are confined and put to a painful death as we wait for the cycle to end.

State and federal laws are being enacted to increase penalties for non-violent liberation actions, making effective forms of non-violent opposition less of an option for those who risk life and liberty to end animal abuse. To make matters worse, fur farmers take no caution to shoot unarmed liberators on their farms. Fur farmers and their puppets in government (Representatives Gronemous, Hatch, Feinstein, Petri and others) are making violence inevitable.

We will wait no more for another decade of death at the hands of fur farmers. To begin the season the Anti-fur Task Force of the Justice Department sent out over 100 razor blade booby trap envelopes to fur farmers and fur trade representatives in North America throughout the month of August. Fur farmers with farms previously liberated and still sticking to the business were randomly sent razor blades coated in rat poison.

Included with each envelope was a letter reading:

"You have been targeted. You have until autumn of the year 2000 to release all of your animal captives and get out of the bloody fur trade. If you do not heed our warning your violence will be turned back upon you."

JD/ATF
Justice Department--Anti-fur Task Force

INNOCENT ON ALL CHARGES

SALT LAKE ACTIVISTS SEAN GAUTSCHY, ANDREW BISHOP, ADAM TROY PEACE FREED!

ELLERMAN BROTHERS BETRAYED FRIENDS, ANIMALS.

A federal jury found three animal-rights activists innocent of all charges in the 1997 bombing of a fur farm office that caused nearly $1 million in damage. Animal liberation turn-coat Ellerman has admitted to federal charges in the bombing but failed to implicate others in a bid to save himself.

Clinton Ellerman, 22, pleaded guilty Thursday to one count of making a firearm and two counts of maliciously damaging property with an explosive in the bombing of the Fur Breeders Co-operative in Sandy. Five pipe bombs exploded and a fire was set in the business offices in the attack. There were no injuries. The March 11, 1997, bombing caused an estimated $900,000 in damage to several trucks and a building owned by the Co-operative, which supplies mink farmers in Utah and Idaho.

Ellerman told U.S. District Judge Thomas Greene he was recruited to build the pipe bombs by his younger brother, Joshua Ellerman, 20. The younger Ellerman pleaded guilty last year to helping plant the bombs. He was sentenced to seven years and two months in prison and ordered to pay $750,000 in restitution. The Fur Breeders Co-operative is one of the country's largest and provides mink to hundreds of farmers in the West. Both brothers turned informant for the state, and in an attempt to save their own hides, lied to authorities about the involvement of others in the bombing. Attorneys for the three animal-rights activists that Ellerman alleged took part in the bombing argued that their clients were in court because Joshua Ellerman was desperate to implicate others. "He needed to give them information to avoid doing 35 years in prison," said Fred Metos, who represents Andrew N. Bishop, 34, of Ithaca, N.Y. "He knows he's got to name names, that he's got to do something. Ellerman has plenty of motivation to lie, defence attorneys contend. "Josh is not a truthful person," Metos said in his opening statement to the 12-member federal jury. "He has lied about this consistently."

Sean Gautschy, 23, of Salt Lake City, was on trial for 11 counts and Andrew Bishop, 34, of Ithaca, N.Y., for 13 counts stemming from the bombing. Adam Troy Peace, 21, of Huntington Beach, Calif., was also charged with two counts from an earlier attempt.

—Douglas Joshua Ellerman admitted lying under oath during his guilty plea and has demonstrated a great ability to concoct a story.

Josh Ellerman said that he, Gautschy, Bishop and Alexander Slack -- who committed suicide in June -- broke into the co-op on March 11, 1997. Peace's attorney, Ed Brass, said revenge was on Ellerman's mind when he named Peace in the case after Peace backed out of a plan to help Ellerman escape to Mexico. Under cross-examination, Ellerman admitted authoring an article on how to exact revenge. Both Ellerman brothers gave several inconsistent statements while testifying, including conflicting accounts of who bought the bomb-making materials. Furthermore, Douglas Ellerman admitted lying under oath during his guilty plea and has demonstrated a great ability to concoct a story.

Peace, Gautschy, and Bishop were found innocent of all charges by a federal jury. Family and friends of the defendants cried and hugged each other after the verdicts were read. The 12-member panel took a day and a half to reach a decision. Gautschy testified that on March 10, 1997, the night before the bombing, he was home in a pain-reliever-induced sleep. Earlier that afternoon, his dentist had extracted a tooth. Gautschy's girlfriend said from the witness stand that she had tended him until nearly 2 a.m. the next morning. Defendant Andrew Bishop testified that he was also home that night. His girlfriend, who is now his wife, and his roommate both confirmed Bishop's story. The third defendant, Adam Troy Peace, was accused of helping in an earlier aborted bombing attempt. Defence attorney Ed Brass, argued there was no credible evidence that the first bombing try occurred.

With no physical evidence linking Bishop, Gautschy and Peace to the bombing and an earlier aborted bombing plan, the federal jury acquitted the three of more than 25 charges.

"I think this shows that the government better have more evidence before it puts someone on trial for a crime like this," said Bishop's attorney, Richard Van Wagoner. "We're pleased the jury didn't see fit to convict solely on the testimony of uncorroborated informants." said Ed Brass, Peace's attorney.@

HEGINS PIGEON SHOOT CANCELED!

AUGUST/99HEGINS, Pa. - It's official! The Labour Day Committee, Inc., promoters of the annual Labour Day pigeon shoot held in Hegins, announced that this year's pigeon shoot has been cancelled. The announcement is being hailed as a victory by the dozens of other animal protection organisations that have been working for more than a decade to stop the annual event.

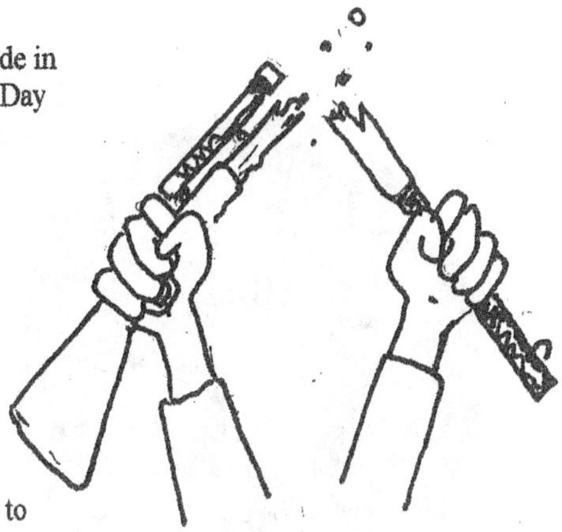

Says Heidi Prescott, National Director of The Fund for Animals, "It has been more than a decade in the making, but we have finally seen a victory for Pennsylvania's pigeons. For the first Labour Day in 66 years, thousands of birds will not be cruelly wounded and killed at Hegins Park."

The voluntary cancellation of the event by the pigeon shoot organisers comes on the heels of last month's unanimous Pennsylvania Supreme Court decision granting Clayton Hulsizer, a humane officer for the Pennsylvania Society for the Prevention of Cruelty to Animals, jurisdiction to enforce Pennsylvania's cruelty to animals law at the Hegins pigeon shoot.

The annual pigeon shoot in Hegins each year attracted hundreds of shooters from around the world, who competed for money and prizes by taking aim at thousands of birds, released one at a time from individual boxes. Investigators documented that approximately 75 percent of the birds were not killed immediately, but rather were wounded and left on the shooting fields to suffer from their injuries. Young children known as "trapper boys" routinely collected wounded birds and killed them by stomping on them, ripping off their heads, banging them against barrels, or throwing them into barrels to suffocate.

Adds Michael Markarian, Executive Vice President of The Fund for Animals, "The Hegins pigeon shoot has often been called the world's cruellest event. It is a hallmark for the humane movement to put an end to this annual atrocity and save thousands of animals from suffering."@

Hillgrove Closed *(Continued from page 7)*

internationally-advertised demonstrations calling for its closure. At least 350 people have been arrested and 21 have been jailed for public order offences, many losing their liberty for a year.

Brown, who has run the breeding centre with his wife Katherine for the past 30 years, turned to the RSPCA to help re-home his stock after informing the charity that he was retiring from the breeding business. A team of RSPCA vets health checked, vaccinated and microchipped all of
the cats, which had been reared in virus-free environments, before 33 of the charity's officers transported them in a fleet of 16 vans to the holding centre. The charity has launched an emergency hotline to appeal for prospective owners to adopt the Hill Grove cats and the thousands of others in its care. The 800 cats were being housed in a purpose-built cattery awaiting neutering before being distributed to the RSPCA's network of animal centres around the country.

Animal activist and television writer Carla Lane said the news of the closure was "magnificent. This is absolutely brilliant. It is a wonderful day for all those who care about animals. I used to go down there to protest about it and this is a victory for the protesters. It is those people we have to thank for this and it means that the people are being heard. That farm was one of our biggest griefs and now it has closed. I am just so happy about it."

Campaigners who had battled for the closure of the farm said they were delighted with the news that Hill Grove cattery had closed down. Heather James, of Save the Hillgrove (correct) Cats, said: "This has never been about us or Christopher Brown, it has been about the cats and their safety. That has always been the priority. We have been calling for the closure for the past two years and we said we would never go away until it was shut and now that day has come. If it had taken another six years we would have still been protesting.

"Without our pressure Mr Brown would not have given up what was a very lucrative business. He could have sold it on for a healthy profit, but now he has been forced to give it all up. This is one of the happiest days of my life"

Robin Webb, a spokesman for the Animal Liberation Front, said: "Mr Brown has always said he wouldn't close the farm, but it is clear that animal rights activists have through constant protest, pickets and raids, encouraged him to end this obscene business that offended everyone." At a demonstration on April 18 last year more than 1,000 protesters from across the country descended on the farm, with many fighting pitched battles against 400 police officers drafted in from five surrounding forces. The escalating violence at the demonstrations forced the police to apply for a five-mile exclusion zone around the farm on July 18 last year - only the second time any such order has been granted on the mainland.@

Bombing of EF! Activists Case to Proceed

Activists say FBI conspired to violate civil rights

A federal appeals court recently ruled that two environmental activists who were nearly killed in a still-unsolved 1990 car bombing may sue the law-enforcement officers who claimed that the activists accidentally bombed themselves.

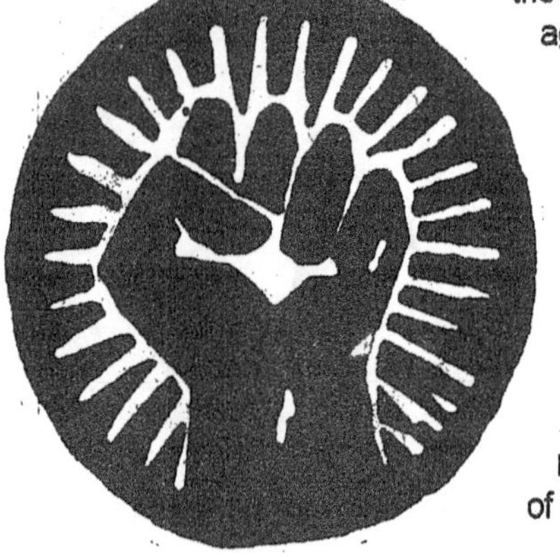

According to the ruling, the Oakland police department conspired with the FBI to falsely arrest Earth First! activists Judi Bari and Darryl Cherney for knowingly transporting a bomb, which the law-enforcement officers said the activists planned to use in a "terrorist" attack against one of several possible targets. The bogus arrests, the court added, may have constituted a violation of the activists' First Amendment rights.

The ruling clears the way for the activists' civil rights lawsuit against the FBI and the Oakland police department, which both responded to the scene of the May 24, 1990 car bombing.

Bari died of breast cancer in 1997. But Cherney said he's looking forward to the upcoming trial. "The FBI needs to be taught a lesson, and our case is at the forefront o holding the FBI accountable for violating activists' constitutional rights," Cherney told media. "We have a golden opportunity with this lawsuit to rid the country of a little bit of oppression, and that is an assignment that we embrace and take very seriously."

The upcoming trial stems from a series of events which preceded and followed the still-unsolved car bombing, which occurred as Bari and Cherney were driving through Oakland on the morning of May 24, 1990. In the weeks prior to the bombing, Bari and Cherney -- the two most prominent organisers in the Earth First! campaign to protect northern California's imperilled redwood forests -- received numerous death threats from opponents of the much-maligned movement.

Boulder's Betty Ball, who was then co-director of the Mendicino County Environmental Center, worked with both Bari and Cherney. One day, Ball recalled, a photograph of Bari with rifle cross-hairs superimposed across her face was found tacked to the center's door. "Judy and I went to the Mendicino County Sheriff's Department to ask them to respond to the death threats," Ball said. "Their response was, 'We're too busy; we don't have time -- if you turn up dead, we'll investigate." A few weeks later, Bari and Cherney almost did turn up dead, as a powerful bomb triggered by a motion device ripped through Bari's Subaru station wagon.

Within minutes of the blast, the FBI appeared on the scene and announced that the two activists had been knowingly transporting the bomb on the floorboard behind the driver's seat and that it had exploded accidentally. Bari, who was nearly killed in the blast, was placed under arrest about three hours later as she struggled for her life in a local hospital.
Cherney, who escaped with minor injuries, was arrested a few hours later.

The FBI and the Oakland police department quickly portrayed Bari and Cherney as violent terrorists to the national and local media. But after seven weeks of investigation -- and an accompanying seven weeks' worth of inflammatory accusations -- the Alameda County District Attorney declined to press charges against the two activists, citing a lack of evidence.

To this day, no one has ever been charged with committing the crime. About a year after the bombing, Bari and Cherney filed a lawsuit against the FBI and the Oakland Police, charging the organisations with false arrest and civil rights violations. The activists' law suit claimed that the FBI and the police knew perfectly well that Bari and Cherney were innocent, and that they were, in fact, victims of an assassination attempt that was never investigated.

The FBI and the Oakland Police department, which have long denied the allegations, have spent the past nine years trying to get th suit dismissed. It was also revealed that the FBI conducted a "bomb school" on land owned by the Louisiana Pacific Lumber Company shortly before the incident in Oakland. According to court documents, FBI agents spent a week on L/P land blowing up cars with pipe bombs and "responding" to the imaginary "crime scenes." The teacher at this "bomb school" was FBI special agen Frank Doyle -- the very same agent who would show up and take charge of the Oakland investigation a few weeks later.

Upon arriving at the scene, according to an official FBI videotape of the incident, Doyle turned to his colleagues -- all of whom had just been his pupils at the "bomb school" -- and said, "This it -- this is the final exam." Doyle was also the agent who claimed that nails taped to the bomb matched were "identical" to a bag of nails found in the trunk of Bari's car.

Given the history of the FBI's notorious COINTELPRO initiative, all agree that it's time to call a halt on this type of harassment once and for all.@

Animal Rights Activist Breaches Security At Top Secret Lab

ENGLAND -- On Saturday 25th September, at a national demonstration against Covance Laboratories, Otley Road, Harrogate an animal rights activist managed to climb a 3 metre security fence and gain access to the company's beagle unit, gaining an insight into the gruesome world of vivisection.

The following statement has been made anonymously by the activist involved: "Upon entering the building I came across the monkey unit but I didn't go in as there was a Biohazard sign on the door and another mentioning rabies experiments. I entered the beagle unit, lots and lots of dogs with no bedding at all. Lots of excrement everywhere. Some of the dogs were cowering with fear. Some of them were just desperate for attention. The sound was astronomical. Some of the dogs were in small cages used in radioactive experiments. Some of them were used in some sort of lavage experiment. Some were used in medical experiments. Many, many different dogs, they're all very affectionate, loving dogs. Unfortunately they remain [at the lab]."

Video footage taken from within the unit revealed appalling conditions with urine and excrement covering the floors of the kennels, flowing out into the walkway between them. Animal feed had been knocked over into the urine rendering it inedible. The dogs were desperate for attention and affection, two things which they will have hardly experienced in their short, miserable lives in the labs.

This footage has come as a major boost to the campaign against this company, which is currently being stepped up. Covance have denied cruelty in the past but we now have concrete evidence that the dogs on site live a life of misery.

The campaign will continue until the laboratories are closed.

Out of 100 activists who attended Saturdays demonstration, two were arrested for public order offences.

The Covance Campaign can be contacted on 07977 637 293.

JUSTIN SAMUEL'S STORY

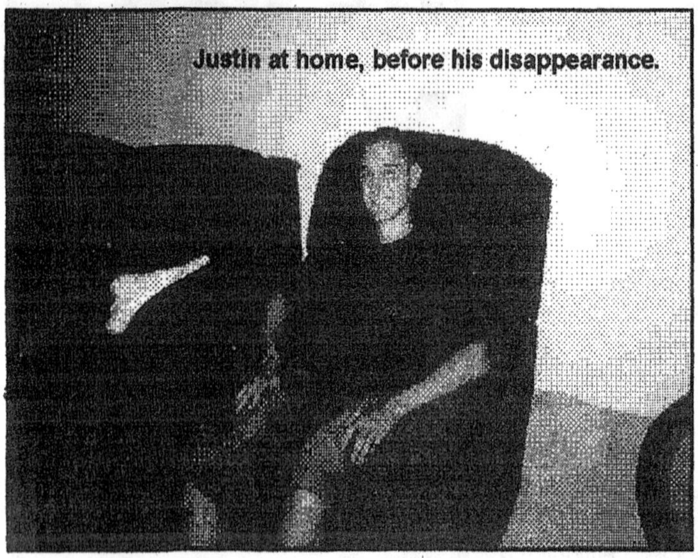
Justin at home, before his disappearance.

SPECIAL TO UNDERGROUND

During October, 1997, persons unknown released several thousand mink imprisoned within fur farms in Independence, Medford, Granton, and Tomahawk, in the state of Wisconsin.

In September, 1998, a Grand Jury in Madison, Wisconsin, was set up to investigate these raids, and indicted two young men, charging them with "animal enterprise terrorism" and "unlawful interference with interstate commerce." The indictment alleges that Peter Young (age 22) from Mercer Island, Washington, and Justin Samuel (age 20) from Snohomish, Washington, attacked at least two of the farms and released 3,600 mink with the intent to cause significant economic damage to the farms. In addition the indictment claims the two undertook "overt acts in three states as part of a conspiracy to engage in extortion by attempting to coerce the farmers to close their business rather than face the threat of further economic losses as a result of their attacks." These alleged overt acts include conducting surveillance on numerous farms and the release of breeding stock.

In all, Peter and Justin face a six-count indictment. Under the Animal Enterprise Protection Act (AEPA) anyone convicted of freeing animals could face a number of years in jail for each count. After the counts were indicted against Peter and Justin the U.S. Attorney's office issued the following statement; "This indictment reflect the determination of the law enforcement community and my office to address criminal activity designed to curtail or shut down a lawful industry, such as the conduct alleged in this indictment."

However despite all the Attorney offices statement they were lacking two things -- their suspects.

For nearly two years nothing was seen of either Peter or Justin. Then on the 4th of September 1999, the news came that Justin had been arrested in Hasselt, Belgium, and is now facing extradition procedures to the USA.

THE ARREST

According to Belgian media, Justin was discovered by authorities in a pub near the military base of Klein Brogel, in Hasselt. Justin had apparently been staying a short time at the home of Pol D'Huyvetter, a leader of the pacifist and ecological movement in Belgium. Pol D'Huyvetter and other Anti-nuclear activists would bring attention to nuclear issues by invading American military bases to search for nuclear bombs. D'Huyvetter was unaware that Justin was wanted on a Federal indictment. At the time of Justin's arrest, a demonstration against the possible presence of US-nuclear weapons was taking place at an American base near the pub he was in. Depsite not having been present at the demo, Justin was discovered when authorities performed a check on his ID. Belgian and Dutch police also looked into the possibility that Justin might have been involved in several mink liberations in the Netherlands (Hasselt, where Justin was arrested is not far from the Dutch border). There was, however, no evidence that Justin was in any way involved with any European mink releases.

Shortly after his arrest, Justin was visited by Joseph M. Pomper, the US Consul. Under the Belgian legal system, Justin is only detained in the country because of a request for provisional arrest and extradition made by the United States government. The case for which he is wanted in the U.S. will not be judged in Belgium. The Belgian's government's role is to ensure that the extradition request is receivable in accordance with the provisions of the extradition treaty signed between Belgium and the United States of America. Once found extraditable, Justin would be picked up by U.S. Marshals to be returned before the appropriate U.S. jurisdiction for trial.

On September 14, Justin was able to leave a voice mail message to his father, in which he thanked everyone supporting him, "Tell everyone I'm doing all right. Thank them for being there for me."

EXTRADITION

An extradition request was submitted to the Belgian authorities in the form of a diplomatic note addressed to the Belgian Ministries of Foreign Affairs and Justice. Under the provisions of the extradition treaty signed between Belgium and the United States of America in 1987, the requesting state has 75 days from the date of arrest to submit the formal extradition request and support documents. The United States Department of Justice is aware of this and has been requested to submit the required documentation as soon as possible. Past experience shows that several months (5-6) are usually required between the date of arrest and the date at which U.S. Marshals pick up the prisoner to return to the United States. In cases where extradition is contested and special proce-

dures need to be initiated in Belgium to show that the extradition request is not receivable, the delay can be increased to over 12 months before extradition actually takes place.
Marlene and Bob Samuel, Justin's parents, have been working very closely with a variety of Animal Liberation Support Organisations in both North America and Europe to work on helping Justin situation. As well, the American Embassy has been very helpful to Justin and his family in establishing communications with each other, ensuring his well being, and helping to get Justin a small amount of money. Both Justin and his parents ask supporters to "please not demonstrate outside the American Embassy" as they are being very supportive of Justin and his efforts to communicate with his family.

SUPPORT

Marlene Samuel had this to say to Justin's supporters: "To all of you, I can't begin to express my appreciation for all you've done, and everything you're doing. I know Justin will be alright with all the support that he is seeing. Thank you, everyone.

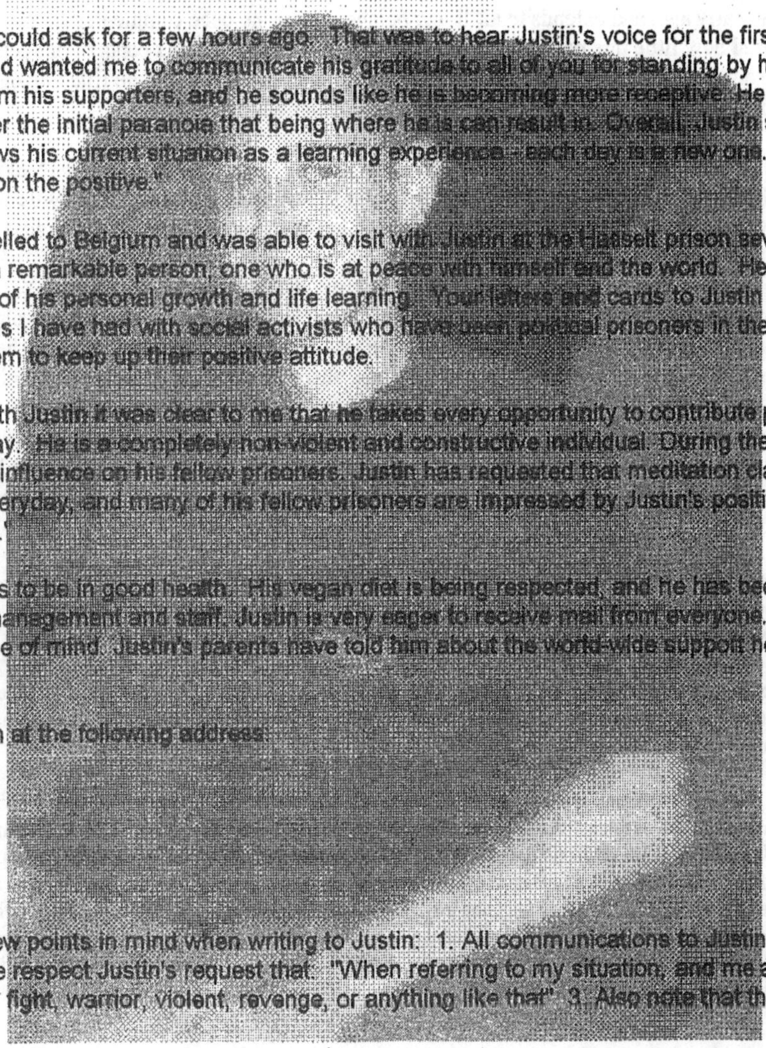

"I had the best phone call I could ask for a few hours ago. That was to hear Justin's voice for the first time in almost two years. He sounds very well, upbeat and wanted me to communicate his gratitude to all of you for standing by him. I talked with him about receiving communications from his supporters, and he sounds like he is becoming more receptive. He did specifically mention that it's taken him a while to get over the initial paranoia that being where he is can result in. Overall, Justin sounds emotionally and mentally sound. He said he views his current situation as a learning experience - each day is a new one. This follows suit with Justin's nature - his ability to focus on the positive."

Justin's father recently travelled to Belgium and was able to visit with Justin at the Hasselt prison several times. Bob reported to supporters, "Justin is truly a remarkable person, one who is at peace with himself and the world. He sees his confinement while awaiting extradition as part of his personal growth and life learning. Your letters and cards to Justin are critical to his ongoing wellbeing. From discussions I have had with social activists who have been political prisoners in the past, support from the outside is very important to help them to keep up their positive attitude.

"In few short hours I was with Justin it was clear to me that he takes every opportunity to contribute positively to our world in a peaceful and meaningful way. He is a completely non-violent and constructive individual. During the four weeks of his imprisonment he has had a positive influence on his fellow prisoners. Justin has requested that meditation classes be started at the Hasselt prison. Justin meditates everyday, and many of his fellow prisoners are impressed by Justin's positive view of life and would like to find a way to share it."

Bob said that Justin appears to be in good health. His vegan diet is being respected, and he has been treated with respect and dignity by the Hasselt prison management and staff. Justin is very eager to receive mail from everyone. His spirit is strong and he's been in a very positive frame of mind. Justin's parents have told him about the world-wide support he has, and preparations for his defence are underway.

Supporters can reach Justin at the following address:

Justin Samuel
Gevangenis Hasselt,
Martelarenlaan, 42
3500 Hasselt, Belgium

Please keep the following few points in mind when writing to Justin: 1. All communications to Justin are monitored, read, and potentially censored. 2. Please respect Justin's request that "When referring to my situation, and me and my case, not to use the words: militant, war, attack, fight, warrior, violent, revenge, or anything like that". 3. Also note that the inmates cannot receive telephone calls at the prison.

There are also several Support Campaigns set up for Justin, which you can write at the following addresses:

JUSTIN SAMUEL LEGAL DEFENSE FUND
Box 22504, Seattle, WA
98122-0504 USA

(This fund is being used to directly pay for Justin's legal defense by his parents. Donations payable to "Justin Samuel Legal Defense Fund").

JUSTIN SAMUEL SUPPORT FUND
(North America)
c/o NA.ALF.SG, Box 69597, 5845 Yonge Street, Willowdale, Ont, M2M 4K3, Canada.

Financial support for Justin Samuel and his family can be made payable to "NAALFSG." Please earmark funds for the Justin's Support Fund.

EUROPE

Justin Samuel Support Fund
c/o Families for Animal & Earth Liberation Prisoners Support
BM Box 2407, London, WC1N 3XX, England
e-mail: family.support@iname.com

A MOTHER'S LOVE

Marlene Samuel

First of all, I would like to thank you for the honor and privilege of telling you about one of the most compassionate people I have had the pleasure of sharing my life with, my son, Justin Samuel. After reading this through, I have strived for the utmost of objectivity. I have had difficulty in making transitions from past to present tense. I'm sure this is largely a result of Justin not having been a part of our family's lives for two years.

Justin's compassion existed from an early age, and extends to all living beings. Someone once commented to me that he should care about people as much as he did animals. I realized how little this person knew Justin. One example of Justin's concern of people were the regular reminders he gave me that we needed to give outgrown clothing to the needy. He kept a bag in his closet that he filled up on a regular basis. This started at an age when most mothers have to plead with their children to cooperate in such an effort.

There was never a time when we had any less than five cats, and up to 11, and a dog. Most of these cats were acquired as strays, and some had to be quarantined due to FIV and FELV. After a number of trips to the thrift stores on half-price days to acquire blankets for the cats, Justin expressed his concern of taking away the opportunity for needy people to purchase the blankets. After that, we started using old towels and smaller items to fill pillowcases for the cats.

Justin was a greatly appreciated volunteer at Providence Hospital in Everett, Washington. The manager of the volunteer staffing office was filled with nothing but praise for Justin in his variety of duties. He completed the tasks that he was asked to do, anywhere from patient transport to filing, always with a cheerful attitude. He enjoyed his involvement there, and shared a lot of inspiring stories with his family.

Academically and intellectually, Justin is blessed, but very humble. When he graduated high school in June of 1995 at the age of 16-1/2, he had already accumulated more than a year's worth of college credit. Along the way, Justin has always been willing to help others. He has never been insecure that if someone knew what he did, he wouldn't be quite as good. He enjoys seeing people succeed. I think about this a lot, as a member of the corporate world, where withholding information for job security is an every day occurrence.

Materialism and consumerism have no place in Justin's life. At holidays and birthdays, he asked his family and friends to make donations to charities, instead of buying gifts for him. Much of his dislike of materialism contributed to his choice to leave the University of Washington. He told me he would never feel comfortable sitting behind a desk in a corporate environment, when he felt his real contribution to this world lay elsewhere.

Justin's love of animals easily led him to a great concern for their welfare. We attended one of PETA's Animal Rights 101 seminars in Seattle in 1988. By the time we left, we could feel the anger toward the perpetrators of all inhumane treatment of animals, and the hurt for the animals themselves. At dinner that night, we announced our commitment to become vegetarians. Midway through high school Justin became vegan.

From the time of that seminar, Justin became a profound crusader for the welfare of animals. He has seized every opportunity as a soundboard to educate people on all issues concerning those that can not speak for themselves. From his efforts in elementary school, turning his art projects into murals of animal cruelty, to more recent one-on-one "discussions" with those who showed indifference, there have been many that felt his impact. One particular incident that comes to mind was returning from a family vacation in September of 1991. As we stood at baggage claim, we both spotted a woman standing across from us, wearing a mink coat. As Justin started moving toward her, her baggage arrived and she left. I could see that he was upset for not going after her. As fate would have it, he got a second chance when she and her husband boarded the same parking shuttle we were on. Justin articulately, and rationally, proceeded to describe the cruelty that produces a fur coat. The woman was definitely flustered by what she was hearing. Her husband verbally attacked Justin for his bringing up the subject, saying that it was a gift from him, which was supposed to justify it. That woman does not know Justin's name, but I'll guarantee that every time she saw that mink coat in her closet, she remembered him.

He was an active volunteer at the Arlington Wildlife Center, and was very devoted to his work there on weekends. He marveled at the animals that he was able to interact with, and was equally appalled by the acts of cruelty that brought many of them there. The center is well-known for rehabilitating birds of prey, who have been wounded by the trigger-happy. No wild animal was turned away. Although every thing that could be to either rehabilitate the animal, or give it a home at the shelter permanently, was done, there were the ones who could not be saved, and Justin accepted that as he knew the effort that went into giving each one its chance.

Justin's personal pets could count themselves among the luckiest creatures on this earth. His request of a pet of his very own came at Christmas 1983. He asked for a "3-colored cat." I was stumped, trying to figure out what a 3-colored cat was. He finally saw there was hope for me when I found a picture of a calico cat, and confirmed that's what he wanted. I finally found one, after searching many shelters, about 5 days before Christmas. She was six months old, and ready to be spayed. I decided that rather than trying to hide her at home for 5 days, I would leave her at the vet for spaying, and pick her up Christmas Eve. I was worried about how Justin would react to seeing her shaved belly, and stitches, but it was unwarranted. To him, she was the most perfect cat in the world.

Justin has the great combination of the gift of conversation, being a good listener, and having an amazing sense of humor. Last week, I told him in our first conversation in 2 years that I felt like I had lost my best buddy, but was glad to have him back. One of my favorite memories of that sense of humor was his rendition of a cat coughing up a hairball at the dinner table. Of course, Justin enjoyed it even more when extended family and guests were amongst the observers.

I was hospitalized in September 1997. He came to see me when I was released from the hospital. He stayed with me for a week, until I was feeling better. Justin cooked three delicious vegan meals for me each day. I wasn't eating much at that time, but he didn't give - he kept cooking. I felt bad for sleeping so much during that time, and when I did get up, I apologized to Justin for not being up to much talking. He didn't feel snubbed at all for his efforts. Justin committed acts of kindness, without further expectation of others.

Every mother's ultimate dream is to see her son or daughter grow up to be a fine human being. I have been blessed with this dream twice. I am extremely proud of Justin, and his brother, Robbie, for having the courage of their convictions. Robbie is a U.S. Marine, something that is no small endeavor and requires tremendous personal sacrifice and risk to defend freedoms we and others enjoy. This has been a hard thing for Justin to accept, being such a conflict to his own pacifist views. Of course, Justin's beliefs have been a source of conflict to Robbie. I am reminded of many conversations their dad and I chanced to hear between these brothers rather pointedly expressing their views. Often having some very serious differences. Yet, this tough Marine was deeply saddened by his brother's disappearance, and shared the concern of the family. Both Justin and Robbie are role models for all of us, they stand for honor, courage, and commitment. I am proud of both of them.

I am proud of Robbie's commitment to his country, but I don't think I'll ever look at an American flag with previously felt patriotism if the outcome of the accusations made against Justin are not found to be unsubstantiated and untrue. I know our judicial system has failed many people, and for that I am sorry. Most of us have read articles or heard stories of how law enforcement officials have told family of victims of heinous crimes how they're doing all they can, but they're resources are limited. I wonder how many of these family members would feel if they were told the truth - that resources were being directed toward pursuing those who have been accused of attempting to end cruelty. The FBI spokesperson, Barry Babler, was recently quoted in the Seattle Times as saying that Justin "acted on his principles, and now has to pay the price", Since when have our American law enforcement officials become the judge and jury?

I am deeply saddened when I think of Justin being confined in Belgium's Hasselt prison awaiting extradition. I am saddened for the toll this may take on Justin, I am selfishly saddened for myself, his father, and his brother, who are denied the ability to hug him, but mostly, I'm saddened for this world. Each day Justin is confined, the world does not benefit from the touch of this incredible person.

Before concluding this, I would like to thank all of you for your support of Justin. It really has been very helpful to Justin, as well as our family. There are those of you who have been working virtually non-stop to call attention to Justin's plight, and I'm not sure if you want me to note your names, but you and I know who you are, and you have helped so much, I will never be able to express enough gratitude. I would also like to send thanks to Justin's dad, Bob, who has been an infinite resource in making things happen, while providing emotional support to me.

Lastly, to Justin, who I couldn't be prouder of, or love any more - I will always be here for you.

Marlene Samuel
AKA "Mom"

JUSTIN WRITES:

Dear everyone,

First of all I want to say thank you for all of the love and support I feel that helps keep me strong and without fear for the future. As of writing this it has been three weeks since my arrest in Belgium, and I'm still here...waiting.

I have not been charged with anything in any country in Europe but am being held in accordance with the request of the U.S. government for my extradition (specifically the international warrant for my arrest issued by a Wisconsin judge last September). At this point the U.S. has 75 days from the time of my arrest (September 5th) to provide an official copy of the arrest warrant, which the Belgian courts require before they will begin extradition proceedings where they will decide whether there are sufficient grounds to grant the request.

There is no way of knowing how long I may be held here after the U.S. does provide the papers. The delay that may slow down any potential extradition would be any investigations, charges or extradition requests here in Europe (such as the Netherlands). There is a lot of media here in Belgium that seems to indicate I am a suspect for just about everything that has happened here recently, and there is no way of knowing how much of this is true and how much is just media sensationalism. So the idea of being here a few months seems a likely guess, but it could be one more week or it could be a year.

When first arrested I did not want to take any chances for affecting my legal case, so I had said I was not receiving support mail at that time. I have realised, though, that any unlikely adverse affect this could have on me is small, and is insignificant in light of the amazing strength that I get from having contact with so many people who support me. So I am now welcoming all letters, postcards, zines and publications anybody wants to send me. Please keep in mind, though, that all of my mail is read, coming in and going out.

As far as my mental state is concerned I'm doing great. The important thing is remaining positive and the support I've been getting helps tremendously. There's also the underlying knowledge of not having done anything wrong, and the bearing of injustice is an inspiration to stay strong. My physical conditions here (Hasselt prison) are OK, too, and I have good access to vegan food, so I can focus my energies on the more important things I have to deal with.

With regards to people writing/speaking/thinking about me, I would like to say that I believe in love, not hate. Compassion, not anger. I would never describe myself or my beliefs as 'violent' or 'militant', and I ask that others not refer to me as these, either. I don't ask this out of concern for any possible effect on my legal case, but instead because I feel they completely misrepresent who I am and what I believe, and I also feel they have a very negative impact on the general understanding of the basic ideas we share. I ask the same for words such as 'war', 'warrior', 'fight', 'attack' and others that, even if not intended to do so, often imply violent (that is, having intent to cause harm to other living beings) actions or ideas. By this I do not intend to disrespect to anyone else's beliefs, or condemn them as wrong, but only feel these words misrepresent me. Anyway, seeing how I have come to represent an alternative viewpoint and lifestyle in the eyes of the public as a result of the media sensationalism (at least here in Belgium) regarding the accusations against me, I have great faith in the corporate/state-controlled media to continue to portray me as a violent terrorist trying to create fear and hurt people, as that is one of their main functions: to limit the acceptable bounds in which people can think by distorting and marginalizing ideas (such as love and non-violence) that threaten the foundations of the power structures of which the media is a tool. I can only hope alternative/support media can refrain from doing the same.

As far as supporting me is concerned, what really gives me strength is to see people continuing to follow their hearts, not deterred by fear or consumed by anger when any one of us is subject to a small piece of the injustice this world has to offer. The important thing is to always remember one's real purpose and not to get caught up in negative emotions that will only leave us drained of energy and inspiration. I do ask that anything being done in support of me and my situation (be it letters written or demonstrations or anything else) be done out of love and compassion, not with any anger or violence in your heart. Understandably, there may be situations where some people react with violence towards others acting out of love, but we can only try to remain grounded in our compassion for the suffering of ALL other beings. Thank you again for all of the love and support. There is an amazing amount of strength I get from knowing I'm not alone. The real freedom is, of course, to not live your life in fear. Tot ziens (Dutch/Flemish 'until we see each other').

Love, Justin

CALIFORNIA ACTIVIST FACES CONTEMPT CHARGES FOR REFUSING TO TALK TO GRAND JURY

Gina Lynn, an animal rights activist from Northern California, was served a subpoena to appear before a federal grand jury in St. Louis this July. "Compliance with this subpoena would be unreasonable and oppressive in that the government has no reasonable belief that the information requested by the subpoena is relevant to its investigation," said Jennifer Brewer, Lynn's attorney. "Rather, the subpoena is intended to harass and intimidate Ms. Lynn from exercising her First Amendment rights by speaking out for the rights of animals." For that reason, Gina refused to cooperate with and did not appear before the grand jury as ordered.

On Sept 10 she was arrested by the FBI at her home and taken into custody. She was held for several days. She was then jailed in St. Louis for "an indefinite period" of time for refusing to cooperate with the grand jury. In a statement issued upon her release from the Oakland jail, Lynn said "I am being persecuted simply for my belief and activism in animal rights. Regardless of the law and although my compliance with this grand jury would fully exonerate me, I have to follow my heart. And my heart will not allow me to aid the FBI in their malicious attempts to destroy the cause that I've devoted my life to."

Anheuser-Busch allegedly received two letters they deemed threatening. One in 1995 and another in 1996. Excerpts read in court by the U.S. Attorney follow: "If you don't release whales from Sea World, violence will come upon you," and "Letters, phone calls, and protests haven't worked. Can you handle terrorism?"

The reasons given by the U.S. Attorney for targeting Gina are that she happened to live in southern California at the time, is an outspoken animal advocate, and an unidentified activist who talked to investigators from the F.B.I. speculated that it might be possible that Gina would be capable of writing such letters. Ms. Lynn categorically denies any involvement with these letters, stating "I'm not even involved in a campaign regarding Sea World. I didn't have anything to do with these letters."

On October 5, Gina was again taken into custody for her refusal to cooperate with the Federal Grand Jury convened in St. Louis. Gina could spend as long as six months in jail unless she relents and provides handwriting samples. Her lawyer, Jennifer Brewer, said Lynn won't change her mind. Gina told supporters and media that she is being harassed because of her animal rights activism. Lynn founded the Animal Rights Direct Action Coalition in Southern California, where she also produces an animal rights newsletter.

In finding her in contempt of court and ordering her to jail, the judge told Lynn that only she can determine how long she stays locked up. If she continues to refuse to provide handwriting samples, she could remain jailed for six months or until the grand jury's term expires. The grand jury hearing the case is set to end in four months, but its term could be extended.

After spending nearly two weeks jailed and on hunger-strike in the St. Louis county jail in protest of her situation, Gina was moved to the jail's infirmary for observation. After refusing to take a (non-vegan) TB test, Gina was placed on lockdown and was no longer allowed to make ANY phone calls. After intense public pressure through protest, phone-calls and faxes, Gina was later returned to the general population. Before long, however, the pressure on the St. Louis County Jail proved to be too much, and Gina was actually KICKED OUT of the Jail (but moved to a new one...)! The staff stated they couldn't get their work done with all the phone calls, so they called the U.S. Marshalls to take her.

Unfortunately the new jail is in worse condition than the last and officials wouldn't let her take the hundreds of letters that she's received, her books or any of her commissary stuff.

When Gina learned of this, she immediately refused to leave the St. Louis County Jail until they agreed to box up a bunch of her stuff to give it her lawyer. Unfortunately, this means she probably won't be able to reply to all the mail she's received. She's also asked that we not send any more books to her until we can figure out something so that she won't lose the books in transit the next time the U.S. Marshalls decide to do something with her.

YOUR SUPPORT IS NEEDED!

Beyond just improving Gina's conditions in jail - we need to get her released! To do this we need to increase the pressure on Judge Sipple. So please keep sending letters to him! Please join activists from around the world in drawing attention to the U.S. Government's unwarranted harassment of this brave activist who has been jailed for little more than being an outspoken advocate for animals. Any one of us could just as easily be in her shoes.

Even if you can only manage a small protest, or doing leafleting, your participation can make a world of difference for Gina. The more pressure we're able to place on the judge and the more media we're able to generate the more likely it becomes that Gina will be released sooner rather than later. Judge Sipple could release Gina at ANY time, this is completely up to his discretion.

Letters may be mailed or FAXed to Judge Sipple at:

Judge Rodney Sipple
US Court and Customs House
1114 Market St.
St. Louis, MO 63101
FAX: (314) 539-7872

Gina Lynn #309515
Saint Clair County Jail
700 North 5th St
Bellville, IL 62221, USA

ANIMAL LIBERATION FRONT

If not you, who?

If not now, when?

DIARY OF ACTIONS

The Diary of Action is intended to report the news of direct action for earth and animal liberation, not to encourage crime, etc. etc. All reports come from communiqués, other publications, the internet and news reports. Some of the actions took place in time periods covered by other issues of *Underground*, but were not known about until recently.

CANADA

AUGUST 25/99: Yarmouth, NS - At least two Canadian fur farmers received threatening letters containing razor blades from the Justice Dept. The return addresses on the envelopes were The Seattle Fur Exchange, New York, N.Y., and Fur Information of America, also of New York.

UNITED STATES

JUNE 23/99: North Brunswick, NJ -- Approximately 40 to 50 fur-trim and full-length fur coats destroyed with a pocket knife at Burlington Coat Factory. -A.L.F.

JUNE 25/99: A.L.F. claimed responsibility for the firebombing of a truck at World-wide Primates, Inc. (7780 NW 53 St., Miami, Florida), the business of modern-day slave trader/primate dealer Matthew Block and his family.

JULY/99: Wiscasset, MA - A.L.F. activists targeted Wiscasset Rod and Gun Club, causing more than $7,000 in damage. Walls were spray-painted with "Animal Liberation Front." Stuffed animal heads and stuffed dead animals in the club were taken and returned to the wilderness "to rest in peace."

JULY 7/99: ?, N.J. -- "Fur Kills" was spray painted on the side of Furs By Guarinos, "ALF" was spray painted on the metal shutter that pulls down over the window as well as on the wall. -A.L.F.

JULY 10/99: Philadelphia, PA -- Flemington Furs billboard on I-95 was paintbombed. - ALF

JULY 27/99 - Berkely, CA -- "The California Croppers" returned to the University of California--Berkeley's (UCB) Gil Tract to organise a late-night tackle football game in the middle of the crop fields. The final score after an enthusiastic match was Croppers 14, UCB 0, as 14 rows of corn used in GE research by two well-known scientists were uprooted. The name of our game may be called, "Preventive harvest!" The crops are the work of Sarah Hake, director of the Plant Gene Expression Center (a collaboration of the U.S. Department of Agriculture and UCB's Department of Plant and Microbial Biology, where she is responsible for about 90 genetics researchers; (510) 559-5907) and biology professor Mike Freeling. These two researchers were targeted because of their dirty work for the multinational corporate titan Novartis at a public institution. This action is in observance of the "GE-Free July" called for by groups in Europe, and in solidarity with groups and individuals across the globe who are taking direct action against genetic-engineering. GE--the ultimate commodification of life itself.

AUGUST 3/99: -- Bristol, WI: Animal rights activists broke into a building at Krieger Farm and released over 3,000 mink, as well as destroying breeding cards for four complete mink sheds. From the communiqué: "The conditions on Krieger's death camp were the worst we have ever seen. There was filth everywhere. The sheds were decrepit and poorly maintained. Throughout the farm there were open ditches full of faeces and urine. In several cages we saw the decomposing corpses of dead mink whom were just left there to lie. These dead mink were surrounded by their fellow inmates." The A.L.F. have also confirmed that Krieger's Far was targeted in large part because of their connection to retail giant Neiman Marcus. Krieger supplies Neiman Marcus with mink pelts.

AUGUST 7/99: Escanaba, MI -- The Earth Liberation Front paid a visit to the home of Jim and Lois Boydston's on Lake Michigan. Their house was positively identified by the "Fur Enough" sign that hung from a post by the road. Their two fishing boats were destroyed by fire. The slogan Fur is Murder was painted on one boat and the garage door. Each slogan was signed "ELF." The two boats are tentatively valued at $15,000 and $25,000. The action was taken to their home to show that they can live away from the destruction and death they are causing, but they cannot hide and wash their hands of the blood. The Boydston's make their money through a mink farm and a veterinary practice. Obviously the Boydston's have no compassion for animals. They have not learned from their veterinary practice that animals suffer. They only care about making money off the backs of others. The Boysdston's property is all stained with the blood of the innocent animals that died to make them rich.

AUGUST 8/99: Plymouth, WI -- the A.L.F. are responsible for releasing all the mink (more than 2000) at Myer's Fur Farm, in a late night raid. Meyer says the damage is done. He will never be able to breed again. "All my records are messed up now, I don't know who's mother is who. "we wait until they fur out and its history, I'm done. I'm not a quitter, but sooner or later you got to give up after you go through something like this." A.L.F. activists report in their communiqué that "Tears came to our eyes as we watched thousands of mink run to their freedom in nearby fields. Once we had finished sweeping the farm, we headed off to United Feeds" where they continued their action...

United Feed mill — out of commission

AUGUST 8/99: Plymouth, WI - A United Feed mill, producers of mink feed for mink fur farms, was burned to the ground by ALF activists. Media reported that United Feeds Inc. is a "total loss" with damage estimates around one million dollars. By the time fire-fighters arrived, there was very little to save of the United Feeds mill -- Wisconsin's largest supplier of mink feed. Activists responsible stated, "We entered the building and checked from top to bottom to ensure that no living thing was inside. After walking throughout the building and seeing the sick huge bins of animal innards and organs, we knew that we had to end this operation. Four incendiaries were strategically placed throughout the building, ensuring that it would burn to the ground." -A.L.F.

AUGUST 13/99: Washington, DC -- Andriana Furs had its locks glued. -A.L.F.

AUGUST 14/99: San Diego, CA -- A dozen or more red paint bombs were splattered over a butcher's shop store front that sold the dead carcasses of innocent animals including Boars and Quails.

AUGUST 16/99: Eugene, OR -- HOBART (meat cutting equipment, meat scales, etc) Doors glued; van in back glued; letters "ALF" spraypainted in back; words "MEAT IS MURDER!" spraypainted on front; 3 windows smashed.

AUGUST 14/99: Salisbury, Maryland - Activists visited Frank Parson's Mink Ranch, and released at least 20 animals. Security alarms went off about 5 a.m. alerting farmers. No arrests.

AUGUST 24/99: Long Island, NY.- Animal liberation activists freed "Annie," a 27-year-old stumptail macaque who had been languishing on display at B.T.J.'s Jungle Pet Shop in West Islip for decades. Annie was well-known to local animal rights activists and concerned animal lovers because of her incarceration and poor living conditions at B.T.J.'s. A veterinarian's deposition on July 11, 1999 described Annie as living in filth and being fed an improper diet. Annie had been housed in isolation for most of her life, denied the opportunity to interact with members of her species.

AUGUST 29/99: Orange County, CA --, forty-six dogs (many injured from surgeries) were liberated by the A.L.F. from Bio-Devices Laboratories. The building, located at Collins and Eckhoff in Orange County, was damaged and many messages were left, such as "Animal Liberation" and "Vivisection is Fraud". This liberation is dedicated to Alex Slack, a true animal liberationist victimised by the federal government, who chose to take his own life rather than betray his friends and the animals. As long as animals are exploited, tortured, and killed for profit there will be an ALF.

SEPTEMBER 1/99: Fulton County, GA -- McDonald's lost a store to an arson attack.

SEPTEMBER 2/99: Goodhue County, MN - Activists from the "Bolt Weevils" destroyed corn at a Novartis Seed Research field, glued locks to the company's corporate offices in Golden Valley. Much of the corn attacked by the Bolt Weevils was labelled as genetically modified with Bt (Bacillus thuregensis), a bacterial insecticide sprayed topically by organic and small scale farmers as a last resort to control problem insects, but now increasingly genetically engineered directly into the DNA of corn, cotton and potatoes, to make plants express the pesticide throughout. Ecologists, farmers and corporate executives alike agree that such widespread exposure to the toxin will eventually create Bt-resistant "super pests", rendering small scale use of the bacteria in spray form obsolete. Additionally, recent research has revealed that Bt pollen has a similar fatal effect on the intestines of the Monarch butterfly as on the corn borer, and scientists have shown that engineered Bt accumulates in the soil and could disrupt soil ecology irreversibly.

SEPTEMBER 14/99: Mankato, MN -- In their second attack this month, the Minnesota Bolt Weevils has destroyed a genetically engineered test crop and other property at Pioneer Hi-Bred's seed research facility. In the attack on Pioneer Hi-Bred, the world's largest seed company, members of the group trampled 50 rows of research corn, damaged company vehicles, spray painted "free the seed" and "stop agribusiness" and changed the Pioneer sign in front of the facility to read "Pioneering Farmageddon." "Our strike against Pioneer is a call to the Weevils and Borers of the world to join the growing resistance to the quickly approaching 'Farmageddon,'" stated the communiqué.

SEPTEMBER 17/99: Davis, CA -- Guerrilla gardeners laid claim to the destruction of experimental sugar beet and corn crops at the University of California, Davis, marking the latest in a string of attacks aimed at genetic engineering of food. The group, "Reclaim the Seeds" said its "plant defenders" wore masks and used "guerrilla gardening gear" to attack a UCD field early Tuesday and uproot a quarter-acre of genetically altered sugar beets.

SEPTEMBER 23/99: Phippsburg, MA - Activists visited the Phippsburg Sportsmen's Association, turned on two coffee pots, left plastic cups on the burners and turned on a gas line. Damage to the clubs was extensive. The words, "Animal Liberation Front" and "No Turkey Shoot" were painted onto walls. "Blood is Dripping" was spray-painted on a refrigerator.

SEPTEMBER 27/99: Maple Grove, MN -- E.L.F. paid a visit to CS McRossan' offices in where they slashed conveyor belts and damaged machinery. From the communiqué, "We see highway 55 as symbolic of the larger system that is strangling us of our air and water. The NAFTA superhighway and the roads into the forests are all a symptom of the sick capitalist system that puts profits before people or ecosystems. As long as the trees continue to fall, so will the profits made of this project. This is just the beginning of a new level of battling against highway 55 and car culture. We urge the elves of MN and the world to unite against the profit hauling infrastructures around the globe. Target machines, offices , and equipment used to build roads. We are everywhere and we are watching. We will be back."

SEPTEMBER 29/99: Davis, CA "Reclaim the Seeds," conducted its fifth action against GE crops at a University of California, destroying five rows of transgenic melons, sixteen rows of transgenic walnut trees, sixty rows of pesticide-ridden tomatoes as well as removing two pieces of research equipment at two UC-Davis GE facilities.

OCTOBER 1/99: Montpelier, IN -- the A.L.F. paid a visit to the Owl Creek Fox Farm where thirty fox at the Montpelier farm had their coats dyed with a harmless red henna to render them worthless to the fur farmer. Breeding cards were also taken causing further economic loss. The raid was apparently thwarted by an undisclosed "disturbance" causing activists to leave the area prematurely. The A.L.F. state that they will return if the farmer does not end his cruelty.

OCTOBER 2/99. Englishtown, NJ. Two windows at Classic Furs shattered by two large rocks. -A.L.F.

OCTOBER 3/99: Minneapolis, MN -- the Earth Liberation Front claimed responsibility for the second attack upon C S McRossan's construction machinery. The ELF entered the construction site on highway 55 where the company is working. Machines that were found with accessible holes had sand poured into the oil, facilitating the draining of them. Three machines had hoses and wires cut before the elves escaped into the night.

OCTOBER 15/99: Long Island, NY -- McDonalds Restaurants in Jericho, Hicksville, Syosset and Garden City had their windows shattered and graffiti scribbled on their walls, including slogans as "Animal Rights Now," "Humans = Animals" and "Animal Liberation Now." The Hicksville restaurant was hit the worst with about $10,000 in damage.

OCTOBER 17: Albuquerque -- The Burger King at 5215 Menaul NE went up in flames and the building was destroyed. Investigators are trying to determine
how the fire was started.

ENGLAND

MAY 1/99: E. London -- Fish shop window smashed in Walthamstow. -A.L.F.

MAY 1/99: E. London -- Butchers van paint-stripped and tyres slashed in Wanstead. -A.L.F.

MAY 1/99: E. London -- Mobile fish van tyres slashed in Leyton. -A.L.F.

MAY 2/99: W. London -- Mobile fish stall paint-stripped and tyres slashed, Greenford. -A.L.F.

MAY 2/99: E. London -- Chicken shop window smashed, Walthamstow. -A.L.F.

MAY 2/99: E. London --Ladbrokes betting shop window smashed, Leyton. -A.L.F.

Mid MAY/99: N. London -- A large butchers refrigerated van in Edmonton, parked near the police station(!) was burnt out by ALF activists.

MAY 20/99: London --ALF took action against the property of Carol and Peter, both prominent players in the British and European fur industry. Many windows were damaged at their north London home. The couple were believed to be out at the time. Peter Bartfeld has recently been exposed by BBC Newsnight as being responsible for the importation of cat and dog fur from China, under the name of Alaska Brokerage, a company for which he is a director. The ALF will continue such actions until every furrier in the UK is out of business and every fur farm is closed.

MAY 27/99: London -- Chicken express, Willesden High Rd - window Smashed. -A.L.F.

JUNE 18/99: London -- On the June 18 demo in the city, at least six NatWest cash point machines (ATMs) were superglued up by ALF activists. NatWest is targeted because of the large loan it gave to Huntingdon Life Sciences when they were in serious financial trouble last year.

JUNE 18/99: Tonbridge - Hildenborough landlord, Robert Hicks received 6in by 10in flat package believed to be a bomb, but actually contained cat excrement. The parcel was the latest in a string of actions on Mr Hicks, who was fined in May for killing his pet cat.

JUNE 28/99: Leytonstone, E London -- Burger bar, Kebab shop, 2 butchers windows smashed.

JUNE 28/99: Essex-- Fresh Fish shop windows smashed.

JUNE 29/99: Hounslow, W London -- McDonald's window smashed.

JUNE 29/99: Chadwell Heath, E London -- Butchers shop window smashed.

JULY 5/99: Mill Hill -- Organic butchers shop near National Institute for Medical Research has window smashed. - A.L.F.

JULY 5/99: Herts - Meat van has tyres slashed, redecorated with slogans and windscreen broken. - A.L.F.

Unigate Dairy is payed a visit by the A.L.F.

JULY 5/99: Crouch End, N London - Meat van has tyres slashed, redecorated and windscreen smashed. -A.L.F.

JULY 6/99: Dalston, E London --Betting shop window smashed.-A.L.F.

JULY 6/99: Dalston, E London --Butchers shop window smashed.-A.L.F.

JULY 6/99: Dalston, E London --Kennedy Fried Chicken window smashed.-A.L.F.

JULY 7/99: Walthamstow, E London -- Steak bar window smashed.-A.L.F.

JULY 7/99: Whipps Cross, E London -- Jellied eel van tyres slashed and slogans daubed.-A.L.F.

JULY 7/99: London Bridge, S London -- Cafe windows smashed.-A.L.F.

JULY 8/99: Kings Cross, N London -- Cafe windows smashed.-A.L.F.

JULY 8/99: Hounslow, W London -- Butchers window smashed.-A

JULY 12/99: Braknell, Berkshire - Anti-genetic modification activists destroyed 115 of the estimated 120 GM poplars which were growing in 2 adjacent test sites at AstraZeneca's research station. Some of the trees have been ringbarked while others have been felled. No one has been arrested in connection with this action.

MID JULY/99: London -- BMC (Botswana Meat Co.) in Tottenham Lane - 2 vans (1 meat, 1 dairy) got spray painted and brake fluid treatment.-A.L.F.

MID JULY/99: London -- A vivisector from the Medical Research Centre, Mill Hill received an anonymous letter put on his car saying he better resign or expect more visits from the ALF. Also, his car was totally spray painted all over, and brake fluid.-A.L.F.

MID JULY/99: London -- Merc Sharpe and Dome sponsor a roundabout on the A10, the posts were graffitied. - A.L.F.

JULY 19/99: London -- Kentucky Fried Chicken, window smashed; JULY 19/99: London -- Kebab shop, window smashed;

JULY 19/99: London -- Betting shop, window smashed;

JULY 19/99: London -- Halal butchers, window smashed.

JULY 20/99: London -- Butcher shop, Forest Gate, windows smashed + slogans spray-painted;

JULY 20/99: London -- McDonalds, Forest Gate, window smashed;

JULY 20/99: London -- KwickSave, window smashed displaying meat advertisement;

JULY 20/99: London -- Lambs cafe, Whippes Cross, windows smashed;

JULY 20/99: London -- Butchers' van, South Woodford, tyres slashed and slogans painted on it."

LATE JULY/99: London -- Roundabout near A10, N London: permanent slogan on brickwork "Merck, Sharp & Dohme kills animals"

LATE JULY/99: London -- Home visit to Doctor at Medical Research Council: 73 Fallows Court Ave. Car trashed - tyres slashed, body spraypainted and brake fluid poured over it. Also a note left on his car that him and others are being watched.

LATE JULY/99: London -- Meat van: tyres slashed and graffitied: Wood Green, N London.

LATE JULY/99: London -- Lab Manager, Medical Research Council. His stairway was spray painted with "Animal abuser lives here". Also area was leafleted.

AUGUST/99: London --Rosebery Avenue: Burger bar window smashed. -A.L.F.

AUGUST/99: London --Tottenham Court Road: Sandwich bar window smashed. -A.L.F.

AUGUST/99: Holborn -- Meat shop window smashed, Burger bar door smashed. -A.L.F.

AUGUST/99: Stratford -- Pet shop window smashed. -A.L.F.

AUGUST/99: Wanstead -- Betting shop window smashed, Butcher's fridge smashed, 10 meat adverts destroyed, slogans painted on. -A.L.F.

AUGUST/99: London --Blackhorse Road: Jellied eel stand has tyres slashed. -A.L.F.

AUGUST/99: London -- Wood Green: Butchers shop window smashed. -A.L.F.

AUGUST/99: Tottenham -- Butchers shop window smashed, Kebab window smashed. -A.L.F.

AUGUST/99: Walthamstow -- Dairy Crest Milk HQ has windows smashed. -A.L.F.

AUGUST/99: Hounslow -- Pizza Hut window smashed. -A.L.F.

AUGUST/99: Ilford -- Butchers shop window smashed. -A.L.F.

AUGUST/99: London --Woodford Green: Butchers shop window smashed. -A.L.F.

AUGUST/99: Acton -- Butchers shop window smashed. -A.L.F.

AUGUST 1/99: Banbury - four meat vehicles were destroyed in an attack at Tadmartin Poultry. Estimated damage is said to be £250,000. Incendiary devices were placed under the lorries. A fifth device underneath a poultry lorry failed to go off.

AUGUST 1/99: Oxford -- An arson attack at Unigate Dairies has caused £1 million damage. Activists planted incendiary devices under lorries at the dairy, causing a large fire, and seventeen vehicles were completely burnt out. Police stated, "We are not sure of the exact value of the damage but we would estimate it at between half a million and a million pounds."

AUGUST 3/99: E. London -- Meat & fish shop, Butchers: Whitechapel windows smashed. -A.L.F.

AUGUST 3/99: E. London -- Butchers, Leather shop: Leyton, windows smashed. -A.L.F.

AUGUST 3/99: E. London -- Chicken shop, Butchers, Cafe: Leytonstone, windows smashed. -A.L.F.

AUGUST 3/99: E. London -- Meat shop: Aldgate, windows smashed. -A.L.F.

AUGUST 6/99: Bristol -- Earth Liberation Front activists (Elves) entered the Waitrose supermarket on Northumbria Drive and symbolically placed a large frozen turkey into a shopping trolley which was then allowed to defrost in the middle of the store. This dead bird symbolised the thousands of birds killed each year by the John Lewis Partnership (the owners of Waitrose) on their shooting estate in Hampshire.

AUGUST 6/99: Preston -- A.L.F. activists raided a mink farm and every one of the 1,500 mink were released from their cages. Large sections of the perimeter fence were removed. Most of the animals released appeared to disperse from the farm area. The action took place on the anniversary of last year's raid on Crow Hill mink farm at Ringwood, Hampshire. - A.L.F.

AUGUST 9/99: Cricklewood -- Grocery store advertising halal meat and poultry - received knock on the window from brick. Restaurant next door selling kebabs and other crap - window was smashed.

AUGUST 24/99: London -- Brick Lane; Leather shop window smashed.-A.L.F.

AUGUST 24/99: London -- Old Street; Betting shop windows smashed.-A.L.F.

AUGUST 24/99: London -- Shoreditch; Betting shop window smashed.-A.L.F.

AUGUST 24/99: London -- Hoxton; Butcher shop window smashed.-A.L.F.

AUGUST 24/99: London -- Woodford Green; Fishing and gun shop locks glued and window smashed.-A.L.F.

AUGUST 24/99: London -- South Woodford; Cancer Research shop locks glued.-A.L.F.

SEPTEMBER 1/99: London - (WHITECHAPEL) windows smashed at the following: Halal butchers, Meat shop, Chicken shop, Leather shop, Kebab shop. -A.L.F.

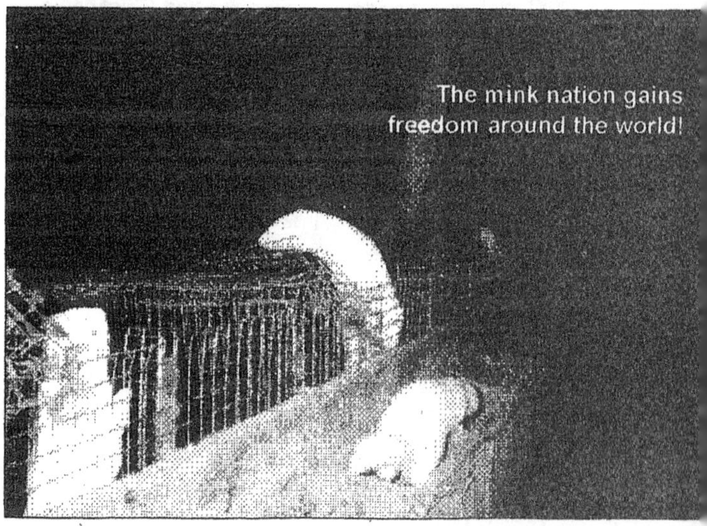

The mink nation gains
freedom around the world!

SEPTEMBER 1/99: London - (WANSTEAD) Betting shop - smashed for a 2nd time after their replacement. A.L.F.

SEPTEMBER 3/99: Burton-on-Trent -- The A.L.F. kick-started the campaign against the Hall family business of breeding and selling Dunkin Guinea Pigs to vivisection laboratories, by liberating six hundred (600) young guinea pigs. ALF activists entered the brand new building - so new in fact that the alarm had not yet been wired up. The sealed doors were breached by drilling out the locks. Once inside, the liberators found thousands of Guinea Pigs in overcrowded, barren floor cages with no bedding or nesting material, many dead and dying babies, and a thick layer of faeces. Documents taken reveal the day to day death rates in their hundreds.

Documents taken during the raid also explain the strict rules about entry into an SPF (Specific Pathogen Free) sterile environment, which the breeding unit was. Of course all those people entering, opening doors, walking around, rifling offices, stealing animals, and filming and photographing, completely breaks the SPF status of this unit and the entire stock. The Halls can no longer sell these animals as sterile, and we do hope they confess this to their customers (we took a customer list too, in case they need approaching). As well as losing 600 baby Guinea Pigs the filthy business has been dealt a financial blow by this breach of the SPF status.

ANIMAL TESTING

SEPTEMBER 15/99: Brixton - Kentucky Fried Chicken, windows smashed. -A.L.F.

SEPTEMBER 15/99: Brixton - Country Chicken, windows smashed.-A.L.F.

SEPTEMBER 15/99: Brixton - Butchers shop, windows smashed.-A.L.F.

SEPTEMBER 15/99: Brixton - Kebab shop, windows smashed.-A.L.F.

SEPTEMBER 15/99: Brixton - McDonalds, sign smashed.-A.L.F.

SEPTEMBER 16/99: Hackney - Chinese Take-away, windows smashed.-A.L.F.

SEPTEMBER 16/99: Hackney - Butchers shop, windows smashed.-A.L.F.

SEPTEMBER 16/99: Hackney - Butchers van, tyres slashed.-A.L.F.

SEPTEMBER 16/99: Wood Green - Butchers shop, windows smashed.-A.L.F.

SEPTEMBER 16/99: Hounslow West - Butchers shop, windows smashed.-A.L.F.

SEPTEMBER 16/99: Acton Town - Butchers shop, windows smashed, Kebab shop windows
Smashed.-A.L.F.

SEPTEMBER 23/99: London -- Activists targeted seven meat-laden lorries parked in the yard of Cherryfield (Croydon) Ltd, in Whistlers Meat Market, Cherry Orchard Road late on Saturday. Petrol Soaked clothing was put under the wheel arches of each lorry and an incendiary device used to start the blaze. Plastic bottles of flammable liquid were also found nearby. Damage was estimated at £500,000. All of the lorries had been loaded with meat ready for transportation the next day.

BELGIUM

JUNE/99: Kontich -- Schots meat company : 1 meat lorry burned.

JULY 11/99: Antwerp -- De Hert and Willemson, a meat processor, had their cold storage lorry torched.

MID JULY/99: Antwerp -- a van belonging to a meat company was burned out. Slogans were sprayed on a wall beside the vans. Police says that at least one of these slogans was sprayed long before the fire, namely when at the same place the van of the meat company Belgameat was set on fire (last year) by the A.L.F.

AUGUST 12/99: Antwerp -- A McDonald' s fast food restaurant was burnt to the ground. "ALF" was painted at the scene. The restaurant was completely destroyed after the roof collapsed. Police stated, "It was the worst destruction we have seen so far." -A.L.F. Red Rooster, Holland

SWITZERLAND

JUNE 19/99: Winterthur - an activist group called "The Heirs of Leonardo da Vinci" slashed 96 tires on twenty meat vans belonging to a slaughter house. Damages reached over 50,000 Swiss Francs.

HOLLAND

JUNE 13/99: Bodegraven -- Five meat trucks parked in the parking lot of a Domberg Vlees slaughterhouse in Bodegraven went up in flames. Four trucks were loaded with meat. The trucks were completely burned out. Damage is estimated at millions of Dutch guilders. It took 40 fire-fighters to tame the fire and the N11 road was cut off for hours because of a massive smoke cloud. The police later recovered some empty petrol cans and firelighters in the vicinity. The ALF communiqué in brief states (and this is translated from Dutch): "Undisturbed we sprinkled gasoline on the meat trucks. Under the tires of each truck we placed one incendiary device, we subsequently left the area...The slaughter of animals will continue unless we don't hit again. This is a warning to all meat companies, this is not personal, it is the start of offensive against ALL murderers of innocent animals. We will strive for justice in an unjust world. As long as inequality and injustice are dominant forces we will strive to fight against it.. Even if the government puts obstacles in our way to thwart our actions others will continue the struggle." - A.L.F.

JULY 5/99: Dedmsvaart -- Seven out of the ten meat trucks outside of poultry slaughterhouse Plukon were set on fire, with damages well into millions of Dutch guilders. The fire also hit the company's storage building which contained paint and spare parts for the meat trucks.

JULY 12/99: Emelo -- A massive fire completely wiped out a poultry processing plant. The fire was noticed at around 4a.m. after a series of explosions rang out. The damage runs into

Some of the nine hens liberated by the ALF

millions of Dutch guilders. 60 fire fighters from 4 towns were called into put out the fire but could not prevent the whole building being burned totally to the ground.

AUGUST 27/99: Zwammerdam - activists from "ALF Commando Roberto Duria" raided a fur farm, releasing 50000 mink. From the communiqué: "We made our own small bridge to reach the farm of fur breeder Verboom. 10-20 metres of fencing was destroyed and cages were opened for 4000-5000 of the 15 000 mink present in the farm. The timing was strategic as in October these animals will be killed and skinned for their pelts.

SEPTEMBER 10/99: Barchem - Animal liberation activists released an estimated 8000 mink from a Dutch fur farm.

POLAND

JUNE/99: Bialystok - unknown activists broke into a McDonalds building site and destroyed equipment. Later a McDonald's billboard was paintbombed.

JUNE/99: Bielsk Podlaski - activists completely destroyed 11 hunting platforms.

DENMARK

JUNE 23/99: Copenhagen -- activists sprayed-painted "Fur is Murder" and lit a fire outside the headquarters of an international fur company. Damage was minor and no one was arrested. "We know where you live" and the Danish name for Animal Liberation Front were painted in red several times on the two-story building housing Saga Fur, a joint marketing company owned by the Nordic fur breeders' associations. The heat caused several windows to explode and the fire singed the building. Saga has a world-wide market share of nearly 70 percent of farm-produced mink, and 90 percent of farmed fox skins.- A.L.F.

JULY 23/99: Overlade -- 3000 mink were released from a farm in the village of Overlade in North-Jylland. Slogans such as "Fur is murder" & "Stop the torture" were sprayed at the farm. Danish Animal Liberation Front takes responsibility for the action.

SWEDEN

April 16/99: Helsingborg - Three big windows on a meat store got smashed. The windows on the staff room on a slaughter house was smashed and the walls were painted black with paint bombs.

April 25/99: Morarp - Nine hens were liberated from Swedens largest battery hen unit Aniagra by the ALF.

April 27/99: Stockholm - A meat company called Kottgrossisten Mikro Meat AB had several windows smashed and "meat is murder" and "ALF" spraypainted.

April 30/99: Malmo - Activists climbed the roof on the meat company Lars Jonsson´s, smashed a window, and threw in a can of fuel that they had lit.

Spring 99: Skane - Several hunting platforms destroyed.

May 8/99: Eksjo - A meat company got slogans painted like "meat is murder" and "murderers".

May 13/99: Helsingborg - The windows on the staff room on the slaughterhouse were smashed again, and paint bombs were thrown inside. An animal transportation truck were covered with slogans, and when the activists were about to cut holes in the wheels, they got spotted and ran away. Slogans were also spraypainted on a meat hop.

May 20/99: Helsingborg - Locks were glued on a meat company. Paint bombs were also thrown on the slaughterhouse, that painted the walls green-black.

May 31/99: Malmo - Several meat companies got windows smashed (one shop in the middle of the day).

June 10/99: Malmo - Malmo hospital's animal lab got windows smashed, and a motion detector alarm went of, so no animals could be rescued.

June 15/99: Southern Sweden - Five hunting platforms were destroyed and a shooting area for hunters were sabotaged (windows smashed, slogans spraypainted and other economical damage).

June 21-27/99: Stockholm - During "XII Symposium of Gnotbiology", a vivisector and main organiser and member of the board on B&K, Tore Midvedt, got his door glued, "animal abuser" was painted next to the door, and red paint were squirted on the door.

July 1/99: Orebro - A McDonalds delivery car got windows smashed, the paint destroyed and the rear-view mirrors destroyed. A loudspeaker for the drive-in also got smashed.

July 4/99: Norrkoping - A McDonalds was spraypainted, and

had neon signs destroyed.

JULY 15/99: Smaland - 24 rabbits were liberated from a rabbit slaughter house by the Swedish ALF. The Furukulls rabbit slaughterhouse in Bredaryd, Varnamo was visited by activists, who discovered the rabbits in terrible condition, with several in need of veterinary care and medicine. The rabbits are now in homes where they receive care, love and a safe future. - ALF"

July 15/99: Orebro - A McDonalds has 15 windows smashed, and a loudspeaker and signs destroyed.

July 16/99: Orebro - A hunting & fishing shop got all seven windows etched with a fluid by the ALF.

July 19/99: Orebro - A skin shop was spraypainted by the ALF.

AUGUST 7/99: Orkelljunga -- An Astra-owned beagle breeder was visited by animal liberationists. Surrounded by a high barb wire fence, the centre breeds dogs for vivisection and is the biggest of its kind in Sweden. The fence was cut and when activists got in to the area, a motion detector alarm was triggered. Searchlights was turned on and sirens started. Despite this, activists got inside and lifted to freedom. Five young beagles now live torture-free, living in loving homes where they will be respected as individuals and not as components in a profit machine. A day will come when people won't have to risk their own freedom to liberate animals from institutes such as this one. -A.L.F.

Vita Fageln chicken trucks destroyed by ALF activists.

August 22/99: Valla - Ten incendiary devices were placed out on the chicken company Vita Fageln by ALF-activists, and one of their trucks were burned to the ground, but nine incendiary devices were disarmed by the police. Damages for $200 000 were made. The company had been in the newspapers earlier in the week, saying that they were expanding their business.

September 1/99: Falkenberg - All cages were opened on Lonestigs mink farm, and 2500 minks left the cages. The farmer said that most of the minks left the area. This was the third raid against the same place.

September 4/99: Morarp - 24 hens were liberated from Aniagra, which was also attacked on April 16, by the ALF/Commando Astrid Lindgren. "Be nice to the animals" were also spraypainted on one house. Astrid Lindgren is a famous Swedish writer, who got a promise on her 80-years birthday that battery hen units should be banned in 1999, but they will still exist because of dispensations.

FINLAND

JUNE/99: Helsinki -- Polar turkis, a fur store, a window smashed.

JULY/99: Helsinki -- Junotex, a fur store, gets one window smashed two times.

JULY/99: Helsinki -- Polar turkis loses another window.

JULY 13/99: Juuka -- Fire destroyed a fur farm storage building, completely destroying it. Finnish A.L.F. claimed responsibility, "We burned down Olavi Kakkinens fur farms storage building, to make the operation of the farm more difficult. Before starting the fire we made sure that the fire wouldn't spread to nearby trees and that the wind wouldn't blow the smoke to the direction of the animals. We also made sure that there were no humans inside the building"

AUGUST 13/99: Kiihtelysvaara - A.L.F. raided a fur farm near Pitkäjärvi. Two guard dogs near the entrance understood whose side the activists were on and let them raid the farm in peace. The farm was in bad shape. Activists opened the back gate of the farm. Several hundred breeding cards were stolen and destroyed. We wish all of the animals a good escape journey!

AUGUST 14/99: Kiihtelysvaara -- Activists raided a fur farm in North Karelia, where an estimated 100 racoon dogs were released from five sheds. Cages were opened or the back net of the cages were cut. Activists also cut down the farm fence to allow the racoon dogs to escape.

AUGUST 20/99: Kontiolahti -- a fur farm was raided and liberators opened several dozens Racoon dog cages and broke equipment. Only a few animals managed to escape but expensive damage was caused by seizing the breeding records.

AUGUST 24/99: Jokioinen -- The farming of angora rabbits for wool is being developed as an intensive trade in the Finnish countryside, so ALF activists decided to make an inspection to check the conditions of the animals at wool producer Arja Simola's farm (Latovainiontie 98, 31629 Latovainio, tel/fax +358-3-4333116). 16 rabbits were liberated. The rabbits were kept in wire floor cages, several of which were covered in dust and urine. Some of the old rabbits were far too fat which is irrdicative of a lack of exercise. Rabbits are not cage animals and they require a lot of exercise. Even though rabbits are herd animals, all of the rabbits were housed in single cages. Several of the rabbits had severe infections caused by the mesh floor of the cages. The infections made the animals ability to move hard Rabbits nails weren't cut and some nails had turned in to the paw like screws.

One of the rabbits had a very severe infection in rear end, it's tail was covered in faeces and had mould inside. The rabbit also had diarrhoea and ticks. The animal couldn't clean itself because the infection has been going on so long. All these problems are clearly the result of neglect.

AUGUST 27/99: Pohjois-Karjala -- 200 fox and racoon cages were opened by activists.

SEPTEMBER 1/99: Luumaki - a fur shop suffered smoke damage in an attempted arson attack. A window in the back of the building was smashed and some flammable substance was thrown inside. When the fire department arrived the sides of the windows were on fire and it was quickly extinguished. Part of the fur coats and equipment suffered smoke damage. The owners of the fur store, Martti and Margit Sipari used to have a fur farm as well, but after it was raided last year, they announced that they will stop farming but will continue selling fur.

SEPTEMBER 23/99: Mäntsälä - The A.L.F. raided the chinchilla farm of Tarmo and Anne Peltola, taking 16 chinchillas, now housed in loving homes. The Peltolas raise chinchillas for fur, with an estimated 130 animals on the farm. The chinchillas were held in very small cages with wire mesh floors, in three levels. Activists took all breeding cards from the cages. Also taken were 83 nutria (coypu) pelts stored on the farm, books with breeding records of the farm since -88 and lots of farm papers and records.

OCTOBER 8/99: Lapinjarvi -- a fox farm was raided and around 200 foxes were released after being dyed with henna. According to media sources, the cages were cut and torn and the damages were estimated to be "significant".

GERMANY

Animal rights activists have destroyed numerous hunting platforms in the following areas (area + number of platforms destroyed):
- Rendsburger Forst: 3 (by "Aktionsfront Sauberer Wald" -- Actionfront
Clean Forest)
- Köln (Cologne): 7
- Bad Schwartau: several
- Hannover: 8
- Hambacher Forst (between Düren and Bergheim): 6

JANUARY 16/99: 7 trucks and one car of the firm "Deutsche See" had tires slashed, windows smashed, and spraying quick/hard drying foam into the cooler and the exhaust pipes. "Deutsche See" is a major firm in Germany, dealing with (dead)fish.

FEBRUARY/99: the windows of six butcher shops have been shot with steel screws. The damage was increased where the screws flew into the interior of the butcheries.

MARCH 20/99: Schwaebish-Hall -- meat and live animal trucks had their tires slashed at the slaughterhouse Wuerstner. It was said that the damage done was more than 100.000 DM (1US$ ~ 1,80 DM).

MARCH 27/99: Moers-Bornheim -- Traps and hunting platforms on a property that hunters use for meetings have been destroyed. Butyric acid was splashed into a hut on the property.

APRIL 4/99: Meckenheim -- Sugar has been poured into the petrol tanks of 34 meat trucks of the firm Rasting. The cleaning of the tanks alone cost 50.000 DM.

APRIL 14/99: Karlruhe -- 30 hens have been liberated from a battery farm . JULY 4/99: Willich -- More than 400 empty cages were destroyed by activists on a mink farm near Duesseldorf. The farmer says he can't afford to buy new cages so he will try to repair the damaged ones, taking a massive hit to profits.

MAY 22/99: Waldfeucht-Selsen -- The "Flinke Marder" released 120 minks from a farm. Fences were cut, cages destroyed and an alarm device/machine which was switched off was taken.

JULY 4/99: Willich -- the group "Nagezahn" damaged/destroyed 400 cages on the mink farm of Manfred Rossberger. Rossberger stated that he can not afford to buy new cages so he will try to repair them. It was said that the damage done was between 40.000 and 100.000DM.

JULY 25/99: Nordrhein-Westfalen -- T.B.F. liberated 20 hens from a so called battery farm. They are now in a place where they can live according to their needs without having to fear for their wellbeing and their life. There they can live as a species whose aim in life is not to be an egg laying machines for humans.

SEPTEMBER 2/99: Rahden -- 8000 minks were freed in a raid on a mink farm. Unclaimed.

NORWARY

AUGUST 8/99: Eidsberg -- Over 70 furbearing animals were released from a fur farmer in Hærland. Anonymous activists opened all the cages at the farm and cut the fence. The farmer, Paul Østby doesn't know how much money he will lose because of this action."

EIRE (REPUBLIC OF IRELAND)

AUGUST 16/99: Cork -- a Genetically Modified sugar beet crop was destroyed by anti-GM activists. The action took place in Midleton, Cork. According to The Times newspaper, this is the second anti-GM action to occur within less than a month in Ireland.

So, how much do you know about U.S. Fur Farm Raids? Afraid you'll be caught short the next time someone quizes you about historical mink liberations? Don't worry! Use this handy **Animal Liberation Front Guide to North American Mink Raids** to expand your knowledge of exciting and inspiring mink farm actions.

KNOWN NORTH AMERICAN MINK RAIDS:

1.August 13, 1995 Annendale, MN Davidson Fur Farm 1 coyote liberated
2.October 24, 1995 Chilliwack, BC Dargatz's Fur Farm 2,400 mink liberated
3.November 14, 1995 Aldergrove, BC Rippin Fur Farm 5,000 mink liberated
4.November 16, 1995 Olympia, WA Jordan Mink Farm 400 mink liberated
5.November 16, 1995 Pleasant View, TN Mac Ellis Fox Farm 30 fox liberated
6.January 15, 1996 Sheboygan, WI Zimbal Minkery 400 mink liberated
7.April 4, 1996 Victor, NY L.W. Bennet Fur Farm 1,700 mink liberated
8.June ?, 1996 Snohomish, WA Brainard Fur Farm 80 mink liberated
9.June 7, 1996 Sandy, UT Fur Breeders Agricultural Co-Op 75 mink liberated
10.June 21, 1996 Riverton, UT Riverton Fur Farm 1,000 mink liberated
11.July 4, 1996 Howard Lake, MN Latzig Mink Ranch 1,000 mink liberated
12.July 4, 1996 Langley, BC Akagami Mink Ranch 400 mink liberated
13.July 17, 1996 South Jordan, UT Holt Mink Ranch 3,000 mink liberated
14.August 9, 1996 Hinsdale, MA Carmel Mink Ranch 1,000 mink liberated
15.August 12, 1996 Alliance, OH Jorney Mink Ranch 2,500 mink liberated
16.September 28, 1996 Alliance, OH Jorney Mink Ranch 8,000 mink liberated
17October 2, 1996 Salem, UT Paul Westwood Fur Farm 1,500 mink liberated
18.October 5, 1996 Lindboro, NH Gauthier Fur Farm 35 fox and 10 mink liberated
19.October 11, 1996 Hinsdale, MA Carmel Mink Ranch 75 mink liberated
20.October 23, 1996 Lebanon, OR Arnold Krohl Fur Farm 2,000 mink liberated
21.October 25, 1996 Coalville, UT Reese Fur Farm 1,500-2,000 mink and 150-200 fox liberated
22.October 29, 1996 Victor, NY Bennett Fur Farm 46 fox liberated
23.November 28, 1997 Hinsdale, MA Carmel Mink Farm 12 mink liberated
24.December 14, 1996 Snohomish, WA Brainard Fur Farm 50 mink liberated
25.December 25, 1996 Bath, MI Jack Brower Fur Farm 150 mink liberated
26.March 15, 1997 Blenheim, Ont. Eberts Fur Farm 240 mink liberated
27.March 30, 1997 Blenheim, Ont. Eberts Fur Farm 1,500 mink liberated
28.April 9, 1997 DeBerry, TX Kelly Fur Farm 10 chinchilla liberated
29.May 11, 1997 Salisbury, MD Parsons Mink Farm 500 mink liberated
30.May 28, 1997 Lebanon, OR Lou Masog Mink Farm 80 mink liberated
31.May 30, 1997 Mt. Angel, OR Arritola Mink Farm 10,000 mink liberated
32.July 4, 1997 Cle Elum, WA David Smith Mink Farm 4,000 mink liberated
33.July 8, 1997 Medina, OH Tom Mohoric Mink Farm 41 mink liberated
34.July ?, 1997 Alliance, OH Unconfirmed raid on Jorney Mink Ranch 500 mink apparently liberated
35.September 1, 1997 Downers Grove, IL Ides Mink Farm 3,500 mink liberated
36.September 20, 1997 Anderson, IN Adams Fox Farm 200 fox liberated
37.October 5, 1997 Crystal Lake, IL Frye Mink Farm 5,000 mink liberated
38.October 6, 1997 Preston, ID Palmer Mink Farm 5,000 mink liberated
39.October 16, 1997 Sioux Ciry, IO Circle K Fur Farm 5,000 mink and 100 fox liberated
40.October 17, 1997 Watertown, SD Turbak Mink Farm 3,000 mink liberated
41.October weekend of the 24th, 1997 Independence, WI Smieja Fur Farm 800 mink liberated
42.October weekend of the 24th, 1997 Tomahawk, WI Ott's Mink Farm 300 mink
liberated
43.October weekend of the 24th, 1997 Medford, WI Jack Dittrich Minkery 3,000 mink liberated
44. October 29, 1997 Hebo, OR Empty mink farm entering the rabbit business
raided 6 rabbits liberated
45.November 5, 1997 Ft. Wayne, IN Blaine Leffers Fox Farm 125 foxes liberated
46. July 3, 1998 Middleton, WI United Vaccines Research Ranch 310 mink liberated
47. July 29, 1998 Sandy, UT Furbreeders Co-op 6 mink liberated
48. July 30, 1998 Sandy, UT Furbreeders Co-op 2 mink liberated
49. August 18, 1998 St. Cloud, MN Mueller Fur Farm 4,000 mink liberated
50. August 20, 1998 Guttenburg, IA Hidden Valley Fur Farms 330 fox liberated
51. August 21 1998 Jewell, IA Isebrand fur farm 3,000 mink liberated
52. August 27, 1998 Beloit, WI Brown Mink Farm 3,000 mink liberated
53. August 28, 1998 Rochester, MN Zumbro River Fur Farm 3,000 mink liberated
54. October 26, 1998 Powers, MI Pipkorn, MI 5,000 mink liberated
55. December 2, 1998 Anderson, IN Adams Fox Farm 150 foxes liberated
56. February 13, 1999 Annendale, MN Davidsons Fur Farm 6 foxes liberated
57. February 23, 1999 Snohomish, WA Brainerd Fur Farm 150 mink liberated
58. Februrary 17, 1999 Richmond, UT Nivison Mink Ranch 9 mink liberated
59. August 3, 1999 Bristol, WI Krieger Fur Farm 3,000 mink liberated
60. August 8, 1999 Plymouth, WI Gene Meyer Mink Farm 2,500 mink liberated

LEFTCOAST *By Adrian Raeside*

LAB ANIMAL LIBERATIONS: AN OVERVIEW

from www.animal-liberation.net factsheets

Liberations of laboratory animals are some of the hardest actions to accomplish, since such tedious preparation is necessary to achieve success. Once animals are brought to safety, they need to be treated by a trusted veterinarian and placed in loving homes.
Often times, A.L.F. volunteers are not able to rescueevery animal, because there aren't enough homes or sanctuaries for them.

Numerous larger liberations took place in the early eighties before technologically advanced security systems were placed in most larger animal laboratories. Plenty of tax payer money is available to vivisectors which allows them to upgrade security on a regular basis. This too becomes a success for animals since money used to purchase animals is re-directed to purchasing new equipment and supplies, while insurance premiums sky rocket.

The first A.L.F. liberation in the North America happened March 14, 1979 at New York Medical Center. One cat, two dogs, and two guinea pigs were liberated. Because A.L.F. volunteers can only take animals that homes have been found for, numbers remained small.

A combination of liberations and economic sabotage began Dec. 1982 in Washington DC; at Howard University, Medical School. Thirty-five cats were liberated, and estimated property damage was $2,640. This combination continued to reap massive rewards for animals since cages had to be replaced, and research was destroyed.

The greatest success of this strategy was illustrated in May 1984 at the University of Pennsylvania, Head Injury Laboratory. $60,000 economic damage, and sixty hours of researcher's videotapes were taken which produced the movie "Unnecessary Fuss" that documented vivisectors taunting and ridiculing sentient animals after horrific experiments were performed.

This evidence recorded by vivisectors themselves, helped to stop funding for the experiments.

Another, famous action, included liberating one hundred fifteen animals (13 cats, 18 rabbits, 21 dogs, 50 mice, and more), along with $500,000 research destruction, and $7,000 damage. The City of Hope, National Research Center, in California never fully recovered from this action on Dec. 1984.

The following year in April 1985, almost 1000 animals were liberated (1 monkey, 21 cats, 9 opossums, 35 rabbits, 38 pigeons, 70 gerbils, 300 mice, rabbits and 460 rats) from the University of California at Riverside. Documents and videotapes were taken with an estimated $700,000 damage caused. These videotapes were shown to the media to expose vivisection at it's worst. A video entitled "Britches" was made to document the success story of one infant primate who was isolated in a steel cage after animal researchers had crudely stitched his eyes shut, for a blindness experiment.

He has since fully recovered after being surrounded with other primates, in a loving environment.

Breeding facilities prove excellent for raids since England has proven that repeated, continual campaigns of direct action can close them permanently. Consort Beagle Breeders in England was closed after repeated A.L.F. actions. One such example saved the lives of 25 dogs that were liberated. The campaign began October of 1996, and nine months later, on June 3, 1997, Consort closed down and emptied the kennels. Fifty beagles were turned over to animal rights activists.

An example for North America is the University of Oregon, Breeding Facility which saw 264 animals (12 hamsters, 28 cats, 24 rabbits, 100 rats and pigeons) rescued October 26, 1986. $120,000 worth of damage was inflicted on the laboratory.

Because of increased security, liberations haven't been as frequent in the 1990's. However, June 19, 1992 at the University of Alberta, Ellerslie Research Station, 29 cats were liberated and $100,000 damage done with documents taken. Activists took boxes of files pertaining to illegal sources of the dogs they used.

More recently, July 4, 1998 at Marmotech Inc. in New York, 150 woodchucks were set free. The A.L.F. took and destroyed the data cards on these cages, logbooks and other information were also confiscated and disposed of, and vials of infectious serum were removed from a refrigerator to spoil.

Despite obstacles such as increased security, and finding enough homes, the Animal Liberation Front will continue to directly stop suffering, by placing their own lives on the front lines for animal liberation.@

FURTHER READING

FURTHER READING

www.ingramcontent.com/pod-product-compliance
Lightning Source LLC
Chambersburg PA
CBHW080810280326
41926CB00091B/4124
* 9 7 8 0 9 8 4 2 8 4 4 4 3 *